Medical Language for Modern Health Care

David M. Allan, MA, MD

Karen D. Lockyer, BS, RHIT, CPC

Michelle A. Buchman, RN, BSN, BC

 **Higher Education**

Boston   Burr Ridge, IL   Dubuque, IA   New York   San Francisco   St. Louis
Bangkok   Bogotá   Caracas   Kuala Lumpur   Lisbon   London   Madrid   Mexico City
Milan   Montreal   New Delhi   Santiago   Seoul   Singapore   Sydney   Taipei   Toronto

Higher Education

MEDICAL LANGUAGE FOR MODERN HEALTH CARE

Published by McGraw-Hill, a business unit of The McGraw-Hill Companies, Inc., 1221 Avenue of the Americas, New York, NY 10020. Copyright © 2008 by The McGraw-Hill Companies, Inc. All rights reserved. No part of this publication may be reproduced or distributed in any form or by any means, or stored in a database or retrieval system, without the prior written consent of The McGraw-Hill Companies, Inc., including, but not limited to, in any network or other electronic storage or transmission, or broadcast for distance learning.

Some ancillaries, including electronic and print components, may not be available to customers outside the United States.

 This book is printed on recycled, acid-free paper containing 10% postconsumer waste.

1 2 3 4 5 6 7 8 9 0 DOW/DOW 0 9 8 7

ISBN 978–0–07–351091–0
MHID 0–07–351091–2

Vice President/Editor-in-Chief: *Elizabeth Haefele*
Vice President/Director of Marketing: *John E. Biernat*
Sponsoring Editor: *Linda Schreiber*
Managing Developmental Editor: *Patricia Hesse*
Senior Marketing Manager: *Nancy Bradshaw*
Lead Media Producer: *Damian Moshak*
Director, Editing/Design/Production: *Jess Ann Kosic*
Lead Project Manager: *Mary E. Powers*
Senior Production Supervisor: *Kara Kudronowicz*
Senior Designer: *David W. Hash*
Cover/Interior Designer: *Maureen McCutcheon*
 (USE) Cover Image: *©The McGraw-Hill Companies, Inc. /Rick Brady, photographer*
Lead Photo Research Coordinator: *Carrie K. Burger*
Photo Research: *Ralph Plastino/Pronk & Associates*
Freelance Editorial Consultant: *Adrianne Rippinger*
Freelance Developmental Editor: *Patricia Gillivan, Triple SSS Press*
Instructional Design: *Teleologic Learning Company*
Compositor: *Electronic Publishing Services Inc., NYC*
Typeface: *10.5/12 ITC Giovanni*
Printer: *R. R. Donnelley Willard, OH*

The credits section for this book begins on page C-1 and is considered an extension of the copyright page.

Library of Congress Cataloging-in-Publication Data

Allan, David, 1942-
 Medical language for modern health care / David Allan, Karen Lockyer, Michelle Buchman. -- 1st ed.
    p. cm.
 Includes index.
 ISBN 978–0–07–351091–0 --- ISBN 0–07–351091–2 (hard copy : alk. paper)
   1. Medicine--Terminology--Programmed instruction. I. Lockyer, Karen. II. Buchman, Michelle. III. Title.
 [DNLM: 1. Medicine. 2. Terminology. WB 100 A417m 2008]
 R123.A43 2008
 610.1'4--dc22
                                                  2006035998

www.mhhe.com

DAVID ALLAN

David Allan received his medical training at Cambridge University and Guy's Hospital in England. He was Chief Resident in Pediatrics at Bellevue Hospital in New York City before moving to San Diego, California.

Dr. Allan has worked as a family physician in England, a pediatrician in San Diego, and Associate Dean at the University of California, San Diego School of Medicine. He has designed, written, and produced more than 100 award-winning multimedia programs with virtual reality as their conceptual base. Dr. Allan resides happily in San Diego and walks the beach most days.

KAREN LOCKYER

Karen Lockyer holds a degree in Health Information (RHIT), a national coding certification (CPC), and a BS from Rutgers University. She is also a credentialed member of AHIMA (American Health Information Management Association) and AAPC (American Academy of Professional Coders).

Mrs. Lockyer has worked in medical practice administration and the Health Information Management fields for many years. She has taught medical terminology for high school, community college, and workforce development areas at the National Institutes of Health and the federal government's Office of Personnel Management. She has also taught coding and billing for undergraduate and certificate programs at the community college level.

Residing in Southlake, Texas, Karen enjoys the sights and flavors of the Southwest.

MICHELLE BUCHMAN

Michelle Buchman is part owner of Educational Support Services, LLC, and the Nursing Director at St. John's Marian Center, Springfield, Missouri. She earned her Nursing Diploma from Burge School of Nursing and her Bachelor of Science Degree in Nursing from Missouri State University.

Mrs. Buchman was formerly employed by Corinthian Colleges, Inc., as an Associate Dean and served as a Captain in the Army as a medical surgical and critical care nurse.

BRIEF CONTENTS

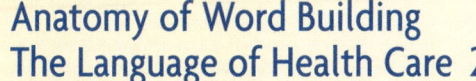

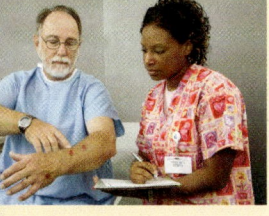

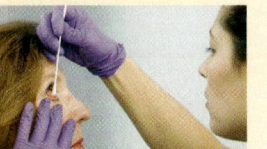

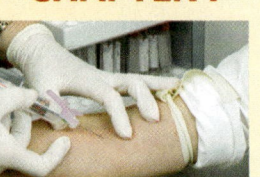
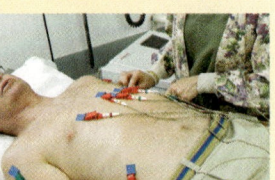

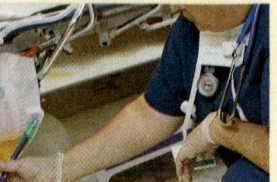
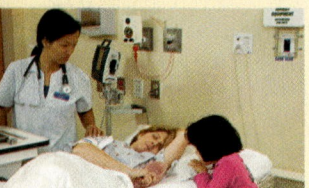

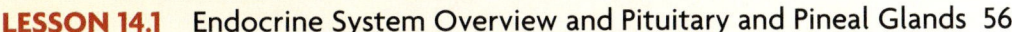

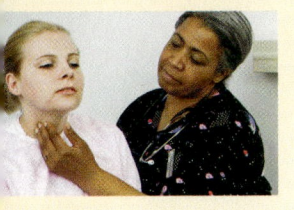

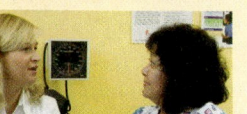
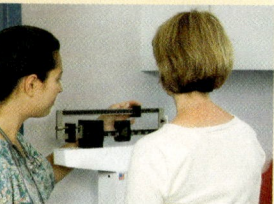

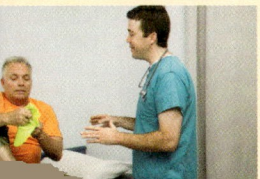

Medical Language for Modern Health Care is designed for you. The development of many medical terminology textbooks and learning programs begins with the question, "What topics should this book or program cover?" This question has been the basis of a host of textbooks available today. There is only one problem: where do *you*, the student, fit into this question?

To put the focus back on the student, a new question guided the design and writing of *Medical Language for Modern Health Care*:

What medical terminology knowledge and skills do students preparing for careers in modern health care need to be successful?

Time and time again, instructors and students alike have indicated their belief that students learn medical language best when it is connected to real life: real health professionals interacting with real patients in a real medical setting. Just as one of the best ways to learn a foreign language is to be immersed in the language and culture of the country where it is spoken, one of the best ways to learn medical language is to be immersed within a vibrant, authentic, modern health care community.

Medical Language for Modern Health Care helps students learn the terminology and language of modern health care in a way that bridges the gap between the classroom and the clinical setting.

HOW STUDENTS' NEEDS ARE MET

This book was designed with your needs in mind. You are a student preparing for a career as an allied health professional. You may have already had a few health care–related courses, or you may just be beginning your studies in the field. While your background and interests may differ, you share the need to understand medical terminology.

To make sure your needs were addressed in this book, we asked both students and experienced medical terminology instructors, "What helps students learn medical terminology?" Overwhelmingly, the responses pointed to three common factors:

- motivation to learn
- retention of the material
- opportunities for application and practice

THIS TEXTBOOK INCORPORATES FEATURES DESIGNED TO ADDRESS THESE THREE FACTORS.

Motivation to learn	→	In order for students to be motivated to learn, what they are learning must be meaningful and relevant. To ensure the chapters in *Medical Language for Modern Health Care* fit these criteria, the student is asked to step into the role of an allied health professional in each chapter. Authentic patient cases are used to illustrate how medical language is used on the job.
Retention of the material	→	To learn and remember something new, students must associate it with something they already know or have experienced. As the old saying goes, "Experience is the best teacher." When students encounter new medical terms within the context of a patient case, they are able to remember it more effectively. In addition, each chapter presents medical terms from one body system or medical specialty, which further serves to "tie it all together" to help students retain the knowledge and skills.
Opportunities for application and practice	→	Practice makes perfect. This is especially true for learning medical terminology. This textbook provides many opportunities for students to apply what they are learning. Exercises are included in the lessons, as well as at the end of each chapter. Additional exercises are available on the student CD-ROM and Online Learning Center.

HOW INSTRUCTORS' NEEDS ARE MET

When you use *Medical Language for Modern Health Care*, you will be supported at every point in the program. Each chapter in the book is broken down into lessons, and the Instructor's Manual provides lesson plans and additional materials for each lesson. Following are features of the textbook designed to address student needs:

Lesson-Based Approach

Each chapter of *Medical Language for Modern Health Care* is divided into lessons covering different aspects of the overall chapter subject. Lessons within a chapter break down into topics. Each topic is designed so your students will not have to flip back and forth when completing exercises or looking at figures, tables, and boxes. All main concepts and ideas presented in topics begin and end within a two-page "spread." These spreads help learning flow smoothly by ensuring that valuable class and reading time is not wasted on flipping pages.

You Are . . . Your Patient Is . . . Case Scenarios

Each chapter begins by immediately placing your students in the role of an allied health professional faced with a situation in which medical communication is necessary. Many different professional allied health and LPN-level nursing roles are utilized so your students can "experience" various specialties and positions. The patient cases introduced at the beginning of the chapters are referenced throughout the lessons to further unify the students' experience.

Chapter Outcomes and Lesson Objectives

The major learning outcomes for each chapter are previewed in the beginning so you and your students can focus on what they need to know and be able to do by the end of the chapter. Each lesson has outcome-based learning objectives. Accomplishing each lesson's objectives helps ensure students will be able to achieve the chapter outcomes and, ultimately, the goal of the textbook: to help them learn the terminology and language of modern health care.

Word Analysis and Definition Tables (WAD)

Each lesson contains tables listing important medical terms and their pronunciation, elements, and definition. Prefixes, suffixes, and combining forms are color-coded. These tables provide your students with an at-a-glance view of the terms covered. The tables are excellent for reference as well as for studying and reviewing.

End-of-Lesson and End-of-Chapter Exercises

At the end of each lesson is a series of exercises. The end-of-lesson exercises provide your students with immediate practice using the terms in the lesson. These exercises focus on basic understanding and ability to apply the terms. They are an excellent foundation for the end-of-chapter exercises, which are often based on authentic situations, such as interactions with patients, physicians, or medical documentation. The end-of-chapter exercises will require your students to understand, accurately apply, and think critically about the medical language they use. Throughout the text, frequent opportunities for application and reinforcement of medical language skills and concepts are provided to help your students build confidence and knowledge. A wide variety of exercises and activities is included to address different medical settings and levels of learning (including knowledge, comprehension, application, analysis, synthesis, and evaluation).

ACKNOWLEDGMENTS

The uniqueness, beauty, and high standards of this book are due to the skills and devotion of a team of people who worked closely and happily together. The team includes: Adrianne Rippinger, William Thomas and Jennifer Murphy of the Teleologic Learning Company, Patricia Gillivan of Triple SSS Press Media Development, and many talented people from McGraw-Hill Higher Education editorial and production. Our deepest thanks to all of them.

We would also like to thank the dedicated staff of Greater Annapolis Medical Group, Annapolis, Maryland, for opening their practice to our photography team.

David Allan

Karen Lockyer

Michelle Buchman

For insightful reviews, criticisms, helpful suggestions, and information, we would like to acknowledge the following:

Anita Dupre Althans, RNC, MSN
Our Lady of Holy Cross College
New Orleans, LA

Summer Aulich, CMA, BS
Ivy Tech State College
Evansville, IN

Christina L. Baumer, RN, Ph.D.,
CNOR, CHES
Lancaster General College of Nursing
and Health Sciences
Lancaster, PA

Nina Beaman, MS, BA, CMA, RN
Bryant and Stratton College
Richmond, VA

Paula Bostwick, RN, MSN
Ivy Tech State College—Northeast
Fort Wayne, IN

Teresa Bruno. BA
EduTek College
Stow, OH

Marcella Bucknam, BA
Clarkson College
Omaha, NE

William, J. Burke, BA
Madison Area Technical College
Madison, WI
Blackhawk Area Technical College
Monroe, WI

Denise Carsillo, RMA, MS
Lincoln College of Technology
West Palm Beach, FL

Jean M. Chenu, MS, BS
Genesee Community College
Batavia, NY

Sheila Maxell Cook, MT, LMT
Red Mountain Institute, Inc.
Homeland, AL

Barbara S. Desch, LVN, CPC, AHI
San Joaquin Valley College
Visalia, CA

Sheryl Daniel, BA, CMT, NMT, BMT
Infinite Healing Massage Therapy
Ft. Collins, CO

Angela Edwards, RN, BSN
Community Care College
Tulsa, OK

Pallavi Eswara, MS
Freelance Science Editor and Writer
State College, PA

Mary Fabink, MSN, M.Ed., RN, CEN
Milligan College
Milligan College, TN

George Fakhoury, MD, DORCP, CMA
Heald College
San Francisco, CA

Penny Fedje, RHIT
North Dakota State College of Science
Wahpeton, ND

Melinda J. Fernandez, AA, EMT-P,
NR-CMA, NR-RPT, B-Radiologist
Keiser Career College
Pembroke Pines, FL

Kathie Folsom, MS, BSN, RN
Whidbey Island Campus, Skagit Valley
College
Oak Harbor, WA

Mark W. Forquer, BS
Advanced Career Training
Jacksonville, FL

Margaret Schell Frazier, CMA, RN, BS
Formerly of Ivy Tech State College—
Northeast,
Ft. Wayne, IN

Eugenia M. Fulcher, RN, BSN, EdD, CMA
Eastern New Mexico University,
Roswell, NM

Tracie Fuqua, BS, CMA
Wallace State Community College
Hanceville, AL

Ron Gaines, MS, BS
Cameron University
Lawton, OK

Mary A. Harmon, BS, CMA, CPC
Med Tech College
Indianapolis, IN

Katherine Harper
Pellissippi State Technical Community
College
Knoxvile, TN

Katherine Hawkins, BS
Ivy Tech Community College
of Indiana
Columbus, IN

Barbara J. Hogg, MLT, RN, BSN
South Arkansas Community College
El Dorado, AR

Janet R. Hunter, MBA, MS, ABD
Northland Pioneer College
Holbrook, AZ

Judy Hurtt, M.Ed.
East Central Community College
Decatur, MS

Frances C. Hutson, MSN, RN
Louisiana Technical College
Natchitoches, LA

Sherry Jones, COTA/L
Sinclair Community College
Dayton, OH

Contextual Approach Promotes Active Learning

Chapters in the textbook are organized by body system in accordance with an overall anatomy and physiology (A & P) approach. Lessons introduce and define terminology through the context of A & P, pathology, and clinical and diagnostic procedures/tests. The organization of the body systems into chapters is based on an "outside to inside" sequence that reflects a physician's differential diagnosis method used during an examination.

To provide students with an authentic context, the medical specialty associated with each body area or system is introduced along with relevant anatomy and physiology. Students actually step into the role of an allied health professional associated with each specialty. Patient cases and documentation are used to illustrate the real-life application of medical terminology in modern health care: to care for and communicate with patients and to interact with other members of the health care team.

The A & P organizational approach, used in conjunction with an authentic medical setting and patient cases, encourages student motivation and facilitates active, engaged learning.

Innovative Pedagogical Aids Provide a Coherent Learning Program

Each chapter is structured around a consistent and unique framework of pedagogic devices. No matter what the subject matter of a chapter, the structure enables students to develop a consistent learning strategy, making *Medical Language for Modern Health Care* a superior learning tool.

YOU ARE . . . YOUR PATIENT IS

Each chapter opens by placing the student in the role of an allied health professional related to the specialty and associated body systems/areas covered by the chapter. The student is also introduced to a patient and given information about the patient's case.

LEARNING OUTCOMES

At the same time, **Learning Outcomes** are presented to let students know what they will learn in the chapter. This technique immediately engages students, motivating them to read on to learn how this patient's case (and their role in the patient's care) relates to the medical terminology being introduced in the chapter.

LESSON-BASED ORGANIZATION

The chapter content is broken down into chunks, or lessons, to help students digest new information and relate it to previously learned information. Rather than containing many various topics within a chapter, these lessons group the chapter material into logical, streamlined learning units designed to help students achieve the chapter outcomes. Lessons within a chapter build on one another to form a cohesive, coherent experience for the learner.

Each lesson is based on specific **Lesson Objectives** designed to support the students' achievement of the overall chapter outcomes.

Each lesson in a chapter contains an Introduction, Lesson Objectives, Lesson Topics, Word Analysis and Definition Tables, and Lesson Exercises. Within each lesson, all topics and information are presented in **self-contained two-page spreads**. This means students will no longer have to flip back and forth to see figures on one page that are described on another.

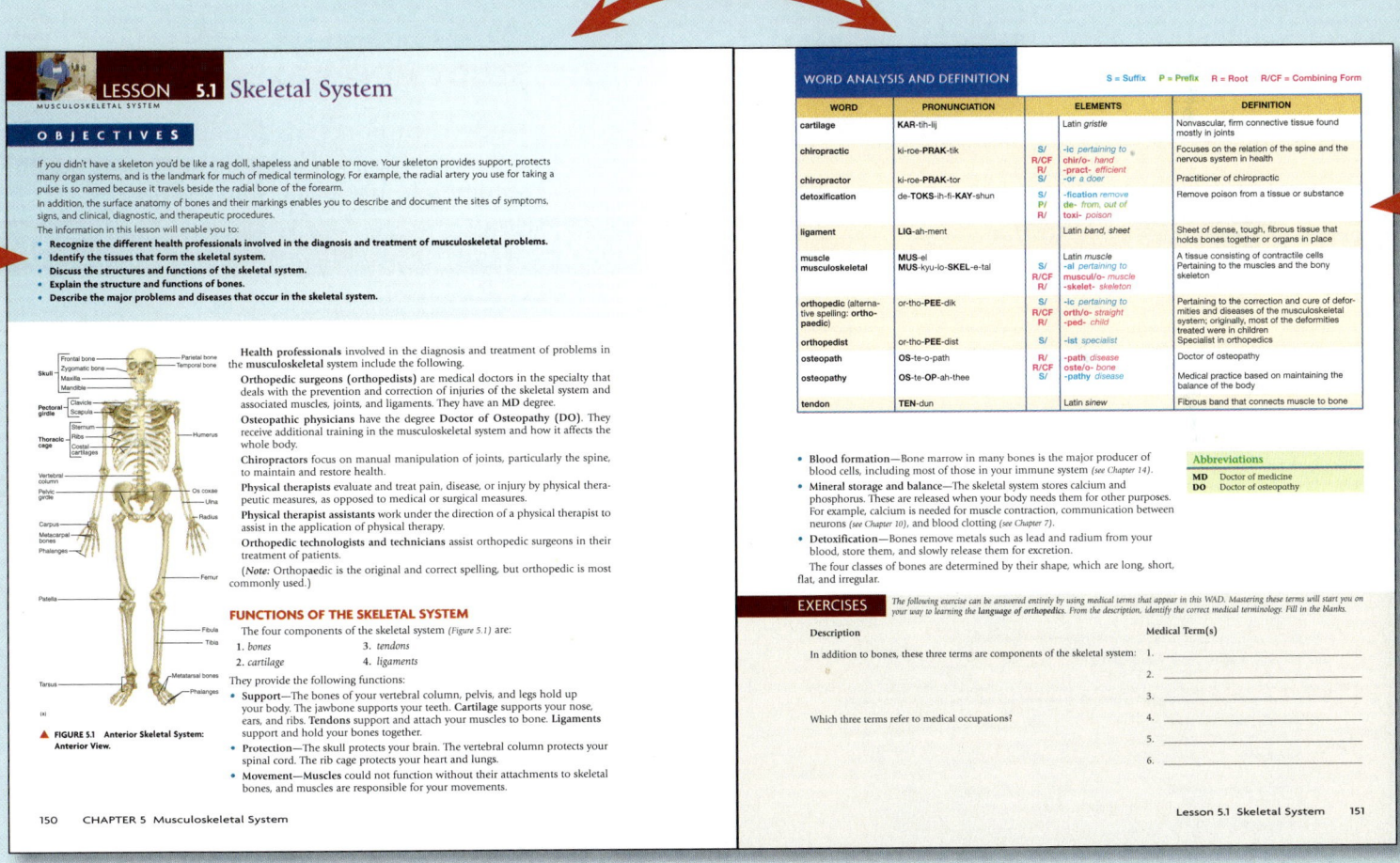

WORD ANALYSIS AND DEFINITION TABLES

The medical terms covered in each lesson are introduced in context, either within a patient case or in the lesson topics. To facilitate easy reference and review, the terms are also listed in tables as a group. The **Word Analysis and Definition (WAD) Tables** list the term and its pronunciation, elements, and definition in a concise, color-coded, at-a-glance format.

LESSON AND CHAPTER-END EXERCISES

Each lesson within a chapter ends with exercises designed to allow students to check their basic understanding of the terms they just learned. These "checkpoints" can be used by instructors as assignments or for self-evaluation by students.

At the end of each chapter you will find 10-15 pages of exercises that ask students to apply what they learned in all lessons of a chapter. These chapter-end exercises reinforce learning and help students go beyond mere memorization to think critically about the medical language they use. In addition to reviewing and recalling the definitions of terms learned in the chapter, students are asked to use medical terms in new and different ways to ensure a thorough understanding.

EXERCISES *After you deconstruct the following medical terms into their basic elements, provide a brief definition for each term. Fill in the chart, then fill in the blanks at the end of the exercise.*

Medical term	Prefix	Root/CF	Suffix	Definition of medical term
reduction				
alignment				
malunion				
hematoma				

Demonstrate your understanding of the terms by finishing this exercise.

1. Use *both* the terms **reduction** and **alignment** in *one* sentence.

2. The suffix **oma** also means *tumor*. Briefly explain why a hematoma is not a tumor.

3. Explain the difference between a **malunion** and a **nonunion** of a fracture.

STUDY HINT BOXES

Study Hint boxes are found throughout the review exercises. They reinforce and remind students to use basic study skills.

CHAPTER 5 REVIEW
MUSCULOSKELETAL SYSTEM

T. Choose the correct medical term(s) from the list to complete the sentence. You will not use all the terms.

striation	synthesis	detoxification	intervertebral discs
DMD	orthotic	opposition	pelvis
retinaculum	shoulder girdle	fascicle	acetabulum
popliteal fossa	traction	steroids	fibromyalgia

1. Line or streak across a muscle is called a _____.

2. Transverse, fibrous band on the wrist: _____

3. _____ support and cushion the vertebral column.

4. _____ has no known etiology, no laboratory tests for it, and no known treatment except pain management.

5. Movement that enables the thumb to touch the tips of the other fingers is called _____.

6. Cartilaginous joint between two bones: _____

7. Bundle of muscle fibers: _____

8. Dr. Stannard ordered continuous application of weight to the patient's broken leg. He has been placed in _____.

9. _____ cause skeletal muscle to hypertrophy.

10. The hollow at the back of the knee is called the _____.

U. Build your orthopedic terminology by completing the medical terms defined here. After you fill in the element on the line, write the type of element (prefix, root, combining form, suffix) you have used below the line. Fill in the blanks.

1. removing poison from tissue   de/ _____ / _____

2. bone disease   osteo/_____

3. projection above the condyle   _____ /condyle

4. membrane surrounding a bone   peri/ _____ / _____

5. region between diaphysis and epiphysis   _____ /physis

6. bones lacking in calcium   osteo/ _____

7. inflammation of bone tissue   osteo/ _____ /itis

8. collection of blood in tissues   _____ /oma

9. moving toward the midline   _____ /ion

10. fixation of a joint with surgery   arthro/ _____

V. Knowing the exact number of certain body parts, and their relative positions, will ensure precision in your medical documentation. Match the correct number to the correct term. Use one answer twice.

1. number of lumbar vertebrae _____   A. 7

2. number of bones in the vertebral column _____   B. 5

3. number of cervical vertebrae _____   C. 3

4. number of components in the axial skeleton _____   D. 12

5. number of regions in the vertebral column _____   E. 26

6. number of thoracic vertebrae _____

W. Could you explain the difference among these abnormal spinal curvatures to a patient if they ask?

Lordosis _____

Scoliosis _____

Kyphosis _____

Which one is the most common defect? _____

Which defect is seen in patients with osteoporosis? _____

> **Study Hint**
> Anything that is referred to as the most powerful, largest, smallest, most common, etc., is probably going to be a test question.

X. Functions of skeletal muscles: (add this to your outline) Bones and joints would get us nowhere without the muscles to move them. Illustrate how each of these functions is accomplished with skeletal muscles.

Function	How Function is Effected
Movement	
Posture	
Body Heat	
Respiration	
Communication	

> **Study Hint**
> To help you remember the functions, make up a sentence with each word (mnemonic) starting with the letters M, P, B, R, and C. *Example: Mr. Parker's Body Heat Rose Considerably.*

Y. Employ the *language of orthopedics* to answer the following questions about muscles.

1. What is muscle tone?

2. What is muscle contraction?

3. What is the difference between muscle atrophy and hypertrophy?

VIVID ILLUSTRATIONS AND PHOTOS

Colorful, precise anatomical illustrations and photos lend a realistic view of body structures and correlate to the clinical context of the lessons.

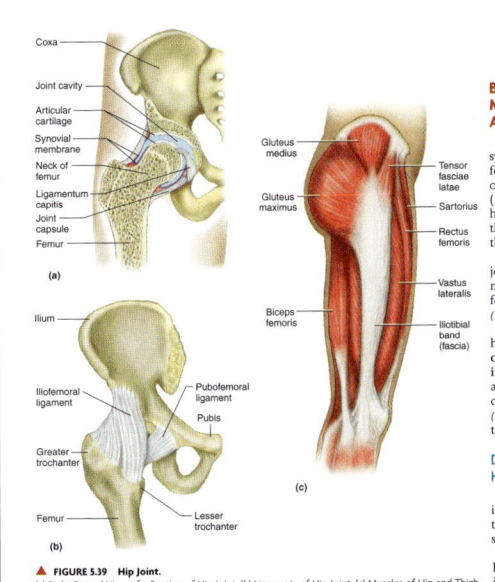

(a)

(b)

(c)

▲ **FIGURE 5.39 Hip Joint.**
(a) Right Frontal View of a Section of Hip Joint. (b) Ligaments of Hip Joint. (c) Muscles of Hip and Thigh (Lateral View).

BONES, JOINTS, AND MUSCLES OF THE HIP AND THIGH

The **hip joint** is a **ball-and-socket** synovial joint between the head of the femur and the cup-shaped **acetabulum** of the hip bone *(Figure 5.39a)*. A ligament (ligamentum capitis) attached to the head of the femur from the lining of the acetabulum carries blood vessels to the head of the femur to nourish it.

The joint is held in place by a thick joint **capsule** reinforced by strong ligaments that connect the neck of the femur to the rim of the acetabulum *(Figure 5.39b)*.

Powerful muscles that support the hip joint and move the thigh have their **origins** on the pelvic girdle and their **insertions** into the femur. Prominent among them are the three **gluteus** muscles, **maximus, medius,** and **minimus** *(Figure 5.39c)*, and the **adductor** muscles that run down the inner thigh.

Disorders and Injuries of the Hip Joint

Hip pointer, usually a football-related injury, is a blow to the rim of the pelvis that leads to bruising of the bone and surrounding tissues.

Osteoarthritis is common in the hip as a result of aging, weight bearing, and repetitive use of the joint. The cartilage on both the acetabulum and the head of the femur degenerates, and eventually there is total loss of the cartilage cushion. The resulting friction between the bones of the head of the femur and the acetabulum leads to pain and loss of mobility.

Rheumatoid arthritis can also affect the hip, beginning in the synovial membrane and progressing to destroy cartilage and bone.

Avascular necrosis of the femoral head is the necrosis (death) of bone tissue when the blood supply becomes avascular (is cut off), usually as a result of trauma.

Fractures of the neck of the femur occur as a result of a fall, most commonly in

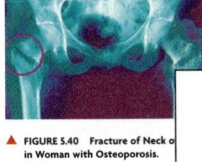

▲ FIGURE 5.40 Fracture of Neck of ... in Woman with Osteoporosis.

186   CHAPTER 5 Musc...

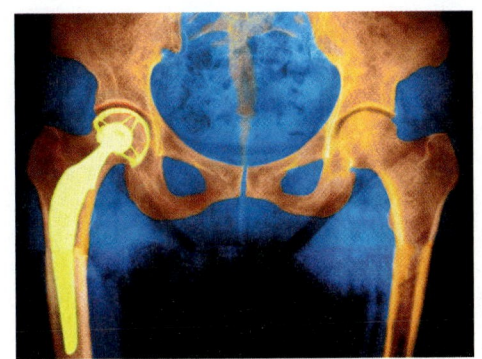

▲ **FIGURE 5.41   Total Hip Replacement.**
Colored X-Ray of Prosthetic Hip.

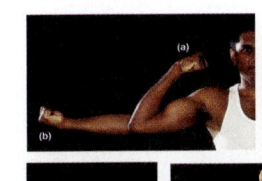

(a)

(b)

(c)

(d)

(e)

(f)

Abduction Adduction Abduction Adduction Abduction Adduction

Medial rotation Lateral rotation

Pronation Supination Circumduction

Eversion Inversion

▲ **FIGURE 5.15a, b   Movement of the Limbs**
(a) Abduction and adduction of the upper limb. (b) Abduction and adduction of the fingers.
FIGURE 5.15c
(c) Medial and Lateral Rotation of the Arm.
FIGURE 5.15d
(d) Circumduction.
FIGURE 5.15e
(e) Pronation and Supination of the Hand.
FIGURE 5.15f
(f) Eversion and Inversion of the Foot.

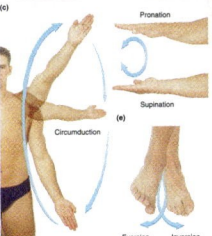

(a) (b) (d) (e) (f) (g) (h)

▲ Figure 5.14   Joint Flexion and Extension. (a) Flexion of the elbow. (b) Extension of the elbow. (c) extension of the wrist. (d) Neutral position of the wrist. (e) Flexion of the wrist. (f) Flexion of the spine. (g) Flexion of the shoulder. (h) Extension of shoulder.

JOINT MOVEMENT

Flexion and Extension of Joints

Flexion (bending) and **extension** (straightening) are shown in the elbow joint *(Figure 5.14a and b)*, in the wrist joint *(Figure 5.14c, d, and e)*, and in the shoulder joint *(Figure 5.14g and h)*.

For most of the rest of the body, flexion is movement of a body part *anterior* to the **coronal plane** *(see Chapter 2)*. Extension is movement *posterior* to the coronal plane. For example, when you bend your trunk forward, that is flexion *(Figure 5.14g)*. When you bend your trunk backward, that is extension *(see Figure 5.14g)*. When you bend your trunk sideways to the right or left, that is called *lateral flexion.*

Abduction and Adduction of Joints

Abduction is movement away from the midline. **Adduction** is movement toward the midline. Abduction of your arm is moving it sideways away from your trunk. Adduction is bringing it back to the side of your trunk *(Figure 5.15a)*. Abduction of your fingers is spreading them apart away from the middle finger. Adduction is bringing them back together *(Figure 5.15b)*.

Rotation of Joints

Rotation is to turn around an axis. Medial rotation of the upper arm bone, the humerus, with the elbow flexed brings the palm of the hand toward the body. Lateral rotation moves the palm away from the body *(Figure 5.15c)*.

Pronation and Supination

When you lie flat on the ground face down on your belly with your palms touching the ground, you are **prone**. When you lie flat on your back with your spine on the floor and your palms facing up, you are **supine**.

162   CHAPTER 5 Musculoskeletal System

TABLES

Meaningful tables aid in summarizing concepts and lesson topics.

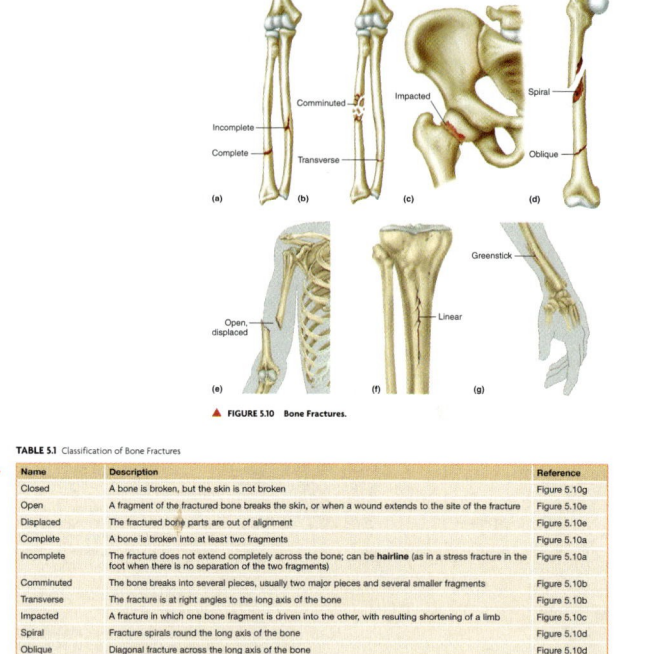

▲ FIGURE 5.10 Bone Fractures.

TABLE 5.1 Classification of Bone Fractures

Name	Description	Reference
Closed	A bone is broken, but the skin is not broken	Figure 5.10g
Open	A fragment of the fractured bone breaks the skin, or when a wound extends to the site of the fracture	Figure 5.10e
Displaced	The fractured bone parts are out of alignment	Figure 5.10e
Complete	A bone is broken into at least two fragments	Figure 5.10a
Incomplete	The fracture does not extend completely across the bone; can be **hairline** (as in a stress fracture in the foot when there is no separation of the two fragments)	Figure 5.10a
Comminuted	The bone breaks into several pieces, usually two major pieces and several smaller fragments	Figure 5.10b
Transverse	The fracture is at right angles to the long axis of the bone	Figure 5.10b
Impacted	A fracture in which one bone fragment is driven into the other, with resulting shortening of a limb	Figure 5.10c
Spiral	Fracture spirals round the long axis of the bone	Figure 5.10d
Oblique	Diagonal fracture across the long axis of the bone	Figure 5.10d
Linear	Fracture runs parallel to the long axis of the bone	Figure 5.10f
Greenstick (closed)	Partial fracture: one side breaks, the other bends	Figure 5.10g
Pathologic	Fracture occurs in an area of bone weakened by disease (such as cancer)	—
Compression	Fracture occurs in a vertebra from trauma or pathology leading to the vertebra being crushed	—

158   CHAPTER 5 Musculoskeletal System

KEYNOTES AND ABBREVIATIONS

Keynotes and Abbreviations offer students additional information correlating to the lesson.

BONE GROWTH AND STRUCTURE

Keynote

Minerals are deposited in bone when the supply is ample and released when they are needed elsewhere.

Factors that affect bone growth include:

1. **Genes**—determine the size and shape of bones and the ultimate adult height.
2. **Nutrition**—calcium and phosphorus are needed to develop good bone density.
3. **Exercise**—increases bone density and total bone mass.
4. **Mineral deposition**—calcium and phosphate are taken from plasma and deposited in bone.
5. **Mineral resorption**—calcium and phosphate are released from bone back into the plasma when they are needed elsewhere. For example, calcium is needed for muscle contraction, communication between neurons, and blood clotting. Phosphate is a component of DNA and RNA.
6. **Vitamins**—vitamin A activates osteoblasts; vitamin C is essential for collagen synthesis; vitamin D stimulates absorption, transport, and deposition of calcium and phosphate into bones *(see Chapter 21)*.
7. **Hormones**—for example, growth hormone stimulates the epiphyseal plate to calcify, and estrogen and testosterone accelerate bone growth after puberty and maintain bone density *(see Chapter 13)*.

Structure of Bones

Long bones are the most common type of bone in the body *(Figure 5.2)*.

The shaft of a long bone is called the **diaphysis**. Each end of the bone is called the **epiphysis** and is expanded to provide extra surface area for the attachment of ligaments and tendons.

Sandwiched between the diaphysis and epiphysis is a thin area called the **metaphysis**. Thin layers of cartilage cells in the **epiphyseal plate** enable the diaphysis (bone shaft) to grow in length. When growth stops, compact bone grows into the epiphyseal plate and forms the **epiphyseal line**.

A tough connective tissue sheath called **periosteum** covers the outer surface of all bones and is attached to the compact or **cortical** bone by tough collagen fibers. The periosteum protects the bone and anchors blood vessels and nerves to the surface of the bone.

The hollow cylinder inside the diaphysis is called the **medullary cavity**. It contains bone **marrow** and is lined by a thin membrane called the **endosteum**. The marrow is a fatty tissue that contains blood cells in different stages of development *(see Chapter 7)*.

The endosteum and periosteum contain **osteoblasts,** cells that produce the matrix of new bone tissue. This is called **osteogenesis**. Bone **matrix** consists of cells, collagen fibers, a gel that supports and suspends the fibers, and calcium phosphate crystals to give bone its hardness.

When osteoblasts are incorporated into the new bone, they become **osteocytes**. These cells, which maintain the matrix, reside in small spaces in the matrix called **lacunae**.

Osteoclasts are produced by the bone marrow. They dissolve calcium, phosphorus, and the organic components of the bone matrix. There is a continual balancing act going on as osteoclasts remove matrix and osteoblasts produce matrix. If osteoclasts out-perform the osteoblasts, then **osteoporosis** occurs, as with Mrs. Vargas in the case report.

All bones are well supplied with blood *(Figure 5.3)*. The blood vessels travel through the bone in a system of small **haversian (central) canals**. Because of its good blood supply, bone heals well.

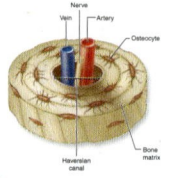

▲ FIGURE 5.2 Femur: Long Bone of the Thigh.

(a) Anterior view   (b) Interior view

▲ FIGURE 5.3 Blood Supply to Bone.

152   CHAPTER 5 Musculoskeletal System

Case Report 5.1 (continued)

On questioning, Mrs. Vargas demonstrated many of the risk factors for osteoporosis, including a family history, lack of exercise, cigarette smoking, inadequate diet, postmenopause, and increasing age.

DISEASES OF BONE

Osteoporosis results from a loss of bone density *(Figure 5.4)* when the rate of bone **resorption** exceeds the rate of bone **formation**. It is more common in women than in men, and its incidence increases with age. Ten million people in the United States already have osteoporosis, and 18 million more have low bone density (**osteopenia**) and are at risk for developing osteoporosis.

In women, production of the hormone estrogen decreases after menopause, and its protection against osteoclast activity is lost. This leads to fragile, brittle bones. In men, reduction in testosterone has a similar but less marked effect.

Women at risk for osteoporosis should have bone mineral density (**BMD**) screening using a dual-energy x-ray absorptiometry (**DEXA**) scan. Men and women over age 50 should take 1200 mg of calcium daily and 400 to 600 international units (**IU**) of vitamin D or expose the body to the sun for 15 minutes daily. Chapter 22 covers nutritional needs.

There are several U.S. Food and Drug Administration (**FDA**)–approved medications available for the treatment of osteoporosis. Most inhibit osteoclast activity.

Osteomyelitis is an inflammation of an area of bone due to bacterial infection, usually with a staphylococcus. Untreated tuberculosis can spread from its original infection in the lungs to bones via the blood stream to produce tuberculous osteomyelitis.

Osteomalacia, known as **rickets** in children, is a disease caused by vitamin D deficiency. When bones lack calcium, they become soft and flexible. They are not strong enough to bear weight and become bowed. Osteomalacia occurs in some developing nations and occasionally in this country when children drink soft drinks instead of milk fortified with vitamin D.

Achondroplasia occurs when the long bones stop growing in childhood but the bones of the axial skeleton are not affected *(Figure 5.5)*. This leads to short stature individuals who are about four feet tall. Intelligence and life span are normal. It is caused by a spontaneous gene mutation that then becomes a dominant gene for succeeding generations.

Osteogenic sarcoma is the most common malignant bone tumor. Peak incidence is between 10 and 15 years of age, and the tumor often occurs around the knee joint.

Osteogenesis imperfecta is a rare genetic disorder, producing very brittle bones that are easily fractured, often **in utero** (while inside the uterus) *(Figure 5.6)*.

▲ FIGURE 5.4 Normal Bone and Osteoporotic Bone.

▲ FIGURE 5.5 Achondroplastic Dwarf with College Roommate.

Abbreviations

BMD	bone mineral density
DEXA	dual energy x-ray absorptiometry
FDA	U.S. Food and Drug Administration
IU	international unit(s)

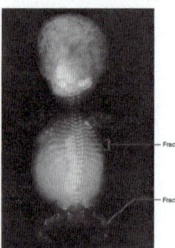

FIGURE 5.6 Osteogenesis Imperfecta *in utero* Showing Fractured Rib and Thigh Bones. ▶

154   CHAPTER 5 Musculoskeletal System

ONLINE LEARNING CENTER (OLC)

www.mhhe.com/allanmedlanguage

This online resource offers an extensive array of quizzing and learning tools that will help students master the topics covered in their textbook.

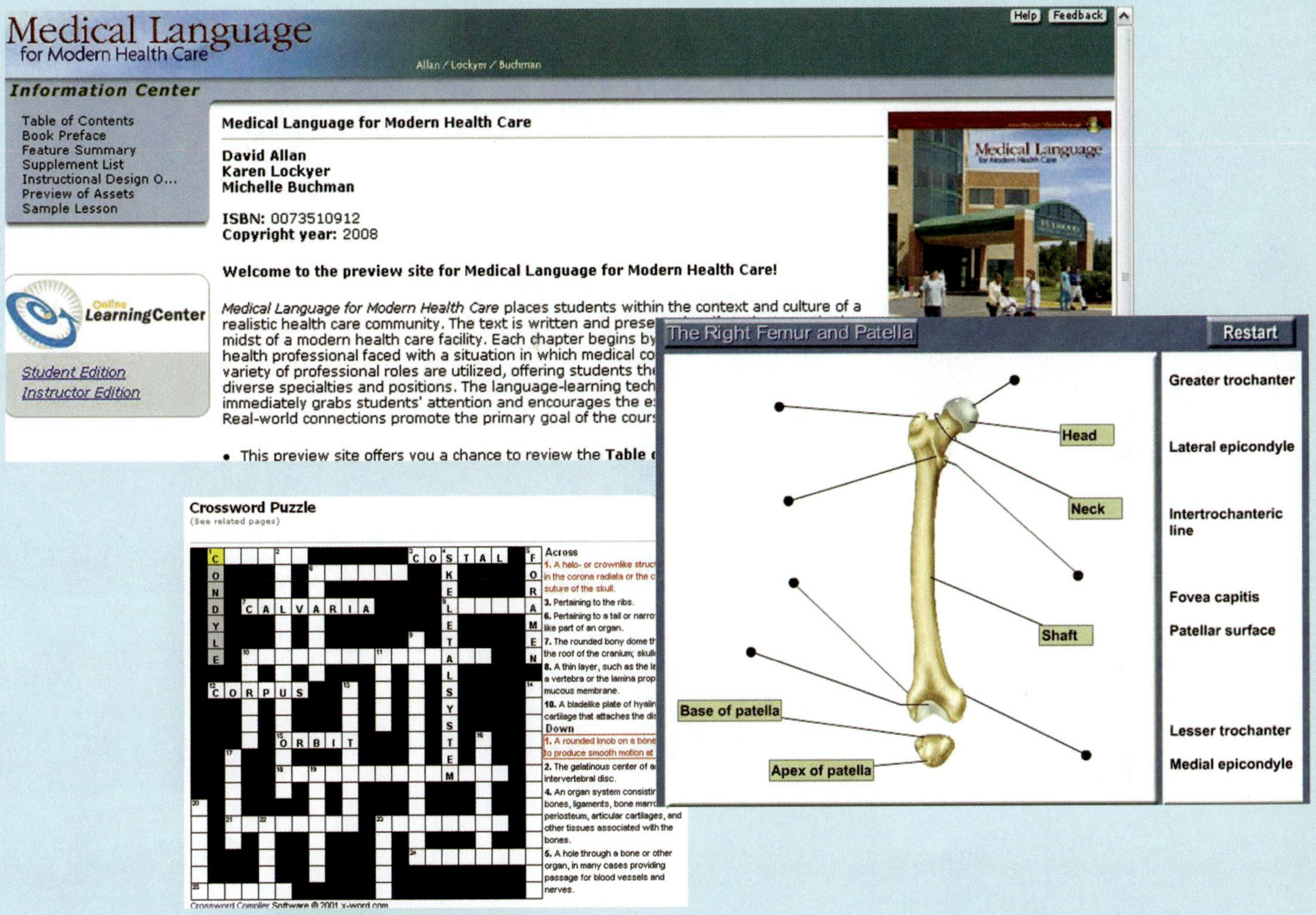

STUDENT CD-ROM

Consider this student CD-ROM to be a personal study partner for medical terminology. This study tool is packed with hundreds of learning exercises designed to help students learn what they need to learn. The exercises are not assessments. They will, however, provide multiple opportunities for practice and the mastery of core concepts.

The student CD is designed to:

- Help students learn medical terms, including specifically their definitions, roots, prefixes and suffixes, plus accurate spelling.
- Help students understand the meaning and use of medical terms.
- Help students learn how and when to correctly apply medical terms in written and verbal communication.

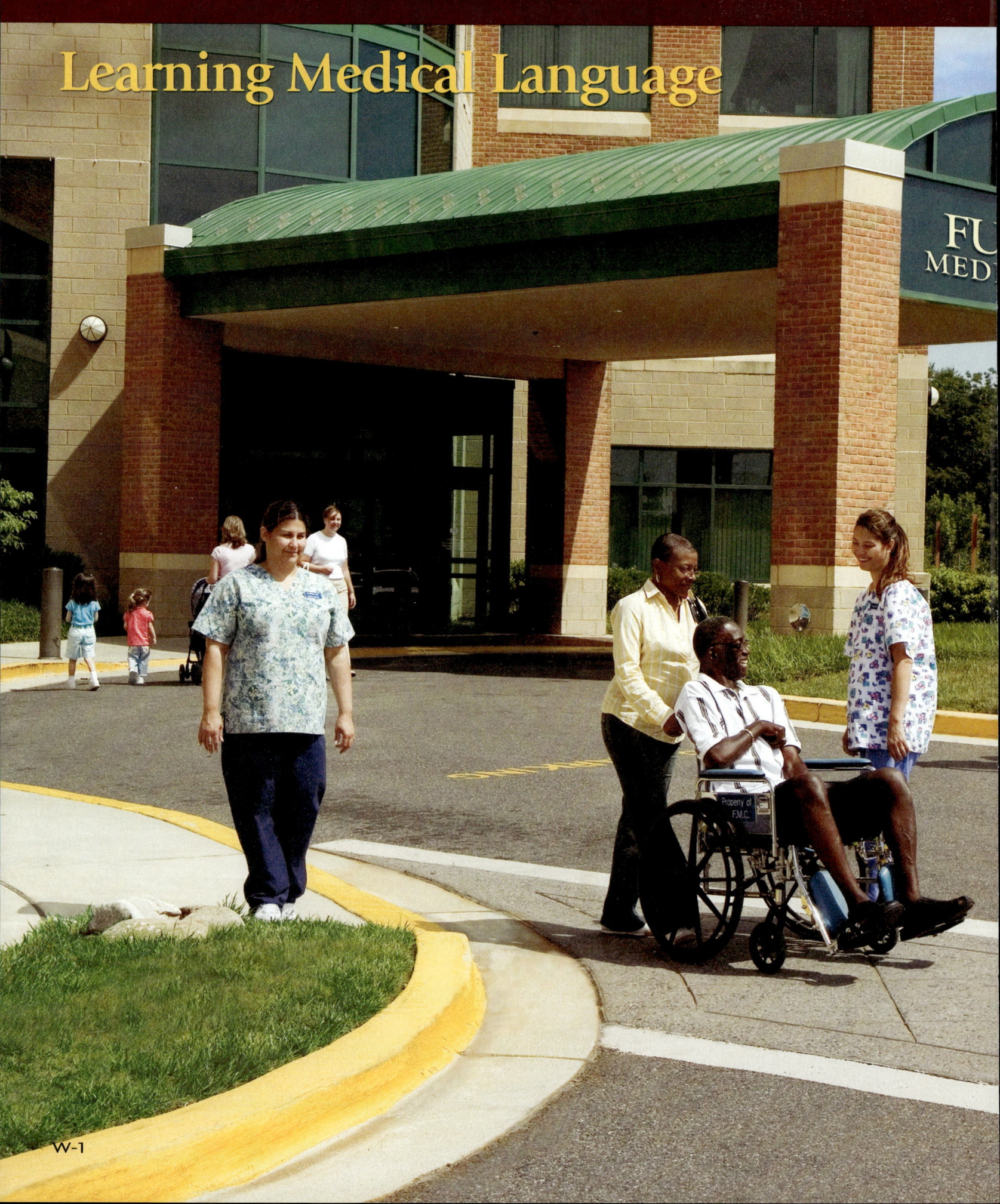

Learning Medical Language

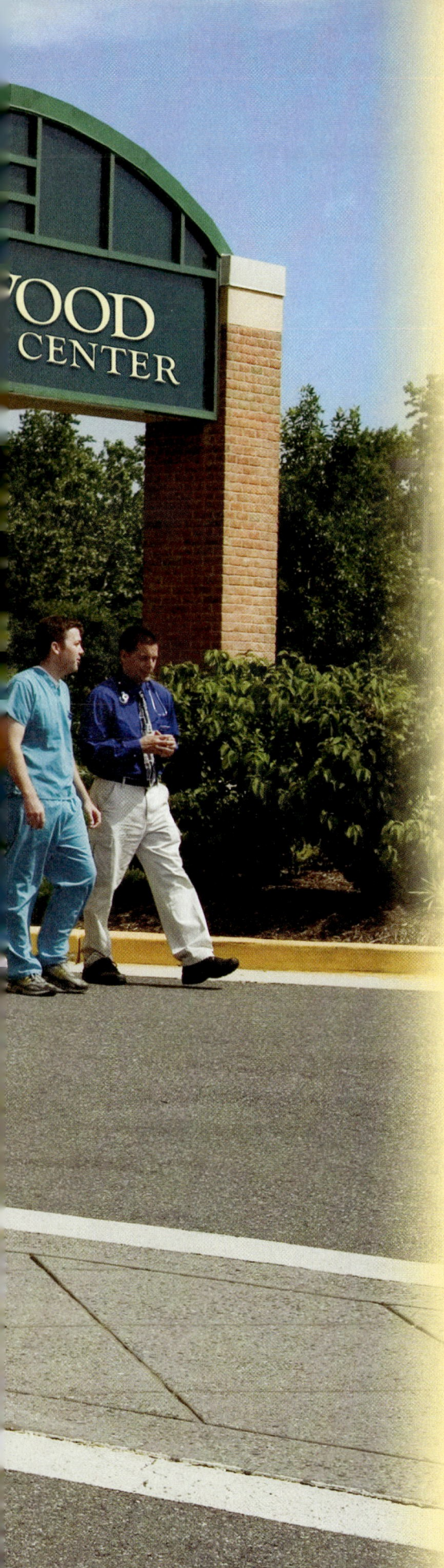

Welcome

CASE REPORT W.1

You are

. . . a student preparing for a career as an allied health professional. As a part of your training program, you must complete a supervised externship. You have just arrived at Fulwood Medical Center for your first day as an extern. You are glad to have this opportunity: Fulwood is a busy center with highly skilled, compassionate staff members. Between attending classes at night, working during the day, and raising two children, you have a full schedule. However, the knowledge and skills you are learning in your studies, and at Fulwood, will prepare you for a successful future.

Learning Outcomes

Your journey through this book, and your externship at Fulwood Medical Center, begin with getting to know the surroundings in which you will experience medical language. In order to get the most out of your experience, you need to:

- Understand the role of various members of the health care team so that you can progress through the medical specialties covered in this book.

- Become familiar with the realistic health care context used in this book to help you learn medical terminology.

- Comprehend the value of learning medical terminology in a realistic setting.

- Recognize the importance of effective study and organizational strategies to becoming a lifelong learner.

- Develop effective study habits.

LESSON W.1 Orientation to Fulwood Medical Center

OBJECTIVES

The information in this lesson will enable you to:

- **Identify members of the health care team.**
- **Recognize the distinguishing features of Fulwood Medical Center and its role in your study of medical terminology.**
- **Explain the importance of learning medical terminology in a realistic setting.**

▲ **FIGURE W.1** A Busy Medical Practice at Fulwood Medical Center.

▲ **FIGURE W.2** The primary care physician refers patients to specialists when necessary.

▲ **FIGURE W.3** Physicians and medical assistants provide direct care to patients.

THE HEALTH CARE TEAM

Fulwood Medical Center is a realistic health care setting *(Figure W.1)* that allows you to experience the use of medical language. Each chapter in this book focuses on the medical terminology used in a specific medical specialty and the body systems, pathology, and medical procedures related to that specialty. A variety of health care professionals make up the teams caring for patients in each medical specialty.

As an **allied health professional,** you are part of a team of medical and other professionals who provide health care services designed to improve the health and well-being of their patients.

The team leader is a medical doctor, or physician, who can be an **MD** (doctor of medicine) or a **DO** (doctor of osteopathy). Most **managed care systems** require the patient to have a **primary care physician** *(Figure W.2)*. This physician can be a **family practitioner, internist,** or **pediatrician** (for children) and is responsible for the continuing overall care of the patient. In managed care, the primary care physician acts as the "gatekeeper" for the patient to enter the system, supervising all care the patient receives.

If needed medical care is beyond the expertise of the primary care physician, the patient is referred to a medical specialist whose expertise is based on a specific body system or even a part of a body system. For example, a **cardiologist** has expertise in diseases of the heart and vascular system, whereas a **dermatologist** specializes in diseases of the skin and an **orthopedist** in problems with the musculoskeletal system. A **gastroenterologist** is an expert in diseases of the whole digestive system, whereas a **colorectal surgeon** specializes only in diseases of the lower gastrointestinal tract.

Other health professionals work under the supervision of the physician and provide direct care to the patient *(Figure W.3)*. These can include a **physician assistant, nurse practitioner, medical assistant,** and, in specialty areas, a variety of therapists, technologists, and technicians with expertise in the use of specific therapeutic and diagnostic tools.

Still other health professionals on the team provide indirect patient care *(Figure W.4)*. These include **administrative medical assistants, transcriptionists, health information technicians, medical insurance billers,** and **coders,** all of whom are essential to providing high-quality patient care.

As you study the language of each medical specialty at Fulwood Medical Center, you will also meet the members of each specialty's health care team and learn more about their roles in caring for the patient.

FIGURE W.4 Administrative medical assistants ▶ are among the health care professionals who provide indirect care to patients.

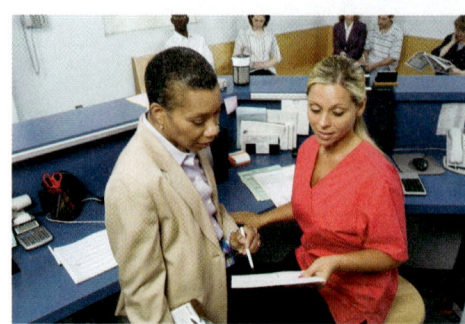

Case Report W.1 (continued)

In the lobby, the Supervisor of Externship Programs welcomes you and tells you about Fulwood Medical Center. You learn that Fulwood consists of this medical office building and the attached 250-bed hospital. The office building houses physicians practicing primary care, the major medical specialties, and some complementary medicine therapies—in all nearly 100 physicians in 25 specialty areas. The hospital and the medical offices share, pharmacy, laboratory, radiology, physical therapy, health education, and cafeteria facilities, but they have separate main entrances. The supervisor points out the directory on the wall, which lists all of the departments and doctors (Figure W.5). This orientation to Fulwood Medical Center makes you realize how fortunate you are to be here, learning and practicing your skills in a wide variety of medical settings and with a diverse group of patients and health care team members. You can't wait to get started.

This book goes beyond simply presenting and defining new medical terms. Fulwood Medical Center, with its wide range of patient cases, health professionals, and realistic medical environment, allows you to encounter and discover terms the way they are used in real life: in the different medical settings. Experiencing medical language in this context bridges the gap between what you learn in the classroom and what really happens in the clinical setting.

As you progress through this book,

- You will encounter, and be asked to interact with, patients and health care professionals.
- You will analyze medical records and documentation.
- You will be introduced to diagnostic and therapeutic methods, and the pathophysiology of disease.

Ultimately, you will be able to see how all of these activities depend upon effective communication, accurate comprehension, and precise use of medical language.

FIGURE W.5 The office directory can help orient visitors within the medical office complex.

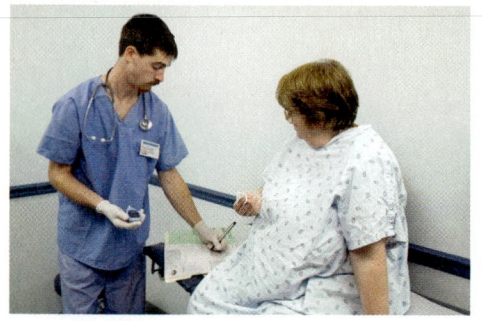

▲ **FIGURE W.6** The CMA interviews the patient to learn more about her condition.

ACTIVELY EXPERIENCING MEDICAL LANGUAGE

Medical terms were created to provide health care professionals a way to communicate with each other and to document the care they provide. To provide effective patient care, all health care professionals must be fluent in medical language. One misused or misspelled medical term on a patient record can cause errors that can result in injury or death to patients, incorrect coding or billing of medical claims, and possible fraud charges.

When medical terms are separated from their intended context, as they are in other medical terminology textbooks, it is easy to lose sight of how important it is to use them accurately and precisely. Learning medical terminology in the context of the medical setting reinforces the importance of correct usage.

During your externship at Fulwood Medical Center, you will *experience* medical language. Just like in a real medical center, you will encounter and apply medical terminology in a variety of ways. Actively experiencing medical language will help ensure you are truly learning, and not simply memorizing, the medical terms in each chapter. Memorizing a term allows you to use it in the same situation (e.g., repeating a definition) but doesn't help you apply it in new situations. Whether you are reading chart notes in a patient's medical record or a description of the treatment prescribed by a physician, you will see medical terms being used for the purpose they were intended.

Here are just a few examples you witness on your first day at Fulwood while observing a patient encounter between Luis Guitterez, a Certified Medical Assistant (CMA), and Mrs. Jones, a patient.

Listening and Speaking

You will:

- Listen to patients describing their medical history and explaining their symptoms *(Figure W.6)*. A sample conversation between a medical assistant and patient follows:

> **Luis Guitterez, CMA:** "Mrs. Jones, I'm Luis, an assistant to Dr. Lee. The receptionist noticed that you were looking pale and sweaty and notified Dr. Lee."
>
> **Mrs. Jones:** "In the rush to get here this morning, Luis, I didn't have time to eat breakfast. I'm not feeling so well right now...I'm diabetic, you know."
>
> **Luis Guitterez, CMA:** "Dr. Lee has asked me to test your blood sugar. As a diabetic, I'm sure you've done this many times yourself."

- Listen to and carry out physicians' instructions and information concerning patient care.
- Speak to physicians and other health care professionals to report information and ask questions.
- Talk with patients in the course of patient encounters and phone calls, giving instructions and answering questions about the physician's prescribed treatment plans.

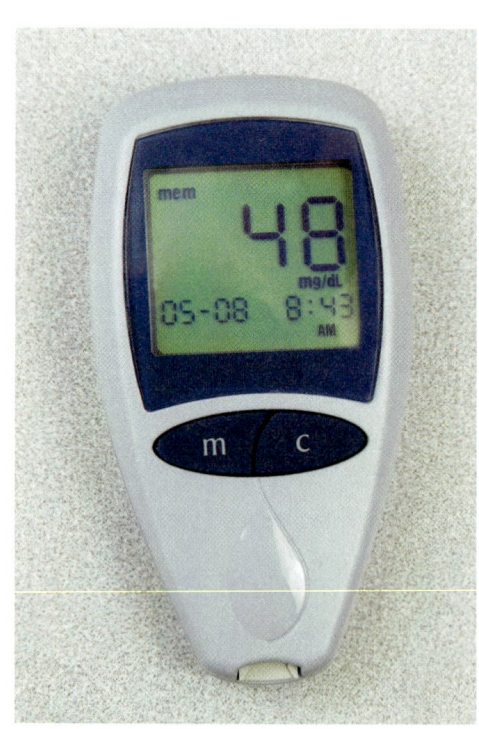

▲ **FIGURE W.7** One of your responsibilities may be to read the results of diagnostic tests.

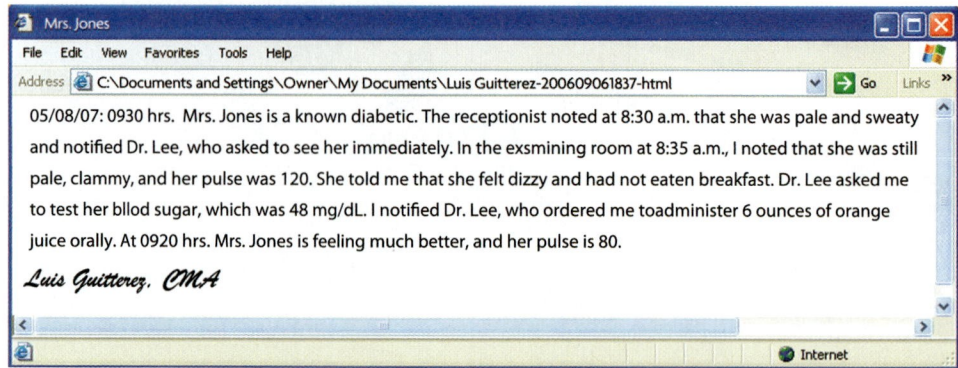

05/08/07: 0930 hrs. Mrs. Jones is a known diabetic. The receptionist noted at 8:30 a.m. that she was pale and sweaty and notified Dr. Lee, who asked to see her immediately. In the exsmining room at 8:35 a.m., I noted that she was still pale, clammy, and her pulse was 120. She told me that she felt dizzy and had not eaten breakfast. Dr. Lee asked me to test her bllod sugar, which was 48 mg/dL. I notified Dr. Lee, who ordered me toadminister 6 ounces of orange juice orally. At 0920 hrs. Mrs. Jones is feeling much better, and her pulse is 80.

Luis Guitterez, CMA

▲ **FIGURE W.8** It is important to proofread documentation to ensure its accuracy.

Reading

You will:

- Read physicians' comments and treatment plans in patient medical records and case reports.
- Read the results of physical examinations, procedures, and laboratory and diagnostic tests *(Figure W.7)*.

Writing

You will:

- Document actions taken by yourself and other members of the health care team *(Figure W.8)*.
- Proofread medical documentation to ensure its accuracy.

Thinking Critically

You will:

- Evaluate medical documentation for accuracy *(Figure W.9)*.
- Translate technical medical communication into words patients can understand.
- Analyze unfamiliar medical terms using the strategies presented in this book.

Learning from Patient Cases

You will encounter realistic patient cases throughout this book. These cases ask you to step into the role of a health care professional *(You are…)* and focus on a real patient with real health care needs *(Your patient is…)*.

Taking full advantage of the patient cases in this book allows you to:

- Experience various allied health care careers.
- Examine the roles you may fill to provide care for patients.
- See the types of documentation needed in these situations.
- Become acquainted with medical terminology in real-life settings.

Applying What You Learn

Throughout each chapter, you will be asked to apply and practice what you are learning. These application opportunities are designed to give you practice using medical terms in a variety of ways and for a variety of purposes. Specifically, the exercises will require you to perform tasks you would perform on the job, such as *listening and speaking, reading, writing,* and *thinking critically*. They are designed to help you move beyond simple memorization and become fluent in the language of modern health care.

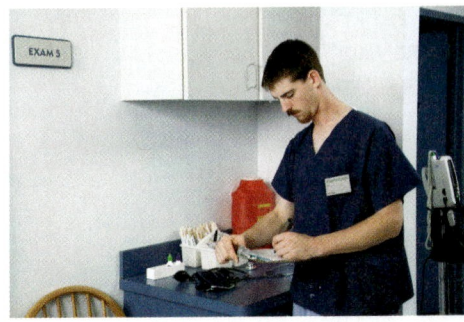

▲ **FIGURE W.9** Your knowledge of medical terminology will help you understand your patients' medical records.

EXERCISE

Each encounter with medical language improves your ability to (a) understand the medical terms you hear, (b) speak accurately and precisely using medical terms, (c) write accurately and precisely using medical terms, (d) read and understand medical terms, and (e) think critically about the medical terms you experience. These five skills are very important for all health care professionals. It is important to be able to identify experiences that build your knowledge and skill with medical language. Write the letter of the skill or skills being used in each blank below. More than one skill may be needed for each activity.

Skills: a. understand spoken medical terms

      b. speak accurately and precisely with medical terms

      c. read and understand medical terms

      d. write accurately and precisely with medical terms

      e. think critically about medical language

      f. translate medical terms into nonmedical language

_____ 1. answering a patient's questions about the physician's diagnosis and instructions

_____ 2. taking a phone message when a specialist calls from another facility and has information concerning one of the patients of a physician in your facility

_____ 3. proofreading an insurance claim form

_____ 4. teaching a patient with special nutritional needs how to modify her diet

_____ 5. using the Internet and textbooks to learn more about a family member's disease or condition

LESSON W.2 Learning Medical Language

OBJECTIVES

The information in this lesson will enable you to:

- **Recognize the need for a solid understanding of medical terminology.**
- **Justify the need to become a lifelong learner.**
- **Apply organizational and study strategies to help you succeed.**

FIGURE W.10 Electronic report of a patient's condition.

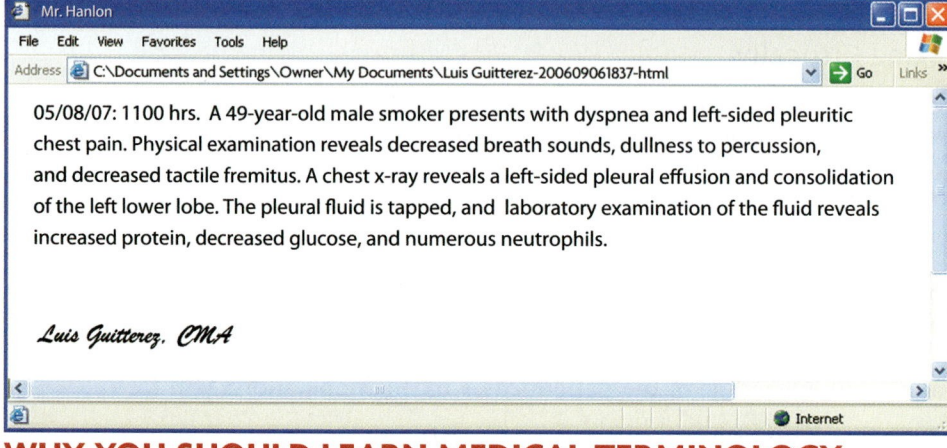

05/08/07: 1100 hrs. A 49-year-old male smoker presents with dyspnea and left-sided pleuritic chest pain. Physical examination reveals decreased breath sounds, dullness to percussion, and decreased tactile fremitus. A chest x-ray reveals a left-sided pleural effusion and consolidation of the left lower lobe. The pleural fluid is tapped, and laboratory examination of the fluid reveals increased protein, decreased glucose, and numerous neutrophils.

Luis Guitterez, CMA

WHY YOU SHOULD LEARN MEDICAL TERMINOLOGY

Medical terminology is not just another subject for which you memorize the facts and then forget them when you move on to the next course. Medical language will be used throughout your studies, as well as every day on your job. Nothing you hear or read in your studies or in a health care setting will make sense without an understanding of medical terminology. Once you learn the language, however, the world of health care is open to you to explore—and understand.

Even beyond your career goals, everyone is a patient at one time or another. You may also accompany an elderly parent, friend, or child to a doctor or emergency room. Knowing medical terminology makes it easier for you to communicate with physicians and use the Internet to research health information—and ultimately to become a proactive medical consumer.

Figure W.10 shows an electronic report of a patient's condition: something you have to understand as a health professional. Terms like **dyspnea, pleuritic, effusion,** and **neutrophils** are used every day in medical language.

Healthcare professionals use specific terms to describe and talk about objects and situations they encounter each day. Like every language, medical terminology is changing as new knowledge is discovered. For example, in genetics, today's terminology was unheard of a decade ago. Medical terms become outdated as new knowledge explodes. **Consumption** is now known as **tuberculosis, grippe** as **influenza,** and **whooping cough** as **pertussis.**

Modern medical terminology is an artificial language constructed over centuries by using words and elements from Greek and Latin origins as its building blocks. Some 15,000 or more words are formed from 1200 Greek and Latin roots. It serves as an international language, enabling medical scientists from different countries and in different medical fields to communicate with a common understanding.

In your world as a health care professional, medical terminology enables you to communicate with your team leader, with the other health care professionals on your team, and with other professionals in different disciplines outside your team. Understanding medical terminology also enables you to translate the medical terms into language your patients can understand, improving the quality of their care and demonstrating your professionalism.

In short, if you can't speak the language, you can't join the club *(Figure W.11)*.

▲ **FIGURE W.11** Every profession has its own language. You may have difficulty understanding your auto mechanic when he tells you that the expansion valve, evaporator core, and orifice tubes in your air-conditioning system need to be replaced.

Lifelong Learning

No matter where you are in your life's journey—an infant trying to walk, a child beginning school, an adolescent working in your first job, a parent changing a diaper, an adult watching television, a grandparent playing with your grandchild—every day provides numerous opportunities for learning. If you actively absorb each piece of learning as it becomes available, you form a foundation on which you can build your continually increasing body of knowledge and experience *(Figure W.12)*.

Your current training in medical terminology is necessary for you to be able to continue your education in health care, but it is important to realize that school is just one of the many places where you acquire knowledge. Each time you solve a problem in life, such as working through an argument with a friend or helping your child perform better in school, the knowledge you gain is *your own* answer to *your own* problem. This type of knowledge—discovered through experience—is genuine, real, and trustworthy for you. It is not like what you learned in school, which was determined by some distant authority. Your medical terminology instructor isn't likely to ask a test question on how to unclog your sink. Instead, this type of learning is driven by your needs and goals. The authentic knowledge you gain from solving your own problems, whether by yourself or with the help of other people or resources, motivates you to acquire still more knowledge and helps you grow as a person and as a professional.

When working as a health care professional, your ongoing education is an integral and inseparable part of your work activities. Additional classroom training will be needed to keep your skills and professional knowledge up to date. You will also continue to learn on your own through experience. As a health care professional, every time you interact with a patient, read a report, or talk with your team leader or peers, you are given another opportunity to learn.

Everything you do in life results in learning. Your own experience and judgment become your most valuable resources to make your life vivid, strong, creative, and ultimately, what *you* want it to be. Take advantage of these resources, and use them to maximize your professional and personal success.

As novelist Lillian Smith once said, *"When you stop learning, stop listening, stop looking and asking questions, always new questions, then it is time to die."*

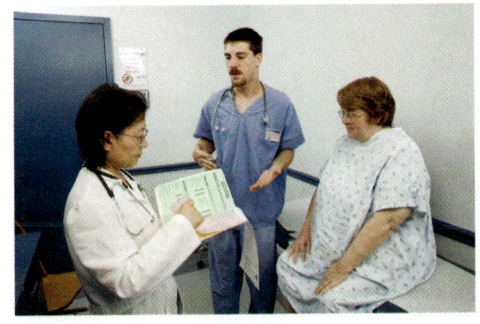

▲ **FIGURE W.12** Learning doesn't stop when you leave the classroom; every time you interact with other health care professionals and patients, you have the opportunity to learn something.

| **EXERCISE** | *Reflect on the idea of "lifelong learning" and how you can make it work for you to enrich your life's experience. Think about one instance in your life when something you learned (by yourself, from another person, from research, etc.) became the foundation upon which you built further learning and information. Some examples are how to paint a room, clean a fish, use a computer, and cook a meal. Briefly describe that here.* |

_____

_____

_____

Now describe why you need to be committed to learning from everyday experiences on the job, and how that can help you in your career.

_____

_____

_____

▲ An Evening at Home.

Case Report W.1 (continued)

Your first day at Fulwood Medical Center went very well. The supervisor gave you a tour of the facilities and introduced you to several health care professionals with whom you will be working. You and she talked about your duties and expectations, as well as your plan for keeping up with your studies. Now it's 7:15 p.m., and you have yet to feed your kids and get them into bed, not to mention pick up around the house, pay some bills, and, oh yes, review a whole chapter in your medical terminology textbook to prepare for a test at class tomorrow night. How are you going to do all of this?

STUDY STRATEGIES

- Recognize the stresses you are under.
- Determine what you can change because the situation, people, and events are making excessive demands on you.
- Prioritize mentally and handle each task in the order of importance.

In this case, eat a healthy meal with your kids, enjoy putting them to bed, pay the bills, then take some deep breaths to relax (or meditate) for 10 minutes. When you feel more relaxed, settle down to review the text, and then go to bed at a reasonable hour. Picking up the house will have to wait since studying and sleeping are a higher priority. Sound too easy? What other choices do you have to be able to study in an effective way?

- Find ways to give yourself a break from stressful situations.

If you know you have a test every Thursday night, ask your spouse, mother, your sister, a friend, or someone in your support group to come and put the kids to bed Wednesday night while you go to their house or to the library and study. If nothing else is possible, just squeezing in 10 minutes to sit quietly and relax can make a difference in your stress level. A support group from family and friends is essential to your success, so look for ways to surround yourself with people you can trust and rely upon.

This lesson contains strategies you can use to get focused. It will help you learn how to manage your time and your studies to succeed—but this lesson can't do it alone. You are what you put into your studies. You have a lot of time and money invested in your education. Don't blow it now by only putting in half of the effort this class requires. Succeeding in this class, and in life, requires the following:

- Committing with your time and perseverance
- Knowing and motivating yourself
- Getting organized
- Scheduling and managing your time
- Being an active learner

The rest of this lesson will help you learn how to be effective in these areas so that, as you encounter new learning situations during your externship at Fulwood, you will be prepared to handle them.

Committing with Your Time and Perseverance

Understanding—and mastering—what you learn in the classroom and during your externship at Fulwood Medical Center will take time, as well as patience. Nothing worthwhile comes easily. Be committed to your studies, and you will reap the benefits in the long run.

Consider this: your training in health care is building the foundation for your future career. Sloppy and hurried craftsmanship now will only lead to difficulties later. A few years of committed study time now is nothing compared to the lifetime that awaits you.

Knowing and Motivating Yourself

What type of learner are you? When are you most productive? Know yourself and your limits, and work within them *(Figure W.13)*. Know how to motivate yourself to give your all to your studies and achieve your goals. You are the one who benefits most from your success. If you lack self-motivation and drive, you are the first person who suffers.

Know yourself. Just as there are many types of learners, there is no right or wrong way of learning. Into which category do you fall?

Visual learner—You respond best to "seeing" processes and information. Take advantage of the strengths of your learning style by doing the following:

- Focus on text illustrations and charts, as well as course handouts.
- Check to see if there are animations on the course or text website to help you.
- Consider drawing diagrams in your notes to illustrate concepts.
- Use the contextual and labeling exercises on the interactive student CD-ROM.

Auditory learner—You work best by listening to processes and information. Take advantage of the strengths of your learning style by doing the following:

- Listen carefully to—and possibly tape record (with instructor permission)— the lecture.
- Talk information through with a study partner.
- Listen to audio pronunciations of terms on the interactive student CD-ROM.

Tactile/kinesthetic learner—You learn best by working "hands on." Take advantage of the strengths of your learning style by doing the following:

- Apply what you have learned in a role play or realistic scenario.
- Think of ways to apply your critical thinking skills in application-based ways.
- The course text website and interactive student CD-ROM will also help you.

In addition to these suggestions, here are a few helpful hints for students of all learning styles:

- Ask questions to make sure you understand what you hear, read, and do.
- Rephrase what you have heard in lecture and read in the text as you talk with your peers.
- Study with a partner to help you stay committed and double-check your understanding of concepts.

▲ **FIGURE W.13** Identify your own personal preferences for learning, and seek out the resources that will best help you with your studies. Recognize your weaknesses, and try to compensate for or work to improve them.

| EXERCISE | *Take time to assess your learning style and use that to aid your study and classroom habits. Briefly describe the type of learner you are, and which of those strengths in that style work best for you:* |

I am a _____ learner.

This works best for me:

_____

_____

_____

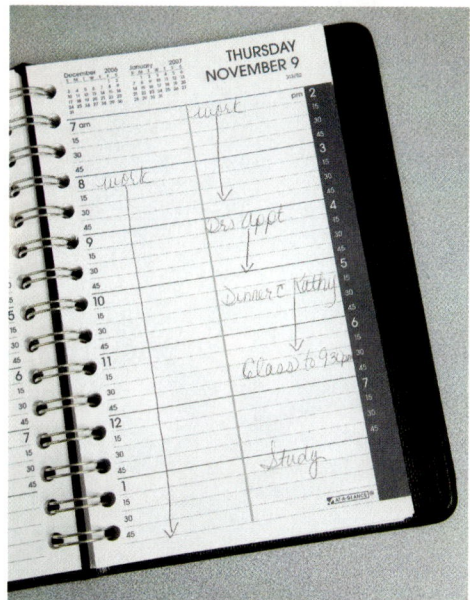

FIGURE W.14 Use a daily planner to organize school, work, family, and leisure time.

Getting Organized

It seems the more organized you are, the easier things come. This will definitely be the case as you proceed through this class and your externship at Fulwood. Take time now to look around and analyze your life and your study habits. Get organized now, and you'll find you have a little more time—and a lot less stress.

Find a calendar system that works for you.   The best kind is one that you can take with you everywhere. To be truly organized, you should integrate all aspects of your life into this one calendar—school, work, family, and leisure *(Figure W.14)*. Some people also find it helpful to have an additional monthly calendar posted in a convenient place (e.g., on the refrigerator) for "at a glance" dates and to have a visual of what is to come. If you do this, be sure you are consistently synchronizing both calendars so you do not miss anything. (More tips for organizing your calendar can be found in the Scheduling and Managing Your Time section below.) Some sample entries follow:

Thursday

- Work from 8:00 a.m. to 3:30 p.m.
- Doctor's appointment from 4:00 to 4:45
- Dinner from 5:15 to 6:15
- Class from 6:30 to 9:30
- Study from 10:00 to 10:30

Keep everything for your course or courses in one place—and at your fingertips.   A three-ring binder works well because it allows you to add or organize handouts and notes from class in any order you prefer. Incorporating your own custom tabs helps you flip instantly to the material you need.

Find your space.   Find a place that helps you be organized and focused. If it is a desk or table at home, keep it clean. Clutter adds confusion and stress, and it wastes time. If there are small children in your home, be sure your study materials are kept out of reach. If your "space" is at the library or a relative's house, keep a backpack or bag fully stocked with your text, binder or notes, pens, highlighters, sticky notes, phone numbers of study partners, and anything else you might need.

Scheduling and Managing Your Time

There is never enough time in the week to get everything done. This makes managing your time one of the most difficult tasks to successfully master.

Valuable time can easily be lost. Here are just a few ways time slips away unnoticed:

- **Procrastination**—putting off tasks simply because you don't feel in the mood to do them right away.
- **Distraction**—getting sidetracked by the endless variety of other things that seem easier (or more fun) to do.
- **Underestimating the value of small bits of time**—thinking it isn't worth doing any work because you have something else to do, or someplace else to be, in 20 minutes or so.

We all lead busy lives, but we all make choices as to how we spend our time. Choose wisely, and make the most of every minute you have.

Just as you make choices about where to spend your money and how to get the best value for your dollar, you do the same with your time. In order to get the most out of your externship at Fulwood Medical Center and out of your life in general, you have to spend your time wisely. Unlike money, however, time passes whether or not it is what you want. You may be able to save money for future use; but, unfortunately, you can't store away time to use later. However, you *can* plan how you will spend your time in a way that maximizes the quality and the quantity of things you can get done in a day, week, month, or year. If you're like most people, you may not have a good idea of how your time is actually being used.

EXERCISE

Write out all of your activities for a typical week. On average, how many hours each week do you spend sleeping, grooming, eating, working, running errands, studying, attending your children's activities, and watching TV. Add all of the hours up. There are 168 hours in the week. How many hours do you have left for studying? A sample budget is shown below.

Activity	Number of Hours per Day	Number of Days per Week	Number of Hours per Week
Sleeping	8	7	56
Grooming	1	7	7
Meals: preparation, eating, cleanup	1	7	7
Cleaning, laundry	1	3	3
Commuting to and from school	1	5	5
In class	4	5	20
Doing errands	1	3	3
Family time	3	7	21
Church, workout, hobbies			5
Job			30
Friends, going out, TV, entertainment			6
TOTAL			163
TOTAL HOURS IN A WEEK			168
Hours remaining for study			5

• Are five hours enough for study?

• When are they available?

• What can you do to increase them?

Study hours should be spent in a setting that allows you to concentrate on your work and not be distracted. Turn off your cell phone and TV. The biggest question to ask yourself is: "Am I investing my time wisely?" If not, how can you budget your time differently so more time is spent on higher priority activities?

STUDY STRATEGIES (continued)

Ten Steps to a Study Schedule that Works   Making a study schedule you will actually follow means knowing yourself and your limits. Implement the following tips to develop a schedule that works for you. Or, if success in the class is not important to you, skip to the next section containing strategies for self-sabotage.

1. **Study when you are most productive.** When are you most productive? Are you a night owl or an early bird? Plan to study when you are most alert and can have uninterrupted segments of time. This could include a quick five-minute review before class or a one-hour problem-solving study session with a friend.

2. **Create a set study time for yourself daily.** Having a set schedule for yourself means making a commitment to studying. Write your study time on your calendar, and do not schedule other activities during this time.

3. **Schedule study time using shorter, focused blocks with small breaks.** Studying a little each day rather than cramming the night before a test is a much more effective use of your time. Doing this helps you learn the material and store it in your long-term memory, not just memorize it and forget it after the test. Also, you will be less fatigued and less likely to procrastinate.

4. **Plan time for family, leisure, friends, exercise, and sleep.** Studying should be your main focus, but you need to balance your time—and your life.

5. **Log your projects and homework deadlines.** Record all due dates, tests, and projects in your personal calendar so you know what is coming. If you have a large project, break the assignment down into smaller targets. Set a goal for the first draft, second draft, and final copy, and record each of these deadlines in your calendar.

6. **Try to complete tasks ahead of schedule.** This will give you a chance to carefully review your work before you hand it in. You'll feel less stressed in the end.

7. **Prioritize.** In your calendar or planner, highlight or number key projects. Do them first, then cross them off when they are complete. Give yourself a pat on the back for getting them done.

8. **Review and reprioritize daily.** Check your scheduled activities each day, and adjust them if priorities have changed.

9. **Resist distractions.** Don't let unscheduled activities take you away from designated study time. The Internet is a notorious time-waster. It is easy to lose hours surfing the Web or instant messaging. It's just as easy to let a five-minute phone call with a friend turn into a three-hour conversation. Stick to your schedule.

10. **Multitask when possible.** You may find a lot of extra time you didn't think you had. Review material or deconstruct medical terms in your head while walking to class, doing laundry, or during "mental down time." (***Note:*** Mental down time does *not* mean in the middle of lecture.)

How to Sabotage Yourself   If you are determined to **fail**, just follow these simple instructions:

1. Skip class, or, if you do attend, arrive fashionably late.

2. Don't bother studying if you have to be someplace in 20 minutes; that's not enough time to get anything done.

3. Big test coming up? Beat the stress by relaxing with friends, going out for a few beers, or hanging out in an Internet chat room. Be sure to complain to your chat room friends about how there is no way you can pass the test tomorrow.

4. Don't ask questions in class. You are probably the only one who doesn't know the answer, and everyone else will think you are stupid.

5. Don't visit the instructor in his or her office; instructors don't want to be bothered.

6. Be sure to pull an all-nighter before the exam; you don't have time to sleep.

7. The time to begin studying for an exam is the day before the test. Four hours ought to be plenty.

8. When reading the book, yellow highlight most of it. If it's not important, it wouldn't be in the book; and, if it is important, you need to highlight it.

9. Don't take notes in lecture. You can't get it all down anyway, and it would be better just to sit back and listen.

10. Stop reading this book now. Do not continue to the next page to find out how to be an active learner and increase your chances of success in the course.

EXERCISE	*Be honest with yourself and self-assess. Are you guilty of any of the tendencies described above? If so, determine to change at least one bad habit before this course begins.*

The habit I would most like to change is:

_____

_____

_____

I recognize that if I change this habit, the *benefit* to me will be:

_____

_____

_____

Remember: Your instructor puts time and effort into preparing this class and marking tests. You need to devote your time and energy to the class as well.

STUDY STRATEGIES (continued)

Being an Active Learner

As you will find out in your externship at Fulwood Medical Center, true learning is active. You can't sit back and let someone else pour knowledge into your head. You need to authentically assume the various allied health care professional roles you'll play at Fulwood and work to get as much from them as you can. Simply attending your Medical Terminology class is another valuable thing you can do to help yourself. However, it doesn't end there. Here are more ways you can be an active learner and get the most out of your studies.

Getting the Most Out of Lectures

1. **Prepare.** You'll be amazed at how much easier it is to understand the material when you have previewed the chapter before going to class. If you find it difficult to carve out the time, simply arrive at class 5 to 15 minutes earlier than usual and skim the chapter before lecture begins. This will at least give you an overview of what may be discussed.

2. **Be a good listener.** Most people think they are good listeners, but few really are *(Figure W.15)*. Are you?
   - You can't listen if you are talking or text messaging or looking at your cellphone.
   - You can't listen if you are daydreaming or dozing.
   - Listening and comprehending are two different things. If you don't understand something the instructor is saying, ask a question or jot a note and visit the instructor after class. Don't feel intimidated: you probably aren't the only person who "doesn't get it."

3. **Take good notes.** Here are some tips for successful note-taking:
   - Use a standard-size notebook or, better yet, a three-ring binder with loose leaf notepaper. The binder will allow you to organize and integrate your notes and handouts.
   - Use a standard black or blue ink pen to take your initial notes. You can annotate later using a pencil, which can be erased if necessary.
   - Start a new page with each lecture or note-taking session.
   - Label each page of your notes with the date and a heading.
   - Focus on the main points and try to use an outline format to take notes. This will help you capture key ideas and organize subpoints.
   - Review and edit your notes shortly after class—at least within 24 hours—to make sure they make sense. You may also want to compare your notes with those of a study partner later to make sure neither of you have missed anything.

Getting the Most Out of Reading

1. **Concentrate on what you are reading.** Survey the titles, outcomes, objectives, and headings in each chapter, and look at the visuals to identify what the chapter is all about.

2. **Use the SQ3R method** (see Study Hint) to help you read actively.

3. **Take notes on key ideas** in the reading.

4. **Write down any questions** you have.

5. **Discuss what you have read** with your study partner.

FIGURE W.15 Being a good listener is important to success.

Study Hint

The SQ3R Model for Reading is a successful equation for studying.

*S*urvey what you are going to read.

*Q*uestion what you are going to learn after the preview.

*R*ead—Read the assignment.

*R*ecite—Stop every once in a while, look up from the book, and put what you've just read into your own words.

*R*eview—After you've finished, review the main points.

Performing Well on Tests

1. **Always read the directions.** If you are unsure, ask. Find out if there is a penalty for guessing. If there is not, try to answer every question on the test even if you have to guess at some.

2. **Before you begin, scan the entire test** so you know how long it is and what types of activities it contains.

3. **Answer the easy questions or sections first** so you get as much of the exam finished as possible if difficult questions slow you down.

   - When answering multiple-choice questions, eliminate each incorrect option until you are left with the answer that seems most correct to you.

   - When answering matching questions, match all items you know first, then do your best with the ones that remain.

   - When answering essay questions, reword the question as a statement to be sure you have answered it. Give enough examples and explanation to support your points.

4. **Once you have finished the test, use any extra time to check that you have answered all questions.** If you still have time after checking for completion, reread the questions and recheck your answers.

▲ **FIGURE W.16** Studying with a partner can help you succeed, and it can be fun.

Studying with a Partner or Group

1. **Get a study partner.** Schedule set study dates. Talk through the concepts, compare notes, and quiz each other *(Figure W.16)*. Studying with a partner can be fun. Think of it this way: you are multitasking, layering study time and social time. Just be sure the social time doesn't squeeze out the study time.

2. **Don't take advantage of your study partner.** If you can't make a study date or attend a class, let your partner know. You won't have a study partner—or a friend—much longer if it isn't a mutually beneficial arrangement.

3. **Establish a study group.** Choose a few students in the class, including your study partner, with whom to study on a regular basis. Having a group in addition to a study partner ensures you will still be able to study with others if your partner has to miss a session.

EXERCISE

Budgeting your time is key to being able to take care of your priorities. Follow these steps with the list of tasks you need to get done:

1. Rank each of the tasks in the table in order of its priority (e.g., 1 is the highest priority, 2 is next highest, and so on).

2. On a separate sheet of paper, plan a weekly schedule that would help you accomplish these tasks. Include all seven days of the week, and block off the days in hourly increments.

3. Keep in mind that while some activities have set times, others can be flexible. Also consider that activities like studying and household tasks will need to be done for a period of time *every day*, not just once a week.

(Note: There is no one "correct" answer to this exercise; however, it is beneficial to see how other students in the class chose to budget their time. Be creative but realistic. Don't forget to budget for travel time between tasks if needed.)

Weekly Tasks

Studying for Medical Terminology _____	Errands (groceries, etc.) _____	Leisure time _____
Sleep _____	Family time _____	Household chores _____
Medical Terminology Class (Tuesday and Thursday 6:30–9:30 p.m.) _____	Work (8:00–3:30 daily) _____	Meals, including preparation & cleanup _____
Church and/or hobbies _____	Exercise _____	Grooming _____

Armed with an understanding of what it takes to be successful, you are now ready to move through this textbook as if engaged in an externship at Fulwood Medical Center.

Anatomy of Word Building

The Language of Health Care

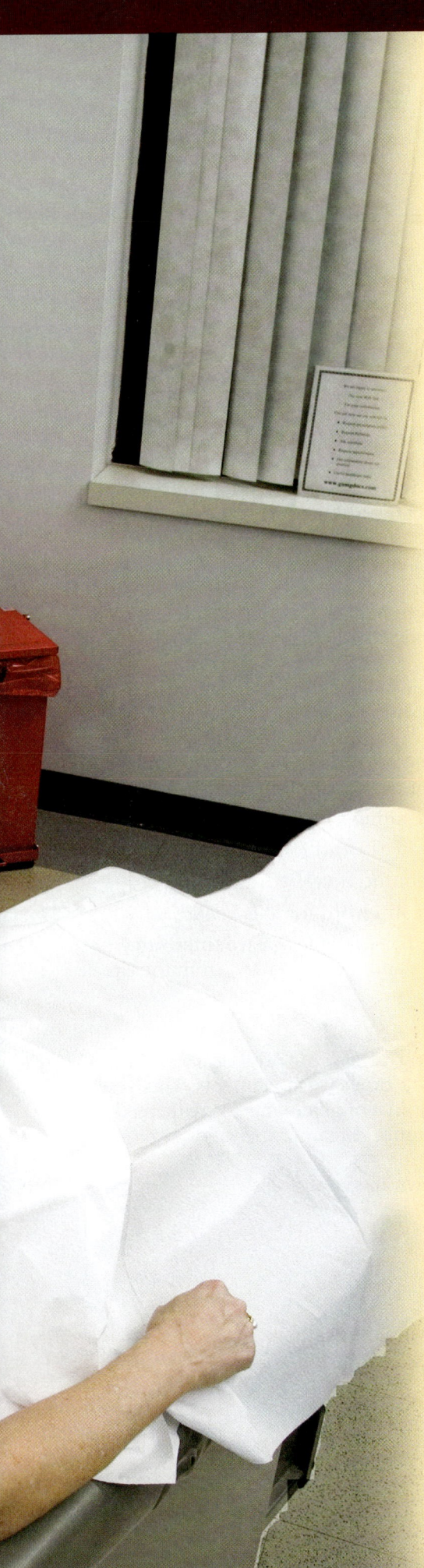

CASE REPORT 1.1

You are

. . . a medical assistant working for Russell Gordon, MD, a primary care physician at Fulwood Medical Center.

Your patient is

. . . Mrs. Connie Bishop, a 55-year-old woman who presents with a swelling in her lower abdomen and shortness of breath. She has no gynecologic or gastroenterologic symptoms. Her previous medical history shows recurrent dermatitis of her hands since a teenager and an arthroscopy for a knee injury at age 40. Physical examination reveals a circular mass 6 inches in diameter in the left lower quadrant of her abdomen. There is no abnormality in her respiratory or cardiovascular systems.

Your role is to maintain her medical record and document her care, assist Dr. Gordon during his examinations, explain the examination and treatment procedures to Mrs. Bishop, and facilitate her referral for specialist care.

Learning Outcomes

Review the various case reports shown in this chapter. Pay close attention to the terms and language contained in them. You will see that medicine has its own language. This language provides all the health professionals involved in the care of a patient with the ability to communicate with each other by using medical terms with precise meanings. This chapter is designed to give you tools that will enable you to:

- Understand the logic of the language of medicine and relate it to your practice as a health care professional.

- Construct medical terms using prefixes, roots, combining forms, and suffixes.

- Use roots, combining forms, prefixes, and suffixes so that you can analyze, deconstruct, and determine the meaning of medical terms.

- Comprehend, spell, and write medical terms so that you communicate and document accurately and precisely in any health care setting.

- Recognize and pronounce medical terms so that you communicate verbally with accuracy and precision in any health care setting.

- Explain the meaning of medical terms to people with no medical training.

Roots and Combining Forms

The technical language of medicine has not arisen at random but has been developed logically from Latin and Greek roots. The first steps to take to understand the logic of the language are to:

- **Select the root of each medical term.**
- **Identify the meaning of the roots of commonly used medical terms.**
- **Define the terms combining vowel and combining form.**
- **Construct combining forms for commonly used medical terms.**
- **Identify the combining vowel and combining form of commonly used medical terms.**

THE ELEMENTS OF A MEDICAL TERM ARE:

- prefix — the beginning of some words
- root — the foundation of the word that provides its meaning
- combining vowel — vowel that joins a root to another root or to a suffix
- combining form — combination of a root and a combining vowel
- suffix — the ending of some words

ROOTS:

- the constant, unchanging foundation of a medical term
- usually of Greek or Latin origin
- nearly all medical terms have one or more roots

COMBINING VOWEL:

- has no meaning of its own
- joins a root to another root
- joins a root to a suffix
- makes a word easier to pronounce
- "o" is the most common combining vowel, followed by "a"

UNDERSTANDING MEDICAL TERMINOLOGY

To understand and be comfortable with the technical language of medicine is an important key to your successful career as a health professional. Your ability to use the language to communicate verbally and in writing is essential for patient safety, high quality patient care, interaction with other health care professionals, and your own self-esteem as a health care professional.

Your confidence in using the medical terms will increase as you understand the logic of how these terms are built from their individual parts, or **elements.** In addition, understanding the logic will enable you to analyze or "deconstruct" a word, break it down into its elements or its "anatomy," and construct the pieces into a whole to understand its meaning.

The core element of any term is its root. You can use the following information about "roots" to help you understand Mrs. Bishop's case report.

Nearly every medical term has at least one root, the element that bears the core meaning of the word. Ninety percent of these roots arise from Greek and Latin words, and many of them have been in use for over 2,000 years. For example:

Gynecologic uses the Greek root gynec-, meaning *female.*

Dermatitis has the root dermat- from the Greek word for *skin.*

Arthroscopy has the root arthr- derived from the Greek word for *joint.*

Respiratory uses the root respir- from the Latin word for *to breathe.*

Many words contain more than one root. For example, **gastroenterology** has the root gastr- from the Greek word for *stomach* and the root enter- from the Greek word for *intestine.*

Combining Vowels

You build medical terms on the foundation of a root. Adding a combining vowel onto the end of a root joins that root to other word elements. This vowel has no meaning of its own. It is the vehicle to join word elements to create medical terms. It also makes the word easier to pronounce. Creating the medical terms is like assembling pieces of a jigsaw puzzle.

The vowel "o" is a combining vowel as shown in gynecologist:

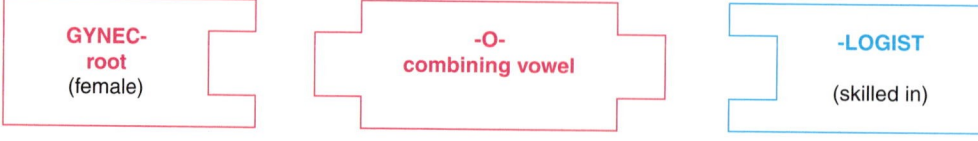

| GYNEC-
root
(female) | -O-
combining vowel | -LOGIST
(skilled in) |

The vowel "a" is a combining vowel as shown in respiratory:

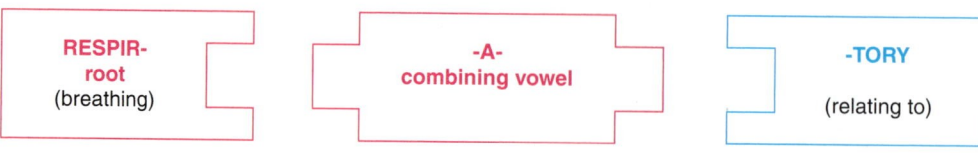

| RESPIR-
root
(breathing) | -A-
combining vowel | -TORY
(relating to) |

"**O**" is the most common combining vowel. The vowels "**a**" "**i**" and "**u**" are used less frequently.

Some words have more than one combining vowel. Gastr**o**enter**o**logy has two "**o**" combining vowels attached to different roots.

A combining vowel can be used to link two roots even when the second root begins with a vowel, as shown in gastr**o**enterology.

Combining Forms

A root with a combining vowel added to it is called a **combining form**. For example, the root **abd-** + the vowel "**o**," or **abd/o-**, meaning *belly*, is the combining form for the word **abd/o-men**, or **abdomen**.

Examples of **combining forms** are:

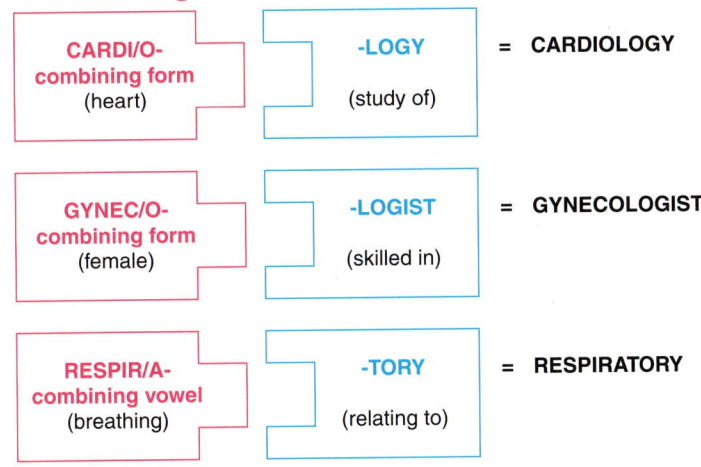

CARDI/O- combining form (heart) + **-LOGY** (study of) = **CARDIOLOGY**

GYNEC/O- combining form (female) + **-LOGIST** (skilled in) = **GYNECOLOGIST**

RESPIR/A- combining vowel (breathing) + **-TORY** (relating to) = **RESPIRATORY**

> **COMBINING FORMS:**
> - combine a **root** and a **combining vowel**
> - can be attached to another **root** or **combining form**
> - can precede a **suffix**

Keynote

Throughout the book, in word analysis tables, for a **combining form** the root will always be separated from the **combining vowel** by a /.

An example of a word with two **combining forms** is **gastroenterology**, the elements of which can be pieced together like this:

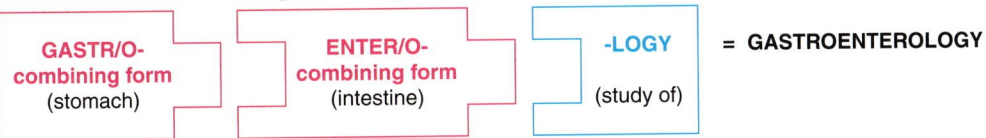

GASTR/O- combining form (stomach) + **ENTER/O-** combining form (intestine) + **-LOGY** (study of) = **GASTROENTEROLOGY**

EXERCISES

The jigsaw pieces are your visual aid to understanding the logic of how elements form medical terms. Number the puzzle pieces with each statement that pertains to that part of the puzzle. Each puzzle piece will have several numbers. Fill in the blanks.

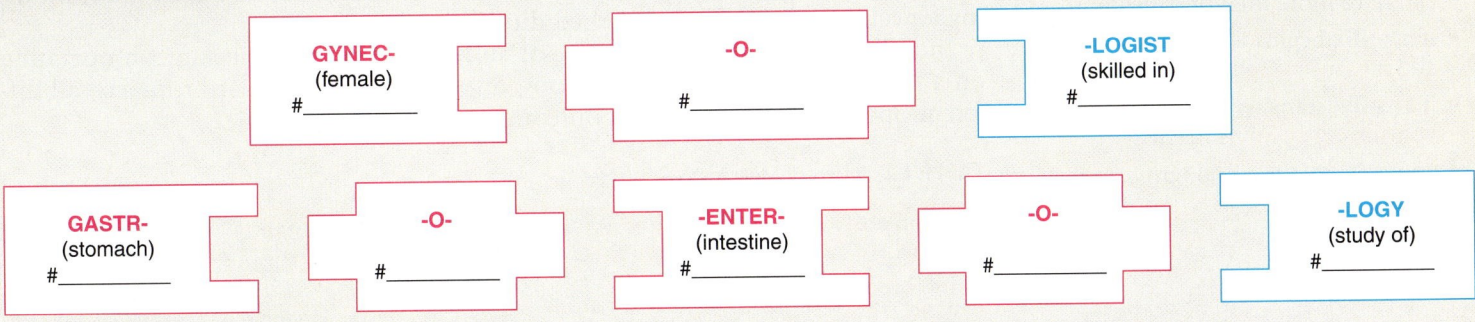

GYNEC- (female) #_____   **-O-** #_____   **-LOGIST** (skilled in) #_____

GASTR- (stomach) #_____   **-O-** #_____   **-ENTER-** (intestine) #_____   **-O-** #_____   **-LOGY** (study of) #_____

Place the numbers of the following statements into the correct puzzle piece.

1. This piece is a root.
2. This piece is a combining vowel.
3. This piece is the end of the term, or the suffix.
4. This piece needs to be in every term.
5. This piece may not be in every term.

6. This piece attaches to a root.
7. This piece comes before a suffix.
8. This piece has no meaning of its own.
9. This piece is usually of Greek or Latin origin.
10. This piece is the core of every medical term.

A root + combining vowel = _____ , which in these puzzles is the element _____.

OBJECTIVES

Adding a different **suffix** to the end of the same **root**, enables you to build a whole new set of words, all with different meanings. Adding a different **prefix** in front of the root also helps to build more medical terms. This lesson will increase your medical word building power by enabling you to:

- **Define the term suffix.**
- **Identify the suffixes of commonly used medical terms and their meanings.**
- **Define the term prefix.**
- **Identify the prefixes of commonly used medical terms and their meanings.**
- **Link word elements together to construct medical terms.**
- **Dissect word elements to deconstruct medical terms.**

Keynote

A **suffix** is added to the end of a root or combining form to give it a new meaning.

SUFFIX:

- a group of letters
- positioned at the end of a medical term
- attaches to the end of a **root** or **combining form**
- can have more than one meaning
- if a **suffix** begins with a consonant, add a **combining vowel** to the **root**
- if a **suffix** starts with a vowel, no **combining vowel** is needed
- an occasional medical term can have two **suffixes**

SUFFIXES AND PREFIXES

Suffixes

You add a suffix onto the end of a word to modify the core of the root and give it a new meaning.

For example, in the medical specialty of cardio**logy**, a cardio**logist** will often diagnose a cardio**pathy**.

Another example of the use of suffixes is in the medical specialty of dermato**logy**, when a dermato**logist** will often diagnose a dermat**itis** (Table 1.1).

TABLE 1.1 Use of Suffixes

Complete Word	Combining Form	Suffix	Meaning of Suffix	Meaning of Word
dermatitis	dermat- (root)	-itis	*inflammation*	*inflammation of the skin*
dermatologist	dermat/o-	-logist	*one who studies*	*one who studies the skin*
dermatology	dermat/o-	-logy	*study of*	*study of the skin*

In dermatitis, the suffix -itis starts with a vowel so there is no need for a combining vowel, and the suffix is attached directly to the root.

In a different example of the use of suffixes, an orthopedic surgeon operating on a joint can perform an arthro**scopy**, an arthro**desis**, or an arthro**plasty**, all different operations with different outcomes as shown in Table 1.2.

TABLE 1.2 Different Meanings of Suffixes

Complete Word	Combining Form	Suffix	Meaning of Suffix	Meaning of Word
arthroscopy	arthr/o-	-scopy	*visual examination*	*visual examination of a joint*
arthrodesis	arthr/o-	-desis	*fixation*	*fixation of a joint*
arthroplasty	arthr/o-	-plasty	*repair*	*repair of a joint*

You always need a combining vowel before a suffix that begins with a consonant (e.g., dermat**o**logy, arthr**o**plasty).

Prefixes

To continue expanding terms derived from the core root of a medical term, you can place a **prefix** at the beginning of the **root**. **Prefixes** are added directly to the **root** or **combining form** and do not require a combining vowel.

For example, you can add the different prefixes **peri-** and **endo-** to the same root, **cardi-**, to produce the different words **peri**cardium and **endo**cardium, which have very different meanings, as shown in Table 1.3.

Note that **-um** is a **suffix** meaning *structure*.

TABLE 1.3 Use of Prefixes

Complete Word	Prefix	Meaning of Prefix	Meaning of Word
pericardium	**peri-**	around	structure around the heart
endocardium	**endo-**	inside	structure inside the heart

Similarly, **epi**gastric, **hypo**gastric, and **endo**gastric all have the same root, **gastr-**, but because of the different prefixes, **epi-**, **hypo-**, and **endo-** have very different meanings, as shown in Table 1.4. Note that **-ic** is a **suffix** meaning *pertaining to*.

TABLE 1.4 Different Meanings of Prefixes

Complete Word	Prefix	Meaning of Prefix	Meaning of Word
epigastric	**epi-**	above	pertaining to above the stomach
hypogastric	**hypo-**	below	pertaining to below the stomach
endogastric	**endo-**	inside	pertaining to inside the stomach

EXERCISES

Building onto the elements of roots, combining vowels and combining forms are the prefixes and suffixes of medical terminology. Prefixes and suffixes are additional word elements that give further meaning to a root or combining form. Develop your knowledge of more word elements with the following exercise. Circle the correct answer, then rewrite any false statement(s) to be correct on the lines below.

1. In a medical term, the suffix will always appear at the end. T F

2. Every medical term has to have a prefix. T F

3. In the terms **arthroscopy** and **arthrodesis**, the combining form is the same, but the suffix is different. T F

4. In the term **endocarditis**, the prefix means above. T F

5. If a suffix begins with a consonant, you will need a combining vowel before it. T F

6. A prefix will always come at the beginning of the term. T F

Corrected statements:

_____

_____

_____

_____

_____

_____

Plurals and Pronunciations

OBJECTIVES

As a health professional, the correct, precise pronunciation of medical terms is an essential part of your daily life and of your self-esteem. It is also critical for patient safety and high-quality patient care. The information in this lesson will enable you to:

- **Connect the singular and plural components of medical terms.**
- **Employ the system for describing pronunciation used in the textbook.**
- **Verbalize the pronunciation of medical terms written in the textbook by utilizing the textbook CD as the reference and standard for pronunciation.**

PLURALS AND PRONUNCIATIONS

Plurals

When you change a medical term from singular to plural, it is not as simple as adding an "s," as you often can in the English language. Unfortunately, in medical terms, the end of the word changes in ways that were logical in Latin and Greek but have to be learned by memory in English. This is shown in Table 1.5.

TABLE 1.5 Singular and Plural Forms

Singular Ending	Plural Ending	Examples	Singular Ending	Plural Ending	Examples
-a	-ae	axilla	-on	-a	ganglion
		axillae			ganglia
-ax	-aces	thorax	-um	-a	septum
		thoraces			septa
-en	-ina	lumen	-us	-era	viscus
		lumina			viscera
-ex	-ices	cortex	-us	-i	villus
		cortices			villi
-is	-es	diagnosis	-us	-ora	corpus
		diagnoses			corpora
-is	-ides	epididymis	-x	-ges	phalanx
		epididymides			phalanges
-ix	-ices	appendix	-y	-ies	ovary
		appendices			ovaries
-ma	-mata	carcinoma	-yx	-ices	calyx
		carcinomata			calices

Adapted from *Anatomy and Physiology*, 3rd ed. by Kenneth S. Saladin. Copyright © 2004 The McGraw-Hill Companies, Inc. Reprinted with permission.

Pronunciations

As an allied health professional, pronouncing medical terms correctly and precisely is not only about understanding a conversation when you talk to your peers or your physician. It is a matter of patient safety and providing high-quality patient care. One "small error" in writing ileum as ilium, for example, changes the meaning entirely from a segment of the small intestine to a bone in the pelvis. In most regions, both ilium and ileum are pronounced **ILL**-ee-um, which is confusing.

Correct pronunciation is essential so that the other health professionals with whom you are working can understand what you are saying. Throughout this textbook, the pronunciation of each medical term will be written out phonetically using modern English language forms. The part(s) of the word to which you give the strongest, or primary, emphasis is written in bold, uppercase letters.

For example, the term **gastroenterology** will be phonetically written **GAS**-troh-en-ter-**OL**-oh-gee, whereas the term **gastritis,** inflammation of the stomach, will be written as gas-**TRY**-tis. **Hemorrhage** will be written as **HEM**-oh-raj, whereas the term **hemostasis,** the stopping of bleeding, will be written he-moh-**STAY**-sis.

The only way you can learn how to pronounce medical terms is to say them repeatedly and have your pronunciation checked against a standard.

The CD-ROM that comes with your book is an integral part of your learning program. The terms listed on the Word Analysis and Definition tables can be easily accessed and listened to as you repeat the term.

Keynote

Check your pronunciation with the standard on the CD.

EXERCISES   *Forming plurals of medical terms can be less difficult if you follow the rules and apply them correctly. The rule is given to you in the following chart—practice changing the medical terms from singular to plural. Fill in the chart.*

Singular	Plural	Singular term	Plural term	Singular	Plural	Singular term	Plural term
-a	-ae	axilla		-on	-a	ganglion	
-ax	-aces	thorax		-um	-a	septum	
-en	-ina	lumen		-us *	-era	viscus	
-ex	-ices	cortex		-us *	-i	villus	
-is *	-es	diagnosis		-us *	-ora	corpus	
-is *	-ides	epididymis		-x	-ges	phalanx	
-ix	-ices	appendix		-y	-ies	ovary	
-ma	-mata	carcinoma		-yx	-ices	calyx	

Note: In the case of the rules with an asterisk (*), both singular terms can end in -is. You have to know on a case-by-case basis which singular terms change to -es and which ones change to -ides. The same applies to the singular terms ending in -us—some will form plurals with -era, -i, or -ora.

LESSON 1.4 Word Analysis

When you see a medical term you do not understand, the first step you can take to analyze, decipher, or deconstruct the term is to break it down into its component elements or parts. In this lesson you will learn to:

- **Break down or deconstruct a medical term into its word elements**
- **Use the word elements to analyze and identify the medical term**

CASE REPORT 1.2

You are

. . . an emergency medical technician **(EMT)** employed in the Emergency Department at Fulwood Medical Center.

Your patient is

. . . Barbara Rotelli, a 17-year-old woman, who presents with **pyrexia** and shaking chills. On her medical record, you read that her physical examination reveals splinter **hemorrhages** under her fingernails and a heart **murmur**. There is blood in her urine. She had **dental** surgery four days ago. A provisional diagnosis is made of acute **endocarditis**. You are to prepare her for admission to intensive care.

TO ANALYZE, BREAKDOWN, OR DECONSTRUCT MEDICAL TERMS:

- recognize any suffix at the end of the word and define its meaning
- recognize any prefix at the beginning of the word and define its meaning
- recognize the root and define its meaning
- assemble these meanings together to define the word

Abbreviation

EMT	emergency medical technician

WORD ANALYSIS, DEFINITION, AND PRONUNCIATION

For words you need to define, first identify the suffix.

For example, in the term **endocarditis**, the suffix at the end of the word is -itis, which you have learned means *inflammation*.

That leaves **endocard-**. You have learned that card- is a root meaning *heart*. So, now you have *inflammation of the heart*.

$$\text{Card} + \text{itis} = \text{inflammation of the heart}$$

That leaves endo-, which you have learned is a prefix meaning *inside*. So, now you can assemble the pieces together to form the word meaning *inflammation of the inside of the heart*.

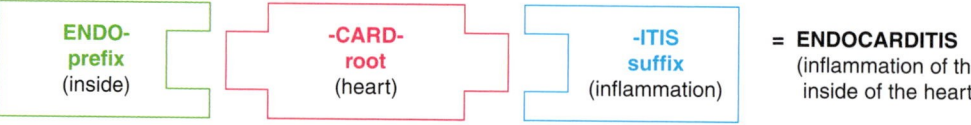

You also have learned that the suffix -um means *a structure*. So, the **endocardium** would be the structure that lines the inside of the heart.

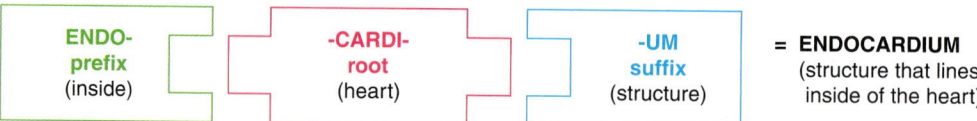

Therefore, you can understand that **endocarditis** is used to mean that the endocardium lining the heart has become inflamed or infected. Both card- and cardi- are roots meaning *heart*.

Another example is the word **hemorrhage** used in Case Report 1.2. The suffix -rrhage following the combining vowel "o" is borrowed from the Greek word meaning *to flow profusely*. The root hem- is from the Greek word for *blood*. The elements of the medical term **hemorrhage** are assembled together and used to mean *a profuse flow of blood*.

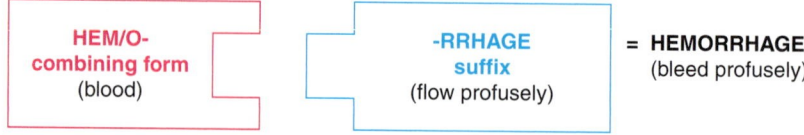

In this book, when the medical terms are broken down into their elements, a hyphen is used to isolate each major element and to identify its position in the whole word.

When a combining form is used, the combining vowel is separated from the root by a slash (/).

One of the key design concepts of this book is that all the textual and visual information you need for any given topic will be on the two-page spread open in front of you. As part of this, in the top right-hand quarter of the two-page spread will be a box designed to give you the elements, definition, and pronunciation of every new medical term that appears in the two pages you are reviewing. For example, the box will look like the following as it refers to the medical terms used on these two pages.

WORD ANALYSIS AND DEFINITION

WORD	PRONUNCIATION	ELEMENTS		DEFINITION
dental	**DEN**-tal	S/ R/	-al *pertaining to* dent- *tooth*	Pertaining to the teeth
dentist dentistry (**Note:** This word has two suffixes and one root.)	**DEN**-tist **DEN**-tis-tree	S/ S/ S/ R/	-ist *specialist* -ry *occupation* -ist- *specialist* dent- *tooth*	Legally qualified specialist in dentistry Evaluation, diagnosis, prevention, and treatment of conditions of the oral cavity and associated structures
endocarditis	**EN**-doh-kar-**DIE**-tis	S/ P/ R/	-itis *inflammation* endo- *within, inner* -card- *heart*	Inflammation of the lining of the heart
endocardium	**EN**-doh-kar-**DEE**-um	S/ R/	-um *structure* cardi- *heart*	The lining of the heart
hemorrhage	**HEM**-oh-raj	S/ R/CF	-rrhage *to flow profusely* hem/o- *blood*	To bleed profusely
murmur	**MUR**-mur		Latin *murmur*	Abnormal sound heard with a stethoscope when a valve closes or opens abnormally
pyrexia	pie-**REK**-see-ah	S/ R/	-ia *condition* pyrex- *fever, heat*	An abnormally high body temperature or fever

Many of the exercises at the end of each spread are based on information found in the Word Analysis and Definition (WAD) box or in the spread.

EXERCISES

*To analyze a medical term, simply break the elements down (deconstruct them) into their basic forms. To construct a new term, take the appropriate elements, put them in the correct position in the term, and build your term. **Note:** Remember that not every term will have all elements present at the same time.*

1. **To deconstruct:** Take the medical term **endocarditis** and break it down into elements. It will help you visually to put a slash (/) between the word elements in the term.

    endocarditis

    The prefix _____ means _____ .

    The root _____ means _____ .

    The suffix _____ means _____ .

    The term **endocarditis** means _____ .

    This term has three word elements only. Write the name of the element under the appropriate place it occupies in the slashed term.

    Endocarditis: endo /   card /   itis

    _____ / _____ / _____

2. **To construct:** Take the following elements and construct a new term with them.

    The element "**um**" means _____ . What type of word element is this? _____

    The element "**endo**" means _____ . What type of word element is this? _____

    The element "**cardi**" means _____ . What type of word element is this? _____

    This term is _____ and means_____ .

    This term has three word elements only. Take the elements you have identified above, and construct the new term by placing the elements in the correct place in the term below.

    _____ / _____ / _____
       P   R   S

OBJECTIVES

This year in the United States, more than 400,000 people will die because of drug reactions and medical errors. Many of these deaths are due to inaccurate or imprecise written or verbal communications between the different members of the health care team. You can avoid making errors in your own communications and this lesson will help you do that by enabling you to:

- **Communicate with precision both verbally and in writing.**
- **Utilize word analysis to help assure the precise use of words.**

You are

. . . a radiology technician (RT) working in the Radiology Department of Fulwood Medical Center.

Your patient is

. . . Mrs. Matilda Morones, a 38-year-old woman who presents with sudden onset of severe colicky right flank pain, and pain in her urethra as she passes urine.

CASE REPORT 1.3

Physical examination has revealed a woman in severe distress with marked tenderness in the right costovertebral angle and in the right lower quadrant of her abdomen. Microscopy of her urine showed numerous red blood cells. The stat x-ray you have taken reveals a radiopaque stone in the right ureter. She has now become faint and hypotensive.

How are you going to communicate Mrs. Morones' condition as you ask for help and then document her condition and your response?

PRECISION IN COMMUNICATION

In Case Report 1.3, if **hypotension** (low blood pressure) were confused with **hypertension** (high blood pressure), incorrect treatments could be prescribed.

If the patient's **ureter** (the tube from the kidney to the bladder) were confused with the **urethra** (the tube from the bladder to the outside), the consequences could be disastrous.

There are several other examples where medical terms can be confused.

The **trapezius** is a back muscle, whereas the **trapezium** is a bone in the wrist.

The **malleus** is a small bone in the middle ear. The **malleolus** is a bony protuberance of your ankle.

Neurology is the study of diseases of the nervous system. **Urology** is the study of diseases of the kidney and bladder and the male reproductive system.

Being a health professional requires the utmost attention to detail and precision, both in written documentation and verbal communication. A patient's life could be in your hands. In addition, the medical record in which you document a patient's care and your actions is a legal document. It can be used in court as evidence in professional medical liability cases. Any incorrect spelling can reflect badly on the whole health care team.

> **Keynote**
>
> Communicate verbally and in writing with attention to detail, accuracy and precision.

> **Keynote**
>
> When you understand the individual word elements that make up a medical term, you are better able to understand clearly the medical terms you are using.

USE OF WORD ANALYSIS

In Case Report 1.3, **ureter** (you-RET-er) and **urethra** (you-REE-thra) are both simple words with no prefix, combining vowel, or suffix. They are derived from the Greek word for *urine*. They are similar words, but have very different anatomical locations *(Chapter 11)*.

For the word **hypotension** (high-po-TEN-shun) you start with the suffix **-ion** which means *a condition*. Next, the prefix **hypo-** means below or less than normal. The root **tens-** is from the Latin word for *pressure*. So you can place the pieces together to form a word meaning *condition of below normal pressure*, or low blood pressure.

In **hypertension** (high-per-TEN-shun), the prefix **hyper-** means excessive. So, when you assemble the pieces together, you have a *condition of excessive pressure*, or high blood pressure.

Your ability to identify the different prefixes of **hypo-** and **hyper-** helps to assure precision in your written and verbal communications.

In the term **costovertebral** (koss-toh-ver-TEE-bral), you start with the suffix **-al**, which means *pertaining to*. Then, separated by the combining vowel "o," are two roots, **cost-** and **vertebr-**. The combining form **cost/o-** is from the Latin word for *a rib*. **Vertebr-** is from the Latin word for *backbone or spine*. So you have *pertaining to the rib and the spine*.

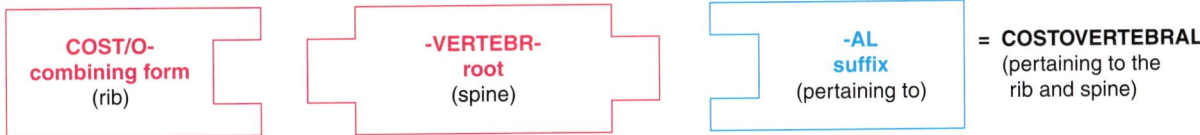

The **costovertebral angle** is the angle pertaining to or between the twelfth rib and the spine. This angle is a surface anatomy marking for the kidney.

EXERCISES

Precision in Communication: *Verbal and written communication must always be precise and accurate for patient safety and legal requirements. Develop your eyes' and ears' ability to distinguish correct pronunciations, correct word choice, and spelling to ensure documentation/communication accuracy. Fill in the following blanks.*

1. If the doctor tells you a patient's blood pressure readings were elevated, does the patient have hypertension or hypotension?

   _____

2. If the patient has a problem with his malleolus, would you send him to see an orthopedist (bone specialist) or an ENT (ear, nose and throat) specialist?

   _____

3. If a patient fell off a ladder and injured his back, would it most likely be his trapezius or his trapezium that was hurt?

   _____

4. Does a patient with a kidney infection need to see a urologist or a neurologist?

   _____

5. What is the difference in anatomical location of the ureter and the urethra?

   The ureter is _____ .

   The urethra is _____

6. Do you remember what is unusual about the elements of the words **ureter** and **urethra**?

   They have no _____ .

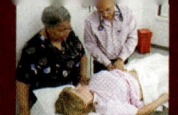

ANATOMY OF WORD BUILDING

CHALLENGE YOUR KNOWLEDGE

A. **Understanding word elements is the key to medical terminology.** Assess your knowledge of word elements by completing the following exercise. Read statements 1 through 15. Each statement applies to a specific word element–root (R), combining vowel (CV), combining form (CF), prefix (P), or suffix (S). Write the number of the statement beside the element to which it applies. The first one is done for you. Every word element in the following list will have more than one correct answer on the line beside it.

Root: #_____

Combining vowel: #_____

Combining form: #___1_____

Prefix: #_____

Suffix: #_____

1. Combination of a root and a combining vowel.
2. Different types of surgical procedures can be noted with this element.
3. Usually "o" and "a," but occasionally "i" and "u."
4. "Ic" and "um" are this type of element.
5. Core meaning of the term.
6. In the term **gastroenterology**, which element is present twice?
7. "**Endo**" is this type of element.
8. Some terms can have more than one.
9. Used to link two roots even when the second root begins with a vowel.
10. In the terms **cardiology, cardiopathy,** and **cardiologist**, which element does not change?
11. "**Abd/o**" is this type of element.
12. Every medical term has at least one.
13. Although opposites, "**hyper**" and "**hypo**" are both this same type of element.
14. Most derive from Greek and Latin words.
15. Can link two roots.

B. **True or False:** Circle the correct answer. On the lines below, rewrite any false answer to be correct.

1. A term never has more than one root.   T   F

2. Some terms will have no combining vowel.   T   F

3. Modification may be necessary to make a word easier to pronounce. T   F

4. A vowel must always be present in a combining form.   T   F

Corrected statements:

_____

_____

_____

_____

_____

C. **Root = core meaning of the term and the foundation upon which the term is built.** Find the root in each of the following terms, and define it.

Term	Root	Meaning of the root
cardiology	_____	_____
gynecologic	_____	_____
dermatitis	_____	_____
arthroscopy	_____	_____

D. **Root + combining vowel = combining form.** Determine the correct combining form (CF) in the following list of medical terms. Finding the root(s) first will put you on the right track. Fill in the blanks.

Term	Root(s)	Combining vowel	Combining form
cardiology	_____	_____	_____
gynecologic	_____	_____	_____
dermatology	_____	_____	_____
arthroscopy	_____	_____	_____

E. **A prefix appears at the beginning of the term, but not every term will have a prefix.** Keeping the same prefix but changing the root and other elements will produce new terms. First, underline the prefix in every term. Then use your knowledge of the meaning of prefixes to fill in the blanks.

1. An **endoscope** is an instrument for looking _____ the body.

    An **endotracheal** tube is inserted _____ the trachea.

2. The **pericardium** is the structure _____ the heart.

    The **perirectal** area is the tissue _____ the rectum.

3. **Epigastric** is the area _____ the stomach.

    Epidermal is the layer of skin _____ the dermal layer.

4. **Hypotension** is _____ blood pressure.

    Hypothyroidism is a condition that occurs when the level of thyroid hormone in your blood is _____ .

5. **Hypertension** is _____ blood pressure.

    Hyperglycemia is _____ sugar content in the blood.

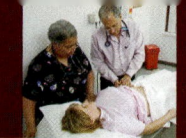

F. **A suffix appears at the end of the term.** Its purpose is to modify the core of the root or combining form and give it new meaning. Your knowledge of suffixes will help you complete this exercise. Circle the correct choice, and finish filling in the blanks. *A hint for the suffix is bolded in each statement.*

1. A **disease** of the heart is cardi/o _____ .

    -logy   -pathy   -plasty

2. Surgical **repair** of a joint is an arthr/o _____ .

    -plasty   -desis   -scopy

3. A **specialist** in the study of skin is a dermat/o _____ .

    -itis   -logy   -logist

4. Visual **examination** of a joint is an arthr/o _____ .

    -plasty   -scopy   -desis

5. A **structure** around the heart is the pericardi _____ .

    -osis   -itis   -um

6. Gastr _____ is an **inflammation** of the stomach.

    -logy   -plasty   -itis

7. The **study of** the skin is called dermat/o _____

    -pathy   -tosis   -logy

G. **The suffix in this exercise remains the same, but changing the root will change the specialist.** You are looking for a position as a medical assistant. The following practices have advertised on the County Medical Society's job hotline. What are their specialties? (Use your dictionary or glossary if needed.)

Type of Physician	Medical Specialty
urologist	_____
gynecologist	_____
gastroenterologist	_____
hematologist	_____
cardiologist	_____
dermatologist	_____
neurologist	_____

H. **Recognizing word elements will help you "dissect," or deconstruct, a term.** The following terms have an element set in bold. Identify the type of element, and give a brief definition of its meaning.

Term	Prefix, root, CF, suffix	Meaning of the element
arthro**plasty**	_____	_____
endocarditis	_____	_____
hemo**rrhage**	_____	_____
hypotension	_____	_____
hyper**gastric**	_____	_____

I. **To help you master plurals, practice changing singular endings to plural and plural endings to singular in the following exercise.** If you are given a singular word, change it to plural. If you are given a plural word, change it back to singular. The first one is done for you. Fill in the chart, then pick any two terms (singular or plural) and write a sentence for each term on the lines below.

Word	Singular	Plural
carcinomata	*carcinoma*	
ovary		
ganglia		
lumen		
villi		
cortices		
calyx		
epididymis		
axilla		
viscus		
appendices		
corpora		
septum		
diagnosis		
thorax		
phalanges		

1. _____

2. _____

J. **Word elements are the building blocks of medical terminology.** Being able to define word elements will help you use them correctly. Identify the element by placing a check mark (✓) in the correct column, then define the meaning of the element. In the last column, give an example of a medical term containing that element. Fill in the chart.

Element	Prefix	Root/CF	Suffix	Meaning of element	Medical term
cardi					
entero					
dermat					
logy					
gastro					
scopy					
itis					
gynec					
logist					

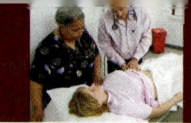
K. **Using the elements from the list in Exercise J, answer the following questions.**

1. Who is the specialist in the stomach and intestines? _____

2. What is study of the heart called? _____

3. What is inflammation of the skin called? _____

4. What specialist would you see for an inflammation of the skin? _____

5. What is inserting a tube into the stomach for an examination called? _____

L. **Spelling is most important in medical terminology.** For example, **ilium** and **ileum** may be similar in appearance, but the difference of one letter makes it a different body part. Choose the correct spelling for the following terms. Fill in the blanks.

1. A Pap smear is part of a _____ exam.

   gynecologik   gyneckologic   gynecologic

2. After a difficult delivery, the patient started to _____ .

   hemorage   hemmorhage   hemorrhage

3. Inflammation of the heart is _____ .

   carditus   carditis   cardiitis

4. A muscle in the back is the _____ .

   trapeze   trapezium   trapezius

5. A bony protuberance in the ankle is your _____ .

   maleus   malius   malleolus

M. **Speak and spell with precision in medical communication.** All terms in the Word Analysis and Definition boxes are spelled phonetically to make them easier for you to learn to pronounce. Be sure you can speak them correctly as well as spell them correctly! Practice, practice, practice. Circle the best answer, then fill in the blanks.

1. The correct pronunciation for an inflammation of the heart is:

   a. EN-do-kar-di-tis

   b. en-DO-kard-itis

   c. EN-doh-kar-DIE-tis

   The correct spelling of this term is _____ .

2. An abnormally high body temperature is:

   a. pie-REK-see-ah

   b. PIE-rek-seeah

   c. pie-REK-see-AH

   The correct spelling of this term is _____ .

3. Profuse bleeding is termed a:

   a. HEM-oh-raj

   b. hem-OH-raj

   c. HEM-oh-RAJ

Study Hint
Remember to start with the suffix and work back in the term.

   The correct spelling of this term is _____ .

N. Constructing terms is taking the building blocks of elements and correctly arranging them to form the term you need. Employ your knowledge of prefixes, roots, combining forms, and suffixes to construct the term required. Fill in the chart.

Meaning	Prefix	Root/Roots	Combining Form	Suffix	Term
Inflammation of the stomach and intestines	_____	_____	_____	_____	_____
Pertaining to the rib and spine	_____	_____	_____	_____	_____
Inflammation of a joint	_____	_____	_____	_____	_____
Visual examination of the stomach	_____	_____	_____	_____	_____
Blood bursting forth	_____	_____	_____	_____	_____
Pertaining to on top of the skin	_____	_____	_____	_____	_____
One who studies the heart	_____	_____	_____	_____	_____
Pertaining to (an injection) under the skin	_____	_____	_____	_____	_____
Visual examination within the body	_____	_____	_____	_____	_____

O. Analyze the following medical terms, based on your knowledge of elements. Put a slash (/) between each element of the terms listed in 1–5, then write the definition of each term.

   1. Enteric _____

   2. Abdominopelvic _____

   3. Arthroplasty _____

   4. Gastric _____

   5. Costovertebral _____

P. The following three elements have something in common. Fill in the blanks.

Study Hint
Learning elements in groups will help you remember them.

   "Epi" means _____ .

   "Hypo" means _____ .

   "Endo" means _____ .

   1. These are all (circle one: prefixes   roots   combining forms   suffixes).

   2. They can be grouped by (circle one: color   size   location).

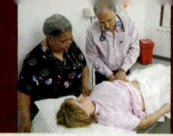

Q. **Precision is the mark of an educated professional.** Review these statements for accuracy, and correct where necessary. The sentence may contain a spelling or a factual error. Some sentences are correct. Rewrite the incorrect statements on the lines below.

1. Patient has a bad case of the hives. I referred her to a neurologist.
2. Discharge diagnosis: resolving cardiitis and cardiopathy.
3. Because of a possible bowel obstruction, I have asked a gastroenterologist to see the patient.
4. Patient is suffering from a topical dermatitis.
5. Due to prolonged hemmorrhaging, the patient needed a blood transfusion.
6. Patient will be scheduled for gastrodesis of her knee on Monday.

Corrected statements:

_____

_____

_____

_____

_____

R. **Terminology Challenge:** Fill in the blanks.

1. Which two prefixes in this chapter are opposites, and what do they mean?

   _____ means _____ , and _____ means _____ .

2. Name two suffixes in this chapter that mean *pertaining to* _____ and _____ .

3. List two medical specialties that were mentioned in this chapter. _____ and _____ .

4. What is the medical term for stopping bleeding? _____ . (*Watch your spelling!*)

S. **Analyze your word choice to be precise.** Errors in medical documentation are a threat to patient safety and a legal liability. Circle the correct answer.

1. A visual **examination** of the stomach is a:

   gastroscopy   gastropexy   gastrodesis   gastroplasty

2. A **sternum** would be:

   an inflammation   a structure   a lining   an extremity

3. An **abdominoplasty** would be a surgical:

   fusion   fixation   repair   examination

4. **Endogastric** would be:

   above the stomach   below the stomach   within the stomach   outside the stomach

5. **Arthropathy** would be a disease of:

   skin   joints   arteries   blood vessels

6. If you have a painful **skin** rash, what type of specialist do you need?

   cardiologist   urologist   neurologist   dermatologist

7. The root **respir-** means:

   to walk   to hear   to breathe   to feel

8. If **rhino** means *nose,* what is a surgical repair of a broken nose called?

      rhinodesis   rhinoscopy   rhinoplasty   rhinopexy

9. Which condition would likely affect your heart?

      arthritis   gastritis   dermatitis   carditis

10. Which of these conditions would a neurologist treat?

      migraine   endocarditis   urinary infection   arthritis

Example:

The prefix **hypo-** means _____ ; it can also mean _____ .

1. In hypogastric, hypo- means _____ .

2. In hypotension, hypo- means _____ .

T. **Case Report Questions:** This case report is taken from the beginning of Chapter 1. You should feel more comfortable with the medical terminology now. Read the report again, and you will be able to answer the questions. Fill in the blanks.

> 💡 *Study Hint*
> Many elements have more than one meaning. You must know both of them because that will make a difference in the use of the medical term.

CASE REPORT 1.1

You are

. . . A medical assistant employed by Russell Gordon, MD, a primary care physician at Fulwood Medical Center.

Your patient is

. . . Mrs. Connie Bishop, a 55-year-old woman who presents with a swelling in her lower abdomen and shortness of breath. She has no gynecologic or gastroenterologic symptoms. Her previous medical history shows recurrent dermatitis of her hands since a teenager and an arthroscopy for a knee injury at age 40. Physical examination reveals a circular mass 6 inches in diameter in the left lower quadrant of her abdomen. There is no abnormality in her respiratory or cardiovascular systems.

Your role is to maintain her medical record and document her care, assist Dr. Gordon during his examinations, explain the examination and treatment procedures to Mrs. Bishop, and facilitate her referral for specialist care.

1. What type of skin problem has Mrs. Bishop had since she was a teenager? _____

_____

2. She "has no gynecologic or gastroenterologic symptoms." _____

Define **gynecologic** _____

Define **gastroenterologic** _____

3. Her knee injury required what type of procedure? _____

Describe this procedure. _____

4. She shows "no abnormality in her respiratory or cardiovascular systems." Explain this in layman's terms.

_____

_____

5. What symptoms does Mrs. Bishop have that brought her to Dr. Gordon? _____

_____

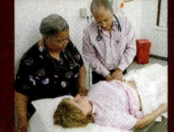

CHAPTER SUMMARY EXERCISE

1. *Listen to the pronunciation of the medical terms as given by your instructor.*
2. *Circle the correct spelling of the medical term.*
3. *Match the correctly spelled terms to the brief descriptions below.*
4. *Write a sentence for each of the 15 terms that appear in this exercise.*

A. SPELLING COMPREHENSION: *Circle the correct spelling of the term.*

1. abdomin	abdumin	abdomen	addumen	adumen
2. cardilogist	cardelogist	cardiologist	cardeologist	cardiollogist
3. respiratory	rispiratory	risperatory	resspiratory	resperatory
4. hemorrhege	hemorrage	hemmorrhage	hemmorage	hemorrhage
5. gastroenterology	gastricenterology	gastrioenterology	gastrology	gastraenterology
6. arthroedisis	artredesis	arthredessis	arthrodesis	arthridisis
7. cardeopathy	cardeeopathy	cardeopathie	cardiopathy	cardiopethy
8. arthriscopy	arthroscopy	artroscopy	arterioscopy	arterioscopie
9. hemostassis	hemostasis	hemmostassis	hematsasis	hemastasis
10. gyneckologic	gynecologic	gynicologic	gynickologic	gynekologic
11. eurology	urology	urrology	eurologie	urologie
12. perricardium	parecardium	perrecardium	paricardium	pericardium
13. cardiovescular	cardiovascular	cardeovascular	cardivascular	cardeoviscular
14. endugastric	endogastric	endegastric	endogasstric	endegestric
15. dermatitis	dermettitis	dermattitis	dermatites	dermatitiss

B. MATCH THE NUMBER OF THE CORRECT TERM IN PART A WITH THE BRIEF DESCRIPTION OF THE TERM BELOW.

a. stomach and intestines _____

b. visual examination of a joint _____

c. stopping bleeding _____

d. pertaining to the heart and blood vessels _____

e. study of diseases of kidney and bladder _____

f. relating to within the stomach _____

g. specialist in treating heart problems _____

h. Latin word for belly _____

i. structure around the heart _____

j. skin inflammation _____

k. lungs _____

l. surgical fixation of a joint _____

m. root means *female* _____

n. bursting forth of blood _____

o. disease of the heart _____

C. USING YOUR KNOWLEDGE OF TERMS 1–15 IN PART A AND THEIR CORRECT SPELLING, WRITE A BRIEF SENTENCE FOR EACH OF THE TERMS AS IT MIGHT APPEAR IN PATIENT DOCUMENTATION.

1. _____

2. _____

3. _____

4. _____

5. _____

6. _____

7. _____

8. _____

9. _____

10. _____

11. _____

12. _____

13. _____

14. _____

15. _____

D. GO TO THE STUDENT CD. OPEN THE GLOSSARY AND PRACTICE YOUR PRONUNCIATION OF THE TERMS IN PART A OF THIS EXERCISE.

The Body As a Whole
The Language of Anatomy

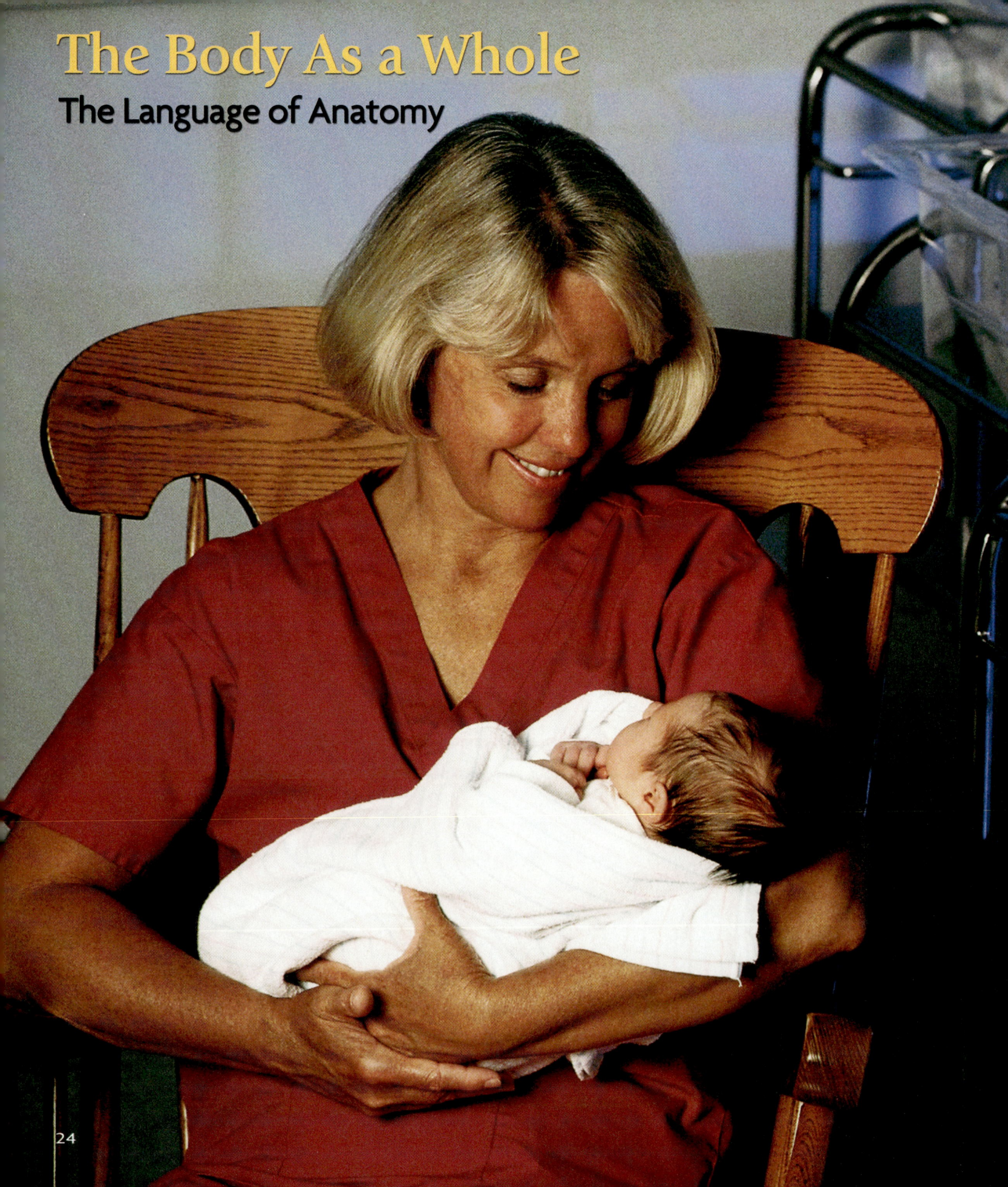

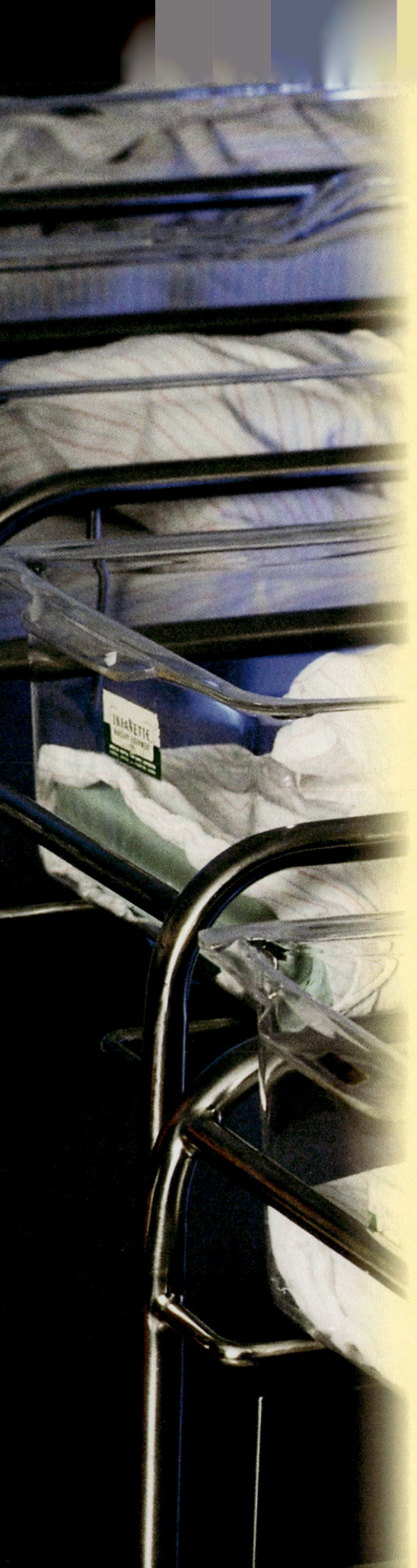

2

You are

. . . a certified medical assistant (CMA) employed as an in vitro fertilization coordinator in the Assisted Reproduction Clinic at Fulwood Medical Center.

Your patient is

. . . Mrs. Mary Arnold, a 35-year-old woman who was unable to conceive. **In vitro fertilization (IVF)** was recommended. After hormone therapy, several healthy and mature eggs were recovered from her ovary. The eggs were combined with her husband's sperm in a laboratory dish where fertilization occurred to form a single cell, called a **zygote**. The cells were allowed to divide for 5 days to become **blastocysts**, and then 4 cells were implanted in her uterus.

Your role is to guide, counsel, and support Mrs. Arnold and her husband through the decision, implementation, and follow-up for the IVF process.

Learning Outcomes

Each of us begins as a zygote and becomes a whole person. Effective medical treatment recognizes that each organ, tissue, and cell in your body functions in harmony with and affects every other organ, tissue, and cell. Your whole body also includes your thoughts, emotions, and perceptions that affect your health, disease, and recovery. This concept of treating the body as a whole is called **holistic** and requires you to be able to:

- Apply correct medical terms to the anatomy and physiology of the body as a whole.

- Integrate individual body systems into the organization and function of the body as a whole.

- Comprehend, spell, and write medical terms pertaining to the body as a whole so that you communicate and document accurately and precisely in any health care setting.

- Recognize and pronounce medical terms pertaining to the body as a whole so that you communicate verbally with accuracy and precision in any health care setting.

All the elements of your body interact with each other to enable your body to be in constant change as it reacts to the environment and to the nourishment you give it.

To understand the structure and function of your body, you need to be able to:

- **Identify the structure and functions of the components of a cell.**
- **List the four primary groups of tissue, and describe their functions.**
- **Identify a major organ, and list the smaller organs contained within it.**
- **Name the medical terms associated with cells, tissues, and organs.**

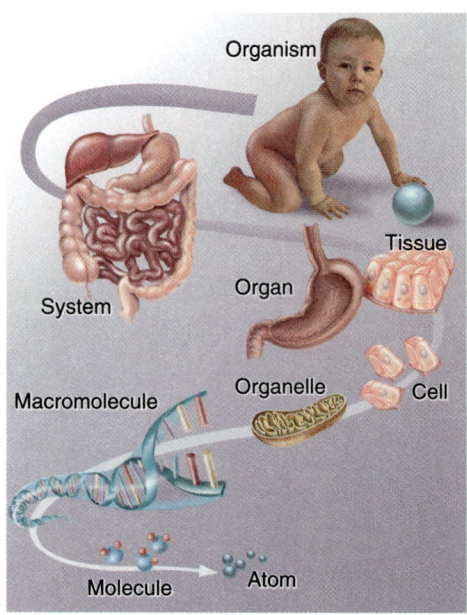

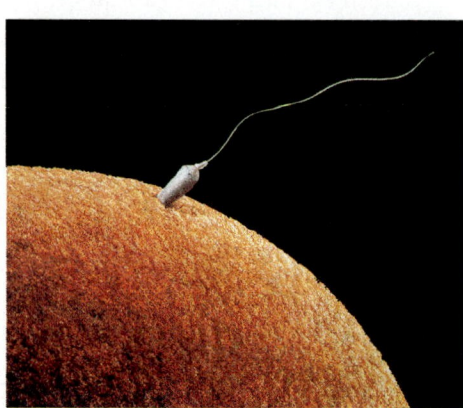

Abbreviation

IVF in vitro fertilization

COMPOSITION OF THE BODY

- The whole body or organism is composed of **organ** systems,
  - organ systems are composed of organs,
    - organs are composed of **tissues**,
      - tissues are composed of cells,
        - cells are composed in part of **organelles**,
          - organelles are composed of **molecules**,
            - molecules are composed of **atoms**.

THE CELL

This single fertilized cell, the **zygote**, is the result of the **fertilization** of an egg by a sperm and is the origin of every cell in your body *(Figures 2.1 and 2.2)*. It divides and multiplies into millions of cells that are the basic unit of every tissue and organ. The structure and all of the functions of your tissues and organs are due to their cells. The **cell** is the basic unit of life. **Cytology** is the study of this cell structure and function. Your understanding of the cell will form the basis for your knowledge of the anatomy and physiology of every tissue and organ.

▲ **FIGURE 2.2 Fertilization of Egg by Single Sperm.**

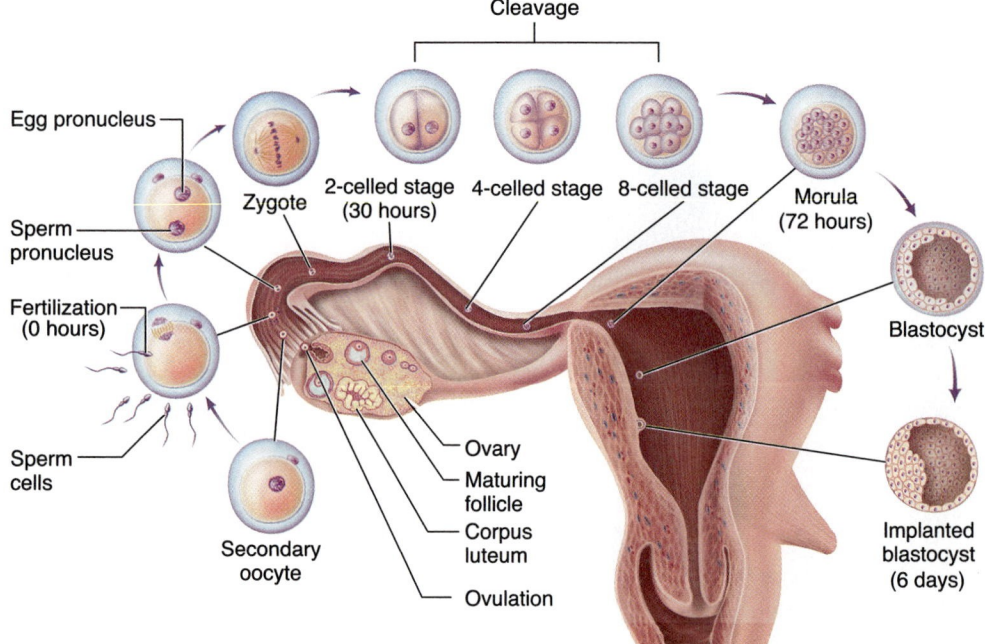

▲ **FIGURE 2.1 Beginning of Life.**

S = Suffix   P = Prefix   R = Root   R/CF = Combining Form

WORD	PRONUNCIATION	ELEMENTS		DEFINITION
atom	**AT**-om		Greek *indivisible*	A small unit of matter
blastocyst	**BLAS**-toe-sist	P/ R/	**blasto-** *dividing* **-cyst** *sac, cell*	First two weeks of the developing embryo
cell	SELL		Latin *a storeroom*	The smallest unit capable of independent existence
cellular (adj)	**SELL**-you-lar	S/ R/	**-ar** *pertaining to* **cellul-** *small cell*	Pertaining to a cell
cytology	**SIGH**-tol-oh-gee	S/ R/CF	**-logy** *study of* **cyt/o-** *cell*	Study of the cell
fertilization fertilize (verb)	fer-til-eye-**ZAY**-shun **FER**-til-ize	S/ R/	**-ation** *action* **fertiliz-** *to bear*	Union of a male sperm and a female egg
holistic	ho-**LIS**-tik	S/ R/	**-ic** *pertaining to* **holist-** *whole*	Pertaining to the care of the whole person in physical, mental, emotional, and spiritual dimensions
molecule molecular (adj)	**MOLL**-eh-kyul mo-**LEK**-you-lar	S/ R/	**-ule** *small* **molec-** *mass*	Very small particle
organ	**OR**-gan		Latin *instrument, tool*	Structure with specific functions in a body system
organelle	**OR**-gah-nell	S/ R/	**-elle** *small* **organ-** *organ*	Part of a cell having specialized function(s)
tissue	**TISH**-you		Latin *to weave*	Collection of similar cells
vitro in vitro fertilization (IVF)	**VEE**-tro IN **VEE**-tro **FER**-til-ih-**ZAY**-shun		Latin *glass*	Process of combining sperm and egg in a laboratory dish and placing resulting embryos inside uterus
zygote	**ZYE**-goat		Greek *yolk*	Cell resulting from the union of the sperm and egg

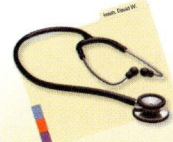

Case Report 2.1 (continued)

Mrs. Arnold achieved pregnancy and delivered a healthy girl at term.

EXERCISES

As you begin your study of medical language, it is important to realize the logic of how terms are formed. Elements are building blocks. You may not see a root in the same position in every term. Not every term requires a prefix and/or a suffix. Build your terms after first reviewing the Word Analysis and Definition (WAD) box. Fill in the blanks.

1. First two weeks of the developing embryo   blasto/ _____
                                                P   R

   This term does have a prefix and the root is the end of the word, not a suffix.

2. Pertaining to a small cell   cellul/_____
                               R   S

   This term does not start with a prefix; it starts with a root and ends with a suffix.

3. Study of the cell   cyto/_____ ;
                      CF   S

   This term begins with a combining form, which is a root plus a combining vowel. The term ends with a suffix.

   The five elements used to build medical terms are: _____, _____, _____, _____, and _____.

> **Study Hint**
> Notice the position of the root in questions 1 and 2. A root can appear at the end of a term, or at the beginning of a term, as well as in the middle of a term (its usual place).

STRUCTURE AND FUNCTIONS OF CELLS

As the zygote divides, every cell derived from it becomes a small, complex factory that carries out these basic functions of life:

- *manufacture* of proteins and lipids
- *production* and use of energy
- *communication* with other cells
- *replication* of deoxyribonucleic acid (**DNA**)
- *reproduction*

All your cells contain a fluid called **cytoplasm (intracellular** fluid) surrounded by a **cell membrane** *(Figure 2.3)*. A single cell may have 10 billion protein molecules inside it.

The cell membrane is made of proteins and lipids and allows water, oxygen, glucose, **electrolytes, steroids,** and alcohol to pass through it. On the outside of the cell membrane are receptors that bind to chemical messengers, such as **hormones** sent by other cells. These are the chemical signals by which your cells communicate with each other. The cytoplasm is a clear, gelatinous substance crowded with different organelles. **Organelles** are small structures that carry out special **metabolic** tasks, the chemical processes that occur in the cell. Examples of organelles are:

- Nucleus
- Endoplasmic reticulum
- Golgi complex or apparatus
- **Mitochondria**

- Nucleolus
- Ribosomes
- Lysosomes
- Centrioles

These are defined and their functions detailed in the succeeding pages.

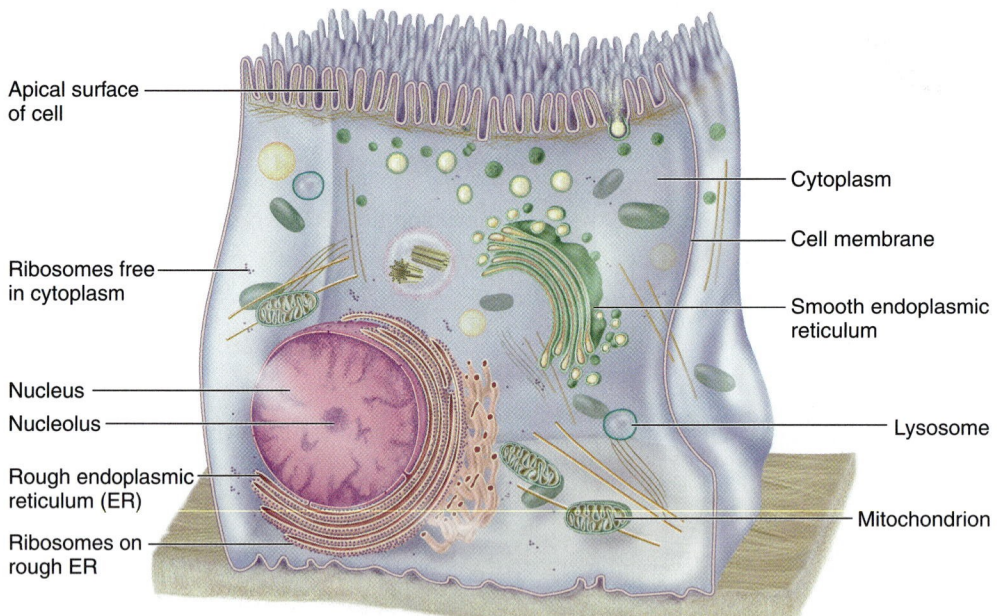

Apical surface of cell

Ribosomes free in cytoplasm

Nucleus

Nucleolus

Rough endoplasmic reticulum (ER)

Ribosomes on rough ER

Cytoplasm

Cell membrane

Smooth endoplasmic reticulum

Lysosome

Mitochondrion

▲ **FIGURE 2.3   Structure of a Representative Cell.**

WORD	PRONUNCIATION		ELEMENTS	DEFINITION
cytoplasm	SIGH-toe-plazm	S/ R/CF	-plasm *something formed* cyt/o- *cell*	Clear, gelatinous substance that forms the substance of a cell except for the nucleus
deoxyribonucleic acid (DNA)	dee-OCK-see-RYE-boh-noo-KLEE-ik AS-id		deoxyribose *sugar* nucleic acid *protein*	Source of hereditary characteristics found in chromosomes
electrolyte	ee-LEK-troh-lite	S/ R/CF	-lyte *soluble* electr/o- *electric*	Substance that, when dissolved in a suitable medium, forms electrically charged particles
hormone hormonal (adj)	HOR-mohn hor-MOHN-al		Greek *set in motion*	Chemical formed in one tissue or organ and carried by the blood to stimulate or inhibit a function of another tissue or organ
intracellular	in-trah-SELL-you-lar	S/ P/ R/	-ar *pertaining to* intra- *within* -cellul- *small cell*	Within the cell
membrane membranous (adj)	MEM-brain MEM-brah-nus		Latin *parchment*	Thin layer of tissue covering a structure or cavity
metabolism metabolic (adj)	meh-TAB-oh-lizm met-ah-BOL-ik	S/ R/ S/	-ism *condition* metabol- *change* -ic *pertaining to*	The constantly changing physical and chemical processes occurring in the cell
mitochondrion mitochondria (pl)	my-toe-KON-dree-on my-toe-KON-dree-ah	S/ R/CF R/	-ion *action, condition* mit/o- *thread* -chondr- *granule*	Organelle that generates, stores, and releases energy for cell activities
organelle	OR-gah-nell	S/ R/	-elle *small* organ- *organ*	Part of a cell having a specialized function(s)
steroid steroidal (adj)	STER-oyd STER-oy-dal	S/ R/	-oid *resemble* ster- *solid*	Large family of chemical substances found in many drugs, hormones, and body components

EXERCISES

Continue building your knowledge of elements. Fill in the blanks.

1. Within the cell   _____/cellul/_____

   Add the elements that will complete this medical term. Write under the line the element(s) you have used (P = prefix, R = root, CF = combining form, S = suffix).

2. Substance of a cell except for the nucleus   _____/ _____/plasm

   Add the elements that will complete this medical term. Write under the line the element you have used (P, R, CF, S).

   What makes the difference between a root and a combining form _____

3. Chemical substance found in drugs   _____/ _____ /oid

   Add the elements that will complete this medical term. Write under the line the element you have used (P, R, CF, S).

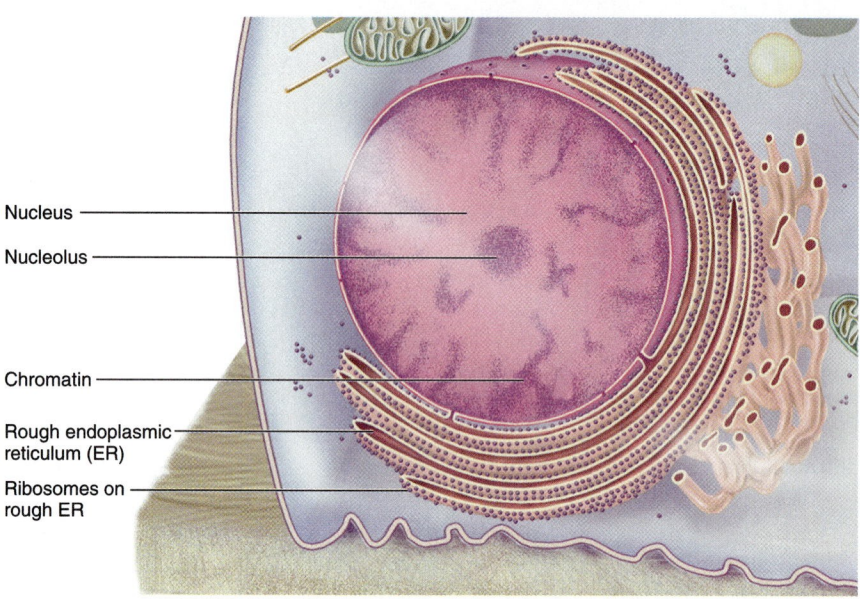

Nucleus

Nucleolus

Chromatin

Rough endoplasmic
reticulum (ER)

Ribosomes on
rough ER

▲ **FIGURE 2.4   The Nucleus.**

STRUCTURE AND FUNCTON OF CELLS (continued)

Organelles

The **nucleus** is the largest organelle *(Figure 2.4)*. It directs all the activities of the cell. Most of your cells have one nucleus; red blood cells have none, and some liver cells and muscle cells contain many nuclei. The nucleus is surrounded by its own membrane, which has small openings called pores. Every minute, hundreds of molecules pass through the pores. These molecules include the raw materials for the DNA and RNA synthesis that is ongoing inside the nucleus. (The functions of DNA and RNA are covered in *Chapter 21.*)

Forty-six molecules of DNA and their associated **proteins** are packed into each nucleus as thin strands called **chromatin.** When cells divide, the chromatin condenses to form 46 more densely coiled bodies called **chromosomes** *(Figure 2.5)*. Each chromosome consists of two **chromatids** joined at a pinched spot called the **centromere.** When the cell divides, the two chromatids separate, and each becomes a chromosome in the new cell.

Each nucleus contains a **nucleolus,** a small dense body composed of RNA and protein. It manufactures ribosomes that migrate through the nuclear membrane pores into the cytoplasm.

Ribosomes are organelles involved in the manufacture of protein from simple materials. This process is called **anabolism.**

The **endoplasmic reticulum** is an organelle that manufactures steroids, cholesterol and other lipids, and proteins. It also detoxifies alcohol and other drugs.

The **Golgi complex** (apparatus) synthesizes **carbohydrates** and packages proteins with carbohydrates to form **glycoproteins.**

Lysosomes are organelles that are the garbage disposal units of the cell. They digest and dispose of worn-out organelles as part of the process of cell death. They also digest foreign particles and bacteria.

Mitochondria are the powerhouses of the cells. They extract energy by breaking down compounds such as glucose and fat. This process is called **catabolism.** The energy is used to do the work of the cell; for example, to make a muscle contract.

- **Metabolism**—the sum of the physical and chemical processes in a cell.
- **Anabolism**—constructive metabolism, the build up from simple substances to complex substances needed in the cell.
- **Catabolism**—destructive metabolism, the breakdown of complex substances to release energy.

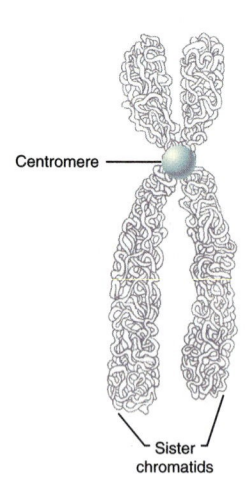

Centromere

Sister
chromatids

▲ **FIGURE 2.5
Chromosome Structure.**

WORD	PRONUNCIATION	ELEMENTS		DEFINITION
anabolism	an-**AB**-oh-lizm	S/ R/	-ism *condition* anabol- *build up*	The buildup of complex substances in the cell from simpler ones as a part of metabolism
carbohydrate	kar-bo-**HIGH**-drate	S/ R/CF R/	-ate *use, action* carb/o- *carbon* -hydr- *water*	Group of organic food compounds that includes sugars, starch, glycogen, and cellulose
catabolism	kah-**TAB**-oh-lizm	S/ R/	-ism *condition* catabol- *break down*	Breakdown of complex substances into simpler ones as a part of metabolism
centromere	**SEN**-troh-mere	P/ R/	centro- *central* -mere *part*	Junction that holds the two chromatids together to form a chromosome
chromatid	**KROH**-ma-tid	S/ R/	-id *having a particular quality* chromat- *color*	One of the two strands of a chromosome
chromatin	**KROH**-ma-tin	S/ R/	-in *in, pertaining to* chromat- *color*	Composed of DNA and RNA and forms chromosomes during cell division
chromosome	**KROH**-moh-sohm	S/ R/CF	-some *body* chrom/o- *color*	Body in the nucleus that contains DNA and genes
endoplasmic reticulum	**EN**-doh-**PLAZ**-mik reh-**TIC**-you-lum	S/ P/ R/ S/ R/	-ic *pertaining to* endo- *inside* -plasm- *something formed* -um *structure* reticul- *network*	Structure inside a cell that synthesizes steroids, detoxifies drugs, and manufactures cell membranes
glycoprotein	**GLYE**-koh-**PRO**-teen	R/CF R/	glyc/o- *sugar* -protein *protein*	Combination of carbohydrate and protein
Golgi complex	**GOAL**-jee **KOM**-pleks	 R/	Camillo Golgi, Italian physician, 1843–1926 complex *woven together*	Organelle involved in synthesis of carbohydrates and glycoproteins
lysosome	**LIE**-soh-sohm	S/ R/CF	-some *body* lys/o- *decompose*	Enzyme that digests foreign material
nucleus nuclear (adj)	**NYU**-klee-us **NYU**-klee-ar	S/ R/	-us *pertaining to* nucle- *nucleus*	Functional center of a cell or structure
nucleolus	nyu-**KLEE**-oh-lus	S/ R/CF	-lus *small* nucle/o- *nucleus*	Small mass within the nucleus
protein	**PRO**-teen	S/ R/CF	-in *in* prot/e- *first*	Class of food substances based on amino acids
ribosome	**RYE**-bo-sohm	S/ R/CF	-some *body* rib/o- *like a rib*	Structure in the cell that assembles amino acids into protein

EXERCISES   *Continue analyzing the logic of medical language. Add the element that will complete this medical term. Write under the line the element you have used (P, R, CF, S). Fill in the blanks.*

1. Combination of carbohydrate + protein   _____/protein

   What is unusual about this term? _____

   This term has no _____ .

2. Pertaining to something formed inside (the cell)   endo/_____/ _____

   This word contains the main building block elements for a medical term.

3. Find a term in the WAD that contains an element that means water.

   _____

CASE REPORT 2.2

Using arthroscopy, the orthopedic surgeon removed his torn **anterior cruciate ligament (ACL)** and replaced it with a **graft** from his patellar ligament. The torn medial collateral ligament was sutured together. The tear in his medial **meniscus** was repaired. Rehabilitation focused on strengthening the **muscles** around his knee joint and regaining joint mobility.

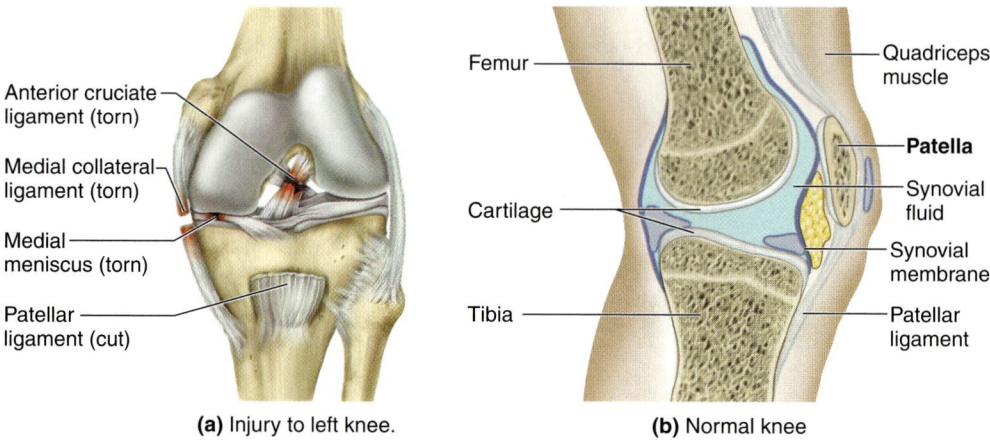

Anterior cruciate ligament (torn)
Medial collateral ligament (torn)
Medial meniscus (torn)
Patellar ligament (cut)

Femur
Cartilage
Tibia

Quadriceps muscle
Patella
Synovial fluid
Synovial membrane
Patellar ligament

(a) Injury to left knee.

(b) Normal knee

▲ **FIGURE 2.6   Knee Anatomy.**

Keynote

Different tissues are made of specialized cells with unique materials around them that are manufactured by the cells.

Abbreviation	
ACL	anterior cruciate ligament

TISSUES

The knee contains examples of all the different major groups of tissue and will be used in this lesson to illustrate the relation of structure to function in the different tissues. To understand the condition of the 22-year-old in the case report, you need a knowledge of tissue structure and function. Ultimately, this is important for your understanding of the anatomy and physiology of organs, organ systems, and the whole body.

Tissues hold your body together. The many tissues of your body have different structures for specialized functions. The different tissues are made of similar cells with unique materials around them that are manufactured by the cells. **Histology** is the study of the structure and function of tissues. The primary tissue groups are outlined in *Table 2.1*.

TABLE 2.1 The Four Primary Tissue Groups

Type	Function	Location
Connective	Bind, support, protect, fill spaces, store fat	Widely distributed throughout the body; for example, in blood, bone, cartilage, and fat
Epithelial	Protect, **secrete**, absorb, **excrete**	Cover body surface, cover and line internal organs, compose glands
Muscle	Movement	Attached to bones, in the walls of hollow internal organs, in the heart
Nervous	Transmit impulses for **coordination**, sensory reception	Brain, spinal cord, nerves

Adapted from *Hole's Human Anatomy and Physiology,* 10th ed. by Shier, Butler, and Lewis. Copyright © 2004 The McGraw-Hill Companies, Inc. Reprinted with permission.

WORD	PRONUNCIATION		ELEMENTS	DEFINITION
anterior (opposite of posterior)	an-**TER**-ee-or	S/ R/	**-ior** *pertaining to* **anter-** *coming before*	Front surface of body; situated in front
coordinate **coordination** (noun)	ko-**OR**-din-ate ko-**OR**-di-**NAY**-shun	S/ P/ R/	**-ate** *action* **co-** *together* **-ordin-** *arrange*	To bring together different structures into a harmonious function
cruciate	**KRU**-she-ate		Latin *cross*	Shaped like a cross
epithelium	ep-ih-**THEE**-lee-um	S/ P/ R/	**-um** *structure* **epi-** *upon* **-theli-** *nipple*	Tissue that covers surfaces or lines cavities
epithelial (adj)	ep-ih-**THEE**-lee-al	S/	**-al** *pertaining to*	
excrete **excretion** (noun)	eks-**KREET** eks-**KREE**-shun		Latin *separate*	To pass out of the body waste products of metabolism Removal of waste products of metabolism out of the body
graft	GRAFT		French *transplant*	Transplantation of living tissue
histology **histologist**	his-**TOL**-oh-jee his-**TOL**-oh-jist	S/ R/CF S/	**-logy** *study of* **hist/o-** *tissue* **-logist** *one who studies*	Structure and function of cells, tissues, and organs
ligament	**LIG**-ah-ment		Latin *band*	Band of fibrous tissue connecting two structures
medial (opposite of lateral)	**ME**-dee-al		Latin *middle*	Nearer to the middle of the body
meniscus **menisci** (pl)	meh-**NISS**-kuss meh-**NISS**-key		Greek *crescent*	Disc of connective tissue cartilage between the bones of a joint; for example, in the knee joint
muscle	**MUSS**-el		Latin *muscle*	A tissue consisting of contractile cells
patella	pah-**TELL**-ah		Latin *small plate*	Thin, circular bone in front of the knee joint and embedded in the patellar tendon. Also called the kneecap
secrete **secretion** (noun)	se-**KREET** se-**KREE**-shun		Latin *release*	To produce a chemical substance in a cell and release it from the cell

EXERCISES

Change the elements, change the word. Find a set of terms in the WAD for which changing a single element will change the meaning of the term. Fill in the blanks.

1. _____/ _____/ _____ means _____ .
       P   R/CF   S

  _____/ _____/ _____ means_____ .
       P   R/CF   S

The element that changed was the _____.

Examples of opposite terms are given in the WAD. Write the terms and their opposites below.

2. _____ is the opposite of_____ .

3. _____ is the opposite of_____ .

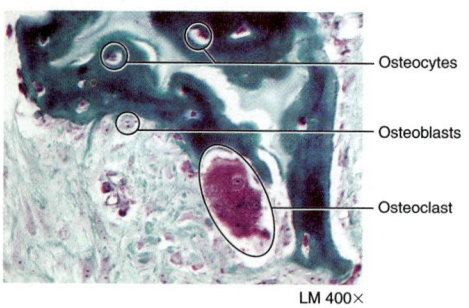

LM 400×

▲ **FIGURE 2.7   Bone Tissue.**

Osteocytes
Osteoblasts
Osteoclast

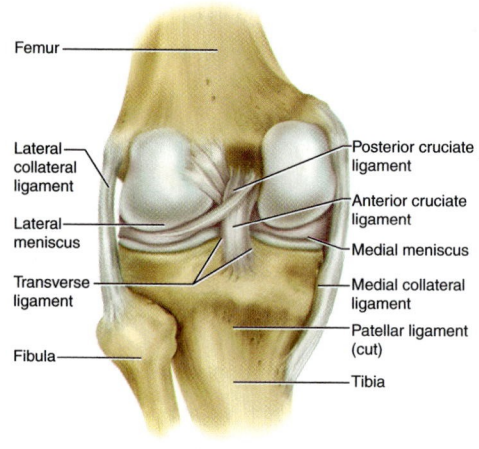

Femur

Lateral collateral ligament

Lateral meniscus

Transverse ligament

Fibula

Posterior cruciate ligament

Anterior cruciate ligament

Medial meniscus

Medial collateral ligament

Patellar ligament (cut)

Tibia

Anterior view

▲ **FIGURE 2.8   Ligaments of the Knee Joint.**

CONNECTIVE TISSUES IN THE KNEE JOINT

- **Bones** of the knee joint are the femur, tibia, and patella. Bone is the hardest connective tissue due to the presence of calcium mineral salts, mostly calcium phosphate. Bone **matrix** is deposited by bone cells, **osteoblasts,** in concentric patterns around a central canal containing a blood vessel *(Figure 2.7)*. As a result, every osteoblast is close to a supply of **nutrients** from the blood. This enables bones to heal after being fractured. **Osteocytes** are former osteoblasts that maintain the bone matrix. **Osteoclasts** dissolve the bone matrix to release calcium and phosphate into the blood when they are needed elsewhere. Bones as a whole are covered with a thick fibrous tissue called the **periosteum.**

- **Cartilage** has a flexible, rubbery matrix that allows it, as a meniscus, to function as a shock absorber, and as a gliding surface at **articulations** where two bones meet to form a joint. Cartilage has very few blood vessels and heals poorly or not at all. When it is injured or torn, surgical repair is usually necessary. Sometimes, for example in osteoarthritis, it cannot be repaired. Cartilage also forms the shape of your ear, the tip of your nose, and your larynx.

- **Ligaments** are strips or bands of fibrous connective tissue *(Figure 2.8)*. Cells called **fibroblasts** form a gelatinous (jelly-like) matrix and closely packed, parallel **collagen** fibers. These fibers provide the strength the ligament needs. The knee joint has a complex array of eleven ligaments that hold it together, prevent it from rotating when we stand upright, and help prevent dislocations. Their blood supply is poor, so they do not heal well without surgery.

- **Tendons** are thick, strong ligaments that attach muscles to bone.

- The **joint capsule** of the knee joint is attached to the tibia and femur, encloses the joint cavity, and is made of thin, collagen fibrous connective tissue. It is strengthened by fibers that extend over it from the ligaments and muscles surrounding the knee joint. These features are common to most joints.

- The inner surface of many joint capsules is lined with **synovial membrane** that secretes **synovial fluid.** This fluid is a slippery lubricant retained in the joint cavity by the capsule. It has a texture similar to raw egg white. It makes joint movement almost friction free and distributes nutrients to the cartilage on the joint surfaces of bone.

- **Muscle tissue** stabilizes the knee joint. Extensions of the tendons of the *quadriceps femoris,* the large muscle in front of the thigh, and of the *semimembranosus muscle* on the rear of the thigh, are major stabilizers. The muscles themselves respectively extend and flex the joint. The structure and functions of these and other skeletal muscles are described in *Chapter 5*.

- **Nervous tissue** extensively supplies all the knee structures, which is why a knee injury is excruciatingly painful. The structure and functions of nervous tissue are described in *Chapter 10*.

WORD ANALYSIS AND DEFINITION

WORD	PRONUNCIATION	ELEMENTS		DEFINITION
articulate articulation (noun)	ar-**TIK**-you-late ar-tik-you-**LAY**-shun		Latin *jointed*	Two bones have formed a joint. The joint formed permits movement between two parts
capsule capsular (adj)	**KAP**-syul **KAP**-syu-lar	S/ R/	-ule *little* caps- *box*	Fibrous tissue layer surrounding a joint or other structure
cartilage	**KAR**-tih-lage		Latin *gristle*	Nonvascular firm, connective tissue found mostly in joints
collagen	**KOL**-ah-jen	S/ R/	-gen *producing* colla- *glue*	Major protein of connective tissue, cartilage, and bone
fibroblast	**FIE**-bro-blast	S/ R/CF	-blast *germ cell* fibr/o- *fiber*	Cell that forms collagen fibers
matrix	**MAY**-triks		Latin "mater" *mother*	Substance that surrounds cells, is manufactured by the cells, and holds them together
nutrient	**NYU**-tree-ent	S/ R/	-ent *end result* nutri- *nourish*	A substance in food required for normal physiological function
osteoblast	**OS**-tee-oh-blast	S/ R/CF	-blast *germ cell* oste/o- *bone*	Bone-forming cell
osteoclast osteocyte	**OS**-tee-oh-klast **OS**-tee-oh-site	S/ S/	-clast *break* -cyte *cell*	Bone-removing cell Bone-maintaining cell
periosteum	**PER**-ee-**OSS**-tee-um	S/ P/ R/CF	-um *tissue* peri- *around* -ost/e- *bone*	Fibrous membrane covering a bone
synovial	si-**NOH**-vee-al	S/ P/ R/CF	-al *pertaining to* syn- *together* -ov/i- *egg*	Pertaining to synovial fluid and synovial membrane

---

EXERCISES

Understanding elements is the key to a large medical vocabulary. Work with the following exercise to increase your knowledge of the medical language. Fill in the blanks.

osteo**blast**   osteo**clast**   osteo**cyte**

1. These terms all have the same (circle one: P   R   CF   S   ) Be careful!

   This element means _____ .

2. Underline the element that changes in every term.

   The element that changes is the (circle one: P   R   CF   S   )

3. Osteo**blast** means_____ .

   Osteo**clast** means _____ .

   Osteo**cyte** means_____ .

4. The difference between a **fibroblast** and an **osteoblast** is:

   _____

   _____

5. In question 4, this element has changed _____, and this element has remained the same: _____ .

CASE REPORT 2.3

Fulwood Medical Center

An 84-year-old man with advanced **Parkinson disease** was having difficulty breathing because his stooped posture was compressing his lungs and his loss of muscle control made respiration more difficult. A bout of influenza increased his breathing difficulty, and a **tracheostomy** tube was inserted to help him breathe. He then became unable to swallow, and a feeding tube was inserted. Because of **hypertrophy** of his prostate, he developed a **urinary** tract infection. This led to **septicemia.** The bloodborne infection attacked his kidneys, heart, and lungs, leading to failure of these organs and their organ systems and, ultimately, death.

As described in the case report, when organs and organ systems do not function in an **integrated** way, a person can die.

An **organ** is a structure composed of several tissues that work together to carry out specific functions. For example, the skin is an organ that has different tissues in it such as epithelial cells, hair, nails, and glands.

An **organ system** is a group of organs with a specific collective function, such as digestion, circulation, or respiration. For example, the nose, pharynx, larynx, trachea, and bronchi work together to achieve the total function of respiration.

Organ Systems

The body has eleven organ systems, shown in *Table 2.2*. Muscular and skeletal are considered one organ system, the musculoskeletal system.

All your organ systems work together to ensure that your body's internal environment remains relatively constant. This process is called **homeostasis.** For example, your digestive, respiratory, and circulatory organ systems work together so that (a) every cell in your body receives adequate nutrients and oxygen and (b) waste products from the breakdown of these nutrients during cell metabolism are removed. Your cells can then function normally. Disease affecting an organ or organ system disrupts this game plan of homeostasis.

Keynote

Homeostasis is the coordinated response of all the organs to maintain the internal physiological stability of an organism.

TABLE 2.2 Organ Systems

Organ System	Major Organs	Major Functions
Integumentary	Skin, hair, nails, sweat glands, sebaceous glands	Protect tissues, regulate body temperature, support sensory receptors
Skeletal	Bones, ligaments, cartilages	Provide framework, protect soft tissues, provide attachments for muscles, produce blood cells, store inorganic salts
Muscular	Muscles	Cause movements, maintain posture, produce body heat
Nervous	Brain, spinal cord, nerves, sense organs	Detect changes, receive and interpret sensory information, stimulate muscles and glands
Endocrine	Glands that secrete hormones: pituitary, thyroid, parathyroid, adrenal gland, pancreas, ovaries, testes, pineal gland, thymus	Control metabolic activities of organs and structures
Cardiovascular	Heart, blood vessels	Move blood and transport substances throughout body
Lymphatic	Lymph vessels and nodes, thymus, spleen	Return tissue fluid to the blood, carry certain absorbed food molecules, defend body against infection
Digestive	Mouth, tongue, teeth, salivary glands, pharynx, esophagus, stomach, liver, gallbladder, pancreas, small and large intestines	Receive, break down, and absorb food, eliminate unabsorbed material
Respiratory	Nasal cavity, pharynx, larynx, trachea, bronchi, lungs	Intake and output air, exchange gases between air and blood
Urinary	Kidneys, ureters, urinary bladder, urethra	Remove wastes from blood, maintain water and electrolyte balance, store and transport urine
Reproductive	*Male:* scrotum, testes, epididymides, vasa deferentia, seminal vesicles, prostate, bulbourethral glands, urethra, penis	Produce and maintain sperm cells, transfer sperm cells into female reproductive tract
	Female: ovaries, uterine (fallopian) tubes, uterus, vagina, vulva	Produce and maintain egg cells, receive sperm cells, support development of an embryo, function in birth process

Adapted from *Hole's Human Anatomy and Physiology,* 10th ed., by Shier, Butler, and Lewis. Copyright © 2004 The McGraw-Hill Companies, Inc. Reprinted with permission..

WORD	PRONUNCIATION	ELEMENTS		DEFINITION
homeostasis (**Note:** Hemostasis is very different.)	ho-mee-oh-**STAY**-sis	S/ R/CF	**-stasis** *standing, control* **home/o-** *the same*	Maintaining the stability or equilibrium of a system or the body's internal environment
hypertrophy	high-**PER**-troh-fee	P/ R/	**hyper-** *excessive* **-trophy** *development*	Increase in size, but not in number, of an individual tissue element
integrate **integration** (noun)	**IN**-teh-grate in-teh-**GRAY**-shun	S/ R/	**-ate** *action* **integr-** *whole*	To bring together a complete and harmonious whole
organ	**OR**-gan		Greek *instrument*	Structure with specific functions in a body system
Parkinson disease	**PAR**-kin-son diz-**EEZ**		James Parkinson, British physician, 1755–1824	Disease of muscular rigidity, tremors, and a masklike facial expression
septicemia	sep-tih-**SEE**-mee-ah	S/ R/	**-emia** *blood condition* **septic-** *infected*	Microorganisms circulating in, and infecting, the blood (blood poisoning)
tracheostomy	tray-kee-**OST**-oh-me	S/ R/CF	**-stomy** *new opening* **trache/o-** *windpipe*	Incision into the windpipe, usually so that a tube can be inserted to assist breathing
urinary	**YUR**-in-ary	S/ R/	**-ary** *pertaining to* **urin-** *urine*	Pertaining to urine

Organs

In *Table 2.2*, you can see that each organ system contains several organs. An organ is composed of two or more tissue types that perform a particular function. Each organ has well-defined anatomical boundaries separating it from adjacent structures. The different organs in an organ system are usually interconnected. For example, in the urinary organ system, the organs are the kidneys, ureters, bladder, and urethra, and they are all connected *(Figure 2.9)*.

EXERCISES	Use your knowledge of the building blocks of terms, and **deconstruct** the following terms into their basic elements. This will give you a better picture of how the words were formed. Fill in the blanks.

Medical Term	Prefix	Root and/or combining form	Suffix	Meaning of Term
homeostasis				
hypertrophy				
septicemia				
tracheostomy				
urinary				

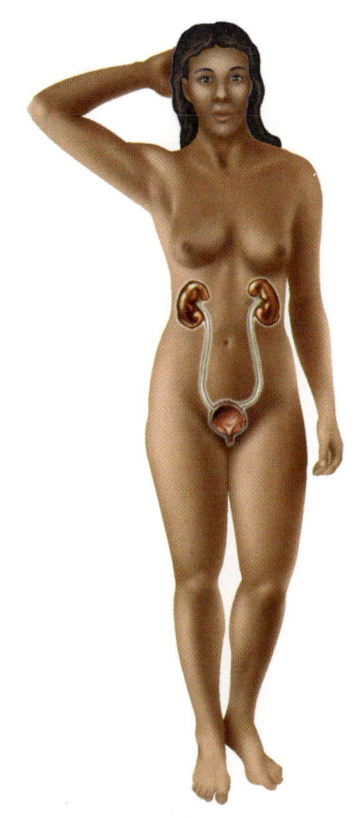

▲ **FIGURE 2.9 Urinary System.**

Anatomical Positions, Planes, and Directions

Terms have been developed over the past several thousand years to enable you to describe clearly where different anatomical structures and lesions are in relation to each other. To communicate effectively with other health professionals, it is critical that you are able to use the terminology to describe these positions and relative positions. To do this, you need to be able to:

- **Define the fundamental anatomical position on which all descriptions of anatomical locations are based.**
- **Describe the different anatomical planes and directions.**
- **Locate the body cavities.**
- **Identify the four abdominal quadrants and three regions.**

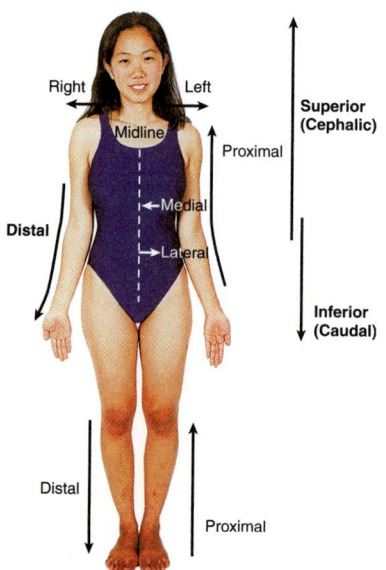

▲ **FIGURE 2.10   Anatomical Position with Directional Terms.**

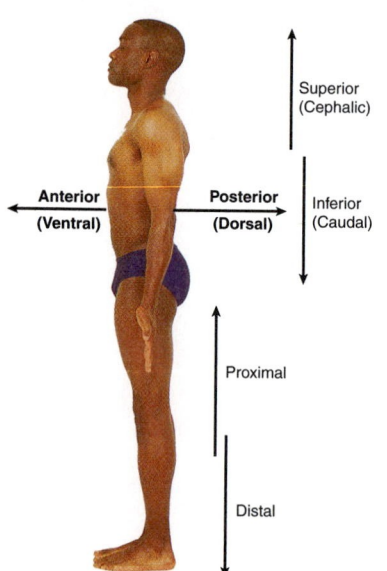

▲ **FIGURE 2.11   Directional Terms.**

ANATOMICAL POSITION

When all anatomic descriptions are used, it is assumed that the body is in the anatomical position. The body is standing erect with feet flat on the floor, face and eyes are facing forward, arms are at the sides with the palms facing forward *(Figure 2.10)*.

When your palms face forward, the forearm is **supine.** When you lie down flat on your back, you are supine. When your palms face backwards, the forearm is **prone.** When you lie down flat on your belly you are prone.

DIRECTIONAL TERMS

Directional terms describe the position of one structure or part of the body relative to another. These directional terms are shown in *Figures 2.10 and 2.11*.

ANATOMIC PLANES

Different views of the body are based on imaginary "slices" producing flat surfaces that pass through the body *(Figure 2.12)*. The three major anatomic planes are:

- **Transverse** or **horizontal**—a plane passing across the body parallel to the floor and perpendicular to the body's long axis. It divides the body into an upper (**superior**) portion and a lower (**inferior**) portion.
- **Sagittal**—a vertical plane that divides the body into right and left portions.
- **Frontal** or **coronal**—a vertical plane that divides the body into front (**anterior**) and back (**posterior**) portions.

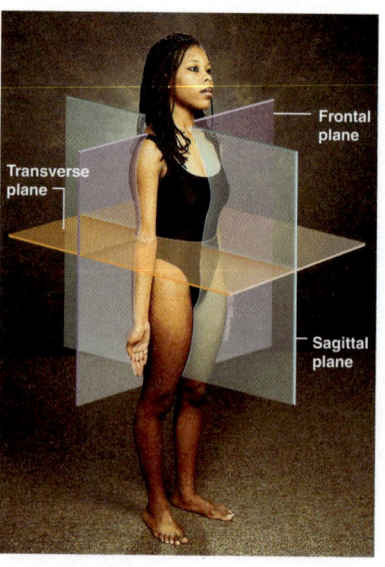

FIGURE 2.12   Anatomic Planes. ▶

WORD	PRONUNCIATION	ELEMENTS		DEFINITION
anterior (opposite of posterior)	an-**TER**-ee-or	S/ R/	**-ior** *pertaining to* **anter-** *coming before*	Front surface of body; situated in front
caudal (opposite of cephalic)	**KAW**-dal	S/ R/	**-al** *pertaining to* **caud-** *tail*	Pertaining to or nearer to the tail
cephalic (opposite of caudal)	se-**FAL**-ik	S/ R/	**-ic** *pertaining to* **cephal-** *cranial*	Pertaining to or nearer to the head
coronal (equivalent of frontal)	**KOR**-oh-nal	S/ R/	**-al** *pertaining to* **coron-** *crown*	Vertical plane dividing body into anterior and posterior portions
distal (opposite of proximal)	**DISS**-tal	S/ R/	**-al** *pertaining to* **dist-** *away from the center*	Situated away from the center of the body
dorsal (equivalent to posterior)	**DOR**-sal	S/ R/	**-al** *pertaining to* **dors-** *back*	Pertaining to the back or situated behind
frontal (equivalent to coronal)	**FRON**-tal	S/ R/	**-al** *pertaining to* **front-** *front*	Vertical plane dividing the body into anterior and posterior portions
inferior (opposite of superior)	in-**FEE**-ree-or	S/ R/	**-ior** *pertaining to* **infer-** *below*	Situated below
posterior (opposite of anterior)	pos-**TER**-ee-or	S/ R/	**-ior** *pertaining to* **poster-** *coming behind*	Back surface of the body; situated behind
prone (opposite of supine)	PRONE		Latin *bending forward*	Lying face down, flat on your belly
proximal (opposite of distal)	**PROK**-sih-mal	S/ R/	**-al** *pertaining to* **proxim-** *nearest*	Situated nearest the center of the body
sagittal	**SAJ**-ih-tal	S/ R/	**-al** *pertaining to* **sagitt-** *arrow*	Plane vertically through the body dividing it into right and left portions
superior (opposite of inferior)	soo-**PEE**-ree-or	S/ R/	**-ior** *pertaining to* **super-** *above*	Situated above
supine (opposite of prone)	soo-**PINE**		Lain *bend backward*	Lying face up, flat on your spine
transverse	trans-**VERS**		Latin *crosswise*	Horizontal plane dividing the body into upper and lower portions
ventral (equivalent to anterior)	**VEN**-tral	S/ R/	**-al** *pertaining to* **ventr-** *belly*	Pertaining to the belly or situated nearer the surface of the belly

> **Study Hint**
> The terms in the WAD will be easier to remember if you study them in *pairs*, since most of them are *opposites*.

EXERCISES

The following list of terms from the WAD has one element in bold. You need to identify what type of element this is, and define its meaning. Then answer the questions. Fill in the blanks.

1. poster**ior**   Type of element: _____   Meaning: _____

2. **caud**al   Type of element: _____   Meaning: _____

3. cephal**ic**   Type of element: _____   Meaning: _____

4. **dist**al   Type of element: _____   Meaning: _____

5. **infer**ior   Type of element: _____   Meaning: _____

6. The three elements with the same meaning are _____, _____, and _____.

7. They all mean _____.

8. Every term in the WAD that can be deconstructed is composed of (types of element) _____.

BODY CAVITIES

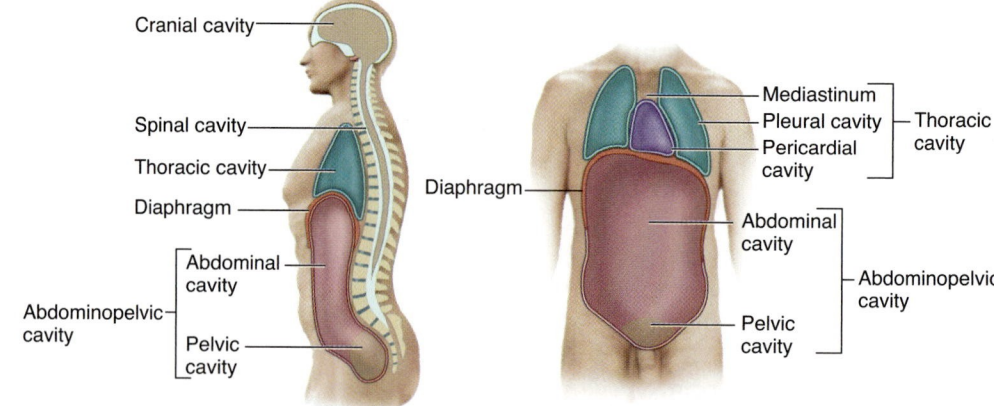

FIGURE 2.13 Body Cavities. ▶

The body contains many **cavities**. Some, like the nasal cavity, open to the outside. Four cavities do not open to the outside and are shown in *Figure 2.13*.

- **Cranial cavity**—contains the brain within the skull.
- **Thoracic cavity**—contains the heart, lungs, thymus gland, trachea, esophagus, and numerous blood vessels and nerves.
- **Abdominal cavity**—is separated from the thoracic cavity by the **diaphragm** and contains the stomach, intestines, liver, spleen, pancreas, and kidneys.
- **Pelvic cavity**—is surrounded by the pelvic bones and contains the urinary bladder, part of the large intestine, rectum, anus, and the internal reproductive organs.
- **Spinal cavity**—contains the spinal cord.

The abdominal cavity and pelvic cavity are collectively referred to as the **abdominopelvic cavity.**

Abbreviations

LLQ	left lower quadrant
LUQ	left upper quadrant
RLQ	right lower quadrant
RUQ	right upper quadrant

ABDOMINAL QUADRANTS

One way of referring to the locations of abdominal structures and to the site of abdominal pain and other abnormalities is to divide the abdominal region into **quadrants,** as shown in *Figure 2.14a*. The locations are: **right upper quadrant**

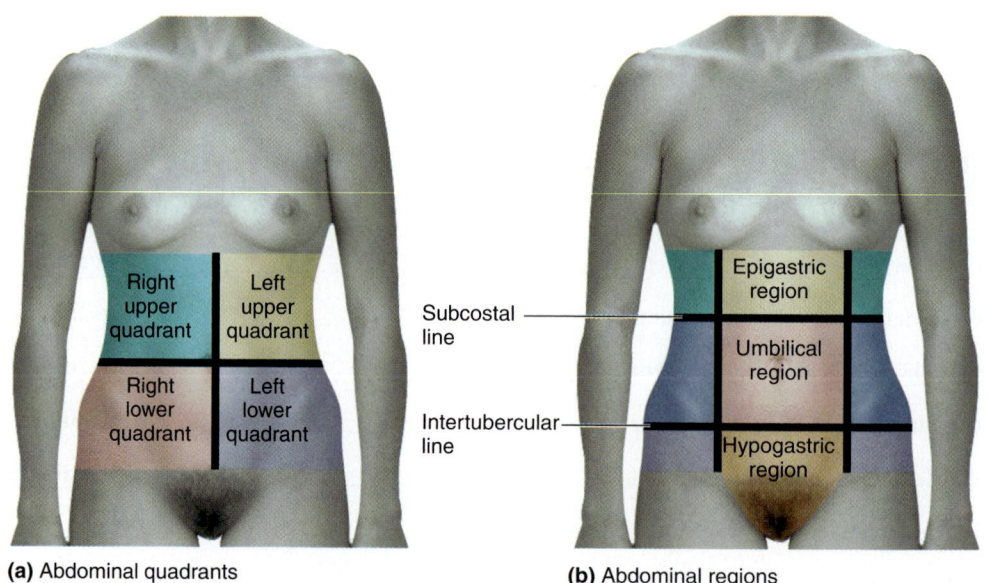

(a) Abdominal quadrants

(b) Abdominal regions

▲ **FIGURE 2.14   Regional anatomy.**

WORD	PRONUNCIATION	ELEMENTS		DEFINITION
abdominopelvic	ab-**DOM**-ih-no-**PEL**-vik	S/ R/CF R/	-ic *pertaining to* abdomin/o- *abdomen* -pelv- *pelvis*	Pertaining to the abdomen and pelvis
cavity cavities (pl)	**KAV**-ih-tee **KAV**-ih-tees		Latin *hollow place*	Hollow space or body compartment
diaphragm	**DIE**-ah-fram		Greek *diaphragm, fence*	Musculo-ligamentous partition separating the abdominal and thoracic cavities.
epigastric epigastrium (noun)	ep-ih-**GAS**-trik ep-ih-**GAS**-tree-um	S/ P/ R/	-ic *pertaining to* epi- *above* -gastr- *stomach*	Abdominal region above the stomach
hypogastric	high-poh-**GAS**-trik	S/ P/ R/	-ic *pertaining to* hypo- *below* -gastr- *stomach*	Abdominal region below the stomach
quadrant	**KWAD**-rant		Latin *one quarter*	One-quarter of a circle
umbilical umbilicus (noun)	um-**BIL**-ih-kal um-**BIL**-ih-kuss	S/ R/	-al *pertaining to* umbilic- *belly button* (navel)	Pertaining to the umbilicus or the center of the abdomen

(RUQ), **left upper quadrant (LUQ)**, **right lower quadrant (RLQ)** and **left lower quadrant (LLQ)**.

In addition, there are three regions in the middle of the abdomen as shown in *Figure 2.14b*. The upper **epigastric region**, the central **umbilical region**, and the lower **hypogastric region**.

EXERCISES

Take a closer look at the breakdown of medical terms. The medical term is given to you. Break it down into elements with a slash (/). Below each element, write the meaning of the element. See how the combination of elements will give you the meaning of the entire term. The first one is done for you. Fill in the blanks.

Study Hint
Remember to start with the suffix and work back to the front of the word.

1. **abdominopelvic**

   abdomino/ ___ pelv ___ / ___ ic ___
   abdomen   pelvis   pertaining to

   Meaning of **abdominopelvic**: _pertaining to the abdomen and pelvis_____

2. **epigastric**   _____/ _____ / _____

   Meaning of **epigastric**: _____

3. **hypogastric**   _____/ _____ / _____

   Meaning of **hypogastric**: _____

4. **umbilical**   _____/ _____ / _____

   Meaning of **umbilical**: _____

THE BODY AS A WHOLE

CHALLENGE YOUR KNOWLEDGE

A. **Word Elements:** These elements are grouped together to make them easier for you to review. There is a space on the table between each different group of elements. Insert the correct name for the type of element (P, R, CF, S) in the heading of the first column for that group, give the meaning of each element, and **construct** a term using each element.

> *Study Hint*
> Notice that there are several elements with the same meanings.

Element group =	Meaning of element	Example of medical term using that element
endo		
epi		
co		
hyper		
hypo		
intra		
syn		

Element group =	Meaning of element	Example of medical term using that element
blasto		
fibro		
histo		
homeo		
mito		
osteo		
theli		
tracheo		
chromo		
ovi		

Element group =	Meaning of element	Example of medical term using that element
al		
ar		
ary		
ation		
elle		
emia		
oid		
ic		
logy		
stomy		
ule		
um		

B. **Apply your knowledge of the body as a whole with the following exercise.** Fill in the following blanks to build the composition of the whole body *from the lowest to the highest order* of the anatomic hierarchy. Two of the blanks have been filled in to help you start the chart.

Atoms   build   *molecules*

_____ build _____ .

_____ build _____ .

_____ build _____ .

_____ build _____ .

_____ build _____ .

_____ build _____ .

_____ build _____ .

A small unit of matter is the _____ .

G. If you understand the terms in this chapter, you can describe correctly the difference between cytology and histology.

The difference is:

_____

_____

_____

_____

_____

H. Knowing the meaning of word elements will help you to deconstruct the following terms to explain the differences in their meaning. First, divide the word into its elements with slashes (/). Circle the suffix, and then fill in the table.

Term	Meaning of Root(s)/CF	Meaning of Suffix	Meaning of Term
homeostasis			
anabolism			
catabolism			
metabolism			
nucleus			
nucleolus			
ribosome			
lysosome			

I. **Terminology Challenge:** Pick what you think are the three most difficult words to spell in this chapter. Write them, pronounce them, and define them here:

1. _____ means. _____

2. _____ means. _____

3. _____ means _____ .

Have you checked your spelling? Can you spell them without looking at the book? You will probably see them again on a test.

J. Organs and Body Systems: Knowledge of the body's systems will help you master medical terminology. Assign the following organs to an organ system, and describe one major function of that system.

Organ	Organ system	System function
blood vessels		
cartilage		
epididymides		
fallopian tubes		
hair		
larynx		
liver		
muscles		
spinal cord		
spleen		
sweat glands		
teeth		
thymus		
thyroid gland		

K. Apply this knowledge of organ systems to answer the following questions. Circle your choice, but remember to rewrite any false information to be correct on the blanks at the end of the exercise.

1. Organs make basic functions happen in an organ system.   T   F

2. Glands that secrete hormones are in the endocrine system.   T   F

3. There are 13 different body systems.   T   F

4. An organ system will have more than one organ.   T   F

5. Organ systems that are not functioning correctly can disrupt homeostasis.   T   F

Rewrite any false statement(s) with correct information.

_____

_____

THE BODY AS A WHOLE

L. **Build medical terms using your knowledge of elements and their proper position in a medical term.** Fill in the blanks.

1. small mass   molec/ _____

2. pertaining to below the stomach   _____ / _____ /ic

3. instrument for viewing a joint   _____ /scope

4. pertaining to urine   urin/ _____

5. a change of condition   _____ /ism

6. small organ   organ/ _____

7. small nucleus   nucleo/ _____

8. enzyme that digests foreign material   lyso/ _____

Note: More than one element can have the same meaning. List the elements in this exercise that have the same meaning.

_____ all mean _____ .

_____ all mean _____ .

M. **Anatomic Positions and Planes:** You must know anatomic positions to prepare a patient for any type of procedure or surgery. Anatomic planes can help define radiologic studies. Using this knowledge, complete the following.

1. The surgeon needs his patient in the _____ position to remove a lesion on his back.

2. To prepare for a knee arthroscopy, the patient will be in the _____ position.

3. The body is standing erect with feet flat on the floor, the face and eyes are facing forward, and the arms are at the side with the palms facing forward in the _____ position.

4. A plane that divides the body into an upper, or superior, portion and a lower, or inferior, portion is called a _____ plane.

5. A frontal plane can also be called a _____ plane.

N. **Directional Terms:** Along with planes, body cavities, and quadrants, you must know body directional terms in order to be able to document and communicate accurately.

> **Study Hint**
> Learn these terms in pairs of opposites. The acronym "PADS" will help you remember the pairs.

Proximal and distal: proximal means _____; distal means _____ .

Anterior and posterior: anterior means_____; posterior means _____ .

Dorsal and ventral: dorsal means_____; ventral means _____ .

Superior and inferior: superior means_____; inferior means _____ .

O. Demonstrate your knowledge of directional terms and abbreviations by circling the correct choice.

1. The epigastric region is (above/below) the stomach. Therefore, it is (superior/inferior) to the stomach.

2. The umbilical region is so named because it is in the (center/back) of the abdomen and (inferior/superior) to the epigastric region.

3. The hypogastric region is between the (RUQ/LUQ) and the (RLQ/LLQ).

4. In the abbreviation LLQ, the first "L" means (lower/left).

5. The nose is (superior/inferior) to the chin.

6. The spine is (anterior/posterior) to the heart.

7. The umbilicus is (dorsal/ventral) to the spine.

8. The toes are (distal/proximal) to the knee.

P. **Recall and Review:** How well do you remember these word elements from the previous chapter? Try to answer without first looking back to check. Fill in the blanks.

Element	Types of element (P, R, R/CF, S)	Meaning of element
gynec		
um		
entero		
pathy		
endo		

Q. **Body Cavities:** The organ is given to you. Challenge yourself to place the organ in the correct body cavity, and then place the organ in the correct body system. Fill in the blanks.

Organ	Body cavity	Body system
brain		
gallbladder		
heart		
kidneys		
lungs		
pituitary		
ribs		
spleen		
uterus		

THE BODY AS A WHOLE

R. **Classroom Discussion:** Pick one topic, and prepare a five sentence brief summary of your thoughts on the topic. The questions given are only an example of what you might choose to discuss. Turn your preparation notes in to the instructor.

    1. Explain the holistic approach to medical treatment. What does this encompass? Do only certain physicians believe in this method? How does one locate this type of physician?

    2. Why is homeostasis important to a normally functioning body? What exactly is homeostasis? How is it disrupted? How is it restored?

S. **Latin and Greek Terms:** There is no easy way to remember these—you just have to know them so you can relate to their meanings. Match the terms in 1–10 to the meanings in A–J. Fill in the blanks.

_____ 1. atom	_____ 6. matrix	A. a storeroom	F. indivisible
_____ 2. graft	_____ 7. cruciate	B. cross	G. mother
_____ 3. hormone	_____ 8. membrane	C. yolk	H. to set in motion
_____ 4. ligament	_____ 9. meniscus	D. crescent	I. transplant
_____ 5. cell	_____ 10. zygote	E. band	J. parchment

T. **Knowledge of anatomic locations on the body will make your communications with other health professionals precise.** Challenge yourself with the following questions. Circle true or false, then rewrite the false answers correctly on the blank lines.

    1. Standing erect with feet flat on the floor, face and eyes facing forward, and arms at the side with palms facing forward is the "anatomical position."   T   F

    2. Transverse is a horizontal plane.   T   F

    3. Frontal and sagittal are both vertical planes.   T   F

    4. Inferior is situated above another part of the body.   T   F

    5. Dorsal means the same as **anterior.**   T   F

    6. The abdominal cavity contains the urinary bladder.   T   F

    7. The thoracic cavity is superior to the pelvic cavity, and the pelvic cavity is inferior to the abdominal cavity.   T   F

    8. The diaphragm divides the pelvic cavity and the abdominal cavity.   T   F

    9. In RUQ, "Q" means quadrant.   T   F

    10. The RUQ and the LUQ can be divided by a sagittal plane.   T   F

    Corrected statements:

    _____

    _____

    _____

    _____

    _____

    _____

U. Multiple choice is the format used for most national certification examinations.

    1. The single, fertilized cell is called the:

        a. mitochondria   **d.** zygote

        b. ribosome   **e.** blastocyst

        c. organelle

2. The word membrane means:

   a. small organ

   b. fluid inside a cell

   c. thin layer of tissue

   d. chemical substance

   e. molecule with electrical charge

Study Hint
Best test-taking strategy: Read the question first, then read *all* the possible answers before making your choice. Finally, go back and read the question again. Your first choice may look good, but sometimes another choice is the best answer.

3. Patella is the medical term for:

   a. ankle

   b. muscle

   c. kneecap

   d. ligament

   e. meniscus

4. Which structure functions as a shock absorber?

   a. cartilage

   b. muscle

   c. tendon

   d. ligament

   e. blood vessel

5. The prefix endo- means:

   a. outside

   b. within

   c. around

   d. behind

   e. across

6. The study of the function of tissues is called:

   a. cytology

   b. cardiology

   c. dermatology

   d. histology

   e. gastroenterology

7. Two bones that have formed a joint are called:

   a. graft

   b. articulation

   c. homeostasis

   d. metabolism

   e. cartilage

8. How many quadrants are in the body?

   a. one

   b. two

   c. three

   d. four

   e. five

9. **Hypogastric** refers to a:

   a. body region

   b. directional term

   c. body quadrant

   d. a and b

   e. a and c

10. What separates the thoracic and abdominal cavities?

    a. a tendon

    b. the diaphragm

    c. a ligament

    d. the pelvic cavity

    e. the upper quadrant

THE BODY AS A WHOLE

V. **Short Answer and/or Class Discussion:** Building up to larger components in the body, expand your knowledge of cells and tissues to organs and organ systems. Write a short answer to each question, and be prepared to discuss your answers with the instructor and class.

1. Define an **organ**.

_____

_____

2. What is the difference between an organ and an organ system?

_____

_____

_____

3. It is difficult to imagine skin as an "organ" because it is not a compact size like a liver or heart. Based on the above answers, why, then is skin an organ?

_____

_____

_____

4. Which body system has skin as a major organ?

_____

_____

_____

5. There can be smaller organs within a large organ. Name the smaller organs within the skin and some of their functions.

_____

_____

_____

6. List all the organ systems in the body.

_____

_____

_____

_____

_____

_____

_____

W. Now that you have had some practice with the new medical terms, you are ready to read again the following case report from earlier in this chapter. Underline all the medical terms, then answer all the questions. Fill in the blanks.

CASE REPORT 2.2

You are

...A physical therapy assistant employed by the Rehabilitation Unit in Fulwood Medical Center.

Your patient is

...Richard Josen, a 22-year-old man who injured tissues in his left knee playing football. Using arthroscopy, the orthopedic surgeon removed his torn anterior cruciate ligament (ACL) and replaced it with a graft from his patellar ligament. The torn medial collateral ligament was sutured together. The tear in his medial meniscus was repaired. Rehabilitation focused on strengthening the muscles around his knee joint and regaining joint mobility.

1. Define **arthroscopy**. _____

2. What type of specialist will use an **arthroscope**? _____

3. **ACL** is the abbreviation for _____ .

4. What is a **graft**? _____

5. What does a **meniscus** resemble? _____

THE BODY AS A WHOLE

CHAPTER SUMMARY EXERCISE

1. *Listen to the pronunciation of the medical terms as given by your instructor.*
2. *Circle the correct spelling of the medical term.*
3. *Match the correctly spelled terms to the brief descriptions below.*
4. *Write a sentence for each of the 15 terms that appear in this exercise.*

A. SPELLING COMPREHENSION: *Circle the correct spelling of the term.*

1. organale	orgenele	organelle	orgenelle	organel
2. sinovial	sinnovial	synoveal	synevial	synovial
3. rybosome	ribosonme	rhibosome	ribosome	rhybosone
4. diaphram	diaphrame	diaphragm	deaphragm	diafragm
5. tracheotomy	trackeostomy	trachiostomy	treckeostomy	tracheostomy
6. nucklii	nucleei	nuclei	neuclei	nucklie
7. zygoat	zigote	zygote	zigotte	zygoate
8. endockrine	endocrine	endoccrine	endockryne	endocrin
9. meniscus	menniscus	menickus	meniskus	meniscuss
10. historyology	histology	hystology	hestology	historology
11. septicemia	seppticemia	septicemmia	septisemia	septum
12. matrex	mitrex	matrixx	matrrix	matrix
13. chytoplism	cytoplasm	citoplasme	cytaplasm	citoplasm
14. cartilage	kartiledge	carttilege	kartilege	cartiledge
15. articulate	arrticulate	arkticulate	artickulate	articculate

B. MATCH THE NUMBER OF THE CORRECT TERM IN PART A WITH THE BRIEF DESCRIPTION OF THE TERM BELOW.

a. manufacture protein _____

b. substance of a cell minus the nucleus _____

c. from the Latin for *mother* _____

d. infection of the blood _____

e. plural of nucleus _____

f. opening for tube to assist in breathing _____

g. suffix means *small* _____

h. protector of bones in joints _____

i. separates two body cavities _____

j. gland   _____

k. study of function of tissues   _____

l. origin of every cell in body   _____

m. crescent-shaped   _____

n. lubricant   _____

o. from the Latin root meaning *jointed*   _____

C. USING YOUR KNOWLEDGE OF TERMS 1–15 IN PART A AND THEIR CORRECT SPELLING, WRITE A BRIEF SENTENCE FOR EACH OF THE TERMS AS IT MIGHT APPEAR IN PATIENT DOCUMENTATION.

1. _____

2. _____

3. _____

4. _____

5. _____

6. _____

7. _____

8. _____

9. _____

10. _____

11. _____

12. _____

13. _____

14. _____

15. _____

D. GO TO THE STUDENT CD. OPEN THE GLOSSARY AND PRACTICE YOUR PRONUNCIATION OF THE TERMS IN PART A OF THIS EXERCISE.

Integumentary System
The Language of Dermatology

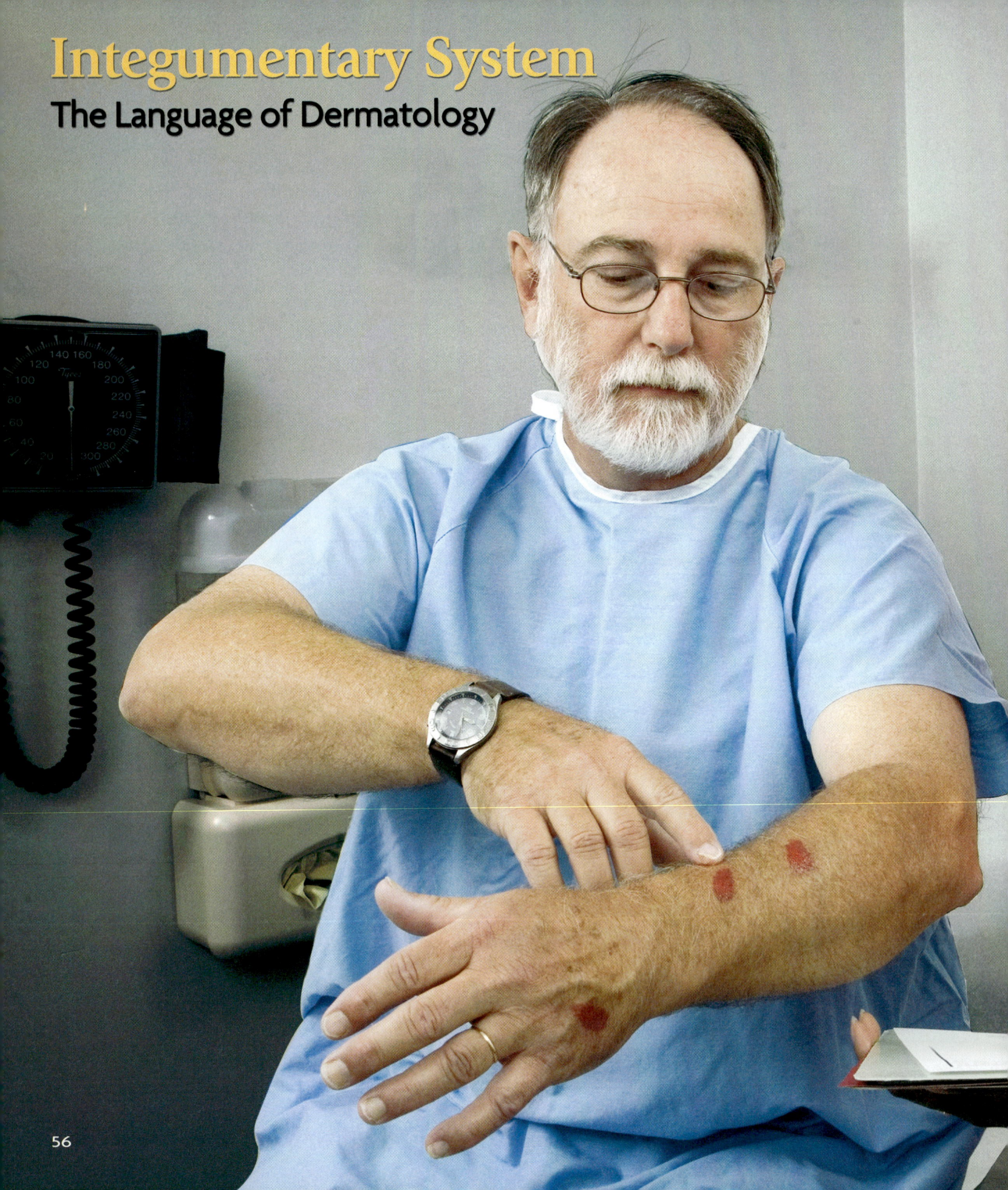

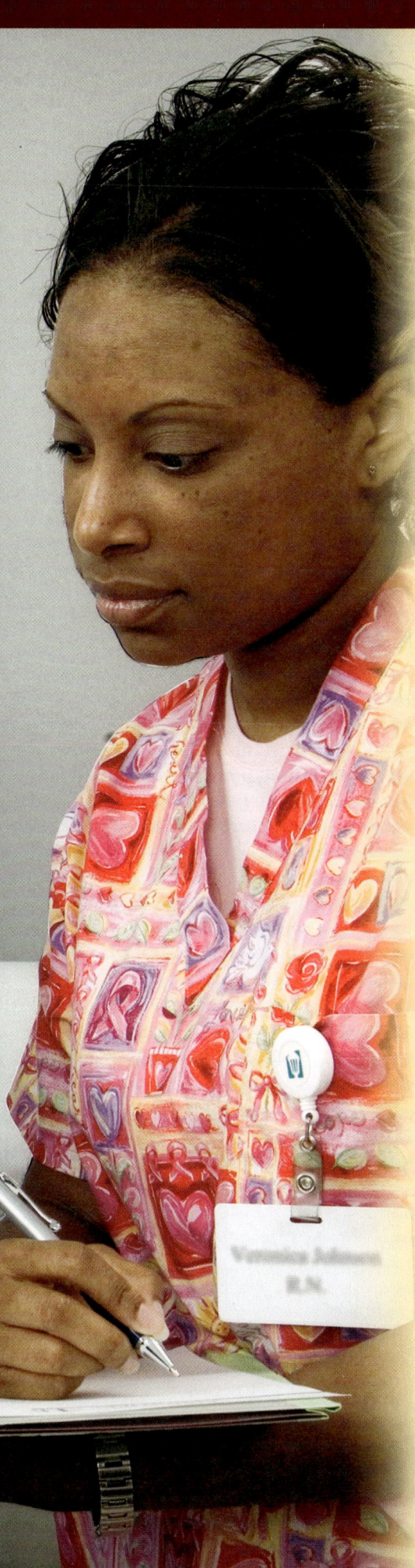

3

CASE REPORT 3.1

You are

. . . a clinical medical assistant working in the office of dermatologist Dr. Lenore Echols, a member of the Fulwood Medical Group.

Your patient is

. . . Mr. Rod Andrews, a 60-year-old man, who shows you three skin lesions, two on his left forearm and one on the back of his left hand. On questioning him, you learn that he has been living for the past ten years in Arizona and has come back home to be near his daughter and young grandchildren. You find no other skin lesions on his body.

Learning Outcomes

In addition to anticipating Dr. Echols' needs for equipment to **biopsy,** diagnose, and treat the **lesions,** you also have to be able to communicate clearly with her in medical terms and to understand her language as she communicates with you and the patient about the etiology (cause) and structure of the lesions. You will then need to document the medical history and treatment and communicate clearly with Mr. Andrews about the treatment of his lesions and their **prognosis.**

To perform these tasks, you must be able to:

- Apply the language of dermatology to the anatomy and physiology of the skin and its associated organs.

- Comprehend, analyze, spell, and write the medical terms of dermatology so you can communicate and document accurately and precisely in any health care setting.

- Recognize and pronounce the medical terms of dermatology so you can communicate verbally with accuracy and precision in any health care setting.

- Understand the etiology and prognosis of common dermatologic conditions.

Functions and Structure of the Skin

The three lesions on Mr. Andrews' arm and hand developed in the superficial layer of the skin called the **epidermis.** This lesson looks at the structure and function of the skin and diseases of the epidermis so that you will be able to:

- **List the layers of the skin.**
- **Name the tissues in the different layers of the skin.**
- **Identify the functions of the different layers.**
- **Describe certain disorders affecting the superficial layers of the skin, including cancers.**
- **Apply correct medical terminology to the anatomy, physiology, and disorders of the superficial layers of the skin.**

Case Report 3.1 (continued)

When Dr. Echols examined Mr. Andrews, she determined clinically that two of his lesions were basal cell **carcinomas** and treated these with **cryosurgery.** She believed that the third lesion was a **squamous cell** carcinoma and performed a **biopsy removal** of the **lesion.** You sent this to the laboratory with a request for **pathological** diagnosis and determination whether the lesion had been completely removed. This is done by ensuring that a normal skin margin completely surrounds the lesion when it is examined under the **microscope.**

FUNCTIONS AND STRUCTURE OF THE SKIN

Keynote

The skin is the largest and most vulnerable organ in the body.

The **integumentary organ system** consists of the skin and its associated organs *(Figure 3.1)*. The study and treatment of the integumentary system is called **dermatology.** This organ system receives more medical and personal attention than any other organ system. Your understanding of its structures and functions will be used every day in your professional and personal life.

The skin is the largest organ in your body and accounts for 7 to 8% of your body weight. The skin is the most vulnerable of all your organs because it is continually exposed to chemicals, trauma, infection, radiation, and all the pollution of modern life. Your skin is an important part of your own self-image and an important part of total patient care.

Keynote

There are four combining forms for skin:
- cutane/o
- derm/a
- dermat/o
- derm/o

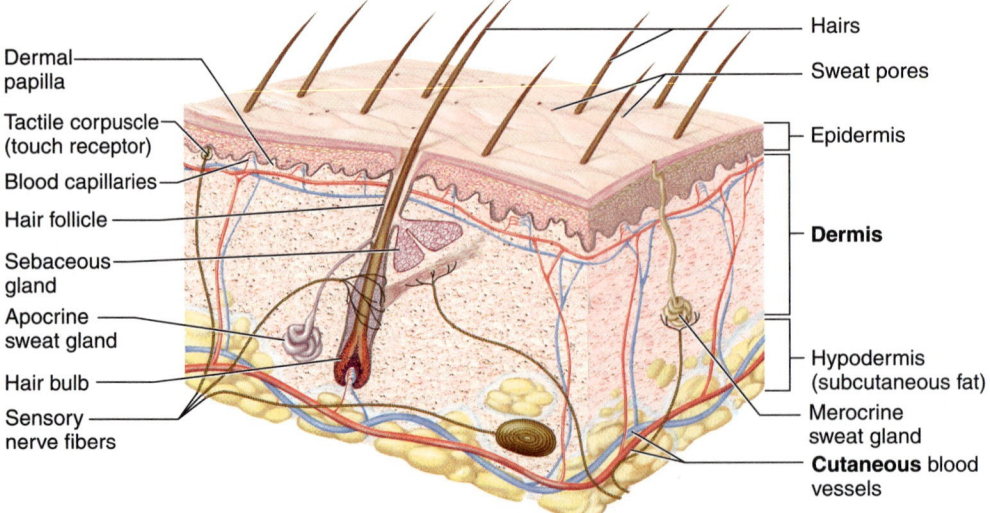

Dermal papilla
Tactile corpuscle (touch receptor)
Blood capillaries
Hair follicle
Sebaceous gland
Apocrine sweat gland
Hair bulb
Sensory nerve fibers

Hairs
Sweat pores
Epidermis
Dermis
Hypodermis (subcutaneous fat)
Merocrine sweat gland
Cutaneous blood vessels

▲ **FIGURE 3.1   Structure of the Skin and Subcutaneous Tissue.**

WORD ANALYSIS AND DEFINITION

S = Suffix   P = Prefix   R = Root   R/CF = Combining Form

WORD	PRONUNCIATION	ELEMENTS		DEFINITION
biopsy	BI-op-see	S/	-opsy *to view*	Removing tissue from a living person for laboratory examination
biopsy removal (also called **excisional biopsy**)	BI-op-see re-**MUV**-al	R/CF	bi/o- *life*	Used for small tumors when complete removal provides tissue for a biopsy and cures the lesion
carcinoma	kar-sih-**NOH**-mah	S/ R/	-oma *tumor, mass* carcin- *cancer*	A malignant and invasive **epithelial** tumor
cryosurgery	cry-oh-**SUR**-jer-ee	P/ R/	cryo- *icy cold* -surgery *surgery*	Use of liquid nitrogen or argon gas in a probe to freeze and kill abnormal tissue
cutaneous	kyu-**TAY**-nee-us	S/ R/CF	-ous *pertaining to* cutan/e- *skin*	Pertaining to the skin
dermis dermal (adj)	**DER**-miss **DER**-mal		Greek *skin*	Connective tissue layer of the skin beneath the epidermis
dermatology dermatologist	der-mah-**TOL**-oh-jee der-mah-**TOL**-oh-jist	S/ R/CF S/	-logy *study of* dermat/o- *skin* -logist *one who studies*	Medical specialty concerned with disorders of the skin Medical specialist in diseases of the skin
epidermis	ep-ih-**DER**-miss	P/ R/	epi- *upon* -dermis *skin*	Top layer of the skin
epithelium epithelial (adj)	ep-ih-**THEE**-lee-um ep-ih-**THEE**-lee-al	S/ P/ R/	-um *tissue* epi- *upon* theli- *nipple*	Tissue that covers surfaces or lines cavities
integument integumentary (adj)	in-**TEG**-you-ment in-teg-you-**MEN**-tah-ree	S/	Latin *a covering* -ary *pertaining to*	Organ system that covers the body, the skin being the main organ within the system
lesion	**LEE**-zhun		Latin *injury*	Pathological change or injury in a tissue
microscope	**MY**-kroh-skope	P/ R/	micro- *small* -scope *instrument for viewing*	Instrument for viewing something small that cannot be seen in detail by the naked eye
microscopic (adj)	**MY**-kroh-**SKOP**-ik	S/	-ic *pertaining to*	Visible only with the aid of a microscope
pathology pathological (adj)	pa-**THOL**-oh-jee path-oh-**LOJ**-ik-al	S/ R/CF	-logy *study of* path/o- *disease*	Medical specialty dealing with the structural and functional changes of a disease process or the cause, development, and structural changes in disease
prognosis	prog-**NO**-sis	P/ R/	pro- *projecting forward* -gnosis *knowledge*	Forecasting of the probable course of a disease
squamous cell	**SKWAY**-mus SELL		Latin *scaly*	Flat, scalelike epithelial cell

EXERCISES

Review the Word Analysis and Definition box (WAD) before starting this exercise. Build your knowledge of the elements in the language of dermatology. Circle the best answer.

1. In the term **epidermis, epi-** is a:

   root   combining form   prefix

2. The suffix **-oma** can mean tumor or:

   gland   mass   cancer

3. Circle the term that means *study of*:

   dermatology   dermatologist   dermatitis

4. The term **epithelium** has a:

   prefix + root   prefix + root + suffix   combining form + suffix

5. **Cryo-** is a prefix that signifies:

   color   temperature   location

6. The term **cutaneous** means pertaining to:

   skin   mass   tumor

7. The root in **carcinoma** means:

   surgery   tumor   cancer

8. In the term **microscope,** the prefix signifies:

   size   shape   position

9. The root in **prognosis** means:

   Specialist   study of   knowledge

10. The suffix **-opsy** means:

   to view   to cut   to repair

FUNCTIONS OF THE SKIN

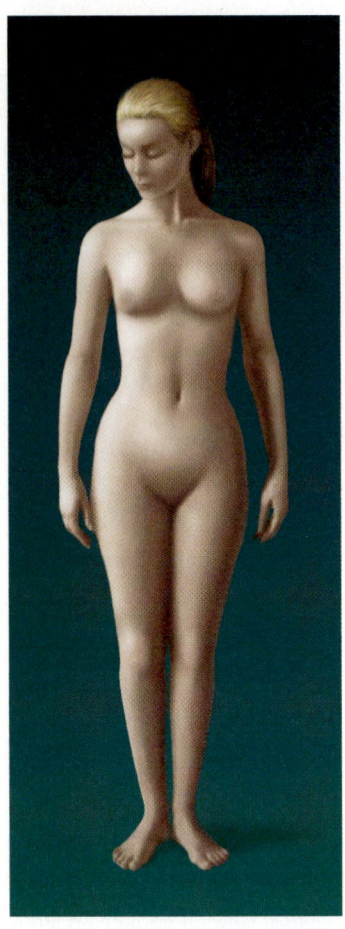

- **Protection**—a physical barrier against injury, chemicals, ultraviolet rays, microbes, and toxins *(Figure 3.2)*.

- **Water resistance**—you don't swell up every time you take a bath because your skin is water resistant. It also prevents water from leaking out from the body tissues.

- **Temperature regulation**—a network of **capillaries** in the skin opens up or dilates **(vasodilation)** when your body is too hot so that the blood flow increases and the heat from the blood dissipates through your skin. When your body is cold, the capillary network narrows, **(vasoconstriction),** blood flow decreases and heat is retained in your body *(Chapter 8)*.

- **Vitamin D synthesis**—as little as 15 to 30 minutes of sunlight daily allows your skin cells to initiate the metabolism of vitamin D, which is essential for bone growth and maintenance.

- **Sensation**—nerve endings that detect touch, pressure, heat, cold, pain, vibration, and tissue injury are particularly numerous on your face, fingers, palms, soles, nipples, and genitals.

- **Excretion and secretion**—water and small amounts of waste products from cell metabolism are lost through the skin by **excretion** (the process of removal of waste products from the body) and by **secretion** (the process of producing and releasing a substance by a tissue or organ of the body) from your sweat glands.

- **Social functions**—the skin reflects your emotions, blushing when you are self-conscious, going pale when you are frightened, wrinkling when you dislike something.

▲ **FIGURE 3.2 Integumentary System.**
The skin provides protection, contains sensory organs, and helps control body temperature.

SKIN AS A BARRIER

The skin is a barrier that is not easily broken. Few infectious organisms can penetrate the skin on their own. Those that do use accidental breaks in the skin or rely on animals such as mosquitoes, fleas, or ticks to puncture the skin to allow access for the infectious organisms. The skin is also a barrier to solar radiation, including ultraviolet (UV) rays.

Blood receives 1 to 2% of its oxygen from diffusion through the skin and it releases through the skin some carbon dioxide and organic chemicals that attract mosquitoes and other insects to people.

WORD	PRONUNCIATION	ELEMENTS		DEFINITION
excrete	eks-**KREET**		Latin *remove*	To pass out of the body waste products of metabolism
excretion (noun)	eks-**KREE**-shun			Removal of waste products of metabolism out of the body
function	**FUNK**-shun		Latin *to perform*	The ability of an organ or tissue to perform its special work
protection	pro-**TEK**-shun	S/	**-ion** *action, condition*	Defense against attack or invasion
protect (verb)		P/	**pro-** *before*	
		R/	**-tect-** *to shelter*	
regulation	reg-you-**LAY**-shun	S/	**-ation** *process*	Control of the way in which a process progresses
regulate (verb)		R/	**regul-** *to rule*	
resistance	ree-**ZIS**-tants	S/	**-ance** *state of*	Ability of an organism to withstand the effects of an antagonistic agent
resist (verb)		R	**resist-** *to withstand*	
secrete	se-**KREET**		Latin *to separate*	To produce a chemical substance in a cell and release it from the cell
secretion (noun)	se-**KREE**-shun			
sensation	sen-**SAY**-shun	S/	**-ation** *process*	The conscious feeling of the effects of a stimulation
sense (verb)		R	**sens-** *to feel*	
synthesis	**SIN**-the-sis	P/	**syn-** *together*	The process of building a compound from different elements
synthesize (verb)	**SIN**-the-size	R/	**-thesis** *to arrange*	

EXERCISES

The following are functions of the skin—assign one to each statement by filling in the blanks.

protection   water resistance   temperature regulation   vitamin D synthesis

sensation   excretion   secretion   social function

1. water and waste products lost through the skin_____

2. nerve endings detect touch, pressure, heat _____

3. prevents leakage from body tissues _____

4. vasoconstriction or vasodilation _____

5. production of sweat glands_____

6. works with sunlight to metabolize_____

7. blushing_____

8. physical barrier against toxins_____

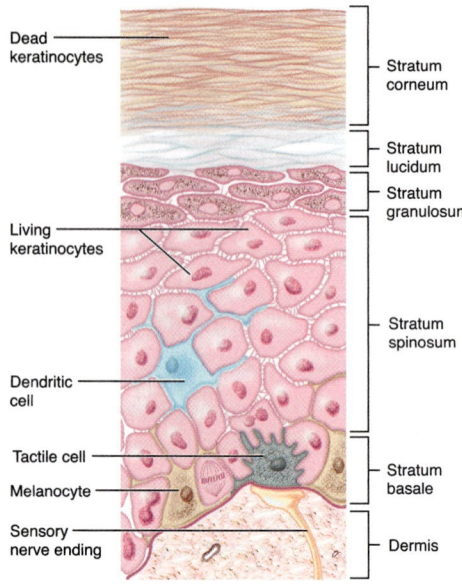

▲ FIGURE 3.3 Epidermis.

Labels on figure:
- Dead keratinocytes
- Living keratinocytes
- Dendritic cell
- Tactile cell
- Melanocyte
- Sensory nerve ending
- Stratum corneum
- Stratum lucidum
- Stratum granulosum
- Stratum spinosum
- Stratum basale
- Dermis

Keynote

The stratum granulosum waterproofs the skin.

Keynote

The stratum spinosum holds the epidermis together.

STRUCTURE OF THE SKIN: EPIDERMIS

The three lesions that Mr. Andrews had were present in the **epidermis,** the most superficial layer of his skin. This layer:

- **protects** underlying structures,
- **withstands** the toxic pollution of modern life,
- **sheds** its superficial cells and renews them continually throughout life, and
- **provides** a waterproof barrier,

The outer layer of the epidermis, the **stratum corneum** *(Figure 3.3)*, is a layer of compact, dead cells packed with **keratin.** These dead cells have no nuclei and are continually shed. **Dandruff** is clumps of these cells stuck together with **sebum,** oil from **sebaceous** glands. Keratin is a tough, scaly protein that is also the basis for hair and nails.

Underneath the stratum corneum on the thick skin of the palms, soles, fingers, and toes is a thin translucent layer of cells, the **stratum lucidum.** These cells are filled with a protein that becomes keratin and are called **keratinocytes.**

In the next layer down, the **stratum granulosum,** these keratinocytes produce a fatty mixture that covers the surface of the cells and waterproofs them. This waterproof barrier not only stops water getting in and out, it also cuts off the supply of nutrients to the keratinocytes above it and they die.

In the next layer, the **stratum spinosum,** the keratinocytes contain nuclei and are firmly attached to each other by numerous spines (hence "spinosum"). This enables the epidermis to be firm and strong.

The **squamous cell carcinoma** *(Figure 3.4)* that Mr. Andrews had on his hand arises from keratinocytes in the stratum spinosum in skin on the back of the hand, face, and ears, areas exposed to sunlight. It responds well to surgical removal but can **metastasize** (spread) to lymph glands if neglected.

The bottom layer of the epidermis, the **stratum basale,** is a single layer of cells that form the keratinocytes. This layer also contains **melanocytes,** which produce the dark pigment **melanin,** and **tactile** (touch) cells attached to sensory nerve fibers. The process by which keratinocytes migrate from this layer to when they are shed as dead cells from your skin surface takes about a month.

Mr. Andrews' **basal cell carcinoma** *(Figure 3.5)* began in the cells of the stratum basale and invaded the dermis and epidermis. It is the most common skin cancer and is also the least dangerous because it does not metastasize.

Malignant melanoma *(Figure 3.6)* is the least common skin cancer but is the most deadly. It arises from the melanocytes in the stratum basale. It metastasizes quickly and is fatal if neglected.

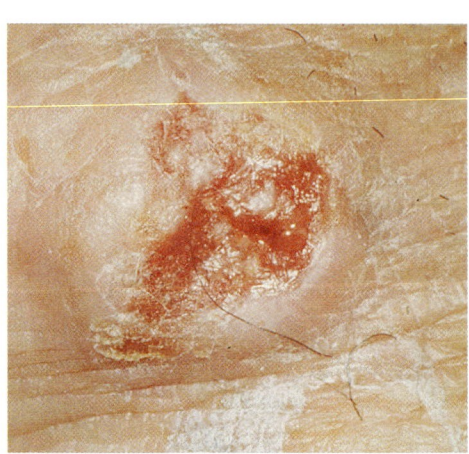

▲ FIGURE 3.4 Squamous Cell Carcinoma.

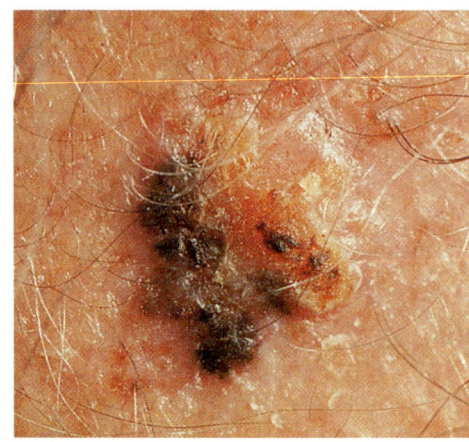

▲ FIGURE 3.5 Basal Cell Carcinoma.

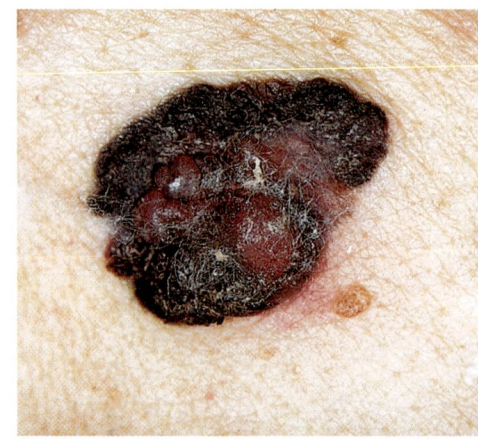

▲ FIGURE 3.6 Malignant Melanoma.

WORD	PRONUNCIATION		ELEMENTS	DEFINITION
keratin	**KER**-ah-tin		Greek *keratin*	Protein found in the dead outer layer of skin and in nails and hair
keratinocyte	ke-**RAT**-in-oh-site	S/ R/CF	-cyte *cell* keratin/o- *keratin*	Cell producing a tough, horny protein (keratin) in the process of differentiating into the dead cells of the stratum corneum
macule	**MAK**-yul		Latin *spot*	Small, flat spot or patch on the skin
macular (adj)	**MAK**-yu-lar			
malignant	mah-**LIG**-nant	S/ R/	-ant *forming* malign- *harmful*	Tumor that invades surrounding tissues and metastasizes to distant organs
melanin	**MEL**-ah-nin		Greek *black*	Black pigment found in skin, hair, retina
melanocyte	**MEL**-ann-oh-cyte	S/ R/CF	-cyte *cell* melan/o- *melanin*	Cell that forms melanin
melanoma	**MEL**-ah-**NO**-mah	S/	-oma *tumor, mass*	Malignant neoplasm formed from cells that produce melanin
metastasis	meh-**TAS**-tah-sis	P/	meta- *between, beyond*	Spread of disease from one part of the body to another
metastasize (verb)	meh-**TAS**-tah-size	R/	-stasis *placement*	
metastatic (adj)	**MET**-ah-**STAT**-ic			
sebaceous glands	se-**BAY**-shus GLANZ	S/ R/CF	-ous *pertaining to* sebac/e- *wax*	Glands in the dermis that open into hair follicles and secrete an oily fluid called sebum
sebum	**SEE**-bum			Waxy secretion of the sebaceous glands
stratum basale	**STRAH**-tum ba-**SAL**-eh	S/ R/ R/	-um *tissue* strat- *layer* basale *deeper*	Deepest layer of the epidermis, from which the other cells originate and migrate
tactile	**TAK**-tile		Latin *to touch*	Relating to touch

Case Report 3.1 (continued)

Dr. Echols learned that Mr. Andrews had driven extensively in Arizona while wearing a short-sleeved shirt. His left forearm and hand were exposed to sunlight through the untinted car window to his left. This was an important factor in causing his skin cancers, all of which responded to treatment.

EXERCISES

Apply the correct rule for plurals and form the plural of the term **stratum**. *Demonstrate that you know the difference in terms by using each form in a sentence.*

1. Singular: *stratum*
   Sentence:

   _____

2. Plural: _____
   Sentence:

   _____

> **Study Hint**
> Whenever there are two or more terms with the same meaning, you must know all of them.

Medical terms that are nouns can also have an *adjectival form,* as seen in **macule** and **macular.** Use the correct form of each term in the following sentences.

3. The report from pathology diagnosed the lesion as a _____.

4. The _____ tissue was removed in the biopsy.

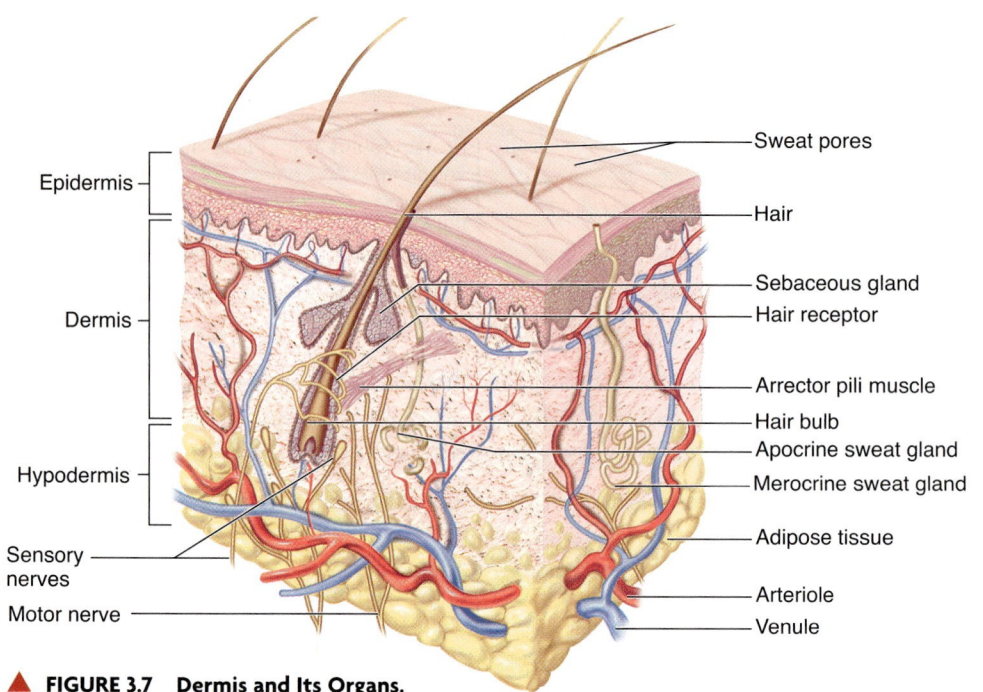

▲ FIGURE 3.7   Dermis and Its Organs.

Epidermis

Dermis

Hypodermis

Sensory nerves

Motor nerve

Sweat pores

Hair

Sebaceous gland

Hair receptor

Arrector pili muscle

Hair bulb

Apocrine sweat gland

Merocrine sweat gland

Adipose tissue

Arteriole

Venule

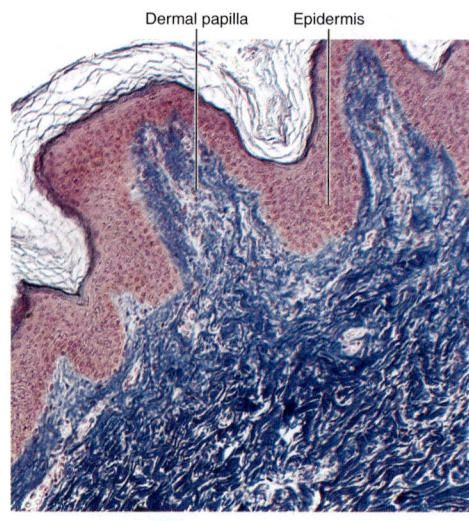

Dermal papilla   Epidermis

▲ FIGURE 3.8   Interlocking Edge of Dermis and Epidermis.

STRUCTURE OF SKIN: DERMIS

Figure 3.7 shows that the **dermis** is a much thicker connective tissue layer than the epidermis. It consists mostly of **collagen,** with fibers and fibroblasts. It is well supplied with blood vessels and nerves and contains the other **skin organs: sweat glands, sebaceous glands, hair follicles,** and **nail roots.**

The boundary between the dermis and epidermis is distinct and irregular *(Figure 3.8)*. Upward projections of the dermis, dermal **papillae,** and downward projections of the epidermis, epidermal ridges, interlock to prevent the epidermis from slipping on the dermis. They also produce the ridges and furrows on your skin that are used for fingerprinting.

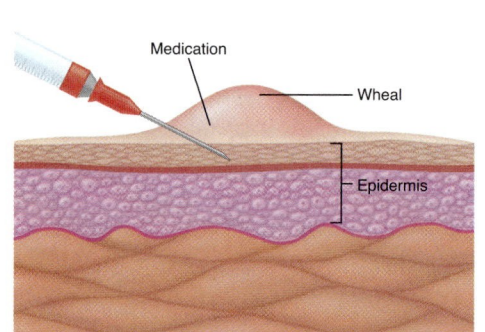

Medication

Wheal

Epidermis

▲ FIGURE 3.9   Intradermal Injection.

HYPODERMIS

This layer beneath the dermis is the site of **subcutaneous** fat (**adipose** tissue). It is also called the **subcutaneous tissue layer.**

CLINICAL APPLICATIONS

Giving Injections

Another important reason why you should be able to identify the layers of the skin is to understand the different sites for giving injections. You will need this information both for documentation and, in some states after appropriate training, for you to be able to give the injections.

The three types of injection are:

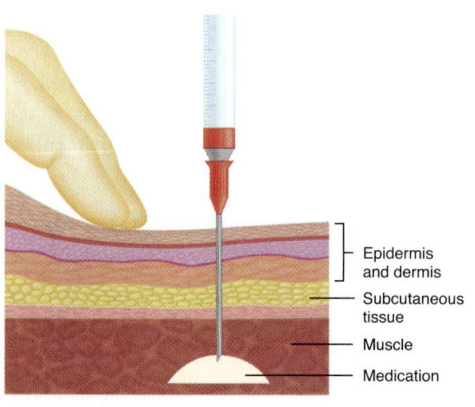

Epidermis and dermis

Subcutaneous tissue

Muscle

Medication

▲ FIGURE 3.10   Intramuscular Injection.

- **Intradermal** *(Figure 3.9)*—a short, thin needle is introduced into the epidermis between the stratum corneum and the stratum basale. Injected into this site, the medication raises a small **wheal.** This site is used for allergy testing or a **tuberculosis (TB)** test.
- **Subcutaneous (SC)**—a longer needle pierces the epidermis and dermis to reach the hypodermis or subcutaneous layer. This site is used for insulin injections.
- **Intramuscular (IM)** *(Figure 3.10)*—a long needle pierces the epidermis, dermis, and subcutaneous layer into the muscles underneath. Some antibiotics can be given by this route.

WORD	PRONUNCIATION	ELEMENTS		DEFINITION
adipose	**ADD**-i-pose	S/ R/	-ose *condition* adip- *fat*	Containing fat
collagen	**KOL**-ah-jen		Greek *producing glue*	Major protein of connective tissue, cartilage, and bone
follicle	**FOLL**-ih-kull		Latin *small sac*	Spherical mass of cells containing a cavity or a small cul-de-sac, such as a hair follicle
hypodermis hypodermic (adj)	high-poh-**DER**-miss high-poh-**DER**-mik	P/ R/	hypo- *below* -dermis *skin*	Tissue layer below the dermis
intradermal	in-trah-**DER**-mal	S/ P/ R/	-al *pertaining to* intra- *within* -derm- *skin*	Within the epidermis
intramuscular	in-trah-**MUSS**-kew-lar	S/ P/ R/	-ar *pertaining to* intra- *within* -muscul- *muscle*	Within the muscle
papilla papillae (pl) papilloma	pah-**PILL**-ah pah-**PILL**-ee pap-ih-**LOH**-mah	S/ R/CF	Latin *small pimple* -oma *tumor, mass* papill/o- *pimple*	Any small projection Benign projection of epithelial cells
papule	**PAP**-yul	S/	-ule *small*	Small, circumscribed elevation on the skin
semipermeable membrane	sem-ee-**PER**-me-ah-bull **MEM**-brain	S/ P/ R/CF R/	-able *capable of* semi- *half* -perm/e- *pass through* membrane *cover, skin*	A membrane that allows only certain substances to pass through it
subcutaneous (same as hypodermic)	sub-kew-**TAY**-nee-us	S/ P/ R/CF	-ous *pertaining to* sub- *below* -cutan/e- *skin*	Below the skin
transdermal	trans-**DER**-mal	S/ P/ R/	-al *pertaining to* trans- *across, through* -derm- *skin*	Going across or through the skin
wheal (also called **hives**)	WHEEL		Old English *wheal*	Small, itchy swelling of the skin. Wheals raised by an injection do not itch

Transdermal Applications

Some medications can be administered through the skin by an adhesive **transdermal** patch that is applied to the skin. In the patch, a small reservoir contains medication that leaves the reservoir at a known rate through a **semipermeable membrane.** The medication diffuses across the epidermis and enters the blood vessels in the dermis. Medications for motion sickness and cardiac problems, testosterone, birth control hormones, and the chemical nicotine are administered by transdermal patches.

Abbreviations

IM	intramuscular
SC	subcutaneous
TB	tuberculosis

EXERCISES   *The following definitions represent medical terms found in this WAD. Find the missing elements and build the terms. Fill in the blanks.*

1. going across the skin   trans/_____/ _____

2. pertaining to wax   sebace/_____

3. pertaining to within muscle   _____/_____/ar

4. pertaining to below the skin   _____/dermic

5. pertaining to below the skin   _____/cutane/_____

> *Study Hint*
> There are many different suffixes that mean *pertaining to.* Some have been introduced in this WAD. Start keeping a list of them in the back of your book, with an example of each in a medical term.

OBJECTIVES

- Describe common diseases of the skin.
- Identify the different types of infections of the skin.
- Define the types of pharmacologic agents used in the treatment of skin disorders.
- Apply correct medical terminology to describe disorders of the skin.

CASE REPORT 3.2

Fulwood Medical Center

Mrs. Rose McGinnis, a 72-year-old widow, has been in a nursing home for the past six months. She has been unable to get out of bed following surgery to repair a broken hip. She has been depressed and difficult to feed and nurse. Two months ago, she developed decubitus ulcers over her buttocks and left heel. The ulcer over her buttocks became infected with a methicillin-resistant *Staphylococcus aureus* (MRSA). Staphylococcal septicemia ensued, and she died.

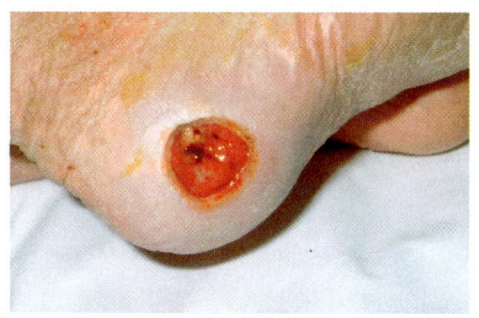

▲ **FIGURE 3.11 Decubitus Ulcer on Heel.**

DISORDERS OF THE SKIN

When a patient lies in one position for a long period, the pressure between the bed and bony body projections, like the lower spine or heel, cuts off the blood supply to the skin and **decubitus (pressure) ulcers** can appear *(Figure 3.11)*. The protective function of the skin is broken, and germs can enter the body.

Other major factors in the breakdown of Rose's skin were that it was thin and dry because of aging. Also, her poor nutritional status had depleted the fatty protective layer in the hypodermis under the skin.

The skin shows the same types of disease as most organs—infections, tumors, **malignancies**—but, in addition, its protective function makes it the first responder to many irritant and allergenic agents.

CASE REPORT 3.3

Fulwood Medical Center

Ms. Cheryl Fox is a 37-year-old nursing assistant working in a surgical unit in Fulwood Medical Center. Recently her fingers have become red and itchy, with occasional **vesicles.** She has also noticed irritation and swelling of her ear lobes and a generalized pruritus. Over the weekends, both the itching and the rash on her hands worsen. A patch test by her dermatologist showed her to be allergic to nickel in rings that she wears on both hands and in her earrings. She wears these on weekends and not during her workdays.

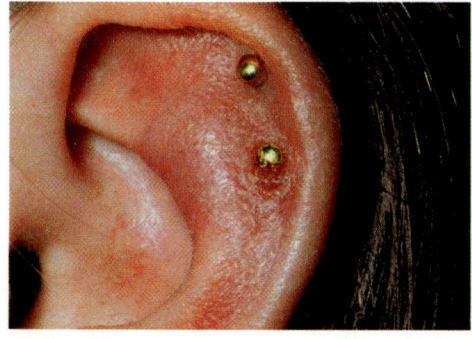

▲ **FIGURE 3.12 Dermatitis of Ear Due to Nickel Sensitivity.**

Ms. Fox had a **dermatitis** *(Figure 3.12)*, resulting from direct exposure to an irritating agent. In her case, it was not just a reaction to an irritant. Her form of **atopic (allergic) dermatitis** develops when the body becomes sensitive to an **allergen** such as **latex,** nickel in jewelry, or poison ivy. This whole-body involvement was shown by her systemic symptoms of **pruritus** distant from the local irritant site. She has stopped wearing the rings and earrings.

Eczema is a general term used for inflamed, itchy skin conditions. When the itchy skin is scratched, it becomes **excoriated** and produces the dry, red, scaly patches characteristic of eczema. The atopic dermatitis that Ms. Fox developed to nickel is a common form of eczema.

WORD	PRONUNCIATION	ELEMENTS		DEFINITION
allergen allergenic (adj) allergy allergic (adj)	**AL**-er-jen al-er-**JEN**-ik **AL**-er-jee a-**LER**-jik	S/ R/	-gen *producing* aller- *allergy*	Substance producing a hypersensitivity (allergic) reaction Hypersensitivity to an allergen
atopy atopic (adj)	**AY**-toh-pee ay-**TOP**-ik		Greek *strangeness*	State of hypersensitivity to an allergen—allergic
decubitus ulcer	de-**KYU**-bit-us **UL**-ser	P/ R/ R/	de- *from* -cubitus *lying down* ulcer *sore*	Sore caused by lying down for long periods of time
dermatitis	der-mah-**TYE**-tis	S/ R/	-itis *inflammation* dermat- *skin*	Inflammation of the skin
eczema eczematous (adj)	**EK**-zeh-mah **EK**-zem-ah-tus	 S/ R/CF	Greek *to boil or ferment* -tous *pertaining to* eczem/a- *eczema*	Inflammatory skin disease often with a **serous** discharge
excoriate excoriation (noun)	eks-**KOR**-ee-ate eks-**KOR**-ee-**AY**-shun	S/ P/ R/	-ate *action* ex- *away from, out of* -cori- *skin*	To scratch Scratch marks
latex	**LAY**-tecks		Latin *liquid*	Manufactured from the milky liquid in rubber plants; used for gloves in patient care
mole	MOLE		Latin *spot*	Benign localized area of melanin-producing cells
nevus nevi (pl)	**NEE**-vus **NEE**-vie		Latin *mole, birthmark*	Congenital lesion of the skin
pruritus pruritic (adj)	proo-**RYE**-tus proo-**RIT**-ik		Latin *to itch*	Itching Itchy
serous	**SEER**-us		Latin *serum*	Thicker and less transparent than water
vesicle	**VES**-ih-kull		Latin *small sac*	Small sac containing liquid; for example, a blister

Sunlight can also be an irritant to the skin, not only to burn it but by leading to cancer when there is excessive exposure, as it did for Mr. Rod Andrews.

Any congenital lesion of the skin, including various types of birthmarks and all **moles,** is referred to as a **nevus.**

Abbreviation

MRSA methicillin-resistant *Staphylococcus aureus*

EXERCISES

Medical terms can have small differences that make them entirely new words. Underline the root of these terms, which stays the same; then focus on how they are different. Insert the correct term in the blanks.

allergen   allergenic   allergy   allergic

1. After many _____ tests, it was determined that she was _____ to mold.

2. There were too many _____ substances in the carpet, and it was removed from the room.

3. Dust mites, peanuts, and pollen are _____.

One of the terms below is a noun (person, place, or thing), and the other term is a verb (action). Identify the noun and verb, then use each term in a sentence.

4. Excoriate: noun or verb: _____

5. Sentence: _____

6. Excoriation: noun or verb: _____

7. Sentence: _____

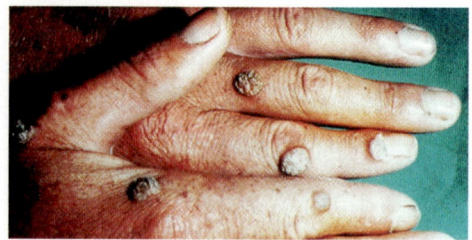
▲ FIGURE 3.13   Warts of Hands.

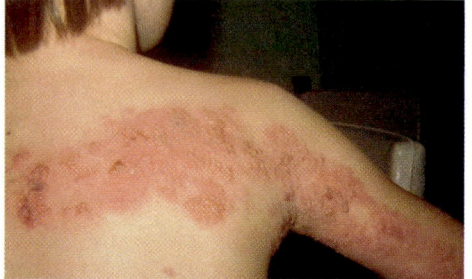
▲ FIGURE 3.14   Shingles.

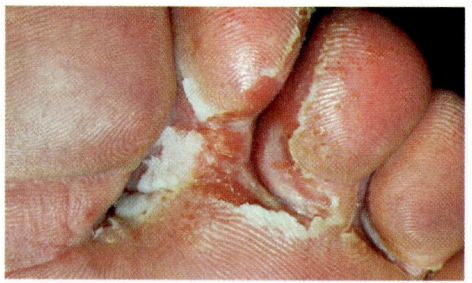
▲ FIGURE 3.15   Tinea Pedis - between Toes.

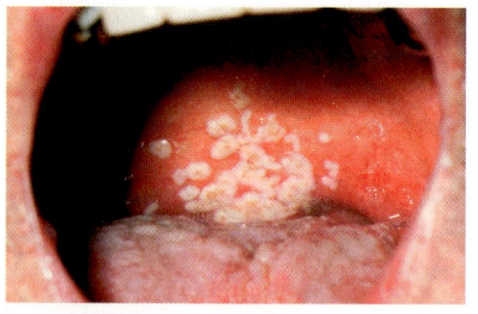
▲ FIGURE 3.16   Oral Thrush.

▲ FIGURE 3.17   House Dust Mite.

INFECTIONS OF THE SKIN

The skin is also susceptible to the many different types of infections. The following descriptions are examples.

Viral Infections

Warts (**verrucas**) are caused by the human **papillomavirus** invading the epidermis and causing the outer epidermal cells to produce a roughened projection from the skin surface *(Figure 3.13)*. Human papillomavirus is discussed extensively in *Chapter 13*.

Varicella-zoster virus causes **chickenpox** in unvaccinated people, forming **macules, papules,** and **vesicles.** The virus can then remain dormant in the peripheral nerves for decades before erupting as the painful vesicles of **herpes zoster (shingles)** *(Figure 3.14)*.

Fungal Infections

Tinea is a general term for a group of related skin infections caused by different species of fungi. The fungi live on and are strictly confined to the nonliving stratum corneum and its derivatives, hair and nails, where keratin provides their food. The different types of tinea take their name from the location of the infection.

Tinea pedis, athlete's foot, causes itching, redness, and peeling of the foot, particularly between the toes *(Figure 3.15)*. **Tinea capitis** describes infection of the scalp (ringworm); **tinea corporis** is the name for infections of the body. **Tinea cruris** ("jock itch") is the name for infections of the groin. The fungus spreads from animals, the soil, and by direct contact with infected individuals. **Tinea versicolor** is characterized by brown and white patches on the trunk.

A yeast-like fungus, *Candida,* can produce **recurrent** infections of the skin, nails, and **mucous membranes.** The first sign can be a recurrent diaper rash or thrush in infants. Older children can show recurrent or **persistent** lesions on the scalp. In adults, chronic **candidiasis** can affect the mouth (**thrush**) *(Figure 3.16)* and vagina, as well as the skin. It can also be associated with diseases of the immune system *(see Chapter 14)*.

Parasitic Infestations

A **parasite** is an organism that lives in contact with and feeds off another organism (host). This process is called an **infestation**. It is different from an **infection**.

Lice are small, wingless, blood-sucking parasites that produce the disease **pediculosis** by attaching their eggs (nits) to hair and clothing *(Table 3.1)*.

"Itch mites" (**scabies**) produce an intense, itching rash, often in the genital area, waist, breast, and armpits. The mites live and lay eggs under the skin.

The skin normally sheds its cells. These tiny specks form some of the dust on our furniture, floors, and carpets. The house dust mite *(Figure 3.17)* thrives on the keratin of these cells and lives well on carpets, upholstery, pillows, and mattresses. Many people are allergic to the inhaled feces of these parasites.

Bacterial Infections

Staphylococcus aureus (commonly called "staph") is the most common **bacterium** to invade the skin and is the cause of pimples, boils, **carbuncles,** and **impetigo**. It can infect hair follicles and the surrounding tissues to produce **furuncles** and carbuncles. Staph can cause a **cellulitis** of the epidermis and dermis.

TABLE 3.1 Pediculosis

Louse (lice, pl)	Attachment of Eggs	Disease
Pediculus capitis	hair of scalp	pediculosis capitis
Phthirus pubis (crab-shaped)	pubic hair	pediculosis cruris (crabs)
Pediculus humanus	clothing, body hair	pediculosis corporis

WORD ANALYSIS AND DEFINITION

S = Suffix   P = Prefix   R = Root   R/CF = Combining Form

Word	Pronunciation		Elements	Definition
Candida	**KAN**-did-ah		Latin *dazzling white*	A yeastlike fungus
candidiasis thrush	can-dih-**DIE**-ah-sis THRUSH	S/ R/	-iasis *condition* candid- *Candida*	Infection with the yeastlike fungus, *Candida* Infection with *Candida albicans*
carbuncle	**KAR**-bunk-ul		Latin *carbuncle*	Infection of many furuncles in a small area, often on the back of the neck
cellulitis	sell-you-**LIE**-tis	S/ R/	-itis *inflammation* cellul- *cell*	Infection of subcutaneous connective tissue
furuncle	**FU**-rung-kel		Latin *a boil*	An infected hair follicle that spreads into the tissues around the follicle
herpes zoster (also called **shingles**)	**HER**-pees **ZOS**-ter		**herpes** *to creep or spread* **zoster** *belt, girdle*	Painful eruption of vesicles that follows a dermatome or nerve root on one side of the body
impetigo	im-peh-**TIE**-go		Latin *scabby eruption*	Infection of the skin producing thick, yellow crusts
infection	in-**FEK**-shun	S/ R/	-ion *action* infect- *tainted*	Invasion of the body by disease-producing microorganisms
infestation	in-fes-**TAY**-shun	S/ R/	-ation *action* infest- *invade*	Act of being invaded on the skin by a troublesome other species, such as a parasite
louse lice (pl)	LOWSE LICE		Old English *louse*	Parasitic insect
parasite	**PAR**-ah-site		Greek *guest*	An organism that attaches itself to, lives on or in, and derives its nutrition from another species
pediculosis	peh-dick-you-**LOH**-sis	S/ R/	-osis *condition* pedicul- *louse*	An infestation with lice
scabies	**SKAY**-bees		Latin *to scratch*	Skin disease produced by mites
tinea	**TIN**-ee-ah		Latin *worm*	General term for a group of related skin infections caused by different species of fungi
verruca	ver-**ROO**-cah		Latin *wart*	Wart caused by a virus
vesicle	**VES**-ih-kull		Latin *blister*	Small sac containing liquid; for example, a blister

EXERCISES

Make the WADs work for you. As you read each WAD, notice any elements that may have the same meaning; highlight them, or keep a separate list in the back of your book. This WAD contains two sets of elements, each with the same meaning. Find the sets of elements, and define them.

1. _____ and _____ both mean _____.

2. _____ and _____ both mean _____.

Match the correct Latin or Greek term to its medical term. Circle the best answer.

1. impetigo: carbuncle   boil   scabby eruption

2. verruca: ulcer   furuncle   wart

3. vesicle: carbuncle   blister   boil

4. scabies: to bleed   to cut   to scratch

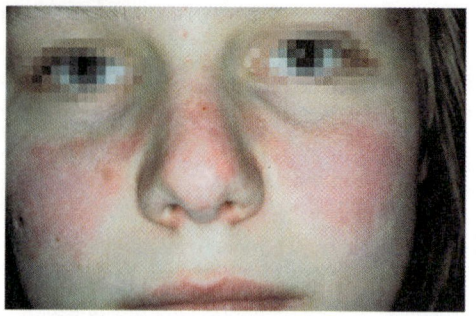

▲ **FIGURE 3.18** **Systemic Lupus Erythematosus.**

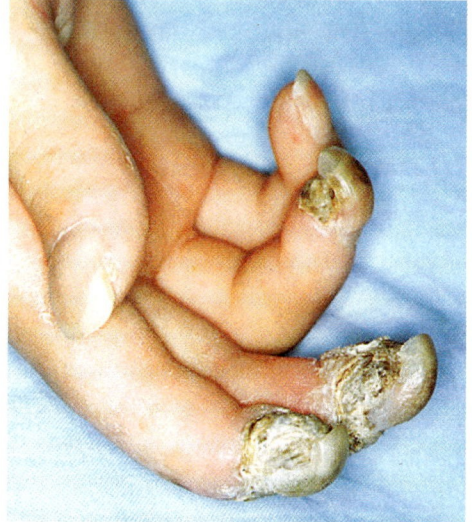

▲ **FIGURE 3.19** **Scleroderma.**

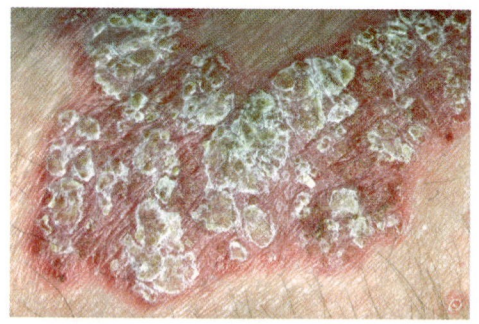

▲ **FIGURE 3.20** **Psoriasis.**

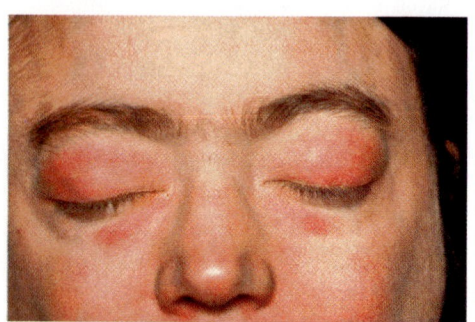

▲ **FIGURE 3.21** **Periorbital Rash of Dermatomyositis.**

DISEASES OF THE SKIN

Collagen Diseases

Collagen, a fibrous protein, comprises 30% of the total body protein. Therefore, collagen diseases can have a dramatic effect all over the body. Collagen diseases, **autoimmune** or otherwise, attack collagen or other components of connective tissue.

Systemic lupus erythematosus (SLE), an autoimmune disease, occurs most commonly in women and produces characteristic skin lesions. A butterfly-shaped, red rash on both cheeks joined across the bridge of the nose is commonly seen *(Figure 3.18)*. It is associated with fever, fatigue, joint pains, and multiple internal organ involvement.

Rosacea produces a similar facial rash to SLE, and the underlying capillaries become enlarged and show through the skin. It is thought to be worsened by alcohol and spicy food. Its etiology is unknown. It has no **systemic** complications.

Scleroderma is a chronic, persistent autoimmune disease, occurring more often in women and characterized by hardening and shrinking of the skin to make it feel leathery *(Figure 3.19)*. Joints show swelling, pain, and stiffness. Internal organs such as the heart, lungs, kidneys, and digestive tract can be involved in a similar process. The etiology is unknown, and there is no effective treatment.

Other Skin Diseases

Psoriasis *(Figure 3.20)* is marked by itchy, flaky, red patches of skin of various sizes covered with white or silvery scales. It appears most commonly on the scalp, elbows, and knees. Its cause is unknown.

Vitiligo produces pale, irregular patches of skin. Its etiology is unknown, and it has no cure.

Skin Manifestations of Internal Disease

The presence of cancer inside the body is often shown by skin lesions, even before the cancer has produced **symptoms** or been diagnosed.

Dermatomyositis *(Figure 3.21)* is often associated with ovarian cancer, which can appear within four to five years after the skin disease is diagnosed.

Pharmacology

No matter what the cause of skin lesions, a wide range of **topical pharmacologic agents** of different types can be used in their treatment, either to relieve symptoms or to cure the disease.

- **Antipruritics**—topical lotions, ointments, creams, or sprays to relieve itching. **Corticosteroids** such as hydrocortisone are most frequently used.

- **Antibacterials**—topical agents that eliminate the bacteria that cause epidermal infections. The antibiotic neomycin is frequently used in ointments for this purpose.

- **Antifungals**—topical agents that eliminate or inhibit the growth of fungi. Lamisil is used as a cream, gel, or spray.

- **Parasiticides**—topical agents to kill parasites living on the skin. Lindane 1% is in a lotion or shampoo used to kill lice.

- **Keratolytics**—topical agents that peel the stratum corneum away from the other epidermal layers. Salicylic acid is used for this purpose.

- **Anesthetics**—topical agents to relieve pain or itching on the skin's surface. Benzocaine is used for this purpose.

- **Retinoids**—derivatives of **retinoic acid** are used in the treatment of acne, although the exact mode of action is unknown.

WORD	PRONUNCIATION	ELEMENTS		DEFINITION
anesthetic anesthesia (noun)	an-es-**THET**-ic an-es-**THEE**-zee-ah	S/ P/ R/	-ic *pertaining to* an- *without* -esthet- *sensation*	Substance that takes away feeling and pain Complete loss of sensation

antipruritic
  pruritus (noun)
  pruritic (adj)
	AN-tee-pru-**RIT**-ik
	proo-**RYE**-tus
	proo-**RIT**-ik
		S/
		P/
		R/
			-ic *pertaining to*
			anti- *against*
			-prurit- *itch*
				Medication against itching
				Itching
				Itchy

corticosteroid	**KOR**-tih-koh-**STEHR**-oyd	S/ R/CF R/	-oid *resembling* cortic/o- *cortisone* ster- *steroid*	A hormone produced by the adrenal cortex
dermatomyositis	**DER**-mah-toe-**MY**-oh-site-is	S/ R/CF R/	-itis *inflammation* dermat/o- *skin* -myos- *muscle*	Inflammation of the skin and muscles
pharmacology pharmacologic (adj) pharmacist pharmacy	far-mah-**KOLL**-oh-jee far-mah-ko-**LOJ**-ik **FAR**-mah-sist **FAR**-mah-see	S/ R/CF S/	-logy *study of* pharmac/o- *drug* -ist *specialist*	Science of the preparation, uses, and effects of drugs Person licensed by the state to prepare and dispense drugs Facility licensed to prepare and dispense drugs
psoriasis	so-**RYE**-ah-sis		Greek *the itch*	Rash characterized by reddish, silver-scaled patches
retinoid	**RET**-ih-noyd		Derived from retinoic acid	A class of keratolytic agents
rosacea	roh-**ZAY**-she-ah		Latin *rosy*	Persistent erythematous rash of the central face
scleroderma	sklair-oh-**DERM**-ah	S/ R/CF	-derma *skin* scler/o- *hard*	Thickening and hardening of the skin due to new collagen formation
systemic lupus erythematosus	sis-**TEM**-ik **LOO**-pus er-ih-**THEE**-mah-toe-sus	S/ R/ S/ R/	-ic *pertaining to* system- *the body as a whole* lupus *wolf* -osus *condition* erythemat- *redness*	Inflammatory connective tissue disease affecting the whole body
topical	**TOP**-ih-kal	S/ R/	-al *pertaining to* topic- *local*	Medication applied to the skin to obtain a local effect
vitiligo	vit-ill-**EYE**-go		Latin *skin blemish*	Nonpigmented white patches on otherwise normal skin

EXERCISES

Building medical terms and taking them apart forces you to focus on the elements they contain. Understanding elements is the key to increasing your medical vocabulary. Deconstruct the following terms to increase your knowledge of their elements. Fill in the blanks.

Medical term	Meaning of Prefix	Meaning of Root	Meaning of Combining Form	Meaning of Suffix
anesthetic				
antipruritic				
corticosteroid				
dermatomyositis				
pharmacology				
scleroderma				
systemic				
topical				

Which term refers to a color? _____

LESSON 3.3 Accessory Skin Organs

OBJECTIVES

Hair follicles and their associated sebaceous glands, sweat glands, and nails are organs located in your skin. They each have specific anatomic and physiologic characteristics. You must understand their roles in the different functions of the skin and in diseases that affect the skin. This lesson will enable you to:

- **Name the associated skin organs.**
- **Link the structures of the different organs to their functions.**
- **Describe certain disorders affecting the associated skin organs.**
- **Explain the etiology of certain disorders affecting the associated skin organs.**
- **Apply correct medical terminology to the anatomy, physiology, and disorders of the associated skin organs.**

You are

. . . a medical assistant working with Lenore Echols, MD, a dermatologist in Fulwood Medical Center.

Your patient is

. . . Wayne Winter, an 18-year-old man, who has been accepted to college in the fall.

CASE REPORT 3.4

He has had acne since the age of 15 and has tried numerous over-the-counter products. Retinoic acid has also been unsuccessful. He has numerous comedones, papules, pustules, and scars on his face and forehead with severe **cystic** lesions and scars on his back. His social life is nonexistent, and he is teased by his peers. He wishes to change all this before he gets to college.

Your role is to document his care and explain to him how to use the medications Dr. Echols prescribes, what their effects will be, and his prognosis.

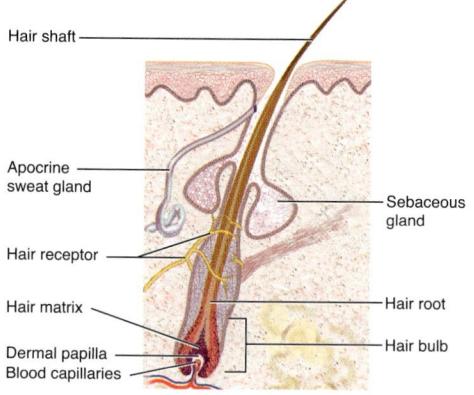

Hair shaft

Apocrine sweat gland

Sebaceous gland

Hair receptor

Hair matrix

Hair root

Dermal papilla
Blood capillaries

Hair bulb

▲ **FIGURE 3.22** **Hair Follicle and Sebaceous Gland.**

HAIR FOLLICLES AND SEBACEOUS GLANDS

Each hair follicle has a **sebaceous gland** opening into it *(Figure 3.22)*. The gland secretes into the follicle a mixture of oily, acidic **sebum** and broken-down cells from the base of the gland.

Around puberty, **androgens** are thought to trigger excessive production of sebum from the glands, which then brings excessive numbers of broken-down cells toward the skin surface. This blocks the follicle, forming a **comedo** (whitehead or blackhead). These can stay closed, leading to **papules,** or rupture, allowing bacteria to get in and produce **pustules.** These are the classic signs of **acne,** which is said to affect, in different degrees, about 85% of people between 12 and 25 years *(Figure 3.23)*.

A different skin problem involving the sebaceous glands is **seborrheic dermatitis.** The glands are thought to be inflamed and to produce a different sebum. The skin around the face and scalp is reddened and covered with yellow, greasy scales. In infants, this condition is called cradle cap. Seborrheic dermatitis of the scalp produces **dandruff.**

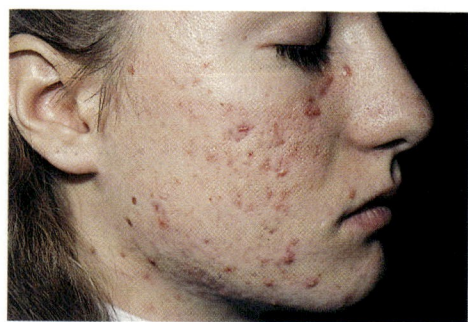

▲ **FIGURE 3.23** **Acne.**

WORD ANALYSIS AND DEFINITION

WORD	PRONUNCIATION	ELEMENTS		DEFINITION
acne	AK-nee		Greek *point*	Inflammatory disease of sebaceous glands and hair follicles
androgen	AN-droh-jen	S/ R/CF	**-gen** *to produce* **andr/o-** *male*	Hormone that promotes masculine characteristics
comedo comedones (pl)	KOM-ee-doh		Latin *eat up*	A whitehead or blackhead caused by too much sebum and too many keratin cells blocking the hair follicle
cyst cystic (adj)	SIST SIS-tik		Greek *sac, bladder*	An abnormal, fluid-containing sac Relating to a cyst
dandruff	DAN-druff		Old English *scurf*	Seborrheic scales from the scalp
pustule	PUS-tyul		Latin *pustule*	Small protuberance on the skin that contains pus
sebum	SEE-bum		Latin *wax*	Waxy secretion of the sebaceous glands
seborrhea seborrheic (adj)	seb-oh-REE-ah seb-oh-REE-ik	S/ R/CF	**-rrhea** *flow* **seb/o-** *sebum*	Excessive amount of sebum

EXERCISES

Match the Greek or Latin term to its medical meaning.

_____ 1. sebum

_____ 2. cyst

_____ 3. pustule

_____ 4. acne

_____ 5. comedone

A. point

B. containing pus

C. eat up

D. wax

E. sac, bladder

Deconstruct the following terms into their elements. Write the meaning of the element below the lines.

6. androgen _____/ _____ / _____

7. seborrhea _____/ _____ / _____

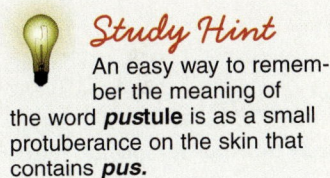

Study Hint

An easy way to remember the meaning of the word **pustule** is as a small protuberance on the skin that contains **pus.**

Study Hint

Make an extra effort to learn the correct spelling of the terms sebo**rrh**ea and sebo**rrh**eic. The "rrh" combination occurs in other medical terms as well—diarrhea, hemorrhage, menorrhagia, herniorrhaphy, etc. Be alert to this combination of letters in terms. You can be sure these terms will appear on a test.

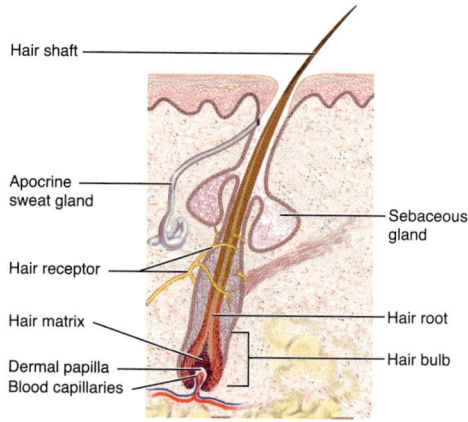

Hair shaft

Apocrine sweat gland

Hair receptor

Hair matrix

Dermal papilla
Blood capillaries

Sebaceous gland

Hair root

Hair bulb

▲ **FIGURE 3.24   Hair Follicle.**

Keynote

Genes, hormones, and pigment determine hair characteristics.

Keynote

Body hair has no specific function.

ACCESSORY SKIN ORGANS

Hair

Each hair, no matter where it is on your body or scalp, originates from epidermal cells at the base (matrix) of a hair follicle. As these cells divide and grow, they push older cells upward away from the source of nutrition in the hair papilla *(Figure 3.24)*. The cells become keratinized and die. They rest for a while; and, when a new hair is formed, the old, dead hair is pushed out and drops off.

In cross-section, each hair has three layers *(Figure 3.25a)*. Its core, the **medulla,** is composed of loosely arranged cells containing a flexible keratin. The **cortex** is composed of densely packed cells with a harder keratin that gives hair its stiffness. These cells also contain pigment. The outer **cuticle** is a single layer of scaly, dead keratin cells.

Straight hair is round in cross-section *(Figure 3.25a and b)*. Curly hair is oval *(Figure 3.25c and d)*. Two pigments derived from melanin give hair its natural color. Black and dark brown hair has a lot of a dark form of the pigment **melanin** in the cells of the cortex *(Figure 3.25b)*. Blonde hair has little of this dark pigment but a moderate amount of a lighter form of melanin *(Figure 3.25a)*. Red hair has a lot of the lighter pigment *(Figure 3.25c)*. White or gray hair has no pigment *(Figure 3.25d)*.

A problem with the scalp hair follicle occurs in men when a combination of genetic influence and excess testosterone produces "top of the head" baldness. In most people, aging causes **alopecia,** thinning of the hair and baldness as the follicles shrink and produce thin wispy hairs.

Scalp hair is thick enough to retain heat. Body hair has no specific function in our present evolution because, in most people, it is too thin to retain heat. Beard, pubic, and **axillary** (armpit) hair reflect sexual maturity. Stronger hairs guard the nostrils and ears to prevent foreign particles from entering. Similarly, eyelashes protect the eyes, and eyebrows help keep perspiration from running into the eyes.

Melanin is in the black skin melanocytes of dark-skinned people and is the pigment generated by sunbathing and tanning. The absence of melanin produces **albinism**.

(a)

(b)

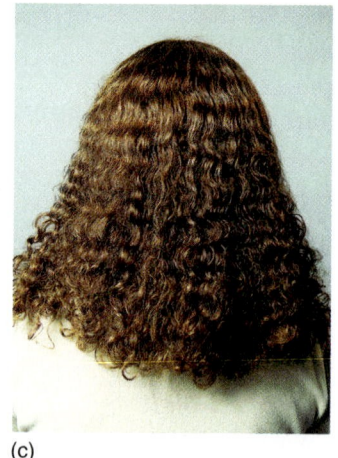

(c)

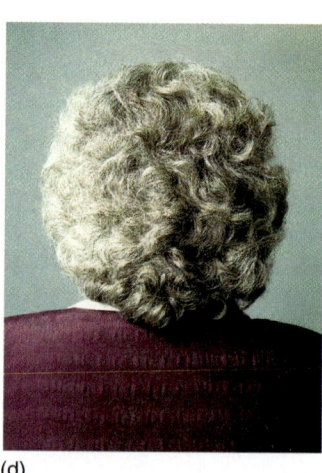

(d)

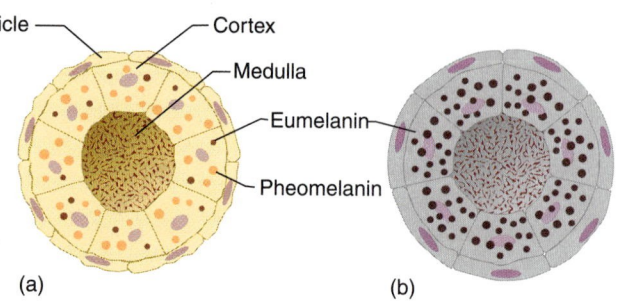

Cuticle

Cortex

Medulla

Eumelanin

Pheomelanin

(a)

(b)

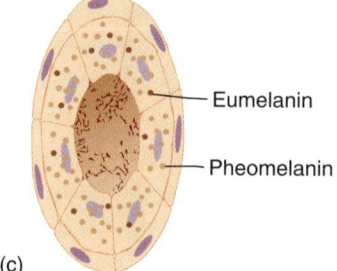

Eumelanin

Pheomelanin

(c)

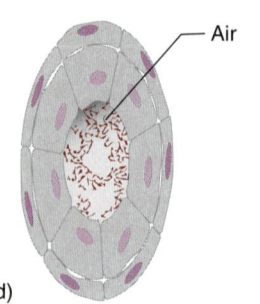

Air

(d)

▲ **FIGURE 3.25   Basis of Hair Color and Texture.**

WORD	PRONUNCIATION		ELEMENTS	DEFINITION
albinism albino	**AL**-bih-nizm al-**BY**-no	S/ R/	-ism *condition* albin- *white*	Genetic disorder with lack of melanin Person with albinism
alopecia	al-oh-**PEE**-shah		Greek *mange*	Partial or complete loss of hair, naturally or from medication
axilla axillae (pl) axillary (adj)	**AK**-sill-ah **AK**-sill-ee **AK**-sill-air-ee		Greek *region under a bird's wing*	Medical name for the armpit
cortex cortical (adj) cortices (pl)	**KOR**-teks **KOR**-tih-kal **KOR**-tih-sees		Latin *outer covering*	Outer portion of an organ, such as bone. Gray covering of cerebral hemispheres
cuticle	**KEW**-tih-cul		Diminutive of **cutis** *skin*	Nonliving epidermis at the base of the finger and toe nails
medulla medullary (adj)	meh-**DULL**-ah meh-**DULL**-eh-ree		French *middle*	Central portion of a structure surrounded by cortex
melanin	**MEL**-ah-nin		Greek *black*	Black pigment found in skin, hair, retina

EXERCISES

*A good review of the WAD will aid you in answering the following questions about the **language of dermatology**. Fill in the blanks.*

1. The root _____ denotes the color _____.

2. The medical term for **armpit** is _____.

3. The plural form of **cortex** is _____.

4. The central portion of a structure is the _____, which means _____.

5. The outer portion of an organ is the _____.

6. **Alopecia** can result from natural causes or from _____.

7. Adjectival forms of medical terms that are nouns can have different endings.

   Three terms that are adjectives appear in this Word Analysis and Definition box. Their endings are: _____, _____, and _____.

8. The medical term for baldness is _____.

The following nouns all have an adjectival form. Fill in the blanks.

9. Noun: axilla   Adjective: _____

10. Noun: cortex   Adjective: _____

11. Noun: medulla   Adjective: _____

12. Use any one of these adjectives in a sentence.

_____

_____

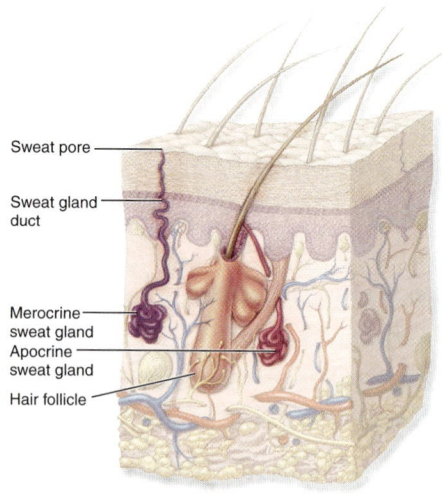

▲ FIGURE 3.26   Sweat Glands.

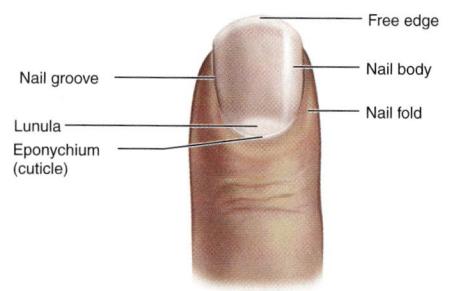

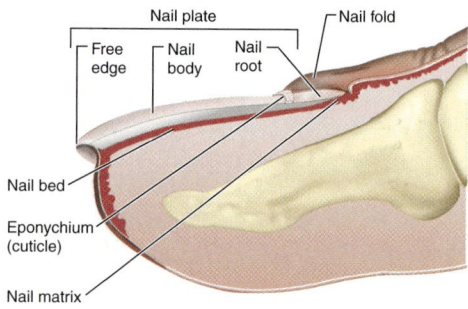

▲ FIGURE 3.27   Anatomy of a Fingernail.

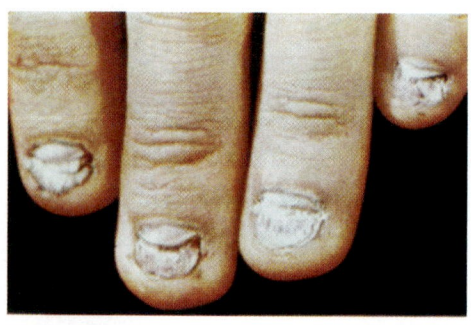

▲ FIGURE 3.28   Onychomycosis (Fungal Infection).

Sweat Glands

You have three to four million **merocrine (eccrine) sweat glands** scattered all over your skin, with concentrations on your palms, soles, and forehead (Figure 3.26).

Their main function is to produce the watery perspiration (sweat) that cools your body. Your sweat is 99% water; the rest is made up of electrolytes such as sodium chloride, which gives the sweat its salty taste. Some waste products of cell metabolism are also secreted.

In the dermis the sweat gland is a coiled tube lined with epithelial cells that secrete the sweat. Around the tube, muscle cells contract to squeeze the sweat up the tube directly to the surface of the skin.

In your armpits (**axillae**), around your nipples, in your groin, and around your anus, **apocrine sweat glands** produce a thick, cloudy secretion that interacts with normal skin bacteria to produce a distinct, noticeable smell. The ducts of these glands lead directly into hair follicles (see Figure 3.26). They respond to sexual stimulation and stress and secrete chemicals called **pheromones**, which have an effect on the sexual behavior of other people.

Ceruminous glands are found in the external ear canal, where their secretions combine with sebum and dead epidermal cells to form earwax. This wax waterproofs the external ear canal and kills bacteria.

Sweat glands have no specific diseases that only affect them. They can be involved in the infections that engulf the nearby hair follicles and sebaceous glands.

Mammary glands, a type of modified sweat gland, serve a distinct purpose in reproduction and are therefore discussed in *Chapter 12* under the female reproductive system.

Nails

Nails are formed from the stratum corneum of the epidermis. They consist of closely packed, thin, dead cells that are filled with parallel fibers of hard keratin.

Fingernails grow at about 1 mm per week. New cells are added by cell division in the nail **matrix,** which is protected by the nail fold of skin and the cuticle at the base of the nail (Figure 3.27). The nail rests on the nail bed, which consists of the living layers of the epidermis, the strata basale, spinosum, and granulosum.

Diseases of Nails   Fifty percent of all nail disorders are caused by fungal infections and are labeled **onychomycosis** (Figure 3.28). They begin in nails constantly exposed to moisture and warmth, for example in warm shoes when associated with poor foot hygiene, in the hands of a restaurant dishwasher, under artificial fingernails, and in pedicure bowls if they are not sanitized. The fungus grows under the nail and leads to brittle cracked nails that separate from the underlying nail bed.

Paronychia (Figure 3.29) is a bacterial infection, usually staphylococcal, of the base of the nail. The nail fold and cuticle become swollen, red, and painful, and pus forms under the nail and can escape at the side of the nail.

The big toe nail can grow into the skin at the side of the nail, particularly if pressured by tight, narrow shoes. Infection can then get underneath this ingrown toenail.

The nails can reflect systemic illness. In anemia, the nail bed is pale, and the nails can become spoon-shaped. In conditions producing chronic **hypoxia**, the fingers, toes, and nails become clubbed. Malnutrition or severe illness can produce horizontal white lines in the nails.

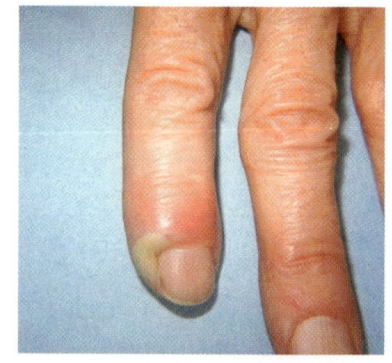

▲ FIGURE 3.29   Paronychia, with Pus at the Corner of the Nail Bed.

WORD	PRONUNCIATION	ELEMENTS		DEFINITION
apocrine	AP-oh-krin	P/ R/	apo- *different from* -crine *hair*	Apocrine sweat glands open into the hair follicle
cerumen ceruminous (adj)	seh-ROO-men seh-ROO-mih-nus		Latin *wax*	Waxy secretion of the cereminous glands of the external ear
eccrine	EK-rin		Greek *to secrete*	Coiled sweat gland that occurs in skin all over the body
hypoxia hypoxic (adj)	high-POCK-see-ah high-POCK-sik	P/ R/	hypo- *deficient* -oxia *oxygen* (**Note:** The vowel "o" at the end of hypo- is dropped. It is unnecessary and cumbersome.)	Below normal levels of oxygen in tissues, gases, or blood Deficient in oxygen
matrix	MAY-triks		Latin *womb*	Substance that surrounds cells, is manufactured by the cells, and holds them together
merocrine	MARE-oh-krin	P/ R/	mero- *partial* -crine *hair*	Another name for eccrine
onychomycosis	oh-ni-koh-my-KOH-sis	S/ R/CF R/	-osis *condition* onych/o- *nail* -myc- *fungus*	Condition of a fungus infection in a nail
paronychia	par-oh-NICK-ee-ah	S/ P/ R/	-ia *pertaining to* para- *alongside* onych- *nail* (**Note:** The vowel "a" at the end of para- is dropped to make the composite word flow more easily.)	Infection alongside the nail
pheromone	FER-oh-moan	P/ R/	pher- *carrying* -omone *excite, stimulate*	Substance that carries and generates a physical attraction for other people

EXERCISES

Work on understanding the meanings of the elements. Dissect the medical terms into their elements, and show that you know their meanings. Fill in the blanks.

Medical term	Prefix	Meaning of Prefix	Root/CF	Meaning of Root/CF	Suffix	Meaning of Suffix
pheromone						
apocrine						
hypoxia						
merocrine						
onychomycosis						
paronychia						

Answer the following questions about the medical terms in this WAD.

A plural form of a term has been intentionally left out of the Word Analysis and Definition box shown above. Find the term, form its plural, and write the rule that applies to that ending.

1. Singular term: _____ Plural term: _____

2. Rule: _____. *Note:* Go back and write the plural form in the Word Analysis and Definition box under the singular term.

> **Study Hint**
> This WAD contains another suffix meaning *pertaining to.* Add that to your ongoing list.

LESSON 3.4 Burns and Injuries to the Skin

OBJECTIVES

You have learned that a major role of the skin is protection of your internal organs. In the previous lessons, you have seen the effects of infectious agents on the skin. In this lesson, you will learn the effects of direct injury to the skin, and you will be able to:

- **Distinguish the four types of burns.**
- **Describe the inflammatory process of the skin when it is injured.**
- **Explain the process of healing and repair of the skin.**
- **Select the correct medical terminology to describe wounds, burns, and the process of healing and repair.**

You are

. . . a burn technologist employed in the Burn Unit at Fulwood Medical Center.

Your patient is

. . . Mr. Steven Hapgood, a 52-year-old man, admitted to the Fulwood Burn Unit with severe burns over his face, chest, and abdomen.

CASE REPORT 3.5

After an evening of drinking, he had been smoking in bed and fell asleep. His next-door neighbors in the apartment building smelled smoke and called 911. In the burn unit, his initial treatment included large volumes of intravenous fluids to prevent **shock.**

Your role will be to participate in his care as a member of the Burn Unit team and to document the care and his response to it.

Keynote

Sunburn causes a first-degree burn.

Scalds can cause second-degree burns.

House fires with prolonged flame contact can cause third-degree burns.

High voltage electrical injury can cause fourth-degree burns.

BURNS

Burns are the leading cause of accidental death. The immediate threats to life are from fluid loss, infection, and the systemic effects of burned dead tissue.

Burns are classified according to the depth of tissue involved *(Figure 3.30)*:

- **First-degree (superficial) burns** involve only the epidermis to produce redness, pain, and slight **edema.** Healing occurs in 3 to 5 days without scarring.
- **Second-degree (partial thickness) burns** involve the epidermis and dermis but leave some of the dermis intact. They produce redness, blisters, and more severe pain. Healing occurs in 2 to 3 weeks with minimal scarring.
- **Third-degree (or full-thickness) burns** involve the epidermis, dermis, and subcutaneous tissues, which are often completely destroyed. Healing takes a long time and involves using skin grafts.
- **Fourth-degree burns** destroy all layers of the skin and involve tendons, muscles, and sometimes bones.

Burn injury to the lungs through damage from heat or smoke inhalation is responsible for 60% or more of fatalities from burns.

In partial-thickness burns, **regeneration** of the skin can occur from remaining cells in the stratum basale, from residual hair follicles and sweat glands, and from

▼ **FIGURE 3.30**

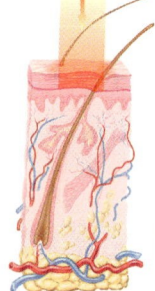 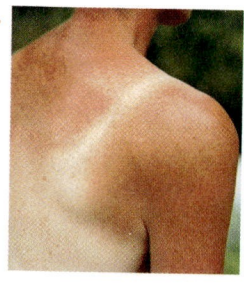

(a) First degree (partial thickness)

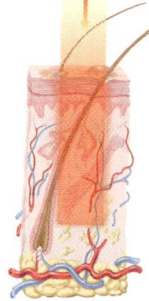 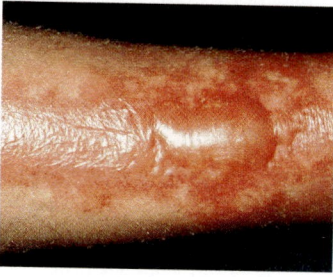

(b) Second degree (partial thickness)

 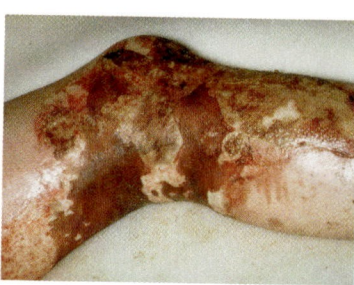

(c) Third degree (full thickness)

WORD	PRONUNCIATION	ELEMENTS		DEFINITION
allograft	**AL**-oh-graft	P/	allo *other*	Skin graft from another person or cadaver
		R/	-graft *transplant*	
homograft	**HOH**-moh-graft	P/	homo- *same, alike*	
autograft	**AWE**-toe-graft	P/	auto- *self*	A graft using tissue taken from the same individual who is receiving the graft
		R/	-graft *transplant*	
debridement	day-**BREED**-mon	S/	-ment *resulting state*	The removal of injured or necrotic tissue
		P/	de- *take away*	
		R/	-bride- *rubbish*	
edema	ee-**DEE**-mah		Greek *swelling*	Excessive collection of fluid in cells and tissues
edematous (adj)	ee-**DEM**-ah-tus			Marked by edema
eschar	**ESS**-kar		Greek *scab of a burn*	The burnt, dead tissue lying on top of third-degree burns
regenerate	re-**JEN**-eh-rate	S/	-ate *action*	Reconstitution of a lost part
regeneration (noun)	re-**JEN**-eh-**RAY**-shun	P/	re- *again*	
		R/	-gener- *produce*	
shock	SHOCK		German *to clash*	Sudden physical or mental collapse or circulatory collapse
xenograft	**ZEN**-oh-graft	P/	xeno- *foreign*	A graft from another species
		R/	-graft *transplant*	
heterograft	**HET**-er-oh-graft	P/	hetero- *different*	

Case-Report 3.5 *(continued)*

Mr. Hapgood's burns were mostly third degree. The protective ability of the skin to prevent water loss had been removed, as had the skin barrier against infection. The burned, dead tissue forms an **eschar** that can have toxic effects on the digestive, respiratory, and cardiovascular systems. The eschar was surgically removed by **debridement**.

the edges of the burned area. In full-thickness burns there is no dermal tissue left for regeneration, and skin grafts are needed. The ideal graft is an **autograft** taken from another location on the patient. It is not rejected by the immune system. Mr. Hapgood had autografts taken from his unburned legs and back.

If the patient's burns are too extensive, **allografts** from another person are needed. These are provided by skin banks and taken from deceased people. A **homograft** is another name for an allograft. A **xenograft**, or **heterograft**, is a graft from another species; for example, pigs.

Artificial skin is being developed commercially and can stimulate the growth of connective tissues from the patient's underlying tissue.

Keynote

In third-and fourth-degree burns, there is no dermal tissue left for regeneration, and skin grafts are necessary.

EXERCISES

*Continue your work with elements from the **language of dermatology**. Match the element in 1–12 to its correct meaning in A–L. Fill in the blanks.*

Study Hint
Pay special attention to the graft prefixes.

_____ 1. homo-   _____ 7. -gener-   A. again   G. action

_____ 2. -bride-   _____ 8. -graft-   B. foreign   H. resulting state

_____ 3. -ate   _____ 9. auto-   C. produce   I. rubbish

_____ 4. allo-   _____ 10. de-   D. same, like   J. transplant

_____ 5. -ment   _____ 11. re-   E. different   K. self

_____ 6. zeno-   _____ 12. hetero-   F. other   L. take away

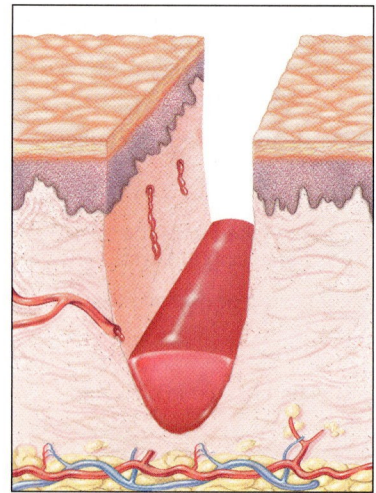

(a) Bleeding into the wound

▲ **FIGURE 3.31** **Wound Healing.**

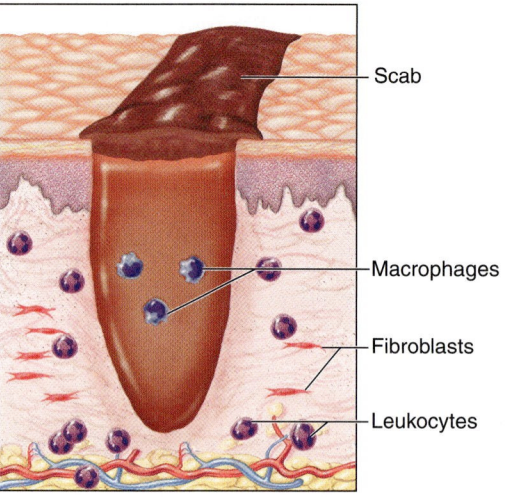

Scab

Macrophages

Fibroblasts

Leukocytes

(b) Scab formation and macrophage activity

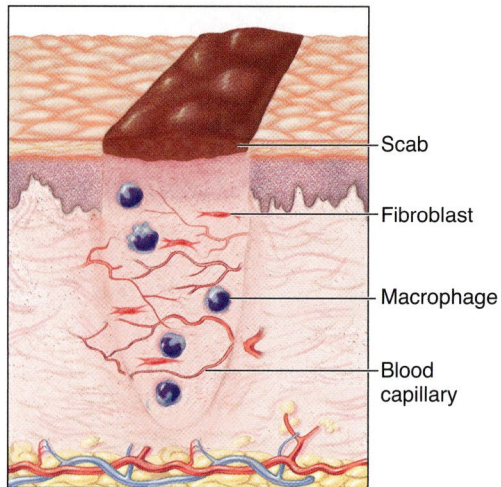

Scab

Fibroblast

Macrophage

Blood capillary

▲ **FIGURE 3.32** **Formation of Granulation Tissue.**

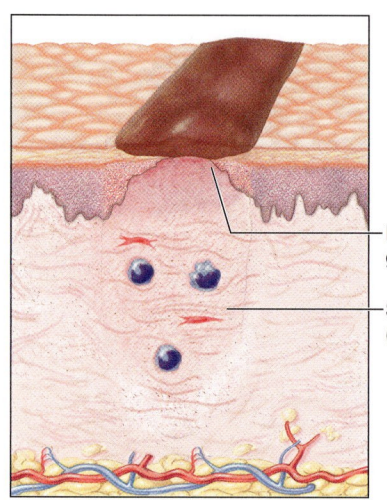

Epidermal growth

Scar tissue (fibrosis)

▲ **FIGURE 3.33** **Scar Formation.**

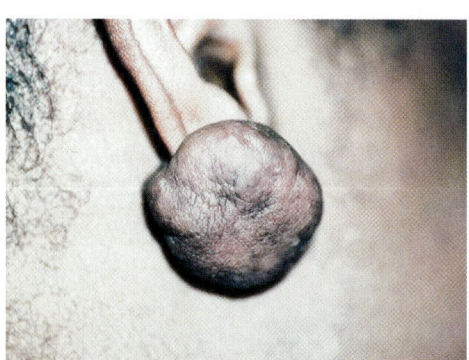

▲ **FIGURE 3.34** **A Keloid of the Earlobe.**
This scar resulted from piercing the ear for earrings.

WOUNDS AND TISSUE REPAIR

If you cut yourself with paper to produce a shallow **laceration** primarily in the epidermis, the epithelial cells along its edges will divide rapidly and fill in the gap. An adhesive bandage helps the process by pulling the edges together.

If you cut yourself more deeply, extending the **wound** into the dermis or hypodermis, or if a surgeon operates on you, then blood vessels in the dermis break and blood escapes into the wound *(Figure 3.31a)*.

This escaped blood forms a **clot** in the wound. The clot consists of the protein (**fibrin**) together with **platelets,** blood cells, and dried tissue fluids trapped in the fibers. **Macrophages** come into the wound with the escaped blood. They digest and clean up the tissue debris. The surface of the clot dries and hardens in the air to form a **scab.** The scab seals and protects the wound from becoming infected *(Figure 3.31b)*.

The clot begins to be invaded by new capillaries from the surrounding dermis. Three or four days after the injury, fibroblasts migrate into the wound and form new collagen fibers that pull the wound together. This soft tissue in the wound is called **granulation tissue** and in unsutured wounds takes a couple of weeks to completely form *(Figure 3.32)*.

As healing continues, surface epithelial cells from the edges of the wound migrate into the area underneath the scab. As this new epithelium thickens, the scab loosens and falls off. Inside the wound, new collagen fibers formed by the fibroblasts form a **scar** to replace the granulation tissue *(Figure 3.33)*. In unsutured wounds, this takes up to a month to complete.

Suturing brings together the edges of the wound to enhance tissue healing. It also reduces the risk of infection and the amount of scarring. A liquid skin adhesive can sometimes be used in place of sutures. Some sutures eventually dissolve, avoiding the need for suture removal. The scar formation and remodeling process may go on for more than a year.

In some people, there is excessive fibrosis and scar tissue formation, producing raised, irregular, lumpy, shiny scars called **keloids** *(Figure 3.34)*. They can extend beyond the edges of the original wound and often return if they are surgically removed. They are most common on the upper body and earlobes.

Surgery on the skin is now being performed using light beams called **lasers.** These beams of light can be focused precisely to vaporize specific lesions on the superficial layers of the skin. The beam removes lesions and creates a fresh surface over which new skin can grow. Healing takes 10 to 15 days and goes through the process described above, with clotting and scabbing.

A superficial scraping of the skin, a mucous membrane, or the cornea *(see Chapter 4)* is called an **abrasion.**

WORD	PRONUNCIATION		ELEMENTS	DEFINITION
abrasion	ah-**BRAY**-shun		Latin *to scrape*	Area of skin or mucous membrane that has been scraped off
clot	KLOT		German *to block*	The mass of fibrin and cells that is produced in a wound
fibrin	**FIE**-brin		Latin *fiber*	Stringy protein fiber that is a component of a blood clot
fibrous (adj)	**FIE**-brus			Tissue containing fibroblasts and fibers
granulation	gran-you-**LAY**-shun	S/ R/	**-ation** *action* **granul-** *small grain*	New fibrous tissue formed during wound healing
keloid	**KEY**-loyd		Greek *stain*	Raised, irregular lumpy, shiny scar due to excess collagen fiber production during healing of a wound
laceration	lass-eh-**RAY**-shun	S/ R/	**-ation** *action* **lacer-** *to tear*	A tear of the skin
laser	**LAY**-zer		acronym for *l*ight *a*mplification by *s*timulated *e*mission of *r*adiation	Intense, narrow beam of monochromatic light
macrophage	**MAK**-roh-fayj	P R/	**macro-** *large* **-phage** *to eat*	Large white blood cell that removes bacteria, foreign particles, and dead cells
platelet (also called thrombocyte)	**PLAYT**-let		Greek *small plate*	Cell fragment involved in clotting process
scab	SKAB		Old English *crust*	Crust that forms over a wound or sore during healing
scar	SKAR		Greek *scab*	Fibrotic seam that forms when a wound heals
suture	**SOO**-chur		Latin *seam*	Stitch to hold the edges of a wound together
wound	WOOND		Old English *wound*	Any injury that interrupts the continuity of skin or a mucous membrane

EXERCISES

Review the WAD before starting this exercise—the elements and definitions will help you work out the answers. Put on your thinking cap. Fill in the blanks.

1. Reorder these terms into the order of their occurrence.

　scab　　　scar　　　laceration　　　clot　　　wound

_____

2. How are a *keloid* and a *scar* different?

_____

3. What is the soft tissue in the wound-healing process called?

_____

4　What's the relationship between a *clot* and a *scab*?

_____

5. What is another name for a stitch used to close a wound?

_____

Congratulations! You have mastered these terms.

INTEGUMENTARY SYSTEM
CHALLENGE YOUR KNOWLEDGE

A. **Apply your knowledge of the language of dermatology to the following case report from this chapter.** Read the case report out loud for pronunciation practice. Underline the medical terms, and be sure you understand them. Answer the questions.

CASE REPORT 3.3

Ms. Cheryl Fox is a 37-year-old nursing assistant working in a surgical unit in Fulwood Medical Center. Recently her fingers have become red and itchy, with occasional vesicles. She has also noticed irritation and swelling of her ear lobes and a generalized pruritus. Over the weekends, both the itching and the rash on her hands worsen. A patch test by her dermatologist showed her to be allergic to nickel in rings that she wears on both hands and in her earrings. She wears these on weekends and not during her workdays.

1. What diagnostic test did Ms. Fox have to determine the cause of her condition?

   _____

2. List Ms. Fox's symptoms.

   _____

   _____

3. What part of her body was *edematous?*

   _____

4. **Pruritus** is a medical term for _____

5. Describe a vesicle. _____

6. What is the *allergen* that Ms. Fox is allergic to? _____

7. A likely diagnosis for Ms. Fox would be: (circle one)

   melanoma   dermatitis   vitiligo   candidiasis

B. **Identify the following group of elements.** Define each element, and use each in a medical term. Complete the analysis by giving the meaning of each medical term. Fill in the chart below.

Element	Meaning of element	Medical term	Meaning of medical term
an			
anti			
apo			
bi			
cryo			
de			
epi			

Element	Meaning of element	Medical term	Meaning of medical term
hypo			
intra			
macro			
melan			
para			
peri			
pro			
re			
semi			
sub			
trans			

This entire group is what type of element? _____

C. **To give you a better understanding of the integumentary system, you must know the** layers of skin and its tissue components, as well as its functions. Fill in the following blanks.

Name the three layers of skin, and which type of tissue is found in that layer.

1. Skin layer: _____

   Tissue(s): _____

2. Skin layer: _____

   Tissue(s): _____

3. Skin layer: _____

   Tissue(s): _____

CHAPTER 3 REVIEW

INTEGUMENTARY SYSTEM

D. **Plurals:** Form the plurals for the following terms.

1. papilla   Plural: _____

2. matrix   Plural: _____

3. cortex   Plural: _____

4. axilla   Plural: _____

E. **Translate to Layman's Terms:** Expressing yourself verbally is something you will have to do every day on the job. Your patient is asking about the following procedures. In the space given, briefly define each procedure in terms the patient will understand.

1. Cryosurgery:

    _____

    _____

2. Biopsy removal:

    _____

    _____

3. Debridement:

    _____

    _____

F. **Each of the following medical terms has something in common.** Use your knowledge of the *language of dermatology* to determine what links them together. The first one is done for you. Fill in the blanks.

1. epidermis, dermis and hypodermis   *Are all layers of skin* _____

2. melanoma, malignancy, metastasis _____

3. bee stings, peanuts, cats, pollen _____

4. intradermal, subcutaneous, intramuscular _____

5. merocrine, apocrine, ceruminous _____

6. mole, papule, macule _____

G. **Diagnoses:** Determining the root(s) of the following diagnoses will help you understand the meaning of the medical term. First, determine the root(s), give the meaning of the root(s), then provide a brief description of the meaning of the term. Fill in the chart below.

Diagnosis	Root(s)	Meaning of Root	Meaning of Term
candidiasis			
carcinoma			
decubitus ulcer			
dermatitis			
dermatomyositis			
hypoxia			
impetigo			
onychomycosis			
paronychia			
pediculosis			
pruritus			
scleroderma			

H. **Also Known As:** Some medical terms may be known by a more common term. You need to know both. Fill in the blanks with the alternate terms.

1. decubitus ulcer = _____

2. cradle cap = _____

3. herpes zoster = _____

4. *Staphylococcus* = _____

5. armpit = _____

6. baldness = _____

7. wax = _____

8. whitehead or blackhead = _____

9. athlete's foot = _____

INTEGUMENTARY SYSTEM

I. **Medical vocabulary is filled with terms taken directly from Greek and Latin.** The medical term is given to you—write the definition beside it.

1. dermis _____

2. integument _____

3. mole _____

4. squamous _____

5. collagen _____

6. follicle _____

7. vesicle _____

8. edema _____

9. nevus _____

10. boil _____

J. **Recall and Review:** How well do you remember these word elements from the previous chapter? Try to answer without first looking back to check. Fill in the blanks.

Element	Type of Element (P, R, CF, S)	Meaning of Element
ism	_____	_____
elle	_____	_____
chromat	_____	_____
endo	_____	_____
cyte	_____	_____

K. **Label Exercise:** Identify the integumentary term in phrases 1–6, and write the terms on the correct lines A–F in the illustration.

1. Open into hair follicles

2. Also called subcutaneous tissue layer

3. Top layer of the skin

4. Concentrated on palms, soles of feet and forehead

5. Layer of skin below epidermis

6. Secrete chemicals called pheromones

B. _____

D. _____

F. _____

A. _____

E. _____

C. _____

L. **The following chart of elements is not complete.** In some cases you are given the element to begin with, in some cases you are given the term that you end with. Work with your integumentary system vocabulary to fill in the missing blanks. There should be an answer in every space of every column.

Element	Type of element	Meaning of element	Medical term using this element
adip		*Fat or suet*	
	prefix		antigen
oma	suffix		
ment			debridement
	prefix	*Icy cold*	
		two/twice	
	suffix	*structure*	
	suffix		androgen
sclero			
		broken	
ox			hypoxia
ation	suffix		
		cell	
		cause	
melan		*becoming black*	

M. **Make a connection from a medical term to an English word.** Fill in the chart below.

Fungal infections that cause human disease are named tinea. Which three body areas host this fungus?

Body area	Medical Term is	Correlate to an English word
1.		pedal
2.		capital/capitol
3.		corporal

Study Hint
Try to match the term to an English word with the same sense or meaning.

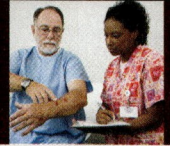

CHAPTER 3 REVIEW

INTEGUMENTARY SYSTEM

X. Continue applying your knowledge of the *language of dermatology* to the integumentary system. Circle the best choice.

1. A congenital lesion of the skin, including birthmarks and moles, is called a:

   a. macule

   b. papule

   c. vesicle

   d. nevus

   e. melanoma

2. Another name for a pressure ulcer is:

   a. eczema

   b. excoriation

   c. decubitus

   d. edematous

   e. serous

3. Strep enzymes digest connective tissue and spread into muscle layers in:

   a. lesions

   b. atopic dermatitis

   c. cellulitis

   d. ulcers

   e. necrotizing fasciitis

4. The medical term for shingles is:

   a. erysipelas

   b. herpes zoster

   c. impetigo

   d. candidiasis

   e. pediculosis

5. Kaposi sarcoma is associated with:

   a. SC

   b. HIV

   c. SLE

   d. TB

   e. MRSA

Y. **Medical terms that are nouns can also have an adjectival form that must be used in some cases.** Test your knowledge of the correct form of the term to use in the following sentences. Circle the best choice.

1. This puncture wound has completely penetrated the (dermis/dermal).

2. This puncture wound has completely penetrated the (dermis/dermal) layer of skin.

3. Please take this specimen to the (pathological/pathology) department.

4. The (pathology/pathological) diagnosis has not been determined yet.

5. The general (anesthesia/anesthetic) caused the patient to lose consciousness.

6. The (anesthesia/anesthetic) properties of the aloe lotion reduced the pain in the sunburn.

Z. **The skin is the largest organ in the body.** Build your knowledge of Chapter 3 terminology with the following exercise. Deconstruct the following medical terms into their word elements. Fill in the chart for each term, and then answer the questions.

Medical term	Prefix	Root/combining form	Suffix	Meaning of Medical Term
biopsy				
carcinoma				
corneum				
cryosurgery				
dermatologist				
epidermis				
integumentary				
keratinocyte				
metastasis				
microscope				
pathological				
prognosis				

1. List the terms that are procedures: _____

2. Write the term for a specialist: _____

3. Name the body system: _____

4. Identify the instrument a pathologist uses: _____

5. Name the top layer of the skin: _____

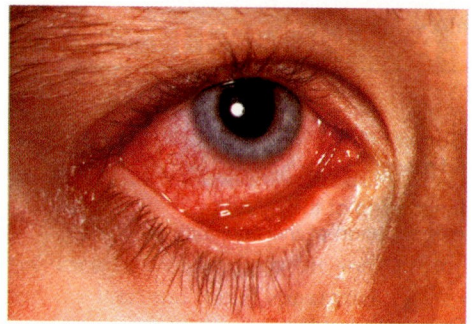

▲ **FIGURE 4.3   Conjunctivitis.**

Stye

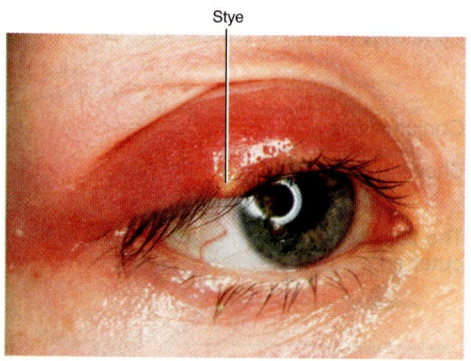

▲ **FIGURE 4.4   Stye Showing Pus-Filled Cyst.**

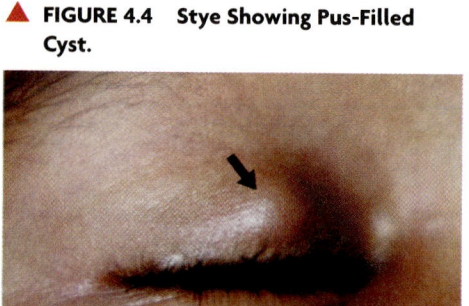

▲ **FIGURE 4.5   Chalazion in Upper Eyelid.**

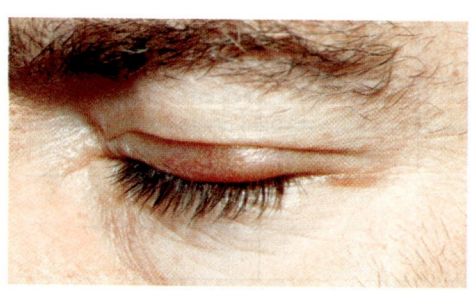

▲ **FIGURE 4.6   Blepharitis.**

DISORDERS OF THE ACCESSORY GLANDS

Conjunctivitis *(Figure 4.3)*, inflammation of the conjunctiva, is more commonly viral than bacterial, and can also be caused by irritants such as chlorine, soaps, fumes, and smoke.

Eyelid edema, generalized swelling of the eyelids, is often produced by an allergic reaction *(see Chapter 15)* due to cosmetics, pollen in the air, or stings and bites from insects.

A **stye,** or **hordeolum,** is an infection of an eyelash follicle producing an abscess *(Figure 4.4)*, with localized pain, swelling, redness, and pus formation at the edge of the eyelid.

A **chalazion** is a small painless, localized, whitish swelling inside the lid when a tarsal gland becomes blocked *(Figure 4.5)*. It can disappear spontaneously or require surgical removal.

Blepharitis occurs when multiple eyelash follicles and tarsal glands become infected. The margin of the eyelid shows persistent redness and crusting and may become ulcerated *(Figure 4.6)*. The infection is usually staphylococcal *(see Chapter 20)*. It is treated with antibiotic ointments.

Dacryostenosis is blockage of the drainage of tears, usually due to narrowing of the nasolacrimal ducts.

Dacryocystitis is an infection of the lacrimal sac, with swelling and pus at the medial corner of the eye.

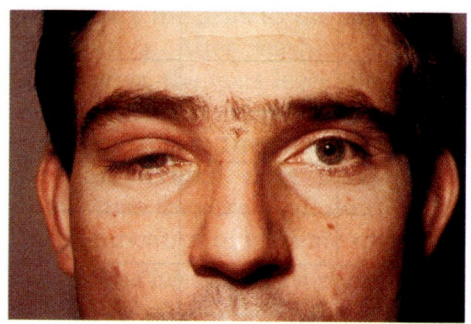

▲ **FIGURE 4.7   Ptosis of Right Eyelid.**

Ptosis occurs when the upper eyelid is constantly drooped over the eye due to **paresis** (partial paralysis) of the muscle that raises the upper lid *(Figure 4.7)*. It can be associated with diabetes, myasthenia gravis, brain tumor, and muscular dystrophy, all of which are described in subsequent chapters. The term **blepharoptosis** is used for sagging of the eyelids due to excess skin. The plastic surgery procedure of **blepharoplasty** is used for the repair of the eyelid.

WORD	PRONUNCIATION		ELEMENTS	DEFINITION
antibiotic	AN-tih-bye-OT-ik	S/ P/ R/	-ic *pertaining to* anti- *against* -biot- *life*	A substance that has the capacity to destroy bacteria and other microorganisms
blepharitis	blef-ah-RYE-tis	S/ R/	-itis *inflammation* blephar- *eyelid*	Inflammation of the eyelid
blepharoptosis	BLEF-ah-ROP-toe-sis	S/ R/CF	-ptosis *drooping* blephar/o- *eyelid*	Drooping of the upper eyelid
blepharoplasty	BLEF-ah-ro-plas-tee	S/	-plasty *surgical repair*	Surgical repair of the eyelid
chalazion	kah-LAY-zee-on		Greek *lump*	Cyst on the outer edge of an eyelid
contagious	kon-TAY-jus		Latin *touch closely*	Infection can be transmitted from person to person or from person to a surface to a person
contaminate contamination (noun)	kon-TAM-in-ate KON-tam-ih-NAY-shun	S/ P/ R/	-ate *action* con- *together* -tamin- *touch*	To cause the presence of an infectious agent to be on any surface Presence of an infectious agent on a surface or in substances
dacryocystitis	DAK-re-oh-sis-TIE-tis	S/ R/CF R/	-itis *inflammation* dacry/o- *tears* -cyst- *sac*	Inflammation of the lacrimal sac
dacryostenosis	DAK-re-oh-ste-NO-sis	S/ R/	-osis *condition* -sten- *narrowing*	Narrowing of the nasolacrimal duct
hordeolum (also called stye)	hor-DEE-oh-lum		Latin *stye in the eye*	Abscess in an eyelash follicle
paresis	par-EE-sis		Greek *paralysis*	Partial paralysis
photophobia photophobic (adj)	foh-toe-FOH-bee-ah foh-toe-FOH-bik	S/ R/CF	-phobia *fear* phot/o- *light*	Fear of the light because it hurts the eyes
ptosis (**Note:** When a word begins with two consonants, the first is silent.)	TOE-sis		Greek *drooping*	Sinking down of an eyelid or an organ

EXERCISES

Disorders: *The accessory structures of the eye have their own disorders. The patient conditions are described in column 1, match the condition with the correct medical term (column 2) from this lesson. Fill in the blanks.*

_____ 1. allergic reaction to pollen

_____ 2. upper eyelid droops over eye

_____ 3. infection of the lacrimal sac

_____ 4. produced by a blocked tarsal gland

_____ 5. blockage of the drainage of tears

_____ 6. eyelid is red, crusted, and ulcerated

_____ 7. pus at the edge of the eyelid

A. chalazion

B. hordeolum

C. dacryostenosis

D. blepharitis

E. eyelid edema

F. dacryocystitis

G. ptosis

LESSON 4.2 The Eyeball and Seeing

SPECIAL SENSES OF
THE EYE AND EAR

OBJECTIVES

The eyeball is a hollow sphere about one inch in diameter. Knowledge of its terminology, structure, and function enables you to understand how we see and what major problems and disorders can arise.

In this lesson, the information will enable you to:

- **Identify the principal components of the eyeball and their functions.**
- **Explain the role of the cornea and the problems that can occur in that structure.**
- **Describe the structure and functions of the lens and its associated structures.**
- **Link the different components of the retina to their functions.**
- **Discuss common disorders of the eyeball and its components.**
- **Apply correct medical terminology to the anatomy, physiology, and disorders of the eyeball.**

THE EYEBALL (GLOBE)

The functions of the eyeball are to:

- *adjust* continuously the amount of light it lets in to reach the retina
- *focus* continuously on near and distant objects
- *produce images* continuously of those objects and instantly transmit them to the brain

The front of the eyeball (except for the cornea) is covered by the conjunctiva, a thin layer of tissue that covers the inside of the eyelids and curves over the eyeball to meet the **sclera,** the tough, white outer layer of the eye.

The center of the front of the eye is a transparent, dome-shaped membrane called the **cornea.** The cornea has no blood supply and obtains its nutrients from tears and from fluid in the **anterior chamber** behind it.

When light rays strike the eye, they pass through the cornea. Because of its domed curvature, those rays striking the edge of the cornea are bent toward its center. The light rays then go through the **pupil,** the black opening in the center of the colored area (the **iris**) in the front of the eye.

The pupil controls the amount of light entering the eye. When you are in a dark place, the pupil opens (dilates) to allow more light to enter. When you are in bright light, the pupil closes (constricts) to admit less light. The **sphincter pupillae muscle** *(Figure 4.11)* opens and closes the pupil.

After passing through the pupil, the light rays pass through the transparent **lens.** The ciliary muscle of the **ciliary body** makes the lens thicker and thinner, enabling it to bend the light rays and focus them on the **retina** at the back of the eye. This process of changing focus is called **accommodation.** The process of bending the light rays by the cornea and lens is called **refraction.**

Keynote

The cornea protects the eye and, by changing shape, provides about 60% of the eye's focusing power.

The pupil controls the amount of light entering the eye.

The lens changes its shape to focus rays of light onto the retina.

FIGURE 4.11   Anatomy of the Eyeball. ▼

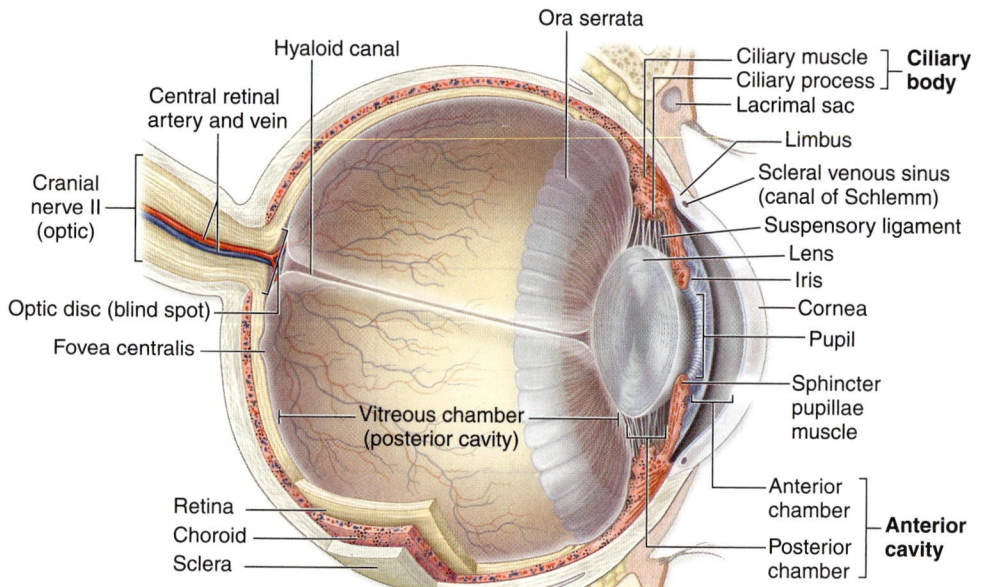

Ora serrata
Hyaloid canal
Central retinal artery and vein
Cranial nerve II (optic)
Optic disc (blind spot)
Fovea centralis
Vitreous chamber (posterior cavity)
Retina
Choroid
Sclera
Ciliary muscle ⎤ **Ciliary**
Ciliary process ⎦ **body**
Lacrimal sac
Limbus
Scleral venous sinus (canal of Schlemm)
Suspensory ligament
Lens
Iris
Cornea
Pupil
Sphincter pupillae muscle
Anterior chamber
Posterior chamber ⎦ **Anterior cavity**

WORD ANALYSIS AND DEFINITION

WORD	PRONUNCIATION	ELEMENTS		DEFINITION
ciliary body	SILL-ee-ary BOD-ee	S R/ R/	-ary *pertaining to* cili- *eyelid* body *mass*	Muscles that make the lens thicker and thinner
cornea corneal (adj)	KOR-nee-ah KOR-nee-al		Latin *web, tunic*	The central, transparent part of the outer coat of the eye covering the iris and pupil
iris	EYE-ris		Greek *diaphragm of the eye*	Colored portion of the eye with the pupil in its center
lens	LENZ		Latin *lentil shape*	Transparent refractive structure behind the iris
presbyopia	prez-bee-OH-pee-ah	S/ R/	-opia *sight* presby- *old man*	Difficulty in nearsighted vision occurring in middle and old age
pupil pupillae (pl) pupillary (adj)	PYU-pill pyu-PILL-ee PYU-pill-AH-ree		Latin *pupil*	The opening in the center of the iris that allows light to reach the lens
refract (verb) refraction (noun)	ree-FRACT ree-FRAK-shun		Latin *break up*	Make a change in direction of, or to bend, a ray of light
retina retinal (adj)	RET-ih-nah RET-ih-nal		Latin *net*	Light-sensitive innermost layer of eyeball
sclera scleral (adj)	SKLAIR-ah SKLAIR-al	S/ R/	-al *pertaining to* scler- *sclera*	Fibrous outer covering of the eyeball and the white of the eye
scleritis	sklair-RI-tis	S/	-itis *inflammation*	Inflammation of the sclera
sphincter	SFINK-ter		Greek *band*	Band of muscle that encircles an opening; when it contracts, the opening squeezes closed

The lens has no supply of blood vessels or nerves. With increasing age, the lens loses its elasticity. When you reach your forties, your eyes may have difficulty focusing on near objects, and the telephone directory can become unreadable without spectacles, a condition called **presbyopia.**

Medical shorthand for a quick normal eye examination can be **PERRLA,** which means *p*upils *e*qual, *r*ound, *r*eactive to *l*ight and *a*ccommodation.

Keynote:

Both the cornea and lens refract light rays. Neither has a blood supply, which compromises healing from injury or disease.

EXERCISES

Components of the Eyeball: *Enhance your knowledge of the components of the eyeball and their functions. This will help you to understand the vision process. Match the phrase in column 1 with the appropriate medical term in column 2.*

_____ 1. colored portion of the eye

_____ 2. change direction of a ray of light

_____ 3. opening in the iris

_____ 4. band of muscle that encircles an opening

_____ 5. transparent, refractive structure

_____ 6. difficulty in near-sighted vision

_____ 7. innermost layer of eyeball

_____ 8. white of the eye

_____ 9. operate the lens

_____ 10. normal eye examination

A. lens

B. retina

C. sphincter

D. pupil

E. ciliary body

F. PERRLA

G. refract

H. iris

I. presbyopia

J. sclera

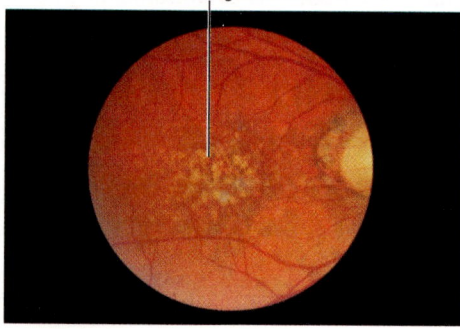

Macular degeneration

▲ **FIGURE 4.22   Ophthalmoscopic View Macular Degeneration.**

▲ **FIGURE 4.23   Vision with Macular Degeneration.**

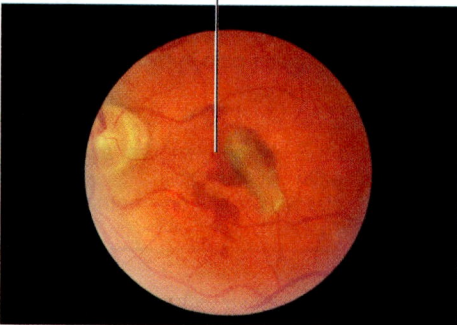

Hemorrhage

▲ **FIGURE 4.24   Ophthalmoscopic View Diabetic Retinopathy.**

▲ **FIGURE 4.25   Vision with Diabetic Retinopathy.**

DISEASES OF THE RETINA

Macular Degeneration

Degeneration of the central macula results in loss of visual acuity, with a dark blurry area of vision loss in the center of the visual field *(Figures 4.22 and 4.23)*.

There is photoreceptor cell loss and bleeding, with capillary proliferation and scar formation. It can progress to blindness. Most cases occur in people over age 55.

At this time, there is no known cure, but laser **photocoagulation** destroys the abnormal capillaries, which slows the pace of the visual loss.

Retinal Detachment

Separation of the retina from its underlying choroid layer may be partial or complete and produces a retinal tear or hole. The detachment can happen suddenly, without pain. The patient sees a dark shadow invading his peripheral vision. The detachment can be seen on **ophthalmoscopic** examination.

When the retina is detached, photoreceptor cells can die; this condition is a surgical emergency. Treatment of small lesions is by **laser surgery**. The laser creates tiny burns around the tear to "weld" the retina back in place. Another form of treatment, **cryopexy,** freezes the area around the hole to help it reattach to the surrounding retina.

Diabetic Retinopathy

The disease occurs most frequently in diabetics who cannot control their blood sugar levels. Some fifty percent of diabetics have **retinopathy.**

In the early stages, **microaneurysms** (balloonlike swellings) of the small retinal blood vessels form. There are usually no symptoms. Later hemorrhages can occur, leading to destruction of the photoreceptor cells (rods and cones) and visual difficulties.

Ophthalmoscopic examination shows the disease *(Figure 4.24)*, and **fluorescein angiography** with pictures taken as the dye passes through the retina reveals more details.

Laser photocoagulation is usually effective in controlling the lesions; but, once vision is lost from an area of the retina, it usually does not return *(Figure 4.25)*.

Papilledema

Papilledema is swelling of the optic disc due to increased **intracranial** pressure. It is not a diagnosis, but a sign of some underlying pathology. It is seen on ophthalmoscopic examination.

Cancer of the Eye

Tumors of the skin of the eyelids include the **squamous cell** and **basal cell carcinomas** and **melanoma** described in *Chapter 3.*

Retinoblastoma is the most common cancer in children and is diagnosed most commonly around 18 months of age. Twenty percent have the cancer in both eyes. The condition can be hereditary.

The first symptom is a white appearance of the pupil **(leukocoria).** With early detection and aggressive treatment based on chemotherapy and laser surgery, 90% are cured.

In adults, the most common cancers are **metastases** to the eye from cancer of the lung in men and the breast in women.

S = Suffix   **P** = Prefix   **R** = Root   **R/CF** = Combining Form

WORD	PRONUNCIATION	ELEMENTS		DEFINITION
angiography	an-jee-**OG**-rah-fee	S/ R/CF	-graphy *to write* angi/o- *blood vessel*	Radiography of vessels after injection of contrast material
angiogram	**AN**-jee-oh-gram	S/	-gram *a record*	Radiograph obtained after injection of radiopaque contrast material into blood vessels
cryopexy	cry-oh-**PEX**-ee	S/ R/CF	-pexy *fixation* cry/o- *icy cold*	Fix the detached retina by freezing it to surrounding tissue
intracranial	in-trah-**KRAY**-nee-al	S/ P/ R/	-al *pertaining to* intra- *inside* -crani- *skull*	Within the cranium (skull)
laser surgery	**LAY**-zer **SUR**-jer-ee	S/ R/	laser *acronym for light amplification by stimulated emission of radiation* -ery *process of* surg- *operation*	Use of a concentrated, intense narrow beam of electromagnetic radiation for surgery
leukocoria	loo-koh-**KOH**-ree-ah	S/ R/CF R/	-ia *condition* -leuk/o- *white* cor- *pupil*	Reflection in pupil of white mass in the eye
metastasis metastases (pl)	meh-**TAS**-tah-sis meh-**TAS**-tah-sees	R/ R/	meta- *beyond, change* -stasis *placement*	Spread of disease from one part of the body to another
microaneurysm	my-kroh-**AN**-yu-rizm	P/ R/	micro- *small* -aneurysm *dilation*	Focal dilation of retinal capillaries
ophthalmoscope	off-**THAL**-moh-skope	S/	-scope *instrument for viewing*	Instrument for viewing the retina
ophthalmoscopy	**OFF**-thal-**MOS**-koh-pee	S/ R/CF	-scopy *the process of viewing* ophthalm/o- *eye*	The process of viewing the retina
ophthalmoscopic	**OFF**-thal-**MOS**-koh-pik	S/	-ic *pertaining to*	Pertaining to the use of an ophthalmoscope
papilledema	pah-pill-eh-**DEE**-mah	S/ R/	-edema *swelling* papill- *small pimple*	Swelling of the optic disc in the retina
photocoagulation	foh-toe-koh-ag-you-**LAY**-shun	S/ P/ R/	-ation *action* photo- *light* -coagul- *clot*	Using light (laser beam) to form a clot
retinoblastoma	**RET**-in-oh-blas-**TOE**-mah	S/ R/CF R/	-oma *tumor, mass* retin/o- *retina* -blast- *germ cell*	Malignant neoplasm of primitive retinal cells
retinopathy	ret-ih-**NOP**-ah-thee	S/	-pathy *disease*	Degenerative disease of the retina

EXERCISES

*Continue your work with elements to help build your knowledge of the **language of ophthalmology**. One element in each of the following medical terms is in bold letters in column 1. Identify the type of element (P, R, CF, S) in column 2, then write the meaning of the element in column 3. Fill in the blanks.*

Medical Term	Type of Element	Meaning of Element
retino**blast**oma		
metastasis		
intracranial		
cryo**pexy**		
microaneurysm		
ophthalmoscope		
angio**graphy**		
photo**coagul**ation		
retino**pathy**		

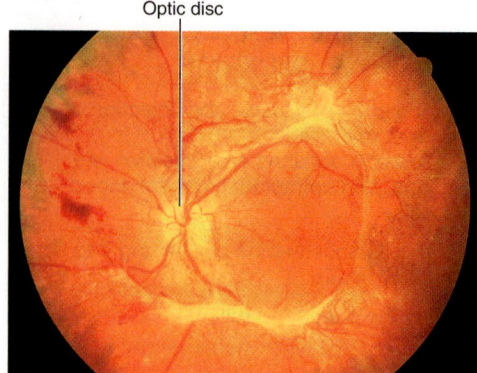

Optic disc

▲ **FIGURE 4.26 Ophthalmoscopic Examination of the Eye.**

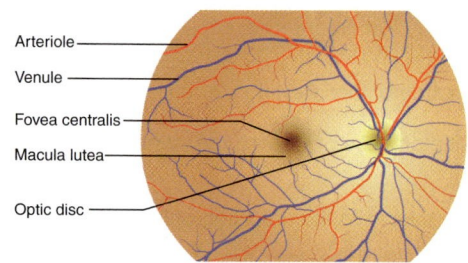

Arteriole
Venule
Fovea centralis
Macula lutea
Optic disc

▲ **FIGURE 4.27 Anatomy of the Fundus.**

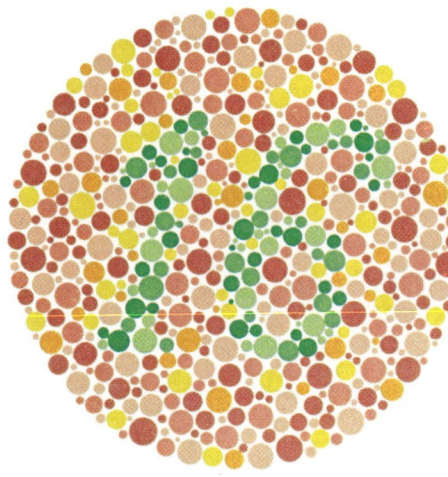

▲ **FIGURE 4.28 Test for Color Blindness.**
Reproduced with permission from Ishihara's Tests for Color Deficiency published by Kanehara Trading Inc., Tokyo, Japan. Tests for color deficiency cannot be conducted with this figure. For accurate testing, the original plates should be used.

FIGURE 4.29 Visual Acuity Tests.
(a) Snellen letter chart for distance vision.
(b) Jaeger reading card.

OPHTHALMIC PROCEDURES

As an ophthalmic assistant, you may be trained to perform the following procedures.

Examination of the Retina

When you perform a **fundoscopy** and examine the retina with an **ophthalmoscope,** you can first identify the **optic disc** ((Figure 4.26). This is where the optic nerve leaves the back of the eye. The optic disc has no receptor cells and therefore produces a blind spot in the visual field of each eye. In the middle of the disc, a retinal artery enters to supply the **intraocular** structures, and a retinal vein leaves the eye.

Lateral to the optic disc is a yellowish area called the **macula lutea** (Figure 4.27). In the center of the macula is the tiny pit called the **fovea centralis.** This pit is the area of your sharpest vision. The arteries and veins of the retina can also be seen and provide clues about vascular diseases (see Chapter 7).

Color Vision

Use illustrations such as those from the **Ishihara color system.** In this example (Figure 4.28), people with red-green color blindness would not be able to see the number 16 among the colored dots.

Distance Vision

Use the **Snellen letter chart** to test distance vision (Figure 4.29a). The results are recorded as a fraction. For example, when the chart is viewed from twenty feet, line 8 is the smallest line a person with standard vision can read. This is recorded as 20/20. If the patient using her left eye misses two letters on line 8, document it as O.S. 20/20 − 2.

Near Vision

Use hand held charts or **Jaeger reading cards** with printed paragraphs of different sizes of print to test near vision (Figure 4.29b).

Visual Fields

Sit two feet in front of your patient, who covers one eye. Cover your own opposite eye and bring a pencil into the horizontal and vertical fields. The field is mapped on a visual field grid.

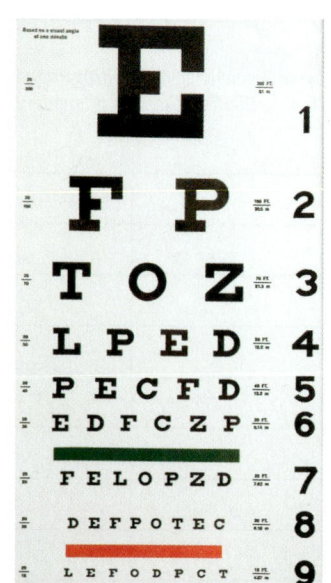

(a)

(b)

WORD	PRONUNCIATION		ELEMENTS	DEFINITION
fundus	**FUN**-dus		Latin *bottom*	Part farthest from the opening of a hollow organ
		S/	**-scopy** *to examine*	
fundoscopy	fun-**DOS**-koh-pee	R/CF	**fund/o-** *fundus*	Examination of the fundus (retina) of the eye
fundoscopic (adj)	fun-do-**SKOP**-ik	S/	**-ic** *pertaining to*	
Ishihara color system	ish-ee-**HAR**-ah		Shinobu Ishihara, Japanese ophthalmologist, 1879–1963	Test for color vision defects
Jaeger reading cards	**YA**-ger		Edward Jaeger, Austrian ophthalmologist, 1818–1884	Type of different sizes of print for testing near vision
peripheral vision	peh-**RIF**-er-al **VIZH**-un	S/	**-al** *pertaining to*	Ability to see objects as they come into the outer edges of the visual field
		R/	**peripher-** *external boundary*	
Snellen letter chart	**SNEL**-en		Hermann Snellen, Dutch ophthalmologist, 1834–1908	Test for acuity of distant vision
tonometer	toe-**NOM**-eh-ter	S/	**-meter** *measure*	Instrument for determining intraocular pressure
		R/CF	**ton/o-** *pressure, tension*	
tonometry	toe-**NOM**-eh-tree	S/	**-metry** *measurement*	The measurement of intraocular pressure

Glaucoma

Measure the intraocular pressure with a **tonometer** *(Figure 4.30)*, which determines the eyeball's resistance to indentation or tension.

Administration of Medication

When you are trained as an ophthalmic technician, you will be able to administer eye drops, creams, or ointments and to irrigate the eye to remove a foreign body.

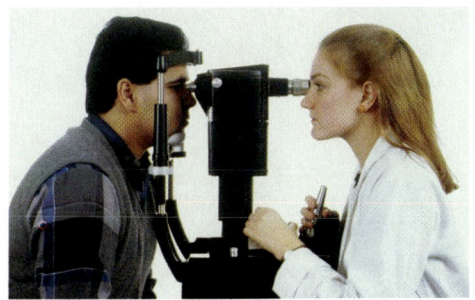

▲ **FIGURE 4.30   Tonometer.**

EXERCISES

The OT in Dr. Chun's office needs to be familiar with all these terms in order to communicate with Dr. Chun and her patients. Show your understanding of the terms by circling the correct answers.

1. Instrument(s) used in an ophthalmologist's office:
   a. tonometer
   b. cystoscope
   c. ophthalmoscope
   d. a and b
   e. a and c

2. Test used to measure color blindness:
   a. Snellen
   b. Jaeger
   c. Ishihara
   d. visual fields
   e. otoscope

3. Peripheral vision measures the outer edge of:
   a. anterior segment
   b. vitreous body
   c. aqueous humor
   d. posterior segment
   e. visual field

4. A test for near vision is:
   a. Snellen chart
   b. ophthalmoscope
   c. Jaeger cards
   d. Ishihara
   e. visual fields

5. Tonometry measures:
   a. interocular pressure
   b. arterial pressure
   c. venous pressure
   d. intraocular pressure
   e. capillary pressure

6. The part farthest from the opening of a hollow organ:
   a. apex
   b. base
   c. fundus
   d. intraocular
   e. peripheral

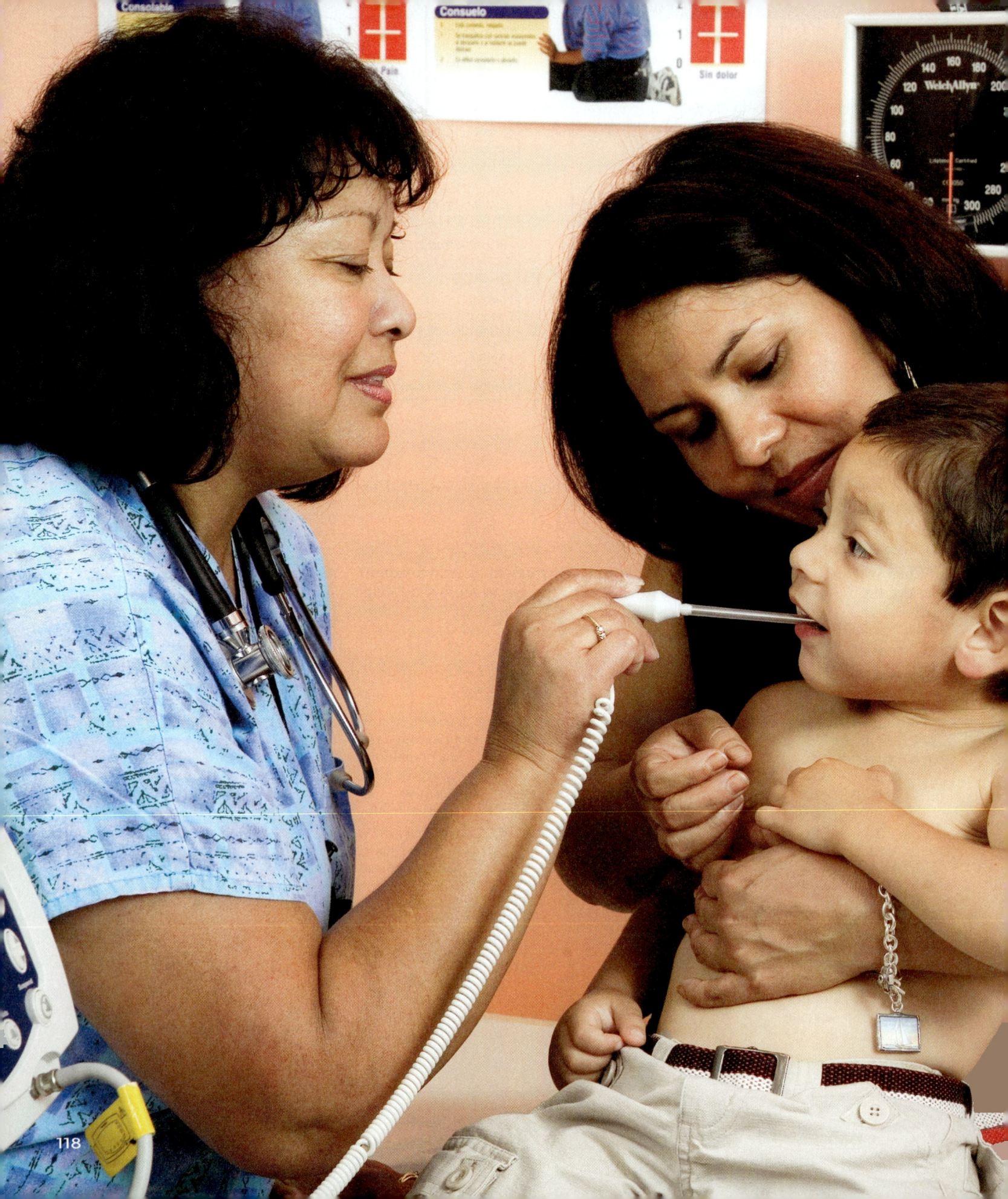

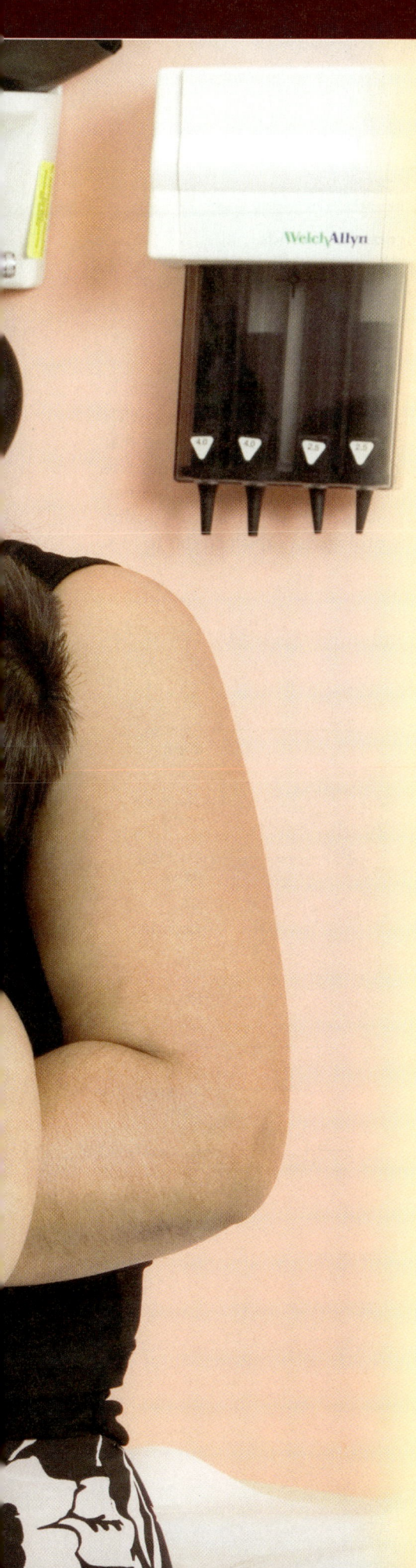

You are

. . . a medical assistant working with primary care physician Susan Lee, MD, of the Fulwood Medical Group.

Your patient is

. . . 3-year-old Eddie Cardenas. Mrs. Carmen Cardenas has brought in her son, Eddie. She tells you that he has had a cold for a couple of days. Early this morning he woke up screaming, felt hot, and was tugging his ears. She gave him **acetaminophen** with some orange juice, and he threw up. She also tells you this is the third similar episode in the past year. Since the last time, she is concerned that he is not hearing normally. You see a worried mother and a very unhappy, restless, toddler with a green nasal discharge. His oral temperature taken with an electronic digital thermometer is 102.4°F, pulse 100. You tell her that Dr. Lee will be in to see Eddie as soon as possible.

Learning Outcomes

In order to understand what is going on with Eddie, to communicate with Dr. Lee about him, to respond to the mother's concerns, and to document the office visit, you need to be able to:

- Apply the language of otology to the anatomy and physiology of the ear.

- Comprehend, analyze, spell and write the medical terms of otology so that you can communicate and document accurately and precisely in any health care setting.

- Recognize and pronounce the medical terms of otology so that you can communicate verbally with accuracy and precision in any health care setting.

- Discuss the cause, appearance, diagnosis and treatment of common disorders of the ear that lead to hearing loss.

- Describe the cause, appearance, diagnosis and treatment of common disorders of the ear that lead to difficulty with equilibrium and balance.

LESSON 4.3 The Ear and Hearing

SPECIAL SENSES OF THE EYE AND EAR

OBJECTIVES

To understand your patient's specific problem, you must be able to:

- **Describe the structures and functions of the three regions of the ear.**
- **Explain how sound waves progress through the ear and are transferred to the brain and recognized as sounds.**
- **Identify how common diseases of the ear interfere with the process of hearing.**
- **Apply the correct medical terminology to the anatomy, physiology, and disorders of the ear.**

Case Report 4.3 (continued)

Progress Note. 05/10/06
Examination by Dr. Lee showed that Eddie has a **bilateral acute otitis media** with an upper respiratory infection. Dr Lee is also concerned that Eddie has a **chronic** otitis media with **effusion** that is giving him a hearing loss. She prescribed amoxicillin 250 mg q.i.d. with acetaminophen 160 mg p.r.n. for 10 days, when she will see Eddie again. If, after the acute infection subsides, there remains an effusion with hearing loss, she may need to refer Eddie to an **otologist**. I explained this to Mrs. Cardenas. Signed, Luis Guittierez, CMA. 1115 hrs.

The ear has three sections: external, middle, and inner *(Figure 4.31)*.

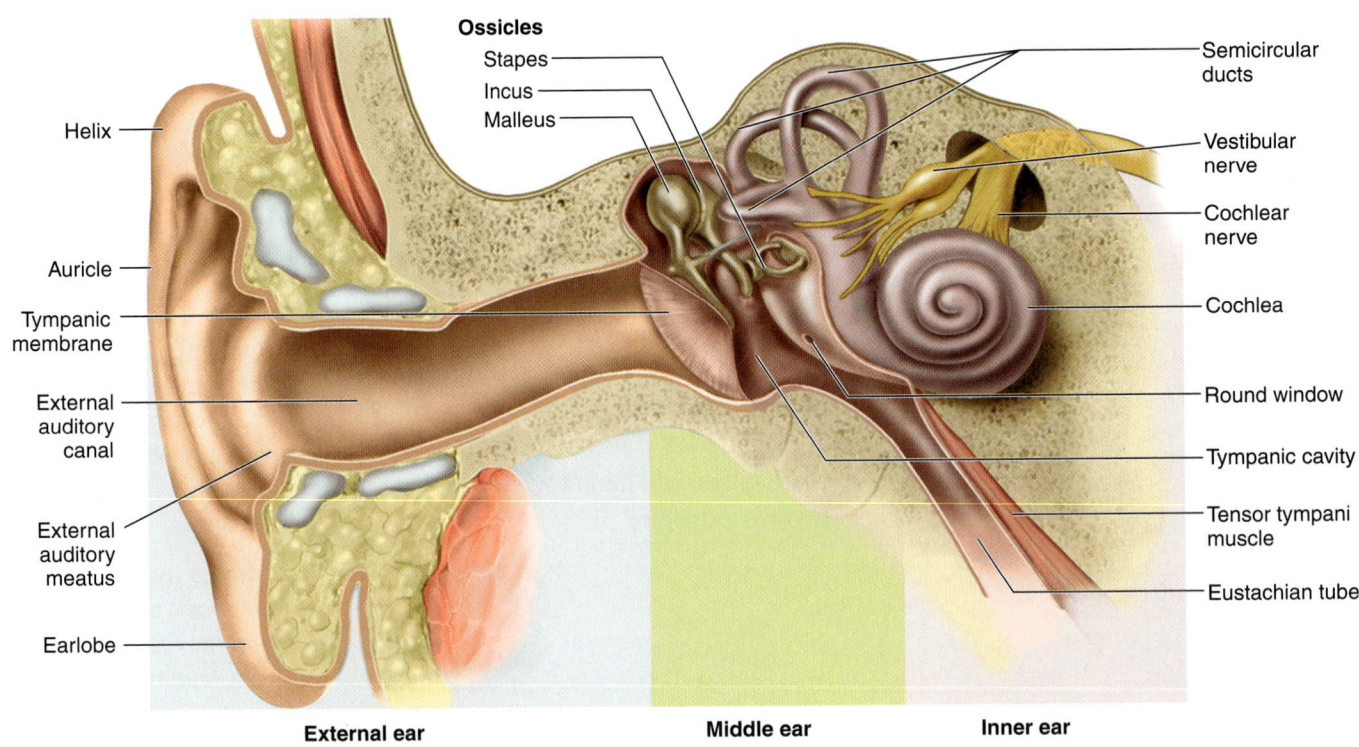

▲ **FIGURE 4.31   Anatomic Regions of the Ear.**

WORD	PRONUNCIATION		ELEMENTS	DEFINITION
acetaminophen	ah-seat-ah-**MIN**-oh-fen		generic drug name	Medication that is an **analgesic** and an **antipyretic**
acute	ah-**KYUT**		Latin *sharp*	Disease of sudden onset
analgesia analgesic	an-al-**JEE**-ze-ah an-al-**JEE**-zic	P/ R/ S/	**an-** *without* **-algesia** *pain* **-ic** *pertaining to*	State in which pain is reduced Substance that reduces the response to pain
antipyretic	**AN**-tee-pie-**RET**-ik	S/ P/ R/	**-ic** *pertaining to* **anti-** *against* **-pyret-** *fever*	Agent that reduces fever
bilateral	by-**LAT**-er-al	P/ R/ S/	**bi-** *two, twice* **-later** *side* **-al** *pertaining to*	On two sides; for example, in both ears
chronic	**KRON**-ik		Greek *time*	The term to describe a persistent, long-term disease
effusion	eh-**FYU**-shun		Latin *pouring out*	Collection of fluid that has escaped from blood vessels into a cavity or tissues
otitis media	oh-**TIE**-tis **ME**-dee-ah	S/ R/ R/	**-itis** *inflammation* **ot-** *ear* **media** *middle*	Inflammation of the middle ear
otologist	oh-**TOL**-oh-jist	S/ R/CF	**-logist** *skilled in the study of; specialist* **ot/o-** *ear*	Medical specialist in diseases of the ear
otology otorhinolaryngologist	oh-**TOL**-oh-jee oh-toe-rhino-lah-rin-**GOL**-oh-jist	S/ R/CF R/CF	**-logy** *study of* **-rhin/o-** *nose* **-laryng/o-** *larynx*	Study of the function and diseases of the ear Ear, nose, and throat medical specialist

Abbreviations

mg milligram
p.r.n. when necessary
q.i.d. four times each day
q.4.h. every four hours.

EXERCISES

Break these medical terms down into their basic elements. Analyzing each term will help you answer the following questions. Fill in the blanks.

Medical Term	Prefix	Root(s)/CF	Suffix
analgesia			
bilateral			
otitis media			
otologist			
otorhinolaryngologist			

1. A medication that is an analgesic reduces _____.

2. Name another body part that is bilateral: _____.

3. What is the difference between an otologist and an otorhinolargyngologist?

_____

4. Where in the ear does otitis media occur? _____

5. Which element is a prefix referring to a number? _____ means _____.

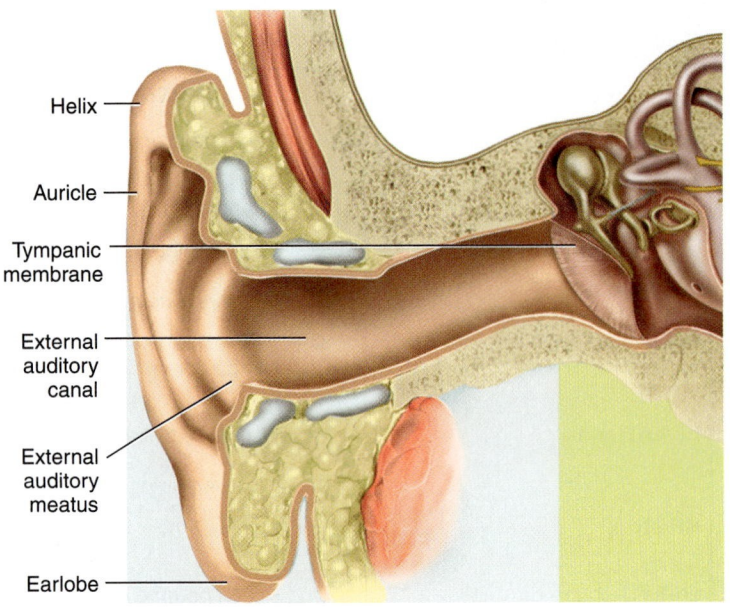

Helix

Auricle

Tympanic
membrane

External
auditory
canal

External
auditory
meatus

Earlobe

▲ **FIGURE 4.32 External Ear.**

EXTERNAL EAR

The **auricle**, or **pinna**, is a wing-shaped structure that directs sound waves coming through the air into the **external auditory meatus** and **external auditory canal.** This in turn ends at the **tympanic membrane** *(Figure 4.32)*. The external auditory canal not only protects the middle and inner ears, but also acts as a resonator to augment the transmission of sound to the middle and inner ears.

The external auditory canal is the only skin-lined cul-de-sac in the body. Its interior is dark, warm, and prone to become moist. These are ideal conditions for bacterial and fungal growth.

The meatus and canal are lined with skin that contains many modified sweat glands called ceruminous glands, which secrete **cerumen.** The cerumen and hairs growing in the meatus help to keep out foreign objects. Cerumen combines with dead skin cells to form **earwax.** Overproduction of cerumen can completely block the meatus, causing hearing loss and preventing examination of the tympanic membrane with an **otoscope.**

If a foreign body, such as a small bead, does get into the canal, or if cerumen becomes **impacted** in the canal, then hearing loss can result.

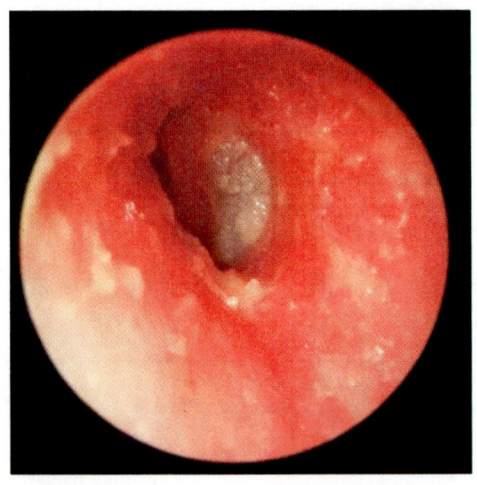

▲ **FIGURE 4.33 Otoscopic View of Otitis Externa with Purulent Exudate.**

Disorders of External Ear

Otitis externa *(Figure 4.33)* is an infection of the lining of the external auditory canal. It produces a painful, red, swollen ear canal, sometimes with purulent drainage. The infection can be bacterial or fungal. Fungal infections are responsible for 10% of otitis externa cases and are called **otomycoses.**

Conditions helping to cause otitis externa include trauma to the canal during attempts to self-clean it; use of unclean earplugs, earphones, or hearing aids; and the presence of other skin diseases, such as seborrhea and psoriasis *(see Chapter 3)*.

Treatment is with thorough cleansing of the canal, acidification with a topical solution of 2% acetic acid in a hydrocortisone solution, and the use of antibiotic drops. Occasionally a wick is needed to enable the topical medications to penetrate down the canal.

Swimmer's ear is a form of otitis externa that comes on after swimming, particularly if the water is polluted.

Excessive earwax can be removed in your physician's office by ear **irrigation** or with a **curette,** a small metal ring at the end of a handle.

WORD ANALYSIS AND DEFINITION

WORD	PRONUNCIATION		ELEMENTS	DEFINITION
auditory	AW-dih-tor-ee		Latin *hearing*	Pertaining to the sense or organs of hearing
audiology	aw-dee-OL-oh-jee	S/	-logy *study of*	Study of hearing disorders
		R/CF	audi/o- *hearing*	
audiologist	aw-dee-OL-oh-jist	S/	-logist *one who studies*	Specialist in evaluation of hearing function
auricle	AW-ri-kul		Latin *ear*	The shell-like external ear
cerumen	seh-ROO-men		Latin *wax*	Waxy secretion of ceruminous glands of external ear
curette	kyu-RET	S/	-ette *little*	Scoop-shaped instrument for scraping the interior of a cavity or removal of new growths
		R/	cur- *cleanse, cure*	
curettage	kyu-reh-TAHZH	S/	-age *related to*	
			(**Note:** The final "e" of **curette** is dropped because the suffix -age begins with a vowel.)	Scraping the interior of a cavity
impacted	im-PAK-ted		Latin *driven in*	Immovably wedged, as with ear wax blocking the external canal
irrigation	ih-rih-GAY-shun	S/	-ation *process*	Use of water to clean wax out of the external ear canal
		P/	-ir *in*	
		R/	-rig *water*	
meatus	me-AY-tus	.	Latin *go through*	Passage or channel; also used to denote the external opening of a passage
meatal (adj)	me-AY-tal			
otomycosis	OH-toe-my-KOH-sis	S/	-sis *condition*	Fungal infection of the external ear
		R/CF	ot/o- *ear*	
		R/CF	-myc/o- *fungus*	
otoscope	OH-toe-skope	S/	-scope *instrument for viewing*	Instrument for examining the ear
		R/CF	ot/o- *ear*	
otoscopy	oh-TOS-koh-pee	S/	-scopy *to examine*	Examination of the ear
pinna	PIN-ah		Latin *wing*	Another name for auricle
pinnae (pl)	PIN-ee			
tympanic	tim-PAN-ick	S/	-ic *pertaining to*	Pertaining to the tympanic membrane or tympanic cavity
		R/	tympan- *drum*	

EXERCISES

*Every part of the body has its own specialized vocabulary. Test your knowledge of the **language of otology** by matching correct answers. Match the phrase in column 1 with the appropriate medical term in column 2.*

_____ 1. external ear fungal infection

_____ 2. external opening of a passage

_____ 3. instrument for viewing the ear

_____ 4. procedure for scraping or removing growths

_____ 5. scoop-shaped instrument

_____ 6. shell-like external ear

_____ 7. "driven in"

_____ 8. another name for auricle

_____ 9. pertaining to the sense or organs of hearing

_____ 10. earwax

_____ 11. pertaining to the tympanic membrane or cavity

A. pinna

B. curette

C. auditory

D. auricle

E. tympanic

F. otomycosis

G. curettage

H. meatus

I. otoscope

J. impacted

K. cerumen

FIGURE 4.34   Middle Ear.   ▶

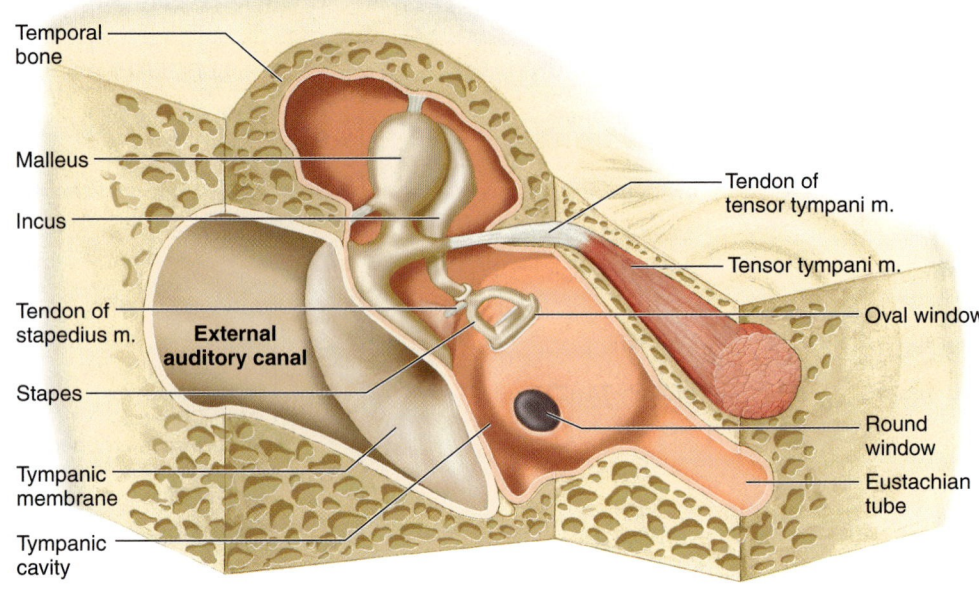

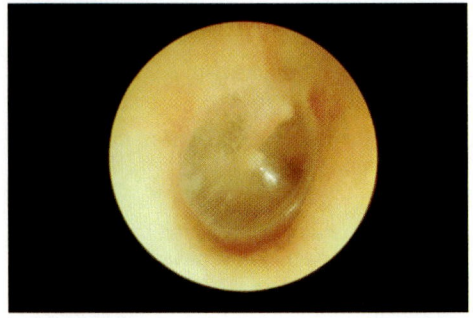

FIGURE 4.35   Otoscopic View of Normal Tympanic Membrane.

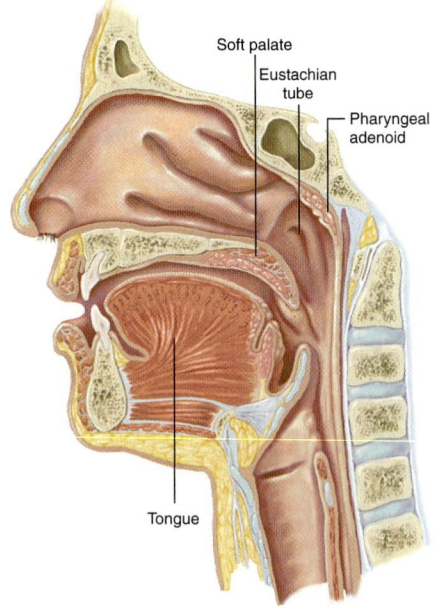

▲ **FIGURE 4.36   Nasopharynx (Throat).**

Keynote

The three ossicles amplify sound so that soft sounds can be heard.

MIDDLE EAR

The middle ear has four components: the tympanic membrane, the tympanic cavity, the **eustachian** (auditory) **tube**, and the ossicles *(Figure 4.34)*.

1. The **tympanic membrane (eardrum)** is located at the inner end of the external auditory canal. It is suspended in a bony groove, is concave on its outer surface, and vibrates freely as sound waves hit it. It has a good nerve supply and is very sensitive to pain. When examined through the otoscope, it is transparent and reflects light *(Figure 4.35)*.

2. The **tympanic cavity** is immediately behind the tympanic membrane. It is filled with air that enters through the eustachian (auditory) tube, and the cavity is continuous with the **mastoid** air cells in the bone behind it. The presence of air in the cavity maintains equal air pressure on both sides of the tympanic membrane, which is essential for normal hearing. The cavity contains the ossicles.

3. The eustachian (auditory) tube connects the middle ear with the **nasopharynx** (throat), into which it opens close to the pharyngeal **tonsil (adenoid)** *(Figure 4.36)*. In children under 5 years, the tube is not fully developed. It is short and horizontal, and the valvelike flaps in the throat that protect it are not developed. When you are landing in an airplane and moving from a high altitude to a lower one, the air pressure in the external auditory canal increases and pushes the tympanic membrane inward. If your eustachian (auditory) tube is blocked, no air can get into the middle ear to equalize the pressure, and your eardrum is painful. If you can force some air up the eustachian (auditory) tube by chewing or swallowing, then your ear "pops" as the tympanic membrane moves back to its normal position.

4. The three **ossicles**, the **malleus, incus,** and **stapes,** are attached to the wall of the tympanic cavity by tiny ligaments that are covered by a mucous membrane. The malleus is attached to the tympanic membrane and vibrates with the membrane when sound waves hit it. The malleus is attached to the incus, which also vibrates and passes the vibrations onto the stapes. The stapes is attached to the oval window, an opening that transmits the vibrations to the inner ear. The stapes is the smallest bone in the body.

WORD	PRONUNCIATION		ELEMENTS	DEFINITION
adenoid	ADD-eh-noyd	S/ R/	-oid *resembling* aden- *gland*	Single mass of lymphoid tissue in the mid-line at the back of the throat
eustachian tube (also called the auditory tube)	you-STAY-shun TYUB		Bartolommeo Eustachio, Italian anatomist, 1524–1574	Tube that connects the middle ear to the nasopharynx
incus	IN-cuss		Latin *anvil*	Middle one of the three ossicles in the mid-dle ear; shaped like an anvil
malleus	MAL-ee-us		Latin *hammer*	Outer (lateral) one of the three ossicles in the middle ear; shaped like a hammer
mastoid	MASS-toyd	S/ R/	-oid *resembling* mast- *breast*	Small bony protrusion immediately behind the ear
nasopharynx	NAY-zoh-FAIR-inks	R/CF R/	nas/o- *nose* -pharynx *throat*	Region of the pharynx at the back of the nose and above the soft palate
ossicle	OS-ih-kel	S/ R/CF	-cle *small* oss/i- *bone*	A small bone, particularly relating to the three bones in the middle ear
stapes	STAY-peas		Latin *stirrup*	Inner (medial) one of the three ossicles of the middle ear; shaped like a stirrup
tonsil tonsillar (adj)	TON-sill TON-sih-lar		Latin *tonsil*	Mass of lymphoid tissue on either side of the throat at the back of the tongue

EXERCISES

Answers to the following questions can all be found in the WAD shown above. Review the terms before you start this exercise. Pay special attention to the spelling. Circle the best choice.

1. In the term **mastoid**, the suffix means:

   condition   resembling   inflammation

2. The element **mast** means:

   throat   breast   ear

3. The **stapes** is:

   gland   ossicle   mastoid

4. The element **pharynx** means:

   throat   nose   gland

5. The term **nasopharynx** is composed of:

   (prefix + suffix)   (root + root)   (combining form + root)

6. This type of tissue is found in an adenoid:

   mucoid   connective   lymphoid

7. The _____ is shaped like a hammer.

   malleus   malleolus   maleus

8. The element **aden** in adenoid is a:

   prefix   root   combining form

9. One of the names for the tube that connects the middle ear to the nasopharynx is the _____ tube.

   eusstachian   eustashian   eustachian

10. The _____ is shaped like an anvil.

   incus   stapes   adenoid

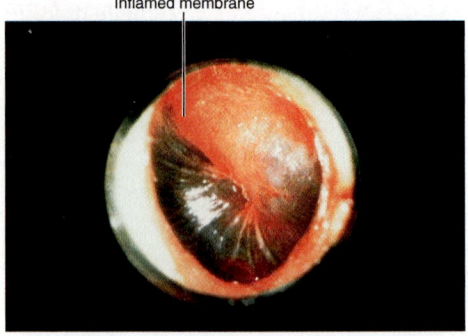
Inflamed membrane

▲ **FIGURE 4.37   Otoscopic View of Otitis Media (Acute) Showing Inflamed Tympanic Membrane.**

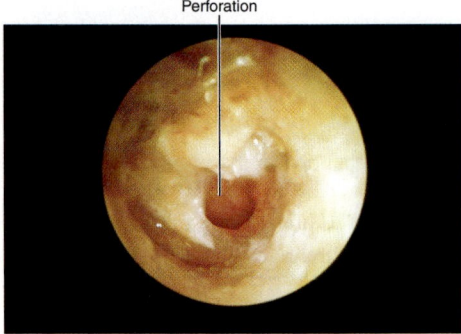
Perforation

▲ **FIGURE 4.38   Otoscopic View of Otitis Media (Chronic) with Perforated Tympanic Membrane.**

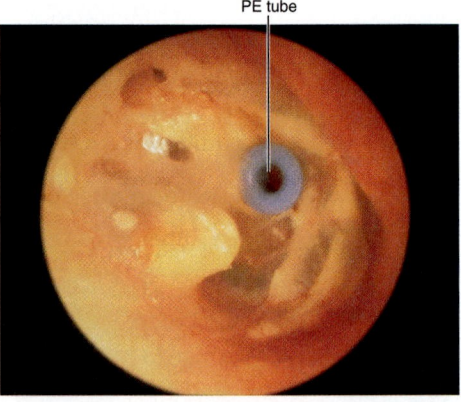
PE tube

▲ **FIGURE 4.39   Pressure-Equalization (PE) Tube in Tympanic Membrane.**

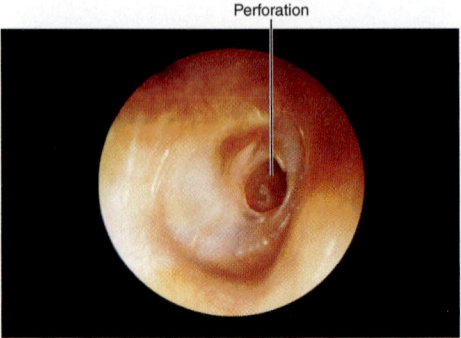
Perforation

▲ **FIGURE 4.40   Perforated Tympanic Membrane.**

DISORDERS OF MIDDLE EAR

Acute otitis media (AOM) is the presence of pus in the middle ear with pain in the ear, fever, and redness of the tympanic membrane. This occurs most often in the first 2 to 4 years of age because:

- Eustachian tubes in children are shorter and more horizontal than in adults, making it easier for bacteria and viruses to find their way into the middle ear from the nasopharynx.
- Adenoids at the back of the nasopharynx near the eustachian tubes can block the opening of the eustachian tubes.
- Children's immune systems are not fully developed until seven years of age, and they have difficulty fighting infections.

If the infections are viral, they will go away on their own. If bacterial, oral antibiotics may be necessary.

Chronic otitis media occurs when the acute infection subsides but the eustachian tube is still blocked. The **effusion** (fluid) in the middle ear cannot drain out and gradually becomes stickier. This is called **chronic otitis media with effusion (OME)** and produces hearing loss because the sticky fluid prevents the ossicles from vibrating. You can see the fluid through the otoscope *(Figure 4.38)*. Dr. Lee was concerned that this had happened to Eddie in his previous ear infection.

If the sticky fluid persists, a **myringotomy** can be performed whereby a small, hollow plastic tube is inserted through the tympanic membrane to allow the effusion to drain. These ear tubes have several names: **tympanostomy tubes, pressure equalization tubes,** or, most commonly, **PE tubes** *(Figure 4.39)*. The tubes are inserted under general anesthesia as an outpatient surgery. They remain in the ear for 6 to 18 months before they drop out on their own.

A **perforated tympanic membrane** can occur in acute otitis media when pus in the middle ear cannot escape down the eustachian tube. It builds up pressure and perforates the ear drum *(Figure 4.40)*. Most perforations will heal spontaneously in a month with a small scar. Other causes of perforation include a puncture by a cotton swab, an open-handed slap to the ear, or large pressure changes (as may be induced in scuba diving).

Cholesteatoma is a complication of chronic otitis media with effusion. Chronically inflamed cells in the middle ear multiply and collect into a tumor. They damage the ossicles and can spread to the inner ear. Surgical removal is required.

Otosclerosis is a middle ear disease that usually affects people between 18 and 35 years of age. It can affect one ear or both and produces a gradual hearing loss for low and soft sounds. Its etiology is unknown. Spongy bone forms around the junction of the oval window and stapes, preventing the stapes from conducting the sound vibrations to the inner ear. The only treatment is to replace the stapes with a metal or plastic **prosthesis**.

WORD	PRONUNCIATION	ELEMENTS		DEFINITION
cholesteatoma	koh-less-tee-ah-**TOE**-mah	S/ R/CF R/	**-oma** *tumor, mass* **chol/e-** *bile* **-steat-** *fat*	Yellow, waxy tumor arising in the middle ear
coryza (also called rhinitis)	ko-**RYE**-zah		Greek *catarrh*	Viral inflammation of the mucous membrane of the nose
effusion	eh-**FYU**-shun		Latin *pouring out*	Collection of fluid that has escaped from blood vessels into a cavity or tissues
myringotomy	mir-in-**GOT**-oh-me	S/ R/CF	**-tomy** *incision* **myring/o-** *tympanic membrane*	Incision in the tympanic membrane
otosclerosis	oh-toe-sklair-**OH**-sis	S/ R/CF R/CF	**-sis** *condition* **-scler/o-** *hardening* **ot/o-** *ear*	Hardening at the junction of the stapes and oval window that causes loss of hearing
perforated	**PER**-foh-ray-ted		Latin *to bore through*	Punctured with one or more holes
prosthesis	**PROS**-thee-sis		Greek *addition*	Manufactured substitute for a missing part of the body
tympanic	tim-**PAN**-ik	S/ R/	**-ic** *pertaining to* **tympan-** *drum*	Pertaining to the tympanic membrane or tympanic cavity
tympanostomy	tim-pan-**OS**-toe-me	S/ R/CF	**-stomy** *new opening* **tympan/o-** *drum*	Surgically created new opening in the tympanic membrane to allow fluid to drain from the middle ear

Abbreviations

AOM acute otitis media
OME otitis media with effusion
PE   pressure-equalization tube
URI upper respiratory infection

EXERCISES

Build Medical Terms. *This is a two-step exercise. Fill in the blanks with the correct element to complete the terms in questions 1–5. Then match the terms in questions 6–9 to their meanings.*

1. pertaining to the eardrum   _____/ic

2. hardening at the junction of the stapes and oval window

   oto/_____/sis

3. small bones in the middle ear ossi/_____

4. incision into the tympanic membrane   myringo/_____

5. yellow, waxy tumor in middle ear

   _____ / _____oma

Match the following terms to their meanings

_____ 6. manufactured body part   A. coryza

_____ 7. fluid in a cavity   B. perforated

_____ 8. common cold   C. prosthesis

_____ 9. punctured   D. effusion

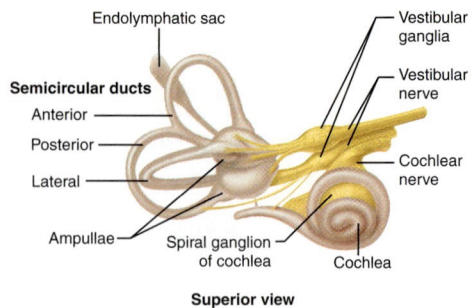

Semicircular ducts
Endolymphatic sac
Anterior
Posterior
Lateral
Ampullae
Spiral ganglion of cochlea
Vestibular ganglia
Vestibular nerve
Cochlear nerve
Cochlea

Superior view

▲ **FIGURE 4.41   Inner Ear.**

Keynote

Repeated exposure to loud noise causes hearing loss in young people as well as in older people.

INNER EAR FOR HEARING

The inner ear is a **labyrinth** of complex, intricate systems of passages. The passages in the **cochlea,** a part of the labyrinth *(Figure 4.41),* contain receptors to translate vibrations into nerve impulses so that the brain can interpret them as different sounds.

The membrane of the oval window separates the middle ear from the vestibule of the inner ear. The stapes (② in *Figure 4.42)* moves the membrane to generate pressure waves in the fluid inside the cochlea ③. The pressure waves cause **vestibular** and **basilar membranes** inside the cochlea to vibrate ④ and sway fine hair cells attached to the basilar membrane ⑤. The hair cells convert this motion into nerve impulses, which travel via the **cochlear nerve** to the brain. The excess pressure waves in the cochlear escape the inner ear via the round window ⑥).

Today, the most common cause of hearing loss is damage to the fine hairs in the cochlea by exposure to repeated loud noise, either related to work (for example, jackhammers, leaf blowers) or to leisure activities (such as amplified music at concerts, personal listening devices, and motorcycles). This is a **sensorineural hearing loss.**

Hearing aids are becoming more sophisticated and smaller, but they do not help people with cochlear damage. **Cochlear implants** are used to bypass the damaged hair cells and directly stimulate cochlear nerve endings.

A **conductive hearing loss** occurs when sound is not conducted efficiently through the external auditory canal to the tympanic membrane and the ossicles. Causes include:

- middle ear pathology, such as acute otitis media, otitis media with effusion, perforated ear drum
- impacted cerumen
- infected external auditory canal
- foreign body in the external canal

Hearing Test Procedures

Whispered Speech Testing.   Ask the patient to cover one ear. Stand two feet away from the uncovered ear, whisper words, and ask the patient to repeat them. If the patient cannot repeat them, say the words more loudly. This is a simple screening method.

Weber Test.   Strike the tuning fork against your elbow to make a tone, place the tuning fork in the middle of the patient's forehead and ask whether the tone is louder in one ear or equal on both sides. This determines on which side a hearing loss is located.

Rinne Test.   Place the vibrating tuning fork on the mastoid process behind the opening of the ear canal. Then hold it opposite the ear canal. Ask the patient where the tone was louder and/or lasted longer. Normally, sound is heard longer by air conduction at the ear canal than by bone conduction at the mastoid process. The reverse indicates a conductive hearing loss.

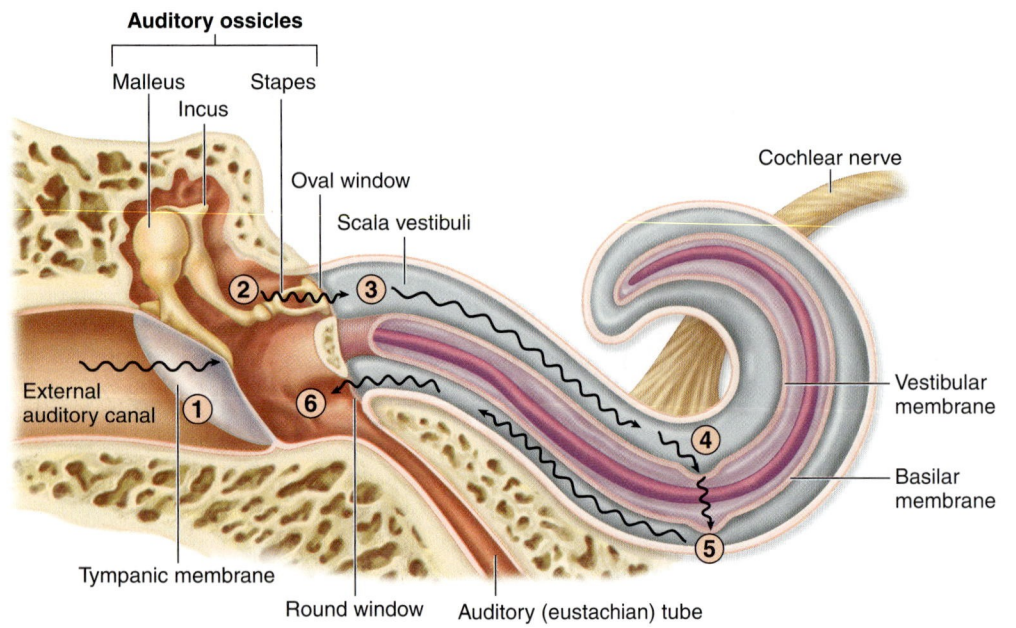

Auditory ossicles
Malleus   Stapes
Incus
Oval window
Scala vestibuli
Cochlear nerve
External auditory canal ①
② ③ ⑥ ④ ⑤
Vestibular membrane
Basilar membrane
Tympanic membrane
Round window   Auditory (eustachian) tube

▲ **FIGURE 4.42   Hearing Process in the Inner Ear.**

WORD	PRONUNCIATION	ELEMENTS		DEFINITION
audiometer	aw-dee-**OM**-ee-ter	S/ R/CF	-**meter** *measure* **audi/o**- *hearing*	Instrument to measure hearing
audiometric (adj)	**AW**-dee-oh-**MET**-rik	S/ R/	-**ic** *pertaining to* **metr**- *measure*	Pertaining to the measurement of hearing
basilar	**BAS**-ih-lar	S/ R/	-**ar** *pertaining to* **basil**- *base, support*	Pertaining to the base of a structure
cochlea cochlear (adj)	**KOK**-lee-ah **KOK**-lee-ar		Latin *snail shell*	An intricate combination of passages; used to describe the part of the inner ear used in hearing
conductive hearing loss	kon-**DUK**-tiv		Latin *to lead*	Hearing loss caused by lesions in the outer ear or middle ear
implant	im-**PLANT**		Latin *to plant*	To insert material into tissues, or the material inserted into tissues
labyrinth labyrinthitis	**LAB**-ih-rinth **LAB**-ih-rin-**THI**-tis	S/	Greek *labyrinth* -**itis** *inflammation*	The inner ear Inflammation of the inner ear
Rinne test	**RIN**-eh TEST		Friedrich Rinne, German otologist, 1819–1868	Test for conductive hearing loss
sensorineural hearing loss	**SEN**-sor-ih-**NYUR**-al	S/ R/CF R/	-**al** *pertaining to* **sensor/i**- *sensory* -**neur**- *nerve*	Hearing loss caused by lesions of the inner ear or the auditory nerve
vestibule vestibular (adj)	**VES**-tih-byul ves-**TIB**-you-lar		Latin *entrance*	Space at the entrance to a canal
Weber test	**VA**-ber TEST		Ernst Weber, German physiologist, 1794–1878	Test for sensorineural hearing loss

Audiometer. After proper training, use an audiometer to test for hearing loss. The audiometer is an electronic device that generates sounds in different frequencies and intensities and can print out the patient's responses.

When recording the results of hearing testing, **A.D.** is shorthand for the right ear, **A.S.** for the left ear, and **A.U.** for both ears. (*Note:* To avoid confusion with similar abbreviations, the **JCAHO** recommends writing out the full terms.)

Abbreviations

A.D.   right ear
A.S.   left ear
A.U.   both ears
JCAHO Joint Commission on Accreditation of Healthcare Organizations

EXERCISES

*Increase your knowledge of the **language of otology** by correctly answering the following questions. Review the WAD, then circle the best answer.*

1. In the term **basilar**, "basil" is a:

   prefix   root   combining form

2. The entrance to the inner ear is the:

   vestibule   labyrinth   cochlea

3. **Labyrinthitis** is:

   procedure   condition   inflammation

4. The element **neur** means:

   never   nerve   nose

5. An **audiometer** is used to:

   measure   scan   examine

6. An intricate combination of passages in the ear is the:

   cochlea   vestibule   labyrinth

7. The root meaning *hearing* can be found in the word:

   vestibule   audiometric   otology

8. Hearing loss caused by lesions of the inner ear is called _____ hearing loss.

   auditory   basilar   sensorineural

9. The suffix meaning *pertaining to* is found in the term:

   vestibular   labyrinthitis   audiometer

You are

... Sonia Ramos, a medical assistant working with Sylvia Thompson, MD, an otolaryngologist at Fulwood Medical Center.

Your patient is

... Mr. Ernesto Santiago, a 44-year-old man who was referred to Dr. Thompson because of recurrent attacks of nausea, vomiting, a sense of spinning or whirling, and ringing in his ears.

CASE REPORT 4.4

The attacks last about 24 hours and are getting more frequent. He has been having trouble hearing quiet speech on his left side.

Your role is to document his investigation, diagnosis, and care and to act as translator between Mr. Santiago and Dr. Thompson.

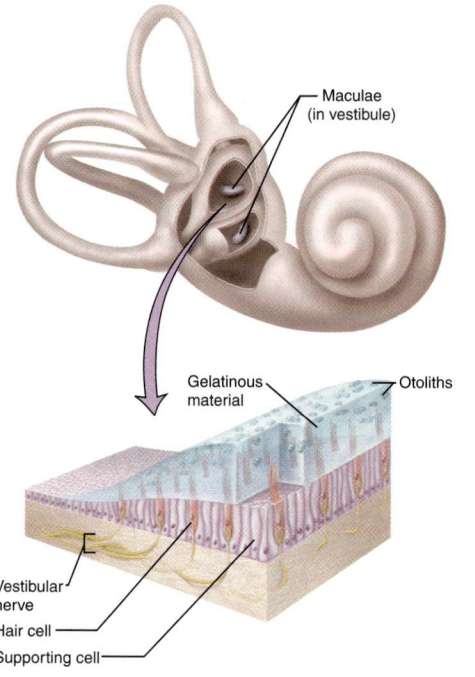

▲ FIGURE 4.43   Vestibule and Maculae.

INNER EAR FOR EQUILIBRIUM AND BALANCE

The **vestibule** and the three **semicircular canals** *(Figure 4.43)* are the organs of balance.

Inside the fluid-filled vestibule are two raised, flat areas (**maculae**) covered with hair cells and a gelatinous material. This gelatinous material contains crystals of calcium and protein called **otoliths**. The position of the head alters the pressure applied to the hair cells by the gelatinous mass. The hair cells respond to horizontal and vertical changes and send impulses to the brain indicating the position to which the head has tilted.

Each of the three fluid-filled semicircular canals has a dilated end called an **ampulla** that contains a mound of hair cells embedded in a gelatinous material that together are called a **crista ampullaris** *(Figure 4.44)*. They detect rotational movements of the head that distort the hair cells and lead to stimulation of connected nerve cells. The nerve impulses travel via the vestibular nerve and go to the brain. From the brain, nerve impulses travel to the muscles to maintain **equilibrium** and balance.

The sensation of spinning or whirling that Mr. Santiago experiences is called **vertigo,** often described by patients as dizziness. The ringing in his ears is called **tinnitus.** Both sensations arise in the inner ear.

Benign paroxysmal positional vertigo (BPPV) is another type of episodic vertigo caused by fragments of the otoliths in the vestibule migrating into the semicircular canals. There they brush against the hair cells, sending conflicting signals to the brain and thereby producing vertigo.

Acute labyrinthitis is an acute viral infection of the labyrinth, producing extreme vertigo, nausea, and vomiting. It usually lasts one to two weeks.

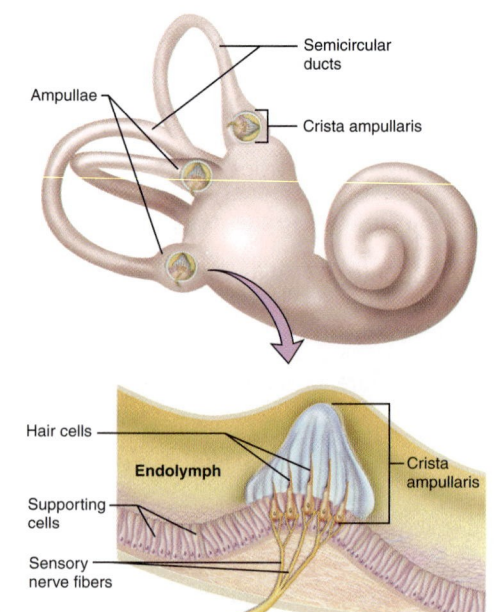

Figure 4.44   Semicircular Ducts. ▶

WORD	PRONUNCIATION	ELEMENTS		DEFINITION
ampulla crista ampullaris	am-**PULL**-ah **KRIS**-tah am-**PULL**-air-is	R/ S/ R/	Latin *two handled bottle* **crista** *crest* **-aris** *pertaining to* **ampull-** *bottle-shaped*	Dilated portion of canal or duct Mound of hair cells and gelatinous material in the ampulla of a semicircular canal
equilibrium	ee-kwi-**LIB**-ree-um	P/ R/	**equi-** *equal* **-librium** *balance*	Being evenly balanced
macula maculae (pl)	**MAK**-you-lah **MAK**-you-lee		Latin *small spot*	Small area of special function, in this case a sensory receptor
Ménière disease	men-**YEAR** diz-**EEZ**		Prosper Ménière, French physican, 1799–1862	Disorder of inner ear with cluster of symptoms of acute attacks of tinnitus, vertigo, and hearing loss
otolith	**OH**-toe-lith	S/ R/CF	**-lith** *stone* **ot/o-** *ear*	A calcium particle in the vestibule of the inner ear
paroxysmal	par-ock-**SIZ**-mal	S/ R/	**-al** *pertaining to* **-paroxysm-** *irritation*	Occurring in sharp, spasmodic episodes
tinnitus	**TIN**-ih-tus		Latin *jingle*	Persistent ringing, whistling, clicking, or booming noise in the ears
vertigo	**VER**-tih-go		Latin *dizziness*	Sensation of spinning or whirling

Case Report 4.4 (continued)

The recurrent attacks that Mr. Santiago suffered are called **Ménière disease**. The disease involves the destruction of inner ear hair cells, but the etiology is unknown, and there is no cure. Dr. Thompson prescribed medication to control his nausea and vomiting.

Abbreviation

BPPV benign paroxysmal positional vertigo

EXERCISES

Challenge your knowledge of the ear by filling in the correct terms for the following definitions. Demonstrate your understanding of the terms by using any one of them correctly in a sentence of your choice. Fill in the blanks.

Definitions	Medical Term
1. persistent ringing in the ears	_____
2. sensation of spinning or whirling	_____
3. something that begins and goes away suddenly	_____
4. evenly balanced	_____
5. dilated portion of a canal or duct	_____
6. small area of special function	_____
7. calcium particle in the vestibule	_____
8. mound of hair cells found in ampulla	_____

9. Use any one of these terms in a sentence of your choice that is *not* a definition.

_____

_____

SPECIAL SENSES OF THE EYE AND EAR

CHALLENGE YOUR KNOWLEDGE

A. Apply your knowledge of medical terminology to change this paragraph from layman's terms into medical communication. Then practice reading the entire paragraph aloud.

Preoperative Diagnosis: Diabetic _____ (disorder of the retinal blood vessels) with vitreous _____ (sudden discharge of blood), left eye

Procedure Performed: Laser _____ (clotting together with light) _____ _____ with (surgical removal of vitreous), left eye

After suitable anesthesia, the patient was prepped and draped in the usual manner. The _____ (inner lining of the eyelid) was well irrigated to remove any debris from the field. A slit _____ (cutting into) was made at four different sites on the _____ (white, outer covering of the eyeball), and the central vitreous cavity was entered. The origin of the bleeding was confined to the _____ _____ (area of sharpest vision). The blood vessels were cauterized with the laser. Fortunately, the _____ _____ (inner lining of the eye) had not become detached, although the vitreous had separated. This was removed in pieces. All operative sites were closed routinely. Ointment, patch, and shield were applied to the affected eye. Patient returned to the postanesthesia care unit for discharge. Patient will be given prescriptions for _____ (medication to destroy bacteria) to be filled when she leaves the hospital. She will follow up with me in the office in one week.

B. **Suffixes:** The following terms all have a suffix with a common meaning. Circle the suffix, then identify the common meaning, and define each term.

1. periorbital _____

2. lacrimal _____

3. bactericidal _____

4. intraocular _____

5. neural _____

6. optic _____

7. tarsal _____

8. macular _____

9. retinal _____

10. corneal _____

These suffixes all mean: _____

C. **Visual Pathway:** In order to better understand the visual pathway, trace its route by putting the following terms in the correct order.

visual cortex   optic chiasm   optic radiation

optic tract   optic foramen   cerebral hemisphere

1. _____

2. _____

3. _____

4. _____

5. _____

6. _____

D. **Diagnosis:** You are preparing to code the claim forms for various patients seen in the clinic today. The doctor has given the diagnosis in general terms on the charge slip. Not every term in the *ICD-9-CM Index* is cross-referenced, so you must know the medical term to find the code. Write the correct medical term for each general term.

1. pink eye _____

2. sensitivity to light _____

3. near-sighted _____

4. scratched cornea _____

5. inflammation of the iris _____

6. "lazy eye" _____

7. far-sighted _____

8. inflammed eyelash and tarsal gland _____

9. droopy eyelid _____

10. cross-eyed _____

E. **Build medical terms from the following elements.** Identify the type of element, its meaning, and a medical term containing that element. The first one is done for you. Fill in the chart.

Element	Prefix	Root/CF	Suffix	Meaning of Element	Example of Medical Term
naso	_____	CF	_____	*nose*	*nasolacrimal*
zyme	_____	_____	_____	_____	_____
ophthalmo	_____	_____	_____	_____	_____
pur	_____	_____	_____	_____	_____
biot	_____	_____	_____	_____	_____
blephar	_____	_____	_____	_____	_____
cidal	_____	_____	_____	_____	_____
phobia	_____	_____	_____	_____	_____
ulcer	_____	_____	_____	_____	_____
con	_____	_____	_____	_____	_____
opia	_____	_____	_____	_____	_____
opto	_____	_____	_____	_____	_____

F. **Terminology Challenge:** What medical term in this chapter is also applicable to Chapter 5, the Musculoskeletal System? The same word can mean two different body parts. Explain.

Hint: Check the Word Analysis and Definition boxes.

_____

_____

_____

G. **Word Elements:** Learning word elements is your most valuable tool for increasing your medical vocabulary. Use your knowledge of word elements to answer the following questions. Circle the correct answer.

1. The root for **tear** is:

    a. blephar

    b. tamin

    c. commodat

    d. strab

    e. lacrim

2. The root of this word means *letting go* and is used to indicate partial paralysis:

    a. parietal

    b. periorbital

    c. paresis

    d. ptosis

    e. presbyopia

3. Based on its suffix, you can tell that a **keratotomy** is:

    a. body part

    b. procedure

    c. diagnosis

    d. medication

    e. infection

4. The prefix in **microaneurysm** tells you that this aneurysm is:

    a. large

    b. black

    c. small

    d. painful

    e. red

5. In the term **amblyopia, "opia"** means:

   a. sound

   b. light

   c. sight

   d. movement

   e. pain

6. **In situ** is a Latin phrase which means: *(Be precise!)*

   a. in this place

   b. in another place

   c. in its original place

   d. in the place

   e. in place of

7. In the terms **retinoblastoma** and **retinopathy,** the combining form tells you that both these terms concern the:

   a. cornea

   b. iris

   c. lens

   d. vitreous body

   e. retina

8. **Angiography** is a radiography of:

   a. organ

   b. bone

   c. blood vessel

   d. muscle

   e. gland

9. In the term **antibiotic, "anti"** is a prefix that means:

   a. within

   b. outside

   c. on top of

   d. against

   e. around

SPECIAL SENSES OF THE EYE AND EAR

H. **Patient Education:** Your patient is confused by some medical terms the doctor has used. Explain to her in simple language the difference between:

1. hyperopia and myopia _____

_____

_____

2. dacryocystitis and dacryostenosis _____

_____

_____

I. **Prefixes:** Use your knowledge of prefixes to deconstruct the terms below, then write the definition of the term. The first one is done for you.

Term	Prefix	Meaning of Prefix	Define term
periorbital	*peri*	*around*	*pertaining to around the orbit*
esotropia			
astigmatism			
contaminate			
accommodation			
exotropia			
bilateral			
analgesic			
intraocular			

J. **Master your documentation—it is a legal record.** Circle the most appropriate choice, and insert the correct abbreviation where indicated.

1. Patient complains of sticky eyelids with (purulent/perulent) discharge, both eyes (_____[abbreviation]) Diagnosis: (scleritis/conjunctivitis)

2. (Refraction/accommodation) reveals patient's vision now 20/40 in the right eye, with correction.

3. The (diagnosis/prognosis) for Mr. Baker is continued decreasing vision in his right eye (_____[abbreviation]) if his diabetes remains uncontrolled and his (retinopathy/retinoblastoma) worsens.

4. (Opthalmoscopic/ophthalmoscopic) examination of the left eye (_____[abbreviation]) reveals (microaneurisms/microaneurysms) forming. (Fluoreseen/fluorescein) angiography ordered for more details.

K. Discussion Question: Prepare a brief discussion that will address the following questions about Case Report 4.1:

Why was Mrs. Jenny Hughes asked to wash her hands before signing the sign-in sheet?

If she hadn't washed her hands, what could possibly happen?

What sanitary precautions must you take when you work with patients?

What types of precautions could Mrs. Hughes use at home to keep her contagious disease from spreading to the rest of her family?

L. Deconstruct the following medical terms into their word elements and meanings. This group of terms has something in common. What is it? Fill in the blanks.

Medical term	Prefix	Root/Combining Form	Suffix	Meaning of Medical Term
phacoemulsification				
photocoagulation				
cryopexy				

This group of terms is similar because: _____

M. Match the Latin and Greek terms in column 1 to their meanings in column 2.

_____	1. orbit	A.	flat
_____	2. extrinsic	B.	falling
_____	3. chalazion	C.	on the outer side
_____	4. cornea	D.	paralysis
_____	5. cortex	E.	lump
_____	6. ptosis	F.	corner of the eye
_____	7. canthus	G.	web
_____	8. contagious	H.	circle
_____	9. tarsus	I.	outer shell
_____	10. paresis	J.	touch closely

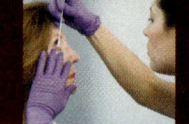

SPECIAL SENSES OF THE EYE AND EAR

N. **Patient Documentation**

1. Read the following patient documentation out loud to practice your pronunciation.

2. Certain medical terms are underlined for you. On the lines below, write a definition for each term on the line provided.

Fulwood Medical Center
3333 Medical Parkway, Fulwood, MI 01234
555-247-6100

Department of: Otology

June 16, 2006

Dear Dr. Lee:

I had the pleasure of seeing your patient, Elizabeth Dano, in consultation for the first time on June 14, 2006.

This is an 86-year-old woman, who comes in with the chief complaint of intermittent vertigo. The patient has known otosclerosis and began having hearing loss in her twenties. Approximately 40 years ago the patient underwent a right stapedectomy, which was not successful. She also states that her hearing continues to get worse each year.

About 3 years ago she begn having attacks of dizziness that come on without warning. These lingering feelings of dizziness may last as long as 3 days. Most recently, she had an attack in her doctor's office, which precipitated this consultation.

Her examination in the office today was relatively unremarkable. She specifically had a negative subjective fistula test so that the possibility of this being due to a perilymphatic fistula secondary to the stapedectomy is not very likely. She may indeed have mild *Ménière's disease*, which is more common in patients with otosclerosis, but since her attacks are relatively mild, I do not think that any intervention is required at this time. We also know that patients with a known autoimmune disorder such as rheumatoid arthritis can develop immune-mediated inner ear disease, but this usually is a more insidious and chronic problem, rather than a temporary one. Finally, I think that all things considered, I would not recommend any particular further testing or intervention at this time. I would mention that if her left hearing loss becomes so great that her hearing aid is no longer effective, then we consider doing a stapedotomy on that ear to once again make her able to use her hearing aid. Obviously, this woud be a last ditch effort, which is not required at this time.

It was a pleasure seeing your patient and if something new develops, I would be happy to see her in follow-up.

Sincerely,

Albert Aran, M.D.

Definitions: Use your dictionary or glossary for unfamiliar terms. Write the definition for the term on the blank next to it. Then divide the terms with an asterisk (*) into their word elements with a slash.

vertigo _____

otosclerosis* _____

stapedectomy* _____

Ménière disease _____

stapedotomy* _____

O. Patient Documentation: You must be precise in your use of abbreviations for documentation. Demonstrate your knowledge of abbreviations by filling in the blanks. You are given the medical language—translate it into an abbreviation.

1. The prescription read: 150 _____ (milligrams) of Cipro, _____ (four times a day).

2. The patient was diagnosed with _____ (otitis media with effusion) secondary to a _____ (upper respiratory infection).

3. Since the _____ (acute otitis media) was resolving, the pain medication was used _____ (when necessary).

P. Build terms from the *language of otology*. Identify the following elements by checking the appropriate column. Give the meaning of the element, then give an example of a medical term containing that element. The first one is done for you. Fill in the chart.

Element	Prefix	Root/CF	Suffix	Meaning of Element	Medical Term
algesia	_____	_____	_____	_____	_____
anti	_____	_____	✓	*pain*	*analgesia*
ette	_____	_____	_____	_____	_____
bi	_____	_____	_____	_____	_____
ot	_____	_____	_____	_____	_____
rhino	_____	_____	_____	_____	_____
laryngo	_____	_____	_____	_____	_____
tympan	_____	_____	_____	_____	_____
aden	_____	_____	_____	_____	_____
stomy	_____	_____	_____	_____	_____
sclero	_____	_____	_____	_____	_____
audio	_____	_____	_____	_____	_____

Q. Teamwork: You are helping with the orientation of a new medical assistant in the otorhinolaryngologist's office where you work. Can you explain to her the office use for an:

1. otoscope _____

_____

2. audiometer _____

_____

3. tonometer _____

_____

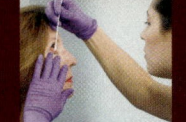
SPECIAL SENSES OF THE EYE AND EAR

Y. **Patient Education**: Patients will ask you for clarification of certain terms they do not understand or for more explanation of body processes. Be prepared to answer the following questions for your patients.

1. Andrew Baker has severe otosclerosis in his left ear. Dr. Lee has recommended replacement of his stapes with a plastic prosthesis. Explain to Mr. Baker what a prosthesis is, and compare it to other body part replacements he may already have.

Look up **prosthesis** in the glossary. Define **prosthesis**: _____

Name three other types of prostheses that can be inserted into the body. _____

Why can a prosthesis also be considered a "foreign body"?_____

_____

_____

2. Caroline Mason has had many ear problems since she was a child. Frequent infections necessitated myringotomy tubes at a young age. Even after tube removal, she continued to have frequent URIs, tonsillitis, middle ear infections, impacted cerumen, labyrinthitis, and vertigo later in life.

Can you explain to her the cumulative effect all these previous conditions have had on her hearing loss?

_____

_____

Trace for her the pathway of sound waves through the ear to the brain in order to be recognized as sounds.

_____

_____

_____

How have her previous ear problems interfered with this process?

_____

_____

_____

Z. **Regions of the Ear:** Identify whether the statement references the external, middle, or inner ear by placing a check (✓) in the correct column.

Reference	External Ear	Middle Ear	Inner Ear
swimmer's ear			
otosclerosis			
labyrinthitis			
tympanic membrane			
myringotomy tubes			
otitis externa			
eustachian (auditory) tube			
good nerve supply; very sensitive to			
pain			
ossicles			
cochlear implants			

SPECIAL SENSES OF THE EYE AND EAR

CHAPTER SUMMARY EXERCISE

1. *Listen to the pronunciation of the medical terms as given by your instructor.*
2. *Circle the correct spelling of the medical term.*
3. *Match the correctly spelled terms to the brief descriptions below.*
4. *Write a sentence for each of the 15 terms that appear in this exercise.*

A. SPELLING COMPREHENSION: CIRCLE THE CORRECT SPELLING OF THE TERM.

1. chalazion	chelezion	chalezian	chalaziun	chalezium
2. optholmologist	ophtalmologist	optolmologist	ophthalmologist	optalmologist
3. prbyopia	prisbiopia	prisbyopia	pressbiopia	presbyopia
4. blephritis	belpharitis	blepharitis	bleperitis	blephartis
5. strebissmus	strabbismus	strubismis	strabismus	strabithmus
6. amblyopia	ambilopia	amblopia	amblyupia	amblopea
7. petosis	putosis	ptosis	ptysosis	phytosis
8. chiasm	ciasum	ciassum	chesum	chasm
9. antipyrretic	antypiretic	antipyretic	antepiretic	antipieretic
10. yustachian	eustachian	eustacian	eusstacyan	yustachien
11. prosstethis	prosthesis	prothesis	prothessis	prosisus
12. youvietis	yuveitis	uvyeitis	uvitis	uveitis
13. cholesteatoma	colestotoma	chollestiotoma	colestioma	cholestioma
14. perulent	purulent	prulent	pureyulent	pruyulent
15. auricle	aurricle	aurickle	aurrickle	aurykicle

B. MATCH THE NUMBER OF THE CORRECT TERM IN PART A WITH THE BRIEF DESCRIPTION OF THE TERM BELOW.

a. substance that reduces fever _____

b. vision not developed equally in both eyes _____

c. squinting _____

d. manufactured substitute for a missing part of the body _____

e. cyst on the outer edge of an eyelid _____

f. connects middle ear to nasopharynx _____

g. nearsighted vision _____

h. treats diseases of the eye and prescribes medication _____

i. inflammation of the uvea _____

j. inflammation of the eyelid   _____

k. external ear   _____

l. two optic nerves cross at the base of the brain   _____

m. showing or containing a lot of pus   _____

n. falling or drooping of an eyelid (or organ)   _____

o. yellow, waxy tumor arising in the middle ear   _____

C. USING YOUR KNOWLEDGE OF TERMS 1–15 IN PART A AND THEIR CORRECT SPELLING, WRITE A BRIEF SENTENCE FOR EACH OF THE TERMS AS IT MIGHT APPEAR IN PATIENT DOCUMENTATION.

1 _____

2. _____

3. _____

4. _____

5. _____

6. _____

7. _____

8. _____

9. _____

10. _____

11. _____

12. _____

13. _____

14. _____

15. _____

D. GO TO THE STUDENT CD. OPEN THE GLOSSARY AND PRACTICE YOUR PRONUNCIATION OF THE TERMS IN PART A OF THIS EXERCISE.

Musculoskeletal System

The Language of Orthopedics

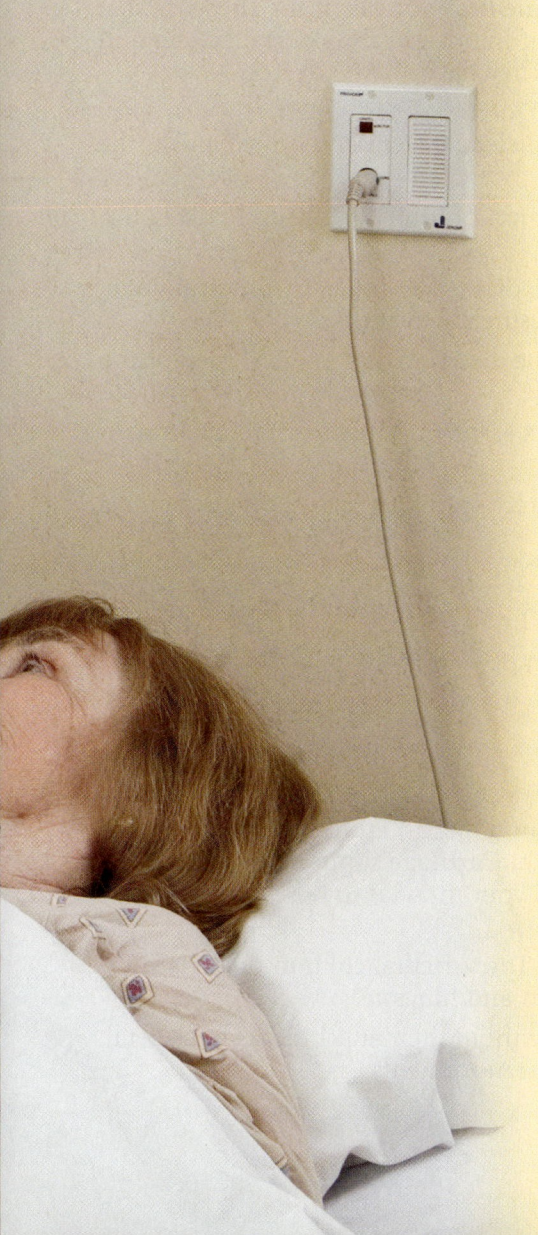

5

CASE REPORT 5.1

You are

. . . an orthopedic technologist working with Kevin Stannard, MD, an orthopedist in the Fulwood Medical Group.

Your patient is

. . . Mrs. Amy Vargas, a 70-year-old housewife, who tripped going down the front steps from her house. She has severe pain in her right hip and is unable to stand. An x-ray showed a hip fracture and marked osteoporosis. Dr Stannard examined her in the Emergency Department and has admitted her for a hip replacement.

In order for you to work with Dr. Stannard to give optimal care to Mrs. Vargas and to help her and her family understand the significance of her bone disorder and injury, you will need to be familiar with the terminology of bone structure and function and its disorders.

Learning Outcomes

This chapter will review the whole musculoskeletal system and will enable you to:

- Apply the language of orthopedics to the anatomy and physiology of bones, joints, and muscles.

- Comprehend, analyze, spell, and write the medical terms of orthopedics so that you can communicate accurately and precisely in any health care setting.

- Recognize and pronounce the medical terms of orthopedics so that you can communicate verbally with accuracy and precision in any health care setting.

- Understand the cause, appearance, methods of diagnosis, and treatment of common disorders of the musculoskeletal system.

OBJECTIVES

If you didn't have a skeleton you'd be like a rag doll, shapeless and unable to move. Your skeleton provides support, protects many organ systems, and is the landmark for much of medical terminology. For example, the radial artery you use for taking a pulse is so named because it travels beside the radial bone of the forearm.

In addition, the surface anatomy of bones and their markings enables you to describe and document the sites of symptoms, signs, and clinical, diagnostic, and therapeutic procedures.

The information in this lesson will enable you to:

- **Recognize the different health professionals involved in the diagnosis and treatment of musculoskeletal problems.**
- **Identify the tissues that form the skeletal system.**
- **Discuss the structures and functions of the skeletal system.**
- **Explain the structure and functions of bones.**
- **Describe the major problems and diseases that occur in the skeletal system.**

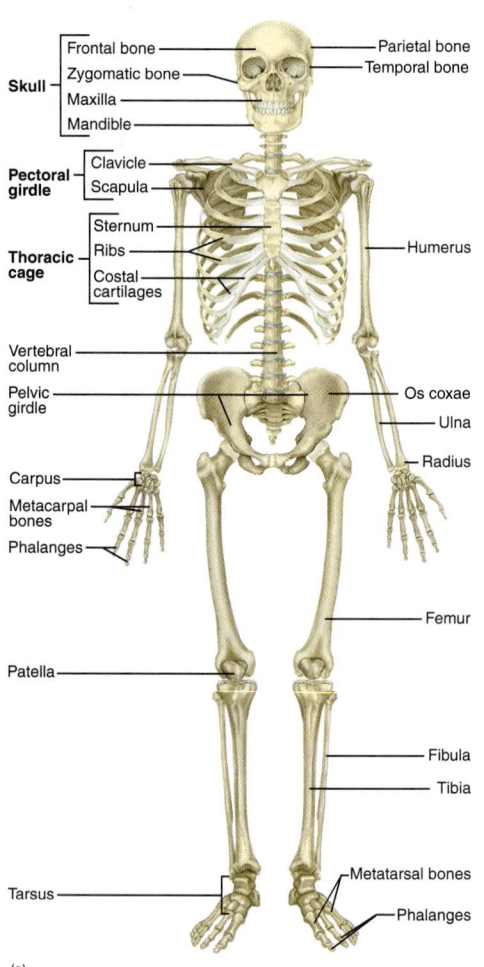

Skull — Frontal bone, Zygomatic bone, Maxilla, Mandible
Parietal bone
Temporal bone
Pectoral girdle — Clavicle, Scapula
Thoracic cage — Sternum, Ribs, Costal cartilages
Humerus
Vertebral column
Pelvic girdle
Os coxae
Ulna
Radius
Carpus
Metacarpal bones
Phalanges
Femur
Patella
Fibula
Tibia
Metatarsal bones
Tarsus
Phalanges

(a)

▲ **FIGURE 5.1   Anterior Skeletal System: Anterior View.**

Health professionals involved in the diagnosis and treatment of problems in the **musculoskeletal** system include the following.

Orthopedic surgeons (orthopedists) are medical doctors in the specialty that deals with the prevention and correction of injuries of the skeletal system and associated muscles, joints, and ligaments. They have an **MD** degree.

Osteopathic physicians have the degree **Doctor of Osteopathy (DO)**. They receive additional training in the musculoskeletal system and how it affects the whole body.

Chiropractors focus on manual manipulation of joints, particularly the spine, to maintain and restore health.

Physical therapists evaluate and treat pain, disease, or injury by physical therapeutic measures, as opposed to medical or surgical measures.

Physical therapist assistants work under the direction of a physical therapist to assist in the application of physical therapy.

Orthopedic technologists and technicians assist orthopedic surgeons in their treatment of patients.

(*Note:* Orthopaedic is the original and correct spelling, but orthopedic is most commonly used.)

FUNCTIONS OF THE SKELETAL SYSTEM

The four components of the skeletal system (*Figure 5.1*) are:

1. *bones*   3. *tendons*
2. *cartilage*   4. *ligaments*

They provide the following functions:

- **Support**—The bones of your vertebral column, pelvis, and legs hold up your body. The jawbone supports your teeth. **Cartilage** supports your nose, ears, and ribs. **Tendons** support and attach your muscles to bone. **Ligaments** support and hold your bones together.
- **Protection**—The skull protects your brain. The vertebral column protects your spinal cord. The rib cage protects your heart and lungs.
- **Movement**—**Muscles** could not function without their attachments to skeletal bones, and muscles are responsible for your movements.

WORD ANALYSIS AND DEFINITION

WORD	PRONUNCIATION	ELEMENTS		DEFINITION
cartilage	**KAR**-tih-lage		Latin *gristle*	Nonvascular, firm connective tissue found mostly in joints
chiropractic	kye-roh-**PRAK**-tik	S/ R/CF R/	**-ic** *pertaining to* **chir/o-** *hand* **-pract-** *efficient*	Diagnosis, treatment, and prevention of mechanical disorders of the musculoskeletal system
chiropractor	kye-roh-**PRAK**-tor	S/	**-or** *a doer*	Practitioner of chiropractic
detoxification	de-**TOKS**-ih-fi-**KAY**-shun	S/ P/ R/	**-fication** *remove* **de-** *from, out of* **toxi-** *poison*	Remove poison from a tissue or substance
ligament	**LIG**-ah-ment		Latin *band, sheet*	Band of fibrous tissue connecting two structures
muscle musculoskeletal	**MUSS**-el **MUSS**-kyu-loh-**SKEL**-eh-tal	S/ R/CF R/	Latin *muscle* **-al** *pertaining to* **muscul/o-** *muscle* **-skelet-** *skeleton*	A tissue consisting of contractile cells Pertaining to the muscles and the bony skeleton
orthopedic (also spelled: orthopaedic)	or-tho-**PEE**-dik	S/ R/CF R/	**-ic** *pertaining to* **orth/o-** *straight* **-ped-** *child*	Pertaining to the correction and cure of deformities and diseases of the musculoskeletal system; originally, most of the deformities treated were in children
orthopedist	or-tho-**PEE**-dist	S/	**-ist** *specialist*	Specialist in orthopedics
osteopath	**OS**-tee-oh-path	R/ R/CF	**-path** *disease* **oste/o-** *bone*	Practitioner of osteopathy
osteopathy	**OS**-tee-**OP**-ah-thee	S/	**-pathy** *disease*	Medical practice based on maintaining the balance of the body
tendon	**TEN**-dun		Latin *sinew*	Fibrous band that connects muscle to bone

- **Blood formation**—Bone marrow in many bones is the major producer of blood cells, including most of those in your immune system *(see Chapter 14)*.
- **Mineral storage and balance**—The skeletal system stores calcium and phosphorus. These are released when your body needs them for other purposes. For example, calcium is needed for muscle contraction, communication between neurons *(see Chapter 10)*, and blood clotting *(see Chapter 7)*.
- **Detoxification**—Bones remove metals such as lead and radium from your blood, store them, and slowly release them for excretion.

The four classes of bones are determined by their shape, which are long, short, flat, and irregular.

Abbreviations

MD	Doctor of medicine
DO	Doctor of osteopathy

EXERCISES

*The following exercise can be answered entirely by using medical terms that appear in this WAD. Mastering these terms will start you on your way to learning the **language of orthopedics**. From the description, identify the correct medical terminology. Fill in the blanks.*

Description	Medical Term(s)
In addition to bones, these three terms are components of the skeletal system:	1. _____
	2. _____
	3. _____
Which three terms refer to medical occupations?	4. _____
	5. _____
	6. _____

BONE GROWTH AND STRUCTURE

Factors that affect bone growth include:

1. **Genes**—determine the size and shape of bones and the ultimate adult height.
2. **Nutrition**—calcium and phosphorus are needed to develop good bone density.
3. **Exercise**—increases bone density and total bone mass.
4. **Mineral deposition**—calcium and phosphate are taken from plasma and deposited in bone.
5. **Mineral resorption**—calcium and phosphate are released from bone back into the plasma when they are needed elsewhere. For example, calcium is needed for muscle contraction, communication between neurons, and blood clotting. Phosphate is a component of DNA and RNA.
6. **Vitamins**—vitamin A activates osteoblasts; vitamin C is essential for collagen synthesis; vitamin D stimulates absorption, transport, and deposition of calcium and phosphate into bones *(see Chapter 21)*.
7. **Hormones**—for example, growth hormone stimulates the epiphyseal plate to calcify, and estrogen and testosterone accelerate bone growth after puberty and maintain bone density *(see Chapter 13)*.

Structure of Bones

Long bones are the most common type of bone in the body *(Figure 5.2)*.

The shaft of a long bone is called the **diaphysis.** Each end of the bone is called the **epiphysis** and is expanded to provide extra surface area for the attachment of ligaments and tendons.

Sandwiched between the diaphysis and epiphysis is a thin area called the **metaphysis.** Thin layers of cartilage cells in the **epiphyseal plate** enable the diaphysis (bone shaft) to grow in length. When growth stops, compact bone grows into the epiphyseal plate and forms the **epiphyseal line.**

A tough connective tissue sheath called **periosteum** covers the outer surface of all bones and is attached to the compact or **cortical** bone by tough collagen fibers. The periosteum protects the bone and anchors blood vessels and nerves to the surface of the bone.

The hollow cylinder inside the diaphysis is called the **medullary cavity.** It contains bone **marrow** and is lined by a thin membrane called the **endosteum.** The marrow is a fatty tissue that contains blood cells in different stages of development *(see Chapter 7)*.

The endosteum and periosteum contain **osteoblasts,** cells that produce the matrix of new bone tissue. This is called **osteogenesis.** Bone **matrix** consists of cells, collagen fibers, a gel that supports and suspends the fibers, and calcium phosphate crystals to give bone its hardness.

When osteoblasts are incorporated into the new bone, they become **osteocytes.** These cells, which maintain the matrix, reside in small spaces in the matrix called **lacunae.**

Osteoclasts are produced by the bone marrow. They dissolve calcium, phosphorus, and the organic components of the bone matrix. There is a continual balancing act going on as osteoclasts remove matrix and osteoblasts produce matrix. If osteoclasts out-perform the osteoblasts, then **osteoporosis** occurs, as with Mrs. Vargas in the case report.

All bones are well supplied with blood *(Figure 5.3)*. The blood vessels travel through the bone in a system of small **haversian (central) canals.** Because of its good blood supply, bone heals well.

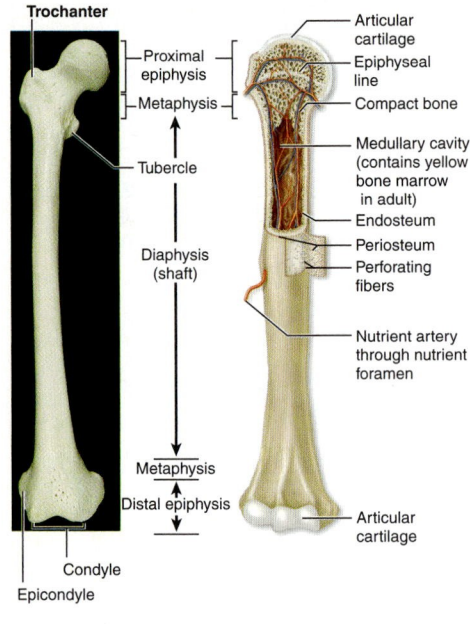

▲ **FIGURE 5.2   Femur: Long Bone of the Thigh.**

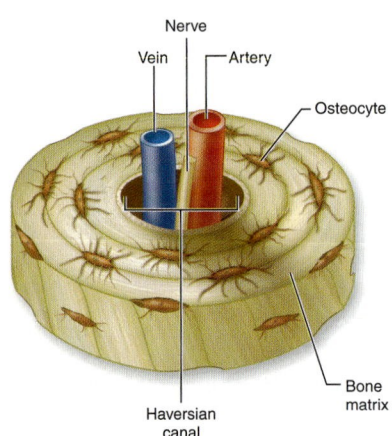

▲ **FIGURE 5.3   Blood Supply to Bone.**

WORD	PRONUNCIATION		ELEMENTS	DEFINITION
cortex cortical (adj)	**KOR**-teks **KOR**-ti-cal		Latin *bark*	Outer portion of an organ, such as bone
diaphysis	die-**AF**-ih-sis		Greek *growing between*	The shaft of a long bone
endosteum	en-**DOSS**-tee-um	S/ P/ R/	**-um** *tissue* **end-** *within* **osteo-** *bone*	A membrane of tissue lining the inner (medullary) cavity of a long bone
epiphysis	eh-**PIF**-ih-sis	P/ R/	**epi-** *upon, above* **-physis** *growth*	Expanded area at the proximal and distal ends of a long bone to provide increased surface area for attachment of ligaments and tendons
epiphyseal plate	eh-**PIF**-ih-see-al PLATE	S/ R/CF	**-al** *pertaining to* **epiphys/i-** *growth*	Layer of cartilage between epiphysis and metaphysis where bone growth occurs
haversian canals (also called **central canals**)	hah-**VER**-shan ka-**NALS**		Clopton Havers, English physician, 1655–1702	Vascular canals in bone
lacuna lacunae (pl)	la-**KOO**-nah la-**KOO**-nee		Latin *a pit, lake*	Small space or cavity within the matrix of bone
marrow	**MAH**-roe		Old English *marrow*	Fatty, blood-forming tissue in the cavities of long bones
matrix	**MAY**-triks		Latin *mother, womb*	Substance that surrounds cells, is manufactured by cells, and holds them together
medulla medullary (adj)	meh-**DULL**-ah **MED**-ul-ah-ree		Latin *marrow*	Central portion of a structure surrounded by cortex
metaphysis	meh-**TAF**-ih-sis	P/ R/	**meta-** *beyond, making change* **-physis** *growth*	Region between the diaphysis and the epiphysis where bone growth occurs
osteoblast	**OS**-tee-oh-blast	S/ R/CF	**-blast** *embryo* **oste/o-** *bone*	Bone-forming cell
osteoclast	**OS**-tee-oh-clast	S/ R/CF	**-clast** *break down* **oste/o-** *bone*	Bone-removing cell
osteocyte	**OS**-tee-oh-site	S/ R/CF	**-cyte** *cell* **oste/o-** *bone*	Bone-maintaining cell
osteogenesis osteogenic (adj)	**OS**-tee-oh-**JEN**-eh-sis **OS**-tee-oh-**JEN**-ik	S/ R/CF	**-genesis** *creation* **oste/o-** *bone*	Creation of new bone
osteoporosis	**OS**-tee-oh-poh-**ROE**-sis	S/ R/CF R/	**-osis** *condition* **oste/o-** *bone* **-por-** *open*	Condition in which the bones become more porous, brittle, fragile, and more likely to fracture
periosteum periosteal (adj)	**PER**-ee-**OSS**-tee-um **PER**-ee-**OSS**-tee-al	S/ P/ R/	**-um** *structure* **peri-** *around* **oste-** *bone*	Strong membrane surrounding a bone
trochanter	troh-**KAN**-ter		Greek *runner*	One of two bony prominences near the head of the femur

EXERCISES

The combining form oste/o- means bone and is the main element in each of the following terms. You choose the correct suffix to complete the term. Fill in the blanks.

blast   **cyte**   **genesis**   **clast**   **genic**   **porosis**

The osteo_____ process begins with osteo_____, which produce the matrix of new bone tissue. Osteo_____ has begun. Once these cells incorporate into new bone, they are termed osteo_____. These cells maintain the matrix. Osteo_____ are produced by bone marrow. A delicate balance must be maintained between cells that remove matrix and cells that produce matrix. If more matrix is removed than produced, osteo_____ will result.

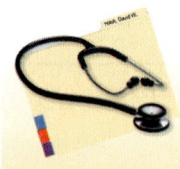

Case Report 5.1 (continued)

On questioning, Mrs. Vargas demonstrated many of the risk factors for osteoporosis, including a family history, lack of exercise, cigarette smoking, inadequate diet, postmenopause, and increasing age.

Normal bone   Osteoporotic bone

LM 5×

▲ **FIGURE 5.4   Normal Bone and Osteoporotic Bone.**

DISEASES OF BONE

Osteoporosis results from a loss of bone density *(Figure 5.4)* when the rate of bone **resorption** exceeds the rate of bone **formation**. It is more common in women than in men, and its incidence increases with age. Ten million people in the United States already have osteoporosis, and 18 million more have low bone density (**osteopenia**) and are at risk for developing osteoporosis.

In women, production of the hormone estrogen decreases after menopause, and its protection against osteoclast activity is lost. This leads to fragile, brittle bones. In men, reduction in testosterone has a similar but less marked effect.

Women at risk for osteoporosis should have bone mineral density (**BMD**) screening using a dual-energy x-ray absorptiometry (**DEXA**) scan. Men and women over age 50 should take 1200 mg of calcium daily and 400 to 600 international units (**IU**) of vitamin D or expose the body to the sun for 15 minutes daily. Chapter 22 covers nutritional needs.

There are several U.S. Food and Drug Administration (**FDA**)–approved medications available for the treatment of osteoporosis. Most inhibit osteoclast activity.

Osteomyelitis is an inflammation of an area of bone due to bacterial infection, usually with a staphylococcus. Untreated tuberculosis can spread from its original infection in the lungs to bones via the blood stream to produce tuberculous osteomyelitis.

Osteomalacia, known as **rickets** in children, is a disease caused by vitamin D deficiency. When bones lack calcium, they become soft and flexible. They are not strong enough to bear weight and become bowed. Osteomalacia occurs in some developing nations and occasionally in this country when children drink soft drinks instead of milk fortified with vitamin D.

Achondroplasia occurs when the long bones stop growing in childhood but the bones of the axial skeleton are not affected *(Figure 5.5)*. This leads to short stature individuals who are about four feet tall. Intelligence and life span are normal. It is caused by a spontaneous gene mutation that then becomes a dominant gene for succeeding generations.

Osteogenic sarcoma is the most common malignant bone tumor. Peak incidence is between 10 and 15 years of age, and the tumor often occurs around the knee joint.

Osteogenesis imperfecta is a rare genetic disorder, producing very brittle bones that are easily fractured, often **in utero** (while inside the uterus) *(Figure 5.6)*.

▲ **FIGURE 5.5   Achondroplastic Dwarf with College Roommate.**

Abbreviations

BMD   bone mineral density
DEXA   dual energy x-ray absorptiometry
FDA   U.S. Food and Drug Administration
IU   international unit(s)

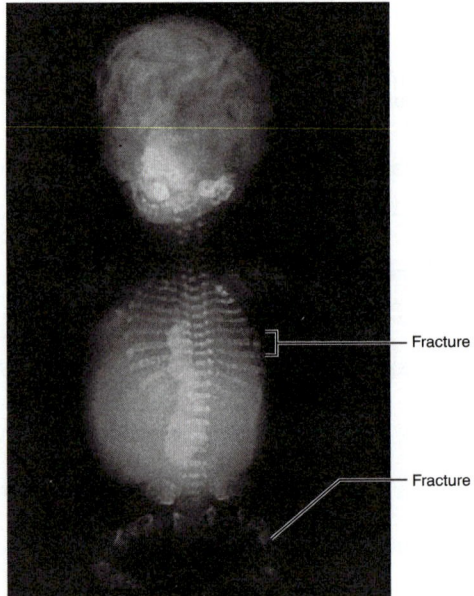

— Fracture

— Fracture

FIGURE 5.6   Osteogenesis Imperfecta *in utero* **Showing Fractured Rib and Thigh Bones.** ▶

WORD	PRONUNCIATION		ELEMENTS	DEFINITION
achondroplasia	a-kon-dro-**PLA**-ze-ah	S/ P/ R/CF	**-plasia** *formation* **a-** *without* **-chondr/o-** *cartilage*	Condition with abnormal conversion of cartilage into bone, leading to dwarfism
in utero	in **YOU**-ter-oh		Latin *uterus*	Within the womb; not yet born
osteogenesis imperfecta	**OS**-tee-oh-**JEN**-eh-sis im-per-**FEK**-tah	S/ R/CF R/	**-genesis** *creation* **oste/o-** *bone* **imperfecta** *unfinished*	Inherited condition when bone formation is incomplete, leading to fragile, easily broken bones
osteomalacia	**OS**-tee-oh-mah-**LAY**-she-ah	S/ R/CF	**-malacia** *softness* **oste/o-** *bone*	Soft, flexible bones lacking in calcium (rickets)
osteomyelitis	**OS**-tee-oh-my-eh-**LIE**-tis	S/ R/CF R/	**-itis** *inflammation* **oste/o-** *bone* **-myel-** *bone marrow*	Inflammation of bone tissue
osteopenia	**OS**-tee-oh-**PEE**-nee-ah	S/ R/CF	**-penia** *deficient* **oste/o-** *bone*	Decreased calcification of bone
resorption	ree-**SORP**-shun		Latin *to suck back*	Loss of substance, in this case bone
rickets	**RICK**-ets		Old English *to twist*	Disease due to vitamin D deficiency producing soft, flexible bones
sarcoma osteogenic sarcoma	sar-**KOH**-mah **OS**-tee-oh-**JEN**-ik sar-**KOH**-mah	S/ R/	**-oma** *tumor, mass* **sarc-** *flesh*	A malignant tumor originating in connective tissue Malignant tumor originating in bone-producing cells

EXERCISES

Bone diseases can strike at any age. Refer to the preceding WAD for the correct terminology to identify the disease. Fill in the blanks, then answer the questions.

Identify the disease.

1. Inflammation of an area of bone, usually due to staph infection _____

2. Bone disease in children caused by vitamin D deficiency_____

3. Leads to short stature (height)_____

4. Genetic bone disorder _____

5. Decreased calcification of bone _____

6. Most common malignant bone tumor _____

7. Also known as "rickets" in children _____

Questions 8 to 10 relate to the answers in questions 1 to 7 above.

8. Which root means *bone marrow?* _____

9. Which combining form means *cartilage?* _____

10. Which suffix means *formation?* _____

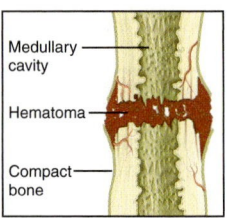
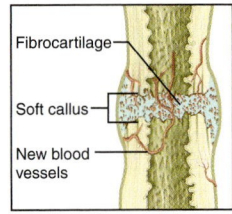

(a)　(b)

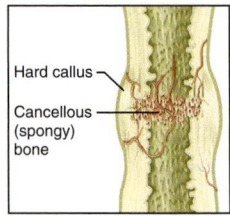
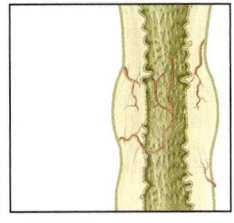

(c)　(d)

▲ **FIGURE 5.7   Healing of Bone Fracture.**

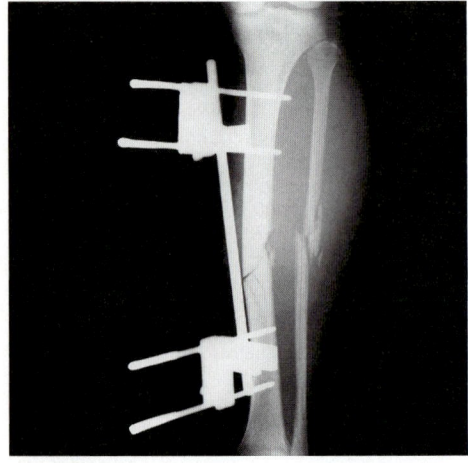

▲ **FIGURE 5.8   Radiograph of Fractured Limb.**
X-Ray of Lower Leg Fracture Set with Steel Pins and External Plate.

▼ **FIGURE 5.9   Internal Fixation of Fractures with Screws and Plate.**

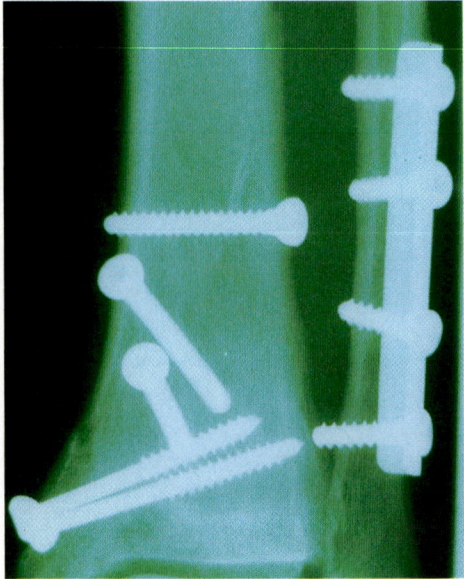

BONE FRACTURES

Healing of Fractures

Step 1: When a bone is fractured, blood vessels bleed into the fracture site, forming a **hematoma** *(Figure 5.7a)*.

Step 2: A few days after the fracture (Fx), osteoblasts move into the hematoma and start to produce new bone. This is called a **callus** *(Figure 5.7b)*.

Step 3: Osteoblasts produce immature, lacy, **cancellous** (spongy) bone that replaces the callus *(Figure 5.7c)*.

Step 4: Osteoblasts continue to produce bone cells. They produce compact bone and fuse the bone segments together *(Figure 5.7d)*.

Uncomplicated fractures take 8 to 12 weeks to heal.

Surgical Procedures for Repairing Fractures

The initial goal of fracture treatment is to bring the ends of the bone at the break back opposite each other so that they fit together as they did in the original bone. This is called **alignment**.

External manipulation is used frequently. The bone is pulled from the distal end back into alignment. This process is called **reduction**. Anesthesia may be used.

External fixation. The alignment is maintained by immobilizing the bone through the use of:

- **Plaster and fiberglass casts**
- **Splints**
- **Traction**—the gentle but continuous application of a pulling force that can align a fracture, reduce muscle spasm, and relieve pain.
- **External fixators**—by which the bone fragments are secured to a strong external steel rod or plate by means of steel pins *(Figure 5.8)*.

Internal fixation with materials such as stainless steel and titanium, which are compatible with tissues, enables the patient to return to function quicker and reduces the incidence of **nonunion** and **malunion** (improper healing). The types of internal fixation are:

- **Wires**—used as sutures to "sew" the bone fragments together; this method is often used in the hand.
- **Plates**—extend along both or all fragments of bone and are held in place by screws.
- **Rods**—can be inserted through the medullary cavity of both fragments to align the bones.
- **Screws**—can be used on their own as well as with plates; these are probably the most common form of internal fixation *(Figure 5.9)*.
- **Pins**—a long thick, metal pin can be driven down the shaft of a bone from one end.

WORD	PRONUNCIATION	ELEMENTS		DEFINITION
alignment	a-**LINE**-ment	S/ P/ R/	-ment *resulting state* a- (variant of **ad-**) *into* -lign- *line*	Having a structure in its correct position relative to other structures
callus (**Note:** *Callous* is a nonmedical word meaning *insensitive*.)	**KAL**-us		Latin *hard skin*	The mass of fibrous connective tissue that forms at a fracture site and becomes the foundation for the formation of new bone
cancellous	**KAN**-sell-us		Latin *lattice*	Bone that has a spongy or latticelike structure
hematoma	he-mah-**TOH**-mah	S/ R/	-oma *tumor, mass* hemat- *blood*	Collection of blood that has escaped from the blood vessels into tissue
malunion	mal-**YOU**-nee-un	S/ P/ R/	-ion *process* mal- *bad* -un- *one*	When the two bony ends of the fracture fail to heal together correctly
nonunion	non-**YOU**-nee-un	P/	non- *not*	Total failure of healing of a fracture
reduction	ree-**DUCK**-shun	S/ P/ R/	-ion *process* re- *backward* -duct- *lead*	Restore a structure to its normal position

EXERCISES

After you deconstruct the following medical terms into their basic elements, provide a brief definition for each term. Fill in the chart, then fill in the blanks at the end of the exercise.

Medical term	Prefix	Root/CF	Suffix	Definition of medical term
reduction				
alignment				
malunion				
hematoma				

Demonstrate your understanding of the terms by finishing this exercise.

1. Use *both* the terms **reduction** and **alignment** in *one sentence*.

_____

_____

2. The suffix **oma** also means *tumor.* Briefly explain why a hematoma is not a tumor.

_____

_____

3. Explain the difference between a **malunion** and a **nonunion** of a fracture.

_____

_____

_____

_____

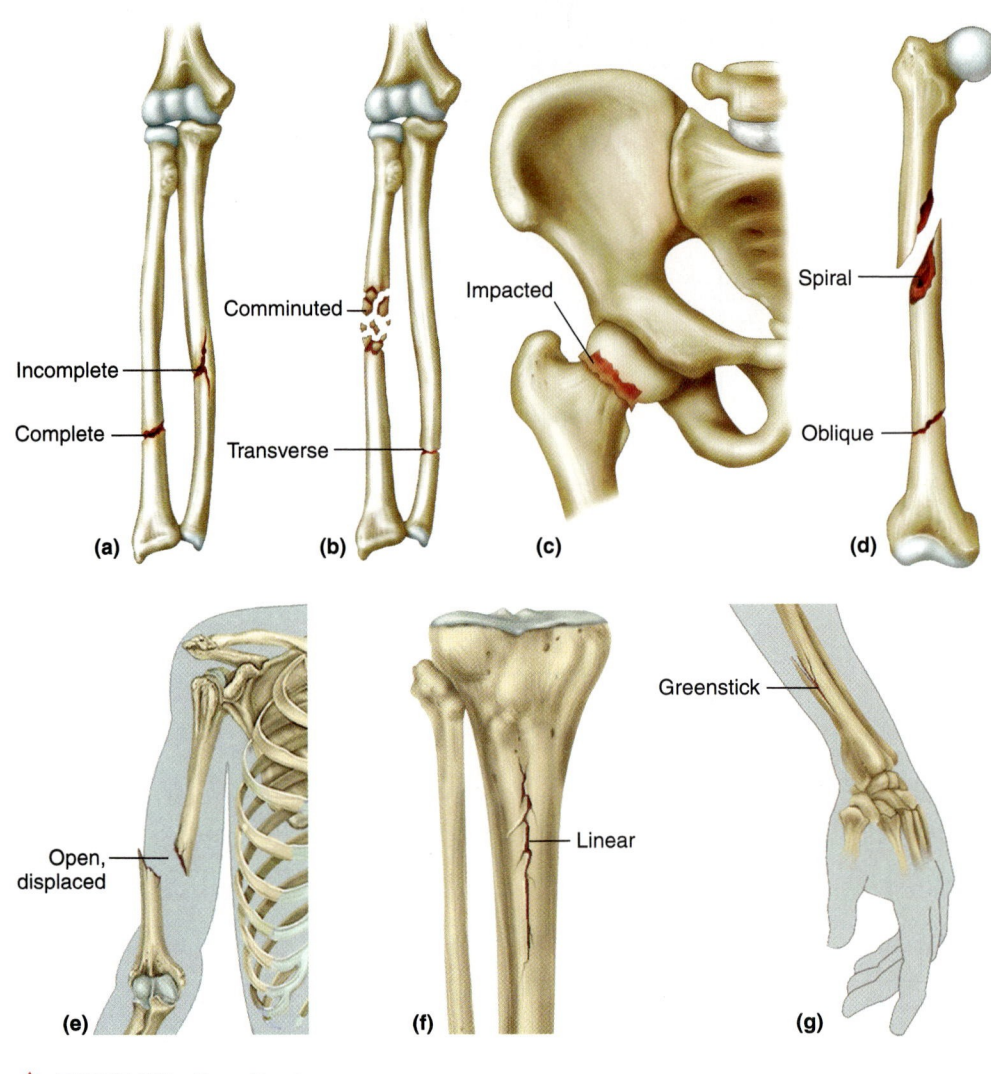

Incomplete

Complete

(a)

Comminuted

Transverse

(b)

Impacted

(c)

Spiral

Oblique

(d)

Open, displaced

(e)

Linear

(f)

Greenstick

(g)

▲ **FIGURE 5.10   Bone Fractures.**

TABLE 5.1 Classification of Bone Fractures

Name	Description	Reference
Closed	A bone is broken, but the skin is not broken	Figure 5.10g
Open	A fragment of the fractured bone breaks the skin, or when a wound extends to the site of the fracture	Figure 5.10e
Displaced	The fractured bone parts are out of alignment	Figure 5.10e
Complete	A bone is broken into at least two fragments	Figure 5.10a
Incomplete	The fracture does not extend completely across the bone; can be **hairline** (as in a stress fracture in the foot when there is no separation of the two fragments)	Figure 5.10a
Comminuted	The bone breaks into several pieces, usually two major pieces and several smaller fragments	Figure 5.10b
Transverse	The fracture is at right angles to the long axis of the bone	Figure 5.10b
Impacted	A fracture in which one bone fragment is driven into the other, with resulting shortening of a limb	Figure 5.10c
Spiral	Fracture spirals round the long axis of the bone	Figure 5.10d
Oblique	Diagonal fracture across the long axis of the bone	Figure 5.10d
Linear	Fracture runs parallel to the long axis of the bone	Figure 5.10f
Greenstick (closed)	Partial fracture: one side breaks, the other bends	Figure 5.10g
Pathologic	Fracture occurs in an area of bone weakened by disease (such as cancer)	—
Compression	Fracture occurs in a vertebra from trauma or pathology leading to the vertebra being crushed	—

WORD	PRONUNCIATION		ELEMENTS	DEFINITION
closed fracture (opposite of open)	KLOSD **FRAK**-chur	S/ R/	**closed** Latin *hard skin* -ure *result of* **fract-** *break up*	A bone is broken but the skin over it is intact
comminuted fracture	**KOM**-ih-nyu-ted	S/ R/	**-ed** *pertaining to* **comminut-** *break into small pieces*	A fracture in which the bone is broken into pieces
complete fracture	kom-**PLEET**		Latin *fill up*	A bone is fractured into two separate pieces
compression fracture	kom-**PRESH**-un	S/ R/	**-ion** *condition, action* **compress-** *press*	Fracture of a vertebra causing loss of height of the vertebra
displaced fracture	dis-**PLAYSD**	P/ R/	**dis-** *apart, away* **-placed** *in an area*	A fracture in which the fragments are separated and are not in alignment
greenstick fracture	**GREEN**-stik	R/ R/	**green-** *green* **-stick** *branch twig*	A fracture in which one side of the bone is partially broken and the other side is bent. Occurs mostly in children
hairline fracture	**HAIR**-line		Old English *hair* **line** Latin *a mark*	A fracture without separation of the fragments
impacted fracture	im-**PAK**-ted	S/ P/ R/	**-ed** *pertaining to* **im-** *in* **-pact** *driven in*	A fracture in which one bone fragment is driven into the other
incomplete fracture	in-kom-**PLEET**	P/ R/	**in-** *in* **-complete** *fill in*	A fracture that does not extend across the bone, as in a hairline fracture
linear fracture	**LIN**-ee-ar	S/ R/	**-ar** *pertaining to* **line-** *a mark*	A fracture running parallel to the length of the bone
oblique fracture	ob-**LEEK**		Latin *slanting*	A diagonal fracture across the long axis of the bone
open fracture	**OH**-pen		Old English *not enclosed*	The skin over the fracture is broken
spiral fracture	**SPY**-ral	S/ R/	**-al** *pertaining to* **spir-** *a coil*	A fracture in the shape of a coil
transverse fracture	trans-**VERS**	P/ R/	**trans-** *across* **-verse** *travel*	A fracture perpendicular to the long axis of the bone

EXERCISES

Fractures (Fxs). You are working as the new radiology technician in the Radiology Department at the hospital. You are attempting to identify the type of fracture with the picture you see on the film. Use the descriptions below to identify the type of fractures.

Fracture seen on the film	Type of fracture
Fx at right angles to the long axis of the radius	
the femur is broken into two clean pieces	
cancer patient with vertebral Fx	
broken ankle, but no broken skin	
diagonal Fx across the long axis of the femur	
fractured hand with bone fragments sticking out	
Fx runs parallel to the long axis of the bone	
fractured elbow, misaligned	

1. Which one is an open fracture?. _____

2. Which one is a closed fracture?. _____

LESSON 5.2 Joints

MUSCULOSKELETAL SYSTEM

OBJECTIVES

Without joints you would be a statue. Joints allow you to move, but movable parts that rub together can wear out. Damage or disease in a joint can make movement very difficult and painful. The structure of any joint, or **articulation,** is directly related to its mobility and function.

In order for you to understand, describe and document your patient's joint problems, you need to be able to:

- **Classify the different types of joints.**
- **Identify the tissues that form the different joints.**
- **Link structure to the functions of the different joints.**
- **Demonstrate an understanding of the major problems and diseases that occur in joints.**

You are

. . . an orthopedic technologist working for orthopedic surgeon, Kenneth Stannard, MD, at Fulwood Medical Center.

Your patient is

. . . Mr. Hank Johnson, a 63-year-old white male. Mr. Johnson has been active all his life.

CASE REPORT 5.2

In his youth Mr. Johnson played football and baseball. As an adult, he has played racquetball weekly and jogged three to four miles most mornings on the streets of his neighborhood. For the past year he has had lower back stiffness and pain, particularly in the mornings. Six months ago while out hiking, he slid down a mountain on his left side for about 100 feet. He is now having pain in his left groin and thigh, with difficulty walking and climbing stairs.

You are responsible for documenting the doctor's diagnostic procedures and treatment and for making sure that the patient understands the significance of the diagnostic findings and the recommendations for his treatment.

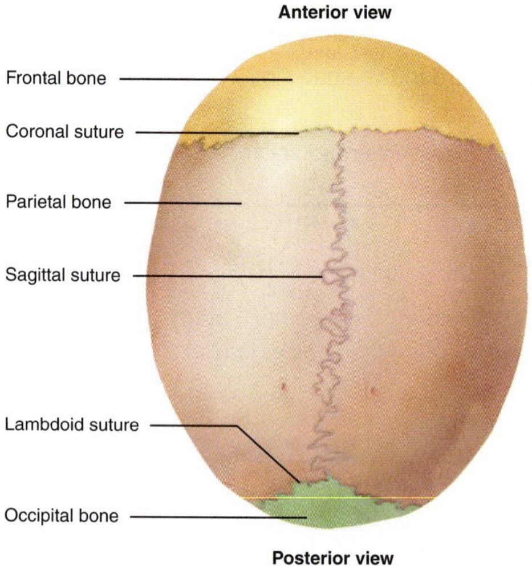

Anterior view

Frontal bone

Coronal suture

Parietal bone

Sagittal suture

Lambdoid suture

Occipital bone

Posterior view

▲ **FIGURE 5.11   Sutures of Skull: Superior View.**

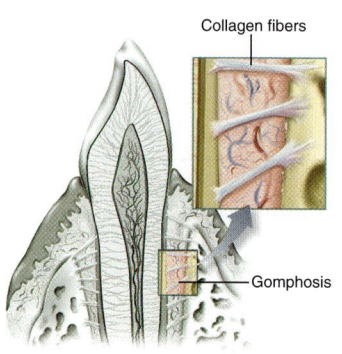

Collagen fibers

Gomphosis

◀ **FIGURE 5.12   Gomphosis Between Tooth and Jaw Socket.**

CLASSES OF JOINTS

Joints are classified structurally as three types:

1. **Fibrous** joints are two bones tightly bound together by bands of fibrous tissue with no joint space. They come in three varieties:

   a. **Sutures** between the bones of the skull *(Figure 5.11);* the two opposing bones have interlocking processes to add stability to the joint. The **periosteum** on the outer and inner surfaces of the two bones is continuous and holds the joint together.

   b. **Syndesmosis,** a joining of two bones with fibrous ligaments. Their movement is minimal. An example is above the ankle where the tibia and fibula are attached.

   c. **Gomphoses** are pegs that fit into sockets and are held in place by fine collagen fibers. Examples are the joints between teeth and their sockets *(Figure 5.12).*

2. **Cartilaginous** joints join two bones with cartilage:

   a. **Synchondroses** join the two bones with **hyaline** cartilage, which allows little or no movement between them, as between your ribs and costal cartilages.

   b. **Symphyses** join two bones with **fibrocartilage.** An example is the symphysis pubis where your two pubic bones meet at the front of your pelvis.

WORD ANALYSIS AND DEFINITION

WORD	PRONUNCIATION		ELEMENTS	DEFINITION
articulation articulate (verb) articular (adj)	ar-tic-you-**LAY**-shun ar-**TIK**-you-late ar-**TIK**-you-lar	S/ R/	**-ation** *process, being* **articul-** *joint*	A joint
bursa	**BURR**-sah		Latin *purse*	A closed sac containing synovial fluid
fibrocartilage	fie-bro-**KAR**-til-age	R/CF R/	**fibr/o-** *fiber* **-cartilage** *cartilage*	Cartilage containing collagen fibers
gomphosis gomphoses (pl)	gom-**FOE**-sis gom-**FOE**-sees	S/ R/	**-osis** *condition* **gomph-** *bolt, nail*	Joint formed by a peg and socket
hyaline	**HIGH**-ah-line		Greek *glass*	Cartilage that looks like frosted glass and contains fine collagen fibers
meniscus menisci (pl)	meh-**NISS**-kuss meh-**NISS**-key		Greek *crescent*	Disc of connective tissue cartilage between the bones of a joint, for example, in the knee joint
suture sutures (pl)	**SOO**-chur		Latin *a seam*	Two bones are joined together by a fibrous band continuous with their periosteum, as in the skull
symphysis symphyses (pl)	**SIM**-feh-sis **SIM**-feh-sees		Greek *growing together*	Two bones joined by fibrocartilage
synchondrosis synchondroses (pl)	sin-kon-**DROH**-sis sin-kon-**DROH**-sees	S/ P/ R/	**-osis** *condition* **syn-** *together* **-chondr-** *cartilage*	Binding together of joint with cartilage
syndesmosis syndesmoses (pl)	sin-dez-**MOH**-sis sin-dez-**MOH**-sees	S/ R/	**-osis** *condition* **syndesm-** *bind together*	Binding together of two bones with ligaments
synovial	si-**NOH**-vee-al	S/ P/ R/CF	**-al** *pertaining to* **syn-** *together* **-ov/i-** *egg*	Pertaining to synovial fluid and synovial membrane

3. **Synovial** joints contain synovial fluid as a lubricant and allow considerable movement *(Figure 5.13)*. Most joints in the legs and arms are synovial joints. The ends of the bones are covered with hyaline **articular** cartilage. In some joints, an additional plate of fibrocartilage is located between the two bones. In the knee, this plate is incomplete and is called a **meniscus**.
A **bursa** is an extension of the synovial joint that forms a cushion between structures that otherwise would rub against each other; for example, in the knee joint between the patellar tendon and the patellar and tibial bones *(Figure 5.13)*.

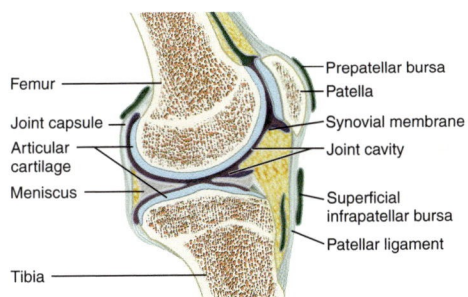

▲ **FIGURE 5.13   Synovial Joint.**

EXERCISES

You must be able to recognize a medical term in its singular or plural form. In the following chart check (✓) in the appropriate column whether the given term is singular or plural. If you have checked singular, write the plural form of the term in the appropriate column; if you have checked plural, write the singular form of the term in the appropriate column. Fill in the chart, then write the definitions.

Medical term	Singular	Plural
syndesmoses		
suture		
gomphosis		
menisci		

Define any two of these terms in a sentence.

1. _____

2. _____

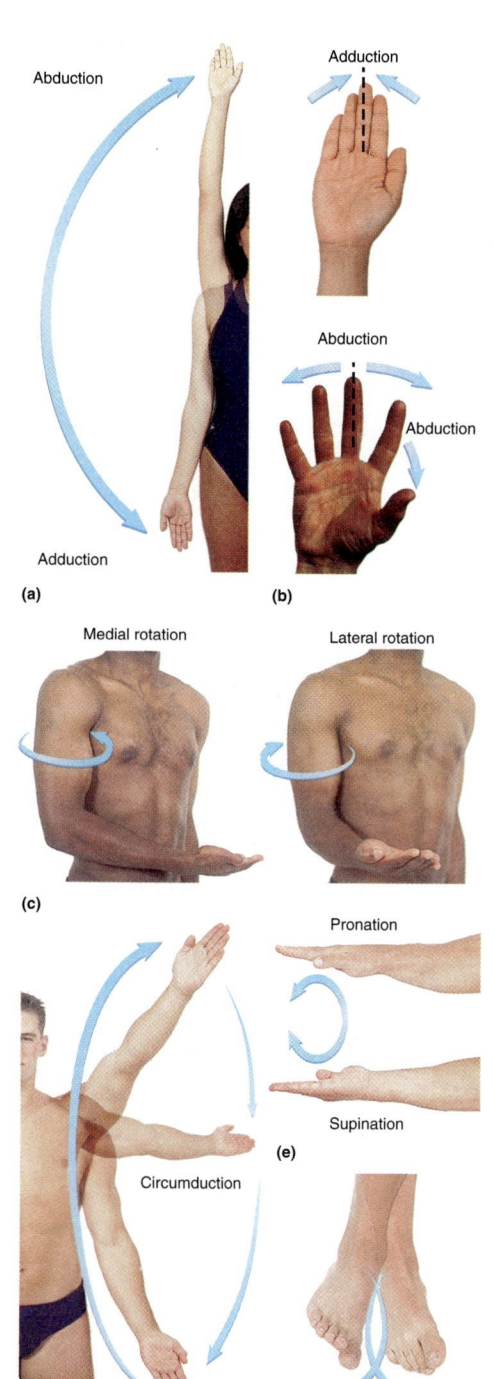

▲ **FIGURE 5.15a, b   Movement of the Limbs**
(a) Abduction and adduction of the upper limb. (b) Abduction and adduction of the fingers.
FIGURE 5.15c
(c) Medial and Lateral Rotation of the Arm.
FIGURE 5.15d
(d) Circumduction.
FIGURE 5.15e
(e) Pronation and Supination of the Hand.
FIGURE 5.15f
(f) Eversion and Inversion of the Foot.

▲ **Figure 5.14   Joint Flexion and Extension.** (a) Flexion of the elbow. (b) Extension of the elbow. (c) extension of the wrist. (d) Neutral position of the wrist. (e) Flexion of the wrist. (f) Flexion of the spine. (g) Flexion of the shoulder. (h) Extension of shoulder.

JOINT MOVEMENT

Flexion and Extension of Joints

Flexion (bending) and **extension** (straightening) are shown in the elbow joint (*Figure 5.14a and b*), in the wrist joint (*Figure 5.14c, d, and e*), and in the shoulder joint (*Figure 5.14g and h*).

For most of the rest of the body, flexion is movement of a body part *anterior* to the **coronal plane** (*see Chapter 2*). Extension is movement *posterior* to the coronal plane. For example, when you bend your trunk forward, that is flexion (*Figure 5.14f*). When you bend your trunk backward, that is extension (*see Figure 5.14g*). When you bend your trunk sideways to the right or left, that is called *lateral flexion*.

Abduction and Adduction of Joints

Abduction is movement away from the midline. **Adduction** is movement toward the midline. Abduction of your arm is moving it sideways away from your trunk. Adduction is bringing it back to the side of your trunk (*Figure 5.15a*). Abduction of your fingers is spreading them apart away from the middle finger. Adduction is bringing them back together (*Figure 5.15b*).

Rotation of Joints

Rotation is to turn around an axis. Medial rotation of the upper arm bone, the humerus, with the elbow flexed brings the palm of the hand toward the body. Lateral rotation moves the palm away from the body (*Figure 5.15c*).

Pronation and Supination

When you lie flat on the ground face down on your belly with your palms touching the ground, you are **prone.** When you lie flat on your back with your spine on the floor and your palms facing up, you are **supine.**

WORD	PRONUNCIATION	ELEMENTS		DEFINITION
abduction abduct (verb)	ab-**DUCK**-shun ab-**DUKT**	S/ P/ R/	-ion *process, action* **ab-** *away from* -duct- *lead*	Action of moving away from the midline
adduction adduct (verb)	ah-**DUCK**-shun ah-**DUCKT**	S/ P/ R/	-ion *process, action* **ad-** *toward* -duct- *lead*	Action of moving toward the midline
circumduction circumduct (verb)	ser-kum-**DUCK**-shun ser-kum-**DUCKT**	S/ P/ R/	-ion *process, action* **circum-** *around* -duct- *lead*	Movement of an extremity in a circular motion
coronal plane	**KOR**-oh-nal PLAIN	S/ R/	-al *pertaining to* **coron-** *crown* **plane,** Latin *flat*	Vertical plane dividing the body into anterior and posterior portions
eversion evert (verb)	ee-**VER**-shun ee-**VERT**		Latin *overturn*	Turn outward
extension	eks-**TEN**-shun		Latin *stretch out*	Straighten a joint to increase its angle
flexion	**FLEK**-shun		Latin *to bend*	Bend a joint to decrease its angle
inversion invert (verb)	in-**VER**-shun in -**VERT**		Latin *to turn about*	Turn inward
prone pronation pronate (verb)	PRONE pro-**NAY**-shun **PRO**-nate	S/ R/ S/	Latin *prone, lying down* **pronat-** *bend down* -ion *process, action*	Lying face down, flat on your belly Process of lying face down or of turning a hand or foot with the volar (palm or sole) surface down
supine supination	soo-**PINE** soo-pih-**NAY**-shun	S/ R/	Latin *supine, lying face up* -ion *process, action* **supinat-** *bend backward*	Lying face up, flat on your spine Process of lying face upward or turning an arm or foot so that the palm or sole is facing up

When you rotate your forearm so that your palm faces the floor, that is **pronation**. When you rotate the forearm so that your palm is facing upwards, that is **supination** *(Figure 5.15d)*.

Circumduction of Joints

Circumduction of the shoulder is moving it in a circular movement so that it forms a cone, with the shoulder joint as the apex of the cone *(Figure 5.15d)*.

Inversion and Eversion

When you turn your ankle so that the sole of your foot faces toward the opposite foot, that is supination or **inversion**. When you turn your ankle so that the sole of the foot faces laterally away from the other foot, that is pronation or **eversion** *(Figure 5.15f)*.

> ### Study Hint
> In English, to "abduct" someone is to lead them *away from* (their family) or to kidnap them. Abduction is moving *away from* the midline of the body. Adduction is the *opposite* of abduction.

EXERCISES

Some medical terms can act as both a verb (action) and/or a noun (person, place or thing). The following pairs of terms are both verbs and nouns. Write the correct form of the term in the blank(s).

1. circumduct   circumduction

   The baseball pitcher was unable to

   _____ his arm to wind up his pitch.

2. invert   inversion

   A club foot would be an _____ of the foot.

3. abduct   abduction

   Moving away from the midline of the body is called

   _____.

4. evert   eversion

   The patient was unable to _____ his ankle due to great pain.

5. adduct   adduction

   The patient was asked to _____ his arms from a horizontal plane toward the center of his chest.

Abbreviations

DJD	degenerative joint disease
MCP	metacarpophalangeal
OA	osteoarthritis
PIP	proximal interphalangeal
THR	total hip replacement
RA	rheumatoid arthritis

Case Report 5.2 (continued)

By age 65, more than 80% of people have some degree of joint degeneration. Mr. Johnson had always been very physically active, putting a lot of pressure on his weight-bearing joints. At different times in his life he had been overweight, adding to the pressure.

X-rays of his lower back showed **osteoarthritis** of his lower lumbar intervertebral joints and marked osteoarthritis of his left hip joint (Figures 5.16a and b). He received a left total hip replacement **(THR)** and physiotherapy for his lower back.

DISEASES OF JOINTS

Osteoarthritis (OA) is caused by the breakdown and eventual destruction of cartilage in a joint. It develops as a result of wear and tear and is most common in the weight-bearing joints, the knee, hip, and lower back *(Figure 5.16)*. Because it is a wear-and-tear disease, it is sometimes called **degenerative joint disease (DJD)**. The degenerative process begins in the articular cartilage, which cracks and frays, eventually exposing the underlying bone.

Rheumatoid arthritis (RA) is a chronic, inflammatory disease that can affect many joints, causing deformity and disability. In *Figure 5.16c*, the hand deformities of RA, swelling of the **metacarpophalangeal (MCP)** and **proximal interphalangeal (PIP)** joints with **ulnar deviation** of the fingers are shown. The disease process initially causes inflammation of the synovial membrane and then spreads to all other parts of the joint. In *Figure 5.16d*, the x-ray shows the digestion of bone and cartilage. Rheumatoid arthritis is three times as common in women and often begins in the thirties and forties.

Bursitis is inflammation of a **bursa** that can result from overuse of a joint, repeated trauma, or diseases such as RA.

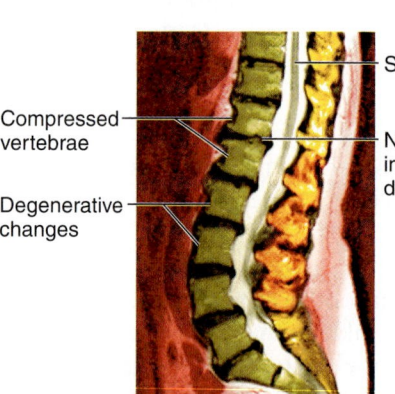

(a) Lumbar vertebrae

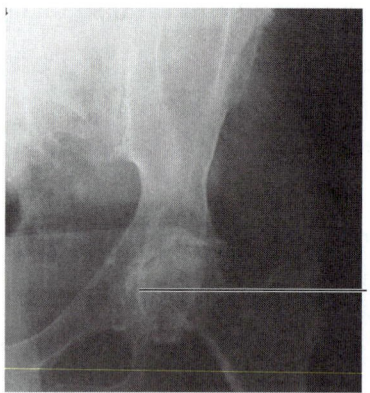

(b) Hip joint

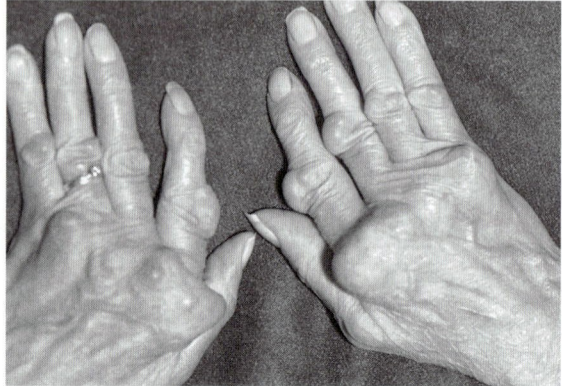

(c)

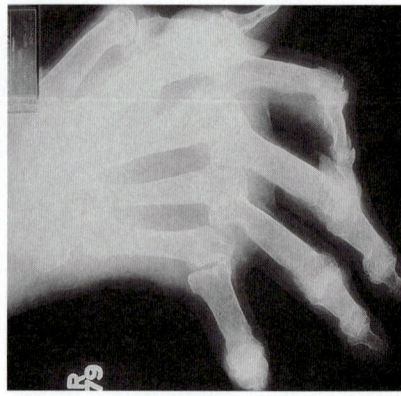

(d)

FIGURE 5.16 Arthritis.
(*a*) MRI Scan of Lumbar Vertebrae Showing Degenerative Changes Due to Osteoarthritis. (*b*) Osteoarthritis of hip. (*c* and *d*) Rheumatoid arthritis.

WORD	PRONUNCIATION	ELEMENTS		DEFINITION
arthrocentesis	AR-throw-sen-TEE-sis	S/ R/	-centesis *to puncture* arthr/o- *joint*	Withdrawal of fluid from a joint through a needle
arthrodesis	ar-THROW-dee-sis	S/ R/CF	-desis *bind together* arthr/o- *joint*	Fixation or stiffening of a joint by surgery
arthrography	ar-THROG-ra-fee	S/ R/CF	-graphy *record* arthr/o- *joint*	X-ray of a joint taken after the injection of a contrast medium into the joint
arthroplasty	AR-throw-plas-tee	S/ R/CF	-plasty *repair* arthr/o- *joint*	Surgery to restore as far as possible the function of a joint
arthroscopy	ar-THROS-koh-pee	S/ R/CF	-scopy *examine* arthr/o- *joint*	Visual examination of the interior of a joint
arthroscope	AR-thro-skope	S/	-scope *instrument*	Endoscope used to examine the interior of a joint
bursa bursitis	BURR-sah burr-SIGH-tis	S/	Latin *purse* -itis *inflammation*	A closed sac containing synovial fluid Inflammation of a bursa
degenerative	dee-JEN-er-a-tiv	S/ R/	-ive *quality of* degenerat- *deteriorate*	Relating to the deterioration of a structure
deviation	de-ve-A-shun		Latin *turn from straight path*	Turn aside from normal course
interphalangeal	IN-ter-fay-LAN-jee-al	S/ P/ R/CF	-al *pertaining to* inter- *between* -phalang/e- *phalanx*	Finger or toe joint between two phalanges
metacarpophalangeal	MET-ah-KAR-poh-fay-LAN-jee-al	S/ R/CF P/ R/CF	-al *pertaining to* -phalang/e- *phalanx, finger, toe* meta- *after, transition* -carp/o- *wrist*	The articulations (joints) between the metacarpal bones and phalanges
osteoarthritis	OS-tee-oh-ar-THRI-tis	S/ R/CF R/	-itis *inflammation* oste/o- *bone* -arthr- *joint*	Chronic inflammatory disease of the joints with pain and loss of function
rheumatoid arthritis (RA)	RU-mah-toyd ar-THRI-tis	S/ P/	-oid *resemblance* rheumat- *rheumatism*	Disease of connective tissue, with arthritis as a major manifestation
ulna	UL-na	R/	ulna *forearm bone*	The medial and larger of the bones of the forearm
ulnar	UL-nar	S/ R/	-ar *pertaining to* uln- *forearm bone*	Pertaining to the ulna or any of the structures (artery, vein, nerve) named after it

EXERCISES

There are seven terms in this WAD all using the root or combining form arthr/arthro-. For questions 1 through 5, match the description of the procedure for which each patient is scheduled in column 1 with the name of the procedure the doctor has ordered in column 2. Then fill in the blanks.

_____ 1. x-ray of a joint after contrast medium injection

_____ 2. withdrawal of fluid from the joint with a needle

_____ 3. surgery to restore/repair joint function

_____ 4. surgical fixation of the joint

_____ 5. visual examination of the interior of the joint

A. arthrodesis

B. arthroplasty

C. arthroscopy

D. arthrography

E. arthrocentesis

6. The procedure in question 5 will use an arthro _____.

7. The diagnosis for all these patients could be arthr _____.

LESSON 5.3 Muscles and Tendons

OBJECTIVES

In the previous two lessons in this chapter, you have learned how bones of the skeleton support the body and how joints provide mobility. Neither of these functions can occur without muscles to provide both posture and movement. Information in this lesson will enable you to:

- **Identify the functions of skeletal muscle and tendons.**
- **Describe the structure of skeletal muscle and tendons.**
- **Demonstrate an understanding of the major problems and diseases that occur in muscles and tendons.**

You are

...a medical assistant working with Susan Lee, MD, a primary care physician at Fulwood Medical Center.

Your patient is

...Mrs. Mary Carr, a 65-year-old white, retired librarian, who had been in good health until a month ago when she had sudden onset of pain in the muscles of her shoulders and hips.

CASE REPORT 5.3

The pain has become more severe and spread into Mrs. Carr's upper arms, thighs, and lower back. She cannot turn over in bed and cannot get into her car. She has lost ten pounds in weight and feels constantly tired.

Dr. Lee has diagnosed **polymyalgia rheumatica** and prescribed prednisone, 5 mg t.i.d. (three times daily). There has been a marked improvement in her symptoms.

Your role as Dr. Lee's assistant is to ensure that Mrs. Carr understands the use of her medication and to document changes in her symptoms.

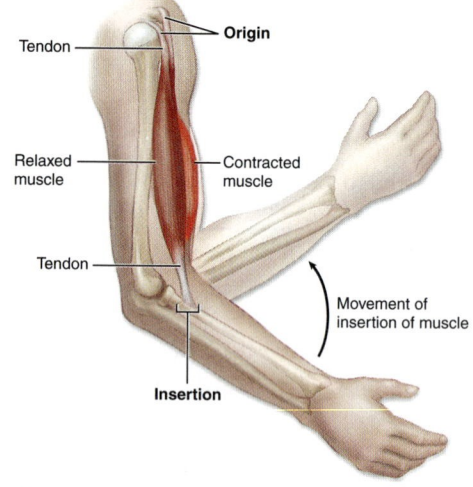

▲ **FIGURE 5.17 Muscle Contraction.**

Tendon — Origin
Relaxed muscle — Contracted muscle
Tendon —
Movement of insertion of muscle
Insertion

Abbreviation

t.i.d. (Latin *ter in die*) three times a day

FUNCTIONS AND STRUCTURE OF SKELETAL MUSCLE

Functions of Skeletal Muscle

Skeletal muscle is attached to one or more bones. It is called **voluntary** because it is under conscious control. Because of their length, muscle cells are usually called muscle **fibers.** Each skeletal muscle consists of bundles of muscle fibers, blood vessels, and nerves, with connective tissue sheets that hold the fibers together and connect the muscle to bone.

Skeletal muscle has the following functions:

1. **Movement**—All skeletal muscles are attached to bones, and when a muscle **contracts** it causes movement of the bones to which it is attached *(Figure 5.17)*. This enables you to walk, run, and work with your hands.
2. **Posture**—The **tone** of skeletal muscles holds you straight when sitting, standing, or moving.
3. **Body heat**—When skeletal muscles contract, heat is produced as a by-product of the energy reaction. This heat is essential to maintain your body temperature.
4. **Respiration**—Skeletal muscles move the chest wall as you breathe.
5. **Communication**—Skeletal muscles enable you to speak, write, type, gesture, and grimace.

Structure of Skeletal Muscle

Skeletal **fibers** are narrow and long, up to 1½ inches (approximately 3.7 cm) in length. Each muscle fiber has a thin layer of connective tissue around it. Bundles of muscle fibers are grouped together into **fascicles** that are also surrounded by a layer of connective tissue. Skeletal muscle fibers contain alternating dark and light bands (**striations**) created by the pattern of protein filaments responsible for

WORD	PRONUNCIATION	ELEMENTS		DEFINITION
atrophy	**AT**-roh-fee	P/ R/	a- *without* -trophy *nourishment*	Wasting or diminished volume of a tissue or organ
contract	kon-**TRAKT**	P/ R/	con- *with, together* -tract *draw*	Draw together or shorten
fascia	**FASH**-ee-ah		Latin *a band*	Sheet of fibrous connective tissue
fascicle	**FAS**-ih-kull		Latin *small bundle*	Bundle of muscle fibers
fiber	**FIE**-bur		Latin *fiber*	A strand or filament
hypertrophy	high-**PER**-troh-fee	P/ R/	hyper- *excessive* -trophy *nourishment*	Increase in size, but not in number, of an individual tissue element
polymyalgia rheumatica	poll-ee-my-**AL**-jee-ah rue-**MAT**-ick-ah	S/ P/ R/ S/ R/	-algia *pain* poly- *many* -my- *muscle* -ica *pertaining to* rheumat- *rheumatism*	Pain in several muscle groups with systemic symptoms
striation striated muscle	stri-**AY**-shun **STRI**-ay-ted **MUSS**-el		Latin *stripe*	Stripes Another term for skeletal muscle
tone	TONE		Greek *tone*	Tension present in resting muscles
voluntary muscle	**VOL**-un-tare-ee **MUSS**-el	S/ R/	-ary *pertaining to* volunt- *free will*	Muscle that is under the control of the will

muscle contraction. Skeletal muscle can be referred to as **striated muscle**.

Bundles of fascicles form a muscle that is separated from adjacent muscles and kept in position by a dense layer of connective tissue called **fascia** *(Figure 5.18)*. Fascia extends beyond the muscle to form a tendon. The tendon attaches to the periosteum of a bone at the origin and insertion of the muscle.

You have the same number of muscle fibers as an adult that you had in late childhood. When you exercise and/or lift weights and your muscles enlarge or **hypertrophy**, you have increased the thickness of each muscle fiber. If you do not use your muscles, the reverse happens, and the muscles **atrophy**.

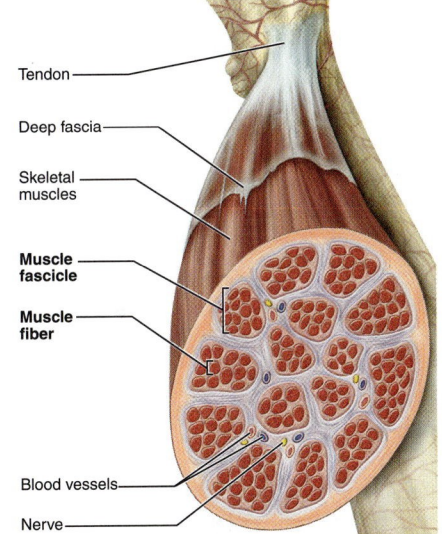

Tendon
Deep fascia
Skeletal muscles
Muscle fascicle
Muscle fiber
Blood vessels
Nerve

FIGURE 5.18   Structure of Skeletal Muscle.

EXERCISES

Deconstruct the following medical terms from the WAD into their basic elements, then define each element. Fill in the chart, then answer the questions about the prefixes and suffixes.

Medical term	Prefix	Meaning of Prefix	Root(s)/CF	Meaning of Root(s)/CF	Suffix	Meaning of Suffix
hypertrophy						
contract						
polymyalgia						
atrophy						
rheumatica						

1. Which term has no prefix? _____

2. Which terms have no suffix? _____

DISORDERS OF SKELETAL MUSCLES

Muscle soreness may be a result of vigorous exercise, particularly if your muscles are not used to it. Exercise causes build up of lactic acid in muscle fibers, and the resulting inflammation of them and their surrounding connective tissue produces soreness.

Muscle cramps are sudden, painful contractions of a muscle or group of muscles. They are usually of short duration. The etiology of cramp is unknown, but low blood potassium, calcium and magnesium levels, use of caffeine and tobacco, and diminished blood supply are possible causes. There are no effective medications available. The cramp is usually self-limiting.

Muscle strains range from a simple stretch in the muscle or **tendon** to a partial or complete tear in the muscle or muscle-tendon combination. Most strains heal with "R.I.C.E" (rest, ice, compression [elastic bandage] and elevation) *(Figure 5.19)*, followed by simple exercises to relieve pain and restore mobility. A complete tear may require surgical repair.

A **sprain** is a stretch or tear of a ligament, often of the ankle, knee, or wrist. It is also treated by R.I.C.E.

Anabolic steroids are related to testosterone but have been altered so that their main effect is to cause skeletal muscle to hypertrophy. They are used illegally in many sports to increase muscle strength. They have marked, often irreversible side effects, including stunting the height of growing adolescents, shrinking testes and sperm counts, masculinizing women, delusions, and paranoid jealousy. In the long term, there are increased risks of heart attacks and strokes, kidney failure, and liver tumors.

Fibromyalgia affects muscles and tendons all over the body, causing chronic pain associated with fatigue and depression. Its etiology is unknown. There are no laboratory tests for it and no specific treatment except pain management, physiotherapy, and stress reduction.

Myasthenia gravis is a chronic autoimmune disease *(see Chapter 15)* characterized by varying degrees of weakness of the skeletal muscles. The weakness increases with activity and decreases with rest. Facial muscles are often involved, causing problems with eye and eyelid movements, chewing, and talking. Antibodies produced by the body's own immune system block the passage of **neurotransmitters** from motor nerves to muscles. **Thymectomy** is usually recommended. **Cholinesterase inhibitors** *(Chapter 10)* such as Prostigmin are also used.

Muscular dystrophy is a general term for a group of hereditary, progressive disorders affecting skeletal muscles. **Duchenne muscular dystrophy (DMD)** is the most common, beginning with difficulty walking in boys around the age of three. Generalized muscle weakness and atrophy progress, and few live beyond twenty years. There is no effective treatment.

Rhabdomyolysis is the breakdown of muscle fibers. This releases a protein pigment called **myoglobin** into the bloodstream. Myoglobin breaks down into toxic compounds that cause kidney failure. Rhabdomyolysis can be caused by muscle trauma, severe exertion (marathon running), alcoholism, and use of cocaine, heroin, amphetamines, or phencyclidine (**PCP**).

Tenosynovitis is inflammation of the sheath that surrounds a **tendon**. It is usually related to repetitive use and occurs commonly in the wrist and hands. It produces pain, tenderness in the tendon, and difficulty in movement of a joint. Treatment is rest, immobilization, nonsteroidal anti-inflammatory drugs (**NSAIDs**), local corticosteroid injections, and, occasionally, surgery.

▲ **FIGURE 5.19   R.I.C.E. Treatment.**

Abbreviations

DMD   Duchenne muscular dystrophy
NSAID   nonsteroidal anti-inflammatory drug
PCP   phencyclidine (angel dust)
R.I.C.E.   rest, ice, compression and elevation

WORD	PRONUNCIATION	ELEMENTS		DEFINITION
Duchenne muscular dystrophy	**DOO**-shen **MUSS**-kyu-lar **DISS**-troh-fee		Guillaume Benjamin Duchenne, French neurologist, 1806–1875	Symmetrical weakness and wasting of pelvic, shoulder, and proximal limb muscles
		P/	dys- *bad, difficult*	
		R/	-trophy *nourishment*	
fibromyalgia	fie-bro-my-**AL**-jee-ah	S/	-algia *pain*	Pain in the muscle fibers
		R/CF	fibr/o- *fiber*	
		R/	-my- *muscle*	
myoglobin	**MY**-oh-**GLOW**-bin	S/	-in *substance*	Protein of muscle that stores and transports oxygen
		R/CF	my/o- *muscle*	
		R/	-glob- *globe*	
neurotransmitter (***Note:*** Transmitter is a word in itself and begins with a prefix.)	**NYUR**-oh-trans-**MIT**-er	S/	-er *doer*	Chemical agent that relays messages from one nerve cell to the next
		R/	neuro- *nerve*	
		P/	-trans- *across*	
		R/	-mitt- *send*	
rhabdomyolysis	**RAB**-doh-my-oh-**LIE**-sis	S/	-lysis *break down, dissolve*	Destruction of muscle to produce myoglobin
		R/CF	rhabd/o- *rod shaped*	
		R/CF	-my/o- *muscle*	
sprain	SPRAIN		root unknown	A wrench or tear in a ligament
strain	STRAIN		Latin *to bind*	Overstretch or tear in a muscle or tendon
tendon tendinitis (also spelled tendonitis)	**TEN**-dun ten-dih-**NYE**-tis	S/ R/	Latin *sinew* -itis *inflammation* tendin- *tendon*	Fibrous band that connects muscle to bone Inflammation of a tendon
tenosynovitis	**TEN**-oh-sin-oh-**VIE**-tis	S/	-itis *inflammation*	Inflammation of a tendon and its surrounding sheath
		R/CF	ten/o- *tendon*	
		R/	-synov- *synovial membrane*	
thymectomy	thigh-**MEK**-toe-me	S/	-ectomy *surgical excision*	Surgical removal of the thyroid gland
		R/	thym- *thymus gland*	

EXERCISES

The following elements are all contained in the WAD shown above. Circle the best answer.

1. The suffix -**itis** means: condition disease inflammation

2. **Dys** is a: suffix prefix root

3. The root **trophy-** means: condition procedure nourishment

4. **Fibro** is a: combining form root suffix

5. The root **my-** means: tendon ligament muscle

6. The suffix -**algia** means: inflammation pain swelling

7. **Fibro** means: fascia fascicle fiber

8. **Dys** means: painful bad excessive

9. **Teno** is a: prefix root combining form

LESSON 5.4 Axial Skeleton

OBJECTIVES

In order to treat patients with spinal injuries and educate them about their problems, you must have a complete knowledge about the structure and functions of their vertebral columns and joints and muscles.

The vertebral column is part of the axial skeleton. In this lesson, information about the axial skeleton with its joints and the muscles that function in an integrated manner will enable you to:

- **Name the regions and bones of the vertebral column.**
- **Describe an intervertebral joint.**
- **Identify the major muscles that hold the vertebral column erect.**
- **Explain the major problems and diseases that affect the vertebral column.**
- **Name the bones of the skull.**
- **Identify the major muscles of mastication and respiration.**

You are

. . . a physical therapist assistant working in the physical therapy department of Fulwood Medical Center.

Your patient is

. . . Ms. Nancy Cardenas, a 27-year-old jeweler. Ms. Cardenas was waiting in her car at a traffic light three days ago when her car was rear-ended.

CASE REPORT 5.4

She now has severe neck pain radiating down her left arm, with dizziness and headaches. She is unable to go to work. Dr. Stannard has examined her and diagnosed her as a whiplash injury. An MRI (magnetic resonance image) shows **herniation** of intervertebral discs between C5–C6 and C6–C7. Your role is to implement a regime of physiotherapy, including range of motion (ROM) exercises for her neck joints.

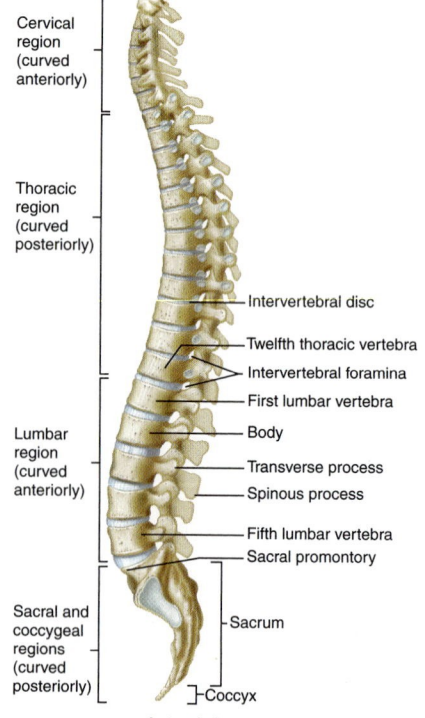

Cervical region (curved anteriorly)

Thoracic region (curved posteriorly)

Intervertebral disc
Twelfth thoracic vertebra
Intervertebral foramina
First lumbar vertebra
Body
Transverse process
Spinous process

Lumbar region (curved anteriorly)

Fifth lumbar vertebra
Sacral promontory

Sacral and coccygeal regions (curved posteriorly)

Sacrum

Coccyx

Lateral view

▲ **FIGURE 5.20 Vertebral Column.**

STRUCTURE OF AXIAL SKELETON

The axial skeleton comprises the:

1. vertebral column
2. skull
3. rib cage

The axial skeleton is the upright axis of the body and protects the brain, spinal cord, heart, and lungs—most of the major centers of our physiology.

Vertebral column has 26 bones divided into five regions *(Figure 5.20)*:

1. **cervical** region with seven vertebrae, labeled C1 to C7 and curved anteriorly.
2. **thoracic** region with 12 vertebrae, labeled T1 to T12 and curved posteriorly.
3. **lumbar** region with five vertebrae, labeled L1 to L5 and curved anteriorly
4. **sacral** region with one bone curved posteriorly
5. **coccyx** (tail bone) with one bone curved posteriorly

The **spinal cord** lies protected in the vertebral canal. Spinal nerves leave the spinal cord through the **intervertebral foramina** to travel to other parts of the body.

Intervertebral discs consist of fibrocartilage and inhabit the intervertebral space between the bodies of adjacent vertebrae. They provide additional support and cushioning for the vertebral column. The center of the disc is a gelatinous nucleus pulposus.

WORD ANALYSIS AND DEFINITION

WORD	PRONUNCIATION	ELEMENTS		DEFINITION
cervical	**SER**-vih-kal	S/ R/	-al *pertaining to* cervic- *neck*	Pertaining to the neck region
coccyx	**KOK**-sicks		Greek *coccyx*	Small tailbone at the lowest end of the vertebral column
foramen foramina (pl)	fo-**RAY**-men fo-**RAM**-in-ah		Latin *an aperture*	An opening through a structure
herniation herniate (verb)	**HER**-nee-ay-shun **HER**-nee-ate	S/ R/	-tion *action* hernia- *rupture*	Protrusion of an anatomical structure from its normal position.
intervertebral	**IN**-ter-**VER**-teh-bral	S/ P/ R/	-al *pertaining to* inter- *between* -vertebr- *vertebra*	The space between two vertebrae
kyphosis kyphotic (adj)	ki-**FOH**-sis ki-**FOT**-ik		French *humpbacked*	An exaggerated posterior curve of the thoracic spine
lordosis lordotic (adj)	lore-**DOH**-sis lore-**DOT**-ik		Greek *bend backward*	An exaggerated forward curvature of the lumbar spine
sacrum sacral (adj)	**SAY**-crum **SAY**-kral		Latin *sacred*	Segment of the vertebral column that forms part of the pelvis
scoliosis scoliotic (adj)	sko-lee-**OH**-sis **SKO**-lee-**OT**-ik		Greek *crooked*	An abnormal lateral curvature of the vertebral column
spine spinal (adj)	**SPINE** **SPY**-nal		Latin *spine*	Vertebral column *or* a short projection from a bone
thorax thoracic (adj)	**THO**-racks **THOR**-ass-ik		Greek *breastplate*	The part of the trunk between the abdomen and neck
vertebra vertebrae (pl) vertebral (adj)	**VER**-teh-brah **VER**-teh-bray **VER**-teh-bral		Latin *spinal joint*	One of the bones of the spinal column

Abnormal spinal curvatures can result from disease, poor posture, or congenital defects in the vertebrae. The defect that is most common is called **scoliosis,** an abnormal lateral curve in the thoracic region *(Figure 5.21a)*. In older people, particularly with osteoporosis, an exaggerated thoracic curvature is called **kyphosis** *(Figure 5.21b)*. An exaggerated lumbar curve is called **lordosis** *(Figure 5.21c)*.

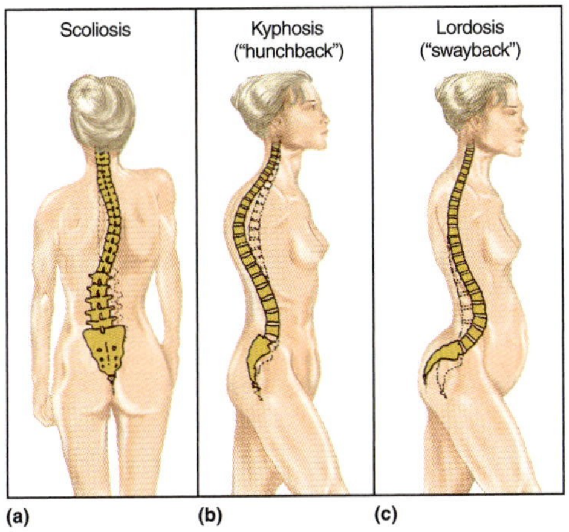

FIGURE 5.21   Abnormal Spinal Curvatures.
(*a*) Scoliosis. (*b*) Kyphosis. (*c*) Lordosis.

EXERCISES

Build your knowledge of the medical terms relating to the spinal column. All the following questions can be answered with medical terms appearing in the WAD. Fill in the blanks.

1. Two terms that apply to opposite ends of the spinal column are _____ and _____.

2. Common neck injury after an automobile accident: _____.

3. The part of the trunk between the abdomen and neck: _____.

4. A specialist who operates on this part of the body is a _____ surgeon.

5. Another name for the vertebral column: _____.

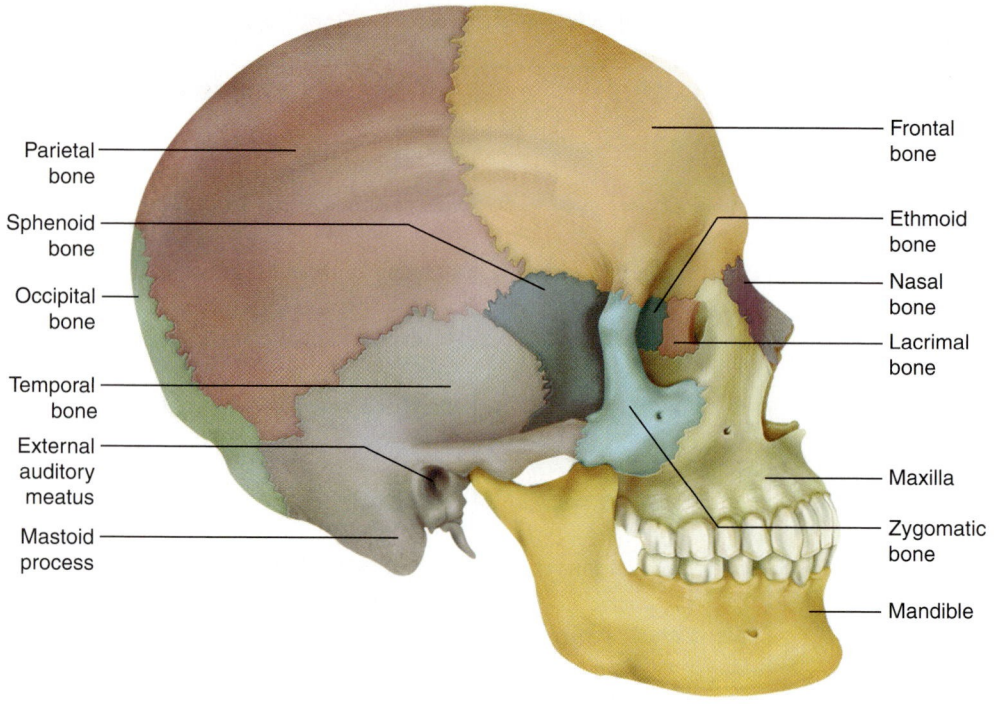

Parietal bone
Sphenoid bone
Occipital bone
Temporal bone
External auditory meatus
Mastoid process

Frontal bone
Ethmoid bone
Nasal bone
Lacrimal bone
Maxilla
Zygomatic bone
Mandible

▲ **FIGURE 5.22** **Skull: Right Lateral View.**

Nasal bone
Vomer
Palatine bone
Maxilla
Mandible

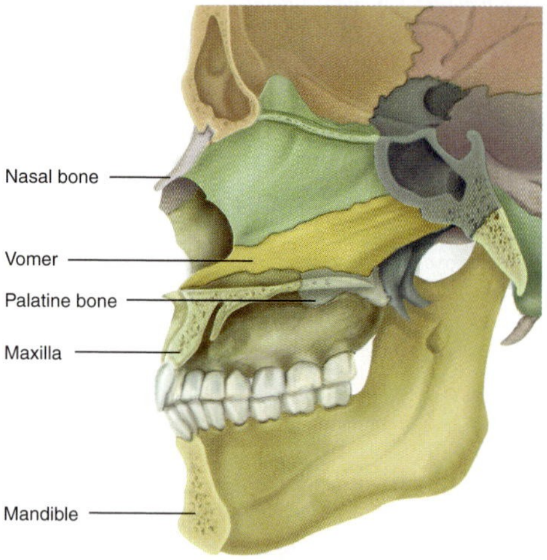

▲ **FIGURE 5.23** **Facial Bones.**

Temporalis
Buccinator
Masseter (cut)

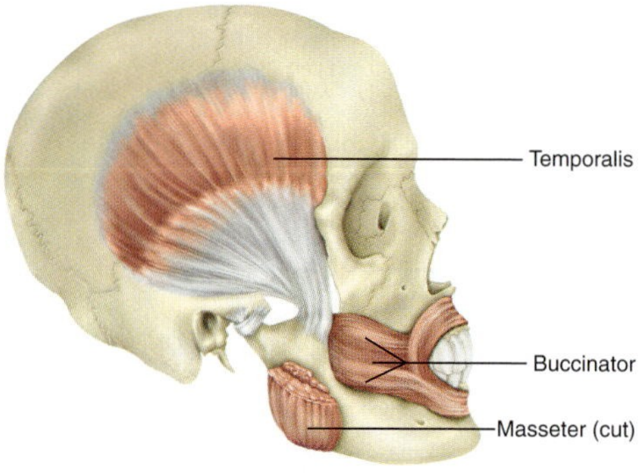

▲ **FIGURE 5.24** **Muscles of Chewing.**

THE SKULL

The human skull has 22 bones, eight of which make up the **cranium,** the upper part of the skull that encloses the **cranial cavity** and protects the brain *(Figure 5.22)*. The bones of the cranium are:

1. **Frontal** bone—forms the forehead and the roofs of the orbits and contains a pair of right and left frontal sinuses above the orbits.

2. **Parietal** bones (2)—form the bulging sides and roof of the cranium.

3. **Occipital** bone—forms the back of and part of the base of the cranium.

4. **Temporal** bones (2)—form the sides and part of the base of the cranium.

5. **Sphenoid** bone—forms part of the base of the cranium and the orbits.

6. **Ethmoid** bone—forms parts of the nose and the orbits and is hollow, forming the ethmoid sinuses.

The bones of the cranium are joined together by **sutures,** joints that appear as seams, covered on the inside and outside by a thin layer of connective tissue.

The lower anterior part of the skull comprises the 14 bones of the facial skeleton *(Figure 5.23; see also Figure 5.22):*

1. **Maxillary** bones (2)—form the upper jaw, hold the upper teeth, and are hollow, forming the maxillary sinuses.

2. **Palatine** bones (2)—are located behind the maxilla.

3. **Zygomatic** bones (2)—form the prominences of the cheeks below the eyes.

4. **Lacrimal** bones (2)—form the medial wall of each eye orbit.

5. **Nasal** bones (2)—form the sides and bridge of the nose.

6. **Vomer** bone—separates the two nasal cavities *(see Figure 5.23)*.

7. Inferior nasal **conchae** (2)—fragile bones in the lower nasal cavity.

8. **Mandible**—the lower jawbone, which holds the lower teeth.

The third component of the axial skeleton, the rib cage, is discussed in *Chapter 8*.

Bones, Joints, and Muscles of Mastication

The **temporomandibular joint (TMJ)** connects the condyle of the mandible to a fossa in the temporal bone at the base of the skull. The joint acts like a hinge when you open and close your mouth.

The muscles you use to chew food include:

1. The **masseter,** which raises the jaw bone and controls the rate at which you lower it *(Figure 5.24)*.

2. The **temporalis,** a fan-shaped muscle that raises the jawbone.

3. Medial **pterygoid,** which closes the jaw and moves it from side to side.

4. Lateral pterygoid, which opens the mouth and moves the jawbone from side to side.

WORD	PRONUNCIATION		ELEMENTS	DEFINITION
concha conchae (pl)	**KON**-kah **KON**-key		Latin *a shell*	Shell-shaped bone on medial wall of nasal cavity
cranium	**KRAY**-nee-um		Greek *skull*	The upper part of the skull that encloses and protects the brain
cranial (adj)	**KRAY**-nee-al			Pertaining to the skull
ethmoid	**ETH**-moyd	S/ R/	**-oid** *resembling* **ethm-** *sieve*	Forms the back of the nose and encloses numerous air cells
mandible mandibular (adj)	**MAN**-di-bel man-**DIB**-you-lar		Latin *jaw*	Lower jawbone
masseter	**MASS**-eh-ter		Greek *to chew*	Muscle that closes the mouth
maxilla maxillary (adj)	mak-**SILL**-ah mak-**SILL**-ary		Latin *jawbone*	Upper jawbone, containing right and left maxillary sinuses
occipital	ock-**SIP**-it-al		Latin *occiput*	The back of the skull
palatine	**PAL**-ah-tine		Latin *palate*	Bone that forms the hard palate and parts of the nose and orbits
parietal	pah-**RYE**-eh-tal	S/ R/	**-al** *pertaining to* **pariet-** *wall*	The two bones forming the sidewalls and roof of the cranium
pterygoid	**TER**-ih-goyd	S/ R/	**-oid** *resemble* **pteryg-** *wing*	Pterygoid muscles are two wing-shaped muscles that open and close the mouth
sphenoid	**SFEE**-noyd	S/ R/	**-oid** *resemble* **sphen-** *wedge*	Wedge-shaped bone at the base of the skull
temporal	**TEM**-por-al	S/ R/	**-al** *pertaining to* **tempor-** *temple, side of head*	Bone that forms part of the base and sides of the skull
temporalis muscle	tem-poh-**RAHL**-is **MUSS**-el	S/	**-alis** *pertaining to*	Muscle attached to temporal bone that opens and closes the jaw
temporomandibular joint (TMJ)	**TEM**-por-oh-man-**DIB**-you-lar JOYNT	S/ R/CF R/	**-ar** *pertaining to* **tempor/o-** *temple* **-mandibul-** *mandible, jaw bone*	The joint between the temporal bone and the mandible
vomer	**VOH**-mer		Latin *ploughshare*	Lower nasal septum
zygoma zygomatic (adj)	zye-**GOH**-mah zye-goh-**MAT**-ic		French *yoke*	Bone that forms the prominence of the cheek

EXERCISES

The following medical terms from this WAD are alike in that they have similar suffixes, but their roots will make them different terms. Define each term after you have defined the suffix. Fill in the blanks.

1. -Oid means _____

   Ethmoid   means: _____

   Sphenoid   _____

   Pterygoid   _____

2. -Al means _____

   Cranial   means: _____

   Parietal   _____

   Temporal   _____

Appendicular Skeleton, Joints, and Muscles

OBJECTIVES

Attached to the axial skeleton through joints and muscles is the appendicular skeleton, the bones of the upper limb and the shoulder girdle and those of the lower limb and its pelvic girdle. These limbs carry out many of the commands issued by your brain in response to changes in your body and in your external environment, particularly in terms of mobility and the manipulation of objects.

An understanding of the terminology, anatomy, and physiology of the bones, joints, and muscles of the limbs and their disorders is a vital part of your overall knowledge of the human body in your work as a health care professional.

Information in this lesson will enable you to:

- **Describe the structure and functions of the bones, joints, and muscles of the shoulder girdle and upper limbs.**
- **Describe the structure and functions of the bones, joints, and muscles of the pelvic girdle and lower limbs.**
- **Explain the major problems and diseases that affect mobility and other functions of the limbs.**

You are

. . . an emergency technician working in the Emergency Department at Fulwood Medical Center.

Your patient is

. . . Mr. Bruce Adams, a 55-year-old construction worker. Mr. Adams presents with severe pain in his right shoulder that has made him leave work and seek relief.

CASE REPORT 5.5

The pain began three or four months ago; it is worse at the end of the workday and when he has to work with his arm above the shoulder. In the past week, the pain has awakened him from sleep.

A month ago, Mr. Adams reported the symptoms to his employer and was referred to the company physician, who treated him with anti-inflammatory medication and a heating pad. He believes the diagnosis was a shoulder bursitis. He has no previous history of work injuries.

Physical examination shows marked limitation by pain of all passive and active movements of the right shoulder and weakness in all lifting movements.

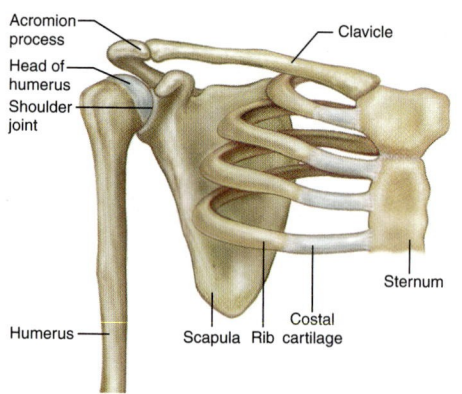

Acromion process
Head of humerus
Shoulder joint
Clavicle
Sternum
Humerus
Scapula Rib Costal cartilage

▲ **FIGURE 5.25 Pectoral Girdle.**

SHOULDER GIRDLE AND UPPER ARM

The **pectoral** (shoulder) **girdle** connects the axial skeleton to the upper limbs and helps with movements of the upper limb.

The bones of the pectoral girdle are the **scapulae** (shoulder blades) and **clavicles** *(Figure 5.25)*. The scapula extends over the top of the joint to form a roof called the **acromion**. The acromion is attached to the clavicle at the **acromioclavicular (AC)** joint. This also provides a connection between the axial skeleton, pectoral girdle, and upper arm.

The joint that connects the pectoral girdle to the upper limb is the shoulder joint, located between the scapula and the **humerus** bone of the upper arm *(see Figure 5.25)*. This joint is a ball-and-socket joint in which the head of the humerus allows the greatest range of motion of any joint in the body. Because of this, the shoulder joint also is the most unstable joint and is liable to **dislocation**.

Several ligaments hold together the articulating surfaces of the humerus and scapula.

Muscles around the shoulder joint are essential for its stability. Four muscles that originate on the scapula wrap around the joint and fuse to form one large tendon, the **rotator cuff**, which is inserted into the humerus *(Figure 5.26)*. This tendon keeps the ball of the humerus tightly in the socket of the scapula and provides the strength that baseball pitchers need. These muscles are:

1. Subscapularis
2. Supraspinatus
3. Infraspinatus
4. Teres minor

Common Disorders of the Shoulder

Rotator cuff tears are the result of the wear and tear of overuse in work situations or in throwing athletes like baseball pitchers. The tears can be partial or

WORD	PRONUNCIATION	ELEMENTS		DEFINITION
acromion acromioclavicular (AC)	ah-**CROW**-mee-on ah-**CROW**-mee-oh- kla-**VICK**-you-lar	S/ R/ S/ R/CF R/	**-ion** *action* **acrom-** *extremity* **-ar** *pertaining to* **acromi/o-** *acromion* **-clavicul-** *clavicle*	Lateral end of the scapula, extending over the shoulder joint The joint between the acromion and the clavicle
clavicle clavicular (adj)	**KLAV**-ih-kul kla-**VICK**-you-lar		Latin *collar bone*	Curved bone that forms the anterior part of the pectoral girdle
dislocation	dis-low-**KAY**-shun	S/ P/ R/	**-ion** *action* **dis-** *apart* **-locat-** *place*	Completely out of joint
humerus	**HYU**-mer-us		Latin *shoulder*	Single bone of the upper arm
pectoral pectoral girdle	**PEK**-tor-al **PEK**-tor-al **GIR**-del	S/ R/	**-al** *pertaining to* **pector-** *chest* **girdle** Old English *encircle*	Pertaining to the chest Incomplete bony ring that attaches the upper limb to the axial skeleton
rotator cuff	roh-**TAY**-tor CUFF	S/ R/	**-or** *one who* **rotat-** *rotates* **cuff** Old English *band*	Part of the capsule of the shoulder joint
scapula scapulae (pl)	**SKAP**-you-lah **SKAP**-you-lee		Latin *shoulder blade*	Shoulder blade
subluxation	sub-luck-**SAY**-shun	S/ P/ R/	**-ion** *action* **sub-** *under, slightly* **-luxat-** *dislocate*	An incomplete dislocation when some contact between the joint surfaces remains

Case Report 5.5 (continued)

When Mr. Adams was evaluated by Dr. Stannard, an x-ray (which looks for bony abnormalities) revealed no shoulder abnormality. An MRI, which shows slices of all tissues, revealed a full thickness tear of the rotator cuff.

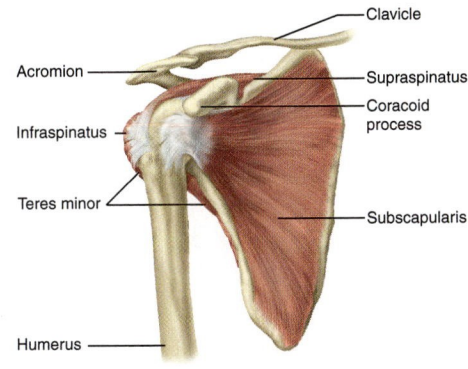

▲ **FIGURE 5.26   Rotator Cuff Muscles.**

complete, and usally require surgical repair.

Shoulder separation is a dislocation of the acromioclavicular (AC) joint, usually due to a fall on the point of the shoulder.

Shoulder dislocation is when the ball of the humerus slips out of the socket of the scapula, usually anteriorly.

Shoulder subluxation is when the ball of the humerus slips partially out of position and then moves back in.

EXERCISES

*Use your knowledge of the **language of orthopedics** to complete the following medical terms. The term is defined and partially complete. Add the rest of the elements to complete the term, and write under the line the element(s) you have used. The first one is done for you. Fill in the blanks.*

1. incomplete dislocation $\dfrac{sub}{P}$ / $\dfrac{luxat}{R/CF}$ / $\dfrac{ion}{S}$

2. joint between acromion and clavicle   _____ / _____ / $\dfrac{ar}{}$

3. completely out of joint $\dfrac{dis}{}$ / _____ / _____

4. Pertaining to the chest   _____ / _____ / $\dfrac{al}{}$

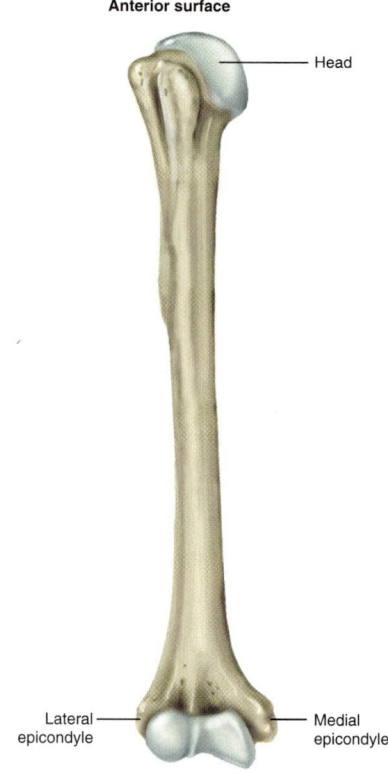

Anterior surface

Head

Lateral epicondyle — Medial epicondyle

▲ **FIGURE 5.27** Humerus.

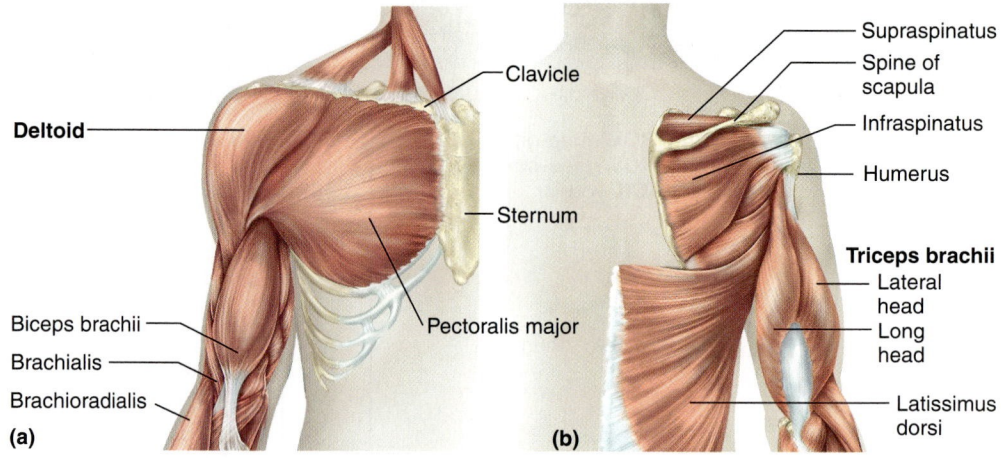

Deltoid

Biceps brachii

Brachialis

Brachioradialis

(a)

Clavicle

Sternum

Pectoralis major

Supraspinatus

Spine of scapula

Infraspinatus

Humerus

Triceps brachii

Lateral head

Long head

Latissimus dorsi

(b)

▲ **FIGURE 5.28** **Muscles Joining Arm to Body.**
(a) Anterior View. (b) Posterior View.

UPPER ARM AND ELBOW JOINT

The **humerus** is the long bone of the upper arm *(Figure 5.27)*. It extends from the scapula to the elbow joint. Muscles connect it to the pectoral girdle, vertebral column, and ribs. These muscles enable the arm to be freely movable at the shoulder joint. The major anterior muscles are the **deltoid** and **pectoralis major** *(Figure 5.28a)*, and among the major posterior muscles is the **latissimus dorsi** *(Figure 5.28b)*.

The elbow joint has two **articulations:**

1. a hinge joint between the humerus and **ulna** bone of the forearm, which allows flexion and extension of the elbow.

2. a gliding joint between the humerus and **radius** bone of the forearm, which allows pronation and supination of the forearm and hand.

A joint capsule and ligaments hold the two articulations together.

Muscles that move the elbow joint and forearm have their **origins** on the humerus or pectoral girdle and are **inserted** into the bones of the forearm. On the front of the arm, a group of three muscles (the **biceps brachii, brachialis,** and **brachioradialis**) flexes the forearm at the elbow joint and rotates the forearm and hand laterally (supination) *(Figure 5.29)*. On the back of the arm, a single muscle, the **triceps brachii,** extends the elbow joint and forearm *(Figure 5.28b)*.

Common Disorders of Elbow

Tennis elbow is caused by overuse of the elbow joint or poor techniques playing tennis or golf. Tendons of upper arm and forearm muscles are inserted into the medial and lateral **epicondyles** of the humerus just above the elbow joint *(Figure 5.28)*. Small tears in the tendons at their attachments occur with overuse, and eventually enough tears accumulate to cause pain and restrict elbow movement. The pain occurs when straightening the elbow or opening and closing the fingers. Treatment is rest, ice, pain medication, massage, and stretching exercises.

Ligament strains and **bone fractures** due to a heavy fall or a blow to the elbow are also common injuries.

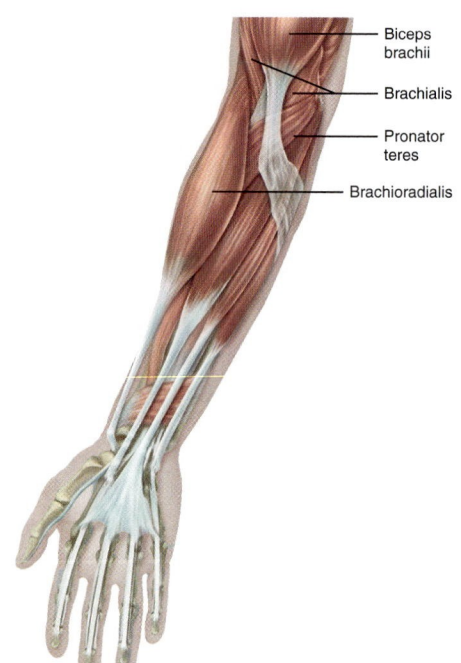

Biceps brachii

Brachialis

Pronator teres

Brachioradialis

▲ **FIGURE 5.29** **Muscles of Elbow Joint.**

S = Suffix   P = Prefix   R = Root   R/CF = Combining Form

WORD	PRONUNCIATION	ELEMENTS		DEFINITION
biceps brachii	BYE-sepz BRAY-key-eye	P/ R/ R/	bi- *two* -ceps *head* brachii *of the arm*	A muscle of the arm that has two heads or points of origin on the scapula
brachialis (Note: Has two suffixes.)	BRAY-kee-al-is	S/ S/ R/	-is *belonging to* -al- *pertaining to* brachi- *arm*	Muscle that lies underneath the biceps and is the strongest flexor of the forearm
brachioradialis	BRAY-kee-oh-RAY-dee-al-is	S/ R/CF R/	-is *belonging to* brachi/o- *arm* -radial- *radius*	Muscle that helps flex the forearm
deltoid	DEL-toyd	S/ R/	-oid *resembling* delt- *Greek letter delta*	Large, fan-shaped muscle connecting the scapula and clavicle to the humerus
epicondyle	ep-ih-KON-dile	P/ R/	epi- *above* -condyle *knuckle*	Projection above the condyle for attachment of a ligament or tendon
insertion	in-SIR-shun	S/ R/	-ion *process* insert- *put together*	The insertion of a muscle is the attachment of a muscle to a more movable part of the skeleton, as distinct from origin
latissimus dorsi	la-TISS-ih-muss DOOR-sigh	S/ R/ R/	-imus *most* latiss- *wide* dorsi *of the back*	The widest (broadest) muscle in the back
origin	OR-ih-gin		Latin *source of*	Fixed source of a muscle at its attachment to bone
radius	RAY-dee-us		Latin *spoke of a wheel*	The forearm bone on the thumb side
triceps brachii	TRY-sepz BRAY-key-eye	P/ R/ R/	tri- *three* -ceps *head* brachii *of the arm*	Muscle of the arm that has three heads or points of origin

EXERCISES

There would be no movement without bones and muscles. Take the terminology of these muscles, and reduce it to the basic elements. Fill in the chart, then fill in the blanks with the terms from the chart.

Muscle	Prefix	Root/CF	Suffix
biceps brachii			
brachialis			
brachioradialis			
deltoid			
latissimus dorsi			
triceps brachii			

Using the terms from the chart, write the name of the correct muscle on the line next to its description.

1. three heads or points of origin _____

2. strongest flexor of the forearm _____

3. fan-shaped muscle _____

4. helps flex the forearm _____

5. two points of origin on the scapula _____

6. broadest muscle of the back _____

CASE REPORT 5.6

The office accounting system is computerized, and Ms. Baker works at a keyboard all day, inputting charges and payments. For the past three months, she has had constant pain in her right hand, arm, and shoulder. She has numbness and tingling in her fingers and drops things out of her right hand. She is now unable to work.

Dr. Stannard has diagnosed tenosynovitis of the wrist. He has prescribed an anti-inflammatory medication, physiotherapy (PT), and a brace for the wrist. Ms. Baker is to ask for an **ergonomic** keyboard for her computer.

She requires help in filling out her worker's compensation form. (This task is an exercise at the end of the chapter.)

Abbreviation	
PT	physiotherapy

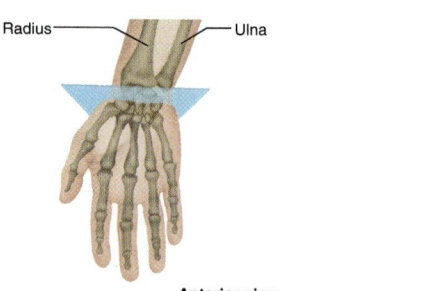

Anterior view

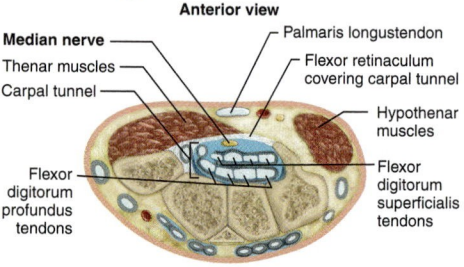

Posterior view

▲ **FIGURE 5.30   Carpal Tunnel: Transverse Section.**

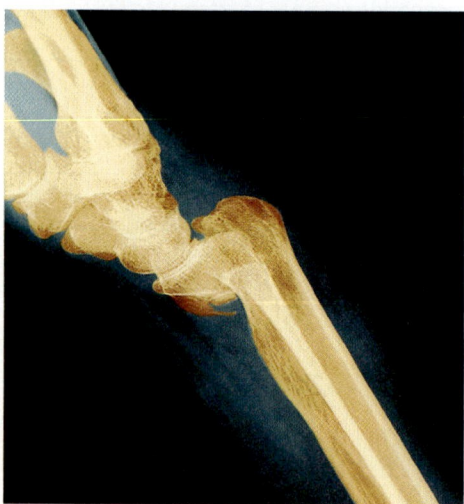

▲ **FIGURE 5.31   X-Ray of Colles Fracture with Radius and Ulna Involved.**
Colles Fracture of Radius with Hand and Wrist Displaced.

FOREARM AND WRIST

The forearm has two bones, the **radius** on the thumb side and the **ulna** on the little finger side. They articulate at the wrist joint with the small **carpal** bones. The muscles of the forearm **supinate** and **pronate** the forearm, flex and extend the wrist joint and hand, and move the hand medially and laterally.

Your forearm is bigger near the elbow because the fleshy bellies of the forearm muscles are bulky. Your wrist is much thinner because the muscles have become tendons that pass over the wrist on the way to being inserted into the bones of the fingers. As the tendons pass over the wrist they are surrounded by sheaths of synovial membrane and held in place on the wrist by a transverse, thick, fibrous band called a **retinaculum** (Figure 5.30).

Common Disorders of the Wrist

Ganglion cysts are fluid-filled cysts arising when the synovial tendon sheaths that run over the back of the wrist are irritated or inflamed. They often disappear spontaneously.

Stenosing tenosynovitis is inflammation of the synovial sheaths on the back of the wrist that causes pressure to develop under the retinaculum, producing pain in the wrist. This is what happened to Ms. Baker.

Carpal tunnel syndrome (Figure 5.30) develops similarly on the front of the wrist as a result of inflammation and swelling of tendon sheaths arising from overuse of the repetitive movements, such as with computer keyboard operation. The swelling compresses the **median nerve** between the carpal bones and the retinaculum. This causes "pins and needles" or pain and loss of muscle power in the thumb-side of the hand. The retinaculum may need to be incised and released (**fasciotomy**).

Colles fracture is a common fracture of the radius just above the wrist joint. It occurs when a person tries to break a fall with an out-stretched hand. The distal radius just proximal to the wrist is broken. In some cases, the distal ulnar is also fractured and the wrist joint dislocated. The fracture is diagnosed with an x-ray (Figure 5.31).

WORD	PRONUNCIATION		ELEMENTS	DEFINITION
carpus carpal (adj)	**KAR**-pus **KAR**-pal	S/ R/	Greek *wrist* **-al** *pertaining to* **carp-** *wrist*	Collective term for the eight carpal bones of the wrist Pertaining to the wrist
cyst	SIST		Greek *bladder*	An abnormal, fluid-containing sac
ergonomic	err-go-**NOM**-ick	S/ R/CF R/	**-ic** *pertaining to* **erg/o-** *work* **-nom-** *law*	Describes a workplace tool or equipment designed to prevent worker injury and discomfort
fascia fasciotomy fasciectomy	**FASH**-ee-ah fash-ee-**OT**-oh-me fash-ee-**EK**-toe-me	 S R/CF S/	Latin *band* **-otomy** *incision* **fasc/i-** *fascia* **-ectomy** *excision*	Sheet of fibrous connective tissue An incision through a band of fascia, usually to relieve pressure on underlying structures Surgical removal of fascia
ganglion ganglionic (adj)	**GANG**-lee-on gang-**LEE**-on-ik		Greek *swelling*	Fluid-containing swelling attached to the synovial sheath of a tendon
pronate	**PRO**-nate		Latin *bend forward*	Rotate the forearm so that the surface of the palm faces posteriorly in the anatomic position
retinaculum	ret-ih-**NACK**-you-lum	S/ R/	**-um** *structure* **retinacul-** *hold back*	Fibrous ligament that keeps the tendons in place on the wrist so that they do not "bowstring" when the forearm muscles contract
stenosis	ste-**NOH**-sis		Greek *narrowing*	Narrowing of a passage
supinate	**SOO**-pih-nate		Latin *face up*	Rotate the forearm so that the surface of the palm faces anteriorly in the anatomic position

EXERCISES

Insert the correct orthopedic terminology from the WAD into the following exercise. You may use a term only one time. Fill in the blanks.

1. Because the patient has _____ tunnel syndrome, she will require a(n) _____ keyboard for her computer at work.

2. The two terms in this WAD that are opposites are _____ and _____.

3. Inflammation of a tendon is tendinitis, but inflammation of a cyst is _____.

4. Constriction produces the narrowing of a passage; _____ will do the same.

5. A fasciectomy is removal of the _____; a cystectomy would be removal of a _____.

6. A _____ will attach to the synovial sheath of a tendon.

7. The _____ is the fibrous ligament that keeps the tendons in place on the wrist.

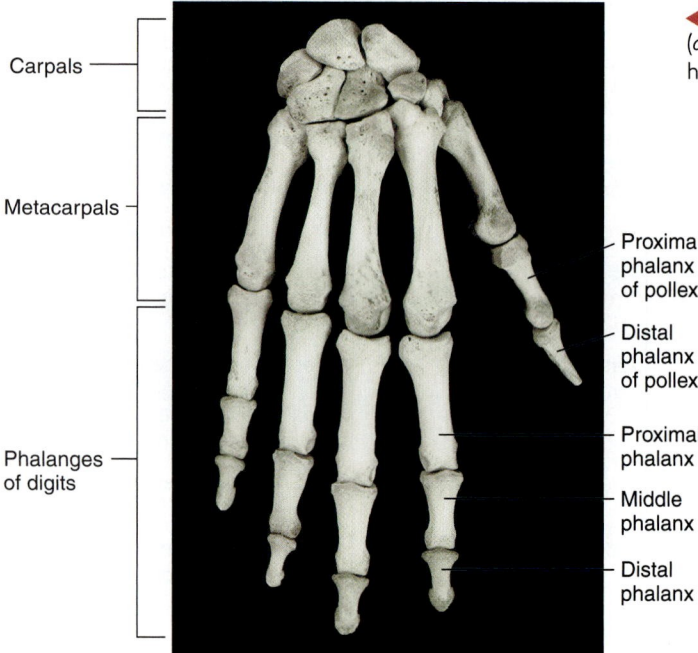

Carpals

Metacarpals

Phalanges of digits

Proximal phalanx of pollex

Distal phalanx of pollex

Proximal phalanx

Middle phalanx

Distal phalanx

(a)

◀ **FIGURE 5.32   The Hand.**
(a) Bones of the hand (b) Muscles and tendons of the palm of the hand. (c) Muscles and tendons of the dorsum of the hand.

THE HAND

Disorders of and injuries to the hand are among the most common reasons for office and emergency department visits and for ambulatory surgical procedures.

The complex structure of the hand *(Figure 5.32)* has evolved in response to the complicated and often very fine movements that modern-day activities require the hand to perform. Examples are making jewelry, repairing a watch, and sewing an artery or nerve back together.

When you look at the **palmar** surface of your hand, at the base of the thumb is a prominent pad of muscles called the **thenar eminence.** A smaller pad of muscles at the base of the little finger is called the **hypothenar eminence** *(Figure 5.33)* The back of the hand is called the **dorsum.**

The five fingers of one hand together have 14 bones called **phalanges.** The thumb has two phalanges. The remaining four fingers have three *(see Figure 5.32a).*

In the palm of the hand, the five bones proximal to the fingers are **metacarpals,** which connect at the wrist to eight small **carpal** bones. These in turn connect the hand to the bones of the forearm *(see Figure 5.32a).*

All these bones require numerous joints with ligaments to connect and stabilize them. The movements of the hand are accomplished by three sets of muscles and tendons.

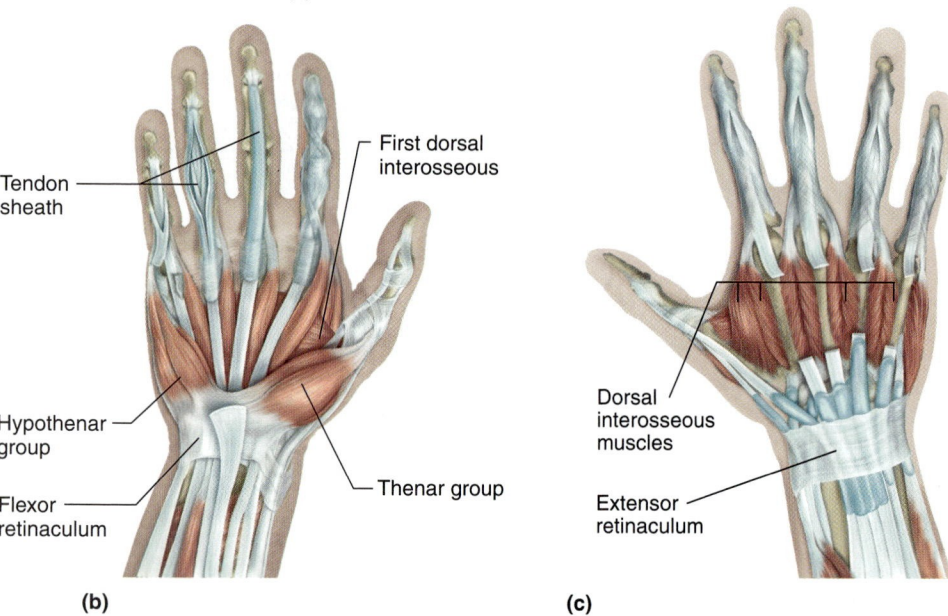

Tendon sheath

First dorsal interosseous

Hypothenar group

Flexor retinaculum

Thenar group

Dorsal interosseous muscles

Extensor retinaculum

(b)

(c)

▼ **FIGURE 5.33   Palmar Surface of Hand.**

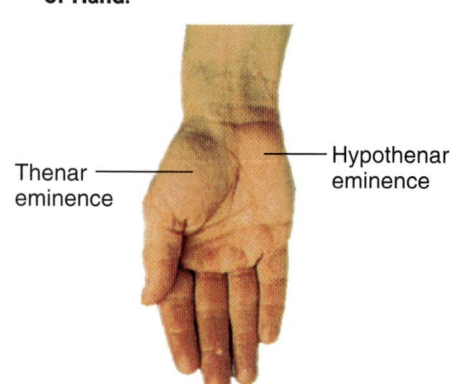

Thenar eminence

Hypothenar eminence

1. The flexor muscles that bend the fingers are located on the front of the forearm and attached by tendons to the phalanges on the palmar surfaces *(see Figure 5.32b).*

2. The extensor muscles are located on the back of the forearm and are attached by tendons to the dorsal surfaces of the phalanges *(see Figure 5.32c).*

3. Small muscles that originate and insert on the hand are located entirely within the palm and include the **interosseous muscles** between the metacarpals *(see Figures 5.32b and c).* These muscles assist in flexion and extension of the fingers but also adduct and abduct them and enable the thumb to touch the tips of the other fingers, a movement called **opposition.**

WORD	PRONUNCIATION		ELEMENTS	DEFINITION
dorsum dorsal (adj)	**DOR**-sum **DOR**-sal		Latin *back*	Upper, posterior, or back surface Pertaining to the back or situated behind
eminence	**EM**-ih-nens		Latin *stand out*	A higher place or part
hypothenar	high-poh-**THAY**-nar	P/ R/	**hypo-** *below, smaller* **-thenar** *palm*	Eminence at the base of the little finger
interosseous	in-ter-**OSS**-ee-us	S/ P/ R/CF	**ous-** *full of* **inter-** *between* **-oss/e-** *bone*	A structure between bones, in this case muscles
metacarpal	**MET**-ah-**KAR**-pal	S/ P/ R/	**-al** *pertaining to* **meta-** *after* **-carp-** *wrist*	The five bones between the carpus and the fingers
opposition	op-oh-**SIH**-shun		Old English *to set against*	The movement of the thumb across the palm of the hand to touch the tips of the other fingers
palm palmar (adj)	PAHLM **PAHL**-mah		Latin *palm*	Palm of the hand
phalanx phalanges (pl)	**FAY**-lanks **FAY**-lan-jeez		Greek *line of soldiers*	A bone of a finger or toe
thenar	**THAY**-nar		Greek *palm*	The thenar eminence is the fleshy mass at the base of the thumb

EXERCISES

Because the body has 206 bones, there is an extensive amount of orthopedic vocabulary. Build your knowledge of hand terminology with the following exercise. Circle your best choice.

1. The term **dorsum** means: front   back   middle   end

2. The prefix **inter-** means: between   before   behind   beneath

3. The suffix **-ous** means: process   action   full of   pertaining to

4. The prefix **hypo-** means: smaller   larger   twisted   excess

5. The term **metacarpal** refers to: arm   elbow   forearm   hand

6. The suffix **-al** means: pertaining to   one who does   study of   condition

7. The element **osse** refers to: blood   wrist   knuckle   bone

8. Bone of a finger *or* toe is: carpus   fascia   eminence   phalanx

9. The prefix **meta-** means: before   during   after   middle

10. Flesh at the base of the thumb is: thenar   metacarpal   hypothenar   phalanges

11. Higher place or part: emmenince   emminence   eminence   emenince

12. The root **thenar-** means: finger   hand   palm   wrist

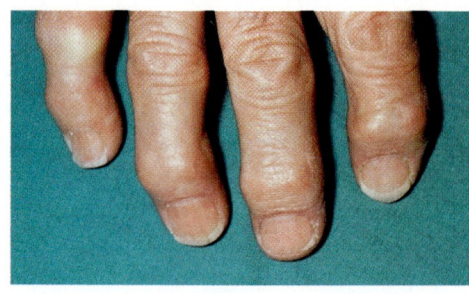

▲ FIGURE 5.34　Hand with Osteoarthritis. Osteoarthritis of Hands Showing Heberden Nodes.

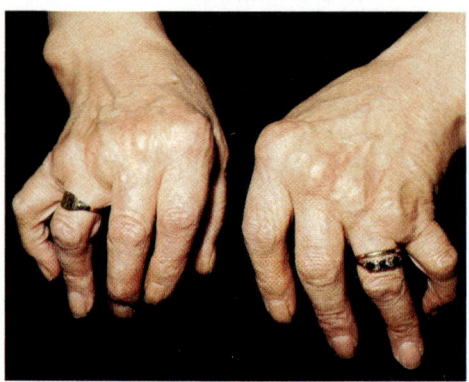

▲ FIGURE 5.35　Hands with Rheumatoid Arthritis.

Abbreviations	
JRA	juvenile rheumatoid arthritis
RA	rheumatoid arthritis

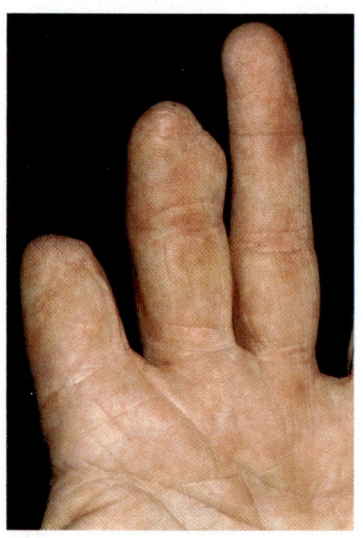

▲ FIGURE 5.36　Healed Partial Amputation of Two Fingers.

THE HAND (continued)

Disorders of the Hand

Osteoarthritis in the hand joints occurs from wear and tear, particularly in the joint at the base of the thumb. As a finger joint deteriorates, small bony spurs called Heberden nodes form over it *(Figure 5.34)*. William Heberden (1710–1801), a surgeon in Cambridge, England, first described these nodes.

Rheumatoid arthritis (RA), with destruction of joint surfaces, joint capsule, and ligaments, leads to marked **deformity** and joint **instability** *(Figure 5.35)*. It occurs mostly in women, with onset between ages 20 and 50.

The great majority of patients have involvement of the hands where the disease affects the synovial membrane that lines joints and tendons. The abnormal synovial membrane can invade the smooth, gliding joint surfaces to destroy them and can invade the surrounding joint capsule and ligaments to cause deformity and joint instability. Lumps known as **rheumatic nodules** form over the small joints of the hand and wrist. The metacarpophalangeal joints can be affected, and this leads to drift of the fingers away from the thumb, called **ulnar deviation.**

Juvenile rheumatoid arthritis (JRA) affects children under the age of 17 with inflammation and stiffness of joints. Many children grow out of it.

Dupuytren contracture is a progressive thickening and contracture of the skin and connective tissues of the palm of the hand.

Injuries of the Hand

Flexor tendon injuries occur as a result of lacerations. Because the flexor tendons lie just beneath the skin on the palmar surfaces of the fingers, they are very **susceptible** to injury even with a shallow laceration. Even after repair, there can be **residual** stiffness and limited motion of the fingers.

Open fractures of hand bones, when the skin is broken and the broken bone penetrates through the break in the skin, can lead to infection of hand tissues.

Partial amputation of a fingertip is a common type of injury particularly in people who work with sharp tools *(Figure 5.36)*. This type of wound also produces an open phalangeal fracture.

Surgical Procedures of the Hand

Fasciectomy is a surgical removal of the hypertrophied connective tissue to release a contracture.

Tendon reconstruction stitches the two ends of a lacerated tendon back together or inserts a tendon graft.

Arthrodesis is the surgical fixation of a joint to prevent motion. Bone graft, wires, screws, or a plate can be used to stabilize the joint.

Arthroplasty in this setting is the complete replacement of a damaged finger joint with an artificial joint made of silicone rubber.

Reattachment of amputated fingers is performed frequently. The bones are rejoined with plates, wires, or screws. The tendons are reconstructed. Nerves and blood vessels are joined back together using microsurgical instruments.

WORD ANALYSIS AND DEFINITION

WORD	PRONUNCIATION		ELEMENTS	DEFINITION
amputation amputate (verb) amputee (noun)	am-pyu-**TAY**-shun **AM**-pyu-tate **AM**-pyu-tee		Latin *cut, prune*	Process of removing a limb, part of a limb, a breast, or other projecting part A person with an amputation
contracture	kon-**TRAK**-chur	S/ R/	**-ure** *process* **contract-** *draw together*	Muscle shortening due to spasm or fibrosis
deformity	de-**FOR**-mih-tee	S/ P/ R/	**-ity** *condition* **de-** *change of* **-form-** *form, appearance*	A permanent structural deviation from the normal
Dupuytren	du-pwe-**TRAHN**		Guillaume Dupuytren, French surgeon, 1777–1835	Dupuytren contracture is thickening and shortening of fibrous bands in the palm of the hand
flexor flex	**FLEK**-sor FLEKS		Latin *to bend*	Muscle or tendon that flexes a joint To bend a joint so that the two parts come together
instability	in-stah-**BIL**-ih-tee	S/ P/ R/	**-ity** *condition* **in-** *not* **-stabil-** *stand firm*	Abnormal tendency of a joint to partially or fully dislocate
juvenile	**JU**-ven-ile		Latin *youthful*	Between the ages of 2 and 17 years
nodule	**NOD**-yule		Latin *small knot*	Small node or knotlike swelling
residual residue (noun)	re-**ZID**-you-al **REZ**-ih-dyu	S/ R/CF	**-al** *pertaining to* **resid/u-** *what is left over*	Pertaining to anything left over
rheumatism rheumatic (adj) rheumatoid arthritis	**RU**-mat-izm ru-**MAT**-ik **RU**-mah-toyd ar-**THRI**-tis	S/ R/ S/ S/	**-ism** *condition* **rheumat-** *a flow* **-ic** *pertaining to* **-oid** *resembling*	Pain in various parts of the musculoskeletal system Disease of connective tissue, with arthritis as a major manifestation
susceptible	suh-**SEP**-tih-bill		Latin *to take up*	Capable of being affected by

---

EXERCISES

Demonstrate your knowledge of the difference between these similar terms. Use the correct form of the term in the appropriate place. Fill in the blanks.

amputation   **amputate**   **amputee**

1. The surgeon has decided to _____ the patient's left leg below the knee. The _____ will be

   performed as soon as possible. Following the surgery, the _____ will be fitted for a new leg prosthesis.

flex   **flexor**

2. The _____ tendon _____ a joint so the two parts of the joint can come together.

residual   **residue**

3. The _____ in the bottom of the test beaker can be referred to as the _____.

rheumatic   **rheumatoid arthritis**   **rheumatism**

4. _____ is a generic term for _____ pain in various parts of the musculoskeletal system.

   However, _____ is a specific systemic disease affecting many joints.

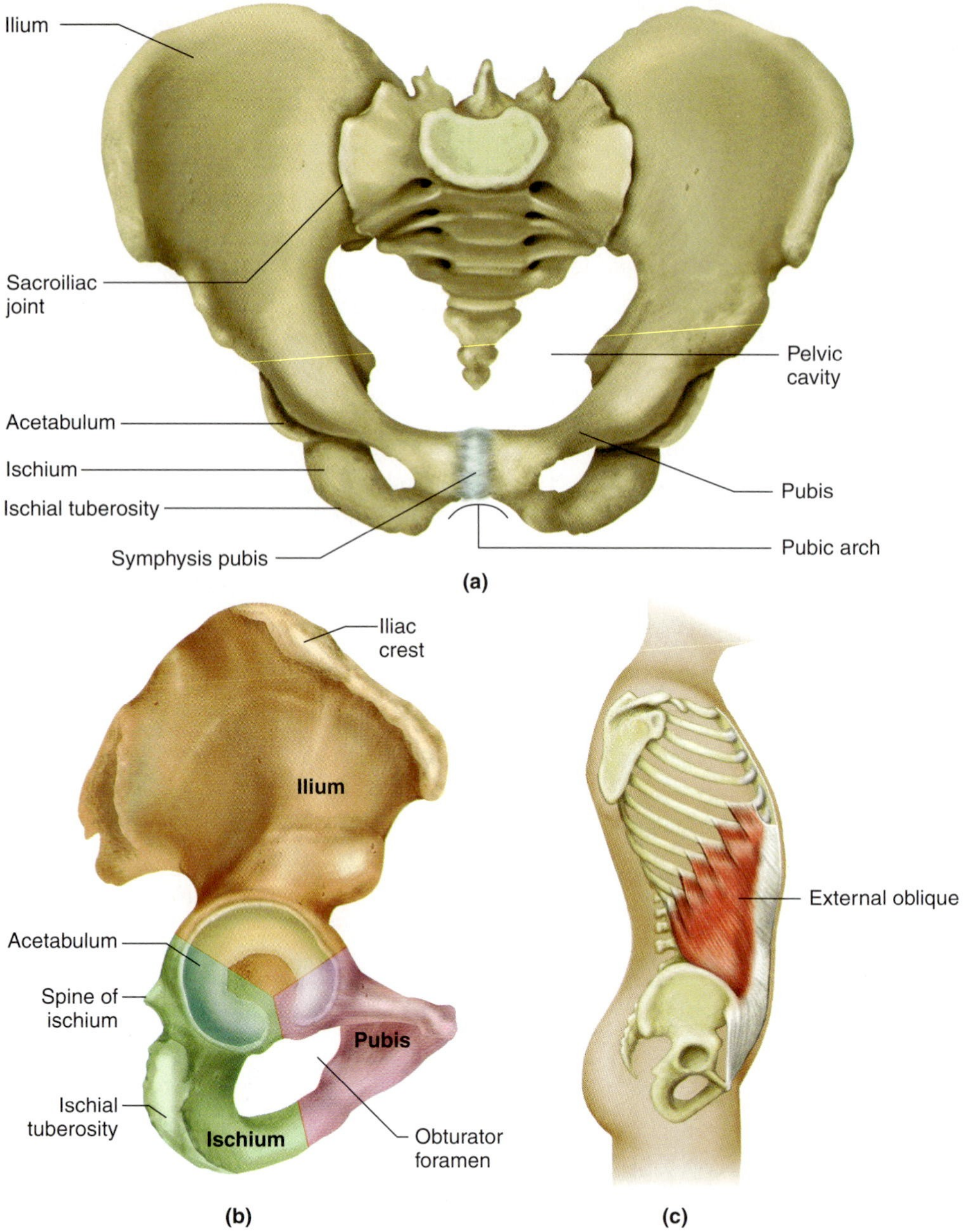

PELVIC GIRDLE

The pelvic girdle (*Figure 5.37*) is the two hip bones that articulate anteriorly with each other at the **symphysis pubis** and posteriorly with the **sacrum** to form the bowl-shaped **pelvis**. The two joints between the **coxae** (hipbones) and the sacrum are the **sacroiliac joints**.

The pelvic girdle has the following functions:

1. supports the axial skeleton
2. transmits the body's weight through to the lower limbs
3. provides attachments for the lower limbs
4. protects the internal reproductive organs, urinary bladder, and distal end of the large intestine.

Each **os coxa** (hipbone) is a fusion of three bones, the **ilium**, **ischium**, and **pubis** (*Figure 5.37a*). The fusion takes place in the region of the **acetabulum,** a cup-shaped cavity on the lateral surface of each os coxa that receives the **head** of the **femur** (thigh bone, *Figure 5.37b*).

The lower part of the pelvis is formed by the lower ilium, ischium, and pubic bones that surround a short canal-like cavity. This opening is larger in females than males to allow the infant to pass through during childbirth. The outlet from the cavity is spanned by strong muscular layers through which the rectum, vagina, and urethra pass (*Figure 5.38*).

Muscles anchor the pelvic girdle to the vertebrae and ribs of the axial skeleton. Anteriorly, these are the abdominal muscles that are inserted into the ilium and pubis (*Figure 5.37c*).

Figure 5.37 labels

(a) Front view: Ilium, Sacroiliac joint, Acetabulum, Ischium, Ischial tuberosity, Symphysis pubis, Pelvic cavity, Pubis, Pubic arch

(b) Side view: Iliac crest, Ilium, Acetabulum, Spine of ischium, Ischial tuberosity, Ischium, Pubis, Obturator foramen

(c) External oblique

▲ **FIGURE 5.37**

(a) Pelvic Girdle: Front View. *(b)* Pelvic Girdle: Side View. *(c)* Abdominal Muscles Support the Pelvic Girdle.

Abbreviation	
SI	sacroiliac

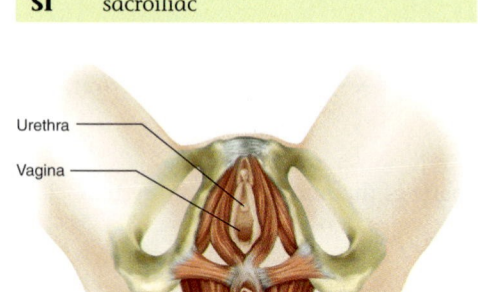

Urethra
Vagina
Anus

▲ **FIGURE 5.38 Female Pelvic Outlet.**

Disorders of the Pelvic Girdle

Sacroiliac joint (SI joint) strain is a common cause of lower back pain. Unlike most joints, the SI joint is only designed to move 1/4 inch (approximately 6 mm) during weight bearing and forward flexion. Its main function is to provide shock absorption for the spine.

During pregnancy, hormones enable connective tissue to relax so that the pelvis can expand enough to allow birth. The stretching in the SI joint ligaments makes it "over-mobile" and susceptible to wear-and-tear painful arthritis.

Another cause of pain in the SI joint is trauma, with tearing of the joint ligaments generating too much motion and pain. The pain is felt in the low back, in the buttock, and sometimes in the back and front of the thigh.

A diagnosis of sacroiliac pain can be made by clinical examination, joint x-ray, and CT scan. **Fluoroscopic** injection of local anesthetic into the joint can relieve the pain temporarily. Treatment is usually **stabilization** of the joint with a **brace** and physical therapy to strengthen the low back muscles. Occasionally, **arthrodesis** of the joint is necessary.

WORD	PRONUNCIATION		ELEMENTS	DEFINITION
acetabulum	as-eh-**TAB**-you-lum		Latin *vinegar cup*	The cup-shaped cavity of the hipbone that receives the head of the femur to form the hip joint
brace	BRACE		Old English *to fasten*	Appliance to support a part of the body in its correct position
coxa coxae (pl)	**COCK**-sah **COCK**-see		Latin *hipbone*	Hipbone
diastasis	die-**ASS**-tah-sis		Greek *separation*	Separation of normally joined parts
femur femoral (adj)	**FEE**-mur **FEM**-oh-ral		Latin *thigh*	The thigh bone
fluoroscopy fluoroscopic (adj)	flor-**OS**-koh-pee flor-oh-**SKOP**-ik	S/ R/CF S/	-scopy *use of an instrument to examine* fluor/o- *x-ray beam* -ic *pertaining to*	Examination of structures of the body by x-rays
head	HED		Old English *head*	The rounded extremity of a bone
ilium (**Note:** The ileum is a section of the small intestine [Chapter 6].) ilia (pl)	**ILL**-ee-um **ILL**-ee-ah		Latin *groin*	Large wing-shaped bone at the upper and posterior part of the pelvis
ischium ischial (adj) ischia (pl)	**ISS**-kee-um **ISS**-kee-al **ISS**-kee-ah		Greek *hip*	Lower and posterior part of the hipbone
pelvis pelvic (adj)	**PEL**-viss **PEL**-vic		Latin *basin*	A cup-shaped ring of bone; also a cup-shaped cavity, as in the pelvis of the kidney
pubis pubic (adj)	**PYU**-bis **PYU**-bik		Latin *pubis*	Alternative name for the pubic bone
sacrum sacral (adj) sacroiliac joint	**SAY**-crum **SAY**-kral say-kroh-**ILL**-ih-ak JOINT	 S/ R/CF R/	Latin *sacred* -ac *pertaining to* sacr/o- *sacrum* -ili- *ilium*	Segment of the vertebral column that forms part of the pelvis In the neighborhood of the sacrum The joint between the sacrum and ilium

Diastasis symphysis pubis is another result of the stretching of pelvic ligaments during pregnancy. The softening and stretching of the ligaments of the symphysis pubis stretches the joint between the two pubic bones and leads to pain over the joint, difficulty in walking, climbing stairs, and turning over in bed.

EXERCISES   *Match the language of the pelvic girdle to its correct definition. Fill in the blanks.*

_____ 1. receives head of femur

_____ 2. cup-shaped ring of bones

_____ 3. posterior part of hip bone

_____ 4. separation of normally joined parts

_____ 5. wing-shaped bone; upper part of pelvis

_____ 6. segment of vertebral column

_____ 7. thigh bone

A. sacrum

B. ilium

C. diastasis

D. femur

E. pelvis

F. ischium

G. acetabulum

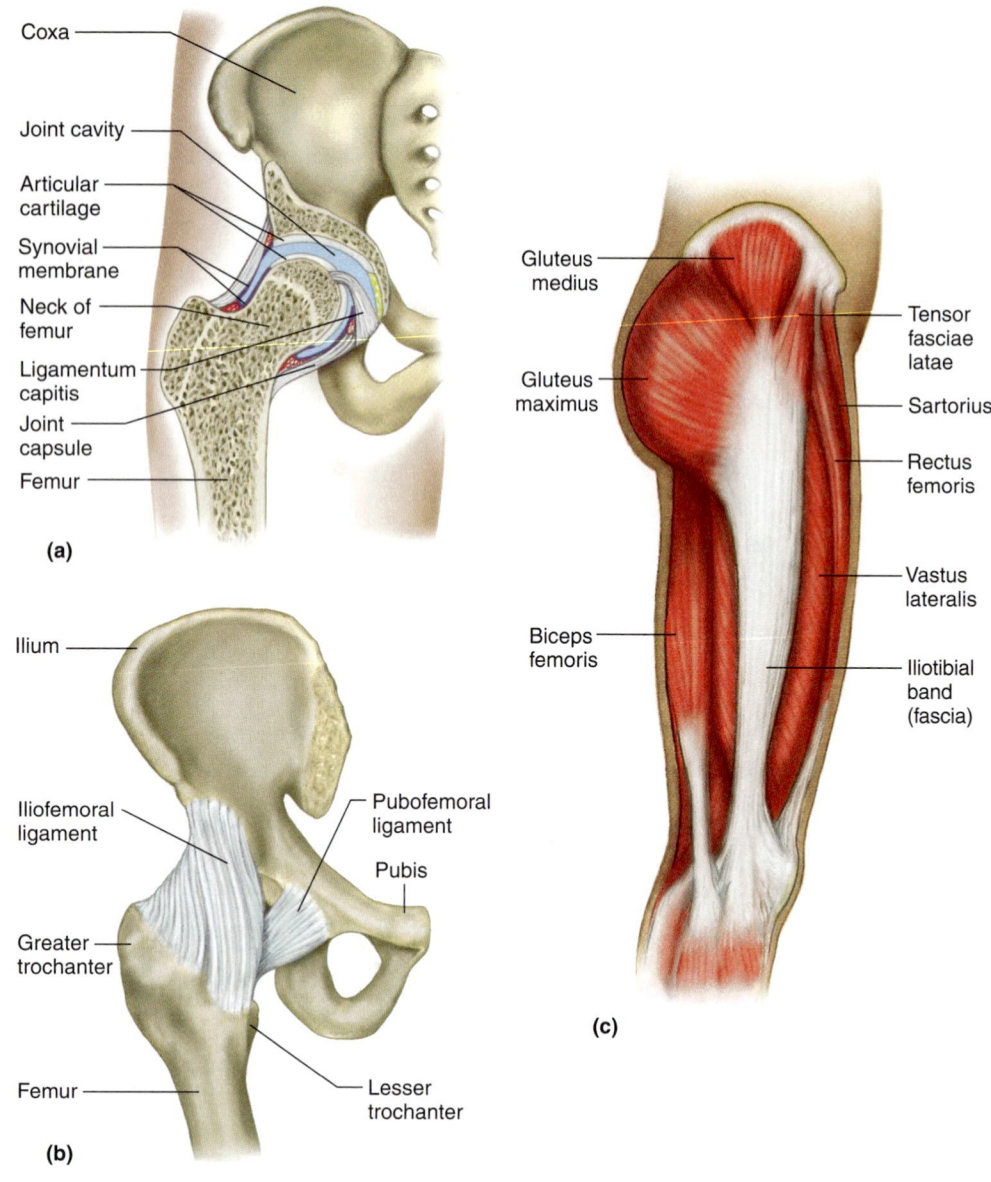

(a)

- Coxa
- Joint cavity
- Articular cartilage
- Synovial membrane
- Neck of femur
- Ligamentum capitis
- Joint capsule
- Femur

(b)

- Ilium
- Iliofemoral ligament
- Greater trochanter
- Femur
- Pubofemoral ligament
- Pubis
- Lesser trochanter

(c)

- Gluteus medius
- Gluteus maximus
- Biceps femoris
- Tensor fasciae latae
- Sartorius
- Rectus femoris
- Vastus lateralis
- Iliotibial band (fascia)

▲ **FIGURE 5.39   Hip Joint.**
(a) Right Frontal View of a Section of Hip Joint. (b) Ligaments of Hip Joint. (c) Muscles of Hip and Thigh (Lateral View).

BONES, JOINTS, AND MUSCLES OF THE HIP AND THIGH

The **hip joint** is a **ball-and-socket** synovial joint between the head of the femur and the cup-shaped **acetabulum** of the hipbone (*Figure 5.39a*). A ligament (ligamentum capitis) attached to the head of the femur from the lining of the acetabulum carries blood vessels to the head of the femur to nourish it.

The joint is held in place by a thick joint **capsule** reinforced by strong ligaments that connect the neck of the femur to the rim of the acetabulum (*Figure 5.39b*).

Powerful muscles that support the hip joint and move the thigh have their **origins** on the pelvic girdle and their **insertions** into the femur. Prominent among them are the three **gluteus** muscles, **maximus, medius,** and **minimus** (*Figure 5.39c*), and the **adductor** muscles that run down the inner thigh.

Disorders and Injuries of the Hip Joint

Hip pointer, usually a football-related injury, is a blow to the rim of the pelvis that leads to bruising of the bone and surrounding tissues.

Osteoarthritis is common in the hip as a result of aging, weight bearing, and repetitive use of the joint. The cartilage on both the acetabulum and the head of the femur degenerates, and eventually there is total loss of the cartilage cushion. The resulting friction between the bones of the head of the femur and the acetabulum leads to pain and loss of mobility.

Rheumatoid arthritis can also affect the hip, beginning in the synovial membrane and progressing to destroy cartilage and bone.

Avascular necrosis of the femoral head is the necrosis (death) of bone tissue when the blood supply becomes avascular (is cut off), usually as a result of trauma.

Fractures of the neck of the femur occur as a result of a fall, most commonly in elderly women with osteoporosis. This is shown in (*Figure 5.40*).

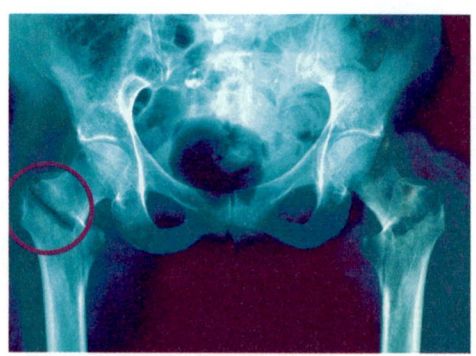

▲ **FIGURE 5.40   Fracture of Neck of Femur in Woman with Osteoporosis.**

WORD	PRONUNCIATION	ELEMENTS		DEFINITION
avascular	a-**VAS**-cue-lar	S/ P/ R/	**-ar** *pertaining to* **a-** *without* **vascul-** *blood vessel*	Without a blood supply
gluteus	**GLU**-tee-us		Greek *buttocks*	Refers to a muscle in the buttocks
maximus	**MAKS**-ih-mus		Latin *the biggest or the greatest*	The gluteus maximus muscle is the largest muscle in the body, covering a large part of each buttock
medius	**ME**-dee-us		Latin *middle*	The gluteus medius muscle is partly covered by the gluteus maximus; it originates on the ilium and is inserted into the femur
minimus	**MIN**-ih-mus		Latin *smallest*	The gluteus minimus is the smallest of the gluteal muscles and lies under the gluteus medius
necrosis necrotic (adj)	neh-**KROH**-sis neh-**KROT**-ik		Greek *death*	Pathologic death of cells or tissue Affected by necrosis
prosthesis	**PROS**-thee-sis		Greek *addition*	Manufactured substitute for a missing part of the body

Surgical Procedures

Arthroplasty, a total replacement of the hip joint with a metal **prosthesis** is the most common hip surgery today; 150,000 total hip replacements are performed each year in the United States, mostly for osteoarthritis of the hip joint. The diseased parts of the joint are removed and replaced with artificial parts made of titanium, other metals, and ceramics *(Figure 5.41)*.

Arthrocentesis, the aspiration of fluid from the hip joint and replacement of the fluid with a steroid solution, is also performed frequently for osteoarthritis.

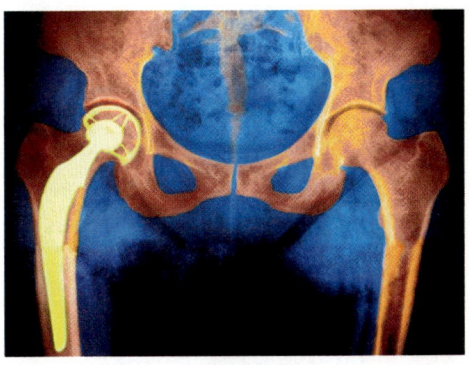

▲ **FIGURE 5.41   Total Hip Replacement.**
Colored X-Ray of Prosthetic Hip.

EXERCISES   *Continue working with the **language of orthopedics**. Circle the best answer in questions 1 through 5 and demonstrate your knowledge of the terms. Use that knowledge to construct a sentence for question 6.*

1. Maximus, medius and minimus are all:

    bones   muscles   tendons   ligaments   phalanges

2. Gluteus refers to the:

    wrist   hand   buttocks   hip   spine

3. If tissue is dead, it is:

    necrotic   sacral   rheumatic   degenerative   fibrotic

4. Avascular means no:

    living tissue   tendon support   movement   blood supply   inflammation

5. A prosthesis is a(n):

    procedure   cast   diagnostic test   brace   artificial body part

Choose any one term, from questions 1 to 5 and use it in a sentence that is not a definition.

6. _____

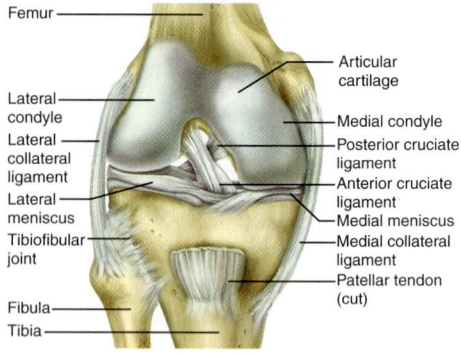

(a)

(b)

▲ **FIGURE 5.42**
(a) Section of Knee Joint (b) Right Knee Joint: Anterior View.

Abbreviations

ACL   anterior cruciate ligament
PCL   posterior cruciate ligament

BONES, JOINTS, AND MUSCLES OF THE KNEE AND THIGH

Knee Joint

The knee is a hinged joint formed with four bones:

1. The lower end of the **femur,** shaped like a horseshoe. The two ends of the horseshoe are the medial and lateral femoral **condyles** *(Figure 5.42b).*

2. The flat upper end of the **tibia.**

3. The flat triangular bone, the **patella** (kneecap), is embedded in the **patellar tendon** and articulates with the femur between its two **condyles** *(Figure 5.42a).*

4. The **fibula,** which forms a separate joint by articulating with the tibia. This is called the **tibiofibular joint** *(see Figure 5.42b).*

Mechanically, the role of the patella is to provide an increase of about 30% in the strength of extension of the knee joint.

Within the knee joint, two crescent-shaped pads of cartilage lie on top of the tibia to articulate with the femoral condyles. They are the **medial** and **lateral menisci.** Their function is to distribute weight more evenly across the joint surface to minimize wear and tear. They play a crucial role in joint stability, lubrication, and transmission of force.

The knee joint has a **fibrous capsule** lined with **synovial membrane** to secrete **synovial fluid,** which provides lubrication for the joint. The joint is held together by **ligaments.** The two ligaments outside the joint are the **medial** and **lateral collateral ligaments.** Two other ligaments are located inside the joint cavity and are called the **anterior cruciate ligament (ACL)** and the **posterior cruciate ligament (PCL).** They cross over each other to form an "X" *(Figure 5.42b).* There are numerous bursae associated with the knee joint *(Figure 5.42a).* Their function is to aid the movement of the patella and the patellar tendon over the bones of the joint.

Thigh Muscles

The thigh muscles move the knee joint and lower leg. The anterior thigh is composed of the large **quadriceps femoris** muscle, which has four heads and is the most powerful muscle in the body. The four muscles converge into the **quadriceps tendon,** which contains the patella, and continue as the patellar tendon to insert into the tibia *(Figure 5.42a).* The quadriceps muscle extends (straightens) the knee joint and, because of the weight of the lower leg, has to be a powerful muscle.

The posterior thigh is composed mostly of the three **hamstring muscles:** the **biceps femoris, semimembranosus,** and **semitendinosus.** They flex (bend) the knee joint and rotate the leg. The hollow at the back of the knee between the hamstring tendons is called the **popliteal fossa.**

WORD ANALYSIS AND DEFINITION

WORD	PRONUNCIATION	ELEMENTS		DEFINITION
collateral	koh-**LAT**-er-al	S/ P/ R/	-al *pertaining to* co- *together* -later- *side*	Situated at the side to bypass an obstruction
condyle	**KON**-dile		Latin *knuckle*	Large, smooth rounded expansion of the end of a bone to form a joint with another bone
cruciate	**KRU**-she-ate		Latin *cross*	Shaped like a cross
fibula fibular (adj)	**FIB**-you-lah **FIB**-you-lar		Latin *clasp or buckle*	The smaller of the two bones of the lower leg
patella (knee cap) patellae (pl) patellar (adj)	pah-**TELL**-ah pah-**TELL**-ee pah-**TELL**-ar		Latin *small plate*	Thin, circular bone in front of the knee joint and embedded in the patellar tendon
popliteal fossa	pop-**LIT**-ee-al **FOSS**-ah	S/ R/CF	-al *pertaining to* poplit/e- *ham* fossa Latin *ditch*	The hollow at the back of the knee
quadriceps femoris	**KWAD**-rih-seps **FEM**-or-is	P/ R/ S/ R/	quadri- *four* -ceps *head* -is *belonging to* femor- *femur*	An anterior thigh muscle with four heads
tibia tibial (adj)	**TIB**-ee-ah **TIB**-ee-al		Latin *large shinbone*	The larger bone of the lower leg

---

EXERCISES

A medical term must be spelled correctly. Work with a fellow student on this exercise. Close your text while the other student dictates the terms in this WAD to you. Do your best to spell them correctly in column 1. When you are finished, open your book and check your spelling in column 2. If you have made any errors, rewrite the correct spelling in column 2.

Spelling	Corrections
1. _____	_____
2. _____	_____
3. _____	_____
4. _____	_____
5. _____	_____
6. _____	_____
7. _____	_____
8. _____	_____
9. _____	_____
10. _____	_____
11. _____	_____
12. _____	_____

Case Report 5.7 (continued)

Gail Griffith, a 17-year-old, landed awkwardly after jumping for a ball during a basketball game. "My knee kinda popped as I landed." She had to be assisted off the court. In the emergency room, the knee was swollen and unstable. An MRI showed a complete tear of medial collateral ligament, a complete tear of the anterior cruciate ligament, and a partial tear (**avulsion**) of the medial meniscus. Gail decided to have surgery, even though full recovery would take six months to one year of rehabilitation.

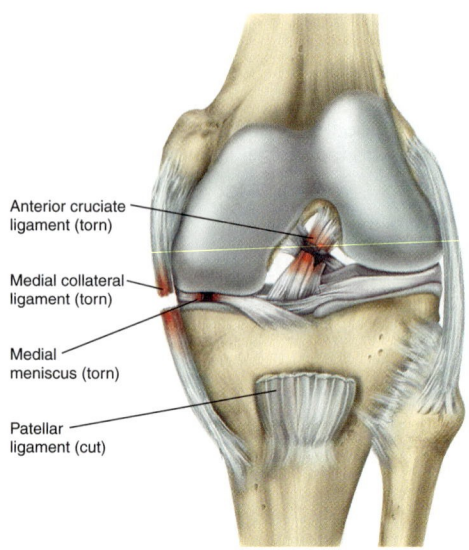

Anterior cruciate ligament (torn)

Medial collateral ligament (torn)

Medial meniscus (torn)

Patellar ligament (cut)

▲ **FIGURE 5.43   Gail Griffith's Knee Injuries.**

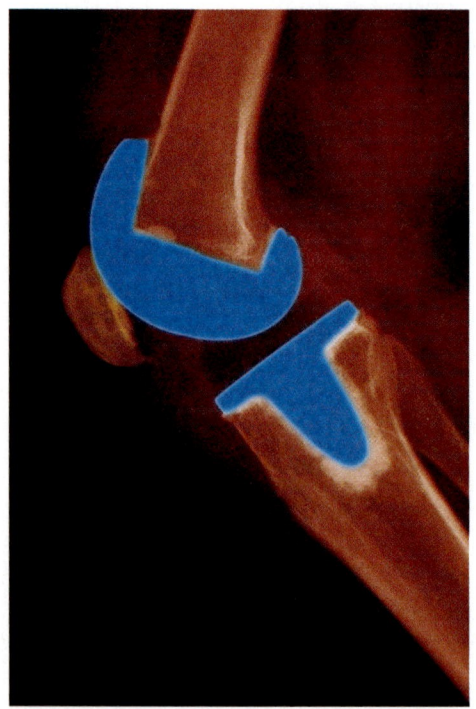

▲ **FIGURE 5.44   Total Knee Replacement.**
Colored X-Ray of Total Knee Replacement Left Knee.

THE KNEE JOINT

Injuries to The Knee Joint

The **anterior cruciate ligament (ACL)** is the most commonly injured ligament in the knee *(Figure 5.43)*, particularly in female athletes. The injury is often caused by a sudden **hyperflexion** of the knee joint when landing awkwardly on flat ground as in Gail's injury. Because of its poor vascular supply, once torn the ligament does not heal. The knee becomes unstable, risking further joint damage and arthritis. The torn ligament has to be stitched back together surgically. If the ACL has been torn away from its bony insertions, the surgeon will harvest a thin portion of a hamstring or patellar tendon and screw the ends into the tibia and femur. This is a **tendon autograft.** If donated tissue from a tissue bank were used for the graft it would be called an **allograft.** If tissue from another species is used for a graft, it is called a **xenograft** or a **heterograft.**

Other major ligaments that are commonly injured are the medial and lateral collateral ligaments and the posterior cruciate ligament.

Meniscus injuries result from a twist to the knee. Pain and locking are the result of the torn meniscus flipping in and out of the joint as it moves. Because loss of a meniscus leads to arthritic changes, repair of the meniscus, as in Gail's case, rather than removal is preferred. Removal of a meniscus is a **meniscectomy.**

Patellar problems produce pain that is noticed particularly when descending stairs. The force on the patella when descending stairs is about seven times body weight compared to about two times body weight when ascending stairs.

Chondromalacia patellae (runner's knee) is caused by irritation of the undersurface of the patella.

Patellar subluxation or dislocation produces an unstable painful kneecap.

Prepatellar bursitis (housemaid's knee) produces painful swelling over the bursa at the front of the knee and is seen in people who kneel for extended periods of time, such as carpet layers.

Tendinitis of the patellar tendon is produced by overuse during such activities as cycling, running, or dancing. Pain is felt where the tendon is inserted into the tibia. It is treated by R.I.C.E.

Rupture of the patellar tendon can occur in the elderly when trying to break a fall or in athletes such as basketball players with their repeated jumping. An MRI can confirm the tear, which may need to be repaired surgically.

Surgical Procedures of the Knee Joint

Arthrocentesis, aspiration of fluid from the knee joint, is used to establish a diagnosis by laboratory examination of the fluid, drain off infected fluid.

Diagnostic arthroscopy is an exploratory procedure performed using an arthroscope to examine the internal compartments of the knee joint.

Surgical arthroscopy, performed through an arthroscope, can be a **debridement** or removal of torn tissue such as a meniscus or a ligament. It can also be repair of a torn ligament by suturing, tendon autograft, or repair of a torn meniscus.

Arthroplasty involves a total replacement of the knee joint *(Figure 5.44)*, usually because of osteoarthritis of the joint. The lower end of the femur is replaced with a metal shell. The upper end of the tibia is replaced with a metal trough lined with plastic and the back of the patella can be replaced with a plastic button.

S = Suffix   P = Prefix   R = Root   R/CF = Combining Form

WORD	PRONUNCIATION	ELEMENTS		DEFINITION
allograft	**AL**-oh-graft	P/ R/	**allo-** *different* **-graft** *splice*	Skin graft from another person or cadaver
autograft	**AWE**-toe-graft	P/ R/	**auto-** *self, same* **-graft** *splice*	A graft using tissue taken from the same individual who is receiving the graft
avulsion	a-**VUL**-shun		Latin *to tear away*	Forcible separation or tearing away, often of a tendon from bone
chondromalacia	**KON**-dro-mah-**LAY**-she-ah	S/ R/CF	**-malacia** *softness* **chondr/o-** *cartilage*	Softening and degeneration of cartilage
debridement	day-**BREED**-mon	S/ P/ R/	**-ment** *action* **de-** *away from* **-bride-** *rubble*	The removal of injured or necrotic tissue
heterograft (also known as **xenograft**)	**HET**-er-oh-graft	P/ R/	**hetero-** *different* **-graft** *splice*	A graft using tissue taken from another species
hyperflexion	high-per-**FLEK**-shun	S/ P/ R/	**-ion** *process* **hyper-** *excess* **-flex-** *bend*	Flexion of a limb or part beyond the normal limits
meniscectomy	men-ih-**SEK**-toh-me	S/ R/	**-ectomy** *excision* **menisc-** *crescent,* *meniscus*	Excision (cutting out) all or part of a meniscus
prepatellar	pree-pah-**TELL**-ar	S/ P/ R/	**-ar** *pertaining to* **pre-** *before, in front of* **-patell-** *patella*	In front of the patella
rupture	**RUP**-tyur		Latin *break*	Break or tear of any organ or body part
tendinitis (also spelled **tendonitis**)	ten-dih-**NYE**-tis	S/ R/	**-itis** *inflammation* **tendin-** *tendon*	Inflammation of a tendon
xenograft (also known as **heterograft**)	**ZEN**-oh-graft	R/CF R/	**xen/o-** *foreign material* **-graft** *splice*	A graft from another species

---

EXERCISES   *Recognition of word elements will help you understand the medical term. In each of the following terms, a specific element is in bold. Identify the type of element, then define that element on the lines provided. Fill in the blanks.*

Medical Term	Type of Element (P, R, CF, S)	Definition of Element
prepatellar		
tendin**itis**		
hyper**flex**ion		
de**brid**ement		
autograft		
chondromalacia		
meniscectomy		
heterograft		
allo**graft**		

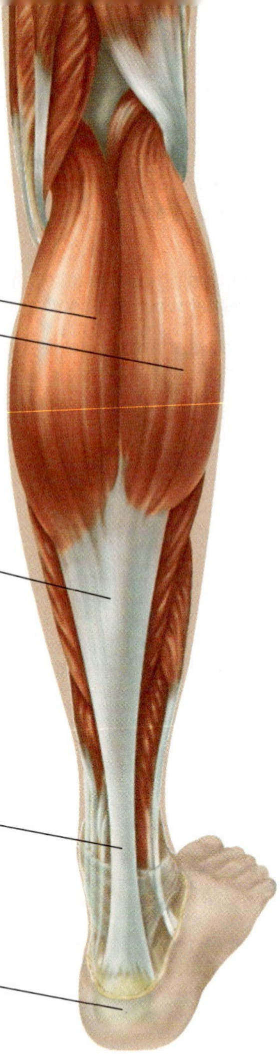

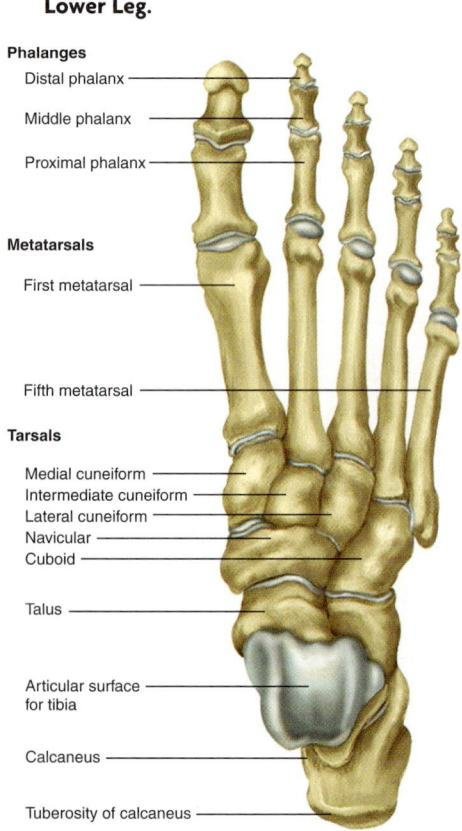

Gastrocnemius
Medial head
Lateral head

Tendon of gastrocnemius

Achilles (calcaneal) tendon

Calcaneus

▲ **FIGURE 5.45 Muscles of Back of Right Lower Leg.**

Phalanges
Distal phalanx
Middle phalanx
Proximal phalanx

Metatarsals
First metatarsal

Fifth metatarsal

Tarsals
Medial cuneiform
Intermediate cuneiform
Lateral cuneiform
Navicular
Cuboid

Talus

Articular surface for tibia

Calcaneus

Tuberosity of calcaneus

▲ **FIGURE 5.46   Bones of Right Foot.**

BONES, JOINTS, AND MUSCLES OF THE LOWER LEG, ANKLE, AND FOOT

The two bones of the lower leg are the larger and medial **tibia** and the thinner and lateral **fibula.** The lower end of the tibia on its medial border forms a prominent process called the medial **malleolus.** The lower end of the fibula forms the lateral malleolus. You can **palpate** both these prominences at your own ankle.

The muscles of the lower leg move the ankle, foot, and toes. Those on the front of the leg are in a compartment between the tibia and fibula. They **dorsiflex** the foot at the ankle and extend the toes. Those on the lateral side of the leg **evert** the foot.

Those on the back of the leg **plantar flex** the foot at the ankle, flex the toes, and **invert** the foot *(Figure 5.45)*. The **gastrocnemius** muscle forms a large part of the calf. The distal end of it joins with the tendon of the **soleus** muscle to form the **Achilles (calcaneal) tendon,** which is attached to the heel bone (**calcaneus**). The gastrocnemius muscle and the Achilles tendon enable you to "push off" and start running or jumping.

The ankle has two joints:

1. one between the lateral malleolus of the fibula and the talus

2. one between the medial malleolus of the tibia and the talus

The **talus** is the most superior of the seven **tarsal** bones of the ankle and proximal foot *(Figure 5.46)*, and its trochlear surface articulates with the tibia. The tarsal bones help the ankle bear the body's weight. Strong ligaments on both sides of the ankle joint hold it together.

Attached to the tarsal bones are the five parallel **metatarsal** bones that form the instep and then fan out to form the ball of the foot, where they bear weight. The toes each have three **phalanges,** except for the big toe, which has only two. This is identical to the thumb and its relation to the hand. The tendons of the leg muscles are inserted into the phalanges.

Disorders and Injuries of the Ankle and Foot

Podiatry is a health care specialty concerned with the diagnosis and treatment of disorders and injuries of the foot.

Bunions occur usually at the base of the big toe and are swellings of the bones that cause the metatarsophalangeal joint to be misaligned and stick out medially. This deformity is called **hallux valgus.**

Strains and sprains are more common in the ankle ligaments than in any other joint in the body. Some severe sprains with tearing of the ligament may require surgical repair.

Pott fracture is a term applied to a variety of fractures in which there is a fracture of the fibula near the ankle, often accompanied by a fracture of the medial malleolus of the tibia *(Figure 5.47)*.

Achilles tendinitis results from a small stretch injury that causes the tendon to become swollen and painful. A larger partial or complete **tear** leads to loss of function with difficulty in walking and no ability to "push off."

Plantar fasciitis is overstretching or tearing of the dense sheet of fascia that supports the arch of the foot. If the plantar fascia is weak, **pes planus** (flatfoot), can be present.

Ingrown toenails are nails that grow into the skin folds on either side of the toe. They are often infected and painful and may need surgical repair.

Clubfoot, a type of **talipes,** (deformity affecting the talus) is a congenital deformity in which the feet are adducted and plantar flexed *(see Chapter 2)* so that the soles are turned medially *(Figure 5.48)*.

WORD	PRONUNCIATION		ELEMENTS	DEFINITION
Achilles tendon (also called **calcaneal tendon**)	ah-**KILL**-eeze		a Greek warrior	A tendon formed from gastrocnemius and soleus muscles and inserted into the calcaneus
bunion	**BUN**-yun		French *bump*	A swelling at the base of the big toe
calcaneus **calcaneal** (adj)	kal-**KAY**-knee-us kal-**KAY**-knee-al		Latin *the heel*	Bone of the tarsus that forms the heel
gastrocnemius	gas-trok-**NEE**-me-us	S/ R/	**-ius** *pertaining to* **gastrocnem-** *calf of leg*	Major muscle in back of the lower leg (the calf)
hallux valgus	**HAL**-uks **VAL**-gus		**hallux** *big toe* **valgus** *turn out*	Deviation of the big toe toward the lateral side of the foot
metatarsus **metatarsal** (adj)	**MET**-ah-**TAR**-sus **MET**-ah-**TAR**-sal	P/ R/ S/	**meta-** *behind* **-tarsus** *flat surface* **-al** *pertaining to*	A collective term referring to the five parallel bones of the foot between the tarsus and the phalanges
pes planus	PES **PLAY**-nuss		**pes** *foot* **planus** *flat surface*	A flat foot with no plantar arch
podiatry **podiatrist**	po-**DIE**-ah-tree po-**DIE**-ah-trist	S/ R/ S/	**-iatry** *treatment* **pod-** *foot* **-iatrist** *practitioner*	The diagnosis and treatment of disorders and injuries of the foot Practitioner of podiatry
Pott fracture	POT **FRAK**-shur		Percival Pott, London surgeon, 1714–1788	Fracture of lower end of fibula, often with fracture of tibial malleolus
soleus	**SO**-lee-us		From Latin for "sole of foot"	Large muscle of the calf
talipes	**TAL**-ip-eze	R/ R/	**-pes** *foot* **tali-** *ankle bone*	Deformity of the foot involving the talus
talus	**TAY**-luss		Latin *heel bone*	The tarsal bone that articulates with the tibia to form the ankle joint
tarsus **tarsal** (adj)	**TAR**-sus **TAR**-sal		Latin *flat surface*	The collection of seven bones in the foot that form the ankle and instep

EXERCISES

Complete your knowledge of the skeleton by matching the statement in Column 1 to the appropriate term in Column 2.

_____ 1. forms ankle joint

_____ 2. flatfoot

_____ 3. forms ankle and instep

_____ 4. heel bone

_____ 5. large muscle of calf

_____ 6. deviation of big toe

_____ 7. swelling at base of big toe

_____ 8. five parallel bones in the foot

_____ 9. foot deformity involving talus

_____ 10. major muscle in calf

A. hallux valgus

B. gastrocnemius

C. soleus

D. tarsus

E. talipes

F. pes planus

G. metatarsus

H. talus

I. calcaneus

J. bunion

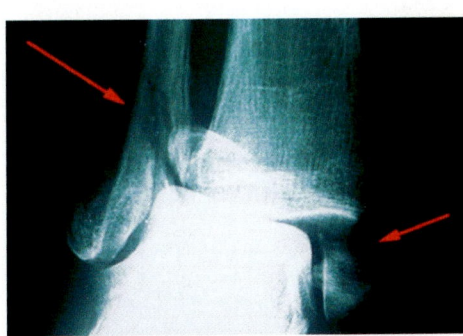

▲ **FIGURE 5.47   Pott Fracture Involving Lower End of Fibula and Medial Malleolus of Tibia.**

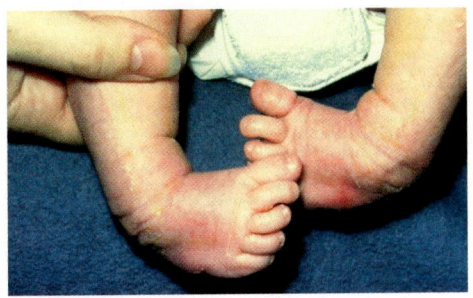

▲ **FIGURE 5.48   Clubfoot (Talipes).**

MUSCULOSKELETAL SYSTEM

CHALLENGE YOUR KNOWLEDGE

A. **Fill out the disability form for Ms. Lara Baker.** Use the information provided in Case Report 5.6, with these additional facts:

1. Ms. Baker must complete her physiotherapy (PT) first, and then return to see Dr. Stannard.

2. Ms. Baker is to remain off work until she has completed PT and returned to see Dr. Stannard in three weeks.

3. Dr. Stannard is an MD.

4. Ms. Baker has no other current medical problems.

5. The disability insurance carrier is Empire Insurance Company.

6. On examination, Dr. Stannard has found pain, swelling, numbness, tingling, and reduced grip in Ms. Baker's right hand.

7. The office phone number is on the letterhead, and Dr. Stannard takes calls from 8 to 9 a.m. and again from 3 to 4 p.m., Monday through Friday.

Fulwood Medical Center
3333 Medical Parkway, Fulwood, MI 01234
555-247-6100

Department of Orthopedics
Dr. Stannard (555)-247-6100

Doctor's report of occupational injury or illness

Patient name:_____

Patient address:_____

Occupation:_____

Employer:_____

Employer's insurance company:_____

(Please provide insurance claim form to billing manager)_____

Date of onset of illness: (*back date from date seen*)_____

Date seen: (*use current date*)_____

Date last worked: (*use current date*)_____

_____

Patient's description of how injury occurred:_____

Patient's chief complaints:_____

Doctor's findings:_____

Diagnosis:_____

Treatment Plan_____

_____

_____

Any special equipment ordered? No_____Yes_____

If yes, describe equipment: _____

Is there any other current condition that will delay recovery from this injury/illness?

No _____ Yes _____ If yes, describe_____

Is further treatment required? No _____ Yes _____

Followup appointment? No _____ Yes _____

When?_____

Can patient return to work at this time?

YES	NO
No modifications _____	Still in treatment _____
With modification _____	Unable to return to this job _____
Describe restrictions: No lifting _____ No standing _____ No sitting for extended periods of time _____ Other_____	
Full time _____	
Part time only _____	

May we call you concerning this patient? No _____Yes_____ Best time:_____

Doctor's name and degree:_____

License number:_____Tax ID#_____

Doctor's signature: (stamped signature not acceptable)

_____

B. Show your understanding of orthopedic terminology by providing the meaning of the elements for the terms below and then using the term in a sentence. Slash (/) the terms into elements before you start the exercise.

1. **orthopedic** The combining form is _____ and means _____.
    Sentence:

    _____

    _____

2. **endosteum** The prefix is _____ and means _____.
    Sentence:

    _____

    _____

3. **epiphysis** The root is _____ and means _____.
    Sentence:

    _____

    _____

4. **articulation** The suffix is _____ and means _____.
    Sentence:

    _____

    _____

5. **degenerative** The root is _____ and means _____.
    Sentence:

    _____

    _____

6. **arthrodesis** The suffix is _____ and means _____.
    Sentence:

    _____

    _____

7. **fibromyalgia** The combining form is _____ and means _____.
    Sentence:

    _____

    _____

MUSCULOSKELETAL SYSTEM

C. **The skeleton effects movement and provides support and protection for the entire body.** Help build your knowledge of the skeleton and orthopedic terminology with this mini-outline.

The four components of the skeletal system are:

1. _____

2. _____

3. _____

4. _____

These components have the following functions:

1. _____

2. _____

3. _____

4. _____

5. _____

6. _____

Factors that affect bone growth:

1. _____

2. _____

3. _____

4. _____

5. _____

6. _____

7. _____

The most common type of bone in the body is the long bone. Define these terms related to long bones:

1. epiphysis: _____

_____

2. diaphysis: _____

_____

3. metaphysis: _____

_____

4. Covers outer surface of all bones: _____

5. Cartilage cells in the _____ enable bone shaft to grow in length.

6. The _____ _____ contains the bone marrow and is lined with the membrane

called the _____.

D. **Abbreviations in medical documentation save time for the writer.** You must be sure, however, to interpret them correctly for patient safety. Write the full meaning of the abbreviation on the blank.

1. Eventual treatment for Mrs. Vargas's THR (_____) will involve either an orthopedist or a DO (_____). The PT (_____ _____) department will also provide follow-up care to improve her ROM (_____) and mobility after the surgery. Mrs. Vargas will also take medication to avoid any further DJD (_____ _____).

2. The patient's prescription for pain medication was written for 150 mg (_____) to be taken two times a day. This was not helping her pain so Dr. Stannard increased the frequency to three times a day (_____).

3. BMD (_____) tests and DEXA (_____) scans will determine if osteoporosis is present. If it is, increased IU (_____) of vitamin D may help. There is also FDA-(_____) approved medication available.

4. The patient's MRI (_____) confirmed herniation at her C5–C6 (hint: location _____ _____) vertebral discs.

5. TMJ (_____) syndrome can be diagnosed with an electromyelogram.

MUSCULOSKELETAL SYSTEM

E. **Many professional certification exams are given in multiple choice format.** Begin deciding on the answer by quickly eliminating the answers you know to be incorrect. Then decide which of the remaining answers is the *best* choice.

1. For an open reduction, internal fixation (ORIF) of a fracture, what surgical hardware could be needed:

   a. wires

   b. rods

   c. plates

   d. screws

   e. any of the above

2. Bone growth occurs at the:

   a. origin

   b. epiphyseal plate

   c. diaphysis

   d. epicondyle

   e. lacuna

3. Inherited condition in which bone formation is incomplete:

   a. osteoarthritis

   b. osteomalacia

   c. osteomyelitis

   d. osteogenesis imperfecta

   e. osteopenia

4. Lubricant for joint movement:

   a. mucin

   b. mucus

   c. mucous

   d. synovial

   e. meniscus

5. Where two bones come together at a joint:

   a. articulation

   b. reduction

   c. mastication

   d. striation

   e. herniation

6. An extension of synovial membrane that forms a cushion to prevent structures from rubbing together:

a. tendon

b. periosteum

c. ligament

d. bursa

e. muscle

7. Pulling a bone from the distal end back into alignment:

a. subluxation

b. dislocation

c. reduction

d. resorption

e. external fixation

8. The process of lying face upward, flat on your spine is:

a. pronation

b. abduction

c. adduction

d. supination

e. inversion

9. Overstretching or tearing of the dense sheet of tissue that supports the arch of the foot:

a. pes planus

b. plantar fasciitis

c. hallux valgus

d. Achilles tendonitis

e. exostosis

10. Joints between the teeth and their sockets are called:

a. symphyses

b. gomphoses

c. sutures

d. syndesmoses

e. synchondroses

Digestive System
The Language of Gastroenterology

CASE REPORT 6.1

You are

... a medical transcriptionist at Fulwood Medical Center.

One of your Physicians

... Dr. Stewart Walsh, has dictated this letter to request authorization for a procedure:

Fulwood Medical Center
3333 Medical Parkway, Fulwood, MI 01234
555-247-6100

Department of: Bariatric Surgery

To: Charles Leavenworth, MD
Medical Director
Lombard Insurance Company

From: Stewart Walsh, MD, FACS
Chief of Surgery
Center for Bariatric Surgery
Fulwood Medical Center

10/06/06

Dear Doctor Leavenworth,
     Request for authorization of Surgery

     Re: Mrs. Martha Jones
     Subscriber ID 056437

Mrs. Jones is a 52-year-old former waitress, recently divorced. She is 5 feet 4 inches tall and weighs 275 pounds. She has type 2 diabetes with frequent episodes of hypoglycemia and also ketoacidosis, requiring three different hospitalizations. She now has diabetic retinopathy and peripheral vasculitis. Complicating this is hypertension (185/110), coronary artery disease, and pulmonary edema. Exercise is out of the question because she has marked osteoarthritis of her knees and hips. Mrs. Jones is now housebound, dependent on transportation to our medical center. In spite of monthly meetings with our nutritionist, she has gained 25 pounds in the past six months.

At a case conference earlier today, we all recognized that unless we were able to reduce and control her weight, we had no hope of controlling any of her other multiple problems.

Therefore, I am proposing to perform a Roux-en-Y **gastric** bypass using a laparoscopic approach. We will need to admit her two days prior to surgery to control her blood sugar and cardiovascular problems and anticipate that she will remain in the hospital for two days after surgery, barring any complications. My surgical technologist and I have spent time with Mrs. Jones explaining the procedure and its risks, and she is aware and accepting of these. She is also very aware of the necessary followup to the procedure and the counseling required for a new lifestyle.

We believe not only that this is an essential procedure medically, but that it will reduce in the long term the financial burden of her multiple therapies and improve the quality of the patient's life. Enclosed is supportive documentation of her current history and medical problems.

Your company has designated our hospital as a Center of Excellence for weight-loss surgery, and I look forward to your prompt agreement with this approach for this patient.

Sincerely,

Stewart Walsh, MD, FACS
Chief of Surgery
Fulwood Medical Center

Learning Outcomes

As a medical transcriptionist, you and all health professionals directly and indirectly involved with Mrs. Jones' care need to be able to:

- Apply the language of gastroenterology to the anatomy and physiology of the gastrointestinal tract, liver, gallbladder, and pancreas.

- Comprehend, analyze, spell, and write the medical terms of gastroenterology so that you can communicate and document accurately and precisely in any health care setting.

- Recognize and pronounce the medical terms of gastroenterology so that you can communicate verbally with accuracy and precision in any health care setting.

- Understand the tests and procedures performed to diagnose and treat gastrointestinal disorders.

In Mrs. Martha Jones' case, the **Roux-en-Y** procedure reduced the size of her available stomach from two quarts to two ounces. This resulted in her being able to eat less and to absorb less. She had no complications from the **laparoscopic** procedure. In the succeeding two months, she lost 15 pounds in weight.

LESSON 6.1 The Digestive System

OBJECTIVES

There are basic elements of anatomy, physiology, and medical terminology that apply throughout the different parts of the digestive system. These elements are discussed in this lesson. That information will enable you to:

- **List the organs and accessory organs of the digestive system.**
- **Describe the functions of the digestive system.**
- **Identify the layers of the alimentary canal.**
- **Discuss the basic processes of digestion.**
- **Select the correct medical terminology to describe the structure and functions of the digestive system.**

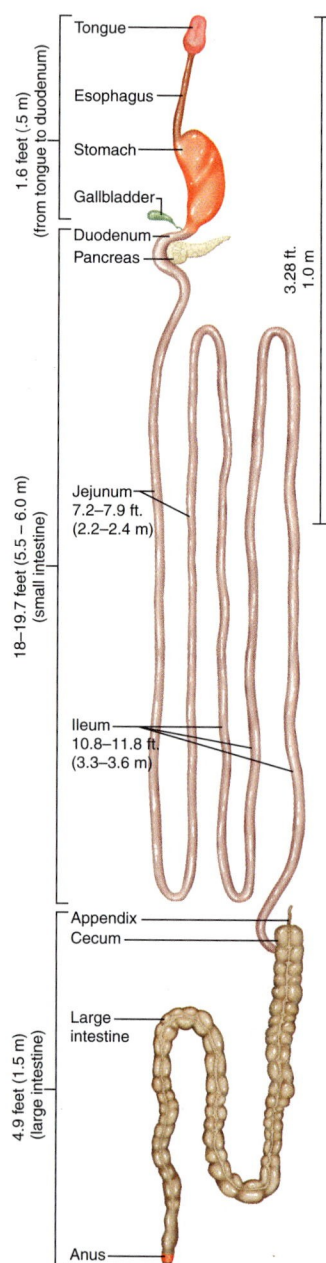

▲ FIGURE 6.1
Alimentary Canal.

ALIMENTARY CANAL AND ACCESSORY ORGANS

Every cell in your body requires a constant supply of nourishment. The cells cannot travel, so the nourishment has to be brought to them in a form that can be absorbed across their cell membrane. The foods that you **ingest** cannot be used in their existing form by the cells. The digestive system, through its alimentary canal, breaks down the nutrients in the food into elements that can be transported to the cells via the blood and **lymphatics.** These elements can then be transported across the cell membrane into the cell.

The **digestive system** consists of the **alimentary canal** (digestive tract), which extends from the **mouth** to the **anus,** and **accessory organs** connected to the canal to assist in digestion.

The term **gastrointestinal (GI)** technically refers to the stomach and **intestines,** but is often used to mean the whole digestive system. **Gastroenterology** is the study of the digestive system. A **gastroenterologist** is a physician who specializes in the digestive system.

The **alimentary canal** (*Figure 6.1*) includes the:

- mouth
- **esophagus**
- small intestine
- pharynx
- stomach
- large intestine

The **accessory organs** of digestion include the:

- teeth
- salivary glands
- gallbladder
- tongue
- liver
- pancreas

Abbreviation

GI gastrointestinal

WORD ANALYSIS AND DEFINITION

S = Suffix   P = Prefix   R = Root   R/CF = Combining Form

WORD	PRONUNCIATION		ELEMENTS	DEFINITION
alimentary	al-ih-**MEN**-tar-ee	S/ R/	**-ary** *pertaining to* **aliment-** *nourishment*	Pertaining to the digestive tract
bariatric	bar-ee-**AT**-rik	S/ R/	**-atric** *treatment* **bari-** *weight*	Treatment of obesity
digestion	die-**JEST**-shun	S/ R/	**-ion** *action* **digest-** *to break down*	Breakdown of food into elements suitable for cell metabolism
digestive (adj)	die-**JEST**-iv	S/	**-ive** *nature of*	Relating to digestion
esophagus	ee-**SOF**-ah-gus		Greek *gullet*	Tube linking the pharynx and the stomach
gastric	**GAS**-trik	S/ R/	**-ic** *pertaining to* **gastr-** *stomach*	Pertaining to the stomach
gastroenterology	**GAS**-troh-en-ter-**OL**-oh-gee	S/ R/CF R/CF	**-logy** *study of* **gastr/o-** *stomach* **-enter/o-** *intestine*	Medical specialty of the stomach and intestines
gastroenterologist gastrointestinal (GI)	**GAS**-troh-en-ter-**OL**-oh-jist **GAS**-troh-in-**TESS**-tin-al	S/ S/ R/CF R/	**-logist** *one who studies* **-al** *pertaining to* **gastr/o-** *stomach* **-intestin-** *gut*	Medical specialist in gastroenterology Relating to the stomach and intestines
intestine intestinal (adj)	in-**TES**-tin in-**TES**-tin-al	 S/	Latin *intestine, gut* **-al** *pertaining to*	The digestive tube from stomach to anus
laparoscopy	lap-ah-**ROS**-koh-pee	S/ R/CF	**-scopy** *to view* **lapar/o-** *abdomen in general*	Examination of the contents of the abdomen using an endoscope
laparoscope	**LAP**-ah-roh-skope	S/	**-scope** *instrument*	Instrument (endoscope) used for viewing the abdominal contents
laparoscopic (adj)	**LAP**-ah-rah-**SKOP**-ik			
lymph lymphatic (adj)	LIMF lim-**FAT**-ik	 S/ R/	Latin *spring water* **-ic** *pertaining to* **lymphat-** *lymph*	A clear fluid collected from tissues and transported by vessels to venous circulation Pertaining to lymph
mouth	MOWTH		Old English *mouth*	External opening of a cavity or canal
Roux-en-Y	**ROO**-on-Y		César Roux, a Swiss surgeon, 1857–1934	Surgical procedure to reduce the size of the stomach

EXERCISES

Analyzing the elements can tell you a lot about a medical term. Look closely at the medical terms shown above, and let the elements be your guide. Review the Word Analysis and Definition box (WAD) before you start the exercise. Fill in the blanks.

1. Based on the root, the term **gastric** pertains to the _____.

2. Analyzing the two combining forms, the term **gastroenterology** pertains to the _____ and

   the _____.

3. In the term **gastric**, the root _____ has the same meaning as the combining

   form _____ in the term **gastroenterology**.

4. A laparoscope would be inserted into the _____ for examination or biopsy.

5. Mrs. Jones's gastric bypass will attempt to reduce the size of her _____.

Use some of the above terms to fill in the following blanks.

6. _____ symptoms pertain to the stomach only. Because the patient had stomach and intestinal problems,

   her symptoms can be described as _____. For this condition, she will need a specialist in the study of

   the stomach and intestines, a field known as _____. This type of physician is referred to as

   a _____.

FUNCTIONS OF THE DIGESTIVE SYSTEM

1. **Ingestion**—the selective intake of food into the mouth; alternatively, food can be inserted directly into the stomach via a **nasogastric** or stomach tube.

2. **Propulsion**—the mechanical movement of food from the mouth to the anus (Figure 6.2). Normally, this takes 24 to 36 hours. **Mastication** (chewing) breaks down the food into smaller particles so that **digestive enzymes** have a larger surface area with which to interact. **Deglutition**, or swallowing, moves the **bolus** of food from the mouth into the esophagus. **Peristalsis**, or waves of contraction and relaxation, moves material through most of the alimentary canal. **Segmental contractions** in the small intestine move food back and forth to mix it with digestive secretions.

3. **Digestion**—the breakdown of foods into forms that can be transported to and absorbed into cells. This process has two components.

   a. Mechanical digestion breaks larger pieces of food into smaller ones without altering their chemical composition. This process exposes a larger surface area of the food to the action of digestive enzymes.

   b. Chemical digestion breaks down large molecules of food into smaller and simpler chemicals. This process is carried out by digestive enzymes produced by the salivary glands, stomach, small intestine, and pancreas.

   The digestive enzymes have three main groups:

   - **amylases** that digest carbohydrates
   - **lipases** that digest fats
   - **proteases** that digest proteins

4. **Secretion**—the addition throughout the digestive tract of secretions that lubricate, liquefy, and digest the food. Mucus lubricates the food and the lining of the tract. Water liquefies the food to make it easier to digest and absorb. Enzymes break down the food.

5. **Absorption**—the movement of nutrient molecules out of the digestive tract and through the epithelial cells lining the tract into the blood or lymph for transportation to body cells.

6. **Elimination**—the process by which the undigested residue of food is removed from the body.

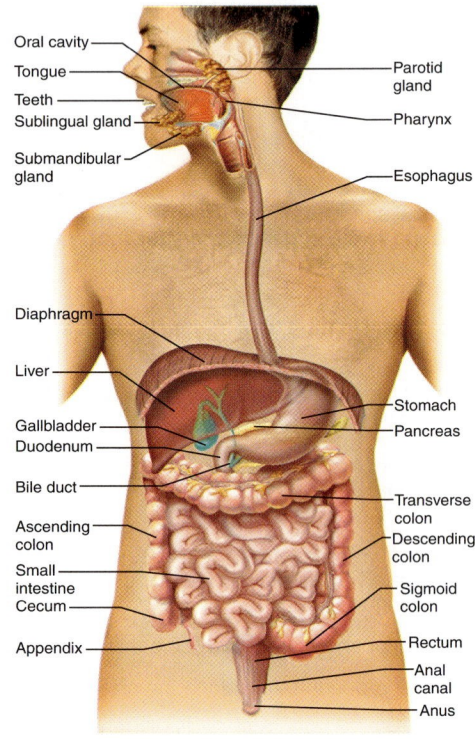

Oral cavity
Tongue
Teeth
Sublingual gland
Submandibular gland
Parotid gland
Pharynx
Esophagus
Diaphragm
Liver
Gallbladder
Duodenum
Bile duct
Ascending colon
Small intestine
Cecum
Appendix
Stomach
Pancreas
Transverse colon
Descending colon
Sigmoid colon
Rectum
Anal canal
Anus

▲ **FIGURE 6.2   The Digestive System.**

WORD ANALYSIS AND DEFINITION

S = Suffix P = Prefix R = Root R/CF = Combining Form

WORD	PRONUNCIATION	ELEMENTS		DEFINITION
absorption **absorb (verb)**	ab-**SORP**-shun ab-**SORB**		Latin *to swallow*	Uptake of nutrients by cells in the GI tract
amylase	**AM**-il-aze	S/ R/	**-ase** *enzyme* **amyl-** *starch*	One of a group of enzymes that break down starch
bolus	**BOH**-lus		Greek *lump*	Single mass of a substance
deglutition	dee-glue-**TISH**-un	S/ R/	**-ion** *action* **deglutit-** *to swallow*	The act of swallowing
elimination	e-lim-ih-**NAY**-shun	S/ R/	**-ation** *process* **elimin-** *throw away*	Removal of waste material from the digestive tract
ingestion	in-**JEST**-shun	S/ R/	**-ion** *action* **ingest-** *carry in*	Intake of food, either by mouth or through a nasogastric tube
lipase	**LIE**-paze	S/ R/	**-ase** *enzyme* **lip-** *fat*	Enzyme that breaks down fat
nasogastric	**NAY**-zoh-**GAS**-trik	S/ R/CF R/	**-ic** *pertaining to* **nas/o-** *nose* **-gastr-** *stomach*	Pertaining to the nose and stomach
peristalsis	per-ih-**STAL**-sis	P/ R/	**peri-** *around* **-stalsis** *constrict*	Wave of alternate contraction and relaxation of intestinal wall to move food along
protease	**PRO**-tee-aze	S/ R/CF	**-ase** *enzyme* **prot/e-** *protein*	Group of enzymes that break down protein
secrete **secretion (noun)**	se-**KREET** se-**KREE**-shun		Latin *to separate*	To produce a chemical substance in a cell and release it from the cell
segment **segmental (adj)**	**SEG**-ment **SEG**-ment-al	 S/ R/	Latin *to cut* **-al** *pertaining to* **segment-** *to cut*	A section of an organ or structure

EXERCISES

The suffixes ation and ion both mean action. The body process or action has been described for you. Match the definition in column 1 to the correct medical term in column 2.

____	1. swallowing	A. mastication
____	2. releasing products of metabolism	B. elimination
____	3. chewing	C. deglutition
____	4. removal of waste material	D. secretion

Build the medical terms by filling in their missing elements.

5. enzymes that break down protein ________ /ase
6. the action of throwing away ________ /ation
7. enzyme that breaks down fat lip/ ________
8. enzyme to break down starch ________ /ase
9. pertaining to a section of an organ ________ /al
10. waves that move food in intestines peri/ ________
11. Based on their suffixes name the three enzymes in this WAD ____________________, ____________________, and ____________________ all end in ____________________.

Mouth, Pharynx, and Esophagus

OBJECTIVES

When you pop a piece of chicken and some vegetable into your mouth, you start a cascade of digestive tract events that occurs during the following 24 to 36 hours. In this chapter, you will follow a meal of chicken and vegetables as it goes through the digestive tract. In this lesson, you will review the first stages in the cascade while the food is in the mouth and then is swallowed. The information in this lesson will enable you to:

- **Identify the structure and functions of the teeth, tongue, and salivary glands.**
- **Describe the composition and functions of saliva.**
- **Document the process and outcomes of mastication and deglutition.**
- **Discuss some common disorders of the mouth, pharynx, and esophagus.**
- **Select the correct medical terminology to describe the anatomy, physiology, and disorders of the mouth, pharynx, and esophagus.**

You are

. . . a medical assistant working with Susan Lee, MD, a primary care physician at Fulwood Medical Center.

Your patient is

. . . Mrs. Helen Schreiber, a 45-year-old high school principal. Your task is to document her care.

CASE REPORT 6.2

Documentation.

Mrs. Helen Schreiber, a 45-year-old high school principal, presents with a six-month history of dry mouth, bleeding gums, and difficulty in chewing and swallowing food.

Questioning by Dr. Susan Lee, her primary care physician, reveals that she also has dry eyes, is having pain in some joints of both hands, and has felt fatigued. Her previous medical history is uneventful. Physical examination shows a dry mouth, mild **gingivitis**, and an ulcer on the back of the lower lip. Her salivary glands are not swollen. Her eyes show no ulceration or conjunctivitis. The metacarpophalangeal joints of both index fingers are swollen, stiff, and tender. All other systems show no abnormality.

Initial laboratory reports show anemia, decreased **WBC** count and an elevated **ESR**. Dr. Lee made a provisional diagnosis of **Sjögren syndrome**. The results of blood studies for **SSA** and **SSB** antibodies (Sjögren syndrome antibodies A and B) and rheumatoid factor titers are pending, as are X-rays of her hands.

Mrs. Schreiber was given advice about symptomatic treatment for her dry mouth and will be seen again in one week.

Signed: Luis Guitterez, **CMA** 06/12/06, 1530 hrs

THE MOUTH AND MASTICATION

The mouth, or **oral** cavity *(Figure 6.3)*, is the entrance to your digestive tract and is the first site of mechanical digestion (through **mastication,** or chewing) and of chemical digestion (through an **enzyme** in saliva).

The cheeks contain the **buccinator** muscles. These muscles hold the chicken and vegetable in place while you chew and your teeth crush and tear them.

The roof of the mouth is called the **palate.** The anterior two-thirds is the bony hard palate. The posterior one-third is the muscular soft palate. The hard palate is covered with folds of epithelium called rugae, which assist the tongue to manipulate food prior to swallowing. The skeletal muscle of the soft palate has a projection called the **uvula** that closes off the nasopharynx during swallowing.

The **tongue** *(Figure 6.4)* moves food around your mouth and helps the cheeks, lips, and gums hold the food in place while you chew it. Small, rough, raised areas on the tongue, called **papillae,** contain some 4,000 **taste buds** that react to the chemical nature of the food to give you the different sensations of taste. A taste bud cell lives for 7 to 10 days and is then replaced.

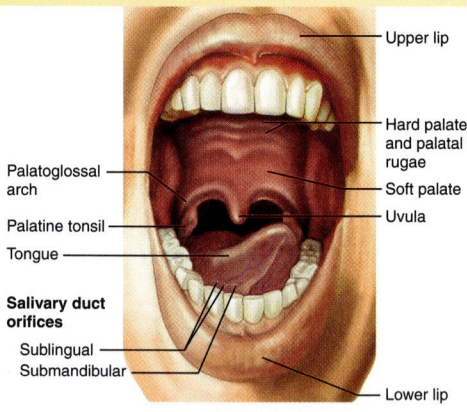

Palatoglossal arch
Palatine tonsil
Tongue

Salivary duct orifices
Sublingual
Submandibular

Upper lip
Hard palate and palatal rugae
Soft palate
Uvula
Lower lip

▲ **FIGURE 6.3   Mouth (Oral Cavity).**

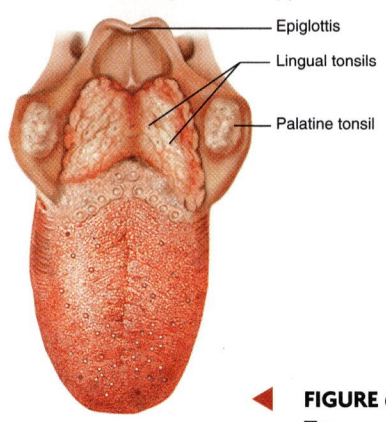

Epiglottis
Lingual tonsils
Palatine tonsil

◀ **FIGURE 6.4
Tongue.**

WORD ANALYSIS AND DEFINITION

S = Suffix   P = Prefix   R = Root   R/CF = Combining Form

WORD	PRONUNCIATION	ELEMENTS		DEFINITION
buccinator	**BUCK**-sin-a-tor	S/ R/	-ator *agent* **buccin-** *the cheek*	Buccinator muscle is the muscle in the cheek
enzyme	**EN**-zime	P/ R/	en- *in* -zyme *fermenting*	Protein that induces changes in other substances
gingivitis	jin-jih-**VI**-tis	S/ R/	-itis *inflammation* gingiv- *gum*	Inflammation of the gums
masticate mastication (noun)	**MAS**-tih-kate mas-tih-**KAY**-shun	S/ R/	-ate *action* **mastic-** *chew*	To chew
oral	**OR**-al	S/ R/	-al *pertaining to* or- (os) *mouth*	Pertaining to the mouth
palate	**PAL**-uht		Latin *palate*	Roof of the mouth
papilla papillae (pl)	pah-**PILL**-ah pah-**PILL**-ee		Latin *small pimple*	Any small projection
Sjögren syndrome	**SHOW**-gren **SIN**-drome		Henrik Sjögren, 1899–1986, Swedish ophthalmologist	Autoimmune disease that attacks the glands that produce saliva and tears
taste	TAYST		Latin *to taste*	Sensation from chemicals on the taste buds
tongue	TUNG		Latin *tongue*	Mobile muscle mass in mouth; bears the taste buds
uvula	**YOU**-vyu-lah		Latin *grape*	Fleshy projection of the soft palate

Abbreviations

CMA	Certified Medical Assistant
ESR	erythrocyte sedimentation rate
SSA	Sjögren syndrome antibodies A
SSB	Sjögren syndrome antibodies B
WBC	white blood cell

EXERCISES

Practice your terms associated with the digestive system by matching the definitions in column 1 with the correct medical terms in column 2. You have more answers than you will need. Fill in the blanks.

_____ 1. fleshy projection of the soft palate

_____ 2. inflammation of the gums

_____ 3. bears the taste buds

_____ 4. any small projection

_____ 5. autoimmune disease that attacks salivary glands

_____ 6. protein that introduces changes in other substances

_____ 7. to chew

_____ 8. cheek muscle

_____ 9. roof of the mouth

_____ 10. pertaining to the mouth

A. Sjögren syndrome

B. gastrocnemius

C. oral

D. uvula

E. palate

F. buccinator

G. papilla

H. gingivitis

I. gastroenteritis

J. tongue

K. enzyme

L. masticate

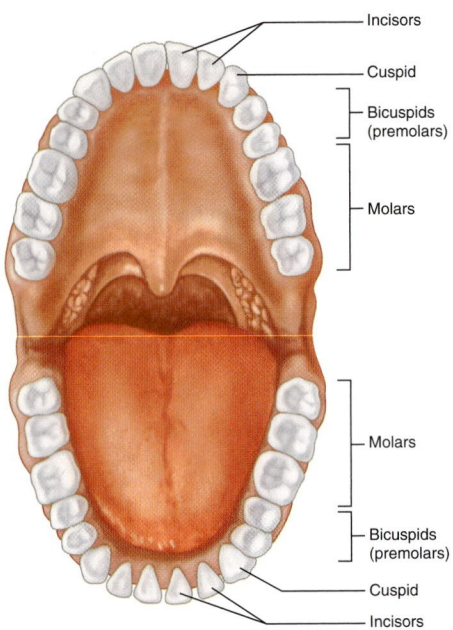

FIGURE 6.5 Adult Teeth.

Labels: Incisors, Cuspid, Bicuspids (premolars), Molars, Molars, Bicuspids (premolars), Cuspid, Incisors

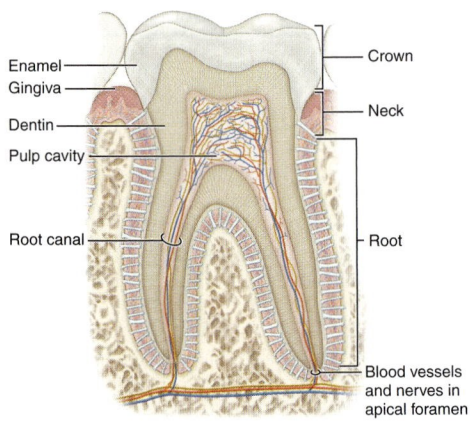

FIGURE 6.6 Anatomy of a Molar.

Labels: Enamel, Gingiva, Dentin, Pulp cavity, Root canal, Crown, Neck, Root, Blood vessels and nerves in apical foramen

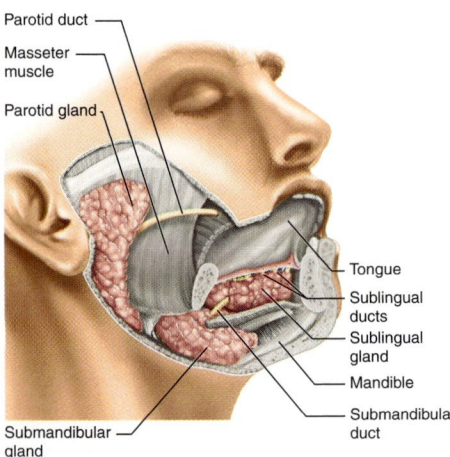

FIGURE 6.7 Salivary Glands.

Labels: Parotid duct, Masseter muscle, Parotid gland, Submandibular gland, Tongue, Sublingual ducts, Sublingual gland, Mandible, Submandibular duct

MOUTH, PHARYNX, AND ESOPHAGUS

Adult Teeth

The normal adult has 32 teeth, 16 rooted in the upper jaw (maxilla) and 16 in the lower jaw (mandible). The teeth are the hardest structures in your body, and different teeth *(Figure 6.5)* are designed to handle food in different ways. The eight **incisors** are shaped like a chisel to slice and cut into food. The four **cuspids** have a pointed tip for puncturing and tearing. The eight **bicuspids** and twelve **molars** have flattened surfaces for grinding and crushing food. Your wisdom teeth are molars.

Each tooth has two main parts:

- the **crown**, which projects above the gum and is covered in **enamel**, the hardest substance in the body.
- the **root**, which anchors the tooth to the jaw.

The bulk of the tooth is composed of **dentin**, a substance like bone but harder *(Figure 6.6)*. The dentin surrounds a central **pulp cavity** that contains blood vessels, nerves, and connective tissue. The blood vessels and nerves reach this cavity from the jaw through tubular **root canals.**

Salivary Glands

Salivary glands secrete saliva. The two **parotid** glands, the two **submandibular** glands, the two **sublingual glands** *(Figure 6.7)*, and numerous minor salivary glands scattered in the mucosa of the tongue and cheeks secrete more than a quart of saliva each day.

Saliva is 95% water and its functions are to:

- begin starch digestion with the enzyme **amylase**
- begin fat digestion through an enzyme **lipase**
- prevent the growth of bacteria in the mouth through an enzyme **lysozyme** and the protective **immunoglobulin A (IgA)** *(see Chapter 14)*
- produce **mucus** to lubricate food to make it easier to swallow

Case Report 6.2 (continued)

Mrs. Helen Schreiber has Sjögren syndrome, an autoimmune disease (*see Chapter 15*) that affects her salivary glands, stopping production of saliva. This leads to a dry mouth, difficulty in swallowing, and increased bacterial activity in the mouth, causing gingivitis. It is associated with dry eyes and with rheumatoid arthritis, which is beginning in her hands. There is no known cure, and treatment is **symptomatic**.

WORD ANALYSIS AND DEFINITION

WORD	PRONUNCIATION	ELEMENTS		DEFINITION
bicuspid (also called **premolar**)	by-**KUSS**-pid	S/ P/ R/	-id *having a particular quality* bi- *two* -cusp- *point*	Having two points; a bicuspid (premolar) tooth has two points
crown	KROWN		Latin *crown*	Part of tooth above the gum
cuspid	**KUSS**-pid	S/ R/	-id *having a particular quality* -cusp- *point*	Tooth with one point
dentin (also spelled dentine)	**DEN**-tin	S/ R/	-in *pertaining to* dent- *tooth*	Dense, ivorylike substance located under enamel in a tooth
enamel	ee-**NAM**-el		French *enamel*	Hard substance covering a tooth
incisor	in-**SIGH**-zor		Latin *to cut into*	Chisel-shaped tooth
lysozyme	**LIE**-soh-zime	S/ R/CF	-zyme *enzyme* lys/o- *dissolve*	Enzyme that dissolves the cell walls of bacteria
molar	**MO**-lar		Latin *millstone*	One of six teeth in each jaw that grind food
parotid	pah-**ROT**-id	S/ P/ R/	-id *having a particular quality* par- *beside* -ot- *ear*	Parotid gland is the salivary gland beside the ear
pulp	PULP		Latin *flesh*	Dental pulp is the connective tissue in the cavity in the center of the tooth
root	ROOT		Old English *beginning*	Fundamental or beginning part of a structure
saliva salivary (adj)	sa-**LIE**-vah **SAL**-ih-var-ee	 S/ R/	Latin *spit* -ary *pertaining to* saliv- *saliva*	Secretion in mouth from salivary glands
sublingual	sub-**LING**-wal	S/ P/ R/	-al *pertaining to* sub- *underneath* -lingu- *tongue*	Underneath the tongue
submandibular	sub-man-**DIB**-you-lar	S/ P/ R/	-ar *pertaining to* sub- *underneath* -mandibul- *mandible*	Underneath the mandible
symptom symptomatic	**SIMP**-tum simp-toe-**MAT**-ik	 S/ R/	Greek *sign* -ic *pertaining to* symptomat- *symptom*	Departure from the normal experienced by a patient Relating to the symptoms of a disease

EXERCISES

Analyze and define the following terms, and determine what makes them similar and what makes them different. Fill in the blanks.

Study Hint
Write these terms in the back of your book.

1. submandibular   Definition: _____

2. salivary   Definition: _____

3. dentine   Definition: _____

4. sublingual   Definition: _____

5. symptomatic   Definition: _____

6. After writing the definition of each term, it should be obvious what is similar. The similarity is:

_____

7. What makes the terms different? _____

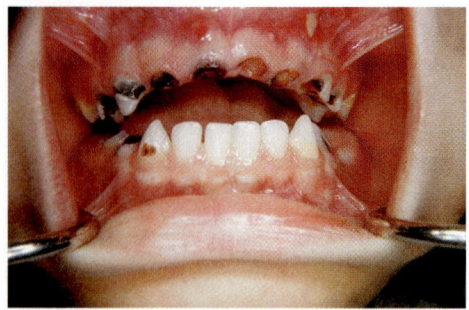

▲ **FIGURE 6.8 Dental Caries.**
Child with Dental Caries.

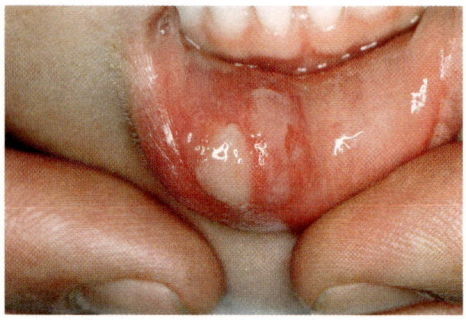

▲ **FIGURE 6.9 Cold Sores.**
Ulcer Inside Lower Lip.

Abbreviations

HSV-1 herpes simplex virus, type 1
HIV   human immunodeficiency virus

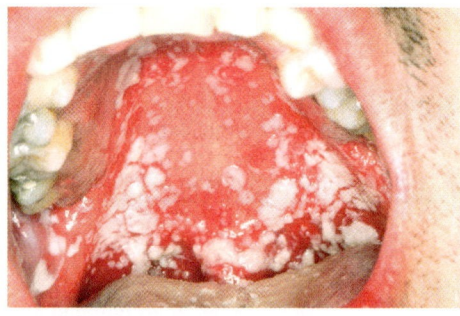

▲ **FIGURE 6.10 Oral Thrush.**

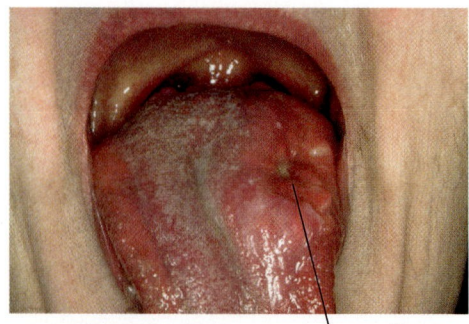

— Cancer

▲ **FIGURE 6.11 Oral Cancer.**
Cancer of the Tongue.

DISORDERS OF THE MOUTH

An accumulation of dental **plaque** (a collection of oral microorganisms and their products) or **dental calculus (tartar)** (calcified deposits at the gingival margin of the teeth) is a precursor to dental disease.

Dental caries, tooth **decay** and **cavity** formation, is an erosion of the tooth surface caused by bacteria *(Figure 6.8)*. If untreated it can lead to an abscess at the root of the tooth. **Gingivitis** is an infection of the gums. **Periodontal disease** occurs when the gums and the jaw bone are involved in a disease process. In **periodontitis,** infection causes the gums to pull away from the teeth, forming pockets that become infected. The infection can spread to the underlying bone. Infection of the gums with a purulent discharge is called **pyorrhea.**

The term **stomatitis** is used for any infection of the mouth. The most common infections are:

- **Mouth ulcers,** also called **canker** sores, are erosions of the mucous membrane lining the mouth. The most common type are **aphthous** ulcers, which occur in clusters of small ulcers and last for 3 or 4 days. They are usually related to stress or illness. Ulcers can also be caused by trauma.

- **Cold sores,** *also known as fever blisters (Figure 6.9)*, are recurrent ulcers of the lips, lining of the mouth, and gums due to infection with the virus **herpes simplex type 1 (HSV-1).** Acyclovir is a treatment used, but the ulcers usually clear spontaneously.

- **Thrush** *(Figure 6.10)* is an infection occurring anywhere in the mouth and is caused by the fungus *Candida albicans.* This fungus typically is found in the mouth, but it can multiply out of control as a result of prolonged antibiotic or steroid treatment, cancer chemotherapy, or diabetes. A newborn baby can acquire oral thrush from the mother's vaginal yeast infection during the birth process. Treatment with antifungal agents, such as nystatin or clotrimazole, is usually successful *(see Chapter 19)*.

- **Leukoplakia** is a white plaque seen anywhere in the mouth. It is more common in the elderly, is often associated with smoking or chewing tobacco, and approximately 3% turn into oral cancer. Patients whose immune systems are compromised (for example, with **human immunodeficiency virus [HIV]**), are susceptible to leukoplakia.

- **Oral cancer** *(Figure 6.11)* is mostly a squamous cell carcinoma, occurring often on the lip. Eighty percent of oral cancers are associated with smoking or chewing tobacco. Metastasis occurs to lymph nodes, bone, lung, and liver. The five-year-survival rate is only 51%.

- **Halitosis** is the medical term for bad breath, which can be found in association with any of the above mouth disorders.

- **Glossodynia** is a painful burning sensation of the tongue. It occurs in postmenopausal women. Its etiology is unknown, and there is no successful treatment.

WORD	PRONUNCIATION		ELEMENTS	DEFINITION
aphthous	**AF**-thus		Greek *ulcer*	Painful small oral ulcers (canker sores)
canker (also called mouth ulcer)	**KANG**-ker		Latin *crab*	Nonmedical term for aphthous ulcer
caries	**KARE**-eez		Latin *dry rot*	Bacterial destruction of teeth
gingiva gingival (adj) gingivitis gingivectomy	**JIN**-jih-vah **JIN**-jih-vul jin-ji-**VI**-tis jin-jih-**VEC**-toe-me	R/ S/ S/	Latin *gum* gingiv- *gum* -itis *inflammation* -ectomy *surgical excision*	Tissue surrounding teeth and covering the jaw Inflammation of the gums Surgical removal of diseased gum tissue
glossodynia	gloss-oh-**DIN**-ee-ah	S/ R/CF	-dynia *pain* gloss/o- *tongue*	Painful, burning tongue
halitosis	hal-ih-**TOE**-sis	S/ R/	-osis *condition* halit- *breath*	Bad odor of the breath
leukoplakia	loo-koh-**PLAY**-kee-ah	S/ P/ R/	-ia *condition* leuko- *white* -plak- *plate, plaque*	White patch on oral mucous membrane, often precancerous
periodontal	**PER**-ee-oh-**DON**-tal	S/ P/ R/	-al *pertaining to* peri- *around* -odont- *tooth*	Around a tooth
periodontics	**PER**-ee-oh-**DON**-tiks	S/	-ics *pertaining to*	Branch of dentistry specializing in disorders of tissues around the teeth
periodontist periodontitis	**PER**-ee-oh-**DON**-tist **PER**-ee-oh-don-**TIE**-tis	S/ S/	-ist *specialist* -itis *inflammation*	Specialist in periodontics Inflammation of tissues around a tooth
plaque	PLAK		French *plate*	Patch of abnormal tissue
tartar (also called dental calculus)	**TAR**-tar		Latin *crust on wine casks*	Calcified deposit at the gingival margin of the teeth
thrush	THRUSH		Root unknown	Infection with *Candida albicans*

EXERCISES

Find the correct suffix to complete the medical terms. Use each suffix only one time. Fill in the blanks, then answer the questions.

1. inflammation of the gums   gingiv/ _____

2. specialized branch of dentistry   periodont/ _____

3. painful, burning tongue   glosso/ _____

4. around a tooth   periodont/ _____

5. bad breath   halit/ _____

6. surgical removal of diseased gums   gingiv/ _____

7. precancerous white patches   leukoplak/ _____

8. one who specializes in periodontics   periodont/ _____

9. Aphthous, oral, and ulcer are all terms connected with _____ _____.

10. Dental calculus is another name for _____.

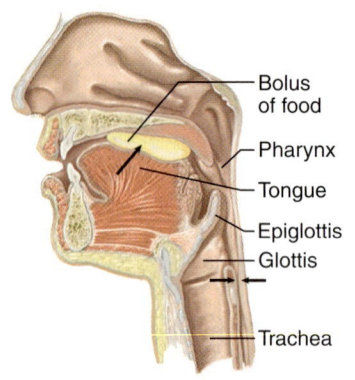

▲ **FIGURE 6.12** Deglutition (Swallowing): Phase One.

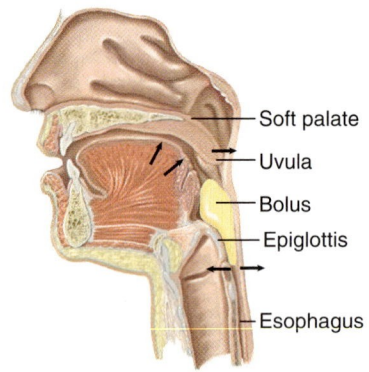

▲ **FIGURE 6.13** Deglutition (Swallowing): Phase Two.

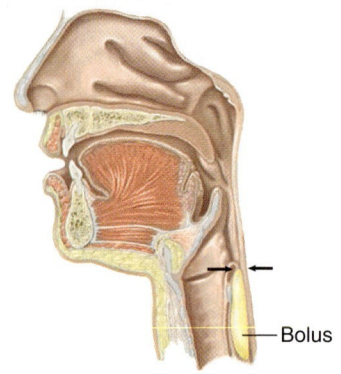

▲ **FIGURE 6.14** Deglutition (Swallowing): Phase Three.

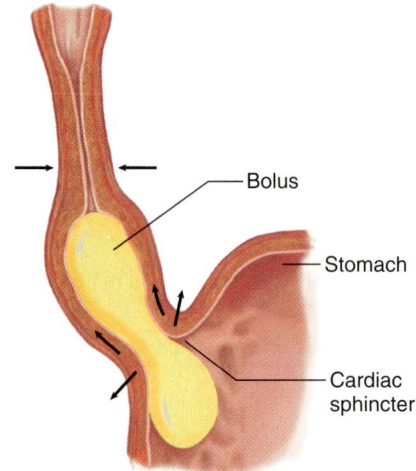

▲ **FIGURE 6.15** Deglutition (Swallowing): Phase Four.

Abbreviation

GERD gastroesophageal reflux disease

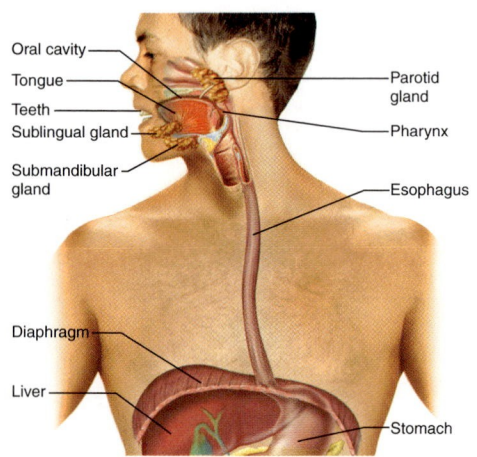

▲ **FIGURE 6.16** Esophagus.

DEGLUTITION (SWALLOWING)—PHARYNX AND ESOPHAGUS

The pieces of chicken and vegetable that you ingested have now been sliced and ground into small particles by the teeth, partly digested and lubricated by saliva, and rolled into a bolus between the tongue and the hard palate, the bony roof of the mouth. The bolus is now ready to be swallowed (**deglutition**).

- **Phase One**—As you swallow, the bolus of food is pushed backward by your tongue into the **oropharynx.** Once the bolus is in your oropharynx, the tongue pushes up the soft palate and **uvula** to close off the **nasopharynx** at the back of the nose. This prevents food from going up into your nasopharynx and nose *(Figure 6.12)*.

- **Phase Two**—Surrounding the oropharynx are circular muscles called **constrictors.** These muscles contract, forcing the bolus down through the laryngopharynx toward the **esophagus** and pushing the **epiglottis** closed so that food cannot enter the **larynx** and **trachea** *(Figure 6.13)*.

- **Phase Three**—When the bolus reaches the lower end of the **pharynx,** the upper esophageal sphincter relaxes and the bolus enters the esophagus, where contractions of the muscles in the wall move the bolus toward the stomach *(Figure 6.14)*.

- **Phase Four**—The esophageal sphincter at the lower end of the esophagus (**cardiac sphincter**) relaxes to allow the bolus to enter the stomach *(Figure 6.15)*.

The **esophagus** *(Figure 6.16)* is a tube 9 to 10 inches long; it pierces the diaphragm at the esophageal **hiatus** to go from the thoracic cavity to the abdominal cavity *(see Chapter 2)*.

Disorders of the Esophagus

Esophagitis is inflammation of the lining of the esophagus that produces a **postprandial** burning chest pain (**heartburn**), pain on swallowing, and occasional vomiting of blood (**hematemesis**). The most common cause is **reflux** of the stomach's acid contents into the esophagus, **gastroesophageal reflux disease (GERD).** **Regurgitation** of stomach contents into the mouth (**water brash**) can occur with resulting hypersalivation.

Hiatal hernia occurs when a portion of the stomach protrudes through the diaphragm alongside the esophagus at the esophageal hiatus. Reflux of acid stomach contents into the esophagus causes an esophagitis. Surgical repair sometimes is necessary and is called a **herniorrhaphy.**

Esophageal varices are **varicose** veins of the esophagus. They are **asymptomatic** until they rupture, causing massive bleeding and hematemesis. They are a complication of cirrhosis of the liver *(Lesson 6.4)*.

Cancer of the esophagus arises from the lining of the tube. Symptoms are difficulty in swallowing (**dysphagia**), a burning sensation in the chest, and weight loss. Risk factors include cigarettes, alcohol, betel nut chewing, and esophageal reflux. The cancer metastasizes to liver, bone, and lung.

WORD ANALYSIS AND DEFINITION

S = Suffix **P** = Prefix **R** = Root **R/CF** = Combining Form

WORD	PRONUNCIATION		ELEMENTS	DEFINITION
deglutition	dee-glue-**TISH**-un		Latin *to swallow*	The act of swallowing
dysphagia	dis-**FAY**-jee-ah	P/ R/	**dys-** *difficulty* **-phagia** *swallowing*	Difficulty in swallowing
emesis	**EM**-eh-sis	S/ R/	**-sis** *condition* **eme-** *to vomit*	Vomit
hematemesis	he-mah-**TEM**-eh-sis	R/	**hemat-** *blood*	Vomiting of red blood
epiglottis	ep-ih-**GLOT**-is	P/ R/	**epi-** *above* **-glottis** *windpipe*	Leaf-shaped plate of cartilage that shuts off larynx during swallowing
esophagus esophageal (adj)	ee-**SOF**-ah-gus ee-**SOF**-ah-**JEE**-al	S/ R/CF	Greek *gullet* **-al** *pertaining to* **esophag/e-** *esophagus*	Tube linking the pharynx and stomach
esophagitis	ee-**SOF**-ah-**JI**-tis	S/	**-itis** *inflammation*	Inflammation of the lining of the esophagus
hernia	**HER**-nee-ah		Latin *rupture*	Protrusion of a structure through the tissue that normally contains it
herniorrhaphy	**HER**-nee-**OR**-ah-fee	S/ R/CF	**-rrhaphy** *suture* **herni/o-** *hernia*	Repair of a hernia
herniate (verb)	**HER**-nee-ate	S/	**-ate** *pertaining to*	To protrude
hiatus hiatal (adj)	high-**AY**-tus high-**AY**-tal		Latin *an aperture*	An opening through a structure
larynx	**LAIR**-inks		Latin *larynx*	Organ of voice production
nasopharynx	**NAY**-zoh-**FAIR**-inks	R/CF R/	**nas/o-** *nose* **-pharynx** *throat*	Region of the pharynx at the back of the nose and above the soft palate
oropharynx	**OR**-oh-fair-inks	R/CF R/	**oro-** *mouth* **-pharynx** *throat*	Region at the back of the mouth between the soft palate and the tip of the epiglottis
pharynx	**FAIR**-inks		Greek *throat*	Air tube from the back of the nose to the larynx
postprandial	post-**PRAN**-dee-al	S/ P/ R/CF	**-al** *pertaining to* **post-** *after* **-prand/i-** *breakfast*	Following a meal
reflux	**REE**-fluks	P/ R/	**re-** *back* **-flux** *flow*	Backward flow
regurgitation	ree-gur-jih-**TAY**-shun	S/ P/ R/	**-ation** *action* **re-** *back* **-gurgit-** *flood*	Expel contents of the stomach into the mouth, short of vomiting
trachea	**TRAY**-kee-ah		Greek *windpipe*	Air tube from the larynx to the bronchi
varix varices (pl) varicose (adj)	**VAIR**-iks **VAIR**-ih-seez **VAIR**-ih-kos		Latin *dilated vein*	Dilated, tortuous vein Characterized by varices

EXERCISES

Some of the terms in this chapter are particularly hard to spell and pronounce. Work with your student CD for pronunciation practice, and remember that spelling is important! Read these sentences aloud when you have circled your choices.

1. The (nasopharynx/nasopharyix) is at the back of the nose and above the soft palate.

2. (Hyatus/Hiatus) is the Latin word for *opening* and is the opening through the diaphragm for the (esophagis/esophagus).

3. The (eppiglotis/epiglottis) is a leaf-shaped plate of cartilage that acts to cover the opening of the (larynix/larynx) during deglutition.

4. Medication may be ordered (postprandial/postperandial), meaning *taken after meals.*

5. (Hemotemasis/Hematemesis) is the (vomiting/vomitting) of blood.

6. (Esophageal/Esophogeal) (varices/varixes) can be caused by reflux disease.

7. Throat cancer would produce (dysphagia/dyspagia).

8. (Varricces/Varices) is the plural of (varix/varex) and means *dilated, tortuous vein.* The adjective is (varicose/varricose).

LESSON 6.3 Digestion—Stomach and Small Intestine

OBJECTIVES

The bolus of food that you swallowed has passed down the esophagus. It now enters the stomach, and the process of digestion begins in earnest. The stomach continues the mechanical breakdown of the food particles and begins the chemical digestion of protein and fats. It is in the small intestine that the greatest amount of digestion and absorption occurs. The information in this lesson will enable you to:

- **Describe the secretions of the stomach and their functions.**
- **Discuss the secretions of the small intestine and their functions.**
- **Explain how food is propelled through the stomach and small intestine.**
- **Detail how the breakdown products of digestion are absorbed from the small intestine.**
- **Use the correct medical terminology to describe the process of digestion in the small intestine.**

You Are

. . . an EMT-1 working in the Emergency Department at Fulwood Medical Center.

Your Patient Is

. . . Mrs. Jan Stark, a 36-year-old pottery maker. Your task is to document her visit.

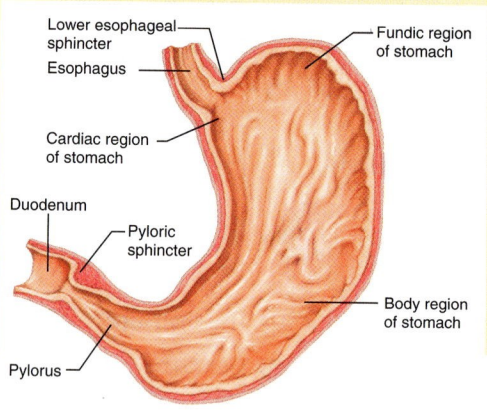

▲ **FIGURE 6.17 Stomach.**

Labels: Lower esophageal sphincter; Esophagus; Cardiac region of stomach; Duodenum; Pyloric sphincter; Pylorus; Fundic region of stomach; Body region of stomach

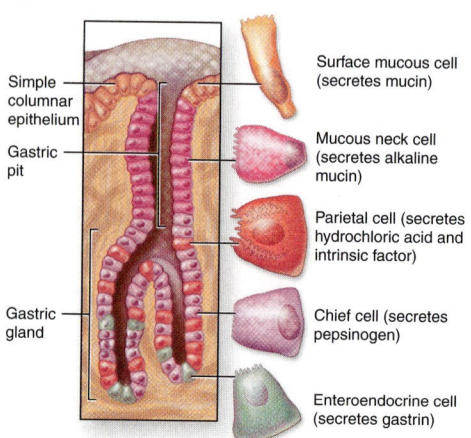

Labels: Simple columnar epithelium; Gastric pit; Gastric gland; Surface mucous cell (secretes mucin); Mucous neck cell (secretes alkaline mucin); Parietal cell (secretes hydrochloric acid and intrinsic factor); Chief cell (secretes pepsinogen); Enteroendocrine cell (secretes gastrin)

▲ **FIGURE 6.18 Gastric Cells and Their Secretions.**

CASE REPORT 6.3

Documentation.

Mrs. Jan Stark, a 36-year-old pottery maker, was admitted to the emergency department at 2015 hrs.

She stated the she had passed between 20 and 30 watery, gray stools in the previous 24 hours. She had not passed urine for more than 12 hours. She was markedly dehydrated and responded well to infusion of lactated Ringer solution and then D5NS (5% dextrose in normal 0.9% saline).

Questioning revealed that, for the past ten years, she has had spasmodic episodes of diarrhea and flatulence associated with severe headaches and fatigue. During those episodes her stools were greasy and pale. In the recent three or four months, she has had some difficulties with fine movements as she works on her pottery wheel and has had tingling in her fingers and toes.

Dr. Homer Hilinski, emergency physician, believes her dehydration is a result of a **malabsorption syndrome**. An appointment has been made for her to see Dr. Cameron Grabowski, gastroenterologist, tomorrow. She was discharged to her husband's care at midnight. She has been advised to stay on fluids only and to return to the **ER** (emergency room) if the diarrhea returns.

Signed: Sunil Patel, EMT-1. 06/21/06, 0100 hrs.

DIGESTION: THE STOMACH

The stomach's peristaltic contractions mix different boluses of food together and also push the more liquid contents toward the **pylorus** *(Figure 6.17)*. These contractions and the digestive process work on the boluses of food to produce a mixture of semidigested food called **chyme**.

The cells of the lining of the stomach secrete the following *(Figure 6.18)*:

- **Mucin**—continues to lubricate food and protects the stomach lining.
- **Hydrochloric acid (HCl)**—breaks up the connective tissue of the chicken and the cell walls of the vegetable that you ingested a few seconds ago.
- **Pepsinogen**—hydrochloric acid converts pepsinogen to **pepsin**, an active enzyme that starts to digest the protein in the chicken and vegetable.
- **Intrinsic factor**—is essential for the absorption of vitamin B_{12} in the small intestine *(see Chapter 21)*. Neither chicken nor vegetables contain this factor.
- **Chemical messengers**—stimulate other cells in the gastric mucosa. One of these messengers, **gastrin**, stimulates both the production of HCl and pepsinogen by the stomach cells and the peristaltic contractions of the stomach.

WORD ANALYSIS AND DEFINITION

WORD	PRONUNCIATION		ELEMENTS	DEFINITION
chyme	KYME		Greek *juice*	Semifluid, partially digested food passed from the stomach into the duodenum
duodenum duodenal (adj)	du-oh-**DEE**-num du-oh-**DEE**-nal	S/ R/	-um *structure* duoden- Latin for *twelve*	The duodenum is the first part of the small intestine and is approximately twelve finger-breadths (9 to 10 inches) in length
gastrin	**GAS**-trin	S/ R/	-in *in* gastr- *stomach*	Hormone secreted in the stomach that stimulates secretion of HCl and increases gastric motility
hydrochloric acid (HCl)	high-droh-**KLOR**-ic **ASS**-id	S/ R/CF R/	-ic *pertaining to* hydr/o- *water* -chlor- *green*	HCl is the acid of gastric juice
intrinsic factor	in-**TRIN**-sik **FAK**-tor	S/ R/ R/	-ic *pertaining to* intrins- *on the inside* factor *maker*	Makes the absorption of vitamin B₁₂ happen
malabsorption	mal-ab-**SORP**-shun	S/ P/ R/	-ion *process* mal- *bad* -absorpt- *to swallow*	Inadequate gastrointestinal absorption of nutrients
mucus mucous (adj) mucin	**MYU**-kus **MYU**-kus **MYU**-sin		Latin *slime*	Sticky secretion of cells in mucous membranes Relating to mucus or the mucosa Protein element of mucus
pepsin pepsinogen	**PEP**-sin pep-**SIN**-oh-jen	 S/ R/CF	Greek *to digest* -gen *produce* pepsin/o- *pepsin*	Enzyme produced by the stomach that breaks down protein Converted by HCl in stomach to pepsin
pylorus pyloric (adj)	pie-**LOR**-us pie-**LOR**-ik	S/ R/	-us *warder* pylor- *gate*	Exit area of the stomach

Liquids exit the stomach within 1½ to 2 hours after ingestion. A typical meal like your chicken and vegetable takes 3 to 4 hours to exit. The resulting chyme is held in the pylorus. Peristaltic waves squirt 2 to 3 mL of the chyme at a time through the **pyloric sphincter** into the **duodenum**.

Abbreviations

ER	emergency room
HCl	hydrochloric acid

EXERCISES

*Continue your work with elements from the **language of gastroenterology**. In the following exercise, every medical term has an element in bold. Identify the type of element, and write the meaning of the element in the appropriate box. Then answer the questions.*

Term	Type of Element	Meaning of Element
malab**sorption**		
pepsinogen		
gastrin		
intrinsic		
duodenum		
hydrochloric		

Which term is a part of the small intestine? _____

Which term is the acid of gastric juice? _____

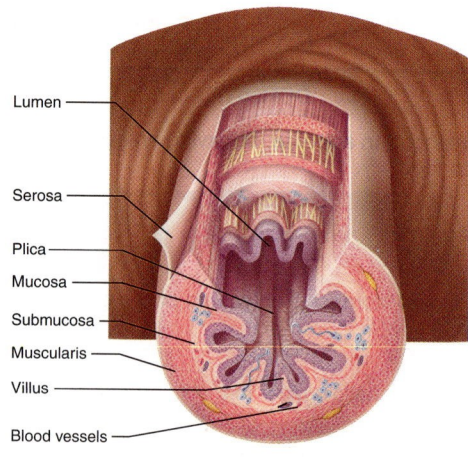

Labels for Figure 6.20:
Lumen
Serosa
Plica
Mucosa
Submucosa
Muscularis
Villus
Blood vessels

▲ **FIGURE 6.20 Tissue Layers of Digestive Tract.**
An example of the most typical histological structure of the tract.

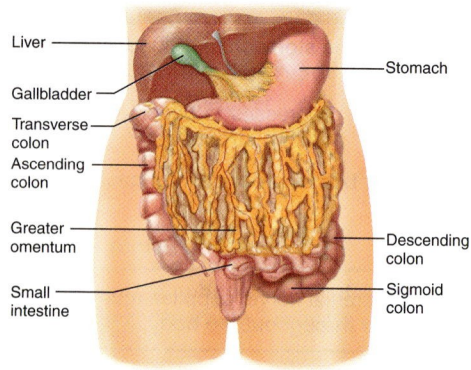

Labels for Figure 6.21:
Liver
Gallbladder
Transverse colon
Ascending colon
Greater omentum
Small intestine
Stomach
Descending colon
Sigmoid colon

▲ **FIGURE 6.21 Greater Omentum.**

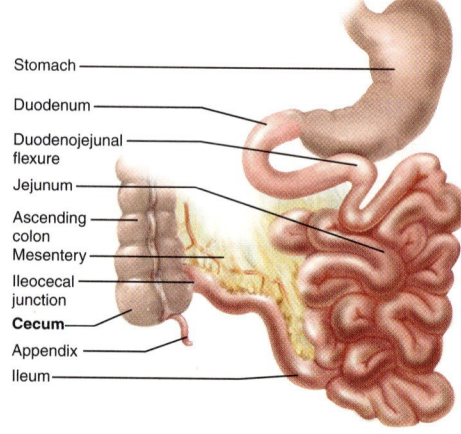

Labels for Figure 6.22:
Stomach
Duodenum
Duodenojejunal flexure
Jejunum
Ascending colon
Mesentery
Ileocecal junction
Cecum
Appendix
Ileum

▲ **FIGURE 6.22 Small Intestine.**

SMALL INTESTINE

The small intestine, called "small" because of its diameter, finishes the process of chemical digestion and is responsible for the absorption of most of the nutrients.

Four major layers are present in the wall of the small intestine and in all areas of the digestive tract *(Figure 6.20)*:

1. **Mucosa,** or mucous membrane—contains the epithelial cells that line the tract, intestinal glands that secrete the digestive enzymes, and supportive connective tissue. Fingerlike shapes of mucosa called **villi** project into the lumen of the intestine.

2. **Submucosa**—a thick connective tissue layer containing blood vessels, lymphatic vessels, and nerves.

3. **Muscularis**—an inner, circular layer of **smooth muscle** and an outer longitudinal layer of smooth muscle. When the inner circular layer contracts, it decreases the diameter of the tract. When the outer longitudinal layer contracts, it shortens the tract. These two movements create peristalsis and segmental contractions.

4. **Serosa**—an outermost layer of thin connective tissue and a single layer of epithelial cells.

Most of the digestive organs lie within the abdominal cavity *(see Chapter 2)*, which is lined by a moist serous membrane called the **peritoneum. Parietal** peritoneum lines the wall of the abdominal cavity. **Visceral** peritoneum (a serosa) covers the external surface of the digestive organs.

The intestines are suspended from the back wall of the abdominal cavity by a **translucent** membrane called the **mesentery,** a continuation of the peritoneum. A fatty portion of the mesentery, called the **greater omentum** *(Figure 6.21)*, hangs like an apron in front of all the intestines.

The small intestine *(Figure 6.22)* occupies much of the abdominal cavity, extends from the pylorus of the stomach to the beginning of the large intestine, and has three segments:

1. The **duodenum** is the first 9 to 10 inches of the small intestine. It receives chyme from the stomach, together with pancreatic juices and bile. Here, stomach acid is neutralized, fats are broken up by the bile acids, and pancreatic enzymes take over chemical digestion.

2. The **jejunum** makes up about 40% of the small intestine's length. It is the primary region for chemical digestion and nutrient absorption.

3. The **ileum** makes up about 55% of the small intestine's length. It ends at the **ileocecal** valve, a sphincter that controls entry into the large intestine.

From the duodenum to the middle of the ileum, the lining of the small intestine is thrown into circular folds, called **plicae.** Along their surface, the plicae have tiny finger-like villi. The plicae and villi increase the surface area over which secretions can act on the food and through which nutrients can be absorbed. The folds also act as "speed bumps" to slow down the movement of chyme through the small intestine. The cells at the tip of the villi are shed and renewed every three or four days.

Digestion in the Small Intestine

After leaving the stomach as chyme, the food spends 3 to 5 hours in the small intestine, from where most of the nutrients are absorbed.

Secretion from the small intestine cells is mostly water, mucus, and enzymes. Peristaltic movements of the small intestine have three functions:

1. mix chyme with intestinal and pancreatic juices and with bile

2. churn chyme to make contact with the mucosa for digestion and absorption

3. move the residue toward the large intestine

S = Suffix   P = Prefix   R = Root   R/CF = Combining Form

WORD	PRONUNCIATION	ELEMENTS		DEFINITION
cecum	**SEE**-kum		Latin *blind*	Blind pouch that is the first part of the large intestine
ileum ileocecal	**ILL**-ee-um **ILL**-ee-oh-**SEE**-cal	S/ R/CF R/	Latin *to roll up* **-al** *pertaining to* **ile/o-** *ileum* **-cec** *cecum*	Third portion of the small intestine Junction of the ileum and cecum
jejunum jejunal (adj)	je-**JEW**-num je-**JEW**-nal		Latin *empty*	Segment of small intestine between the duodenum and the ileum where most of the nutrients are absorbed
mesentery mesenteric (adj)	**MESS**-en-ter-ree **MESS**-en-ter-ik	P/ R/ S/	**mes-** *middle* **-entery** *intestine* **-ic** *pertaining to*	A double layer of peritoneum enclosing the abdominal viscera
mucosa (another name for **mucous membrane**) mucosal (adj)	myu-**KOH**-sah myu-**KOH**-sal		Latin *mucus*	Lining of a tubular structure
muscularis	muss-kyu-**LAR**-is	S/ R/	**-aris** *pertaining to* **muscul-** *muscle*	The muscular layer of a hollow organ or tube
omentum omental (adj)	oh-**MEN**-tum oh-**MEN**-tal		Latin *membrane that encloses the bowels*	Membrane that encloses the bowels
pancreas	**PAN**-kree-as		Greek *sweetbread*	Lobulated gland, the head of which is tucked into the curve of the duodenum
peritoneum peritoneal (adj)	per-ih-toe-**NEE**-um per-ih-toe-**NEE**-al		Latin *to stretch over*	Membrane that lines the abdominal cavity
plica plicae (pl)	**PLEE**-cah **PLEE**-key		Latin *fold*	Fold in a mucous membrane
serosa serosal (adj)	seh-**ROH**-sa seh-**ROH**-sal		Latin *serous*	Outermost covering of the alimentary tract
submucosa	sub-mew-**KOH**-sa	S/ R/	**sub-** *under* **-mucosa** *mucus*	Tissue layer underneath the mucosa
villus villi (pl)	**VILL**-us **VILL**-eye		Latin *shaggy hair*	Thin, hairlike projection, particularly of a mucous membrane lining a cavity
viscus (**Note: Viscous** is pronounced the same but means something *sticky*.) viscera (pl) visceral (adj)	**VISS**-kus **VISS**-er-ah **VISS**-er-al		Latin *internal organ* Latin *soft internal organs*	Hollow, walled, internal organ Internal organs, particularly in the abdomen Pertaining to the internal organs

EXERCISES

Greek and Latin terms do not deconstruct into basic elements, so you must know them for what they are. Build your knowledge of these terms by matching the phrase in column 1 to the correct medical term in column 2.

1. to roll up _____   A. viscus

2. membrance that encloses bowels _____   B. peritoneum

3. serous _____   C. mucosa

4. shaggy hair _____   D. plica

5. internal organ _____   E. cecum

6. fold _____   F. omentum

7. empty _____   G. ileum

8. to stretch over _____   H. serosa

9. mucus _____   I. villus

10. blind _____   J. jejunum

LESSON 6.3 Digestion—Stomach and Small Intestine   231

Digestion—Liver, Gallbladder, and Pancreas

OBJECTIVES

The liver and pancreas secrete enzymes that are responsible for most of the digestion that occurs in the small intestine. It is essential to understand the function of these enzymes as they relate to digestion, and you will need to be able to:

- **Identify the functions of the liver, gallbladder, bile ducts, and pancreas.**
- **Describe the functions of the digestive secretions of the liver and pancreas.**
- **Explain common disorders of the liver, gallbladder, bile ducts, and pancreas.**
- **Apply the correct medical terminology to describe the anatomy, physiology, and the common disorders of the liver, gallbladder, bile ducts, and pancreas.**

You are

...a medical assistant working with Susan Lee, MD, a primary care physician at Fulwood Medical Center.

Your patient is

...Mrs. Sandra Jacobs, a 46-year-old mother of four. Your task is to document her care.

CASE REPORT 6.4

Mrs. Sandra Jacobs, a 46-year-old mother of four, presents in Dr. Susan Lee's primary care clinic with episodes of crampy pain in her right upper quadrant associated with nausea and vomiting. The pain often occurs after eating fast food. She has not noticed fever or jaundice. Physical examination reveals an obese white woman with a positive **Murphy sign.** Her BP (blood pressure) is 170/90, and she has slight pedal edema. A provisional diagnosis of **gallstones** has been made. She has been referred for an ultrasound examination, and an appointment has been made to see Dr. Stewart Walsh in the surgery department.

I explained to her the etiology of her gallstones, the need for surgical removal of the stones, and discussed with her a low-fat, 1500-calorie diet sheet.

Signed: Luis Guitterez, CMA. 06/12/06, 1430 hrs.

LIVER

The **liver,** the body's largest internal organ, is a complex structure located under the right ribs and below the diaphragm *(Figure 6.23)*.

The liver has multiple functions, including those to:

- **Manufacture** and excrete **bile.** Although it contains no digestive enzymes, bile plays key roles in digestion. It neutralizes the acidic chyme so that pancreatic enzymes can function. Bile salts **emulsify** fat. Bile acids are synthesized from **cholesterol,** and bile also contains cholesterol and fat-soluble vitamins.
- **Remove** the pigment **bilirubin** from the blood stream and excrete it in bile. Bilirubin is produced as a breakdown product of hemoglobin during phagocytosis by macrophages in the spleen and liver. It is dark yellow and is responsible for the brown color of feces and for the yellow color of skin in **jaundice.**
- **Remove** excess glucose (sugar) from the blood and store it as **glycogen** and release glucose when needed by the body.
- **Convert** proteins and fats into glucose, a process called **gluconeogenesis.**
- **Store** fat and fat-soluble vitamins A, D, E, and K.
- **Manufacture** blood proteins, including those necessary for clotting *(see Chapter 7).*
- **Remove** toxins from the blood.

A major reason that the liver can perform all these functions is that venous blood is returned from all the intestines to join into the **portal** vein that takes the blood directly to the liver.

The liver cells secrete bile into narrow channels that converge on the underside of the liver to form the common **hepatic duct.**

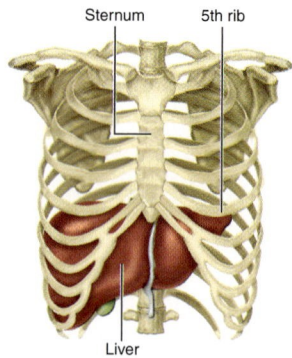

Sternum   5th rib

Liver

▲ **FIGURE 6.23 Location of Liver.**

Keynote

Only the production of bile relates the liver to digestion.

S = Suffix   P = Prefix   R = Root   R/CF = Combining Form

WORD	PRONUNCIATION		ELEMENTS	DEFINITION
bile bile acids biliary (adj)	BILE BILE **AH**-sids **BILL**-ee-air-ee	 S/ R/CF	Latin *bile* **-ary** *pertaining to* **bil/i-** *bile*	Fluid secreted by the liver into the duodenum Steroids synthesized from cholesterol
bilirubin	bill-ee-**RU**-bin	S/ R/CF	**-rubin** *rust colored* **bil/i-** *bile*	Bile pigment formed from hemoglobin
cholesterol	koh-**LESS**-ter-ol	R/CF R/	**chol/e-** *bile* **-sterol** *steroid*	Formed in liver cells; is the most abundant steroid in tissues and circulates in the plasma attached to proteins of different densities
emulsify emulsion (noun)	ee-**MUL**-sih-fye ee-**MUL**-shun	S/ R/	**-ify** *to become* **emuls-** *milk*	Break up into very small droplets to suspend in a solution (emulsion)
gallstone	**GAWL**-stone	R/ R/	**gall-** *bile* **stone** *pebble*	Hard mass of cholesterol, calcium, and bilirubin that can be formed in gallbladder and bile duct
gluconeogenesis	**GLU**-ko-nee-oh-**JEN**-eh-sis	S/ R/CF R/	**-genesis** *creation* **gluc/o-** *sugar* **-neo-** *new*	Formation of glucose from noncarbohydrate sources
glycogen	**GLYE**-koh-gen	S/ R/CF	**-gen** *produce, create* **glyc/o-** *sugar*	The body's principal carbohydrate reserve, stored in the liver and skeletal muscle
hepatic hepatitis	hep-**AT**-ik hep-ah-**TIE**-tis	S/ R/ S/	**-ic** *pertaining to* **hepat-** *liver* **-itis** *inflammation*	Pertaining to the liver Inflammation of the liver
jaundice	**JAWN**-dis		French *yellow*	Yellow staining of tissues with bile pigments, including bilirubin
liver	**LIV**-er		Old English *liver*	Body's largest organ located in right upper quadrant of abdomen
Murphy sign	**MUR**-fee SINE		John B. Murphy, Chicago surgeon, 1857–1916	Tenderness in the right subcostal area on inspiration associated with acute cholecystitis
portal	**POR**-tal		Latin *gate*	The vein that brings blood from the intestines to the liver

EXERCISES

Use this exercise as a quick review of the elements in the WAD. Circle the correct choice.

1. In the term **hepatic**, the root means:

   pancreas   stomach   liver

2. The term **gallstone** is composed of:

   root + combining form   root + root   root + suffix

3. The term **biliary** is composed of a:

   prefix + root   root + suffix   combining form + suffix

4. To break up into small droplets suspended in a solution is to:

   emulsify   secrete   liquefy

5. In the term **gallstone**, one of the roots means:

   enzyme   acid   bile

6. Which is formed in the liver cells?

   cholesterol   gallstone   insulin

7. In the term **gluconeogenesis**, *neo* means:

   never   new   negative

8. The combining form in the term **glycogen** means:

   sugar   enzyme   bile

DISORDERS OF THE LIVER

Hepatitis is an inflammation of the liver causing jaundice. Viral hepatitis is the most common cause of hepatitis and is related to three major types of virus:

1. **Hepatitis A virus (HAV)** is highly contagious and causes a mild to severe infection. It is transmitted by the **fecal-oral route** through contaminated food. It frequently occurs in schools, camps, and institutions.

2. **Hepatitis B virus (HBV)**, or serum hepatitis, is transmitted through contact with blood, semen, vaginal secretions, saliva, or a needle prick, and sharing contaminated needles. Some people become chronic carriers of the virus in their blood.

3. **Hepatitis C virus (HCV)** is the most common blood-borne infection in the United States. The disease is transmitted by blood and body fluids. Many carriers are asymptomatic, but others show a chronic hepatitis and progress to cirrhosis.

In addition, **hepatitis D** can occur in association with hepatitis B, making the infection worse. **Hepatitis E** is similar to hepatitis A and occurs mostly in under-developed countries.

Other causes of hepatitis include abuse of alcohol; autoimmune diseases, such as Sjögren syndrome and type 1 diabetes; other viruses, such as mononucleosis and cytomegalovirus *(see Chapter 20)*; and drugs such as acetaminophen.

Symptoms include nausea, vomiting and loss of appetite, joint pain, and sore muscles. Signs include jaundice, fever and tenderness in the right upper quadrant of the abdomen.

Chronic hepatitis occurs when the acute hepatitis is not healed after six months. It progresses slowly, can last for years, and is difficult to treat.

Cirrhosis of the liver is a chronic, irreversible disease, replacing normal liver cells with hard, fibrous scar tissue *(Figure 6.24)*. It is the seventh leading cause of death in the United States. The most common cause of **cirrhosis** is alcoholism. In cirrhosis, the

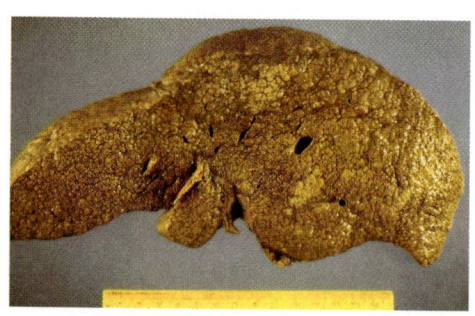

▲ **FIGURE 6.24** Cirrhosis of Liver.

Abbreviations

ALP	alkaline phosphatase
ALT	alanine aminotransferase (also known as SGPT)
AST	aspartate aminotransferase (also known as SGOT)
GGT	gamma-glutamyl transpeptidase
HAV	hepatitis A virus
HBV	hepatitis B virus
HCV	hepatitis C virus
LFT	liver function test
PT	prothrombin time
SGOT	serum glutamic oxaloacetic acid transaminase (also known as AST)
SGPT	serum glutamic-pyruvic transaminase (also known as ALT)

Liver Function Tests

Liver Function Tests (LFTs) are a group of tests to show how well your liver is functioning. They are divided into four categories:

1. **Measuring liver proteins in blood serum**

   - Total proteins, albumin, and globulin (*see Chapter 7*) are low when there is liver damage.

2. **Measuring liver enzymes in blood serum**

   - Enzymes made in the liver, known as **transaminases**, include **alanine aminotransferase (ALT;** also known as **serum glutamic-pyruvic transaminase,** or **SGPT)** and **aspartate aminotransferase (AST;** also known as **serum glutamic oxaloacetic acid transaminase,** or **SGOT).** Elevated levels of these enzymes in the blood indicate liver damage.

   - **Prothrombin** is a protein involved in blood clotting that is made in the liver. Low blood levels resulting from liver disease increase the time it takes blood to clot, and the **prothrombin time (PT)** test is elevated (*see Chapter 7*).

3. **Measuring cholestatic liver enzymes in the blood serum**

   - **Alkaline phosphatase (ALP)** metabolizes phosphorus and makes energy available for the body. Elevated blood levels are found in liver and biliary tract disorders.

   - **Gamma-glutamyl transpeptidase (GGT)** is elevated in liver disease.

4. **Measuring bilirubin in the blood stream**

   - **Bilirubin** is formed in the liver from hemoglobin and secreted into the biliary system. If the liver is damaged, bilirubin can leak out into the blood stream, producing elevated levels and jaundice.

WORD	PRONUNCIATION		ELEMENTS	DEFINITION
alanine aminotransferase (ALT) aspartate aminotransferase (AST)	AL-ah-neen ah-ME-no-TRANS-fer-aze as-PAR-tate ah-me-no-TRANS-fer-aze	S/ R/CF R/	alanine *an amino acid* -ase *enzyme* amin/o- *ammonia-based compound* -transfer- *carry* aspartate *an amino acid*	Enzymes that are found in liver cells and leak out into the bloodstream when the cells are damaged, enabling liver damage to be diagnosed
ascites	ah-SIGH-teez	S/ R/	-ites *associated with* asc- *belly*	Accumulation of fluid in the abdominal cavity
cholestatic	koh-les-TAT-ik	S/ R/ R/CF	-ic *pertaining to* -stat- *stand still* chol/e- *bile*	Stopping the flow of bile
cirrhosis	sir-ROE-sis	S/ R/	-osis *condition* cirrh- *yellow*	Extensive fibrotic liver disease
hemangioma	he-MAN-jee-o-mah	S/ R/ R/CF	-oma *tumor, mass* hem- *blood* -ang/i- *blood vessel*	Mass of proliferating blood vessels
hemochromatosis	HE-mah-krom-ah-TOE-sis	S/ R/ R/CF	-osis *condition* -chromat- *color* hem/o- *blood*	Dangerously high levels of iron in the body with deposition of iron pigments in tissues
phosphatase	FOS-fah-tase	S/ R/	-ase *enzyme* phosphat- *phosphorus*	Enzyme that liberates phosphorus
prothrombin	pro-THROM-bin	P/ R/	pro- *before* -thrombin *clot*	Protein formed by liver and converted to thrombin in the blood-clotting mechanism

damage sustained to the liver is irreversible, and there is no known cure. Treatment is symptomatic. When cirrhosis blocks the flow of blood in the portal vein, the back-pressure produces **ascites,** an accumulation of fluid in the abdominal cavity.

Cancer of the liver as a primary cancer typically arises in patients with chronic liver disease, usually from HBV infection. A more common form of liver cancer is secondary deposits of metastases from a primary cancer in colon, lung, breast, or prostate.

Benign liver tumors are often small and symptom free and include **hepatocellular adenoma** and **hemangioma.**

Hemochromatosis is caused by the absorption of too much iron, which is stored throughout the body mostly in the liver, and can lead to liver failure.

Wilson disease is the retention of too much copper in the liver and can also lead to liver failure.

EXERCISES

Work on recognizing the elements contained in this lesson's WAD. Know the medical terms in which they will appear. Fill in the chart. The first one is done for you.

Element	Meaning of element	Type of element (prefix, root, combining form, suffix)	Example of medical term containing this element
pro	*before*	*P*	*prothrombin*
osis			
hemo			
asc			
cirrh			
stat			
ase			
thrombin			

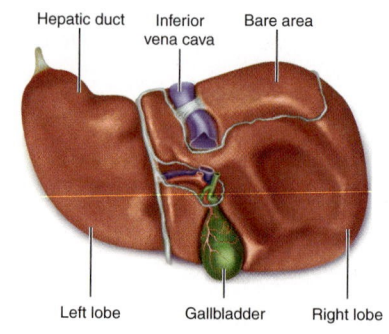

(a)

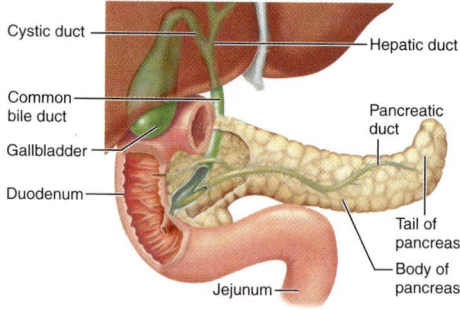

(b)

▲ **FIGURE 6.25**

(a) Underside of liver; *(b)* Anatomy of gallbladder, pancreas, and biliary tract

▲ **FIGURE 6.26** Gallstones.

Abbreviations

ERCP endoscopic retrograde cholangio-pancreatography
ESWL extracorporeal shock wave lithotripsy
RBC red blood cell

GALLBLADDER AND BILIARY TRACT

On the underside of the liver is the **gallbladder** *(Figure 6.25a)*, which stores and concentrates the bile that the liver produces. The **cystic duct** from the gallbladder joins with the **hepatic duct** to form the **common bile duct**. The system of ducts to get the bile from the liver to the duodenum is called the **biliary tract** *(Figure 6.25b)*

When acid and fat arrive in the duodenum, cells in the lining of the duodenum secrete a hormone, **cholecystokinin,** which causes the gallbladder to contract and force bile into the bile duct and, from there, into the duodenum. Cholecystokinin also stimulates the production of pancreatic enzymes.

Disorders of the Gallbladder

Gallstones (cholelithiasis) can form in the gallbladder from excess cholesterol, bile salts, and bile pigment *(Figure 6.26)*. The stones can vary in size and number. Risk factors are **obesity**, high-cholesterol diets, multiple pregnancies, and rapid weight loss. Mrs. Jacobs presented in the emergency department with the classic gallstone symptoms of severe waves of right upper quadrant pain (**biliary colic**), nausea, and vomiting. If small stones become impacted in the common bile duct, this is called **choledocholithiasis**. This can cause biliary colic and jaundice (see below).

Cholecystitis is an acute or chronic inflammation of the gallbladder usually associated with cholelithiasis and obstruction of the cystic duct with a stone. Acute colicky pain in the right upper quadrant with nausea and vomiting are followed by jaundice, dark urine (because bilirubin backs up into the blood and is excreted by the kidneys), and pale-colored stools (because bilirubin cannot get into the duodenum).

Jaundice (icterus) is a symptom of many different diseases in the biliary tract and liver. It is a yellow discoloration of the skin and sclera of the eyes *(see Chapter 3)* caused by deposits of bilirubin just below the outer layers of the skin. Bilirubin is a breakdown product of hemoglobin that occurs as old **red blood cells (RBCs)** are destroyed. Bilirubin is removed from the bloodstream by the liver and excreted in bile.

Jaundice occurs when there is an increased concentration of bilirubin circulating in the bloodstream. There are three categories of disease that cause jaundice:

1. **Obstructive jaundice** is a result of the blockage of bile between the liver and duodenum, usually due to gallstones in the common bile duct or to a carcinoma of the head of the pancreas invading the common duct.

2. **Hemolytic jaundice** results from an accelerated destruction of red blood cells such that the liver cannot remove the excess bilirubin fast enough. This is most often seen in newborn infants with hemolytic jaundice due to blood group incompatibility between mother and infant.

3. **Hepatocellular jaundice** is when an infection or poison injures the liver cells, preventing the removal of bilirubin from the blood. This occurs in viral hepatitis.

Procedures for the Biliary System

- **Cholangiography** requires injection of a dye intravenously followed by X-ray of the biliary system so that the biliary system can be visualized.

- **Cholecystectomy** is surgical removal of the gallbladder through open cholecystectomy or laparoscopic cholecystectomy. A method to remove stones and leave the gallbladder intact involves using **endoscopic retrograde cholangiopancreatography (ERCP)**. An endoscope is passed orally into the duodenum and a guide wire inserted into the cystic duct and gallbladder. This is followed by **extracorporeal shock wave lithotripsy (ESWL)** and infusion of a solvent to dissolve the stones.

WORD	PRONUNCIATION	ELEMENTS		DEFINITION
cholangiography	KOH-lan-jee-OG-rah-fee	S/ R/ R/CF	-graphy *to write* chol- *bile* -angi/o- *vessel*	Use of a contrast medium to radiographically visualize the bile ducts
cholecystectomy	KOH-leh-sis-TECK-toe-me	S/ R/CF R/	-ectomy *surgical excision* chol/e- *bile* -cyst- *bladder*	Surgical removal of the gallbladder
cholecystitis	KOH-leh-sis-TIE-tis	S/ R/CF R/	-itis *inflammation* chol/e- *bile* -cyst- *bladder*	Inflammation of the gallbladder
cholecystokinin	KOH-leh-sis-toe-KIE-nin	S/ R/CF R/CF	-kinin *move in* chol/e- *bile* -cyst/o- *bladder*	Hormone secreted by the lining of the intestine that stimulates secretion of pancreatic enzymes and contraction of the gallbladder
choledocholithiasis	koh-leh-DOH-koh-li-THIGH-ah-sis	S/ R/CF R/	-iasis *condition* choledoch/o- *common bile duct* -lith- *stone*	Presence of a gallstone in the common bile duct
cholelithiasis	KOH-leh-lih-THIGH-ah-sis	S/ R/CF R/	-iasis *condition* chol/e- *bile* -lith- *stone*	Condition of having bile (gall) stones
extracorporeal	EKS-tra-kor-PO-ree-al	S/ P/ R/CF	-al *pertaining to* extra- *outside* corpor/e- *body*	Outside the body
gallbladder	GAWL-blad-er	R/	gall- *bile* Old English bladder	Receptacle on inferior surface of liver for bile
hemolysis	he-MOL-ih-sis	S/ R/CF	-lysis *destroy* hem/o- *blood*	Destruction of red blood cells so that hemoglobin is liberated
hemolytic (adj)	he-moh-LIT-ik	S/ R/	-tic *pertaining to* -ly- *breakdown*	Pertaining to the process of destruction of red blood cells
hepatocellular	HEP-ah-toe-SELL-you-lar	S/ R/ R/CF	-ar *pertaining to* -cellul- *small cell* hepat/o- *liver*	Pertaining to liver cells
lithotripsy	LITH-oh-trip-see	S/ R/CF	-tripsy *crush* lith/o- *stone*	Crushing stones by sound waves
obesity	oh-BEE-sih-tee		Latin *fat*	Excessive amount of fat in the body

EXERCISES

In this exercise the root or combining form remains the same, but the addition of other elements will construct entirely different medical terms. Use this group of elements, in addition to "chol/e" to form the medical terms that are defined. Some elements you will use more than once; some elements you will not use at all. Fill in the blanks.

The element "**chol/e**" means: _____.

Add these elements to "chol/e" to form the medical terms defined below:

lith	**choledoch/o**	**iasis**	**chol**	**graphy**
ectomy	**osis**	**cyst**	**angi/o**	**kinin**
chol/e	**cyst/o**	**hemat/o**	**tripsy**	**itis**

1. condition of bile (gall)stones _____

2. surgical removal of gallbladder _____

3. inflammation of the gallbladder _____

4. gallstone in the common bile duct _____

5. using contrast medium to see bile ducts _____

6. hormone that stimulates gallbladder contraction _____

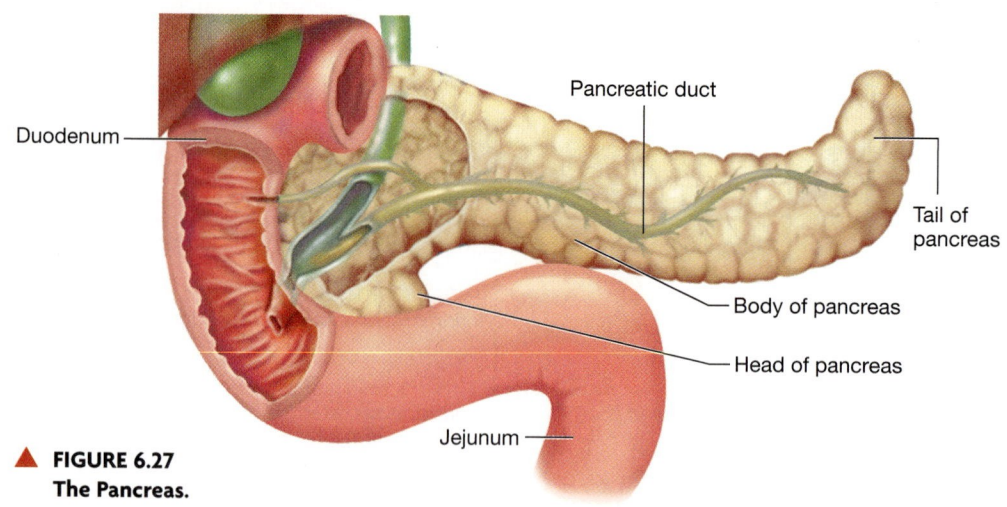

FIGURE 6.27
The Pancreas.

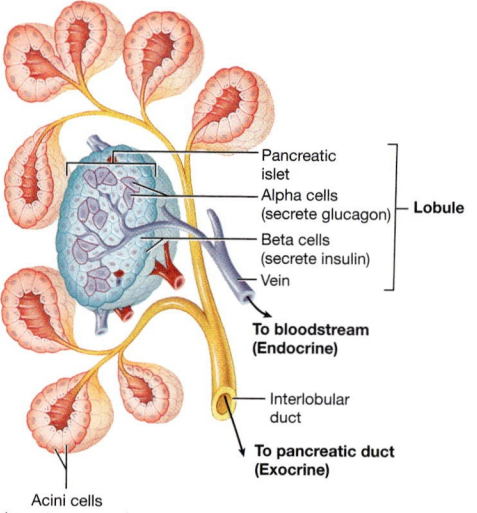

FIGURE 6.28 **Exocrine and Endocrine Aspects of Pancreas.**

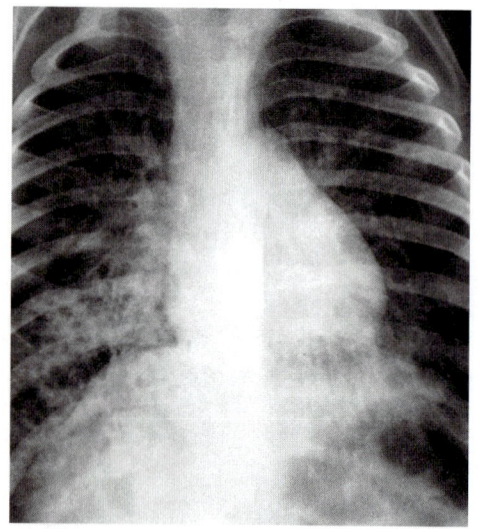

FIGURE 6.29 **Cystic Fibrosis.**

PANCREAS

The pancreas is a spongy gland, the head of which is encircled by the duodenum. Most of the pancreas secretes digestive juices, but a smaller area of pancreatic islet cells secretes **insulin** and **glucagon** that regulate blood sugar levels *(see Chapter 13).*

The pancreas is called an **exocrine** gland, and the pancreatic digestive juices formed in the **acinar cells** are excreted through the pancreatic duct. The pancreatic duct joins the common bile duct shortly before it opens into the duodenum *(Figure 6.27).* Pancreatic and bile juices then enter the duodenum.

In the same parts of the pancreas as pancreatic enzymes are produced, pancreatic **islet cells** secrete the hormones insulin and glucagon *(see Chapter 14),* which go directly into the bloodstream. This part of the pancreas is an **endocrine** gland *(Figure 6.28).*

Pancreatic juices contain:

1. **Electrolytes,** including the alkaline sodium bicarbonate, that make the pancreatic juice alkaline and help neutralize the acid chyme as it comes from the stomach.

2. **Enzymes:**
   - **amylase** breaks down the **polysaccharide** starch into **disaccharides** and **monosaccharides**
   - **lipase** breaks down **triglyceride** fat molecules into **fatty acids** and **monoglycerides**
   - **trypsin, chymotrypsin,** and **carboxypeptidase** split proteins into their amino acids.

Pancreatic secretions are regulated by both the nervous and endocrine systems. While food is being digested in the stomach, nervous impulses stimulate the pancreas to produce its juices. When chyme enters the duodenum, the hormone **secretin,** produced in the duodenal mucosa, stimulates the pancreas to produce large volumes of watery fluid. Another hormone, **cholecystokinin,** is produced in the intestinal mucosa to stimulate production of pancreatic enzymes. Both hormones travel from the intestine via the blood stream to the pancreas.

Disorders of the Pancreas

Pancreatitis is inflammation of the pancreas. The acute disease ranges from a mild, self-limiting episode to an acute life-threatening emergency with severe abdominal pain, nausea, vomiting, and a rapid fall in blood pressure. In the **chronic** form, there is a progressive destruction of pancreatic tissue leading to **malabsorption** and diabetes. Factors in the development of pancreatitis are biliary tract disease, gallstones, and alcoholism. The pancreatic enzyme **trypsin** builds up and digests parts of the pancreas causing the intense pain.

Pancreatic cancer is the fourth leading cause of cancer-related death. It occurs twice as often in males as in females. Incidence peaks in the 40- to 60-year-old range. The cancer can be asymptomatic in its early stages and is difficult to detect. The treatment is surgical resection of the cancer. The prognosis is poor with only a 15 to 20% five-year-survival rate.

Diabetes, in which insulin production is shut down or severely reduced or its effects are resisted by body cells, is discussed in Chapter 14.

Cystic fibrosis (CF) is an inherited disease that becomes apparent in infancy or childhood *(Figure 6.29).* It affects exocrine glands in multiple body systems, including the respiratory and digestive systems.

WORD	PRONUNCIATION		ELEMENTS	DEFINITION
acinar cells	ASS-in-ar SELLS	S/ R/	-ar *pertaining to* acin- *grape*	Enzyme-secreting cells of the pancreas
carboxypeptidase	kar-box-ee-PEP-tide-ase	S/ R/ R/	-ase *enzyme* carboxy- *group of organic compounds* -peptid- *digestion*	Enzyme that breaks down protein
disaccharide	die-SACK-ah-ride	S/ P/ R/	-ide *having a particular quality* di- *two* -sacchar- *sugar*	A combination of two monosaccharides; for example, table sugar
endocrine	EN-doh-krin	P/ R/	endo- *within* -crine *secrete*	A gland that produces an internal or hormonal secretion
exocrine	EK-soh-krin	P/ R/	exo- *outward* -crine *secrete*	A gland that secretes outwardly through excretory ducts
fatty acid	FAT-ee ASS-id		Old English *fat* Latin *sour*	An acid obtained from the hydrolysis of fats
islet cells	I-let SELLS		islet *small island*	Hormone-secreting cells of the pancreas
monoglyceride	mon-oh-GLISS-eh-ride	S/ P/ R/	-ide *having a particular quality* mono- *one* -glycer- *glycerol*	A fatty substance with a single fatty acid
diglyceride triglyceride	die-GLISS-eh-ride tri-GLISS-eh-ride	P/ P/	di- *two* tri- *three*	Has two fatty acids Has three fatty acids
monosaccharide	MON-oh-SACK-ah-ride	P/ R/	mono- *one* -sacchar- *sugar*	Simplest form of sugar; for example, glucose
polysaccharide	pol-ee-SACK-ah-ride	P/ S/	poly- *many* -ide *having a particular quality*	A combination of many saccharides; for example, starch
pancreas	PAN-kree-as		Greek *sweetbread*	Lobulated gland, the head of which is tucked into the curve of the duodenum
pancreatic (adj)	pan-kree-AT-ik	S/ R/	-ic *pertaining to* pancreat- *pancreas*	
pancreatitis	PAN-kree-ah-TIE-tis	S/	-itis *inflammation*	Inflammation of the pancreas
secretin	se-KREE-tin	S/ R/	-in *in* secret- *separate*	Hormone produced by duodenum to stimulate pancreatic juice
trypsin	TRIP-sin	S/ R/	-in *in* tryps- *friction*	Enzyme that breaks down protein
chymotrypsin	kye-moh-TRIP-sin	R/CF	chym/o- *chyme*	Trypsin found in chyme

EXERCISES

Grouping elements of similar meaning or category will help you remember them. The following exercise contains all prefixes of number. Fill in the number for the element, define the medical terms, then define the English terms with the same elements. Fill in the blanks.

Prefixes indicating numbers:

1. mono = (number) _____

2. di = _____

3. tri = _____

4. poly = _____

Medical terms:

5. monoglyceride: _____

6. disaccharide: _____

7. triglyceride: _____

8. polysaccharide: _____

English terms:

9. Monorail: _____

10. Divide: _____

11. Triangle: _____

12. Polygon: _____

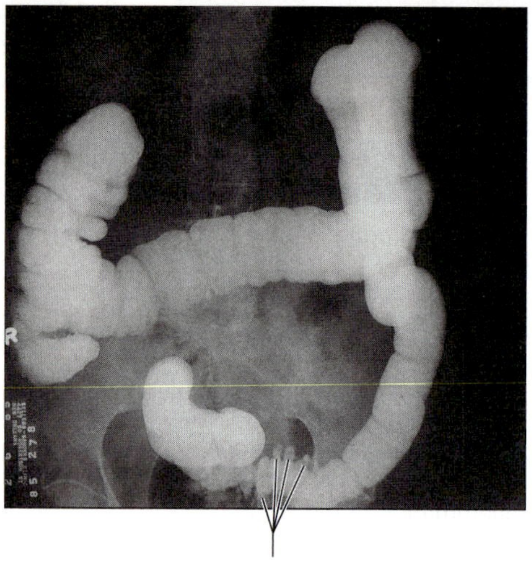

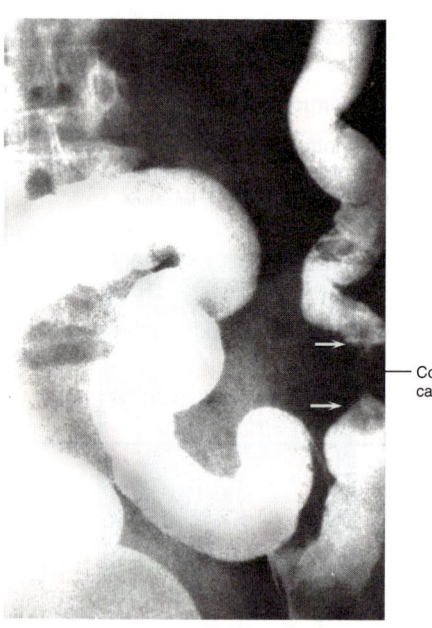

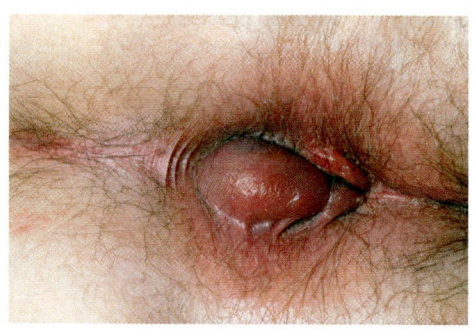

DISORDERS OF THE LARGE INTESTINE AND ANAL CANAL

Disorders of the Large Intestine

Appendicitis is the most common cause of acute abdominal pain in the right lower quadrant. On palpation, tenderness over **McBurney point** (one-third the distance from the anterior superior iliac crest to the umbilicus) *(see Chapter 5)* suggests appendicitis. If neglected, the inflamed appendix can rupture leading to **peritonitis.** This is strongly suggested by the presence of **rebound tenderness,** in which a stab of severe pain is produced when the abdominal wall which has been pressed in slowly, is released rapidly. A surgical appendectomy, usually performed through laparoscopy, is the treatment for appendicitis.

Diverticulosis is the presence of small pouches bulging outward through weak spots in the lining of the large intestine *(Figure 6.35).* They are asymptomatic until the pouches become infected and inflamed, a condition called **diverticulitis.** This condition causes abdominal pain, vomiting, constipation, and fever. Complications, such as perforation and abscess formation, can occur. The most likely cause of diverticular disease (diverticulosis and diverticulitis) is a low-fiber diet.

Ulcerative colitis is an extensive inflammation and ulceration of the lining of the large intestine. It produces bouts of bloody diarrhea, crampy pain, and often weight loss and electrolyte imbalance.

Irritable bowel syndrome (IBS) is an increasingly common large **bowel** disorder, presenting with crampy pains, gas, and changes in bowel habits to either constipation or diarrhea. There are no anatomical changes seen in the bowel, and the cause is unknown.

Polyps are masses of tissue arising from the wall of the large intestine that protrude into the bowel **lumen.** They vary in size and shape. Most are benign. Endoscopic biopsy can determine if they are **precancerous** or cancerous.

Colon and **rectal cancers** *(Figure 6.36)* are the second leading cause of cancer deaths after lung cancer. The majority occur in the rectum and sigmoid colon. These cancers spread by:

1. direct extension through the bowel wall
2. **metastasis** to regional lymph nodes
3. moving down the lumen of the bowel
4. blood-borne **metastases** to liver, lung, bone, and brain.

Obstruction of the large bowel can be caused by cancers, large polyps, or diverticulitis.

Intussusception is a form of obstruction whereby a tumor in the lumen of the bowel, together with its segment of bowel, is telescoped into the immediately distal segment of bowel.

Proctitis is inflammation of the lining of the rectum, often associated with ulcerative colitis, Crohn disease, or radiation therapy. Symptoms are **anorectal** pain, rectal bleeding, and excess mucus in the **stool.**

Disorders of the Anal Canal

Hemorrhoids are dilated veins in the submucosa of the anal canal, often associated with pregnancy, chronic **constipation,** diarrhea, or aging. They protrude into the anal canal (internal hemorrhoid) or bulge out along the edge of the anus (external hemorrhoid, *Figure 6.37*), producing pain and bright red blood from the anus. A **thrombosed** hemorrhoid, in which blood has clotted, is very painful.

Anal fissures are tears in the lining of the anal canal, such as may occur with difficult bowel movements (**BMs**).

Anal fistulas occur following abscesses in the anal glands. The anal canal has six or seven glands in the posterior canal that secrete mucus to lubricate the canal. If the glands become infected, abscesses form that, when they heal, can form a passage (fistula) between the anal canal and the skin outside the anus.

▲ **FIGURE 6.35 Barium Enema Showing Diverticulosis**

▲ **FIGURE 6.36 Barium Enema Showing Colon Cancer.**

▲ **FIGURE 6.37 External Hemorrhoid.** Hemorrhoid Protruding From Anus.

WORD	PRONUNCIATION		ELEMENTS	DEFINITION
bowel	BOUGH-el		Latin *sausage*	Another name for intestine
diverticulum	di-ver-TICK-you-lum	S/	-um *tissue*	A pouchlike opening or sac from a tubular structure (e.g., gut)
diverticula (pl)	di-ver-TICK-you-lah	R/	diverticul- *by-road*	
diverticulosis	DIE-ver-tick-you-LOW-sis	S/	-osis *condition*	Presence of a number of small pouches in the wall of the large intestine
diverticulitis	DIE-ver-tick-you-LIE-tis	S/	-itis *inflammation*	Inflammation of the diverticula
fissure	FISH-ur		Latin *slit*	Deep furrow or cleft
fistula	FIS-tyu-lah		Latin *pipe, tube*	Abnormal passage
hemorrhoid	HEM-oh-royd	S/	-rrhoid *flow*	Dilated rectal vein producing painful anal swelling
hemorrhoids (pl)		R/CF	hem/o- *blood*	
hemorrhoidectomy	HEM-oh-roy-DEK-toh-me	S/	-ectomy *excision*	Surgical removal of hemorrhoids
intussusception	IN-tuss-sus-SEP-shun	S/	-ion *action*	The slipping of one part of bowel inside another to cause obstruction
		P/	intus- *within*	
		R/	-suscept- *to take up*	
lumen	LOO-men		Latin *light, window*	The interior space of a tubelike structure
McBurney point	mack-BUR-nee POYNT		Charles McBurney, New York surgeon, 1845–1913	One-third the distance from anterior superior iliac spine to umbilicus
metastasis	meh-TAS-tah-sis	P/	meta- *in the midst of*	Spread of a disease from one part of the body to another
metastases (pl)	meh-TAS-tah-seez	R/	-stasis *to place*	
peritoneum	per-ih-toe-NEE-um	S/	-um *tissue*	Membrane that lines the abdominal cavity
		R/CF	periton/e- *stretch over*	
peritoneal (adj)	PER-ih-toe-NEE-al	S/	-al *pertaining to*	Pertaining to the peritoneum
peritonitis	PER-ih-toe-NIE-tis	S/	-itis *inflammation*	Inflammation of the peritoneum
polyp	POL-ip		Latin *foot, stalk*	Mass of tissue that projects into the lumen of bowel
		R/	polyp- *polyp*	
polyposis	pol-ih-POH-sis	S/	-osis *condition*	Presence of several polyps
polypectomy	pol-ip-ECK-to-mee	S/	-ectomy *excision*	Excision or removal of a polyp
precancerous	pree-KAN-sir-us	S/	-ous *pertaining to*	Lesion from which a cancer can develop
		P/	pre- *before*	
		R/	-cancer- *cancer*	
proctitis	prok-TIE-tis	S/	-itis *inflammation*	Inflammation of the lining of the rectum
		R/	proct- *rectum*	
ulcerative	UL-sir-ah-tiv	S/	-ative *quality of*	Marked by an ulcer or ulcers
		R/	ulcer- *a sore*	

Abbreviations

BM bowel movement
IBS irritable bowel syndrome

EXERCISES

This exercise focuses on the suffixes in this WAD. The suffix is your first clue to the meaning of a medical term. Challenge your knowledge of suffixes by filling in the blanks. Some answers you will use twice because more than one suffix can have the same meaning.

_____ 1. -um

_____ 2. -ous

_____ 3. -osis

_____ 4. -ion

_____ 5. -itis

_____ 6. -rrhoid

_____ 7. -ative

_____ 8. -al

_____ 9. -ectomy

A. flow

B. action

C. inflammation

D. tissue

E. pertaining to

F. condition

G. excision

H. quality of

Risk factors that can cause GI bleeding
include alcohol, smoking, and a low-fiber
diet.

GASTROINTESTINAL (GI) BLEEDING

Bleeding can occur anywhere in the gastrointestinal tract from a variety of causes, as described in the preceding sections. The bleeding can be internal and painless. It can present in different ways to provide a clue as to the site of bleeding:

- **Hematemesis**—the vomiting of bright red blood, which indicates an upper GI source of bleeding (esophagus, stomach, duodenum).

- **Vomiting of "coffee-grounds"**—occurs when bleeding from an upper GI source has slowed or stopped; red hemoglobin has been converted to brown hematin by gastric acids.

- **Hematochezia**—the passage of bright red bloody stools; usually indicates lower GI bowel bleeding from the sigmoid colon, rectum, or anus.

- **Melena**—the passage of black tarry stools; usually indicates upper GI bleeding. The blood is digested and hemoglobin is oxidized as it passes through the intestine to produce the black color. Melena can continue for several days after a severe hemorrhage.

- **Occult blood**—no bleeding can be seen in the stool, but a chemical fecal occult blood test (**Hemoccult test**) is positive. The chronic source of the bleeding can be anywhere in the GI tract.

Consuming black licorice, Pepto-Bismol, or blueberries can produce black stools.

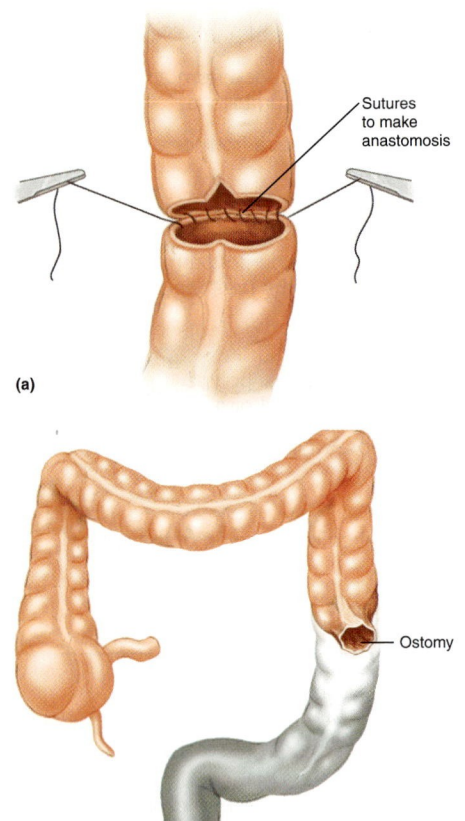

Sutures to make anastomosis

Ostomy

▲ **FIGURE 6.38   Intestinal Resections.**
(*a*) Anastomosis. (*b*) Ostomy.

Common Diagnostic and Therapeutic Procedures

- **Fecal occult blood test** (Hemoccult)—used to detect the presence of blood not visible to the naked eye.

- **Nasogastric aspiration and lavage**—the presence of bright red blood indicates active upper GI bleeding; "coffee-grounds" indicate the bleeding has slowed or stopped.

- **Upper GI barium x-rays** are less accurate than endoscopy at identifying the bleeding lesion.

- **Barium enema**—a radiographic contrast material is injected into the large intestine as an enema and X-ray films are taken (see Figures 6.33b, 6.35, and 6.36).

- **Endoscopy**—enables direct visual examination of the intestine with a flexible tube containing light-transmitting glass fibers or a video transmitter that sends back an enlarged image. **Panendoscopy** examines the esophagus, stomach, and duodenum and provides the highest yield of information to establish the source of upper GI bleeding. Endoscopy can also be used to perform a biopsy, remove polyps (**polypectomy**), and **coagulate** bleeding lesions.

- **Anoscopy**—examines the anus and lower rectum with a rigid instrument.

- **Flexible sigmoidoscopy** examines the rectum and sigmoid colon.

- **Colonoscopy** examines the whole length of the colon.

- **Gastroscopy** examines the stomach.

- **Intestinal resections**—used to surgically remove diseased portions of the intestine. The remaining portions of the intestine can be joined together through an **anastomosis** (Figure 6.38a). If there is insufficient bowel remaining, an **ostomy** (Figure 6.38b) can be performed, where the end of the bowel opens onto the skin at a **stoma. Ileostomy** and **colostomy** are two common procedures.

- **Digital rectal exam**—the physician palpates the rectum and prostate gland with an index finger.

WORD ANALYSIS AND DEFINITION

S = Suffix   P = Prefix   R = Root   R/CF = Combining Form

WORD	PRONUNCIATION	ELEMENTS		DEFINITION
anastomosis anastomoses (pl)	ah-**NAS**-to-**MO**-sis ah-**NAS**-to-**MO**-sez	S/ R/	-osis *condition* anastom- *provide a mouth*	A surgically made union between two tubular structures
coagulate	koh-**AG**-you-late	S/ R/	-ate *action* coagul- *clot*	Form a clot
endoscope	**EN**-doh-skope	P/	endo- *within, inside*	Instrument to examine the inside of a tubular or hollow organ
endosopic (adj) endoscopy anoscopy colonoscopy	**EN**-doh-**SKOP**-ik en-**DOS**-koh-pee **A**-nos-koh-pee koh-lon-**OSS**-koh-pee	S/ S/ R/CF R/CF	-scope *instrument* -scopy *examine* an/o- *anus* colon/o- *colon*	The use of an endoscope Endoscopic examination of the anus Examination of the inside of the colon by endoscopy
gastroscopy ileoscopy proctoscopy	gas-**TROS**-koh-pee ill-ee-**OS**-koh-pee prok-**TOSS**-koh-pee	R/CF R/CF R/CF	gastr/o- *stomach* ile/o- *ileum* proct/o- *anus*	Endoscopic examination of the stomach Endoscopic examination of the ileum Examination of the inside of the anus by endoscopy
sigmoidoscopy	sig-moi-**DOS**-koh-pee	R/CF	sigmoid/o- *sigmoid colon*	Endoscopic examination of the sigmoid colon
enema	**EN**-eh-mah		Greek *injection*	An injection of fluid into the rectum
hematochezia	he-mat-oh-**KEY**-zee-ah	S/ R/CF	-chezia *pass a stool* hemat/o- *blood*	The passage of red, bloody stools
melena	mel-**EN**-ah		Greek *black*	The passage of black, tarry stools
occult Hemoccult test	o-**KULT** **HEEM**-o-kult TEST		Latin *to hide*	Not visible on the surface *Hemoccult* (trade name for a fecal occult blood test)
ostomy	**OS**-toe-me	S/ R/	-stomy *new opening* os- *mouth*	Artificial opening into a tubular structure
colostomy	ko-**LOSS**-toe-me	R/	col- *colon*	Artificial opening from colon to the outside of the body
ileostomy	ill-ee-**OS**-toe-me	R/	ile- *ileum*	Artificial opening from the ileum to the outside of the body
stoma	**STOW**-mah		Greek *mouth*	Artificial opening

EXERCISES

"Scope" and "scopy" are two suffixes you will see attached to many medical terms you will meet in later chapters. "Scope" is the actual instrument used in the procedure. The procedure itself is the "scopy." Utilize your medical vocabulary to fill in the blanks for this exercise.

Instrument	Procedure Term	Definition of Procedure
endoscope		
colonoscope		
proctoscope		
anoscope		
gastroscope		
ileoscope		
sigmoidoscope		

*Note: **Endoscope** is a generic (general) term that means any instrument used to examine the inside of a tubular or hollow organ. The instrument obtains its specific name from the organ it is used to examine. Thus, an instrument used to view a bronchus is a bronchoscope specifically, but it is also an endoscope in general.*

DIGESTIVE SYSTEM
CHALLENGE YOUR KNOWLEDGE

A. **Can you interpret the following colonoscopy report for this patient?** First, read the report out loud. Underline the medical terminology. If you need to, consult a dictionary or your glossary for additional help. Fill in the blanks.

> **Preoperative Diagnosis:** History of (H/O) multiple colonic polyps
>
> **Postoperative Diagnosis:** Normal colon
> In the left lateral position, the colonoscope was advanced into the rectum without difficulty. Examination of the rectum was normal. The sigmoid and descending colon revealed extensive diverticular disease but no evidence of colonic polyp disease. The transverse colon was examined to the hepatic flexure. There were no abnormalities of the transverse colon. The ascending colon was examined to the ileocecal valve. This was confirmed by abdominal wall transillumination. There were no abnormalities of the ascending colon. The patient tolerated the procedure well and was discharged from the endoscopy suite in good condition. In view of his age and a clean colonoscopy, I have recommended no further surveillance.

1. Based on the prefixes, what is the difference between the pre- and postoperative diagnosis?

    pre- = _____ post- = _____
    Why are the diagnoses sometimes different?

    _____

2. Describe the left lateral position. _____

3. What instrument was used for this procedure? _____

4. Give another adjective meaning *extensive*. _____

5. Deconstruct **diverticulosis,** and write its meaning. _____

6. Define **polyp:** _____

7. Based on the prefix trans-, in which direction does the transverse colon lie? _____

8. Again, using the prefix trans-, what does **transillumination** mean? _____

9. What does a "clean colonoscopy" mean? _____

10. Is it good or bad that the physician is recommending "no further surveillance." Explain your answer.

    _____

B. **While every medical term does not need a prefix, most medical terms will have a suffix, which appears at the end of the term.** Remember that *there can be more than one suffix with the same meaning.* Fill in the chart.

Suffix	Meaning of Suffix	Example of Medical Term Using This Suffix
-al		
-ar		
-ary		
-ase		
-dynia		

Suffix	Meaning of Suffix	Example of Medical Term Using This Suffix
-ectomy		
-ia		
-ics		
-id		
-ist		
-itis		
-osis		
-zyme		

C. **Patient Education: In Your Own Words** If you had to explain each of the specific functions of the digestive system to a patient, what would you say? Translate the medical terms into language the patient can understand. Fill in the blanks.

1. ingestion: _____

2. propulsion: _____

3. digestion: _____

4. secretion: _____

5. absorption: _____

6. elimination: _____

D. **Using all the terms in part C, trace the path of digestion in a paragraph.** The exercise has been started for you. Underline all the terms in your writing to make sure you have used every one.

The path of digestion begins in the mouth where (go on from here)

_____

_____

_____

_____

_____

DIGESTIVE SYSTEM

E. **Dental assistants, or anyone working in an Oral Surgery Department need to have a thorough knowledge of the mouth and the mastication process.** Your knowledge of medical terms will help you communicate with the dentist or oral surgeon and their patients. Match the correct answer to the statements below.

_____ 1. grind and crush food

_____ 2. projects above the gum/covered with enamel

_____ 3. cheek muscles

_____ 4. destroys tooth enamel and dentin

_____ 5. contains blood vessels, nerves, tissue

_____ 6. harder than bone

_____ 7. oral cavity

_____ 8. dental decay

_____ 9. anchors tooth to jaw

_____ 10. inflammation of the gum

_____ 11. nerves reach jaw through this

_____ 12. contain the taste buds

A. mouth

B. pulp cavity

C. root canal

D. caries

E. root

F. gingivitis

G. papillae

H. crown

I. tartar

J. buccinator

K. bicuspids and molars

L. dentin

F. **Be aware of singular and plural terms.** Insert the correct medical terms in the blanks; watch for spelling. You will not use all the terms.

diverticulitis   diverticulum   diverticulosis   diverticula

1. What starts out as a single _____, if left untreated, can lead to many _____.

   The condition of having a number of these small pouches in the wall of the large intestine is known

   as _____. Should these pouches become inflamed, _____ will result.

metastasses   metastases   metastize   metastasis

2. What was originally thought to be a single _____ to the patient's lung was proven to be multiple

   _____ to lung, kidney, and bone.

polypectomy   polyposis   polyp (singular)

3. The first polyp was found on sigmoidoscopy. A follow-up colonoscopy six months later found several more

   (plural) _____ in the large intestine. Diagnosis is _____. Proposed treat-

   ment is _____.

peritoneum   peritonitis   peritoneal

4. The _____ laceration sliced completely through the _____. Because of an

   infection in the wound, the patient developed _____.

G. **Deconstruct and Define:** The following medical terms can all designate a diagnosis or a condition. Use your knowledge of basic elements to deconstruct these terms and determine their meanings. First, slash (/) the terms into elements, then fill in the chart.

Medical Term	Prefix	Root/CF	Suffix	Meaning of Medical Term
dysphagia				
esophagitis				
hematemesis				
pyrosis				
reflux				
regurgitation				

H. **Abbreviations:** Choose the abbreviation that is best described in the statement, and fill it in on the blank provided. On the line below the statement, write out the meaning of the abbreviation you have chosen. There are more answers than questions. The first one is done for you. Fill in the blanks.

GI   SSA   GERD   HAV   ESWL   SGOT   CF   BM

1. Destroys calculi or stones   Abbreviation___*ESWL*_____

   Meaning: _____*extracorporeal shock wave lithotripsy*_____

2. Backing up into the esophagus   Abbreviation: _____

   Meaning: _____

3. Digestive system component   Abbreviation: _____

   Meaning: _____

4. Liver disease   Abbreviation: _____

   Meaning: _____

5. Inherited disease affects exocrine glands   Abbreviation: _____

   Meaning: _____

6. Final act of elimination   Abbreviation: _____

   Meaning: _____

I. **Group Recall:** The following colors all have a Latin or Greek term associated with them. Fill in the blanks with the element or term, and provide a medical term where it is used.

White:_____   Term: _____

Yellow: _____   Term: _____

Rust: _____   Term: _____

DIGESTIVE SYSTEM

J. **Word elements are the keys to unlocking medical terms.** Assess your knowledge of elements with the following exercise:

1. Where is the inflammation in **hepatitis**?

    a. the belly

    b. the liver

    c. the pancreas

    d. the mouth

    e. the intestine

2. In the term **submucosa,** the prefix means:

    a. over

    b. under

    c. around

    d. inside

    e. across

3. The color denoted in the term **leukoplakia** is:

    a. green

    b. black

    c. white

    d. yellow

    e. red

4. The element "**os**" means:

    a. stomach

    b. mouth

    c. eye

    d. liver

    e. ear

5. If the root cyst means *bladder,* what is a **cystectomy**?

    a. bladder irrigation

    b. bladder removal

    c. bladder examination

    d. bladder laceration

    e. bladder hemorrhage

6. If a medication is given **postprandial**, you will take it after:

   a. exercise

   b. drinking water

   c. meals

   d. a vitamin

   e. waking up

7. **Gingivitis** has a root that means:

   a. opening

   b. teeth

   c. gum

   d. decay

   e. enzyme

8. A **cholecystectomy** is:

   a. procedure

   b. diagnosis

   c. inflammation

   d. discharge

   e. instrument

9. What is the adjective used to describe a dilated, tortuous vein?

   a. adipose

   b. varicose

   c. edematous

   d. pyloric

   e. segmental

10. Based on the suffix, you know that the **peritoneum** will be:

   a. opening

   b. incision

   c. structure

   d. tumor

   e. matrix

DIGESTIVE SYSTEM

K. **Element:** The following elements are a mixture of the prefixes, roots, combining forms, and suffixes contained in this chapter. In your study of medical terminology, it is important for you to be able to identify the types of elements and their definitions. This will aid you in determining the meaning of the medical term. Fill in the chart.

Identify each element with a check mark (✓) in the proper column. Then provide a meaning for the element. The first one is done for you.

Element	Prefix	Root/CF	Suffix	Meaning of element
al	_____	_____	✓	*pertaining to* _____
atric	_____	_____	_____	_____
bari	_____	_____	_____	_____
bi	_____	_____	_____	_____
cusp	_____	_____	_____	_____
dynia	_____	_____	_____	_____
glosso	_____	_____	_____	_____
id	_____	_____	_____	_____
lingu	_____	_____	_____	_____
peri	_____	_____	_____	_____
stalsis	_____	_____	_____	_____
sub	_____	_____	_____	_____

Now take any combination of elements from this chart and form a complete medical term. Define the term based on the meaning of the elements given in the chart.

Medical term: _____ / _____ / _____

                      Prefix   Root/CF   Suffix

Meaning of medical term: _____

L. **Discussion Questions:** Draw on your knowledge of the *language of gastroenterology* to discuss the following questions. Prepare a short answer. Be certain you can define every term you are using.

1. What is the bony roof of the mouth called? _____

   What birth defect is associated with this part of the body? _____

   What large facial bone is connected to this part of the body? (*Hint:* see Chapter 5) _____

2. Why do teeth have to be the hardest structures in your body?

   _____

   _____

3. Remember what you learned in Chapter 5 about the role of muscles in the body. What are the buccinator muscles responsible for, and how does that tie in with question 2?

   _____

   _____

M. **Recall and Review:** The following exercise on word elements contains some elements from this chapter and the previous chapter. Try to recall the previous elements without turning back in your book. Check (✓) the type of element, then write its meaning. Fill in the blanks.

Element	Prefix	Root/CF	Suffix	Meaning of Element
clast	_____	_____	_____	_____
de	_____	_____	_____	_____
hydr	_____	_____	_____	_____
lacte	_____	_____	_____	_____
malacia	_____	_____	_____	_____

N. **Patient Education: In Your Own Words** Your knowledge of medical terminology usually must be translated into layman's terms if you are going to explain something the patient can comprehend. Prepare a short answer that will help your patient understand the *difference* between:

1. A polypectomy and enteroscopy

_____

_____

_____

2. Sublingual and subcutaneous medication (*Hint:* Think back to Chapter 3.)

_____

_____

_____

O. **Deconstruct.** No matter how long or how short the medical term, reducing it to elements will provide the meaning. Deconstruct with slashes the following two medical terms into their elemental meanings. Fill in the blanks. Divide and conquer your terms!

esophagogastroduodenoscopy

Prefix	Meaning of Prefix	Root(s)/CF	Meaning of Root(s)/CF	Suffix	Meaning of Suffix

1. The meaning of esophagogastroduodenoscopy is:

_____

_____

_____

oral

Prefix	Meaning of Prefix	Root(s)/CF	Meaning of Root(s)/CF	Suffix	Meaning of Suffix

2. The meaning of oral is:

_____

DIGESTIVE SYSTEM

P. As a body system, the digestive system has a lot of different disorders. Can you pair the correct organ with its disease or condition and write a brief definition of the term? Fill in the chart.

Term	Organ	Definition
aphthous ulcers	_____	_____
cholecystitis	_____	_____
choledocholithiasis	_____	_____
cirrhosis	_____	_____
Crohn disease	_____	_____
diverticulitis	_____	_____
dysphagia	_____	_____
GERD	_____	_____
IBS	_____	_____
liver	_____	_____
intussusception	_____	_____
pancreatitis	_____	_____
proctitis	_____	_____

Q. Medical terms that are nouns can also have an adjective form. The statement has the noun form in parentheses: you must fill in the correct form of the adjective on the blank. Fill in the blanks.

1. The patient's (digestion) _____ symptoms were resolved with the new medication.

2. Due to an obstruction, the (pylorus) _____ sphincter was necrotic.

3. The (lymph) _____ tissues were sent to the pathologist for examination.

4. The patient is suffering from (pancreas) _____ cancer.

5. The (saliva) _____ gland was removed and sent to pathology.

6. Due to infection, the patient's (intestine) _____ surgery has been postponed until next week.

7. (Hemolysis) _____ jaundice results from RBC destruction and excess bilirubin.

8. The patient's (esophagus) _____ varices were bleeding.

9. The (laparoscope) _____ surgery poses less risk to the patient.

10. The (segment) _____ resection of the intestine is scheduled for later today.

R. Supply the missing element(s) that will complete the medical term. Beneath the line, write the type of word element(s) you have used. Some terms may require more than one element. Fill in the blanks. The first one is done for you.

1. Inflammation of the appendix

    appendic*itis*_____

    Suffix

2. Part of the colon shaped like an "S"

    sigm_____

3. Pertaining to the anus   an_____

4. Excessive amount of gas   flatul _____

5. To bend back   _____ flex

6. Inflammation of the colon   col _____

7. Pertaining to the anus and rectum   ano _____ al

8. Evacuation of feces from rectum and anus   de_____

9. An edge or a border   _____ meter

10. Pertaining to the colon   _____ic

S. **The following medical terms have their origins in Greek and Latin.** Give a definition for each term, then use any three terms in sentences of your choice. Fill in the blanks.

Medical Term	Definition
bolus	
incisor	
uvula	
ulcer	
lymph	
saliva	
canker	
esophagus	
pulp	
caries	
palate	

1. _____

_____

2. _____

_____

3. _____

_____

DIGESTIVE SYSTEM

T.   Documentation:

> Mrs. Helen Schreiber, a 45-year-old high school principal, presents with a six-month history of dry mouth, bleeding gums, and difficulty in chewing and swallowing food. Questioning by Dr. Susan Lee, her primary care physician, reveals that she also has dry eyes, is having pain in some joints of both hands, and has felt fatigued.
>
> Her previous medical history is uneventful. Physical examination shows a dry mouth, mild gingivitis, and an ulcer on the back of the lower lip. Her salivary glands are not swollen. Her eyes show no ulceration or conjunctivitis. The metacarpo-phalangeal joints of both index fingers are swollen, stiff, and tender. All other systems show no abnormality.
>
> Initial laboratory reports show anemia, decreased WBC count, and an elevated ESR. Dr. Lee made a provisional diagnosis of Sjögren syndrome. The results of blood studies for SSA and SSB antibodies and for rheumatoid factor titers are pending, as are X-rays of her hands. Mrs. Schreiber was given advice about symptomatic treatment for her dry mouth and will be seen again in one week.
>
> Signed: Luis Guitterez, CMA 06/12/06, 1530 hrs.

Helen Schreiber's medical record of her visit to Dr. Susan Lee contains terms from this and previous chapters. Reinforce your knowledge of the language of medicine by answering the following questions based on this scenario. Fill in the blanks.

1.   List all of Mrs. Schreiber's signs and symptoms.

   _____

   _____

   _____

2.   Which symptoms pertain to the digestive system? _____

3.   Which other body systems are presenting symptoms? _____

4.   Examination of Mrs. Schreiber's eyes revealed no conjunctivitis. What is conjunctivitis?

   _____

U.   **Terminology Challenge:** Dr. Lee made a *"provisional"* diagnosis for Mrs. Schreiber of Sjögren syndrome. Use your school library or a medical dictionary online to learn the meaning of the term **provisional diagnosis.** Write your notes here.

   _____

   _____

   _____

   _____

   _____

V.   **Precision in Documentation:** Get the stone in the right place: **cholelithiasis** or **choledocholithiasis?** Make the correct choice of medical terminology. Fill in the blanks.

   1.   Patient's films revealed a stone in the common bile duct.

      Diagnosis: _____

   2.   The presence of a stone in the patient's gallbladder was confirmed by the radiologist.

      Diagnosis: _____

W. **Build your knowledge of the digestive system by correctly answering the following questions.** Circle the best choice.

1. What lines the wall of the abdominal cavity?

   a. omentum

   b. periosteum

   c. viscera

   d. parietal peritoneum

   e. serosa

2. Medical term for the act of swallowing:

   a. micturition

   b. digestion

   c. mastication

   d. deglutition

   e. absorption

3. **Peristalsis** means:

   a. waves of contractions

   b. segment of the intestine

   c. an enzyme

   d. chewing food

   e. ingestion

4. Which of the following is *not* a component of the digestive system?

   a. alimentary canal

   b. digestive tract

   c. salivary glands

   d. pancreas

   e. trachea

5. Mechanical movement of food from the mouth to the anus:

   a. digestion

   b. elimination

   c. propulsion

   d. mastication

   e. ingestion

DIGESTIVE SYSTEM

X. **Prefixes make the difference in precision.** Analyze the two pairs of medical terms. Write a brief description of how they differ, based on their prefixes.

1. emesis and hematemesis

_____

_____

2. symptomatic and asymptomatic

_____

_____

Y. **Precision in Documentation:** You may someday find yourself doing medical transcription in a hospital or physician's office. Proofread the letter Dr. Walsh has sent to the patient's insurance company, asking for preauthorization for her surgery. Underline or highlight all the errors, then rewrite the correct terms on the lines below the dictation. Then add a brief definition of each term.

> Dear Doctor Leavenworth,
>
> Request for Authorization of Surgery
>
> Re: Mrs. Martha Jones
>
> Subscriber ID # 056437
>
> Mrs. Jones is a 52-year-old former waitress, recently divorced. She is 5 feet 4 inches tall and weighs 275 pounds. She has type 2 diabeetes with frequent episodes of hyperglycemia and also ketoacidoses, requiring three different hospitalizations. She now has diabetick retinnopathy and peripheral vascullitis. Complicating this is hypertension (185/110), coronery artery disease, and pulmonary edema. Exercise is out of the question because she has marked osteoarrthritis of her knees and hips. Mrs. Jones is now housebound, dependent on her daughter for transportation to our medical center. In spite of monthly meetings with our nutritionist, she has gained 25 pounds in the past 6 months.

Write the correct form of the misspelled words with a brief definition for each term here:

_____

_____

_____

_____

_____

_____

_____

_____

_____

_____

_____

Z. Your knowledge of medical terminology will increase if you focus on similarities and differences in medical terms. Fill in the blanks.

1. One word element makes lactose different from lactase.

   The word element is a _____ .

   Lactose means: _____

   Lactase means: _____

2. One word element makes an enteroscope different from an endoscope.

   The word element is a _____ .

   An enteroscope is: _____

   An endoscope is: _____

AA. Check the accuracy of your chart documentation. The following patients have presented to the gastroenterology clinic today. Can you correctly complete their documentation?

1. Caroline Mason presents today with severe symptoms of _____ (difficult swallowing), which

   has been getting progressively worse. _____ (pertaining to looking within by a scope)

   reveals _____-atous (swollen) _____ (pertaining to the

   esophagus) _____ (dilated veins). She will be scheduled for esophageal _____

   (enlargement) early next week.

2. Andrew Baker reported to the Fulwood Emergency Room yesterday with _____ (signs)

   of _____ (following a meal) burning chest pain and _____ (vomiting of

   blood). Dr. Lee admitted him to the GI service for further diagnostic tests and possible surgery.

BB. Many medical terms that are nouns also have an adjectival form. Correctly apply these six medical terms to the following sentences. Fill in the blanks.

mucous	mucin	mucus	mucosal	mucosa	submucosa

1. The lining of a tubular structure is referred to as the _____ .

2. A sticky film containing mucin is _____ .

3. The term for *pertaining to* the mucosa is _____ .

4. The tissue layer beneath the mucosa would be the _____ .

5. _____ is a secretion from the mucosal glands.

6. _____ means *relating to mucus or the mucosa.*

7. Which two terms have similar meanings? _____ and _____

8. Which two terms are pronounced the same but spelled differently? _____

   and _____

CHAPTER 6 REVIEW

DIGESTIVE SYSTEM

CHAPTER SUMMARY EXERCISE

1. *Listen to the pronunciation of the medical terms as given by your instructor or on the student CD.*
2. *Circle the correct spelling of the medical term.*
3. *Match the correctly spelled terms to the brief descriptions below.*
4. *Write a sentence for each of the 15 terms that appear in this exercise.*

A. SPELLING COMPREHENSION: CIRCLE THE CORRECT SPELLING OF THE TERM.

1. laperoscopie   laparoscopy   leperoscopie   leporoscopy   laporoscopie

2. hematemesis   hemmatemisis   hematimisis   hematemis   hematimisus

3. parrotid   paratid   poratid   parotid   parritid

4. jegjunum   jejuunum   jedgejunum   jeghjunem   jejunum

5. mesentery   mesantery   mesenterie   mesanterie   messantery

6. hematochezia   hemetocizia   hemmatocizia   hemocizia   hematocizia

7. leukoplakkia   leukopakia   leukopiccia   leukoplakia   leukkophakia

8. degluetition   deglutition   deeglutition   deglutation   deglutation

9. varices   varixes   verixces   vericces   varicces

10. aphous   aphtous   appthous   aphthous   affthous

11. cirosis   chirosis   chirosus   chirrhosis   cirrhosis

12. alimentary   elementary   alementary   elementarie   alimenterie

13. ickteris   ichterus   icterus   eckterus   ecterrus

14. sphinchter   spinchter   spinkter   sphenter   sphincter

15. peristallsis   perastalssis   peristalsis   perostalis   peritallsis

B. MATCH THE NUMBER OF THE CORRECT TERM IN PART A WITH THE BRIEF DESCRIPTION OF THE TERM BELOW.

a. act of swallowing _____

b. double layer of peritoneum enclosing viscera _____

c. small ulcer in the mouth _____

d. vomiting of blood _____

e. examining abdomen with an endoscope _____

f. dilated, tortuous veins _____

g. moves digestive contents onward _____

h. most nutrients absorbed here _____

i. extensive liver disease _____

j. band of muscle that encircles a tube _____

k. the digestive tract _____

l. jaundice _____

m. white plaque in the mouth _____

n. red, bloody stools _____

o. salivary gland beside the ear _____

C. USING YOUR KNOWLEDGE OF TERMS 1-15 IN PART A AND THEIR CORRECT SPELLING, WRITE A BRIEF SENTENCE FOR EACH OF THE TERMS AS IT MIGHT APPEAR IN PATIENT DOCUMENTATION.

1. _____

2. _____

3. _____

4. _____

5. _____

6. _____

7. _____

8. _____

9. _____

10. _____

11. _____

12. _____

13. _____

14. _____

15. _____

D. GO TO THE STUDENT CD. OPEN THE GLOSSARY AND PRACTICE YOUR PRONUNCIATION OF THE TERMS IN PART A OF THIS EXERCISE.

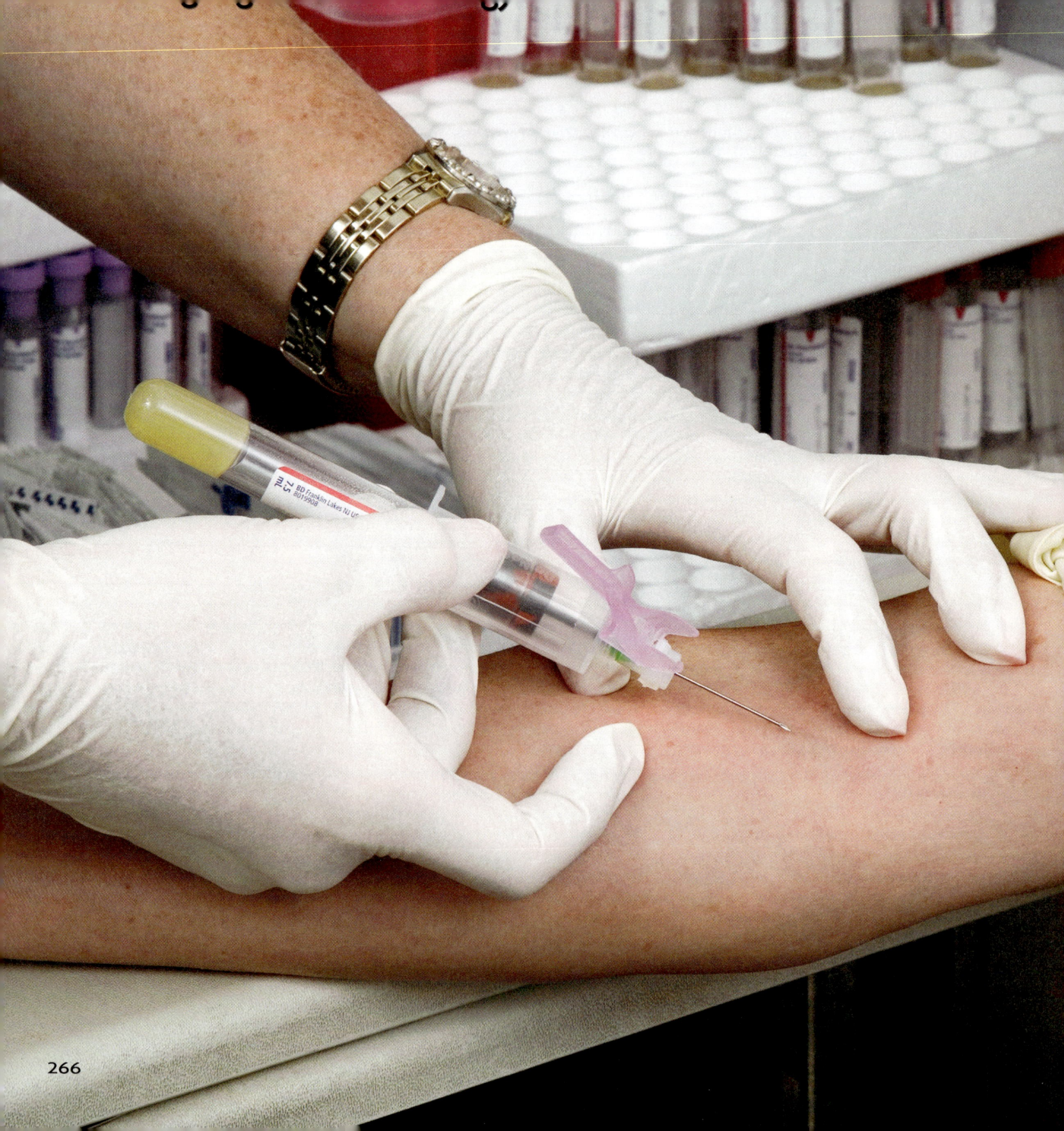

CASE REPORT 7.1

You are

. . . a medical assistant working with Susan Lee, MD, a primary care physician at Fulwood Medical Center

Your patient is

. . . Mrs. Luisa Sosin, a 47-year-old woman who presented a week ago with fatigue, lethargy, and muscle weakness. Physical examination revealed pallor of her skin, a pulse rate of 90, and a respiratory rate of 20. Dr. Lee referred her for extensive blood work. Dr. Lee also determined that the patient had been taking aspirin and **NSAIDs (nonsteroidal anti-inflammatory drugs)** for the past six months for low back pain.

You are responsible for documenting her investigation and care. She is your next patient, and you are reviewing this laboratory report:

Learning Outcomes

In order to understand this report, to be able to communicate intelligently with Dr. Lee about the patient, and to document Mrs. Sosin's medical care, you need to have knowledge of the anatomy, physiology, and the medical terminology of **hematology.**

This chapter will provide you with information that enables you to:

- Apply the language of hematology to the anatomy and physiology of the blood.

- Comprehend, analyze, spell, and write the medical terms of hematology so that you can communicate and document accurately and precisely in any health care setting.

- Recognize and pronounce the medical terms of hematology so that you can communicate verbally with accuracy and precision in any health care setting.

- Explain the effects of common disorders of the blood on health.

Laboratory Report

Luisa Sosin, ID # 7248412
Blood smear: Red blood cells are **microcytic**, **hypochromic**, and **poikilocytic**.

Red Blood Cell **Index**	Patient's Result	Reference Range
Hemoglobin Concentration	10.4g/dL	12–16 g/**dL** (grams per deciliter)
Mean **Corpuscular** Volume (**MCV**)	71 fL	86–98 **fL** (femtoliters)
Mean **Corpuscular** Hemoglobin (**MCH**)	21.5 **pg**/cell (picograms per cell)	26–32 g/dL
Mean Corpuscular Hemoglobin Concentration (**MCHC**)	27.5%	32–36%
Serum Iron	35 μg/100 mL	50-150 **μg**/100 mL (micrograms per 100 milliliters)
Serum Ferritin	20 μg/100 mL	5-280 μg/100 mL
Total Iron-Binding Capacity (**TIBC**)	500 μg/100 mL	250–410 μg/100 mL

The reference range is the usual range of test values for a healthy population.

LESSON 7.1 Components of Blood

OBJECTIVES

The information in this lesson relates to the composition, functions, and uses of blood and will enable you to:

- **Identify the components of blood.**
- **Describe plasma and its functions.**
- **Explain the functions of blood.**

Abbreviations

dL	deciliter; one-tenth of a liter
fL	femtoliter; one-quadrillionth of a liter
L	liter
Hct	hematocrit
MCH	mean corpuscular hemoglobin; the average amount of hemoglobin in the average red blood cell
MCHC	mean corpuscular hemoglobin concentration; the average concentration of hemoglobin in a given volume of red blood cells
MCV	mean corpuscular volume, the average volume of a red blood cell
μg	microgram; one-millionth of a gram; sometimes written as mcg
NSAID	nonsteroidal anti-inflammatory drug
pg	picogram, one-trillionth of a gram
RBC	red blood cell
TIBC	total iron-binding capacity; the amount of iron needed to saturate transferrin, the protein that transports iron in the blood
WBC	white blood cell

COMPONENTS OF BLOOD

Blood is a type of connective tissue and consists of cells contained in a liquid matrix.

Blood volume varies with your body size and the amount of adipose tissue. An average-sized adult has about 5 L (10 pints) of blood that represents some 8% of body weight.

If a specimen of blood is collected in a tube and centrifuged, the cells of the blood are packed into the bottom of the tube *(Figure 7.1)*. These cells are called the formed elements of blood and consist of 99% red blood cells (**RBCs**), together with white blood cells (**WBCs**) and platelets. The blood sample is normally about 45% formed elements.

The **hematocrit (Hct)** is the percentage of total blood volume composed of red blood cells. The red blood cells can account for 40 to 54% of the total blood volume in normal males and 38 to 47% in females.

Plasma is the remaining 55% of the blood sample. It is a clear, yellowish liquid that is 91% water. Plasma is the fluid noncellular part of blood. Plasma is a **colloid**, a liquid that contains suspended particles, most of which are plasma proteins:

- **Albumin**—makes up 58% of the proteins.

- **Globulin**—makes up 38% of the plasma proteins. Antibodies are globulins *(see Chapter 15)*.

- **Fibrinogen**—makes up 4% of the plasma proteins and is part of the mechanism for blood clotting *(see Lesson 7.4)*.

Nutrients, waste products, hormones, and **enzymes** are dissolved in plasma for transportation.

When blood is allowed to clot and the solid clot is removed, **serum** is left. Serum is identical to plasma except for the absence of clotting proteins.

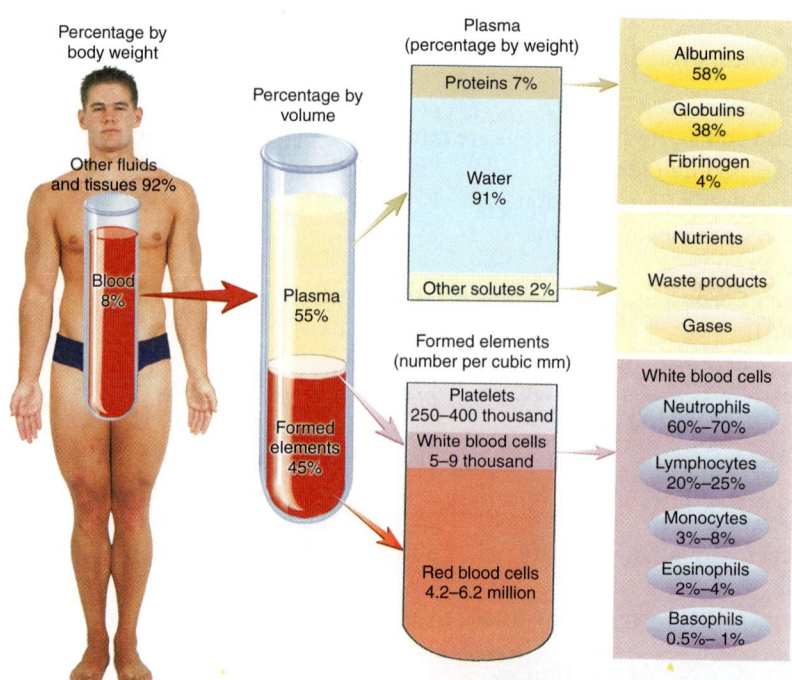

FIGURE 7.1 Components of Blood.

WORD ANALYSIS AND DEFINITION

S = Suffix   P = Prefix   R = Root   R/CF = Combining Form

WORD	PRONUNCIATION		ELEMENTS	DEFINITION
albumin	al-**BYU**-min		Latin *white of an egg*	Simple, soluble protein
colloid	**COLL**-oyd	S/ R/	-oid *appearance of* coll- *glue*	Liquid containing suspended particles
corpuscle corpuscular (adj)	**KOR**-pus-ul kor-**PUS**-kyu-lar	S/ R/	-cle *small thing* corpus- *body*	A blood cell
ferritin	**FER**-ih-tin	S/ R/	-in *chemical* ferrit- *iron*	Iron–protein complex that regulates iron storage and transport
fibrin	**FIE**-brin		Latin *fiber*	Stringy protein fiber that is a component of a blood clot
fibrinogen	fie-**BRIN**-oh-jen	S/ R/CF	-gen *create, produce* fibrin/o- *fibrin*	Precursor of fibrin in blood-clotting process
globulin	**GLOB**-you-lin		Latin *globule*	Family of blood proteins
hematocrit (Hct)	**HE**-mat-oh-krit	S/ R/CF	-crit *to separate* hemat/o- *blood*	Percentage of red blood cells in blood
hematology hematologist	he-mah-**TOL**-oh-jee he-mah-**TOL**-oh-jist	S/ S/	-logy *study of* -logist *specialist*	Medical specialty of disorders of blood Specialist in hematology
hemoglobin	**HE**-moh-**GLOW**-bin	S/ R/CF	-globin *protein* hem/o- *blood*	Red-pigmented protein that is the main component of red blood cells
hypochromic	high-poh-**CROW**-mik	S/ P/ R/	-ic *pertaining to* hypo- *deficient, below* -chrom- *color*	Pale in color, as in RBCs when hemoglobin is deficient
index indices (pl)	**IN**-deks **IN**-di-seez		Latin *one that points out*	A standard indicator of measurement
microcytic	my-kroh-**SIT**-ik	S/ P/ R/	-ic *pertaining to* micro- *small* -cyt- *cell*	Pertaining to a small cell
plasma	**PLAZ**-mah		Greek *something formed*	Fluid, noncellular component of blood
poikilocytic	**POY**-key-low-**SIT**-ik	S/ P/ R/	-ic *pertaining to* poikilo- *irregular* -cyt- *cell*	Pertaining to an irregular-shaped RBC
serum	**SEER**-um		Latin *whey*	Fluid remaining after removal of cells and fibrin clot

EXERCISES

Know your elements—they will increase your medical vocabulary! The following exercise consists of elements taken from this Word Analysis and Definition box (WAD). Match the element to its correct meaning.

_____ 1. hemo   A. small

_____ 2. logy   B. color

_____ 3. oid   C. deficient, below

_____ 4. micro   D. iron

_____ 5. cyt   E. create, produce

_____ 6. crit   F. blood

_____ 7. chrom   G. appearance of

_____ 8. hypo   H. to separate

_____ 9. gen   I. cell

_____ 10. ferrit   J. study of

11. Which of these elements are prefixes? _____

FUNCTIONS OF BLOOD

The functions of the blood are to:

1. **Maintain the body's homeostasis** *(see Chapter 2)*.

2. **Maintain body temperature.** Warm blood is transported from the interior of the body to its surface, where heat is released from the blood.

3. **Transport nutrients, vitamins, and minerals** from digestive system and storage areas to organs and cells where they are needed. Examples of nutrients are glucose and amino acids *(see Chapter 6)*.

4. **Transport waste products** from cells and organs to the liver and kidneys for detoxification and excretion. Examples are **creatinine, urea,** bilirubin and lactic acid *(see Chapter 11)*.

5. **Transport hormones** from endocrine glands to the target cells. Examples are insulin and thyroxin *(see Chapter 14)*.

6. **Transport gases** to and from the lungs and cells. Examples are oxygen and carbon dioxide *(see Chapter 7)*.

7. **Protect against foreign substances.** Cells and chemicals in the blood are an important part of the immune system to deal with microorganisms and toxins *(see Chapter 15)*.

8. **Form clots.** This provides protection against blood loss and is the first step in tissue repair and restoration of normal function.

9. **Regulate pH and osmosis.**

Hydrogen ion concentration is measured using a **pH** scale to show the balance between **acid** and **alkaline** in any solution. Pure water is the neutral solution and has a pH of 7.0. Solutions with a pH less than 7 are acidic. Solutions with a pH greater than 7 are alkaline (or basic). Blood has a pH between 7.35 and 7.45 and must be maintained within that range for life to continue. **Buffer** systems in the blood are used to maintain the correct pH range. Examples of buffer systems are bicarbonate and phosphate.

Osmosis is the passage of water through a selectively permeable membrane, such as a cell membrane, from the "more watery" side to the "less watery" side. All cells exchange water by osmosis, and red blood cells exchange 100 times their own volume across the cell membrane every second.

Viscosity, the resistance of a fluid to flow, is an important element that affects the blood's ability to flow through blood vessels. Whole blood is five times as viscous as water. If this viscosity decreases because red blood cells are deficient (as in **anemia**), it enables blood to flow more easily and puts a strain on the heart because of the increased amount of blood being returned to it in a unit of time.

Keynote

Failure to maintain the normal pH range of the blood between 7.35 and 7.45 can cause paralysis and death.

Abbreviations

CBC	complete blood count
ESR	erythrocyte sedimentation rate
pH	hydrogen ion concentration

Laboratory Studies for Blood

- **A complete blood count (CBC)** is a combination of

  1. red blood cell count **(RBC)** and indices

  2. white blood cell count **(WBC)** and differential WBC count

  3. platelet count
     In some laboratories a CBC does not include the differential white blood cell count. This may need to be requested separately. White blood cells are addressed in Lesson 7.3.

- **Erythrocyte sedimentation rate (ESR)** is a nonspecific measure of inflammation. This test is falling out of use as other more specific tests are developed.

WORD ANALYSIS AND DEFINITION

S = Suffix   P = Prefix   R = Root   R/CF = Combining Form

WORD	PRONUNCIATION		ELEMENTS	DEFINITION
acid	**ASS**-id		Latin *sour*	Substance with a pH below 7.0
alkaline (also called basic)	**AL**-kah-line	S/ R/	-ine *pertaining to* alkal- *base*	Substance with a pH above 7.0
anemia	ah-**NEE**-me-ah	P/ R/	an- *without* -emia *blood*	Decreased number of red blood cells
buffer	**BUFF**-er		Latin *cushion*	Substance that resists a change in pH
creatinine	kree-**AT**-ih-neen	S/ R/	-ine *pertaining to* creatin- *flesh*	Breakdown product of the skeletal muscle protein creatine
erythrocyte	eh-**RITH**-ro-site	S/ R/CF	-cyte *cell* erythr/o- *red blood cell*	Another name for a red blood cell
homeostasis	ho-mee-oh-**STAY**-sis	S/ R/CF	-stasis *to stand* home/o- *the same*	Maintaining the stability or equilibrium of a system or the body's internal environment
osmosis	oz-**MO**-sis	S/ R/	-sis *process* osmo- *push*	The passage of water across a cell membrane
sediment	**SED**-ih-ment	S/ R/	Latin *to settle* -ation *action* sediment- *a settling*	Insoluble material that settles to the bottom of a liquid
sedimentation	**SED**-ih-men-**TAY**-shun			Formation of a sediment
urea	you-**REE**-ah		Greek *urine*	End product of nitrogen metabolism
viscous viscosity	**VISS**-kus vis-**KOS**-ih-tee		Latin *sticky*	Sticky fluid that is resistant to flow The resistance of a fluid to flow

EXERCISES

You will help yourself in this exercise if you first slash (/) the bold medical terms into their elements. Review the WAD before you start to fill in the blanks.

1. In the term **sedimentation**, the suffix means _____.

2. If something is a buffer, it acts as a _____

3. Viscous is a term meaning _____.

4. In the term **erythrocyte**, the suffix means _____.

5. *A state of equilibrium* means something remains _____.

6. The suffix in **homeostasis** means _____.

7. Urea comes from the Greek meaning _____.

8. The opposite of acid is _____.

9. The prefix in **anemia** means _____.

10. In the term **osmosis**, the root means _____.

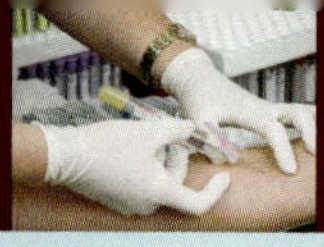

LESSON 7.2 Red Blood Cells (Erythrocytes)

OBJECTIVES

In your bloodstream at this moment are approximately 25 trillion red blood cells (RBCs). Approximately 2.5 million of them are being destroyed every second. This means that 1% of your red blood cells are destroyed and replaced every day of your life.

It is crucial to understand the reasons for this dynamic process and to be familiar with the critical role that the red blood cells play in maintaining life. This lesson will provide you with the information to:

- **Link the structure of red blood cells to their functions.**
- **Identify the roles of hemoglobin in maintaining homeostasis.**
- **Describe the life history of red blood cells.**
- **Recognize some common disorders of red blood cells.**

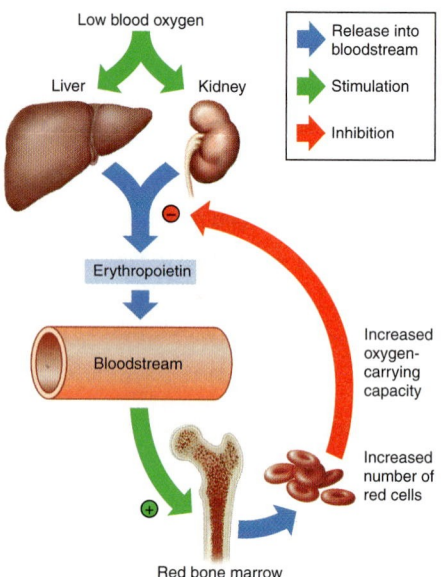

▲ **FIGURE 7.3 Control of RBC Production.**

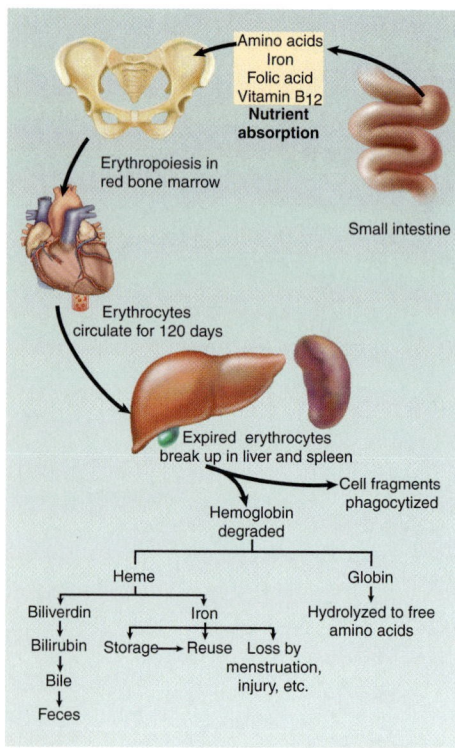

▲ **FIGURE 7.4 Life and Death of RBCs.**

FIGURE 7.2 Red Blood Cells. ▶

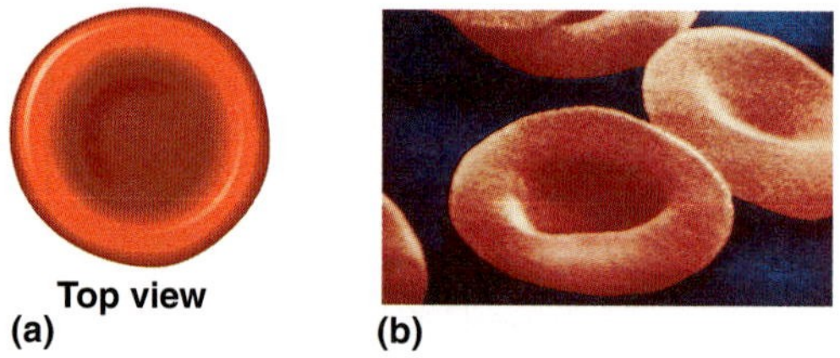

Top view
(a)   (b)

STRUCTURE AND FUNCTION OF RED BLOOD CELLS

Structure of Red Blood Cells

The main component of RBCs is **hemoglobin (Hb)**, which gives the cell its red color. Hemoglobin occupies about one-third of the total cell volume and is composed of the iron-containing pigment **heme** bound to a protein called globin. The rest of the red blood cell consists of the cell membrane, water, electrolytes, and enzymes. Mature RBCs do not have a nucleus.

Each RBC is a **biconcave** disc with edges that are thicker than the center (*Figure 7.2*). This biconcave shape gives the disc a larger surface area than if it were a sphere. The biconcave surface area enables a more rapid flow of gases into and out of the RBC.

Red blood cells are unable to move themselves and are dependent on the heart and blood vessels to move them around the body.

Function of Red Blood Cells

The functions of the RBCs are to:

1. **Transport oxygen (O_2)** from the lungs to cells all over the body. Oxygen is transported in combination with hemoglobin (**oxyhemoglobin**).
2. **Transport carbon dioxide (CO_2)** from the tissue cells to the lungs for excretion.
3. **Transport nitric oxide (NO)**, a gas produced by cells lining the blood vessels that signals smooth muscle to relax and is also a transmitter of signals between nerve cells.

Life History of Red Blood Cells

Red blood cell formation (**erythropoiesis**) occurs in the spaces in bones filled with red bone marrow. **Hematopoietic stem cells** become nucleated **erythroblasts** and then non-nucleated erythrocytes, which are released into the blood stream.

A hormone, **erythropoietin,** produced by the kidneys and liver, controls the rate of RBC production (*Figure 7.3*). A lack of oxygen in the body's tissues triggers the release of erythropoietin, which travels in the blood to the red bone marrow to stimulate RBC production.

Red blood cell production is also influenced by the availability of iron, the B vitamins B_{12} and folic acid, and amino acids through absorption from the digestive tract (*Figure 7.4*).

WORD	PRONUNCIATION		ELEMENTS	DEFINITION
biconcave	bi-**KON**-cave	P/ R/	**bi-** *two, double* **-concave** *arched*	Hollowed surface on both sides of a structure
erythroblast	eh-**RITH**-ro-blast	S/ R/CF	**-blast** *germ cell* **erythr/o-** *red blood cell*	Precursor to a red blood cell
erythropoiesis	eh-**RITH**-ro-poy-**EE**-sis	S/ R/CF	**-poiesis** *to make* **erythr/o-** *red blood cell*	The formation of red blood cells
erythropoietin	eh-**RITH**-ro-**POY**-ee-tin	S/ R/CF	**-poietin** *the maker* **erythr/o-** *red blood cell*	Protein secreted by the kidney that stimulates red blood cell production
hematopoietic	**HE**-mah-toh-poy-**ET**-ick	S/ S/ R/CF	**-ic** *pertaining to* **-poiet-** *the making* **hemat/o-** *blood*	Pertaining to the making of red blood cells
heme	HEEM		Greek *blood*	The iron-based component of hemoglobin that carries oxygen
macrophage	**MAK**-roh-fayj	P/ R/	**macro-** *large* **-phage** *to eat*	Large white blood cell that removes bacteria, foreign particles, and dead cells
oxyhemoglobin	**OCK**-see-he-moh-**GLOW**-bin	P/ R/CF R/	**oxy-** *oxygen* **hem/o-** *blood* **-globin-** *protein*	Hemoglobin in combination with oxygen

The average life span of an RBC is 120 days, during which time the cell has circulated through the body about 75,000 times. With age, the cells become more fragile, and squeezing through tiny capillaries ruptures them. **Macrophages** in the liver and spleen take up the hemoglobin that is released and break it down into its components heme and globin. The heme is broken down into iron and into a rust-colored pigment called bilirubin *(see Chapter 6.)*

Abbreviations

CO_2	carbon dioxide
Hb	hemoglobin; may also be written as Hgb
NO	nitric oxide
O_2	oxygen

EXERCISES

Some of the medical terms from this WAD are defined for you. One word in the definition is in bold; find the element in the term that has the same meaning. **The first one is done for you.** *Fill in the blanks.*

1. **Macrophage:**   Element _____*macro*_____ = _____*large*_____

   Definition: **large** white blood cell that removes bacteria and dead cells

2. **Erythroblast:**   Element _____ = _____

   Definition: **precursor** to red blood cell

3. **Biconcave:**   Element _____ = _____

   Definition: hollowed surface on **both** sides of a structure

4. **Erythropoiesis:**   Element _____ = _____

   Definition: the **formation** of red blood cells

5. **Hemoglobin:**   Element _____ = _____

   Definition: red color and oxygen transporter of red **blood** cells

6. **Erythropoietin**   Element _____ = _____

   Definition: protein that is secreted by kidney and stimulates **red blood cell** production

7. **Hematopoietic:**   Element _____ = _____

   Definition: **pertaining to** the making of red blood cells

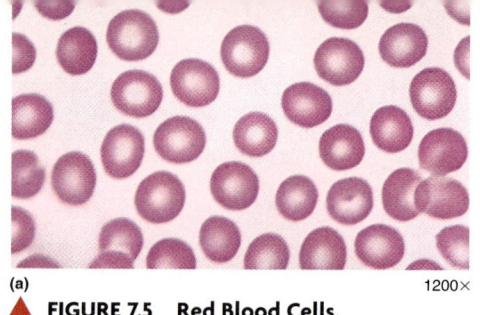

(a)   1200×

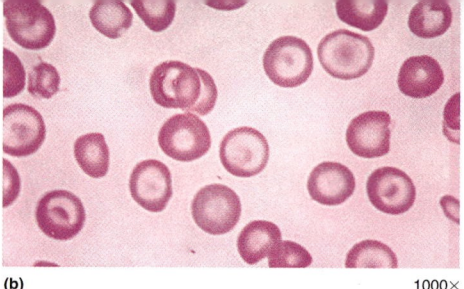

(b)   1000×

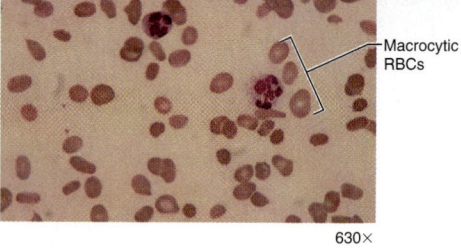

Macrocytic RBCs

630×

▲ **FIGURE 7.5   Red Blood Cells.**
(*a*) Normal RBCs. (*b*) Hypochromic RBCs.

▲ **FIGURE 7.6   Macrocytic Cells in Pernicious Anemia.**

Keynote

Anemia reduces the oxygen-carrying capacity of blood.
Hemolysis liberates hemoglobin from RBCs.

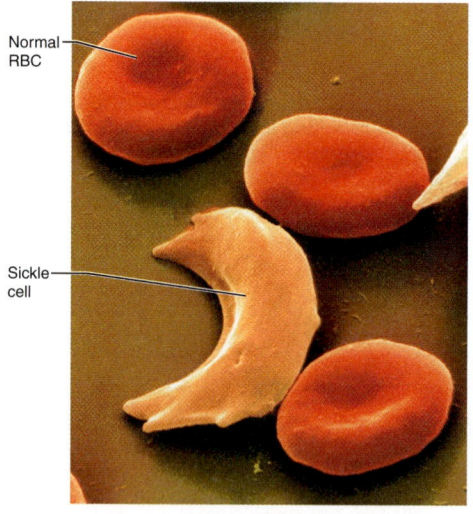

Normal RBC

Sickle cell

▲ **FIGURE 7.7   Sickle Cell Anemia.**

DISORDERS OF RED BLOOD CELLS

Anemia is a reduction in the number of RBCs or in the amount of hemoglobin each RBC contains (*Figure 7.5*). Both of these conditions reduce the oxygen-carrying capacity of the blood and produce the symptoms of shortness of breath (SOB) and fatigue. They also produce **pallor** because of the deficiency of the red-colored oxyhemoglobin, the combination of oxygen and hemoglobin.

There are several types of anemia:

- **Iron-deficiency anemia** is the diagnosis for Mrs. Luisa Sosin. In her case, the cause was chronic bleeding from her gastrointestinal tract due to the aspirin and other painkillers she was taking. Her stools were positive for occult blood. Other causes can be from heavy menstrual bleeding or a diet deficient in iron.

- **Pernicious anemia (PA)** is due to vitamin B_{12} deficiency. This is caused by a shortage of *intrinsic factor* (*see Chapter 6*), which is normally secreted by cells in the lining of the stomach and binds with vitamin B_{12}; this complex is absorbed into the blood stream. Without vitamin B_{12}, hemoglobin cannot be formed. The RBCs decrease in number and in hemoglobin concentration and increase in size (**macrocytic**, *Figure 7.6*).

- **Sickle cell anemia** (also called sickle cell disease) is a genetic disorder found most commonly in African Americans, Africans, and some Mediterranean populations. It results from the production of an abnormal hemoglobin that causes the RBCs to form a rigid sickle cell shape (*Figure 7.7*). The abnormal cells are sticky, clump together (**agglutinate**), and block small capillaries. This causes intense pain in the **hypoxic** tissues (a sickle cell crisis) and can cause stroke and kidney and heart failure.

  There is a minor form of the disease, sickle cell trait, in which symptoms rarely occur and do not progress to the full-blown disease.

- **Hemolytic anemia** is due to excessive destruction of normal and abnormal RBCs. **Hemolysis** can be caused by such toxic substances as snake and spider venoms, mushroom toxins, and drug reactions. Trauma to RBCs by hemodialysis or heart–lung machines can produce a hemolytic anemia.

Hemoglobinopathies, such as sickle cell disease and **thalassemia**, with their inherited abnormal hemoglobins are an important cause of hemolysis.

Hemolysis can also occur through **incompatible** blood transfusions or maternal–fetal incompatibilities (*see Lesson 7.5*). Jaundice is a complication.

Polycythemia vera is an overproduction of RBCs and WBCs due to an unknown cause.

Case Report 7.1 (continued)

Because Mrs. Luisa Sosin was deficient in iron and hemoglobin, her RBCs were small (microcytic), lacked the red color of oxyhemoglobin (hypochromic; see Figure 7.5), and some were irregular-shaped (poikilocytic) rather than the normal, round shape. The volume of each cell, mean corpuscular volume (MCV), and the amount of hemoglobin in each cell, mean corpuscular hemoglobin (MCH), were decreased. The amount of iron in her blood (serum iron) and the amount of ferritin in her serum were decreased. Her total iron-binding capacity was raised because the shortage of iron resulted in an increased availability of the protein to which iron is bound in the bloodstream.

WORD	PRONUNCIATION	ELEMENTS		DEFINITION
agglutinate	ah-**GLUE**-tin-ate	S/ P/ R/	-ate *action* ag- *to* -glutin- *stick*	Stick together to form clumps
hemoglobinopathy	**HE**-mo-**GLOW**-bih-**NOP**-ah-thee	S/ R/CF R/CF	-pathy *disease* hem/o- *blood* -globin/o- *protein*	Disease caused by the presence of an abnormal hemoglobin in the red blood cells
hemolysis	he-**MOL**-ih-sis	S/ R/CF	-lysis *destruction* hem/o- *blood*	Destruction of red blood cells so that hemo-globin is liberated
hemolytic (adj)	he-moh-**LIT**-ik	S/ R/	-ic *pertaining to* -lyt- *destroy*	Pertaining to the process of destruction of red blood cells
hypoxic (*Note:* The surplus "o" is not used.)	high-**POCK**-sik	S/ P/ R/	-ic *pertaining to* hypo- *deficient* -ox- *oxygen*	Deficient in oxygen
incompatible	in-kom-**PAT**-ih-bul	S/ P/ R/	-ible *can do* in- *not* -compat- *tolerate*	Substances that interfere with each other physiologically
macrocyte	**MAK**-roh-site	P/ R/	macro- *large* -cyte *cell*	Large red blood cell
macrocytic (adj)	mak-roh-**SIT**-ik	S/	-ic *pertaining to*	Pertaining to macrocytes
pallor	**PAL**-or		Latin *paleness*	Paleness of the skin
pernicious anemia (PA)	per-**NISH**-us ah-**NEE**-me-ah	 P/ R/	pernicious Latin *destructive* an- *without* -emia *blood*	Chronic anemia due to lack of vitamin B$_{12}$
polycythemia vera	**POL**-ee-sigh-**THEE**-me-ah	P/ R/ R/	poly- *many, much* -cyth- *cell* -emia *blood* Vera Latin *truth*	Chronic disease with bone marrow hyper-plasia, increase in number of RBCs and in blood volume
thalassemia	thal-ah-**SEE**-me-ah	S/ R/	-emia *blood condition* thalass- *sea*	Group of inherited blood disorders that pro-duce a hemolytic anemia

EXERCISES   *Deconstruct the medical term that appears in the first column. Separate out the basic elements that form the term. Fill in the chart.*

Medical Term	Prefix	Root(s)/CF	Suffix
agglutinate			
hemoglobinopathy			
hemolysis			
hypoxic			
incompatible			
macrocyte			
polycythemia			
thalassemia			

White Blood Cells (Leukocytes)

OBJECTIVES

The information in this lesson will enable you to:

- **Distinguish the different types of white blood cells.**
- **Explain the functions of the different types of white blood cells.**
- **Describe white blood cell counts and differential white blood cell counts.**
- **Describe the effect of common disorders of white blood cells on health.**

You are

...a laboratory technician reviewing a peripheral blood smear.

Your patient is

...Mrs. Latisha Masters, a 27-year-old student who presented with a five-day history of fatigue, low-grade fever, and sore throat.

CASE REPORT 7.2

Physical examination showed tonsillitis with bilateral, enlarged, tender cervical lymph nodes and an enlarged spleen.

The white blood cell count (WBC) count you performed showed 9200 cells per cubic millimeter. The peripheral smear you are looking at is reported as showing the presence of atypical mononuclear cells with abundant cytoplasm.

Keynote

Neutrophils, eosinophils, and basophils are granulocytes.

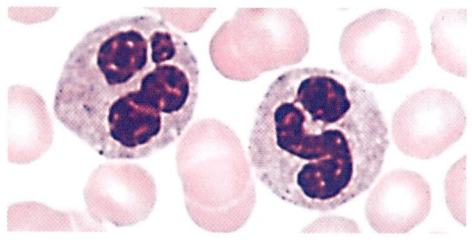

▲ **FIGURE 7.8** Neutrophils Are Granulocytes.

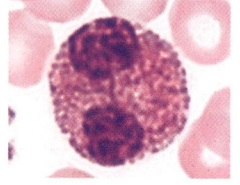

▲ **FIGURE 7.9** Eosinophils Are Granulocytes.

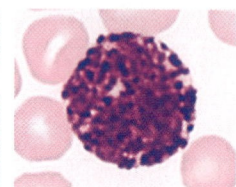

▲ **FIGURE 7.10** Basophils Are Granulocytes.

FIGURE 7.11 Monocytes Are Agranulocytes. ▶

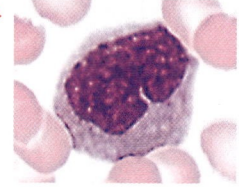

TYPES OF WHITE BLOOD CELLS

Granulocytes

1. **Neutrophils** *(Figure 7.8)* are normally 50 to 70% of the total WBC count. They are also called **polymorphonuclear leukocytes (PMNL).** These cells phagocytize bacteria, fungi, and some viruses and secrete a group of enzymes called lysozymes, which destroy some bacteria. In bacterial infections, the number and percentage of neutrophils increase dramatically. In **neutropenia,** the number of neutrophils is diminished below normal.

2. **Eosinophils** *(Figure 7.9)* are normally 2 to 4% of the total WBC count. They are mobile cells that leave the bloodstream to enter tissue undergoing an allergic response. In allergic reactions, the number and percentage of eosinophils increase.

3. **Basophils** *(Figure 7.10)* are normally less than 1% of the total WBC count. Basophils migrate to damaged tissues, where they release histamine (which increases blood flow) and **heparin** (which prevents blood clotting).

Because of their granular cytoplasm, the above three types of WBCs are called **granulocytes.** Their granules are the sites for production of enzymes and chemicals.

Agranulocytes

Because monocytes and lymphocytes have no granules in their cytoplasm, they are called **agranulocytes.**

4. **Monocytes** *(Figure 7.11)* are the largest blood cell and are normally 3 to 8% of the total WBC count. Monocytes leave the bloodstream and become macrophages that phagocytize bacteria, dead neutrophils, and dead cells in the tissues.

5. **Lymphocytes** *(Figure 7.12)* are normally 25 to 35% of the total WBC count. They are the smallest type of WBC. Lymphocytes are produced in red bone marrow and migrate through the blood stream to lymphatic tissues—lymph nodes, tonsils, spleen, and thymus—where they proliferate.

WORD	PRONUNCIATION	ELEMENTS		DEFINITION
agranulocyte	a-**GRAN**-you-lo-site	S/ P/ R/CF	-cyte *cell* a- *without, not* -granul/o- *granule*	A white blood cell without any granules in its cytoplasm
antibody antibodies (pl)	**AN**-tih-body	P/ R/	anti- *against* body- *structure*	Protein produced in response to an antigen
basophil	**BAY**-so-fill	S/ R/CF	-phil *attraction* bas/o- *basic*	A basophil's granules attract a basic blue stain in the laboratory
differential	dif-er-**EN**-shal	S/ R/	-ial *pertaining to* different- *not identical*	A differential white blood cell count lists percentages of the different leukocytes in a blood sample
eosinophil	ee-oh-**SIN**-oh-fill	S/ R/CF	-phil *attraction* eosin/o- *dawn*	An eosinophil's granules attract a rosy-red color on staining
granulocyte	**GRAN**-you-loh-site	S/ R/CF	-cyte *cell* granul/o- *small grain*	A white blood cell that contains multiple small granules in its cytoplasm
heparin	**HEP**-ah-rin	S/ R/	-in *in* hepar- *liver*	An anticoagulant secreted particularly by liver cells
immunoglobulin	**IM**-you-noh-**GLOB**-you-lin	S/ R/CF R/	-in *substance* immun/o- *immune response* -globul- *globe-shaped*	Specific protein evoked by an antigen. All antibodies are immunoglobulins
leukocyte (alternative spelling leucocyte)	**LOO**-koh-site	S/ R/CF	-cyte *cell* leuk/o- *white*	Another term for a white blood cell
leukocytosis leukopenia	**LOO**-koh-sigh-toe-sis loo-koh-**PEE**-nee-ah	S/ S/	-osis *condition* -penia *deficiency*	An excessive number of white blood cells A deficient number of white blood cells
lymphocyte	**LIM**-fo-site	S/ R/CF	-cyte *cell* lymph/o- *lymph*	Small white blood cell with a large nucleus
monocyte	**MON**-oh-site	R/ P/	-cyte *cell* mono- *single*	Large white blood cell with a single nucleus
neutrophil neutropenia	**NEW**-troh-fill **NEW**-troh-**PEE**-nee-uh	S/ R/CF S/	-phil *attraction* neutr/o- *neutral* -penia *deficiency*	A neutrophil's granules take up (purple) stain equally whether the stain is acid or alkaline A deficiency of neutrophils
polymorphonuclear	**POL**-ee-more-foh-**NEW**-klee-ur	S/ P/ R/CF R/	-ar *pertaining to* poly- *many* morph/o- *shape* -nucle- *nucleus*	White blood cell with a multi-lobed nucleus

There are two main types of lymphocyte:

a. **B cells** that differentiate into plasma cells. These are stimulated by bacteria or toxins to produce **antibodies,** or **immunoglobulins (Ig).**

b. **T cells** that attach directly to foreign antigen-bearing cells such as bacteria, which they kill with toxins they secrete.

In a laboratory report, a **differential white blood cell count (DIFF)** lists the percentages of the different leukocytes in a blood sample.

Abbreviations

DIFF	differential white blood cell count
Ig	immunoglobulin
PMNL	polymorphonuclear leukocyte

FIGURE 7.12 ▶
Lymphocytes are Agranulocytes.

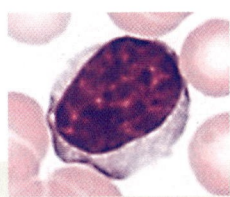

EXERCISES

Pick the correct suffix to complete the medical term. One element will remain the same in each group of terms. Review the WAD before you start the exercise. Fill in the blanks.

-penia   -cyte   -cytosis

1. An excessive number of white blood cells is: _____ .

2. Another term for a white blood cell is: _____ .

3. A deficient number of white blood cells is: _____ .

Case Report 7.2 (continued)

Latisha Masters' blood smear indicated a diagnosis of infectious **mononucleosis** caused by the **Epstein-Barr virus (EBV)**. This virus infects WBCs. A positive **heterophile reaction (Monospot test)** was present.

Infectious mononucleosis occurs in the 15- to 25-year-old population. Its cause, the Epstein-Barr virus (EBV), is a very common virus, a member of the herpesvirus family *(see Chapter 20)*. The EBV is transmitted by exchange of saliva, as in kissing. In patients with symptoms compatible with infectious mononucleosis, a positive Monospot test is diagnostic.

Keynote

Leukocytosis is the presence of too many white blood cells.

Leukopenia is the presence of too few white blood cells.

Pancytopenia is the presence of too few RBCs, WBCs, and platelets.

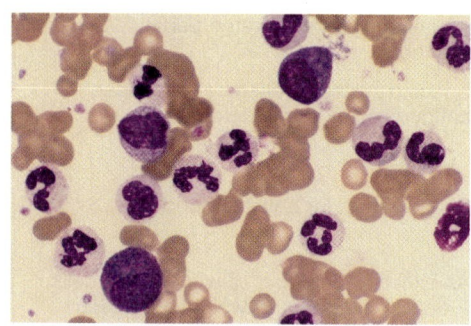

▲ **FIGURE 7.13** **Myeloid Leukemia.**

Keynote

Acute lymphoblastic leukemia is the most common leukemia in children.

DISORDERS OF WHITE BLOOD CELLS

Normally a cubic millimeter (**mm³**) of blood contains 5000 to 10,000 white blood cells.

Leukocytosis is defined as having a total WBC count exceeding 10,000/mm³. When the majority of the increased cells are neutrophils (polymorphonuclear leukocytes), an acute infection is usually present; for example, appendicitis or bacterial pneumonia.

Allergic reactions increase the number of eosinophils. Typhoid fever, malaria, and tuberculosis increase the number of monocytes. Whooping cough and infectious mononucleosis increase the number of lymphocytes.

Leukemia is cancer of the hematopoietic tissues and produces a high number of leukocytes and their **precursors** in the WBC count. As the **leukemic** cells proliferate, they take over the bone marrow and cause a deficiency of normal RBCs, WBCs, and **platelets.** This makes the patient anemic and vulnerable to infection and bleeding.

Myeloid leukemia is characterized by uncontrolled production of granulocytes and their precursors *(Figure 7.13)*. It can be in an acute or chronic form.

Lymphoid leukemia is characterized by uncontrolled production of lymphocytes. It can be in an acute or chronic form. **Acute lymphoblastic leukemia (ALL)** is the most common form of childhood cancer and is curable with modern treatments, such as chemotherapy, bone marrow and umbilical cord **stem cell** transplants.

Leukopenia results when the WBC count drops below 5000 cells/mm³ of blood. Leukopenia is seen in viral infections such as measles, mumps, chickenpox, poliomyelitis, and AIDS.

Pancytopenia occurs when the erythrocytes (RBCs), leukocytes (WBCs), and thrombocytes (**platelets**) in the circulating blood are all markedly reduced. This can occur with cancer chemotherapy.

Abbreviations

ALL	acute lymphocytic leukemia
EBV	Epstein-Barr virus
HLA	human leukocyte antigen
mm³	cubic millimeter

Procedures

- **Bone marrow biopsy** or **aspiration** is often performed as part of the diagnostic work-up in patients with aplastic anemia, leukemias, lymphomas, and/or multiple myeloma. The specimen is usually taken from the posterior iliac crest of the pelvis *(see Chapter 5)*.

- **Bone marrow transplant** is the transfer of bone marrow from a healthy, compatible donor to a patient with aplastic anemia, leukemia, lymphoma, multiple myeloma, and other diseases. Compatibility requires having the same type of **human leukocyte antigen (HLA)** in a blood sample.

WORD	PRONUNCIATION		ELEMENTS	DEFINITION
heterophile	HET-er-oh-file	S/ R/CF	-phile *attraction* heter/o- *different*	Antibodies not directed against the causative organism but seen during the disease
leukemia leukemic (adj)	loo-KEE-mee-ah loo-KEE-mick	S/ R/	-emia *blood* leuk- *white*	Disease when the blood is taken over by white blood cells and their precursors
lymphoid	LIM-foid	S/ R/	-oid *resembling* lymph- *lymph*	Resembling lymphatic tissue
mononucleosis	MON-oh-nyu-klee-OH-sis	S/ P/ R/	-osis *condition* mono- *single* -nucle- *nucleus*	Presence of large numbers of mononuclear leukocytes
Monospot test	MON-oh-spot TEST		Trade name	Detects heterophile antibodies in infectious mononucleosis
myeloid	MY-eh-loyd	S/ R/	-oid *resembling* myel- *bone marrow*	Resembling cells derived from bone marrow
pancytopenia	PAN-site-oh-PEE-nee-uh	S/ P/ R/CF	-penia *deficiency* pan- *all* -cyt/o- *cell*	Deficiency of all types of blood cells
platelet (also called thrombocyte)	PLAYT-let	S/ R/	-let *small* plate- *flat*	Cell fragment involved in clotting process
precursor	pree-KUR-sir	P/ R/	pre- *before* -cursor *run*	Cell or substance formed earlier in the development of the cell or substance
stem cell	STEM SELL		stem *Old English stalk of a plant*	Undifferentiated cell found in a differentiated tissue that can divide to yield the specialized cells in that tissue

EXERCISES

Demonstrate that you know whether the element is a prefix, root, combining form, or suffix by placing a check (✓) in the appropriate column. Do not forget to write the meaning of the element as well. Fill in the chart.

Element	Prefix	Root(s)	Combining form	Suffix	Meaning of Element
cursor					
cyto					
emia					
hetero					
leuk					
mono					
myel					
oid					
osis					
pan					
pre					

LESSON 7.4 Hemostasis

OBJECTIVES

When you are employed in any clinical area in health care—in an office, in a hospital, or out in the field—at many times in your career, you will be faced with a patient who is bleeding.

Before you can take blood for laboratory examination, you need to have an awareness of the medical terminology for possible diagnoses and the appropriate tests that will be performed. In this lesson, information will be available for you to:

- **Identify the functions of platelets.**
- **Specify the body's mechanisms for controlling bleeding.**
- **Describe the methods of producing blood clots.**
- **Explain some disorders of blood clotting.**

You are

. . . an **emergency medical technician (EMT)** employed in the Fulwood Medical Center Emergency Department.

Your patient is

. . . Janis Tierney, a 17-year-old high school student, who presents with fainting at school.

CASE REPORT 7.3

She is pale. Her pulse is 90. Blood pressure is 100/60. She tells you that she is having a menstrual period with excessive bleeding. Her physical examination is otherwise unremarkable. She has a past history of easy bruising and recurrent nosebleeds and an episode of severe bleeding after a tooth extraction.

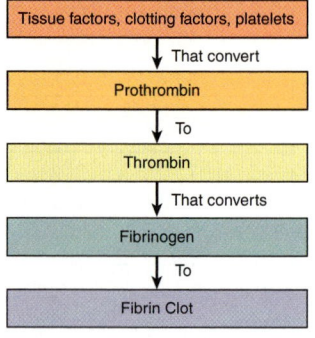

▲ **FIGURE 7.14   Blood Coagulation.**

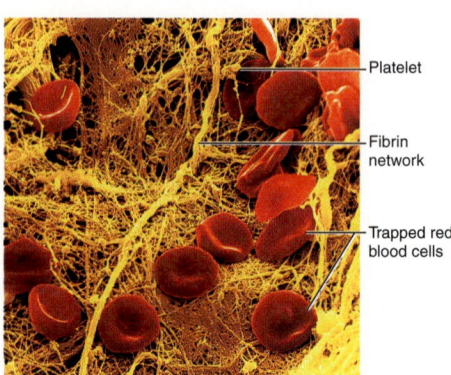

SEM 1400×

▲ **FIGURE 7.15   Blood Clot.**

Hemostasis, the control of bleeding, is a vital issue in maintaining homeostasis, the state of equilibrium of the body. Uncontrolled bleeding can take the body out of balance by decreasing blood volume and lowering blood pressure, leading to death.

Platelets (also called **thrombocytes)** play a key role in hemostasis. They are minute fragments of large bone marrow cells called **megakaryocytes**. They consist of a small amount of granular cytoplasm surrounded by a plasma membrane and have no nucleus. Platelet granules secrete chemicals that are critical to hemostasis:

- **coagulation factors**—proteins and enzymes that initiate the process.
- **vasoconstrictors**—cause constriction in injured blood vessels.
- **chemicals** that attract neutrophils and monocytes to sites of inflammation.

Hemostasis is achieved through a three-step mechanism:

1. **Vascular spasm**—an immediate but temporary constriction of the injured blood vessel.
2. **Platelet plug formation**—an accumulation of platelets that bind themselves together and adhere to surrounding tissues. The binding and adhesion of platelets is mediated through **von Willebrand factor (vWF)**, a protein produced by the cells lining blood vessels.
3. **Blood coagulation**—the process beginning with the production of molecules that make **prothrombin** and **thrombin** and finishing with the formation of a blood clot that traps blood cells, platelets, and tissue fluid in a network of fibrin *(Figures 7.14 and 7.15)*.

After a blood clot forms, platelets adhere to strands of fibrin and contract to pull the fibers closer together. As the blood clot shrinks, it pulls the edges of the broken blood vessel together. **Fibroblasts** invade the clot to produce a fibrous connective tissue that seals the blood vessel.

WORD ANALYSIS AND DEFINITION

S = Suffix   P = Prefix   R = Root   R/CF = Combining Form

WORD	PRONUNCIATION	ELEMENTS		DEFINITION
anticoagulant	AN-tee-ko-AG-you-lant	S/ P/ R/	-ant *forming* anti- *against* -coagul- *clump*	Substance that prevents clotting
coagulation	koh-ag-you-LAY-shun	S/	-ation *action*	The process of blood clotting
fibroblast	FIE-bro-blast	S/ R/	-blast *immature cell* fibro- *fiber*	Cell that forms collagen fibers
hemostasis (*Note:* Homeostasis has a very different meaning.)	he-moh-STAY-sis	S/ R/	-stasis *control, stop* hemo- *blood*	Control of or stopping bleeding
megakaryocyte	MEG-ah-kair-ee-oh-site	S/ P/ R/CF	-cyte *cell* mega- *large* kary/o- *nucleus*	Large cell with large nucleus. Parts of the cytoplasm break off to form platelets
platelet (also called **thrombocyte**)	PLAYT-let	S/ R/	-let *small* plate- *flat*	Cell fragment involved in clotting process
prothrombin	pro-THROM-bin	P/ R/	pro- *before* -thrombin *clot*	Protein formed by the liver and converted to thrombin in the blood-clotting mechanism
thrombin thrombocyte (also called **platelet**) thrombus thrombosis	THROM-bin THROM-boh-site THROM-bus throm-BOH-sis	S/ R/CF	Greek *clot* -cyte *cell* thromb/o- *clot*	Enzyme that forms fibrin Another name for a platelet A clot attached to a diseased blood vessel or heart lining Formation of a thrombus.

Case Report 7.3 *(continued)*

Janis Tierney, who presented in the ER with heavy menstrual bleeding, has a deficiency of von Willebrand factor (vWF). Her platelets are unable to stick together or adhere to the wall of an injured blood vessel, and a platelet plug cannot form in the lining of her uterus to help end her menstrual flow. Von Willebrand disease (vWD) is the most common hereditary bleeding disorder. It affects at least 1% of the population and both sexes equally.

Abbreviations

EMT emergency medical technician
vWD von Willebrand disease
vWF von Willebrand factor

EXERCISES

*Employ your knowledge of the **language of hematology** to answer the following questions about the medical terms and elements in this WAD. Circle the best answer.*

1. In the term **hemostasis**, the suffix means

   blood   condition   control

2. **Prothrombin** is a:

   drug   protein   white blood cell

3. The process of blood clotting is called:

   homeostasis   coagulation   hemostasis

4. The combining form **thrombo-** means:

   cell   clot   clump

5. The term **prothrombin** has no:

   prefix   root/CF   suffix

6. A substance used to prevent blood clotting is called:

   anticoagulant   thrombocyte   thrombus

7. The suffix -**ation** signifies:

   an action   a condition   a deficiency

8. The root **coagul-** means:

   clump   clot   condition

9. A **thrombocyte** is a:

   red blood cell   white blood cell   platelet

10. The enzyme that forms fibrin is:

   fibrinogen   thrombin   prothrombin

Abbreviations

aPTT	activated partial thromboplastin time
DIC	disseminated intravascular coagulation
HUS	hemolytic–uremic syndrome
INR	international normalized ratio
ITP	idiopathic (or immunologic) thrombocytopenic purpura
PT	prothrombin time
tPA	tissue plasminogen activator
TTP	thrombotic thrombocytopenic purpura

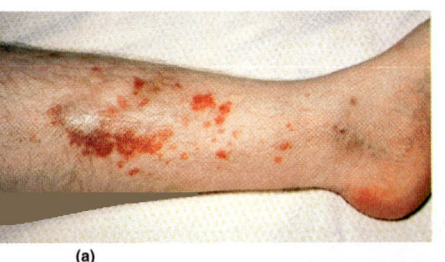
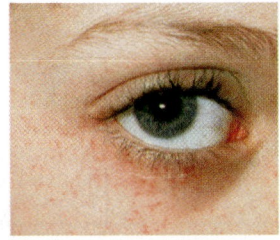
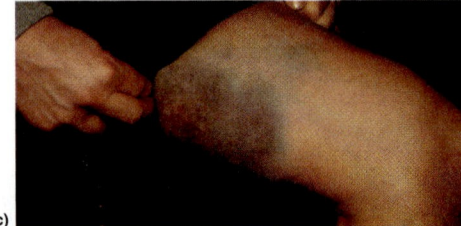

(a)

(b)

FIGURE 7.16 ▲
Subsurface Bleeding.
(a) Purpura.
(b) Petechiae.
(c) Bruises.

(c)

DISORDERS OF COAGULATION (COAGULOPATHIES)

Hemophilia in its classical form (hemophilia A) is a disease males inherit from their mothers and is due to a deficiency of a coagulation factor, called factor VIII. The disorder causes painful bleeding into skin, joints, and muscles. Concentrated factor VIII is given intravenously to reduce the symptoms.

Von Willebrand disease (vWD) is a deficiency of a specific protein of the factor VIII complex that is different from the part involved in hemophilia.

Disseminated intravascular coagulation (DIC) occurs when the clotting mechanism is activated simultaneously throughout the cardiovascular system. The trigger is usually a severe bacterial infection. Small clots form and obstruct blood flow into tissues and organs, particularly the kidney, leading to renal failure. As the clotting mechanisms are overwhelmed, severe bleeding occurs.

Thrombus formation (**thrombosis**) is a clot that forms attached to diseased or damaged areas on the walls of blood vessels or the heart. If part of the thrombus breaks loose and moves through the circulation, it is called an **embolus**.

Thrombocytopenia is a low platelet count (below a 100,000/mm^3 of blood). It occurs when bone marrow is destroyed by radiation, chemotherapy, or leukemia. Small capillary hemorrhages called petechiae and bruises can be seen in the skin. **Idiopathic (immunologic) thrombocytopenic purpura (ITP)** is an acute self-limiting form of the disease usually seen in children.

Thrombotic thrombocytopenic purpura (TTP) and **hemolytic–uremic syndrome (HUS)** are acute, potentially fatal disorders in which loose strands of fibrin are deposited in numerous small blood vessels. This causes damage to platelets and RBCs, causing thrombocytopenia and hemolytic anemia.

Henoch-Schönlein purpura (anaphylactoid purpura) is a disorder involving purpura, joint pain, and **glomerulonephritis** *(see Chapter 11)*. The etiology is unknown. Most cases resolve spontaneously.

Purpura is bleeding into the skin from small arterioles to produce a larger individual lesion than petechiae from capillary bleeding *(Figure 7.16)*. **Bruises** (or **hematomas**) are **extravasations** of blood from all types of blood vessels.

Laboratory Tests to Evaluate Blood Coagulation

- **Platelet count** has a normal range of 130,000 to 400,000 platelets/mm^3 of blood.

- **Prothrombin time (PT)** is prolonged in deficiencies of some coagulation factors and fibrinogen. It is used to monitor the dose of **warfarin (Coumadin).** It is now reported as an **international normalized ratio (INR)** instead of in seconds.

- **Activated partial thromboplastin time (aPTT)** is prolonged in deficiencies of certain coagulation factors, including factor VIII and fibrinogen. It is used to monitor the dose of heparin.

Pharmacology of Blood Clotting

- **Aspirin** reduces platelet adherence and aggregation. It is used in 81-mg doses to reduce the incidence of heart attacks.

- **Heparin** is a polysaccharide that prevents prothrombin and fibrin formation. It has to be given **parenterally** (not through the digestive tract), and recently a form of heparin that can be given subcutaneously has been approved. Its dose is monitored by activated partial thromboplastin time (aPTT).

- **Hirudin** is a potent anticoagulant, produced by **recombinant DNA technology.** It blocks thrombin formation.

- **Warfarin (Coumadin)** inhibits the synthesis of prothrombin and other coagulation factors so acts as an anticoagulant. It is given by mouth and its dose monitored by prothrombin times, which are reported as an International Normalized Ratio (INR).

- **Streptokinase,** derived from hemolytic streptococci, dissolves the fibrin in blood clots. Given intravenously within three to four hours of a heart attack, it is often effective in dissolving the clot that has caused the heart attack.

- **Tissue plasminogen activator (tPA)** binds strongly to fibrin and dissolves clots that have caused heart attacks. It is similar in effect and use to streptokinase. Reteplase and urokinase are forms of tPA.

S = Suffix   P = Prefix   R = Root   R/CF = Combining Form

WORD	PRONUNCIATION	ELEMENTS		DEFINITION
coagulopathy coagulopathies (pl)	koh-ag-you-**LOP**-ah-thee	S/ R/CF	-pathy *disease* coagul/o- *clotting*	Disorder of blood clotting
disseminate	dih-**SEM**-in-ate	S/ P/ R/	-ate *action* dis- *apart* -semin- *scatter seed*	Widely scattered throughout the body or an organ
embolus	**EM**-bo-lus		Greek *plug, stopper*	Detached piece of thrombus, a mass of bacteria, quantity of air, or foreign body that blocks a blood vessel
extravasate	eks-**TRAV**-ah-sate	S/ P/ R/	-ate *action* extra- *out of* -vas- *vessel*	To ooze out from a vessel into the tissues
hematoma (also called bruise)	he-mah-**TOH**-mah	S/ R/	-oma *mass, tumor* hemat- *blood*	Collection of blood that has escaped from the blood vessels into tissue
hemophilia	he-moh-**FILL**-ee-ah	S/ R/CF	-philia *attraction* hem/o- *blood*	An inherited disease from a deficiency of clotting factor VIII
recombinant DNA	ree-**KOM**-bin-ant dee-en-a	S/ P/ R/	-ant *forming* re- *again* -combin- *combine*	DNA (deoxyribonucleic acid) altered by inserting a new sequence of DNA into the chain
streptokinase	strep-toe-**KI**-nase	P/ R/	strepto- *curved* -kinase *enzyme*	An enzyme that dissolves clots
thrombocytopenia	**THROM**-boh-site-oh-**PEE**-nee-uh	S/ R/CF R/CF	-penia *deficiency* thromb/o- *clot* -cyt/o- *cell*	Deficiency of platelets in circulating blood
warfarin	**WAR**-fuh-rin		Named after *Wisconsin Alumni Research Foundation*, which funded its discovery	Anticoagulant; also used as rat poison

EXERCISES

Form the correct plurals for the following three terms. Then use each term (singular or plural) in a sentence that is not a definition. Practice pronouncing both the singular and plural forms, and check your spelling! Fill in the blanks.

1. Singular: **coagulopathy**   plural: _____

   Sentence: _____

   _____

2. Singular: **embolus**   plural: _____

   Sentence: _____

   _____

3. Singular: **hematoma**   plural: _____

   Sentence: _____

   _____

Word Association.

The medical term **purpura** looks and sounds like the English word for the color purple. What structure turns this color? _____

_____

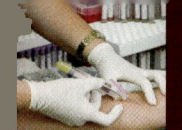

LESSON 7.5 Blood Groups and Transfusions

OBJECTIVES

In order to make an appropriate decision it is critical that you are able to:

- **List the different blood groups.**
- **Explain what determines a person's ABO blood type and how this relates to transfusion compatibility.**
- **Describe the effect of an incompatibility between mother and fetus in the Rh blood type.**

You are

...an emergency medical technician–paramedic (EMT-P) working in the Level One Trauma Unit at Fulwood Medical Center.

CASE REPORT 7.4

Miss Rodi is receiving a blood transfusion. You document that her temperature has risen to 102°F and her respirations to 24 per minute, and she has chills. You take her blood pressure; it has fallen to 90/60. What should you do?

Your patient is

...Miss Joanne Rodi, an 18-year-old student, who has been admitted to the unit from the operating room after surgery for multiple fractures in a car accident.

Abbreviations

HDN hemolytic disease of the newborn
Rh rhesus
Rho-GAM rhesus immune globulin

Keynote

All blood groups are inherited.

Rh factor is an antigen on the surface of a red blood cell.

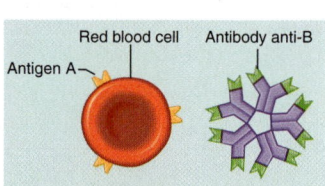

(a) Type A blood

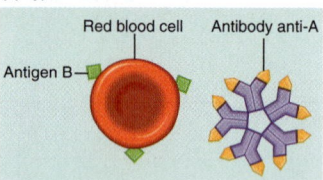

(b) Type B blood

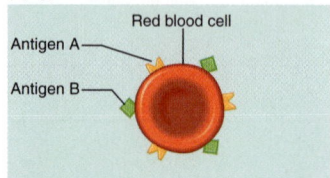

(c) Type AB blood

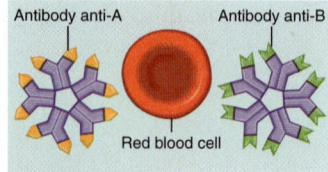

(d) Type O blood

▲ **FIGURE 7.17 Blood Types.**

RED CELL ANTIGENS

On the surfaces of red blood cells are molecules called antigens. In the plasma, antibodies are present. Each antibody can only combine with a specific antigen. If the plasma antibodies combine with a red cell antigen, bridges are formed that connect the red cells together. This is called **agglutination,** or clumping, of the cells. Hemolysis (rupture) of the cells also occurs.

The antigens on the surfaces of the cells have been categorized into groups, of which two are the most important. These are the ABO and Rh blood groups.

ABO Blood Group

The two major antigens on the cell surface are antigen A and antigen B *(Figure 7.17).*

A person with only antigen A has *type A* blood.

A person with only antigen B has *type B* blood.

A person with both antigen A and antigen B has *type AB* blood.

A person with neither antigen has *type O* blood.

Figure 7.17 shows the different combinations of antigens and antibodies in the different blood types.

A **transfusion** of blood or packed red blood cells replaces lost red blood cells to restore the blood's oxygen-carrying capacity. **Autologous** donation and transfusion is when people donate their own blood ahead of time to be given to them if necessary during a surgical procedure.

Case Report 7.4 *(continued)*

In Miss Rodi's case, she has type A blood and, by mistake, received blood of type AB, which agglutinated in the presence of her anti-B antibodies. Your immediate response is to stop the transfusion, replace it with a saline **infusion,** call your supervisor, and notify the doctor.

WORD	PRONUNCIATION	ELEMENTS		DEFINITION
agglutination	ah-glue-tih-**NAY**-shun	S/ P/ R/	-ation *action* ag- *to* -glutin- *glue*	Process by which cells or other particles adhere to each other to form clumps
autologous	awe-**TOL**-oh-gus	P/ R/	auto- *self, same* -logous *relation*	Blood transfusion with the same person as donor and recipient
erythroblastosis	eh-**RITH**-ro-blast-oh-sis	S/ R/CF R/	-osis *condition* erythr/o- *red blood cell* -blast- *germ cell*	Condition of many immature red cells in blood
fetalis	fee-**TAH**-lis	S/ R/	-is *of the* fetal- *fetus*	Erythroblastosis fetalis is a hemolytic disease of the newborn
infusion	in-**FYU**-zhun	P/ R/	in- *in* -fusion *to pour*	Introduction of a substance other than blood intravenously
spherocyte	**SFEAR**-oh-site	S/ R/CF	-cyte *cell* spher/o- *sphere*	A spherical cell
spherocytosis	**SFEAR**-oh-site-oh-sis	S/	-osis *condition*	Presence of spherocytes in blood
transfusion	trans-**FYU**-zhun	P/ R/	trans- *across* -fusion *to pour*	Transfer of blood or a blood component from donor to recipient

Rh Blood Group

If an **Rh** antigen is present on an RBC surface, the blood is said to be Rh-positive (Rh⁺). If there is no Rh antigen on the surface, the blood is Rh-negative (Rh⁻). The presence or absence of Rh antigen is inherited.

If an Rh-negative person receives a transfusion of Rh-positive blood, anti-Rh antibodies will be produced. This can cause RBC agglutination and hemolysis.

If an Rh-negative woman and an Rh-positive man conceive an Rh-positive child *(Figure 7.18a)*, the placenta normally prevents maternal and fetal blood from mixing. However, at birth or during a miscarriage, fetal cells can enter the mother's blood stream. These Rh-positive cells stimulate the mother's tissues to produce Rh-antibodies *(Figure 7.18b)*.

If the mother becomes pregnant with a second Rh-positive fetus, her Rh-antibodies can cross the placenta and agglutinate and hemolyze the fetal RBCs *(Figure 7.18c)*. This causes hemolytic disease of the newborn **(HDN, or erythroblastosis fetalis)**.

Hemolytic disease of the newborn due to Rh-incompatibility can be prevented. The Rh-negative mother giving birth to an Rh-positive child should be given Rh-immuno globulin (RhoGAM).

Other causes of hemolytic disease in the newborn include ABO incompatibility, incompatibility in other blood group systems, hereditary **spherocytosis**, and some infections acquired before birth.

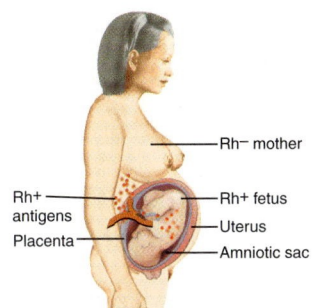

Rh⁻ mother
Rh+ antigens
Rh+ fetus
Placenta
Uterus
Amniotic sac

(a) First pregnancy

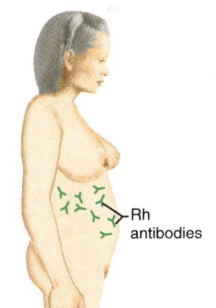

Rh antibodies

(b) Between pregnancies

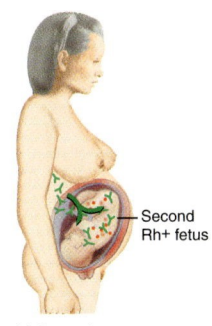

Second Rh+ fetus

(c) Second pregnancy

▲ **FIGURE 7.18   Hemolytic Disease of the Newborn.**

EXERCISES	*Review the elements in this WAD before starting this exercise. Match the elements in column 1 with the correct meanings in column 2.*

_____ 1. logous   A. poison

_____ 2. fusion   B. self

_____ 3. trans   C. to pour

_____ 4. blast   D. across

_____ 5. virus   E. relation

_____ 6. auto   F. germ cell

BLOOD

CHALLENGE YOUR KNOWLEDGE

A. **Patient Education:** Mrs. Sosin has asked you to interpret the results of her blood work for her. Use your knowledge of blood to explain in your own words her test results.

> Examination of her peripheral smear reveals her RBCs to be microcytic, hypochromic, and poikilocytic. Laboratory examination reveals a hemoglobin concentration of l0.4 g/dL (normal range 12–16 g/dL).

1. Define for the Patient:

    RBC: _____

    microcytic: _____

    hypochromic: _____

    poikilocytic: _____

    hemoglobin _____

2. In your own words, describe to the patient the role of hemoglobin in the blood.

    _____

    _____

    _____

3. Is Mrs. Sosin's hemoglobin within normal limits (WNL)? _____

B. **Recall:** The following elements are grouped according to type. Write the meaning of the element, give a medical term containing that element, and briefly define the medical term. Then identify the group as either prefixes, roots/CF, or suffixes. Fill in the chart.

Element	Meaning of Element	Medical Term	Meaning of Medical Term
emia			
globin			
in			
ine			
lysis			
oid			
penia			
poiesis			
sis			

This is a group of _____ .

C. Choose the appropriate abbreviation, or meaning of abbreviation, to fill in the patient documentation.

1. The patient's _____ (Hct) last week showed normal _____ (RBCs), but the (CBC) _____ showed an abnormal count of _____(WBCs). Her blood values this week were _____ (WNL).

2. The patient's _____ (MCV) and _____ (MCH) both showed decreased values on his recent blood test.

3. Laboratory work proved Latisha's mononucleosis to be caused by the _____ (EBV).

4. Orders for this patient's preop testing before her surgery will include a _____ (PT) and an _____ (aPTT).

5. Possible admitting diagnoses for this patient include: _____ (vWD), or _____ (ALL).

6. This patient was given a drug containing _____ (tPA) in the emergency room following his heart attack.

D. **With the possible exception of the appendix, everything in the body has a function.** The functions are listed below. Assign them a letter for the blood component that performs the function.

A. a function of a red blood cell (RBC)
B. a function of a white blood cell (WBC)
C. a function of a platelet
D. a function of plasma

1. Transport oxygen _____

2. Help maintain hemostasis _____

3. Migrate to damaged tissues and release histamine _____

4. Carry nutrients, hormones, and enzymes to cells _____

5. Dissolve cellular waste products _____

6. Secrete lysozymes _____

7. Transport carbon dioxide _____

8. Seal off injury and hemorrhage _____

9. Provide fluid environment to formed elements _____

10. Transport nitric oxide _____

BLOOD

E. Medical terminology is a language of small nuances that make a difference.

Determine the difference between the pairs of terms listed below. Underline the element that makes the difference in the term, then provide a brief definition for each term.

1. transfusion and infusion

_____

_____

_____

2. hemostasis and homeostasis

_____

_____

_____

3. pancytopenia and thrombocytopenia

_____

_____

_____

4. In the group of terms in questions 1 through 3, the _____ (type of element) stays the same.

F. **Build medical terms from the following group of elements.** The definition is given to you; fill in the medical term. You will not use every element. Fill in the blanks.

Use a combination of these elements to complete the terms:

plasm	**osis**	**ar**
ic	**hypo**	**a**
blast	**crit**	**toxo**
micro	**ox**	**macro**
auto	**ary**	**al**

1. Condition of many immature red cells in blood: erythro _____

2. Pertaining to a small cell: _____cyt_____

3. Blood transfusion with the same person as both donor and recipient: _____logous

4. Large red blood cell: _____cyte

5. Percentage of red blood cells in blood: hemato _____

6. Deficient in oxygen: _____ic

G. **Definition:** The following medical terms come directly from Latin, Greek, or French **roots.** You must know their definitions. Fill in the chart, then compose your sentences.

Medical Term	Meaning of Element	Medical Definition
acid		
albumin		
heme		
index		
viscous		
occult		
pallor		
plasma		
urea		
sediment		
thrombus		

Choose any three terms from this chart, and use each term in a sentence that is not a definition.

1. _____

_____

_____

2. _____

_____

_____

3. _____

_____

_____

BLOOD

H. Multiple Choice: Use the *language of hematology* to answer the following questions. Remember in the case of multiple choice, there is only one *best* answer.

1. Blood volume varies with:

   a. your body size

   b. the amount of your adipose tissue

   c. only b

   d. only a

   e. both a and b

2. The percentage of formed elements in a blood sample is called the:

   a. hemoglobin

   b. hematocrit

   c. hematemesis

   d. hemolysis

   e. hemostasis

3. In the term **hypochromic**, the root means:

   a. blood

   b. center

   c. color

   d. glue

   e. air

4. How many types of WBCs also qualify as granulocytes?

   a. one

   b. two

   c. three

   d. four

   e. five

5. **Myeloid leukemia** is a disorder of:

   a. RBCs

   b. WBCs

   c. platelets

   d. plasma

   e. hemoglobin

6. In the term **erythrocyte**, the combining form means:

   a. yellow

   b. red

   c. white

   d. black

   e. blue

7. **Heparin** is:

   a. antidepressant

   b. antihistamine

   c. antibody

   d. anticoagulant

   e. antigen

8. Which of these terms can be connected with blood?

   a. liquid matrix

   b. connective tissue

   c. formed elements

   d. a and c

   e. a, b, and c

9. The largest white blood cell is:

   a. monocyte

   b. macrophage

   c. eosinophil

   d. basophil

   e. neutrophil

10. What is plasma minus its protein fibrinogen?

    a. hemoglobin

    b. antithrombin

    c. plasmin

    d. serum

    e. a formed element

BLOOD

I. Team Exercise: Pair with a fellow student or group of students. Choose three medical terms in this chapter that you find the most difficult to remember or understand. Write them, pronounce them, and then use each term in a brief sentence that is a definition. Place a check mark (✓) on the appropriate line once you have practiced the pronunciations. Take turns quizzing the other students on your terms, and see if you can answer their term questions. Track if there is a pattern of certain terms that you all find difficult. *Use this exercise as a study review.*

1. Term:_____   Pronunciation practiced: _____

    Definition:

    _____

    _____

2. Term: _____   Pronunciation practiced: _____

    Definition:

    _____

    _____

3. Term: _____   Pronunciation practiced: _____

    Definition:

    _____

    _____

J. Medical terms may be similar in appearance. You need to use your knowledge of prefixes, roots, and suffixes to help determine the difference between similar terms. Using the terms below, correctly insert them into the following paragraph.

erythrocyte   **erythroblast**   **erythroblastosis**   **erythropoiesis**   **erythropoietin**

The immature RBC (_____) undergoes the process of formation (_____) in the red bone marrow.

Too many immature cells result in a condition known as _____. A mature RBC is called an _____.

The hormone _____ controls the rate of RBC production.

K. Discussion Questions: Prepare a brief discussion on either topic.

1. What is the major concern in transfusions? What types of safeguards can be used to prevent a patient getting the wrong blood in a transfusion? Why is it a good thing to know your own blood type?

2. What is the function of buffer systems in the blood? Give some examples. What is the pH range of blood?

L. Terminology Challenge:

erythrocyte   **leukemia**   **purpura**

This group of medical terms has something in common. What is it?_____

M. **Meet the lesson and chapter objectives** by testing your knowledge of the blood and its components. *Use this exercise as a study review before a test.* Fill in the blanks.

1. Name the functions of blood:

    a. _____

    b. _____

    c. _____

    d. _____

    e. _____

    f. _____

    g. _____

    h. _____

    i. _____

2. List the components of blood and give one function for each:

    a. Component: _____ Function: _____

    b. Component: _____ Function: _____

    c. Component: _____ Function: _____

3. Plasma transports:

    a. _____

    b. _____

    c. _____

    d. _____

4. The different types of WBCs are:

    a. _____

    b. _____

    c. _____

    d. _____

    e. _____

5. List the different blood groups:

    a. _____

    b. _____

    c. _____

    d. _____

BLOOD

N. **There are many diseases associated with the various components of blood.** Circle the correct choice in the descriptions below; then, on the blanks, write in which blood component is associated with the disease you circled. Use RBC, WBC, and P (for platelet) for blood component notations.

Blood Component

1. Chronic bleeding from the gastrointestinal tract can cause:
    iron-deficiency anemia   pernicious anemia   sickle cell anemia   _____

2. Deficiency of a specific protein of the factor VIII complex:
    Thrombus   von Willebrand disease   iron-deficiency anemia   _____

3. Cancer of the hematopoietic tissues is called:
    leukemia   lukemia   lukemmia   _____

4. Disease resulting from a vitamin B_{12} deficiency:
    pernicious anemia   hemolytic anemia   polycythemia vera   _____

5. A disease males inherit from their mothers:
    hemmaphilia   hemophilia   hemmophilia   _____

6. Hereditary disease found mostly in people of African descent:
    sickle cell anemia   iron-deficiency anemia   polycythemia vera   _____

7. Numerous small clots form and obstruct blood flow into organs:
    DIC   vWD   tPA   _____

8. Seen in viral infections such as measles and mumps:
    leukopenia   leukocytosis   leukemia   _____

9. Low blood cell count that produces a tendency to bleed:
    thrombocitopenia   thrombocytopenia   thrombocytopennia   _____

10. Destruction of blood cells by toxic substances:
    polycythemia vera   hemolytic anemia   pernicious anemia   _____

O. **Pharmacology of Blood Clotting:** Anyone working with patients must have a knowledge of prescribed drugs and their function. Match the correct drug to its purpose.

_____ 1. dissolves fibrin in blood clots   A. heparin

_____ 2. reduces platelet adherence   B. tPA

_____ 3. prevents prothrombin and fibrin formation   C. Coumadin

_____ 4. binds strongly to fibrin   D. streptokinase

_____ 5. inhibits synthesis of coagulation factors   E. aspirin

P. **Recall and Review:** How well do you remember these word elements from the previous chapter? Try to answer without first looking back to check. Fill in the blanks.

Element	Type of Element (P, R, CF, S)	Meaning of Element
laparo	_____	_____
zyme	_____	_____
gingiv	_____	_____
phagia	_____	_____
hydro	_____	_____

Q. **Demonstrate your knowledge of word elements by deconstructing the following medical terms.** Then write the term next to the statements below.

Term	Prefix	Root/CF	Suffix
leukocytosis			
hypochromic			
vasoconstrictor			
poikilocytic			
precursor			
anemia			
microcytic			
osmosis			
hemoglobin			
pancytopenia			

1. that which comes before something _____

2. pertaining to a small cell _____

3. decreased number of red blood cells _____

4. passage of water across a cell membrane _____

5. pigmented protein in RBCs _____

6. excessively high WBC count _____

7. deficiency of all formed elements in the blood _____

8. agent that causes narrowing of blood vessels _____

9. pertaining to an RBC of irregular shape _____

10. pale in color _____

BLOOD

R. **Test your knowledge of blood, blood groups, and Rh factor by choosing the correct answer to the following questions.** Circle the best answer.

1. A person with both antigen A and antigen B will have:

   a. blood type O

   b. blood type A

   c. blood type B

   d. blood type AB

   e. none of these blood types

2. Where are antibodies synthesized after birth?

   a. in the heart

   b. in the blood

   c. in the arteries

   d. in the plasma

   e. in the veins

3. What normally prevents maternal and fetal blood from mixing?

   a. cell membranes

   b. the peritoneum

   c. the placenta

   d. the amniotic sac

   e. the matrix

4. Blood is said to be Rh-positive if:

   a. the Rh antigen is present on the RBC surface

   b. the Rh antibody is present in the blood type

   c. the Rh antibody is present in the plasma

   d. the Rh antigen is present on the WBCs

   e. the blood type is AB

5. **Agglutination** occurs when:

   a. you have not been vaccinated

   b. you are given the wrong blood type

   c. your antibodies are low

   d. your hematocrit is high

   e. you are Rh-positive

6. The term **transfusion** is only used for:

   a. plasma

   b. whole blood

   c. blood or a blood component

   d. saline solution

   e. intravenous (IV) antibiotics

S. Word Association:

The medical term **viscous** means _____. Equate this to something seen in everyday life that has the same consistency.

Example: _____

T. How well do you understand what you read? First, read the paragraph aloud to check your pronunciation. Then, read the paragraph again and underline the medical terms. Enter the term in column one of the chart next to its correct meaning.

When a lab tech takes a blood sample, they spin it in a centrifuge. Formed elements are separated from the colloidal suspension and are packed into the bottom of the tube. The patient's hematocrit can be determined from this test. Whole blood contains all the formed elements. Transfusions can be done with either whole blood or only certain portions of the formed elements—only transfusing RBCs or platelets, for instance. The remaining (55%) of a blood sample is the plasma, which is mostly water. Plasma provides the fluid transport for the formed elements as well as nutrients, hormones and enzymes for body cells. Waste cell products dissolve in plasma and are excreted through the kidneys and liver.

Term	Meaning
	To dispose of
	Liquid containing particles that do not settle
	Introduction of blood or a blood component into a vein
	Something life sustaining
	Blood clotting cell
	Instrument for separating a blood sample
	Stimulates function of an organ or tissue
	Erythrocyte
	Liquid transport system
	Induces chemical changes in other substances
	Percentage of RBCs in the blood

BLOOD

CHAPTER SUMMARY EXERCISE

1. *Listen to the pronunciation of the medical terms as given by your instructor.*
2. *Circle the correct spelling of the medical term.*
3. *Match the correctly spelled terms to the brief descriptions below.*
4. *Write a sentence for each of the 15 terms that appear in this exercise.*

A. SPELLING COMPREHENSION: CIRCLE THE CORRECT SPELLING OF THE TERM.

1. autollogus	autologis	autoligus	autologous	autolagus
2. creatinnine	creatinine	creatynine	creatonin	creatyine
3. erythropoesis	errythropoesis	erythropoisus	erythropuesis	erythropoiesis
4. leukocytusis	leukocytosis	lukocytosis	leukocitosis	lukocitossis
5. feretin	ferrittin	ferriten	ferritin	feriton
6. pitichia	petickia	petechia	petikia	peteckia
7. centrifuje	centerfuge	senterfuge	centrifuge	sentrifuge
8. ossmosis	ossmossis	osmosis	osmoses	osmossus
9. apherises	apheresis	aperisis	aperhisis	apherisus
10. agluetinate	agglutenate	aguentinate	agglutonate	agglutinate
11. billirubin	bellirubin	belarubin	bilirubin	bilireuben
12. thalassemia	thelassimia	thalasimia	thelasemia	thalasemia
13. viscus	visscus	viscuss	vescus	viscous
14. megacaryocyte	megakaryocyte	megakareocyte	meggakariocyte	megakaryosyte
15. poikilocytic	poykillocytec	polykilocytic	poikelocyte	polkilocytic

B. MATCH THE NUMBER OF THE CORRECT TERM IN PART A WITH THE BRIEF DESCRIPTION OF THE TERM BELOW.

_____ a. passage of fluid across a cell membrane

_____ b. sticky or thick consistency

_____ c. removing only platelets and returning the rest to the donor

_____ d. inherited disorder causes hemolysis

_____ e. regulates iron storage and transport

_____ f. separates particles in a suspension

_____ g. formation of red blood cells

_____ h. donating your own blood for your surgery

_____ i. minute hemorrhage in the skin

_____ j. large cell with large nucleus

_____ k. breakdown product of RBCs

_____ l. clump together

_____ m. pertaining to irregularly shaped red blood cells

_____ n. excessive number of WBCs

_____ o. protein found in skeletal muscle

C. USING YOUR KNOWLEDGE OF TERMS 1-15 IN PART A AND THEIR CORRECT SPELLING, WRITE A BRIEF SENTENCE FOR EACH OF THE TERMS AS IT MIGHT APPEAR IN PATIENT DOCUMENTATION.

1. _____

2. _____

3. _____

4. _____

5. _____

6. _____

7. _____

8. _____

9. _____

10. _____

11. _____

12. _____

13. _____

14. _____

15. _____

D. GO TO THE STUDENT CD. OPEN THE GLOSSARY AND PRACTICE YOUR PRONOUNCIATION OF THE TERMS IN PART A OF THIS EXERCISE.

Cardiovascular System
The Language of Cardiology

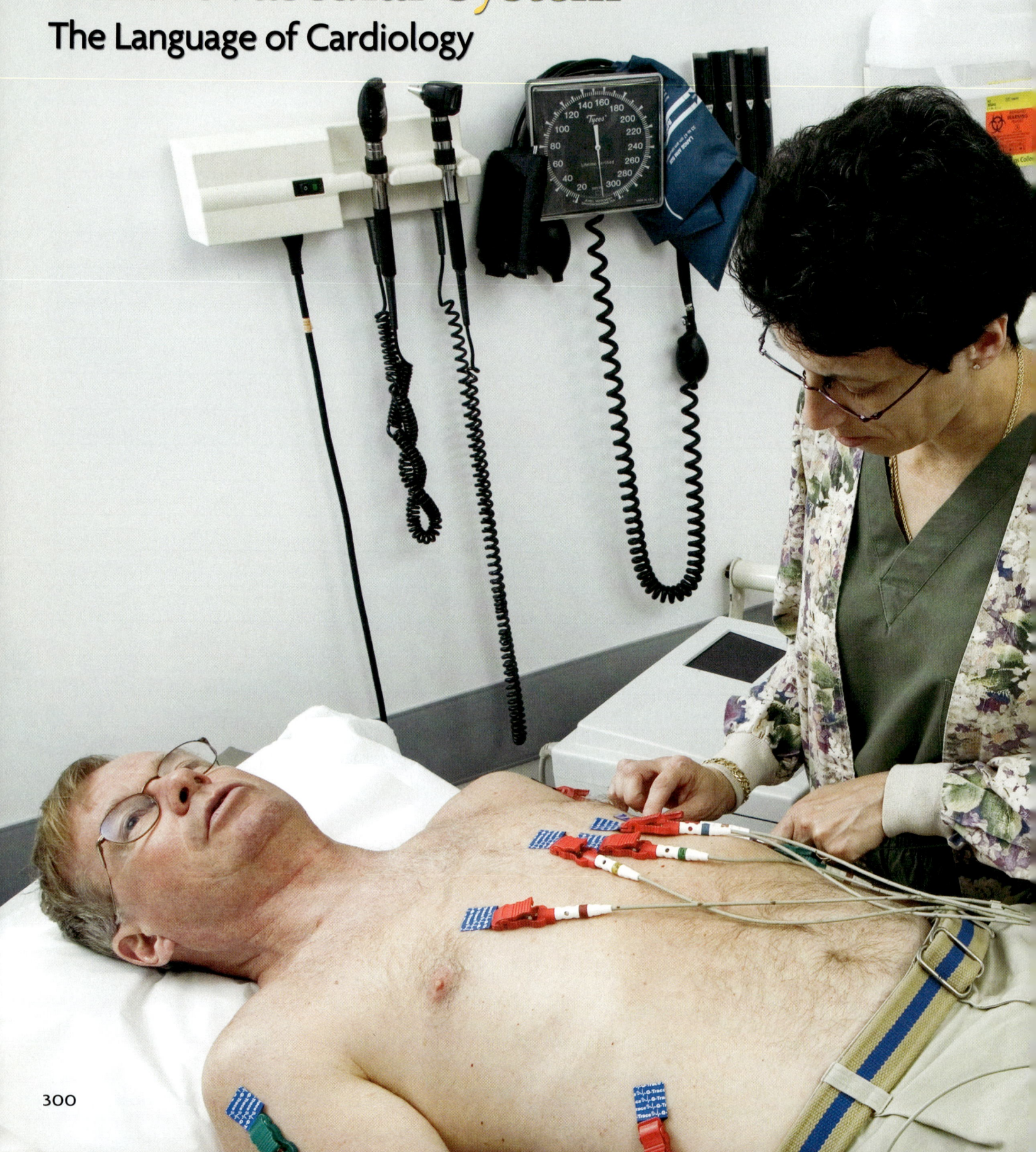

8

CASE REPORT 8.1

You are

. . . a cardiovascular technologist (**CVT**) employed by the **cardiology** department at Fulwood Medical Center. You have been called to the emergency department **STAT** to take an electrocardiogram (**ECG or EKG**).

Your patient is

. . . Mr. Hank Johnson. From his medical records, you see that he is the 64-year-old owner of a printing company.

Eight months previously, he had a left total hip replacement. In the past three months, Mr. Johnson has returned to his daily workouts. This morning while riding his exercise bike, he felt tightness in his chest. He kept on cycling and developed pain in the center of his chest radiating down his left arm and up into his jaw. He became **diaphoretic**. His personal trainer called 911.

You perform the ECG and the automatic report describes abnormalities in the chest leads.

As you remove the electrodes, Mr. Johnson complains that he is feeling faint and short of breath (**SOB**). You are the only person in the room.

Learning Outcomes

In order to understand the ECG report and to determine what you do next, you need to have knowledge of the heart's pumping mechanisms, its blood supply, the electrical properties of cardiac muscle, and the medical terminology to communicate and understand that information. No matter in which discipline or setting an allied health professional works, the condition of the patient's heart will always be a factor during diagnosis, treatment, and communication. You need to be able to:

- Apply the language of cardiology to the anatomy and physiology of the **cardiovascular** system.

- Comprehend, analyze, spell, and write the terms of cardiology so that you communicate and document accurately and precisely in any health care setting.

- Recognize and pronounce the medical terms of cardiology so that you communicate and document verbally with accuracy and precision in any health care setting.

- Explain the effects of common disorders of the cardiovascular system on health.

LESSON 8.1 Heart

CARDIOVASCULAR SYSTEM

OBJECTIVES

If you have a healthy heart rate of 60 beats per minute and you live to be 80 years old, your heart will beat (contract and relax) at least 2,522,880,000 times. Your heart pumps approximately 2,000 gallons of blood each day. In 80 years of life, it will have pumped a total of 58,400,000 gallons of blood. If your heart is unable to maintain this ability to pump blood for just a few minutes, your life is in danger.

When the heart fails, there is no circulation of blood, tissues are deprived of oxygen and nutrients, and metabolic wastes accumulate. Your cells die.

The information in this lesson will enable you to use correct medical terminology to:

- **Describe the location of the heart and its relation to other structures.**
- **Discuss the functions of the heart.**
- **Identify the chambers of the heart and the pathway blood takes through them.**
- **Explain the causes of the sounds of the heartbeat heard through a stethoscope.**
- **Specify the blood supply to the heart muscle.**
- **Distinguish between contraction and relaxation during the heart cycle.**
- **Detail the electrical properties of the heart.**

Abbreviations

CPR	cardiopulmonary resuscitation
CVT	cardiovascular technician
ECG	electrocardiogram
EKG	electrocardiogram
SOB	shortness of breath
STAT	immediately

ANATOMY OF THE HEART

Location of the Heart

It is important to know the position of the heart so that you can perform effective **cardiopulmonary resuscitation (CPR),** position a **stethoscope** to hear heart sounds, or position the **electrodes** correctly for an **electrocardiogram (ECG or EKG).**

The heart is roughly the size of your fist and weighs around 10 ounces. The heart is a blunt cone, pointing down and to the left. It lies obliquely between the lungs, with one-third of its mass behind the **sternum** and two-thirds to the left of the sternum *(Figure 8.1a)*. The **apex** can normally be palpated in the fifth **intercostal** space, between the fifth and sixth ribs. The base of the heart lies behind the sternum and the second intercostal space, between the second and third ribs. The region of the thoracic cavity in which the heart lies is called the **mediastinum.** *(Figure 8.1b)*

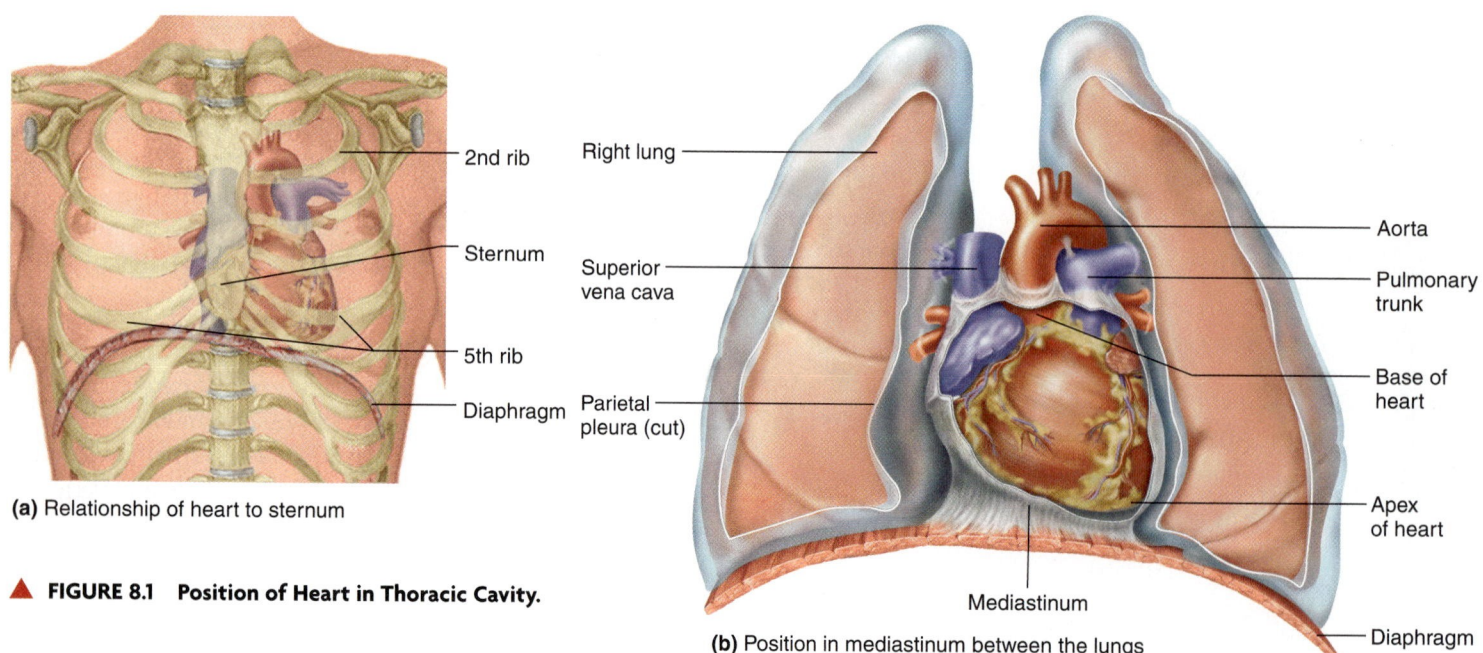

(a) Relationship of heart to sternum

Labels: 2nd rib, Sternum, 5th rib, Diaphragm

▲ **FIGURE 8.1** **Position of Heart in Thoracic Cavity.**

Labels: Right lung, Superior vena cava, Parietal pleura (cut), Aorta, Pulmonary trunk, Base of heart, Apex of heart, Mediastinum, Diaphragm

(b) Position in mediastinum between the lungs

WORD ANALYSIS AND DEFINITION

S = Suffix   **P = Prefix**   **R = Root**   **R/CF = Combining Form**

WORD	PRONUNCIATION		ELEMENTS	DEFINITION
apex	**A**-peks		Latin *summit or tip*	Tip or end of cone-shaped heart
cardiac	**KAR**-dee-ak	S/ R/	**-ac** *pertaining to* **cardi-** *heart*	Pertaining to the heart
cardiogenic	**KAR**-dee-oh-**JEN**-ik	S/ S/	**-ic** *pertaining to* **-gen** *that which produces*	Of cardiac origin
cardiologist	kar-dee-**OL**-oh-jist	R/CF S/	**cardi/o-** *heart* **-logist** *one who specializes*	A medical specialist in diagnosis and treatment of the heart (cardiology)
cardiology	kar-dee-**OL**-oh-jee	S/	**-logy** *study of*	Medical specialty of diseases of the heart
cardiopulmonary resuscitation	**KAR**-dee-oh-**PUL**-mo-nary ree-sus-ih-**TAY**-shun	S/ R/CF R/ S/ R/	**-ary** *pertaining to* **cardi/o-** *heart* **-pulmon-** *lung* **-ation** *process* **resuscitat-** *revival from apparent death*	The attempt to restore cardiac and pulmonary function
cardiovascular	**KAR**-dee-oh-**VAS**-kyu-lar	S/ R/CF R/	**-ar** *pertaining to* **cardio-** *heart* **-vascul-** *vessel*	Pertaining to the heart and blood vessels
diaphoretic (adj) diaphoresis (noun)	**DIE**-ah-fo-**RET**-ic **DIE**-ah-fo-**REE**-sis	S/ R/	**-ic** *pertaining to* **diaphoret-** *sweat*	Pertaining to sweat or perspiration
electrocardiogram (ECG or EKG)	ee-lek-troh-**KAR**-dee-oh-gram	S/ R/CF R/CF	**-gram** *a record* **electr/o-** *electricity* **-cardi/o-** *heart*	Record of the electrical signals of the heart
electrocardiograph electrocardiography	ee-lek-troh-**KAR**-dee-oh-graf ee-**LEK**-troh-kar-dee-**OG**-rah-fee	S/ S/	**-graph** *to record* **-graphy** *recording*	Machine that makes the electrocardiogram Interpretation of electrocardiograms
electrode	ee-**LEK**-trode	S/ R/	**-ode** *way, road* **electr-** *electricity*	A device for conducting electricity
intercostal	**IN**-ter-**KOS**-tal	S/ P/ R/	**-al** *pertaining to* **inter-** *between* **-cost-** *rib*	The space between two ribs
mediastinum	**ME**-dee-ass-**TIE**-num		Latin *median*	Area between the lungs containing the heart, aorta, venae cavae, esophagus, and trachea
sternum	**STIR**-num		Latin *chest*	Long, flat bone forming the center of the anterior wall of the chest
stethoscope	**STETH**-oh-skope	S/ R/CF	**-scope** *instrument* **steth/o-** *chest*	Instrument for listening to cardiac and respiratory sounds

EXERCISES

Build your **language of cardiology** by completing the following documentation. There is only one best answer for each blank. There is one extra answer you will not use in the first paragraph.

cardiopulmonary   **cardiology**   **cardiovascular**   **cardiologist**   **cardiac**

1. The universal root/combining form in these terms is _____, which means _____.

2. The _____ department sent a specialist to examine the patient in the Emergency Room. The _____ ordered an angioplasty, which showed three obstructed arteries in the patient's heart, so the _____ surgeon was notified immediately to perform _____ surgery.

electrode   **electrocardiogram**   **electrocardiograph**   **electrocardiography**

3. The universal root/combining form in these terms is _____ (meaning _____) and _____ (meaning _____).

4. The patient was scheduled for _____ today. The CVT attached the _____ to the patient's chest and proceeded to turn on the _____. Unfortunately, a malfunction of the machine prevented him from obtaining the _____. This study will have to be rescheduled for the patient.

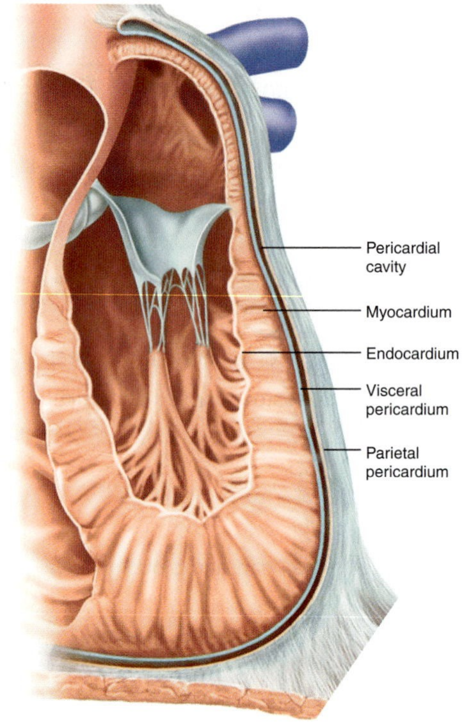
Pericardial cavity
Myocardium
Endocardium
Visceral pericardium
Parietal pericardium

▲ **FIGURE 8.2 Heart Wall.**

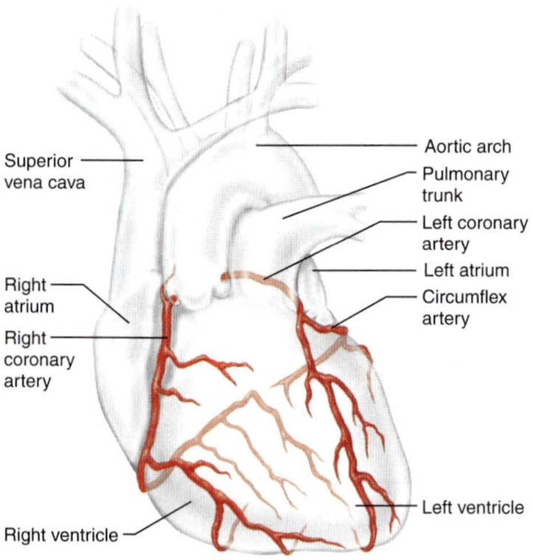
Superior vena cava
Aortic arch
Pulmonary trunk
Left coronary artery
Left atrium
Circumflex artery
Right atrium
Right coronary artery
Left ventricle
Right ventricle

▲ **FIGURE 8.3 Coronary Arterial Circulation.**

Abbreviation	
MI	myocardial infarction ("heart attack")

FUNCTIONS AND STRUCTURE OF THE HEART

Functions of the Heart

1. **Pump blood.** Contractions of the heart generate the pressure to produce movement of blood through the blood vessels.
2. **Route blood.** The heart can be described as two pumps: a pump on the right side of the heart that sends blood through the **pulmonary** circulation of the lungs and back to the pump on the left side, which sends blood through the **systemic** circulation of the body. The valves of the heart ensure this one-way flow of blood.
3. **Regulate blood supply.** The changing metabolic needs of tissues and organs (for example, when you exercise) are met by changes in the rate and force of the heart's contraction.

Structure of the Heart

The heart wall consists of three layers *(Figure 8.2)*:

1. **endocardium**—a single layer of cells over a thin layer of connective tissue lining the heart.
2. **myocardium**—cardiac muscle cells that enable the heart to contract.
3. **pericardium**—a connective tissue sac that surrounds and protects the heart. It consists of an inner **visceral** and outer **parietal** layer, between which is the **pericardial** cavity. The cavity contains a **lubricant** fluid that allows the heart to beat with very little friction around it.

Blood Supply to Heart Muscle Because the heart beats continually and strongly, it requires an abundant supply of oxygen and nutrients. To meet this need, the cardiac muscle has its own blood circulation, the **coronary circulation** *(Figure 8.3)*.

Immediately above the aortic valve in the root of the aorta, the right and left **coronary arteries** exit from the aorta and divide into branches to begin the coronary circulation.

After the blood has flowed through the arteries into the capillaries of the myocardium, it drains into veins that flow into the right atrium, where the blood mixes with deoxygenated blood from the body.

If any of the coronary arteries become blocked, the blood supply to a part of the cardiac muscle is cut off **(ischemia)**, and those cells supplied by that artery die (undergo **necrosis**) within minutes. This is a **myocardial infarction (MI)**, what many call a "heart attack."

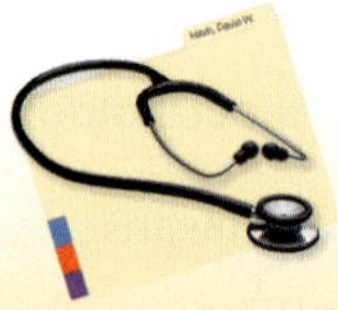

Case Report 8.1 (continued)

Changes on Mr. Johnson's ECG show he was having a myocardial infarction. Cardiac muscle cells have very limited capability to replicate, and the repair of muscle cell death is mainly by **fibrosis.** This limits cardiac function and will contribute to a diminished ability of Mr. Johnson's heart muscle to contract normally after he recovers from the heart attack.

WORD	PRONUNCIATION	ELEMENTS		DEFINITION
coronary circulation	**KOR**-oh-nair-ee **SER**-kyu-**LAY**-shun	S/ R/	-ary *pertaining to* coron- *crown*	Blood vessels supplying the heart
endocardium endocardial (adj)	**EN**-doh-kar-**DEE**-um **EN**-doh-kar-**DEE**-al	S/ P/ R/	-um *structure* endo- *inside* -cardi- *heart*	The lining of the heart
fibrosis fibrotic (adj)	fie-**BRO**-sis fie-**BROT**-ik	S/ R/	-sis *condition* fibro- *fiber*	Repair of dead tissue cells by formation of fibrous tissue
infarct infarction	in-**FARKT** in-**FARK**-shun	S/ P/ R/	-ion *process* in- *in* -farct- *stuff*	Area of cell death resulting from an infarction Sudden blockage of an artery
ischemia ischemic (adj)	is-**KEE**-me-ah is-**KEE**-mik	S/ R/	-emia *blood* isch- *to keep back*	Lack of blood supply to a tissue
lubricant	**LOO**-bri-cant	S/ R/	-ant *forming* lubric- *make slippery*	Substance for reducing friction
myocardium myocardial (adj)	**MY**-oh-**KAR**-dee-um **MY**-oh-**KAR**-dee-al	S/ P/ R/ S/	-um *structure* myo- *muscle* -cardi- *heart* -al *pertaining to*	All the heart muscle
necrosis necrotic (adj)	neh-**KROH**-sis neh-**KROT**-ik	S/ R/ S/ R/CF	-osis *condition* necr- *death* -tic *pertaining to* necr/o- *death*	Pathologic death of tissue or cells Affected by necrosis
parietal	pah-**RYE**-eh-tal	S/ R/	-al *pertaining to* pariet- *wall*	Pertaining to the outer layer of the pericardium and other body cavities
pericardium pericardial (adj)	per-ih-**KAR**-dee-um per-ih-**KAR**-dee-al	S/ P/ R/ S/	-um *structure* peri- *around* -cardi- *heart* -al *pertaining to*	The tissue covering the heart
pulmonary	**PUL**-moh-nar-ee	S/ R/	-ary *pertaining to* pulmon- *lung*	Pertaining to the lungs and their blood supply
systemic	sis-**TEM**-ik	S/ R/	-ic *pertaining to* system- *body as a whole*	Relating to the entire organism
visceral	**VISS**-er-al	S/ R/	-al *pertaining to* viscer- *an organ*	Pertaining to the internal organs

EXERCISES

Deconstruct the following medical terms into their basic elements by filling in the chart. Knowledge of elements will help increase your medical vocabulary.

Medical Term	Prefix	Root/CF	Suffix	Meaning of Term
coronary				
endocardium				
fibrosis				
infarction				
ischemia				
myocardium				
parietal				
pericardium				
pulmonary				
visceral				

DISORDERS OF THE HEART

Abnormal Heart Rhythms

Arrhythmias are abnormal or irregular heartbeats, and four types are commonly seen:

1. **Premature** beats occur most often in elderly people and are often associated with caffeine and stress.

2. **Atrial fibrillation** occurs when the two atria quiver rather than contract correctly to pump blood. This causes blood to pool in the atria and sometimes clot. **Paroxysmal atrial tachycardia (PAT)** presents with periods of rapid, regular heart beats that originate in the atrium. The episodes begin and end abruptly. The heart rate speeds up to 160 to 200 beats per minute.

3. **Ventricular arrhythmias. Ventricular tachycardia** is a rapid heartbeat arising in the ventricles. **Premature ventricular contractions (PVCs)** occur when extra impulses arise from a ventricle. **Ventricular fibrillation (V-fib)** is characterized by ventricles going out of control, quivering, and beating ineffectively instead of pumping.

4. **Heart block** occurs when interference in cardiac electrical conduction causes the contractions of the atria to fail to coordinate with the contractions of the ventricles.

Palpitations are unpleasant sensations of a rapid or irregular heartbeat that last a few seconds or minutes. They can be brought on by exercise, anxiety, and stimulants like caffeine. Occasionally they can be due to an arrhythmia.

The arrhythmias can be treated with medications, but some patients require mechanical **pacemakers.** These artificial pacemakers consist of a battery, electronic circuits, and computer memory to generate electronic signals. The signals are carried along thin, insulated wires to the heart muscle. The most common need for a pacemaker is a very slow heart rate (bradycardia).

People with life-threatening arrhythmias may need an **implantable cardioverter/ defibrillator (ICD),** which senses abnormal rhythms and gives the heart a small electrical shock to return the rhythm to normal.

In emergency situations, external **cardioversion** is performed through **automatic external defibrillators (AED)** *(Figure 8.11)* that send an electrical shock to the heart to restore a normal contraction rhythm.

Abbreviations

AED	automatic external defibrillator
ICD	implantable cardiovertor/defibrillator
PAT	paroxysmal atrial tachycardia
PVC	premature ventricular contraction
V-fib	ventricular fibrillation

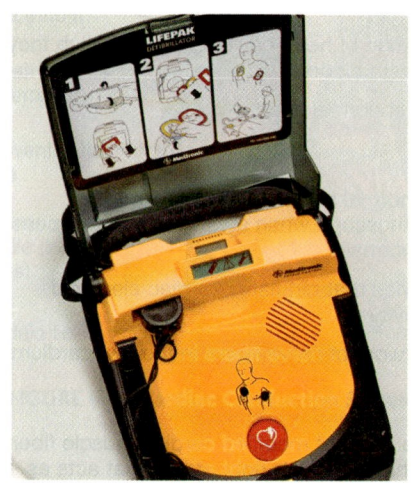

▲ **FIGURE 8.11   Automatic External Defibrillator.**

S = Suffix   P = Prefix   R = Root   R/CF = Combining Form

WORD	PRONUNCIATION	ELEMENTS		DEFINITION
cardioversion (also called defibrillation)	KAR-dee-oh-VER-shun	R/CF R/	cardi/o- *heart* -version *change*	Use electric shock to change abnormal heart rhythm back to normal rhythm
cardioverter	KAR-dee-oh-VER-ter			Device used to generate electric shock
defibrillation	de-fib-rih-LAY-shun	S/ P/ R/	-ation *action* de- *without, away from* -fibrill- *small fiber*	Restoration of uncontrolled twitching of cardiac muscle fibers to normal rhythm
defibrillator	de-fib-rih-LAY-tor	S/	-ator *instrument*	Instrument for defibrillation
fibrillation	fi-brih-LAY-shun	S/ R/	-ation *action* fibrill- *small fiber*	Uncontrolled quivering or twitching of the heart muscle
implantable	im-PLAN-tah-bul	S/ P/ R/	-able *capable* im- *in* -plant- *insert*	A device that can be inserted into tissues
palpitation	pal-pih-TAY-shun	S/ R/	-ation *action* palpit- *throb*	Forcible, rapid beat of the heart felt by the patient
paroxysmal	par-ock-SIZ-mal	S/ R/	-al *pertaining to* paroxysm- *irritate*	Occurring in sharp, spasmodic episodes

EXERCISES

The definitions for the medical terms in this Word Analysis and Definition box (WAD) are given to you—break the term down into its basic elements. Notice in particular which terms do not have prefixes or suffixes. Every term must have a root and/or combining form.

1. forceful, rapid beat of the heart   _____/_____/_____
                                                      P   R/CF   S

2. uncontrolled heart muscle twitching   _____/_____/_____
                                                      P   R/CF   S

3. changes abnormal rhythm to normal   _____/_____/_____
                                                      P   R/CF   S

4. device inserted into body tissues   _____/_____/_____
                                                      P   R/CF   S

5. sharp, spasmodic episodes   _____/_____/_____
                                                      P   R/CF   S

6. establishes normal heart rate and rhythm   _____/_____/_____
                                                      P   R/CF   S

Use one of the terms in a sentence that is not a definition.

7. Sentence: _____

     _____

     _____

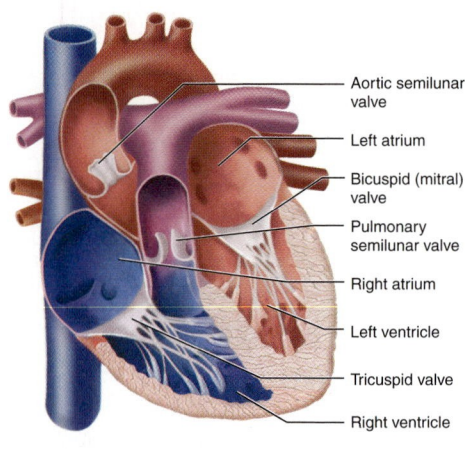

Aortic semilunar valve

Left atrium

Bicuspid (mitral) valve

Pulmonary semilunar valve

Right atrium

Left ventricle

Tricuspid valve

Right ventricle

▲ **FIGURE 8.12   Heart Valves.**

DISORDERS OF THE HEART (continued)

Disorders of the Heart Valves

Heart valves can **malfunction** in two basic ways:

1. **Stenosis**—when the valve does not open fully, and its opening is narrowed (constricted). Blood cannot flow freely through the valve and accumulates behind the valve.

2. **Incompetence** or **insufficiency**—when the valve cannot close fully, and blood can **regurgitate** (flow back) through the valve to the chamber from which it started.

Mitral valve stenosis can occur following rheumatic fever. Because the blood cannot flow freely through the valve, the left atrium becomes dilated. Eventually, **chronic heart failure** results. *(Figure 8.12* enables you to review the locations of the valves and chambers.)

Mitral valve incompetence occurs when there is leakage back through the valve as the left ventricle contracts. The left atrium becomes dilated. Again, chronic heart failure results.

Mitral valve prolapse occurs when the cusps of the valve bulge back into the left atrium when the left ventricle contracts. This allows blood to flow back into the atrium.

Aortic valve stenosis is common in the elderly when the valves become calcified due to **atherosclerosis.** Blood flow into the systemic circuit is diminished, leading to dizziness and fainting. The left ventricle dilates, hypertrophies, and ultimately fails.

Aortic valve incompetence initially produces few symptoms other than a murmur, but eventually the left ventricle fails.

Malfunctions of the valves on the right side of the heart are much less common.

A prolapsed or incompetent mitral valve can often be repaired. If a valve replacement is necessary, there are two types of artificial valves to choose from:

1. **A mechanical (prosthetic) valve**—various models and designs are made from different metal alloys and plastics.

2. **Tissue valve**—can come from a pig or cow (occasionally from a human), or a valve can be constructed of tissue from the patient's own pericardium.

Rheumatic fever is an inflammatory disease. If a sore throat caused by group A beta-hemolytic streptococcus *(see Chapter 20)* is not treated with a complete course of antibiotics, antibodies to the bacteria can develop and attack normal tissue. Multiple joints are inflamed, and an endocarditis can affect the function of the heart valves, particularly the mitral and aortic valves.

Disorders of the Heart Wall

Endocarditis is inflammation of the lining of the heart. It is usually secondary to an infection elsewhere. Intravenous drug users and people with damaged heart valves are at high risk for endocarditis.

Myocarditis is inflammation of the heart muscle. It can be bacterial, viral, or fungal in origin or a complication of other diseases such as influenza.

Pericarditis is inflammation of the covering of the heart. The inflammation causes an exudate (pericardial **effusion**) to be released into the pericardial space. This interferes with the heart's ability to contract and expand normally, and cardiac output falls—a condition called **cardiac tamponade.**

Cardiomyopathy is a weakening of the heart muscle so that it pumps inadequately. The etiology can be viral, idiopathic (when the cause is unknown), or alcoholic.

It causes **cardiomegaly** and heart failure.

Cor pulmonale is failure of the right ventricle to pump properly. Almost any chronic lung disease causing low blood oxygen (**hypoxia**) can cause this disorder.

WORD ANALYSIS AND DEFINITION

WORD	PRONUNCIATION	ELEMENTS		DEFINITION
cardiomegaly	KAR-dee-oh-MEG-ah-lee	S/ R/CF	-megaly *enlargement* cardi/o- *heart*	Enlargement of the heart
cardiomyopathy	KAR-dee-oh-my-OP-ah-thee	S/ R/CF R/CF	-pathy *disease* cardi/o- *heart* -my/o- *muscle*	Disease of heart muscle, the myocardium
cor pulmonale	KOR pul-moh-NAH-lee	S/ R/ R/	-ale *pertaining to* cor *heart* pulmon- *lung*	Right-sided heart failure arising from chronic lung disease
effusion	eh-FYU-shun		Latin *pouring out*	Collection of fluid that has escaped from blood vessels into a cavity or tissues
endocarditis	EN-doh-kar-DIE-tis	S/ P/ R/	-itis *inflammation* endo- *within* -card- *heart*	Inflammation of the lining of the heart
incompetence	in-KOM-peh-tense	S/ P/ R/	-ence *quality of* in- *not* -compet- *strive together*	Failure of valves to close completely
insufficiency	in-suh-FISH-en-see	S/ P/ R/CF	-ency *quality of* in- *not* -suffic/i- *enough*	Lack of completeness of function; in this case, for a valve to close properly
malfunction	mal-FUNK-shun	S/ P/ R/	-ion *action, condition* mal- *bad, inadequate* -funct- *perform*	Inadequate or abnormal function
myocarditis	MY-oh-kar-DIE-tis	S/ R/CF R/	-itis *inflammation* my/o- *muscle* -card- *heart*	Inflammation of the heart muscle
pericarditis	PER-ih-kar-DIE-tis	S/ P/ R/	-itis *inflammation* peri- *around* -card- *heart*	Inflammation of the pericardium, the covering of the heart
prolapse	pro-LAPS		Latin *a falling*	An organ slips out of its normal position
prosthesis prosthetic (adj)	PROS-thee-sis pros-THET-ik		Greek *an addition*	Manufactured substitute for a missing part of the body
regurgitate	ree-GUR-jih-tate	S/ P/ R/	-ate *action* re- *back* -gurgit- *flood*	To flow backwards; in this case, through a heart valve
tamponade	tam-po-NAID	S/ R/	-ade *pertaining to* tampon- *plug*	Pathologic compression of an organ such as the heart

---

EXERCISES

*Use your knowledge of the **language of cardiology** to match the description in column 1 with the correct medical term in column 2. Fill in the blanks.*

_____ 1. weakening of heart muscle

_____ 2. inflammation that causes exudates

_____ 3. cusps of valve bulge back into atrium

_____ 4. constricted valve opening

_____ 5. failure of right ventricle to pump properly

_____ 6. cardiomyopathy can be the cause

_____ 7. inflammation of heart lining

_____ 8. causes valve regurgitation

_____ 9. inflammation of heart muscle

_____ 10. inflammatory heart disease

A. incompetence

B. cardiomegaly

C. cor pulmonale

D. pericarditis

E. rheumatic fever

F. myocarditis

G. cardiomyopathy

H. prolapse

I. endocarditis

J. stenosis

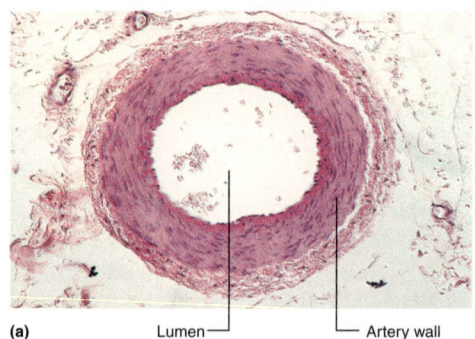

(a) Lumen — Artery wall

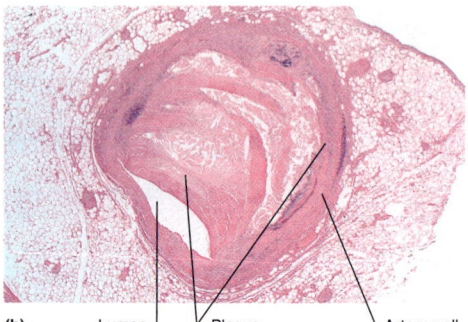

(b) Lumen — Plaque — Artery wall

▲ **FIGURE 8.13 Arterial Structure.**
(*a*) Normal coronary artery. (*b*) Advanced atherosclerosis.

Abbreviations

ASHD arteriosclerotic heart disease
CAD coronary artery disease
MI myocardial infarction

Keynote

All these risk factors can be reduced by changes in life style.

Case Report 8.1 *(continued)*

For Mr. Johnson in the emergency room, the ECG indicated that he was having a myocardial infarction (MI) that was affecting the anterior wall of his left ventricle. The cardiovascular technician did not want to leave the patient and used the call system to obtain nursing and medical help.

DISORDERS OF THE HEART (continued)

Coronary Artery Disease (CAD)

The arteries supplying the myocardium become narrowed by atherosclerotic **plaques,** called **atheroma.** As the atheroma increases, the lumen of the artery becomes more and more narrow (*Compare Figures 8.13a and b*). The blood supplied to the cardiac muscle by the artery is reduced. Platelet aggregation can occur on the plaque to form a blood clot (**coronary thrombosis**). **Atherosclerosis** is the most common form of **arteriosclerosis** (hardening of the arteries) and can lead to **arteriosclerotic heart disease (ASHD).**

Angina pectoris, pain in the chest on exertion, is often the first symptom of reduced oxygen supply to the myocardium. The pain goes away if the exertion is stopped or if a **nitroglycerin** tablet is placed under the tongue (**sublingually**).

Myocardial infarction (MI) is the death of myocardial cells caused by the lack of blood supply (ischemia) when an artery eventually becomes blocked (**occluded**). Sudden, severe, crushing **substernal** or left chest pain is experienced. If the ischemia is not reversed within four to six hours, the muscle cells die (undergo **necrosis**).

Cardiogenic shock occurs when the heart fails to pump effectively and organs and tissues are **perfused** inadequately. The pulse is weak and rapid, and blood pressure drops. The patient becomes pale, cold, sweaty, and anxious.

The other form of circulatory shock is **hypovolemic shock,** in which there is a loss of blood volume, often from hemorrhage or dehydration.

Cardiac arrest is the sudden cessation of cardiac activity resulting from **anoxia.** The ECG shows a flat line, **asystole** (*Figure 8.14*).

Risk factors for CAD include:

- Obesity
- Lack of exercise (**sedentary**)
- Tobacco
- Diabetes mellitus
- High blood pressure (**hypertension**)
- Elevated serum cholesterol
  (*see Chapter 20*)
- Stress

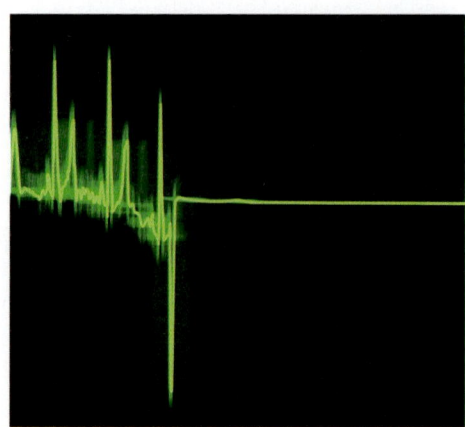

▲ **FIGURE 8.14 Electrocardiogram (ECG) Showing Asystole.**

WORD	PRONUNCIATION		ELEMENTS	DEFINITION
anoxia anoxic (adj)	an-OCK-see-ah an-OCK-sik	S/ P/ R/	-ia *condition* an- *without* -ox *oxygen*	Without oxygen
arteriosclerosis arteriosclerotic (adj)	ar-TIER-e-oh-skler-OH-sis ar-TIER-e-oh-skler-OT-ic	S/ R/CF R/CF S/	-sis *condition* arteri/o *artery* -scler/o- *hardness* -tic *pertaining to*	Hardening of the arteries
asystole	a-SIS-toe-lee	P/ R/	a- *without* -systole *contraction*	Absence of contractions of the heart
atheroma atherectomy atherosclerosis	ath-er-ROE-mah ath-er-EK-toe-me ATH-er-oh-skler-OH-sis	S/ R/ S/ R/CF S/ R/CF	-oma *tumor* ather- *porridge, gruel* -ectomy *excision* ather/o- *porridge, gruel* -sis *condition* -scler/o- *hardness*	Lipid deposit in the lining of an artery Surgical removal of the atheroma Atheroma in arteries
occlude (verb) occlusion (noun)	o-KLUDE o-KLU-zhun		Latin *to close*	To close, plug, or completely obstruct
perfuse	per-FYUSE		Latin *to pour*	To force blood to flow through a lumen or a vascular bed
plaque	PLAK		French *a plate*	Patch of abnormal tissue
sedentary	sed-en-TER-ee	S/ R/	-ary *pertaining to* sedent- *sitting*	Accustomed to little exercise or movement
sublingual	sub-LING-wal	S/ P/ R/	-al *pertaining to* sub- *under* -lingu- *tongue*	Underneath the tongue
substernal	sub-STER-nal	S/ P/ R/	-al *pertaining to* sub- *under* -stern- *chest*	Under the sternum or breastbone

EXERCISES

Consult this WAD for the best medical term to complete the following sentences in patient documentation. Fill in the blanks.

1. The _____ (underneath the tongue) medication did not dissolve completely, so liquid medication was given to the patient instead.

2. The patient's _____ (hardening of the arteries) puts him at risk for a stroke. I have ordered a blood thinner.

3. His _____ (little exercise or movement) lifestyle, coupled with obesity, increases his risk factors for a heart attack.

4. Schedule the patient for a(n) _____ (surgical removal of lipid deposit in artery lining) as soon as possible.

5. _____ (absence of heart contractions) occurred at 2251 hrs, and the patient was pronounced dead.

6. Angioplasty showed a large clot _____ (completely obstructing) his left coronary artery.

7. The bullet entered his left _____ (under the breastbone) area and exited his back.

8. _____ (being without oxygen) has caused permanent brain damage to this infant.

9. The patient's diagnostic studies show clear evidence of _____ (patch of abnormal tissue) in the coronary heart muscle.

10. Cardiogenic shock occurred and the patient's tissues were not _____ (forcing blood through a vascular bed or lumen) adequately.

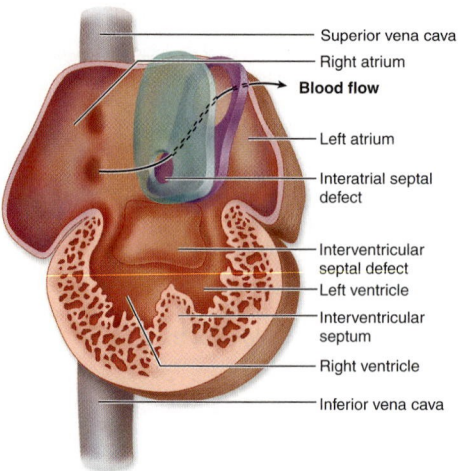

FIGURE 8.15 Atrial and Ventricular Septal Defects.

Keynote

Hypertension is the major cause of heart failure, stroke, and kidney failure.

All these risk factors can be reduced by changes in lifestyle.

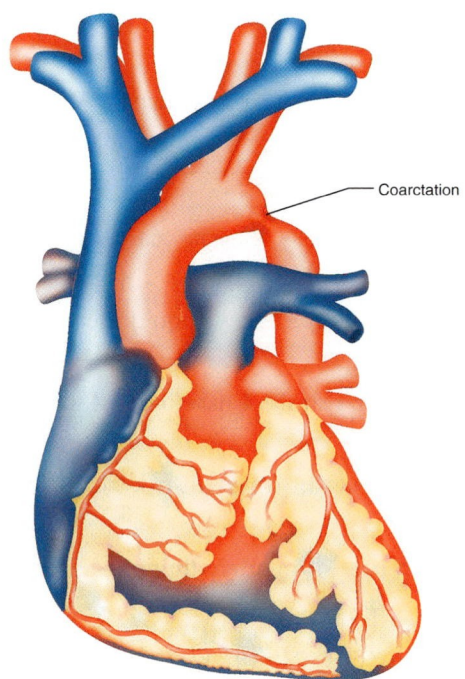

FIGURE 8.16 Coarctation of Aorta

Abbreviations

ASD	atrial septal defect
CHD	congenital heart disease
CHF	congestive heart failure
Hg	mercury
PDA	patent ductus arteriosus
TOF	tetralogy of Fallot
VSD	ventricular septal defect

DISORDERS OF THE HEART (continued)

Hypertensive Heart Disease

Hypertension is the most common cardiovascular disorder in this country, affecting more than 20% of the adult population. It results from a prolonged elevated blood pressure throughout the vascular system. The high pressure forces the ventricles to work harder to pump blood. Eventually, the myocardium becomes strained and less efficient. It is the major cause of heart failure, stroke, and kidney failure.

High blood pressure is currently defined as a blood pressure reading at or above 140/90 mm **Hg** (mercury). A normal blood pressure is below 120/80 mm Hg. The first number, or **systolic** reading, reflects the blood pressure when the heart is contracting. The second number, or **diastolic** reading, reflects blood pressure when the heart is relaxed between contractions.

Primary (essential) hypertension is the most common type of hypertension. Its etiology is unknown. Its risk factors are:

- overweight
- tobacco
- stress
- lack of exercise
- alcohol

Secondary hypertension results from other diseases such as kidney disease, atherosclerosis, and hyperthyroidism.

Malignant hypertension is a rare, severe, life-threatening form of hypertension in which the blood pressure reading can be greater than 200/120 mm Hg. Aggressive intervention is indicated to reduce the blood pressure.

Prehypertension, with a systolic pressure between 120 and 139 mm Hg and a diastolic pressure between 80 and 90 mm Hg, may indicate an increased risk for cardiovascular disease.

Congestive Heart Failure (CHF)

Congestive heart failure occurs with the inability of the heart to supply enough cardiac output to meet the body's metabolic needs.

The most common conditions leading to CHF are:

- cardiac ischemia
- valvular regurgitation
- cardiomyopathy
- severe hypertension
- aortic **stenosis**
- chronic lung disease

Congenital Heart Disease (CHD)

Congenital heart disease is the result of abnormal development of the heart in the fetus.

Common congenital defects include:

- **Atrial septal defect (ASD)**—a hole in the interatrial septum allows blood to **shunt** from the higher pressure left atrium to the lower pressure right atrium *(Figure 8.15)*.
- **Ventricular septal defect (VSD)**—a hole in the interventricular septum allows blood to shunt from the higher pressure left ventricle to the lower pressure right ventricle *(see Figure 8.15)*.
- **Patent ductus arteriosus (PDA)**—the ductus arteriosus is a normal blood vessel in the fetus that usually closes within 24 hours of birth. When the artery remains open (patent), blood can shunt from the aorta to the pulmonary artery, and the higher pressure causes damage to the lungs.
- **Coarctation of the aorta**—a narrowing of the aorta shortly after the artery to the left arm branches from the aorta *(Figure 8.16)*. This causes **hypertension** in the arms behind the narrowing and **hypotension** in the lower limbs and organs like the kidney below the narrowing.
- **Tetralogy of Fallot (TOF)** is a syndrome with four congenital heart defects. All these congenital abnormalities can be surgically repaired.

WORD ANALYSIS AND DEFINITION

WORD	PRONUNCIATION		ELEMENTS	DEFINITION
coarctation	koh-ark-**TAY**-shun	S/ R/	**-ation** *action* **coarct-** *press together*	Constriction stenosis, particularly of the aorta
congenital	kon-**JEN**-ih-tal	S/ P/ R/	**-al** *pertaining to* **con-** *together, with* **-genit-** *bring forth*	Present at birth, either inherited or due to an event during gestation up to the moment of birth
defect	**DEE**-fect		Latin *to lack*	An absence, malformation, or imperfection
hypertension	**HIGH**-per-**TEN**-shun	S/ P/ R/	**-ion** *process* **hyper-** *excessive* **-tens-** *pressure*	Persistent high arterial blood pressure
hypotension prehypertension	**HIGH**-poh-**TEN**-shun pree-**HIGH**-per-**TEN**-shun	P/ P/	**hypo-** *low* **pre-** *before*	Persistent low arterial blood pressure Precursor to hypertension
patent ductus arteriosus	**PAY**-tent **DUK**-tus ar-**TER**-ee-oh-sus	R/ R/ R/	**patent** *lie open* **ductus** *leading* **arteriosus** *artery*	An open channel between the aorta and the pulmonary artery
shunt	SHUNT		Middle English *divert*	A bypass or diversion of fluid; in this case, blood
stenosis	ste-**NOH**-sis	S/ R/CF	**-sis** *condition* **sten/o-** *narrow*	Narrowing of a passage
tetralogy of Fallot (TOF)	te-**TRAL**-oh-jee fah-**LOW**	 P/ R/	Etienne-Louis Fallot, French physician 1850–1911 **tetra-** *four* **-logy** *study of*	Set of four congenital heart defects occurring together

EXERCISES

Abbreviations need to be used carefully so that you communicate exactly what is necessary. The following sentences both contain abbreviations—translate the abbreviations into their correct medical terms. Rewrite the sentences without the abbreviations and convey the same message. Check your spelling!

1. ASD, TOF, VSD, and PDA are all examples of CHD.

_____

_____

_____

2. CHF occurs with the inability of the heart to supply enough cardiac output to meet the body's metabolic needs.

_____

_____

_____

3. High blood pressure is a reading at or above 140/90 mm Hg.

_____

_____

_____

CARDIOLOGIC TESTS

Blood Tests

Lipid profile helps determine the risk of CAD and comprises:

- total cholesterol
- **high-density lipoprotein (HDL)** ("good cholesterol")
- **low-density lipoprotein (LDL)** ("bad cholesterol")
- **triglycerides**

These are discussed in Chapter 22.

B-type natriuretic peptide (BNP), a brain hormone, is used to diagnose and monitor congestive heart failure and to predict the course of end-stage heart failure.

C-reactive protein (CRP), produced by the endothelial cells of arteries, has been identified as a risk factor for atherosclerosis and CAD.

Homocysteine is an amino acid in the blood. Elevated levels are related to a higher risk of CAD, stroke, and peripheral vascular disease.

Creatine kinase (CK) is an enzyme released into the blood by dead myocardial cells in MI.

Troponin I and T are part of a protein complex in muscle that is released into the blood during myocardial injury. Troponin I is found in heart muscle but not in skeletal muscle. Its presence in blood is therefore a highly sensitive indicator of a recent MI. Both CK and Troponin I and T are used to confirm a suspected MI.

Diagnostic Tests

Electrocardiogram (ECG or EKG) is a paper record of the electrical signals of your heart.

Cardiac stress testing is an exercise tolerance test to raise your heart rate and monitor its effect on cardiac function. **Nuclear imaging** of the heart, using an injection of a radioactive substance, can be used with the stress test.

Persantine/thallium exercise testing is used for people unable to engage in physical exercise. It combines nuclear imaging with a drug that increases the demand on the heart.

Echocardiography uses ultrasound waves to study cardiac function. The test is performed by a **sonographer,** who places a **transducer** on the patient's chest.

Transesophageal echocardiography (TEE) involves insertion of a small probe into your esophagus to record the anatomy and function of heart valves.

Holter monitor is a continuous ECG recorded on a tape recorder cassette as you work, play, and rest.

Event monitor is used for patients whose symptoms occur sporadically. A monitor is held over the chest when an event occurs. The data is stored and transmitted by telephone to a monitoring station.

Ambulatory blood pressure monitor provides a record of your blood pressure over a 24-hour period as you go about your daily activities.

Electron beam tomography (EBT) is a scan that identifies calcium deposits in arteries.

Magnetic resonance imaging (MRI) can produce detailed images of the heart and identify sections of cardiac muscle that are not receiving an adequate blood supply.

Cardiac catheterization detects patterns of pressures and blood flows in the heart. A thin tube is guided into the heart under x-ray guidance after being inserted into a vein or artery.

Coronary angiogram uses a contrast dye injected during cardiac catheterization to identify coronary artery blockages.

Abbreviations	
BNP	B-type natriuretic peptide
CK	creatine kinase
CRP	C-reactive protein
EBT	electron beam tomography
HDL	high-density lipoprotein
LDL	low-density lipoprotein
MRI	magnetic resonance imaging
TEE	transesophageal echocardiography

WORD	PRONUNCIATION	ELEMENTS		DEFINITION
catheter	KATH-eh-ter		Greek *to send down*	Hollow tube to allow passage of fluid into or out of a body cavity, organ, or vessel
catheterize (verb)	KATH-eh-teh-RIZE	S/ R/	-ize *action* catheter- *catheter*	To introduce a catheter
catheterization	KATH-eh-ter-ih-ZAY-shun	S/	-ation *action*	Introduction of a catheter
creatine kinase	KREE-ah-teen KI-naze	S/ R/ S/ R/	-ine *pertaining to* creat- *flesh* -ase *enzyme* kin- *motion*	Enzyme elevated in plasma following heart muscle damage in myocardial infarction
echocardiography	EK-oh-kar-dee-OG-rah-fee	S/ R/ R/CF	-graphy *recording* echo- *sound* -cardi/o- *heart*	Ultrasound recording of heart function
homocysteine	ho-moh-SIS-teen	P/ R	homo- *same* -cysteine *an amino acid*	An amino acid similar to cysteine
lipoprotein	LIE-poh-pro-teen	R/CF R/	lip/o- *fat* -protein *protein*	Molecules made of combinations of fat and protein
natriuretic peptide	NAH-tree-you-RET-ik PEP-tide	S/ R/ R/ S/ R/	-ic *pertaining to* natri- *sodium* -uret- *ureter* -ide *particular quality* pept- *amino acid*	Protein that increases the excretion of sodium
sonograph	SON-oh-graf	S/ R/	-graph *to record* sono- *sound*	Instrument that uses sound waves to create images of structures
sonographer sonogram	so-NOG-rah-fer SON-oh-gram	S/ S/	-grapher *one who records* -gram *a record*	The technician who performs a sonogram Image obtained by using a sonograph
tomography	toe-MOG-rah-fee	S/ R/CF	-graphy *recording* tom/o- *section*	Radiographic image of a selected slice of tissue
transducer	trans-DYU-sir	P/ R/	trans- *across* -ducer *to lead*	Device that converts energy from one form to another
triglyceride	tri-GLISS-eh-ride	S/ P/ R/	-ide *having a specific quality* tri- *three* -glycer- *sweet*	Has three fatty acids

EXERCISES

Identify the type of element and its meaning in the appropriate column. The first one is done for you. Fill in the blanks.

Element	Meaning of Prefix	Meaning of Root/CF	Meaning of Suffix
ase			*Enzyme*
cardio			
creat			
cysteine			
echo			
graphy			
homo			
ic			
ide			
ine			

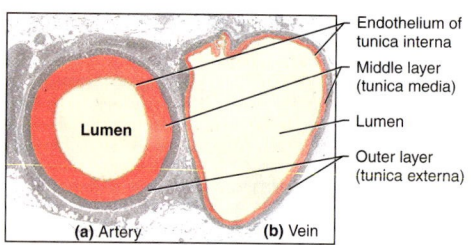

▲ FIGURE 8.22 Anatomy of an Artery and Vein.

BLOOD VESSEL FUNCTION RELATED TO STRUCTURE

Except for the capillaries and venules, all the blood vessel walls show a basic structure of three layers *(Figure 8.22)*:

1. **Tunica intima (interna)**—the innermost layer of endothelial cells, with thin layers of fibrous and elastic connective tissue supporting them.
2. **Tunica media**—a middle layer of smooth muscle cells arranged circularly around the blood vessel. A membrane of elastic tissue separates the tunica media from the outer layer of the wall.
3. **Tunica adventitia (externa)**—an outer connective tissue layer of varying density and thickness.

The larger arteries near the heart, the aorta and its major branches, have to cope with large quantities of blood and fluctuating pressures between systole and diastole. Therefore, these arteries have a large number of elastic fibers and a relatively small number of muscle fibers.

The functions of the medium-sized and smaller arteries are to regulate the blood supply to the different regions of the body and to ensure that the blood pressure in the arteries is at an appropriate level. The tunica media of these arteries contains 25 to 40 layers of smooth muscle to enable the muscles to contract (**vasoconstriction**) and to relax (**vasodilation**) to increase flow.

The function of the veins is to return the blood from the periphery to the heart in a low-pressure system. For example, by the time blood reaches the venules, its pressure has dropped from the 120 mm Hg of systole to around 15 mm Hg. By the time the blood is in the venae cavae, the **central venous pressure (CVP)** is down to around 4 to 5 mm Hg.

Veins have a much thinner tunica media than arteries, with few muscle cells and elastic fibers *(Figure 8.22)*. They have a larger lumen and a thick tunica adventitia that merges with the connective tissue of surrounding structures. In the limbs, the veins are surrounded and massaged by muscles to squeeze the blood along the veins. One-way valves in the veins allow the blood to flow toward the heart but not away from the heart. They are shaped like and function like the semilunar valves of the heart.

Space Medicine

Normally, gravity helps the blood circulate in the lower limbs. When astronauts are weightless for long periods of time, blood pools in the central and upper areas of the body and there appears to be an excess blood volume. The kidney compensates by excreting more fluid, leading to a 10 to 20% decrease in blood volume and a low blood pressure. Astronauts compensate for this by wearing lower-body suction suits, which apply a vacuum force to draw blood into the lower limbs.

Arterial Pulses

The pulse is always part of a clinical examination because it can show heart rate, rhythm, and the state of the arterial wall by **palpation**. There are nine locations on each side of the body where large arteries are close to the surface and can be palpated. *(Figure 8.23)*.

The most easily accessible is the **radial artery** at the wrist, where the pulse is usually taken. The **brachial artery** at the elbow is used for taking blood pressure readings. All the pulse sites can be used as **pressure points** to temporarily reduce arterial bleeding in an emergency.

The two places in the foot where a pulse can be felt are called the **pedal** pulses.

Blood Pressure (BP)

Blood pressure is the force the blood exerts on arterial walls as it is pumped around the circulatory system by the left ventricle. The pressure is measured using a **sphygmomanometer** and a stethoscope.

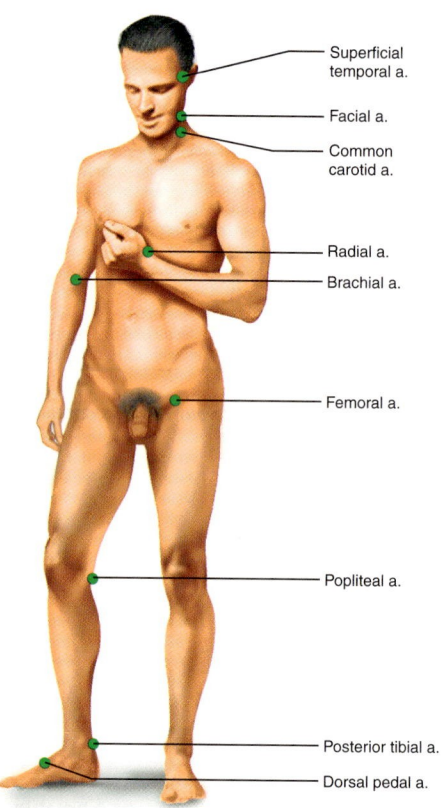

▲ FIGURE 8.23 Arterial Pulses.
(*a.* = artery)

Abbreviations

BP	blood pressure
CVP	central venous pressure

WORD	PRONUNCIATION	ELEMENTS		DEFINITION
adventitia	ad-ven-**TISH**-ah		Latin *from outside*	Outer layer of connective tissue covering blood vessels or organs
intima	**IN**-tih-ma		Latin *inmost*	Inner layer of a structure, particularly a blood vessel
media	**ME**-dee-ah		Latin *middle*	Middle layer of a structure, particularly a blood vessel
palpate palpation (noun)	**PAL**-pate pal-**PAY**-shun		Latin *touch, stroke*	To examine with the fingers and hands
pedal	**PEED**-al	S/ R/	-al *pertaining to* ped- *foot*	Pertaining to the foot
radial	**RAY**-dee-al	S/ R/	-al *pertaining to* radi- *radius (forearm bone)*	Pertaining to the forearm
sphygmomanometer	**SFIG**-moh-mah-**NOM**-ih-ter	S/ R/CF R/CF	-meter *instrument to measure* sphygm/o- *pulse* -man/o- *pressure*	Instrument for measuring arterial blood pressure
tunica	**TYU**-nih-kah		Latin *coat*	A layer in the wall of a blood vessel or other tubular structure
vasoconstriction	**VAY**-soh-con-**STRIK**-shun	S/ R/CF R/	-ion *process* vas/o- *vessel* -constrict- *narrow*	Reduction in diameter of a blood vessel
vasodilation	**VAY**-soh-di-**LAY**-shun	S/ R/CF R/	-ion *process* vas/o- *vessel* -dilat- *open up*	Increase in diameter of a blood vessel

EXERCISES

Match the definition in column 1 with the correct medical term in column 2.

_____ 1. to examine by feeling with fingers and hands

_____ 2. reduction in diameter of a blood vessel

_____ 3. inner layer of a structure

_____ 4. Latin for *coat*

_____ 5. outer tissue covering of an organ

_____ 6. instrument to measure blood pressure

_____ 7. pertaining to the foot

_____ 8. increase in diameter of a blood vessel

_____ 9. middle layer of a structure

_____ 10. pertaining to the forearm

A. radial

B. vasodilation

C. adventitia

D. pedal

E. vasoconstriction

F. media

G. intima

H. sphygmomanometer

I. palpate

J. tunica

Case Report 8.2 (continued)

Mrs. Martha Jones, who had been referred to Dr. Bannerjee's cardiovascular clinic, has several circulatory problems related to her diabetes and obesity. She has been diagnosed previously with hypertension, CAD, and diabetic retinopathy. She now has severe pain in her legs on walking.

Her ankle/brachial index (**ABI**), which measures the ratio of the blood pressure in her ankle to that in her arm, showed significant blockage of blood flow. Doppler studies confirmed this. This blockage produces the pain on walking (intermittent claudication). It is due to arteriosclerosis of the large arteries in her legs. Angiograms showed several atherosclerotic areas in her popliteal artery.

The ulcers on the edges of her big toes result from thickening of the walls of her capillaries and arterioles and the resulting poor circulation to her feet. Again, this is due to her diabetes.

In the venous system of her legs, the tender cordlike lesion is due to thrombophlebitis of a superficial vein in her left leg. Pain in the calf on flexion of the ankle (Homans sign) indicates that she may have a deep vein thrombosis (**DVT**). A venogram confirmed this diagnosis.

CIRCULATORY DISORDERS

Disorders of Veins

Thrombophlebitis is an inflammation of the lining of a vein (tunica intima), allowing clots (thrombi) to form.

Deep vein thrombosis (DVT) is thrombus formation in a deep vein, often due to reduced blood flow. Risk factors include immobility, surgery, prolonged travel, and contraception (estrogen). The increased pressure in the capillaries due to back-pressure from the blocked blood flow in the veins causes an increase in the flow of fluid from the capillaries to the interstitial spaces. The collection of fluid is called **edema.**

A major complication of thrombus formation is that a piece of the clot can break off and be carried in the bloodstream to lodge in a blood vessel in another organ and block blood flow. The piece that breaks of is called an **embolus.** It often lodges in the lungs, causing a pulmonary embolus *(see Chapter 9).*

Varicose veins are superficial veins that have lost their elasticity and appear swollen and tortuous *(Figure 8.24).* Their valves become incompetent, and blood flows backward and pools. Smaller, more superficial varicose veins are called **spider veins.** Varicose veins are associated with a family history, obesity, and prolonged standing. Treatments offered include laser technology and **sclerotherapy,** where solutions that scar the veins are injected into them. **Collateral** circulations develop to take the blood through alternative routes.

A **phlebotomist** is a technician who draws blood. The procedure is called **phlebotomy.**

Disorders of Arteries

An **aneurysm** is a localized dilation of an artery as a result of a localized weakness of the vessel wall. Common sites occur along the aorta, mostly the abdominal aorta. They can rupture, leading to severe bleeding and hypovolemic shock. Surgical repair consists of excision of the aneurysm and replacement with a synthetic graft.

Intracranial aneurysms, particularly at the base of the brain, are an important cause of bleeds into the cranial cavity *(see Chapter 10).*

Thromboangiitis obliterans (Buerger disease) is an inflammatory disease of the arteries with clot formation, usually in the legs. The occlusion of arteries and impaired circulation leads to intermittent claudication.

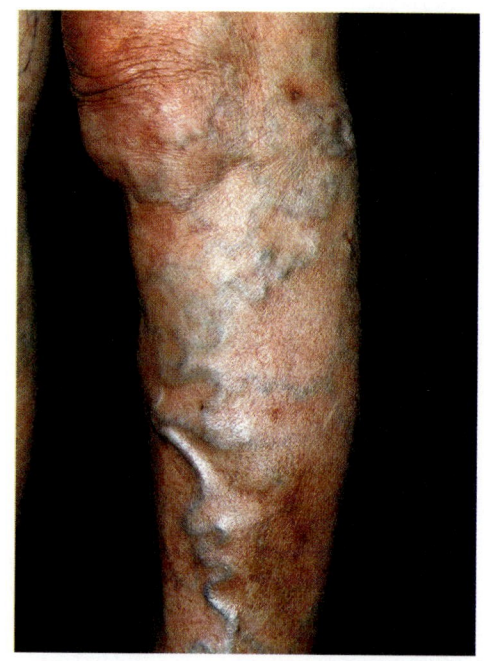

▲ **FIGURE 8.24** **Varicose Veins of Leg.**

Abbreviations	
ABI	ankle/brachial index
DVT	deep vein thrombosis
PVD	peripheral vascular disease

WORD	PRONUNCIATION		ELEMENTS	DEFINITION
aneurysm	**AN**-yur-izm		Greek *dilation*	Small, circumscribed dilation of an artery or cardiac chamber
collateral	koh-**LAT**-er-al	P/ R/	**col-** *before* **-lateral** *at the side*	Situated at the side to bypass an obstruction
edema edematous (adj) pitting edema	ee-**DEE**-mah ee-**DEM**-ah-tus		Greek *swelling*	Excessive accumulation of fluid in cells and tissues Marked by edema An indentation made by a finger in an edematous area persists for a long time
embolus	**EM**-bo-lus		Greek *plug, stopped*	Detached piece of thrombus, a mass of bacteria, quantity of air, or foreign body that blocks a blood vessel
endarterectomy	**END**-ar-ter-**EK**-toe-me	S/ P/ R/	**-ectomy-** *surgical excision* **end-** *within* **-arter-** *artery*	Surgical removal of plaque from an artery
phlebitis	fleh-**BIE**-tis	S/ R/	**-itis** *inflammation* **phleb-** *vein*	Inflammation of a vein
phlebotomist phlebotomy	fleh-**BOT**-oh-mist fleh-**BOT**-oh-me	S/ R/CF R/ S/	**-ist** *specialist in* **phleb/o-** *vein* **-tom-** *incision* **-tomy** *make an incision*	Person skilled in taking blood from veins Taking blood from a vein
sclerotherapy sclerose (verb)	**SKLAIR**-oh-**THAIR**-ah-pee skle-**ROZE**	S/ R/CF	**-therapy** *treatment* **scler/o-** *hardening*	Injection of a solution into a vein to thrombose it
thromboembolism thromboembolic (adj) thrombophlebitis	**THROM**-boh-**EM**-boh-lizm **THROM**-boh-**EM**-**BOL**-ik **THROM**-boh-fleh-**BY**-tis	S/ R/ R/ S/ R/ R/	**-ism-** *condition* **thromb/o-** *clot* **-embol-** *plug* **-itis** *inflammation* **thromb/o-** *clot* **-phleb-** *vein*	A piece of detached blood clot (embolus) blocking a distant blood vessel Inflammation of a vein with clot formation

Carotid artery disease affects the two major arteries supplying the brain. They can be involved in arteriosclerosis and the deposition of plaque, which puts the patient at risk for a stroke. If an artery is more than 70% blocked, a carotid **endarterectomy** can be performed to surgically remove the plaque.

Peripheral vascular disease (PVD) is a general term describing all the disorders of the systemic arterial and venous systems.

EXERCISES

*Apply the **language of the cardiovascular system** and circle the best answer.*

1. The suffix tells you that **thrombophlebitis** is a(n):

   clot   inflammation   excision

2. **Endarterectomy** means the plaque has been:

   incised   excised   repaired

3. The combining form *phlebo-* means:

   artery   vein   capillary

4. **Collateral** means:

   at the front   in the middle   at the side

5. The symptom of **edema** is:

   a rash   a swelling   a lesion

6. **Aneurysm** describes a blood vessel that is:

   dilated   constricted   collapsed

7. The combining form *sclero-* describes a:

   softening   clotting   hardening

8. The suffix tells you that **thromboembolism** is a(n):

   condition   procedure   infection

9. The combining form *thrombo-* means:

   clot   lump   plug

10. The prefix *end-* signifies:

   within   without   beside

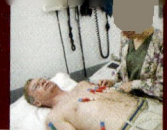

CARDIOVASCULAR SYSTEM

CHALLENGE YOUR KNOWLEDGE

A. **How well do you understand what you read?** Interpret the following paragraph from a patient's chest x-ray report, and answer the questions in parts B and C.

> The left ventricle is slightly enlarged. Right atrium and right ventricle appear to be dilated. There is tortuosity of the thoracic aorta, with arteriosclerosis. The hilar and interstitial structures are somewhat accentuated. There are large pericardial fat pads. Tricuspid and pulmonic valves appear normal but are not well seen. Mitral valve appears grossly normal for age. Aortic valve appears grossly normal for age.

B. **Definitions: Define** the following medical terms either by looking them up in a WAD or by breaking them down into elements and defining the elements to give you the meaning of the term:

ventricle _____

atrium _____

dilated _____

thoracic aorta _____

arteriosclerosis _____

interstitial _____

tricuspid _____

pulmonic _____

mitral _____

aortic _____

C. **Using your knowledge of the terminology in the preceding scenario, circle the correct answer for the following questions.**

1. Where are the pericardial fat pads?

    a. in the heart

    b. around the heart

    c. below the heart

    d. beside the heart

    e. above the heart

2. What is a likely diagnosis for this patient?

    a. CABG

    b. ASHD

    c. PTCA

    d. DVT

    e. MI

3. Which two heart chambers have a somewhat similar appearance?

    a. right and left ventricle

    b. right and left atrium

    c. left atrium and right ventricle

    d. right atrium and left ventricle

    e. right atrium and right ventricle

4. What is another spelling and pronunciation for *dilation?*

    a. dillation

    b. dilatation

    c. dillatation

    d. diletation

    e. dilletation

5. **Interstitial** means:

    a. space between the cells of a structure or organ

    b. cavity between the cells of a structure or organ

    c. fluid between the cells of a structure or organ

    d. membrane between the cells of a structure or organ

    e. wall between the cells of a structure or organ

D. **Build your knowledge of heart terms by working with the following word elements.** Fill in the table, then answer the questions below.

Element	Type of Element (prefix, root, combining form, suffix)	Meaning of Element
graphy		
cardio		
ar		
logy		
gram		
ary		
logist		
vascul		
electro		
graph		
pulmon		

CARDIOVASCULAR SYSTEM

E. Using elements in the chart in question D, form medical terms to fill in the blanks.

1. A _____ is a specialist in the study of the heart.

2. In the abbreviation CPR, the "C" stands for: _____.

3. The abbreviation ECG stands for: _____.

4. The study of the heart is the specialty called: _____.

5. The term that means *pertaining to the heart and blood vessels* is: _____.

6. Instrument used for taking an ECG: _____.

7. A specialist in the study of lung diseases: _____.

F. Label: On the line next to the statements below, write the medical term for the body part it refers to. Then take the medical term, and write it on the correct line in the illustration.

1. "pacemaker of the heart" _____

2. distribute electrical stimuli, which cause contraction of the ventricular myocardium _____

3. electrical gateway to the ventricles _____

4. supply both ventricles _____

5. superior and inferior venae cavae open into this atrium _____

6. electrical signals leaving the AV node reach the ventricles through this _____

7. blood from pulmonary veins flows into this atrium _____

G. **Knowing your word elements will always help you to deconstruct a medical term.** Test your knowledge of word elements by defining the following medical terms.

Prefix: sub = _____

subclavian   _____

substernal   _____

sublingual   _____

subaortic   _____

Suffixes: Underline the suffix in each term, then write a brief definition of that term.

sonographer   _____

sonogram   _____

sonography   _____

sonograph   _____

H. **To better understand the peripheral circulations and their functions, complete the following mini-outline.**

The two major peripheral circulations are the:

1. _____

2. _____

Their functions are the same:

1. _____

2. _____

3. _____

4. _____

How are they different? Complete the table below to show in which circulation each event occurs.

Event	Pulmonary Circulation	Systemic Circulation
Oxygenated blood carried by		
Deoxygenated blood carried by		
Blood goes to all areas of the body		
Gas exchange occurs between lungs and blood		
Takes blood to left atrium		
Coronary circulation branches from here		
Removes carbon dioxide from blood		
Blood exits lung through these veins		
Ventricle pumps to aorta		

Study Hint
Use this outline for test review.

CARDIOVASCULAR SYSTEM

I. **Build your knowledge of the heart's location and function by correctly answering the following questions.**

1. Which of the following is *not* a function of the heart:

    a. pulmonary circulation

    b. maintain respiration

    c. systemic circulation

    d. regulate blood supply

    e. pump blood

2. The heart lies in the thoracic cavity between the lungs in an area called the:

    a. sternum

    b. mediastinum

    c. ventricle

    d. atrium

    e. vena cava

3. If the *base* of the heart is the upper end of the heart, what is the tip (or other end) of the heart called?

    a. tricuspid

    b. atrium

    c. aorta

    d. semilunar

    e. apex

4. The rate and force of heart contraction can be changed by:

    a. blood flow

    b. exercise

    c. body temperature

    d. all of the above

    e. none of the above

5. What is responsible for ensuring the one-way flow of blood in the heart?

    a. blood vessels

    b. pulmonary circulation

    c. coronary circulation

    d. valves

    e. blood pressure

J. **Translate:** Rewrite the sentences using medical terms instead of the abbreviations. Make sure you are communicating the same message either way. Check (✓) your spelling! Fill in the blanks.

1. The CVT started CPR after checking the patient's ECG. He paged the doctor STAT. Apparently, the patient had had an MI.

_____

_____

_____

_____

_____

2. Because of the patient's PVD, the doctor ordered special stockings to prevent DVT.

_____

_____

_____

_____

K. **Use your medical terminology to provide a short answer** to the following questions:

1. The peripheral circulation makes use of which types of blood vessels?

_____

_____

2. In addition to the peripheral circulation, what is the third type of circulation in the body, and what does it do?

_____

_____

_____

_____

3. Explain the term **collateral circulation** and describe its function.

_____

_____

_____

_____

_____

_____

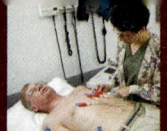

CARDIOVASCULAR SYSTEM

L. **Procedures:** You have passed your certification examination and have been hired as the coder for the Cardiology Department in Fulwood Medical Center. You are coding the claims for the following tests performed in the department. How much do you know about cardiology testing? Match the letter to the numbered blank.

_____ 1. thallium testing

_____ 2. EKG, also known as

_____ 3. continuous ECG recorded on tape

_____ 4. cardiac stress testing

_____ 5. TEE

_____ 6. helps determine risk of CAD

_____ 7. event monitor

_____ 8. sound waves study heart function

_____ 9. electron beam CT

_____ 10. cardiac catheterization

_____ 11. radioactive substance injected

_____ 12. can identify ischemic muscle

_____ 13. dye injected to find heart blockage

A. MRI

B. through esophagus to see heart valves

C. echocardiography

D. detects patterns of pressure in the heart

E. people unable to do physical exercise

F. coronary angiogram

G. exercise tolerance test

H. sporadic symptoms

I. lipid profile

J. ECG

K. Holter monitor

L. identifies calcium in arteries

M. nuclear imaging

M. **The diagnostic tests in question L may yield results that indicate a procedure should be performed.** Match up the following cardiac procedures.

_____ 1. catheter inflates and compresses plaque

_____ 2. converting an arrhythmia to normal rhythm

_____ 3. prevents artery from closing up again

_____ 4. donor to recipient

_____ 5. electrode used to destroy cells that produce arrhythmia

_____ 6. sands away plaque

_____ 7. injection of clot-busting drugs

_____ 8. harvested healthy vessels replace blocked ones

_____ 9. restores normal function to heart and lungs

_____ 10. artificial regulator of cardiac activity

A. CABG

B. rotational atherectomy

C. CPR

D. thrombolysis

E. PTCA

F. cardioversion

G. heart transplant

H. pacemaker implantation

I. radiofrequency ablation

J. stent placement

N. **Recall and Review:** The following exercise on word elements contains some elements from this chapter and the previous chapter. Try to recall the previous elements without turning back in your book. Check the type of element, then write its meaning. Fill in the blanks.

Element	Prefix	Root/CF	Suffix	Meaning of Element
de	_____	_____	_____	_____
emia	_____	_____	_____	_____
erythro	_____	_____	_____	_____
hemato	_____	_____	_____	_____
inter	_____	_____	_____	_____
mal	_____	_____	_____	_____
scope	_____	_____	_____	_____
tri	_____	_____	_____	_____
um	_____	_____	_____	_____

O. **In Your Own Words:** Identify one procedure or type of service performed by the following occupations.

CVT: _____

phlebotomist: _____

cardiologist: _____

sonographer: _____

cardiovascular surgeon: _____

P. **Terminology Challenge:** What does a perfusionist do? (Use the Internet or a dictionary if you need to.)

_____

_____

_____

_____

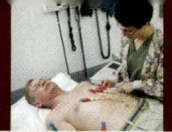

CARDIOVASCULAR SYSTEM

Q. **The following procedures could all be performed by a cardiovascular surgeon.** First, slash the term into its elements. Use the suffix to help you analyze the meaning of the term. Write a brief description of the procedure on the lines below. Fill in the blanks.

1. ablation: _____/ _____ / _____
                    P   R/CF   S

   Description: _____

2. angioplasty: _____/ _____ / _____
                    P   R/CF   S

   Description: _____

3. endarterectomy: _____/ _____ / _____
                    P   R/CF   S

   Description: _____

4. sclerotherapy: _____/ _____ / _____
                    P   R/CF   S

   Description: _____

5. atherectomy: _____/ _____ / _____
                    P   R/CF   S

   Description: _____

R. **Test your knowledge of the heart by circling the correct answer.**

1. The long, flat bone forming the center of the anterior wall of the chest is the:

   a. mediastinum

   b. sternum

   c. myocardium

   d. apex

   e. pericardium

2. The area of cell death caused by the sudden blockage of a blood vessel is termed:

   a. fibrosis

   b. infarct

   c. coronary

   d. sinus

   e. visceral

3. The term **sinus rhythm** refers to:

   a. the AV node

   b. normal heartbeat

   c. dysrhythmias

   d. arrthythmias

   e. a pacemaker

4. Pathologic compression of the heart is known as:

   a. endocarditis

   b. prolapse

   c. tamponade

   d. regurgitation

   e. effusion

5. The abbreviations that represent cardiac diagnoses are:

   a. SOB and EKG

   b. MI and PAT

   c. CPR and CVT

   d. STAT and SA

   e. AED and ID

6. What is the purpose of the four valves in the heart?

   a. blood flows in only one direction

   b. blood gets oxygenated

   c. the heart muscle can rest between beats

   d. prevents infection

   e. gateway to the heart

7. In the term **cardioversion,** the suffix -ion means:

   a. a structure

   b. a process

   c. to pour

   d. pertaining to

   e. small

CARDIOVASCULAR SYSTEM

S. Test your knowledge of the heart with the following questions:

1. Tissue heart valves can come from:

    a. pigs

    b. cows

    c. occasional humans

    d. all of the above

    e. none of the above

2. Abnormality in valve closure produces:

    a. exudate

    b. infarct

    c. murmur

    d. necrosis

    e. fibrillation

3. The cordlike tendons that anchor the mitral and tricuspid heart valves to the floor of the ventricles are:

    a. semilunar

    b. intraventricular

    c. mesenteric

    d. chordae tendinae

    e. fibrotic

4. The pacemaker of heart rhythm is the:

    a. AV node

    b. bundle branch

    c. SA node

    d. coronary sinus

    e. PVC

5. **Marginal, interventricular,** and **circumflex** are all terms applied to heart:

    a. veins

    b. capillaries

    c. arteries

    d. tendons

    e. muscles

6. Components of a pacemaker:

    a. battery

    b. electronic circuits

    c. computer memory

    d. all of the above

    e. none of the above

7. The term **visceral** pertains to:

    a. an artery

    b. a vein

    c. a capillary

    d. the aorta

    e. an internal organ

8. Capillary exchange occurs by:

    a. infusion

    b. transfusion

    c. perfusion

    d. diffusion

    e. effusion

T. **Each of the following medical terms is defined—you need to fill in the missing element(s) to complete the word for the last column.** Fill in the blanks.

Definition	Prefix	Root/CF	Suffix	Complete Medical Term
Increases urine production	di		ic	
Affects contractility of cardiac muscle			tropic	
Relating to autonomic nervous system		adren		
Ultrasound to record cardiac function		echo		
One who records sound waves		sono		
Agents that affect heart rate			tropic	
Surgical destruction of a tissue's function			ion	
Surgical intervention on a blood vessel		angio		

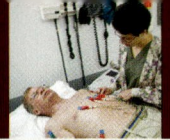

CARDIOVASCULAR SYSTEM

U. **Knowledge of pharmacology is essential to be certain your patients are receiving the correct drugs for their conditions.** Listed below are six types of cardiac drugs in use. List the main function for each drug, then give an example of that type of drug.

Drug Type	Function of the Drug	Example
vasodilators		
inotropic drugs		
anticoagulants		
antiarrhythmic drugs		
chronotropic drugs		
diuretics		

V. Determine which type of drug listed in exercise U. would be prescribed for the following conditions:

1. Patient has hypertension _____

2. Patient suffers from atrial fibrillation _____

3. Patient has excessive platelets _____
    (*Critical thinking:* Based on your knowledge of Chapter 7, what then is likely to form, and is that a problem?

    _____)

    _____

4. Based on studies, patient has poor cardiac output _____

5. Patient has tachycardia: this drug attempts to alter that rate _____

6. Patient has CHF and needs a _____ to reduce fluid volume.

W. **Discussion Question: Regurgitation** means to *flow backward*. In this chapter, regurgitation through the heart valve is discussed. What previous chapter discusses regurgitation of another type? What body system is that present in? Describe that regurgitation as compared with cardiac regurgitation. How are they similar? How are they different? Write your notes below.

_____

_____

_____

X. **The cardiac cycle can be heard through the stethoscope.** Apply the correct terms in the appropriate place to describe what happens in the chambers of the heart during the cardiac cycle. One term you will use twice. Three terms you will not use at all.

atrial diastole	relax	heartbeat	atrial systole	ventricular systole
atria	ventricular diastole	contraction	contract	murmur

1. When the atria _____, called _____ (atrial emptying), the ventricles _____, called _____ (or ventricular filling).

2. When the atria relax, called _____, the ventricles _____, called _____.

3. Then the atria and ventricles all relax briefly. This series of events is the complete cardiac cycle or _____.

Y. **The following elements are all roots or combining forms.** Write the meaning of the root/CF, then demonstrate its use with a medical term containing that element. Fill in the blanks.

Root/Combining Form	Meaning of Root/CF	Medical Term Containing that Root/CF
coron		
cost		
diaphoret		
isch		
lun		
palpit		
resuscitat		
stetho		
tampon		
viscer		

CARDIOVASCULAR SYSTEM

Z. **You are mentoring a new CVT who has just been hired in the Cardiology Department in Fulwood Medical Center.** Because you have been on the job for a while, you should be able to explain to him the difference between:

1. Heart valve stenosis and heart valve incompetency

   _____

   _____

   _____

   _____

   _____

2. A thrombus and an embolus

   _____

   _____

   _____

   _____

   _____

3. Essential hypertension, secondary hypertension, and malignant hypertension

   _____

   _____

   _____

   _____

   _____

AA. Cardiac terminology can be complex. Test yourself on the following terms to demonstrate your understanding of the medical language. Use some answers more than once. This exercise will self-correct.

_____ 1. fluid from tissue or capillary   R. artery

_____ 2. heart attack   Y. exudate

_____ 3. death of cells   C. valve

_____ 4. cut off blood supply   T. coronary sinus

_____ 5. blood goes from here to a capillary   E. parietal pericardium

_____ 6. serous cells are here   U. necrosis

_____ 7. murmur signifies abnormal   O. myocardial infarction

_____ 8. ischemia + necrosis =   A. ischemia

_____ 9. circumflex

_____ 10. interventricular

_____ 11. attached inferiorly to diaphragm

_____ 12. prevents backflow of blood

_____ 13. opens into right atrium

BB. Abbreviations are present throughout medical documentation and you must be absolutely certain you are interpreting them correctly. Fill in the correct abbreviation in the following patient documentation. All of the abbreviations contain some combination of the following letters. You will have to use some letters more than once.

A   C   D   F   H   I   M   P   S   V   O

1. Studies show the patient has a hole in the interventricular septum allowing blood to shunt from the higher pressure left ventricle to the lower pressure right ventricle. Abbreviation for the diagnosis: _____

2. The pediatric cardiologist was called to the Neonatal Unit because the baby's fetal blood vessel had not closed normally. He was diagnosed with _____.

3. The patient's arterial vessels have become dangerously narrowed due to his _____, and an angioplasty will be scheduled.

4. Due to her sedentary lifestyle, obesity, hypertension, and smoking history, the patient is at great risk for _____.

5. This patient's left ventricle is failing because it cannot pump out the blood it receives. He is going into _____.

6. Infant male was born with Tetralogy of Fallot (_____) syndrome. This is a form of _____.

7. This patient's ischemic attack resulted in occlusion of her coronary artery and a(n) _____ followed.

Upper Respiratory Tract

OBJECTIVES

The **upper respiratory tract** consists of the nose, pharynx, and trachea. It is the first site that brings air and its pollutants inside your bodies. As health professionals, it's important that you understand the roles of the upper respiratory tract in trying to protect you, as well as enabling you to live by transporting oxygen into your body.

The information in this lesson will enable you to:

- **Trace the flow of air from the nose through the pharynx and larynx.**
- **Relate the function of any segment of the upper airway to its structure.**
- **Define the protective mechanisms of the upper respiratory tract.**
- **Describe how sound is produced.**
- **Explain how smells are recognized.**
- **Describe common disorders of the upper respiratory tract.**

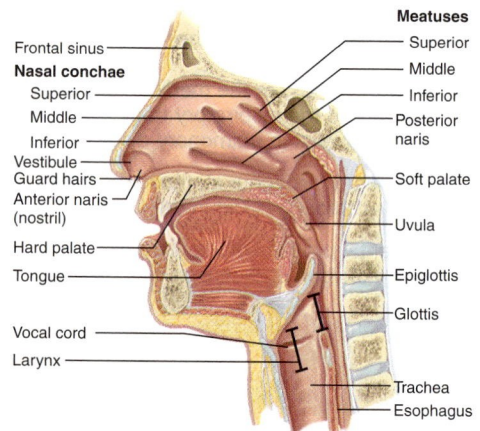

▲ **FIGURE 9.3   Upper Respiratory Tract.**

Keynote

Your nose is the first line of defense against pollutants.

NOSE

When you breathe in air through your nose, the air goes through the nostrils (**nares**) into the **vestibule** of the **nasal cavity.** The nares are guarded by internal hairs to prevent the entry of large particles.

The nasal cavity is divided by the nasal **septum** into right and left compartments. On the lateral wall of each nasal cavity, three bony ridges called **conchae (turbinate bones)** stick out into each cavity. Beneath each **concha** is a passageway called a **meatus** *(Figure 9.3).* The palate *(see Chapter 6)* forms the floor of the nose.

The nasal cavity is lined with a mucous membrane (mucosa) containing goblet cells that secrete mucus. Mucus forms a protective layer that can trap particles of dust and solid pollutants.

The **paranasal,** frontal, and maxillary sinuses open into the nose. Because they are hollow, the functions of these sinuses are to reduce the weight of the skull and to act as resonating chambers for the sounds of the voice. If your sinuses are congested your voice loses its normal quality.

Functions of the Nose

- **Passageway for air**—the palate is the floor of the nasal cavity that separates it from the mouth and enables you to breathe even with food in your mouth.
- **Air cleanser**—the hairs in the vestibule trap some of the large particles in the air.
- **Air moisturizer**—moisture from nasal mucus and from tears that drain into the cavity through the nasolacrimal duct *(see Chapter 4)* is added to the air.
- **Air warmer**—the blood flowing through the nasal cavity beneath the mucous membrane also warms the air. This prevents damage from the cold to the more fragile lower respiratory passages.
- **Sense of smell (olfaction)**—the olfactory region recognizes some 4000 separate smells.

Disorders of the Nose

Common cold is a viral **upper respiratory infection (URI).** It is contagious, being transmitted from person to person in airborne droplets from coughing and sneezing. There is no proven effective treatment.

Rhinitis is an inflammation of the nasal mucosa, usually viral in origin. It is also called **coryza.**

Allergic rhinitis affects 15 to 20% of the population. There is swelling of the mucous membranes of the nose, pharynx, and sinuses, with a clear watery discharge.

Sinusitis is an infection of the paranasal sinuses, often following a cold. The infection can be bacterial, producing a **mucopurulent** discharge from the nose. Treatment with **antibiotics** and decongestants is indicated.

Abbreviation	
URI	upper respiratory infection

WORD	PRONUNCIATION	ELEMENTS		DEFINITION
cautery	KAW-ter-ee		Greek *a branding iron*	Agent or device used to burn or scar a tissue
concha conchae (pl)	KON-kah KON-kee		Latin *shell*	Shell-shaped bone on the medial wall of the nasal cavity
coryza (also called rhinitis)	ko-RYE-zah		Greek *catarrh*	Viral inflammation of the mucous membrane of the nose
epistaxis	ep-ih-STAK-sis	S/ P/ R/	-is *condition* epi- *above, over* -stax- *fall in drops*	Nosebleed
meatus	me-AY-tus		Latin *a passage*	Passage or channel; also used to denote the external opening of a passage
mucopurulent	myu-koh-PYUR-you-lent	S/ R/CF R/	-ent *forming* muc/o- *mucus* -purul- *pus*	Mixture of pus and mucus
naris nares (pl)	NAH-ris NAH-rez		Latin *nostril*	Nostril
nasal	NAY-zal	S/ R/	-al *pertaining to* nas- *nose*	Pertaining to the nose
paranasal	PAR-ah NAY-zal	P/	para- *adjacent to*	Adjacent to the nose
rhinitis (also called coryza)	rye-NI-tis	S/ R/	-itis *inflammation* rhin- *nose*	Inflammation of the nasal mucosa
turbinate	TUR-bin-ate		Latin *shaped like a top*	Another name for the nasal conchae on the lateral walls of the nasal cavity

Deviated nasal septum occurs when the partition between the two nostrils is pushed to one side, leading to a partially obstructed airway in one nostril.

Epistaxis is bleeding from the septum of the nose, usually from trauma. If pinching the nose or packing the nostril with gauze does not stop the bleeding, **cautery** (burning and scarring) with silver nitrate or electrical cautery is indicated.

EXERCISES

Elements. *Work with elements to build your knowledge of the* **language of pulmonology**. *One element in each of the following medical terms is bold, italic. Identify the type of element (P, R, CF, S) in column 2, then write the meaning of that element in column 3. Fill in the blanks.*

Medical Term	Type of Element	Meaning of Element
epis*tax*is		
*rhin*itis		
muco*purul*ent		
*para*nasal		
*nas*al		

There are two elements in this list with the same meaning. What are they?

_____ and _____ .

Both mean: _____ .

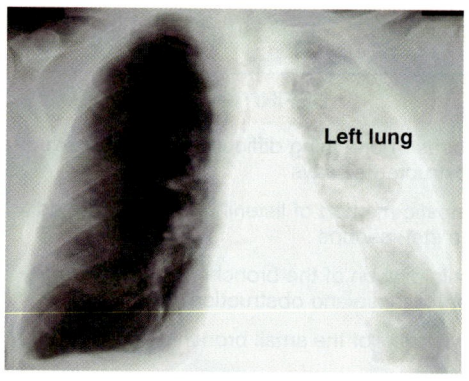

▲ FIGURE 9.18 Chest x-ray of Patient with Pneumonia in the Left Lung. A normal lung appears as a black space on an x-ray because its spongy structure is filled with air. In contrast, a pneumonic lung appears white or opaque on an x-ray as a result of accumulation of fluid and cells in the alveoli.

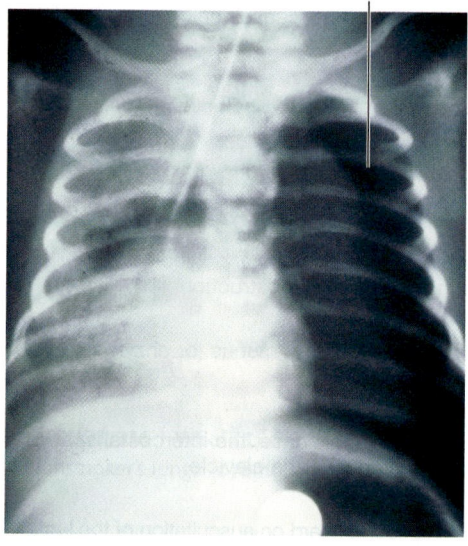

▲ FIGURE 9.19 Left Pneumothorax. There are no lung markings seen in the area of the pneumothorax.

Abbreviations

ARDS adult respiratory distress syndrome
ARF acute respiratory failure
NRDS neonatal respiratory distress syndrome

DISORDERS OF LOWER RESPIRATORY TRACT (continued)

Pneumonia is an acute infection affecting the alveoli and lung parenchyma *(Figure 9.18)*. Bacterial infections focus on the alveoli, viral infections on the parenchyma. **Lobar pneumonia** is an infection limited to one lung lobe. **Bronchopneumonia** is used to describe an infection in the bronchioles that spreads to the alveoli.

When an area of the lung (**segment**) or a lobe becomes airless as a result of the infection, the lung is **consolidated.** When an area of the lung collapses as a result of bronchial obstruction, it is called **atelectasis.**

Pleurisy, an inflammation of the pleurae, can be a complication of pneumonia. This condition is very painful on breathing because the parietal pleura is very pain sensitive. The inflammation often leads to an exudate accumulating in the pleural cavity. This is a **pleural effusion.** If the pleural effusion contains pus, it is called **empyema.** If it contains blood, it is called **hemothorax.** When pleural fluid is drawn off therapeutically or for laboratory analysis, the procedure is **aspiration** or **thoracentesis.**

Lung abscess can be a complication of bacterial pneumonia or cancer. Long-term antibiotics are used and surgical resection of the abscess may be required.

Pneumothorax is the entry of air into the pleural cavity *(Figure 9.19)*. The cause can be unknown (**spontaneous pneumothorax),** but it often results from trauma when a fractured rib, knife blade, or bullet lacerates the parietal pleura.

Thromboembolism is caused by an embolus, usually arising in the deep vein of the calf and lodging in a branch of the pulmonary artery. This cuts off the blood supply to an area of the lung. The symptoms are chest pain, dyspnea, tachypnea (increased respiratory rate) and a reduction in blood oxygen levels.

Adult respiratory distress syndrome (ARDS) is sudden life-threatening lung failure caused by a variety of underlying conditions, from major trauma to sepsis. The alveoli fill with fluid and collapse, and gas exchange is shut down. Hypoxia results. Mechanical ventilation has to be provided. The mortality is from 35 to 50%.

Neonatal respiratory distress syndrome (NRDS) is seen in premature babies whose lungs have not matured enough to produce surfactant. The alveoli collapse, and mechanical ventilation is needed to keep them open.

Chronic infections of the lung parenchyma are the result of prolonged exposure to infection or to occupational irritant dusts or droplets. These disorders are called **pneumoconioses.** Levels of dust inhalation overwhelm the airways' particle-clearing abilities; the dust particles accumulate in the alveoli and parenchyma, leading to fibrosis. **Asbestosis** is from inhaling asbestos particles and can lead to a cancer (**mesothelioma**) in the pleura. **Silicosis** from silica particles is called stone mason's disease. **Anthracosis** from coal dust particles is called coal miners' disease. **Sarcoidosis** is an idiopathic fibrotic disorder of the lung parenchyma.

Pulmonary tuberculosis is a chronic, infectious disease of the lungs *(see Chapter 20).*

Lung cancer, related to tobacco use, used to be a male disease, but now fatalities in women from lung cancer exceed those from breast cancer. Ninety percent of lung cancers arise in the mucous membranes of the larger bronchi and are called **bronchogenic carcinomas.** The tumor obstructs the bronchus, spreads into the surrounding lung tissues, and metastasizes to lymph nodes, liver, brain, and bone.

Flail chest occurs when a segment of the chest wall is separated from the rest of the thoracic cage. A free or separated segment occurs when there are two fractures in each of three adjoining ribs. This free segment flails and is unable to contribute to chest expansion. Flail chest is produced by blunt trauma, such as in a motor vehicle accident, and is associated with underlying damage to the lung.

Acute respiratory failure (ARF) is abnormal respiratory function resulting in inadequate tissue oxygenation or carbon dioxide elimination that is severe enough to impair vital organ functions. Causes of ARF include congestive heart failure (CHF); COPD; chest trauma with resultant flail chest; spinal cord injury; and neuromuscular disorders when the muscles of respiration are paralyzed. Endotracheal intubation and mechanical ventilation are used until the underlying cause is treated, if possible.

WORD ANALYSIS AND DEFINITION

WORD	PRONUNCIATION	ELEMENTS		DEFINITION
anthracosis	an-thra-**KOH**-sis	S/	-osis *condition*	Lung disease caused by the inhalation of coal dust
		R/	anthrac- *coal*	
asbestosis	as-bes-**TOE**-sis	S/	-osis *condition*	Lung disease caused by the inhalation of asbestos particles
		R/	asbest- *asbestos*	
aspiration	**AS**-pih-**RAY**-shun	S/	-ion *process*	Removal by suction of fluid or gas from a body cavity
		R/	aspirat- *to breathe*	
atelectasis	at-el-**ECK**-tah-sis	S/	-ectasis *dilation*	Collapse of part of a lung
		R/	atel- *incomplete*	
bronchogenic	brong-koh-**JEN**-ik	S/	-genic *creation*	Arising from a bronchus
		R/CF	bronch/o- *bronchus*	
bronchopneumonia	**BRONG**-koh-new-**MOH**-nee-ah	S/	-ia *condition*	Acute inflammation of the walls of smaller bronchioles with spread to lung parenchyma
		R/	-pneumon- *air, lung*	
		R/CF	bronch/o- *bronchus*	
empyema	**EM**-pie-**EE**-mah	S/	-ema *result*	Pus in a body cavity, particularly in the pleural cavity
		P/	em- *in*	
		R/	-py- *pus*	
hemothorax	he-moh-**THOR**-ax	R/CF	hem/o- *blood*	Blood in the pleural cavity
		R/	-thorax *chest*	
mesothelioma	**MEZ**-oh-thee-lee-**OH**-mah	S/	-oma *tumor, mass*	Cancer arising from the cells lining the pleura or peritoneum
		P/	meso- *middle*	
		R/CF	-thel/i- *lining*	
pneumonia	new-**MOH**-nee-ah	S/	-ia *condition*	Inflammation of the lung parenchyma
		R/	-pneumon- *air, lung*	
pneumonitis (syn)	nu-moh-**NI**-tis	S/	-itis *inflammation*	
pneumoconiosis	new-moh-koh-nee-**OH**-sis	S/	-osis *condition*	Fibrotic lung disease caused by the inhalation of different dusts
		R/	-coni- *dust*	
		R/CF	pneum/o- *air, lung*	
pneumothorax	new-moh-**THOR**-ax	R/CF	pneum/o- *air, lung*	Air in the pleural cavity
		R/	-thorax *chest*	
sarcoidosis (*Note:* Two suffixes.)	sar-koy-**DOH**-sis	S/	-osis *condition*	Granulomatous lesions of lungs and other organs; cause is unknown
		S/	-oid- *resembling*	
		R/	sarc- *sarcoma*	
silicosis	sil-ih-**KOH**-sis	S/	-osis *condition*	Fibrotic lung disease from inhaling silica particles
		R/	silic- *silicon*	
thoracentesis (also called **pleural tap**)	**THOR**-ah-sen-**TEE**-sis	S/	-centesis *puncture*	Insertion of a needle into the pleural cavity to withdraw fluid or air
		R/	thora- *chest*	
thromboembolism	**THROM**-boh-**EM**-boh-lizm	S/	-ism *condition*	A piece of detached blood clot (embolus) blocking a distant blood vessel
		R/CF	thromb/o- *blood clot*	
		R/	-embol- *plug*	
tuberculosis	too-**BER**-kyu-**LOW**-sis	S/	-osis *condition*	Infectious disease that can infect any organ or tissue
		R/	tubercul- *nodule*	

EXERCISES

Suffixes. *This WAD contains a lot of suffixes you will see again in later chapters for other medical terms. Confirm your knowledge of suffixes by filling in the chart with the correct meaning for the element.*

Suffix	Meaning of Suffix	Medical Term with This Suffix
-centesis		
-ectasis		
-ema		
-genic		
-ia		

PULMONARY FUNCTION TESTS (PFTs)

A **spirometer** is a device to measure the **volume** of air that moves in and out of the respiratory system *(Figure 9.20)*. You ask the patient to breathe in as deeply as possible and then breathe out as rapidly and completely as possible through the spirometer. The volume of air expired at the end of the test is the patient's **forced vital capacity (FVC)**.

The spirometer also measures **flow rates**. The **forced expiratory volume in one second (FEV_1)** is the amount of air expired in the first second of the test.

In obstructive lung disorders such as asthma or COPD, the lumina of the airways are constricted and resistant to airflow. This will cause a reduction in the FEV_1.

In restrictive lung disorders in which the lung tissue is fibrotic or scarred and resists expansion, there will be a reduction in the FVC.

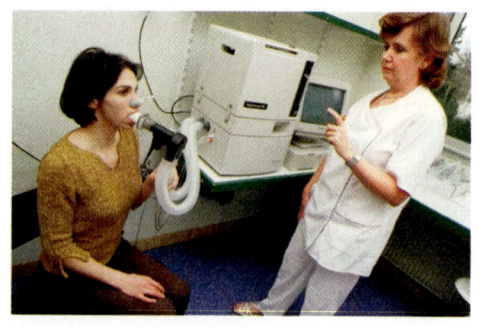

▲ **FIGURE 9.20   Spirometer.**

Keynote

Measure pulmonary function with spirometer, peak flow meter, and arterial blood gases.

Abbreviations

FEV_1	forced expiratory volume in one second
FVC	forced vital capacity
PEFR	peak expiratory flow rate
PFT	pulmonary function test

Case Report 9.1 (continued)

In Mr. Jacobs, his FEV_1 was only 40% of the predicted value for a man of his age, height, and weight. Mr. Jacobs' FVC was also reduced because of the fibrotic effects of repeated infections on his lung tissues reducing the volume in his airways. Off oxygen, Mr Jacobs' oxygen levels were below 50% of normal. Even with nasal prongs and oxygen, his blood oxygen levels were only 75% of normal.

A **peak flow meter** records the greatest flow of air that can be sustained for 10 milliseconds on forced expiration, the **peak expiratory flow rate (PEFR)**. It is of value in following the course of asthma and in postoperative care to monitor the return of lung function after anesthesia.

Arterial blood gases, the measurement of the levels of oxygen and carbon dioxide in the blood, are good indicators of respiratory function.

Pulmonary Pharmacology

- **Bronchodilators** relax the smooth muscles of the bronchioles. Examples are theophylline, $beta_2$-agonists (such as salbutamol and terbutaline), and anticholinergics (such as ipratropium bromide).

- **Anti-inflammatory** drugs, such as corticosteroids, are best given by inhalation but can be used orally or intravenously in acute episodes of asthma or COPD.

- **Mucolytics** are agents that break up mucus to allow it to be cleared more effectively from the airways. Examples are guaifenesin (common in over-the-counter cough medications), potassium iodide, and *N*-acetylcysteine taken through a **nebulizer.**

- **Antibiotics** are used when a bacterial infection is present. Penicillin, erythromycin, cefotaxime, and flucloxacillin are frequently used.

- **Oxygen** is used in hypoxia and can be given by nasal **cannula** or by mask and intubation. Patients with severe, chronic COPD can be attached to a portable cylinder of oxygen.

WORD	PRONUNCIATION	ELEMENTS		DEFINITION
bronchodilator	**BRONG**-koh-die-**LAY**-tor	S/ R/CF R/	**-or** *one who does* **bronch/o-** *bronchus* **-dilat-** *expand*	Agent that increases the diameter of a bronchus
cannula	**KAN**-you-lah		Latin *reed*	Tube inserted into a blood vessel or cavity as a channel for fluid
mucolytic	**MYU**-koh-**LIT**-ik	S/ R/CF R/	**-ic** *pertaining to* **muc/o-** *mucus* **-lyt-** *dissolve*	Agent capable of dissolving or liquefying mucus
nebulizer	**NEB**-you-liz-er	S/ R/	**-izer** *line of action* **nebul-** *cloud*	Device used to deliver liquid medicine in a fine mist
oxygen	**OCK**-see-jen	S/ R/	**-gen** *form, create* **oxy-** *sharp, acid*	The gas essential for life
spirometer	spy-**ROM**-eh-ter	S/ R/CF	**-meter** *measure* **spir/o-** *breathe*	An instrument used to measure respiratory volumes

EXERCISES

Deconstruct each of these medical terms into basic elements. Define the elements, then use each in a sentence that is not a definition to demonstrate that you understand the term's meaning. Fill in the blanks.

Medical Term	Meaning of Prefix	Meaning of Root/CF	Meaning of Suffix
nebulizer			
oxygen			
mucolytic			
bronchodilator			

1. _____

   _____

2. _____

   _____

3. _____

   _____

4. _____

   _____

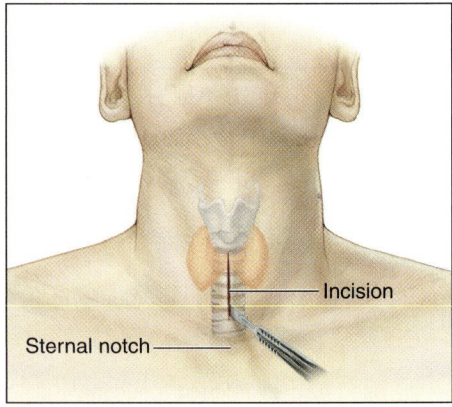

① Tracheotomy incision is made superior to sternal notch.

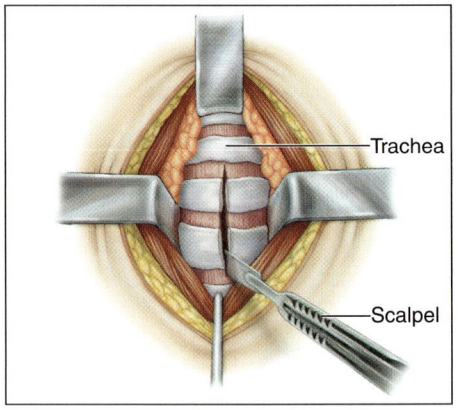

② Retractors separate the tissue, and an incision is made through the third and fourth tracheal rings.

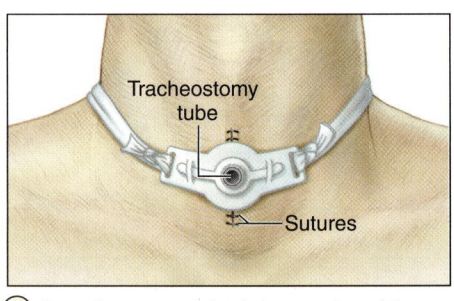

③ A tracheostomy tube is inserted, and the remaining incision is sutured closed.

▲ **FIGURE 9.21 Tracheostomy Procedure.**

Abbreviations

AP	anteroposterior
CPAP	continuous positive airway pressure
CT	computed tomography
CXR	chest x-ray
MRA	magnetic resonance angiography
PA	posteroanterior
PDT	postural drainage therapy
PEEP	positive end-expiratory pressure
PET	positron emission tomography

DIAGNOSTIC AND THERAPEUTIC PROCEDURES

Diagnostic Procedures

Chest x-ray (CXR) is a radiograph image of the chest taken in **anteroposterior (AP)**, **posteroanterior (PA)**, lateral, and sometimes oblique and lateral decubitus positions.

Computed tomography (CT), **angiography** of the pulmonary circulation using contrast materials, **magnetic resonance angiography (MRA)** to define emboli in the pulmonary arteries, and **ultrasonography** of the pleural space are chest imaging techniques in current use. **Positron emission tomography (PET)** can sometimes distinguish benign from malignant lesions.

Bronchoscopy is a procedure to insert a fiber-optic endoscope into the bronchial tubes to visually examine the tubes, take a tissue biopsy, or a wash for secretions.

Mediastinoscopy is used to stage lung cancer and diagnose mediastinal masses. The mediastinoscope is inserted through an incision in the sternal notch.

Tracheal aspiration uses a soft catheter that allows brushings and washings to be performed to remove cells and secretions from the trachea and main bronchi. It can be passed through a tracheostomy or **endotracheal** tube or through the mouth or nose.

Thoracentesis is the insertion of a needle through an intercostal space to remove fluid from a pleural effusion for laboratory study or to relieve pressure. It is also called a **pleural tap.**

Thoracotomy is used to obtain an open biopsy of tissue from the lung, hilum, pleura, or mediastinum. It is performed through an intercostal incision under general anesthesia.

Therapeutic Procedures

Pulmonary rehabilitation includes education, breathing exercises and retraining, exercises for the upper and lower extremities, and psychosocial support.

Nutritional support is critical for patients who have difficulty breathing or who lose a lot of weight.

Immunizations are available against influenza and the pneumococcus bacterium, the most common cause of bacterial pneumonia.

Postural drainage therapy (PDT) uses gravity to promote drainage of secretions from lung segments by positioning and tilting the patient. Chest percussion (tapping) can help loosen, mobilize, and drain the retained secretions.

Continuous positive airway pressure (CPAP) is an attempt to keep alveoli open by maintaining a positive pressure in the airways. A mask is fitted over the nose and mouth and attached to a ventilator. This can be used at night when sleeping or used in acute situations in COPD.

Positive end-expiratory pressure (PEEP) is a technique in ventilation to keep the alveoli from collapsing in ARDS and NRDS.

Intubation uses an oropharyngeal airway in the unconscious patient during bag and mask ventilation to maintain an open airway. A tube is inserted to prevent the tongue from falling back to obstruct the airway and facilitates suctioning the airway. An **endotracheal intubation** involves the placement of a tube into the trachea. This allows patients to be placed on a ventilator and their breathing controlled.

Pulmonary resection is the surgical removal of lung tissue.

- **Wedge resection** is the removal of a small localized area of diseased lung.
- **Segmentectomy** is removal of lung tissue attached to a bronchus.
- **Lobectomy** is removal of a lobe.
- **Pneumonectomy** is removal of an entire lung.

Tracheotomy is an incision made into the trachea (windpipe) so that a temporary or permanent opening into the windpipe called a **tracheostomy** is created *(Figure 9.21)*. A tube is placed into the opening to provide an airway. A tracheostomy is used to maintain an airway when there is obstruction or paralysis in the respiratory structures above it.

Mechanical ventilation is a process by which gases are moved into and out of the lungs via a device that is set to meet the respiratory requirements of the patient. It requires a tracheostomy or endotracheal tube to be attached to the mechanical device (ventilator). It can augment or replace the patient's own ventilatory efforts.

WORD	PRONUNCIATION	ELEMENTS		DEFINITION
bronchoscope	**BRONG**-koh-skope	S/ R/CF	**-scope** *instrument used to examine*	Endoscope used for bronchoscopy
bronchoscopy	brong-**KOS**-koh-pee	S/	**bronch/o-** *bronchus* **-scopy** *examine*	Examination of the interior of the tracheo-bronchial tree with an endoscope
endotracheal	en-doh-**TRAY**-kee-al	S/ P/ R/CF	**-al** *pertaining to* **endo-** *inside* **-trach/e-** *trachea*	Pertaining to being inside the trachea
lobectomy	low-**BECK**-toe-me	S/ R/	**-ectomy** *surgical removal* **lob-** *lobe*	Surgical removal of a lobe of the lungs
mediastinoscopy	**ME**-dee-ass-tie-**NOS**-koh-pee	S/ R/CF	**-scopy** *examine* **mediastin/o-** *mediastinum*	Examination of the mediastinum using an endoscope
pneumonectomy	**NEW**-moh-**NECK**-toe-me	S/ R/	**-ectomy** *surgical removal* **pneumon-** *lung, air*	Surgical removal of a lung
resection	ree-**SEK**-shun	S/ P/ R/	**-ion** *action* **re-** *back* **-sect-** *cut off*	Removal of a specific part of an organ or structure
segmentectomy	seg-men-**TEK**-toe-me	S/ R/	**-ectomy** *surgical excision* **segment-** *a section*	Surgical excision of a segment of a tissue or organ
thoracotomy	thor-ah-**KOT**-oh-me	S/ R/CF	**-tomy** *incision* **thorac/o-** *chest*	Incision through the chest wall
tomography	toe-**MOG**-rah-fee	S/ R/	**-graphy** *recording* **tomo-** *slice*	Radiographic image of a selected slice of tissue
tracheostomy	tray-kee-**OST**-oh-me	S/ R/CF	**-stomy** *new opening* **trache/o-** *trachea*	Incision into the windpipe, usually so that a tube can be inserted to assist breathing
tracheotomy	tray-kee-**OT**-oh-me	S/	**-tomy** *surgical incision*	Incision made into the trachea to create a tracheostomy
ultrasonography	**UL**-trah-soh-**NOG**-rah-fee	S/ P/ R/CF	**-graphy** *recording* **ultra-** *beyond* **-son/o-** *sound*	Delineation of deep structures using sound waves

EXERCISES

Put the following elements into the right combinations to form medical terms for the definitions provided. Some elements you will use more than once; some elements you will not use at all. Fill in the blanks.

endo-	-ectomy	trans-	bronch/o-	-trache/o-	mediastin/o-
lob-	-al	-ator	pharyng/e-	pneumon-	immuniz-
-ation	-son/o-	-tomy	-trach/e-	in-	-scopy
-sect-	tomo-	re-	thorac/o-	-iasis	ventil-
-graphy	-ic	-stomy	hyper-	ultra-	-ion

1. surgical removal of a lung _____

2. examination of a bronchus _____

3. radiographic image of a selected slice of tissue _____

4. image of deep structures using sound waves _____

5. pertaining to being inside the trachea _____

6. removal of a specific part of an organ _____

7. incision through the chest wall _____

8. new opening in the neck to the trachea _____

RESPIRATORY SYSTEM

CHALLENGE YOUR KNOWLEDGE

A. **Interpretation:** Use your knowledge of the **language of pulmonology** to understand the case report and answer the following questions. Fill in the blanks.

> **CASE REPORT**
>
> Mr. Jude Jacobs, a 68-year-old white male, a retired mail carrier, is known to have COPD and is on continual oxygen by nasal prongs. He has smoked two packs a day for his adult life. Last night, he was unable to sleep because of increased shortness of breath and cough. His cough produced yellow sputum. He had to sit upright in bed to be able to breathe.
>
> Vital signs are: Temperature (T) 101.6°F, pulse (P) 98, respirations (R) 36, blood pressue (BP) 150/90. On examination, he was cyanotic, frightened, and had nasal prongs in his nose. Air entry is diminished in both lungs, and there are rales at both bases. You have been ordered to draw blood for arterial blood gases (ABGs) and to measure the amount of air entering and leaving his lungs using spirometry.

1. What disease appears in Mr. Jacobs' history?

   _____

2. Which particular symptom indicates Mr. Jacobs has an infection?

   _____

3. **Cyanotic** indicates an outward sign the physician can detect. What is it?

   _____

4. Rales heard through a stethoscope indicate the presence of what in the lungs?

   _____

5. What measure has been taken to restore the level of oxygen in Mr. Jacobs' blood?

   _____

6. What will be used to measure Mr. Jacobs' inspiration and expiration volumes?

   _____

B. **Word elements will always remain the best tool for deconstructing medical terminology.** Test your knowledge of respiratory word elements by breaking down the following medical terms. Fill in the chart.

Medical Term	Prefix	Root/CF	Suffix	Meaning of Term
hemothorax				
aspiration				
pneumonia				
bronchitis				
empyema				
pneumoconiosis				
mesothelioma				

Medical Term	Prefix	Root/CF	Suffix	Meaning of Term
tachypnea				
bronchogenic				
tracheotomy				

Choose the correct five of the preceding terms, to complete the following sentences.

1. This disease arises from the lining cells of the pleura: _____ .

2. Rapid breathing is also called: _____ .

3. Pleural effusion containing pus is also termed: _____ .

4. Anthracosis is a form of _____ .

5. Bloody pleural effusion is also termed: _____ .

C. **Terminology Challenge:** Remembering terminology from a previous body system studied—what is the difference between:

Hemoptysis

_____

Hematemesis

_____

What do both these terms have in common? _____

What two different body systems do they represent? _____ and _____ .

D. **Pharmacology:** For any body system, it is important to know the various types of medications and when they might be prescribed. Demonstrate your knowledge of pharmacology for the respiratory system by assigning the correct drug category in column 2 to the statements in column 1. The first one is done for you.

___D___ 1. Example: penicillin   A. bronchodilators

_____ 2. relax smooth muscles of the bronchioles   B. anti-inflammatories

_____ 3. corticosteroids   C. mucolytics

_____ 4. Example: potassium iodide   D. antibiotics

_____ 5. used in hypoxia   E. oxygen

_____ 6. used when a bacterial infection is present

_____ 7. Example: theophylline

_____ 8. best given by inhalation

_____ 9. administered by nasal cannula

_____ 10. breaks up mucus

_____ 11. used in acute episodes of asthma or COPD

_____ 12. can be administered using a nebulizer

CHAPTER 9 REVIEW

RESPIRATORY SYSTEM

Study Hint

When there are two elements with the same meaning, you must know them both and how to apply them.

E. **Roots:** Sometimes in medical terminology there can be two roots or combining forms with the same meaning. Pneum/o- and pulmon/o- are examples. These forms are not interchangeable—the medical term takes either one combining form or the other. Demonstrate your knowledge of the difference between the two elements by choosing the correct form for the terms listed below.

1. PFT is the abbreviation for what diagnostic test? _____

2. Acute infection affecting the alveoli and lung parenchyma: _____.

3. Entry of air into the pleural cavity is called: _____.

4. A specialist in the study of the lung is called a _____.

5. Surgical removal of a lung: _____.

6. COPD is the abbreviation for what lung disease? _____

7. Sarcoidosis is a form of which disease? _____

8. Study of the lungs and lung diseases is: _____

F. **In Your Own Words:** Do you understand the following terms well enough to explain the difference to patients if they should ask?

What is the difference between:

1. inspiration

   _____

   expiration

   _____

   aspiration

   _____

2. pneumothorax

   _____

   hemothorax

   _____

3. wedge resection

   _____

   segmentectomy

   _____

G. **Discussion Question:** Be prepared to discuss and define the **anatomical dead space.** Go online to see if you can find and print an illustration of this area to use in your discussion. Describe the process of inspiration and how the lung inflates. Be prepared to name all the organs in the thoracic cavity. Outline your discussion below.

_____

_____

_____

_____

_____

H. **Spelling:** The following terms come directly from Latin and Greek. A hint is given to you—choose the correct spelling. Circle the best answer.

1.	reed:	cannula	canula	canulla
2.	passage:	miatus	meatis	meatus
3.	shell:	conca	conka	concha
4.	branding iron:	cautiry	cautery	cautary
5.	lack of breath:	apenea	apnea	apnia
6.	throat:	pharynix	parynix	pharynx
7.	ring:	cricoid	crickoid	crecoid
8.	creaking sound:	strideor	stridore	stridor
9.	oblong shield:	thyrhoid	thiroyd	thyroid
10.	nerves enter and leave this area:	hylum	hilum	hylim

I. **Trace the Pathway:** The tracheobronchial tree begins with the trachea, which starts air on its pathway all the way down to the alveoli where gas exchange can occur. Trace this path by sequentially lettering the following choices A through H. The first one is done for you.

1. Each secondary bronchus divides into tertiary bronchi. _____

2. Bronchioles divide into several alveoli. _____

3. Bronchi enter the lung at the hilum. _____

4. Bronchioles divide into terminal bronchioles. _____

5. Main bronchi divide into a secondary bronchus for each lobe. _____

6. Tertiary bronchi divide into bronchioles. _____

7. Terminal bronchioles divide into smaller respiratory bronchioles. _____

8. At the carina, the trachea divides into right and left main bronchi. __A__

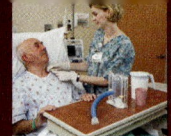
RESPIRATORY SYSTEM

J. **Interpretation:** How well do you understand what the physician has written? Translate this physician's order into plain English without any abbreviations. Fill in the blanks.

This patient is to have AP and lateral CXRs, followed by a CT, MRI, and PET scan STAT.

_____

_____

_____

K. **Build Terms:** The suffix -itis is one that you will meet over and over again in these chapters. Build the correct medical term to match its definition. Fill in the blanks.

1. inflammation of the bronchus   _____itis

2. inflammation of the organ of voice production   _____itis

3. inflammation of the tonsils   _____itis

4. inflammation of the throat   _____itis

5. inflammation of the nose   _____itis

6. inflammation of the epiglottis   _____itis

7. croup   _____itis

8. inflammation of the small bronchioles   _____itis

9. inflammation of the lungs   _____itis

L. **Recall and Review:** How well do you remember these word elements from the previous chapter? Try to answer without first looking back to check. Fill in the blanks.

Element	Type of Element (P, R, CF, S)	Meaning of Element
viscer		
inter		
um		
semi		
myo		

M. **Language of Pulmonology:** You are a new student in the Respiratory Therapy program. The following questions contain terminology you will use every day on the job. Answer the following questions correctly by circling the choice.

1. **Cyanosis** signals deficient oxygenation of blood and will turn nail beds:

    a. yellow

    b. red

    c. black

    d. white

    e. blue

2. The term **respiration** can mean:

    a. ventilation

    b. cellular metabolism

    c. exchange of gases

    d. all of these

    e. none of these

3. Shell-shaped bone in the nose:

    a. meatus

    b. concha

    c. nares

    d. vestibule

    e. choana

4. Which medical term can be associated with mucopurulent discharge?

    a. pleurisy

    b. sinusitis

    c. epistaxis

    d. pneumonia

    e. nasal polyps

5. A segment of the chest wall separates from the rest of the thoracic cage in:

    a. pneumoconiosis

    b. epiglottitis

    c. flail chest

    d. thoracentesis

    e. ARF

6. **Cautery** can be performed electrically or chemically. What is its purpose?

    a. to burn a tissue

    b. to scar a tissue

    c. to stop bleeding

    d. all of the above

    e. none of the above

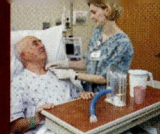
RESPIRATORY SYSTEM

N. Analyze: Knowledge of medical terms includes choosing the correct term for the meaning you want to convey either verbally or in documentation. Analyze the suffixes to help you choose the term. Use the following medical terms to fill in the statements all relating to the bronchus.

bronchogenic	**bronchi**	**bronchopneumonia**	**bronchioles**	**bronchiolitis**
bronchus	**bronchial asthma**	**bronchial**	**bronchitis**	**bronchiectasis**

> ### Study Hint
> In the term **broncho-pneumonia**, the combining form is used, and it is one word. In the term **bronchial asthma**, the suffix -al makes it an adjective, and the two words are separated.

1. Greek word for *windpipe*: _____

2. Plural of the word in question 1: _____

3. Pertaining to the windpipe: _____

4. Tertiary bronchi divide into these: _____

5. Inflammation of the bronchus: _____

6. Abnormal dilation of bronchioles due to repeated infections: _____

7. Infection in the bronchioles that usually spreads to the alveoli: _____

8. Inflammation of the bronchioles: _____

9. Recurrent acute episodes of bronchial obstruction due to constriction: _____

10. Arising from a bronchus: _____

Now, using the word elements below, build new terms relating to the bronchus. Your root or combining form will still be bronch/o-.

malacia	**stenosis**	**plasty**
scope	**pathy**	**pulmonary**
staxis	**scopy**	**dilator**
dilation	**gram**	**ostomy**

1. An instrument used to see into the bronchus: _____

2. Drug meant to open bronchial passages: _____

3. A softening or deficiency in the wall of a bronchus: _____

4. Surgical procedure doing plastic repair on a bronchus: _____

5. Any disease of a bronchus: _____

6. Pertaining to the bronchus and the lung: _____

7. Widening the area of the bronchus: _____

8. Bleeding in the bronchus: _____

9. The procedure of viewing into the bronchus: _____

10. Constriction or narrowing of the bronchus: _____

11. The record obtained by bronchography: _____

12. Surgical creation of an opening into the bronchus: _____

O. **Procedures.** You are the coder in the General Surgery department at Fulwood Medical Center. Using your medical terminology skills, fill in the correct codes for the following procedures.

Procedure	CPT Code
bronchoscopy	31622
laryngectomy	31360
lobectomy	32480
mediastinoscopy	39400
pneumonectomy	32440
polypectomy	31237
thoracentesis	32000
thoracotomy	32100
tonsillectomy	42825
tracheostomy	31600

1. Patient was admitted for removal of lymphatic tissue at the back of his throat: _____

2. A new airway was created for the patient: _____

3. Benign growths from the mucosa were removed: _____

4. Diagnostic procedure with cell washings: _____

5. Pleural fluid was drawn off for lab analysis: _____

6. Entire lung was removed due to metastasis: _____

7. Examination for lung cancer staging and possible masses: _____

8. Left lower lobe removed from lung: _____

9. Patient's chest was entered to explore for cause of bleeding: _____

10. Tumor was removed; vocal cords were sacrificed: _____

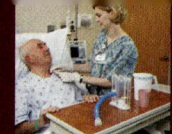

CHAPTER 9 REVIEW

RESPIRATORY SYSTEM

P. **Translate from medical language to layman's language.** Take the following statement and translate it into layman's language. First, write a simple version of the medical terms in italics. Then reconstruct the sentence in language a nonmedical person could understand. Use your glossary or search online for any terms you can't recall. Fill in the blanks.

1. *Sarcoidosis* is an *idiopathic fibrotic* disorder of the lung *parenchyma*.

   sarcoidosis _____

   idiopathic _____

   fibrotic _____

   parenchyma _____

   Sentence:

   _____

   _____

   _____

Q. **Abbreviations are meant to save time, but you must interpret them correctly.** Write out the meaning for the abbreviations in the following exercise.

1. You have been ordered to draw blood for Mr. Jacobs' ABGs.

   _____

2. Increased viscosity of secretions from the lungs leads to the conclusion this patient has CF.

   _____

3. PEEP is a technique in ventilation to keep the alveoli from collapsing.

   _____

4. Patient suffers from dyspnea and is SOB.

   _____

5. Mrs. White was prescribed medication for her URI.

   _____

6. This patient has been on a ventilator for a week; diagnosis is either ARDS or ARF.

   _____

7. PA view of the chest is all that is needed right now.

   _____

8. Mrs. Black is experiencing CAO due to her COPD.

   _____

R. **Test-taking skills.** Employ your test-taking skills when you answer multiple choice questions. Start by immediately crossing off answers you know to be incorrect. With the choices you have left, one answer will clearly be the *best* choice. Circle the best choice.

1. The hair-like structures in the nasal cavity are called:

   a. polyps

   b. cilia

   c. adenoids

   d. bullae

   e. trachealis

2. What is the total number of lobes in *both* lungs?

   a. 4

   b. 5

   c. 6

   d. 2

   e. 3

3. What exactly is a lobe?

   a. an opening into an organ

   b. an exit from an organ

   c. a subdivision of an organ

   d. a blood reservoir in an organ

   e. a pathway through an organ

4. An instrument used to measure breathing volume is called:

   a. bronchoscope

   b. spirometer

   c. endoscope

   d. tenometer

   e. sphygmomanometer

5. What is a surfactant?

   a. creates surface tension

   b. a detergent-like substance

   c. keeps alveolar sacs from collapsing

   d. all of the above

   e. none of the above

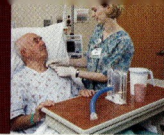
RESPIRATORY SYSTEM

S. **Test-taking skills.** Employ your test-taking skills when you answer multiple choice questions. Start by immediately crossing off answers you know to be incorrect. With the choices you have left, one answer will clearly be the *best* choice. Circle the best choice.

1. The measure of the capacity of a chamber or hollow viscus to expand is called:

   a. expectorate

   b. idiopathic

   c. compliance

   d. postural drainage

   e. consolidation

2. What is another name for the nasal **conchae** on the lateral wall of each nasal cavity?

   a. meatus

   b. choana

   c. nares

   d. turbinates

   e. septum

3. A bubblelike structure is called a:

   a. bronchiole

   b. barbiturate

   c. bulla

   d. bronchus

   e. bradypnea

4. Cellular metabolism is another name for:

   a. external respiration

   b. aspiration

   c. internal respiration

   d. exhalation

   e. olfaction

5. What is another term for heart failure?

   a. cyanosis

   b. conchae

   c. choana

   d. cor pulmonale

   e. chordae tendinae

6. Laryngeal polyps are:

    a. benign tumors of the larynx

    b. treated by excision

    c. papillomas

    d. all of the above

    e. none of the above

7. The medical term for the nostrils is:

    a. nares

    b. adenoids

    c. polyps

    d. tonsils

    e. papillomas

T. **Plurals.** Refresh your memory for the rules of plurals with the following exercise. Check (✓) whether the given medical term is the singular or plural form. If it is singular, fill in the plural; if it is plural, fill in the singular form. Then write the meaning of the term. Fill in the chart.

Medical Term	Singular	Plural	Meaning of Medical Term
alveolus			
cilia			
rale			
conchae			
naris			
bulla			
rhonchi			

CRANIAL NERVES

To function, the brain must communicate with the rest of the body, and it does this through the spinal cord and the **cranial nerves.** Twelve pairs of cranial nerves arise from the base of the brain *(Figure 10.12).*

The two pairs of nerves for smell and vision contain only sensory fibers. The other ten pairs are mixed nerves containing sensory and motor and parasympathetic fibers. The cranial nerves have, from front to back, both names and numbers. The latter are always written in Roman numerals *(Table 10.1).*

FIGURE 10.12   Cranial Nerves. ▶
Base of brain showing origins of the 12 cranial nerves.

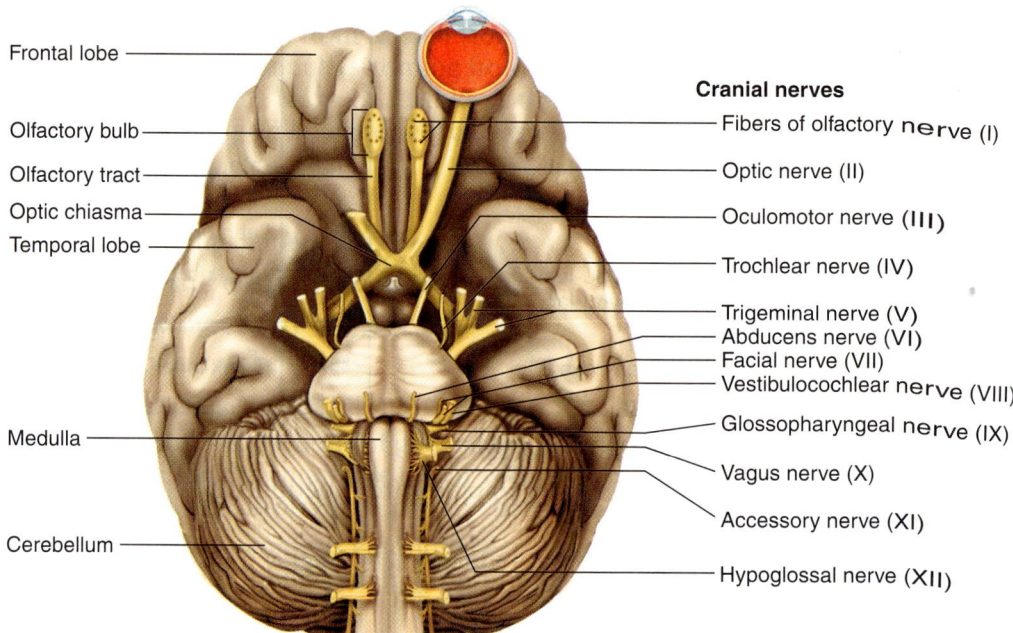

Frontal lobe

Olfactory bulb
Olfactory tract
Optic chiasma
Temporal lobe

Medulla

Cerebellum

Cranial nerves
Fibers of olfactory nerve (I)
Optic nerve (II)
Oculomotor nerve (III)
Trochlear nerve (IV)
Trigeminal nerve (V)
Abducens nerve (VI)
Facial nerve (VII)
Vestibulocochlear nerve (VIII)
Glossopharyngeal nerve (IX)
Vagus nerve (X)
Accessory nerve (XI)
Hypoglossal nerve (XII)

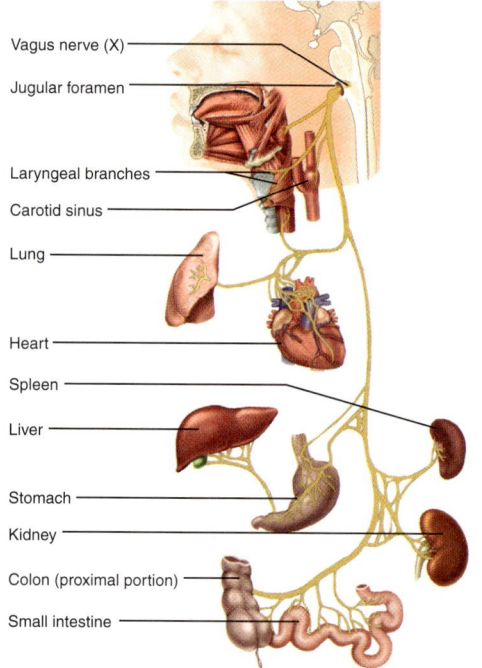

Vagus nerve (X)
Jugular foramen
Laryngeal branches
Carotid sinus
Lung
Heart
Spleen
Liver
Stomach
Kidney
Colon (proximal portion)
Small intestine

▲ **FIGURE 10.13   Left Vagus Nerve.**

TABLE 10.1 Cranial Nerves

Roman Numeral	Name	Description
I	**Olfactory** nerves	Sensory nerves for smell
II	**Optic** nerves	Sensory nerves for vision
III	**Oculomotor** nerves	Predominantly motor nerves for eye movement and pupil size
IV	**Trochlear** nerves	Predominantly motor nerves for eye movement
V	**Trigeminal** nerves	Sensory and motor nerves responsible for face, nose, and mouth sensations and for chewing
VI	**Abducens** nerves	Predominantly motor nerves responsible for eye movement
VII	**Facial** nerves	Mixed nerves associated with taste (sensory), facial expression (motor), and production of tears and saliva (parasympathetic fibers of motor nerves)
VIII	**Vestibulocochlear (auditory)** nerves	Predominantly sensory nerves associated with hearing and balance
IX	**Glossopharyngeal** nerves	Mixed nerves for sensation and swallowing in the pharynx
X	**Vagus** nerves	Mixed sensory and parasympathetic nerves supplying the pharynx, larynx (speech), and the viscera of the thorax and abdomen *(Figure 10.13)*
XI	**Accessory** nerves	Predominantly motor nerves supplying neck muscles, pharynx, and larynx.
XII	**Hypoglossal** nerves	Predominantly motor nerves that move the tongue in speaking, chewing, and swallowing

WORD	PRONUNCIATION	ELEMENTS		DEFINITION
abducens	ab-**DYU**-senz		Latin *abduct, draw away from*	Sixth (VI) cranial nerve; responsible for eye movement
accessory	ack-**SESS**-oh-ree		Latin *move toward*	Eleventh (XI) cranial nerve; supplying neck muscles, pharynx, and larynx
auditory	**AW**-dih-tor-ee	S/ R/	-ory *resembles* **audit-** *hearing*	Pertaining to the sense or the organs of hearing
cranial	**KRAY**-nee-al	S/ R/	-al *pertaining to* **crani-** *skull, cranium*	Pertaining to the skull
facial	**FAY**-shal		Latin *face*	Seventh (VII) cranial nerve; supplying the forehead, nose, eyes, mouth, and jaws
glossopharyngeal	**GLOSS**-oh-fah-**RIN**-jee-al	S/ R/CF R/	-eal *pertaining to* **gloss/o-** *tongue* **-pharyng-** *pharynx*	Ninth (IX) cranial nerve; supplying the tongue and pharynx
hypoglossal	high-poh-**GLOSS**-al	S/ P/ R/	-al *pertaining to* **hypo-** *below, under* **-gloss-** *tongue*	Twelfth (XII) cranial nerve; supplying muscles of the tongue
oculomotor	**OCK**-you-loh-**MOH**-tor	S/ R/CF R/	-or *doer* **ocul/o-** *eye* **-mot-** *move*	Third (III) cranial nerve; moves the eye
olfactory	ol-**FAK**-toh-ree	S/ R/	-ory *resembles* **olfact-** *smell*	First (I) cranial nerve; carries information related to the sense of smell
optic	**OP**-tick		Greek *eye*	Second (II) cranial nerve; carries visual information
trigeminal	try-**GEM**-in-al	S/ P/ R/	-al *pertaining to* **tri-** *three* **-gemin-** *group, twins*	Fifth (V) cranial nerve, with its three different branches supplying the face
trochlear	**TROHK**-lee-are	S/ R/	-ar *pertaining to* **trochle-** *pulley*	Fourth (IV) cranial nerve; supplies one muscle of the eye
vagus	**VAY**-gus		Latin *to wander*	Tenth (X) cranial nerve; supplies many different organs throughout the body
vestibulocochlear (**Note:** This term starts with a combining form, not a prefix.)	ves-**TIB**-you-loh-**KOK**-lee-ar	S/ R/CF R/	-ar *pertaining to* **vestibul/o-** *vestibule of inner ear* **-cochle-** *cochlea*	Eighth (VIII) cranial nerve; carrying information for the senses of hearing and balance

EXERCISES

Elements: *Continue your work with elements to help build your knowledge of the **language of neurology**. One element in each of the following medical terms is set in bold. Identify the type of element (P, R, CF, S) in column 2, then write the meaning of the element in column 3. Fill in the blanks.*

> *Study Hint*
> Note that some terms can start with a root or combining form instead of a prefix.

Medical Term	Type of Element	Meaning of Element
glosso**pharyngeal**		
hypo**glossal**		
trochlear		
oculo**motor**		
trigeminal		
auditory		
olfactory		
vestibulo**cochlear**		

LESSON 10.3 Disorders of the Nervous System

OBJECTIVES

When patients communicate with you as a health professional, they will often enhance your continual, on-going learning by informing you and reinforcing your knowledge about a specific disorder.

Information in this lesson will enable you to:

- Relate common disorders of the brain and cranial nerves to normal and abnormal anatomy and physiology.
- Contrast the normal anatomy and physiology of the brain and cranial nerves with the abnormal anatomy and physiology that produce disorders.
- Describe common disorders of the brain and cranial nerves.
- Select the correct terminology to communicate about the brain and cranial nerves and their disorders with patients and other health professionals.

You are

. . . a medical assistant working with Dr. Raoul Cardenas, a neurologist at Fulwood Medical Center.

Your patient is

. . . Mr. Lester Rood, a 75-year-old man who was diagnosed a year ago as having dementia.

CASE REPORT 10.2

Mr. Rood lives with his daughter, Judy, and she is with him today.

Patient Interview:

Mr. Lester Rood:

"How am I feeling? Scared stiff. Sometimes I don't know where I am. Most times I'm pretty sure I'm living with my daughter. I get so messed up. I can't cook anymore. I forget what I'm doing, can't get things straight. I find myself in the street and don't know how I got there. Judy has to help me shower and remind me to go to the bathroom. And it's only going to get worse. I don't want to be a burden. I used to have 100 people work for me. It's so frustrating, so frightening."

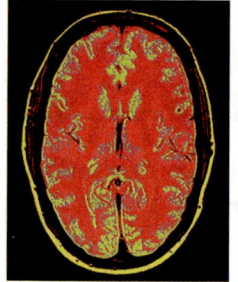 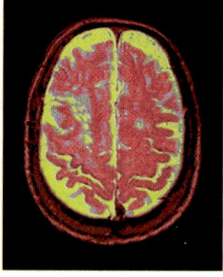

(a)   (b)

▲ **FIGURE 10.18   Brain Sections.**
(a) MRI Scan of Normal Brain. *(b)* MRI Scan of Alzheimer Disease Showing Cerebral Atrophy *(yellow).*

BRAIN

Dementia

Your **empathy** allowed Mr. Rood to talk without interruption. He reminded you that the symptoms of **dementia** include short-term memory loss, inability to solve problems, confusion, inappropriate behavior (such as wandering away), and impaired intellectual function that interferes with normal activities and relationships. In its early stages it is a very frightening and frustrating situation for the patient. It requires a lot of **sympathy** from family and caregivers.

Dementia is *not* a normal part of aging and is *not* a specific disease. It is a term used for a collection of symptoms that can be caused by a number of disorders affecting the brain.

Alzheimer disease is the most common form of dementia. It affects 10% of the population over 65 and 50% of the population over 85. Nerve cells in the areas of the brain associated with memory and cognition are replaced by abnormal clumps and tangles of a protein *(Figure 10.18).*

Vascular dementia is the second most common form of dementia. It can come on gradually when arteries supplying the brain become arteriosclerotic (narrowed or blocked), depriving the brain of oxygen, or can occur suddenly after a **stroke** *(see Chapter 7).*

Confusion is used to describe people who cannot process information normally. For example, they cannot answer questions appropriately, understand where they are, or remember important facts. Confusion is often part of dementia or delirium.

WORD	PRONUNCIATION	ELEMENTS		DEFINITION
Alzheimer disease	AWLZ-high-mer diz-EEZ		Alois Alzheimer, German neurologist, 1864–1915	Common form of dementia
confusion	kon-FEW-zhun	S/ R/	-ion *process* confus- *bewildered*	Mental state in which environmental stimuli are not processed appropriately
delirium	de-LIR-ee-um	S/ R/	-um *structure* deliri- *crazy*	Acute altered state of consciousness with agitation and disorientation; condition is reversible
dementia	de-MEN-she-ah	S/ P/ R/	-ia *condition* de- *removal* -ment- *mind*	Chronic, progressive, irreversible loss of the mind's cognitive and intellectual functions
empathy	EM-pa-thee	P/ R/	em- *into* -pathy *emotion, disease*	Ability to place yourself into the feelings, emotions, and reactions of another person
sympathy	SIM-pa-thee	P/	sym- *together*	Appreciation and concern for another person's mental and emotional state
stroke	STROHK		Old English *to strike*	Acute clinical event caused by an impaired cerebral circulation

Delirium is the sudden onset of disorientation, an inability to think clearly or pay attention. There is a change in the level of consciousness, varying from increased wakefulness to drowsiness. It is a mental state, not a disease. It can be part of dementia or a stroke.

Other conditions causing dementia are often treatable. They include:

- **Reactions to medications** (e.g., sedatives, antiarthritics)
- **Metabolic abnormalities** (e.g., hypoglycemia)
- **Nutritional deficiencies** (e.g., vitamins B_1 and B_6)
- **Emotional problems** (e.g., depression in the elderly)
- **Infections** (e.g., AIDS, encephalitis)

EXERCISES

Identify the elements in each medical term, and unlock the meaning of the word. Fill in the chart, then use one of the terms in a sentence of your choice.

Medical Term	Meaning of Prefix	Meaning of Root/ CF	Meaning of Suffix	Meaning of the Term
dementia				
sympathy				
delirium				
confusion				
empathy				

Sentence:

_____

_____

TRAUMATIC BRAIN INJURY

Traumatic brain injury (TBI) causes damage to the brain. Over 1 million people are seen by medical doctors each year following a blow to the head. Of these, 50,000 to 100,000 will have prolonged problems affecting their work and their **activities of daily living (ADLs)**.

If you are driving your car at 50 miles per hour and are hit head-on, your brain goes from 50 miles per hour to zero instantly. Your soft brain tissue is propelled forward and squished against the front of your hard skull (**coup**). Then the brain and the rest of your body rebound backwards. The soft brain is then squished against the back of your rigid skull (**contrecoup**). The squished front and back areas are at least bruised. This bruise is called a **contusion** *(Figure 10.22)*.

If the process is more severe, blood vessels tear, and blood flows into the brain. In addition, the brain itself can tear and cut brain connections and signals. In any injury, brain swelling can occur. Because the skull is hard and rigid, it cannot expand to cope with this extra volume. So the soft brain tissue is compressed, and some areas can stop working.

A mild head injury is called a **concussion.** You may feel dazed or have a period of confusion during which you do not recall the event that caused the concussion. In more severe cases, you may lose consciousness for a brief period of time and have no memory of the event. Repeated concussions have a cumulative effect with loss of mental ability and/or traumatically induced Parkinson disease (as happened with professional boxer Muhammad Ali).

In more severe TBIs, the symptoms will depend on the area of the brain damaged. Some symptoms, such as difficulty with memory or concentration, irritability, aggression, **insomnia**, or depression, can be long-term. Traumatic brain injury has become a signature wound of the war in Iraq.

The residual effects of brain damage, whether due to trauma or stroke, have a terminology.

Impairment is a deviation from normal function; for example, not being able to control an unwanted muscle movement.

Disability is a restriction in the ability to perform a normal activity of daily living (ADL); for example, a three-year-old who cannot walk independently.

Handicap is defined as having a disability that prevents a child or adult from achieving a normal role in society commensurate with age and sociocultural setting; for example, a 16-year-old who cannot take care of personal toiletry and hygienic needs.

Shaken baby syndrome (SBS) is a type of TBI produced when a baby is violently shaken. The baby has weak neck muscles and a heavy head. Shaking makes the brain bounce back and forth in the skull, leading to severe brain damage. Other injuries include retinal hemorrhages, damage to the spinal cord, and fractures of the ribs and limb bones. This syndrome usually occurs in children younger than two years.

Abbreviations

ADLs activities of daily living
SBS shaken baby syndrome
TBI traumatic brain injury

▼ **FIGURE 10.22 Contusions Caused by Back-and-Forth Movement of Brain in Skull.**

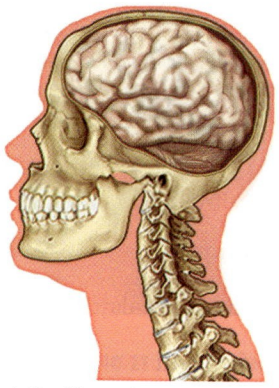
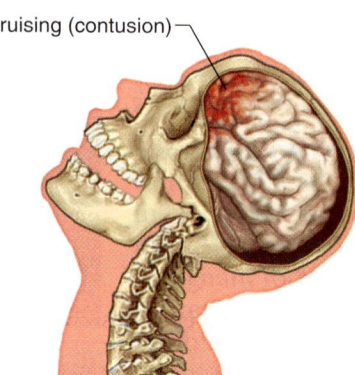
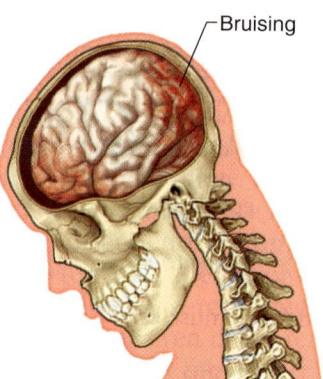
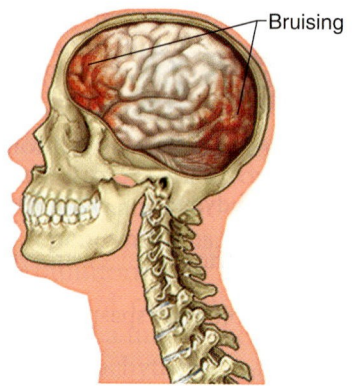

1. Position prior to impact. 2. Impact from behind. 3. Contrecoup action. 4. Subsequent coup contrecoup injury.

WORD ANALYSIS AND DEFINITION

S = Suffix   P = Prefix   R = Root   R/CF = Combining Form

WORD	PRONUNCIATION		ELEMENTS	DEFINITION
activities of daily living (ADLs)	ak-**TIV**-ih-tees of **DAY**-lee **LIV**-ing	S/ R/ S/ R/ S/ R/	**-ity** *condition* **activ-** *perform* **-ly** *every* **dai-** *day* **-ing** *quality of* **liv-** *life*	Daily routines for mobility and personal care, bathing, dressing, eating, and moving
concussion	kon-**KUSH**-un	S/ R/	**-ion** *process* **concuss-** *shake violently*	Mild head injury
contusion	kon-**TOO**-zhun	S/ R/	**-ion** *process* **contus-** *bruise*	Bruising of a tissue, including the brain
coup	KOO		French *a blow*	Injury to the brain occurring directly under the skull at the point of impact
contrecoup	**KON**-tre-koo		French *counter-blow*	Injury to the brain at a point directly opposite the point of original contact
disability	dis-ah-**BILL**-ih-tee	P/ R/	**dis-** *away from* **-ability** *competence*	Diminished capacity to perform certain activities or functions
handicap	**HAND**-ee-cap		French *assess before a race*	Condition that interferes with a person's ability to function normally
insomnia	in-**SOM**-nee-ah	S/ P/ R/	**-ia** *condition* **in-** *in* **-somn-** *sleep*	Inability to sleep

EXERCISES

Apply the correct medical language from this WAD to the sentences below. Remember to check your spelling when you are finished. Fill in the blanks.

1. A TBI can cause problems with the (abbreviation) _____

2. Rewrite sentence 1 without using the abbreviations. (Spell them out.)

   _____

   _____

3. Diminished capacity to perform certain activities or functions is _____.

4. A condition that interferes with a person's ability to function normally is _____.

5. A mild head injury can be termed _____.

6. Bruising of a tissue, including the brain, is _____.

7. List briefly some of the activities of daily living: _____.

8. The two terms in this WAD that are diagnoses you might see on an Emergency Room record are: _____ and

   _____.

PAIN MANAGEMENT

Pain persisting longer than three months is said to be **chronic.** It can be caused by cancer, arthritis, fibromyalgia, low back or neck problems, headache, or injuries that are said to have healed. Normal activities can be restricted or be impossible.

Six million to 10 million Americans are affected by fibromyalgia, 5 million are disabled by back problems, 8 million experience chronic neck and facial pain, and 40 million suffer from chronic recurrent headaches. In modern health care, chronic pain management has become essential and often uses a **multidisciplinary** approach. Pain management is now a board-certified subspecialty for **anesthesiologists.**

Medications are the cornerstone of pain management, and the following can be used based on the severity of the pain:

- Mild pain—**analgesics** (such as acetaminophen) and **nonsteroidal anti-inflammatory drugs (NSAIDs)** (such as ibuprofen) are used.

- Moderate pain—**opiate** medications used in combination with acetaminophen or NSAIDs are used. Some opiates used in combination medications are codeine, hydrocodone, and oxycodone. Examples are hydrocodone/acetaminophen (Vicodin), oxycodone/acetaminophen (Percocet), and oxycodone/aspirin (Percodan).

- Severe pain—higher doses of opiates are used, often not as combination products. These include **morphine,** fentanyl, oxy- and hydromorphone. The opiates can be taken orally, by patch, sublingually, by **intravenous (IV)** infusion, or by continuous delivery systems.

Central sensitization pain is a new concept describing how neurons in the spinal cord sending messages to the brain become excitable. They exaggerate the pain response in tissues they supply. The input can be somatic from skeletal muscles (as in fibromyalgia) or visceral (as in irritable bowel syndrome).

Interventional pain management, particularly for pain originating in the spine and spinal nerves, is being increasingly used. Examples are:

- **Epidural** or **facet nerve blocks**—anesthetic or anti-inflammatory agents are injected into an area surrounding the pain-generating nerve.

- **Radiofrequency (RF) nerve ablation**—a probe heats the area around a pain-generating spinal nerve and temporarily deactivates it.

- **Cryoneurolysis**—peripheral nerves outside the spine are treated with extremely low temperatures to temporarily deactivate them.

- **Spinal infusion pump**—pain medications such as morphine are delivered through an indwelling catheter into the **intrathecal** CSF surrounding the spinal cord. A pump delivery device is inserted under the skin of the abdomen.

Phantom limb pain occurs following the **amputation** of a limb or part of a limb. Any stimulation of the remaining intact portion of the sensory pathway coming originally from the limb is interpreted by the brain as coming from the original limb. The pain can be severe and debilitating or just an insatiable urge to scratch an itch.

Referred pain is when pain in the viscera is felt in the skin or other superficial sites *(Figure 10.23)*. An example is the pain of a heart attack felt along the front of the left shoulder and down the underside of the left arm. This is because spinal cord segments T1 to T5 receive sensory input from the heart, as well as from the skin of the shoulder and arm. This input is transmitted to the brain. The brain cannot distinguish the true source of the pain. It assumes it is coming from the skin, which has more pain receptors than the heart and is injured more often.

Abbreviations	
IV	intravenous
NSAIDs	nonsteroidal anti-inflammatory drugs
RF	radiofrequency
T1	first thoracic vertebra or nerve
T5	fifth thoracic vertebra or nerve

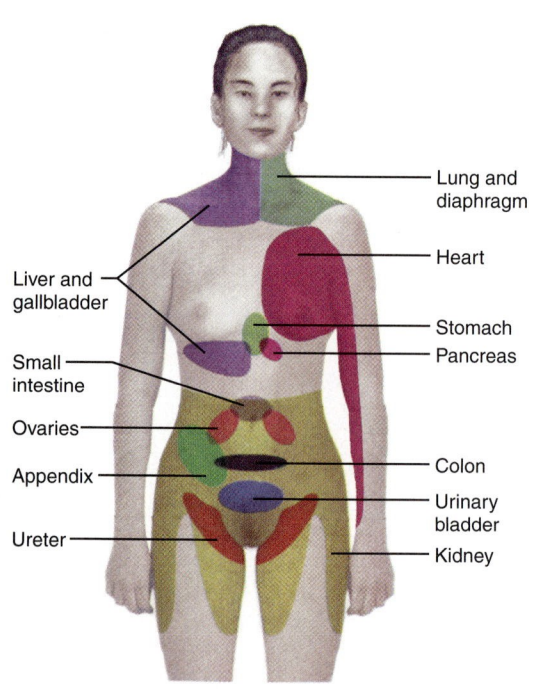

Liver and gallbladder
Small intestine
Ovaries
Appendix
Ureter

Lung and diaphragm
Heart
Stomach
Pancreas
Colon
Urinary bladder
Kidney

▲ **FIGURE 10.23   Referred Pain.**

WORD	PRONUNCIATION	ELEMENTS		DEFINITION
ablation	ab-**LAY**-shun	S/ P/ R/	-ion *process* ab- *away* -lat- *to take*	Removal of tissue to destroy its function
amputation	am-pyu-**TAY**-shun	S/ R/	-ion *process* amputat- *to prune, lop off*	Process of removing a limb, part of a limb, a breast, or other projecting part
analgesia	an-al-**JEE**-ze-ah	S/ P/ R/	-ia *condition* an- *without* -alges- *sensation of pain*	State in which pain is reduced
analgesic	an-al-**JEE**-sic	S/	-ic *pertaining to*	Substance that produces analgesia
anesthesia	an-es-**THEE**-zee-ah	S/ P/ R/	-ia *condition* an- *without* -esthes- *sensation*	Complete loss of sensation
anesthesiologist anesthesiology	**AN**-es-thee-zee-**OL**-oh-jist **AN**-es-thee-zee-**OL**-oh-jee	S/ S/ P/ R/CF	-logist *one who studies* -logy *study of* an- *without* -esthesi/o- *feeling, sensation*	Medical specialist in anesthesia Medical specialty related to anesthesia
anesthetic	an-es-**THET**-ic	S/ P/ R/	-ic *pertaining to* an- *without* -esthet- *feeling sensation*	An agent that causes absence of feeling or sensation
chronic	**KRON**-ic	S/ R/	-ic *pertaining to* chron- *time*	Term to describe a persistent long-term disease
cryoneurolysis	cry-oh-**NYUR**-oh-lie-sis	S/ P/ R/CF	-lysis *destruction* cryo- *cold* -neur/o- *nerve*	Temporary deactivation of nerve tissue using extreme cold
facet	**FAS**-et		French *little face*	Small area around a pain-producing nerve
intrathecal	**IN**-trah-**THEE**-kal	S/ P/ R/	-al *pertaining to* intra- *within* -thec- *sheath*	Within the subarachnoid or subdural space
morphine	**MOR**-feen		Latin *god of dreams*	Derivative of opium used as an analgesic or sedative
multidisciplinary	mul-tee-**DIS**-ih-plin-**NAR**-ee	S/ P/ R/	-ary *pertaining to* multi- *many* -disciplin- *disciple*	Involving health care providers from more than one profession
opiate	**OH**-pee-ate		Latin *bringing sleep*	A drug derived from opium

EXERCISES

*Deconstruct the following **language of neurology**. Write the meaning of each element to see how it will aid you in understanding the meaning of the complete term. Fill in the chart.*

Medical Term	Meaning of Prefix	Meaning of Root/CF	Meaning of Suffix	Meaning of Term
chronic				
ablation				
analgesia				
anesthesia				
amputation				
cryoneurolysis				
multidisciplinary				

Remember: Every term does not need a prefix!

LESSON 10.4 Disorders of the Spinal Cord and Peripheral Nerves

OBJECTIVES

There are many disorders of the nervous system that affect the spinal cord and the peripheral nerves without affecting the brain. In this lesson, the information will enable you to:

- **Discuss disorders of the spinal cord and peripheral nerves.**
- **Distinguish between different diagnostic tests used for nervous system disorders.**
- **Define methods by which nervous system medications influence disease processes.**
- **Recognize common congenital disorders of the nervous system.**
- **Select the correct terminology to communicate about the nervous system and its disorders with patients and other health professionals.**

You are

. . . Tanisha Colis, an electroneuro-diagnostic technologist working with Raul Cardenas, MD, a neurologist at Fulwood Medical Center.

Your patient is

. . . Mrs. Suzanne Kalish, a 42-year-old social worker employed by the medical center.

CASE REPORT 10.3

Mrs. Kalish has recently had an exacerbation of her symptoms due to multiple sclerosis **(MS)**. She is going to have a visual evoked potential **(VEP)** test, followed by an MRI of her brain and spinal cord.

Patient Interview:

Tanisha: "Good morning, Mrs. Kalish, I'm Tanisha Colis, the technologist who'll be performing your visual evoked potential test. How are you feeling?"

Mrs. Kalish: "I've been doing OK for the last four or five years. Then, a few weeks ago, I started dragging my right foot like a wounded witch. I've got to hang on to the walls to stay vertical. I'm tired out, can't come to work. It's a struggle to walk the few yards just to pick up the mail."

Tanisha: "The MRI you are going to have today will give us a lot of information about what's going on."

Mrs. Kalish: "My mind is going 'wheelchair, wheelchair, wheelchair.' Especially since in the last couple of days the vision in my right eye has got all blurred."

Tanisha: "That's the reason you are having the visual evoked potential test."

Mrs. Kalish: "I hate this disease. If I had cancer, I've got a chance. I'd fight it to the end, whatever that would be. Nobody's ever beat MS. You can only lose. It can be kind and leave you for a while, but it's never far away."

Tanisha: "Let me help you up, and we'll go get this test done."

Mrs. Kalish: "I can manage, thank you."

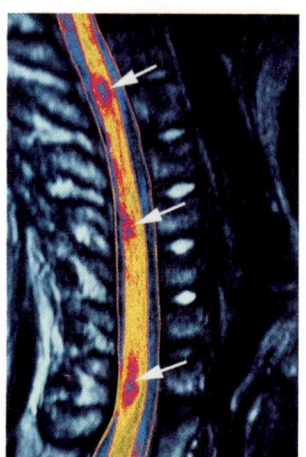

▲ **FIGURE 10.27   Multiple Sclerosis.**
Note areas of spinal cord where myelin sheath has been destroyed (arrows). Normal spinal cord is yellow.

DISORDERS OF THE MYELIN SHEATH OF NERVE FIBERS

When the myelin sheath surrounding nerve fibers is damaged, nerves do not conduct impulses normally. In newborns, many of their nerves have immature myelin sheaths, which is why some of their movements are jerky and uncoordinated.

Demyelination, the destruction of an area of the myelin sheath, can occur in the PNS caused by inflammation, vitamin B_{12} deficiency, poisons, and some medications.

Guillain-Barré syndrome is a disorder of the peripheral nerves in which the body makes antibodies against myelin, leading to loss of nerve conduction, muscle weakness, and **paresthesias** (changes in sensation). Treatment is with corticosteroids, and recovery of neurologic function is slow.

Demyelination of nerve fibers in the brain, spinal cord, and optic nerves can also occur. **Multiple sclerosis (MS)** is the most common of these demyelination disorders. As you can tell from Suzanne Kalish's story, MS is a chronic, progressive disorder. **Intermittent** myelin damage and scarring slows nerve impulses *(Figure 10.27)*. This leads to muscle weakness, pain, numbness, and vision loss. Because different nerve fibers are affected at different times, MS symptoms often worsen (**exacerbations**) or show partial or complete reduction (**remissions**). Suzanne is now in an exacerbation.

MS has an average age of onset between 18 and 35 years and is more common in women. Its cause is unknown, but it is thought to be an autoimmune disease.

WORD	PRONUNCIATION	ELEMENTS		DEFINITION
demyelination	dee-**MY**-eh-lin-**A**-shun	S/ P/ R/	-ation *action* de- *away from* -myelin- *myelin*	Process of losing the myelin sheath of a nerve fiber
encephalitis	en-**SEF**-ah-**LIE**-tis	S/ R/	-itis *inflammation* encephal- *brain*	Inflammation of the brain parenchyma
encephalomyelitis	en-**SEF**-ah-loh-**MY**-eh-lie-tis	R/CF R/	encephal/o- *brain* -myel- *spinal cord*	Inflammation of the brain and spinal cord
exacerbation (opposite of remission)	ek-zas-er-**BAY**-shun	S/ R/	-ation *action* exacerbat- *increase*	Period when there is an increase in the severity of a disease
Guillain-Barré syndrome	**GEE**-yan-bah-**RAY** **SIN**-drom		Georges Guillain (1876–1961) and Jean-Alexandre Barré (1880–1967); French neurologists	Disorder in which the body makes anti-bodies against myelin, disrupting nerve conduction
intermittent	**IN**-ter-**MIT**-ent	S/ P/ R/	-ent *state of* inter- *between* -mitt- *send*	Alternately ceasing and beginning again
modify	**MOD**-ih-fie		Latin *to limit*	Change the form or qualities of something
paresthesia paresthesias (pl)	par-es-**THEE**-ze-ah	S/ P/ R/	-ia *condition* par(a)- *abnormal* -esthes- *sensation*	Abnormal sensation; for example, tingling, burning, prickling
remission (opposite of exacerbation)	ree-**MISH**-un	S/ P/ R/	-ion *process* re- *back* -miss- *send*	Period when there is a lessening or absence of the symptoms of a disease

There is no known cure for MS, but recently developed "**disease-modifying**" drugs appear to have partial success in slowing down the accumulation of disabilities if started when the diagnosis is first made.

Other causes of demyelination in the CNS are injury, ischemia, toxic agents such as chemotherapy or radiotherapy, and congenital disorders such as **Tay Sachs disease** (*see Chapter 22*). After viral infections or vaccinations, **postinfectious encephalomyelitis** is a demyelination process, as is **HIV encephalitis,** which is seen in up to 30% of patients with AIDS.

Abbreviations

MS	multiple sclerosis
VEP	visual evoked potential

EXERCISES

Test yourself on the elements and terms in this WAD. Practice pronouncing the terms before you start the exercise. Circle the best answer.

1. **Guillain–Barré syndrome** disrupts:

    nerve and conduction　　　blood flow

    tissue oxygenation

2. In the term **paresthesia** the prefix means:

    between　　　abnormal　　　many

3. **Remission** is the opposite of:

    intermittent　　　exacerbation　　　demyelination

4. To **modify** something is to:

    dispose of it　　　change it　　　renew it

5. In the term **demyelination** the prefix means:

    away from　　　in front of　　　in between

6. If a disease is **exacerbated**, it is:

    more severe　　　unchanged　　　less severe

 Have you pronounced each word correctly? Did you listen to your CD?

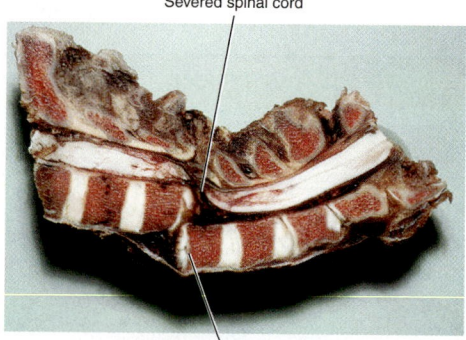

Severed spinal cord

(a)   Fracture-dislocation of vertebra

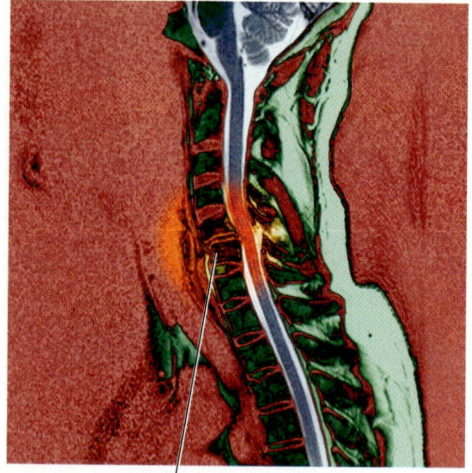

(b)   Fractured vertebra

▲ **FIGURE 10.28   Spinal Cord Injuries.**
(a) Severed Spinal Cord from Fracture -
Dislocation of Vertebra. *(b)* Compressed spinal
cord with vertebral fracture.

DISORDERS OF THE SPINAL CORD

Trauma

The spinal cord is injured in three ways *(Figure 10.28)*:

1. **Severed**

2. **Contused**

3. **Compressed,** by a broken or dislocated vertebra, bleeding or swelling.

Because of its anatomy with nerve fibers and tracts going up and down, to and from the brain, injury to the spinal cord results in loss of function *below the injury.* For example, if the cord is injured in the thoracic region, the arms function normally, but the legs can be **paralyzed.** Both muscle control and sensation are lost.

If the spinal cord is severed, the loss is permanent. Contusions can cause temporary loss lasting days, weeks, or months. Compression injuries may require surgical intervention to relieve the pressure. Compression can also be due to a **herniated** disc.

The first goal of treatment is to prevent further damage, which is why you see football players being carried off the field strapped to a board and carefully padded to prevent even slight shifting of the spine.

Approximately half-a-million people in the USA have **spinal cord injuries (SCI).** There are approximately 8,000 new injuries each year; 82% involve males between the ages of 16 and 30. Quadriplegia is slightly more common than paraplegia.

Compression of the cord can also occur slowly from a tumor in the cord or spine. Cancer or osteoporosis can cause a vertebra to collapse and compress the cord.

- **Cervical spondylosis** is a disorder in which the discs and vertebrae in the neck degenerate, narrow the spinal canal, and compress the spinal cord and/or the spinal nerve roots.

- In **syringomyelia,** fluid-filled cavities grow in the spinal cord and compress nerves that detect pain and temperature. There is no specific cure.

Other Disorders

Acute transverse myelitis is a localized disorder of the spinal cord that blocks transmission of impulses up and down the spinal cord. People who have **Lyme disease, syphilis, or tuberculosis** *(see Chapter 20)* or those who inject heroin or amphetamines intravenously are at risk to develop this disorder. The disorder causes loss of sensation, muscle paralysis, and loss of bladder and bowel control. There is no specific treatment. Most people recover completely.

Subacute combined degeneration of the spinal cord is due to a deficiency of vitamin B_{12}. The sensory nerve fibers in the spinal cord degenerate, producing weakness, clumsiness, tingling, and loss of the position sense as to where limbs are. Treatment is injections of vitamin B_{12}.

Poliomyelitis (polio) is an acute infectious disease, occurring mostly in children, that is caused by the poliovirus. The virus can be asymptomatic in the nasopharynx and **gastrointestinal (GI)** tract. When it spreads to the nervous system, it replicates in the spinal cord and destroys motor neurons. Symptoms are progressive muscle **paralysis;** paralysis of the respiratory muscles can require mechanical ventilation using the **Drinker respirator** (iron lung). Poliomyelitis is preventable by vaccination and has almost been eradicated in the world.

Postpolio syndrome (PPS), in which people develop tired, painful, and weak muscles many years after recovery from polio, is classified as a motor neuron disorder.

Motor neuron disorders occur when motor nerves in the spinal cord and brain progressively deteriorate. This leads to muscle weakness that can progress to paralysis.

Amyotrophic lateral sclerosis (ALS, or Lou Gehrig disease) and its variants, **progressive muscular atrophy** and **primary lateral sclerosis,** are examples. There is no cure.

WORD ANALYSIS AND DEFINITION

WORD	PRONUNCIATION	ELEMENTS		DEFINITION
amyotrophic	a-my-oh-**TRO**-fik	S/ P/ R/CF R/	-ic *pertaining to* a- *without* -my/o- *muscle* -troph- *nourishment,* *development*	Pertaining to muscular atrophy
atrophy	**AT**-roh-fee	P/ R/	a- *without* -trophy *development,* *nourishment*	Wasting or diminished volume of a tissue or organ
compression	kom-**PRESH**-un	S/ P/ R/	-ion *process* com- *together* -press- *squeeze*	Squeeze together to increase density or decrease a dimension of a structure
herniation hernia (noun) herniate (verb)	**HER**-nee-ay-shun **HER**-nee-ah **HER**-nee-ate	S/ R/ S/	-ation *action* herni- *rupture* -ate *composed of*	Protrusion of an anatomical structure from its normal location
Lyme disease	LIME **DIZ**-eez		Named in 1977 after a group of children in Lyme, Connecticut	Disease transmitted by the bite of an infected deer tick
paralyze	**PAR**-ah-lyze	P/ R/	para- *beside, abnormal* -lyze *destruction*	To make incapable of movement
paralysis	pah-**RAL**-ih-sis	R/ R/	-lysis *breaking down* -ly- *break down*	Loss of voluntary movement
paralytic (adj)	par-ah-**LYT**-ik	S/	-tic *pertaining to*	Suffering from paralysis
poliomyelitis polio (abbrev)	**POE**-lee-oh-**MY**-eh-lie-tis	S/ P/ R/	-itis *inflammation* polio- *gray matter* -myel- *spinal cord*	Inflammation of the gray matter of the spinal cord, leading to paralysis of the limbs and muscles of respiration
postpolio syndrome (PPS)	post-**POE**-lee-oh **SIN**-drome	P/ P/ R/	post- *after* syn- *together* -drome *running*	Progressive muscle weakness in a person previously affected by polio
spondylosis	spon-dih-**LOH**-sis	S/ R/	-osis *condition* spondyl- *vertebra*	Degenerative osteoarthritis of the spine
syringomyelia	si-**RING**-oh-my-**EE**-lee-ah	S R R/CF	-ia *condition* myel- *spinal cord* syring/o- *tube, pipe*	Abnormal longitudinal cavities in the spinal cord cause paresthesias and muscle weakness

EXERCISES

Identify the meaning of these elements then provide a medical term that contains the element. Review this WAD before you start the exercise. Fill in the blanks.

Element	Meaning of Element	Medical Term Containing This Element
com		
a		
post		
polio		
para		
herni		
myo		
myel		
itis		
ation		

DISORDERS OF THE PERIPHERAL NERVES

Neuropathy is used here as any disorder affecting one or more peripheral nerves.

Mononeuropathy is damage to a single peripheral nerve. Prolonged pressure on a nerve that runs close to the surface over a bony prominence is a common cause. Examples are:

- **Carpal tunnel syndrome**—the median nerve at the wrist is compressed between the wrist bones and a strong overlying ligament. Numbness, pain, and tingling of the thumb side of the hand are the symptoms. Incision of the ligament relieves the pressure.

- **Ulnar nerve palsy**—from nerve damage as the ulnar nerve crosses close to the surface over the humerus at the back of the elbow. Pins-and-needles sensation and weakness in the hand result. Hitting the ulnar nerve is the cause of pain when you hit your "funny bone."

- **Peroneal nerve palsy**—from nerve damage as the peroneal nerve passes close to the surface near the back of the knee. Compression of the nerve occurs in people who are bedridden or strapped in a wheelchair.

Polyneuropathy is damage to, and the simultaneous malfunction of, many peripheral nerves throughout the body.

Symptoms of acute polyneuropathy include muscle weakness and a pins-and-needles sensation or loss of sensation. The symptoms begin suddenly in the legs and work upwards to the arms.

In diabetic chronic polyneuropathy, only sensation is affected, most commonly in the feet. Pins-and-needles, numbness, and a burning sensation are prominent.

When people with a neuropathy are unable to sense pain, they can injure a joint many times without feeling it. The joint malfunctions and can progress to be permanently destroyed. Joints involved in this **neuropathic joint disease** are called **Charcot joints**.

Herpes zoster (shingles) is an infection of peripheral nerves arising from a reactivation of the primary virus infection in childhood with **chickenpox (varicella)**. During the primary infection of chickenpox, the virus gains entry into sensory dorsal root ganglia. Later in life, for unknown reasons, the virus produces the painful, unilateral dermatome rash of shingles *(Figure 10.29)*.

Postherpetic neuralgia is acute dermatome pain persisting after the acute rash of shingles has subsided. It is debilitating and very difficult to treat *(see Chapter 3)*.

Neuromuscular junction disorders occur where nerves connect with muscle fibers and interfere with the **neurotransmitter acetylcholine**. Examples are:

- **Myasthenia gravis**—the immune system produces antibodies that attack the acetylcholine receptors on the muscle cells. The common symptoms are drooping eyelids; weak eye muscles, causing double vision; difficulty talking and swallowing; and muscle weakness in the limbs. Treatment is with a drug called **pyridostigmine**, which increases the amount of available acetylcholine.

- **Botulism**—a rare, life-threatening, food poisoning caused by toxins from the bacterium *Clostridium botulinum*. These **neurotoxins** paralyze the muscles. In certain seasons, shellfish produce a similar neurotoxin.

- Certain **insecticides (organophosphates)** and nerve gases used in chemical warfare all act on neuromuscular junctions.

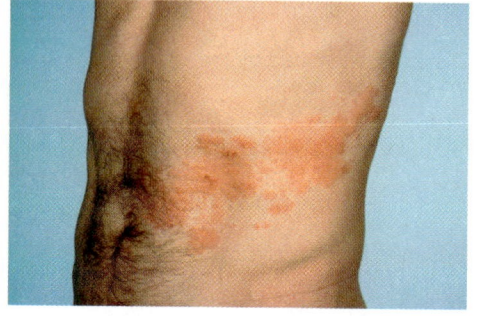

▲ **FIGURE 10.29** Herpes Zoster (Shingles).

Keynote

Herpes zoster occurs in people with depressed immune responses, HIV-infection, cancer, or those on chemotherapy and/or radiation therapy, as well as for no apparent reason.

WORD	PRONUNCIATION	ELEMENTS		DEFINITION
botulism	**BOT**-you-lizm		Latin *sausage*	Food poisoning caused by the neurotoxin produced by *Clostridium botulinum*
botox	**BO**-tox			Neurotoxin injected into muscles of the face to prevent the muscles from contracting and causing wrinkles
Charcot joint	**SHAR**-koh JOYNT		Jean-Martin Charcot, 1825–1893, French neurologist	Bone and joint destruction secondary to a neuropathy and loss of sensation
chickenpox (also called **varicella**)	**CHICK**-en-pocks		Disease originally considered a "chicken" (not dangerous) version of smallpox	Acute, contagious viral disease
Clostridium botulinum	klos-**TRID**-ee-um bot-you-**LIE**-num			Bacterium that causes food poisoning
insecticide	in-**SEK**-tih-side	S/ R/CF	**-cide** *kill* **insect/i-** *insect*	Agent to destroy insects
myasthenia gravis	my-as-**THEE**-nee-ah **GRA**-vis	S/ R/ P/ R/ R/	**-ia** *condition* **my-** *muscle* **-a-** *without* **-sthen-** *strength* **gravis** *serious*	Disorder of fluctuating muscle weakness
neuropathy neuropathic (adj) mononeuropathy polyneuropathy	nyu-**ROP**-ah-thee nyur-oh-**PATH**-ik **MON**-oh-nyu-**ROP**-ah-thee **POL**-ee-nyu-**ROP**-ah-thee	S/ R/CF P/ P/	**-pathy** *disease* **neur/o-** *nerve* **mono-** *one* **poly-** *many*	Any disorder affecting the nervous system Disorder affecting a single nerve Disorder affecting many nerves
neurotoxin	**NYUR**-oh-tock-sin	R/ R/CF	**-toxin** *poison* **neur/o-** *nerve*	Agent that poisons the nervous system
organophosphate	**OR**-ga-no-**FOS**-fate	S/ R/CF R/	**-ate** *use, action* **organ/o-** *organic* **-phosph-** *phosphorus*	Organic phosphorus compound used as an insecticide

EXERCISES

Complete the definition with the correct medical language. Review this WAD for the elements you need to construct the term. Fill in the blanks.

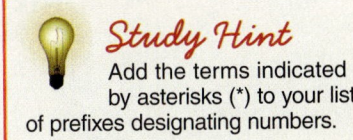

Study Hint
Add the terms indicated by asterisks (*) to your list of prefixes designating numbers.

1. agent to destroy insects   _____ /cide

2. disorder affecting the nervous system   neuro/ _____

3. disorder of fluctuating muscle weakness   my/a/sthen/ _____ _____

4. agent that poisons the nervous system   _____ /toxin

5. disorder affecting many nerves   _____ /neuro/ _____

6. prefix meaning affecting one*   _____

7. prefix meaning affecting many*   _____

8. used as an insecticide   organophosph/ _____

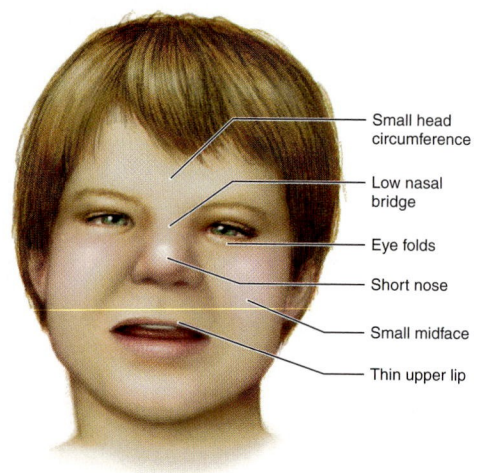

Small head circumference

Low nasal bridge

Eye folds

Short nose

Small midface

Thin upper lip

▲ **FIGURE 10.30   Fetal Alcohol Syndrome.**

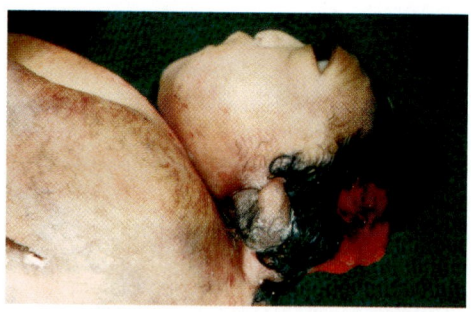

▲ **FIGURE 10.31   Newborn with Anencephaly.**

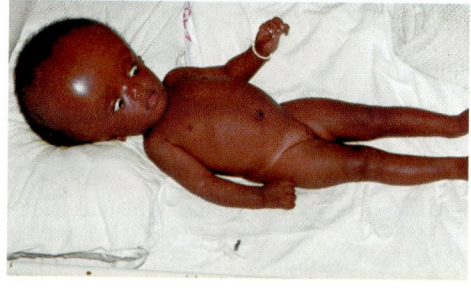

▲ **FIGURE 10.32   Infant with Hydrocephalus.**

Abbreviation

FAS   fetal alcohol syndrome

CONGENITAL ANOMALIES OF THE NERVOUS SYSTEM

Some of the most devastating **congenital neurologic abnormalities** develop in the first 8 to 10 weeks of **gestation**, when the nervous system is in its early stages of formation. These malformations can be detected using **ultrasonography** and **amniocentesis** (see Chapter 13). Many can be prevented by the mother taking 4 mg/day of **folic acid** before conception and during early pregnancy.

A **teratogen** is an agent that can cause malformations of an embryo or fetus (see Chapter 13). It can be a chemical, virus, or radiation. Some teratogens are encountered in the workplace and include textile dyes, photographic chemicals, semi-conductor materials, lead, mercury, and cadmium. One of the early uses of the drug thalidomide was to control morning sickness in pregnancy, but it caused severe limb and other deformities in the baby.

Anencephaly is absence of the cerebral hemispheres and is incompatible with life (Figure 10.31).

Microcephaly, decreased head size, is associated with small cerebral hemispheres and with moderate to severe motor and mental retardation.

Hydrocephalus, ventricular enlargement in the cerebral hemispheres with excessive CSF, is usually due to an obstruction that prevents the CSF from exiting the ventricles to circulate around the spinal cord (Figure 10.32). Treatment typically is to place a **shunt** to drain the CSF from the ventricles to either the peritoneal cavity or an atrium of the heart.

Spina bifida occurs mostly in the lumbar and sacral regions (Figure 10.33). It is very variable in its presentation and symptoms. **Spina bifida occulta** has a small partial defect in the vertebral arch. The spinal cord or meninges does not protrude. Often the only sign is a tuft of hair on the skin overlying the defect.

In **spina bifida cystica**, no vertebral arch is formed. The spinal cord and meninges protrude through the opening and may or may not be covered with a thin layer of skin (Figure 10.33a and b). Protrusion of the meninges only is called a **meningocele**; protrusion of the meninges and spinal cord is called a **meningomyelocele**. Paralysis of the lower limbs may be present. The defect must be closed promptly to preserve spinal cord function and prevent infection. The cause of spina bifida is not known.

Fetal alcohol syndrome (FAS) can occur when a pregnant woman drinks alcohol. The child born with FAS has a small head, narrow eyes, and a flat face and nose (Figure 10.30). Intellect and growth are **impaired**. Fetal alcohol syndrome is the third most common cause of mental retardation in newborns.

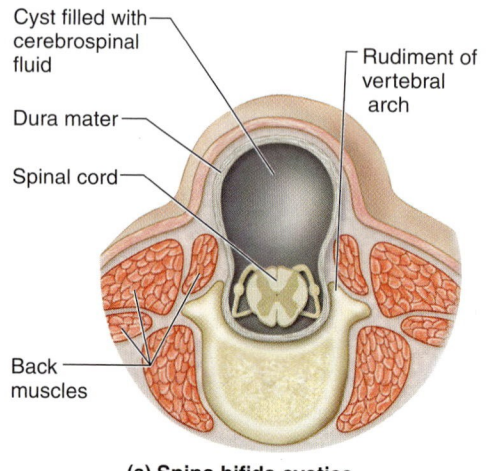

Cyst filled with cerebrospinal fluid

Rudiment of vertebral arch

Dura mater

Spinal cord

Back muscles

(a) Spina bifida cystica

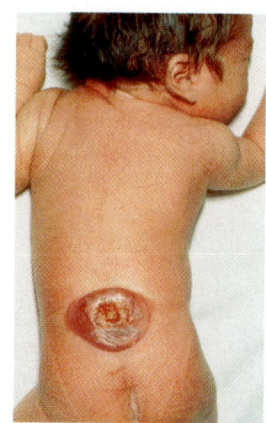

(b) Child with spina bifida cystica

▲ **FIGURE 10.33   Spina Bifida Cystica.**
(a) Cross section of spinal cord. (b) Child with spina bifida cystica.

WORD ANALYSIS AND DEFINITION

WORD	PRONUNCIATION	ELEMENTS		DEFINITION
anencephaly	AN-en-SEF-ah-lee	S/ P/ R/	-aly *condition* an- *without* -enceph- *brain*	Born without cerebral hemispheres
anomaly	ah-NOM-ah-lee		Greek *abnormality*	Structural abnormality present at birth
hydrocephalus	high-droh-SEF-ah-lus	S/ P/ R/	-us *pertaining to* hydro- *water* -cephal- *head*	Enlarged head due to excess CSF in the cerebral ventricles
meningocele	meh-NING-oh-seal	S/ R/CF	-cele *hernia* mening/o- *meninges*	Protrusion of the meninges from the spinal cord or brain through a defect in the vertebral column or cranium
meningomyelocele	meh-nin-go-MY-el-oh-seal	S/ R/CF R/CF	-cele *hernia* -myel/o- *spinal cord* mening/o- *meninges*	Protrusion of the spinal cord and meninges through a defect in the vertebral arch of one or more vertebrae
microcephaly	MY-kro-SEF-ah-lee	P/ R/	micro- *small* -cephaly *head*	An abnormally small head
spina bifida	SPY-nah BIH-fi-dah	R/ P/ R/	spina *spine* bi- *two* -fida *split*	Failure of one or more vertebral arches to close during fetal development
spina bifida cystica	SIS-tik-ah	S/ R/	-ica *pertaining to* cyst- *cyst*	Meninges and spinal cord protruding through the absent vertebral arch and having the appearance of a cyst
spina bifida occulta	OH-kul-tah	R/	occulta *hidden*	The deformity is not apparent from the surface
teratogen teratogenic (adj) (*Note:* Has two suffixes.)	TER-ah-toe-jen TER-ah-toe-jen-ik	S/ S/ R/CF	-ic *pertaining to* -gen *produce, create* terat/o- *monster*	Agent that produces fetal deformities

EXERCISES

Search and find the correct term for the element you are given. Circle the best answer.

1. Find the term with the prefix meaning *without:*

   hydrocephalus   anencephaly   impairment

2. Find the term with the root meaning *cyst:*

   meningocele   cystica   teratogen

3. Find the term with the root meaning *monster:*

   teratogen   spina   myelomeningocele

4. Find the term with the prefix meaning *water:*

   teratogenic   hydrocephalus myelomeningocele

5. Find the term with the suffix meaning *hernia:*

   meningocele   hydrocephalus   anomaly

6. Find the term with the root meaning *split:*

   bifida   occulta   cystica

7. Find the term with the root meaning *head:*

   anomaly   hydrocephalus   meningocele

8. Find the term with the root meaning *hidden:*

   spina bifida   spina bifida cystica   spina bifida occulta

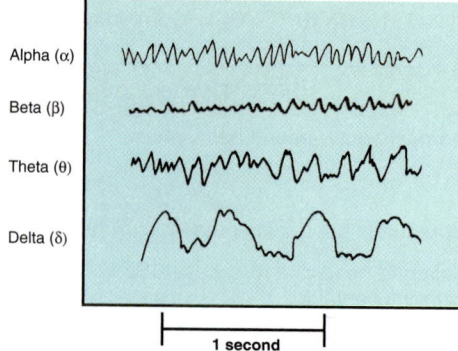

▲ FIGURE 10.34 Four Classes of Brain Waves on EEG

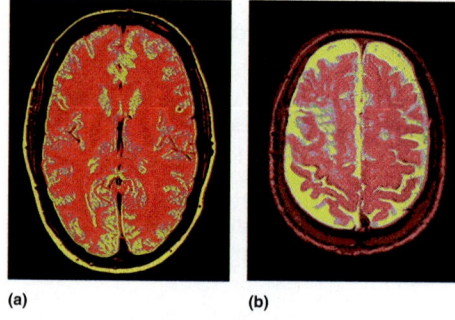

(a)   (b)

▲ FIGURE 10.35 Brain Sections.
(a) MRI Scan of Normal Brain. *(b)* MRI Scan of Alzheimer Disease Showing Cerebral Atrophy *(yellow)*.

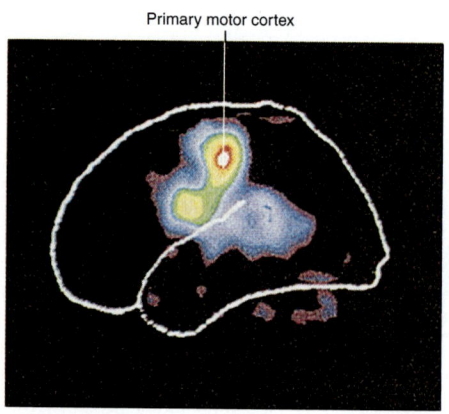

▲ FIGURE 10.36 PET Scan of the Brain Showing the Motor Cortex.

DIAGNOSTIC PROCEDURES IN NEUROLOGY

Lumbar puncture (spinal tap) has been shown earlier. Laboratory examination of the CSF that shows white blood cells suggests meningitis. High protein levels indicate meningitis or damage to the brain or spinal cord. Blood suggests a brain hemorrhage or a traumatic tap.

Electroencephalography records the brain's electrical activity and helps identify seizure disorders, sleep disturbances, degenerative brain disorders, and brain damage *(Figure 10.34)*.

Computed tomography (CT), a computer-enhanced x-ray technique, generates images of slices of the brain and can detect a wide range of brain and spinal cord disorders, including tumors, areas of dead brain tissue due to stroke, and birth defects.

Magnetic resonance imaging (MRI) produces highly detailed anatomic images of most neurologic disorders, including strokes, brain tumors, and myelin sheath damage *(Figure 10.35)*.

Magnetic resonance angiography uses an injection of a radiopaque dye to produce images of blood vessels of the head and neck during MRI.

Cerebral angiography is an invasive procedure to inject a radiopaque dye into the blood vessels of the neck and brain. It can detect blood vessels that are partially or completely blocked, aneurysms, or arteriovenous malformations.

Color Doppler ultrasonography uses high-frequency sound (ultrasound) waves to show different rates of blood flow through the arteries of the neck or the base of the brain. This evaluates TIAs and the risk of a full-blown stroke.

Echoencephalography uses ultrasound waves to produce an image of the brain in children under the age of two because their skulls are thin enough for the waves to pass through them.

Positron emission tomography (PET) involves attaching radioactive molecules onto a substance necessary for brain function (for example, the sugar glucose). As the molecules circulate in the brain, the radioactive labels give off positively charged signals that can be recorded *(Figure 10.36)*.

Myelography is the use of x-rays of the spinal cord that are taken after a radiopaque dye has been injected into the CSF by spinal tap. It has been replaced by MRI when that is available.

Evoked responses are when stimuli for vision, sound, and touch are used to activate specific areas of the brain and their responses are measured with EEG or PET scans. This provides information about how that specific area of the brain is functioning in disorders such as MS.

Electromyography involves placing small needles into a muscle to record its electrical activity at rest and during contraction. It is used to provide information in disorders of muscles, peripheral nerves, and the **neuromuscular** junction.

Nerve conduction studies measure the speed at which motor or sensory nerves conduct impulses. It excludes disorders of the brain, spinal cord, and muscles and focuses on the peripheral nerves.

WORD	PRONUNCIATION	ELEMENTS		DEFINITION
Doppler	**DOP**-ler		Johann Christian Doppler, 1803–1853, Austrian mathematician and physicist	Diagnostic instrument that sends an ultrasonic beam into the body
Doppler ultrasonography color Doppler ultrasonography	**DOP**-ler **UL**-trah-soh-**NOG**-rah-fee	S/ P/ R/CF	-graphy *recording* ultra- *beyond* -son/o- *sound*	Detects direction, velocity, and turbulence of blood flow; used in workup of stroke patients Computer-generated color image to show directions of blood flow
echoencephalography	**EK**-oh-en-sef-ah-**LOG**-rah-fee	S/ R/CF P/ R/CF	-graphy *recording* ech/o- *sound wave* -en- *in* -cephal/o- *head*	Use of ultrasound in the diagnosis of intracranial lesions
electromyography	ee-**LEK**-troh-my-**OG**-rah-fee	S/ R/CF R/CF	-graphy *recording* electr/o- *electricity* -my/o- *muscle*	Recording of electrical activity in muscle
myelography	my-eh-**LOG**-rah-fee	S/ R/CF	-graphy *recording* myel/o- *spinal cord*	Radiography of the spinal cord and nerve roots after injection of contrast medium into the subarachnoid space
nerve conduction study	NERV kon-**DUK**-shun **STUD**-ee	R/ S/ P/ R/ R/	nerve *nerve* -ion *action* con- *with, together* -duct- *lead* study *inquiry*	Procedure to measure the speed at which an electrical impulse travels along a nerve
neuromuscular	**NYUR**-oh-**MUSS**-kyu-lar	S/ R/CF R/	-ar *pertaining to* neur/o- *nerve* -muscul- *muscle*	A junction where a nerve supplies muscle tissue

EXERCISES

Analyze the following diagnostic procedures based on their elements alone, then answer the questions. Fill in the blanks.

1. echoencephalography

   The combining form _____ tells me this is a diagnostic procedure on the _____

2. electromyography

   The combining form _____ tells me this is a diagnostic procedure on the _____

3. myelography

   The combining form _____ tells me this is a diagnostic procedure on the _____

4. Each of the three procedures listed above ends with the suffix _____, which

   means _____.

5. Change the suffix in each of these terms to -gram, which means the actual record produced by the diagnostic procedure. Write the new terms below.

   _____   _____   _____

You have now learned six new terms related to diagnostic procedures in neurology!

Pharmacology of the Nervous System

The transmission of impulses from one neuron to another and from a neuron to a cell is achieved by **neurotransmitters at synaptic connections**. Drugs that affect the nervous system, called psychoactive drugs, target this synaptic mechanism.

Psychoactive drugs are able to change mood, behavior, cognition, and anxiety. They can be classified into several families:

1. **Stimulants. Caffeine, nicotine, amphetamines**, and **cocaine** enhance the stimulation provided by the **sympathetic nervous system**. They cause the level of **dopamine** to rise in the synapses, leading to the pleasurable effects associated with these drugs.

2. **Sedatives. Ethanol** (beverage alcohol), **barbiturates**, and **meprobamate** decrease the sensitivity of the postsynaptic neurons to quiet the nervous excitement. They also act on the sleep centers to induce sleep.

3. **Inhaled anesthetics** such as isoflurane act similarly to but are more powerfull than sedatives.

4. **Opiates. Morphine, codeine, heroin, methadone**, and **oxycodone** depress nerve transmission in sensory pathways of the brain and spinal cord. They also inhibit centers in the brain controlling coughing, breathing, and intestinal motility. Codeine is used in cough medicines. Constipation is a side-effect for all of these drugs. Opiates are **addictive** because they produce **tolerance** and physical dependence.

5. **Opiate antagonists**, such as **naloxone** and **naltrexone**, prevent opiates from acting in the synapses. They can be used in drug overdose and to help recovering heroin addicts stay drug free.

6. **Tranquilizers** such as **chlorpromazine, haloperidol**, and the **enzodiazapines** (Librium, Valium, Xanax) act like sedatives but without their sleep-inducing effect.

7. **Antidepressants** all increase the amount of **serotonin** at the synapses where it is a neurotransmitter. Zoloft and Prozac are examples.

8. **Antiepileptics** act in different ways on the synaptic junction to prevent stimuli passing across the synapse. Phenytoin and carbamazepine are examples.

9. **Psychedelics** distort sensory perceptions, particularly sight and sound. They can be natural plant products, such as mescaline, psilocybin, and dimethyltryptamine. They can be **synthetic**, such as **lysergic acid diethylamide (LSD)**, **methylemedioxymethamphetamine (MDMA** or "ecstasy"), and **phencyclidine (PCP** or "angel dust"). They increase the amount of serotonin in the synaptic junctions, and some have an additional amphetamine stimulation.

10. **Marijuana** has the active ingredient **tetrahydrocannabinol (THC)**. It produces the drowsiness of sedatives like alcohol, the dulling of pain like opiates, and, in high doses, the perception distortions of the psychedelics. Unlike opiates or sedatives, tolerance does not occur.

Abbreviations

LSD	lysergic acid diethylamide
MDMA	methylenedioxymethamphetamine (ecstasy)
PCP	phencyclidine (angel dust)
THC	tetrahydrocannabinol (marijuana)

WORD ANALYSIS AND DEFINITION

S = Suffix   P = Prefix   R = Root   R/CF = Combining Form

WORD	PRONUNCIATION		ELEMENTS	DEFINITION
addict	AD-ikt	P/ R/	ad- *to* -dict *consent*	One who cannot live without a substance or practice
addiction	ah-DIK-shun	S/	-ion *condition. action*	Habitual psychologic and physiologic dependence on a substance or practice
addictive	ah-DIK-tiv	S/	-ive *pertaining to*	Producing or causing addiction
antagonist	an-TAG-oh-nist	S/ P/ R/	-ist *agent* ant- *against* -agon- *contend against*	An opposing structure, agent, disease, or process
antagonism	an-TAG-oh-nizm	S/	-ism *a process*	Situation of opposing
marijuana	mar-ih-HWAN-ah		Mexican Spanish *María Juana*	Dried, flowering leaves of the plant *Cannabis sativa*
psychedelic	sigh-keh-DEL-ik	S/ R/ R/	-ic *pertaining to* psyche- *mind, soul* -del- *visible*	Agent that intensifies sensory perception
psychoactive	sigh-koh-AK-tiv	S/ R/CF R/	-ive *quality of* psych/o- *mind, soul* -act- *to do*	An agent able to alter mood, behavior, and/or cognition
sedative sedation	SED-ah-tiv se-DAY-shun	S/ R/ S/	-ive *pertaining to* sedat- *to calm* -ion *condition, action*	Agent that calms nervous excitement State of being calmed
stimulant stimulate (verb) stimulation	STIM-you-lant STIM-you-late stim-you-LAY-shun	S/ R/	-ant *forming* stimul- *excite, strengthen*	Agent that excites or strengthens functional activity Arousal to increased functional activity
synthetic synthesis (noun)	sin-THET-ik SIN-the-sis	S/ P/ R/ S/	-ic *pertaining to* syn- *together* -thet- *place, arrange* -esis *condition*	Built up or put together from simpler compounds The process of building a compound from different elements
tolerance	TOL-er-ants	S/ R/	-ance *state of* toler- *endure*	Become accustomed to a stimulus or drug
tranquilizer	TRANG-kwih-lie-zer	S/ R/	-izer *affects in a particular way* tranquil- *calm*	Agent that calms without sedating or depressing

EXERCISES

*Deconstruct this **language of neurology** into its basic elements to help you understand the meaning of the term. Write the elements between the slashes. The first one is done for you. Every term does not need every element, so you will have some blanks.*

1. antagonist   _____ant_____ / _____agon_____ / _____ist_____

2. addict   _____ / _____ / _____

3. tranquilizer   _____ / _____ / _____

4. stimulant   _____ / _____ / _____

5. synthetic   _____ / _____ / _____

6. pyschedelic   _____ / _____ / _____

7. tolerance   _____ / _____ / _____

8. psychoactive   _____ / _____ / _____

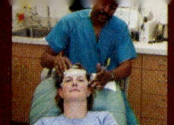

NERVOUS SYSTEM
CHALLENGE YOUR KNOWLEDGE

A. Proofread Your Documentation: The radiologist has just dictated the following report for a patient of the Fulwood Neurology Clinic. Before you print a final copy, always proofread the document for errors. Can you find the errors in the report? Circle the incorrect words in the report, then write the corrected words on the lines below, and include a brief definition for each correct word.

> CT of the head: CT of the head performed without IV contrast demonstrates mild dilutation of the venticular system. The sulcuses are also prominent. These findings are consistent with mild atrophie.
> No intracerbral hemorhage, subdaral, or epedural hemetoma is noted. No shift of the midline structures is noted.
> IMPRESSION: mild cerebral atrohy.

_____

_____

_____

_____

_____

_____

_____

_____

_____

B. Word elements are the building blocks of every medical term. Fill in the chart below by deconstructing the medical terms into their basic elements and meanings. Start with the suffix. The meaning of the entire term will then be self-evident by combining the meanings of the elements. The first term is done for you.

Term	Prefix	Root/CF	Suffix	Meaning of Element
amyotrophic			Ic	*Pertaining to*
	A			*Without*
		Myo		*Muscle*
		Troph		*Development*
neurotransmitter			Er	
	Trans			
		Mitt		
		Neuro		
endarterectomy			Ectomy	
	End			
		Arter		

Term	Prefix	Root/CF	Suffix	Meaning of Element
microangiopathy			Pathy	
	Micro			
		Angio		
cryoneurolysis			Lysis	
		Neuro		
	Cryo			
mononeuropathy			Pathy	
	Mono			
		Neuro		
compression			Ion	
		Press		
	Com			

C. **Roots and combining forms remain the core of a medical term.** Reinforce your knowledge of this element with the following exercise. Match the correct root or combining form in column 1 to its meaning in column 2.

_____ 1. -pathy

_____ 2. cephalo-

_____ 3. -algesia

_____ 4. syringo-

_____ 5. audit-

_____ 6. -trophy

_____ 7. proto-

_____ 8. pleg-

_____ 9. somn-

_____ 10. angio-

A. hearing

B. first

C. sleep

D. vessel

E. tube, pipe

F. disease

G. development

H. head

I. sensation of pain

J. paralysis

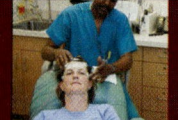
NERVOUS SYSTEM

D. **Word Building Skills:** Combine your knowledge of word elements and medical terminology construction, together with the power of your millions of brain cells, to answer the following questions.

1. In the term **neuralgia**, the suffix is _____, which means _____. If the element "**ceph**"

    means *head*, what does the term **cephalgia** mean? _____ .

    What does the term **arthralgia** mean? _____. If the element "**caus**" means *burning*, what is **causalgia?**

    _____ .

2. Exacerbation and remission are both processes, as defined by their _____ (which word element?). Using their Latin roots, explain the difference between these two processes.

    Exacerbation means: _____

    Remission means: _____

E. **Similar but Different:** The following medical language contains a similar root, but the suffixes change the meaning of the terms. Use the correct form of these terms in the following sentences. Fill in the blanks.

| **neurosurgery** | **neurologic** | **neurologist** | **neurosurgeon** | **neurology** |

The _____ from the Fulwood _____ Department referred the patient to

a _____ for surgical consultation. The patient's _____ condition was deterio-

rating rapidly, and she would probably need _____.

F. **Plurals:** Refresh your memory on the rules for plurals. Precision in communication depends on this. The singular form is given; circle the best answer for the plural form.

1. **ganglion:**   ganglius   ganglia   gangli

2. **plexus:**   plexuses   plexuia   plexui

3. **sulcus:**   sulces   sulci   sulcia

4. **gyrus:**   gyri   gryia   gryuses

G. **Prefixes can be a very important part of a medical term.** Challenge your knowledge of this chapter's prefixes by correctly filling in the following chart. You are given either the meaning or the prefix—complete the rest of the chart.

Prefix	Meaning of Prefix	Medical Term Containing that Prefix	Meaning of Medical Term
dis			
con			
	self		
re			
	together		
an			
de			

H. Medical Language: The nervous system is a complicated one and has a large range of vocabulary. Assess your knowledge of the nervous system by circling the correct answer in the questions below.

1. Abnormal movements marked by rapid contraction and relaxation of a muscle or muscle groups is called:

   a. compression

   b. clonus

   c. coma

   d. contusion

   e. concussion

2. Astrocytes, oligodendrocytes, microglia, ependymal, Schwann, and satellite are all terms relating to:

   a. capillaries

   b. tumors

   c. hematomas

   d. neuroglia

   e. ganglia

3. Body temperature is regulated by the:

   a. thalamus

   b. hypothalamus

   c. limbic system

   d. pons

   e. cerebellum

4. Centers that control vital visceral activities are located in the:

   a. pons

   b. corpus

   c. medulla oblongata

   d. hypothalamus

   e. CSF

NERVOUS SYSTEM

I. **Medical Language:** The nervous system is a complicated one and has a large range of vocabulary. Assess your knowledge of the nervous system by circling the correct answer in the questions below.

1. An agent capable of preventing or arresting epilepsy is called an:

   a. antidiuretic

   b. antibiotic

   c. antiepileptic

   d. antidepressant

   e. antibody

2. Administration of tPA is given for:

   a. ALS

   b. thrombolysis

   c. seizures

   d. dementia

   e. meningitis

3. **Hypoglossal** refers to structures that can be found under the:

   a. diaphragm

   b. tongue

   c. jawbone

   d. bronchus

   e. alveoli

4. In simple terms, a **synapse** is a:

   a. malformation

   b. birth defect

   c. junction

   d. seizure

   e. vesicle

5. Implantation of radioactive pellets directly into a tumor is called:

   a. bradytherapy

   b. bradycardia

   c. brachytherapy

   d. brachial plexus

   e. none of the above

6. A state of deep unconsciousness is called:

   a. coma

   b. seizure

   c. sulcus

   d. dementia

   e. hypoperfusion

7. Groove that separates gyri:

   a. gyrus

   b. cortex

   c. fissure

   d. sulcus

   e. dermatome

8. The cerebral hemispheres are covered by a thin layer of gray matter called the:

   a. basal ganglia

   b. corpus callosum

   c. frontal lobe

   d. cerebral cortex

   e. cerebellum

9. The abbreviation for short-term, small strokes is:

   a. EEG

   b. HACE

   c. TIA

   d. PET

   e. SBS

10. The medical term that means pertaining to or caused by a seizure is:

    a. clonic

    b. ictal

    c. tonic

    d. visceral

    e. synaptic

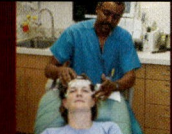

NERVOUS SYSTEM

J. **Terminology Challenge:** The difference in one or two letters makes for precision in medical language. Brady- and brachy- have two different meanings. Define them below, and give an example of their use in a term.

Brady- means: _____ Example:_____

Brachy- means: _____ Example:_____

K. **Recall and Review:** The following exercise on word elements contains some elements from this chapter and the previous chapter. Try to recall the previous elements without turning back in your book. Check the type of element, then write its meaning. Fill in the blanks.

Element	Prefix	Root/CF	Suffix	Meaning of Element
cyan	_____	_____	_____	_____
arachn	_____	_____	_____	_____
ar	_____	_____	_____	_____
pulmono	_____	_____	_____	_____
pleg	_____	_____	_____	_____
ectomy	_____	_____	_____	_____
purul	_____	_____	_____	_____
cervic	_____	_____	_____	_____
oro	_____	_____	_____	_____
plasty	_____	_____	_____	_____

L. **Abbreviations are only helpful if you know what they are meant to communicate.** Rewrite the following sentences without their abbreviations, but communicate the same message.

1. PPS can appear an unspecified number of years after the patient has had polio.

    _____

    _____

2. Because the mother is an alcoholic, the infant's symptoms have been diagnosed as FAS.

    _____

    _____

3. The patient's CVA has affected her PNS.

    _____

    _____

4. The BBB exists to protect brain tissue.

_____

_____

5. The patient's CSF will be tested today with an LP.

_____

_____

M. **In Your Own Words:** Translate into layman's terms these sentences directly from this chapter. How well do you understand what you read? Can you explain these sentences in nonmedical language?

1. Brain **abscess** is most often a direct spread of infection from **sinusitis**, **otitis media** or **mastoiditis**.
   Rewrite this sentence in your own words.

   _____

   _____

2. **Carotid endarterectomy** may be necessary if a carotid **artery** is significantly **occluded** with **plaque**.
   Rewrite this sentence in your own words.

   _____

   _____

3. Risk factors for **hemorrhagic strokes** are **hypertension, cerebral arteriovenous malformation**, and cerebral **aneurysms**.
   Rewrite this sentence in your own words.

   _____

   _____

   _____

   What exactly is a **risk factor?**

   _____

   _____

NERVOUS SYSTEM

N. Test-Taking Strategy Practice: Use your knowledge of medical terminology to insert the correct term in the appropriate statement. Not all answers will be used, and no answer will be used more than once.

hemiplegia   somatic   afferent

meningitis   meningioma   quadriplegia

festinant   comatose   visceral

neurotransmitters   dendrite   dementia

Study Hint
Start by answering the questions where you are sure of the correct answer. Cross off the answer in the column after you insert it in the statement, and then answer the rest of the questions from the choices you have left. You will then be working with a smaller and smaller group of choices, which will make it easier to spot the correct answer.

1. _____ nerves carry signals from major organs such as the heart, lungs, stomach, and intestines.

2. State of deep unconsciousness: _____

3. A process, or extension of a neuron is a(n) _____.

4. Shuffling gait: _____

5. Loss of the mind's cognitive functions: _____

6. Paralysis of all four limbs: _____

7. Chemicals that cross the synapse to another neuron are called _____.

8. _____ nerves carry signals from the skin, muscles, bones, and joints.

O. Precision of Medical Language: Medical language has many terms that look and sound similar. You must use the precise term in spoken and written medical communication and documentation. If a patient were to ask, you should be able to explain to him/her the difference between the pairs of words shown below. Write a short answer.

1. concussion and contusion:

   _____

   _____

   _____

2. meningitis and meningioma:

   _____

   _____

   _____

3. cerebellum and cerebrum:

   _____

   _____

   _____

P. **Construct the proper medical terms for the statements.** You have an assortment of prefixes, roots, combining forms, and suffixes with which to construct your terms. Fill in the blanks.

hydro	lepsy	cryo
narco	lysis	esthesia
algia	occulta	a
neur/o	itis	para
an	trophy	post

1. Recurring episodes of falling asleep during the day: _____

2. Complete loss of sensation: _____

3. Temporary deactivation of nerve tissue using extreme cold: _____

4. Pain in the distribution of a nerve: _____

5. Wasting away of tissue: _____

6. Derived from a word meaning *hidden:* _____

Brain Teaser: From previous chapters, what is the term for microscopic (hidden) blood in stool? _____

Q. **Diseases and Disorders:** The Fulwood Neurology Clinic treats patients with varied diseases and disorders of the nervous system. Are you familiar enough with their terminology and symptoms to match the correct disease/disorder with the appropriate statement for each patient? Circle the correct choice.

1. Patient has had a hemorrhagic stroke. Another name for this is:

   intercranial hemorrhage   intercerebral hemorrhage   intracranial hemorrhage

2. Patient bumped head on low doorway:

   concussion   seizure   convulsion

3. Patient has inflammation of the parenchyma of the brain:

   meningitis   encephalitis   vasculitis

4. Infection of the peripheral nerves arising from a reactivation of the chickenpox (varicella) virus:

   herpes simplex   shingles   post herpetic neuralgia

5. Infant has motor impairment resulting from brain damage at birth:

   Bell palsy   cerebral palsy   palsy

6. Patient had very bad dental infection that resulted in blood-borne pathogens lodging in her brain:

   brain tumor   brain abscess   brain hematoma

7. Patient complains of intermittent, shooting pain in the area of the face and head:

   trigeminal neuralgia   peripheral neuropathy   neuritis

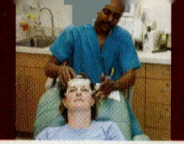

NERVOUS SYSTEM

R. Latin and Greek terms do not deconstruct like some medical terms. Test your knowledge of these terms with this exercise. Match the terms in column 1 to their correct meaning in column 2.

____1. epilepsy   A. stroke

____2. sulcus   B. braid

____3. efferent   C. swelling

____4. cerebrum   D. seizure

____5. ictal   E. brain

____6. plexus   F. ditch, furrow

____7. ganglion   G. away from

S. Pharmacology of Pain Management: Chronic pain management is a relatively new specialty of medicine. Medications are the cornerstone of this treatment. Demonstrate your knowledge of pain medications and their uses by filling in the chart. Place a checkmark (✓) in the correct column.

Medication	Prescribed for		
	Mild pain	Moderate pain	Severe pain
Percodan			
fentanyl			
Vicodin			
oxy- and hydromorphone			
continuous delivery system for drugs (pumps)			
hydrocodone			
acetaminophen			
oxycodone			
opiates combined with acetaminophen and NSAIDs			
NSAIDs			
morphine			

Discussion questions:

1. Name a diagnosis for which pain medication would be prescribed.

    _____. What type of medication might be prescribed? _____.

2. Name three pain medications that are available OTC (over-the-counter; that is, available without a prescription) in any pharmacy.

    _____

    _____

T. **Diagnostic Testing:** You are responsible for scheduling diagnostic procedures for patients in the Neurology Clinic at Fulwood Medical Center. Practice your *language of neurology* by scheduling these patients appropriately, using the tests listed below.

CT scan	**angiography**
myelography	**magnetic resonance imaging**
evoked responses	**nerve conduction studies**
electromyography	**electroencephalogram**
lumbar puncture or spinal tap	**magnetic resonance angiography**

Patient Needs/Symptoms:	Schedule Patient for:
Dr. Solis would like to measure the speed at which a patient's motor nerves conduct impulses.	
Doctor has ordered a recording of the electrical activity of the patient's brain.	
Dr. Solis suspects a tumor and needs to see a highly detailed anatomic image of the brain.	
Patient needs x-rays of the spinal cord taken after dye has been injected into it.	
Dr. Solis wants a sample of the patient's CSF.	
Patient has to schedule a study with contrast to image the cerebral blood vessels.	
Patient has a blocked carotid artery.	
Patient has possibly had a stroke; study will be looking for areas of dead brain tissue.	
Sensory stimuli will be used to activate specific areas of the brain and measure responses with EEG.	
Doctor wants to test and record the electrical activity of a patient's muscle at rest and during contractions	

U. **Precision in Documentation:** One of the six terms below is clearly the best choice for your answer—Circle it, and explain why it is the best choice.

Astrocytoma, ependymoma, and **oligodendroglioma** are all:

tumors   primary tumors   secondary tumors   primary brain tumors   secondary brain tumors

The most precise term is _____ because _____

_____ .

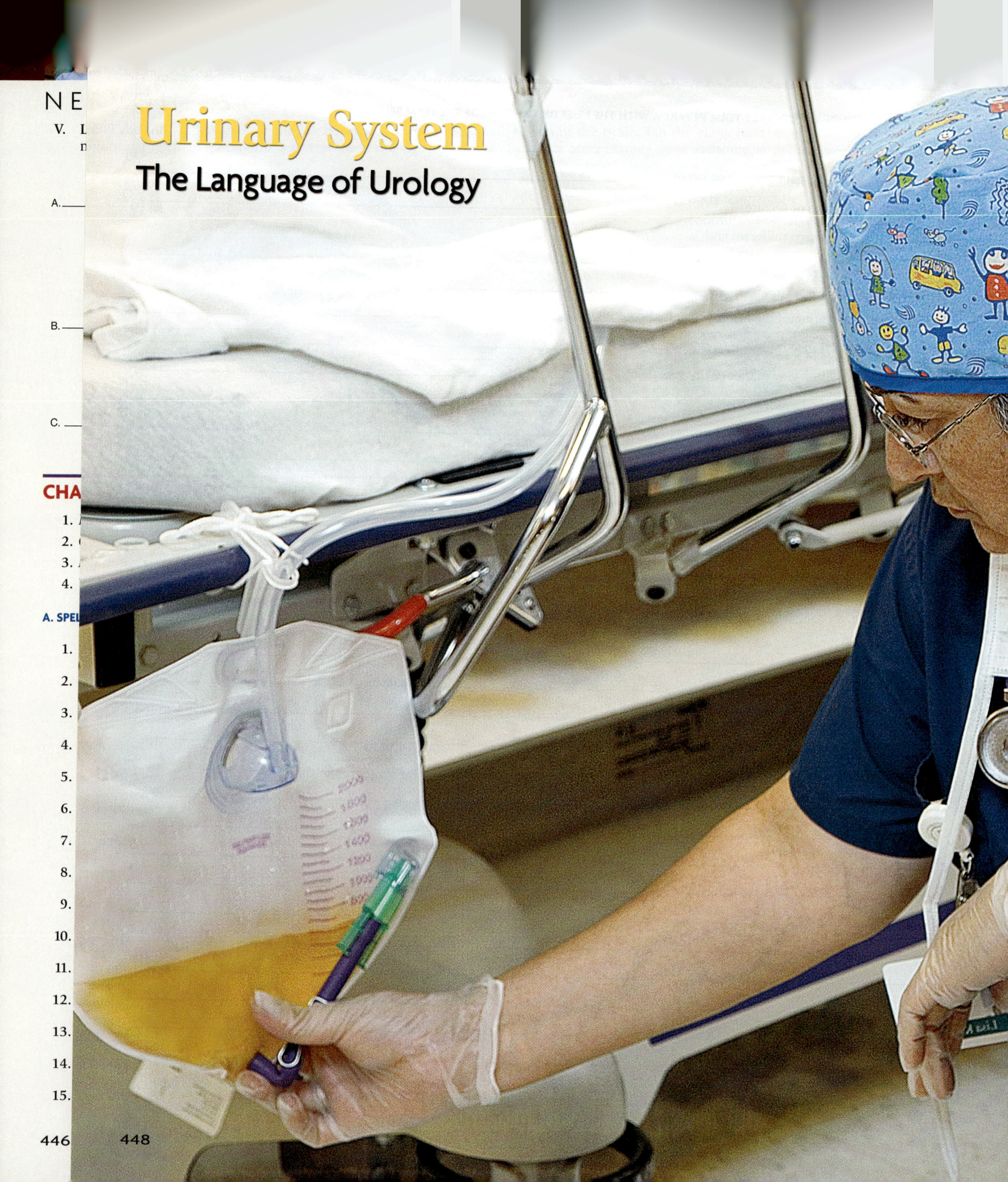

Urinary System
The Language of Urology

CASE REPORT 11.1

You are

. . . a surgical physician assistant working with **urologist** Phillip Johnson, MD, at Fulwood Medical Center.

Your patient is

. . . Mr. Nelson Hughes, a 58-year-old school principal. You are making your afternoon hospital visits to Dr. Johnson's patients. Earlier today you assisted at Mr. Hughes' surgery. A **laparoscopic radical nephrectomy** for a **TNM stage II renal** cell carcinoma (cancer) with no evidence of local invasion or lymph node involvement (metastasis) was performed.

Your job is to assess Mr. Hughes' postoperative state and determine whether post-operative complications exist.

Learning Outcomes

In order to define and understand these areas of concern, communicate with Dr. Johnson and the patient, and document Mr. Hughes' progress, you need to be able to:

- Apply the language of **urology** to the anatomy and physiology of the urinary system.

- Comprehend, analyze, spell, and write the medical terms of urology so that you communicate and document accurately and precisely in any health care setting.

- Recognize and pronounce the medical terms of urology so that you communicate verbally with accuracy and precision in any health care setting.

- Explain the effects of common urinary disorders on health.

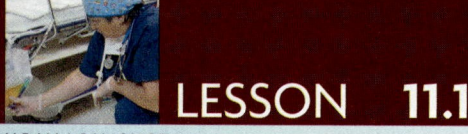

LESSON 11.1 Urinary System, Kidneys and Ureters

OBJECTIVES

While the respiratory system (see Chapter 9) **excretes** carbon dioxide and water, the integumentary system (see Chapter 3) excretes water, inorganic salts, and lactic acid in sweat, and the digestive tract (see Chapter 6) excretes water, salts, lipids, bile pigments, and other wastes, the urinary system carries the major burden of excretion.

Within the urinary system, the kidney is the agent that eliminates the waste products. If the kidneys fail to function, the other three systems of excretion are not able to replace it. Therefore, the kidney is a vital organ to be understood, and it brings with it a whole new set of terminology.

In this lesson, the information will enable you to:

- **Identify the location and anatomical features of the kidney.**
- **List the functions of the kidney.**
- **Trace the flow of fluid through the renal filtration process.**
- **Describe the functional anatomy of the ureters and urinary bladder.**
- **Explain how common disorders of the kidneys and ureters affect health.**
- **Apply correct medical terminology to the anatomy, physiology, and disorders of the kidneys and ureters.**

Keynote

The kidney is the major organ that eliminates the waste products of cellular metabolism.

Abbreviation

TNM *tumor-node-metastasis system of staging for cancer*

URINARY SYSTEM

The urinary system *(Figure 11.1)* consists of six organs:

- two **kidneys**
- a single **urinary bladder**
- two **ureters**
- a single **urethra**

The process of removing metabolic waste is called **excretion**. It is an essential process in maintaining **homeostasis** *(see Chapter 2)*. The metabolic wastes include carbon dioxide from cellular respiration, excess water and electrolytes, **nitrogenous** compounds from the breakdown of proteins, and **urea**. If these wastes are not eliminated, they poison the whole body.

In the body's cells, protein is broken down *(see Chapter 2)* into amino acids. When an amino acid is broken down, **ammonia** is produced. Ammonia is extremely toxic to cells. The liver quickly converts it to the less toxic urea, which is excreted by the kidneys.

FIGURE 11.1 (*a*) The Urinary System. (*b*) Structures of the urinary system are visible in this colored x-ray.

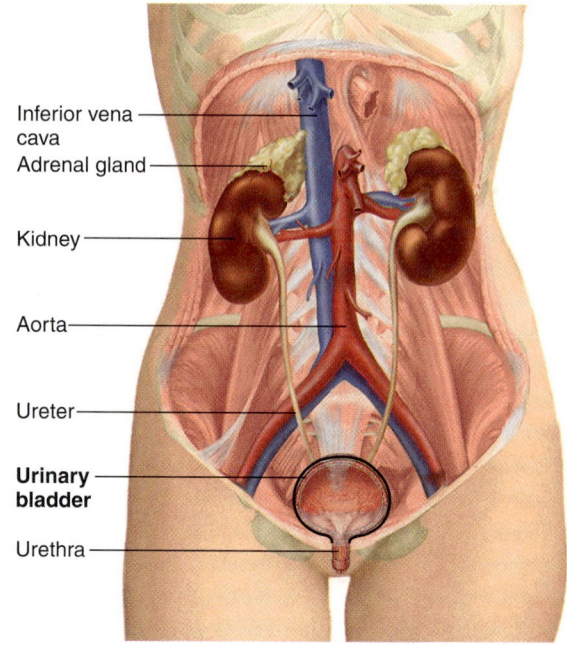
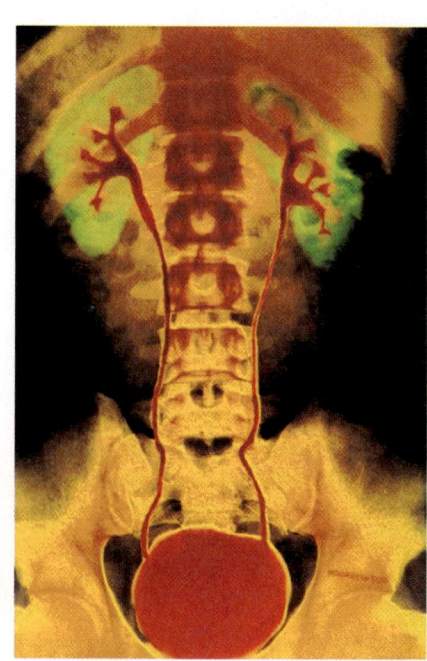

Inferior vena cava
Adrenal gland
Kidney
Aorta
Ureter
Urinary bladder
Urethra

(a)

(b)

WORD	PRONUNCIATION	ELEMENTS		DEFINITION
ammonia	ah-**MOAN**-ih-ah	R/	**-ia** suffix *condition* **ammon-** *ammonia*	Toxic breakdown product of amino acids
bladder	**BLAD**-er		Old English *bladder*	Hollow sac that holds fluid; for example, urine or bile
excretion	eks-**KREE**-shun		Latin *remove*	Removal of waste products of metabolism out of the body
excrete (verb)	eks-**KREET**			To pass out of the body the waste products of metabolism
kidney	**KID**-nee		Greek *kidney*	Organ of excretion
nephrectomy	neh-**FREK**-toe-me	S/ R/CF	**-ectomy** *surgical excision* **nephr/o-** *kidney*	Surgical removal of a kidney
nephrology	neh-**FROL**-oh-jee	S/	**-logy** *study of*	Medical specialty of diseases of the kidney
nephrologist	neh-**FROL**-oh-jist	S/	**-logist** *one who studies*	Medical specialist in disorders of the kidney
nitrogenous	ni-**TROJ**-en-us	S/ R/CF R/	**-ous** *pertaining to* **nitr/o-** *nitrogen* **-gen-** *create*	Containing or generating nitrogen
radical	**RAD**-ih-cal		Latin *root*	Extensive removal of disease process
renal	**REE**-nal	S/ R/	**-al** *pertaining to* **ren-** *kidney*	Pertaining to the kidney
urea urethra (***Note:*** One "e" = one tube.)	you-**REE**-ah you-**REE**-thra		Greek *urine* Greek *urethra*	End product of nitrogen metabolism Canal leading from the bladder to outside (***Note:*** The roots for **urethra** and **ureter** are different.)
urethral (adj)	you-**REE**-thral	S/ R/	**-al** *pertaining to* **urethr-** *urethra*	
urethritis	you-ree-**THRI**-tis	S/	**-itis** *inflammation*	Inflammation of the urethra (***Note:*** The roots for **urethra** and **ureter** are different.)
ureter (***Note:*** Two "e's" = two tubes.)	you-**RET**-er		Greek *urinary canal*	Tube that connects the kidney to the urinary bladder
ureteral (adj)	you-ree-**TER**-al	S/ R/	**-al** *pertaining to* **ureter-** *ureter*	
urine	**YUR**-in		Latin *urine*	Fluid and dissolved substances excreted by kidney
urinary (adj)	**YUR**-in-ary	S/ R/	**-ary** *pertaining to* **urin-** *urine*	Pertaining to urine
urinate (verb) urination	**YUR**-in-ate yur-ih-**NAY**-shun	S/ S/	**-ate** *action* **-ation** *action*	To pass urine The act of passing urine
urology	you-**ROL**-oh-jee	S/ R/CF	**-logy** *study of* **ur/o-** *urinary system*	Medical specialty of disorders of the urinary system
urologist	you-**ROL**-oh-jist	S/	**-logist** *one who studies*	Medical specialist in disorders of the urinary system

The Same but Different. *More than one word element can have the same meaning. In this body system,* **nephr-** *and* **ren-** *both mean kidney. The elements are not interchangeable—one particular element will be used for a specific term. You need to know them individually. Fill in the blanks. Read carefully!*

1. surgical removal of a kidney: _____/_____/_____

2. medical specialist in kidney treatment: _____/_____/_____

3. medical specialty in kidney diseases: _____/_____/_____

4. pertaining to the kidney: _____/_____/_____

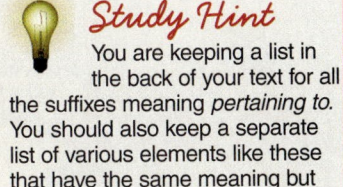

Study Hint

You are keeping a list in the back of your text for all the suffixes meaning *pertaining to*. You should also keep a separate list of various elements like these that have the same meaning but generate their own vocabulary.

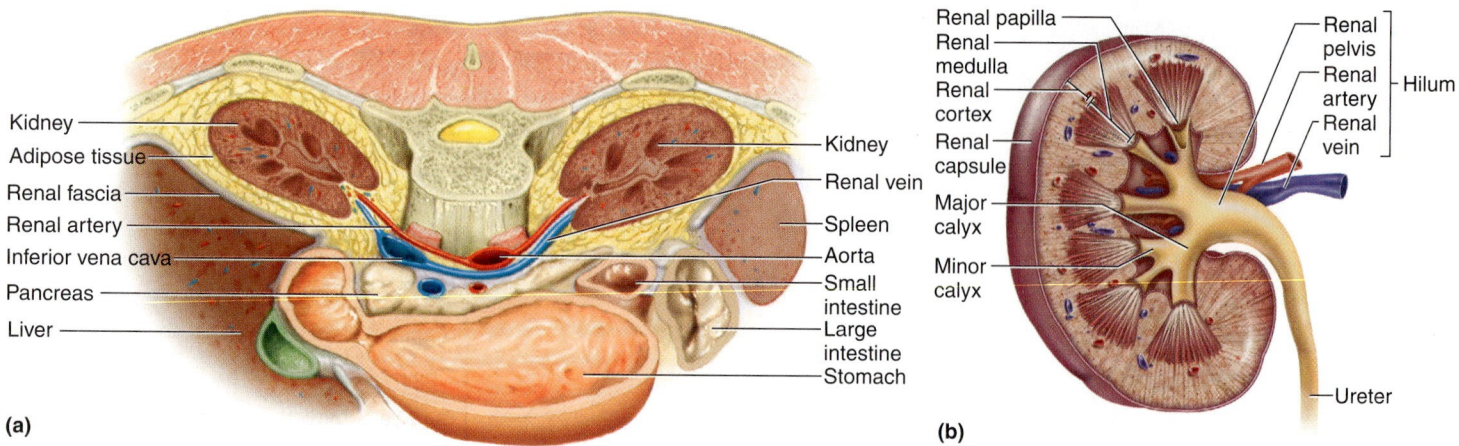

(a)

Kidney
Adipose tissue
Renal fascia
Renal artery
Inferior vena cava
Pancreas
Liver

Kidney
Renal vein
Spleen
Aorta
Small intestine
Large intestine
Stomach

(b)

Renal papilla
Renal medulla
Renal cortex
Renal capsule
Major calyx
Minor calyx

Renal pelvis
Renal artery — Hilum
Renal vein

Ureter

▲ **FIGURE 11.2   Kidney.**
(a) Transverse section of abdomen to show position of kidneys. (b) Longitudinal section of a kidney.

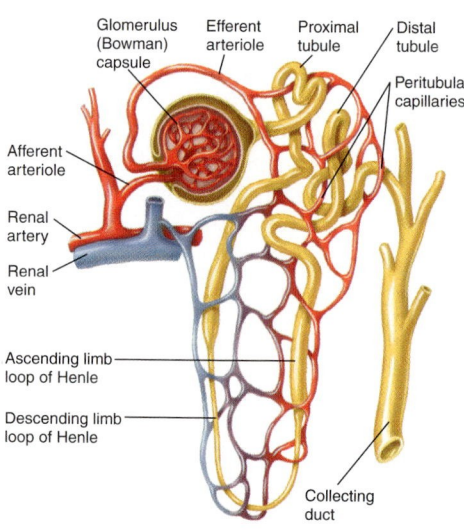

Glomerulus (Bowman) capsule
Efferent arteriole
Proximal tubule
Distal tubule
Peritubular capillaries
Afferent arteriole
Renal artery
Renal vein
Ascending limb loop of Henle
Descending limb loop of Henle
Collecting duct

▲ **FIGURE 11.3   Glomerulus and Renal Tubule.**

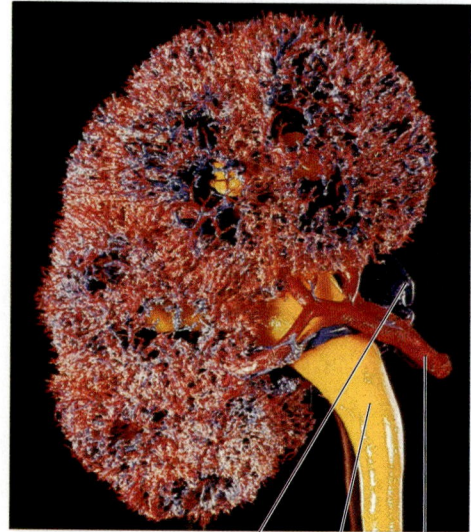

Renal vein   Ureter   Renal artery

▲ **FIGURE 11.4   Cast of Renal Arterial System.**

ANATOMY AND PHYSIOLOGY OF THE KIDNEYS

Each kidney is a bean-shaped organ about the size of a clenched fist. It is located on either side of the vertebral column behind the peritoneum and lies against the deep muscles of the back. The left kidney is behind the spleen, and the right kidney behind and below the liver *(Figure 11.2a).*

Waste-laden blood enters the kidney at its **hilum** *(Figure 11.2b)* through the renal artery. Excess water, urea, and other waste products are **filtered** from the blood by the kidney, collected in the ureter, and carried off to the bladder. The filtered blood exits through the renal vein at the hilum.

Each kidney has three regions *(Figure 11.2b):*

* an outer renal **cortex**—contains the **nephrons,** the basic filtration unit.

* an inner renal **medulla**—contains the collecting ducts, which merge together to form about 30 papillary ducts, that enter into a **calyx.**

* a central renal **pelvis**—a funnel-shaped structure into which the calyces open that forms the ureter.

In the cortex, the renal artery divides into smaller and smaller arterioles, each of which enters a nephron and divides into a network of approximately 50 capillaries, known as a **glomerulus.** The glomerulus is encased in the **glomerular capsule (Bowman capsule).** Because the blood is under pressure and the capillaries and glomerular capsule are **permeable,** much of the fluid from the blood filters through the capillary wall and glomerular capsule into the renal tubule, which includes the **loop of Henle** *(Figure 11.3).*

This **filtrate** entering the renal tubule contains water, urea, glucose, electrolytes, amino acids, and vitamins. Red blood cells, platelets, and plasma proteins are too large to pass through the capillary membrane, and they remain in the blood.

Approximately 180 liters (45 gallons) of filtrate are formed each day. As the filtrate passes down the renal tubule, over 90% of the water is returned to the blood by **reabsorption.** Glucose and minerals are also returned to the blood. Some residual wastes in the blood are **secreted** from the blood into the tubule. These interchanges between the filtrate in the tubule and the blood are made possible by a mesh of capillaries that surrounds the renal tubule *(Figure 11.3).* The material that remains in the tubule is urine. It consists of excess water, electrolytes, and urea.

The renal tubules merge to form collecting ducts *(Figure 11.3)* that merge into the calyces, then form the **renal pelvis** and become the **ureter.**

Purified blood is returned from the **peritubular** mesh of capillaries *(Figure 11.4)* to the circulatory system through the renal vein.

Functions of the kidneys are to:

* **filter** blood to eliminate wastes

* **regulate** blood volume and pressure by eliminating or conserving water as necessary

* **maintain homeostasis** by controlling the quantities of water and electrolytes

that are eliminated

WORD	PRONUNCIATION		ELEMENTS	DEFINITION
calyx calyces (pl)	KAY-licks KAY-lih-sees		Greek *cup of a flower*	Funnel-shaped structure
cortex cortices (pl) cortical (adj)	KOR-teks KOR-tih-sees KOR-tih-kal	S/ R/	-ical *pertaining to* cort- *cortex*	Outer portion of an organ
filtrate filter (verb) filtration	FIL-trate fil-TRAY-shun	S/ R/ S/	-ate *action* filtr- *strain through* -ation *action*	That which has passed through a filter Process of passing liquid through a filter
glomerulus glomeruli (pl) glomerular (adj)	glo-MER-you-lus glo-MER-you-lee glo-MER-you-lar		Latin *small ball of yarn*	Plexus of capillaries; part of a nephron
hilum hila (pl)	HIGH-lum HIGH-lah		Latin *small bit*	The part where the nerves and blood vessels enter and leave an organ
loop of Henle	LOOP of HEN-lee		Friedrich Henle, 1809–1885, German anatomist, pathologist, and histologist	Part of the renal tubule where reabsorption occurs
nephron	NEF-ron		Greek *kidney*	Filtration unit of the kidney; glomerulus + renal tubule
pelvis	PEL-vis		Latin *basin*	A cup-shaped cavity, as in the pelvis of the kidney
peritubular	PER-ih-too-BYU-lar	S/ P/ R/	-ar *pertaining to* peri- *around* -tubul- *small tube*	Surrounding the small renal tubules
permeable semipermeable impermeable	PER-me-ah-bull sem-ee-PER-me-ah-bull im-PER-me-ah-bull	S/ R/CF P/ P/	-able *capable* perm/e- *pass through* semi- *half* im- *not*	Allows passage of substances through a membrane Freely permeable to water but not to solutes Does not allow passage of anything
reabsorption (*Note:* This term has two prefixes.)	ree-ab-SORP-shun	S/ P/ P/ R/	-ion *process* re- *back* ab- *away from* -sorpt- *swallow*	Take back into the blood substances that had previously been filtered out from it
renin	REE-nin	S/ R/	-in *in* ren- *kidney*	Enzyme secreted by the kidney that causes vasoconstriction

- **secrete** the enzyme **renin;** if blood pressure falls in the kidney so that blood flow decreases, renin is produced and leads to widespread contraction of arterioles, which raises arterial pressure throughout the body
- **secrete** the hormone **erythropoietin,** which acts on the bone marrow to release red blood cells
- **synthesize vitamin D** to contribute to maintaining normal blood calcium levels

Keynote

Kidneys remove waste products from the blood by a process of **filtration.**

The renal cortex contains about one million nephrons, the functional unit of the kidney.

A nephron is the combination of a glomerulus and the renal tubule.

EXERCISES

Define and deconstruct *the following medical terms into their basic elements. Write the name of the element on the line below the slash. Fill in the blanks.*

1. passage of a substance through a membrane: _____ / _____ / _____

2. enzyme that causes vasconstriction: _____ / _____ / _____

3. surrounding the small kidney tubules: _____ / _____ / _____

4. blood takes back previously filtered substances: _____ / _____ / _____

Keynote:

Twenty-five to 30% of all renal cancers relate directly to smoking.

As little as one milliliter of blood will turn the urine red.

Keynote:

Hematuria can be caused by a lesion anywhere in the urinary system.

Keynote:

The acute form of glomerulonephritis has 100% recovery.

Acute interstitial nephritis causes 15% of cases of acute renal failure.

DISORDERS OF THE KIDNEYS

Renal cell carcinoma is the most common form of kidney cancer and occurs twice as often in men as in women. The cancer develops in the lining cells of the renal tubules, which is why Mr. Hughes had hematuria. Radical **nephrectomy** is the most common treatment for renal cell carcinoma.

Wilms tumor, or **nephroblastoma,** is a malignant kidney tumor of childhood, usually appearing between ages 3 and 8 years, that is treated effectively with a combination of surgery and chemotherapy.

Benign kidney tumors, such as **renal adenoma,** are usually asymptomatic, are discovered incidentally, and are not life-threatening.

Hematuria, blood in the urine, can be caused by lesions anywhere in the urinary system; this includes trauma (including long-distance running), infections, medications (such as quinine and phenytoin), and congenital diseases (such as sickle cell anemia). In **microscopic hematuria,** the urine is not red, and red blood cells can only be seen under a microscope or identified by a urine dipstick. Normal urine contains no blood. Excessive consumption of beets, rhubarb, and red food coloring can cause urine to be colored red. This is not hematuria. Also, in the collection of urine from a woman during menstruation, the urine can be contaminated with blood, giving the impression of hematuria.

Acute glomerulonephritis is an inflammation of the glomerulus. It damages the glomerular capillaries, allows protein and red blood cells to leak into the urine, and interferes with the clearance of waste products. In its acute form, it can develop rapidly after an episode of strep throat infection, most often in children. The *Streptococcus* bacteria do not invade the kidney but stimulate the immune system to overproduce antibodies that damage the glomeruli.

Chronic glomerulonephritis can occur with no history of kidney disease and present as kidney failure. It also occurs in **diabetic nephropathy** and can be associated with autoimmune diseases such as lupus erythematosus; HIV can cause glomerular disease even before developing AIDS.

Nephrotic syndrome involves large amounts of protein leaking out into the urine so that the level of protein in the blood falls. In children it nearly always responds to treatment with steroids. The causes of nephrotic syndrome are described in *Table 11.1.* The most obvious symptom is fluid retention with edema of the ankles and legs. This is treated with **diuretics,** restricting salt in the diet, and reducing fluid intake.

Interstitial nephritis is an inflammation of the spaces between the renal tubules. Most often it is acute and temporary. It can be an allergic reaction to or a side effect of drugs such as penicillin or ampicillin, NSAIDs, and diuretics. Treatment is directed to the underlying disease. Temporary **dialysis** may be necessary.

Pyelonephritis is an infection of the renal pelvis. Most often it occurs as part of a total **urinary tract infection (UTI),** commencing in the urinary bladder. It has a high mortality rate in the elderly and in people with a compromised immune system *(see Chapter 15).* It requires aggressive antibiotic therapy.

WORD	PRONUNCIATION	ELEMENTS		DEFINITION
dialysis	die-**AL**-ih-sis	S/ R/	-lysis *to separate* dia- *complete*	An artificial method of filtration to remove excess waste materials and water from the body
diuretic (adj)	die-you-**RET**-ik	S/ P/ R/	-etic *pertaining to* di- *complete* -ur- *urine*	Agent that increases urine output
diuresis (noun)	die-you-**REE**-sis	S/	-esis *condition*	Excretion of large volumes of urine
glomerulonephritis	glo-**MER**-you-low-nef-**RYE**-tis	S/ R/CF R/	-itis *inflammation* glomerul/o- *glomerulus* -nephr- *kidney*	Infection of the glomeruli of the kidney
hematuria	he-mah-**TYU**-ree-ah	S/ R/	-uria *urine* hemat- *blood*	Blood in the urine
interstitial	in-ter-**STISH**-al	S/ P/ R/	-ial *pertaining to* inter- *between* -stit- *space*	Pertaining to the spaces between cells in a tissue or organ
nephritis	neh-**FRY**-tis	S/ R/	-itis *inflammation* nephr- *kidney*	Inflammation of the kidney
nephropathy	neh-**FROP**-ah-thee	S/ R/CF	-pathy *disease* nephr/o- *kidney*	Any disease of the kidney
nephrotic syndrome	neh-**FROT**-ik **SIN**-drome	S/ R/CF	-tic *pertaining to* nephr/o- *kidney*	Glomerular disease with marked loss of protein
nephrosis (syn)	neh-**FRO**-sis	S/	-osis *condition*	
pyelonephritis	**PIE**-eh-loh-neh-**FRY**-tis	S/ R/CF R/	-itis *inflammation* pyel/o- *renal pelvis* -nephr- *kidney*	Inflammation of the kidney and renal pelvis
Wilms tumor	WILMZ **TOO**-mor		Max Wilms, 1867–1918, German surgeon	Cancerous kidney tumor of childhood
nephroblastoma (syn)	**NEF**-roh-blas-**TOE**-mah	S/ R/CF R/	-oma *tumor, mass* nephr/o- *kidney* -blast- *embryonic*	

TABLE 11.1 Types of Nephrotic Syndrome

Disease (as seen on biopsy)	Description
minimal change disease	Most common in children; responds to steroids
focal segmental glomerulosclerosis (FSGS)	Cause unknown; little response to treatment
membranous nephropathy	Cause unknown; may respond to immunosuppressive treatment
diabetes	Occurs if blood sugar has been poorly controlled

EXERCISES

Word elements will help you analyze the following medical terms for the urinary system. Divide the medical term into elements using a slash (/) and answer the questions by using your knowledge of these elements to fill in the blanks.

1. pyelonephritis   What does the suffix mean? _____

2. hematuria   Where is the blood? _____

3. interstitial   This prefix specifies a location—where is *interstitial* located? _____

4. nephropathy   Which organ has this disease? _____

5. nephritis   How is this term different from **pyelonephritis?** _____

6. Which suffixes appearing in this WAD have a similar meaning? _____, _____, and _____ all mean *pertaining to*. Add them to your list.

DISORDERS OF THE KIDNEYS (continued)

Hypertension, with its high blood pressure, can damage the renal arterioles and glomeruli, causing them to thicken and narrow. This reduces their capability to remove wastes and excess water, which can cause the blood pressure to rise even more. If the cause of hypertension is not known, it is called **primary (or essential) hypertension** *(see Chapter 8)*.

Polycystic kidney disease (PKD) is an inherited disease. Large, fluid-filled cysts grow within the kidneys and press against the kidney tissue. Finally, the kidneys cannot function effectively.

Acute renal failure (ARF) makes the kidneys suddenly stop filtering waste products from the blood. The signs and symptoms can include: **oliguria**—reduction of urine output, **anuria**—cessation of urine output, confusion, seizures, coma.

The causes of acute renal failure include:

- **Severe burns, trauma, or complicated surgery**—with a drastic drop in blood pressure and the release of myoglobin from injured muscles *(see Chapter 5)*. Myoglobin lodges in the renal tubules and blocks the flow of urine.

- **Drugs**—including pain medications such as aspirin and ibuprofen, antibiotics such as streptomycin and gentamicin, and contrast dyes used in angiography.

- **Toxins**—such as heavy metals (mercury is one) and excessive alcohol.

- **Systemic infections** (septicemia)

- **Blood disorders** such as idiopathic thrombocytic purpura (ITP) or disseminated intravascular coagulopathy (DIC) *(see Chapter 7)*.

In treatment of ARF, the goal is to treat the underlying disease. Dialysis may be necessary while the kidneys are healing.

Chronic renal failure (CRF), or **chronic kidney disease (CKD)**, is a gradual loss of renal function. Symptoms and signs may not appear until kidney function is less than 25% of normal.

The causes of chronic renal failure include:

- **Diabetes**—type 1 and type 2 *(see Chapter 14)*, **hypertension, kidney diseases, lead poisoning.**

Azotemia is the build up of nitrogenous waste products in the blood. **Uremia** is the complex of symptoms resulting from excess nitrogenous waste products in the blood, as seen in renal failure.

End-stage renal disease (ESRD) means the kidneys are functioning at less than 10% of their normal capacity. At this point, life cannot be sustained, and either dialysis or kidney **transplant** is needed.

Dialysis is an artificial method of removing waste materials and excess fluid from the blood. It is not a cure but can prolong life. There are several types of kidney dialysis:

- **Hemodialysis** *(Figure 11.7)* filters your blood through an artificial kidney machine (**dialyzer**). Most patients require 12 hours of hemodialysis a week, usually in three sessions.

- **Peritoneal dialysis** uses a dialysis solution that is infused into and drained out of your abdominal cavity through a small, flexible, **implanted** catheter. The dialysis solution extracts wastes and excess fluid from the network of capillaries in the peritoneal lining of the abdominal cavity.

- **Continuous ambulatory peritoneal dialysis (CAPD)** is performed by the patient at home through an implanted abdominal catheter *(Figure 11.8)*, usually four times a day, seven days a week.

Abbreviations

ARF	acute renal failure
CAPD	continuous ambulatory peritoneal dialysis
CKD	chronic kidney disease; also known as chronic renal failure
CRF	chronic renal failure; also known as chronic kidney disease
ESRD	end-stage renal disease
PKD	polycystic kidney disease

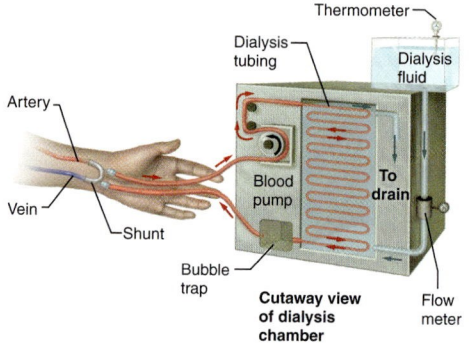

▲ **FIGURE 11.7 Hemodialysis.**

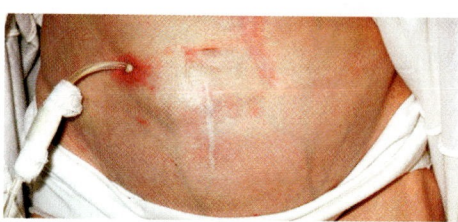

▲ **FIGURE 11.8 Continuous Ambulatory Peritoneal Dialysis.**

WORD	PRONUNCIATION	ELEMENTS		DEFINITION
anuria	an-**YOU**-ree-ah	P/ R/	an- *lack of* -uria *urine*	Absence of urine production
azotemia	azo-**TEE**-me-ah	S/ R/	-emia *blood condition* azot- *nitrogen*	Excess nitrogenous waste products in the blood
dialysis dialyzer	die-**AL**-ih-sis **DIE**-ah-lie-zer	S/ R/	-lysis *to separate* dia- *complete*	An artificial method of filtration to remove excess waste materials and water from the body Machine for dialysis
hemodialysis	**HE**-moh-die-**AL**-ih-sis	S/ P/ R/CF	-lysis *to separate* -dia- *complete* hem/o- *blood*	An artificial method of filtration to remove excess waste materials and water directly from the blood
implant	im-**PLANT**	P/ R/	im- *in* -plant *insert or plant*	To insert material into tissues, or the material inserted into tissues
oliguria	ol-ih-**GYUR**-ee-ah	P/ R/	olig- *scanty* -uria *urine*	Scanty production of urine
polycystic	pol-ee-**SIS**-tik	S/ P/ R/	-ic *pertaining to* poly- *many* -cyst- *bladder, cyst*	Composed of many cysts
sibling	**SIB**-ling	S/ R/	-ling *small* sib- *relative*	Brother or sister
transplant	**TRANZ**-plant	P/ R/	trans- *across* -plant *insert, plant*	The act of transferring tissue from one person to another
uremia	you-**REE**-me-ah	S/ R/	-emia *blood condition* ur- *urine*	The complex of symptoms arising from renal failure

- **Continuous cycling peritoneal dialysis** uses a machine to automatically infuse dialysis solution into and out of the abdominal cavity during sleep.

Kidney transplant provides a better quality of life than dialysis—if a suitable donor can be found. The donor has to match the recipient's blood type, cell surface proteins, and antibodies *(see Chapter 15)*. A **sibling** or a blood relative can often qualify as a donor. If not, tissue banks across the country can search for a kidney from an accident victim or a donor who has died.

EXERCISES

Build your knowledge of the elements contained in the **language of urology.** *Specific elements in each term are set in bold. Identify the type of element, and provide a meaning for the element. Fill in the blanks.*

Term	Type of Element (P, R, CF, S)	Meaning of Element
hemo**dialysis**	_____	_____
azot**emia**	_____	_____
trans**plant**	_____	_____
olig**uria**	_____	_____
poly**cystic**	_____	_____
ur**emia**	_____	_____

Remember: Every element at the beginning of a medical term is not necessarily a prefix!

Give an example from this exercise: _____

DISORDERS OF THE URINARY BLADDER AND URETHRA

Urinary Tract Infection

A **urinary tract infection (UTI)** occurs when bacteria invade and multiply in the urinary tract. The **portal** of entry for the bacteria is through the urethra. Because the female urethra is shorter than the male and opens to the surface near the anus (*Figure 11.11*), bacteria from the **gastrointestinal (GI)** tract, such as *Escherichia coli (E. coli)* can more easily invade the female urethra. This is why women are more prone than men to UTIs. Once UTIs have occurred, they often recur.

Infection of the urethra is called urethritis; infection of the urinary bladder is cystitis. If cystitis is untreated, infection can spread up the ureters to the renal pelvis, causing **pyelitis,** and carry on to reach the renal cortex and nephrons, causing **pyelonephritis.**

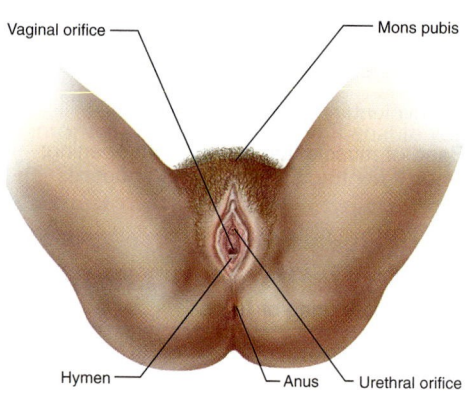

▲ FIGURE 11.11   Female External Genitalia.

Vaginal orifice — *Mons pubis*
Hymen — *Anus* — *Urethral orifice*

Case Report 11.3 (continued)

Mrs. Dobson described many of the symptoms of cystitis. She had **suprapubic** and low back pain. She had increased **frequency** of micturition with **dysuria,** and difficulty in and burning on micturition. Her pink urine is probably hematuria.

The diagnosis can be made through urinalysis. Culture of the organism and testing of its sensitivity to different antibiotics enables appropriate antibiotic therapy to be prescribed. Cranberry juice makes the urine more acid.

Urinary Incontinence

Loss of control of your bladder is called **urinary incontinence.** The result is wet clothes. About 12 million adults in America have urinary incontinence. It is most common in women over the age of 50 years.

There are four types of urinary incontinence:

- **Stress incontinence**—urine leaks because of sudden pressure on the lower stomach muscles when you cough, laugh, sneeze, lift something heavy, or exercise. It is most common in women, with previous pregnancy and childbirth being risk factors.

- **Urge incontinence**—the need to urinate comes on too fast for you to get to the toilet. It is often **idiopathic,** but can be associated with UTI, diabetes, stroke, Alzheimer and Parkinson disease, or bladder cancer.

- **Overflow incontinence**—small amounts of urine leak from a bladder that is always full because you cannot empty it. This occurs when an enlarged prostate gland or tumor blocks the outflow of urine from the bladder, in spinal cord injuries, and as a side effect of some medications.

- **Functional incontinence**—you have normal bladder control but cannot get to the toilet in time because of arthritis or any other disease that makes moving around difficult.

Treatment depends on the cause. If a medical or surgical problem is present, then the incontinence can go away when the problem is treated. **Bladder training** and **biofeedback** *(see Chapter 23)* lengthen the time between the urges to go to the toilet. **Kegel exercises** strengthen the muscles of the pelvic floor. Medications, for example, oxybutynin are used for urge incontinence. Surgery can pull up the bladder and secure it if pelvic floor muscles are weak **(cystopexy).** Absorbent underclothing is available.

Urinary retention is the abnormal, involuntary holding of urine in the bladder. **Acute retention** can be caused by an obstruction in the urinary system; for example, an enlarged prostate in the male *(see Chapter 12)* or neurological problems such as multiple sclerosis. It can be a side effect of anticholinergic drugs that include tricyclic antidepressants *(see Chapter 19).* **Chronic retention** can be caused by untreated obstructions in the urinary tract such as an enlarged prostate.

Bladder cancer is more common in men than women. It is the fourth most common cancer in men and the eighth in women *(see Chapter 24).*

Abbreviations

GI	gastrointestinal
E. coli	*Escherichia coli*
UTI	urinary tract infection

WORD	PRONUNCIATION	ELEMENTS		DEFINITION
cystopexy	SIS-toh-pek-see	S/ R/CF	-pexy *fixation* cyst/o- *bladder*	Surgical procedure to support the urinary bladder
cystoscope	SIS-toh-skope	S/ R/CF	-scope *instrument* cyst/o- *bladder*	An endoscope inserted to view the inside of the bladder
cystoscopy	sis-TOS-koh-pee		-scopy *to examine*	The process of using a cystoscope
dysuria	dis-YOU-ree-ah	S/ P/ R/	-ia *condition* dys- *bad, difficult* -ur *urine*	Difficulty or pain with urination
frequency	FREE-kwen-see	S/ R/	-ency *state of* frequ- *repeated, often*	The number of times something happens in a given time (e.g., passing urine)
idiopathic	ID-ih-oh-PATH-ik	S/ R/CF R/	-ic *pertaining to* idi/o- *unknown* -path- *disease, suffering*	Pertaining to a disease of unknown etiology
incontinence incontinent	in-KON-tin-ence in-KON-tin-ent	S/ P/ R/	-ence *state of* in- *in* -contin- *hold together*	Inability to prevent discharge of urine or feces
Kegel exercises	KEG-al EKS-er-size-ez		Arnold Kegel (1894–1981) American gynecologist	Contraction and relaxation of the pelvic floor muscles to improve urethral and rectal sphincter function
portal	POR-tal		Latin *gate*	The vein that brings blood from the intestines to the liver
pyelitis	pie-eh-LYE-tis	S/ R/	-itis *inflammation* pyel- *renal pelvis*	Inflammation of renal pelvis
retention	ree-TEN-shun		Latin *hold back*	Holding back in the body what should normally be discharged (e.g., urine)
suprapubic	SOO-prah-pyu-bik	S/ P/ R/	-ic *pertaining to* supra- *above* -pub- *pubis*	Above the symphysis pubis

Transitional cell carcinoma is the most common type of bladder cancer, arising in the transitional cells of the lining of the bladder. Its primary symptom is hematuria. It is diagnosed by:

- **urinalysis** to detect microscopic hematuria
- **NMP22®BladderChek®**, which detects elevated levels of a specific protein in the urine even in the early stages
- **imaging tests** such as IVP, CT scan, MRI scan, and ultrasound
- **cystoscopy with biopsy** is the definitive test.

The cancer is **staged** using the **TNM system (tumor, node, metastasis)** *(see Chapter 22)*.

EXERCISES

Deconstruct the **language of urology** *found in this WAD. Knowledge of elements is your best key to understanding the meaning of the term. Fill in the chart.*

Medical Term	Meaning of Prefix	Meaning of Root/CF	Meaning of Suffix
incontinence			
cystopexy			
dysuria			
idiopathic			
pyelitis			
suprapubic			

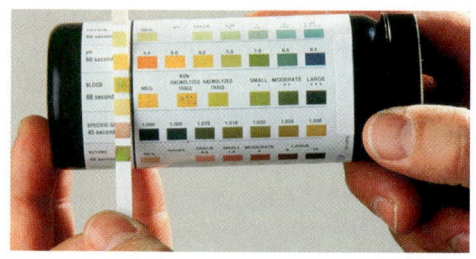

▲ **FIGURE 11.12 Urinalysis Dipstick Being Compared Against Color Chart on Container.**

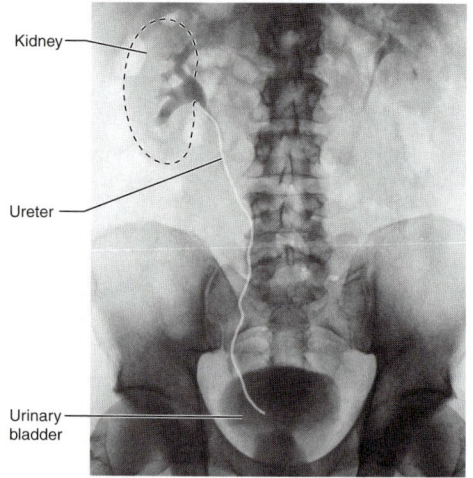

▲ **FIGURE 11.13 Intravenous Pyelogram (IVP).**

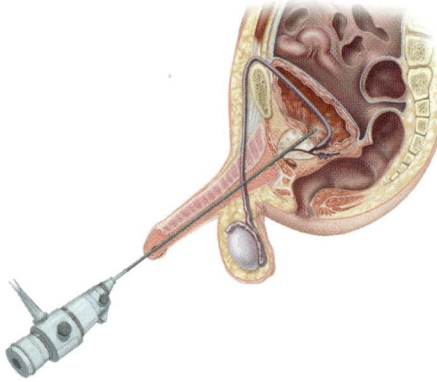

▲ **FIGURE 11.14 Cystoscopy.**

DIAGNOSTIC PROCEDURES

Urinalysis

Dipstick (a plastic strip bearing paper squares of reagent) is the most cost-effective method to screen urine *(Figure 11.12)*. After dipping the stick in the urine specimen, the color change in each segment of the dipstick is compared to a color chart on the container. Dipsticks can screen for pH, specific gravity, protein, blood, glucose, ketones, bilirubin, **nitrite,** and leukocyte esterase (see below).

Routine urinalysis (UA) in the laboratory can include the following tests:

- **Visual observation**—examines **color** and **clarity.** Normal urine is pale yellow or amber in color and clear. Cloudiness indicates excess cells or cellular material. Red and cloudy indicates red blood cells.
- **Odor**—Normal urine has a slight "nutty" odor. Infected urine has a foul odor. **Ketosis** gives urine a fruity odor.
- **pH**—measures how acidic or alkaline urine is *(see Chapter 2).*
- **Specific gravity (SG)** measures how dilute or concentrated the urine is.
- **Protein** is not detected normally in urine. Its presence (**proteinuria**) indicates infection or urinary tract disease.
- **Glucose** in the urine (**glycosuria**) is a spill-over into the urine when the nephrons are damaged or diseased or blood sugar is high in uncontrolled diabetes.
- **Ketones** are present in the urine in **diabetic ketoacidosis** *(see Chapter 14)* or in starvation *(see Chapter 22).*
- **Leukocyte esterase** indicates the presence of white blood cells in the urine, which in turn can indicate a UTI.
- **Urine culture** from a clean-catch specimen (see box) is the definitive test for a UTI.

Microscopic urinalysis is performed on the solids deposited by centrifuging a specimen of urine. It can reveal:

- **red blood cells (RBCs), white blood cells (WBCs),** and renal tubular epithelial cells stuck together to form **casts,** WBCs stuck together to form casts, and bacteria can be seen.

Other Diagnostic Procedures

- **KUB**—an x-ray of the abdomen to show your kidneys, ureters, and bladder.
- **Intravenous pyelogram (IVP)**—a contrast material containing iodine is injected intravenously, and its progress through the urinary tract is then recorded on a series of rapid x-ray images *(Figure 11.13).*
- **Retrograde pyelogram**—contrast material is injected through a urinary catheter into the ureters to locate stones and other obstructions.
- **Voiding cystourethrogram (VCUG)**—contrast material is inserted into the bladder through a catheter and x-rays taken as you void.
- **CT scan**—x-ray images to show cross-sectional views of the kidneys and bladder.
- **MRI**—magnetic fields are used to generate cross-sectional images of the urinary tract.
- **Ultrasound imaging**—high-frequency sound waves and a computer generate noninvasive images of kidneys.
- **Renal angiogram**—x-rays with contrast material to assess blood flow to the kidneys.
- **Cystoscopy**—a pencil-thin, flexible, tubelike optical instrument is inserted through the urethra into the bladder to examine directly the lining of the bladder and to take a biopsy if needed *(Figure 11.14).*

WORD	PRONUNCIATION		ELEMENTS	DEFINITION
cast	KAST		Latin *pure*	A cylindrical mold formed by materials in kidney tubules
cystourethrogram	sis-toh-you-**REETH**-roe-gram	S/ R/CF R/CF	**-gram** *a record* **cyst/o-** *bladder* **-urethr/o-** *urethra*	X-ray image during voiding to show structure and function of bladder and urethra
glycosuria	**GLYE**-koh-**SYU**-ree-ah	S/ R/CF R/	**-ia** *condition* **glyc/os-** *glucose* **-ur-** *urine*	Presence of glucose in urine
ketone	**KEY**-tone		Greek *acetone*	Chemical formed in uncontrolled diabetes or in starvation
ketosis	key-**TOE**-sis	S/ R/CF R/CF	**-sis** *condition* **ket/o-** *ketones* **-acid/o-** *acid*	Excess production of ketones
ketoacidosis	**KEY**-toe-as-ih-**DOE**-sis			Excessive ketones in blood, making it acid
nitrite	**NI**-trite		Greek *niter, saltpeter*	Chemical formed in urine by *E. coli* and other microorganisms
proteinuria	pro-tee-**NYU**-ree-ah	R/ R/	**-uria** *urine* **protein-** *protein*	Presence of protein in urine
retrograde	**RET**-roh-grade	P/ R/	**retro-** *backward* **-grade** *going*	Reversal of a normal flow; for example, back from the bladder into the ureters
urinalysis	you-rih-**NAL**-ih-sis	S/ R/CF	**-lysis** *to separate* **urin/a-** *urine*	Examination of urine to separate it into its elements and define their kind and/or quantity

Methods of Urine Collection

- **Random collection** is taken with no precautions regarding contamination. It is often used for collecting samples for drug testing.

- **Early morning collection** is used to determine the ability of the kidneys to concentrate urine following overnight dehydration.

- **Clean-catch, midstream specimen** is collected after the external urethral meatus is cleaned. The first part of the urine is passed, and the sterile collecting vessel is introduced into the urinary stream to collect the last part.

- **Twenty-four–hour collection** is used to determine the amount of protein being excreted and to estimate the kidneys' filtration ability.

- **Suprapubic transabdominal needle aspiration** of the bladder is used in newborns and small infants to obtain a pure sample of urine.

- **Catheterization of the bladder** can be used as a last resort to obtain a urine specimen. A soft plastic or rubber tube (catheter) is inserted through the urethra into the bladder to drain and collect urine (*Figure 11.15*).

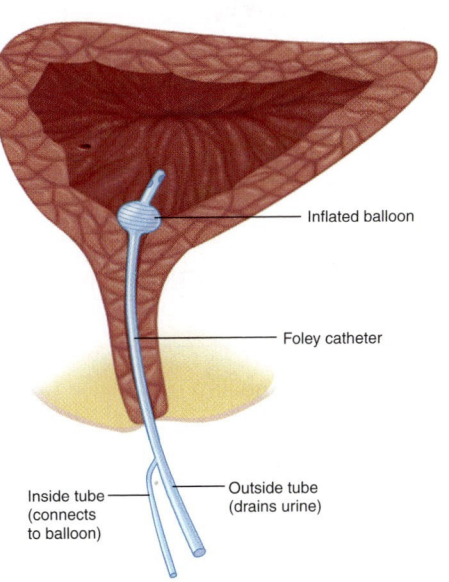

Inflated balloon

Foley catheter

Inside tube
(connects
to balloon)

Outside tube
(drains urine)

▲ **FIGURE 11.15   Foley Catheter.**

EXERCISES

Apply your knowledge of medical language to the following exercise. All the questions can be answered using terms from this spread. Circle the best answer.

1. An x-ray image taken during voiding:

   retrograde pyelogram   KUB   cystourethrogram

2. Presence of glucose in urine:

   hematuria   polyuria   glycosuria

3. Urine colection method to test for proteinuria:

   catheterization   24 hour   clean catch

4. Reversal of normal flow:

   reflex   retrograde   regenerate

5. Excessive ketones in the blood, making it acid:

   ketosis   ketoacidosis   ketone

6. Separate urine into its elements:

   urinalysis   cystourethrogram   retrograde pyelogram

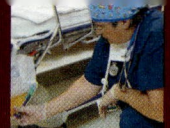

CHAPTER 11 REVIEW

URINARY SYSTEM

CHALLENGE YOUR KNOWLEDGE

A. Patient Documentation:

1. *Read the following case history aloud.*
2. *Go through the paragraph and underline all the medical terms.*
3. *Answer the questions.*

> A 68-year-old female presents with hematuria, dysuria, and left flank pain. I ordered a KUB and an IVP to ascertain the possibility or extent of obstruction. Test results indicate one large and several small calculi impacted in her left ureter just below the renal artery. Patient would prefer ESWL, but surgical laparoscopy, I think, will offer better and quicker results to alleviate her pain. Patient will proceed with surgery tomorrow.

1. What are the patient's symptoms?

   _____

2. Define KUB.

   _____

3. Define IVP.

   _____

4. What is the singular of calculi? _____

5. What does **impacted** mean?

   _____

6. What is obstructing the ureter?

   _____

7. Define ESWL.

   _____

8. What is a laparoscopy?

   _____

9. What type of doctor performs laparascopy for renal calculi?

   _____

10. What is a preoperative diagnosis for this patient?

    _____

B. Brain Teaser: Taken directly from your text: "The peristaltic waves are intermittent, which is why Justin's pain was spasmodic."

1. Define **peristaltic.** _____

2. Which previous body system that you have already studied in this text also mentions peristalsis? _____

   Is it the same type of process?_____

C. **Elements:** Roots and combining forms may stay the same in similar terms, but you will notice that the suffix can change the entire meaning of the medical term. Insert the correct suffix on the term to provide the precise meaning. Pick the correct ending from among the following choices; you have more choices than you will need. Fill in the blanks.

-al	-lysis
-ectomy	-osis
-emia	-pexy
-gen	-scope
-iasis	-scopy
-ion	-tomy
-logist	-tripsy
-logy	-uria

1. study of the kidney   nephro _____

2. dilation of pelvis and calyces of a kidney   hydronephr _____ _

3. instrument for viewing inside a kidney   nephro _____

4. presence of a kidney stone   nephrolith _____

5. process of eliminating waste products of metabolism   excret _____

6. surgical removal of a kidney   nephr _____

7. incision for removal of a kidney stone   nephrolitho _____

8. separating urine for examination of elements   urina_____

9. medical specialist in disorders of the urinary system   uro _____

10. crushing a renal stone with sound waves   litho _____

D. **Seek and Find:** How many medical terms ending in -itis have you found in this chapter? List them here, and give a brief definition for each term. Fill in the blanks.

1. _____itis

    Definition: _____

2. _____itis

    Definition: _____

3. _____itis

    Definition: _____

4. _____itis

    Definition: _____

5. _____itis

    Definition: _____

6. _____itis

    Definition: _____

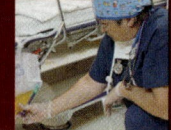

URINARY SYSTEM

E. **Documentation.** The scenario in this lesson presents all the information you need to fill out the HPI (history of present illness) form for the patient's medical record. *You are translating the patient's own words into medical terminology.* First read the scenario about Mrs. Dobson, then read the questions you need to answer. Go back and read the scenario again, underlining what you think is important information. This will help you to fill in the blanks in the HPI form. The last part of the exercise involves asking Mrs. Dobson additional questions you think will provide helpful information for the doctor. Use the correct medical term whenever possible, and be prepared to define each term you use.

Fulwood Medical Center
3333 Medical Parkway, Fulwood, MI 01234
555-247-6100

Medical record number: # _____   Date of visit: _____

Patient Name: _____   Patient age or DOB: _____

Physician: _____   Department: _____

History of Present Illness:

Onset: _____

Chief complaint(s) and duration: _____

_____

_____

Recurrent problem? _____

Current medications: _____

What other additional questions could the medical assistant ask Mrs. Dobson that would provide helpful information for Dr. Lee?

1. _____

2. _____

F. **Recall and Review:** One or more roots or combining forms can have the same meaning. Demonstrate that you can use these elements correctly. *Remember: they are not interchangeable.* One particular root or combining form goes with a specific suffix. Fill in the blanks.

1. Respiratory system: _____ and _____ both mean lung.

2. Urinary system: _____ and _____ both mean kidney.

Take the following suffixes and attach them to the correct roots/combining forms for lung or kidney to form the exact medical terms. You will use some elements twice. Fill in the blanks.

-al -in -ary -logist -ectomy -itis -otomy -logy

3. pertaining to the lung: _____

4. removal of the lung: _____

5. inflammation of the lung: _____

6. study of the lung: _____

7. specialist in lung diseases: _____

8. incision into the kidney: _____

9. pertaining to the kidney: _____

10. removal of the kidney: _____

11. kidney enzyme that causes vasoconstriction: _____

12. inflammation of the kidney: _____

13. study of the kidney: _____

14. specialist in kidney diseases: _____

G. **Short Answer.** You will often be called upon to express yourself in writing documentation. Practice writing clear, concise answers to the following questions. Always be sure to check your spelling!

1. Explain the body's process of reabsorption of water.

_____

_____

_____

_____

2. The kidneys secrete both an enzyme and a hormone. What are they called, and what are the functions of each?

Enzyme: _____

_____

_____

Hormone: _____

_____

_____

URINARY SYSTEM

H. **System Review.** Understanding the structure and function of the urinary system will give you a better grasp of the terminology. Circle the correct answers to the following questions.

1. Where does waste-laden blood enter the kidney?

   a. the fascia

   b. the glomerulus

   c. the hilum

   d. the renal vein

   e. the portal vein

2. The medical term to describe urine being forced back up the ureter to the kidneys is:

   a. reflux

   b. filtration

   c. excretion

   d. absorption

   e. micturition

3. What results if the kidney produces too much renin?

   a. hematuria

   b. oliguria

   c. primary hypertension

   d. anuria

   e. secondary hypertension

4. What is the end product of nitrogen metabolism?

   a. ammonia

   b. nitrogen

   c. urea

   d. nitrates

   e. renin

5. What do urethritis, cystitis, pyelitis, and pyelonephritis all have in common?

   a. infection

   b. inflammation

   c. the same suffix

   d. the same body system

   e. all of these

6. Each kidney is the size of a(n):

    a. orange

    b. golf ball

    c. clenched fist

    d. bean

    e. ping-pong ball

7. What protects the kidney?

    a. adipose tissue

    b. renal fascia

    c. renal capsule

    d. none of these

    e. all of these

8. The external opening of a passage is called:

    a. meatus

    b. urethra

    c. ureter

    d. bladder

    e. trigone

9. The glomerulus is encased in:

    a. a blood vessel

    b. a muscle

    c. renal fascia

    d. Bowman capsule

    e. urethra

10. Nephrotic syndrome leads to:

    a. acute renal failure

    b. primary hypertension

    c. secondary hypertension

    d. chronic renal failure

    e. oliguria

CHAPTER 11 REVIEW

URINARY SYSTEM

I. **System Review.** Understanding the structure and function of the urinary system will give you a better grasp of the terminology. Circle the correct answers to the following questions.

1. *Muscular tube, about 10 inches long, that carries urine to bladder.* This describes:

   a. the ureter

   b. the urethra

   c. the portal vein

   d. the renal vein

   e. the aorta

2. Another name for a kidney stone:

   a. UTI

   b. calculus

   c. tumor

   d. hematuria

   e. lithotripsy

3. Water is returned to the blood by:

   a. excretion

   b. filtration

   c. absorption

   d. elimination

   e. reabsorption

4. What gets released from crushed muscles?

   a. myoglobin

   b. hemoglobin

   c. hematuria

   d. ammonia

   e. enzymes

5. **Peritoneal** and **continuous cycling** are terms that apply to:

   a. incontinence

   b. azotemia

   c. dialysis

   d. nephrectomy

   e. transplants

J. **Terminology Challenge.** Medical terminology is full of vocabulary that sounds and looks similar but has very different meanings. Think about the following terms, and explain in plain language how they are different. **Notice** that these two terms differ by only one letter—this is where precision comes in! Fill in the blanks.

1. Reflex: _____

2. Reflux: _____

K. **Word elements remain your key for understanding a medical term.** Deconstruct the following medical terms into their basic elements, then write the meaning of the term. It will be visually helpful to you to put a slash (/) between each element in every term before you start. Fill in the chart.

Medical Term	Prefix	Root/CF	Suffix	Meaning of Term
hemodialysis				
hydronephrosis				
incontinence				
nephrectomy				
nephrolithiasis				
nephrolithotomy				
peritubular				
uremia				

L. **Plurals:** Precision in communication requires the correct use of the singular and/or plural form of the medical term. If the singular form is given, write in the plural form or vice versa. Be sure to define the term. Fill in the chart.

Medical Term	Singular	Plural	Meaning of term
calculus			
calyces			
cortex			
glomeruli			
hila			

Precision in communication is the mark of a professional.

URINARY SYSTEM

M. Common Denominator. Each of the following groups of terms has something in common. Your knowledge of the terminology and functional anatomy of the urinary system will help you determine the common denominator for each group. Fill in the blanks.

1. filter, regulate, maintain, secrete, synthesize, detoxify

   All are: _____

2. urination, micturition, voiding

   All are: _____

3. sibling, blood relative, accident victim, cadaver

   All are: _____

4. ESWL, ureteroscopy, percutaneous nephrolithotomy

   All are: _____

5. stress, urge, overflow, functional

   All are: _____

6. random, clean-catch, catheterization, early morning, 24-hour

   All are: _____

N. Matching: Confirm that your knowledge of the **language of the urinary system** and its functions is accurate. Match the statements in column 1 to the correct answers in column 2.

_____ 1. vessels and nerves enter and leave   A. uremia

_____ 2. outside the body   B. permeable

_____ 3. donor organ to recipient   C. azotemia

_____ 4. reversal of normal flow   D. flank

_____ 5. identified by dipstick   E. extracorporeal

_____ 6. loss of bladder control   F. dialyzer

_____ 7. disease state resulting from renal failure   G. radical

_____ 8. extensive removal of disease process   H. incontinence

_____ 9. side of body between ribs and pelvis   I. hilum

_____ 10. artificial kidney machine   J. transplant

_____ 11. allows substance to pass through membrane   K. retrograde

_____ 12. excess waste products in urine   L. microscopic hematuria

O. Differences. Being able to explain how terms are different means you understand exactly what they mean. These terms all have the same suffix, but their other elements define them. Fill in the blanks.

1. A **nephroscopy** is: _____

2. A **ureteroscopy** is: _____

3. A **cystoscopy** is: _____

4. The suffix in each term is _____ and means _____.

P. **Abbreviations are not helpful if you do not understand their meaning and cannot use them to communicate safely and effectively.** The following abbreviations are from this chapter and earlier chapters. Demonstrate that you can put the appropriate abbreviation in the correct context. You will not use every abbreviation listed to fill in the blanks.

ARF	ESWL	KUB	TNM
BUN	GRF	PKD	UA
CRF	IV	SG	UTI
ESRD	IVP	SPA	VCUG

1. Dr. Lee ordered the medication _____ stat.

2. Patient informed me that there is a history of _____ in his family.

3. The patient with the kidney stone is scheduled for _____ early tomorrow morning.

4. Patient's renal carcinoma was staged using the _____ method.

5. Patient returns with her second _____ this month. Medication prescribed.

6. Dr. Johnson ordered the following radiologic diagnostic tests for the patient: _____, _____,

   and _____.

7. Patient's _____ progressed to _____

   and _____ resulted.

Q. **Discussion Questions:** Discussions with patients require effort to get your thoughts organized about what you want to say. Prepare for these discussions by:

- making a mini outline of what you want to say OR
- making a list of keywords that will help your memory OR
- making a list of short notes to keep your thoughts on track—try to confine your list/outline to a large index card

Use any of these methods to prepare a short discussion on one of the following topics:

1. The functions of the kidney: pick any two functions of the kidney, and be prepared to explain what these functions are, how important they are, what other systems may be involved with this function or impacted by it, what urinary structures are involved with this function, etc. *Be sure that you can define/explain to your classmates any terms you use in your discussion.*

2. Trace the flow of fluid through the renal filtration process. This particular discussion may benefit from a simple illustration you might want to prepare. Research this on the Internet.

3. Explain the various methods of dialysis. Be prepared to explain which type of dialysis you would choose if you were in a condition where you needed it. Give reasons why this would be your choice rather than the other options. Search the Internet for illustrations of this type of dialysis. Perhaps you know someone who is on dialysis—interview them.

Notes: _____

_____

_____

_____

_____

_____

URINARY SYSTEM

R. Roots and Combining Forms: Form the foundation of a medical term. All these terms have the same suffix. Differentiate their meanings by analyzing the rest of the term. Every one of these terms could be a diagnosis for your next patient. Fill in the blanks.

Medical Term	Meaning of Prefix	Meaning of Root/CF	Meaning of Suffix
anuria			
dysuria			
glycosuria			
hematuria			
oliguria			
proteinuria			

Can you determine the meaning of these two terms after analyzing the rest of their elements?

1. If **py** means *pus*, then **pyuria** means _____ .

2. If **noct** means *night,* then **nocturia** means _____ .

S. Tests and Procedures: Patients with urinary problems will be sent for various renal function tests and diagnostic procedures that may result in a surgical procedure. If any of the following procedures were ordered for your patient, do you know their purpose? Can you define these procedures? Fill in the blanks.

_____ 1. contrast material injected to locate stones

_____ 2. used to collect bladder sample in newborns

_____ 3. incision for removal of kidney stone

_____ 4. iodine injected and recorded

_____ 5. crushing renal stone by sound waves

_____ 6. assess blood flow to the kidneys

_____ 7. tissue bank matches donor to recipient

_____ 8. treatment for renal cell carcinoma

_____ 9. x-ray of the abdominal urinary organs

_____ 10. viewing the bladder through a scope

A. lithotripsy

B. transplant

C. KUB

D. retrograde pyelogram

E. cystoscopy

F. nephrolithotomy

G. nephrectomy

H. IVP

I. needle aspiration

J. renal angiogram

Study Hint

Create a study hint for yourself that will make it easy to remember exactly what an IVP is.

Write your hint here:

_____
_____
_____
_____
_____
_____

T. Labeling: Demonstrate your knowledge of urinary anatomy and use of medical terminology by labeling the following exercise. The suffix in the term for each label tells you these diagnoses are all an *inflammation of* a particular part of the urinary system.

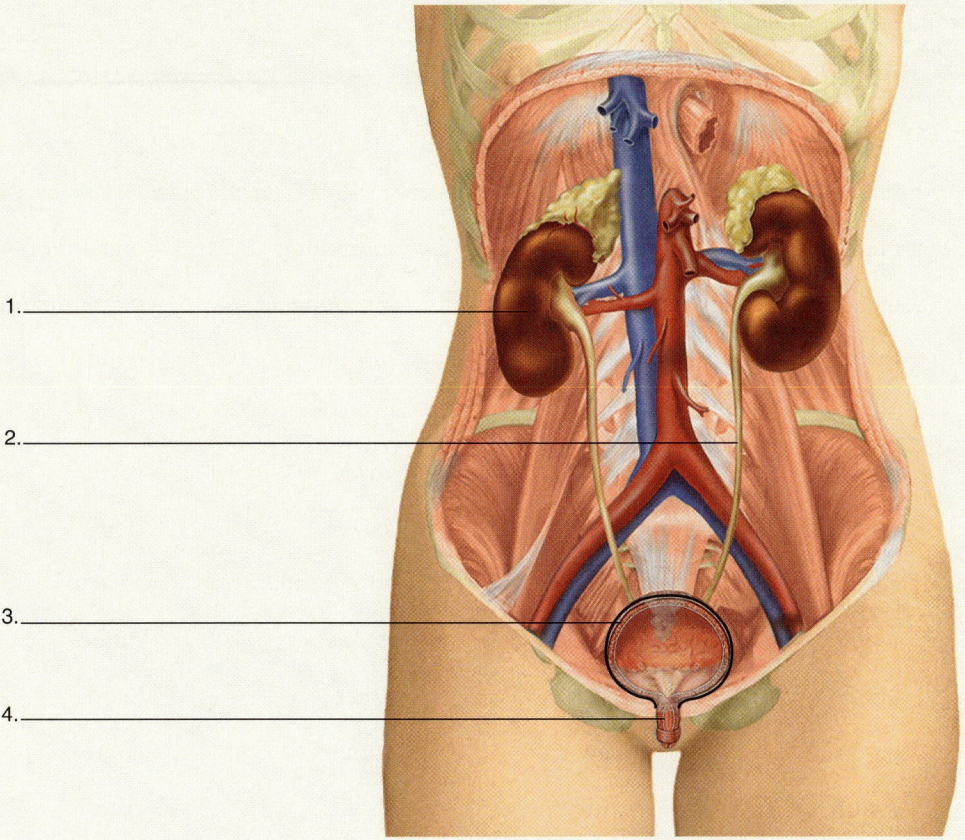

1._____

2._____

3._____

4._____

Diagnoses are lettered A through D in the table below.

1. Put the letter of the diagnosis and write the term (from column 1) on the correct line in the illustration that shows the part of the anatomy connected to that diagnosis.

2. In column 2 of the table, write the layman's definition of the medical term.

Label these in the illustration:

Diagnosis	Layman's Terms
a. urethritis	
b. cystitis	
c. nephritis	
d. ureteritis	

These sites are not in the illustration, but describe what part(s) of the urinary system are affected by:

1. glomerulonephritis _____

2. pyelonephritis _____

3. pyelitis _____

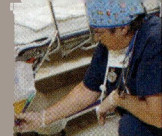

URINARY SYSTEM

CHAPTER SUMMARY EXERCISE

1. *Listen to the pronunciation of the medical terms as given by your instructor.*
2. *Circle the correct spelling of the medical term.*
3. *Match the correctly spelled terms to the brief descriptions below.*
4. *Write a sentence for each of the 15 terms that appear in this exercise.*

A. SPELLING COMPREHENSION: CIRCLE THE CORRECT SPELLING OF THE TERM. *Listen to the pronunciation of the medical terms as given by your instructor.*

1. micktutrition	mictrition	mickterition	micterition	micturition
2. incontenince	incontenance	incontinence	incontinance	inccontinance
3. pilitis	pylitis	pyelitis	phylitis	pulitis
4. ureea	uria	urea	urrea	uremia
5. voyd	void	voyid	vuyde	voyde
6. kalyx	calyxx	calyx	kalyxx	calix
7. adventitia	adventishia	adventusa	adventechia	adventia
8. reninne	renine	renin	rynine	rinine
9. Kegelle	Kegele	Keggle	Kegel	Kegale
10. groin	groun	groan	grunne	grune
11. cystitis	cysitis	cistitis	cistytis	cistiitis
12. disurria	dysurria	disurea	dissureia	dysuria
13. callculus	calcules	calculus	calckulus	calckules
14. supprapubic	suprapubic	suprapublic	superpublic	suprapubick
15. detrussor	detressor	distressor	detrusor	distrusore

B. MATCH THE NUMBER OF THE CORRECT TERM IN PART A WITH THE BRIEF DESCRIPTION OF THE TERM BELOW.

a. crease where thigh joins abdomen _____

b. funnel-shaped structure _____

c. causes vasoconstriction _____

d. a muscle that acts to expel something _____

e. above the symphysis pubis _____

f. end product of nitrogen metabolism _____

g. inflammation of the renal pelvis _____

h. act of passing urine _____

i. inflammation of the urinary bladder _____

j. outermost connective tissue layer of any structure _____

k. painful, difficult urination _____

l. exercises to strengthen muscles of pelvic floor _____

m. to evacuate urine or feces _____

n. loss of control of the bladder _____

o. small stone _____

C. USING YOUR KNOWLEDGE OF TERMS 1-15 IN PART A AND THEIR CORRECT SPELLING, WRITE A BRIEF SENTENCE AS IT MIGHT APPEAR IN PATIENT DOCUMENTATION.

1. _____

2. _____

3. _____

4. _____

5. _____

6. _____

7. _____

8. _____

9. _____

10. _____

11. _____

12. _____

13. _____

14. _____

15. _____

D. GO TO THE STUDENT CD. OPEN THE GLOSSARY AND PRACTICE YOUR PRONUNCIATION OF THE TERMS IN PART A OF THIS EXERCISE.

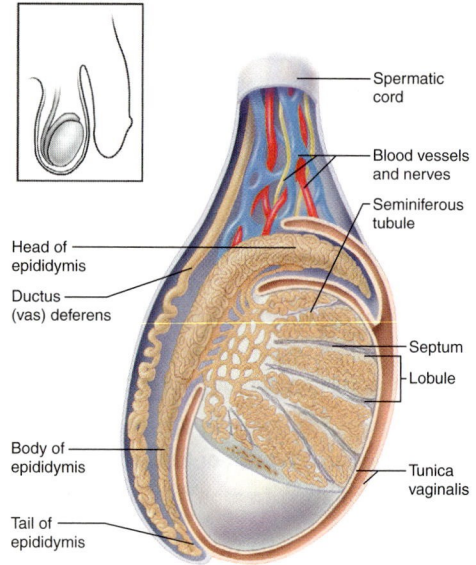

Spermatic cord

Blood vessels and nerves

Seminiferous tubule

Head of epididymis

Ductus (vas) deferens

Septum

Lobule

Body of epididymis

Tunica vaginalis

Tail of epididymis

▲ **FIGURE 12.3   The Testis and Associated Structures.**

Keynote

The male testes produce up to 100,000,000 sperm per day.

Abbreviation
BMR basal metabolic rate

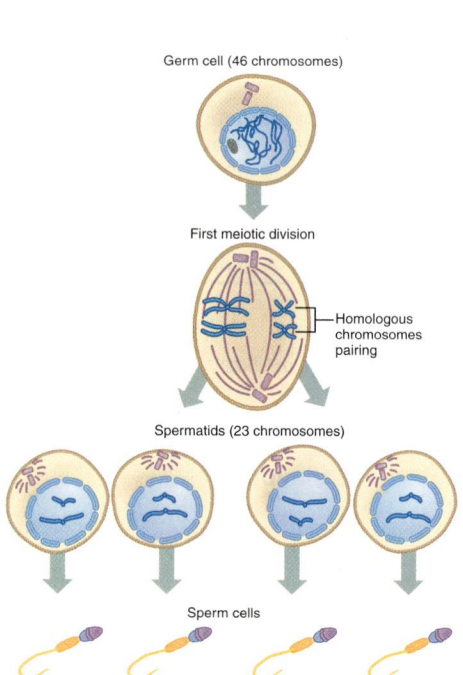

Germ cell (46 chromosomes)

First meiotic division

Homologous chromosomes pairing

Spermatids (23 chromosomes)

Sperm cells

▲ **FIGURE 12.4   Spermatogenesis.**

TESTES AND SPERMATIC CORD

In the adult male, each testis is a small, oval organ about 2 inches (5 cm) long and 3/4 inch (2 cm) in width *(Figure 12.3)*. Each testis is covered by a serous membrane, the **tunica vaginalis,** which has an outer parietal layer and an inner visceral layer separated by serous fluid.

Inside the testis, thin septa subdivide the testis into some 250 lobules *(Figure 12.3)*. Each lobule contains three or four **seminiferous tubules** in which several layers of germ cells are in the process of becoming sperm.

Between the seminiferous tubules are the interstitial cells. They produce hormones called **androgens.**

Testosterone is the major androgen produced by the interstitial cells of the testes. It has the following effects:

- **sustains** the male reproductive tract throughout adulthood
- **stimulates** spermatogenesis; testosterone levels peak at age 20, and then decline steadily to one-third of that level at age 65
- **inhibits** the secretion of female hormones
- **stimulates** the development of male secondary sex characteristics at puberty
- **enlarges** the spermatic ducts and accessory glands of the male reproductive system
- **stimulates** a burst of growth at puberty—including increased muscle mass, higher **basal metabolic rate (BMR),** and larger larynx (this last effect deepens the voice).
- **stimulates** erythropoiesis, giving men a higher red blood cell (RBC) count than women
- **stimulates** the brain to increase **libido** (sex drive) in the male.

Spermatic Cord

The blood vessels and nerves to the testis arise in the abdominal cavity. They pass through the inguinal canal, where they join with connective tissue to form a spermatic cord that suspends each testis in the scrotum *(see Figure 12.3)*. The left testis is suspended lower than the right. Within the cord are an artery, a plexus of veins, nerves, a thin muscle, and the ductus (vas) deferens (the passage into which sperm go when they leave the testis).

Spermatogenesis

Spermatogenesis is the process in which the germ cells of the seminiferous tubules mature and divide (**mitosis**) and then undergo two divisions called **meiosis.** The four daughter cells differentiate into **spermatids** and then **spermatozoa (sperm)** *(Figure 12.4)*. The germ cells have 23 pairs of chromosomes (a total of 46). Because of meiosis, each sperm has only 23 chromosomes that can combine at fertilization with the 23 chromosomes in a female **oocyte** (egg).

The mature sperm has a pear-shaped head and a long tail. The nucleus of the head contains 23 chromosomes.

The tail (**flagellum**) provides the movement as the sperm swims up the female reproductive tract.

Head

Nucleus

Basal body

Mitochondria

Midpiece (body)

Principal piece

Tail

Endpiece

▲ **FIGURE 12.5   Mature Sperm.**

WORD ANALYSIS AND DEFINITION

WORD	PRONUNCIATION	ELEMENTS		DEFINITION
androgen	**AN**-droh-jen	S/ R/CF	**-gen** *formation* **andr/o-** *masculine*	Hormone that promotes masculine characteristics
flagellum flagella (pl)	fla-**JELL**-um fla-**JELL**-ah		Latin *small whip*	Tail of a sperm
libido	li-**BEE**-doh		Latin *lust*	Sexual desire
meiosis	my-**OH**-sis	S/ R/	**-osis** *condition* **mei-** *lessening*	Two rapid cell divisions, resulting in half the number of chromosomes
mitosis	my-**TOE**-sis	S/ R/	**-osis** *condition* **mit-** *threadlike structure*	Cell division to create two identical cells, each with 46 chromosomes
oocyte	**OH**-oh-site	S/ R/CF	**-cyte** *cell* **o/o-** *egg*	Female egg cell
oogenesis	oh-oh-**JEN**-eh-sis	R/ S/	**-gen-** *origin, source* **-esis** *condition*	Development of female egg cell
puberty	**PYU**-ber-tee		Latin *grown up*	Process of maturing from child to young adult
seminiferous tubule	sem-ih-**NIF**-er-us **TU**-byul	S/ R/CF R/	**-ous** *pertaining to* **semin/is-** *sperm* **-fer-** *to bear*	Coiled tubes in the testes that produce sperm
sperm (also called **sper-matozoon**)	SPERM		Greek *seed*	Mature male sex cell
spermatozoa (pl)	**SPER**-mat-oh-**ZOH**-ah	S/ R/CF	**-zoa** *animals* **spermat/o-** *sperm*	Sperm (plural of spermatozoon)
spermatid	**SPER**-ma-tid	S/ R/	**-id** *having a particular quality* **spermat-** *sperm*	A cell late in the development process of sperm
spermatogenesis (*Note:* This term has no prefix or suffix.)	**SPER**-mat-oh-**JEN**-eh-sis	R/ R/CF	**-genesis** *origin* **spermat/o-** *sperm*	The process by which male germ cells differentiate into sperm
testosterone (*Note:* This term has no prefix or suffix.)	tes-**TOSS**-ter-own	R/ R/CF	**-sterone** *sterol* **test/o-** *testis*	Powerful androgen produced by the testes
tunica vaginalis	**TYU**-nih-kah vaj-ih-**NAHL**-iss	S/ R/	*tunica* Latin *coat* **-alis** *pertaining to* **vagin-** *sheath*	Covering, particularly of a tubular structure. The tunica vaginalis is the sheath of the testis and epididymis

EXERCISES

Deconstruction of medical terms is a tool for analyzing the meaning. In the following chart, you are given a medical term. Deconstruct the term into its root (or combining form) and suffix. Note that none of these terms have prefixes, and not all of the terms have a suffix. Write the element in the appropriate column and the meaning of each element in the last column. The first one is done for you. Then answer the question at the end of the exercise.

Term	Root/CF	Suffix	Meaning of Element
vaginalis	*vagin*	*alis*	*sheath, pertaining to*
testosterone			
androgen			
spermatid			
spermatogenesis			

In your opinion, which two terms are the most unusual in this Word Analysis and Definition box (WAD), and why? (**Hint:** Think of the elements.)

DISORDERS OF THE TESTES

Testicular torsion is the twisting of a testis on its spermatic cord. As the testis twists, the spermatic cord has to twist because it is fixed in the abdomen. The testicular artery in the twisted cord becomes blocked, and the blood supply to the testis is cut off. The condition occurs in men between puberty and age 25. In half the cases, it starts in bed at night.

Varicocele is a condition in which the veins in the spermatic cord become dilated and tortuous as varicose veins. If it is uncomfortable, it can be treated by surgically tying off the affected veins.

Hydrocele is a collection of excess fluid in the space between the visceral and parietal layers of the tunica vaginalis of the testis. It is most common after age 40. The diagnosis can be confirmed by transillumination, shining a bright light on the swelling to see the shape of the testis through the translucent excess fluid (*Figure 12.6*). Surgical removal is performed for large hydroceles.

Spermatocele is a collection of sperm in a sac formed in the epididymis. It occurs in about 30% of men, is benign, and rarely causes symptoms. It does not require treatment unless it becomes bothersome.

Cryptorchism occurs when a testis fails to descend from the abdomen into the scrotum before the boy is 12 months old. In the **embryo,** the testes develop inside the abdomen at the level of the kidney. They must then migrate down the abdomen into the scrotum. As undescended testicles have a higher risk of infertility and cancer, **orchiopexy** is performed to bring the testis into the scrotum.

Epididymitis and **epididymoorchitis (orchitis).** Epididymitis is inflammation of the epididymis; epididymoorchitis is inflammation of the epididymis and testis. Orchitis is usually a consequence of epididymitis. They are most commonly caused by a bacterial infection spreading from a urinary tract infection or infection of the prostate. They can also be caused by **sexually transmitted diseases (STDs),** such as gonorrhea or chlamydia (*see Chapter 20*).

A viral cause of orchitis is mumps. In males past puberty who develop mumps, 30% will develop orchitis, and 30% of those will develop resulting testicular atrophy. If the testicular infection is bilateral, **infertility** can result. Mumps is avoidable by immunization during childhood (*see Chapter 16*).

Testicular cancer usually develops in men younger than 40.

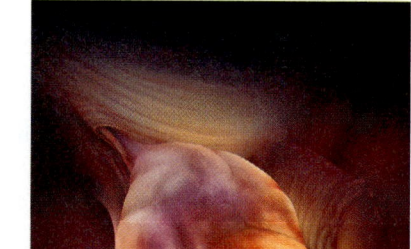

Spermatic cord

Testis

▲ **FIGURE 12.6   Transillumination of Hydrocele Showing Testis and Spermatic Cord.**

Abbreviations

SET	self-examination of the testes
STD	sexually transmitted disease

Forty percent of testicular cancers are **seminomas,** made up of immature germ cells. Nonseminomas occur in different combinations of **choriocarcinoma, embryonal cell,** and **teratoma.** Lance Armstrong's cancer was 60% choriocarcinoma, and 40% embryonal cell. The initial treatment for testicular cancer is surgical removal of the affected testis (**orchiectomy**), followed by chemotherapy and sometimes radiation therapy.

WORD	PRONUNCIATION	ELEMENTS		DEFINITION
choriocarcinoma	**KOH**-ree-oh-kar-sih-**NOH**-mah	S/ R/CF R/	-oma *tumor* chori/o- *membrane* -carcin- *cancer*	Highly malignant cancer in a testis or ovary
cryptorchism	krip-**TOR**-kizm	S/ R/ R/	-ism *condition* crypt- *hidden* -orch- *testicle*	Failure of one or both testes to descend into the scrotum
epididymis	ep-ih-**DID**-ih-mis	P/ R/	epi- *above* -didymis *testis*	Coiled tube attached to the testis
epididymitis	**EP**-ih-did-ih-**MY**-tis	S/	-itis *inflammation*	Inflammation of the epididymis
epididymoorchitis (syn: orchitis)	ep-ih-**DID**-ih-mo-or-**KIE**-tis	S/ P/ R/CF R/	-itis *inflammation* epi- *above* -didym/o- *testis* -orch- *testicle*	Inflammation of the epididymis and testicle
hydrocele	**HIGH**-droh-seal	S/ R/CF	-cele *swelling* hydr/o- *water*	Collection of fluid in the space of the tunica vaginalis
infertility	in-fer-**TIL**-ih-tee	S/ P/ R/	-ity *condition* in- *not* -fertil- *able to conceive*	Failure to conceive
orchiectomy	or-kee-**ECK**-toe-me	S/ R/	-ectomy *surgical excision* orchi- *testicle*	Removal of one or both testes
orchitis (syn: epididymoorchitis)	or-**KIE**-tis	S/ R/	-itis *inflammation* orch- *testicle*	Inflammation of the testis
orchiopexy	**OR**-key-oh-**PEK**-see	S/ R/	-pexy *surgical fixation* orchi/o- *testis*	Surgical fixation of a testis in the scrotum
seminoma	sem-ih-**NO**-mah	S/ R/	-oma *tumor, mass* semin- *seed*	Neoplasm of germ cells of a testis
spermatocele	**SPER**-mat-oh-seal	S/ R/CF	-cele *cave* spermat/o- *sperm*	Cyst of epididymis that contains sperm
teratoma	ter-ah-**TOE**-mah	S/ R/	-oma *tumor, mass* terat- *monster*	Neoplasm of a testis or ovary containing multiple tissues from other sites in the body
varicocele	**VAIR**-ih-koh-seal	S/ R/CF	-cele *cave* varic/o- *varicosity*	Varicose veins of the spermatic cord

EXERCISES

Build your knowledge of the **language of urology** by correctly answering the following questions regarding the elements in the terms. *Before you attempt to answer the question, divide the term into its components with a slash (/). This will help you identify the element to which the question is referring. Circle the best answer.*

1. In the term *teratoma*, the root means:

   monster   multiple   neoplasm

2. In the term *choriocarcinoma*, the CF means:

   hidden   membrane   above

3. In the term *hydrocele*, the root/CF means:

   testis   water   sperm

4. In the term *cryptorchism*, one of the roots means:

   outside of   behind   hidden

5. In the term *orchiopexy*, the suffix means:

   removal   incision   fixation

6. In the term a *seminoma*, the suffix means:

   cyst   tumor   vesicle

MALE REPRODUCTIVE SYSTEM

F. **Language of Urology:** Every day on the job in the urology clinic you will be asked to apply the **language of urology** to the anatomy and physiology of the male reproductive system. Circle the correct choice.

1. The prostate, seminal vesicles, and bulbourethral glands are all:

    a. gonads

    b. primary sex organs

    c. accessory glands

    d. secondary sex organs

    e. none of the above

2. Surgical procedure that makes a male sterile:

    a. nephrectomy

    b. vasovasostomy

    c. orchiopexy

    d. vasectomy

    e. lithotripsy

3. Shining a bright light on a swelling to see the shape of the testes:

    a. maturation

    b. micturition

    c. vasoepididymostomy

    d. orchiopexy

    e. transillumination

4. Scarring that narrows the urethra is called:

    a. UTI

    b. urethral stricture

    c. ureteroscope

    d. urethrotomy

    e. urethropexy

5. The diamond-shaped region between the thighs is called:

    a. rete testis

    b. perineum

    c. median septum

    d. ductus deferens

    e. anal triangle

6. Androgens are:

   a. enzymes

   b. vitamins

   c. hormones

   d. special nerve cells

   e. flagellum

7. The penis, scrotum, and testes collectively are known as:

   a. primary sex organs

   b. accessory glands

   c. secondary sex organs

   d. external genitalia

   e. none of the above

8. Measured in a blood test to check for prostate cancer:

   a. BPH

   b. TURP

   c. BMR

   d. PSA

   e. ED

9. A female egg cell is called:

   a. flagellum

   b. spermatozoa

   c. spermatid

   d. oocyte

   e. varicocele

10. The distinct ridge in the scrotum is called the:

    a. dartos

    b. raphe

    c. hydrocele

    d. epididymis

    e. cavernosa

MALE REPRODUCTIVE SYSTEM

G. **Language of Urology:** Every day on the job in the urology clinic you will be asked to apply the **language of urology** to the anatomy and physiology of the male reproductive system. Circle the correct choice.

1. Transports the sperm away from the testes:

    a. spermatic cord

    b. autonomic nerves

    c. ductus deferens

    d. bulbourethral glands

    e. seminal vesicle

2. Suspends each testis in the scrotum:

    a. spermatic cord

    b. ductus deferens

    c. dartos muscle

    d. interstitial cells

    e. tunica

3. An endoscope that is inserted into the urethra to remove excess prostatic tissue is a:

    a. cystoscope

    b. ureteroscope

    c. resectoscope

    d. hysteroscope

    e. none of the above

4. The ductus deferens is also known as the:

    a. sustentacular cells

    b. seminiferous tubules

    c. tunica vaginalis

    d. tubuloalveolar glands

    e. vas deferens

5. **Hypogonadism** is a term meaning:

    a. undescended testis

    b. low sperm count

    c. testosterone deficiency

    d. male infertility

    e. premature ejaculation

H. Roots: The following medical terms all share the same root. Employ your knowledge of the other elements to determine the correct term for the sentence. First, slash (/) each term so you can identify the elements. Then fill in the blanks.

cryptorchism   orchitis   epididymoorchitis   orchiopexy   orchiectomy   anorchism

1. Patient has inflammation of the epididymis and testicle on the right side. Diagnosis: _____.

2. Patient was born without testes. Diagnosis: _____

3. Patient had one diseased testicle removed. Procedure: _____

4. Patient had testicular torsion repaired. Procedure: _____

5. Patient has inflammation of both testicles. Diagnosis: _____

6. Patient was born with an undescended right testicle. Diagnosis: _____

I. Study Review: Taking a test on any body system involves remembering a lot of information and terminology. Making short lists for yourself to study from is easier than trying to remember facts in paragraph context. There are three answers to each of the following questions. Fill in the blanks.

1. The head of a mature sperm has three segments—name the accessory glands.

   a. _____

   b. _____

   c. _____

2. The tail of a sperm is divided into three segments—name them.

   a. _____

   b. _____

   c. _____

3. What are the three main types of prostatitis? (Specify acute or chronic.)

   a. _____

   b. _____

   c. _____

4. The shaft of the penis contains three erectile vascular bodies—name them.

   a. _____

   b. _____

   c. _____

5. What are the three disorders which can affect the prepuce?

   a. _____

   b. _____

   c. _____

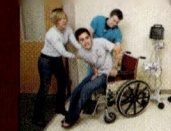

MALE REPRODUCTIVE SYSTEM

J. **Terminology Challenge: Cryptorchism** means *hidden* testicle because the testicle has failed to descend from the abdomen.

Find an element from a previous chapter that also means hidden.

1. The element _____ means _____.

2. Use this other element in a sentence.

_____

_____

_____

_____

K. **Patient Education:** Patients will always have questions that you must be able to answer professionally. How well could you explain to your patient the difference between:

1. The surgical procedures of vasectomy and vasovasostomy:

_____

_____

_____

2. A radical prostatectomy and a TURP:

_____

_____

_____

L. **Recall and Review:** How well do you remember these word elements from the previous chapter? Try to answer without first looking back to check. Fill in the blanks.

Element	Type of Element (P, R, CF, S)	Meaning of Element
ren		
ex		
peri		
hydro		
litho		

M. **Disorder/Disease:** Complete the diagnosis documentation for the following patients. Finish filling in the blanks with the correct medical term for the disorder or disease mentioned in each statement.

1. Excess fluid has collected in the space between the visceral and parietal layers of the tunica vaginalis of the patient's right

   testis: hydro_____

2. Noncancerous enlargement compressing the prostatic urethra: benign _____plasia.

3. Marked curvature of the erect penis caused by fibrous tissue: _____ disease

4. Undescended testicles in a 10-month-old male: _____ism

5. Inability to have a satisfactory erection: _____ dys_____

6. Veins in the spermatic cord become tortuous and dilated: varico_____

7. Opening of the urethra is on the undersurface of the penis instead of at the head of the glans:

   hypo_____

8. Yeast infection of the glans and foreskin: _____itis

9. Foreskin is tight and cannot be retracted over the glans for cleaning: _____sis

10. Inflammation of the epididymis: _____itis

N. **Brain Teaser:** Why is a resectoscope also an endoscope?

_____

_____

O. **Abbreviations are another form of precise communication.** Demonstrate that you know the meanings of the abbreviations in the following exercise. Circle the best answer.

1. Diagnosis for a type of prostate disease:

   a. BPH

   b. TURP

   c. PSA

2. Can produce condylomata acuminata:

   a. STD

   b. UTI

   c. ED

3. The abbreviation **BMR** relates to:

   a. metabolism

   b. bowel movement

   c. bulbourethral glands

4. **SET** refers to:

   a. a diagnostic test

   b. something you do yourself

   c. a surgical procedure

P. **Prefixes can be a critical clue to the meaning of a medical term.** Challenge your knowledge of prefixes with the following exercise. Write the meaning of the prefix, a medical term containing that prefix, and the meaning of the medical term. Fill in the blanks.

Prefix	Meaning of Prefix	Medical Term with Prefix	Meaning of Medical Term
an-			
circum-			
contra-			
crypt-			
epi-			
noct-			
para-			
poly-			

MALE REPRODUCTIVE SYSTEM

CHAPTER SUMMARY EXERCISE

1. *Listen to the pronunciation of the medical terms as given by your instructor.*
2. *Circle the correct spelling of the medical term.*
3. *Match the correctly spelled terms to the brief descriptions below.*
4. *Write a sentence for each of the 15 terms that appear in this exercise.*

A. SPELLING COMPREHENSION: CIRCLE THE CORRECT SPELLING OF THE TERM.

1. gonad — gonnad — gonade — gunad — gunade
2. perikneal — perikneeal — perineal — perrineal — peraneal
3. coriocarcinoma — corriocarcinoma — choriacarcinoma — choriocarcinoma — corheacarcinoma
4. insemination — insemmination — insimination — insimmination — insimation
5. tortion — torsion — tortsion — tortcion — tostion
6. epidydimis — epidydimus — epididymis — epididymus — epodidymis
7. frinulum — frenullum — frenulum — frennulum — frenulumn
8. tistosterune — testosterine — testosterone — tistosterone — testosteron
9. priaprism — piaprism — priapism — prapism — piapresm
10. flagilla — flaggila — flagella — flaggela — flaggilla
11. genitaleia — genitailia — genitalia — ginitalea — gennitalia
12. vessicle — vessickle — vesickle — vissicle — vesicle
13. siphillus — syphylis — syphilis — syphillus — syphylus
14. puberty — pubberty — pubertie — pubbirty — pubirty
15. bubolurethral — bulbourethral — bulboureteral — bulbouritheral — buboureteral

B. MATCH THE NUMBER OF THE CORRECT TERM IN PART A WITH THE BRIEF DESCRIPTION OF THE TERM BELOW.

a. pertaining to the bulbous penis and urethra _____

b. androgen produced by testis _____

c. highly malignant cancer in testis or ovary _____

d. process of maturing from child to young adult _____

e. Plural: tail of sperm _____

f. the act or result of twisting _____

g. deposition of semen in female reproductive tract _____

h. pertaining to the area between the thighs _____

i. testis or ovary _____

j. external and internal organs of reproduction _____

k. small sac containing liquid _____

l. sexually transmitted disease _____

m. structure on posterior surface of testis _____

n. persistent, painful erection _____

o. fold of mucous membrane _____

C. USING YOUR KNOWLEDGE OF TERMS 1-15 IN PART A AND THEIR CORRECT SPELLING, WRITE A BRIEF SENTENCE AS IT MIGHT APPEAR IN PATIENT DOCUMENTATION.

1. _____

2. _____

3. _____

4. _____

5. _____

6. _____

7. _____

8. _____

9. _____

10. _____

11. _____

12. _____

13. _____

14. _____

15. _____

D. GO TO THE STUDENT CD. OPEN THE GLOSSARY AND PRACTICE YOUR PRONUNCIATION OF THE TERMS IN PART A OF THIS EXERCISE.

Ovaries, Fallopian (Uterine) Tubes, and Uterus

OBJECTIVES

The female gonads, the primary sex organs, are the ovaries. The female internal accessory organs include a pair of **fallopian (uterine) tubes,** a **uterus,** and a vagina. Women are born with all the eggs (**ova**) that they will release, but it is not until puberty that the eggs mature and start to leave the ovary. The ovarian hormones, estrogen and progesterone, are involved in **menstruation** and **pregnancy (PGY).** The pituitary gland at the base of the brain produces other hormones that control the functions of the ovaries, uterus, and breast (see Chapter 14).

These complex interactions are the core of the human reproductive system and an essential part of understanding the human body. The information in this lesson will enable you to:

- **Describe the structure of an ovary.**
- **Identify the major events of oogenesis.**
- **List the functions of estrogen and progesterone.**
- **Explain the control of the pituitary gland over the female reproductive system.**
- **Detail the anatomy and physiology of the uterus and fallopian (uterine) tubes.**
- **Apply correct medical terminology to the anatomy and physiology of the ovaries, fallopian (uterine) tubes, and uterus.**
- **Evaluate the effects of common disorders of the ovaries, uterine tubes, and uterus on the health of the female.**

You are

. . . a certified health education specialist **(CHES)** employed by Fulwood Medical Center.

Your patient is

. . . Ms. Claire Marcos, a 21-year-old student referred to you by Anna Rusack, MD, a **gynecologist.**

CASE REPORT 13.2

Ms. Marcos has been diagnosed with **polycystic ovarian** syndrome, and your task is to develop a program of self-care as part of her overall plan of therapy.

From her medical record, you see that she presented with irregular, often missed menstrual periods since the beginning of puberty, persistent acne, patches of dark skin on the back of her neck and under her arms, loss of hair from the front of her scalp, and inability to control her weight. She is five feet four inches and weighs 150 pounds.

Her self-care program is to include exercise, diet, and regular use of birth control medication and metformin, both of which have been prescribed.

She has written out a list of questions that she hands to you. These include:
- Why are my periods so irregular?
- Why doesn't my acne respond to all the treatment I've had?
- Am I going bald?
- Will I be able to have children some day?
- Why am I taking birth control pills when I'm not sexually active?
- What are all these other health problems they say I'm at risk for?

At the end of this chapter you will be asked to answer these questions.

Abbreviations

CHES certified health education specialist
PGY pregnancy

WORD	PRONUNCIATION	ELEMENTS		DEFINITION
fallopian tubes (also called **uterine tubes**)	fah-**LOW**-pee-an		Gabriello Fallopio, 1523–1562, Italian anatomist	Uterine tubes connected to the fundus of the uterus
menses	**MEN**-seez		Latin *month*	Monthly uterine bleeding
menstruation (**syn** of **menses**)	men-stru-**A**-shun	S/ R/CF	-ation *action* menstr/u- *menses*	The act of menstruation
menstruate (verb)	**MEN**-stru-ate			
menstrual (adj)	**MEN**-stru-al			
ovary	**OH**-va-ree		Latin *egg*	One of the paired female egg-producing glands
ovum (**syn** of **oocyte**)	**OH**-vum		Latin *egg*	Egg
ova (pl)	**OH**-va			
ovarian (adj)	oh-**VAIR**-ee-an	S/ R/	-an *pertaining to* ovari- *ovary*	Pertaining to the ovary
polycystic	pol-ee-**SIS**-tik	S/ P/ R/	-ic *pertaining to* poly- *many* -cyst- *cyst*	Composed of many cysts
pregnant	**PREG**-nant	S R/	-ant *pertaining to* pregn- *with child*	Having conceived
pregnancy	**PREG**-nan-see	S/	-ancy *state of*	State of being pregnant
gestation	jes-**TAY**-shun	S/ R/	-ion *condition* gestat- *gestation*	From conception to birth
uterus	**YOU**-ter-us		Latin *womb*	Organ in which an egg develops into a fetus
uterine (adj)	**YOU**-ter-ine			

EXERCISES

Elements: *Knowing the meaning of word elements is your best tool for building and analyzing medical terms. Choose from among the following word elements, and insert the correct element in the blank to complete the medical term.*

1. pertaining to many cysts: _____cystic

    mono   poly   cyano   endo

2. pertaining to the ovary: _____an

    gestat   ovari   menstru   pregn

3. This term is synonymous for menstruation: _____

    gynecology   gynecologic   menses   menstrual

4. having conceived: _____ant

    pregn   gyneco   gestat   estra

5. the most potent form of estrogen: _____diol

    menstru   estra   ovari   proges

6. from conception to birth: _____ion

    ovari   gestat   gyneco   menstru

Approximately 20% of women now have their first child when they are aged 35 or older.

In 20 to 30% of female infertility problems, no identifiable cause is found.

FEMALE INFERTILITY

Infertility is the inability to become pregnant after one year of unprotected intercourse. It affects 10 to 15% of all couples. The causes of infertility are due to:

- the female factor alone in 35%
- the male factor alone in 30%
- male and female factors in 20%
- unknown factors in 15%

In women, fertility begins to decrease as early as age 30, and pregnancy rates are very low after age 44.

Causes of infertility in a woman are:

- **Infrequent ovulation** is responsible in 20% of female infertility problems, so that both ovulation and menses occur at intervals of longer than one month. Bulimia, anorexia nervosa, rapid weight loss, excessive exercise training, low body weight, obesity, and polycystic ovarian syndrome are among the causes.

- **Scarring of the fallopian (uterine) tubes** is responsible for 30% of female infertility problems. Scarring can result from previous surgery, previous tubal pregnancy, pelvic inflammatory disease, or endometriosis.

- **Structural abnormalities of the uterus** are responsible for 20% of female infertility problems. Fibroid tumors, uterine polyps, and scarring from infections, abortions, and miscarriages can all produce abnormalities of the uterus.

After a complete physical examination, including vagina and pelvic organs, other diagnostic tools include:

- **hormone blood levels** of progesterone, estrogens, and FSH
- **hysterosalpingogram** in which x-rays of the uterus and fallopian (uterine) tubes are taken after dye is injected into the uterus through a slender catheter
- **ultrasound** of the abdomen can show the shape and size of the uterus, and vaginal ultrasound can show the shape and size of the ovaries
- **hysteroscopy** can visualize the inside of the uterus and be used to take an endometrial biopsy and remove polyps or fibroids
- **laparoscopy** allows inspection of the outside of the uterus and ovaries and removal of any scar tissue blocking tubes
- **postcoital testing** in which the cervix is examined soon after unprotected intercourse to see if sperm can travel through into the uterus

Treatment is of any underlying cause arising from the results of the infertility evaluation. Infrequent ovulation can be treated with hormones to stimulate release of the egg. These include clomiphene citrate and injectable forms of FSH, LH, and GnRH.

Surgical procedures to initiate pregnancy include:

- **Intrauterine insemination**—sperm are inserted directly into the uterus via a special catheter.
- **In vitro fertilization (IVF)**—eggs and sperm are combined in a laboratory dish, and two to four resulting embryos are placed inside the uterus. This can result in twins or triplets.

Keynote

The success rate for IVF is approximately 30% for each egg retrieval.

Abbreviation

IVF	in vitro fertilization

WORD ANALYSIS AND DEFINITION

S = Suffix   P = Prefix   R = Root   R/CF = Combining Form

WORD	PRONUNCIATION	ELEMENTS		DEFINITION
hysterosalpingogram	HIS-ter-oh-sal-PING-oh-gram	S/ R/CF R/CF	-gram *a record* hyster/o- *uterus* -salping/o- *uterine tube*	Radiograph of uterus and uterine tubes after injection of contrast material
hysteroscopy	his-ter-OS-koh-pee	S/ R/CF	-scopy *view or examine* hyster/o- *uterus*	Visual inspection of the uterine cavity using an endoscope
infertility infertile (adj)	in-fer-TIL-ih-tee in-FER-tile	S/ P/ R/	-ity *condition* in- *not* -fertil- *able to conceive*	Failure to conceive
insemination inseminate (verb)	in-sem-ih-NAY-shun in-SEM-ih-nate	S/ P/ R/	-ation *action* in- *in* -semin- *semen*	Introduction of semen into the vagina
intrauterine	IN-trah-YOU-ter-ine	S/ P/ R/	-ine *pertaining to* intra- *inside* -uter- *uterus*	Inside the uterine cavity
in vitro fertilization (IVF)	IN VEE-tro FER-til-ih-ZAY-shun	S/ R/	in vitro *Latin in glass* -ization *process of creating* fertil- *able to conceive*	Process of combining sperm and egg in a laboratory dish and placing the resulting embryos inside the uterus
postcoital	post-KOH-eye-tal	S/ P/ R/	-al *pertaining to* post- *after* -coit- *sexual intercourse*	After sexual intercourse

EXERCISES

Build your knowledge of the meaning of elements. Write the correct element on the line to complete the term.

1. If it occurs after intercourse, it is _____coital.
   (pre   post)

2. Visual inspection of the uterine cavity using an endoscope is a _____scopy.
   (cysto   hystero)

3. Patient is unable to conceive and suffers from _____.
   (infertility   insemination)

4. Inside the uterine cavity is referred to as _____uterine.
   (intra   inter)

5. The process of combining sperm and egg in a laboratory dish is _____ fertilization.
   (intrauterine   in vitro)

6. Introduction of semen into the vagina is _____.
   (infertility   insemination)

7. A radiograph of the uterus and uterine tubes is a _____.
   (hysterogram   hysterosalpingogram)

8. Sperm can be _____ directly into the uterus via a catheter.
   (inseminated   insemination)

▲ **FIGURE 13.21** **Female Condom.**

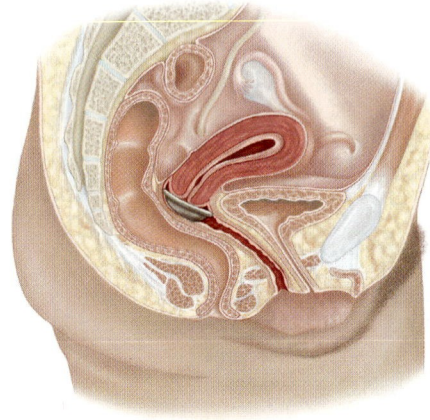

▲ **FIGURE 13.22** **Diaphragm.**

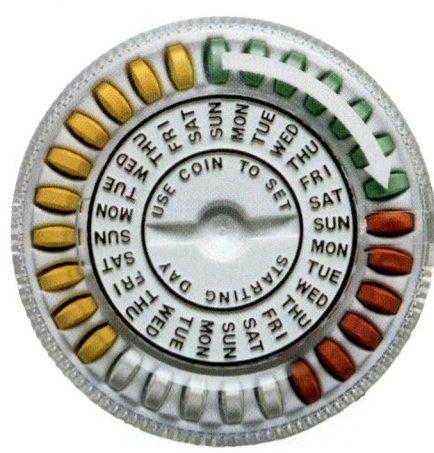

▲ **FIGURE 13.23** **Oral Contraceptives.**

Keynote

Unprotected sex has a failure rate of 85%, with resulting pregnancy.

Abbreviations	
IUD	intrauterine device
RU-486	mifepristone

CONTRACEPTION

Contraception is the prevention of pregnancy. Common methods of contraception include:

Behavioral Methods

- **Abstinence** is reliable if followed consistently.
- **Rhythm method** avoids intercourse near the time of expected ovulation, which is difficult to determine consistently. It has a 25% failure rate.
- **Coitus interruptus** involves the male withdrawing his penis before ejaculation. There is a 20% failure rate.

Barrier Methods

- **Male condom**—a sheath of latex or rubber rolled on over the erect penis.
- **Female condom**—a polyurethane sheath that fits into the vagina with a ring at one end to go over the cervix and a larger ring at the other end to go over the vulva *(Figure 13.21).* Both male and female condoms help protect against STDs. They have a 5 to 10% failure rate.
- **Diaphragm** *(Figure 13.22)* **and cervical cap**—a latex or rubber dome inserted into the vagina and placed over the cervix. When used with a spermicide, they have a 5 to 10% failure rate for pregnancy.
- **Spermicidal foam and gel**—inserted into the vagina. Used on their own, they have a 25% failure rate.

Intrauterine Devices

Intrauterine devices (IUDs) are T-shaped flexible plastic or copper devices inserted into the uterus and left in place for one to four years. Failure rate is less than 3%.

Hormonal Methods

- **Oral contraceptives** (birth control pills) utilize a mixture of estrogen and progesterone to prevent follicular development and ovulation *(Figure 13.23).* They are taken orally and have a 5% failure rate, usually due to inconsistent pill taking.
- **Estrogen/progestin patches** deliver the hormones transdermally. Some are applied monthly, some weekly. Their failure rate is less than 1%.
- **Injected progestins,** such as Depo-Provera, are given by injection every three months. Their failure rate is less than 1%.
- **Implanted progestins,** such as Norplant, are contained in porous silicone tubes that are inserted under the skin and slowly release the progestin for up to five years. Their failure rate is less than 1%.
- **Morning-after pills,** such as Plan B, contain large doses of progestins to inhibit or delay ovulation. They are a backup when taken within 72 hours of unprotected intercourse. Their failure rate is around 10%.
- **Mifepristone (RU-486),** when taken with a prostaglandin, induces a miscarriage. It has an 8% failure rate.

Surgical Methods

- **Tubal ligation** ("getting your tubes tied") is performed with laparoscopy. Both fallopian (uterine) tubes are cut, a segment removed, and the ends tied off and cauterized shut. Failure rate is less than 1%. A **tubal anastomosis** is the procedure to rejoin the tubes if there is a subsequent change of mind.
- **Vasectomy** in the male is discussed in *Chapter 12.*

WORD ANALYSIS AND DEFINITION

WORD	PRONUNCIATION		ELEMENTS	DEFINITION
anastomosis anastomoses (pl)	ah-**NAS**-to-**MO**-sis	S/ R/	**-osis** *condition* **anastom-** *join together*	A surgically made union between two tubular structures
coitus	**KOH**-it-us		Latin *come together*	Sexual intercourse
condom	**KON**-dom		Thought to be named for the eighteenth century English physician who invented it	A sheath or cover for the penis or vagina to prevent conception and infection
contraception	kon-trah-**SEP**-shun	S/ P/ R/	**-ion** *process* **contra-** *against* **-cept-** *receive*	Prevention of pregnancy
contraceptive	kon-trah-**SEP**-tiv	S/	**-ive** *quality of*	An agent that prevents conception
diaphragm (**Note:** Diaphragm also is the term for the muscle that separates the thoracic and abdominal cavities.)	**DIE**-ah-fram		Greek *partition or wall*	A ring and dome-shaped material inserted in the vagina to prevent pregnancy
ligature	**LIG**-ah-chur	S/	Latin *band, tie* **-ion** *action*	Thread or wire tied around a tubal structure to close it
ligation	lie-**GAY**-shun	R/	**ligat-** *tie up*	Using a tie to close a tube
progestin	pro-**JESS**-tin	S/ P/ R/	**-in** *pertaining to* **pro-** *before* **-gest-** *produce*	A synthetic form of progesterone

EXERCISES

Review all the terms in this Word Analysis and Definition box (WAD). With critical thinking, you will be able to answer the following questions using these terms. Fill in the blanks.

1. What is the Latin term for sexual intercourse? _____

2. If a patient has a tubal ligation and later changes her mind, what procedure is necessary to repair this? _____

   _____

   Briefly describe what this term means. _____

   _____

3. Write the two definitions of the word **diaphragm** and one sentence for each meaning.

   Definition 1: _____

   Sentence: _____

   _____

   Definition 2: _____

   Sentence: _____

   _____

4. A contraceptive works against something—what does it work against?

   _____

5. What is the medical term for a thread or wire that is used to close a tube?

   _____

Obstetrics: Pregnancy and Childbirth

OBJECTIVES

The nuclei of the male and female cells unite, their chromosomes mingle. Fertilization (**conception**) is complete, and a **zygote** is formed. So begins the incredible, dramatic, and wondrous development of an embryo and a new human being. This process will be described in this lesson to enable you to:

- **Specify the stages of embryonic development.**
- **Describe the implantation of the embryo in the uterus.**
- **List the functions of the placenta.**
- **Identify the major events of fetal development.**
- **Explain the process of childbirth.**
- **Discuss some of the most common problems of fetal development and childbirth.**
- **Recognize and use appropriately the medical terminology for embryonic and fetal development and childbirth.**

CONCEPTION

When released from the ovary, an egg takes 72 hours to reach the uterus, but it must be **fertilized** *(Figure 13.24)* within 12 to 24 hours to survive. Therefore, **fertilization** must take place in the distal third of the uterine tube.

Between 200 million to 600 million sperm are deposited in the vagina near the cervix. Many are destroyed by the acidity in the vagina or just drain out. Others fail to get through the cervical mucus. Approximately half the survivors will go up the wrong fallopian (uterine) tube. The journey through the uterus into the fallopian (uterine) tube takes about an hour. Some 2,000 to 3,000 sperm reach the egg. Several of these penetrate the outer layers of the egg and clear the path for the one sperm that will penetrate all the way into the egg cytoplasm to fertilize it *(Figure 13.24)*.

Implantation

While still in the uterine tube, the zygote divides, producing a ball of cells called a **morula** *(Figure 13.25)*. Within the morula, a fluid-filled cavity develops, and the morula becomes a **blastocyst.** A week after fertilization, the blastocyst enters the

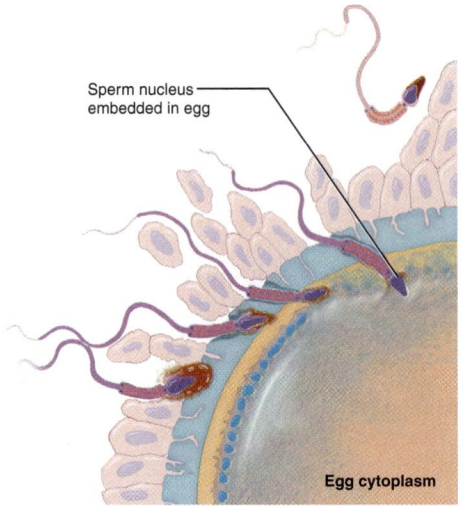

Sperm nucleus embedded in egg

Egg cytoplasm

▲ **FIGURE 13.24   Fertilization.**

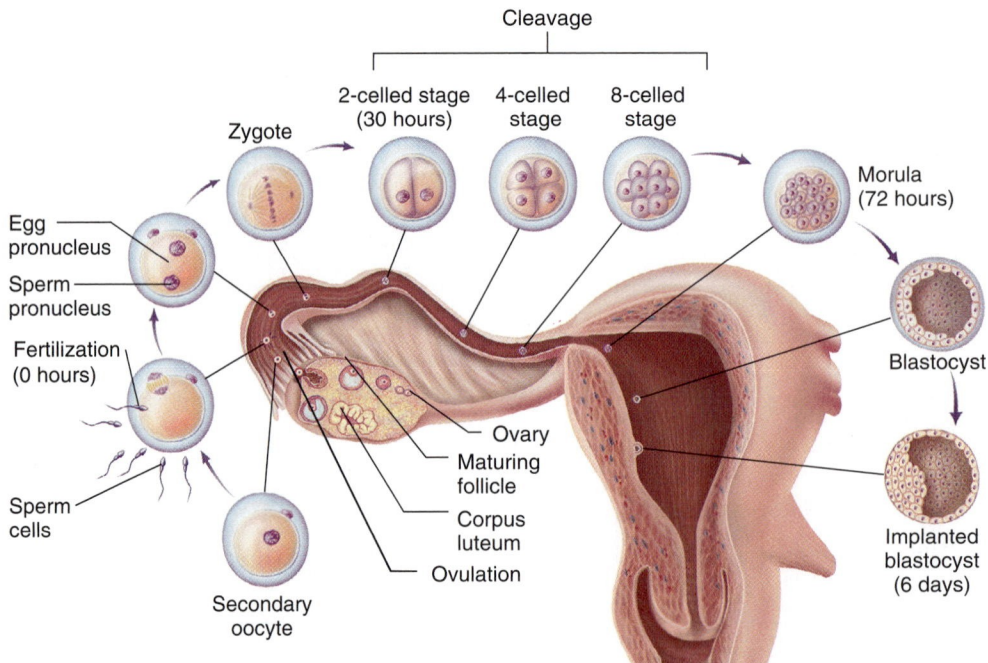

Cleavage

2-celled stage (30 hours)   4-celled stage   8-celled stage

Zygote

Morula (72 hours)

Egg pronucleus

Sperm pronucleus

Fertilization (0 hours)

Blastocyst

Sperm cells

Ovary
Maturing follicle
Corpus luteum
Ovulation

Implanted blastocyst (6 days)

FIGURE 13.25   Early Embryo Development. ▶

Secondary oocyte

WORD	PRONUNCIATION	ELEMENTS		DEFINITION
blastocyst	**BLAS**-toe-sist	S/ R/CF	**-cyst** *bladder* **blast/o-** *germ cell*	First two weeks of the developing embryo
conception	kon-**SEP**-shun		Latin *something received*	Fertilization of the egg by sperm to form a zygote
dizygotic	die-zye-**GOT**-ik	S/ P/ R/	**-ic** *pertaining to* **di-** *two* **-zygot-** *yoked together*	Twins from two separate zygotes
fertilize fertilization	**FER**-til-ize **FER**-til-eye-**ZAY**-shun	S/ R/	Latin *make fruitful* **-ation** *action* **fertiliz-** *make fruitful*	Penetration of the oocyte by sperm Union of a male sperm and a female egg
implantation	im-plan-**TAY**-shun	S/ P/ R/	**-ation** *action* **im-** *in* **-plant-** *to plant*	Attachment of a fertilized egg to the endometrium
monozygotic	**MON**-oh-zye-**GOT**-ik	S/ P/ R/	**-ic** *pertaining to* **mono-** *one* **-zygot-** *yoked together*	Twins from a single zygote
morula	**MOR**-you-lah		Latin *mulberry*	Ball of cells formed from divisions of a zygote
placenta placental (adj)	plah-**SEN**-tah plah-**SEN**-tal		Latin *a cake*	Organ that allows metabolic interchange between the mother and fetus
zygote	**ZYE**-goat		Greek *joined together*	Cell resulting from the union of the sperm and egg

uterine cavity and burrows into the endometrium (**implantation**). A group of cells in the blastocyst, the inner cell mass, differentiate into the germ layers and form the embryo. Other cells from the blastocyst, together with endometrial cells, form the **placenta.**

Twins (and other multiple births) can be produced in two ways:

- **Dizygotic** twins are produced when two eggs are released by the ovary and fertilized by two separate sperm. They can be of different sexes and are only as genetically similar as other siblings would be.

- **Monozygotic** twins are produced when a single egg is fertilized and later two inner cell masses form within a single blastocyst, each producing an embryo. These twins share a single placenta, are genetically identical, are the same sex, and look alike.

EXERCISES

*Analyze the following **language of obstetrics** to determine the meaning of the elements that are in bold. Notice that in some terms, the complete word is in bold. Finish the exercise by defining the medical term. Fill in the blanks.*

Medical Term	Meaning of Element	Meaning of Term
di**zygotic**		
blastocyst		
fertiliz**ation**		
monozygotic		
im**plant**ation		
zygote		
conception		

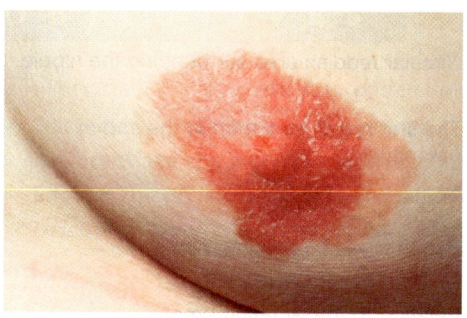

▲ **FIGURE 13.37** Paget Disease of the Nipple is Associated with Breast Cancer.

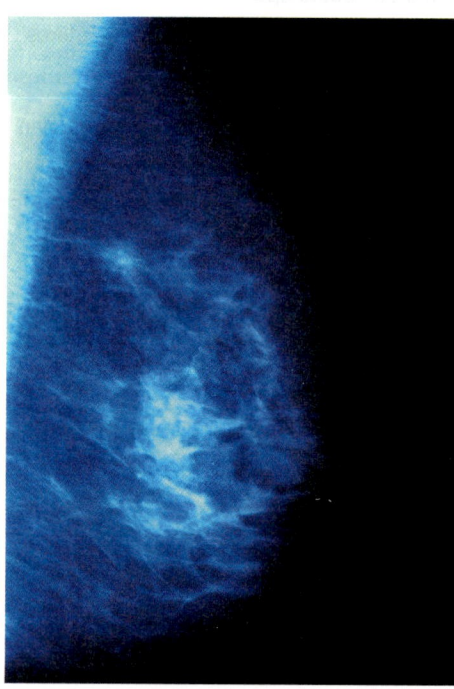

▲ **FIGURE 13.38** Fibrocystic Disease of the Breast.

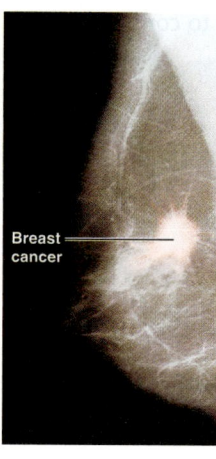

Breast cancer

▲ **FIGURE 13.39** Mammogram Showing Breast Cancer.

DISORDERS OF THE BREAST

Mastitis, inflammation of the breast, can occur in association with breast-feeding if the nipple or areola is cracked or traumatized. It is usually segmental in one of the lobes of the breast and responds well to antibiotics. It is not an indication for stopping breast-feeding.

Mastalgia (breast pain) is the most common benign breast disorder. The pain can be associated with breast tenderness and be part of PMS. If the pain is not relieved by acetaminophen or NSAIDs, danazol or tamoxifen can be used for a short time.

Paget disease of the nipple presents as a scaling, crusting lesion of the nipple, sometimes with a discharge from the nipple *(Figure 13.37)*. It is indicative of an underlying cancer that has to be the focus of diagnosis and treatment.

Nipple discharge, particularly if it is from one breast and bloody, is an indication of an underlying disorder such as breast cancer and warrants investigation.

Fibroadenomas are circumscribed, small, benign tumors that can be either cystic or solid and can be multiple. They can be excised surgically.

Fibrocystic disease of the breast presents as a dense, irregular cobblestone consistency of the breast, often with intermittent breast discomfort *(Figure 13.38)*. It occurs in over 60% of all women and is considered by many doctors as a normal variant.

Breast cancer affects one in eight women in their lifetime. Risk factors include a family history, particularly if a woman carries either the **BRCA1** or **BRCA2 gene,** the use of postmenopausal estrogen therapy, and an early menarche and late menopause.

Most breast cancers are discovered as a lump by the patient, which is why **monthly breast self-examinations (BSE)** are so important. Another 40% are discovered on routine mammogram *(Figure 13.39)*. Routine mammography reduces breast cancer mortality by 25 to 30%.

Most breast cancers occur in the upper and outer quadrant of the breast. If cancer is suspected, biopsy should be planned. This is being performed more and more often as a **stereotactic biopsy,** a needle biopsy performed during mammography.

The surgical treatments for breast cancer include:

- **excisional biopsy** to remove the breast tumor with a surrounding margin of normal breast tissue
- **lumpectomy or quadrantectomy,** which are breast-conserving surgeries
- **simple mastectomy** to remove the breast with skin and nipple *(Figure 13.40)*
- **modified radical mastectomy,** which is a simple mastectomy plus lymph node dissection
- **radical mastectomy,** with complete removal of breast tissue, pectoralis major muscle, and lymph nodes

Additional radiotherapy, combination chemotherapy, Herceptin and Tamoxifen therapy are also used.

Procedures for postoperative breast reconstruction surgery *(Figure 13.41)* include sub-muscular silicone or saline implants and transfer of muscle from the latissimus dorsi. *(see Chapter 5).*

Breast cancer can metastasize to lymph nodes, lungs, liver, bone, brain, and skin.

Galactorrhea is the production of milk when a woman is not breast-feeding. Sometimes the cause cannot be found, but it can occur in association with hormone therapy, antidepressants, tumor of the pituitary gland *(see Chapter 14),* and use of street drugs such as opiates and marijuana. In most cases, the milk production ceases with time.

Gynecomastia, enlargement of the breast, can be unilateral or bilateral and occur in both sexes. It is usually associated with either liver disease, marijuana, or drug therapy such as estrogens, calcium channel blockers, and antineoplastic drugs. It remits or disappears after the drug is withdrawn. Occasionally **suction lipectomy** and/or cosmetic surgery is needed.

WORD	PRONUNCIATION	ELEMENTS		DEFINITION
fibroadenoma	**FIE**-bro-ad-en-**OH**-muh	S/ R/ R/CF	-oma *tumor* -aden- *gland* fibr/o- *fiber*	Benign tumor containing much fibrous tissue
fibrocystic disease	fie-bro-**SIS**-tik diz-**EEZ**	S/ R/CF R/	-ic *pertaining to* fibr/o- *fiber* -cyst- *cyst*	Benign breast disease with multiple tiny lumps
galactorrhea	ga-**LAK**-toe-**REE**-ah	S/ R/CF	- rrhea *flow* galact/o- *milk*	Abnormal flow of milk from the breasts
gynecomastia	**GUY**-nih-koh-**MAS**-tee-ah	S/ R/CF R/	-ia *condition* gynec/o- *female* -mast- *breast*	Enlargement of the breast
lipectomy	lip-**ECK**-toe-me	S/ R/	-ectomy *surgical excision* lip- *fatty tissue*	Surgical removal of adipose tissue
lumpectomy	lump-**ECK**-toe-me	S/ R/	-ectomy *surgical excision* lump- *piece*	Removal of a lesion with preservation of surrounding tissue
mastalgia	mass-**TAL**-jee-uh	S/ R/	-algia *pain* mast- *breast*	Pain in the breast
mastectomy	mass-**TECK**-toe-me	S/ R/	-ectomy *surgical excision* mast- *breast*	Surgical excision of the breast
mastitis	mass-**TIE**-tis	S/ R/	-itis *inflammation* mast- *breast*	Inflammation of the breast
quadrant quadrantectomy	**KWAD**-rant kwad-ran-**TEK**-toe-me	 S/ R/	Latin *quarter* -ectomy *surgical excision* quadrant- *quarter*	One-quarter of a circle Surgical excision of a quadrant of the breast
stereotactic	**STER**-ee-oh-**TAK**-tic	S/ R/ R/CF	-ic *pertaining to* -tact- *orderly arrangement* stere/o- *three dimensional*	A precise three-dimensional method to locate a lesion

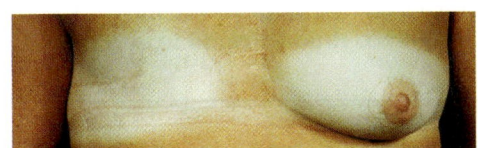

▲ **FIGURE 13.40   Same Patient as in Figure 13.39 After Mastectomy.**

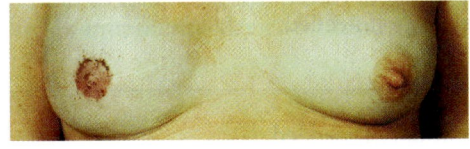

▲ **FIGURE 13.41   Same Patient as in Figure 13.40 After Surgical Breast Reconstruction.**

EXERCISES

Build your knowledge of suffixes, which always provide a big clue to the meaning of a medical term. Review all the terms in this WAD, then answer the following questions. All of these questions can be answered by analyzing the suffix in each term. Which of the term(s) in this WAD mean:

1. *surgical excision?* List them here.

_____

_____

2. *a glandular tumor?* _____

3. *condition of enlarged breasts?* _____

4. *pertaining to?* _____

5. *an inflammation of the breast?* _____

6. *breast pain?* _____

7. *an abnormal flow of milk?* _____

FEMALE REPRODUCTIVE SYSTEM

Q. **Patient Claire Marcos:** Go back and reread the scenario in Case Report 13.2. Now that you have completed this chapter, you should be able to answer her questions in language she will understand. Fill in the blanks.

1. Why are my periods so irregular?

_____

_____

2. Why doesn't my acne respond to all the treatment I've had?

_____

_____

3. Am I going bald?

_____

_____

4. Will I be able to have children some day?

_____

_____

5. Why am I taking birth control pills when I'm not sexually active?

_____

_____

6. What are all these other health problems they say I'm at risk for?

_____

_____

R. **Patient Education:** Breast cancer affects one in eight women in their lifetime. If a patient were to ask, could you give a brief description of each of the following surgical treatments for breast cancer?

1. excisional biopsy:

_____

_____

2. lumpectomy:

_____

_____

3. quadrantectomy:

_____

_____

4. simple mastectomy:

_____

_____

5. modified radical mastectomy:

_____

_____

6. radical mastectomy:

_____

_____

S. **Trace the Pathway of Conception:** The following phrases describe the process of fertilization. List the numbers 1–8 to indicate the correct order of their occurrence.

a. nuclei of male and female cells unite _____

b. morula becomes a blastocyst _____

c. inner cell mass differentiates and forms embryo _____

d. zygote produces morula_____

e. ovary releases egg _____

f. all organ systems present; embryo becomes fetus _____

g. blastocyst implants in the endometrium_____

h. zygote is formed _____

Note: Notice the various terms change as what starts out as the "egg" progresses through different stages and terms to become the "fetus."

List those terms here: _____, _____,

_____, _____

T. **Precision in Documentation:** The roots **recto-** and **retro-** can sound similar but have very different meanings. Demonstrate that you know the difference by using a term containing each element in sentences of your choice.

Sentence using a term containing *"recto-":*

_____

_____

Sentence using a term containing *make "retro-":*

_____

_____

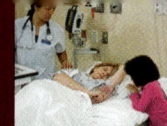

CHAPTER 13 REVIEW

FEMALE REPRODUCTIVE SYSTEM

CHAPTER SUMMARY EXERCISE

1. Listen to the pronunciation of the medical terms as given by your instructor.
2. Circle the correct spelling of the medical term.
3. Match the correctly spelled terms to the brief descriptions below.
4. Write a sentence for each of the 15 terms that appear in this exercise.

A. SPELLING COMPREHENSION: CIRCLE THE CORRECT SPELLING OF THE TERM.

1. mensstuation	menstruation	menstuation	mensstruation	menstrruation
2. Falopian	fallopian	faloppian	fallopean	falopean
3. anteverted	antiverted	anteverrted	antiverrted	antevertted
4. postpubescent	postpubiscient	postpubescient	postpubisent	postpubessient
5. cotus	cottus	coitus	coituss	cutois
6. fimbeia	fimmbria	fembria	fimbrea	fembrea
7. dyspareeunia	dispareunia	dyspareunia	disspariunia	despariunia
8. liomioma	lyomyoma	leiomyoma	liomyoma	leomyoma
9. gonorhea	gonorrhea	gonnorhea	gonorhea	gonorheea
10. epesiotomy	episiotomy	eppesiotomy	epessiotomy	epeziotomy
11. chancre	chankre	chanckree	canckre	canker
12. ammenorhea	amenorhea	amenorrhea	amenorhia	ammenorrhea
13. genitailia	genitalia	genetalia	genetailia	geneetalia
14. ecclampsia	ecclampsea	eclampsia	eclampssia	ecalmpsia
15. autololisus	autolosis	autolysis	autollysis	autolossis

B. MATCH THE NUMBER OF THE CORRECT TERM IN PART A WITH THE BRIEF DESCRIPTION OF THE TERM BELOW.

a. pain during sexual intercourse _____

b. convulsions in a patient with preeclampsia _____

c. synonym for menses _____

d. internal and external organs of reproduction _____

e. uterine tubes _____

f. absence or abnormal cessation of menstrual flow _____

g. fringelike structure _____

h. contagious infection of genital mucosa _____

i. after the age of puberty _____

j. tilted forward _____

k. sexual intercourse   _____

l. benign neoplasm derived from smooth muscle   _____

m. self-digestion   _____

n. surgical incision of the vulva   _____

o. primary lesion of syphilis   _____

C. USING YOUR KNOWLEDGE OF TERMS 1-15 IN PART A AND THEIR CORRECT SPELLING, WRITE A BRIEF SENTENCE FOR EACH OF THE TERMS AS IT MIGHT APPEAR IN PATIENT DOCUMENTATION.

1. _____

2. _____

3. _____

4. _____

5. _____

6. _____

7. _____

8. _____

9. _____

10. _____

11. _____

12. _____

13. _____

14. _____

15. _____

D. GO TO THE STUDENT CD. OPEN THE GLOSSARY AND PRACTICE YOUR PRONUNCIATION OF THE TERMS IN PART A OF THIS EXERCISE.

Endocrine System

The Language of Endocrinology

CASE REPORT 14.1

You are

. . . a registered nurse working with **endocrinologist** Sabina Khalid, MD, in the **endocrinology** clinic at Fulwood Medical Center.

Your patient is

. . . Mrs. Gina Tacher, a 33-year-old schoolteacher. She complains of coarsening of her facial features and enlargement of the bones of her hands. Over the past ten years her nose and jaw have increased in size, and her voice has become husky. She has brought photos of herself at ages 9, 16, and as she is now. She has no other health problems.

Keynote

A hormone is secreted by an organ and is carried by the blood stream to act at distant target sites.

Learning Outcomes

The **endocrine system** is a communication system. The **hormones** it produces circulate in the blood stream, giving them access to all other cells of the body. Hormones are bloodborne messengers secreted by endocrine glands. They are distributed anywhere that blood goes but affect only the target cells that have receptors for them; they alter the metabolism of these cells.

The information in this chapter enables you to:

- Apply the language of endocrinology to the anatomy and physiology of the endocrine system.

- Comprehend, analyze, spell, and write the medical terms of endocrinology so that you can communicate and document accurately and precisely in any health care setting.

- Recognize and pronounce the medical terms of endocrinology so that you communicate verbally with accuracy and precision in any health care setting.

- Explain the effects of common endocrine disorders on health.

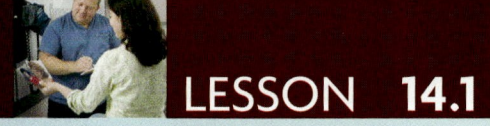

Endocrine System Overview and Pituitary and Pineal Glands

The information in this lesson will enable you to:

- **Name the glands that comprise the endocrine system.**
- **List the hormones produced by the hypothalamus and pituitary gland.**
- **Explain the interactions between the hypothalamus and pituitary gland.**
- **Identify the controls the hypothalamus and pituitary exert over other endocrine glands.**
- **Specify the roles of the pineal gland.**
- **Describe disorders of the hypothalamus, pituitary gland, and pineal gland.**

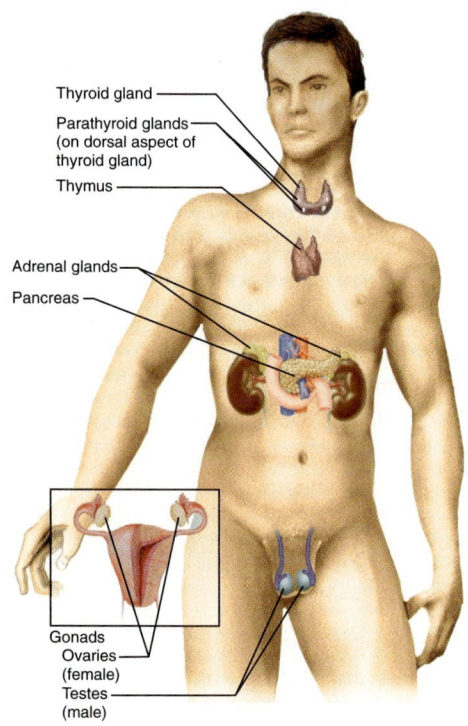

Thyroid gland
Parathyroid glands (on dorsal aspect of thyroid gland)
Thymus
Adrenal glands
Pancreas
Gonads
Ovaries (female)
Testes (male)

▲ **FIGURE 14.1   Major Endocrine Glands.**

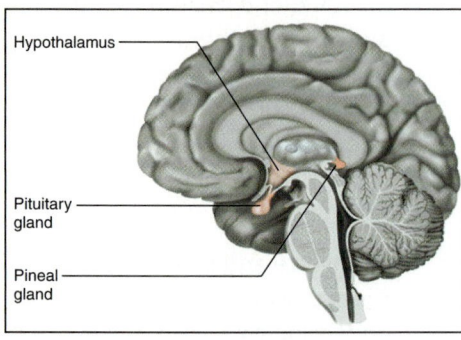

Hypothalamus
Pituitary gland
Pineal gland

▲ **FIGURE 14.2   Hypothalamus, Pituitary Gland, and Pineal Gland.**

Abbreviations

ADH	antidiuretic hormone
SAD	seasonal affective disorder

ENDOCRINE SYSTEM

The endocrine system comprises several major organs *(Figure 14.1)*:

- pituitary gland and the nearby hypothalamus
- pineal gland
- thyroid gland
- parathyroid glands (4)
- thymus gland
- adrenal glands (2)
- pancreas
- gonads: testes (2) in the male; ovaries (2) in the female

In addition, endocrine cells found in tissues all over the body secrete hormones. Examples are:

- **cells in the upper GI tract** secrete the hormone **gastrin**, which stimulates gastric secretions and the hormone **cholecystokinin**, which contracts the gallbladder *(see Chapter 6)*.
- **cells in the kidney** secrete **erythropoietin**, which stimulates erythrocyte production *(see Chapter 7)*.
- **fat cells** secrete **leptin**, which helps suppress appetite. Lack of it can lead to overeating and obesity *(see Chapter 17)*.
- **cells in tissues throughout the body** secrete **prostaglandins**, which act locally to dilate blood vessels, relax airways, stimulate uterine contractions in menstrual cramps or labor, and lower acid secretion in the stomach. When tissues are injured, prostaglandins promote an inflammatory response.

Hypothalamus

The hypothalamus *(Figure 14.2)* forms the floor and walls of the brain's third ventricle *(see Chapter 10)* and produces eight hormones. Six of them are local hormones that regulate the production of hormones by the anterior pituitary gland *(see page 570)*. Two of them, oxytocin and **antidiuretic hormone (ADH)**, are transported to the posterior pituitary, where they are stored until they are needed elsewhere in the body.

Pineal Gland

The pineal gland is located on the roof of the third ventricle of the brain, posterior to the hypothalamus *(Figure 14.2)*. It secretes **serotonin** by day and converts it to **melatonin** at night. The gland reaches its maximum size in childhood and may regulate the timing of puberty. It may also play a role in **seasonal affective disorder (SAD)**, in which people are depressed in the dark days of winter.

WORD	PRONUNCIATION	ELEMENTS		DEFINITION
antidiuretic (*Note:* This term has two prefixes.)	**AN**-tih-die-you-**RET**-ik	S/ P/ P/ R/	-ic *pertaining to* anti- *against* -di- *complete* -uret- *urination*	An agent that decreases urine production
endocrine	**EN**-doh-krin	P/ R/	endo- *within* -crine *secrete*	A gland that produces an internal or hormonal secretion
endocrinology (*Note:* The "e" in "-crine" changes to "o" for easier pronunciation.)	**EN**-doh-kri-**NOL**-oh-jee	S/	-logy *study of*	Medical specialty concerned with the production and effects of hormones
endocrinologist	**EN**-doh-kri-**NOL**-oh-jist	S/	-logist *one who studies*	A medical specialist in endocrinology
hormone **hormonal (adj)**	**HOR**-mohn hor-**MOHN**-al		Greek *to set in motion*	Chemical formed in one tissue or organ and carried by the blood to stimulate or inhibit a function of another tissue or organ
leptin	**LEP**-tin	S/ R/	-in *substance* lept- *thin*	Hormone secreted by adipose tissue
melatonin	mel-ah-**TONE**-in	S/ R/ R/	-in *substance* mela- *black* -ton- *tone*	Hormone formed by the pineal gland
oxytocin	**OCK**-see-toe-sin	S/ P/ R/	-in *substance* oxy- *quick* -toc- *labor*	Pituitary hormone that stimulates the uterus to contract
parathyroid	par-ah-**THY**-royd	S/ P/ R/	-oid *resemble* para- *beside* -thyr- *thyroid*	Endocrine gland embedded in the back of the thyroid
pineal	**PIN**-ee-al		Latin *like a pine cone*	Pertaining to the pineal gland
pituitary	pih-**TYU**-ih-tary	S/ R/	-ary *pertaining to* pituit- *pituitary*	Pertaining to the pituitary gland
prostaglandin	**PROS**-tah-**GLAN**-din	S/ R/CF R/	-in *substance* prost/a- *prostate* -gland- *gland*	Hormone present in many tissues, but first isolated from prostate gland
seasonal affective disorder (*Note:* The abbreviation for this is SAD, which is how you feel with this disorder.)	see-**ZON**-al af-**FEK**-tiv dis-**OR**-der			Depression that occurs at the same time every year, often in winter
serotonin	ser-oh-**TOE**-nin	S/ R/CF R/	-in *substance* ser/o- *serum* -ton- *tension*	A neurotransmitter in the central and peripheral nervous systems

EXERCISES

Elements are listed in column 1. Place a check mark (✓) in the correct column identifying the type of element. Finish the exercise by writing the meaning of the element in the last column.

Element	Prefix	Root/CF	Suffix	Meaning of Element
di	_____	_____	_____	_____
anti	_____	_____	_____	_____
endo	_____	_____	_____	_____
mela	_____	_____	_____	_____
crine	_____	_____	_____	_____
oxy	_____	_____	_____	_____
toc	_____	_____	_____	_____
oid	_____	_____	_____	_____

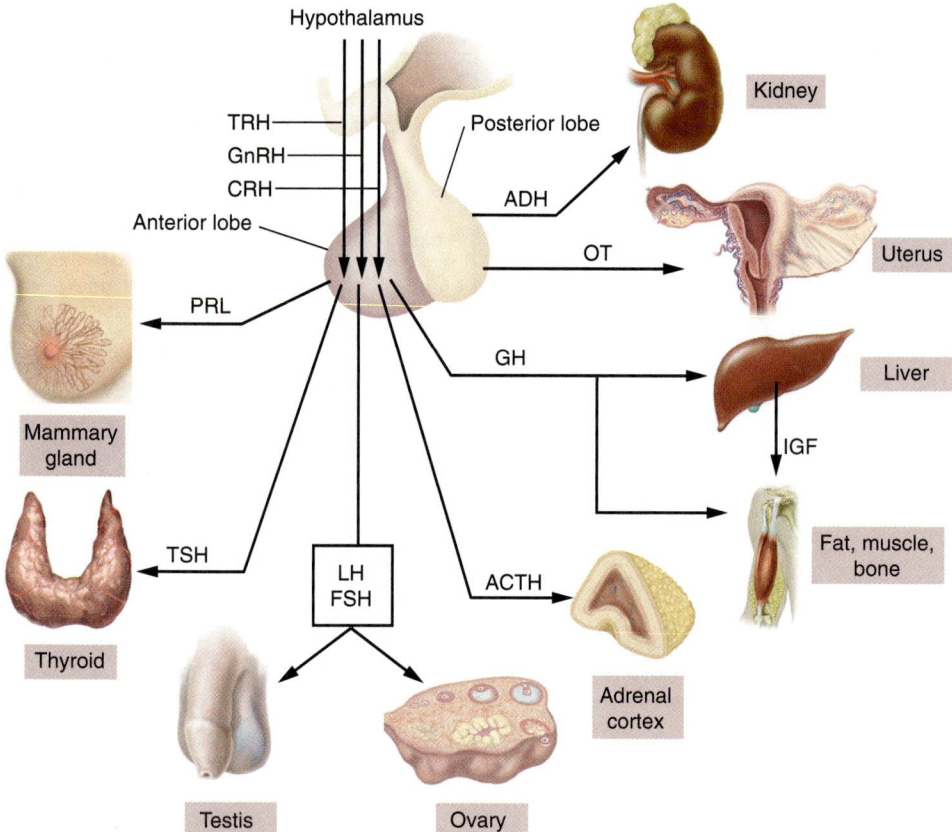

FIGURE 14.3 Hormones of the Pituitary Gland and Their Target Organs.

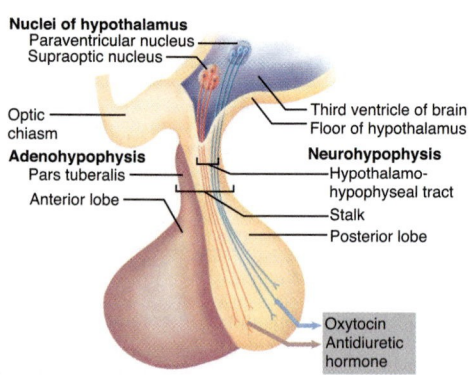

FIGURE 14.4 Hormones of the Posterior Lobe of the Pituitary Gland.

Abbreviations

ACTH adrenocorticotropic hormone
ADH antidiuretic hormone
FSH follicle-stimulating hormone
GH growth hormone
LH luteinizing hormone
OT oxytocin
PRL prolactin
TSH thyroid-stimulating hormone

PITUITARY GLAND

While there is no single conductor of the endocrine orchestra in which each hormone plays its part in maintaining homeostasis, the pituitary gland and the hypothalamus work together and often influence the production of hormones in the other endocrine glands.

The pituitary gland (**hypophysis**) is suspended from the hypothalamus. The gland has two components:

1. a large anterior lobe called the **adenohypophysis**
2. a smaller posterior lobe called the **neurohypophysis**

Anterior lobe hormones are six in number *(Figure 14.3)*:

- **Follicle-stimulating hormone (FSH)** stimulates target cells in the ovaries to develop eggs and stimulates sperm production in the testes.

- **Luteinizing hormone (LH)** stimulates ovulation and the formation of a corpus luteum in the ovary *(see Chapter 13)* to secrete estrogen and progesterone. In the male, LH stimulates production of testosterone *(see Chapter 12)*.

- **Thyroid-stimulating hormone (TSH), or thyrotropin,** stimulates the growth of the thyroid gland and the production of **thyroxine.**

- **Adrenocorticotropic hormone (ACTH), or corticotropin,** stimulates the adrenal glands to produce hormones called **corticosteroids.**

- **Prolactin (PRL)** stimulates the mammary glands after pregnancy to produce milk. In the male, it enhances production of testosterone.

- **Growth hormone (GH), or somatotropin,** is produced in quantities at least a thousand times as great as any other pituitary hormone. It stimulates cells to enlarge and divide, particularly in childhood and adolescence.

Tropic hormones are hormones that stimulate other endocrine glands to produce their hormones. All of the anterior lobe hormones except PRL are tropic hormones.

Posterior lobe hormones are of two types. They are produced by nuclei in the hypothalamus and then stored in and released by in the pituitary posterior lobe *(Figure 14.4)*:

- **Oxytocin (OT)** in childbirth stimulates uterine contractions and in lactation forces milk to flow down ducts to the nipple. In both sexes, its production increases during sexual intercourse to help give the feelings of satisfaction and emotional bonding.

- **Antidiuretic hormone (ADH)** reduces the volume of urine produced by the kidneys. It is also called **vasopressin.**

WORD	PRONUNCIATION	ELEMENTS		DEFINITION
adenohypophysis (*Note:* The prefix hypo- is part of **hypophysis,** which is a term in itself.)	AD-en-oh-hi-**POF**-ih-sis	R/ R/CF P/	-physis *growth* aden/o- *gland* -hypo- *below*	Anterior lobe of the pituitary gland
adrenal gland	ah-**DREE**-nal GLAND	S/ P/ R/	-al *pertaining to* ad- *near, toward* -ren- *kidney*	The suprarenal, or adrenal, gland on the upper pole of each kidney
adrenocorticotropic	ah-**DREE**-noh-**KOR**-tih-koh-**TROH**-pik	S/ R/CF R/CF	-tropic *a turning* adren/o- *adrenal gland* -cortic/o- *cortisone*	Hormone of the anterior pituitary that stimulates cortex of the adrenal gland to produce its own hormones
antidiuretic hormone (ADH) (also called **vasopressin**)	**AN**-tih-die-you-**RET**-ik **HOR**-mohn	S/ P/ P/ R/CF R/	-tic *pertaining to* anti- *against* -di- *complete* -ur/e- *urine* hormone *chemical messenger*	Posterior pituitary hormone that decreases urine output by acting on the kidney
corticosteroid	**KOR**-tih-koh-**STEHR**-oyd	S/ R/CF	-steroid *steroid* cortic/o- *cortisone*	A hormone produced by the adrenal cortex
corticotropin	**KOR**-tih-koh-**TROH**-pin	S/ R/CF	-tropin *a turning* cortic/o- *cortisone*	Pituitary hormone that stimulates the adrenal gland to secrete cortisone
hypophysis	high-**POF**-ih-sis	P/ R/	hypo- *below* -physis *growth*	Another name for the pituitary gland
neurohypophysis	**NYUR**-oh-high-**POF**-ih-sis	R/ R/CF P/	-physis *growth* neur/o- *nervous tissue* -hypo- *below*	Posterior lobe of the pituitary gland
prolactin	pro-**LAK**-tin	S/ P/ R/	-in *substance* pro- *before* -lact- *milk*	Pituitary hormone that stimulates production of milk
somatotropin (also called **growth hormone**)	**SO**-mah-toh-**TROH**-pin	S/ R/CF	-tropin *a turning* somat/o- *the body*	Hormone of the anterior pituitary that stimulates growth of body tissues
thyroid	**THIGH**-royd		Greek *an oblong shield*	Gland in the neck, or a cartilage of the larynx
thyrotropin	thigh-roe-**TROH**-pin	S/ R/CF	-tropin *a turning* thyr/o- *thyroid*	Hormone from the anterior pituitary gland that stimulates function of the thyroid gland
thyroxine	thigh-**ROCK**-sin	S/ R/ R/CF	-ine *chemical compound* -ox- *oxygen* thyr/o- *thyroid*	Thyroid hormone T₄, tetraiodothyronine
tropic (adj) **tropin (noun)**	**TROH**-pik **TROH**-pin		Greek *a turning*	Tropic hormones stimulate other endocrine glands to produce hormones
vasopressin (also called **antidiuretic hormone ADH**)	vay-soh-**PRESS**-in	S/ R/CF R/	-in *substance* vas/o- *blood vessel* -press- *press, close*	Pituitary hormone that constricts blood vessels and decreases urine output

EXERCISES

Many hormones are known by their abbreviation. Match the description in column 1 to the correct abbreviation in column 2.

_____ 1. stimulates formation of corpus luteum   **A.** PRL

_____ 2. stimulates production of corticosteroids   **B.** LH

_____ 3. stimulates uterine contractions   **C.** GH

_____ 4. stimulates ovaries to develop eggs   **D.** ACTH

_____ 5. reduces volume of urine   **E.** TSH

_____ 6. stimulates milk production   **F.** OT

_____ 7. stimulates production of thyroxin   **G.** FSH

_____ 8. stimulates cells to enlarge and divide   **H.** ADH

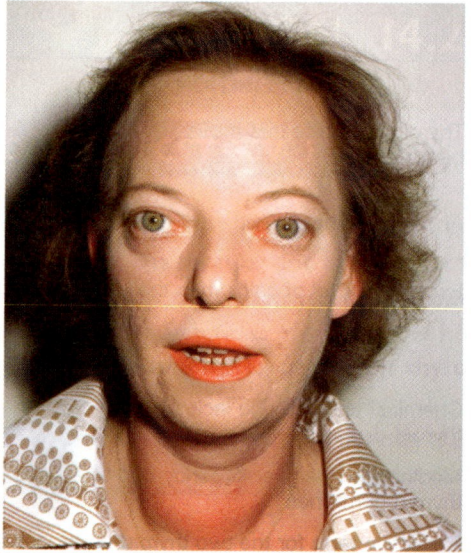

▲ **FIGURE 14.9   Hyperthyroidism May Cause the Eyes to Protrude (Exophthalmos).**

Case Report 14.2 *(continued)*

Thyroid storm is the condition Ms. Norma Leary presented with in the emergency department. It shows severely exaggerated effects of the thyroid hormones. This explains her hyperpyrexia, tachycardia, agitation, and delirium. The weight loss prior to her illness becoming acute was part of her undiagnosed Graves disease. Ms. Leary's immediate treatment included supplemental oxygen, intravenous (IV) fluids with dextrose solutions, ice packs and cooling blanket, propanolol, **antithyroid** medications, and oral iodine compounds.

DISORDERS OF THE THYROID GLAND

Hyperthyroidism (Thyrotoxicosis)

Whatever the cause of **hyperthyroidism,** the symptoms are those of increased body metabolism. These include tachycardia, hypertension, sweating, shakiness, anxiety, weight loss despite increased appetite, and diarrhea.

Graves disease is an autoimmune disorder *(see Chapter 15)* in which an antibody stimulates the thyroid to produce and secrete excessive quantities of thyroid into the blood. It is associated with one or more symptoms of a **goiter** (enlarged thyroid gland), **exophthalmos,** and pretibial **myxedema.**

Exophthalmos, when the eyes bulge outward *(Figure 14.9)*, is caused by a substance that builds up behind the eyes. The same substance is occasionally deposited in the skin over the shins and called pretibial myxedema.

Thyroiditis is an inflammation of the thyroid gland. It presents in three forms:

- **silent lymphocytic thyroiditis**—characterized by some thyroid enlargement and a **self-limiting** hyperthyroid phase of a few weeks, followed by recovery to the normal **euthyroid** state.

- **subacute thyroiditis**—there is a history of an antecedent viral upper respiratory infection (URI) followed by signs of hyperthyroidism with a diffusely enlarged thyroid gland. It is self-limiting.

- **Hashimoto disease** is an autoimmune disease with lymphocytic infiltration of the gland. Hypothyroidism results, necessitating lifelong thyroid hormone replacement therapy.

Toxic thyroid adenoma is a nodule in the gland that produces thyroid hormones without stimulation by the pituitary's TSH. The nodule can be removed surgically.

Goiter *(Figure 14.10)* is an enlargement of the thyroid gland that, as it enlarges, can cause difficulty in swallowing and breathing. It can occur in any of the disorders listed above and also in pregnancy.

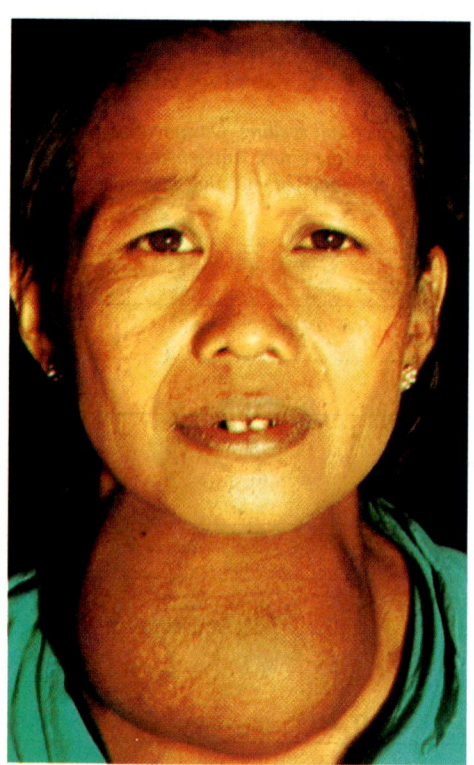

▲ **FIGURE 14.10   Woman with Goiter.**

WORD	PRONUNCIATION	ELEMENTS		DEFINITION
antithyroid	an-tee-**THIGH**-royd	P/ R/	anti- *against* -thyroid *thyroid*	A substance that inhibits production of thyroid hormones
euthyroid	you-**THIGH**-royd	P/ R/	eu- *good* -thyroid *thyroid*	Normal thyroid function
exophthalmos	ek-sof-**THAL**-mos	P/ R/	ex- *out* -ophthalmos *eye*	Protrusion of the eyeball
goiter	**GOY**-ter		Latin *throat*	Enlargement of the thyroid gland
Graves disease	GRAVZ diz-**EEZ**		Robert Graves, 1796–1853, Irish physician	Hyperthyroidism with toxic goiter
Hashimoto disease (also called **Hashimoto thyroiditis**)	hah-shee-**MO**-toe diz-**EEZ**		Hakaru Hashimoto, 1881–1934, Japanese surgeon	Autoimmune disease of the thyroid gland
hyperthyroidism	high-per-**THIGH**-royd-ism	S/ P/ R/	-ism *condition* hyper- *excessive* -thyroid- *thyroid*	Excessive production of thyroid hormones
thyroidectomy	thigh-roy-**DEK**-toe-me	S/ R/	-ectomy *surgical excision* thyroid- *thyroid*	Surgical removal of the thyroid gland
thyroiditis	thigh-roy-**DIE**-tis	S/ R/	-itis *inflammation* thyroid- *thyroid*	Inflammation of the thyroid gland
thyrotoxicosis	**THIGH**-roe-toks-ee-**KOH**-sis	S/ R/CF R/CF	-sis *condition* thyr/o- *thyroid* -toxic/o- *poison*	Disorder produced by excessive thyroid hormone production

EXERCISES

Elements: *One word in each of the descriptions 1 through 7 is in bold. This is your clue to finding the correct medical term in the word bank. Fill in the blanks.*

Word Bank   thyroiditis   euthyroid   antithyroid   exophthalmos

thyroidectomy   thyrotoxicosis   hyperthyroidism

1. **excessive** production of thyroid hormones: _____

2. **removal** of the thyroid gland: _____

3. **inhibits** production of thyroid hormone: _____

4. disorder produced by **excessive** thyroid hormone production: _____

5. **normal** thyroid function: _____

6. **inflammation** of the thyroid gland: _____

7. protrusion of the **eyeball** _____

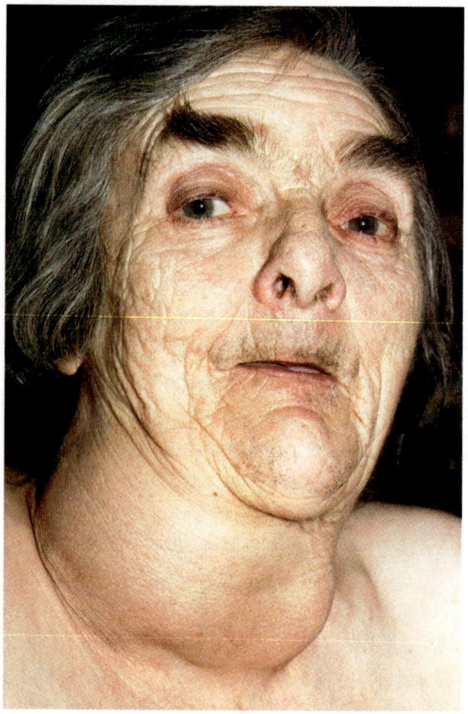

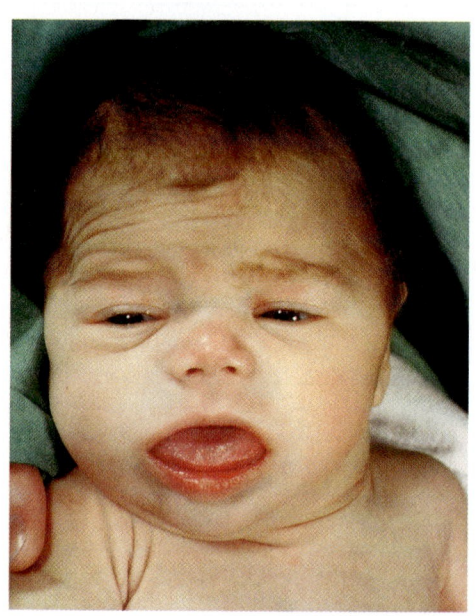

FIGURE 14.11 **Elderly Woman with Hypothyroidism.**

FIGURE 14.12 **Infant with Cretinism.**

DISORDERS OF THE THYROID GLAND (continued)

Hypothyroidism

Hypothyroidism results from an inadequate production of thyroid hormone, leading to a slowing of the body's metabolism. Primary hypothyroidism, in which no specific cause is found, affects 10% of older women. Severe hypothyroidism is called **myxedema.** In developing countries, a common cause is lack of iodine in the diet. In this country, iodine is added to table salt to prevent hypothyroidism, and iodine is also found in dairy products and seafood.

Hypothyroidism causes the body to function slowly. Symptoms develop gradually. They include loss of hair; dry, scaly skin; puffy face and eyes; slow hoarse speech; weight gain; constipation; and inability to tolerate cold *(Figure 14.11)*. If untreated, hypothyroidism can progress to coma, triggered by severe cold or other physical stresses.

Diagnosis of primary hypothyroidism is confirmed with a TSH blood level that is high. Treatment is to replace the thyroid hormone with synthetic T_4 (L-thyroxine), which is started in small doses.

Cretinism *(Figure 14.12)* is a congenital form of thyroid deficiency that severely retards mental and physical growth. If it is diagnosed and treated early with thyroid hormones, significant improvement can be achieved.

Thyroid cancer usually presents as a symptomless nodule in the thyroid gland.

Thyroid Diagnostic Tests

TSH level in the blood: if the thyroid gland is overactive, the level of TSH is low.

Thyroid hormone levels in blood detail the activity of the gland: if the thyroid gland is overactive, thyroid hormones are generally high.

Antithyroid antibodies are associated with autoimmune inflammatory diseases of the thyroid.

Isotopic thyroid scans detail the nature of the thyroid enlargement and the function of the gland.

Serum calcitonin level is elevated in medullary carcinoma.

Needle aspiration biopsy distinguishes benign from malignant lesions.

Ultrasonography reveals the size of the gland and the presence of nodules.

Thyroid Pharmacology

Antithyroids prevent formation of thyroid hormones.

- Propylthiouracil inhibits the uptake of iodine and the conversion of T_4 to T_3.
- Methimazole inhibits uptake of iodine.

Radioactive iodine taken orally reaches the thyroid through the bloodstream and destroys thyroid cells.

Thyroid replacements:

- L-thyroxine—this synthetic T_4 is a preferred replacement.
- Liothyronine sodium—this synthetic T_3 has a rapid turnover and has to be monitored frequently.

WORD	PRONUNCIATION	ELEMENTS		DEFINITION
cretin	**KREH**-tin		French *cretin*	A person with severe congenital hypothyroidism
hypothyroidism	high-poh-**THIGH**-royd-ism	S/ P/ R/	**-ism** *condition* **hypo-** *deficient* **-thyroid-** *thyroid*	Deficient production of thyroid hormones
isotope isotopic (adj)	I-so-tope	P/ R/	**iso-** *equal* **-tope** *part*	Radioactive element used in diagnostic procedures
myxedema	miks-eh-**DEE**-muh	P/ R/	**myx-** *mucus* **-edema** *swelling*	Severe hypothyroidism
radioactive iodine	**RAY**-dee-oh-**AK**-tiv **EYE**-oh-dine	S/ R/CF R/	**-ive** *pertaining to* **radi/o-** *radiation* **-act-** *active* **iodine** *nonmetallic element*	Emitting alpha, beta, or gamma rays
ultrasonography	**UL**-trah-soh-**NOG**-rah-fee	S/ P/ R/CF	**-graphy** *recording* **ultra-** *beyond* **-son/o-** *sound*	Delineation of deep structures using sound waves

EXERCISES *Certain kinds of tests are performed for the purpose of arriving at the correct diagnosis for treatment. Employ the **language of endocrinology** to fill in the blanks with the name of the test that is described.*

1. Associated with autoimmune inflammatory disease of the thyroid: _____

2. Blood test to measure activity of the thyroid gland: _____

3. Level becomes elevated in medullary carcinoma: _____

4. Levels in the blood are generally high if the thyroid gland is overactive: _____

5. Reveals the size of the gland and the presence of nodules: _____

6. Distinguishes benign from malignant lesions: _____

7. Detail the nature of the thyroid enlargement and the function of the gland: _____

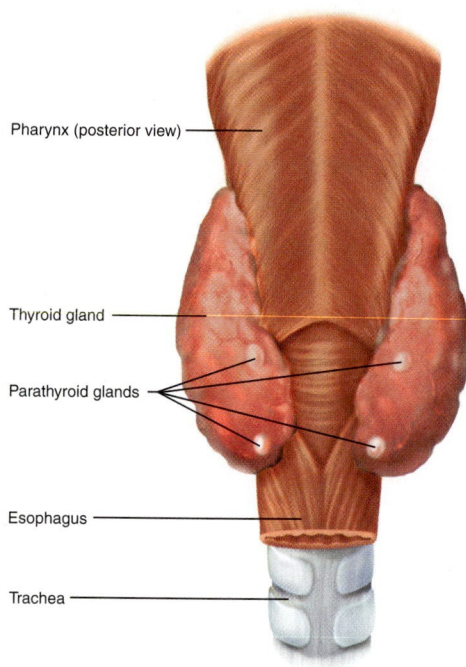

Pharynx (posterior view)

Thyroid gland

Parathyroid glands

Esophagus

Trachea

▲ **FIGURE 14.13   Site of Parathyroid Glands: Posterior View.**

Abbreviation

PTH   parathyroid hormone

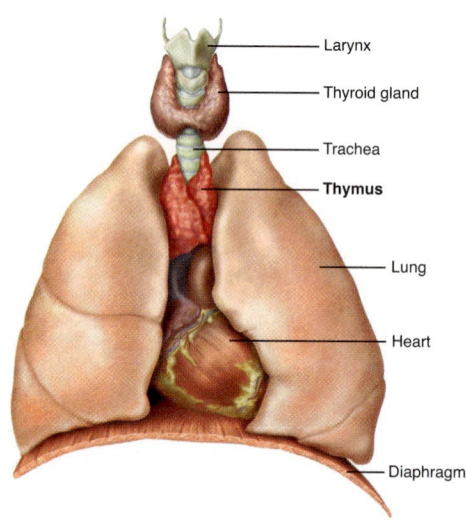

Larynx

Thyroid gland

Trachea

Thymus

Lung

Heart

Diaphragm

▲ **FIGURE 14.14   Position of Thymus Gland in Mediastinum.**

OTHER ENDOCRINE GLANDS

Parathyroid Glands

The **parathyroid glands** are usually four in number and are partially embedded in the posterior surface of the thyroid gland *(Figure 14.13)*. They secrete **parathyroid hormone (PTH)** in response to hypocalcemia. Calcitonin and PTH are antagonistic: PTH stimulates osteoclasts to reabsorb bone and bring calcium back into the blood, while calcitonin takes calcium from the blood and stimulates osteoblasts to lay down bone *(see Chapter 5)*.

Disorders of Parathyroid Glands

Hypoparathyroidism is a deficiency of PTH that lowers levels of blood calcium (hypocalcemia). Most symptoms are neuromuscular, ranging from tingling in the fingers to muscle cramps and the painful muscle spasms of **tetany** (*not* **tetanus**). A genetically engineered recombinant form of PTH is being introduced. Other treatments are a high-calcium diet and calcium and vitamin D supplements.

Hyperparathyroidism is an excess of PTH. It is seen more often than hypoparathyroidism and is usually caused by one of the four glands enlarging and working out of pituitary control. It leads to four major abnormalities:

1. bones are depleted of calcium (osteopenia) and become brittle.
2. high blood calcium levels (hypercalcemia) lead to decreased bowel motility and constipation and to increased gastric acidity and heartburn.
3. extra excretion of calcium in the urine leads to kidney stones (nephrolithiasis).
4. high blood calcium leads to mental symptoms such as depression and fatigue and can lead to coma.

Surgical removal of the enlarged gland is **curative.**

Thymus Gland

The **thymus gland** is located in the mediastinum behind the sternum between the lungs and above the heart *(Figure 14.14)*. It is large in children and decreases in size until, in the elderly, it is mostly fibrous tissue. It secretes a group of hormones that stimulate the production of T lymphocytes *(see Chapter 15)*.

Disorders of Thymus Gland

DiGeorge syndrome is a genetic immunodeficiency disorder *(see Chapter 15)* in which the thymus is underdeveloped or absent at birth. Abnormalities of the thymus and parathyroid glands, heart, and facial structure are present, with few or no T lymphocytes. Transplantation of stem cells or thymus tissue can cure the immunodeficiency.

Thymomas, benign tumors, and **thymic carcinomas** are rare tumors that can be associated with myasthenia gravis *(see Chapter 10)* and other autoimmune syndromes, such as lupus erythematosus, and rheumatoid arthritis. Treatment is usually surgical removal of the tumor or the gland **(thymectomy),** followed by **adjuvant** radiotherapy.

WORD ANALYSIS AND DEFINITION

WORD	PRONUNCIATION	ELEMENTS		DEFINITION
adjuvant	**AD**-joo-vant	S/ R/	**-ant** *pertaining to* **adjuv-** *give help*	Additional treatment after a primary treatment has been used
antagonist	an-**TAG**-oh-nist	S/ P/ R/	**-ist** *agent* **ant-** *against* **-agon-** *to fight*	An opposing structure, agent, disease, or process
antagonistic (adj)	an-**TAG**-oh-nist-ik	S/	**-ic** *pertaining to*	Having an opposite function
curative	**KYUR**-ah-tiv	S/ R/	**-ive** *quality of* **curat-** *to care for*	That which heals or cures
DiGeorge syndrome	dee-**JORJ SIN**-drome		Angelo M. DiGeorge, U.S. pediatrician, described syndrome in 1921	Congenital absence of the thymus gland
hyperparathyroidism	**HIGH**-per-para-**THIGH**-royd-ism	S/ P/ P/ R/	**-ism** *condition* **hyper-** *excessive* **-para-** *adjacent* **-thyroid-** *thyroid*	Excessive levels of parathyroid hormone
hypoparathyroidism	**HIGH**-poh-para-**THIGH**-royd-ism	S/ P/ P/ R/	**-ism** *condition* **hypo-** *deficient* **-para-** *adjacent* **-thyroid-** *thyroid*	Deficient levels of parathyroid hormone
tetany tetanic (adj)	**TET**-ah-nee teh-**TAN**-ik		Greek *convulsive tension*	Severe muscle twitches, cramps, and spasms
thymectomy	thigh-**MEK**-toe-me	S/ R/	**-ectomy** *surgical excision* **thym-** *thymus*	Surgical removal of the thymus gland
thymoma	thigh-**MOH**-mah	S/ R/	**-oma** *tumor, mass* **thym-** *thymus*	Benign tumor of the thymus

---

EXERCISES

*Build your knowledge of the **language of endocrinology** by analyzing the elements in the following terms. Review the Word Analysis and Definition box (WAD) before you fill in the chart. Write a sentence of your choice for any one term in the chart.*

Medical Term	Meaning of Prefix	Meaning of Root/CF	Meaning of Suffix
thymoma			
adjuvant			
antagonist			
hyperparathyroidism			
curative			
thymectomy			
hypoparathyroidism			

Sentence:

_____

_____

_____

LESSON 14.3 Adrenal Glands and Hormones

OBJECTIVES

The information in this lesson will enable you to:

- **Locate the adrenal glands.**
- **Differentiate between the adrenal cortex and medulla.**
- **Identify the functions of the hormones produced by the cortex and medulla.**
- **Detail how the body adapts to stress.**
- **Explain common disorders of the adrenal glands.**

▲ **FIGURE 14.15** John F. Kennedy.

Abbreviation

DHEA dehydroepiandrosterone

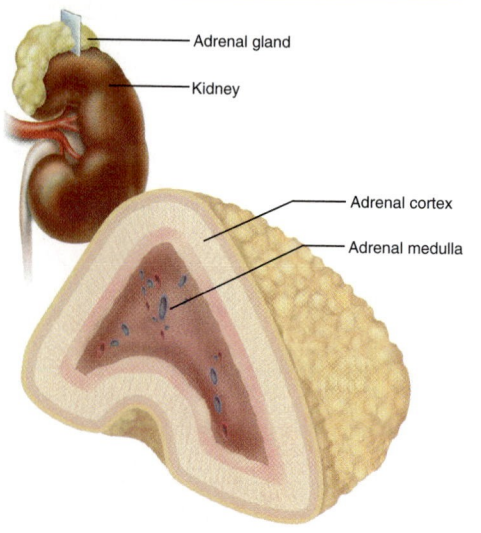

- Adrenal gland
- Kidney
- Adrenal cortex
- Adrenal medulla

▲ **FIGURE 14.16** Adrenal Gland.

CASE REPORT 14.3

John Fitzgerald Kennedy (JFK) (1917–1963) was elected President of the United States of America in 1960 at the age of 43, the youngest person elected to that office (Figure 14.15). Since the age of 13, when he was diagnosed as having colitis, he had had health problems. At age 27, he had low back pain necessitating lower back surgery, and he was then diagnosed as having adrenal gland insufficiency (**Addison disease**) with osteoporosis of his lumbar spine. This required lower back surgery on three more occasions. JFK received adrenal hormone replacement therapy for the rest of his life, together with pain medication for his low back pain, until his assassination in Dallas, Texas, in 1963.

In medical retrospect, instead of colitis, he probably had celiac disease (see Chapter 6), which has strong associations with Addison disease.

ADRENAL GLANDS

An **adrenal (suprarenal) gland** is anchored like a cap on the upper pole of each kidney *(Figure 14.16)*.

The outer layer of the gland, the **adrenal cortex**, synthesizes more than 25 steroid hormones known collectively as **adrenocortical hormones, corticosteroids,** or **corticoids**. There are three groups of corticosteroids:

1. **glucocorticoids**—particularly **hydrocortisone (cortisol)**. These hormones stimulate fat and protein catabolism and help regulate blood glucose levels, particularly as the body resists stress (see next lesson). Hydrocortisone also has an anti-inflammatory effect and is used in ointments to relieve inflammation

2. **mineralocorticoids**—the principal one of which is called **aldosterone**. This hormone promotes sodium retention and potassium excretion by the kidneys.

3. **sex steroids**:
   a. **androgens**—principally **dehydroepiandrosterone (DHEA)**, which is a weak androgen but is converted by other tissues into testosterone *(see Chapter 12)*
   b. **estrogens**—principally estradiol, which is produced in much smaller quantities by the ovaries *(see Chapter 13)*

The inner layer of the adrenal gland, the **adrenal medulla**, secretes hormones called **catecholamines**, principally **epinephrine (adrenaline)** and **norepinephrine**. These hormones prepare the body for physical activity. They raise blood pressure, increase circulation to muscles, increase pulmonary blood flow, and stimulate gluconeogenesis *(see Chapter 6)*.

WORD	PRONUNCIATION	ELEMENTS		DEFINITION
Addison disease	**AD**-ih-son diz-**EEZ**		Thomas Addison, English physician, 1793–1860	An autoimmune disease leading to decreased production of adrenocortical steroids
adrenal gland	ah-**DREE**-nal GLAND	P/	ad- *to*	The suprarenal, or adrenal, gland on the upper pole of each kidney
		R/	-renal- *kidney*	
adrenaline (also called epinephrine)	ah-**DREN**-ah-lin	S/	-ine *a substance*	One of the catecholamines
adrenocortical	ah-dree-noh-**KOR**-tih-kal	S/	-al *pertaining to*	Pertaining to the cortex of the adrenal gland
		R/CF	adren/o- *adrenal*	
		R/	-cortic- *cortex*	
aldosterone	al-**DOS**-ter-own	S/	-one *hormone*	Mineralocorticoid hormone of the adrenal cortex
		R/CF	ald/o- *organic compound*	
		R/	-ster- *steroid*	
catecholamine	kat-eh-**COAL**-ah-meen	S/	-amine *organic compound*	Major element in stress response
		R/	catechol- *benzene derivative*	
corticoid (also called corticosteroid)	**KOR**-tih-koyd	S/	-oid *resemble*	One of the steroid hormones produced by the adrenal cortex
		R/	cortic- *cortisone*	
cortisol (also called hydrocortisone)	**KOR**-tih-sol	S/	-ol *chemical substance*	One of the glucocorticoids produced by the adrenal cortex; has anti-inflammatory effects
		R/	cortis- *cortisone*	
dehydroepian-drosterone (DHEA)	de-**HIGH**-droh-epee-an-**DROS**-ter-own	S/	-one *hormone*	Precursor to testosterone; produced in the adrenal cortex
		P/	-epi- *above*	
		R/	-ster- *steroid*	
		R/CF	-andr/o- *male*	
		P/	de- *without*	
		R/CF	-hydr/o- *water*	
epinephrine (also called **adrenaline**)	ep-ih-**NEF**-rin	S/	-ine *pertaining to*	Main catecholamine produced by the adrenal medulla
		P/	epi- *above*	
		R/	-nephr- *kidney*	
glucocorticoid	glu-co-**KOR**-tih-koyd	S/	-oid *resemble*	Hormone of the adrenal cortex that helps regulate glucose metabolism
		R/	-cortic- *-cortisone*	
		R/CF	gluc/o- *glucose*	
hydrocortisone (also called **cortisol**)	high-droh-**KOR**-tih-sohn	S/	-one *hormone*	Potent glucocorticoid with anti-inflammatory properties
		P/	hydro- *water*	
		R/	-cortis- *cortisone*	
mineralocorticoid	**MIN**-er-al-oh-**KOR**-tih-koyd	S/	-oid *resemble*	Hormone of the adrenal cortex that influences sodium and potassium metabolism
		R/	-cortic- *cortisone*	
		R/CF	mineral/o- *inorganic materials*	
norepinephrine (also called **noradrenaline**)	**NOR**-ep-ih-**NEFF**-rin	S/	-ine *pertaining to*	Parasympathetic neurotransmitter
		P/	nor- *normal*	
		P/	-epi- *above*	
		R/	-nephr- *kidney*	

EXERCISES

Elements are the building blocks of medical terms. Match the elements in 1–10 to their correct meanings in A–J. Review the WAD before you begin the exercise.

_____ 1. hydro-

_____ 2. adren/o-

_____ 3. -oid

_____ 4. epi-

_____ 5. -ster-

_____ 6. andr/o-

_____ 7. gluc/o-

_____ 8. nor-

_____ 9. -one

_____ 10. -nephr-

A. normal

B. resemble

C. hormone

D. glucose

E. water

F. steroid

G. kidney

H. adrenal

I. above

J. male

DISORDERS OF ADRENAL GLANDS

Adrenal cortical hypofunction can be primary when the disorder is in the adrenal cortex (Addison disease) or secondary when there is a lack of ACTH from the pituitary gland.

Addison disease is caused mostly by idiopathic atrophy of the adrenal cortex. It occurs equally in both sexes and in all age groups. Production of the three groups of adrenocortical steroids is diminished or absent.

Decreased cortisol production leads to weakness, fatigue, diminished resistance to stress, increased susceptibility to infection, and weight loss.

Decreased aldosterone production leads to dehydration, decreased circulatory volume, hypotension, and circulatory collapse.

Replacement therapy in Addison disease is with daily hydrocortisone **by mouth (PO).** Additionally, fluorocortisone is given PO to replace aldosterone. Intercurrent infections require the hydrocortisone dose to be doubled. John F. Kennedy received replacement therapy from his late twenties until he died.

Acute adrenocortical insufficiency in patients with Addison disease is called an adrenal crisis. It can be precipitated by an infection or trauma and leads to peripheral vascular collapse and kidney failure. Treatment is with IV fluids and IV hydrocortisone.

Adrenal cortical hyperfunction is due to excessive production of the groups of the corticosteroids.

Hypersecretion of glucocorticoids produces **Cushing syndrome** *(Figure 14.17)*. Clinical manifestations include "moon" **facies,** obesity of the trunk, muscle wasting and weakness, osteoporosis, kidney stones, and reduced resistance to infection. Most cases of Cushing syndrome are due to a pituitary tumor secreting too much ACTH, thereby causing the normal adrenal glands to produce too much cortisol. Other cases of Cushing syndrome are due to benign adenomas of the adrenal gland producing excess cortisol.

Pituitary tumors causing Cushing syndrome are removed surgically. Single, benign adrenal adenomas are removed by **laparoscopic adrenalectomy.**

In a few cases, some of the symptoms of Cushing syndrome can be produced by therapeutic administration of excess cortisol medications *(Figure 14.18)*.

Hypersecretion of aldosterone (aldosteronism, or **Conn syndrome)** leads to sodium retention and potassium loss with increased blood volume, hypertension, excessive thirst, and excessive urination. A benign adenoma **(aldosteronoma)** is the most common cause and can be removed by laparoscopic adrenalectomy.

Hypersecretion of androgens is called **adrenal virilism** or **adrenogenital syndrome.** In adult women, manifestations include **hirsutism,** baldness, acne, deepened voice, decreased breast size, and other signs of masculinization. If a tumor is found by CT or MRI scan, it can be removed surgically.

Pheochromocytoma is a tumor of the adrenal medulla that overproduces the catecholamines epinephrine and norepinephrine. It produces marked hypertension that is difficult to control, with severe headaches, tachycardia, palpitations, and feelings of impending death. Diagnosis is made by measuring the excess catecholamines in blood and 24-hour urine specimens. The tumor is located by scans and angiography and removed by laparoscopic adrenalectomy.

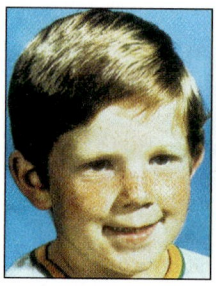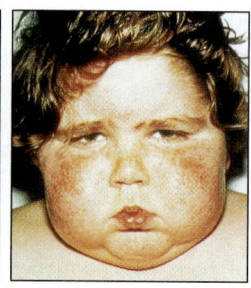

(a)   (b)

▲ **FIGURE 14.17   Cushing Syndrome.**
(a) Patient before onset of the syndrome.
(b) The same boy, only 4 months later, showing the "moon face" characteristic of Cushing syndrome.

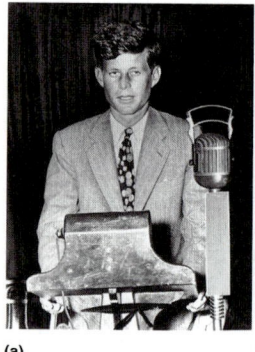

(a)   (b)

▲ **FIGURE 14.18   Treatment Effects of Excess Cortisol Medication May Mimic Symptoms of Cushing Syndrome.**

Stress

Is there an exam at the end of the week? Is the baby-sitter sick? You know what stress is and how it affects your physical and emotional well-being.

Your body reacts to stress in a consistent way called the stress response or general adaptation syndrome.

The initial response is an **alarm reaction** ("fight or flight") initiated by catecholamines that raise blood pressure and increase glucose production from stored

Keynote

Prolonged or repeated stress can cause physical illness.

Stress reduction techniques are an important part of modern life.

WORD	PRONUNCIATION	ELEMENTS		DEFINITION
adrenalectomy	ah-dree-nal-**ECK**-to-me	S/ P/ R/	**-ectomy** *surgical excision* **ad-** *to* **-renal-** *kidney*	Removal of part or whole of an adrenal gland
adrenogenital syndrome	ah-**DREE**-no-**JEN**-it-al **SIN**-drome	S/ R/CF R/	**-al** *pertaining to* **adren/o-** *adrenal gland* **-genit-** *genitalia*	Hypersecretion of androgens from the adrenal gland
aldosteronism (also called **Conn syndrome**)	al-**DOS**-ter-on-izm	S/ R/CF R/CF	**-ism** *condition* **ald/o-** *organic compound* **-ster/on-** *steroid*	Condition caused by excessive secretion of aldosterone
aldosteronoma	al-**DOS**-ter-on-oma	S/	**-oma** *tumor, mass*	Benign adenoma of the adrenal cortex
Conn syndrome (also called **aldosteronism**)	KON **SIN**-drom		Jerome W. Conn, 1907–1981, U.S. endocrinologist	Aldosteronism
Cushing syndrome	**KUSH**-ing **SIN**-drom		Harvey Cushing, 1869–1939, American neurosurgeon	Hypersecretion of cortisol by the adrenal cortex
facies	**FASH**-eez		Latin *appearance*	Facial expression and features
hirsutism	**HER**-sue-tizm		Latin *shaggy*	Excessive body and facial hair
pheochromocytoma	fee-oh-**KRO**-moh-sigh-**TOE**-muh	S/ P/ R/CF R/	**-oma** *tumor* **pheo-** *gray* **-chrom/o-** *color* **-cyt-** *cell*	Adenoma of the adrenal medulla secreting excessive catecholamines
virilism	**VIR**-ih-lizm	S/ R/	**-ism** *condition* **viril-** *masculine*	Development of masculine characteristics by a woman or girl

glycogen. This source of glucose is soon exhausted, and the feelings of anxiety, irritability, and insecurity are replaced by headache and back and neck pain due to the effects of the catecholamines on blood vessels and muscles.

If the stress is allowed to persist, the physical priority is to provide alternative fuels to provide energy. The adrenal gland increases its output of cortisol to stimulate glucose synthesis. Fatigue, indigestion, and diminished sex drive become dominant.

The third stage of a prolonged stress response is exhaustion when glycogen and fat stores have gone. The immune system cannot find the energy to continue functioning. This is when deep physical illness takes over. Body muscle wastes away, and heart and kidney failure or overwhelming infection are the end result.

EXERCISES

Language of Endocrinology. *The meaning of a word element never changes, regardless of the term which contains it. Demonstrate your knowledge of word elements by making the correct choice in the following multiple choice questions.*

1. Based on its suffix, an **aldosteronoma** is a:
   a. condition
   b. facial hair
   c. tumor
   d. facial expression
   e. gland

2. In the term **pheochromocytoma**, the prefix is one of:
   a. size
   b. shape
   c. direction
   d. color
   e. gender

3. Circle the term with a root that means **masculine**:
   a. hirsutism
   b. aldosteronism
   c. facies
   d. virilism
   e. aldosteronoma

4. The suffix in this term means **surgical excision**:
   a. adrenalectomy
   b. virilism
   c. aldosteronoma
   d. facies
   e. pheochromocytoma

LESSON 14.4 Pancreas

OBJECTIVES

The information provided in this lesson will enable you to:

- **Distinguish between the different cells of the pancreas and their secretions.**
- **Identify the functions of the hormones produced by the pancreas.**
- **Explain common disorders of the pancreatic hormones.**

You are

...a medical assistant working with Susan Lee, MD, in her primary care clinic at Fulwood Medical Center.

Your patient is

...Mrs. Martha Jones, who is here for her monthly checkup.

CASE REPORT 14.4

Mrs. Martha Jones is a 53-year-old type 2 diabetic on insulin, with diabetic retinopathy and diabetic neuropathy of her feet. Bariatric surgery has enabled her to reduce her weight from 275 to 156 pounds. The time is 0930 hrs.

She is complaining of having a cold and cough for the past few days. Now she is feeling drowsy and nauseous and has a dry mouth. As you talk with her, you notice that her speech is slurred. She cannot remember if she gave herself her morning insulin. Examination of her lungs reveals rales at her right base.

Her VS: T 97.8°F, P 120, R 20, BP 100/50. You perform her blood glucose measurement. The reading is 525 mg/dL (a recommended value 2 hours after breakfast is < 145 mg/dL).

At the end of this chapter you will be asked to document in SOAP format your encounter with her.

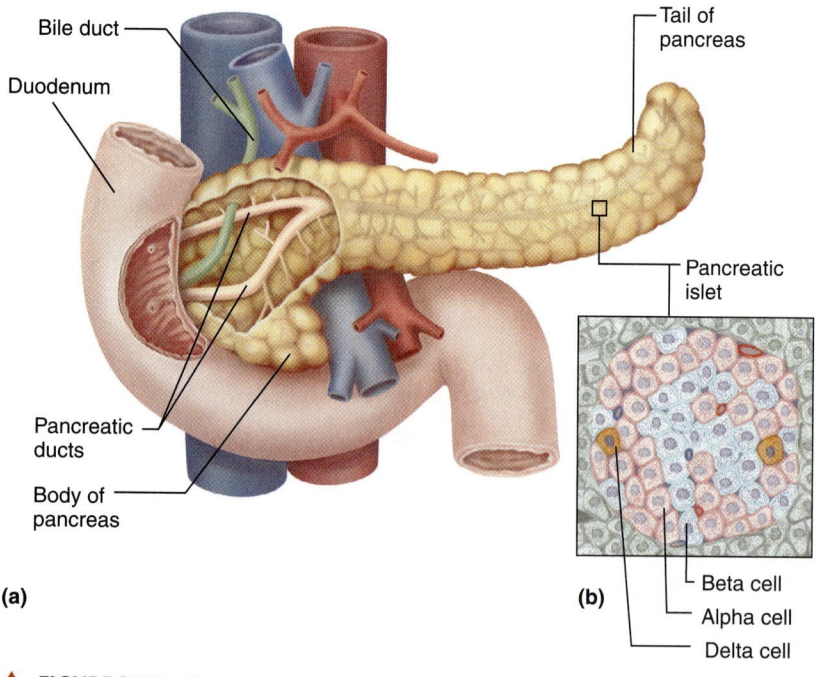

▲ FIGURE 14.19 Pancreas.
(*a*) General anatomy. (*b*) Alpha, beta, and delta cells.

PANCREAS

The location and structure of the pancreas is detailed in *Chapter 6.* Most of the pancreas is an exocrine gland that secretes digestive juices into the duodenum through a duct *(Figure 14.19)*. Scattered throughout the pancreas are clusters of endocrine cells grouped around blood vessels. These clusters are called **pancreatic islets (islets of Langerhans).** Within the islets are three distinct cell types:

1. **alpha cells**—secrete the hormone **glucagon** in response to a low blood glucose. Glucagon's actions are:

   a. in the liver to stimulate **gluconeogenesis, glycogenolysis,** and the release of glucose into the bloodstream

   b. in adipose tissue to stimulate fat catabolism and the release of free fatty acids

2. **beta cells**—secrete **insulin** in response to a high blood glucose. Insulin has the opposite effects of glucagon:

a. in muscle and fat cells to encourage absorption of glucose and to store glycogen and fat

b. in the liver to stimulate the conversion of glucose to glycogen and to inhibit the conversion of noncarbohydrates to glucose

WORD	PRONUNCIATION	ELEMENTS		DEFINITION
glucagon	GLU-kah-gon	S/ R/	-agon *to lead* gluc- *glucose*	Pancreatic hormone that supports blood glucose levels
gluconeogenesis	GLU-ko-nee-oh-JEN-eh-sis	S/ P/ R/CF	-genesis *creation* -neo- *new* gluc/o- *glucose*	Formation of glucose from noncarbohydrate sources
glycogenolysis	GLYE-koh-jen-oh-LYE-sis	S/ R/CF R/CF	-lysis *break down* glyc/o- *glycogen* -gen/o- *creation*	Conversion of glycogen to glucose
pancreas	PAN-kree-ass		Greek *sweetbread*	Lobulated gland, the head of which is tucked into the curve of the duodenum
somatostatin	SO-mah-toe-STAT-in	S/ R/CF	-statin- *inhibit* somat/o- *body*	Hormone that inhibits release of growth hormone and insulin

3. **delta cells**—secrete **somatostatin**, which acts within the pancreas to inhibit the secretion of glucagon and insulin.

Glucagon is not the only hormone that raises blood glucose; epinephrine, cortisol, and growth hormone also have that effect. Insulin is the only hormone that lowers blood glucose.

EXERCISES

Build the correct medical term that matches the definition. When you insert an element on the line, label what type of element it is under the line. Fill in the blanks. Use each term in a sentence of your choice.

1. inhibits release of growth hormone and insulin   _____/_____/statin

   Sentence: _____

   _____

2. conversion of glycogen to glucose   _____/_____/lysis

   Sentence: _____

   _____

3. pancreatic hormone   _____/gluc/_____

   Sentence: _____

   _____

4. formation of glucose from non-carbohydrates   gluco/_____/_____

   Sentence: _____

   _____

Abbreviations

DM	diabetes mellitus
IDDM	insulin-dependent diabetes mellitus
MODY	mature onset diabetes of the young
NIDDM	non-insulin-dependent diabetes mellitus

Diabetes mellitus (DM) is a syndrome characterized by hyperglycemia resulting from an absolute or relative impairment of insulin secretion and/or insulin action. This leads to a disruption of carbohydrate, fat, and protein metabolism. It is the world's most prevalent metabolic disease and the leading cause of blindness, renal failure, and gangrene. There are four categories of diabetes mellitus.

1. **Type 1 diabetes,** also called **insulin-dependent diabetes mellitus (IDDM),** accounts for 10 to 15% of all cases of DM but is the predominant type of DM under the age of 30. When symptoms become apparent, 90% of the pancreatic insulin-producing cells have been destroyed by **autoantibodies.** The incidence of type 1 diabetes is increased in patients with Graves disease, Hashimoto disease, and Addison disease.

2. **Type 2 diabetes,** also called **non-insulin-dependent diabetes mellitus (NIDDM),** accounts for 85 to 90% of all cases of DM. Almost 7% of U.S. residents are diagnosed with type 2 diabetes. Not only is there some impairment of insulin response, but there is decreased insulin effectiveness in stimulating glucose uptake by tissues and in restraining hepatic glucose production. This is called **insulin resistance.** In addition to type 2 diabetes, insulin resistance leads to other common disorders such as obesity, hypertension, hyperlipidemia, and coronary artery disease. Type 2 diabetes can be secondary to Cushing syndrome, acromegaly, pheochromocytoma, and aldosteronism.

   Stress can raise blood glucose levels in type 2 diabetes by a direct effect on insulin response and effectiveness but also by disturbing the patient's pattern of disease management.

3. **Gestational diabetes** is seen in the latter half of 5% of pregnancies. While most cases of gestational diabetes resolve after the pregnancy, a woman who has this complication of pregnancy has a 30% chance of developing type 2 diabetes within ten years.

4. **Maturity onset diabetes of the young (MODY)** is genetically inherited, occurs in thin individuals who are in their teens and twenties, and is comparable to type 2 diabetes in its severity.

Hypoglycemia is present when blood glucose is below 70 mg/dL. Hormonal defense mechanisms (glucagon and adrenaline) are activated as the blood glucose drops below 55mg/dL. Because brain metabolism depends primarily on glucose, the brain is the first organ affected by hypoglycemia. Impaired mental efficiency starts to be seen when the blood glucose falls below 65 mg/dL. It becomes very obvious (shakiness, anxiety, confusion, tremor) around 40 mg/dL, and, below that figure, seizures can occur. If the blood glucose falls below 10 mg/dL, the neurons become electrically silent, resulting in diabetic **coma.** Symptomatic hypoglycemia is sometimes called **insulin shock.**

Low blood glucose can be raised to normal in minutes by taking 10 to 20 grams of carbohydrate (3 to 4 ounces) such as orange, apple, or grape juice. Symptoms should begin to improve in 5 minutes, with full recovery in 10 to 15 minutes. In an emergency, if the patient is not able to take oral sugar, treatment is begun with a rapid IV **bolus** of 25 mL of 50% glucose solution, followed by an IV infusion of glucose.

WORD ANALYSIS AND DEFINITION

S = Suffix   P = Prefix   R = Root   R/CF = Combining Form

WORD	PRONUNCIATION		ELEMENTS	DEFINITION
autoantibody	aw-toe-**AN**-tee-bod-ee	P/ P/ R/	**auto-** *self, same* **-anti-** *against* **-body** *body*	Antibody produced in response to an antigen in the host's own tissue
bolus	**BOH**-lus		Greek *a lump*	Single mass of a substance
coma	**KOH**-mah		Greek *deep sleep*	State of deep unconsciousness
diabetes mellitus	dye-ah-**BEE**-teez **MEL**-ih-tus		**diabetes** Greek *a siphon* **mellitus** Latin *sweetened with honey*	Metabolic syndrome caused by absolute or relative insulin deficiency and/or insulin ineffectiveness
diabetic (adj)	dye-ah-**BET**-ik	S/ R/	**-ic** *pertaining to* **diabet-** *diabetes*	Pertaining to or suffering from diabetes
hypoglycemia	**HIGH**-poh-glie-**SEE**-me-ah	S/ P/ R/	**-emia** *blood condition* **hypo-** *below, deficient* **-glyc-** *glucose*	Low level of glucose (sugar) in the blood

EXERCISES

Diabetes is the world's most prevalent metabolic disease. Many patients have diabetes as a concurrent condition with other health problems—which always makes it a consideration in treatment and prescribing medications. Test your knowledge of this disease by answering the following questions. Circle the correct choice.

1. Diabetes is the leading cause of:

   blindness   renal failure   gangrene   none of these   all of these

2. The first organ affected by hypoglycemia is the:

   kidney   heart   pancreas   brain   liver

3. The predominant type of DM in patients under the age of 30 is:

   type 1   type 2   noninsulin-dependent DM   gestational diabetes type 3

4. Impairment of insulin response and decreased insulin effectiveness is termed insulin:

   production   resistance   autoantibodies   control   conversion

5. Most cases of gestational diabetes resolve after:

   medication   treatment   testing   delivery   surgery

6. Symptomatic hypoglycemia is sometimes called:

   insulin resistance   coma   insulin shock   glucolysis   bolus

7. Type 1 diabetes is also known as:

   IDDM   NIDDM   hypoglycemia   hyperglycemia   coma

DIAGNOSIS AND TREATMENT OF DIABETES MELLITUS

Criteria for the Diagnosis of Diabetes Mellitus

The accepted **criteria** for the diagnosis of DM include either a fasting (8 hours) plasma glucose of 126 mg/dL or greater or symptoms (polyuria, polydipsia, polyphagia, unexplained weight loss) and a random plasma glucose of 200 mg/dL or higher.

An **oral glucose tolerance test (OGTT)** is used occasionally in diagnosing type 2 diabetes.

Treatment of Diabetes Mellitus

The basic principle of diabetes treatment is to avoid hyperglycemia and hypoglycemia. The following are the areas of treatment:

- **Diet and exercise**—to achieve weight reduction of 2 lbs per week in overweight type 2 patients is essential. For insulin-treated diabetics, detailed diet management restricts variations in timing, size, and content of meals.

- **Patient education**—to understand the disease process, to recognize the indications for seeking immediate medical care, and to follow a regimen of foot care.

- **Plasma glucose monitoring**—an essential skill that all diabetics must learn. Patients on insulin must learn to adjust their insulin doses. Home glucose analyzers use a drop of blood obtained by a spring-powered lancet from the fingertip or forearm. The frequency of testing is varied individually. Insulin-treated patients should test their plasma glucose before meals, two hours after meals, and at bedtime.

- **Routine physician visits**—the patient is assessed for symptoms or signs of complications. Skin condition, pulses, and sensation in feet are tested. Urine is tested for **microalbuminuria** using **immunoassays.** This detects smaller increases in urinary albumin than does conventional urine testing.

- **Periodic laboratory evaluation**—includes **blood urea nitrogen (BUN)** and serum creatinine (kidney function), lipid profile, **electrocardiogram (ECG)**, and an annual complete ophthalmologic evaluation.

Glycosylated hemoglobin (Hb A1c) is used to monitor plasma glucose control during the preceding one to three months. It is formed at rates that increase with plasma glucose levels. Normal Hb A1c is less than 6%. In poor control, the value is 9 to 12%.

Fructosamine is formed by glucose combining with plasma protein and reflects plasma glucose control over the preceding one to three weeks. A standard reference range for this test is not available.

Insulin preparations routinely contain 100 U/mL (**U-100 insulin**). The insulin is injected subcutaneously using disposable syringes that hold 0.5 mL. In addition, already prepared mixtures of intermediate and regular insulins in different ratios are available. An **insulin pen** is an injection device that holds several days' dosage.

Continuous subcutaneous insulin infusion is given by a battery-powered, programmable pump that provides continuous insulin through a small needle in the abdominal wall.

Abbreviations

BUN	blood urea nitrogn
ECG	electrocardiogram
Hb A1c	glycosylated hemoglobin (hemoglobin A one-C)
NPH	neutral protamine Hagedorn insulin
OGTT	oral glucose tolerance test
U	unit

TABLE 14.1 Classes of Insulin (*min* = minutes; *h* = hours)

Insulin Type	Onset of Action	Peak of Action	Duration of Action	Examples
Rapid-acting	15 min	30–60 min	3–5 h	Humalog, NovoLog
Regular-acting	30–60 min	100–120 min	5–8 h	Humulin R, Novolin R
Intermediate-acting (NPH)	1–3 h	7–8 h	18–24 h	Humulin N, Novolin N
Long-acting	4–8 h	8–12 h	24–36 h	Humulin U, Lantus

WORD ANALYSIS AND DEFINITION

S = Suffix   P = Prefix   R = Root   R/CF = Combining Form

WORD	PRONUNCIATION		ELEMENTS	DEFINITION
criterion criteria (pl)	kri-**TEER**-ee-on kri-**TEER**-ee-ah		Greek *a standard*	Standard or rule for judging
fructosamine	**FRUK**-toe-sah-meen	S/ R/	**-amine** *organic compound derived from ammonia* **fructos-** *fruit sugar*	Organic compound with fructose as its base
glycosylated hemoglobin (Hb A1c)	**GLYE**-koh-sih-lay-ted **HE**-moh-**GLOW**-bin	R/CF S/	**glyc/o-** *glucose* **-sylated** *linked*	Hemoglobin A fraction linked to glucose; used as index of glucose control
immunoassay	**IM**-you-noh-**ASS**-ay	R/ R/CF	**-assay** *evaluate* **immun/o-** *immune response*	Biochemical test to measure the amount of a substance in a liquid using the reaction of an antibody to its antigen
insulin	**IN**-syu-lin	S/ R/	**-in** *a substance* **insul-** *island*	A hormone secreted by the pancreas
microalbuminuria	**MY**-kroh-al-byu-min-**YOU**-ree-ah	S/ P/ R/ R/	**-ia** *condition* **micro-** *small* **-albumin-** *albumin* **-ur-** *urine*	Presence of very small quantities of albumin in urine that cannot be detected by conventional urine testing
synergist synergistic (adj)	**SIN**-er-jist	S/ P/ R/	**-ist** *specializes in* **syn-** *together* **-erg-** *work*	Agent or process that aids the action of another

Pharmacology

Oral antidiabetic drugs are used for type 2 but not type 1 diabetes. These drugs include:

- **Metformin** acts by decreasing hepatic glucose production. It also promotes weight loss and decreases lipid levels. It is **synergistic** in combination with sulfonylureas.

- **Acarbose** delays carbohydrate digestion and absorption in the intestine and can be used in combination with other drugs.

- **Thiazolidinediones,** such as troglitazone, improve insulin sensitivity in skeletal muscle and suppress hepatic glucose production. It is used in type 2 patients who are on insulin and allows them to reduce their insulin dose.

EXERCISES

Medications: *Diabetics will deal with medications for the rest of their lives. Match the statement to the correct drug by placing a check mark (✓) in the appropriate column with the drug name. Then fill in the blanks below.*

Statement	Metformin	Acarbose	Thiazolidinediones
Delays carbohydrate digestion in intestine			
Improves insulin sensitivity in skeletal muscle			
Decreases hepatic glucose production			
Can be used in combination with other drugs			
Promotes weight loss			
Allows type 2 patients to reduce their insulin dose			
Decreases lipid levels			
Troglitazone is an example			

1. Oral antidiabetic drugs are used for type _____ diabetes but not type _____.

2. Name the four major types of insulin preparations:

a. _____   c. _____

b. _____   d. _____

ENDOCRINE SYSTEM

CHALLENGE YOUR KNOWLEDGE

A. **Written Communication:** Reread the case report on Dr. Lee's patient, Martha Jones. *When you read the report for the second time, try highlighting the important terminology you will use to write your SOAP note.*

Your patient is

. . . Mrs. Martha Jones, who is here for her monthly checkup. She is a 53-year-old type 2 diabetic on insulin, with diabetic retinopathy and diabetic neuropathy of her feet. Bariatric surgery has enabled her to reduce her weight from 275 to 156 pounds. The time is 0930 hrs.

She is complaining of having a cold and cough for the past few days. Now she is feeling drowsy and nauseous and has a dry mouth. As you talk with her, you notice that her speech is slurred. She cannot remember if she gave herself her morning insulin. Examination of her lungs reveals rales at her right base.

Her VS: T 97.8°F, P 120, R 20, BP 100/50. You perform her blood glucose measurement. The reading is 525 mg/dL (a recommended value 2 hours after breakfast is < 145 mg/dL).

Mrs. Martha Jones is in the early stages of a hyperglycemic, nonketotic coma, probably initiated by a right lower lobe pneumonia. A urine specimen was obtained. Dr. Lee was notified. Blood was taken for a full chemistry panel, and arterial blood gases were drawn. An IV infusion bolus of 550 mL of isotonic sodium chloride was given, followed by 1.5 liters of isotonic saline over the next two hours. She was given 10 units of regular insulin IV and was admitted to the hospital.

During your career, any documentation you author will be read by other health care personnel. This is an official document for the patient's chart and must be professional-looking—writing must be legible and neat, and all spelling must be correct.

This part of the exercise is for organizing your thoughts about what to write on the actual documentation. To obtain the form to use after you have completed this exercise, go to the Online Learning Center and print out a blank SOAP form. Transfer your notes from this exercise to the official form and hand it in to your instructor.

Organize your notes in the following manner:

S (*subjective*) What is the patient's chief complaint and symptoms at this visit (from the patient's own words)?

_____

_____

_____

_____

O (*objective*) What can be observed or measured by examination of the patient?

_____

_____

_____

_____

A (*assessment*) What measures (tests, etc.) were taken to determine the cause of this patient's problem? What is the possible/tentative diagnosis?

_____

_____

_____

_____

P (*plan*)   What is being done for this patient now to alleviate her complaint?

_____

_____

_____

_____

B. **Prefixes:** Practice the prefixes contained in endocrine terminology. Write the meaning for each of the prefixes listed below, then give an example of a medical term that begins with that prefix. Finally, pick any three terms, and use them in a sentence of your own choice.

Prefixes	Meaning of Prefix	Medical Term Using that Prefix
ad-		
anti-		
endo-		
eu-		
ex-		
in-		
iso-		
pan-		
par-		
para-		
pheo-		
pro-		

1. _____

_____

2. _____

_____

3. _____

_____

ENDOCRINE SYSTEM

C. **Diseases and Disorders:** Identify the diseases and disorders of the endocrine system as described in the following statements. Special attention to the prefixes will aid you in matching your correct choice.

_____ 1. autoimmune disease with lymphocytic infiltration   A. Graves disease

_____ 2. congenital form of thyroid deficiency   B. thyroid cancer

_____ 3. excess of PTH   C. hypoparathyroidism

_____ 4. severe hypothyroidism   D. thyroiditis

_____ 5. presents as symptomless thyroid nodule   E. Hashimoto disease

_____ 6. inflammation of the thyroid gland   F. goiter

_____ 7. associated with a goiter   G. exophthalmos

_____ 8. deficiency of PTH   H. hyperparathyroidism

_____ 9. enlargement of the thyroid gland   I. myxedema

_____ 10. eyes bulging outward   J. cretinism

D. **Terminology Construction:** Construct the **language of endocrinology**. Build the term for the definition provided. Fill in the blanks.

1. hormone formed by the pineal gland: _____ / _____ / _____

2. protrusion of the eyeball: _____ / _____ / _____

3. hormone produced by adrenal cortex: _____ / _____ / _____

4. deficiency of all the pituitary hormones: _____ / _____ / _____

5. another name for the pituitary gland: _____ / _____ / _____

6. stimulates uterus to contract: _____ / _____ / _____

7. removal of part or all of the adrenal gland: _____ / _____ / _____

8. prolactin-producing tumor: _____ / _____ / _____

9. waxy, nonpitting edema of skin: _____ / _____ / _____

10. excessive growth hormone produces enlarged head: _____ / _____ / _____

E. **Translation:** Rewrite the following sentence—without any abbreviations—into language a patient can understand. Review any terms you need to before you start writing.

"ADH, also called vasopressin, causes vasoconstriction in small arterioles, usually insufficient to cause hypertension."

_____

_____

_____

_____

_____

_____

F. **Recall and Review:** How well do you remember these word elements from the previous chapter? Try to answer without first looking back to check. Fill in the blanks.

Element	Type of Element (P, R, CF, S)	Meaning of Element
estr/o		
poly		
vert		
ovari		
pro		

G. **Language of Endocrinology:** Knowing the endocrine system will aid you in understanding the overall body process of *homeostasis.* Apply the *language of endocrinology* to the following questions about the anatomy and physiology of the endocrine system; circle the correct answer.

1. Which of the following is not a part of the endocrine system?

   a. pancreas

   b. pituitary

   c. pineal

   d. parathyroid

   e. palatine

2. The abnormal production of breast milk is called:

   a. dysmenorrhea

   b. polydipsia

   c. galactorrhea

   d. dysphagia

   e. menorrhagia

3. The speed at which the body's chemical functions proceed is called:

   a. cardiac rate

   b. vasoconstriction

   c. metabolic rate

   d. blood pressure

   e. homeostasis

4. The only hormone that lowers blood glucose is:

   a. glucagon

   b. cortisol

   c. aldosterone

   d. corticosterone

   e. insulin

ENDOCRINE SYSTEM

H. Language of Endocrinology: Apply the *language of endocrinology* to the following questions about the anatomy and physiology of the endocrine system; circle the correct answer.

1. A congenital form of thyroid deficiency that severely retards mental and physical growth is:

   a. goiter

   b. thyroid adenoma

   c. cretinism

   d. pretibial myxedema

   e. hyperthyroidism

2. **Tetany** is:

   a. lockjaw

   b. painful muscle spasm

   c. protrusion of the eyeball

   d. enlargement of the thyroid gland

   e. excessive production of thyroid hormones

3. A condition produced by a pituitary tumor that causes a decline in the production of several hormones at the same time is called:

   a. hypopituitarism

   b. hyperpituitarism

   c. panhypopituitarism

   d. prolactinoma

   e. diabetes mellitus

4. Another name for **epinephrine** is:

   a. corticosteroid

   b. corticosterone

   c. adrenalin

   d. hydrocortisone

   e. cortisol

5. The pineal gland secretes **serotonin** by day and converts it to _____ at night:

   a. melatonin

   b. a vasodilator

   c. vasopressin

   d. prolactin

   e. an enzyme

6. This term can be used to describe the location of the adrenal gland:

   a. infrarenal

   b. interrenal

   c. epirenal

   d. hyporenal

   e. suprarenal

7. In the term **paresthesia,** the root means:

   a. obese

   b. sensation

   c. movement

   d. abnormally thin

   e. body

8. **Hypophysis** is the term for the:

   a. pituitary gland

   b. thyroid gland

   c. pineal gland

   d. parathyroid gland

   e. thymus gland

9. Condition of a forward-projecting jaw is called:

   a. hypercalcemia

   b. goiter

   c. exophthalmos

   d. prognathism

   e. myxedema

10. A needle aspiration biopsy would be done to:

    a. measure size of lesion

    b. determine place of lesion

    c. count numbers of lesions

    d. reduce size of lesion

    e. determine possible malignancy of lesion

ENDOCRINE SYSTEM

I. **Hormones:** Hormones are blood-borne messengers secreted by endocrine glands. Each has a specific function as stated below. Correctly use the following terms or abbreviations to fill in the blanks.

ACTH	FSH	somatotropin	PRL	tropic
insulin	glucocorticoid	melatonin	LH	thyrotropin

1. Hormone that stimulates the growth of the thyroid gland: _____

2. Hormones that stimulate other endocrine glands to produce hormones: _____

3. Hormone that stimulates ovulation and testosterone production: _____

4. Hormone of the adrenal cortex that helps regulate glucose metabolism: _____

5. Hormone that stimulates cells to enlarge and divide: _____

6. Hormone produced by the islet cells of the pancreas: _____

7. Hormone of the anterior pituitary that stimulates cortex of adrenal gland to produce its own hormones: _____

8. Hormone that stimulates target cells in the ovaries and testes: _____

9. Hormone formed by pineal gland: _____

10. Hormone that stimulates the mammary glands after pregnancy to produce milk: _____

J. **Latin and Greek Terms:** Latin and Greek terms cannot be further deconstructed into prefix, root, or suffix. You must know them for what they are. Test your knowledge of these terms with the following exercise. Match the meaning in column l with the correct medical term in column 2.

_____	1. oblong shield	A.	tetany
_____	2. island	B.	coma
_____	3. deep sleep	C.	tropic
_____	4. a turning	D.	thyroid
_____	5. siphon	E.	insulin
_____	6. a lump	F.	facies
_____	7. convulsive tension	G.	hirsutism
_____	8. appearance	H.	bolus
_____	9. shaggy or hairy	I.	hormone
_____	10. to set in motion	J.	diabetes

K. Terminology Challenge: An element may have more than one meaning.

For example: **hypo-** can mean either *below* (location) or *deficient* (less in quantity or number). The following five terms all start with **hypo-**. Write the meaning of each term and check mark (✓) whether the prefix in this case means *below* or *deficient*. Fill in the blanks.

Medical Term	Prefix Means below	Prefix Means deficient	Meaning of Term
hypoglycemia			
hypothyroidism			
hypothalamus			
hypopituitarism			
hypophysis			

L. Plurals: Enhance your command of plurals in medical terminology by completing this exercise. Circle the best choice for the correct form of the plural in the sentence.

1. Patient complains of multiple (paresthesiae/paresthesias) on her left side.

2. There are several (criterion/criteria) by which to judge this patient's recovery.

3. (Catecholamines/Catecholamina) are major elements in stress response.

4. Insulin sensitivity in skeletal muscle is improved by (thiazolidinediones/thiazolidinedionia).

M. Deconstruction: Deconstruct these medical terms into the meanings of their basic elements. Demonstrate you understand the meanings by using one term in a sentence. Fill in the chart.

Medical Term	Meaning of Prefix	Meaning of Root(s)/CF	Meaning of Suffix
polyuria			
parathyroid			
vasopressin			
panhypopituitarism			
prognathism			
polydipsia			
euthyroid			
autoantibody			
hypoglycemia			
polyphagia			
endocrinology			
paresthesia			

Sentence:

_____

_____

ENDOCRINE SYSTEM

CHAPTER SUMMARY EXERCISE

1. *Listen to the pronunciation of the medical terms as given by your instructor.*
2. *Circle the correct spelling of the medical term.*
3. *Match the correctly spelled terms to the brief descriptions below.*
4. *Write a sentence for each of the 15 terms that appear in this exercise.*

A. SPELLING COMPREHENSION: CIRCLE THE CORRECT SPELLING OF THE TERM.

1. hypophysis	hypopersis	hypopisis	hypophsis	hypophses
2. hersutism	hirsutism	herrsutism	hirssutism	hirsutesm
3. emaciated	emmaciated	imaciated	immaciated	emacciated
4. prolacktinomma	prolactinoma	prolictinoma	proliktinoma	prolacktinnoma
5. gooter	gutter	goiter	goiiter	guiter
6. isotope	issotope	eisotope	eissotope	isutope
7. thyroidtoxicosis	thyrotoxicosis	thyroidtoxicossis	thyrodtoxicosis	throidtoxicosis
8. myxxedema	mixxedema	mexidema	myxedema	mixedema
9. uthyroid	euthyroid	euuthroid	uthroid	utthryoid
10. insepidus	insippidus	inseppidus	insipidus	insipides
11. thyridectomy	thyroidectomy	thyrectomy	thirectomy	tiroidectomy
12. leaptin	lepton	lepten	leptine	leptin
13. exoptalmos	exxopthalmos	exophtalmuss	exophthalmos	exophthalmus
14. creetin	crettin	critin	cretin	crretin
15. serrotonnin	serotonin	serutonin	serrutonin	serutonine

B. MATCH THE NUMBER OF THE CORRECT TERM IN PART A WITH THE BRIEF DESCRIPTION OF THE TERM BELOW.

a. hormone secreted by adipose tissue _____

b. normal thyroid function _____

c. protrusion of the eyeball _____

d. person with severe congenital hypothyroidism _____

e. converted at night to melatonin _____

f. excessive body and facial hair _____

g. enlargement of thyroid gland _____

h. another term for pituitary gland _____

i. radioactive element used in diagnostic procedures _____

j. nonpitting edema _____

k. can appear in both men and women   _____

l. removal of the thyroid gland   _____

m. abnormally thin   _____

n. results from decreased production of ADH   _____

o. disorder produced by excessive thyroid hormone production _____

C. USING YOUR KNOWLEDGE OF TERMS 1-15 IN PART A AND THEIR CORRECT SPELLING, WRITE A BRIEF SENTENCE FOR EACH OF THE TERMS AS IT MIGHT APPEAR IN PATIENT DOCUMENTATION.

1. _____

2. _____

3. _____

4. _____

5. _____

6. _____

7. _____

8. _____

9. _____

10. _____

11. _____

12. _____

13. _____

14. _____

15. _____

D. GO TO THE STUDENT CD. OPEN THE GLOSSARY AND PRACTICE YOUR PRONUNCIATION OF THE TERMS IN PART A OF THIS EXERCISE.

LYMPHATIC TISSUES AND CELLS

Keynote

Tissues that are the first line of defense to pathogens, for example the airway passages, have lymphatic tissue in the submucous layers to help protect against invasion.

Abbreviations

CD	cluster domain
Ig	immunoglobulin

Many organs have a sprinkling of lymphocytes in their connective tissues and mucous membranes, particularly in passages that open to the exterior—the respiratory, digestive, urinary, and reproductive tracts—where invaders have access to the body.

In some organs, lymphocytes and other cells form dense clusters called **lymphatic follicles.** These are constant features in lymph nodes, the tonsils, and the ileum.

Lymphatic tissues are composed of a variety of cells that include:

1. **T lymphocytes (T cells).** The "T" stands for *thymus,* where they mature. T lymphocytes make up 75 to 85% of body lymphocytes. There are several types of T cells:

    a. **Cytotoxic or "killer" T cells** destroy target cells. Their cell membrane holds a **coreceptor** that can recognize a specific antigen. Coreceptors are named with the letters "CD" **(cluster domain)** followed by a number, for these cells, CD8.

    b. **Helper T cells** contain the CD4 coreceptor and are called T4 cells. They begin the defensive response against a specific antigen.

    c. **Memory T cells** arise from cytotoxic T lymphocytes that have previously destroyed a foreign cell. If they encounter the same antigen, they can now quickly kill it without initiation by a helper T cell.

    d. **Suppressor T cells** suppress activation of the immune system. Failure of these cells to function properly may result in autoimmune diseases.

2. **B lymphocytes (B cells)** These cells mature in the bone marrow.

    B lymphocytes make up 15 to 25% of lymphocytes. They are activated by helper T cells, respond to a specific antigen, and cause the production of antibodies **(immunoglobulins, Ig).** The activated B cells are called **plasma cells** and secrete large quantities of antibodies that immobilize, neutralize, and prepare the specific antigen for destruction.

3. **Null cells** are large granular lymphocytes that are natural killer cells but lack the specific surface markers of the T and B lymphocytes

4. **Macrophages** develop from monocytes that have migrated from blood. They ingest and destroy tissue debris, bacteria, and other foreign matter **(phagocytosis).**

LYMPHATIC ORGANS

Spleen

The **spleen,** a highly vascular and spongy organ, is the largest lymphatic organ. It is located in the left upper quadrant of the abdomen below the diaphragm and lateral to the kidney *(Figure 15.4).*

The spleen contains two basic types of tissue:

1. **white pulp**—a part of the immune system that produces T cells, B cells, and macrophages. The blood passing through the spleen is monitored for antigens. Antibodies are produced, and the foreign matter removed.

2. **red pulp**—acts as a reservoir for erythrocytes, platelets, and macrophages that remove old and defective erythrocytes.

Thus, the functions of the spleen are to:

- **phagocytize bacteria** and other foreign materials
- **initiate an immune response** when antigens are found in the blood
- **phagocytize old, defective erythrocytes** and platelets (hemolysis)
- **serve as a reservoir** for erythrocytes and platelets

Tonsils

The **tonsils** *(see Chapter 9)* are two masses of lymphatic tissue located at the entrance to the oropharynx, where they entrap inhaled and ingested pathogens.

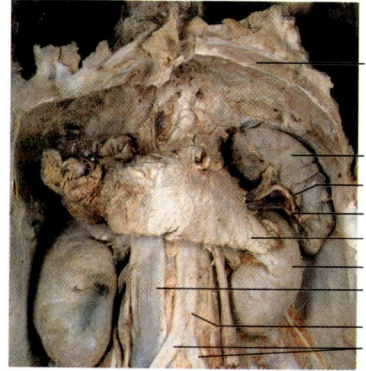

Diaphragm (cut)

Spleen
Splenic artery
Splenic vein
Pancreas
Kidney
Inferior vena cava
Aorta
Common iliac arteries

▲ **FIGURE 15.4   Position of Spleen.**

WORD	PRONUNCIATION		ELEMENTS	DEFINITION
adenoid	**ADD**-eh-noyd	S/ R/	-oid *resemble* aden- *gland*	Single mass of lymphoid tissue in the midline at the back of the throat
coreceptor	koh-ree-**SEP**-tor	S/ P/ R/	-or *a doer* co- *with* -recept- *receive*	Cell surface protein to enhance the sensitivity of an antigen receptor
follicle	**FOLL**-ih-kull		Latin *bellows*	Spherical mass of cells containing a cavity or a small cul-de-sac, such as a hair follicle
macrophage	**MAK**-roh-fayj	P/ R/	macro- *large* -phage *to eat*	Large white blood cell that removes bacteria, foreign particles, and dead cells
null cells	NULL SELLS		**null** Latin *none*	Lymphocytes with no surface markers, unlike T cells or B cells
phagocyte	**FAG**-oh-site	S/ R/CF	-cyte *cell* phag/o- *to eat*	Blood cell that ingests and destroys foreign particles and cells
phagocytosis phagocytic (adj)	FAG-oh-sigh-**TOE**-sis fag-oh-**SIT**-ik	S/ S/	-osis *condition* -ic *pertaining to*	Process of ingestion and destruction
plasma cell	**PLAZ**-mah SELL		**plasma**, Greek, *something formed*	Cell derived from B lymphocytes and active in formation of antibodies
spleen	SPLEEN		Greek *spleen*	Vascular, lymphatic organ in the left upper quadrant of the abdomen
splenectomy splenomegaly (**Note:** The "ee" in **spleen** becomes "e" for easier pronunciation.)	sple-**NECK**-toe-me sple-noh-**MEG**-ah-lee	S/ R/CF S/	-ectomy *excision* splen/o- *spleen* -megaly *enlargement*	Surgical removal of the spleen Enlarged spleen
tonsil tonsillectomy	**TON**-sill ton-sih-**LEC**-toh-me	S/ R/	Latin *tonsil* -ectomy *excision* tonsill- *tonsil*	Mass of lymphoid tissue on either side of the throat at the back of the tongue Surgical removal of the tonsils
tonsillitis	ton-sih-**LIE**-tis	S/	-itis *inflammation*	Inflammation of the tonsils

Adenoids are similar tissue on the posterior wall of the nasopharynx *(see Chapter 9)*. The tonsils and adenoids form lymphocytes and antibodies, trap bacteria and viruses, and drain them into the tonsillar lymph nodes for elimination. They can become infected themselves.

Thymus Gland

The thymus gland has both endocrine *(see Chapter 14)* and lymphatic functions. T cells develop and mature in it and are released into the bloodstream. The thymus is largest in infancy and childhood and reaches its maximum size at puberty. It then regresses and is eventually replaced by fibrous and adipose tissue *(Figure 15.5)*.

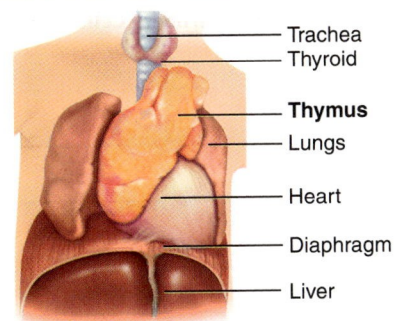

Trachea
Thyroid
Thymus
Lungs
Heart
Diaphragm
Liver

▲ **FIGURE 15.5   Large Thymus in an Infant.**

EXERCISES   Elements. *Knowledge of elements is your best key to understanding medical terminology. Reinforce that knowledge with the following exercise. Circle the best choice.*

1. In the term **adenoid**, one of the elements means:

   tissue   organ   gland

2. The element -osis means:

   a condition   pertaining to   a procedure

3. The prefix in **macrophage** identifies:

   color   location   size

4. The suffix in **phagocyte** means:

   cyst   cell   mass

5. The prefix co- means:

   next to   with   under

6. The root -phage means:

   flow   eat   produce

7. This suffix means *enlargement:*

   -oid   -megaly   -ectomy

OBJECTIVES

The study of the immune system is called **immunology.** The medical specialist involved in the study and research of the immune system and in treating disorders of the immune system is called an **immunologist.** The information in this lesson will enable you to:

- **Define the immune system and its specificity.**
- **Contrast cellular and humoral immunity.**
- **Describe the life histories of B cells and T cells.**
- **Explain the structure and actions of antibodies.**
- **Discuss some common disorders of the immune system, including HIV and AIDS.**

You are

...a laboratory technician working the night shift at Fulwood Medical Center.

Your patient is

...Mr. Michael Cowan, a 40-year-old homeless man and drug addict, who has presented to the emergency department with a high fever for which no cause is obvious on clinical examination.

CASE REPORT 15.2

You are called to the emergency room to take blood from Mr. Cowan. You have inserted the needle into an antecubital vein when he starts jerking his arm around and trying to get off the gurney. In the struggle, the needle comes out of the vein and pricks your hand through your glove.

As you immediately *flush* and *clean* the wound, *report* the incident, seek *immediate medical attention,* and go through your *initial medical evaluation,* it is essential that you have knowledge about your immune system and its response to the potential infection. Then you can make *informed decisions* about your treatment and future employment.

You will be asked to fill out your incident report at the end of this chapter.

Keynote

The immune system is not an organ system, but a group of specialized cells.

Receptors on the surface of T cells and B cells recognize specific nonself antigens.

THE IMMUNE SYSTEM

The immune system is a group of specialized cells in different parts of the body that recognize foreign substances and neutralize them. It is the third line of defense listed at the beginning of this chapter. When the immune system is functioning correctly, it protects the body against bacteria, viruses, cancer cells, and foreign substances. When the immune system is weak, it allows pathogens (including the viruses that cause common colds and "flu") and cancer cells to successfully invade the body.

Three characteristics distinguish immunity from the first two lines of defense:

1. **Specificity**—The immune response is directed against a particular pathogen. Immunity to one pathogen does not confer immunity to others. Specificity has one disadvantage. If a virus or a bacterium changes a component of its genetic code, it will lead to a change in the structure and/or physiology of the microorganism, which then is no longer recognized by the immune system. This **mutation** occurs, for example, with bacteria in response to antibiotics and in HIV's response to anti-HIV drugs (development of **resistance**).

2. **Memory**—When exposure to the same identical pathogen occurs again, the immune system recognizes the pathogen and has its responses ready to act quickly.

3. **Discrimination**—The immune system learns to recognize agents (antigens) that represent **"self"** and agents that are **"nonself"** (foreign). Most of this recognition is developed prior to birth. A variety of disorders occur when this discrimination breaks down. They are known as autoimmune disorders.

WORD	PRONUNCIATION	ELEMENTS		DEFINITION
discrimination	**DIS**-krim-ih-**NAY**-shun	S/ P/ R/	**-ation** *process* **dis-** *away from* **-crimin-** *distinguish*	Ability to distinguish between different things
hapten	**HAP**-ten		Greek *to fasten or bind*	Small molecule that has to bind to a larger molecule to form an antigen
mutation	myu-**TAY**-shun		Latin *to change*	Change in the chemistry of a gene
resistance resistant	ree-**ZIS**-tants ree-**ZIS**-tant	S/ R/ S/	**-ance** *state of* **resist-** *withstand an effect* **-ant** *pertaining to*	Ability of an organism to withstand the effects of an antagonistic agent Able to resist
specific	speh-**SIF**-ik	S/ R/	**-ic** *pertaining to* **specif-** *species*	Relating to a particular entity
specificity	spes-ih-**FIS**-ih-tee	S/	**-ity** *condition, state*	State of having a fixed relation to a particular entity

An **antigen** is any molecule that triggers an immune response. Some antigens are free molecules, such as toxins. Others are components of a cell membrane or a bacterial cell wall. Most antigens are large, complex molecules with a unique structure. It is this uniqueness that enables your body to distinguish its own (self) molecules from foreign (nonself) molecules.

Some small foreign molecules, called **haptens,** are too small to generate their own antigenic response; they attach themselves to host molecules, forming large, unique complexes that the body recognizes as foreign.

Keynote

Haptens are found in cosmetics, detergents, dust particles, industrial chemicals, poison ivy, and animal dander.

EXERCISES

Build your knowledge of elements and their meaning by matching the element in column 1 with the definition in column 2. One answer will be used twice.

_____ 1. -crimin-

_____ 2. -ity

_____ 3. specif-

_____ 4. -ant

_____ 5. dis-

_____ 6. -ation

_____ 7. -ic

_____ 8. -ance

A. species

B. away from

C. distinguish

D. process

E. pertaining to

F. condition, state

G. state of

IMMUNITY

Immunity is classified biologically into two types, though both mechanisms often respond to the same antigen:

1. **Cellular (cell-mediated) immunity**—a direct form of defense based on the actions of lymphocytes to attack foreign and diseased cells and destroy them. The many different types of T cells, B cells, and macrophages described in the previous lesson of this chapter are involved in this style of attack.

2. **Humoral (antibody-mediated) immunity** is an indirect form of attack that employs antibodies produced by plasma cells, which have been developed from B cells. The antibodies bind to an antigen and thus tag them for destruction.

These antibodies are called **immunoglobulins (Ig)**, defensive gamma globulins in the blood plasma and body secretions. There are five classes of antibodies:

- **IgG** makes up about 80% of the antibodies. It is found in plasma and tissue fluids. It crosses the placenta to give the fetus some immunity.

- **IgA** makes up about 13% of the antibodies. It is found in exocrine secretions such as breast milk, tears, saliva, nasal secretions, intestinal juices, bile, and urine.

- **IgM** makes up about 6% of antibodies. It develops in response to antigens in food or bacteria.

- **IgD** is found on the surface of B cells and acts as a receptor for antigens.

- **IgE** is found in exocrine secretions along with IgA.

Once released by plasma cells, the antibodies function in several ways to make antigens harmless, including:

- **Neutralization**—by binding to the antigen and masking it.

- **Agglutination**—an antibody binds to two or more bacteria to prevent them spreading through the tissues.

- **Precipitation**—antibodies create an antigen–antibody complex that is too heavy to stay in solution. The complex precipitates (drops out of solution) and can be ingested and destroyed by phagocytes.

- **Complement fixation**—The complement system is a group of 20 or more proteins continually present in blood plasma; IgG and IgM bind to foreign cells, initiating the **binding of complement** to the cell and leading to its destruction. Complement fixation is the major defense mechanism against bacteria and mismatched blood cells.

Based on the production or acquisition of antibodies, four classes of immunity can be described:

1. **Natural active immunity**—the production of your own antibodies as a result of normal maturation, pregnancy, or an infection.

2. **Artificial active immunity**—the production of your own antibodies as a result of **vaccination** or **immunization**. A vaccine consists of either killed or **attenuated** (weakened) pathogens (antigens).

3. **Natural passive immunity**—a temporary immunity from acquiring antibodies from another individual. This occurs for the fetus through the placenta (IgG) or for the infant through breast milk (IgA).

4. **Artificial passive immunity**—a temporary immunity from the injection of an **immune serum** from another individual or an animal. Immune serum is used to treat snakebite, tetanus, and rabies.

Keynote

The immune system is thought to be able to produce some 2 million different antibodies.

Antibodies do not actively destroy an antigen. They render it harmless and mark it for destruction by phagocytes.

Abbreviations

IgA	immunoglobulin A
IgD	immunoglobulin D
IgE	immunoglobulin E
IgG	immunoglobulin G
IgM	immunoglobulin M

Keynote

Antibodies can be produced naturally in response to an antigen or artificially in response to immunizations and vaccines.

WORD ANALYSIS AND DEFINITION

WORD	PRONUNCIATION	ELEMENTS		DEFINITION
agglutination agglutinate (verb)	ah-glue-tih-**NAY**-shun ah-**GLUE**-tin-ate	S/ R/	**-ation** *process* **agglutin-** *sticking together, clumping*	Process by which cells or other particles adhere to each other to form clumps Stick together to form clumps
attenuate attenuated (adj)	ah-**TEN**-you-ate ah-**TEN**-you-a-ted	S/ R/	**-ate** *action* **attenu-** *to weaken*	Weaken the ability of an organism to produce disease
complement	**KOM**-pleh-ment		Latin *that which completes*	Group of proteins in serum that finish off the work of antibodies to destroy bacteria and other cells
immune serum (also called **antiserum**)	im-**YUNE SEER**-um		**immune,** Latin *protected from* **serum,** Latin *whey*	Serum taken from another human or animal that has antibodies to a disease
vaccine vaccinate (verb) vaccination	**VAK**-seen **VAK**-sin-ate vak-sih-**NAY**-shun	 S/ R/ S/	Latin *relating to a cow* **-ate** *action* **vaccin-** *giving a vaccine* **-ation** *process*	Preparation to generate active immunity To administer a vaccine Administration of a vaccine

EXERCISES

*Organize the important information about immunity. The **language of immunology** will help you understand the questions and provide the answers. Refer to this exercise for test review. Fill in the blanks.*

1. Name the two types of immunity and how they function:

   a. _____

   b. _____

2. Which of the types of immunity in question 1 is a direct defense, and which is an indirect form of attack?

   Direct: _____

   Indirect: _____

3. What type of cells produce antibodies? _____

4. Are antibodies produced in direct or indirect defense? _____

5. What is the correct term for these particular antibodies? _____

6. What are the main functions of antibodies?

   a. _____

   b. _____

   c. _____

   d. _____

DISORDERS OF THE IMMUNE SYSTEM

Hypersensitivity is an excessive immune response to an antigen that would normally be tolerated. Hypersensitivity includes:

- **Allergies,** reactions to environmental antigens such as pollens, molds, and dusts; to foods such as peanuts, shellfish, and eggs; to plants like poison ivy; to drugs such as penicillin; and asthma to inhaled antigens (see below)

- Abnormal reactions to your *own* tissues (**autoimmune disorders**)

- Reactions to tissues **transplanted** from *another* person (**alloimmune disorders**)

In most allergic (hypersensitivity) reactions, allergens (antigens) bind to IgE on the membranes of basophils and mast cells *(see Chapter 7)* and, within seconds of exposure, stimulate the cells to produce histamine. This triggers vasodilation, increased capillary permeability, and smooth muscle spasms. The symptoms produced by these changes include edema, mucus hypersecretion and congestion, watery eyes, hives (urticaria), and sometimes cramps, diarrhea, and vomiting.

Anaphylaxis is an acute, immediate, and severe allergic reaction. It can be relieved by antihistamines.

Anaphylactic shock is more severe and is characterized by dyspnea due to bronchiole constriction, circulatory shock, and sometimes death. It is a life-threatening medical emergency and requires immediate epinephrine and circulatory support.

Asthma is triggered by allergens (as listed above) and by air pollutants, drugs, and emotions. These all stimulate plasma cells to secrete IgE, which binds to cells in the respiratory mucosa and releases a mixture of histamine and interleukins. Within minutes, the bronchioles constrict spasmodically (bronchospasm), leading to the wheezing and coughing of asthma.

Autoimmune disorders are an overvigorous response of the immune system in which the immune system fails to distinguish self-antigens from foreign antigens. These self-antigens produce autoantibodies that attack the body's own tissues. This type of response occurs, for example, in lupus erythematosus, type 1 diabetes, multiple sclerosis, rheumatoid arthritis, and psoriasis.

Immunodeficiency disorders are a deficient response of the immune system in which it fails to respond vigorously enough. They are in three categories:

1. **Congenital** (inborn)—caused by a genetic abnormality that is often sex-linked *(see Chapter 21)*, so that boys are affected more often than girls. An example from among the 20 or more congenital immunodeficiency diseases is **inherited combined immunodeficiency disease** in which there is an absence of both T cells and B cells. These children are very susceptible to opportunistic infections and must live in protective sterile enclosures *(Figure 15.7)*.

2. **Immunosuppression**—is a common side effect of corticosteroids in treatment to prevent transplant rejection and in chemotherapy treatment for cancer. These drugs reduce the numbers of all lymphocytes, making it possible for opportunistic infections to invade the body.

3. **Acquired immunodeficiency**—resulting from diseases such as **acquired immunodeficiency syndrome (AIDS)** that involve a severely depressed immune system from infection with the **human immunodeficiency virus (HIV)**.

▲ **FIGURE 15.7 Boy with Combined Immunodeficiency Disease in Protective Sterile Enclosure.**

Abbreviations

AIDS acquired immunodeficiency syndrome
HIV human immunodeficiency virus

Immunology of Transplantation

The success of any organ transplantation is based on control of the recipient's immune system to prevent rejection of the **allograft,** tissue from another individual of the same species.

Transplant immunity is designed to cause rejection, and both cellular and humoral defense mechanisms are involved. To try and prevent this, recipient and donor must match at both the HLA and ABO *(see Chapter 7)* types. A combination of immunosuppressive drugs is used to control graft rejection, but the drugs have adverse side effects on the recipient. One combination is corticosteroids with cyclosporine or FK506. Other drugs are in clinical trials.

WORD	PRONUNCIATION	ELEMENTS		DEFINITION
allogen allogenic (adj) allograft	**AL**-oh-jen al-oh-**JEN**-ik **AL**-oh-graft	S/ R/CF S/	-gen *producing* all/o- *strange, other* -graft *tissue for transplant*	Antigen from someone else in the same species Skin graft from another person or cadaver
alloimmune	**AL**-oh-im-**YUNE**	P/ R/	allo- *strange, other* -immune *immune response*	Reaction directed against foreign tissue
anaphylaxis anaphylactic (adj)	**AN**-ah-fi-**LAK**-sis	P/ R/	ana- *away from* -phylaxis *protection*	Immediate severe allergic response
autoimmune	aw-toe-im-**YUNE**	P/ R/	auto- *self, same* -immune *immune response*	Immune reaction directed against a person's own tissue
hypersensitivity	**HIGH**-per-sen-sih-**TIV**-ih-tee	S/ P/ R/	-ity *condition* hyper- *excessive* -sensitiv- *feeling*	Exaggerated abnormal reaction to an allergen
immunodeficiency	**IM**-you-noh-dee-**FISH**-en-see	S/ R/CF R/	-ency *quality* immun/o- *immune response* -defici- *failure*	Failure of the immune system
immunosuppression	**IM**-you-noh-suh-**PRESH**-un	S/ R/CF R/	-ion *process* immun/o- *immune response* -suppress- *pressed under*	Failure of the immune system caused by an outside agent
transplant	**TRANZ**-plant	P/ R/	trans- *across* -plant *plant*	The tissue or organ used, or the act of transferring tissue from one person to another
transplantation	**TRANZ**-plan-**TAY**-shun	S/	-ation *process, action*	The moving of tissue or an organ from one person or place to another

---

EXERCISES

Build more medical vocabulary for immunology. Complete the construction of the term by using the following elements to fill in the blanks.

phylaxis	defici	ion	sensitiv	ity	auto
hyper	allo	suppress	logy	histo	ency

1. exaggerated, abnormal reaction to an allergen: _____/_____/ity

2. failure of the immune system: immuno/_____/_____

3. reaction directed against foreign tissue: _____/immune

4. Immediate, severe, allergic response: ana/_____

5. immune reaction directed against self: _____/immune

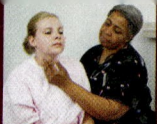

H. Discussion: You may choose from either topic for your discussion/presentation.

1. There are four classes of immunity described in this chapter: natural active, artificial active, natural passive, and artificial passive. Pick any two of these classes, and compare and contrast them. How do you acquire these immunities? Give examples. Prepare a five-minute class presentation on your topic. *You should be able to define any medical terms you use in your presentation.* Hand your notes and outline of your presentation in to the instructor.

2. Your body has three lines of defense mechanisms against foreign organisms that may harm you. Answer the questions: which types of organisms seek to harm you; what are the three lines of defense your body puts up; give examples of each type of defense mechanism, and how they act against foreign organisms. Prepare a five-minute class presentation on your topic. *You should be able to define any medical terms you use in your presentation.* Hand your notes and outline of your presentation in to the instructor.

I. Language of Immunology: Challenge your knowledge of the immune system and employ the *language of immunology* to answer the following questions. Circle the correct choice.

1. Choose the correct pair of spellings:

   a. tonsel   tonselectomy

   b. tonsil   tonsillectomy

   c. tonssil   tonsilectomy

   d. tonsill   tonsilectomy

   e. tonnsil   tonsillectomy

2. This triggers vasodilation in an allergic response:

   a. interferon

   b. complement fixation

   c. histamine

   d. hormones

   e. antihistamine

3. The largest lymphatic vessel is the:

   a. thoracic duct

   b. lymph node

   c. spleen

   d. lymphatic duct

   e. aorta

4. Kaposi sarcoma is a form of:

   a. lymphadenitis

   b. skin cancer

   c. lymphadenopathy

   d. lung cancer

   e. lymphoma

5. Ingestion and destruction of tissue debris and bacteria is called:

   a. lymphadenitis

   b. phagocytosis

   c. lymphadenopathy

   d. filariasis

   e. macrophage

6. Life-threatening medical emergency that cannot be relieved by antihistamines:

   a. asthma

   b. anaphylaxis

   c. Kaposi sarcoma

   d. anaphylactic shock

   e. urticaria

7. An allergic reaction is one of:

   a. hypoglycemia

   b. hypersensitivity

   c. hypotension

   d. hyperglycemia

   e. hypertension

8. White pulp and red pulp can be found in the:

   a. lymph nodes

   b. spleen

   c. lymph vessels

   d. none of these

   e. all of these

9. "Elevated body temperature" is another name for:

   a. pathogen

   b. pyrexia

   c. precipitation

   d. protease

   e. phagocytosis

LYMPHATIC AND IMMUNE SYSTEMS

J. Language of Immunology: Challenge your knowledge of the immune system and employ the *language of immunology* to answer the following questions. Circle the correct choice.

1. Which disease is likely to cause enlarged lymph nodes under the jaw?

   a. tonsillitis

   b. lymphoma

   c. hypersplenism

   d. asthma

   e. urticaria

2. Abnormal, cancerous B cells are known as:

   a. macrophages

   b. osteoblasts

   c. Reed-Sternberg cells

   d. killer cells

   e. phagocytes

3. Lymph nodes accessible for palpation are in the:

   a. neck

   b. axilla

   c. groin

   d. all of these

   e. only a and c

4. Lymphatic capillaries and vessels do not penetrate:

   a. the liver

   b. the CNS

   c. the thoracic duct

   d. the left subclavian vein

   e. the tonsils

5. Immunosuppressive drugs are given after:

   a. organ transplant

   b. anaphylactic shock

   c. retrovirus

   d. opportunistic infection

   e. viral load count

6. Serum used to treat a snakebite is an example of:

   a. natural active immunity

   b. artificial active immunity

   c. natural passive immunity

   d. artificial passive immunity

   e. none of the above

K. **Recall and Review:** How well do you remember these word elements from the previous chapter? Try to answer without first looking back to check. Fill in the blanks.

Element	Type of Element (P, R, CF, S)	Meaning of Element
mela		
ren		
vas/o		
megaly		
pro		

L. **Prefixes:** All of the following terms are lacking their prefix. After you have entered the prefix *on* the line, write the meaning of the prefix *under* the line. Fill in the blanks.

1. reaction directed against foreign tissue: _____/immune

2. substance produced in response to an antigen: _____/body

3. surface protein that enhances sensitivity of antigen receptor: _____/recept/or

4. spleen removes blood components at an excessive rate: _____splen/ism

5. virus with an RNA core: _____/virus

M. **Translation:** First, use your knowledge of medical terminology to understand the statement. Then, organize your thoughts and formulate your answer in layman's terms that a patient could understand. Write an explanation of each sentence on the lines below.

1. Pyrexia is a defense mechanism because it inhibits reproduction of bacteria and viruses and accelerates tissue repair.

   _____

   _____

   _____

2. Intra-abdominal hemorrhage from the ruptured spleen can be extensive, with dramatic hypotension, and is a surgical emergency requiring splenectomy.

   _____

   _____

   _____

N. **Suffixes:** Use your knowledge of word elements from this and previous chapters. Take a basic root/combining form, add a variety of suffixes, and change the meaning different ways to form six new terms. Fill in the chart, then fill in the blanks.

Root/CF	Suffix	Meaning of Term
Lymphaden		Neoplasm of lymphatic tissue
Lymphaden		Inflammation of a lymph node
Lympho		Small white blood cell with large nucleus
Lymphaden		Removal of a lymph node
Lympha		Pertaining to lymph
Lymphadeno		Any disease process affecting a lymph node

1. Which of the above terms would be found in a surgeon's dictation? _____

2. Which of the above terms would a pathologist use? _____

3. Which term would an oncologist use in dictation? _____

4. Which of the above terms is a diagnosis? (There is more than one term.) _____

_____

O. **Patient Documentation:** Apply your knowledge of medical language to the following case report about Mr. Holman.
- Read the complete report.

Your patient is

. . . Mr. Eugene Holman, a 40-year-old male who is known to be HIV-positive and has been receiving treatment with efavirenz, zidovudine, and lamivudine. However, in the past couple of months, he has not been taking his medication regularly. In the previous week, he has noticed a progressive shortness of breath and a nonproductive cough. VS are T 102°F, P 120, R 32, BP 110/60. He is anxious and dyspneic but not cyanotic. His breath sounds are clear, with no rales or rhonci heard. You have called Dr. Vandenberg to see him.

Mr. Holman's chest x-ray showed bilateral, diffuse, fluffy infiltrates spreading out from the hila. Bronchial lavage with laboratory examination showed *Pneumocystis jirovec.* His CD4 count was 140. Mr. Holman had developed an opportunistic infection, which is now thought to be a fungus.

- Read it a second time, underlining the medical terminology that will help you answer the questions.

1. What is the meaning of the abbreviation HIV?

_____

_____

2. For what reason might Mr. Holman not be taking his medication?

_____

_____

3. What symptoms did Mr. Holman note in the previous week?

_____

_____

4. How could the physician tell the patient was not cyanotic?

_____

_____

5. What does **dyspneic** mean?

_____

_____

6. If a cough is *nonproductive,* what does that mean?

_____

_____

7. Describe rales: _____

_____

_____

8. Describe rhonchi: _____

_____

_____

9. How does the physician assess for rales and rhonci? _____

_____

_____

10. Mr. Holman's infiltrate was bilateral—what does that mean?

_____

_____

11. What procedure did Mr. Holman undergo?

_____

_____

12. Why does this patient have an opportunistic infection?

_____

_____

13. There is another abbreviation that could have been inserted in this case report but was not. Rewrite the sentence that could contain an additional abbreviation.

_____

_____

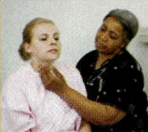

LYMPHATIC AND IMMUNE SYSTEMS

P.   Immunology Terminology: Increase your knowledge of the *language of immunology.* The element's meaning is given to you in column 1. List the element in column 2 and identify the type of element in column 3. In the last column, give an example of a medical term containing that element.

Meaning of Element	Element	Type of Element (P, R, CF, S)	Medical Term Containing That Element
strange, other			
tissue			
across			
backward			
sleep			
fluid			
against			
large			
with			
condition			
disease			
lymphatic vessels			

Q. **Patient Education:** Explain to your patients, in words they can understand, the difference among:

edema: _____

_____

_____

peripheral edema: _____

_____

_____

pitting edema: _____

_____

_____

lymphedema: _____

_____

_____

R. **Latin and Greek elements cannot be further deconstructed into prefix, root, or suffix.** You must know them for what they are. Test your knowledge of these elements with the following exercise. Match the meaning in column 1 with the correct medical term in column 2.

_____	1. protected from	A.	mediate
_____	2. that which completes	B.	hapten
_____	3. none	C.	lymph
_____	4. to fasten or bind	D.	lavage
_____	5. divide in the middle	E.	mutation
_____	6. a knot	F.	complement
_____	7. to change	G.	edema
_____	8. to wash	H.	immune
_____	9. swelling	I.	null
_____	10. clear spring water	J.	node

LYMPHATIC AND IMMUNE SYSTEMS

CHAPTER SUMMARY EXERCISE

1. *Listen to the pronunciation of the medical terms as given by your instructor.*
2. *Circle the correct spelling of the medical term.*
3. *Match the correctly spelled terms to the brief descriptions below.*
4. *Write a sentence for each of the 15 terms that appear in this exercise.*

A. SPELLING COMPREHENSION: CIRCLE THE CORRECT SPELLING OF THE TERM.

1. pagocyossis	phaggocytosis	pagocytosis	phagocytosis	phagocytossis
2. pirexia	pyrexxia	pyirexia	phirexia	pyrexia
3. attenuated	atenuated	atinuated	attinuated	ateenuated
4. addenoid	adinoid	adenoid	adennoid	adinoyd
5. urrtickaria	errticaria	urtickaria	urticaria	urrticaria
6. imunization	immunisation	imunnization	immunization	imunisation
7. pagocytize	phagositize	phagocitize	pagocitize	phagocytize
8. vacination	vacation	vacinnation	vaccination	vackination
9. imunoglobulin	immunogobulin	imunogobulin	immunoglobulin	imunnogobulin
10. interstitial	intersisteal	insterstial	interstissial	interstittial
11. agluetinate	aglutinate	agglutinate	agluetenate	agglutenate
12. sytotoxic	cytotoxxic	sytotoxxic	cytotoxic	cytoxic
13. lymphangiogram	limpangiogram	lymangiogram	lymphangeogram	lymphangiogrim
14. macropage	macrophage	micropage	microphage	maccropage
15. oportunistick	oporrtunistic	opportinistic	opportunistic	opportunistick

B. MATCH THE NUMBER OF THE CORRECT TERM IN PART A WITH THE BRIEF DESCRIPTION OF THE TERM BELOW.

a. killer of cells   _____

b. act of administering a vaccine   _____

c. cell that performs the action in question 7 of part A   _____

d. obtaining immunity by administration of a killed agent   _____

e. an organism or disease in a host with lowered resistance   _____

f. fever   _____

g. stick together to form clumps   _____

h. fluid that surrounds cells   _____

i. to ingest foreign bacteria   _____

j. lymphatic tissue in the nasopharynx   _____

k. radiograph images of lymph vessels after injecting contrast material   _____

l. weakens ability of organism to produce disease   _____

m. ingest and destroy tissue debris and bacteria   _____

n. rash of itchy wheals   _____

o. protein of an antibody   _____

C. USING YOUR KNOWLEDGE OF TERMS 1-15 IN PART A AND THEIR CORRECT SPELLING, WRITE A BRIEF SENTENCE AS IT MIGHT APPEAR IN PATIENT DOCUMENTATION.

1. _____

2. _____

3. _____

4. _____

5. _____

6. _____

7. _____

8. _____

9. _____

10. _____

11. _____

12. _____

13. _____

14. _____

15. _____

D. GO TO THE STUDENT CD. OPEN THE GLOSSARY AND PRACTICE YOUR PRONUNCIATION OF THE TERMS IN PART A OF THIS EXERCISE.

Life Span
The Language of Pediatrics and Gerontology

CASE REPORT 16.1

You are

. . . a pediatric medical assistant working with Sandra Mendes, MD, a pediatrician at Fulwood Medical Center. You are working in her well-baby clinic.

Your patients are

. . . 8-week-old Carol Hotteling and her mother, Mrs. Anna Hotteling, a 35-year-old executive in a book publishing company. Mrs. Hotteling's first baby, was born normally at term, weighed 7 pounds and 2 ounces. She had normal Apgar scores. Carol had persistent jaundice when seen at two weeks of age. She is being breast-fed. Using holidays and sick leave, her mother has managed to obtain three months leave of absence from work.

You ask Mrs. Hotteling if she has any concerns.

Learning Outcomes

In order to understand the growth and development of children, adults, and the elderly and communicate about this with your employer, other health professionals, and patients, you need to be able to:

- Apply the languages of pediatrics and gerontology to the anatomy, physiology, and psychology of human growth and development.

- Comprehend, analyze, spell, and write the medical terms of pediatrics and gerontology so that you communicate and document accurately and precisely in any health care setting.

- Recognize and pronounce the medical terms of pediatrics and gerontology so that you communicate verbally with accuracy and precision in any health care setting.

- Explain the effects of disorders in growth and development on health.

LESSON 16.1 Neonatal Period

OBJECTIVES

In order to be able to understand where **neonates** are in their development and to talk to mothers and other health professionals about this, you need to be able to use correct medical terminology as you:

- **Describe the anatomic and physiologic adaptations that occur at birth.**
- **Discuss the normal neonatal development of anatomic, physiologic, and psychologic functions.**
- **Explain congenital anomalies that interfere with normal anatomic and physiologic development.**
- **Recognize common causes of disorders in growth and development in the neonatal period.**

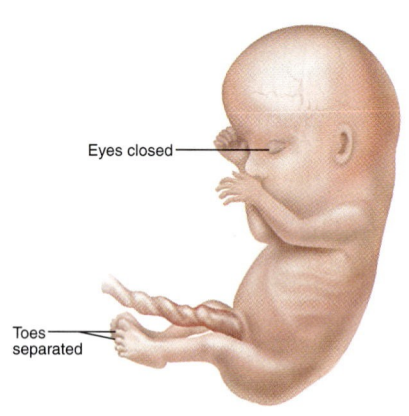

▲ **FIGURE 16.1 Fetus at Eight Weeks (56 Days).**

Eyes closed

Toes separated

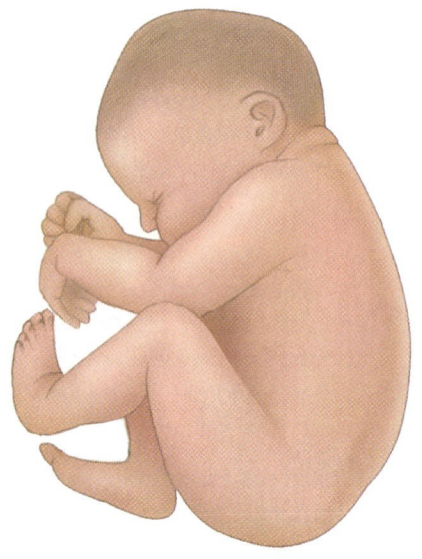

▲ **FIGURE 16.2 Full-Term Infant (38 Weeks).**

Abbreviation

SIDS sudden infant death syndrome

NEONATAL ADAPTATIONS

"It's incredibly disturbing to be pushed out of the warm, dark, liquid environment in which I've lived for nine months. All my food has been supplied, and I've had nobody else to interact with. Suddenly, I'm squeezed down a narrow passage that hurts my head, out into a brightly lit, noisy place. Someone says 'breathe' and cuts off my source of nourishment, my **umbilical cord.** How *do* I breathe? Where do I find the right food? What's going to happen to me next?"

"I'm not even fully developed. I've got to change the way blood circulates through me so that I can get this stuff called oxygen to my cells on my own. My liver and kidneys aren't fully functional, my bones are still developing, and my nervous system isn't mature. What am I expected to do? Am I supposed to know **innately** what it's all about?"

Case Report 16.1 (continued)

Mrs. Anna Hotteling, the mother, has several areas of concern. A friend's baby recently died of **SIDS (sudden infant death syndrome).** How can she prevent this for her child? Carol wants to feed every two to three hours day and night, and she (Anna) is exhausted. How long will this go on, and for how long should she continue breast-feeding? Mrs. Hotteling also wants to know what her baby can see and how she should communicate with her.

Fetal life is a preparation for birth. At the end of the first eight weeks of fetal life, all the organ systems are in place *(Figure 16.1)*. From then until birth, the organs grow and acquire the functional capabilities to support life outside the mother. Sometimes a part of this process will fail, and the fetus can have a developmental abnormality.

At birth, normal organ development is not yet complete, but the neonate suddenly has to **adapt** to a totally different environment *(Figure 16.2)*. Each of the organ systems has to adapt to the new environment and then go on to complete its development during childhood. This developmental process is why children are not just "little adults," and why there is a specialty of **pediatrics** practiced by **pediatricians.**

The first four weeks after birth, the **neonatal period,** is the time for the most rapid adaptations of the organ systems. In this lesson, you will review normal adaptations in the neonatal period and see what effects failure of development and failure of adaptation can have on the neonate.

WORD ANALYSIS AND DEFINITION

WORD	PRONUNCIATION	ELEMENTS		DEFINITION
adaptation adapt (verb)	ad-ap-**TAY**-shun a-**DAPT**	S/ R/	-ation *action* adapt- *to adjust*	Change in function or structure of an organ to meet new conditions
congenital	kon-**JEN**-ih-tal	S/ P/ R/	-al *pertaining to* con- *with* -genit- *birth*	Present at birth, either inherited or due to an event during gestation up to the moment of birth
geriatrics (*Note:* This term consists only of two roots.)	jer-ee-**AT**-riks	R/ R/	-iatrics *healing* ger- *old age*	Medical specialty that deals with the problems of old age
gerontology	jer-on-**TOL**-oh-jee	S/ R/CF	-logy *study of* geront/o- *aging*	Study of the process and problems of aging
gerontologist	jer-on-**TOL**-oh-jist	S/	-logist *one who studies*	Medical specialist in gerontology
innate innately (adj)	ih-**NATE**	P/ R/	in- *in* -nate *birth*	Present at birth; arising from the intellect
neonate	**NEE**-oh-nate	P/ R/	neo- *new* -nate *born*	A newborn infant
neonatal (adj)	**NEE**-oh-**NAY**-tal	S/	-al *pertaining to*	Pertaining to the newborn infant
pediatrics	pee-dee-**AT**-riks	S/ R/ R/	-ics *knowledge* -iatr- *medical treatment* ped- *child*	Medical specialty of treating children during development from birth through adolescence
pediatrician	**PEE**-dee-ah-**TRISH**-an	S/	-ician *expert, specialist*	Medical specialist in pediatrics
umbilicus	um-**BIL**-ih kus		Latin *navel*	Pit in the abdomen where the umbilical cord entered the fetus
umbilical	um-**BIL**-ih-kal	S/ R/	-al *pertaining to* umbilic- *umbilicus*	Pertaining to the umbilicus or the center of the abdomen

EXERCISES

Spelling. *Test your ability to recognize and correctly spell the following medical terms, which come from the **language of pediatrics**. The correct term is given to you in a word scramble in column 1—unscramble the term, and write it on the blank. A brief definition is given in column 2 to help you determine the correct term you need. Remember: The answer is not acceptable unless it is spelled correctly!*

1. otsoitlngrgeo   Medical specialist who treats aged population: _____

2. onteane   Newborn infant: _____

3. olgninaetc   Born with: _____

4. eirciatpdain   Medical specialist in treating children: _____

5. datintapapo   Change in organ function to meet new conditions: _____

6. itnaen   Present at birth: _____

7. iumlbcsui   Site where umbilical cord enters fetus: _____

8. terapiscdi   Medical specialty treating children: _____

9. ontgyrogleo   Study of the aging process: _____

10. dpata   To meet new conditions: _____

Employ the *languages of pediatrics and gerontology* in communication. Choose any three of the above terms and write a brief sentence for each term that is not a definition.

1. _____

2. _____

3. _____

NEONATAL ADAPTATIONS (continued)

Immediately after birth, the neonate is evaluated for her **Apgar score** at one minute and five minutes of life. The Apgar score gives health care providers an immediate assessment of the baby's condition at birth. The five parameters of *A*ctivity, *P*ulse, *G*rimace, *A*ppearance, and *R*espiration are scored on a three-point scale: 0 (poor), 1, or 2 (normal). Scores obtainable are between 0 and 10 *(Table 16.1)*. A score of 7 or above is normal. Below 7, the baby needs special immediate care, including oxygen and further airway **suctioning.**

The Apgar score does not predict long-term health, intellectual status, or outcome.

Cardiovascular System Adaptations

The **cardiovascular system (CVS)** changes from being dependent on the **placenta** and **umbilical cord** to provide oxygen and nutrients and to remove carbon dioxide and fetal wastes to being independent. The fetal heart pumps blood to the placenta through two umbilical arteries. Blood flows back to the fetus by a single umbilical vein. At birth, the two major divisions, the pulmonary and systemic circuits, become separate and operational.

Congenital cardiovascular defects are present in about 1% of births. Before birth an open vessel (**ductus arteriosus**) connects the aorta and pulmonary artery. Normally this closes within a few hours of birth. When it doesn't close, a **patent ductus arteriosus (PDA)** allows blood that should flow through the aorta to nourish the body to return to the lungs *(see Chapter 8)*. These children may grow slowly, tire easily, and catch pneumonia. A small patent ductus can close spontaneously. Medication with indomethacin can constrict the muscle in the wall. A plug can be inserted in the lumen of the PDA by using a **transcatheter.** The ductus can be closed by surgically tying it.

Septal defects occur when the baby is born with an opening in the septum (wall) that separates the right and left sides of the heart ("hole in the heart"). An opening between the two upper chambers is called an **atrial septal defect (ASD).** An opening between the two lower chambers is called a **ventricular septal defect (VSD)** *(see Chapter 8)*. Small defects often close spontaneously during the first year of life. If not, the defects can be closed by open-heart surgery.

Cyanotic heart defects occur when insufficient blood is being pumped to the lungs so that the blood being pumped to the body contains less oxygen than the tissues need. These neonates are called "blue babies" because of their cyanotic blue skin *(Figure 16.3)*. An example is the **tetralogy of Fallot (TOF),** in which four heart defects all shunt blood away from the lungs. These children do not grow normally, are dyspneic, and require open-heart surgery to correct the defects.

Abbreviations

ASD	atrial septal defect
CVS	cardiovascular system
PDA	patent ductus arteriosus
TOF	tetralogy of Fallot
VSD	ventricular septal defect

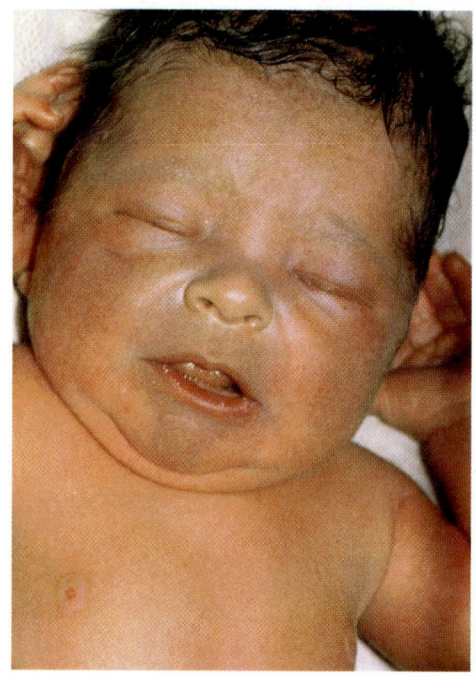

▲ **FIGURE 16.3 Cyanotic ("Blue") Baby.**

TABLE 16.1 Apgar Scoring

Apgar Sign			0	1	2
A		**Activity (muscle tone)**	Limp, no movement	Limbs flexed, little movement	Active spontaneous movement
P		**Pulse**	No pulse	Below 100 beats per minute	Above 100 beats per minute
G		**Grimace (responsiveness)**	No response to airway **suction**	Grimace only to airway suction	Pulls away from airway suction
A		**Appearance (skin color)**	Blue-gray all over	Pink, except hands and feet are bluish	Pink all over
R		**Respiration**	No breathing	Weak cry, gasping	Strong cry, normal breathing effort and rate

WORD	PRONUNCIATION	ELEMENTS		DEFINITION
Apgar score	**AP**-gar SKOR		Virginia Apgar, 1909–1974, U.S. anesthesiologist	Evaluation of newborn status
cyanosis	sigh-ah-**NO**-sis	S/ R/	-osis *condition* cyan- *blue*	Blue discoloration of the skin, lips, and nail beds due to low levels of oxygen in the blood
cyanotic (adj)	sigh-ah-**NOT**-ik	S/ R/CF	-tic *pertaining to* cyan/o- *blue*	Marked by cyanosis
defect defective (adj)	**DEE**-fect dee-**FEK**-tiv		Latin *to lack or fail*	An absence, malformation, or imperfection Imperfect
ductus arteriosus	**DUK**-tus ar-**TEER**-ih-**OH**-sus		Latin *duct that connects two arteries*	Fetal vessel that connects the descending aorta with the left pulmonary artery
Fallot	fah-**LOW**		Étienne-Louis A. Fallot, 1850–1911, French physician	First described this tetralogy of congenital heart defects
patent	**PAY**-tent		Latin *lie open*	Open
placenta	plah-**SEN**-tah		Latin *a cake*	Organ that allows metabolic interchange between the mother and fetus
suction suctioning	**SUK**-shun		Latin *sucking*	Use of a catheter to clear the upper airway or other tubes
tetralogy	te-**TRAL**-oh-jee	S/ R/	-logy *study of* tetra- *four*	A set of four congenital heart defects
transcatheter	trans-**KATH**-eh-ter	P/ R/	trans- *across* -catheter *catheter*	Catheter with a self-expanding mushroom device that is placed and left inside the PDA

EXERCISES

Patient Documentation. *Incorporate your knowledge of abbreviations from this lesson into the following patient documentation. Fill in the blanks, using the following choices. Use each answer only once.*

ASD   TOF   VSD   PDA

1. Diagnostic testing confirms _____, which is an opening between the two lower chambers of the infant's heart. Patient will be scheduled for open heart surgery early next week.

2. Admitting diagnosis: "blue baby," cyanotic heart defect. _____

3. The septal defect in this infant has been confirmed as being between the two upper heart chambers _____.

4. Child has had a history of failure to thrive and tires easily. Possible diagnosis is _____. I am referring him to a pediatric cardiologist.

*Use your knowledge of the **language of pediatrics** to match the statement in column l with the correct terminology in column 2.*

_____ 1. open-heart surgery   A. Apgar parameters

_____ 2. vessel is open before birth   B. umbilical arteries

_____ 3. fetal heart pumps blood to the placenta   C. ductus arteriosus

_____ 4. activity, pulse, grimace, appearance, respiration   D. septal defect

_____ 5. "hole in the heart"   E. repairs septal defects

Meconium is the first stool a baby passes.

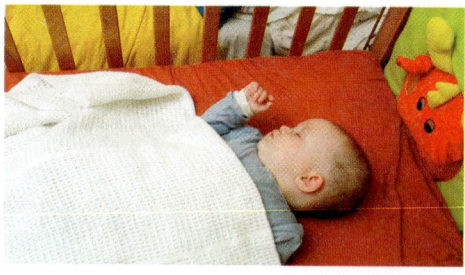

▲ **FIGURE 16.4 Infant Sleeping on Back.**

Abbreviations

CPAP continuous positive airway pressure
HMD hyaline membrane disease
RDS respiratory distress syndrome
SIDS sudden infant death syndrome
TTN transient tachypnea of the newborn

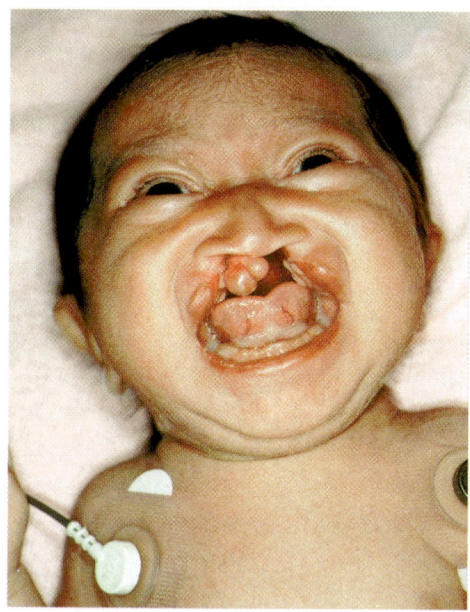

▲ **FIGURE 16.5 Infant with Cleft Lip and Palate.**

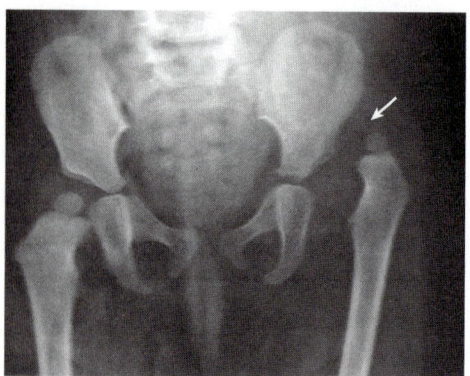

▲ **FIGURE 16.6 Newborn with Congenital Dislocation of the Left Hip.**

NEONATAL ADAPTATIONS (continued)

Respiratory Adaptations

Respiratory adaptations occur immediately at birth, and it is a myth that the baby has to be spanked at birth to stimulate the first breath. Unless the baby's respiratory function is depressed by too much sedation or anesthesia in the mother, the first breath is taken spontaneously.

The development of **surfactant** is a key to the development of fully functioning lungs. When surfactant is deficient, the lung alveoli collapse, and the exchange of gases cannot take place. This deficiency occurs in **premature infants** born before week 37 of gestation and produces **respiratory distress syndrome (RDS)** due to **hyaline membrane disease (HMD).** The more premature, the greater the risk of RDS. Infants with RDS are at risk for cerebral ischemia, hemorrhage, and neonatal death. Treatment of RDS is with respiratory support, including supplemental oxygen and/or **continuous positive airway pressure (CPAP)** when the infant can breathe spontaneously or, for the sicker infants, mechanical ventilation.

Synthetic surfactant instilled into the trachea reduces the severity of RDS.

Bronchopulmonary dysplasia is a chronic lung disorder that occurs in a few infants who have required mechanical ventilation for RDS over a prolonged period of time.

Meconium aspiration syndrome occurs in newborns who are stressed in utero or at the time of delivery. The distress causes the fetus to expel meconium (stool) into the amniotic fluid. Then deep gasping for breath by the distressed fetus causes the aspiration of meconium into the lungs. Treatment is by **intubation** to suck out the meconium-stained fluid.

Transient tachypnea of the newborn (TTN) occurs most often in C-section and **precipitate** (unduly rapid) vaginal deliveries. Amniotic fluid remains in the infant's lungs and causes a self-limiting respiratory distress.

Sudden infant death syndrome (SIDS) is thought to be caused by a failure of cardiorespiratory control mechanisms to mature. It is the sudden death of an infant during sleep for which no cause is found after a thorough investigation and autopsy. Risk of SIDS peaks between two and three months, and it is more common in males. It can be prevented by placing infants on their backs to sleep *(Figure 16.4)*. Soft pillows, mattress, and bedding, and an adult sharing a bed with the infant should be avoided. Pacifiers also have a protective effect.

Musculoskeletal Adaptations

The musculoskeletal system can fail **in utero** and produce congenital abnormalities in different parts of the newborn's body.

Craniofacial malformations are most often **cleft lip** and **cleft palate,** which occur once in 800 births *(Figure 16.5)*. The cleft varies from involvement of the soft palate only to a complete cleft of the soft and hard palates, the alveolar process of the maxilla, and the lip. A cleft palate interferes with feeding and speech development. The end-treatment is surgical closure.

Congenital dislocation of the hip occurs more commonly in female infants and following a breech delivery *(Figure 16.6)*. During a newborn examination, the pediatrician abducts and externally rotates the femur *(see Chapter 5)*. If the hip is dislocated, this produces an audible and palpable "clunk" as the head of the femur enters the acetabulum. Hip ultrasound can confirm the diagnosis. Treatment is with padded diapers to keep the affected femur abducted. Surgery may be necessary.

WORD ANALYSIS AND DEFINITION

WORD	PRONUNCIATION	ELEMENTS		DEFINITION
bronchopulmonary dysplasia	**BRONG**-koh-**PUL**-moh-nair-ee dis-**PLAY**-zee-ah	S/ R/CF R/ S/ P/ R/	-ary *pertaining to* bronch/o- *bronchus* -pulmon- *lung* -ia *condition* dys- *difficult, painful* -plas- *formation*	Chronic lung disorder in premature infants after prolonged mechanical ventilation
cleft lip cleft palate	KLEFT LIP KLEFT **PAL**-ate		**cleft** Latin *fissure, separation of parts*	Congenital defect of the upper lip Congenital defect of the upper palate
craniofacial	**KRAY**-nee-oh-**FAY**-shal	S/ R/CF R/	-al *pertaining to* crani/o- *cranium* -faci- *face*	Pertaining to both the face and cranium
hyaline membrane disease	**HIGH**-ah-line **MEM**-brain dis-**EEZ**	S/ R/ R/ P/ R/	-ine *pertaining to* hyal- *glass* membrane *cover* dis- *apart from* -ease *freedom from pain*	Respiratory distress syndrome of the newborn
intubation	**IN**-tyu-**BAY**-shun	S/ P/ R/	-ion *process* in- *in* -tubat- *tube*	Insertion of a tube into the trachea
in utero	in **YOU**-ter-oh	R/CF	uter/o *uterus*	Within the womb; not yet born
meconium	meh-**KOH**-nee-um		Greek *little poppy*	The first bowel movement of the newborn
precipitate	pree-**SIP**-ih-tate		Latin *to throw down headlong*	Precipitate labor is a very rapid labor and delivery
premature	pree-mah-**TYUR**	P/ R/	pre- *before* -mature *ripe*	Occurring before the expected time; for example, an infant born before 37 weeks of gestation
surfactant	ser-**FAK**-tant	S/ R/	-ant *forming* surfact- *surface*	A protein and fat compound that creates surface tension to hold lung alveolar walls apart

EXERCISES

Elements. *The following exercise will help build your knowledge of the elements in the* **language of pediatrics**. *Fill in the table.*

Medical Term	Meaning of Prefix	Meaning of Root/ CF	Meaning of Suffix	Meaning of Medical Term
dysplasia				
premature				
intubation				
craniofacial				
bronchopulmonary				
hyaline				
surfactant				

NEONATAL ADAPTATIONS (continued)

Brain and Neurological Adaptations

A newborn baby's brain is a work in progress. It is one-quarter of its adult size. The brain's growth is monitored by charting increases in head circumference.

At birth, only the spinal cord and brainstem are well developed. The cortex is primitive. All of the newborn's kicking, grasping, **rooting** (searching for the nipple), and crying behaviors are functions of the brainstem, which is why they are **involuntary** and not well coordinated.

The presence of a well-developed brainstem ensures the **neural** circuits for the most vital bodily functions—breathing, heartbeat, sleeping, sucking, and swallowing—are in place at birth.

Three involuntary newborn reflexes that are tested are brainstem reflexes. The **Moro**, or **startle, reflex** (the baby splays out her arms and slowly closes them in response to sudden movement), the **doll's eye maneuver** (the baby's eyes stay focused forward when her head is turned to one side), and the **stepping reflex** (the baby "walks" when she is held up with her feet touching a surface). Also, babies show a **Babinski sign** or extensor response to the **plantar reflex** when stimulation of the sole of the foot extends the toes upwards and fans them out instead of flexing them inwards. As the cortex develops over the next two to three months, all these reflexes disappear.

Congenital neurological abnormalities include:

- **Anencephaly**—absence of the cerebral hemispheres. This is incompatible with life.

- **Microcephaly**—small cerebral hemispheres, leading to motor and mental retardation.

- **Encephalocele**—a protrusion of nervous tissue and meninges through a defect in the skull.

- **Hydrocephalus**—enlargement of the ventricles with excessive **cerebrospinal fluid (CSF)**. This is the most common cause of a large head in the neonate *(see Chapter 10)*.

- **Spina bifida** is a failure of the vertebral column to close over the spinal cord in the lumbar and sacral regions. **Spina bifida occulta** is when the vertebral arches fail to unite and there is no neurological involvement *(see Chapter 5)*. When the vertebral defect is more open, nervous tissue can protrude through it in a sac. In **spina bifida cystica** *(Figure 16.7)*, the sac can contain meninges (**meningocele**), part of the spinal cord (**myelocele**), or both (**myelomeningocele**) *(see Chapter 5)*.

Neonatal seizures are a common and sometimes serious neonatal disorder. They can be:

- **Primary**—from an intracranial process such as meningitis or a cerebral hemorrhage from a difficult birth.

- **Secondary**—from a systemic or metabolic problem such as hypoxia, hypoglycemia, or hypocalcemia.

Treatment is directed to the underlying pathology. The seizure itself is treated with IV phenobarbital.

Thermoregulation and Adaptation

The infant has a larger ratio of surface area to body volume than an adult. Therefore, the infant loses heat more easily, particularly if the body surface is wet. This is why the newborn is dried, wrapped, and placed in a warmer after birth. Although growing infants accumulate subcutaneous fat to retain heat, their body temperature regulation remains more variable than that of an adult.

Hypothermia is more likely to occur in **premature** or **small for date (SFD)** neonates. Hypothermia is rare in this country but is often seen in rural areas of developing countries, even in full-term babies, when informed neonatal care is lacking.

Abbreviations

CSF	cerebrospinal fluid
SFD	small for date

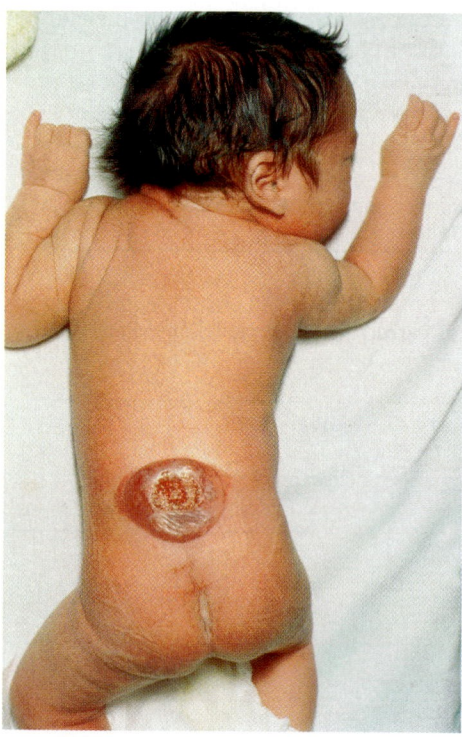

▲ **FIGURE 16.7 Child with Spina Bifida Cystica.**

WORD	PRONUNCIATION	ELEMENTS		DEFINITION
anencephaly	AN-en-SEF-ah-lee	P/ R/	an- *without* -encephaly *condition of the brain*	Born without cerebral hemispheres
Babinski sign	bah-BIN-skee SINE		Joseph Babinski, 1857–1932	Abnormal neurological response to plantar reflex
bifid spina bifida	BI-fid SPY-nah BIH-fi-dah		bifid Latin *split into two* spina Latin *backbone*	Separated into two parts Failure of one or more vertebral arches to close during fetal development
cystic cystica (adj)	SIS-tik		Greek *bladder*	Relating to a cyst
encephalocele	en-SEF-ah-loh-seal	S/ R/CF	-cele *hernia* encephal/o- *brain*	Congenital defect of the cranium with herniation of brain tissue
hydrocephalus	high-droh-SEF-ah-lus	P/ R/	hydro- *water* -cephalus *head*	Enlarged head due to excess CSF in the cerebral ventricles
hypothermia	high-poh-THER-me-ah	S/ P/ R/	-ia *condition* hypo- *below* -therm- *heat*	Very low core body temperature
involuntary	in-VOL-un-tah-ree	S/ P/ R/	-ary *pertaining to* in- *not* -volunt- *willing*	Not under control of the will
meningocele	meh-NING-oh-seal	S/ R/CF	-cele *hernia* mening/o- *meninges*	Protrusion of the meninges from the spinal cord or brain through a defect in the vertebral column or cranium
microcephaly microcephalic (adj)	MY-kroh-SEF-ah-lee	P/ R/	micro- *small* -cephaly *condition of the head*	An abnormally small head
Moro reflex (also called startle reflex)	MOR-oh RE-fleks		Ernst Moro, 1874–1951 reflex Latin *to bend back*	Neonatal brainstem reflex
myelocele myelomeningocele	MY-eh-low-seal MY-eh-low-meh-NING-oh-seal	S/ R/CF R/CF	-cele *hernia* myel/o- *spinal cord* -mening/o- *meninges*	Protrusion of the spinal cord through a defect in the vertebral arch Protrusion of the spinal cord and meninges through a defect in the vertebral arch of one or more vertebrae
neural	NYU-ral	S/ R/	-al *pertaining to* neur- *nerve*	Pertaining to nervous tissue
plantar reflex	PLAN-tar re-FLEKS		plantar Latin *sole of the foot* reflex *to bend back*	Neurological response to stimulation of the sole of the foot
rooting	rue-TING		Latin *seek*	A neonatal reflex to turn toward and open mouth when nipple is placed on cheek

EXERCISES

Build the medical term by filling in the blanks with the correct element(s).

1. born without cerebral hemispheres: _____ / encephaly

2. pertaining to nervous tissue: _____ /al

3. very low core body temperature: hypo/ _____ / _____

4. small head: _____ /cephaly

5. enlarged head due to excess CSF: hydro/ _____

6. protrusion of the meninges: meningo/ _____

7. congenital cranial defect with herniation of brain tissue: _____ /cele

Growth Adaptations

Failure to grow fully in utero is caused by two main factors:

1. **inadequate nutrition** caused by poor placental function. The newborn can be delivered preterm, term, or postterm but is below the 10th percentile of babies of the same gestational age. This is called **small for gestational age (SGA)**. Good nutrition after delivery will enable growth to accelerate to normal.

2. **premature labor** when the infant is born before 37 weeks of gestation. The cause of premature labor is usually unknown. The premature infant weighs less than 5.5 pounds, has little subcutaneous fat or hair, and spontaneous activity is low *(Figure 16.8)*. Surfactant deficiency leads to RDS. Inadequate cerebral perfusion can contribute to cerebral hemorrhage. Immature development of the CNS leads to poor sucking and swallowing. These infants may have to be fed by IV or by **gavage (stomach tube)**.

Occasionally, labor does not start until after 42 weeks gestation and produces a **postmature infant** *(Figure 16.9)*. The problem is that past term the placenta **involutes**, and the fetus receives insufficient nutrition in the days after term. As a result, these infants have decreased subcutaneous fat and dry peeling skin. They are prone to meconium aspiration and to neonatal hypoglycemia because their glycogen stores are depleted.

Normal full-term babies lose up to 10% of their birth weight during the first few days of life. By one month, she should be gaining 2/3 to 1 ounce per day. She will grow 1 to 1.5 inches per month. These changes will be plotted on **growth charts,** which indicate the size and growth patterns of individual children compared to other children in the United States. **Percentiles** are used. For example, a 2-year-old girl whose weight is plotted on the weight chart at the 25th percentile weighs the same or more than 25% of other 2-year-old girls. She also weighs less than 75% of other 2-year-old girls. The function of growth charts is to show how consistent the child's growth pattern is over time. You will be asked to work with growth charts at the end of this chapter.

Failure to thrive (FTT) is the term used for an infant or young child who is not growing and developing as expected. There are two main reasons for the failure:

1. **Organic disorders** such as chronic illness (e.g., celiac disease), genetic (e.g., Down syndrome), metabolic (e.g., **fetal alcohol syndrome [FAS]**), and hormone disorders (e.g., pituitary dwarfism).

2. **Psychosocial disorders** including poverty, lack of education about feeding, neglect or abuse, parental mental illness or substance abuse.

Urinary System Adaptations

Kidneys at birth are not fully developed. Infants cannot concentrate their urine so have a high rate of water loss. They require more fluid intake, relative to body weight, than adults. In the first month of life, an infant will produce five to six wet diapers daily.

Congenital urinary tract disorders include renal **agenesis**, in which one or both kidneys is absent; blockage of urinary flow in utero, causing hydronephrosis of the kidneys; **polycystic kidney disease,** one of the most common genetic disorders; and **hypospadias** of the penis, in which the urethra does not extend to the end of the penis and opens along the underside of the penis. Hypospadias affects nearly 1% of baby boys *(see Chapter 11)*.

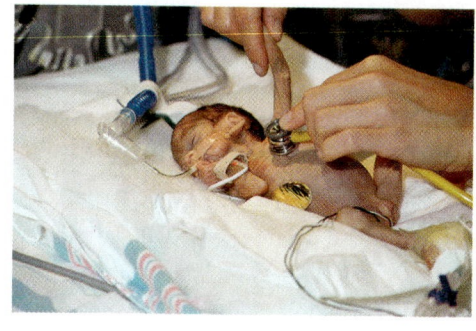

▲ **FIGURE 16.8 Premature Baby.**

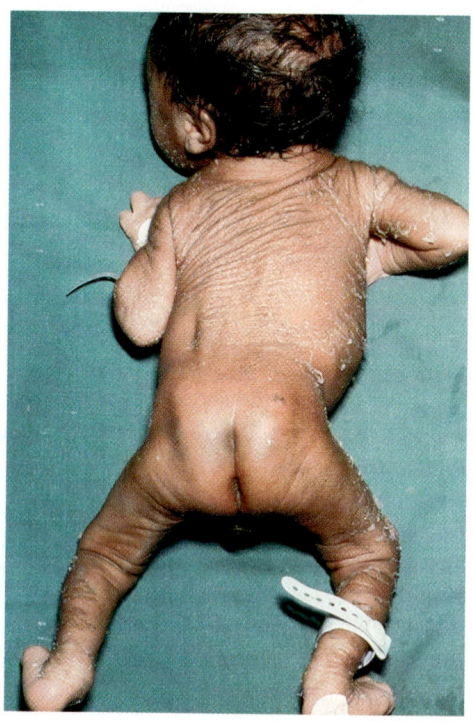

▲ **FIGURE 16.9 Postmature Infant with Skin Changes.**

Abbreviations

FAS	fetal alcohol syndrome
FTT	failure to thrive
SGA	small for gestational age

WORD ANALYSIS AND DEFINITION

WORD	PRONUNCIATION	ELEMENTS		DEFINITION
agenesis	a-**JEN**-eh-sis	P/ R/	a- *without* -genesis *creation or production*	Failure to develop any organ or any part
gavage	guh-**VAHZH**		French *to force feed geese (to make pâté de foie gras)*	To feed by a stomach tube
hypospadias	high-poh-**SPAY**-dee-as	S/ P/ R/	-ias *condition* hypo- *below, under* -spad- *to tear*	Urethral opening more proximal than normal on the ventral surface of the penis
involute	in-voh-**LUTE**	P/ R/	in- *in* -volute *to roll up*	Regressive changes in any tissue, occurring with aging
percentile	per-**SEN**-tile	S/ P/ R/	-ile *capability* per- *through* -cent- *hundred*	One of a hundred groups in a distribution of variables
postmature	post-mah-**TYUR**	P/ R/	post- *after* -mature *fully developed*	Infant born after 42 weeks of gestation

EXERCISES

Documentation. *Use the terminology and abbreviations found on these two pages to correctly fill in the following patient documentation. Then choose any three terms and create patient documentation of your own.*

1. This infant's mother has been an alcoholic for the past year and a half. Infant was born suffering from _____ .

2. This preemie falls below the 10th percentile on a growth chart and is _____ .

3. Starting this evening, this patient is to be fed by gastric _____ .

4. Patient was born with only the right kidney present. Diagnosis: renal _____ .

5. This infant's urethral opening falls short of the tip of his penis. Diagnosis: _____ .

6. Genetic testing has confirmed this patient has _____ .

7. Celiac disease has caused _____ in this patient; she is significantly below normal height and weight for her age group.

Create your own documentation:

8. _____
_____
_____
_____
_____

9. _____
_____
_____
_____

10. _____
_____
_____
_____

Keynote

Breast milk provides valuable antibodies, digestive enzymes, and hormones that infants need. It is nonallergenic.

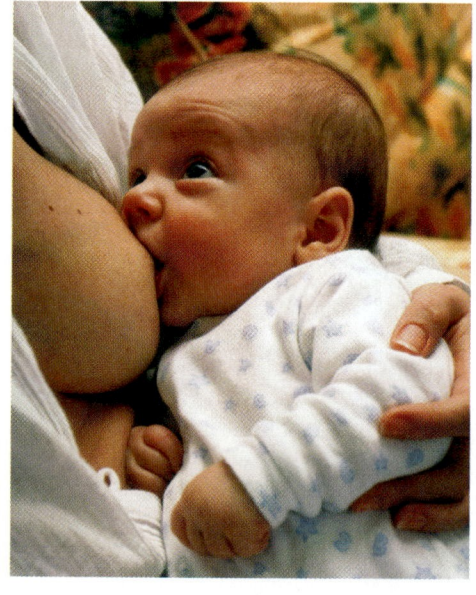

▲ **FIGURE 16.10 One-Month-Old Baby Breast-Feeds and Interacts with Mother.**

Keynote

All newborn babies should receive hearing screening tests before they go home from the hospital.

NEONATAL ADAPTATIONS (continued)

Digestive System Adaptations

Until the baby is 6 months old, she only needs **breast milk** or commercially prepared **infant formula.** At one month of age, a breast-fed baby will be feeding every 2 to 3 hours for about ten minutes each time, and the mother's supply of milk will be adjusting to the baby's needs. The supply is based on the energy and frequency of the baby's sucking. Formula-fed babies will take 3 to 4 ounces every 3 to 4 hours.

Around one month of age, a feeding routine will be established. Breast milk can be pumped out of the breast and stored in the refrigerator for up to a week for other people to help with feeding. By three months, daytime feedings should be around every four hours, and baby should be sleeping through the night.

An immature digestive system may be the cause of **colic,** when the neonate cries for hours at a time until you feel like joining in. Twenty-five percent of all infants have colic. It begins between the third and sixth weeks and goes away on its own by the twelfth week. There is no known treatment.

Food intolerance, totally different from food allergy (see page 650, Immunologic Adaptations), is an adverse digestive system reaction to food. It does not involve the immune system. It can be a metabolic reaction to a digestive enzyme deficiency, such as **lactase deficiency** leading to intolerance to cows' milk. It can be an inability to deal with gluten, as in **celiac disease** *(see Chapter 6)*. The symptoms of food intolerance include feeling irritable and cranky, bloating and flatulence, nausea, vomiting, and diarrhea.

Visual Adaptations

At birth, a nonanesthetized baby is able to see and focus on an object between 8 and 12 inches away. This distance has probably **evolved** because it is the distance between mother's and baby's faces during breast-feeding *(Figure 16.10)*. For color vision, the baby will only see very brightly colored objects. Full color vision comes in at between 3 and 4 months of age. Research has shown that newborns are naturally attracted to human faces, even to rough sketches of faces. This mechanism helps in **bonding,** particularly during breast-feeding.

Hearing Adaptations

The fetus begins to hear loud noises around the beginning of the third trimester (24 weeks). By the seventh month of pregnancy, the fetus can hear maternal speech and remember what is heard after she is born. Fetal experience with sounds and speech can make them more responsive to speech after birth *(Case Report 16.2)*.

Congenital malformations of the external auditory canal and middle ear can result in a conductive hearing loss. Congenital malformations of the inner ear can result in a **sensorineural hearing loss** *(see Chapter 4)*. About 1 in 1000 newborns has a severe hearing loss.

WORD	PRONUNCIATION		ELEMENTS	DEFINITION
bonding	**BON**-ding		Latin *to hold together*	Formation of a close and lasting emotional attachment
celiac disease	**SEE**-lee-ak diz-**EEZ**	S/ R/	**-ac** *pertaining to* **celi-** *abdomen*	Disease caused by sensitivity to gluten
colic	**KOL**-ik	S/ R/	**-ic** *pertaining to* **col-** *colon*	Spasmodic, crampy pains in the abdomen. In young infants, persistent crying and irritability thought to be arising from pain in the intestines
evolve	ee-**VOLV**		Latin *to unfold*	To develop gradually
infant formula	**IN**-fant **FOR**-myu-lah	 S/ R/	**infant** Latin infans *not speaking* **-ula** *small thing* **form-** *form*	Commercial product for infants manufactured from cows' milk or soy milk
intolerance	in-**TOL**-er-ance		Latin *impatient*	Inability of the small intestine to digest and dispose of a particular dietary constituent
lactase	**LAK**-tase	S/ R/	**-ase** *enzyme* **lact-** *milk*	Enzyme that breaks down lactose to glucose and galactose
sensorineural hearing loss	**SEN**-sor-ih-**NYUR**-al	S/ R/CF R/	**-al** *pertaining to* **sensor/i-** *sensation* **-neur-** *nerve*	Hearing loss caused by lesions of the inner ear or the auditory nerve

EXERCISES

Pediatric terminology will help you determine the correct answer for the following questions. Circle the best answer.

1. Breast milk provides:
   a. antibodies
   b. digestive enzymes
   c. hormones
   d. none of these
   e. all of these

2. Bloating, flatulence, nausea, vomiting, and diarrhea are symptoms of:
   a. food allergy
   b. immune response
   c. food intolerance
   d. urinary tract infection
   e. enzyme malabsorption

3. An immature digestive system may be the cause of:
   a. TTN
   b. colic
   c. elevated temperature
   d. FAS
   e. a rash

4. Formation of a close and lasting emotional attachment is called:
   a. independency
   b. visual adaptation
   c. bonding
   d. dependency
   e. intolerance

5. Congenital malformations of the external auditory canal can result in:
   a. FTT
   b. celiac disease
   c. FAS
   d. conductive hearing loss
   e. lactase deficiency

6. Lactase deficiency is:
   a. metabolic reaction to digestive enzyme deficiency
   b. intolerance to cow's milk
   c. food allergy
   d. a and b
   e. a and c

7. Circle the incorrect statement about breast milk:
   a. breast milk is nonallergenic
   b. breast milk contains antibodies that babies need
   c. breast milk can be pumped out of the breast and put in a bottle
   d. breast milk can be stored in the refrigerator
   e. breast milk supply depends on the mother's diet

8. The root *celi* means:
   a. stomach
   b. abdomen
   c. nerve
   d. colon
   e. bowel

Hematologic Adaptations

The newborn infant has an excess of red blood cells (RBCs). When these are broken down, bilirubin is produced *(see Chapter 7)*. In addition, the neonate's liver is immature and cannot process bilirubin quickly. The excess bilirubin is deposited in the tissues, producing jaundice. In the first three days after birth, neonatal jaundice affects 60% of full-term and 80% of premature infants. In most infants, no specific treatment is needed. Sunlight and **phototherapy** with a blue fluorescent light break down the bilirubin and are the mainstay of therapy *(Figure 16.11)*.

Breast-feeding is associated with hyperbilirubinemia in the first few days of life. It is related to breast milk taking a few days to come in to the breast in adequate amounts to maintain hydration of the infant.

Rhesus and ABO incompatibilities that can produce neonatal jaundice and anemia are described in *Chapter 7*.

Immunologic Adaptations

Many of these adaptations occur in the first six months of life. The baby is born with immunoglobulin G (IgG) levels near that of an adult, having acquired them from her mother through the placenta. These levels remain high enough in the first six months to protect the baby against some infectious diseases but not against others, including **whooping cough** (**pertussis**) and **diphtheria**. This is why immunization against these diseases takes place at 2, 4, and 6 months of age. At six months, the IgG levels are at their lowest, and respiratory infections occur more easily.

Major failures of immunologic adaptation are discussed in *Chapter 15*.

In **food allergies,** the body's immune system reacts as though a particular food is harmful (an allergen) and creates IgE antibodies to it. This, in turn, generates chemicals such as histamine that produce symptoms of a runny nose, itchy skin rash, swelling of the lips, or wheezing. The most common allergens are **cow's milk, eggs, wheat, soy,** and **peanuts.** Between 25 and 50% of the children outgrow their food allergies by age three years.

Social Adaptations

Identity. The building blocks of a baby's identity began in the last trimester in utero when she played with her fingers and toes and responded to sounds, music, and voices. Genes and her **inborn temperament** play their roles. At one month of age, her interaction with her caregiver's love, attention, and caring skills are the stimulus for how she reacts to other people. By two to three months, as she plays with her fingers and toes, she will be starting the process of being aware of her own physical identity.

Communication. Crying is the baby's primary communication method. She cries in different ways to say "I'm wet, hungry, lonely, or just overwhelmed by the sights and sounds of this world around me." She'll start to "coo" and gurgle and will enjoy hearing the caregiver respond with the same sounds. When she turns away or closes her eyes, she may just need her own space.

Curiosity. A one-month-old baby can only show interest in what is in front of her, such as a parent's face, or a brightly colored toy. As her eye and neck muscles develop, she can turn her head to see any object that catches her eye. At three months, she'll take swipes at a mobile of shapes hanging over her crib, and she'll look into a child-safe mirror in the crib near her head.

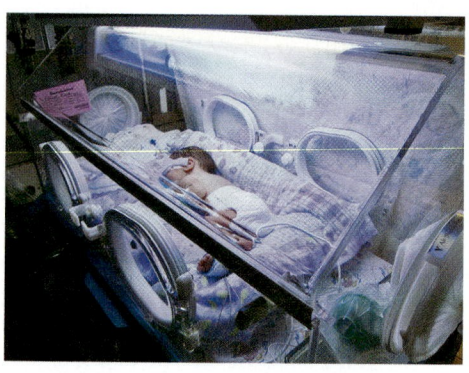

▲ **FIGURE 16.11 One-Day-Old Premature Baby Undergoing Phototherapy.**

Keynote

In the first two years of life, most children have 8 to 10 colds.

Six percent of children under the age of three have food allergies.

Abbreviation	
Ig	immunoglobulin

Keynote

By three months of age, the baby will smile at the sound of a known voice and turn her head to the direction of the sound.

WORD	PRONUNCIATION	ELEMENTS		DEFINITION
diphtheria	dif-**THEER**-ee-ah		Greek *leather*	Disease with a thick, membranous (leathery) coating of the pharynx
pertussis whooping cough (syn)	per-**TUSS**-is **WHO**-ping KAWF	P/ R/	**per-** *intense* **-tussis** *cough*	Infectious disease with spasmodic, intense cough ending on a whoop (stridor)
phototherapy	foh-toe-**THAIR**-ah-pee	R/CF S/	**phot/o-** *light* **-therapy** *treatment*	Treatment using light rays
temperament	**TEM**-per-ah-ment		Latin *disposition*	Predisposition to character or personality

EXERCISES

Analyze and choose the correct medical term to fill in the blanks. Watch your spelling please!

1. Predisposition to character and personality is referred to as your _____ .

(parameter   temperament)

2. Treatment using light rays is called _____ .

(fototherapy   phototherapy)

3. Excess bilirubin in tissues produces _____ .

(jaundice   pertussis)

4. Another name for whooping cough is _____ .

(diphtheria   pertussis)

5. Disease with a thick, leathery coating of pharynx is called _____ .

(pertussis   diphtheria)

For each of the terms above, write a brief sentence explaining the term as if you were talking to a mother.

6. _____

7. _____

_____

8. _____

_____

9. _____

_____

10. _____

_____

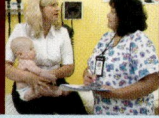

LESSON 16.3 Adulthood, Aging, Senescence, and Death

OBJECTIVES

The information in this lesson will enable you to:

- **Distinguish aging from senescence.**
- **Describe changes that occur with senescence in major organ systems using correct medical terminology.**
- **Outline some theories of senescence.**
- **Discuss preparations for death.**
- **Recognize and reinforce medical terminology used in Chapters 2 through 15.**

You are

. . . a medical assistant working in the geriatric clinic at Fulwood Medical Center.

Your patient is

. . . 85-year-old Mr. Mathew Hickman, who has an early dementia and a slow-growing prostate cancer for which he has opted to have no treatment.

CASE REPORT 16.4

With the help of his two daughters and day care providers, he is struggling to stay at home. His daughter, Sandra Hotteling, is with him.

Mr. Hickman:

"I'm still here, you know, somewhere inside this frail old body. I can remember yesteryear, though I'm a bit hazy about today. I can't hear you like I used to. But, I can still tie my shoes. I'm not frightened of death, but the process of getting there scares the heck out of me. I've lived my life with dignity. I want to live my death the same way, you know, and leave with dry pants".

Keynote

Stage 6 issue: intimacy versus isolation.
Stage 7 issue: others versus self.
Stage 8 issue: fulfillment versus despair.

DEFINITIONS

- **Life span** is the age to which individual humans aspire to live and the process of getting there.
- **Life expectancy** is the average length of life for any given population.
- **Longevity** is living beyond the normal life expectancy.
- **Aging** is the gradual, spontaneous change resulting in maturation through childhood, adolescence, and young adulthood. Changes then decline, rather than mature, through late adulthood and old age.
- **Senescence** is the loss over time of the capacity of cells to divide, grow, and function, a process that terminates in death.

ADULTHOOD

Stage 6: Young Adulthood—Age 19 to 40 years

Your sense of identity that you acquired in adolescence enables you to achieve intimacy with spouse and children and to view your parents in a different light. Without identity, you may well be successful at work, but you will fear commitment, be isolated emotionally, and be unable to depend on anyone else.

Stage 7: Middle Adulthood—Age 40 to 70 years

Your sense of identity enables you to look outside yourself and care for others through parenting or social commitment. You want to create a living legacy. Without this identity, you remain self-centered, stop growing emotionally, wonder why nobody loves you, and become addicted to work or a substance.

Stage 8: Late Adulthood—Age 70 to death

When you look back, has life been filled with satisfaction or disappointment? Do you feel good about yourself? According to Erikson, "Just as a healthy child does not fear life, a healthy adult will not fear death." Otherwise, old age is filled with despair, fear, and sickness.

The medical study, care, and treatment of the elderly is called **geriatrics,** and the medical specialist in geriatrics is called a **geriatrician.**

WORD ANALYSIS AND DEFINITION

WORD	PRONUNCIATION	ELEMENTS		DEFINITION
aging **aged**	**A**-jing **A**-jid		Latin *aging*	The process of human maturation and decline Having lived to an advanced age
geriatrics (***Note:*** This term consists only of two roots.) **geriatrician** **gerontology**	jer-ee-**AT**-riks jer-ee-ah-**TRISH**-an jer-on-**TOL**-oh-jee	S/ R/ R/ S/ S/ R/CF	-ics *knowledge* ger- *old age* -iatr- *medical treatment* -ician *expert* -logy *study of* geront/o- *process of aging*	Medical specialty that deals with the problems of old age Medical specialist in geriatrics Study of the process and problems of aging
life expectancy **life span**	LIFE eck-**SPEK**-tan-see LIFE SPAN	S/ R/	-ancy *state of* expect- *await* life Old English *life* span Old English *stretch or reach*	Statistical determination of the number of years an individual is expected to live The age that a person reaches
longevity	lon-**JEV**-ih-tee	S/ R/	-ity *condition* longev- *long life*	Duration of life beyond the normal expectation
senile **senescence** **senility**	**SEE**-nile se-**NES**-ens se-**NIL**-ih-tee	S/ R/ S/ R/ S/ R/	-ile *pertaining to* sen- *old age* -ence *state of* senesc- *growing old* -ity *condition* senil- *senile*	Characteristic of old age The state of being old Mental disorders occurring in old age

EXERCISES

Complete your description of Erikson's final stages of development by filling in the following table.

Stage	Ages	Major Issue in Development
6		
7		
8		

Pick any one of these stages, and write a two-sentence description of what might happen to a person in this stage.

_____

_____

_____

_____

_____

Good job! You have met the lesson objective.

Visual acuity starts to decline very early in life. Eye exercises can be of value to prevent this.

Exercise and good nutrition help prevent osteopenia.

Exercise and good nutrition help prevent muscle degeneration.

Exercising your brain enhances the quality of life in old age.

Exercise and good nutrition extend **longevity** and enhance the quality of life.

Bronchitis and emphysema, the **chronic obstructive pulmonary diseases (COPDs)**, are the cumulative effects of cigarette smoking and are a leading cause of death in old age.

SENESCENCE OF ORGAN SYSTEMS

Organ systems begin to show signs of senescence at very different ages and do not degenerate at the same speed. For example, **autopsies (postmortem)** in children will often reveal atherosclerosis in the CVS. Most physiologic studies show general peak physical performance appears in the twenties. Autopsies are usually performed by a **pathologist** or a medical examiner.

Integumentary system changes begin in the forties. Melanocytes *(see Chapter 3)* die, and hair becomes gray and thinner. The skin becomes paper thin, loses elasticity, hangs loose, and wrinkles appear *(Figure 16.12)*. Flat brown-black spots, **senile lentigines (age spots)**, appear on the back of the hands and areas exposed to sunlight.

Special senses start to decline in the twenties. Visual acuity declines at that time. In the forties, presbyopia *(see Chapter 4)* begins, and many people develop cataracts in old age. Hearing loss occurs as the ossicles become stiffer and the number of cochlear hair cells *(see Chapter 4)* declines. This was the cause of Mr. Hickman's hearing loss. Taste and smell are blunted late in life as taste cells and olfactory buds decline in number.

Skeletal system changes appear in the thirties, when osteoblasts become less active than osteoclasts. The result is osteopenia, which goes on to become osteoporosis, particularly in postmenopausal women. Joints in the older age groups have less synovial fluid and thinner articular cartilage. Osteoarthritis results *(see Chapter 5)*.

Muscular system changes occur with age as muscle mass is replaced with fat. As muscle **atrophies**, there are fewer muscle fibers to do the work, and the available blood supply is decreased. Tasks that used to be easy become difficult, such as buttoning shirts and tying shoelaces. This was one of Mr. Hickman's triumphs of the day.

Nervous system changes begin around age 30, when the brain weighs twice as much as it does by age 75. Motor coordination, intellectual function, and short-term memory decline more quickly than long-term memory and language skills.

Cardiovascular systems always show coronary artery atherosclerosis from an early age. As a result, when aging myocardial cells die, the heart wall gets thinner and weaker, and cardiac output declines. This causes the decline in physical capabilities with aging. Atherosclerotic plaques narrow arteries and trigger thrombosis, leading to strokes and heart attacks. In veins, valves become weaker, blood flows back and pools in the legs, leading to poor venous return to the heart and heart failure.

Respiratory system changes are noticeable in the thirties when pulmonary ventilation declines, a factor in the gradual loss of stamina. The rib cage becomes less flexible, the lungs less elastic and have fewer alveoli. Respiratory function declines. As respiratory health declines, hypoxic degenerative changes occur in all the other organ systems.

▲ **FIGURE 16.12 Senescence of the Skin.**
Photograph of child from The 1974 Science Year, © 1973 Field Enterprises Educational Corporation. By permission of World Book, Inc. Photograph of aging woman © Stock Photo.

WORD	PRONUNCIATION	ELEMENTS		DEFINITION
atrophy	**AT**-roh-fee	P/ R/	a- *without* -trophy *development, nourishment*	Wasting or diminished volume of a tissue or organ
autopsy	**AWE**-top-see		Greek *see with one's own eyes*	Examination of the body and organs of a dead person to determine the cause of death
postmortem (syn)	post-**MOR**-tem	S/ P/ R/	-em *condition* post- *after* -mort- *death*	
lentigo lentigines (pl)	len-**TIE**-go len-**TIHJ**-ih-neez		Greek *lentil*	Age spot; small, flat, brown-black spot in the skin of older people
pathologist	pa-**THOL**-oh-jist	S/ R/CF	-logist *one who studies* patho- *disease*	A specialist in pathology

Urinary system changes begin in the twenties, when the number of nephrons starts to decline. Later in life, many of the remaining glomeruli become atherosclerotic.

Glomerular filtration rate (GFR) decreases, and the kidneys become less efficient. For example, drug doses in the elderly need to be reduced because they cannot be cleared from the blood as rapidly.

Immune system function declines in the elderly as the amounts of lymphatic tissue and red bone marrow decrease with age. This leads to a reduction in both cellular and humoral (antibody) immunity *(see Chapter 15)*. This means that the elderly have less protection against infectious diseases and cancer.

The **disorders of senescence** and their terminology are described in detail in each of the body system chapters in this book.

Keynote

The kidneys of an 80-year-old only receive half as much blood as those of a 30 year old because of atherosclerosis.

Because of lowered immunity, vaccinations against influenza and other seasonal infections are recommended for the elderly.

Abbreviations

COPD chronic obstructive pulmonary disease

GFR glomerular filtration rate

EXERCISES   *Organ systems show various signs of senescence. Provide one example of a sign of senescence in each organ system listed in the following table. Be sure to use correct medical terminology and be able to explain every term you use. Fill in the blanks.*

Organ System	Sign of Senescence
integumentary	
special senses	
skeletal	
muscular	
nervous	
cardiovascular	
respiratory	
urinary	
immune	

Have you checked your spelling?

THEORIES OF SENESCENCE, DYING, AND DEATH

The causes of senescence are unknown. **Heredity** plays a role because longevity or early death tend to run in families. Theories of senescence include:

- **Protein abnormalities**—One-quarter of the body's protein is collagen. With age, collagen and other proteins show abnormal structures in their cells and tissues and become less soluble and more rigid. The cells accumulate more of these dysfunctional proteins as they age, and their functions are impaired, leading to **senescent** changes.

- **Free radicals**—chemical particles with an extra electron. For example, the stable oxygen molecule has two atoms with many electrons. If it picks up an extra electron through some metabolic reaction, by radiation, or by chemicals, it becomes a free radical. The free radical's life is short because it combines quickly with other molecules that in turn become free radicals with the addition of the extra electron. A chain reaction occurs as more and more molecules become free radicals. Among the damage they cause are cancer, myocardial infarction, and perhaps senescence. They can be neutralized by **antioxidants** (*see Chapter 17*).

- **Autoimmune** altered molecules (*see Chapter 15*) may be recognized as foreign antigens, and an immune response may be generated against the body's own tissues. This theory is helped by the fact that autoimmune diseases such as rheumatoid arthritis are more common in old age.

It is highly likely that senescence has more than one etiology.

Dying and Death

Death is inevitable. Just as fetal life in the womb is a preparation for birth, so living and aging are a preparation for death. You can prepare for death in different ways, all of which are done with your family and many of which necessitate legal assistance.

Medical issues are clearly significant in the process of dying. Your views on the types and extent of the medical treatment you wish to have should be clearly stated. This is done through an **advance medical directive**, which consists of two documents:

1. **Medical (durable) power of attorney**—in which you appoint someone you know and trust as your agent and authorize him/her to make medical decisions for you when you cannot.

2. **Living will**—in which you provide a set of instructions detailing what treatment you do and do not want in a terminal illness, including **hospice** treatment. If there are special instructions, such as "**do not resuscitate (DNR),**" these must be stated clearly. It should also include a Health Insurance Portability and Accountability Act **(HIPAA) authorization** to enable your agent to receive the medical information about you that is necessary for making decisions about treatment. This is needed because the HIPAA act of 1996 (*see Chapter 2*) imposes tough privacy of medical information rules on doctors and hospitals.

Your primary care doctor should have a copy of your advance medical directive and have read the document with you.

The process of dying, rather than death itself, is of concern to most elderly people. Dying should be dignified and free from physical and emotional pain. A hospice provides **palliative care** and provides for the emotional and spiritual needs of terminally ill patients and their loved ones at an inpatient facility or in the patient's home. Palliative care is designed to provide pain and symptom management to maintain the highest quality of life for as long as life remains.

Just as the moment life begins is controversial, there is no universally accepted moment of biological death.

In most states in the United States, death is now defined in terms of **brain death (BD)**, when there is no cerebral or brainstem activity, and the EEG is flat for a specific length of time (*Figure 16.13*). Two other conditions involving brain damage

Abbreviations

BD	brain death
DNR	do not resuscitate
HIPAA	Health Insurance Portability and Accountability Act
MCS	minimally conscious state
PVS	persistent vegetative state

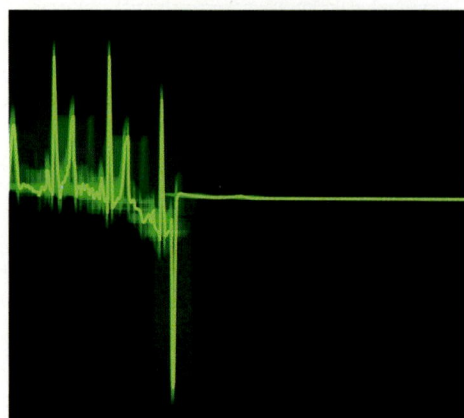

▲ **FIGURE 16.13 Electroencephalogram Shows Brain Death.**

WORD	PRONUNCIATION	ELEMENTS		DEFINITION
advance medical directive	ad-**VANTS MED**-ih-kal die-**REK**-tiv			Legal document signed by the patient dealing with issues of prolonging or ending life in the event of life-threatening illness
antioxidant	an-tee-**OKS**-ih-dant	S/ P/ R/	**-ant** *forming* **anti-** *against* **-oxid-** *oxidize*	Substance that can prevent cell damage by neutralizing free radicals
coma	**KOH**-mah		Greek *deep sleep*	State of deep unconsciousness
death	DETH		Old English *to die*	Total and permanent cessation of all vital functions
free radical	FREE **RAD**-ih-kal	R/ S/ R/	**free-** *free* **-al** *pertaining to* **radic-** *root*	Short-lived product of oxidation in a cell that can be damaging to the cell
heredity	heh-**RED**-ih-tee	S/ R/	**-ity** *state, condition* **hered-** *inherited through genes*	Transmission of characteristics from parents to offspring through genes
hospice	**HOS**-pis		Latin *lodging*	Provides care to the dying and their families
palliative care	**PAL**-ee-ah-tiv KAIR	S/ R/ R/	**-ive** *pertaining to* **palliat-** *reduce suffering* **care** *be responsible for*	To relieve symptoms and pain without curing
vegetative	**VEJ**-eh-tay-tiv	S/ R/	**-ive** *quality of* **vegetat-** *growth*	Functioning unconsciously as plant life is assumed to do

and loss of brain function cause medical difficulty and should be addressed in your living will:

- **Persistent vegetative state (PVS)** occurs in people who suffer enough brain damage that they are unaware of themselves or their surroundings, even though their eyes are open. Yet, they still have certain reflexes and can breathe and pump blood because the brainstem still functions. Even reflex events like crying and smiling and the sleep-wake cycle can be seen. With medical care and artificial feeding, patients can survive for decades.

- **Minimally conscious state (MCS)** describes a condition of severely altered consciousness in which minimal, inconsistent evidence of awareness of self or the surroundings is demonstrated. However, PET scans show cortical function when their loved ones speak to them. They are more likely to improve than are PVS patients.

Keynote

Both PVS and MCS differ from **coma**, in which the individual is unresponsive and keeps eyes closed.

EXERCISES   *Explain the difference among the following terms to a patient's relatives. If you understand it yourself, you can explain it to someone else. Write a brief explanation for each term.*

1. Persistent vegetative state:

_____

_____

2. Minimally conscious state:

_____

_____

3. Coma:

_____

_____

LIFE SPAN

CHALLENGE YOUR KNOWLEDGE

A. **Case Report:** Re-read the following case report, which was presented earlier in this chapter. Use your knowledge of the *language of pediatrics* to answer the following questions. Fill in the blanks.

Your patients are

. . . 7-year-old Carol Hotteling and her mother. You have watched Carol grow over the seven years that you have worked in Dr. Mendes' well-baby clinic. Her mother, Anna, is telling you about her current concerns:

"As you know, she's always been a handful. The neighbors call her a tomboy. She's trashed every room in the house. The other kids' mothers stopped inviting her to parties. Nothing holds her attention for very long. I've lost her a couple of times in the shopping mall when she's darted away. I always thought she'd grow out of it. But, now she's in second grade. The teacher is complaining that she can't sit still, she interferes with the other kids, disrupts the class, and she's having trouble reading and staying focused. It's got to be due to something I did or didn't do?"

1. According to Erikson, what stage of development is Carol Hotteling in now?

_____

2. What is the major issue in this stage of development?

_____

3. What types of problems does Carol have?

_____

_____

_____

4. Based on these symptoms and the descriptions provided by her mother, what disorders could Carol possibly have? _____

_____

B. **Elements:** You need to recognize word elements in and out of context. First, match the meaning in column 1 with the element in column 2. Then, fill in column 3 with the type of element that is next to it in column 2. Fill in the blanks.

Meaning of Element		Element		Type of Element (P, R, CF, S)
1. together	_____	A. drom		_____
2. in	_____	B. ase		_____
3. appetite	_____	C. syn		_____
4. pertaining to	_____	D. rumin		_____
5. without	_____	E. uresis		_____
6. enzyme	_____	F. an		_____
7. running	_____	G. orex		_____
8. the mind	_____	H. ine		_____
9. throat	_____	I. psycho		_____
10. to urinate	_____	J. en		_____

C. **Dictionary:** English words that are not necessarily "medical terminology" can still have an impact on the meaning of a medical term; for example, transient tachypnea of the newborn. Use your dictionary or go online to look up the meaning of the word **transient,** then fill in the blanks:

1. Transient: _____

    Is "transient tachypnea of the newborn" a permanent condition?

    _____

2. Take your knowledge of the definition of transient, and use it to analyze this sentence. "Amniotic fluid remains in the infant's lungs and causes a *self-limiting* respiratory distress."

    a. What does **self-limiting** mean in this context?

    _____

    b. How will this condition resolve?

    _____

D. **Abbreviations:** Regardless of whether you are an administrative or clinical health care worker, you will be reading patient documentation with abbreviations, which can mean a diagnosis, procedure, disease, etc. To interpret this documentation correctly and safely, you must know the meanings of the abbreviations. Challenge yourself to *define* each of the following abbreviations correctly. *Then list the specialist* connected to that medical term. Fill in the chart, then practice your documentation.

Abbreviation	Meaning of Abbreviation	Specialist
BD		
MCS		
PVS		
PDA		
HMD		
SIDS		
SFD		
RDS		
FTT		
LD		

Choose any abbreviation from the table above and write one sentence of patient documentation that might come from that particular specialist.

Abbreviation:_____

Specialist _____

Patient documentation:

_____

_____

_____

LIFE SPAN

E. Discussion: Research in the school library or on the Internet to be able to explain the statement: "Autism is a spectrum of disorders." Be sure you can define any vocabulary you use in your discussion. Briefly organize your thoughts below, or write down the words you need to look up.

_____

_____

_____

_____

_____

_____

_____

_____

_____

_____

_____

_____

_____

_____

_____

_____

_____

F. Education: Take the following sentences and convert them into layman's terms to explain to the parent of a patient.

1. Infants with RDS are at risk for cerebral ischemia, hemorrhage, and neonatal death.

    _____

    _____

    _____

    _____

2. Postmature infants are prone to meconium aspiration and neonatal hypoglycemia.

    _____

    _____

    _____

    _____

G. **Prefixes and suffixes are good clues to the meaning of a medical term.** Analyze each medical term for the meaning of its prefix and suffix. Then give the complete meaning of the medical term in the last column. Every term may not have both a prefix and a suffix. Fill in the table.

Medical Term	Meaning of Prefix	Meaning of Suffix	Meaning of Medical Term
agenesis			
anorexia			
colic			
encephalocele			
enuresis			
pediatric			
psychosocial			
senile			
stereotype			
syndrome			

H. **English and Medical Terminology:** Some of the terminology in this chapter is rooted in Latin or Greek and can be literally translated and used in the English language or the language of medicine. On the line below each sentence, fill in the meaning for the bold word in that particular sentence. Fill in the blanks.

1. My sister is **depressed** and has been on medication for six years.

   _____

   Her immune system is **depressed,** and she is much more susceptible to disease.

   _____

2. Her **precipitate** labor threatened the life of her unborn child.

   _____

   In the centrifuge, the **precipitate** fell to the bottom of the tube.

   _____

   OR—A term may have more than one meaning, but only one meaning is specific to that particular context. Write the correct meaning of the bold word on the line below each of the following sentences.

3. The young child **aspirated** a peanut at the picnic and had to be rushed to the ER.

   _____

   The fluid in the patient's lungs was **aspirated** by a thorocentesis.

   _____

4. The Poison Control Center advised an emetic and **purging** of the child's stomach.

   _____

   Harsh laxatives may cause a **purging** of the intestinal tract.

   _____

LIFE SPAN

I. **Similar but Different:** Terms that appear similar can have very different meanings. When you know the terms well enough, you can briefly explain the difference between these terms. Write a short answer.

1. Food intolerance:

_____

_____

Food allergy:

_____

_____

2. Enuresis:

_____

_____

Encopresis:

_____

_____

J. **Elements:** Even though these elements do not appear in the context of a medical term, you should be able to recognize their meaning out of context. Match the correct element in column 1 with its meaning in column 2. Fill in the blanks.

_____	1. -plasia	**A.**	to adjust
_____	2. neo-	**B.**	old age
_____	3. -faci-	**C.**	forming
_____	4. -therm-	**D.**	relating to medicine
_____	5. -ile	**E.**	without
_____	6. ped-	**F.**	formation
_____	7. adapt-	**G.**	to roll up
_____	8. a- or an-	**H.**	capability
_____	9. -iatric	**I.**	new
_____	10. -ant	**J.**	face
_____	11. -volute-	**K.**	child
_____	12. geronto-	**L.**	heat

K. **Medical Language:** Employ the *language of pediatrics and gerontology* to answer the following multiple choice questions. Circle the correct answer.

1. The term **thermoregulation** has to do with:

    a. body weight

    b. body height

    c. body density

    d. body temperature

    e. body metabolism

2. Which of the following conditions causes a "blue" baby?

    a. cleft lip

    b. cyanosis

    c. hypoglycemia

    d. OCD

    e. encopresis

3. The medical term for feeding through a stomach tube is:

    a. senescence

    b. coma

    c. vegetative

    d. resuscitation

    e. gavage

4. This occurs most frequently in infants from C-sections and precipitate deliveries:

    a. transient tachypnea

    b. dyspnea

    c. enuresis

    d. dysplasia

    e. SIDS

5. Appointing someone you trust to make medical decisions for you is called:

    a. living will

    b. medical power of attorney

    c. DNR order

    d. consent form

    e. HIPAA authorization

LIFE SPAN

L. Medical Language: Employ the *language of pediatrics and gerontology* to answer the following multiple choice questions. Circle the best answer.

1. Neonatal reflex to turn toward and open mouth when nipple is placed on cheek:

   a. Moro reflex

   b. rooting

   c. stepping reflex

   d. startle reflex

   e. doll's eye maneuver

2. Synthetic surfactant is instilled:

   a. intertracheally

   b. subcutaneously

   c. intratracheally

   d. subdermally

   e. by gavage

3. Free radicals can be neutralized by:

   a. T lymphocytes (T cells)

   b. organ systems

   c. antioxidants

   d. enzymes

   e. hormones

4. Hypothermia is more likely to occur in infants who are:

   a. SFD

   b. premature

   c. postmature

   d. a and b

   e. a and c

5. Refusal to maintain a normal body weight is a symptom of:

   a. bulimia

   b. anorexia nervosa

   c. binge eating disorder

   d. dyslexia

   e. pica

6. Fetal distress can cause:

   a. Asperger syndrome

   b. meconium aspiration syndrome

   c. cleft palate

   d. Down syndrome

   e. HMD

7. The development of _____ is the key to the development of fully functioning lungs:

   a. ventilation

   b. surfactant

   c. precipitate

   d. osteoclasts

   e. protein

8. Exercise and good nutrition are helpful in preventing:

   a. cancer

   b. tumors

   c. freckles

   d. osteopenia

   e. COPD

9. Another name for whooping cough is:

   a. OCD

   b. TTN

   c. pertussis

   d. celiac disease

   e. jaundice

10. A milder form of autism is:

    a. Down syndrome

    b. hyaline membrane disease

    c. Asperger syndrome

    d. dyslexia

    e. ODD

LIFE SPAN

M. Deconstruct: The language of any body system can be analyzed by its basic elements. Deconstruct each of the following medical terms into the elements, which will reveal its meaning. Fill in the chart, then use any two of the terms in patient documentation. The first entry on the chart has been done for you.

Medical Term	Prefix/Meaning	Root/CF/Meaning	Suffix/Meaning	Meaning of Term
hydrocephalus	*hydro* water	*cephalus* head		*Enlarged head due to excess CSF in the cerebral ventricles*
involuntary				
anencephaly				
neural				
phototherapy				
pertussis				
neonatal				
microcephaly				
hypospadias				
atrophy				
postmortem				

Patient documentation:

1. _____

   _____

2. _____

   _____

N. Terminology Challenge: Find the synonym for the medical term **autopsy**. Deconstruct each term and provide a definition. Fill in the blanks.

1. The synonym for autopsy is: _____

2. Deconstruct each term into elements with meanings:

   autopsy: _____

   (synonym): _____

3. Definition of the terms: _____

   _____

4. What type of specialist is likely to perform an autopsy? _____

5. What can be learned from an autopsy? _____

   _____

O. **Language of Gerontology:** The following medical terms are all applicable to the *language of gerontology.* Build your knowledge of their meanings by correctly using each term in a sentence of your choice, which is *not a definition that appears in the text.* **Example:** The life expectancy at any given age will be considerably shortened if that person smokes cigarettes.

life span   **life expectancy**   **longevity**   **aging**   **senescence**

1. _____

_____

_____

_____

2. _____

_____

_____

_____

3. _____

_____

_____

_____

4. _____

_____

_____

_____

5. _____

_____

_____

_____

LIFE SPAN

P. **Recall and Review:** How well do you remember these word elements from the previous chapter? Try to answer without first looking back to check. Fill in the blanks.

Element	Type of Element (P, R, CF, S)	Meaning of Element
megaly	_____	_____
oid	_____	_____
ism	_____	_____
agglutin	_____	_____
macro	_____	_____

Q. **Latin and Greek terms cannot be further deconstructed into prefix, root, or suffix.** You must know them for what they are. Test your knowledge of these terms with the following exercise. Match the meaning in column 1 with the correct medical term in column 2.

_____ 1. to bend back	A. rooting
_____ 2. to hang from	B. peer
_____ 3. to grow old	C. bulimia
_____ 4. seek	D. diphtheria
_____ 5. full of manure	E. senescence
_____ 6. equal	F. purge
_____ 7. hunger	G. reflex
_____ 8. disposition	H. encopresis
_____ 9. to cleanse	I. dependent
_____ 10. leather	J. temperament

R. **Brain Teaser:** In a previous chapter you studied the term **lavage.** This chapter presents the term **gavage.** Demonstrate that you can use both terms correctly by first defining each term, and then using each term in a sentence that is not a definition.

1. Definition of lavage:

   _____

   _____

   Sentence:

   _____

   _____

   _____

   _____

2. Definition of gavage:

   _____

   _____

   Sentence:

   _____

   _____

   _____

   _____

LIFE SPAN

CHAPTER SUMMARY EXERCISE

1. Listen to the pronunciation of the medical terms as given by your instructor.
2. Circle the correct spelling of the medical term.
3. Match the correctly spelled terms to the brief descriptions below.
4. Write a sentence for each of the 15 terms that appear in this exercise.

A. SPELLING COMPREHENSION: CIRCLE THE CORRECT SPELLING OF THE TERM.

1. tetrailogy	tettrology	tetralogy	tedtrology	tidtrology
2. bullemia	bulimia	bulemia	buleemia	bulemea
3. jerontelogist	geronntologist	jerontologist	gerontologist	jirontologist
4. seenesence	cenescence	sinescence	ceniscence	senescence
5. purtusis	pertusis	pertussis	putussis	pertuses
6. rumination	rumenation	rummination	rimination	remination
7. hialine	hyline	hyaline	hilyne	hylene
8. innvolude	involute	involude	involede	invelute
9. deptheria	deeptheria	diphtheria	diptheria	dipteria
10. percentile	persentile	pircentile	pirsentile	persentiel
11. adolescence	addolesence	addelescence	adollesence	adolisence
12. entubation	intubation	entudation	intudation	enervation
13. ocuult	ocult	occult	ocullt	occultt
14. befid	bifit	bifid	beffid	befit
15. pediatrician	pidiatrican	patrician	pedeatrican	pediatricean

B. MATCH THE NUMBER OF THE CORRECT TERM IN PART A WITH THE BRIEF DESCRIPTION OF THE TERM BELOW.

a. specialist for infants through adolescents _____

b. not visible on the surface _____

c. disease with thick, leathery coating on the pharynx _____

d. insertion of a tube into the trachea _____

e. split in two parts _____

f. whooping cough _____

g. regressive changes occurring with aging _____

h. thin membrane in lung alveoli _____

i. to bring back food into the mouth to chew over and over_____

j. a set of four congenital heart defects _____

k. medical specialist for aged patient population _____

l. period between puberty and physical maturity _____

m. loss of cell function _____

n. episodic bouts of eating then throwing up _____

o. one of a hundred groups in a distribution of variables_____

C. USING YOUR KNOWLEDGE OF TERMS 1-15 IN PART A AND THEIR CORRECT SPELLING, WRITE A BRIEF SENTENCE AS IT MIGHT APPEAR IN PATIENT DOCUMENTATION.

1. _____

2. _____

3. _____

4. _____

5. _____

6. _____

7. _____

8. _____

9. _____

10. _____

11. _____

12. _____

13. _____

14. _____

15. _____

D. GO TO THE STUDENT CD. OPEN THE GLOSSARY AND PRACTICE YOUR PRONUNCIATION OF THE TERMS IN PART A OF THIS EXERCISE.

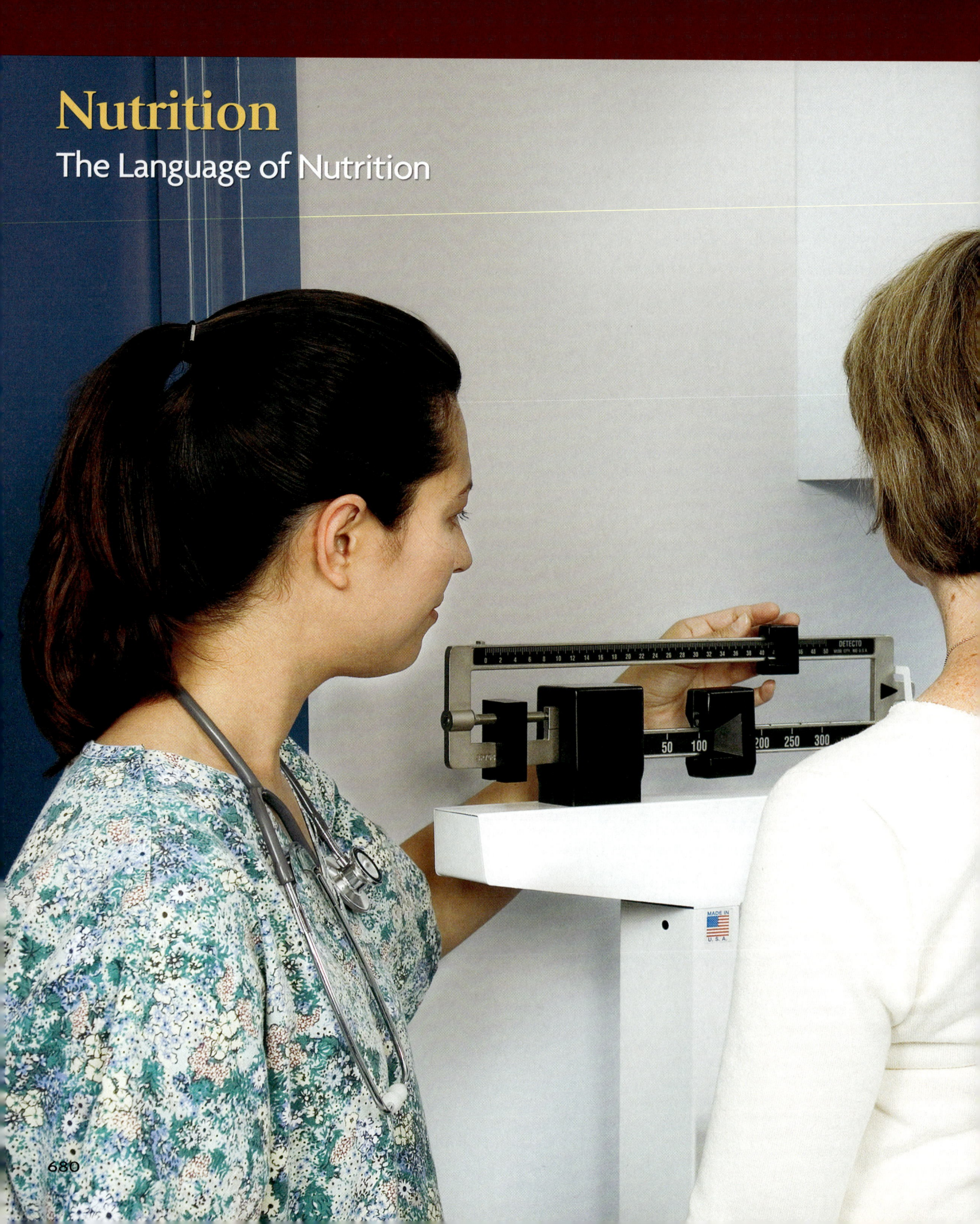

Nutrition
The Language of Nutrition

680

17

CASE REPORT 17.1

You are

. . . a nutrition assistant working with Karen Goodrich, MS, PhD, a **nutritionist** who provides guidance to patients referred from the different clinics at Fulwood Medical Center.

Your patient is

. . . Ms. Karen Johnson, a 20-year-old single woman, who is enrolled in a six-month nursing assistant program. She is concerned about her weight (140 pounds, five feet four inches) and the nutritional life style she should adopt. She has heard that she should be eating a high-carbohydrate **diet**. Her breakfast is a bowl of cereal with skim milk. For lunch, Ms. Johnson brown-bags a turkey sandwich with white bread, lettuce, tomato, and mustard and an 8-ounce bottle of apple juice. Dinner is either a frozen dinner entrée or pasta with a packaged marinara sauce. She snacks on fat-free yogurt and low-fat cookies. Once a week she goes out with her boyfriend and has several light beers and nachos.

Learning Outcomes

In order to be able to provide optimal care and communicate with your patient, other health care professionals, dieticians, and nutritionists, you need to be able to:

- Apply the language of nutrition to the form, function, metabolism, and well-being of the cells, tissues, and organs of the body.

- Describe in correct medical terminology the different nutrients and their roles in cell metabolism.

- Comprehend, analyze, spell, and write the language of nutrition so that you can communicate in writing and document accurately and precisely in any health care setting.

- Recognize and pronounce the language of nutrition so that you can communicate verbally with accuracy and precision in any health care setting.

- Explain the effects of a balanced diet and improper nutrition on health.

LESSON 17.1 Nutrients

Nutrition is the taking in and use of food and other nourishing material by the body. It is a three-part process:

1. The food or drink is consumed (**ingested**) into the digestive system.
2. The food or drink is **digested** and broken down into **nutrients** that are **absorbed** from the digestive tract into the bloodstream.
3. The nutrients are **transported** by the bloodstream to cells all over the body to be used for energy, cell maintenance, reproduction, growth, and repair.

In Chapter 6 (digestive system), you learned how different foods were digested, metabolized into nutrients, and absorbed into the bloodstream. The information in this lesson will enable you to use correct terminology to:

- **Define the term Calorie and the sources of dietary calories.**
- **Identify the major groups of nutrients and their functions.**
- **Describe the food sources of the nutrients.**
- **Discuss the roles of dietary fiber.**
- **Use correct medical terminology to explain the effects of nutrients on body functions.**

Keynote

The term **Calorie** in metabolism always has an uppercase "C" and represents 1,000 calories (lower case "c").

Abbreviations

AI	adequate intake
BMR	basal metabolic rate
g	gram
RDA	recommended dietary allowance

NUTRIENTS

The energy stored by most **nutrients** is taken and used by your body in cellular metabolism. The term **Calorie** is used to express the quantities of energy supplied by foods and to measure the energy needs of your body. Each **gram (g)** of carbohydrate yields 4 Calories of energy. Each gram of protein yields 4 Calories. Each gram of fat yields 9 Calories. This daily input of energy supplied by food should equal your body's metabolic expenditure of energy (*Table 17.1*).

Basal metabolic rate (BMR) is the energy expenditure by your body when at rest. Total energy expenditure depends on the BMR, the energy expended for physical activity, and the energy expended in synthesizing reserves of energy such as glycogen, fat, and protein.

Exercise increases your **metabolic rate,** the total amount of energy produced and used by the body in a unit of time. Walking briskly will use 7 Calories per minute, jogging 13 Calories per minute. If you jog for 40 minutes each day for a week, you can lose a pound of body fat. Exercise is the only component of energy expenditure that you can control. A combination of exercise and dietary control can modify weight.

TABLE 17.1 Caloric Needs per Day

	Caloric Range	
Children	**Sedentary**	**Active**
2–3 years	1,000	1,400
Females		
14–18	1,800	2,400
19–30	1,800	2,400
31–50	1,500	2,200
50 +	1,500	2,000
Males		
14–18	2,200	3,000
19–30	2,400	3,200
31–50	2,200	3,000
50 +	2,000	2,800

Based on U.S. Department of Agriculture (USDA). www.mypyramid.gov, 2005.

WORD	PRONUNCIATION		ELEMENTS	DEFINITION
absorption	ab-**SORP**-shun	S/ R/	-ion *action condition* absorpt- *take in*	Uptake of nutrients and water by cells in the GI tract
basal metabolic rate (BMR)	**BAY**-sal met-ah-**BOL**-ic RATE	S/ R/ S/ R/	-al *pertaining to* bas- *base* -ic *pertaining to* metabol- *change* rate *Latin a reckoning*	Energy the body requires to function at rest
Calorie caloric (adj)	**KAL**-oh-ree kah-**LOR**-ik	S/ R/	Latin *heat* -ic *pertaining to* calor- *heat*	An expression of the energy content of food; capitalize "C" always Pertaining to Calories
diet dietetics dietician (alternative spelling: dietitian)	**DIE**-et die-eh-**TET**-iks die-eh-**TISH**-un	S/ R/ S/	Greek *a way of life* -etics *pertaining to* diet- *a way of life* -ician *one who does*	Specific course of eating and drinking Application of diet to prevention and treatment of disease Licensed professional in dietetics
nutrient nutritive (adj)	**NYU**-tree-ent **NYU**-trih-tiv	S/ R/	Latin *to nourish* -ive *quality of* nutrit- *nourishment*	A substance in food required for normal physiological function Providing nourishment
nutrition nutritionist	nyu-**TRISH**-un nyu-**TRISH**-un-ist	S/ S/ R/	Latin *to nourish* -tion- *a process* -ist *specialist in* nutri- *nourish*	Food and liquid requirements for normal function of the human body Certified professional in nutrition science

The intake of a nutrient that is sufficient to meet the daily needs of 97% of individuals in a specific age and gender group is called the **Recommended Dietary Allowance (RDA)**. If there is insufficient information available to calculate an RDA, the nutrient is given a recommended value called its **Adequate Intake (AI)**.

The six groups of nutrients are carbohydrates, lipids, proteins, vitamins, minerals, and water.

EXERCISES

Language of Nutrition. *This knowledge about nutrition and its specialized vocabulary will aid you in taking better care of your patients and provide you with an awareness of how to improve and maintain your own health. Apply correct medical terminology to fill in each blank.*

1. Nutrition is a three-part process: (briefly define each part)

   a. Ingestion _____

   b. Digestion _____

   c. Transportation _____

2. The term _____ is used to express the quantities of energy supplied by foods and to measure the energy needs of your body.

3. (BMR)_____ is the energy expenditure by the body when at rest.

4. Exercise increases _____ rate—the total amount of energy produced and used by the body in a unit of time.

5. The intake of a nutrient that is sufficient to meet the daily needs of 97% of individuals in a specific age and gender group is called the _____ or _____ (abbreviation).

6. If there is insufficient information available to calculate an RDA, the value given is called _____ (abbreviation).

CARBOHYDRATES

Carbohydrates vary from the complex starch in potatoes to the simple sugars of **glucose, fructose** (fruit sugar), and **sucrose** (table sugar). The simple sugars on their own have calories but no nutrient value. They are said to have **empty calories.**

Most carbohydrates are broken down to glucose, the major source of energy in cells.

Glycogen, the storage form of carbohydrate, is found in the liver and skeletal muscles. Glycogen in muscles supplies glucose during high intensity and endurance exercise.

The RDA of carbohydrates is 130 grams per day for an adult. Most North Americans consume 180 to 300 g/day. The leading sources of carbohydrate intake are bread, soft drinks, cookies, cakes and doughnuts, syrups, jams, and potatoes.

Artificial Sugars

Nutritive sweeteners is a term used for all of the sugars that provide energy as well as sweetness. **High-fructose corn syrup** is manufactured from cornstarch. It is used in many processed foods such as cookies, soft drinks, jam, and jelly. It is mostly fructose and is cheaper than sucrose. **Brown sugar** is sucrose with some **molasses. Maple syrup** is made by boiling down the sap of sugar maple trees. **Honey** is plant nectar broken down by bee enzymes into fructose and glucose. It offers only the same nutritional value as the other sugars.

Sugar alcohols, for example, **sorbitol,** provide energy (3 Calories/g), are absorbed more slowly than sucrose, and they are metabolized to glucose. They are used in sugarless gum, breath mints, and candy.

Alternative or artificial sweeteners provide no energy, only sweetness *(Table 17.2)*. Six are currently available in the United States:

- **Saccharin,** no longer considered a potential cause of cancer, is used in diet drinks.

- **Aspartame,** sold as Nutrasweet and Equal, is used in diet beverages, gelatin desserts, chewing gum, and toppings and fillings in bakery goods and cookies. Because aspartame is made from **phenylalanine,** people with **phenylketonuria (PKU)** *(see Chapter 21)* must avoid it.

- **Neotame** is also a phenylalanine derivative that is heat stable and can be found in cooked products, as well as soft drinks and chewing gum.

- **Acesulfame-K** is heat stable and is found in many baked goods.

- **Sucralose** is derived from sucrose, is heat stable, and is used in baked goods, ice creams, and juices and for tabletop use as Splenda.

- **Stevia** is an herb that is sold as a diet supplement. It is heat stable and can be used in cooking but does not add texture to food.

Abbreviation

PKU	phenylketonuria

TABLE 17.2 Relative Sweetness

Substance	Sweetness Compared to Sucrose
Sucrose (table sugar)	1
Saccharin	300 ×
Aspartame	180–200 ×
Neotame	7000–13,000 ×
Acesulfame-K	200 ×
Sucralose	600 ×
Stevia	150–400 ×

WORD	PRONUNCIATION	ELEMENTS		DEFINITION
carbohydrate	kar-boh-**HIGH**-drate	S/ R/CF R/	-ate *action, composed of* carb/o- *carbon* -hydr- *water*	Group of organic food compounds that includes sugars, starch, glycogen, and cellulose
fructose	**FRUK**-toes	S/ R/	-ose *full of* fruct- *fruit*	Sugar found in fruits and honey
glucose	**GLU**-koes	S/ R/	-ose *full of* gluc- *sugar, glucose*	The final product of carbohydrate digestion and the main sugar in the blood
glycogen	**GLYE**-koh-jen	S/ R/CF	-gen *to produce* glyc/o- *sugar, glucose*	The body's principal carbohydrate reserve, stored in the liver and skeletal muscle
molasses	mo-**LASS**-iz		Latin *honeylike*	Dark-colored syrups produced during the refining of sugar
phenylalanine	fen-il-**AL**-ah-neen	R/ R/	phenyl- *chemical group* -alanine *protein synthesized in muscle*	An amino acid
phenylketonuria	**FEN**-il-**KEE**-toe-**NYU**-ree-ah	S/ R/ R/	-uria *urine* phenyl- *chemical group* -keton- *ketone*	Hereditary disease with accumulation of phenylalanine and urinary excretion of its metabolites; leads to mental retardation if not controlled
sorbitol	**SOR**-bih-tol	S/ R/	-ol *alcohol* sorbit- *fruit of a tree*	Alcohol derivative of glucose
sucrose	**SUE**-krose	S/ R/	-ose *full of* sucr- *table sugar*	Table sugar
sugar	**SHUH**-gar		Latin *sugar*	Basic carbohydrate; term sometimes used for glucose or sucrose

EXERCISES

Deconstruct *the following medical terms into their basic elements. Write the meaning of the medical term in the last column. Remember to answer the question following the table.*

Medical Term	Root/CF	Suffix	Meaning of Medical Term
phenylketonuria			
carbohydrate			
phenylalanine			
sorbitol			

What is one important fact about carbohydrates that you did not know until you read this lesson? _____

_____

CARBOHYDRATES (continued)

Fiber

Keynote

Sources of fiber are whole-grain breads, high-fiber cereals, fruits, vegetables, and beans.

Fiber consists of complex carbohydrates that cannot be broken down by the human digestive process. These carbohydrates are dietary fiber. It is undigested as it leaves the small intestine to enter the colon, where it provides bulk and softness for the stool. Whole grains have their outer covering intact and are a good source of dietary fiber, some vitamins, and magnesium.

Water soluble dietary fiber, including pectin and gum, slows glucose absorption from the small intestine, of value to diabetics and overweight people. It also inhibits absorption of cholesterol, reducing the risk of cardiovascular disease and gallstones. Fruits, vegetables, and beans in general are rich sources of soluble fiber.

Functional fibers are those that can be added to foods. They are plant-based compounds such as **cellulose, pectins,** and gums. Some of these fibers are soluble and are fermented by bacteria in the large intestine to produce gases such as methane.

The AI for fiber is 25 g/day for women and 38 g/day for men. In North America, the average intake is about half these figures.

Keynote

One-third of people over age 45 have diverticulosis.

Lack of fiber in the diet can lead to small, hard stools and constipation. Excessive pressure may be needed for defecation. This high pressure developed in the colon can force parts of the colon wall out between the bands of muscle, producing pouches called diverticula and the asymptomatic disorder called diverticulosis. If the diverticula stay filled with feces, they can become inflamed and painful, a condition called diverticulitis *(see Chapter 6)*.

Choice of Carbohydrates

Simple sugars provide calories but have no nutritional value. Overcrowding the diet with sugar can mean that foods such as fruits and vegetables, that are dense in nutrients, are left out. Foods that are advertised as low-fat and fat-free usually contain lots of added sugar to produce an acceptable taste.

Simple sugars are absorbed rapidly and converted into blood glucose. This rapid blood glucose response is called a high **glycemic index (GI)** and results in a high **glycemic load (GL)** in the body. These high-glycemic-load carbohydrates generate a high insulin output from the pancreas *(see Chapter 14)*. A persistent high insulin output produces numerous ill-effects on the body:

- increased **fat deposits** in adipose tissue
- increased **fat synthesis** in the liver
- high **low-density lipoprotein (LDL)**—"bad cholesterol"—levels and high triglycerides *(see Chapter 6)*
- rapid return of **hunger** after a meal

Complex carbohydrates with a **starch** structure and fiber content are absorbed much more slowly and have a lower glycemic index. Glucose is given a glycemic index of 100. Low GI foods are below 55 and should be chosen when possible. High GI foods are over 70 and should be chosen in minimal quantities, if at all. A glycemic load of 20 is high, 10 or below is low *(Table 17.3)*.

Abbreviations	
GI	glycemic index
GL	glycemic load
LDL	low-density lipoprotein

Case Report 17.1 (continued)

Your training as a nutrition assistant tells you that, from the carbohydrate perspective, Karen Johnson's diet is lacking in fruits and vegetables, and this affects her fiber intake. Also, her bread should be changed to whole-grain to increase her fiber. Her snacks of fat-free yogurt and low-fat cookies will have added simple sugars and will generate a high glycemic load. The snacks should be replaced by fresh produce, such as apples and other fruits and any raw vegetables that she enjoys.

WORD ANALYSIS AND DEFINITION

S = Suffix   P = Prefix   R = Root   R/CF = Combining Form

WORD	PRONUNCIATION	ELEMENTS		DEFINITION
cellulose	SELL-you-lohse	S/ R/	-ose *carbohydrate* cellul- *small cell*	Major constituent of cell walls of plants
fiber	FIE-ber		Latin *fiber*	Carbohydrate not digested by intestinal enzymes; or a strand or filament
glycemic index	glye-SEE-mic IN-deks	S/ R/ R/	-emic *in the blood* glyc- *sugar* index *to declare*	Measure of the rapidity in rise of blood glucose after ingestion of carbohydrates
glycemic load	glye-SEE-mic LOHD	R/	load *to carry*	Takes into account the amount of sugar available in the food to cause the rise in blood sugar
pectin	PEK-tin		Greek *to make solid*	Plant fiber with the ability to thicken and solidify to a gel
starch	STARCH		Anglo-Saxon *stiffen*	Complex carbohydrate made of multiple units of glucose attached together

TABLE 17.3 Glycemic Index and Glycemic Load of Foods

Food	Glycemic Index	Glycemic Load
Glucose	100	50
Potato (baked)	85	26
Honey	73	10
Cheerios	74	15
White rice	72	23
Bread (white or whole-grain), bagel	70	10
Coca Cola	63	16
Carrots	49	3
Apple	38	6
Milk (skim)	32	4
Lentils	30	5
Peanuts	14	2

EXERCISES

Apply your knowledge of elements to the following questions. One element is present in several different terms and has the same meaning in all of them. Fill in the blanks.

1. What do the terms **anemia, uremia,** and **glycemia** all have in common?

_____

_____

2. Which body systems are affected by the conditions described by these terms?

_____

Insert these medical terms in the appropriate places in the following sentence:

diverticulosis   **diverticulitis**   **diverticula**

3. The patient's multiple _____ became infected, and the condition that began as _____ then became _____.

4. The specialist that this patient needs to see for this condition is a(n): _____ .

TABLE 17.4 Food with High Saturated Fat Content

Food Item and Amount	Fat (grams)	Saturated Fat (grams)
T-bone steak, 6 oz.	34	14.0
Hamburger, 4 oz.	20	8.0
Peanuts, oil roasted, ½ cup	35.7	5.0
Doughnut, plain, 1	13.0	3.0

Abbreviations

EFA	*essential fatty acid*
HDL	*high-density lipoprotein*
omega-3	*alpha-linolenic acid*
omega-6	*linolenic acid*

Keynote

Two-thirds of your body cholesterol is made by your cells, and the remaining one-third is derived from your diet. Plant foods do not contain cholesterol.

▲ **FIGURE 17.1 Tastes Great But High in Saturated Fat.**

LIPIDS

Lipids that are solid at room temperature are called **fats;** for example, the solid fat around an uncooked steak. Lipids that are liquid are called **oils.** Lipids do not dissolve in water. For example, the oil in an oil and vinegar salad dressing will not mix with the water-based vinegar.

Triglycerides comprise 95% of the fat in the human diet and have three main categories:

- **saturated fats or fatty acids** are found in meats, dairy products (milk, cheese, butter), and eggs. These are solid at room temperature.
- **unsaturated fats or fatty acids** are found mostly in oils such as olive, peanut, safflower, and canola oil. These are liquid at room temperature.
- **hydrogenated trans fatty acids** are formed commercially by partial hydrogenation of unsaturated vegetable oils to make them solid or semisolid. Trans fatty acids are found in margarine, shortenings, pie crusts, crackers, croissants, and French fries. The labeling of the content of trans fatty acids in food is required. They raise LDL levels, lower **high-density lipoprotein (HDL)** levels *(see Chapter 8)*, and have no role in maintaining body health. They should be avoided as much as possible. Some cities and states are banning their use.

Essential fatty acids (EFAs) are so-called because the body cannot synthesize them and they must be ingested. **Linolenic acid (omega-6)** and **alpha-linolenic acid (omega-3)** are essential fatty acids, which have important roles in cell structure and immune system function. The EFAs are found in plant oils or fatty fish such as salmon, tuna, and sardines.

Cholesterol is a steroid characterized as a lipid because it does not dissolve in water. Cholesterol has the following functions:

- forms part of hormones (such as estrogen and testosterone) and active vitamin D
- precursor of bile acids, which are essential for fat digestion *(see Chapter 6)*
- an essential component of cell membranes
- an essential component of the LDL and HDL particles that transport lipids in the blood *(see Chapter 8)*

Fat Intake

There are no RDAs for fat intake for adults. Most authorities recommend that fat intake should be between 30 and 35% of energy intake, with minimal trans fat and saturated fat intake *(Table 17.4)*. Omega-3 and omega-6 fatty acids should be included in the diet. For a person on a 2000 Calorie diet, this would involve 600 to 700 Calories coming from fat. At 9 Calories/g, this means eating 65 to 80 g of fat per day.

Combining these concepts with what you have learned about carbohydrates, a good diet plan could emphasize vegetables, fruits, plant oils, and whole grains; use fish, poultry, eggs, and dairy products daily but sparingly, and avoid red meats, white rice, white bread, potatoes, pasta, and sweets *(Figure 17.1)*.

Case Report 17.1 (continued)

As a nutrition assistant, you would advise Karen Johnson to avoid nachos, which contain saturated fats and lots of calories, and the processed frozen dinner, which probably contains trans fats.

WORD ANALYSIS AND DEFINITION

S = Suffix   P = Prefix   R = Root   R/CF = Combining Form

WORD	PRONUNCIATION		ELEMENTS	DEFINITION
cholesterol	koh-**LESS**-ter-ol	S/ R/CF	-sterol *steroid* chol/e- *bile*	Formed in liver cells; is the most abundant steroid in tissues and circulates in the plasma attached to proteins of different densities
fat fatty acid	FAT **FAT**-ee **ASS**-id		Old English *fat*	Lipid that is solid at room temperature An acid obtained from the hydrolysis of fats
hydrogenated	**HIGH**-dro-jeh-**NAY**-ted	S/ S/ R/	-ated *action, process* -gen- *producing* hydro- *water*	Addition of hydrogen to unsaturated oils to solidify them and produce trans fats
lipid	**LIP**-id		Greek *fat*	General term for all types of fatty compounds; for example, cholesterol, triglycerides, and fatty acids
saturated fatty acid	satch-you-**RAY**-ted **FAT**-ee **ASS**-id	S/ R/	-ated *action, process* satur- *to fill*	Incapable of absorbing any more hydrogen
trans fatty acid	TRANZ **FAT**-ee **ASS**-id		trans Latin *through, across*	Solid or semisolid product of hydrogenation of unsaturated plant oils
triglyceride	tri-**GLISS**-eh-ride	S/ P/ R/	-ide *having a specific quality* tri- *three* -glycer- *sweet*	Has three fatty acids
unsaturated fatty acid	un-**SATCH**-you-ray-ted **FAT**-ee **ASS**-id	S/ P/ R/	-ated *composed of* un- *not* -satur- *to fill*	Found mostly in oils and is liquid at room temperature

---

EXERCISES   *Elements are the key to learning medical terminology. Build your knowledge of elements with the following exercise. Match the meaning in column l with the correct element in column 2.*

_____ 1. three

_____ 2. not

_____ 3. action, process

_____ 4. water

_____ 5. through, across

_____ 6. sweet

_____ 7. producing

_____ 8. steroid

_____ 9. to fill

_____ 10. bile

A. chol/e-

B. -gen

C. -sterol

D. -glycer-

E. satur-

F. tri-

G. trans-

H. hydro-

I. un-

J. -ated

PROTEINS

Proteins are essential for health. Proteins form the major part of lean body tissue, about 17% of body weight. **Amino acids** are the building blocks of proteins and help build and repair tissue. They consist of carbon linked to nitrogen. Twenty different amino acids are divided into two groups:

1. **essential amino acids,** which the body cannot **synthesize** and therefore have to be obtained in the diet.
2. **nonessential amino acids,** which the body can synthesize from other molecules.

A **complete protein food** contains all **nine** essential amino acids. Examples are meat, fish, poultry, cheese, and eggs. **Incomplete protein foods** do not contain all nine essential amino acids. Examples are grains, leafy green vegetables, and **legumes** (beans and peas). A variety of plant proteins have to be consumed to obtain the different essential amino acids.

Proteins perform numerous functions in the body:

- **Collagen** provides structural strength in connective tissue *(see Chapter 5)*.
- **Keratin** provides structural strength in skin *(see Chapter 3)*.
- **Hormones** regulate physiologic processes by communicating between cells *(see Chapter 14)*.
- **Enzymes** regulate the rate of chemical reactions and function as catalysts *(see Chapter 6)*.
- **Hemoglobin** transports oxygen and carbon dioxide in the blood *(see Chapter 7)*.
- **Antibodies, complement, and lymphokines** are essential components of the immune system *(see Chapter 15)*.
- **Proteins** are a source of energy, providing 4 Calories per gram.
- **Proteins transport** other molecules outside the cell, through the cell membrane, and inside the cell.
- **Proteins bind** cells to each other to keep tissues from falling apart and enable immune cells to bind to cancer cells.

TABLE 17.5 Food Sources of Protein

Food Item and Amount	Protein (Grams)
Roast beef, 3.5 oz.	28.0
Fish, 3.5 oz.	21.0
Hamburger, 3.5 oz.	20.0
Peanut butter, 2 tablespoons	10.0
Baked potato, 8 oz.	9.0
Whole milk, 8 oz.	8.0
Peanuts, 1 oz.	7.3
Cheddar cheese, 1 oz.	7.0
Egg, 1	6.0
Oatmeal, cooked, 1 cup	6.0
Natural cereal, ½ cup	4.0
Whole-grain bread, 1 slice	2.6
Raw vegetables, ½ cup	2.6

WORD	PRONUNCIATION		ELEMENTS	DEFINITION
amino acid	ah-ME-no ASS-id		amino *nitrogen containing*	The basic building block for protein
complete	kom-PLEET	P/ R/	com- *with, together* -plete *filled*	Whole, entire, total
essential	eh-SEN-shal	S/	-ial *pertaining to*	Amino acids that cannot be synthesized by the body
nonessential	NON-ee-SEN-shal	P/ R/	non- *not* -essent- *existence*	Can be synthesized by the body
incomplete (**Note:** This word has two prefixes.)	in-kom-PLEET	P/ P/ R/	in- *not* -com- *with, together* -plete *filled*	Lacking some part
legume	LEG-yoom		Latin *plant with seed-pods*	Family of plants including peas, beans, and lentils
protein	PRO-teen	S/ R/CF	-in *neutral chemical* prot/e- *first*	Class of food substances based on amino acids
synthesis synthesize (verb)	SIN-the-sis SIN-the-size	P/ R/	syn- *together* -thesis *arrange, place*	The process of building a compound from different elements

Protein Intake

The RDA for protein intake is expressed as 0.8 g of protein per kilogram of body weight. This works out to about 56 g of protein per day for a person weighing 154 pounds and 46 g of protein for a person weighing 125 pounds. North American men consume about 95 g protein daily, and women consume about 65 g daily. The excess protein is turned into glucose or fat and used for energy or stored in adipose tissue.

Pregnant women require an extra 10 g of protein daily; lactating women an extra 15 g.

For most North Americans, 70% of protein comes from animal sources. Vegetable sources of protein include soy, nuts, and legumes *(Table 17.5)*. They contain no cholesterol, little saturated fat, and legumes contain soluble fiber.

EXERCISES   **Lesson Objective.** *Meet the lesson objective and relate medical vocabulary to function by matching the correct medical terminology in column 1 with the correct function in column 2.*

_____ 1. hemoglobin

_____ 2. hormones

_____ 3. enzymes

_____ 4. antibodies

_____ 5. keratin

_____ 6. collagen

A. regulate chemical reactions

B. provides structural strength in skin

C. components of the immune system

D. provides structural strength in tissue

E. regulate physiologic processes

F. transports O_2 and CO_2 in blood

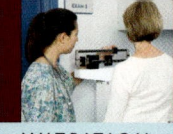

LESSON 17.2 Vitamins and Minerals

NUTRITION

OBJECTIVES

Neither vitamins nor minerals are used as fuel to provide calories, but both are essential to our ability to use the other nutrients and are only needed in small quantities. The information in this lesson will enable you to:

- **Identify the major vitamins and minerals needed by the body.**
- **Describe the sources and functions of the major vitamins and minerals.**
- **Explain the sources and functions of trace minerals.**
- **Use correct medical terminology to describe the effects of vitamins and minerals on body functions.**

Keynote

Only vitamin D and niacin can be synthesized by the body—but in inadequate amounts. Therefore, all vitamins have to be acquired in the diet or through supplements.

Abbreviations

IU	international units
μg	microgram, one-millionth of a gram

VITAMINS

Vitamins are **organic** (carbon-containing) substances that are essential in small amounts for the normal function of cells. Both plant and animal foods supply vitamins. Vitamins synthesized in the laboratory are no different from natural vitamins, except for vitamin E, which is twice as potent in its natural form.

Water-soluble vitamins are vitamin C and the B vitamins.

Fat-soluble vitamins do not dissolve in water and are vitamins A, D, E, and K.

Some of the vitamins in foods can be lost during transport from the field to the store, and cooking in water can remove more. The least contact with water and as short a cooking time as possible preserves more nutrients and vitamins.

Vegetables and fruits frozen soon after picking contain as many nutrients and vitamins as fresh supermarket produce.

FAT-SOLUBLE VITAMINS

Vitamin E Vitamin E functions as an efficient **antioxidant,** preventing the propagation of cell-damaging chain reactions caused by **free radicals**. There is widespread scientific agreement that adequate quantities of fruits and vegetables help to lower the incidence of cancer and cardiovascular disease. It has not yet been proven that this effect is due to antioxidants.

Vitamin E deficiency can occur in premature newborns because only small amounts cross the placenta. Premature newborns can develop anemia and bleeding into the brain and retina. Deficiency is rare among older children and adults.

Excess vitamin E can lead to hemorrhagic stroke, particularly in people taking the anticoagulant Coumadin (warfarin) *(see Chapter 7)*.

Sources of vitamin E are plant oils (e.g., corn, safflower, soybean), asparagus, peanuts, oatmeal, nuts, and seeds (e.g., sunflower seeds) *(Figure 17.2)*. The RDA for vitamin E is 15 mg/day for men and women. This is equivalent to 22 **international units (IU)** of a natural source and 33 IU of a **synthetic** source. Two tablespoons of chunky peanut butter contains 3.6 IU of vitamin E.

▲ **FIGURE 17.2 Plant Oils Are Rich Sources of Vitamin E.**

WORD	PRONUNCIATION	ELEMENTS		DEFINITION
antioxidant	an-tee-**OKS**-ih-dant	S/ P/ R/	-ant *forming* anti- *against* -oxid- *oxidize*	Substance that can prevent cell damage by neutralizing free radicals
free radical	FREE **RAD**-ih-kal	R/ S/ R/	free *free* -al *pertaining to* radic- *root*	Short-lived product of oxidation in a cell that can be damaging to the cell
mineral	**MIN**-er-al	S/ R/	-al *pertaining to* miner- *mines*	Inorganic compound usually found in earth's crust
organic	or-**GAN**-ik		Greek *organ*	Compound with carbon atoms. Food produced without using chemicals
synthetic	sin-**THET**-ik	S/ P/ R/	-ic *pertaining to* syn- *together* -thet- *place, arrange*	Built up or put together from simpler compounds
vitamin	**VYE**-tah-min	R/ R/	vit- *life* -amin *nitrogen containing*	Essential organic substance necessary in small amounts for normal cell function

Vitamin K   Vitamin K is essential for blood clotting and is required for the synthesis of the clotting factors by the liver *(see Chapter 7)*. One example is the formation of prothrombin. Sources of vitamin K are liver, green leafy vegetables, salad greens *(Figure 17.3)*, broccoli, peas, green beans, and vegetable oils. The AI is 90 μg/day for women and 120 μg/day for men. One-half cup cooked green beans contains 49 μg of vitamin K.

Vitamin K deficiency can occur in newborns, and vitamin K is given routinely by injection within six hours of birth. Deficiency can also occur in patients taking antibiotics for a long period of time.

▲ **FIGURE 17.3 Salad Greens.**
A salad containing dark greens (or other green vegetables) each day provides abundant vitamin K for a diet.

EXERCISES

*Build more knowledge of the **language of nutrition**. Answers to all the questions can be found on these two pages. Circle the best answer.*

1. Preventing the propagation of cell-damaging chain reactions caused by free radicals is the function of a(n):
   a. antibiotic
   b. antiemetic
   c. anticonvulsant
   d. antioxidant
   e. anticoagulant

2. Vitamins are supplied by:
   a. plant foods
   b. water
   c. animal foods
   d. only a and c
   e. a, b, and c

3. Which of these will help preserve more of the vitamins in food:
   a. quicker transportation from field to store
   b. shorter cooking time
   c. less contact with water
   d. all of these
   e. only a and b

4. Vitamin K is essential for:
   a. digestion
   b. higher RBC count
   c. blood clotting
   d. strong bones
   e. smoother skin

5. The water-soluble vitamins are:
   a. A
   b. B vitamins
   c. C
   d. all of these
   e. only b and c

6. Name one source of vitamin K:
   a. milk
   b. cheese
   c. liver
   d. nuts
   e. oatmeal

FAT-SOLUBLE VITAMINS (continued)

Vitamin A

Vitamin A is found in two forms.

1. **Carotenoids** are vitamin A precursors and produce the yellow-orange pigment in fruits and vegetables. Carotenoids are also found in green vegetables and fruits *(Figure 17.4)*. **Beta carotene** can be converted to vitamin A and provides the skin with some protection from ultraviolet light damage. **Lutein** and **zeaxanthin,** the yellow pigment in corn, appear to delay the age-related eye diseases macular degeneration and cataracts *(see Chapter 4)*. **Lycopene,** the red pigment in tomatoes, provides some protection against prostate cancer *(see Chapter 12)*. Carotenoids also act as antioxidants *(see Vitamin E)*.

2. **Retinoids** are preformed vitamin A and are found in liver, egg yolk, butter, fish oils, and fortified milk. Vitamin A is needed by the retina to change visual light into nerve signals to the brain and to maintain the cell types in the retina, cornea, and epithelium of the eye. It is also necessary for the function of epithelial cells in the lungs, trachea, gastrointestinal tract, and skin. Because of its effect on skin, forms of **retinoic acid,** such as Retin-A, are used to treat skin damage.

Infants who drink too much carrot juice or eat too much winter squash can turn a yellow-orange color due to high carotenoid deposition in the skin. This **hypercarotenemia** can be mistaken for the **hyperbilirubinemia** of jaundice.

Vitamin A deficiency can lead to impaired dark adaptation and night blindness and to growth retardation in children.

Vitamin D

Skin cells can synthesize vitamin D with exposure to sunlight. This can provide 90% of your needs, except in winter in northern climates and in elderly people when aging decreases production. The most active form of vitamin D is called **calcitriol,** a potent hormone that raises blood calcium concentration.

Dietary sources of vitamin D include fatty fish (such as salmon and sardines), fish oils, and fortified milk. Eight ounces of fortified milk contains 99 IU of vitamin D.

The AI of vitamin D for adults is 200 IU per day; this increases to 400 IU per day for those over 50 years. Infants are born with sufficient vitamin D to last about six months, at which time a breast-fed infant should be exposed to sunlight or given a vitamin D supplement. Breast milk does not come fortified with vitamin D.

Vitamin D's functions relate primarily to calcium and phosphorus metabolism to:

- increase **intestinal absorption of calcium** from foods; this makes calcium available for incorporation into bone and teeth
- **release calcium from bone** if blood calcium levels are low
- **maintain the function of neuromuscular junctions**

Vitamin D deficiency leads to inadequate calcium and phosphorus deposition in bone. In children, this causes **rickets,** in which the weakened leg bones bow under weight-bearing pressure and the pelvis is deformed *(Figure 17.5)*. In adults, this disease is called **osteomalacia:** this is different from osteoporosis, in which the rate of bone resorption exceeds the rate of bone formation and the bones are liable to fracture *(see Chapter 5)*.

▲ **FIGURE 17.4 Carotenoids Are Vitamin A Precursors.**

Many vegetables, such as asparagus and broccoli, are rich in carotenoids.

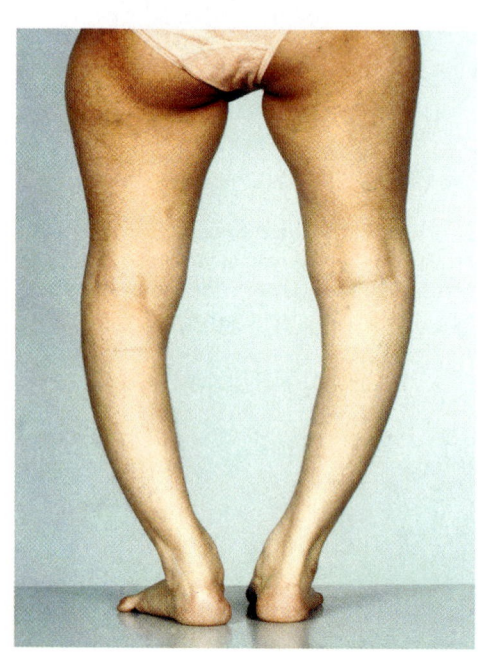

▲ **FIGURE 17.5 Bowed Legs of Rickets.**

WORD ANALYSIS AND DEFINITION

S = Suffix   P = Prefix   R = Root   R/CF = Combining Form

WORD	PRONUNCIATION	ELEMENTS		DEFINITION
beta carotene	BAY-tah KAR-oh-teen	R/ R/	beta *second letter of Greek alphabet* carotene *yellow-red pigment*	Yellow-red pigment in fruits and vegetables
calcitriol (*Note:* The prefix **tri-** relates to the chemical substance.)	KAL-sih-TRY-ol	S/ P/ R/CF	-ol *chemical substance* -tri- *three* calc/i- *calcium*	Potent form of vitamin D that acts as a hormone
carotenoid	kah-ROT-en-oyd	S/ R/	-oid *resemble* caroten- *yellow-red pigment*	Organic pigment occurring naturally in plants
hypercarotenemia (*Note:* The final "e" in -carotene is dropped for easier flow and pronunciation.)	HIGH-per-KAR-o-teh-NEE-me-ah	S/ P/ R/	-emia *blood condition* hyper- *above, excessive* -caroten- *carotene*	Excessive level of the yellow-red pigment carotene in the blood
lutein	LOO-tee-in		Latin *saffron yellow*	Yellow pigment
lycopene	LIE-koh-peen		Latin *tomato*	Carotenoid that gives tomatoes their red color
retinoid	RET-ih-noyd	S/ R/	-oid *resembling* retin- *resin*	A class of keratolytic agents
retinoic acid	ret-ih-NO-ik ASS-id	S/ R/CF	-ic *pertaining to* retin/o- *resin*	
rickets	RICK-ets		Old English *to twist*	Disease due to vitamin D deficiency, producing soft flexible bones
zeaxanthin	ZEE-ah-ZAN-thin	S/ P/ R/	-in *pertaining to* zea- *to live* -xanth- *yellow*	Carotenoid found in pepper, corn, and spinach

EXERCISES

Identify the correct nutritional vocabulary based on the clues given. After you have identified the term, deconstruct the term into its elements, then answer the questions. Fill in the blanks.

1. carotenoid found in pepper, corn, spinach: _____ / _____ / _____

2. organic pigment found naturally in plants: _____ / _____ / _____

3. excessive level of carotene in the blood: _____ / _____ / _____

4. yellow-red pigment in fruits and vegetables: _____ / _____ / _____

5. combining form that means calcium: _____ / _____ / _____

6. List any term that could be a diagnosis: _____

7. List any term that contains elements meaning a color: _____

8. Which term is a potent form of vitamin D that acts as a hormone? _____

9. Write the term that is a carotenoid antioxidant: _____

10. List any term with an element that means a number: _____

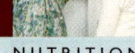

LESSON 17.3 Diets

OBJECTIVES

The information in this lesson will enable you to:

- **Discuss different types of diet that are recommended for different purposes.**
- **Establish an eating plan in balance with different body needs.**
- **Analyze the value of MyPyramid 2005 in providing individual nutrition advice.**
- **Describe some common forms of metabolic and nutritional problems.**
- **Explain what information is on a nutrition label and what it tells you.**

You are

. . . a medical assistant working with Susan Lee, MD, a primary care physician at Fulwood Medical Center.

Your patient is

. . . Mrs. Rosa Costa, a 55-year-old medical transcriptionist working at Fulwood Medical Center.

CASE REPORT 17.2

Since menopause four years ago, Mrs. Costa has put on 15 pounds in weight, mostly around the lower abdomen. A recent examination by Dr. Susan Lee in the primary care clinic showed her abdominal circumference to be 37 inches (Figure 17.10). Her blood pressure was 145/90 mm Hg, triglyceride level 150 mg/dL, a fasting blood glucose level of 100 mg/dL, and an HDL level of 40 mg/dL. Her mother died of type 2 diabetes in her mid-sixties. Dr. Lee made a diagnosis of metabolic syndrome, informed her of its significance, and recommended lifestyle changes.

The changes include losing the 15 pounds of weight she had gained and starting an exercise program including a brisk 30-minute walk each day. Dietary changes should be a 1600 Calorie diet, restricting carbohydrates to no more than 50% of total calories, and eating only complex carbohydrates. Fiber consumption should be increased, together with eating no red meats and minimal saturated and trans fats. Dr. Lee will see her again in six weeks.

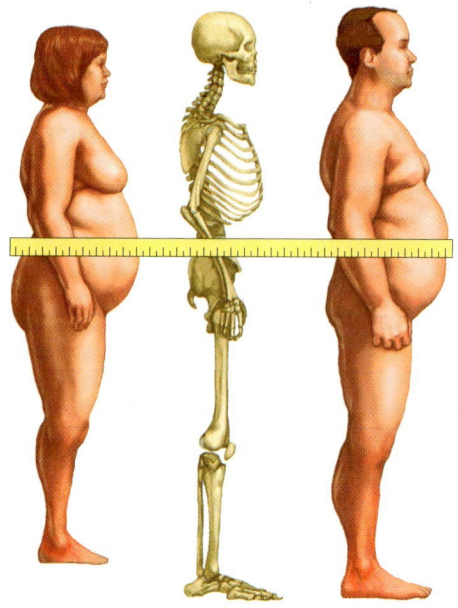

▲ **FIGURE 17.10 Waist Circumference Measurement.**

Place measuring tape, holding it parallel to the floor, around abdomen at the level of the iliac crest. Hold tape snug but do not compress the skin. Measure circumference at end of normal expiration. From *Identification, evaluation, and treatment of overweight and obesity in adults: The practical guide*. Bethesda, MD: National Institutes of Health 2000; NIH publication 00-4064.

DIETS

There is an old saying, "Good food is good medicine." However, good food and nutrition go way beyond medicine and drugs in maintaining and treating the body as a whole. Drugs are brought in to combat a specific problem at a specific site that poor nutrition may have affected. Good nutrition could perhaps have prevented the problem and a return to good nutrition could be a large component in correcting the problem and enabling the drug to function optimally. Good nutrition is a daily need and is an important part of any lifestyle. There is no one diet that is best for everyone.

Case Report 17.2 (continued)

The value of good, individualized nutrition, often in conjunction with exercise, is shown by Dr. Lee's recommendations for Mrs. Costa in treating her metabolic syndrome. She has prescribed no medication.

The protein, carbohydrates, and fat that you eat generate complex hormonal responses. An example of this is insulin. Insulin's role is to take excess glucose from dietary carbohydrates and excess amino acids from dietary protein, store them in adipose tissue as fat, and keep the fat locked in the adipose tissue. High–glycemic carbohydrate loads generate high levels of insulin.

Proponents of a specific type of diet often maintain that the diet is appropriate for everyone. Just as individuals respond differently to medications, so responses to different foods will vary, depending on enzyme concentrations and efficiencies during absorption, transport, and metabolism of the food. You may respond well to a high-carbohydrate diet, others to a low-carbohydrate–high-protein diet, and many to a diet balanced between carbohydrates and protein. All agree that fats in any diet should contain minimal saturated and trans fats.

WORD	PRONUNCIATION	ELEMENTS		DEFINITION
antimicrobial	AN-tee-my-KROH-bee-al	S/ P/ R/CF R/	-al *pertaining to* anti- *against* -micr/o- *small* -bio- *life*	Agent to destroy or prevent multiplication of organisms
fertilizer	FER-tih-lie-zer	S/ R/	-izer *that which creates* fertil- *fruitful*	Substance used to increase the yield of crops
fungicide	FUN-jee-side	S/ R/CF	-cide *to kill* fung/i- *fungus*	Agent to destroy fungi
herbicide	ER-bih-side	S/ R/CF	-cide *to kill* herb/i- *plant*	Agent to destroy plants
insecticide	in-SEK-tih-side	S/ R/CF	-cide *to kill* insect/i- *insect*	Agent to destroy insects
pesticide	PES-tih-side	S/ R/CF	-cide *to kill* pest/i- *nuisance*	Agent for destroying flies, mosquitoes, and other pests

Good food has two other components. The food should contain appropriate levels of nutrients. Since 1950, levels of calcium and magnesium in many vegetables have dropped by one-third. Changes in the soil with the use of commercial **fertilizers** have diminished the concentration of trace minerals, including zinc and chromium. Many fruits and vegetables are picked green. Without exposure to the sun to ripen, antioxidants are not allowed to develop.

There is growing concern about different ways in which small doses of **pesticides** in food can affect people, although these are not well understood. Pesticides include **insecticides** to control insects, **herbicides** to control weeds, **fungicides** to control mold and fungus, and **antimicrobials** to control bacteria *(Figure 17.11)*. The health problems posed by pesticides include birth defects, nerve damage, and cancer, including prostate cancer. Parkinson disease, not caused by genetics or head injury, is much more common in rural areas. Researchers are now tracking farmers to document their exposure to combinations of pesticides and to determine whether there is an increased incidence of Parkinson disease in this population.

▲ **FIGURE 17.11 Spraying Insecticide on Carrots.**

EXERCISES	*"There is no one diet that is good for everyone."* Use what you have learned about nutrition to briefly answer the following questions. Fill in the blanks.

1. What exactly does this statement mean?

_____

_____

_____

_____

2. Based on what you have learned about nutrition, why is this a correct statement?

_____

_____

_____

_____

High-Carbohydrate Diet

A high-carbohydrate diet is based largely on plant foods with starch as the carbohydrate source. The only exception to plants is fruit, in which the carbohydrates are the simple sugars fructose, sucrose, and glucose, as well as pectin, a fiber. Nuts contain 20 to 30% carbohydrate in terms of energy and are part of the diet.

Most high-carbohydrate diets contain 60 to 65% of energy from carbohydrate with 15% of energy from protein and 20 to 25% from fat. *Table 17.11* shows this as grams in different Calorie diets.

The high-carbohydrate diet is rich in fiber, minerals, vitamins, and antioxidants. It is important to keep the intake of simple sugars below 10 to 15% of total energy intake and to use mostly complex, low-glycemic carbohydrates. A high-carbohydrate diet with a high percentage of high-glycemic carbohydrates is one of the reasons for the epidemic of obesity in this country.

TABLE 17.11 High-Carbohydrate Diet

Total Calories	Carbohydrate (% and grams)	Fat (% and grams)	Protein (% and grams)
1600	60% 240 g	25% 44 g	15% 30 g
2500	60% 375 g	25% 70 g	15% 40 g

High-Protein Diet

A high-protein diet usually obtains 30% of its calories from protein, 40% from carbohydrates, and 30% from fat *(Table 17.12)*. Just as in a good high-carbohydrate diet where the type of carbohydrate is important, so in a good high-protein diet the type of protein is important. In both diets, the type of fat is important.

Sources of protein to avoid are beef and red meats, cow's milk, cheese, and protein powders with artificial sweeteners. Good sources of lean protein are fish, free-range poultry (chicken and turkey), buffalo, deer, **spirulina**, the grain **quinoa**, nuts, and beans. The healthy fat intake should avoid saturated fats and trans fats.

A 2005 study showed that a diet with 25% of total calories from protein (half from vegetable protein) was more effective in reducing blood pressure and blood cholesterol than the **Dietary Approaches to Stop Hypertension (DASH)** diet (18% protein) developed by the **National Heart, Lung, and Blood Institute (NHLBI)**.

Abbreviations

DASH **D**ietary **A**pproaches to **S**top **H**ypertension
NHLBI National Heart, Lung, and Blood Institute

TABLE 17.12 High-Protein Diet

Total Calories	Carbohydrate (% and grams)	Fat (% and grams)	Protein (% and grams)
1600	40% 160g	30% 53g	30% 60g
2500	40% 250g	30% 85g	30% 80g

Balanced Diet

A good balanced diet is what is right for you, enables you to maintain the weight you want to be, provides you with the energy you need, and has the food that you enjoy eating. In all diets, which are really a lifestyle, exercise plays an important role. One example of a balanced diet could contain 50% carbohydrate, 25% protein, and 25% fat *(Table 17.13)*. The lean protein should be from both vegetable and animal sources. Carbohydrates should be complex and high-glycemic, and fats should not be saturated or trans fats.

TABLE 17.13 Balanced Diet

Total Calories	Carbohydrate (% and grams)	Fat (% and grams)	Protein (% and grams)
1600	50% 200g	25% 44g	25% 50g
2500	50% 310g	25% 70g	25% 70g

WORD	PRONUNCIATION	ELEMENTS		DEFINITION
lactovegetarian	LAK-toe-VEJ-eh-TAR-ee-an	S/ R/CF R/	-arian *one who is* lact/o- *milk* -veget- *plants*	Person whose diet consists of only plants and dairy products
quinoa	kee-NO-ah		Inca *mother of all grains*	Plant with edible seeds high in protein
spirulina	spy-roo-LEE-nah		Genus of plant	Commercial product of blue-green algae containing 60 to 70% protein
vegan	VEE-gan		Greek *plants*	One who eats plants and no animal or dairy products

Vegetarian Diets

The two major vegetarian styles are:

- **Vegans,** who eat only plant foods
- **Lactovegetarians,** who eat dairy products and plant foods

A vegan diet is low in saturated fat, high in fiber, and rich in antioxidants but must also find sources of vitamins D and B_{12}, calcium, iron, and zinc. Fortified foods or a vitamin and mineral supplement can provide these. Protein is provided by nuts, legumes, seeds and grains, and dairy products, if these are used.

The importance and the quantities of the different foods needed in a vegetarian diet is illustrated by the Vegetarian Diet Pyramid *(Figure 17.12).*

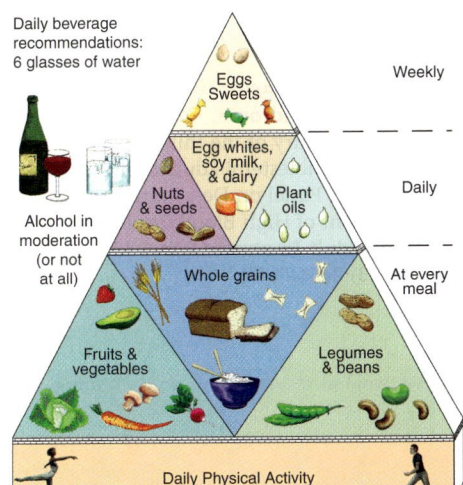

The Traditional Healthy Vegetarian Diet Pyramid

FIGURE 17.12 The Oldways Preservation & Exchange Trust Traditional Vegetarian Diet.
The diet has the advantage of being low in saturated fat, high in fiber, and rich in antioxidants. However, it can pose a risk for an inadequate iron, vitamin D, and vitamin B_{12} intake.

Copyright © 2000 Oldways Preservation & Exchange Trust. www.oldwayspt.org

EXERCISES

Reinforce your knowledge of various diets with the following exercise. Decide whether the statements given apply to a high-carbohydrate, high-protein, or vegetarian diet. Fill in the table.

Statement	High-Carbohydrate Diet	High-Protein Diet	Vegetarian Diet
May include only dairy and plant foods			
Effective in reducing blood pressure and blood cholesterol			
Rich in fiber, minerals, vitamins, and antioxidants			
Based largely on plant foods with starch			
30% of calories from protein, 40% from carbohydrates, and 30% from fat			
May need fortified foods or vitamin supplements			

Figure 17.15 Soup Label

Nutrition Facts		
Serving Size 1 cup (8fl. oz.) 240mL		
Servings Per Container 4		

Amount Per Serving		
Calories 100 Calories from Fat 20		

		% Daily Value*
Total Fat 2g		3%
Saturated Fat 1.5g		6%
Cholesterol 10mg		3%
Sodium 750mg		31%
Total Carbohydrate 16g		5%
Dietary Fiber 1g		4%
Sugars 10g		
Protein 5g		

Vitamin A 10%	•	Vitamin C 4%	
Calcium 15%	•	Iron 2%	

*Percent Daily Values are based on a 2,000 calorie diet. Your daily values may be higher or lower, depending on your calorie needs.

	Calories	2,000	2,500
Total Fat	Less than	65g	80g
Sat Fat	Less than	20g	25g
Cholesterol	Less than	300mg	300mg
Sodium	Less than	2,400mg	2,400mg
Total Carbohydrate		300g	375g
Dietary Fiber		25g	30g

Ingredients: Organic Milk, Filtered Water, Organic Tomato Paste, Organic Cane Sweetener, Organic Caramelized Red Pepper Flavor (Organic Red Peppers, Sea Salt, Organic Butter), Roasted Garlic, Roasted Red Peppers, Sea Salt, Sodium Citrate, Organic Rice Flour, Organic Garlic Powder, Organic Onion Powder

▲ **FIGURE 17.15 Soup Label.**

READING FOOD LABELS

Most foods sold in stores must be labeled with the product name, its manufacturer, the amount of product in the package, its nutritional composition, and its ingredients listed in *descending order by weight*. So, below the label in *Figure 17.15*, the two major ingredients by weight in the soup are milk and water.

Starting at the top of the label, the **serving size** is 1 cup (8 ounces), not a large serving by modern standards. With four servings per container, the **total volume** in the container is $4 \times 8 = 32$ ounces (1 quart). Knowing the total volume enables you to more easily compare prices with competing products.

In the next section, each **serving** contains 100 Calories, with 20 of them being from fat. If you consume 12 ounces (1½ servings) of the soup, you will have consumed 150 calories, with 30 of these calories derived from fat.

The next section shows you the quantities of the main nutrients and relates this to a percentage of the **Daily Value.** The Daily Values are set at the nutrient recommendations for a 2000 Calorie diet with 30% of the Calories derived from fat (one-third of this total from saturated fat), 60% from carbohydrates, and 10% from protein. So, if you are on a low-carbohydrate diet, the carbohydrate percentages on the label will be low.

In this soup, three-quarters of the fat is saturated, reflecting the content of butter and milk. Sixty percent of the carbohydrate (10 out of 16 g) is sugar, reflecting the use of cane syrup as the sweetener. Protein does not have a Daily Value because determining it would require expensive testing by the manufacturer.

The RDA for sodium for adults is 500 mg/day (0.5 g). Most adults ingest 4 to 7 g/day. This soup contains 750 mg per serving.

This soup carries the **USDA organic symbol,** which means that the product contains at least 95% organic ingredients. Organic refers to the way food is grown (or raised in the case of animals) without commercial pesticides, herbicides, or fertilizers. Irradiated or genetically engineered ingredients are not used in organic foods.

The traditional food industry lobbies the **U.S. Department of Agriculture (USDA)** continually to allow synthetic ingredients to be added. The definition of organic may well change.

The label shown in *Figure 17.16* is for a much simpler product, but if you really want to know what you are eating you have to count the chips. Compared to the soup, the chips contain much more total fat but not much more saturated fat, and they have zero cholesterol. There is no hydrogenated oil listed in the ingredients, so there should be no trans fats. Sodium is much lower, and the chips contain small amounts of some B vitamins. There are no sugars.

At the very bottom of the label is the information about the manufacturing crossover with peanut oil. If you are allergic to peanuts, the small amount of peanut oil that might be in this food could set off your allergy.

It's always good to peruse the food label in its entirety.

Nutrition Facts		
Serving Size 1 oz (28g/About 22 chips)		
Servings Per Container 9		

Amount Per Serving		
Calories 150 Calories from Fat 80		

		% Daily Value*
Total Fat 8g		12%
Saturated Fat 2g		10%
Cholesterol 0mg		0%
Sodium 110mg		5%
Total Carbohydrate 18g		6%
Dietary Fiber 1g		4%
Sugars 0g		
Protein 2g		

Vitamin A 0%	•	Vitamin C 10%	
Calcium 15%	•	Iron 2%	
Thiamin 2%	•	Niacin 4%	
Vitamin B6 6%	•	Phosphorus 2%	

*Percent Daily Values are based on a 2,000 calorie diet. Your daily values may be higher or lower, depending on your calorie needs.

	Calories	2,000	2,500
Total Fat	Less than	65g	80g
Sat Fat	Less than	20g	25g
Cholesterol	Less than	300mg	300mg
Sodium	Less than	2,400mg	2,400mg
Total Carbohydrate		300g	375g
Dietary Fiber		25g	30g

Ingredients: Potatoes, Vegetable Oil (Contains One or More of the Following: Corn, Cottonseed, or Sunflower Oil), and Sea Salt

Allergy Information: This product is made on equipment that also makes products containing peanut oil.

▲ **FIGURE 17.16 Potato Chip Label.**

Understand What You Read. *Reading the nutritional facts about the food you are about to consume may lead you to make wiser choices in the supermarket or at the vending machine. Refer to the food labels in Figures 17.15 and 17.16 to answer the following questions. Some answers may surprise you.*

1. Which food product contains more sodium per serving, the soup or the potato chips? _____

2. What is the serving size of potato chips? _____

3. What is the serving size of the soup? _____

4. Which product contains no sugar? _____

5. Which product contains more protein? _____

6. Which product contains less total fat? _____

7. Which product contains no cholesterol? _____

8. How many servings in a container of chips? _____

9. How many servings in the can of soup? _____

10. Which food product contains trace minerals? _____

11. Which product contains a warning on the label? _____

12. If you have a patient with hypertension, which component on the label should be of particular interest to them? _____

Take a moment to think about what you are eating every day and whether or not it contributes to a healthy lifestyle. Answer these questions for yourself.

13. How often in a day do you eat "junk" food? _____

14. How many potato chips do you eat at one time? _____

15. Do you drink soda more than once a day? _____

16. Do you skip meals because of limited time? _____

17. Do you eat a piece of fruit every day? _____

18. What is your "normal" breakfast? _____

19. How many glasses (or bottles) of water do you drink in any one day? _____

20. What is your main source of protein? _____

21. Can you name three things you ate today that contained sugar? _____
_____, and _____

22. Do you think you eat a balanced diet? _____
In not, why not? _____
_____

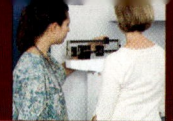

NUTRITION

CHALLENGE YOUR KNOWLEDGE

A. **Case Report:** Re-read the following case report, and use your knowledge of the *language of nutrition* to answer the questions.

Your patient is

. . . Mrs. Rosa Costa, a 55-year-old medical transcriptionist working at Fulwood Medical Center. Since menopause four years ago, she has put on 15 pounds in weight, mostly around the lower abdomen. A recent examination by Dr. Susan Lee in the primary care clinic showed her abdominal circumference to be 37 inches. Her blood pressure was 145/90, triglyceride level 150 mg/dL, a fasting blood glucose level of 100mg/dL, and an HDL level of 40 mg/dL. Her mother died of type 2 diabetes in her mid-sixties. Dr. Lee made a diagnosis of metabolic syndrome, informed her of its significance and recommended significant life-style changes.

The changes include losing the 15 pounds of weight she had gained and starting an exercise program with a brisk 30-minute walk each day. Dietary changes should be a 1600 Calorie diet, restricting carbohydrates to no more than 50% of total calories, and eating only complex carbohydrates. Fiber consumption should be increased, together with eating no red meats and minimal saturated and trans fats. Dr. Lee will see her again in six weeks.

The value of good, individualized nutrition, often in conjunction with exercise, is shown by Dr. Lee's recommendations for Mrs. Costa in treating her metabolic syndrome. She has prescribed no medication.

Mrs. Costa has metabolic syndrome. The diagnostic criteria for this disorder are shown in Figure 17.13. Mrs. Costa meets four of the five criteria, and her plasma triglycerides are borderline. The diet Dr. Lee has prescribed is similar to the balanced diet shown previously. It is important for you as a medical assistant to reinforce the need for the diet and to encourage her weight loss.

1. What is menopause?

   _____

2. At what age did Mrs. Costa reach menopause? _____

3. What significant health risk has developed for Mrs. Costa since menopause?

   _____

4. What significant disease does Mrs. Costa have in her past family history? _____

5. What food does Mrs. Costa need to cut completely out of her diet?

   _____

6. What medication has Dr. Lee prescribed for Mrs. Costa's condition?

   _____

7. What criteria does Mrs. Costa meet that led Dr. Lee to diagnose metabolic syndrome?

   _____

   _____

   _____

8. Define: **syndrome**

   _____

   _____

   _____

B. **Translation:** If you really know something, you are able to explain it to someone else in terms they can understand. To be certain your patient understands the information, translate into layman's terms the following sentences.

1. "Vitamin B$_6$ deficiency results in a microcytic, hypochromic anemia and seborrheic dermatitis."

    _____

    _____

    _____

    _____

2. "Niacin deficiency causes pellagra, characterized by dementia, diarrhea, and dermatitis."

    _____

    _____

    _____

C. **Deconstruct:** Exercise your knowledge of elements in nutritional terms by deconstructing the following *language of nutrition.* Not every term will contain all the elements. Fill in the blanks.

1. dietetics: _____/_____/_____
                              prefix   root/CF   suffix

2. chlorophyll: _____/_____/_____
                              prefix   root/CF   suffix

3. hemochromatosis: _____/_____/_____
                              prefix   root/CF   suffix

4. adiposity: _____/_____/_____
                              prefix   root/CF   suffix

5. retinoid: _____/_____/_____
                              prefix   root/CF   suffix

6. dyslipidemia: _____/_____/_____
                              prefix   root/CF   suffix

7. pyridoxine: _____/_____/_____
                              prefix   root/CF   suffix

8. ascorbic: _____/_____/_____
                              prefix   root/CF   suffix

9. phenylketonuria   _____/_____/_____
                              prefix   root/CF   suffix

10. synthesis   _____/_____/_____
                              prefix   root/CF   suffix

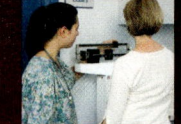

NUTRITION

D. Patient Education: Medical terms often have to be explained to patients so they can better understand their plan of treatment. Your patient has been referred to a nutritionist and told to use artificial sweeteners in her diet. Use your knowledge of the *language of nutrition* to help you explain to your patient the difference between:

1. A dietician and a nutritionist

Dietician: _____

_____

Nutritionist: _____

_____

2. Nutritive sweeteners and alternative or artificial sweeteners

Nutritive sweeteners: _____

_____

Alternative/artificial sweeteners: _____

_____

E. Discussion: You may go online to do additional research to help you present a short talk on either of the following topics. You should address all the questions regarding your chosen topic.

1. **Empty calories:** What are they, where do they come from, do they have any nutritional value, what is their effect on the glycemic index? Name five more examples of foods containing empty calories that were not mentioned in the text.

2. **Fiber:** What is the function of fiber in the intestines, what nutrient group does it come from, what is a good source of fiber, what does fiber have to do with glucose absorption, what is functional fiber? Name five more examples of foods containing fiber that were not mentioned in the text.

Use the lines below to list any new terminology you discover in your research. Be sure to define the new terms you have found.

_____

_____

_____

_____

_____

_____

_____

_____

_____

_____

As a final step to this exercise, search for an article from a health magazine, online website, etc., regarding either empty calories or fiber. Be prepared to discuss this article in class or hand in to your instructor.

F. **Optional Exercise:** Track your food intake for one entire day. Be certain you also note the amount and type of liquids you drink (include plain water). Make a chart listing the six groups of nutrients, and write down what food you eat and the amount of each nutrient you have consumed that day. Ask yourself the following questions:

1. Am I getting nutrients from all six groups on my chart?
2. Is there any nutrient I have not consumed this day?
3. Am I giving my body enough water?
4. Analyze your food pattern—do you eat too much of one or two groups and not enough from the rest of the groups?
5. Are you eating a balanced diet?
6. Think of one small way in which you can start to improve your eating habits.

Write here how you can improve your eating habits in one way.

_____

_____

_____

_____

_____

G. **Diseases:** "You are what you eat," and sometimes lack of proper diet can contribute in some way to a disease. The following diseases can be affected by nutrition. Match the correct disease to the statement. Fill in the blanks.

_____	1. lack of vitamin D in child	A. cretinism
_____	2. thiamine deficiency causes	B. pernicious anemia
_____	3. lack of iodide in pregnancy may cause	C. scurvy
_____	4. folate deficiency is linked to	D. osteomalacia
_____	5. lack of fiber in the diet leads to	E. pellagra
_____	6. deficiency of B_{12} produces	F. rickets
_____	7. too much carrot juice can produce	G. beriberi
_____	8. niacin deficiency causes	H. spina bifida
_____	9. vitamin D deficiency in adults	J. hypercarotenemia
_____	10. lack of vitamin C can produce	K. constipation

NUTRITION

H. Word elements continue to be the best tool for analyzing medical terms. Challenge your knowledge of the nutritional elements to answer the following questions.

1. **Chol-** is a root meaning:

   a. liver

   b. stone

   c. bile

   d. leaf

   e. organ

2. The word element **ose** is a:

   a. suffix

   b. prefix

   c. root

   d. combining form

   e. combining vowel

3. **Cyan/o-** is a combining form of color meaning:

   a. yellow

   b. blue

   c. green

   d. white

   e. red

4. The suffix **-cide** means to:

   a. breathe

   b. kill

   c. cut

   d. repair

   e. bleed

5. The element **oid** is always found:

   a. at the beginning of a term

   b. in the middle of a term

   c. in a Latin term

   d. in a Greek term

   e. at the end of a term

6. The prefix **poly-** means:

   a. under

   b. one

   c. many

   d. none

   e. green

7. The root **scorb-** means:

   a. sticky

   b. scurvy

   c. soap

   d. spirulina

   e. sucrose

8. The root **-flavone** pertains to:

   a. color

   b. size

   c. location

   d. direction

   e. number

9. The prefix **iso-** means:

   a. same

   b. different

   c. heavy

   d. large

   e. equal

10. The suffix **-ician** indicates:

    a. pertaining to life

    b. one who does

    c. study of

    d. knowledge of

    e. to nourish

I. **Prefixes:** Fluids of all types help maintain hemostasis. Your knowledge of prefixes can assist you in correctly answering the following questions. First, find the prefix in each term, and write it in the blank. Then define a body location for each of the fluids listed below. Fill in the blanks.

1. intravascular fluid: prefix = _____

   location: _____

2. interstitial fluid: prefix = _____

   location: _____

3. extracellular fluid: prefix = _____

   location: _____

4. intracellular fluid: prefix = _____

   location: _____

J. What am I?
   - I maintain homeostasis in the body.
   - I serve as a solvent for many chemical compounds.
   - I provide a medium for chemical reactions to occur.
   - I transport nutrients to cells.
   - I contribute to temperature regulation.
   - I remove waste products of cellular metabolism.
   - I contribute to lubricants in the knees and other joints.
   - I form saliva, bile, and amniotic fluid,

   I am _____ .

K. **Nutrients:** Each of the following foods is a source of some type of nutrient. Can you identify what you are eating? Choose your answers from the word bank. There are more answers than questions. Fill in the blanks.

carbohydrates	fatty acids	vitamin D	zinc	copper	potassium
vitamin B$_6$	vitamin C	saturated fats	folate	protein	fiber

1. stevia, aspartame, saccharin: _____

2. salmon, sardines, and fortified milk: _____

3. whole-grain breads, fruits, vegetables, and beans: _____

4. bananas, raisins, fruit juices: _____

5. dark green leafy vegetables and legumes: _____

6. peanut butter, lentils, tuna canned in water, soy milk: _____

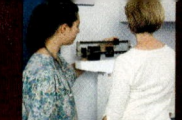

NUTRITION

L. **Optional Exercise:** You are almost three-quarters of the way into this text and have worked your way through numerous types of exercises at chapter ends. *Create a short exercise you will exchange with another student.* Be sure to put your answers on a separate sheet and keep that. Ten questions for the exercise can be short answer, multiple choice, fill in the chart, spelling, word elements, or fill in the blank. Be prepared to hand the sample exercise and the answers in to the instructor.

M. **Diet Plans:** Not all diet plans work for everyone who tries them. Being knowledgeable about what your body needs and what you are providing it, will help you choose a healthy diet plan that will work for you. Write a short answer for each question, describing the basics of each diet plan.

1. Name the two types of vegetarian eating plans and briefly describe what types of food they permit.

   a. _____

   Food consumed: _____

   b. _____

   Food consumed: _____

2. What are the basic elements of a balanced diet?

   _____

   _____

   _____

3. What are the basic elements of a high-carbohydrate diet?

   _____

   _____

   _____

4. What are the basic elements of a high-protein diet?

   _____

   _____

   _____

   _____

5. Generally, most diet plans will tell you to avoid:

   _____

   _____

N. Patient Documentation: Employ your knowledge of the *language of nutrition* to correctly complete the following patient documentation. Fill in the blanks with your correct choice—choose from the answers below the statement.

1. I am prescribing daily use of _____ for the patient's acne. She will return to see me in two weeks so I can check for any improvement in her skin.

   lutein   niacin   retinoic acid   beta carotene

2. What was initially thought to be hyperbilirubinemia has proven on lab results to be _____;
   the patient had ingested a large amount of carrot juice in the past month (which she failed to tell me).

   hypertension   hypercalcemia   hypercarotenemia   hyperketonuria

3. I am treating this patient's osteomalacia with additional supplements of _____.

   vitamin B   vitamin K   vitamin C   vitamin D

4. Because the patient is pregnant, I have recommended an additional daily intake of _____.

   amino acids   carbohydrates   folic acid   lipids

5. Since this patient has been on antibiotics for an extended period of time and liver function lab results are lower than

   normal, I am prescribing additional _____ to boost liver function.

   vitamin B_6 vitamin B_{12} vitamin K   vitamin E

O. Brief Answer: Prepare a six-sentence answer to the following statement, and hand it in to your instructor:

In all diets, which are really a lifestyle, exercise plays an important role.

Three important questions you must address in your answer:

1. What is a lifestyle?
2. Why is it a "lifestyle" and not a "diet"?
3. What is the value of exercise in lifestyle and diet?

P. Recall and Review: How well do you remember these word elements from the previous chapter? Try to answer without first looking back to check. Fill in the blanks.

Element	Type of Element (P, R, CF, S)	Meaning of Element
1. geront/o	_____	_____
2. pulmon/o	_____	_____
3. pre	_____	_____
4. ped	_____	_____
5. an	_____	_____

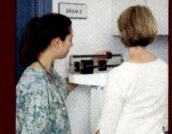
NUTRITION

Q. **Build Your Knowledge of the Language of Nutrition:** Major minerals and trace minerals play a key role in body nutrition. Build your knowledge of the language of nutrition by matching the following statements in column 1 with the correct medical terminology in column 2.

_____ 1. common name for sodium chloride

_____ 2. prevents development of dental caries

_____ 3. too much absorption of iron

_____ 4. magnesium deficiency causes

_____ 5. calcium deficiency appears in

_____ 6. iron deficiency causes pale RBCs

_____ 7. excess blood sodium

_____ 8. can be absorbed into the bloodstream

_____ 9. insufficient iodine intake leads to

_____ 10. low blood potassium

A. hypernatremia

B. bioavailable

C. hypokalemia

D. hypochromic

E. goiter

F. tachycardia

G. salt

H. fluoride

I. hemochromatosis

J. osteoporosis

R. **Terminology Challenge:** Elements you have learned in earlier chapters you see again throughout the text.

Example: In this chapter you have the term **choline.** Deconstruct this term into elements, then list as many other terms from previous chapters that have the *same root.*

choline: prefix means: _____ root means: _____ suffix means: _____

Additional medical terms with this same root, and their meaning.

Medical Term	Meaning of Medical Term

S. **Deconstruct the following terms into their basic elements,** and define the term in column 5. Certain elements have appeared in earlier chapters. Then, in the section below the table, list a different medical term, using the same chart element that has previously appeared in the language of a body system. Define this term as well. Fill in the chart, then fill in the blanks.

Medical Term	Prefix	Root/CF	Suffix	Definition of Medical Term
hemochromatosis				
antimicrobial				
lactovegetarian				
dyslipidemia				
phenylketonuria				
hydrogenated				

List another medical term.

1. List a medical term using a prefix from the above chart that has appeared in any previous chapter.

   Previous term: _____ Term's meaning: _____

2. List a medical term using a root or combining form from the above chart that has appeared in any previous chapter.

   Previous term: _____ Term's meaning: _____

3. List a medical term using a suffix from the above chart which has appeared in any previous chapter.

   Previous term: _____ Term's meaning: _____

T. **Apply the *language of nutrition* to the following exercise.** There are six groups of nutrients, each with specific properties and functions. On the first row across the top of the following chart fill in the name of each one of the six nutrients. After you have done this, read the first column down and place a check mark (✓) in the column for the correct nutrient the statement refers to. Fill in the chart.

Nutrients →						
Constitutes 60% of your body weight						
Breaks down to glucose, major source of cell energy						
Organic substances						
Can be complex starch or simple sugars						
Some vitamins increase the bioavailability of this nutrient						
Do not dissolve in water						
Zinc						
Form major part of lean body tissue						
No caloric value						
Cholesterol						

NUTRITION

U. **Test your knowledge of the** *language of nutrition.* Choose the correct answer for the following questions by circling the best choice.

1. What is the best way to modify weight?

   a. more protein, less fat

   b. herbal supplements and vitamins

   c. exercise and dietary control

   d. fewer carbohydrates, more protein

   e. no sugar

2. Which of the following apply to simple sugars?

   a. glucose, fructose, sucrose

   b. nutrients but no calories

   c. empty calories

   d. a, b, and c

   e. a and c only

3. Which of these inhibits absorption of cholesterol?

   a. carbohydrates

   b. simple sugars

   c. fiber

   d. vitamin K

   e. protein

4. What is the rapid blood glucose response to simple sugar called?

   a. HDL

   b. LDL

   c. GI

   d. EFA

   e. RDA

5. Why is cholesterol characterized as a lipid?

   a. It limits the absorption of calcium.

   b. It does not dissolve in water.

   c. It is a coenzyme involved in the DNA process.

   d. It is an integral part of tissues.

   e. It is not stored in any particular place in the body.

6. What are the building blocks of protein called?

   a. vitamins

   b. minerals

   c. trace minerals

   d. amino acids

   e. electrolytes

7. What are the sources of vitamins in diet?

   a. plant foods

   b. supplements

   c. animal foods

   d. a, b, and c

   e. none of these

8. Which group requires extra protein daily?

   a. anyone over age 60

   b. children under 5 years of age

   c. teenagers

   d. pregnant and lactating mothers

   e. males ages 13 to 18

9. What causes pellagra?

   a. lack of vitamin C

   b. niacin deficiency

   c. lack of vitamin K

   d. low hemoglobin

   e. trace minerals deficiency

10. Which vitamin is also called ascorbic acid?

   a. vitamin A

   b. vitamin B

   c. vitamin C

   d. vitamin D

   e. vitamin K

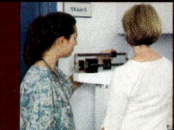
NUTRITION

11. What is the major electrolyte in extracellular fluid?

    a. sodium

    b. potassium

    c. vitamin E

    d. copper

    e. calcium

12. Which term represents excess blood sodium?

    a. hyperglycemia

    b. hypernatremia

    c. hypoglycemia

    d. hyperkalemia

    e. hyponatremia

V. Translate the following sentence from layman's language into medical terminology.
"Excess blood sodium is associated with high blood pressure and kidney stones."

Rewrite using correct medical terminology. _____

_____

_____

_____

_____

_____

W. **True or False:** Not all of the following statements are correct. Check true or false for each statement. Rewrite any false statements to be correct on the lines below.

    1.   Glycogen is the storage form of carbohydrate.   T   F

    2.   Calcium is found in every living cell.   T   F

    3.   Trace minerals do not dissolve in water.   T   F

    4.   Neither vitamins nor minerals are used as fuel to burn Calories.   T   F

    5.   Seventy-five percent of your body weight is water.   T   F

    6.   Major minerals are those for which you need > 100 mg/day.   T   F

    Sentences written to be correct:

_____

_____

_____

_____

_____

_____

_____

_____

_____

_____

X. **Study Hint: Learn to make study hints that work for you.** Make up a good study hint to help you remember:

    Water-soluble vitamins are vitamin C and the B vitamins.

    Fat-soluble vitamins do not dissolve in water and are vitamins A, D, E, and K.

    My study hint: _____

_____

_____

_____

_____

_____

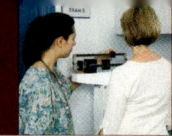

CHAPTER 17 REVIEW

NUTRITION

CHAPTER SUMMARY EXERCISE

1. *Listen to the pronunciation of the medical terms as given by your instructor.*
2. *Circle the correct spelling of the medical term.*
3. *Match the correctly spelled terms to the brief descriptions below.*
4. *Write a sentence for each of the 15 terms that appear in this exercise.*

A. SPELLING COMPREHENSION: CIRCLE THE CORRECT SPELLING OF THE TERM.

1. rickits	rickets	ricketts	ricketes	rickettes
2. colesterol	cholestrol	cholesterol	collesterol	cholisterol
3. nutrieent	nutreint	nutreent	nurtrient	nutrient
4. vegan	vigen	vagen	vagan	vegin
5. defeciency	dificiency	deficiency	defficiency	difficiency
6. pilagra	pellagra	pelagra	pillagra	pellagria
7. scurrvey	scurve	scurvie	surrvey	scurvy
8. glycogen	glicogen	glecogen	gicogen	gilcogen
9. lipid	lippid	lipidd	liped	lepid
10. ribbofavin	riboflavin	ribboflavin	ryboflavin	ribofavin
11. aceetilcoline	acetocholine	acetylcholine	acitocoline	acetyocoline
12. constippation	constipation	constepation	consstipation	consttipation
13. dislipidemia	dyslepidemia	dislepidemia	dyslipidemia	dyslipidimia
14. sackarin	sacharin	saccharin	sakarine	sacarine
15. adipossity	adiposety	adiposity	addiposity	addiposety

B. MATCH THE NUMBER OF THE CORRECT TERM IN PART A WITH THE BRIEF DESCRIPTION OF THE TERM BELOW.

a. vegetarians who eat only plant foods _____

b. neurotransmitter associated with learning and memory _____

c. disease due to lack of dietary niacin _____

d. vitamin B_2 _____

e. excessive accumulation of fat in an organ _____

f. steroid characterized as a lipid _____

g. food compound that does not dissolve in water _____

h. storage form of carbohydrate   _____

 i. artificial sweetener   _____

 j. vitamin D deficiency in children   _____

k. lack of, less than normal   _____

 l. inability to move the bowels   _____

m. food required for normal physiological function   _____

n. abnormal levels of blood lipids   _____

o. lack of vitamin C   _____

C. USING YOUR KNOWLEDGE OF TERMS 1-15 IN PART A AND THEIR CORRECT SPELLING, WRITE A BRIEF SENTENCE FOR EACH OF THE TERMS AS IT MIGHT APPEAR IN PATIENT DOCUMENTATION.

1. _____

2. _____

3. _____

4. _____

5. _____

6. _____

7. _____

8. _____

9. _____

10. _____

11. _____

12. _____

13. _____

14. _____

15. _____

D. GO TO THE STUDENT CD. OPEN THE GLOSSARY AND PRACTICE YOUR PRONUNCIATION OF THE TERMS IN PART A OF THIS EXERCISE.

Restorative Rehabilitation

OBJECTIVES

The information in this lesson will enable you to:

- **Identify the members of the rehabilitation team.**
- **Discuss the purposes of rehabilitation medicine.**
- **Define the goals for a restorative rehabilitation program for specific common problems.**
- **Detail common medical problems that arise during rehabilitation.**

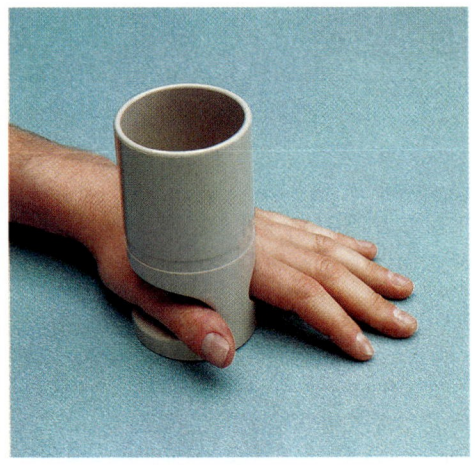

▲ **FIGURE 18.1 Assistive devices for eating.**

Abbreviations

ADL	activities of daily living
IADL	instrumental activity of daily living
IU	international unit
mg	milligram
OT	occupational therapy
PT	physical therapy
PTA	physical therapy assistant
ROM	range of motion

DEFINITIONS

Rehabilitation medicine focuses on **function**. Being able to function is essential for being independent and having a good quality of life.

Restorative rehabilitation restores a function that has been lost. It can be intense and short term. Examples are following a hip fracture, hip replacement, or stroke.

Maintenance rehabilitation strengthens and maintains a function that is gradually being lost. It is less intense and often long term. Examples are in the problems of senescence; for example, difficulty with balance or flexibility.

Rehabilitation medicine is also involved with **prevention** of loss of function and prevention of injury. In sports medicine, an example would be prevention of shoulder and elbow injuries in baseball pitchers.

Rehabilitation Team

Rehabilitation programs involve a **multidisciplinary** team approach. Each member of the team will manage different rehabilitation activities. Team members include:

- **Physiatrist**—a physician specializing in **physical medicine** and rehabilitation. This person is often the team leader.

- **Medical specialists**—manage acute or chronic illnesses and pain.

- **Occupational therapists**—improve performance of the **activities of daily living (ADL)** that are described below and help adapt to visual and other perceptual deficits. They practice **occupational therapy (OT)**.

- **Physical therapists**—improve strength, **range of motion (ROM)**, balance, and endurance and teach the use of assistive devices. They practice **physical therapy (PT)** assisted by **restorative aids.**

- **Rehabilitation psychologists**—specialists in helping people undergoing rehabilitation and those with resulting disabilities to reclaim their sense of belonging, contributing to, and participating in the world around them.

- **Social workers**—provide support and assistance with social issues such as health insurance, care facilities, and employment.

- **Speech therapists**—evaluate and treat communication, speech, and swallowing disorders.

- **Orthotists**—make and fit orthopedic appliances (**orthotics**).

- **Nutritionists**—evaluate and improve nutritional status.

Activities of Daily Living (ADLs) are the routine activities of personal care. The six basic ADLs are eating, bathing, dressing, grooming, toileting, and transferring. **Assistive devices** are designed to make ADLs easier to perform and help maintain independence. Examples are reachers and grabbers, easy-pull sock aids, long shoe horns, jar openers, and eating aids *(Figure 18.1)*. ADLs are also a measurement to assess therapy needs and monitor its effectiveness.

WORD	PRONUNCIATION	ELEMENTS		DEFINITION
assistive device	ah-**SIS**-tiv de-**VICE**	S/ R/	-ive *pertaining to* **assist-** *aid, help* device *an appliance*	Tool, software, or hardware to assist in performing daily activities
multidisciplinary	mul-tee-**DIS**-ih-plih-**NAR**-ee	S/ P/ R/	-ary *pertaining to* **multi-** *many* **-disciplin-** *instruction*	Involving health care providers from more than one profession
occupational therapy	**OCK**-you-**PAY**-shun-al **THAIR**-ah-pee	S/ R/ R/	-al *pertaining to* **occupation-** *work* **therapy** *healing*	Use of work and recreational activities to increase independent function
orthotic	or-**THOT**-ik	S/ R/	-ic *pertaining to* **orthot-** *correct*	Orthopedic appliance to correct an abnormality
orthotist	or-**THOT**-ist	S/	-ist *one who specializes*	Maker and fitter of orthopedic appliances
physiatry **physiatrist**	fih-**ZIE**-ah-tree fih-**ZIE**-ah-trist	 S/ R/ R/	Greek *science of nature* -ist *one who specializes* **phys-** *nature* **-iatr-** *treatment*	Physical medicine Specialist in physical medicine
physical medicine	**FIZ**-ih-cal **MED**-ih-sin	S/ R/	-al *pertaining to* **physic-** *body*	Diagnosis and treatment by means of remedial agents, such as exercises, manipulation, heat, etc.
physical therapy (also known as **physiotherapy**)	**FIZ**-ih-cal **THAIR**-ah-pee	S/ R/ R/	-al *pertaining to* **physic-** *body* **therapy** *healing*	Use of remedial processes to overcome a physical defect
physiotherapy (syn)	**FIZ**-ee-oh-**THAIR**-ah-pee	R/CF	**physi/o-** *body*	Another term for physical therapy
prevention	pree-**VEN**-shun	S/ R/	-ion *action* **prevent-** *prevent*	Process to prevent occurrence of a disease or health problem
rehabilitation	**REE**-hah-bill-ih-**TAY**-shun	S/ P/ R/	-ion *action* **re-** *again* **-habilitat-** *restore*	Therapeutic restoration of an ability to function as before
restorative **rehabilitation**	ree-**STOR**-ah-tiv **REE**-hah-bill-ih-**TAY**-shun	S/ R/	-ative *pertaining to* **restor-** *renew*	Promote renewal of health and strength

    Instrumental Activities of Daily Living (IADLs) relate to independent living. They include managing money, using a telephone, cooking, driving, shopping for groceries and personal items, and doing housework.

EXERCISES

Deconstruct the following medical terms into their word elements. Some terms will not have every element present. Then use any one term in a sentence of your own choice that is not directly from the text. Fill in the blanks.

Medical Term	Prefix	Root/CF	Suffix	Meaning of Term
physiatrist				
rehabilitation				
orthotic				
multidisciplinary				
orthotist				
physiotherapist				

Sentence: _____

_____

You are

. . . a certified occupational therapist assistant (COTA) working in the rehabilitation unit at Fulwood Medical Center.

Your patient is

. . . Mr. Hank Johnson, a 65-year-old owner of a printing shop.

CASE REPORT 18.2

One year ago, Mr. Johnson had an **elective** left total hip replacement for osteoarthritis. Four months later, he had a myocardial infarction. Two weeks ago, while on his exercise bicycle, he had a stroke. His right arm and leg were paralyzed, and he lost his speech and had difficulty swallowing. He was brought to the emergency department within three hours of the stroke and received thrombolytic **therapy** (see Chapter 7). He is now receiving physical therapy, occupational therapy, and speech therapy in the inpatient rehabilitation unit. He is able to say some simple words and has begun to have voluntary movements in the arm and leg.

Your roles are to help him regain function in his arm and leg, and to monitor and record his progress.

Abbreviations

BKA below the knee amputation
COTA certified occupational therapist assistant
PVD peripheral vascular disease

Keynote

Coordinated multidisciplinary evaluation, management, and therapy add significantly to the chances of a good recovery.

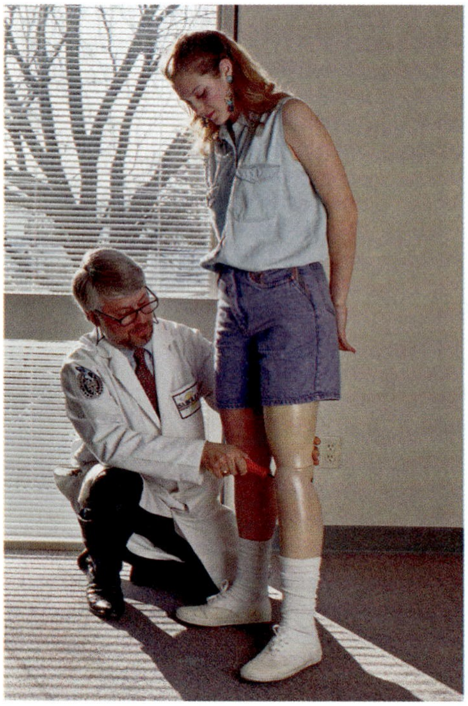

▲ **FIGURE 18.4 Sixteen-Year-Old Being Fitted with Prosthesis.**

STROKE REHABILITATION

The goals of Mr. Johnson's rehabilitation program are to enable him to:

• walk safely using an assistive device
• use his hands with accuracy
• restore his speech abilities
• prevent a second stroke

Because he received thrombolytic therapy *(see Chapter 7)* within three hours of the onset of his stroke, his chance of being left with little or no **residual** difficulty is around 35%, compared to 50% if he had not received the therapy.

Social workers are helping his wife make their home safe for his return and to work with Medicare to obtain the maximum benefits they allow. They will work out the family's need for **adaptive equipment,** such as raised toilet seats, handrails in bath and shower, eating devices, and other equipment to enable Mr. Johnson to perform the activities of daily living as he recovers.

Anyone who has had one stroke is at high risk for having a second stroke. During this rehabilitative period, he will be evaluated for such risk factors as narrowing of his carotid arteries with plaque and thrombosis *(see Chapter 7)* and the presence of atrial fibrillation *(see Chapter 8)*.

AMPUTATIONS

Seventy-five percent of all **amputations** are performed on people over 65 years with **peripheral vascular disease (PVD)** with complications due to arteriosclerosis and diabetes. Most of these are **below the knee amputations (BKA).** The war in Iraq has led to the loss of arms and legs in soldiers due to explosive devices. Rehabilitation after amputation is an increasingly important component in rehabilitation programs.

Immediately after surgery to perform the amputation the objectives are to:

• promote healing of the stump
• strengthen the muscles above the site of the amputation
• strengthen arm muscles to assist in ambulation
• prevent **contractures** of the joints above the amputation (knee and hip for BKAs)
• shrink the stump with elastic cuffs or bandages to fit the socket of a temporary **prosthesis**
• provide emotional, psychological, and family support.

With a temporary leg prosthesis *(Figure 18.4)*, weight bearing and walking can be practiced first on parallel bars *(Figure 18.5)* and then with a walker, crutches, and cane.

WORD	PRONUNCIATION	ELEMENTS		DEFINITION
adapt	a-**DAPT**		Latin *to adjust*	To adjust to different conditions
adaptive equipment	a-**DAP**-tiv ee-**KWIP**-ment	S/ R/ S/ R/	-**ive** *pertaining to* **adapt-** *adjust* -**ment** *action* **equip-** *to fit out*	Devices and supplies that enable a disabled individual to perform specific functions
amputation amputate (verb) amputee	am-pyu-**TAY**-shun am-pyu-**TATE** **AM**-pyu-tee		Latin *to prune*	Process of removing a limb, part of a limb, a breast, or other projecting part A person with an amputation
contracture	kon-**TRAK**-chur	S/ R/	-**ure** *result of* **contract-** *pull together*	Muscle shortening due to spasm or fibrosis
elective	e-**LEK**-tiv	S/ R/	-**ive** *pertaining to* **elect-** *choice*	Surgery that is not urgent or vital
prosthesis	**PROS**-thee-sis		Greek *an addition*	Manufactured substitute for a missing part of the body
residual	re-**ZID**-you-al	S/ R/CF	-**al** *pertaining to* **resid/u-** *left over*	Pertaining to anything left over
therapy	**THAIR**-ah-pee		Greek *medical treatment*	Systematic treatment of a disease, dysfunction, or disorder
therapeutic	**THAIR**-ah-**PYU**-tik	S/ R/	-**ic** *pertaining to* **therapeut-** *treatment*	Relating to the treatment of a disease or disorder

A temporary prosthesis can usually be fitted 4-8 weeks after surgery, and a permanent prosthesis 8 to 12 weeks after surgery. About 75% of older adults with a prosthesis can walk, often without a cane or walker.

For an arm–hand prosthesis, the decision on what type of prosthesis will be needed depends on three factors:

- what natural arms and hands remain
- what functions the patient wants and needs to do
- which kinds of prostheses are available and affordable

The hand or tool of the prosthesis can be a hand, hook, or some other shape to perform specific functions that are needed.

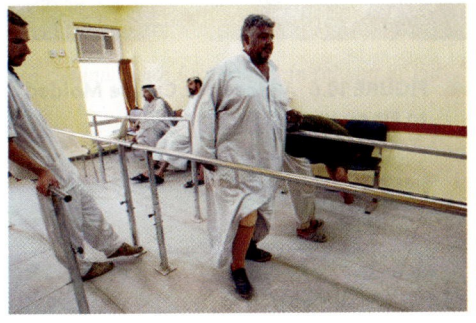

▲ **FIGURE 18.5 Trying Out a New Prosthesis in Iraq.**

EXERCISES

*Utilize the correct **language of rehabilitation** in the following paragraph. The word bank contains the terms you need to use—some terms you may use more than once. When you have finished the exercise, proofread it again to see if it makes sense. Fill in the blanks.*

Word bank

adapt	contracture	amputation(s)	prosthesis
amputee	adaptive equipment	elective	amputate
residual	PVD	assistive	protocol

Seventy-five percent of all _____ are performed on patients over 65 years of age with

_____ complicating arteriosclerosis and diabetes. Loss of blood flow to a limb area produces necrotic

tissue, which in time can become infected or gangrenous and makes the need for this procedure urgent, rather

than _____. A traumatic _____ can occur in an industrial accident, motor vehicle accident,

or household accident. The decision to _____ is a serious one and must be undertaken by a qualified

surgeon. The _____ will require postoperative training in how to _____ to the use of

a _____ and/or _____. Hopefully, there will be no muscle _____

or _____ pain after the surgery.

THERAPEUTIC TECHNIQUES AND TOOLS (continued)

Ultrasound Therapy

Therapeutic ultrasound uses its high frequency, **acoustic** (sound) vibrations to provide deep heating *(Figure 18.8)*. A **transducer** is used to convert electrical energy to sound energy that passes through tissues generating heat.

Treatments are usually started as soon as possible after injury of muscles, tendons, and joints. Ultrasound can also be used to stimulate bone healing.

Phonophoresis uses ultrasound to facilitate delivery of some medications through the skin into tissues by increasing the permeability of the stratum corneum. Hydrocortisone or dexamethasone cream (Decadron) are commonly delivered with this technique.

Light Therapy

Laser is an acronym for **Light Amplification by Stimulated Emission of Radiation**. Low-power lasers seem to be effective in aiding wound healing and reducing pain but have not received FDA approval.

Light emission diode (LED) therapy has received FDA approval. Red LEDs help prevent the skin appearances of aging, amber LEDs trigger pain relief, and blue LEDs treat acne.

Ultraviolet therapy has a limited use for treating dermatologic conditions such as psoriasis, acne, and pressure sores.

Electrical Stimulation

Electrical stimulation is used in two forms:

1. **Functional electrical stimulation** uses an electrical current directed to a muscle. This prevents **atrophy** in muscles that are not being used. It can also help increase the function of previously paralyzed muscles.

2. **Transcutaneous electrical nerve stimulation (TENS)** stimulates peripheral nerves to improve muscle strength and mass *(Figure 18.9)*. It is also used to treat pain associated with the peripheral neuropathy of diabetes and for older adults with herpes zoster (shingles).

Spinal Traction

Traction can be performed mechanically using a machine or a system of ropes and pulleys or performed manually by a therapist. Its function is to increase the space between vertebrae, so it can be used to treat intervertebral disc herniations and lumbar and cervical muscle spasm.

Mechanical lumbar traction can be performed using a lower body harness and a traction device to generate a force equal to half the patient's body weight. Mechanical cervical traction can use a head harness with forces of 20 to 50 pounds *(Figure 18.10)*.

Hyperbaric Oxygen Therapy

Hyperbaric oxygen therapy (HBOT) chambers enable oxygen therapy to be given at pressures greater than atmospheric pressure. This promotes angiogenesis (formation of new blood vessels) and wound healing. In addition to decompression sickness, it is used to improve skin graft and wound healing, treat radiation ulcers, snake bites, acute thermal burns, and foot injuries in diabetics. It also kills certain anaerobic bacteria and prevents the production of some bacterial toxins *(see Chapter 20)*.

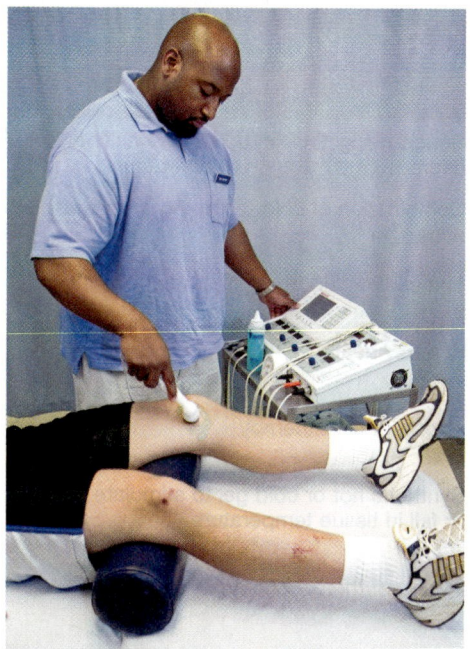

▲ **FIGURE 18.8 Ultrasound Applied Through a Gel-Like Coupling Medium.**

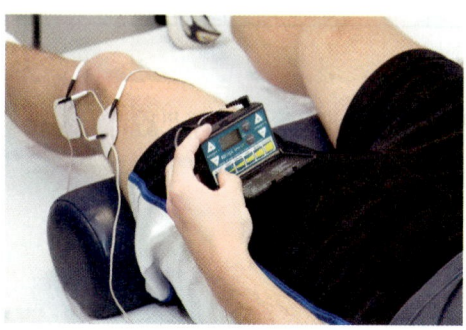

▲ **FIGURE 18.9 Application of Electrodes for TENS Stimulation.**

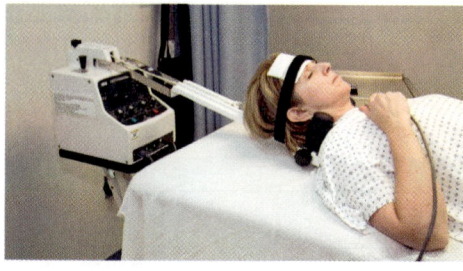

▲ **FIGURE 18.10 Mechanical Cervical Traction.**

Abbreviations

HBOT	hyperbaric oxygen therapy
LASER	light amplification by stimulated emission of radiation
LED	light emission diode
TENS	transcutaneous electrical nerve stimulation

WORD ANALYSIS AND DEFINITION

WORD	PRONUNCIATION	ELEMENTS		DEFINITION
acoustic	ah-**KOOS**-tik	S/ R/	**-tic** *pertaining to* **acous-** *hearing*	Pertaining to hearing
atrophy	**AT**-roh-fee	P/ R/	**a-** *without* **-trophy** *development, nourishment*	Wasting or diminished volume of a tissue or organ
diode	**DIE**-ode	P/ R/	**di-** *two* **-ode** *path*	Allows electrical current to flow in one direction only
hyperbaric	high-per-**BAR**-ik	S/ P/ R/	**-ic** *pertaining to* **hyper-** *above, excessive* **-bar** *pressure*	Pressure greater than atmospheric pressure
phonophoresis	foh-noh-for-**EE**-sis	S/ R/CF R/	**-sis** *condition* **phon/o-** *sound* **-phore-** *carried*	Transport of one substance across the skin through the use of ultrasound
traction	**TRAK**-shun		Latin *to pull*	Pulling or dragging force
transducer	trans-**DYU**-sir	P/ R/	**trans-** *across* **-ducer** *leader*	Device that converts energy from one form to another
ultrasound	**UL**-trah-sownd	P/ R/	**ultra-** *higher, beyond* **-sound** *noise*	Use of very high frequency sound waves
ultraviolet	ul-trah-**VIE**-oh-let	P/ R/	**ultra-** *higher, beyond* **-violet** *bluish purple*	Electromagnetic rays at higher frequency than the violet end of the spectrum

EXERCISES

Demonstrate your knowledge of word elements and definitions for each of the following rehabilitation terms. Circle the correct answer.

1. transducer   The prefix means:

    beneath   beside   on top of   across

2. traction   means to:

    sleep   walk   pull   turn

3. phonophoresis   The combining form means:

    water   that which does   treatment   sound

4. hyperbaric   The root means:

    bar   pressure   fluid   flow

5. ultrasound   The prefix means:

    excessive   above   higher   below

6. diode   The prefix is one of

    size   location   number   color

7. acoustic   The root means:

    smelling   walking   lifting   hearing

8. atrophy   The prefix means:

    two   without   across   above

REHABILITATION MEDICINE

CHALLENGE YOUR KNOWLEDGE

A. **Case Report:** Review again the case of Mr. Hank Johnson. Read carefully and try to identify the occupations of the various health care personnel Mr. Johnson has had taking care of him in the past year. *Do not forget to take into account his P/M/H (past medical history).* List the various specialists and allied health care personnel who may have had treatment responsibilities for Mr. Johnson.

Your patient is

. . . Mr. Hank Johnson, a 65-year-old owner of a printing shop. One year ago, Mr. Johnson had an elective left total hip replacement for osteoarthritis. Four months later, he had a myocardial infarction. Two weeks ago, while on his exercise bicycle, he had a stroke. His right arm and leg were paralyzed, and he lost his speech and had difficulty swallowing. He was brought to the emergency department within three hours of the stroke and received thrombolytic therapy. He is now receiving physical therapy, occupational therapy, and speech therapy in the inpatient rehabilitation unit. He is able to say some simple words and has begun to have voluntary movements in the arm and leg.

Your roles are to help him regain function in his arm and leg and to monitor and record his progress.

The goals of Mr. Johnson's stroke rehabilitation program are to enable him to:

- walk safely using an assistive device
- use his hands with accuracy
- restore his speech abilities
- prevent a second stroke

Health Care Team (Occupation)	Function of This Occupation (How They Could Help Mr. Johnson)

B. **Abbreviations:** An abbreviation is a "short cut" for saving time by not writing out all the words. Rewrite the following sentences in correct medical language *without* using the abbreviations. (Take the abbreviations out of these sentences, and insert the full terms.)

1. Rehab for this stroke patient includes instruction in ADLs and IADLs.

    _____

    _____

    _____

    _____

2. In order to prevent DVT from forming, patient needs to get out of bed and walk one hour in the morning, afternoon, and evening.

    _____

    _____

    _____

    _____

3. The patient's ROM will be assessed by the PT tomorrow.

    _____

    _____

    _____

4. We will try to alleviate this patient's chronic pain with a TENS unit.

    _____

    _____

    _____

    _____

5. Now choose one of the sentences above and rewrite it in nonmedical language.

    _____

    _____

    _____

    _____

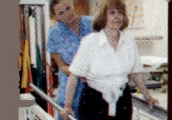

REHABILITATION MEDICINE

C. **Greek and Latin Terms:** A lot of medical terms are formed directly from Greek and Latin terms. You are given the medical term; list its meaning, then define the term. The first one is done for you. Fill in the blanks.

Medical Term	Greek/Latin	Definition
adapt	*to adjust*	*To adjust to different conditions*
amputation		
assist		
elective		
modality		
physiatry		
prosthesis		
protocol		
traction		

Some of these terms can be used in regular English sentences with no medical meaning. *Choose one term,* and write a simple English sentence in which the word has no medical meaning. Write a second sentence that illustrates how the same term is used medically.

Term: _____ .

1. English usage: _____

   _____

   _____

   _____

   _____

2. Medical usage: _____

   _____

   _____

   _____

   _____

D. **Elements:** Identifying word elements will assist you in determining the meaning of the medical term. Test your knowledge of the elements, and circle the correct choice.

1. In the term **physiatrist,** the suffix means:

    a. one who specializes

    b. a condition

    c. an inflammation

    d. one who leads

    e. nature

2. In the term **orthotic,** the root means:

    a. many

    b. correct

    c. move

    d. action

    e. physical

3. In the term **contracture,** the suffix means:

    a. addition

    b. movement

    c. process

    d. energy

    e. result of

4. In the term **transducer,** the root means:

    a. device

    b. pulling

    c. temperature

    d. leader

    e. cold

5. In the term **multidisciplinary,** the prefix means:

    a. one

    b. specialists

    c. many

    d. across

    e. less than

REHABILITATION MEDICINE

P. Research: Use your dictionary, glossary, school library, and/or the Internet to research the medical term **pain threshold**.

1. Write a definition for this term.

_____

_____

_____

2. Write three facts you have learned about this medical term.

_____

_____

_____

_____

_____

_____

_____

_____

_____

_____

_____

_____

3. Use this term in a sentence that is not a definition.

_____

_____

_____

_____

Q. Terminology Challenge: ultrasound versus hyperbaric

Both these prefixes denote some degree of measurement. Give the exact meaning of each prefix, and explain how they are similar and how they are different. Fill in the blanks.

Ultrasound: prefix is _____ and means _____.

Hyperbaric: prefix is _____ and means _____.

Similar but different:

_____

_____

_____

R. **Elements:** Demonstrate your knowledge of word elements and definitions for each of the following rehabilitation terms. Circle the correct answer.

1. **cryotherapy:** "**cryo**" is a:

   suffix   prefix   root   combining form

2. **transducer:** The prefix means:

   beneath   beside   on top of   across

3. **modality:** The term means a:

   condition   method   disease   sound

4. **thermotherapy:** "**thermo**" is a:

   suffix   prefix   root   combining form

5. **Hydrocollator:** "**hydro**" means:

   white   water   heat   excessive

6. **cryokinetics:** The root means:

   motion   collect   being born   leader

7. **traction:** means to:

   sleep   walk   pull   turn

8. **phonophoresis:** The suffix means:

   condition   that which does   treatment   sound

9. **acoustic:** The root means:

   seeing   walking   hearing   standing

10. **atrophy:** The root means:

    development   abnormal   without   beside

Pick one term from above and use it to communicate a message about a patient:

Term:_____

Message: _____

_____

_____

_____

_____

_____

_____

_____

REHABILITATION MEDICINE

S. **Apply the *language of rehabilitation* to the following questions.** Circle the correct answer.

1. Rehabilitation medicine focuses on:

    a. prevention

    b. restoration

    c. function

    d. strength

    e. maintenance

2. A *protocol* is a:

    a. rehabilitation team

    b. treatment plan

    c. medical specialist

    d. special piece of equipment

    e. treatment modality

3. Name one tool of cryotherapy:

    a. subcutaneous injection

    b. heating pad

    c. Hydrocollator

    d. hot wax

    e. acupuncture

4. Name one example of adaptive equipment:

    a. raised toilet seat

    b. walker

    c. prosthesis

    d. orthotic

    e. special shoes

5. How many prongs does a quad cane have?

    a. one

    b. two

    c. three

    d. four

    e. five

6. Can be used to treat decompression sickness, snake bites, and radiation ulcers:

   a. ADL

   b. LED

   c. TENS

   d. ROM

   e. HBOT

7. In a rehabilitation multidisciplinary team, the _____ leads the team:

   a. social worker

   b. orthopedist

   c. physiatrist

   d. orthotist

   e. physical therapist

8. Patients with hip fractures and hip replacements are susceptible to:

   a. BKA

   b. DVT

   c. ADL

   d. ROM

   e. PVD

9. Heat reduces pain and increases:

   a. body metabolism

   b. relaxation of muscle

   c. vasoconstriction of blood vessels

   d. pulse rate

   e. tendon elasticity

10. A maker and fitter of orthopedic appliances is called a(n):

    a. orthopedist

    b. ophthalmologist

    c. histologist

    d. orthotist

    e. physiatrist

REHABILITATION MEDICINE

CHAPTER SUMMARY EXERCISE

1. *Listen to the pronunciation of the medical terms as given by your instructor.*
2. *Circle the correct spelling of the medical term.*
3. *Match the correctly spelled terms to the brief descriptions below.*
4. *Write a sentence for each of the 15 terms that appear in this exercise.*

A. SPELLING COMPREHENSION: CIRCLE THE CORRECT SPELLING OF THE TERM.

1. fonophoresis	phonophoresis	funoporesis	phonoporesis	ponophoresis
2. restoreitive	ristoritive	restorative	ristorative	ristoriteve
3. ultravilet	ultreviolet	ultreeviolet	ultraviolet	ultraviolette
4. pysiatry	phsiatry	physiatrey	phsiatrey	physiatry
5. therapeutic	teraputetic	thereputic	terapeutic	theraputic
6. kryocinetics	cryocinetics	kryokinetics	cryokinetics	criocinetics
7. trackion	tracktion	tracion	treckion	traction
8. rehabilitation	rehabillition	rehavilitation	rehabillitation	rehebiliation
9. orthotic	othotick	ortotic	orthotick	orrthotic
10. hyperberric	hypoberic	hyperbarrick	hyperbaric	hypobaric
11. tranducer	trensducker	transducer	transdusser	trenducer
12. lazer	laser	lasser	lasir	lasere
13. Hydruculator	Hydruckulator	Hydroculator	Hydruckulater	Hydrocollator
14. protocol	protocool	protolcol	protocul	proticule
15. fludiotherapy	fluidterapy	fluidotherapy	fluedtherapy	fluidiotherapy

B. MATCH THE NUMBER OF THE CORRECT TERM IN PART A WITH THE BRIEF DESCRIPTION OF THE TERM BELOW.

a. employs radiation in its use _____

b. detailed regimen of therapy _____

c. pressure greater than atmospheric pressure _____

d. uses ultrasound to facilitate delivery or medication _____

e. combines cold with exercise _____

f. limited use for dermatologic conditions _____

g. uses dry air stream to apply heat _____

h. physical medicine _____

i. focuses on function _____

j. converts energy from one form to another _____

k. corrects an orthopedic abnormality   _____

l. contains hot or cold gel that changes tissue temperature   _____

m. pertaining to treatment   _____

n. to return something to what it was   _____

o. can be manual or mechanical   _____

C. USING YOUR KNOWLEDGE OF TERMS 1-15 IN PART A AND THEIR CORRECT SPELLING, WRITE A BRIEF SENTENCE FOR EACH OF THE TERMS AS IT MIGHT APPEAR IN PATIENT DOCUMENTATION.

1. _____

2. _____

3. _____

4. _____

5. _____

6. _____

7. _____

8. _____

9. _____

10. _____

11. _____

12. _____

13. _____

14. _____

15. _____

D. GO TO THE STUDENT CD. OPEN THE GLOSSARY AND PRACTICE YOUR PRONUNCIATION OF THE TERMS IN PART A OF THIS EXERCISE.

Mental Health and Affective Disorders

Mental health is defined as emotional, behavioral, and social well-being so that an individual can cope with internal and external events. In this lesson, you will be given information about affective disorders, mood disorders, schizophrenia, anxiety disorders, psychosomatic and somatoform disorders.

This lesson and the introduction will enable you to use correct medical terminology to:

- **Distinguish between psychology and psychiatry.**
- **Define mental disorder and insanity.**
- **Discuss affective disorders.**
- **Describe the differences between the two main types of mood disorder.**

DEFINITIONS IN MENTAL HEALTH

Psychology is defined as the scientific study of behavior and mental processes. **Behavior** is anything you do—talking, sleeping, reading, interacting with others. **Mental processes** are your private, internal experiences—thinking, feeling, remembering, dreaming.

A licensed specialist in psychology is called a **psychologist.** Psychologists can have a master's degree or a doctorate in philosophy **(PhD)** or a doctorate in psychology **(PsyD)**. They can practice in many different career specialties, including being a **psychotherapist** or a **psychoanalyst.**

Psychiatry is the medical specialty concerned with the origin, diagnosis, prevention, and treatment of mental, emotional, and behavioral disorders. **Psychiatrists** have an MD or DO degree and a minimum of four years of residency training in the specialty.

Many psychiatrists and psychologists work together in a team approach to therapy. Other health professionals in the mental health team include **clinical social workers, psychiatric nurses, mental health technicians, and psychiatric technicians.**

Mental disorder can be defined as any behavior or emotional state that:

- causes a person to suffer emotional distress (e.g., depression, anxiety).
- is harmful to the individual sufferer (impairs the individual's ability to work, take care of personal needs, or get along with others).
- is self-destructive (e.g., substance abuse, gambling and other addictions, self-injury)
- endangers others or the community (antisocial behaviors, **homicidal** intent, **pyromania** [setting fires]).

Insanity is a *legal* term for a severe mental illness, present at the time a crime was committed, that impaired the defendant's capacity to understand the moral wrong of the act. *It is not a medical diagnosis.*

Mental disorders are numerous and very diverse. A uniform system for classifying and describing them has been developed by the American Psychiatric Association. It is called the *Diagnostic and Statistical Manual of Mental Disorders,* fourth edition, text revision (**DSM-IV-TR**). The "IV" indicates that this is the fourth conceptual revision; "TR" indicates a text revision of the fourth edition. The manual is usually referred to as **the DSM-IV** ("DSM-4").

The DSM-IV provides a detailed description of the symptoms seen in psychiatric disorders. These descriptions allow psychiatric disorders to be classified. It is the disorders that are classified, not the people who have the disorders. Modern mental health terminology does not use the term **schizophrenic,** but uses the phrase "a person with **schizophrenia.**" The DSM-IV contains over 200 diagnoses grouped into 17 major categories.

Keynote

Psychologists are not licensed to prescribe medications.

As physicians, psychiatrists are licensed to prescribe medications.

Abbreviations

DSM-IV-TR	*Diagnostic and Statistical Manual of Mental Disorders,* fourth edition, text revision: referred to as "DSM-IV"
PhD	Doctorate in philosophy
PsyD	Doctorate in psychology

Keynote

The DSM-IV classifies and describes psychiatric disorders.

WORD	PRONUNCIATION	ELEMENTS		DEFINITION
delusion	de-**LOO**-zhun	S/	-ion *condition, process*	Fixed, unyielding, false belief or judgment held despite strong evidence to the contrary
		R/	delus- *deceive*	
delusional (adj)	de-**LOO**-zhun-al	S/	-al *pertaining to*	
hallucination	hah-loo-sih-**NAY**-shun	S/	-ation *process*	Perception of an object or event when there is no such thing present
		R/	hallucin- *imagination*	
homicide	**HOM**-ih-side	R/CF	hom/i- *man*	Killing of one human by another
		R/CF	-cid/e *killing*	
homicidal	hom-ih-**SIDE**-al	S/	-al *pertaining to*	Having a tendency to commit homicide
		R/	-cid- *killing*	
insanity	in-**SAN**-ih-tee	S/	-ity *condition*	Nonmedical term for person unable to be responsible for actions
		P/	in- *not*	
		R/	-san- *sound*	
psychiatry	sigh-**KIGH**-ah-tree	S/	-iatry *treatment*	Diagnosis and treatment of mental disorders
		R/	psych- *mind*	
psychiatric	sigh-kee-**AH**-trik	S/	-ic *pertaining to*	Pertaining to psychiatry
psychiatrist	sigh-**KIGH**-ah-trist	S/	-iatrist *one who treats*	Licensed medical specialist in psychiatry
psychology	sigh-**KOL**-oh-jee	S/	-logy *study of*	Science concerned with the behavior of the human mind
		R/CF	psych/o- *mind*	
psychologic	sigh-koh-**LOJ**-ik	S/	-ic *pertaining to*	Pertaining to psychology
psychologist	sigh-**KOL**-oh-jist	S/	-logist *specialist*	Licensed specialist in psychology
psychoanalysis	sigh-koh-ah-**NAL**-ih-sis	R/	-analysis *process to define*	Method of psychotherapy
psychoanalyst	sigh-koh-**AN**-ah-list	R/	-analyst *one who defines*	Practitioner of psychoanalysis
psychotherapy	sigh-koh-**THAIR**-ah-pee	S/	-therapy *treatment*	Treatment of mental disorders through communication
psychotherapist	sigh-koh-**THAIR**-ah-pist	S/	-therapist *one who treats*	Practitioner of psychotherapy
pyromania	pie-roh-**MAY**-nee-ah	R/CF	pyr/o- *fire*	Morbid impulse to set fires
		R/	-mania *frenzy*	
schizophrenia	skitz-oh-**FREE**-nee-ah	S/	-ia *condition*	Disorder of perception, thought, emotion, and behavior
		R/CF	schiz/o- *to split, cleave*	
		R/	-phren- *mind*	
tangentiality	tan-jen-she-**AL**-ih-tee	S/	-ity *condition*	Thought processes move rapidly and superficially from one topic to another
		S/	-al- *pertaining to*	
tangent	**TAN**-jent	R/CF	tangent/i- *touch*	Sudden change of course

Elements remain your best clue to the meaning of a medical term. Match the element in column l with its correct meaning in column 2.

_____ 1.	psych/o-	A. pertaining to
_____ 2.	-logy	B. condition
_____ 3.	-mania	C. one who studies
_____ 4.	schiz/o-	D. not
_____ 5.	-ity	E. fire
_____ 6.	pyr/o-	F. mind
_____ 7.	-logist	G. to split
_____ 8.	in-	H. frenzy
_____ 9.	-ic	I. treatment
_____ 10.	-iatry	J. study of

PERSONALITY DISORDERS

Personality is defined as an individual's unique and stable patterns of thoughts, feelings, and behaviors. When these patterns become rigid and inflexible in response to different situations, they can cause impairment of the individual's ability to deal with other people (i.e., to function socially).

Borderline personality disorder (BPD) is a frequent diagnosis in people who are impulsive, unstable in mood, and manipulative. They can be exciting, charming and friendly one moment and angry, irritable, and sarcastic the next. Their identity is fragile and insecure, their self-worth low. They can be promiscuous and self-destructive; for example with **self-mutilation (self-injury)** *(Figure 19.5)* or suicide. People with **narcissistic personality disorder** have an exaggerated sense of self-importance and seek constant attention.

Antisocial personality disorder, used interchangeably with the terms **sociopath** and **psychopath,** describes people who lie, cheat, steal, and have no sense of responsibility and no anxiety or guilt about their behavior. The psychopaths have these characteristics but tend to be more violent and anger easily because of little things.

Schizoid and paranoid personality disorders are absorbed with themselves, untrusting, and fearful of closeness with others.

Treatment for personality disorders is not successful. One method is **dialectical behavior therapy,** which encourages acceptance of the person by family while encouraging the person to change.

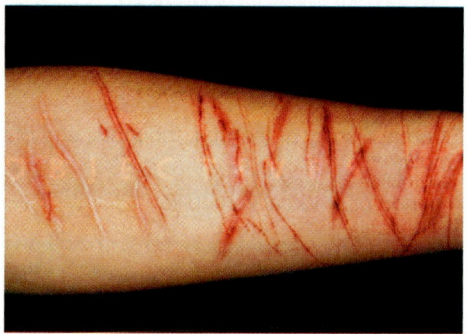

▲ **FIGURE 19.5 Self-Mutilated Arm.**

▲ **FIGURE 19.6 Dissociative Identity Disorder (Multiple Personality Disorder).**

Dissociative Disorders

Dissociative disorders involve a disassociation (splitting apart) of past experiences from present memory or consciousness. Being unable to recall identity is called dissociative amnesia. The development of distinctly separate personalities is called **dissociative identity disorder (DID).** It was formerly called **multiple personality disorder (MPD).**

The basic origin of all these disorders is the need to escape, usually from extreme trauma, and most often from sexual, emotional, or physical abuse in childhood.

The most severe of this group of disorders is DID. Two or more distinct personalities, each with their own memories and behaviors, inhabit the same person at the same time *(Figure 19.6)*. Treatment is with psychotherapy.

Impulse Control Disorders

Impulse control disorders are an inability to resist an impulse to perform an action that is harmful to the individual or to others. These disorders include:

- **Intermittent explosive disorder** is characterized by recurrent episodes of unrestrained aggression toward people, furniture, or property, with violent resistance to attempts to restrain. The etiology is thought to be epileptic-like activity in the brain. Medications that generate some improvement include propranolol, lithium, valproate, and phenytoin.

- **Kleptomania** is characterized by stealing—not for gain, but to satisfy an irresistible urge to steal. Behavior therapy can help, and SSRIs appear to be of value.

- **Trichotillomania (TTM)** is characterized by the repeated urge to pull out scalp, beard, pubic, and other body hair.

- **Substance abuse and chemical dependence** describe continued use of drugs or alcohol despite having had significant problems or distress related to their use. This **addiction** affects the brain and behavior and develops an increased need for the substance and an inability to stop using it.

- **Pyromania** is repeated fire setting with no motive other than a fascination with fire and fire engines. Some pyromaniacs end up as volunteer firefighters. Treatment with behavior therapy is sometimes successful.

- **Pathologic gambling** is a recurrent, compelling fascination to spend time

▲ **FIGURE 19.7 Compulsive Gambler.**

WORD	PRONUNCIATION		ELEMENTS	DEFINITION
addict	**ADD**-ikt	P/ R/	ad- *toward* -dict *surrender*	One who cannot live without a substance or practice
addiction	ah-**DIK**-shun	S/	-ion *condition, action*	Habitual psychologic and physiologic dependence on a substance or practice
antisocial personality disorder	**AN**-tee-**SOH**-shal per-son-**AL**-ih-tee dis-**OR**-der	S/ P/ R/ S/ S/ R/	-al *pertaining to* anti- *against* -soci- *community* -ity *condition* -al *pertaining to* -person- *person*	Describes people who lie, cheat, steal, and have no guilt about their behavior
dialectic dialectical (adj)	die-ah-**LEK**-tik die-ah-**LEK**-tik-al	 S/ R/	Greek *argumentative* -al *pertaining to* dialectic- *argument*	Logical argumentation
dissociative identity disorder	di-**SO**-see-ah-tiv eye-**DEN**-tih-tee dis-**OR**-der	P/ R/ S/	dis- *apart, away from* -soci- *community* -ative *separated*	Part of an individual's personality is separated from the rest, leading to multiple personalities
kleptomania	klep-toe-**MAY**-nee-ah	S/ R/CF	-mania *frenzy* klept/o- *to steal*	Uncontrollable need to steal
narcissism narcissistic (adj)	**NAR**-sih-sizm **NAR**-sih-**SIS**-tik	 S/ R/ S/	Greek mythical character, Narcissos, who was in love with his own reflection in water -ism *a process* narciss- *narcissism* -istic *pertaining to*	Self-love; person interprets everything purely in relation to themselves
pathologic gambling	path-oh-**LOJ**-ik **GAM**-bling	S/ R/ R/	-ic *pertaining to* path/o- *disease* -log- *study of*	Morbid, constant, uncontrollable, destructive gambling
psychopath	**SIGH**-koh-path	S/ R/CF	-path *disease* psych/o- *mind*	Person with antisocial personality disorder
pyromania	pie-roh-**MAY**-nee-ah	R/CF R/	pyr/o- *fire* -mania *frenzy*	Morbid impulse to set fires
schizoid	**SKITZ**-oyd	S/ R/	-oid *resemble* schiz- *split*	Withdrawn, socially isolated
self-mutilation	self-myu-tih-**LAY**-shun	R/ S/ R/	self- *own individual* -ation *action* -mutil- *to maim*	Injury or disfigurement made to one's own body
sociopath	**SO**-see-oh-path	S/ R/CF	-path *disease* soci/o- *social, society*	Person with antisocial personality disorder

and money on gambling, despite ever-mounting losses *(Figure 19.7)*. Gambling becomes the reason for living. Financial ruin does not stop the gambling. Fraud and theft then support it. Treatment with behavior therapy helps, in tandem with participation in Gamblers Anonymous.

Abbreviations

BPD	borderline personality disorder
DID	dissociative identity disorder
MPD	multiple personality disorder
TTM	trichotillomania

EXERCISES

Identify the elements that are in bold in the following medical terms in column l. Define the type of element in column 2. Write the meaning of that bolded element in column 3.

Medical Term	Type of Element (P, R, CF, S)	Meaning of the Element
socio**path**	_____	_____
pyromania	_____	_____
patho**log**ical	_____	_____
klepto**mania**	_____	_____
dissociative	_____	_____
anti**social**	_____	_____

PSYCHOACTIVE DRUGS

Psychoactive drugs are chemicals that change consciousness, awareness, or perception *(Table 19.5)*. The most commonly used drugs are caffeine, tobacco, and alcohol.

Drug abuse refers to drugs that cause emotional or physical harm to an individual as their consumption becomes frequent and compulsive.

Addiction occurs when a person feels compelled to use a drug or perform a certain activity and cannot control the use.

Psychologic dependence is the mental desire or **craving** for the effects produced by a drug.

Physical dependence is the changes in the body processes that make the drug necessary for daily functioning. If the drug is stopped, the withdrawal symptoms include physical pain, as well as intense cravings.

Tolerance is when the body adjusts to the effects of the drug, and higher and higher doses produce less and less effect. The brain, liver, heart, and other organs can be damaged.

Comorbidity is the presence of a combination of mental disorders. It is very common. Alcohol dependence and abuse overlap with almost all other mental disorders including anxiety disorders, mood disorders, and personality disorders. In these cases, stopping drinking alcohol is only the first step in solving the problem.

Keynote

Dependence on drugs can be both psychologic and physical.

TABLE 19.5 Psychoactive Drugs

TYPE/MODE OF ACTION	NAME	COMMON EFFECTS	EFFECTS OF ABUSE
Stimulants ("uppers") Speed up activity in the CNS	caffeine	Wakefulness, shorter reaction time, alertness	Restlessness, insomnia, heartbeat irregularities
	nicotine	Varies from alertness to calmness, appetite for carbohydrates decreases	Heart disease; high blood pressure; vasoconstriction; bronchitis; emphysema; lung, throat, mouth cancer
	amphetamines	Wakefulness, alertness, increased metabolism, decreased appetite	Nervousness, high blood pressure, delusions, psychosis, convulsions, death
	cocaine	**Euphoria**, high energy, illusions of power	Excitability, paranoia, anxiety, panic, depression, heart failure, death
Depressants ("downers") Slow down activity in the CNS	alcohol	**1–2 drinks**—reduces inhibitions and anxiety	Blackouts, mental and neurologic impairment, psychosis, cirrhosis of liver, death
		Many drinks—slow reaction time, poor coordination and memory	Impaired motor and sensory functions, amnesia, loss of consciousness, death
	barbiturates and tranquilizers	Reduce anxiety and tension, sedation	
Narcotics—Mimic the actions of natural **endorphins**	codeine, opium, morphine, heroin	Euphoria, pleasure, relief of pain	High tolerance of pain, nausea, vomiting, constipation, convulsions, coma, death
Psychedelics Disrupt normal thought processes	marijuana	Relaxation, euphoria, increased appetite, pain relief	Sensory distortion, hallucinations, paranoia, throat and lung damage
	LSD, mescaline, MDMA (Ecstasy)	Exhilaration, euphoria, hallucinations, insightful experiences	Panic, extreme delusions, bad "trips," paranoia, psychosis

WORD	PRONUNCIATION	ELEMENTS		DEFINITION
comorbidity	koh-mor-**BID**-ih-tee	S/ P/ R/	-ity *condition* co- *with, together* -morbid- *disease*	Presence of two or more diseases at the same time
craving	**KRAY**-ving		Latin *desire*	Deep longing or desire
dependence	de-**PEN**-dense		Latin *to hang from*	State of needing someone or something
depressant	de-**PRESS**-ant	S/ P/ R/	-ant *agent* de- *away from* -press- *press down*	Substance that diminishes activity, sensation, or tone
endorphin	en-**DOR**-fin	P/ R/	end- *within* -orphin *morphine*	Natural substance in the brain that has same effect as opium
euphoria	yoo-**FOR**-ee-ah	S/ P/ R/	-ia *condition* eu- *normal* -phor- *to bear*	Exaggerated feeling of well-being
narcotic	nar-**KOT**-ik	S/ R/CF	-tic *pertaining to* narc/o- *sleep*	Drug derived from opium or a synthetic drug with similar effects
psychedelic	sigh-keh-**DEL**-ik	S/ R/ R/	-ic *pertaining to* psyche- *mind, soul* -del- *manifest*	Agent that intensifies sensory perception
psychoactive	sigh-koh-**AK**-tiv	S/ R/CF R/	-ive *quality of* psych/o- *mind, soul* -act- *performance*	An agent able to alter mood, behavior, and/or cognition
stimulant	**STIM**-you-lant	S/ R/	-ant *agent* stimul- *to excite*	Agent that excites or strengthens functional activity
tolerance	**TOL**-er-antz	S/ R/	-ance *condition, quality of being* toler- *endure*	Become accustomed to a stimulus or drug

EXERCISES

Review all the new terms you have learned on these two pages. Choose the correct medical terminology to insert into each of the following sentences. You will use some terms twice.

1. Overuse of antibiotics builds up a _____ to certain drugs, and they are no longer effective.

2. A diabetic with high blood pressure has a _____.

3. Caffeine and nicotine can be *both* a _____ and a _____.

4. Marathon runners can experience the natural stimulatory effect from _____.

5. _____ is a state that can be physical or mental.

6. The two opposite terms in this WAD are _____ and _____.

7. An agent able to alter mood, behavior, and/or cognition is _____.

8. A natural substance in the brain that has the same effect as opium is _____.

9. A _____ is an agent that excites or strengthens functional activity.

10. Deep longing or desire is a _____.

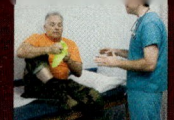
MENTAL HEALTH

C. Difference Between ...: Any health care worker in the mental health field will be interacting with psychologists and psychiatrists. Write a brief answer *in layman's terms* that explains the basic differences between the two practitioners.

1. Psychologist:

_____

_____

_____

2. Psychiatrist:

_____

_____

_____

Meet the lesson objective by explaining the difference between:

3. Mental disorder:

_____

_____

_____

4. Insanity:

_____

_____

_____

5. Is there a listing for insanity in the DSM-IV-TR?

Yes _____ No _____

6. If no, why is it not listed? _____

D. Anxiety and Impulse Control Disorders: Patients with various types of anxiety and impulse control disorders would be seen in the Fulwood Psychiatric Clinic. Determine the specific disorder from the description of the patient and the symptoms in the following documentation. The first one is done for you. Fill in the blanks.

1. Patient suffers sudden bouts of intense fear that cause profuse sweating, nausea, and occasional vomiting.

panic disorder

2. Patient has been arrested for shoplifting but admits to stealing many more items before she was caught today. Patient states

she steals for the "thrill of it." _____

3. Patient's house was destroyed in the flooding following Hurricane Katrina. He barely escaped with his life and now suffers

from almost daily stress headaches and physical aches and pains. _____

4. Patient was locked in closets for hours at a time as a young boy. _____

5. Patient is here today by court order for psychiatric examination. Patient is suspected of setting two fires in the same neighborhood in the last two weeks. _____

6. Patient is so uncomfortable on buses, subways, elevators, and crowded sidewalks that she is unable to get to work.

    _____

7. Patient presents today with severe dermatitis on both hands. Patient states she washes her hands at least 50 times a day to be sure they are germfree. _____

8. Patient's chief complaint today is palpitations and insomnia, which keep him awake most nights. He feels worried and anxious all the time but can give no specific reason for it. _____

E. **Suffixes:** Mental health practitioners can be either *psycho*logists or *psychi*atrists. The root/combining form psych/o- is present in all the following terms. The suffix is what makes the difference. Challenge your knowledge of the *language of mental health* by applying the correct term to the following statements. Fill in the blanks, using the choices below.

psychopath	**psychiatry**	**psychiatric**	**psychotherapy**
psychotic	**psychopharmacotherapy**	**psychoanalysis**	**psychology**
psychiatrist	**psychoanalyst**	**psychologist**	**psychologic**
psychosomatic	**psychotherapist**	**psychosis**	**psychoactive**

1. An agent able to alter mood, behavior, or cognition: _____

2. Treatment of mental disorders through communication is called ._____

3. _____ is the science concerned with the behavior of humans.

4. A licensed specialist in psychology is known as a _____.

5. The patient's _____ state was starting to affect his physical well-being.

6. A method of psychotherapy is _____.

7. What type of technician is the health care worker in the first case report at the beginning of this chapter?

    _____ technician

8. Drug treatment of mental disorders: _____

9. A medical specialist in psychiatry is a _____.

10. A practitioner of psychoanalysis is called a _____.

11. Disorder causing mental disruption and loss of contact with reality: _____

12. _____ is the medical specialty dealing with the diagnosis and treatment of mental disorders.

13. Practitioner of psychotherapy is a _____.

14. Real, physical disorder that, at least in part, has a psychologic cause: _____

15. Pertaining to or affected by psychosis: _____.

16. A serial killer can be termed a _____.

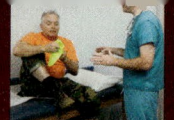

MENTAL HEALTH

J. **Prefixes:** Test your recall of word element meanings by answering the following questions about prefixes. The medical term is given; on the line beside the term, write the prefix, and then circle the meaning of the prefix.

1. **Bipolar:**   Prefix is _____ and means

   a. one

   b. two

   c. three

   d. four

   e. five

2. **Hypochondriasis:**   Prefix is _____ and means

   a. after

   b. around

   c. below

   d. next to

   e. excessive

3. **Depressant:** Prefix is _____ and means

   a. toward

   b. forming

   c. within

   d. away from

   e. around

4. **Catatonia:**   Prefix is _____ and means

   a. up

   b. around

   c. through

   d. down

   e. beside

5. **Addiction:**   Prefix is _____ and means

   a. toward

   b. from

   c. for

   d. with

   e. up

6. **Euphoria:** Prefix is _____ and means _____

 a. marketplace

 b. mind

 c. normal

 d. madness

 e. wound

7. **Paranoia:** Prefix is _____ and means _____

 a. above

 b. excessive

 c. abnormal

 d. condition

 e. study of

8. **Unipolar:** Prefix is _____ and means _____

 a. one

 b. four

 c. many

 d. few

 e. none

9. **Dissociative:** Prefix is _____ and means _____

 a. painful

 b. apart

 c. abnormal

 d. irregular

 e. together

10. **Convulsive:** Prefix is _____ and means _____

 a. in front of

 b. with

 c. next to

 d. yellow

 e. small

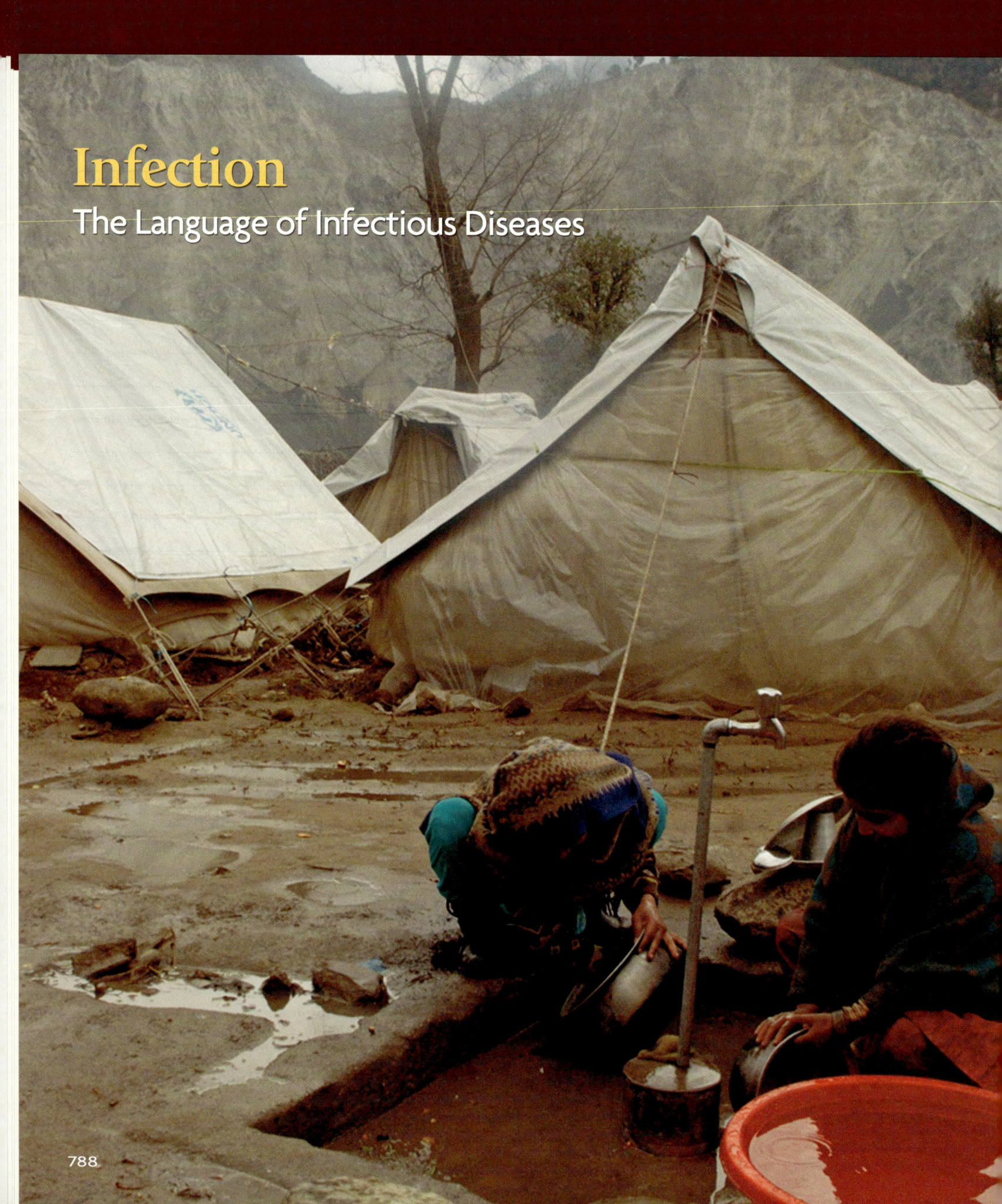

Infection
The Language of Infectious Diseases

20

CASE REPORT 20.1

You are

. . . a physician assistant working as a volunteer with a health care team from Fulwood Medical Center in a tented camp outside Muzaffarabad, the capital of the state of Azad Kashmir in Pakistan. It is close to the epicenter of the earthquake of October 8, 2005, that killed more than 87,000 people and destroyed 70% of the buildings in Muzaffarabad. The tent city holds 1500 people whose homes have been destroyed. It is winter 2006. The temperature is around 0° C (32°F).

Your patients are

. . . Mrs. Uzma Aziz and her 2-year-old daughter Alisha, the youngest of her five children. The woman and child arrived in the tent city two weeks ago from a remote village high in the Himalaya mountains, where their home had been destroyed by the earthquake. The intense cold at the higher altitude made staying in their make-shift tent impossible.

Your interpreter tells you that Alisha was well until three days earlier, when she developed a runny nose, red eyes, and a cough. Today she has developed a rash on her forehead and neck that is spreading down onto her body.

Your examination shows T 104.2°F, P 120, R 24. A rash of red-brown macules is present on her face, neck, and shoulders. She has a bilateral conjunctivitis. As you proceed with your examination, the rash continues to extend down the trunk. On the buccal mucosa inside the mouth are some small red spots with white centers (Koplik spots). You hear rales at the base of her right lung, and her left tympanic membrane is inflamed. She is diagnosed as having measles.

Learning Outcomes

In situations like this where the patient load is high and resources are limited, it is essential to communicate clearly with the other team members. You need to be able to:

- Apply the language of infectious diseases to the causes, treatment, and prevention of infections.

- Comprehend, analyze, spell, and write the medical terms of infectious diseases so that you can communicate and document accurately and precisely in any health care setting.

- Recognize and pronounce the medical terms of infectious diseases so that you can communicate verbally with accuracy and precision in any health care setting.

- Explain the effects of common infectious diseases on health.

Through the interpreter, you learn that none of the five children has been immunized for any disease. When they arrived at the camp, the mother refused to start a program of immunization for the children.

INFECTION

Normal Flora and Defenses Against Infections

OBJECTIVES

The information in this lesson will enable you to:

- **Describe normal flora.**
- **Specify the differences between colonization and infectious disease.**
- **Detail the host defense mechanisms.**
- **Define the mechanisms of infection.**

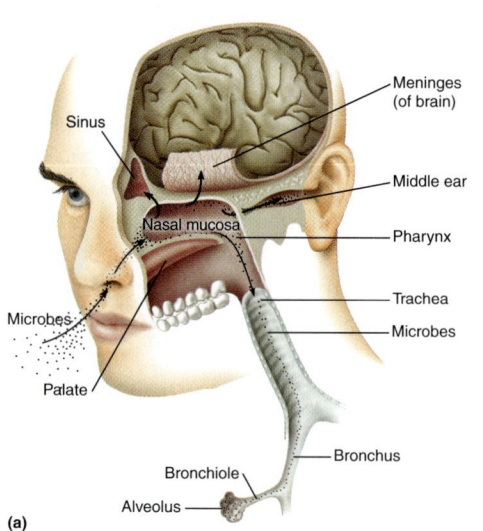

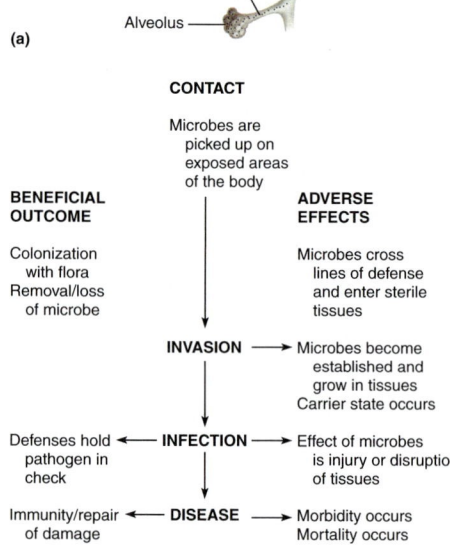

▲ **FIGURE 20.1** **Associations Between Microbes and Humans.**

Keynote

Bacterial pathogens have several specific weapons to invade cells.

NORMAL FLORA AND MECHANISMS OF INFECTION

Normal Flora

Microbes (microorganisms) are everywhere—in the air, water, and soil, where they are essential for the physiology and nutrition of animals (including humans) and plants. Thousands of microbes cover your body and are called **normal flora**, while the human body is called their **host**.

These normal microorganisms are found on your skin, in your nose and respiratory tract, and in your mouth and digestive tract. This is called **colonization**. Areas like the brain and cardiovascular system remain **sterile** (microbe free).

The host tolerates colonization by the organisms of the normal flora but restricts them to areas where they can do no harm. For example, the **bacterium** *Streptococcus pneumoniae* is found in the nasopharynx of many healthy adults. If the microbes invade the body by penetrating the nasal mucosa (*see Chapter 9*) or progressing beyond the nose into sinuses, middle ear, and the respiratory tract, they become pathogens, and an **infection** occurs (*Figure 20.1b*). If the infection causes harm to the host, then an **infectious disease** is present. *Streptococcus pneumoniae* can invade and infect various sites in the respiratory tract and in the meninges (*Figure 20.1a*).

A healthy host defends against these pathogens through the response of the immune system (*see Chapter 15*). These defenses may be able to prevent an infection occurring. If infection does occur, the defenses may stop the process before any harm (disease) is done (*Figure 20.1b*). Other defenses may not come into play until the infectious disease is apparent.

Mechanisms of Infection

Toxins can be formed and released by pathogens to bind to specific adjacent or distant cells' receptors. The toxins can damage or **lyse** the cell membranes and inhibit protein synthesis and other intracellular functions.

Virulence factors in the microorganisms overcome host resistance and cause disease. **Bacterial** proteins can both facilitate local spread in tissues and penetrate intact cells, allowing the bacteria to enter the body through mucosal surfaces. Some bacteria can block antibody production, and others have developed methods to inactivate phagocytosis (*see Chapter 7*).

Microbial **adherence** to different surfaces of the host gives **pathogens** a base from which to invade cells and tissues. Some pathogens, such as *Escherichia coli*, have **fimbriae** that will attach to most human cells. Pathogens can bind to medical devices, such as IV (intravenous) catheters, shunts, stents, and vascular grafts, making them a possible source of infection.

Antimicrobial resistance involves the antibiotics used against the pathogens acting as mutagens (*see Chapter 21*) and causing mutations in the pathogens' DNA. This, in turn, enables the pathogen to become resistant to the antimicrobial agent. This resistance to antibiotics is an increasing problem, particularly in hospitals.

WORD	PRONUNCIATION	ELEMENTS		DEFINITION
adherence adhere (verb)	ad-**HERE**-ents ad-**HERE**		Latin *to stick to*	The act of sticking to something
bacterium bacteria (pl) bacterial (adj)	bak-**TEER**-ee-um bak-**TEER**-ee-ah bak-**TEER**-ee-al	S/ R/	Latin *walking stick* -ial *pertaining to* **bacter-** *bacterium*	A unicellular simple organism Pertaining to bacteria
colonization	**KOL**-on-ih-**ZAY**-shun	S/ R/	-ization *process of creating* **colon-** *colony*	Formation of a population of microorganisms
fimbria fimbriae (pl)	**FIM**-bree-ah **FIM**-bree-ee		Latin *fringe*	A fringelike structure on the surface of a cell or microorganism
flora	**FLO**-rah		Latin *flower*	Microorganisms covering the exterior and interior of a healthy animal
host	HOST		Latin *host*	Organism on which organisms live
infect infection infectious	in-**FEKT** in-**FEK**-shun in-**FEK**-shus	S/ R/ S/ R/CF	Latin *invade internally* -ion *condition* **infect-** *internal invasion* -ous *pertaining to* **infect/i-** *internal invasion*	To invade an organism by a microorganism Invasion of the body by disease-producing microorganisms Capable of being transmitted, or a disease caused by the action of a microorganism
lysis lyse (verb)	**LIE**-sis		Greek *dissolve*	Destruction of a cell
microbe microorganism	**MY**-krohb **MY**-kroh-**OR**-gan-izm	P/ R/ S/ R/	**micro-** *small* -be *life* -ism *process* -organ- *tool, instrument*	Short for microorganism Any organism too small to be seen by the naked eye
pathogen pathogenic (adj)	**PATH**-oh-jen path-oh-**JEN**-ik	S/ R/CF S/	-gen *that which produces* **path/o-** *disease* -ic *pertaining to*	A disease-causing microorganism
resistance	ree-**ZIS**-tants		Latin *to withstand*	Ability of an organism to withstand the effects of an antagonistic agent
sterile sterilize (verb) sterilization	**STER**-isle **STER**-ih-lize **STER**-ih-lih-**ZAY**-shun		Latin *barren*	Free from all living organisms and their spores, or unable to fertilize or reproduce To make sterile Process of making sterile
toxin	**TOK**-sin		Greek *poison*	Poisonous substance formed by a cell or organism
virulent virulence (noun)	**VIR**-you-lent **VIR**-you-lence		Latin *poisonous*	Extremely toxic or pathogenic The power of a toxin or pathogen

EXERCISES

Usage. *Employ the **language of infectious diseases** to convey the correct meaning in the following sentences. You may be asked to fill in the adjective, noun, verb, or plural form of the term. Fill in the blanks. Some terms you may use more than once.*

bacterium   **bacteria**   **bacterial**

1. Lab results showed the myco _____ tuberculosis organism to be positive.

2. Her _____ infection showed major improvement after administration of antibiotics.

3. Lacerated or open skin allows _____ to invade the body.

4. A single _____ can develop into a colony of _____, producing a _____ infection.

sterile   **sterilize**   **sterilization**

5. Operating rooms must be a _____ environment for the patient's safety. For this reason, _____ of

all equipment and instruments is performed. An autoclave is used to _____ surgical instruments.

DEFENSE MECHANISMS

Host defense mechanisms determine whether infection will occur and an infectious disease will be produced. The defense mechanisms are in four main categories:

1. **Innate resistance**
   - **Species** have a resistance to certain **pathogens.** For example, syphilis, gonorrhea, measles, and poliomyelitis affect humans but not lower animals. The canine distemper virus does not affect humans.
   - **Individuals** within the same species have greater or lesser innate resistance to the same pathogen. Reasons for this include age, diet, malnutrition, trauma, intercurrent disease, tobacco use, immunization status, and stress.

2. **Natural barriers**
   - **Skin** *(see Chapter 3)*—effectively prevents invasion by microorganisms unless it is breached by trauma, an incision, IV puncture, or by a lesion such as a bite. Exceptions to this rule are the **human papillomavirus (HPV)** *(see Chapter 13)* that can invade normal tissue to produce warts and cancer and some parasites that can penetrate intact skin *(see Chapter 3)*.
   - **Mucous membranes**—produce secretions containing lysozyme, which has antimicrobial properties, and immunoglobulins **IgG** and **IgA** that block the attachment of microorganisms to host cells *(see Chapter 15)*. Breast milk contains IgA.
   - **Respiratory tract**—has a filter system in the nose and upper airways and a **mucociliary** system to transport microorganisms away from the lung *(Figure 20.2)*. This is helped by coughing and sneezing *(see Chapter 9)*.
   - **Gastrointestinal tract**—is protected by the acid pH of the stomach and the antibacterial activity of intestinal secretions. Bile and pancreatic enzymes are natural barriers to invasion by pathogens *(see Chapter 6)*.
   - **Genitourinary tract**—men are protected by the length of their urethra and women by the acid pH of their vagina *(see Chapters 12 and 13)*.

3. **Specific immune responses**
   The infected host produces a variety of **antibodies (immunoglobulins)** that bind to specific microbial **antigens** *(see Chapter 15)*. The antigen–antibody complexes activate the **complement** system to destroy the cell walls of the microbes *(Figure 20.3)* and stimulate the macrophage system to remove them.

4. **Nonspecific immune responses**
   - **Cytokine production** by macrophages and lymphocytes *(see Chapter 15)* in response to an infection occurs regardless of the nature of the invading microorganism. Cytokine generates fever and an increase in neutrophil production.
   - **Inflammatory responses** *(see Chapter 15)* to infection generate an increased blood supply and increased vascular permeability at the site of the infection. The result is that neutrophils and phagocytes can leave the intravascular compartment and attack the invading microorganism.

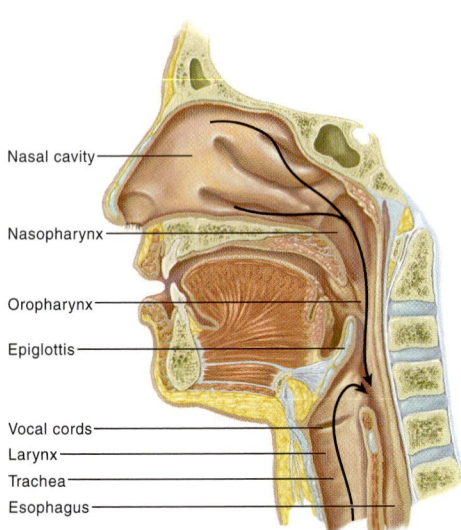

Nasal cavity
Nasopharynx
Oropharynx
Epiglottis
Vocal cords
Larynx
Trachea
Esophagus

▲ **FIGURE 20.2   Filter and Transport System of Upper Respiratory Tract to Prevent Microorganisms and Pollutants from Entering the Lungs.**

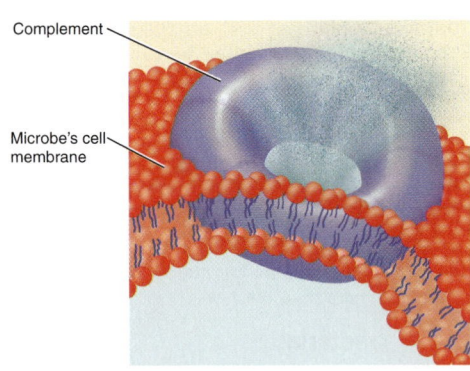

Complement
Microbe's cell membrane

▲ **FIGURE 20.3   Complement System Attacks Microbe's Cell Wall to Cause Its Death.**

Abbreviations

HPV	human papillomavirus
IgA	immunoglobulin A
IgG	immunoglobulin G

Case Report 20.1 (continued)

People, especially children, who have seen their home destroyed in the explosion of an earthquake, who have tried to survive extreme cold in a simple tent, and have had to move into a foreign, primitive environment will be stressed. Their resistance to disease will be low. Add to this the lack of protection from **immunizations,** and the children will be susceptible to all the **contagious** childhood diseases, including the **measles** that Alisha has contracted.

WORD ANALYSIS AND DEFINITION

S = Suffix   P = Prefix   R = Root   R/CF = Combining Form

WORD	PRONUNCIATION	ELEMENTS		DEFINITION
complement	KOM-pleh-ment		Latin *that which completes*	Group of proteins in serum that finish off the work of antibodies to destroy bacteria and other cells
contagious	kon-TAY-jus	S/ P/ R/	-ious *pertaining to* con- *with, together* -tag- *touch*	Infection can be transmitted from person to person or from a person to a surface to a person
cytokine	SIGH-toh-kine	S/ R/CF	-kine *movement* -cyt/o- *cell*	Proteins produced by different cells that communicate with other cells in the immune system
immune	im-YUNE	P/ R/	im- *not* -mune *in service*	Protected from an infectious disease
immunize	IM-you-nize	S/	-ize *affect in a particular way*	To make resistant to an infectious disease
immunization	im-you-nih-ZAY-shun	S/	-ization *the process of creating*	Administration of an agent to provide immunity
innate	ih-NATE	P/ R/	in- *in* -nate *birth*	Present at birth; arising from the intellect
measles (also known as rubeola)	ME-zelz		Old English *measles*	Acute, contagious disease of childhood
mucociliary	MYU-koh-SIL-ih-ah-ree	S/ R/CF R/	-ary *pertaining to* muc/o- *mucus* -cili- *hairlike structure*	Pertaining to the ciliated epithelium lining the bronchial tree
species	SPEE-sheez		Latin *form, kind*	A group of organisms that bear a strong resemblance to each other

EXERCISES

Usage. *Continue to employ the* **language of infectious diseases** *to convey the correct meaning in the following sentences. You may be asked to fill in the adjective, noun, verb, or plural form of the term. Fill in the blanks.*

immune   **immunity**   **immunize**   **immunization**

1. You may be born with a natural _____ against a certain disease. In that case, there is no need for an

_____ to _____ you against the disease. You are already _____ to it.

infected   **infection**   **infectious**

2. The body can be invaded by _____ organisms with the potential to cause disease. The

_____ body part (such as a cut) may be red, swollen, and warm to the touch. Fever can also be a sign

of _____.

Use each of the following three terms in sentences that could be used for patient education. Remember to use language a nonmedical person would understand.

3. contagious: _____

_____

4. innate: _____

_____

5. measles: _____

_____

OBJECTIVES

The information in this lesson will enable you to:

- Identify the characteristics and properties of viruses.
- Describe some of the viral diseases of children.
- Detail some of the viral respiratory diseases.
- Define diagnostic methods for viruses.
- Discuss the prevention of viral infections.

VIRUSES

Viruses are the smallest of microorganisms. They are too small to be seen under an ordinary light microscope but are visible using electron microscopy *(Figure 20.4)*. They are composed of an outer membrane (envelope) of protein and lipid with a nucleic acid core of RNA or DNA enclosed in a **capsid.**

Viruses are not "living" organisms, so they need living cells in order to multiply. The viruses invade cells and redirect the cells from their normal functions to replicate the virus. Viruses stimulate antibody production by the host.

Hundreds of viruses can infect humans and are spread mainly by **respiratory** (coughs, sneezes) *(see Chapter 9)* and **enteric excretions** *(see Chapter 6)* via hands when they are not properly washed. When viruses can spread from person to person, they are said to be contagious.

Some viruses are **oncogenic** (cancer producing). For example, the **Epstein-Barr virus (EBV)** is associated with Hodgkin disease, nasopharyngeal carcinoma, and lymphomas in immunosuppressed patients *(see Chapter 15)*.

Slow viral diseases are characterized by lengthy **incubation** periods and the production of chronic degenerative diseases. An example is the JC (patient's initials) virus that is firmly associated with **progressive multifocal leukoencephalopathy**, with its destruction of brain cells, progressive dementia, and paralysis.

Bovine spongiform encephalopathy (BSE), called mad cow disease, and the associated human **spongiform encephalopathy** called **Creutzfeldt-Jakob disease (CJD),** are not caused by a virus but by a **prion,** a small protein particle in cells capable of causing an infection.

Latency—a long period when the virus is quiescent (dormant)—permits recurrent infection and person-to-person spread. Herpesviruses exhibit latency.

VIRAL DISEASES OF CHILDHOOD

Many viral childhood diseases have a skin rash **(exanthem)** associated with them.

Measles (rubeola), in its **prodromal** phase, produces signs similar to an upper respiratory infection (URI), but inside the mouth on the buccal mucosa are found small red spots with white centers. These are called **Koplik spots** *(Figure 20.5)*. The reddish-brown **macular** rash *(see Chapter 3)* comes out on the face and body on the third or fourth day of the illness. A safe and effective vaccine is available to prevent measles.

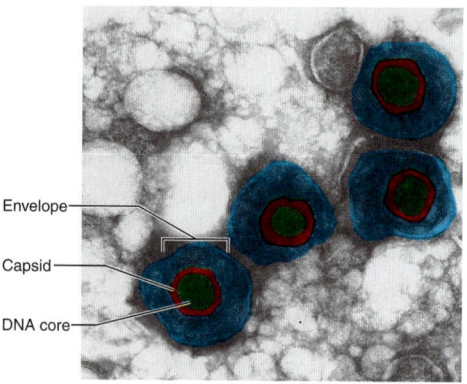

Envelope
Capsid
DNA core

300,000×

▲ **FIGURE 20.4 Electron Microscopy of Herpesvirus.**

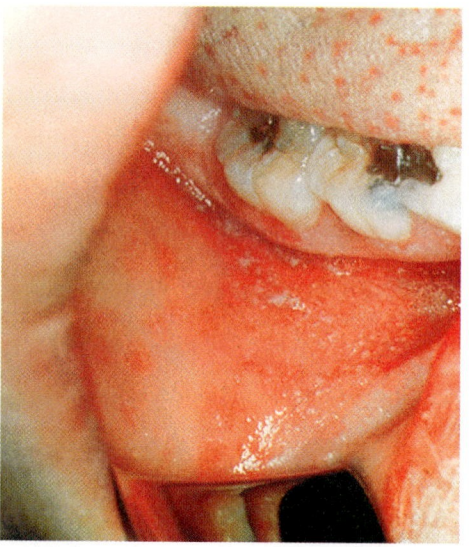

▲ **FIGURE 20.5 Koplik Spots on the Buccal Mucosa Early in Measles.**

Abbreviations

BSE	bovine spongiform encephalopathy
CJD	Creutzfeldt-Jakob disease
EBV	Epstein-Barr virus

Case Report 20.1 (continued)

Alisha had two of the complications of measles. The rales heard at the base of her right lung indicated a right, lower lobe pneumonia, and she had an otitis media. The medical staff wanted to admit Alisha to the hospital set up on the edge of the tent city. Alisha's mother refused to let her be admitted. She was shown how to give antibiotics orally, and they went back to their tent.

S = Suffix   P = Prefix   R = Root   R/CF = Combining Form

WORD	PRONUNCIATION	ELEMENTS		DEFINITION
capsid	**KAP**-sid	S/ R/	-id *having a particular quality* caps- *cover, shell*	Protein shell surrounding the nucleic acid in the core of a virus
enteric	en-**TEHR**-ik	S/ R/	-ic *pertaining to* enter- *bowels*	Pertaining to the intestine
exanthem	ek-**ZAN**-them		Greek *an eruption*	Skin eruption or rash occurring as the outward sign of a viral or bacterial disease
incubation incubate (verb)	in-kyu-**BAY**-shun **IN**-kyu-bate	S/ R/	-ation *process* incub- *lie on*	Process to develop an infection
Koplik spots	**KOP**-lik SPOTZ		Henry Koplik, 1858–1927, American pediatrician	Small red spots with a white center on the buccal mucosa seen early in measles
latent latency (noun)	**LAY**-tent **LAY**-ten-see		Latin *lie hidden*	Dormant, not discernible
leukoencephalopathy	**LOO**-koh-en-sef-ah-**LOP**-ah-thee	S/ R/CF R/CF	-pathy *disease* leuk/o- *white* -encephal/o- *brain*	Disease-producing destruction of white matter of the brain
macule macular (adj)	**MAK**-yul **MAK**-you-lahr		Latin *spot*	Small, flat spot or patch on the skin
multifocal	mul-tee-**FOH**-kal	S/ P/ R/	-al *pertaining to* multi- *many* -foc- *center*	Arising from many centers
oncogenic	**ONG**-koh-**JEN**-ik	S/ R/CF	-genic *producing* onc/o- *tumor*	Capable of producing a neoplasm
prion	**PREE**-on		Derived from *proteinaceous infectious particle*	Small infectious protein particle
prodromal	pro-**DRO**-mal		Greek *running before*	Beginning of disease before signs become overt
spongiform	**SPON**-jih-form	S/ R/CF	-form *shape* spong/i- *sponge*	Looking like a sponge
virus viral (adj)	**VIE**-rus **VIE**-ral	S/ R/	Latin *poison* -al *pertaining to* vir- *virus*	Group of infectious agents that require living cells for growth and reproduction

EXERCISES

Deconstructing a medical term into basic elements will give you clues to the meaning of the term. Fill in the blanks. Then pick any two terms, and use each one in a sentence of your own choice that is not directly from the text.

Medical Term	Prefix	Root/CF	Suffix	Meaning of Term
oncogenic				
capsid				
leukoencephalopathy				
incubation				
spongiform				
enteric				

1. _____

_____

2. _____

_____

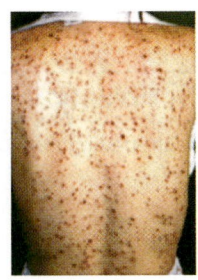

▲ **FIGURE 20.6   Chickenpox.**

VIRAL DISEASES OF CHILDHOOD (continued)

German measles (rubella) is a much milder disease than rubeola. It can also be prevented with an effective vaccine. If a woman develops rubella early in pregnancy, the unborn child can develop serious birth defects, including hearing loss, cataracts, congenital heart disease, and mental retardation.

Chickenpox (varicella) produces an itchy, blistered **rash** that crusts *(Figure 20.6)*. The virus can remain **quiescent** (dormant) in nerve fibers for many years before producing the painful lesions of **herpes zoster (shingles)**. There is an effective **vaccine** to prevent varicella.

Other childhood viral diseases with a rash are **erythema infectiosum (fifth disease), roseola infantum, hand-foot-and-mouth disease,** and **herpangina.**

Mumps causes swelling of the parotid salivary glands and can cause **orchitis** (inflammation of the testis) in the male *(see Chapter 12)*. There is an effective vaccine to prevent the disease.

VIRAL RESPIRATORY DISEASES

The common cold, influenza, pharyngitis, laryngitis, and **laryngotracheobronchitis (croup)** *(see Chapter 9)* are all upper respiratory infections caused by viruses. Symptoms can be more severe in the very young because of the relative narrowness of their respiratory passages and in the very old because of their decreased immune response.

Viral pneumonia *(see Chapter 9)* is common in winter months, can affect small or large areas of the lungs, and is more serious in the very young and very old *(Figure 20.7)*.

Respiratory syncytial virus (RSV) is the most common cause of bronchiolitis and pneumonia in infants and children under one year of age.

Severe acute respiratory syndrome (SARS) is a viral respiratory tract infection that first appeared in China in 2002. Eighty to 90% of cases are mild, but the remaining 10 to 20% develop severe respiratory distress and may require mechanical ventilation. The overall death rate is 3 to 4% of those infected.

Avian influenza (bird flu) is caused by avian influenza viruses that are **endemic** in wild birds worldwide. When domesticated birds such as chickens, turkeys, and ducks are infected, they become very sick and die. It rarely spreads to humans.

A subtype of the avian influenza viruses called **H5N1** virus caused outbreaks of the disease among poultry in Asia in late 2003 and early 2004. One hundred million birds died from the disease or were killed in attempts to control the outbreaks. More than 100 human cases were reported, mostly in poultry workers. In 2005, worries about a **pandemic** were fueled by the disease spreading to Eastern Europe.

West Nile virus (WNV) is established as a seasonal **epidemic** in North America, flaring up in the summer and fall. Mosquitoes become infected when they feed on infected birds and then spread the disease to humans when they bite *(Figure 20.8)*. The fever and aches may last for several weeks. There is no specific treatment.

The prevention of viral diseases is discussed in lesson 20.5 of this chapter.

Most viral diseases do not respond to antibiotics. Many physicians do not prescribe antibiotics to patients with upper respiratory diseases unless a bacterial cause or complication is identified.

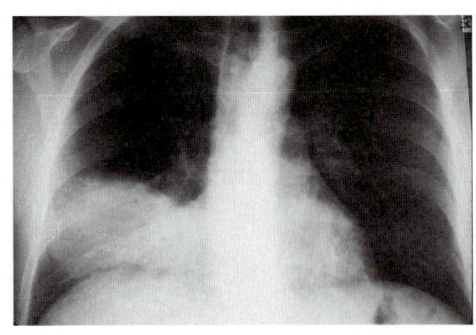

▲ **FIGURE 20.7   X-Ray of Right Middle Lobe in Patient with Viral Pneumonia.**

Abbreviations

H5N1   subtype of avian influenza virus
RSV   respiratory syncytial virus
SARS   severe acute respiratory syndrome
WNV   West Nile virus

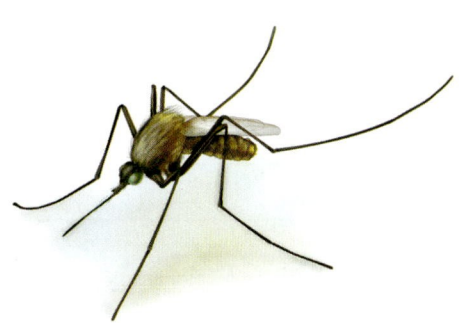

▲ **FIGURE 20.8   Mosquito.**

WORD ANALYSIS AND DEFINITION

S = Suffix   P = Prefix   R = Root   R/CF = Combining Form

WORD	PRONUNCIATION	ELEMENTS		DEFINITION
avian	A-vee-an		Latin *a bird*	Pertaining to birds
epidemic	ep-ih-**DEM**-ik	S/	-ic *pertaining to*	Outbreak in a community of a disease or a health-related behavior
		P/	epi- *above, upon*	
		R/	-dem- *the people*	
endemic	en-**DEM**-ik	P/	en- *in*	Disease always present in a community
pandemic	pan-**DEM**-ik	P/	pan- *all*	Disease attacking the population of a very large area
erythema infectiosum (also called **fifth disease**)	er-ih-**THEE**-mah in-fek-she-**OH**-sum	S/ R/	Greek *flushed skin* -iosum *pertaining to* infect- *infect*	Mild infectious disease of childhood with a flushed cheek appearance
herpangina	her-**PAN**-ji-nah	R/ R/	-angina *sore throat* herp- *blister*	Ulcerative disease of the throat
laryngotracheo-bronchitis (also called **croup**)	lah-**RING**-oh-**TRAY**-kee-oh-brong-**KI**-tis KROOP	S R/CF R/CF R/	-itis *inflammation* laryng/o- *larynx* -trache/o- *trachea* -bronch- *bronchus*	Inflammation of the larynx, trachea, and bronchi Infection of the upper airways in children, characterized by a barking cough
quiescent	kwi-**ESS**-ent		Latin *quiet*	Latent, dormant
rash	RASH		French *skin eruption*	Cutaneous eruption
roseola infantum	roh-**ZEE**-oh-lah in-**FAN**-tum	S/ R/ S/ R/	-ola *small* rose- *rose* -um *structure* infant- *infant*	Disease of infants and young children caused by a herpesvirus
syncytium	sin-**SISH**-ee-um	S/ P/ R/CF	-um *tissue, structure* syn- *together* -cyt/i- *cell*	A multinucleated mass not separated into cells
syncytial (adj)	sin-**SISH**-ee-al	S/	-al *pertaining to*	
vaccine	**VAK**-seen		Latin *relating to a cow*	Preparation to generate active immunity
vaccinate (verb)	**VAK**-sin-ate	S/ R/	-ate *action* vaccin- *giving a vaccine*	To administer a vaccine
vaccination	vak-sih-**NAY**-shun	S/	-ation *process of creating*	Administration of a vaccine

---

EXERCISES

Also Known As. *Medical terms may have more common names that are in frequent usage. You need to know both terms. Match the medical terms in column 1 with their common names in column 2, then answer the questions about childhood diseases.*

_____ 1. varicella

_____ 2. laryngotracheobronchitis

_____ 3. erythema infectiosum

_____ 4. avian influenza

_____ 5. rubella

_____ 6. orchitis

_____ 7. herpes zoster

A. German measles

B. bird flu

C. inflammation of the testis

D. fifth disease

E. chicken pox

F. croup

G. shingles

8. Which of the following childhood diseases does *not* have a rash as a symptom?

    Chickenpox   German measles   roseola   mumps

9. *Laryngotracheobronchitis* is another name for:

    coughing   croup   rubella   herpangina

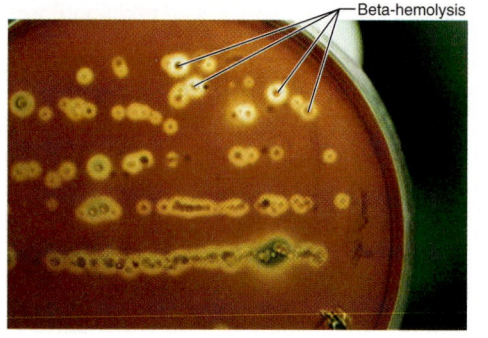

▲ FIGURE 20.10   Blood Agar Plate Growing Bacteria from Human Throat.
Clear areas of hemolysis are shown around beta-hemolytic *Streptococcal* colonies.

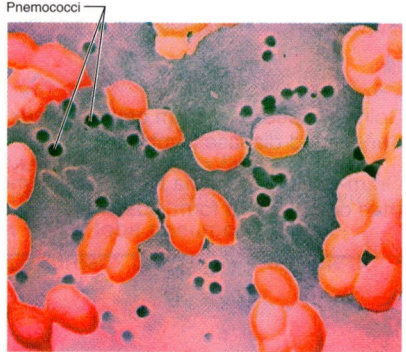

▲ FIGURE 20.11   Spherical Bacteria of *Pneumococcus.*

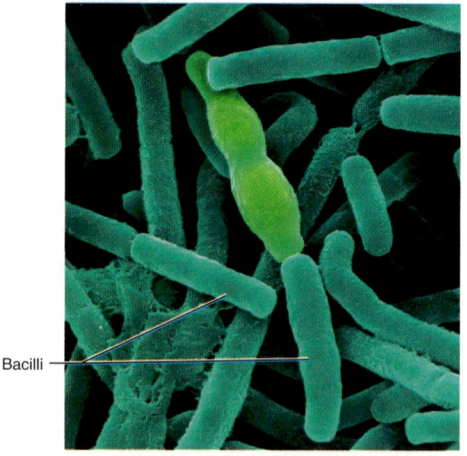

▲ FIGURE 20.12   *Bacillus Anthrax*

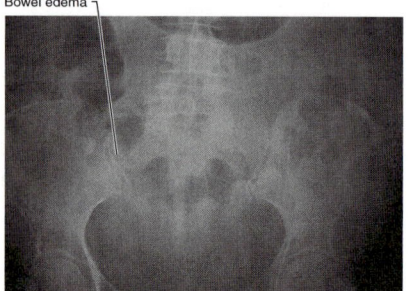

▲ FIGURE 20.13   Abdominal X-Ray Showing Marked Bowel Edema from *Clostridium difficile.*

INFECTIONS CAUSED BY GRAM-POSITIVE COCCI (continued)

Streptococcal Infections

Streptococci are classified according to their reaction when grown on sheep **blood agar.**

Beta-hemolytic streptococci produce an area of clear hemolysis around each colony *(Figure 20.10)*. Diseases produced by beta-hemolytic **strep,** also called *Streptococcus pyogenes,* include:

- tonsillitis, pharyngitis, scarlet fever, glomerulonephritis, septicemia
- wound and skin infections, cellulitis, impetigo, erysipelas
- neonatal sepsis, puerperal sepsis, septic arthritis, endocarditis, toxic shock syndrome, necrotizing fasciitis

Alpha-hemolytic streptococci produce a green area around each colony on the agar plate. Diseases produced by these bacteria, also called *Streptococcus viridans,* include:

- bacterial endocarditis, localized abscesses, cellulitis, and invasive soft tissue infections

Pneumococcal Infections

Pneumococci (*Streptococcus pneumoniae*) are found in the respiratory tract of about 50% of the population in winter and early spring. The organisms spread from person to person by droplets through coughing or sneezing or via the hands *(Figure 20.11)*. Infections caused by pneumococci include:

- **pneumonia,** usually lobar, but occasionally bronchopneumonia *(see Chapter 9)*
- half of the cases of acute otitis media in infants and children *(see Chapter 4)*
- conjunctivitis, sinusitis, meningitis, bacteremia, endocarditis, and septic arthritis

A vaccine against **pneumococcal** disease is available.

INFECTIONS CAUSED BY GRAM-POSITIVE BACILLI

The **spores** of the **anthrax** bacillus (*Bacillus anthracis*) resist destruction by disinfectants and heat *(Figure 20.12)*. They can enter your body through broken skin or, more rarely, be inhaled. Inside the body, the spores germinate in macrophages to produce bacteria that are transported to lymph nodes, where they multiply. The bacteria produce a variety of toxins capable of causing sudden death.

The term "weapons of mass destruction" includes nuclear, chemical, radiologic, and biologic agents. Biologic (germ) warfare is the use of microbiologic agents such as anthrax, smallpox, and botulinum toxin for hostile purposes, though this is against international law. In 2001, anthrax was deliberately spread through the postal system in and around Washington, DC. Twenty-one cases of anthrax were caused.

Clostridium difficile (C. difficile) is a gram-positive anaerobic spore-forming bacillus that is the major cause of antibiotic-associated diarrhea. The antibiotics alter the normal intestinal flora, allowing *C. difficile* to flourish. It produces two exotoxins that generate watery, bloody diarrhea and mucus and promote marked swelling of the bowel wall with edema *(Figure 20.13)*.

Case Report 20.2 *(continued)*

Any patient in a hospital who is on antibiotics and is elderly and frail is suspected of having *C. difficile* disease if they have an onset of diarrhea. A stool sample taken for laboratory analysis from Mr. Geller is positive for *C. difficile*. The bacterium is highly contagious, and patients require isolation. The antibiotics Mr. Geller was taking are discontinued, and he has been started on IV metronidazole (Flagyl).

S = Suffix   P = Prefix   R = Root   R/CF = Combining Form

WORD	PRONUNCIATION		ELEMENTS	DEFINITION
anthrax	**AN**-thraks		Greek *carbuncle*	A severe, malignant infectious disease
Clostridium difficile	klos-**TRID**-ee-um dif-ih-**SEE**-il		***Clostridium*** Greek *a spindle* **difficile** French *difficult*	Gram-positive rod producing powerful exotoxins that cause colitis
pneumococcus **pneumococci (pl)** **pneumococcal (adj)**	new-moh-**KOK**-us new-moh-**KOK**-al	R/ R/CF S/	**-coccus** *berry* **pneum/o-** *lung, air* **-al** *pertaining to*	Gram-positive cocci associated with respiratory infection
pneumonia **pneumonic (adj)**	new-**MOH**-nee-ah new-**MON**-ik	S/ R/CF S/	**-ia** *a condition* **pneum/on-** *lung, air* **-ic** *pertaining to*	Inflammation of the lung parenchyma Relating to pneumonia
pyogenes	**PIE**-o-jen-ese	S/ R/CF	**-genes** *producing* **py/o-** *pus*	Producing pus
spore	SPOR		Greek *seed*	Generic term for any tiny compact cells produced during reproduction by bacteria
Streptococcus **streptococci (pl)** **streptococcal (adj)**	strep-toe-**KOK**-us strep-toe-**KOK**-sigh strep-toe-**KOK**-al	R/CF R/ S/	**strept/o-** *twisted* **-coccus** *berry* **-al** *pertaining to*	Gram-positive bacteria that grow in chains

---

EXERCISES

Elements. *Identify each element in the following exercise. Place a check mark (✓) in the correct column for the element type, then write the meaning of each element.*

Element	Prefix	Root/CF	Suffix	Meaning of Element
coccus				
pneumo				
al				
ia				
mal				
strepto				

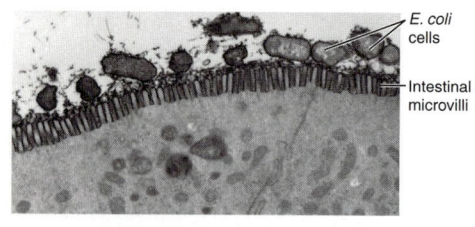

▲ **FIGURE 20.14** **A Row of** *Escherichia coli* **Cells Clinging to the Surface of Intestinal Cells.**

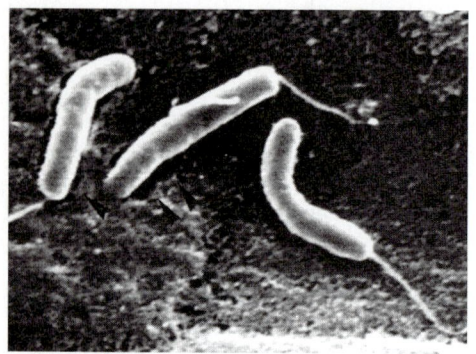

▲ **FIGURE 20.15** **Bacteria That Cause Cholera.**

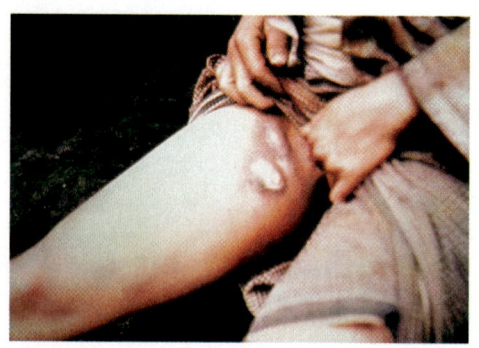

▲ **FIGURE 20.16** **Inguinal Bubo of Bubonic Plague.**

INFECTIONS CAUSED BY GRAM-NEGATIVE BACILLI

Escherichia coli (E. coli) inhabits the gastrointestinal tract of humans and animals *(Figure 20.14)*. Most strains are harmless, but several produce toxins that can cause diarrhea. **Contamination** of meat can occur in the animal slaughtering process. Humans acquire the infection by eating inadequately cooked meat. Person-to-person transmission can occur if infected people do not wash their hands after using the toilet.

Salmonella infections are another cause of gastroenteritis. They result from eating contaminated food, often of animal origin. Thorough cooking kills the germ. *Salmonella typhi (S. typhi)* causes **typhoid fever,** sometimes called **enteric fever.** A few people continue to shed organisms in their stool for longer than a year and are called **chronic enteric carriers.**

Shigellosis (bacillary dysentery) is a severe form of gastroenteritis, with marked diarrhea containing blood, pus, and mucus. It is transmitted in contaminated food or water.

Brucellosis (undulant fever) is an acute febrile illness acquired from infected animals or drinking infected raw milk. Symptoms persist for one to five weeks, remit for 2 to 14 days, and then return. **Remissions (undulations)** can recur over months or years.

Cholera is an acute infection with watery diarrhea, vomiting, dehydration, and collapse *(Figure 20.15)*. It is spread by ingestion of water and foods contaminated with the **excrement** of infected persons. It is endemic in numerous parts of the world where sanitation is poor.

Plague occurs in rats and mice and is transmitted to humans by the bite of an infected flea vector. **Bubonic plague** is characterized by fever and enlarged lymph nodes (**buboes;** *Figure 20.16*). **Pneumonic plague** is characterized by acute respiratory symptoms and pneumonia. The mortality rate is high in any plague epidemic.

Pseudomonas **infections** mostly occur in hospitalized patients who are debilitated or immunosuppressed. They occur in many anatomic sites, particularly where there has been trauma, catheters, or other invasive procedures.

INFECTIONS CAUSED BY GRAM-NEGATIVE, AEROBIC COCCI

Organisms of the *Neisseria* group include:

- *N. meningitides,* which causes meningitis *(see Chapter 10)*
- *N. gonorrhoeae,* which causes **gonorrhea** *(see Chapter 13)*

S = Suffix   **P** = Prefix   **R** = Root   **R/CF** = Combining Form

WORD	PRONUNCIATION	ELEMENTS		DEFINITION
brucellosis	brew-sel-**OH**-sis	S/ R/	**-osis** *condition* **brucell-** *from pathologist David Bruce*	Undulant fever
bubo buboes (pl) bubonic (adj)	**BYU**-bo **BYU**-bose **BYU**-bon-ik		Greek *swelling in groin*	Swollen, inflamed lymph node
cholera	**KOL**-er-ah		Greek *bile*	Acute endemic infectious disease
contamination	**KON**-tam-ih-**NAY**-shun	S/ R/	**-ation** *action* **contamin-** *to corrupt*	Presence of an infectious agent on a surface or in substances
dysentery dysenteric (adj)	**DIS**-en-tare-ee dis-en-**TARE**-ik	P/ R/ S/	**dys-** *bad, difficult, painful* **-entery** *condition of the bowels* **-ic** *pertaining to*	Disease with diarrhea, bowel spasms, fever, and dehydration
Escherichia coli	esh-eh-**RIK**-ee-ah **KOH**-lie		T. Escherich, 1857–1911, a German pediatrician and bacteriologist	Organism in the intestine; releases an exotoxin that causes diarrhea
excrement (noun) excrete (verb)	**EKS**-kreh-ment eks-**KREET**	S/ P/ R/	**-ment** *resulting state* **ex-** *out, away from* **-cre-** *separation*	Waste matter such as feces To pass out of the body waste products of metabolism
gonorrhea *Neisseria gonorrhoeae*	gon-oh-**REE**-ah ni-**SEE**-ree-ah gon-oh-**REE**-ee	S/ R/CF	**-rrhea** *flow* **gon/o-** *seed* Albert Neisser, 1855–1916, German bacteriologist	Specific contagious sexually transmitted infection Bacterium that causes gonorrhea
plague	PLAYG		Latin *stroke, injury*	Infectious disease causing excessive mortality
Pseudomonas	soo-doh-**MOH**-nas	P/ R/	**pseudo-** *false* **-monas** *unit*	Gram-negative aerobic rods
remit remission	ree-**MIT** ree-**MISH**-un	S/ R/	Latin *to send back* **-ion** *action* **remiss-** *send back*	To diminish in intensity Period when there is a lessening or absence of the symptoms of a disease
Salmonella	sal-moh-**NELL**-ah		Daniel Salmon, 1850–1914 U.S. pathologist	Pathogenic gram-negative rods causing dysentery
Shigella shigellosis	she-**GEL**-ah shig-eh-**LOH**-sis	S/	Kiyoshi Shiga, 1870–1957 Japanese bacteriologist **-osis** *condition*	Genus of gram-negative rods Dysentery caused by *Shigella*
typhoid	**TIE**-foyd	S/ R/	**-oid** *resembling* **typh-** *typhus*	Acute infectious disease caused by *Salmonella typhi*

EXERCISES

Apply the **language of infectious diseases** *and match the meaning in column 1 with the correct medical terminology in column 2.*

_____	1. enteric fever	**A.**	plague	
_____	2. occur mostly in hospitalized patients	**B.**	bacillary dysentary	
_____	3. undulant fever	**C.**	shigellosis	
_____	4. another name for shigellosis	**D.**	*E.coli*	
_____	5. transmitted to humans by a vector	**E.**	typhoid	
_____	6. endemic in some parts of the world	**F.**	pseudomonas	
_____	7. severe form of gastroenteritis	**G.**	cholera	
_____	8. most strains are harmless	**H.**	brucellosis	

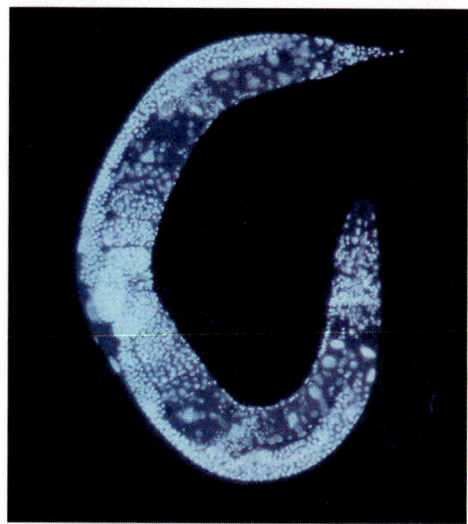

▲ **FIGURE 20.21   Roundworm.**

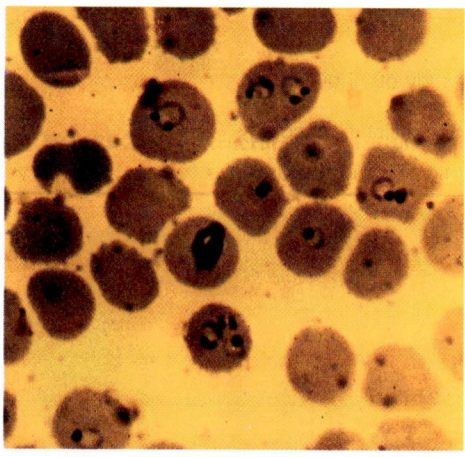

▲ **FIGURE 20.22   Malarial Parasites in Erythrocytes.**

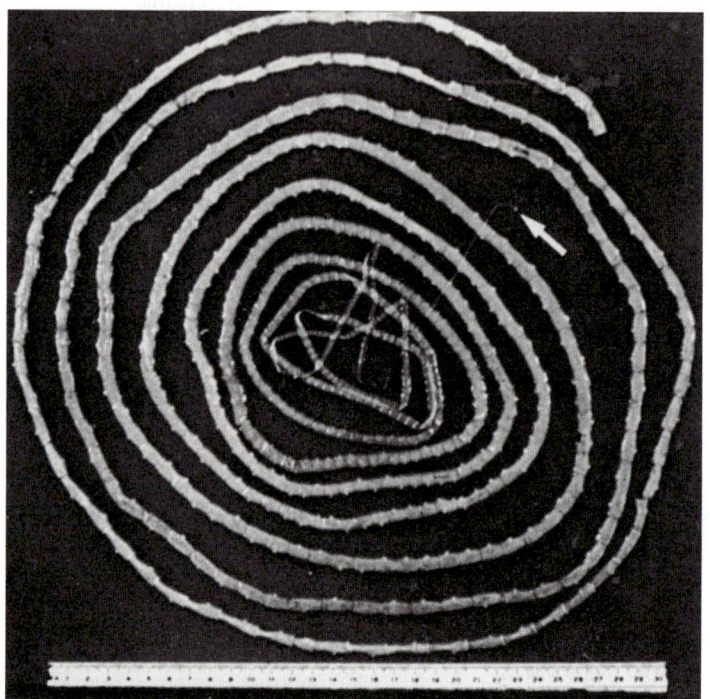

◀ **FIGURE 20.23   Tapeworm.**

PARASITIC INFECTIONS

Parasites are organisms that live on or inside another organism (the host). The more virulent parasites for humans are endemic in rural parts of Africa, Asia, and Latin America. They may be present in food and water. They range in size from tiny single-cell organisms to large worms (*Figure 20.21*). They are being increasingly identified as causes of food-borne illness in the United States.

Parasites that enter through the mouth are swallowed and can remain in the intestine or burrow through the wall to invade other organs. Parasites that enter through the skin can burrow through the skin or be introduced by the bite of an infected insect, the **vector. Malaria** is an example of a vector-borne parasitic infection (*Figure 20.22*). It is caused by the parasite *Plasmodium,* which is transmitted from person to person by the bite of the female *Anopheles* **mosquito;** the mosquito requires blood that it obtains through the bite to nurture her young.

Inside the human host, the malarial parasite takes about 10 to 14 days to mature into a form that can infect a mosquito again when it draws blood. In the mosquito, the parasite develops further and is then able to infect another human.

Malaria kills an African child every 30 seconds. Malaria kills by infecting and destroying red blood cells and by clogging the capillaries that supply the brain. The parasites are developing resistance to drugs, and many insecticides are no longer useful against mosquitoes.

Giardia lamblia is a parasite that causes a disease called **giardiasis,** an infection of the small intestine causing diarrhea, flatulence, and cramps. It is the most common intestinal parasitic infection in the United States and is mostly acquired from contaminated lakes and streams. Direct person-to-person transmission of the parasite can occur in day care centers and between homosexual men.

Pinworms are the most common parasite in children in this country. Pinworm eggs are ingested, hatch in the intestine, and the young worms migrate to the anus where the female deposits her eggs. The eggs can be transferred by fingers from the anus or from infected bedding (**fomites**) to the mouth of the same child or another.

Tapeworms are large, flat worms that live in the intestine and can grow 15 to 30 feet in length (*Figure 20.23*). The parasite is acquired by eating raw or undercooked meat or fish.

Ascaris lumbricoides, an intestinal roundworm (*Figure 20.21*), affects people worldwide in areas of poor sanitation. Adult worms in the intestine range from 6 to 20 inches in length.

Trichinosis is a roundworm infection developed if people eat poorly cooked meat (usually pork) from an animal with the parasite. **Larvae** migrate from the intestine to muscle, where they can produce pain and swelling.

Toxoplasmosis can also be acquired by eating undercooked meat from infected animals or from cats. It can infect the brain of immunosuppressed people.

Amoebiasis is another disease of poor sanitation with fecal contamination of food and water. A few people develop symptoms of an intestinal infection, and it occasionally spreads to other organs, including the brain.

Food and water are often contaminated with parasites in regions of the world where there is poor sanitation and hygiene. The advice given to travelers in these areas is "Cook it, boil it, peel it, or don't eat it." Some parasites survive freezing, and ice cubes made from unpurified water can transmit disease.

WORD	PRONUNCIATION		ELEMENTS	DEFINITION
amoeba	ah-**ME**-bah		Greek *change*	Single-celled organism that changes shape as it moves
amoebiasis	ah-me-**BY**-ah-sis	S/ R/	**-iasis** *condition* **amoeb** *amoeba*	Infection with *Amoeba*
Anopheles	ah-**NOF**-eh-leez	P/ R/	**an-** *not* **-opheles** *be of service*	A type of mosquito
Ascaris lumbricoides	**AS**-kah-ris lum-bri-**KOY**-deez		Greek *intestinal worm*	Large roundworm parasite
fomites	**FO**-my-teez		Latin *to keep warm*	Bedding, clothing, towels, etc., that can harbor and transmit a disease agent
Giardia	jee-**AR**-dee-ah		Alfred Giard, 1846–1908, French biologist	Parasite in the small intestine
giardiasis	jee-ar-**DIE**-ah-sis			Infection with *Giardia*, causing diarrhea
larva larvae (pl)	**LAR**-vah **LAR**-vee		Latin *a mask*	Stage in the development of an insect or intestinal parasite
malaria	mah-**LAIR**-ee-ah	P/ R/	**mal-** *bad* **-aria** *air*	Disease transmitted by the bite of a female *Anopheles* mosquito
mosquito mosquitoes (pl)	mos-**KEY**-toe		Latin *little fly*	Blood-sucking insect
pinworm	**PIN**-worm		Worm thin as a pin	Intestinal parasite
Plasmodium	plaz-**MOH**-dee-um	S/ R/CF	**-dium** *appearance* **plasm/o-** *to form*	Causal agent for malaria
tapeworm	TAPE WORM		tape, Old English *strip* worm, Old English, *worm*	Intestinal parasitic worm
toxoplasmosis	**TOK**-soh-plaz-**MOH**-sis	S/ R/CF R/CF	**-sis** *condition* **tox/o-** *toxic* **-plasm/o-** *to form*	Parasitic infection acquired from undercooked meat from infected animals
trichinosis	trik-ih-**NOH**-sis	S/ R/	**-osis** *condition* **trichin-** *hair*	Disease from ingestion of undercooked pork containing the roundworm
vector	**VEK**-tor		Latin *a carrier*	An animal or insect capable of transmitting an infection

EXERCISES

Apply your knowledge of the elements and terms of infectious diseases. Circle the correct answer.

1. Give an example of a vector-borne parasitic infection:
   a. polio
   b. osteomyelitis
   c. nephritis
   d. malaria
   e. bronchopneumonia

2. Most common parasite in children in this country:
   a. pinworm
   b. toxoplasmosis
   c. tapeworm
   d. amoebiasis
   e. trichinosis

3. Parasitic infection of the small intestine causing diarrhea, flatulence, and cramps:
   a. colic
   b. malaria
   c. giardiasis
   d. plasmodium
   e. colitis

4. This element has the same meaning as "**sis**" and "**osis**":
   a. dium
   b. aria
   c. iasis
   d. an
   e. toxo

5. Malaria kills by infecting and destroying:
   a. WBCs
   b. platelets
   c. RBCs
   d. organelles
   e. none of these

6. Disease that can be caused by eating undercooked pork:
   a. toxoplasmosis
   b. trichinosis
   c. malaria
   d. dysentery
   e. typhoid

LESSON 20.5 Prevention of Infections

OBJECTIVES

The information in this lesson will enable you to:

- **Define the common terms used in infection prevention and control.**
- **Detail the rationale for and use of Standard Precautions and Transmission-based Precautions.**
- **Identify diseases for which there are vaccinations and immunizations.**
- **Discuss the prophylactic use of antibiotics.**
- **Describe methods for preventing the transmission of food-borne and water-borne diseases.**

Case Report 20.2 (continued)

Preventive measures must be taken to inhibit the highly contagious *C. difficile* from spreading to caregivers, patients, and visitors. Caregivers must wash their hands before and after patient contact and wear disposable gloves and gowns. After Mr. Geller has been moved to an **isolation** setting, his room must be vigorously cleaned to remove **spores** that can spread the condition and then disinfected with an EPA-registered hypochlorite-based disinfectant. Handwashing is done with soap and water. Alcohol-based gels are not as effective against spores.

Mr. Geller had a very difficult 10 days, with abdominal distension and circulatory failure, before he gradually improved and was able to be transferred to a skilled nursing facility.

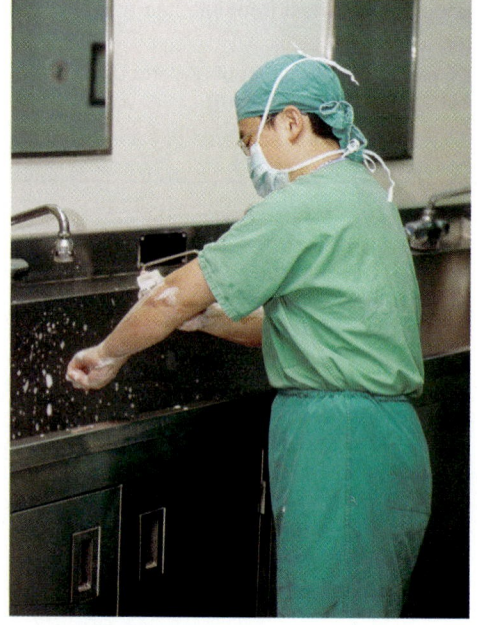

▲ **FIGURE 20.24 Surgical Scrub.**

DEFINITIONS

Cleaning is the process of removing all visible contamination from inanimate objects. It consists of thoroughly washing with soap or detergent and water, rinsing with clean water, and drying.

Sanitization is the process of removing pathogens from surfaces by chemical means, such as chlorine.

Disinfection is the destruction of pathogenic and other microorganisms on surfaces, instruments, and other man-made objects by using **disinfectants.** Commonly used disinfectants include alcohol, hydrogen peroxide, phenols, and hypochlorites.

High-level disinfection (HLD) is a process that eliminates all microorganisms, except some endospores, from inanimate objects by boiling, steaming, or with chemical disinfectants.

Sterilization eliminates all microorganisms, including **endospores,** by high-pressure steam (**autoclave**), dry heat (oven), or radiation.

Antisepsis is the process of reducing the number of microorganisms on skin, mucous membranes, or other tissue by applying an antimicrobial (**antiseptic**) agent. Preoperatively, the agents used are 70% isopropyl alcohol, 0.5% chlorhexidine, or 70% povidone-iodine. Hand antisepsis is achieved with a surgical scrub *(Figure 20.24).*

Asepsis is the process of eliminating all microorganisms on both living surfaces (skin and mucous membranes) and inanimate objects (surgical instruments and other items) to produce a state of sterility.

NOSOCOMIAL INFECTIONS

Nosocomial infections (hospital-acquired infections) are becoming increasingly common. They are estimated to occur in 5 to 10% of acute care hospital admissions. There are some 2 million cases and about 200,000 deaths per year as a result of them.

Nosocomial infections are the result of several factors working together:

- high incidence of pathogens in a hospital

WORD	PRONUNCIATION	ELEMENTS		DEFINITION
antisepsis antiseptic (adj)	an-tih-**SEP**-sis an-tih-**SEP**-tic	P/ R/	anti- *against* -sepsis *decay*	Inhibiting the growth of infectious agents
asepsis aseptic (adj)	a-**SEP**-sis a-**SEP**-tik	P/ R/	a- *without* -sepsis *decay*	Absence of living pathogenic organisms
autoclave	**AW**-toe-klayv	P/ R/	auto- *self* -clave *lock*	Apparatus for sterilization by steam under pressure
clean	KLENE		Old English *pure*	Free from visible contamination
disinfection	dis-in-**FEK**-shun	S/ P/ R/	-ion *process* dis- *apart* -infect- *corrupt*	Process of destruction of microorganisms by chemical agents
disinfectant	dis-in-**FEK**-tant	S/	-ant *pertaining to*	Agent that disinfects
isolate (verb) isolation (noun)	**I**-so-late i-so-**LAY**-shun		Latin *an island*	To separate from others
nosocomial	noh-soh-**KOH**-mee-al	S/ R/CF R/	-ial *pertaining to* nos/o- *disease* -com- *take care of*	Acquired while in the hospital
sanitization	**SAN**-ih-tih-**ZAY**-shun	S/ R/	-ation *process* sanitiz- *make healthy*	Process of using chemicals to remove pathogens from surfaces
sepsis septic (adj)	**SEP**-sis **SEP**-tik		Greek *decay*	Presence of pathogenic organisms or their toxins in blood or tissues
spore	SPOR		Greek *seed*	Generic term for any tiny compact cells produced during reproduction by bacteria
endospore	**EN**-doh-spor	P/ R/	endo- *within* -spore *spore*	Spore produced inside a cell and capable of resisting heat, freezing, radiation, and chemicals

- high incidence of immunocompromised patients
- high incidence of invasive procedures
- high incidence of people close together
- high incidence of pathogens becoming resistant to antibiotics
- routes of transmission of pathogens from individual to individual are in place in hospital settings.

Keynote

Within hours of admission to the hospital, a patient's flora begin to acquire the characteristics of the hospital's infection pool.

EXERCISES

Deconstruct the following medical terminology of infectious diseases into the meaning of each basic element. Fill in the chart, then use any two terms in sentences of your choice to demonstrate your understanding of the terms.

Medical Term	Meaning of Prefix	Meaning of Root/CF	Meaning of Suffix
disinfection			
antisepsis			
nosocomial			
sanitization			
asepsis			
autoclave			

Sentences:

1. _____

2. _____

Abbreviations

BSI	Body Substance Isolation
CDC	Centers for Disease Control and Prevention
SP	Standard Precautions
UP	Universal Precautions

PRECAUTIONS TO PREVENT INFECTION

To reduce the transmission of nosocomial infections to and from patients and to protect caregivers, different systems of precautions have been introduced at different times. In the 1980s, systems called **Universal Precautions (UP)** and **Body Substance Isolation (BSI)** were put in place. As the problems of transmission of infections in a hospital continued to grow, in 1996 the **Centers for Disease Control and Prevention (CDC)** issued a new system, combining UP and BSI, called **Standard Precautions (SP)**.

Standard Precautions

Standard Precautions guidelines are designed for use in all health care facilities all the time for treating all patients, regardless of their presumed diagnosis. The key components of SP address the areas of:

- hand-washing
- gloves
- masks, goggles, face masks
- gowns
- **sharps**
- linens
- patient care equipment
- environmental cleaning
- patient resuscitation
- patient placement

In any health care setting, handwashing is the most important factor in preventing the transmission of infections.

Details of the implementation of each component are not given here, as they do not add to your knowledge of medical terminology and are freely available elsewhere.

Transmission-Based Precautions

In addition to SP, three sets of precautions based on routes of transmission of infections (called **Transmission-based Precautions**) apply to hospitalized patients and those in nursing homes or other types of extended care facilities. The three routes of transmission of pathogens are by:

- **Air** (tuberculosis, chickenpox, measles)
- **Droplet** (flu, mumps, rubella)
- **Contact** (hepatitis A and other enteric pathogens, including *E. coli* and *C. difficile*; staph infections; herpes simplex; skin or eye infections).

The use of transmission-based precautions is designed to reduce the risk of spreading infections between hospitalized patients and health care staff.

Personal health precautions include:
- **wash hands frequently,** particularly before and after food preparation
- **sanitize** food preparation areas
- **avoid** inadequately cooked meat
- **drink only purified water** in endemic areas
- **avoid** leafy vegetables and salads in endemic areas
- **avoid** ice made from nonpurified water in endemic areas

Public health precautions include:
- **purification** of drinking water
- **effective disposal** of **sewage**
- **pasteurization** of milk, juice, and other beverages
- **handwashing laws** for food handlers (*Figure 20.25*)
- **immunization** programs

Keynote

Standard Precautions combines Universal Precautions and Body Substance Isolation in the theoretical assumption that every patient with whom you come into contact has HIV infection.

▲ **FIGURE 20.25** **Employee Washes Hands in Kitchen.**

Keynote

In all cases, Transmission-based Precautions must be used with Standard Precautions.

WORD ANALYSIS AND DEFINITION

S = Suffix   P = Prefix   R = Root   R/CF = Combining Form

WORD	PRONUNCIATION	ELEMENTS		DEFINITION
droplet	**DROP**-let	S/ R/	**-let** *small* **drop-** *liquid globule*	Globule of liquid; for example, that which is ejected from the mouth during speaking, coughing, sneezing
pasteurization	**PAS**-tyur-ih-**ZAY**-shun		Louis Pasteur, 1822–1895, French chemist and bacteriologist	The heating of fluids to moderate temperatures to destroy microorganisms
purification	**PYUR**-if-ih-kay-shun	S/ R/	**-ation** *action* **purific-** *make pure*	Make free from pathogens
sewage	**SOO**-aje		Latin *drain off*	Waste matter from populated areas
sharps	SHARPS	S/	Greek *pointed* **-er** *that which*	Any medical instrument capable of puncturing skin
sharps container	SHARPS kon-**TAY**-ner	P/ R/	**con-** *with* **-tain-** *hold*	Puncture-resistant container for disposal of sharps

EXERCISES

Abbreviations. *Demonstrate your understanding of abbreviations by interpreting them correctly. Translate the following abbreviations—rewrite the sentence without using the abbreviations.*

1. The CDC issued a new system, combining UP and BSI, called SP.

_____

_____

_____

Short Answers. *Any health care worker needs to learn the value of precautions in patient care. This ensures the safety of you and the patient. Employ the* **language of infectious diseases** *to briefly answer the following questions. Fill in the blanks.*

1. What exactly is a *precaution*? (**Hint:** Start with the prefix.)

_____

_____

_____

2. Why are precautions necessary?

_____

_____

_____

3. Give one example of what a precaution might be:

_____

_____

_____

4. What can precautions achieve?

_____

_____

_____

OTHER METHODS OF PREVENTION OF INFECTIONS

Chemoprophylaxis is the use of antimicrobial agents to prevent infection in nonimmune individuals exposed to the infection. These agents can be used against:

- **exogenous pathogens** that are not part of the normal flora before they can invade and attach to cells or produce toxins. An example is the use of 2 grams of amoxicillin one hour before a dental procedure in individuals with a prosthesis such as an artificial hip. Amoxicillin is also effective in preventing Lyme disease after a tick bite. Individuals exposed to the respiratory secretions of patients with meningococcal disease should receive rifampin.

- **endogenous pathogens.** For example, adults with recurrent infections caused by *Staphylococcus aureus* have fewer infections while receiving oral clindamycin. Patients undergoing hemodialysis, intensive chemotherapy, or bone marrow transplantation leading to low neutrophil counts benefit from chemoprophylaxis.

- **latent pathogens** that are microorganisms already residing in the human host but are not causing disease. For example, use of acyclovir significantly reduces the rate and severity of recurrences of genital herpes in infected individuals.

Immunization is one of the primary preventative measures. All health care workers providing direct patient care should be immune to rubella, measles, mumps, varicella, and hepatitis A and B. They should receive **tetanus toxoid.** Caregivers should also receive an annual influenza vaccine, as should the elderly and people with chronic diseases *(Figure 20.26)*. Children also receive immunization against poliomyelitis, pneumococcal disease, and *Haemophilus influenzae* type b. Other vaccines for yellow fever, typhoid, anthrax, and meningococcal disease are available to high-risk populations.

Passive immune prophylaxis is the transfer of immunity to prevent viral infections in exposed but nonimmune individuals. Short-lived immunity is achieved through immunoglobulins (preformed IgG antibodies) prepared from large pools of serum from blood donors. This pooled product is used as prophylaxis against hepatitis A infection and enterovirus infections in neonates and for HIV-infected neonates.

Hyperimmune globulin is immunoglobulin prepared from the serum of individuals who have a high **titer** of antibody to a specific virus. These include:

- **Zoster immune globulin** for prevention of varicella in immunocompromised children and neonates

- **Human rabies immunoglobulin** for an individual bitten by a **rabid** animal

- **Hepatitis B immunoglobulin** for a nonimmune individual exposed to the hepatitis B virus (HBV)

- **RSV immunoglobulin** for treatment of **respiratory syncytial virus (RSV)** in the neonatal period

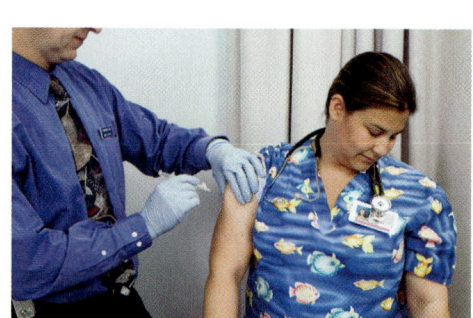

▲ **FIGURE 20.26** **Caregiver Receiving Immunization.**

WORD	PRONUNCIATION	ELEMENTS		DEFINITION
chemoprophylaxis (*Note:* The "c" in prophylac- is dropped.)	**KEEM**-oh-**PRO**-fil-ak-sis	S/ R/CF P/ R/	-xis *condition* chem/o- *chemical* -pro- *before* -phylac- *protect*	Prevent infection by use of chemicals or drugs
endogenous	en-**DOJ**-en-us	S/ P/ R/	-ous *pertaining to* endo- *within* -gen- *production*	Produced within the organism
exogenous	ex-**OJ**-en-us	S/ P/ R/	-ous *pertaining to* exo- *outside* -gen- *production*	Originating outside the organism
hyperimmune globulin	**HIGH**-per-im-**YUNE** **GLOB**-you-lin	P/ R/ S/ R/	hyper- *excessive* -immune *immune response* -in *substance* globul- *protein*	Immunoglobulin prepared from serum of people with high antibody titer to a specific virus
prophylaxis **prophylactic (adj)**	pro-fih-**LAX**-is pro-fih-**LAK**-tik	S/ P/ R/	Greek *to take precautions* -tic *pertaining to* pro- *before* -phylac- *protect*	Prevention of disease The act or the agent that prevents a disease
rabies **rabid**	**RAY**-beez **RAB**-id		Latin *to be mad*	Highly fatal infectious disease transmitted by the bite of infected animals Suffering from rabies
titer	**TIE**-ter		French *standard*	The strength of a substance in a solution as compared to a standard
toxoid	**TOK**-soyd	S/ R/	-oid *resembling* tox- *poison*	Toxin treated to destroy its toxic capability but retain its antigenic capability

EXERCISES

Communication. *Use the* **language of infectious diseases** *to communicate information to your patients, coworkers and fellow students. Provide a brief answer to each of the following questions.*

1. A patient has asked you to explain to him the difference between passive immune prophylaxis and chemoprophylaxis.

   Passive immune prophylaxis:

   _____

   _____

   Chemoprophylaxis:

   _____

   _____

2. The pathologist has explained to you the difference between an exogenous pathogen and an endogenous pathogen. Can you summarize what he said for a fellow student?

   Exogenous pathogen:

   _____

   _____

   Endogenous pathogen:

   _____

   _____

INFECTION

CHALLENGE YOUR KNOWLEDGE

A. **Case Report Revisited:** Apply your knowledge of *all* the medical terminology you have learned up to this point to the questions asked about the following case report.

Your patients are

. . . Mrs. Uzma Aziz and her 2-year-old daughter Alisha, the youngest of her five children.

Your interpreter tells you that Alisha was well until three days earlier, when she developed a runny nose, red eyes, and a cough. Today she has developed a rash on her forehead and neck that is spreading down onto her body.

Your examination shows T 104.2°F, P 120, R 24. A rash of red-brown macules is present on her face, neck, and shoulders. She has a bilateral conjunctivitis. As you proceed with your examination, the rash continues to extend down the trunk. On the buccal mucosa inside the mouth are some small red spots with white centers (Koplik spots). You hear rales at the base of her right lung, and her left tympanic membrane is inflamed. She is diagnosed as having measles.

Through the interpreter, you learn that none of the five children has been immunized for any disease. When they arrived at the camp, the mother refused to start a program of immunization for the children.

1. What are Alisha's symptoms? _____
   _____
   _____
   _____
   _____

2. What are Alisha's signs of measles? _____
   _____
   _____
   _____

3. How do you know Alisha is febrile? _____
   _____
   _____
   _____

4. What does a macule look like? _____
   _____
   _____
   _____

5. What is conjunctivitis? _____
   _____
   _____

6. Exactly where in the mouth is the buccal mucosa? _____
   _____

7. What would you use to hear the rales in her lung? _____

_____

8. What might the rales signify? _____

_____

9. What instrument did you use to discover her left tympanic membrane was inflamed?

_____

_____

10. What childhood disease does Alisha have? _____

11. What could have prevented this? _____

12. What body systems that you have already studied have helped you understand this report? _____

_____

_____

B. **Prefixes:** Not every medical term will have a prefix. When they do have a prefix, it is another clue to the meaning of the entire term. Match the prefix in column l to its correct meaning in column 2.

_____	1.	im-	A.	small
_____	2.	mal-	B.	false
_____	3.	ex-	C.	together
_____	4.	a/an-	D.	bad
_____	5.	dis-	E.	within
_____	6.	micro-	F.	not
_____	7.	endo-	G.	away from
_____	8.	dys-	H.	apart
_____	9.	pseudo-	I.	difficult
_____	10.	syn-	J.	without

C. **Patient Education:** Explain to your patients, in a language they can understand the difference between **contagious** and **infectious**.

Contagious:

_____

_____

Infectious:

_____

_____

INFECTION

D. Elements: The following medical terms are composed of roots, combining forms, and suffixes only. Deconstruct the term into its basic elements, and write the meaning of each element in the proper column. Fill in the blanks.

Medical Term	Root/CF	Meaning of Root/CF	Suffix	Meaning of Suffix
infection				
pathogen				
vaccinate				
aerobic				
hemolysis				
enteric				
gonorrhea				
trichinosis				
toxoid				

E. Disease Process: Understanding the infectious disease process can help us all take better care of our bodies. Apply your knowledge of the **language of infectious diseases** to the following exercise. *Remember: There is only one best answer*—circle it.

1. Innate resistance, natural barriers, nonspecific immune responses, and specific immune responses are all part of:

   a. colonization

   b. host defense mechanisms

   c. mechanisms of infection

   d. virulence factors

   e. inflammatory response

2. If a *mycologist* studies fungus, what does a *toxicologist* study?

   a. viruses

   b. bacteria

   c. poisons

   d. tissues

   e. cells

3. What is the human spongiform encephalopathy associated with BSE?

   a. WNV

   b. SARS

   c. EBV

   d. CJD

   e. RSV

4. Bacteria can be classified by their shapes, use of oxygen, and:

   a. Gram stain color

   b. DNA

   c. size

   d. location

   e. infections they cause

5. What is the most common intestinal parasitic infection in the United States?

   a. toxoplasmosis

   b. giardiasis

   c. trichinosis

   d. amoebiasis

   e. malaria

6. Hand antisepsis is achieved with:

   a. a lotion

   b. extremely hot water

   c. special soap

   d. surgical scrub

   e. fingernail brush

7. A nosocomial infection would be acquired from:

   a. school

   b. dormitory

   c. workplace

   d. airplane

   e. hospital

8. Which pathogen is the major cause of antibiotic-associated diarrhea?

   a. *E. coli*

   b. streptococcus

   c. staphylococcus

   d. *C. difficile*

   e. pneumococci

INFECTION

F. **Disease Process:** Understanding the infectious disease process can help us all take better care of our bodies. Apply your knowledge of the **language of infectious diseases** in this exercise. Remember: *There is only one best answer*—circle it.

1. The smallest of *microorganisms* is:

   a. bacterium

   b. prion

   c. fungus

   d. spores

   e. virus

2. The stage in development in which an insect hatches from an egg:

   a. vector

   b. parasite

   c. larva

   d. plasmodium

   e. colonization

3. The term **exanthem** means:

   a. outside the cells

   b. rash as the outward sign of disease

   c. outside the uterus

   d. bulging eyeball

   e. falling forward of an organ

4. Rubeola, in its prodromal phase, produces signs similar to:

   a. rubella

   b. URI

   c. pharyngitis

   d. varicella

   e. BSE

G. **Latin and Greek terms cannot be further deconstructed into prefix, root, or suffix.** You must know them for what they are. Test your knowledge of these terms with the following exercise. Match the meaning in column l with the correct medical term in column 2.

_____	1. fringe	**A.**	lysis
_____	2. running before	**B.**	bubo
_____	3. poison	**C.**	parasite
_____	4. berry	**D.**	latent

_____	5. dissolve	E.	fimbria
_____	6. swelling in the groin	F.	coccus
_____	7. to take precautions	G.	prodromal
_____	8. a guest	H.	sterile
_____	9. barren	I.	prophylactic
_____	10. lie hidden	J.	toxin

H. **Test Review:** Microbes are everywhere, and they can have a good or bad effect on the body. The *language of infectious diseases* will help you understand the questions and formulate your answers to make a test review sheet for yourself on microbes. Fill in the blanks. *Refer to this exercise for test review.*

1. Give an example of five places on the body where you will find normal flora.

    a. _____

    b. _____

    c. _____

    d. _____

    e. _____

2. What two areas of the body remain microbe-free?

    a. _____

    b. _____

3. What is the medical term for "microbe-free"? _____

4. At what point do normal bacteria become pathogens? _____

5. If an infection causes harm to the host, what is present? _____

6. What helps a healthy host defend itself? _____

7. **Recall question:** What is present inside the skull that contributes to the protection of the brain by preventing cross

    contamination? _____

I. **Research and Discuss:** Pick any one of the natural barriers the body has to resisting infection (skin, mucous membranes, respiratory tract, gastrointestinal tract, genitourinary tract).

1. Review previous chapters on those subjects.
2. Add to that your new knowledge of the infectious disease process, and prepare a five-minute class discussion on any one of the body's natural defense barriers, how they prevent disease, or, if they fail, how the disease process begins. Remember the role of the immune system in this as well.
3. Use your school library and online research to supplement your text material.
4. Make a list of ten key terms you are going to use in your discussion:

    _____

    _____

    _____

    _____

5. Print out your notes, and be prepared to hand them in to your instructor.

INFECTION

J. **Terminology Applied to Coding:** Solid comprehension of medical terminology can make you a better coder. Challenge your knowledge of the medical terms you have studied so far in this text with the following exercise. Each medical code is first listed with the corresponding medical term. In the table that follows, use the *description* of the medical term to determine the appropriate code.

Medical Term	ICD-9-CM code
osteomyelitis	730.20
bacteremia	790.7
furuncle	680.9
pneumonia	486
toxic shock syndrome	040.82
endocarditis	424.90
impetigo	684
rubeola	055.9
herpangina	074.0
malaria	084.6

Description of the Medical Term	Correct ICD-9-CM Code
Infected hair follicle	
Inflammation of the lining of the heart	
Acute, contagious childhood disease	
Ulcerative disease of the throat	
Inflammation of an area of bone due to bacterial infection	
Infection of the skin producing thick, yellow crusts	
Inflammation of the lung parenchyma	
Life-threatening illness caused by toxins circulating in the blood	
Vector-borne parasitic infection	
Presence of bacteria in the blood	

K. **Medical Language:** A good knowledge of medical terminology will enable you to clarify, describe, and explain a term's meaning and use. Using medical language, provide short answers in the following exercise.

1. The term **parasite** comes from the Greek meaning *a guest.* Explain how a parasite becomes "a guest" of the host and what is involved in that relationship.

_____

_____

_____

_____

_____

_____

2. Explain this chapter keynote: "Within hours of admission to the hospital, a patient's flora begin to acquire the characteristics of the hospital's infection pool."

_____

_____

_____

_____

_____

_____

L. **Precautions:** The best defense is often a good offense—so to prevent infections from starting, medical facilities use a variety of methods of infection prevention and control. A brief description is given of each method. Fill in the correct medical term in the blanks.

| asepsis | antisepsis | hand antisepsis | sterilization |
| sanitization | disinfection | HLD | cleaning |

1. boiling, steaming, or using chemical disinfectants on inanimate objects: _____

2. removing pathogens from surfaces by chemical means: _____

3. surgical scrub: _____

4. washing with soap and water, rinsing with clean water, and drying: _____

5. autoclave: _____

6. reducing microorganisms on skin with antimicrobial agents: _____

7. destroying microorganisms with chlorine, alcohol, or hydrogen peroxide: _____

8. eliminating microorganisms on living surfaces and inanimate objects: _____

M. **Terminology Challenge:** For the following three similar medical terms, analyze each prefix. This will help you understand how the terms are different. Write a brief definition that explains the difference in each term.

Epidemic: _____

_____

Endemic: _____

_____

Pandemic: _____

_____

CHAPTER 20 REVIEW

INFECTION

N. **Word Elements:** The better your knowledge of word elements, the easier you will find understanding the meaning of medical terms. Challenge your knowledge of word elements with this exercise. First, listen to the correct pronunciation of each term on the student CD. Then read each of the terms aloud *using your best pronunciation.* Don't forget to circle the correct choice.

1. In the term **endogenous,** the suffix is _____ and means:

   a. pertaining to

   b. within

   c. production

   d. action

   e. outside

2. In the term **anaerobic,** the prefix is _____ and means:

   a. within

   b. without

   c. on top of

   d. behind

   e. underneath

3. In the term **toxin,** the Greek root means:

   a. barren

   b. life

   c. poison

   d. sterile

   e. intestine

4. In the term **contamination,** the root is _____ and means:

   a. to corrupt

   b. bowels

   c. to produce

   d. separation

   e. to change

5. In the term **pyogenes,** the root/combining form is _____ and means:

   a. fever

   b. pus

   c. pain

   d. swelling

   e. rash

6. In the term **prodromal**, the Greek root means:

   a. in the middle

   b. coming before

   c. running after

   d. in between

   e. at the end of

7. In the term **syncytium**, the prefix is _____ and means:

   a. together

   b. apart

   c. beside

   d. on top of

   e. below

8. In the term **antisepsis**, the root is _____ and means:

   a. liquid

   b. decay

   c. chlorine

   d. exempt

   e. precaution

9. In the term **infection**, the suffix is _____ and means:

   a. a process

   b. an action

   c. a condition

   d. a disease

   e. a policy

10. In the term **latent**, the Latin root means:

    a. to produce something

    b. to lie hidden

    c. to come in waves

    d. to push under

    e. to burst forth

INFECTION

O. Language of Infectious Diseases: Apply your knowledge of the terminology of infectious diseases to match the description given in column l with the correct medical term *or* abbreviation in column 2.

_____	1. carried by birds	A. Epstein-Barr
_____	2. viral respiratory tract infection	B. BSE
_____	3. German measles	C. shingles
_____	4. bacillary dysentery	D. WNV
_____	5. an oncogenic virus	E. SARS
_____	6. undulant fever	F. rubella
_____	7. cause of bronchiolitis in infants	G. avian influenza
_____	8. also carried by mosquitoes	H. shigellosis
_____	9. herpes zoster	I. RSV
_____	10. caused by a prion	J. brucellosis

P. Deconstruct the following medical terms into elements. Analyze the elements, and give a layman's definition of the medical term. Fill in the blanks, then use any one term in a sentence that is not directly out of the text.

Medical Term	Prefix	Root/CF	Suffix	Meaning of Term
microorganism				
anaerobic				
oncogenic				
pyogenes				
streptococcus				
exogenous				
prophylactic				
toxoid				
enteric				
herpangina				

Sentence:

_____

_____

_____

Q. Teamwork: Pair up with another student, and prepare answers to the following questions. Make your answers as complete as possible. Take turns asking other teams the questions. How do their answers compare with yours? Note any important additions to the material their answers may have contributed to what you originally wrote. Hand the answers in to the instructor.

1. Excluding the word element, what do *pneumococcus, staphylococcus,* and *streptococcus* all have in common?

   _____

   _____

   _____

2. Nosocomial infections account for approximately 200,000 deaths per year. List six factors that contribute to the spread of nosocomial infections. Your examples must illustrate the factors listed in the text.

   _____   _____

   _____   _____

   _____   _____

3. Give three examples of prophylactic practices to prevent the spread of nosocomial infections.

   _____

   _____

   _____

R. Prefixes: Some, but not all, of the following medical terms have a prefix. Identify each medical term that has a prefix, then write the meaning of the prefix in the last column. If there is no prefix in the term, leave the line blank. Fill in the chart.

Medical Term	Prefix	Meaning of Prefix
dysentery		
malaria		
immunize		
disinfection		
prophylaxis		
antisepsis		
asepsis		
autoclave		

1. Choose any prefix from the chart, and write a medical term *from a different chapter* that has the same prefix: _____

   _____

2. Define the term you chose: _____

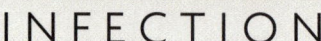

INFECTION

S. Apply your knowledge of the language of infectious diseases. Circle the correct answer.

1. A tell-tale sign of bubonic plague was the appearance of:

   Pseudomonas   *Shigella*   bubo   spore

2. Presence of an infectious agent on a surface is:

   mutation   immunization   contamination   vaccination

3. *E. coli* causes diarrhea by releasing:

   hormone   enzyme   endorphin   exotoxin

4. **Enteric** means pertaining to the:

   feces   intestines   anus   rectum

5. Diarrhea, spasms, fever, and dehydration are symptoms of:

   dysentery   dysentary   dsyentary   dysinteray

6. In the term *Pseudomonas,* pseudo- means:

   difficult   away from   false   painful

7. A fever that comes and goes is termed:

   undulant   infectious   contagious   septic

8. **Spore** is the Greek word for:

   bowel   seed   feces   carbuncle

T. Dictionary Exercise: Use your glossary or a medical dictionary (textbook or online) to define the term.

Virulence:

Then explain this sentence in layman's terms: "Virulence factors assist pathogens to overcome host resistance and cause disease."

_____

_____

_____

_____

_____

_____

U. **Brain Teasers:** Leukoencephalopathy is a term presented in this chapter. Relate the elements in this term to other terms from *previous* chapters that contain the same elements. See how many terms you can enter in the table. The first one is done for you.

Definition of elements:

leuk/o (or leuc/o) means: _____

encephal/o means: _____

pathy means: _____

Element	Another Medical Term Containing This Element	Meaning of This Medical Term
leuk/o (or leuc/o) (*Note:* This element can be spelled two ways.)	*leukoplakia*	*white plaque seen inside the mouth*
encephal/o		
pathy		

What other medical term in this chapter means the same as **latent** or **dormant**? _____

CHAPTER 20 REVIEW

INFECTION

CHAPTER SUMMARY EXERCISE

1. *Listen to the pronunciation of the medical terms as given by your instructor.*
2. *Circle the correct spelling of the medical term.*
3. *Match the correctly spelled terms to the brief descriptions below.*
4. *Write a sentence for each of the 15 terms that appear in this exercise.*

A. SPELLING COMPREHENSION: CIRCLE THE CORRECT SPELLING OF THE TERM.

1. contagius	contagious	kontagius	contajous	contajious
2. varecella	varesella	varicela	varicella	varecela
3. latency	lateincy	laytency	laytincy	lateincey
4. prodromal	prodomal	prodrumal	produmal	prodromel
5. firmbriae	fimbriae	fembriae	fimmbrie	fimbriee
6. anaerobic	anairobic	enairobic	anairobic	anerobic
7. preon	precion	prion	preion	preeon
8. xantem	exantem	xanthem	exanthema	xantum
9. orkitis	orckitus	orchitis	orchitus	orkitus
10. mycroscopy	miscroscopy	microscopy	microscopey	miccroscopy
11. undullant	undullent	undulant	undulent	udulant
12. queesient	quiescent	quiesent	quiescient	quietsent
13. propylaxtic	prophylaxic	prophilaxic	propilaxic	prophylactic
14. lisis	lissus	lysis	lysus	lissis
15. gunorea	gonorhea	gonorrhea	gonorhia	gonnorhea

B. MATCH THE NUMBER OF THE CORRECT TERM IN PART A WITH THE BRIEF DESCRIPTION OF THE TERM BELOW.

a. long quiet period for a virus _____

b. destruction of a cell _____

c. organism can live without oxygen _____

d. can be caused by mumps _____

e. febrile disease that comes and goes _____

f. fringelike structures on the surface of a cell _____

g. sexually transmitted disease _____

h. chickenpox _____

i. examination under a microscope _____

j. skin rash _____

k. spread from person to person   _____

l. prevention of a disease process   _____

m. beginning of disease before overt signs appear   _____

n. not currently active   _____

o. small protein particle can cause infection   _____

C. USING YOUR KNOWLEDGE OF TERMS 1-15 IN PART A AND THEIR CORRECT SPELLING, WRITE A BRIEF SENTENCE FOR EACH OF THE TERMS AS IT MIGHT APPEAR IN PATIENT DOCUMENTATION.

1. _____

2. _____

3. _____

4. _____

5. _____

6. _____

7. _____

8. _____

9. _____

10. _____

11. _____

12. _____

13. _____

14. _____

15. _____

D. GO TO THE STUDENT CD. OPEN THE GLOSSARY AND PRACTICE YOUR PRONUNCIATION OF THE TERMS IN PART A OF THIS EXERCISE.

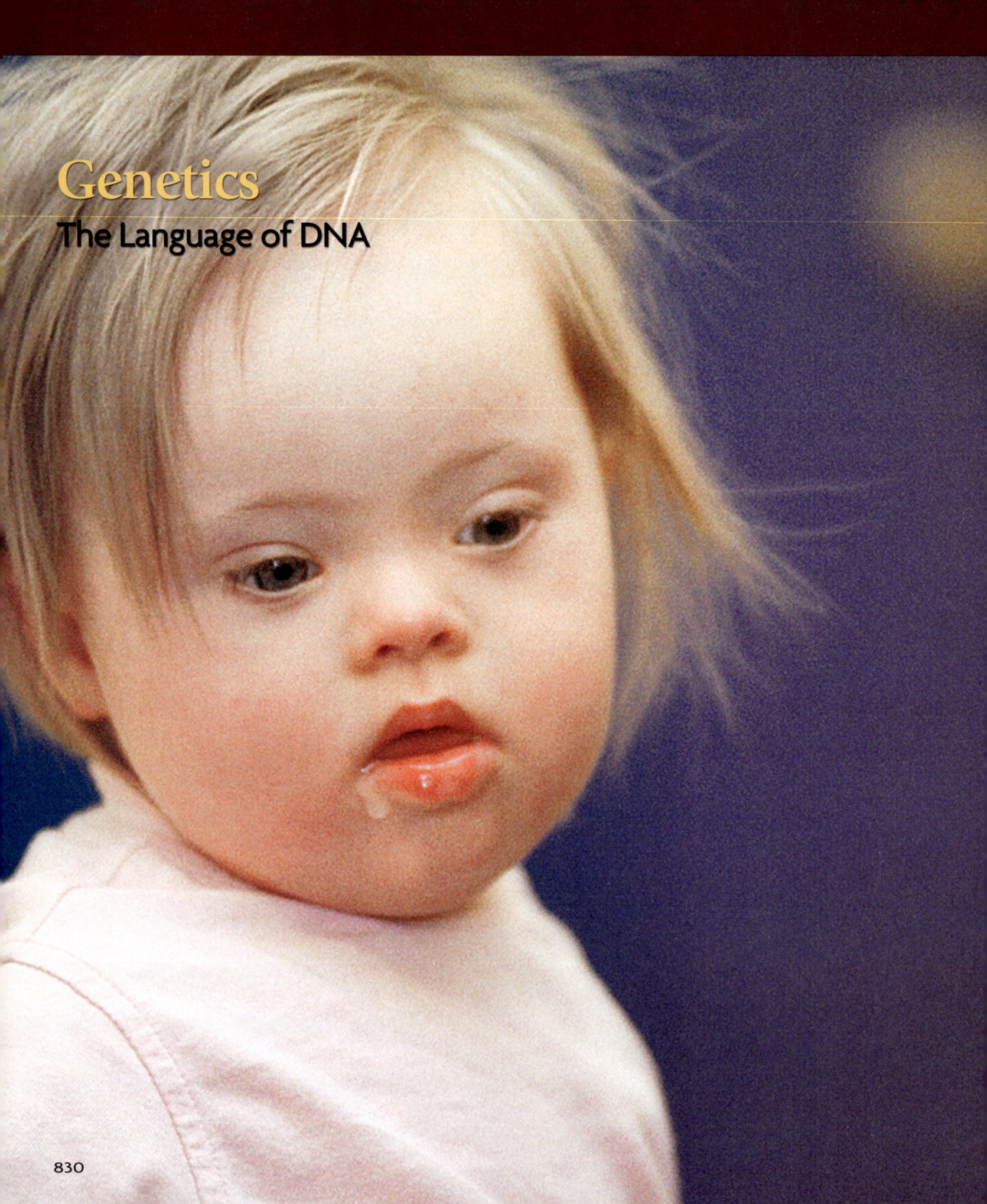

Genetics

The Language of DNA

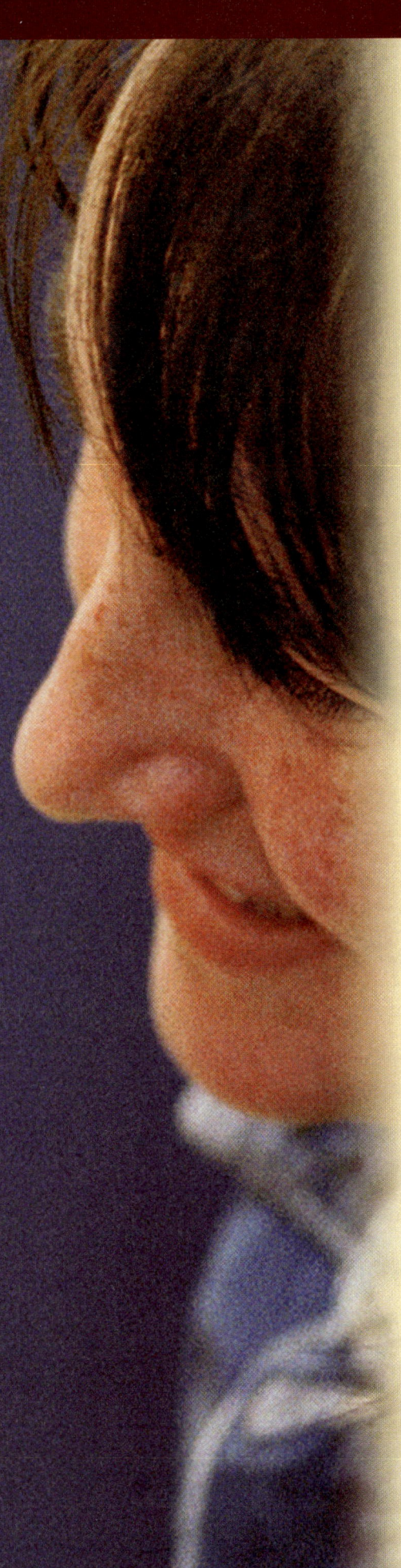

CASE REPORT 21.1

You are

. . . a **genetic** nurse working with **geneticist** Ingrid Hughes, MD, PhD, in the Genetics Department at Fulwood Medical Center.

Your patient is

. . . Mrs. Sharon Fisher, a 37-year-old administrative assistant who has been referred by Susan Lee, MD, in the primary care clinic. She is of **Ashkenazi** Jewish ancestry and has a girl aged 10 and a boy aged 7. Mrs. Fisher tries to live a healthy lifestyle. She does not smoke, drinks alcohol only occasionally, and goes to the gym two or three times per week. Physical examination and a mammogram performed a week ago were normal. Her mother, aged 62, is being treated for ovarian cancer. Her maternal grandmother is believed to have had breast cancer in her forties. Her mother's sister had breast cancer in her thirties and has recently had genetic screening at Fulwood Medical Center. She is carrying a gene mutation associated with breast cancer.

Learning Outcomes

In your role as a genetic nurse, you are a member of the genetic team, and you need to be able to:

- Apply the language of genetics to the anatomy and physiology of genes and chromosomes.

- Comprehend, analyze, spell, and write the medical terms of genetics so that you communicate and document accurately and precisely in any health care setting.

- Recognize and pronounce the medical terms of genetics so that you communicate verbally with accuracy and precision in any health care setting.

- Explain the effects of common genetic modifications on health.

LESSON 21.1 DNA, RNA, and the Genetic Code

OBJECTIVES

In this lesson, the information will enable you to:

- **Describe the structure of a chromosome.**
- **Explain the structure and functions of a gene.**
- **Compare the structures and functions of DNA and RNA.**
- **Discuss the sequencing of the human genome.**
- **Identify genetic causes of breast cancer.**
- **Evaluate the significance of the genetic causes of breast cancer for genetic counseling.**

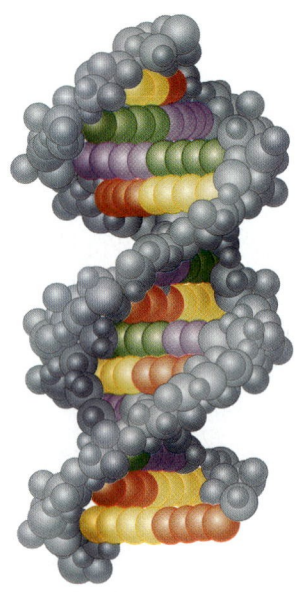

▲ **FIGURE 21.1 DNA Structure.**
A molecular space-filling model of DNA giving some impression of its actual geometry.

Abbreviation

DNA deoxyribonucleic acid

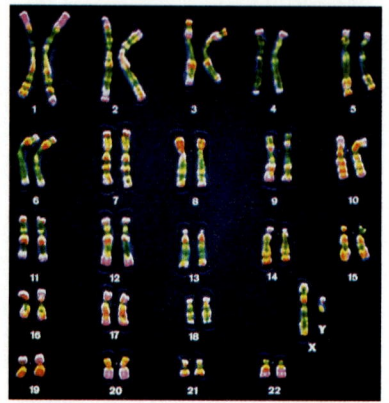

▲ **FIGURE 21.2 Karyotype Showing the Complete Set of Chromosomes of a Normal Male.**

DNA, GENES, AND CHROMOSOMES

Human development depends on genetic and environmental factors. **Genetics** is the study of the transmission of information about the characteristics of our similarities and uniqueness from generation to generation, which is called **heredity.**

Your genetic composition, your **genome,** is established at conception. The genetic information is carried in **genes,** sequences of **DNA** carried on rod-shaped structures called **chromosomes** *(see Chapter 2)*. The transfer of genetic information between generations takes place through genes in the nuclei of the egg and sperm, by the process of meiosis *(see Chapter 2)*.

When your genes are working perfectly, your body develops and functions smoothly. But if a segment(s) of a single gene is abnormal, deformities and disease can result. Chromosomal abnormalities, including deviations from the normal number and structural defects, can also produce disorders. For example, in Down syndrome there is an extra chromosome 21.

DNA (Deoxyribonucleic acid)

Deoxyribonucleic acid (DNA) carries the instructions that enable cells to make proteins. It exists as two long, paired strands, spiraled into a **double helix** *(Figure 21.1)*. Each strand is made up of millions of chemical building blocks called bases. There are only four chemical bases in DNA—**adenine, thymine, cytosine,** and **guanine**—and the order in which the bases appear in the strands codes the necessary information in the same way as the alphabet is used to form words and sentences.

There is DNA in the nucleus of each body cell except for mature red blood cells, which have no nucleus and cannot reproduce. Every cell in the body contains the same DNA and has 46 molecules of double-stranded DNA. Each molecule contains 50 to 250 million bases. The tightly coiled strands of DNA are packaged in paired units called **chromosomes.** Therefore, nondividing cells contain two copies of each chromosome and two copies of every gene. **Mendel's Law of Inheritance** says that during transmission from parent to offspring, the two copies of the gene separate from each other, so that mature sperm and egg cells carry only a single set of 23 chromosomes.

Thus, human cells contain two pairs of chromosomes, one **inherited** from the father, one from the mother. Each set has 23 single chromosomes: 22 **autosomes** and an **X** or **Y sex chromosome,** making a total of 46 chromosomes in a cell. Males inherit an X chromosome from the mother and a Y chromosome from the father. Females inherit an X chromosome from each parent. A chart of the chromosomes is called the **karyotype** *(Figure 21.2)*.

WORD ANALYSIS AND DEFINITION

S = Suffix   P = Prefix   R = Root   R/CF = Combining Form

WORD	PRONUNCIATION		ELEMENTS	DEFINITION
adenine	AD-eh-neen	S/ R/	-ine *pertaining to* aden- *a gland*	One of the chemicals found in both DNA and RNA
Ashkenazi	ASH-ke-NAZ-ih		Hebrew *Germany*	Jews of eastern European ancestry
autosome autosomal (adj)	AWE-toe-soam awe-toe-SO-mal	P/ R/ S/	auto- *self* -some *body* -al *pertaining to*	Any chromosome other than a sex chromosome
chromosome	KROH-moh-some	P/ R/	chromo- *color* -some *body*	Body in the nucleus that contains DNA and genes
cytosine	SIGH-toh-seen	R/CF S/	cyt/o- *cell* -sine *pertaining to*	One of the chemicals found in both DNA and RNA
deoxyribonucleic acid (DNA)	dee-OCK-see-RYE-boh-noo-KLEE-ik ASS-id	S/ P/ R/ R/ R/ R/	-ic *pertaining to* de- *without* oxy- *oxygen* -ribo- *pentose, a sugar* -nucle- *nucleus* acid *acid, low pH*	Source of hereditary characteristics found in chromosomes
gene genetic (adj) genetics geneticist	JEEN jeh-NET-ik jeh-NET-iks jeh-NET-ih-sist	 S/ S/ S/ R/	Greek *birth, origin* -ic *pertaining to* -ics *knowledge* -ist *one who specializes in* genet- *gene*	Functional segment of DNA molecule Science of the inheritance of characteristics A specialist in genetics
genome	JEE-nome	P/ R/	gen- *birth, origin* -ome *body*	Complete set of genes
guanine	GWAH-neen	S/ R/	-ine *pertaining to* guan- *dung*	One of the chemicals found in both DNA and RNA
helix	HE-liks		Greek *a coil*	A line in the shape of a coil
heredity	heh-RED-ih-tee	S/ R/	-ity *states, condition* hered- *inherited through genes*	Transmission of characteristics from parents to offspring through genes
inherited	in-HAIR-it-ed			Acquired through genetic code
karyotype	KAIR-ee-oh-type	S/ R/CF	-type *model* kary/o- *nucleus*	Map of chromosomes of an individual cell
Mendelian	men-DEE-lee-an	S/	-ian *pertaining to* Gregor Johann Mendel, 1822–1884, Austrian geneticist; considered the father of genetics	Described by Gregor Mendel
thymine	THIGH-meen	S/ R/	-ine *pertaining to* thym- *wart*	Chemical found in DNA but not RNA

EXERCISES

*Build your knowledge of the modern **language of genetics** by matching the following terms correctly. These are terms you will see in common usage—not just in the field of medicine, but forensics, law, and journalism as well. Fill in the blanks.*

_____	1. study of heredity	A. autosome
_____	2. prefix means *color*	B. karyotype
_____	3. exists in a double helix	C. genetics
_____	4. complete set of genes	D. chromosome
_____	5. map of chromosomes	E. DNA
_____	6. prefix means *self*	F. genome

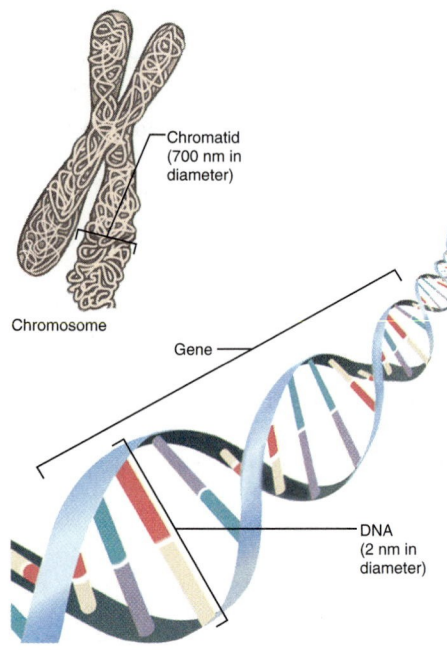

▲ FIGURE 21.3   DNA, Gene, and Chromosome.

Chromatid (700 nm in diameter)

Chromosome

Gene

DNA (2 nm in diameter)

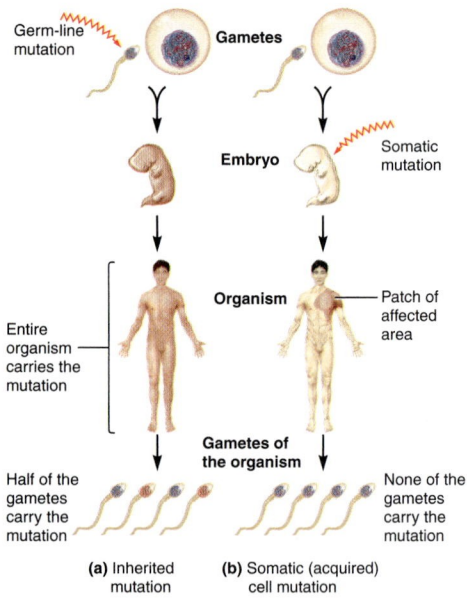

▲ FIGURE 21.4   Genetic Mutations.
(*a*) Hereditary (inherited) mutation. (*b*) Somatic (acquired) mutation. (Gametes are eggs and sperm.)

Germ-line mutation

Gametes

Embryo

Somatic mutation

Organism

Patch of affected area

Entire organism carries the mutation

Gametes of the organism

Half of the gametes carry the mutation

None of the gametes carry the mutation

(a) Inherited mutation

(b) Somatic (acquired) cell mutation

Abbreviation

mRNA messenger RNA

DNA, GENES, AND CHROMOSOMES (continued)

Genes

Genes are the working subunits of DNA (*Figure 21.3*). The DNA in each chromosome contains 25,000 to 30,000 genes (the genome), each made up of thousands of chemical bases to give a total of some 3 billion bases. A gene is any segment along the DNA strand that **encodes** instructions to the cell to make a specific product, usually a protein such as an enzyme that initiates one specific action. Genes, through the proteins they encode, determine all body processes, including the way the body responds to challenges from the environment. A normal cell activates the genes it needs at the moment and shuts down the rest. The **genotype** is the specific genetic makeup (the specific genome) of an individual, in the form of DNA.

RNA (Ribonucleic acid)

For a cell to make a protein, the information from the gene is copied, base chemical by base chemical, from DNA into new strands of **messenger RNA (mRNA).** The newly formed mRNA travels out from the nucleus into the cell cytoplasm to organelles called ribosomes (*see Chapter 2*). In the ribosomes, mRNA directs the assembly of amino acids into a protein molecule. The DNA stays safely behind in the nucleus, directing the operation from there.

With only 70 to 10,000 chemical bases, RNA is much smaller than DNA. It does not contain thymine, which is replaced by **uracil.**

Genes and Mutations

The **Human Genome Project** at the beginning of this century generated a map of specific genes linked to specific locations on chromosomes. Before this, human genetics had focused on single genes and the disorders that **malfunctions** of a single gene produced. Now, there is a new view of physiology as a complex interplay between multiple, interacting genes. This concept is called **genomics.** The complexity of this process is illustrated by looking at the sites where genes function at the organ level. The same genes can function at different sites.

Gene mutations occur frequently and randomly in every cell during cell division. The cells are able to recognize mistakes and correct them. However, the cells' repair ability can become less efficient with age, or it can fail because of environmental stresses such as radiation or toxins like chemotherapy or other chemicals.

When a gene mutates, the protein encoded by that gene will be abnormal. Some protein changes are insignificant, others are disabling. For example, the flawed hemoglobin in sickle-cell anemia (*see Chapter 7*) is able to function but not well enough to carry oxygen normally.

Gene mutations can be inherited or **acquired.**

A hereditary mutation is a mistake that is present in virtually all the cells in the body and can be passed from generation to generation (*Figure 21.4*).

More than 4,000 disorders are thought to arise from mutated genes inherited from a parent. Common disorders, such as heart disease and cancer, arise from this complex interplay between genes and also between genes and factors in the environment.

Acquired mutations, also called **somatic mutations,** are DNA changes that develop during an individual's life. The changes arise in the DNA of individual cells and can be the result of errors during cell division or the result of environmental stresses such as radiation, chemicals, or toxins.

In the 23 pairs of chromosomes, the location of a particular gene is called its **locus.** The locus is normally the same on each chromosome, and each gene is the same. If the genes are not exactly the same, they are called **alleles,** which produce different forms of a particular **trait** or characteristic. If the trait is detectable, it is called a **phenotype,** and the allele producing the phenotype is said to be **dominant.** If the trait is not detectable, the allele is said to be **recessive.**

A phenotype is the manifestation of a trait, such as size, eye color or behavior that varies between individuals. More than one gene may contribute to a single trait.

WORD	PRONUNCIATION		ELEMENTS	DEFINITION
acquired	ah-**KWIRED**		Latin *to obtain*	A condition that arises from environmental influences and is not inherited
allele	ah-**LEEL**		Greek *reciprocal*	Genetic variant found on the same locus of a pair of chromosomes
dominant gene	**DOM**-ih-nant JEEN		Latin *to rule*	Single allele that is expressed as a trait or characteristic
encode	en-**KODE**	P/ R/	**en-** *in* **-code** *information system*	Convert information
genome	**JEE**-nome	R/ R/	**-ome** *body* **gen-** *birth*	Complete set of genes
genomics	jee-**NOME**-iks	S/ R/CF	**-ics** *pertaining to* **gen/o-** *birth*	Study of the interaction of genes
genotype	jee-**NOH**-type	S/	**-type** *particular kind*	Specific genetic constitution of an individual
locus	**LOW**-kus		Latin, *a place*	A specific site; in this instance, the position a gene occupies on a chromosome
mutation mutate (verb)	myu-**TAY**-shun myu-**TATE**		Greek *to change*	Change in the chemistry of a gene
phenotype	**FEE**-noh-type	R/CF R/	**phen/o-** *to display* **-type** *model*	A characteristic of genetic selection
recessive gene	ree-**SESS**-iv JEEN		Latin *withdraw*	Allele that does not manifest as a trait or characteristic
ribonucleic acid (RNA)	**RYE**-boh-nyu-**KLEE**-ik **ASS**-id	S/ R/ R/ R/	**-ic** *pertaining to* **ribo-** *pentose, a sugar* **-nucle-** *nucleus* **acid** *acid, low pH*	Information carrier from DNA in the nucleus to the ribosome to produce specific protein molecules
somatic	soh-**MAT**-ik	S/ R/	**-ic** *pertaining to* **somat-** *body*	Relating to the body in general
trait	TRAYT		Latin *to draw out*	A discrete characteristic that has a known quality
uracil	**YUR**-ah-sil	S/ R/	**-il** *capability* **urac-** *urine*	Chemical found in RNA

EXERCISES

*Apply the correct **language of genetics** in the following exercise. Remember: Correct spelling always counts! Fill in the blanks.*

1. A complete set of genes is called: _____

   genome   allele

2. A characteristic of genetic selection is: _____

   phenotype   fenotype

3. Change in the chemistry of a gene is called: _____

   recessive   mutation

4. If a gene does not manifest as a trait it is: _____

   recessive   dominant

5. RNA stands for: _____ acid.

   ribonucelic   ribonucleic

OBJECTIVES

In order to be involved and helpful to enable patients with abnormal genes to make informed decisions, you must be able to:

- **Explain the different types of prenatal testing.**
- **Discuss the inheritance of different types of genetic disorders.**
- **Describe some of the more common genetic disorders.**

You are

...a genetic nurse working with geneticist Ingrid Hughes, MD, PhD, in the Genetics Department at Fulwood Medical Center.

Your patients are

... Rebecca and Paul Holyfield, a married couple in their early thirties.

CASE REPORT 21.2

The Holyfields have one daughter, Sarah (aged 5), who is doing well. Last year, they lost a son, aged 2, with **cystic fibrosis (CF).** Rebecca is now eight weeks pregnant, and they want to know if the new baby can also have cystic fibrosis. They did not intend to have any more children.

GENETIC TESTING

Genetic testing is the analysis of human DNA, RNA, chromosomes, and proteins to diagnose inheritable diseases and detect vulnerabilities to inherited diseases. In most examples, it involves examining a person's DNA from a sample of blood, hair, skin, or cells from the inside of the cheek, called a **buccal smear.**

Prenatal Diagnostic Testing

The improvement in diagnostic techniques in the past three decades has produced different options that can be used to determine whether a fetus is affected with a specific condition.

- **Ultrasound** *(see Chapter 13)* is a noninvasive test used from the fifth week of pregnancy to determine the presence of more than one fetus, estimate gestational age, and check for birth defects that affect the brain and spinal cord. The baby's sex can be determined around 18 weeks.
- **Chorionic villus** sampling removes placental tissue between 9 and 12 weeks of gestation. Fetal and placental positions are established by ultrasound and a transcervical biopsy taken *(Figure 21.5a)*. The placental cells are a source of DNA and cells for cell culture and further analysis.
- **Amniocentesis** samples amniotic fluid from around the fetus using an aspiration needle. The amniotic fluid contains cells shed by the fetus that contain fetal DNA, which then can be analyzed. The fluid itself can be assayed for components such as **alpha-fetoprotein (AFP)**, the levels of which rise when neural tube defects are present *(see Chapter 10)*. Amniocentesis is a safe procedure that can be performed between 16 and 20 weeks of gestation *(Figure 21.5b)*.
- **Fetal blood** sampling takes a blood sample from the umbilical vein of the fetus using a very fine needle with ultrasound guidance. The sample provides cells for DNA or abnormal protein studies.

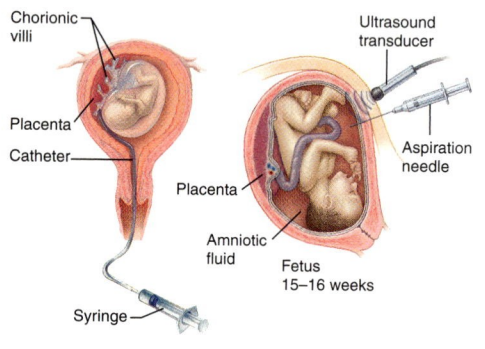

(a) Chorionic villus sampling   (b) Amniocentesis

▲ **FIGURE 21.5   Prenatal Genetic Testing.** (*a*) Chorionic villus biopsy. (*b*) Amniocentesis.

Abbreviations

AFP	alpha-fetoprotein
CF	cystic fibrosis
IVF	in vitro fertilization

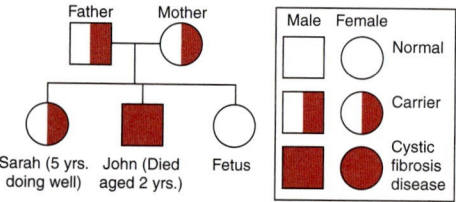

▲ **FIGURE 21.6   The Holyfield Family: Autosomal Recessive Inheritance of Cystic Fibrosis.**

Case Report 21.2 (continued)

When the Holyfield's son was diagnosed with cystic fibrosis, genetic testing showed that both parents carried the Mendelian autosomal recessive gene for CF (Figure 21.6) and that their daughter Sarah was also a **carrier**, or **heterozygote.** The child who died inherited an abnormal gene from each parent and is called a **homozygote.** Chorionic villus testing in the current pregnancy showed a fetal girl who did not carry the gene.

WORD	PRONUNCIATION	ELEMENTS		DEFINITION
alpha-fetoprotein	AL-fah fee-toe-PRO-teen	P/ R/CF R/	alpha- *first letter in Greek alphabet* fet/o- *fetus* -protein *protein*	Protein normally produced only by the fetus
buccal smear	BUCK-al SMEER	S/ R/ R/	-al *pertaining to* bucc- *cheek* smear *spread*	Use of a small brush or cotton swab to collect cells from the inside surface of the cheek
carrier (also called heterozygote)	KAH-ree-er		Latin *vehicle*	In this setting, a person with an autosomal recessive gene for a disease
chorionic villus	koh-ree-ON-ik VILL-us		chorion *membrane* villus *finger-like projection*	Vascular process of the embryonic chorion to form the placenta
heterozygous heterozygote (noun)	HET-er-oh-ZIE-gus HET-er-oh-ZIE-goat	S/ P/ R/	-ous *pertaining to* hetero- *different* -zyg- *zygote*	Carries a different version (allele) of a specific gene on each of the two corresponding chromosomes
homozygous homozygote (noun)	hoh-moh-ZIE-gus hoh-moh-ZIE-goat	S/ P/ R/	-ous *pertaining to* homo- *the same* -zyg- *zygote*	Carries two identical copies of a specific gene on the two corresponding chromosomes

- **Maternal blood** sampling provides a very small number of fetal cells that can be detected in the maternal circulation. Some chemical changes in the maternal blood can suggest the presence of a fetus with Down syndrome.
- **Preimplantation diagnosis** for **in vitro fertilization (IVF)** involves the removal of a single cell from a developing embryo for genetic study prior to implantation.
  Newborn screening is performed using a small blood sample obtained by pricking the heel of a newborn. It is taken to identify genetic disorders that can be treated early in life.

EXERCISES

Deconstruct the following medical terms into the meaning of each element, then answer the questions about the terms. Fill in the blanks.

Medical Term	Meaning of Prefix	Meaning of Root/CF	Meaning of Suffix
homozygous			
alpha-fetoprotein			
heterozygous			
buccal smear			

1. Which two terms are opposites?

_____ and _____

2. **Recall question:** What is a zygote?

_____

3. Use the term **buccal** in a sentence not related to genetics. (This term also appeared in an earlier chapter.)

_____

▲ **FIGURE 21.7   Down Syndrome (Trisomy 21).**

GENETIC DISORDERS

Changes in Chromosome Number

Down syndrome is most often associated with an extra (**trisomy**) copy of chromosome 21, and it is found in about 1 in 660 newborns (*Figure 21.7*). People with Down syndrome are usually short, have **hypotonia,** lax joints, and soft skin. Facial features include a prominent tongue, and obliquely positioned eyes. Almost half show a single crease (**simian crease**) across the palm of the hand. About 40% have congenital heart disease, often a ventricular or atrial septal defect (*see Chapter 8*). Mental retardation occurs in 100%, though many individuals with Down syndrome can learn basic skills and function with independence.

The most important risk factor for conceiving a child with Down syndrome is advanced maternal age. The incidence rises from an incidence of 1:1200 at maternal age 30, to 1:25 at age 45. Prenatal diagnosis uses a combination of ultrasound and the measurement of specific hormones and alpha-fetoprotein levels in maternal blood.

Variations in the number of sex chromosomes in women produce **Turner syndrome.** The most common **anomaly** is the absence of one X chromosome, producing the karyotype 45,XO. Their ovaries do not develop normally and do not produce adequate amounts of hormones. Treatment is to provide the hormones that are deficient.

In males, the presence of an extra X chromosome (45,XXY) produces **Klinefelter syndrome,** in which testicles are small, with few sperms developing. Treatment is with testosterone.

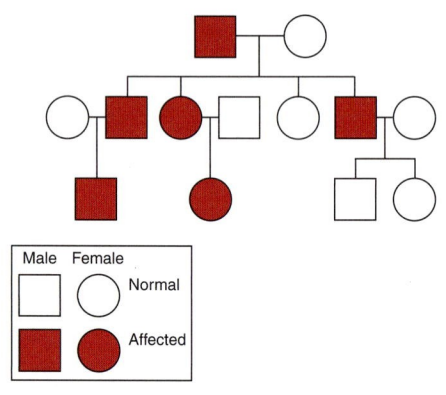

▲ **FIGURE 21.8   Autosomal Dominant Family Tree.**

Autosomal Dominant Conditions

In autosomal dominant inheritance, one autosome carries a gene that expresses a specific trait or characteristic. This person is called a heterozygote. The chance that an individual germ cell will contain the chromosome with the abnormal gene is 50%, and the chance for an affected individual to transmit the abnormal gene is 50% with each conception. Therefore, an average of 50% of the offspring of an affected individual will also be affected (*Figure 21.8*).

Autosomal dominant disorders include:

- **Neurofibromatosis**—neurofibromas arise from the Schwann cells that support nerve fibers (*see Chapter 10*), and "**café-au-lait**" (coffee with cream) macules appear on the skin.
- **Achondroplasia** (*see Chapter 16*)
- **Marfan syndrome**—excessive height due to growth of long bones, together with long fingers, and unstable joints.
- **Huntington disease**—a disorder of the **central nervous system (CNS),** appearing in the third and fourth decades of life with loss of motor control, personality changes, and decreased mental capacity (*see Chapter 10*).

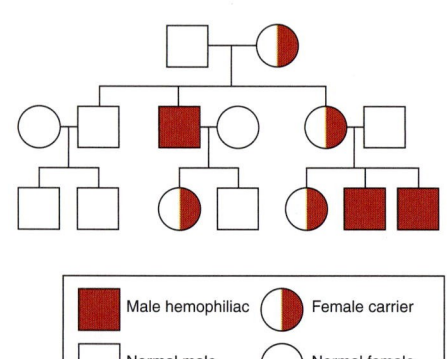

▲ **FIGURE 21.9   Family History of Hemophilia.**

Autosomal Recessive Disorders

Autosomal recessive disorders appear when there is a specific abnormality in a copy of a gene contributed by each parent. The unaffected parents are heterozygotes, and the affected offspring is a homozygote. Because each parent has only one abnormal copy of the gene, there is only a 25% likelihood of each pregnancy resulting in a homozygote.

Autosomal disorders include:

- **Sickle cell disease** (*see Chapter 7*)
- **Gaucher disease**—reflects malfunction in a specific enzyme pathway in protein metabolism. A reliable enzyme replacement therapy is now available.
- **Phenylketonuria**—an important cause of mental retardation and tested for in newborn screening. The basis of treatment is limiting the causative amino acid phenylalanine in the serum by limiting it in the diet.
- **Albinism**—a failure to produce melanin (*see Chapter 3*).

WORD	PRONUNCIATION	ELEMENTS		DEFINITION
albinism	**AL**-bih-nizm	S/	**-ism** *condition*	Genetic disorder with lack of melanin
		R/	**albin-** *white*	
albino	al-**BY**-no	R/CF	**albin/o-** *white*	Person with albinism
anomaly	ah-**NOM**-ah-lee		Greek *irregularity*	Structural abnormality present at birth
café-au-lait (adj)	**KAF**-ay-oh-**LAY**		**café** French *coffee*	Color of skin macules in neurofibromatosis
			au French *with*	
			lait French *milk*	
Down syndrome	DOWN **SIN**-drome		John Down, 1828–1896, English physician	A syndrome with variable abnormalities associated with three chromosomes 21
Huntington disease (also called **Huntington chorea**)	**HUN**-ting-ton diz-**EEZ**		George Huntington, 1851–1916, American neurologist	Progressive, inherited, degenerative, incurable neurologic disease
hypotonia	high-poh-**TOE**-nee-ah	S/	**-ia** *condition*	Diminished muscle tone
hypotonic (adj)	high-poh-**TON**-ik	P/	**hypo-** *below, deficient*	
		R/	**-ton-** *tone*	
Klinefelter syndrome	**KLINE**-fel-ter **SIN**-drome		Harry Klinefelter, Jr., born 1912, Boston physician	Genetic anomaly in males with XXY chromosomes
Marfan syndrome	mahr-**FAN SIN**-drome		Antoine Marfan, 1858–1942, French pediatrician	Genetic condition with malformation of elastic connective tissue
simian crease	sih-**ME**-an KREES	S/	**-an** *pertaining to*	Single crease across the palm of the hand; found in monkeys
		R/	**simi-** *ape, monkey*	
		R/	**crease** *groove*	
trisomy	**TRI**-so-me	P/	**tri-** *three*	Presence of an extra chromosome
		R/CF	**-som/y** *body*	
Turner syndrome	**TER**-ner **SIN**-drome		Henry H. Turner, 1892–1970, American endocrinologist	Syndrome associated with a chromosome count of 45 and only one X chromosome

X-linked disorder occurs when the altered gene is located on the X chromosome. Examples of this type of inheritance are: **Hemophilia A** *(Figure 21.9; see Chapter 7)*; **defective color vision** *(see Chapter 4)*; **Duchenne muscular dystrophy** *(see Chapter 5)*; **fragile-X syndrome,** the most common form of inherited mental retardation, affecting 1 in every 1,000 to 2,000 male individuals.

EXERCISES

Elements will always be your best clues to analyzing a medical term. Identify and give a definition for the element that is in bold in the following exercise.

Medical term	Type of element	Meaning of element
trisomy		
hypotonia		
albinism		
translocation		
simian		

GENETICS

CHALLENGE YOUR KNOWLEDGE

A. **Case Report:** Re-read the following case report from this chapter, and then answer the questions.

Your patients are

. . . Rebecca and Paul Holyfield, a married couple in their early thirties. They have one daughter, Sarah (aged 5), who is doing well. Last year, they lost a son, aged 2, with cystic fibrosis (CF). Rebecca is now eight weeks pregnant, and they want to know if the new baby can also have cystic fibrosis. They did not intend to have any more children.

When the Holyfield's son was diagnosed with cystic fibrosis, genetic testing showed that both parents carried the Mendelian autosomal recessive gene for CF and that their daughter Sarah was also a carrier, or heterozygote. The child who died inherited an abnormal gene from each parent and is called a homozygote. Chorionic villus testing in the current pregnancy showed a fetal girl who did not carry the gene.

1. Explain how chorionic villus testing is done.

   _____

   _____

   _____

2. What is the purpose of this type of testing?

   _____

   _____

   _____

3. Why is the child who died termed a *homozygote,* as opposed to his sister, who is referred to as a *heterozygote?*

   _____

   _____

   _____

4. What should the Holyfield's daughter Sarah consider when she gets married and wants to have a family?

   _____

   _____

   _____

B. **Elements:** To facilitate learning medical terminology, you need to be able to recognize a word element for what it is (prefix, root, combining form, or suffix,) as well as what it means. Test your knowledge by correctly filling in the following chart with a check mark (✓) in the proper element column. Then fill in the meaning of the element and a medical term containing that element.

Element	Prefix	Root/CF	Suffix	Meaning of Element	Medical Term Using That Element
aden	_____	_____	_____	_____	_____
albino	_____	_____	_____	_____	_____
alpha	_____	_____	_____	_____	_____
auto	_____	_____	_____	_____	_____
bucc	_____	_____	_____	_____	_____
chromo	_____	_____	_____	_____	_____
cyst	_____	_____	_____	_____	_____
cyto	_____	_____	_____	_____	_____
de	_____	_____	_____	_____	_____

C. **Abbreviations must be interpreted correctly for safety in communication.** Match the correct abbreviation from the *language of genetics* to its characteristic. Fill in the blanks.

_____ 1. travels from nucleus to ribosome

_____ 2. genetic mutation responsible for breast CA

_____ 3. has uracil instead of thymine

_____ 4. exists as two paired strands in a double helix

_____ 5. not an option for Sharon Fisher

_____ 6. genetic mutation responsible for breast and ovarian CA

_____ 7. protein normally produced only by the fetus

_____ 8. can be detected in utero

A. BRCA 1

B. AFP

C. DNA

D. mRNA

E. CF

F. BRCA2

G. RNA

H. HRT

D. **Terminology Challenge:** Medical terms can have more than one meaning, as you have seen throughout this text. The term **vector** in genetics has a different meaning than the term **vector** in infectious diseases. Compare the two terms. How are they similar, and how are they different?

Vector in genetics means: _____

_____

Vector in infectious diseases means: _____

_____

The terms are similar because: _____

The terms are different because: _____

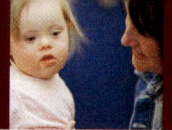
GENETICS

E. **Lesson Objectives:** Each of the following is a lesson objective from Chapter 21. In your own words, provide a short answer to the question. If you are able to illustrate this with a line drawing, or photo downloaded from the Internet, so much the better.

1. Can you describe the structure of a chromosome?

    _____

    _____

    _____

    _____

    _____

2. What are the structure and functions of a gene?

    _____

    _____

    _____

    _____

    _____

F. **Elements:** Continue working with word elements to refine your knowledge of the *language of genetics.*

Element	Prefix	Root/CF	Suffix	Meaning of Element	Medical Term Using that Element
en	_____	_____	_____	_____	_____
feto	_____	_____	_____	_____	_____
gen	_____	_____	_____	_____	_____
hetero	_____	_____	_____	_____	_____
homo	_____	_____	_____	_____	_____
hypo	_____	_____	_____	_____	_____
ia	_____	_____	_____	_____	_____
ine	_____	_____	_____	_____	_____
ism	_____	_____	_____	_____	_____
karyo	_____	_____	_____	_____	_____

G. **Pathology:** The science of genetics has discovered gene mutations that account for very specific hereditary diseases. Finding the cause of a disease can eventually lead to discovering how to cure it. Use the *language of genetics* to answer the following questions. Some questions may only require a "yes" or "no" answer. Fill in the blanks.

1. Are some ethnic groups more prone to certain diseases? _____

2. If you carry a gene mutation, are there any symptoms? _____

3. If both parents carry the same mutated gene, does that increase their chances of having a child born with a hereditary disease? _____

4. *BRCA1* and *BRCA2* are alterations in which type of cancer gene? _____

5. Which hereditary disease is a fatal lipid storage disease? _____

6. What is the treatment for this disease? _____

7. Which hereditary disease is caused by an enzyme deficiency? _____

8. What is the treatment for this disease? _____

9. Which disease produces severe sensory and autonomic dysfunctions? _____

H. The *language of genetics* **will help you understand human development.** Use this terminology to provide the answers to the following questions. Circle the correct choice.

1. What factors affect human development?

   a. dietary and hereditary

   b. genetic and environmental

   c. environmental and dietary

   d. genetic and dietary

   e. none of these

2. What is the only type of body cell where DNA does not exist?

   a. WBCs

   b. leukocyte

   c. osteoblasts

   d. mature RBCs

   e. neutrophils

3. A cell's repair ability is affected by:

   a. age

   b. environmental stress

   c. radiation

   d. chemotherapy

   e. all of these

4. The location of a particular gene is called its:

   a. vector

   b. allele

   c. phenotype

   d. locus

   e. mutation

GENETICS

I. The *language of genetics* will help you understand human development. Use this terminology to provide the answers to the following questions. Circle the correct choice.

1. Another name for your genetic composition is:

   a. phenotype

   b. meiosis

   c. genome

   d. autosome

   e. alleles

2. Hereditary mutations are also called:

   a. somatic mutations

   b. homozygous mutations

   c. inherited mutations

   d. statistical mutations

   e. vector mutations

3. Produce different forms of a particular trait:

   a. gamete

   b. chromosome

   c. gene

   d. ribosome

   e. allele

4. Genetic information is carried in:

   a. adenine

   b. thymine

   c. cytosine

   d. guanine

   e. all of these

5. Messenger RNA travels from the nucleus to:

   a. the bloodstream

   b. the heart

   c. an organelle

   d. a target organ

   e. another nucleus

6. A mutated gene has an abnormally encoded:

   a. nucleus

   b. protein

   c. phenotype

   d. trait

   e. locus

7. Somatic mutations are:

   a. acquired

   b. random

   c. heterozygous

   d. enzyme related

   e. cytogenetic

8. Tightly coiled strands of DNA are packaged in units called:

   a. genes

   b. phenotypes

   c. bases

   d. chromosomes

   e. guanine

9. Delivers the therapeutic gene to the target cell:

   a. vector

   b. karyotype

   c. phenotype

   d. trait

   e. base

10. Adenine, thymine, cytosine, and guanine are:

    a. amino acids

    b. enzymes

    c. vitamins

    d. chemical bases of DNA

    e. hormones

11. *BRCA1* and *BRCA2* mutations can be passed on to men and cause:

   a. colon cancer

   b. breast cancer

   c. prostate cancer

   d. a and c

   e. b and c

J. **Recall and Review:** How well do you remember these word elements from the previous chapter? Try to answer without first looking back to check. Fill in the blanks.

Element	Type of Element (P, R, CF, S)	Meaning of Element
con		
patho		
enter		
micro		
onco		

K. **Discussion Question:** Think about what it was like before genetic counseling was available. No information and, consequently, no choices were available for certain patients. How does genetic counseling enable patients to make an informed choice and be proactive in their health care? Demonstrate your answer by using two examples of circumstances in which genetic counseling can make a difference. Write your thoughts on the lines below, and be prepared to share them with the class.

_____

_____

_____

_____

_____

_____

_____

_____

_____

_____

_____

_____

GENETICS

L. **Latin and Greek terms cannot be further deconstructed into prefix, root, or suffix.** You must know them for what they are. Test your knowledge of these terms with the following exercise. Match the meaning in column 1 with the correct medical term in column 2.

_____	1. withdraw	A.	helix
_____	2. to change	B.	recessive
_____	3. born with	C.	vector
_____	4. a carrier	D.	heredity
_____	5. transferred from generation to generation	E.	mutation
_____	6. a coil	F.	congenital

M. **Patient Education:** You have been doing a clinical rotation in the OB (obstetrics) Clinic. Explain to your patient, in layman's terms, the difference between a congenital and a hereditary disease. Provide an example of each disease.

1. Congenital disease:

    _____

    _____

    _____

    _____

2. Hereditary disease:

    _____

    _____

    _____

    _____

N. **Research Question:** Use your school library or the Internet to do research on the concept of genomics. Prepare a one page, double-spaced paper with your summary, and be prepared to discuss in class. Remember to also search for articles in recent health magazines or the health section of your newspaper.

Answer questions such as:

1. What is the concept of genomics?
2. How is this different from previous thinking about this subject?
3. What type of medical research is being done for this?
4. Who is providing grants for research?
5. What have they discovered so far?
6. How will this research help human development?

O. **Elements:** Finish your review work with the word elements from Chapter 21. Use these charts for study review. Fill in the chart.

Element	Prefix	Root/CF	Suffix	Meaning of Element	Medical Term Using That Element
hypo					
karyo					
ome					
ous					
some					
ton					
trans					
tri					
urac					
zygus					

P. **Translation:** Use your knowledge of medical terms to read and understand the following statements, then provide a brief answer to the question that follows.

"Hereditary traits can be dominant or recessive. If they are not hereditary, they can also be acquired."

In your own words, exactly what information does this communicate?

_____

_____

_____

_____

GENETICS

CHAPTER SUMMARY EXERCISE

1. *Listen to the pronunciation of the medical terms as given by your instructor.*
2. *Circle the correct spelling of the medical term.*
3. *Match the correctly spelled terms to the brief descriptions below.*
4. *Write a sentence for each of the 15 terms that appear in this exercise.*

A. SPELLING COMPREHENSION: CIRCLE THE CORRECT SPELLING OF THE TERM.

1. karytype	keriotype	karyotype	cariotype	carriotipe
2. helix	hellix	heelix	hellex	helick
3. myosis	miosis	meiosis	myoses	mieosis
4. toxsin	toxin	toxsen	toxxin	toxen
5. homozygous	hommozigous	homozigous	hommozygous	homosigous
6. fenotype	penotype	phenyltype	phenotype	feenotype
7. urecell	uracil	uracell	urecil	uresell
8. congenial	congenital	congintial	congential	congeenial
9. Gaucher	Goucher	Gucher	Gowcher	Goucer
10. heridity	hereditty	herredity	heredity	herridity
11. alele	allele	aleele	alelle	alelie
12. autosome	autosum	autosume	autisum	autossum
13. gammete	gamite	gamete	gammite	gamette
14. geniticest	genetcist	geneticist	genitecest	genetecist
15. chromosone	cronosome	crohmosome	cromosome	chromosome

B. MATCH THE NUMBER OF THE CORRECT TERM IN PART A WITH THE BRIEF DESCRIPTION OF THE TERM BELOW.

a. existing at or from birth   _____

b. any chromosome other than a sex chromosome   _____

c. a line in the shape of a coil   _____

d. contained in RNA   _____

e. carries DNA sequences   _____

f. congenital disorder of fat metabolism   _____

g. poison; harmful substance   _____

h. similarities and uniqueness from generation to generation _____

  i. having identical alleles at one gene locus _____

  j. chart of chromosomes _____

  k. detectable trait _____

  l. germ cell _____

m. one of different genes on the same locus _____

n. transfer of genetic information from egg and sperm _____

  o. medical specialist in genetics _____

C. USING YOUR KNOWLEDGE OF TERMS 1-15 IN PART A AND THEIR CORRECT SPELLING, WRITE A BRIEF SENTENCE FOR EACH OF THE TERMS AS IT MIGHT APPEAR IN PATIENT DOCUMENTATION.

1. _____

2. _____

3. _____

4. _____

5. _____

6. _____

7. _____

8. _____

9. _____

10. _____

11. _____

12. _____

13. _____

14. _____

15. _____

D. GO TO THE STUDENT CD. OPEN THE GLOSSARY AND PRACTICE YOUR PRONUNCIATION OF THE TERMS IN PART A OF THIS EXERCISE

Cancer

The Language of Oncology

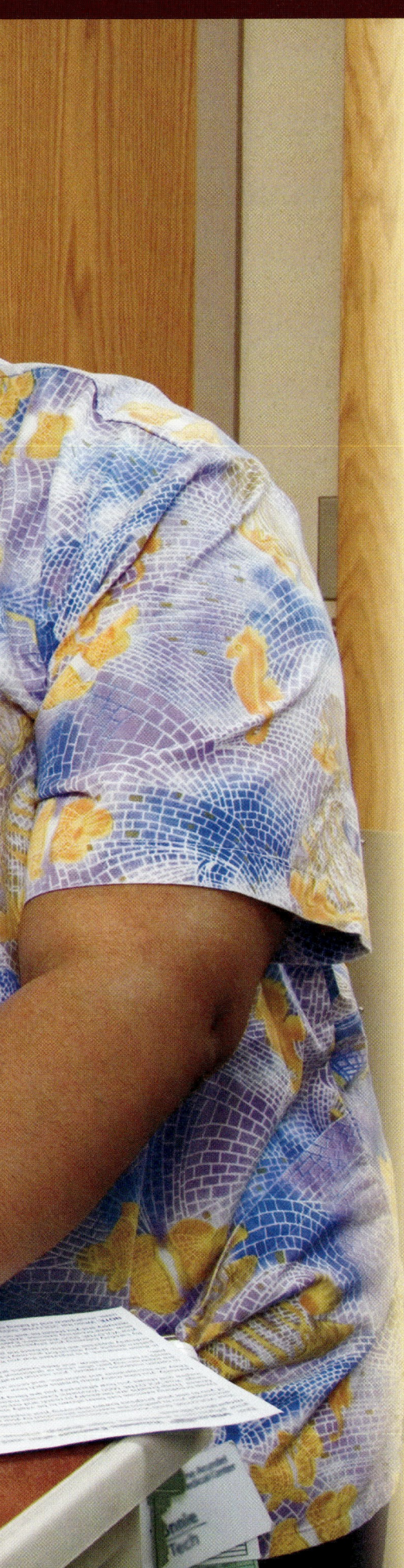

CASE REPORT 22.1

You are

. . . an advanced level respiratory therapist employed by Fulwood Medical Center, working with Tavis Senko, MD, a pulmonologist.

Your patient is

. . . Mrs. Raquel Sacco, a 44-year-old mother of two teenage boys, who is the owner of a quilting fabrics store. She is two days postop from a lobectomy for non–small cell lung cancer. From her records, you see that she has two secondary (2°) metastases in her brain. She has been a non-smoker all her life. Her 70-year-old father is a two-pack-a-day smoker, as is her husband. They both show no evidence of cancer on chest x-rays. Before Mrs. Sacco is discharged, as part of her postoperative respiratory care plan, you are using incentive spirometry—also called **sustained maximal inspiration (SMI)**—to increase her inspiratory volume and improve her inspiratory muscle performance. You will also be taking an arterial blood sample to check her **arterial oxygen pressure (PaO$_2$)**.

Learning Outcomes

In order to understand the possible etiologies of cancer, its pathology and staging, its treatment and prognosis, and to communicate among the health care team as you care for Mrs. Sacco, you will need to be able to:

- Apply the language of oncology to the anatomy and physiology of cancer.

- Comprehend, analyze, spell, and write the medical terms of oncology so that you communicate and document accurately and precisely in any health care setting.

- Recognize and pronounce the medical terms of oncology so that you communicate verbally with accuracy and precision in any health care setting.

- Explain the pathophysiology, diagnosis, and therapies of common types of cancer.

Note: In previous chapters on individual body systems, the terminology of cancers specific to each body system has been detailed. In this chapter, the terminology that relates to cancer in general will be explored using lung cancer as an example.

LESSON 22.1 Types of Cancer

OBJECTIVES

Normal tissue development is a balance between cell growth and cell death. If cells multiply quicker than cells die, tumors (**neoplasms**) are formed. The study of tumors is called **oncology,** and medical specialists in this field are called **oncologists.**

Neoplasms whose cells **proliferate** rapidly and spread to distant sites (**metastasize**) are called **malignant.** Neoplasms that grow slowly, stay localized, do not invade surrounding tissues, and do not metastasize are called **benign.**

The information in this lesson will enable you to:

- **Distinguish between benign and malignant neoplasms.**
- **Classify the types of cancer by the type of cell from which it originates.**
- **Explain the process of carcinogenesis.**
- **Discuss the roles of environmental factors in carcinogenesis.**

TYPES OF CANCER

Cancer (CA) is a class of malignant diseases characterized by uncontrolled cell division. The basic cause of this uncontrolled growth is damage to the cells' DNA. This damage produces mutations to the genes that control cell division. These mutations, which can be inherited or acquired, lead to the uncontrolled cell division and malignant tumor formation.

Thus all cancer is genetic; that is, it develops because something in a cell's genes has changed (mutated). Less than 10% of all cancers are inherited; that is, the genetic change is passed from parent to child. Almost 90% of cancers are acquired—something has caused the gene mutation in specific cells in a particular individual. In cancer, a few genes mutated within a cell nucleus are enough to cause cancer. These gene mutations give the cells a superpower to proliferate in an uncontrolled way.

The Cells of Malignant Tumors

- have unlimited, unregulated growth potential
- grow directly into adjacent tissues (invasion or **infiltration**)
- invade the lymphatic system and are carried to local and distant lymph nodes (*Figure 22.1*)
- invade the blood stream and are carried to other distant organs and tissues (**metastasis;** *Figure 22.1*)

In contrast, benign tumors do not show such unregulated, invasive growth.

The Cells of Benign Tumors

- grow slowly
- are surrounded by a connective tissue capsule
- do not invade or infiltrate adjacent tissues
- do not spread to other organs (metastasize) or to lymph nodes
- can compress surrounding tissues, causing functional problems

In the United States, the three most common causes of death are:

- cardiovascular disease (28.5% of all deaths)
- cancer (22.8% of all deaths)
- cerebrovascular disease, primarily stroke (6.7% of all deaths)

Table 22.1 shows the leading causes of cancer death in the USA, with lung cancer by far the most common.

Environmental factors, particularly cigarette smoke, are associated with many forms of cancer. In this chapter, we will use a case of lung cancer to illustrate the characteristics of an acquired cancer and to discuss methods of detection and treatment.

Abbreviations

CA	cancer
PaO₂	partial pressure of arterial oxygen
2°	secondary
SMI	sustained maximal inspiration

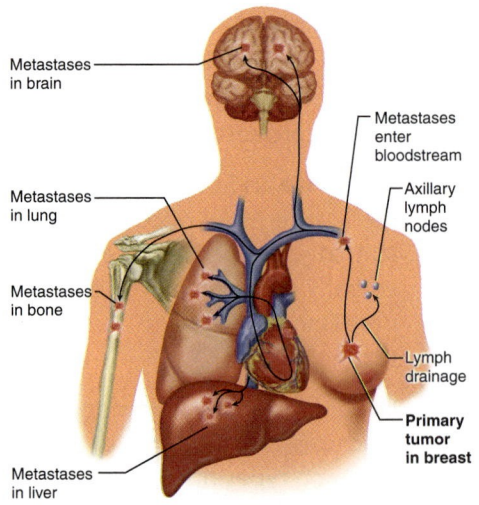

▲ **FIGURE 22.1 Metastases from Primary Breast Cancer.**
Metastasis may be via lymph drainage to the axillary lymph nodes or via the bloodstream to the brain, lung, liver, and bone.

WORD	PRONUNCIATION		ELEMENTS	DEFINITION
benign	bee-**NINE**		Latin *kind*	The nonmalignant character of a neoplasm or illness
cancer	**KAN**-ser		Latin *crab*	General term for a malignant neoplasm
cancerous	**KAN**-ser-ous	S/ R/	-ous *pertaining to* cancer- *cancer*	Pertaining to a malignant neoplasm
infiltrate	**IN**-fil-trate	S/ P/ R/	-ate *action* in- *in* -filtr- *strain through*	To penetrate and invade into a tissue or cell
infiltration	in-fil-**TRAY**-shun	S/	-ation *process*	The invasion into a tissue or cell
malignant (adj)	mah-**LIG**-nant		Latin *hurtful*	Tumor that invades surrounding tissues and metastasizes to distant organs
malignancy (noun)	mah-**LIG**-nan-see	S/ R/	-ancy *state of* malign- *cancer*	Able to be malignant
metastasis (noun)	meh-**TAS**-tah-sis	P/ R/	meta- *after, transition* -stasis *to stand*	Spread of disease from one part of the body to another
metastatic (adj)	met-ah-**STAT**-ik	S/	-ic *pertaining to*	Able to metastasize
metastases (pl)	meh-**TAS**-tah-sez	R/	-stat- *standing still*	
neoplasm (noun)	**NEE**-oh-plazm	P/ R/	neo- *new* -plasm- *growth, thing formed*	A new growth, either a benign or malignant tumor
neoplastic (adj) neoplasia (*Note:* The "m" in -plasm is removed to allow the elements to flow.)	**NEE**-oh-**PLAS**-tic **NEE**-oh-**PLAY**-zee-ah	S/ S/	-tic *pertaining to* -ia *condition*	Pertaining to a neoplasm Process that results in formation of a tumor
oncology	on-**KOL**-oh-jee	S/ R/CF	-logy *study of* onc/o- *tumor*	The science dealing with cancer
oncologist	on-**KOL**-oh-jist	S/	-logist *one who studies*	Medical specialist in oncology
proliferate	pro-**LIF**-eh-rate	S/ R/CF R/	-ate *action* prol/i- *offspring* -fer- *to bear*	To increase in number through reproduction
tumor	**TOO**-mor		Latin *swelling*	Any abnormal swelling

TABLE 22.1 Leading Causes of Cancer Death in the United States

Cause	Percent of Total Cancer Cases	Numbers per Year
lung	30.9%	154,900
colon	9.6%	48,100
breast	8.0%	40,000
prostate	6.0%	30,200

From National Vital Statistics Report, October 2004.

EXERCISES

Demonstrate that you can use various forms of the same term in correct usage. Insert the appropriate medical term in the following blanks.

neoplasm   **neoplastic**   **neoplasia**

1. _____ is a process that results in the formation of a tumor, which can be either malignant or benign.

2. Another name for a tumor is a _____ .

3. The tumor exhibited _____ behavior and was immediately biopsied.

metastases   **metastatic**   **metastasis**

4. A _____ carcinoma is cancer that has spread to a different site than the primary tumor.

5. The patient has _____ in his brain and kidneys.

6. Finding a primary tumor before _____ has occurred increases the chances for a cure.

TYPES OF CANCER (continued)

Within the broad classes of cancer *(Table 22.2)* are many subgroups, depending on the type of cells in the cancer. The term **carcinoma in situ (CIS)** describes an early form of carcinoma in which there is no invasion of surrounding tissues. In many instances, it is a precursor that will transform into an invasive or malignant cancer.

TABLE 22.2 Types of Cancer

Class of Cancer	Cells of Origin	Examples
Carcinoma	epithelial	cervical cancer, stomach cancer, squamous cell skin cancer, lung cancer
Sarcoma	connective tissue, bone cartilage, muscle	**osteosarcoma, chondrosarcoma, rhabdomyosarcoma**
Leukemia	blood-forming tissues	acute lymphocytic leukemia, chronic myelogenous leukemia
Lymphoma	lymph nodes	Hodgkin disease, non-Hodgkin lymphoma
Melanoma	melanocytes (pigment-producing skin cells)	malignant melanoma

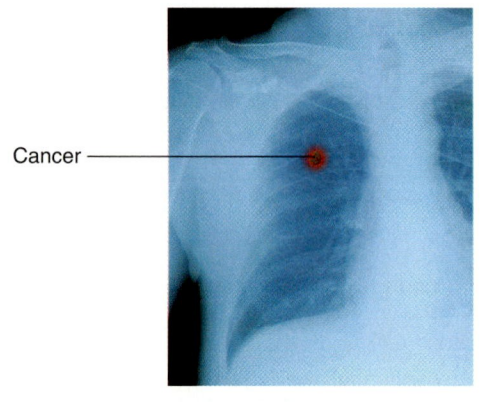

Cancer ————

▲ **FIGURE 22.2 Small-Cell Cancer of Right Upper Lung.**

Abbreviations

CIS	carcinoma in situ
1°	primary

Lung cancer has three main subgroups:

1. **Non–small cell lung cancer**—accounts for 75% of cases, and 80% die within five years of diagnosis. Included in this type are:

   a. **squamous cell carcinoma,** arising from *round cells* that have replaced damaged cells in the epithelial lining cells of a major bronchus. They account for 25 to 40% of lung cancers.

   b. **adenocarcinoma,** arising from the *mucus-producing cells* in the bronchi and accounting for between 30 and 50% of lung cancers. It is the most common lung cancer in women, and its incidence is increasing.

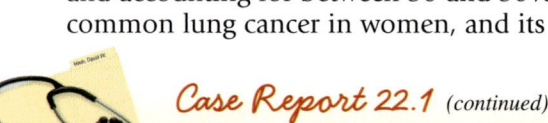

Case Report 22.1 (continued)

Adenocarcinoma was found in Raquel Sacco. It was diagnosed because she had a seizure, and neurological tests revealed the presence of two metastases in her brain, leading to a search for the primary (1°) tumor that was found in her lung (Figure 22.2).

   c. **large cell carcinoma** includes cancers that cannot be identified under the microscope as squamous cell or adenocarcinomas. It accounts for 10 to 20% of lung cancers.

2. **Small cell lung cancer**—like squamous cell carcinoma, this is derived from the epithelial cells of the bronchi but replicates at a faster rate, producing smaller cells. It accounts for 15 to 25% of all lung cancers; most patients die within 18 months of diagnosis.

3. **Mesothelioma**—a rare tumor of the cells lining the pleura that is associated with **asbestosis** and accounts for 5% of lung cancers.

WORD ANALYSIS AND DEFINITION

S = Suffix   P = Prefix   R = Root   R/CF = Combining Form

WORD	PRONUNCIATION	ELEMENTS		DEFINITION
adenocarcinoma	**AD**-eh-noh-kar-sih-**NOH**-mah	S/ R/CF R/	-oma *tumor* aden/o- *gland* -carcin- *cancer*	A cancer arising from glandular epithelial cells
asbestosis	as-bes-**TOE**-sis	S/ R/	-osis *condition* asbest- *asbestos*	Lung disease caused by the inhalation of asbestos particles
carcinoma	kar-sih-**NOH**-mah	S/ R/	-oma *tumor* carcin- *cancer*	A malignant and invasive epithelial tumor
carcinoma in situ (CIS)	kar-sih-**NOH**-mah in **SIGH**-too		in situ *Latin in its place*	Carcinoma that has not invaded surrounding tissues
chondrosarcoma	**KON**-dro-sar-**KOH**-mah	S/ R/CF R/	-oma *tumor* chondr/o- *cartilage* -sarc- *flesh*	Cancer arising from cartilage cells
mesothelioma	**MEZ**-oh-thee-lee-**OH**-mah	S/ P/ R/	-oma *tumor* meso- *middle* -theli- *epithelium*	Cancer arising from the cells lining the pleura or peritoneum
osteosarcoma	**OS**-tee-oh-sar-**KOH**-mah	S/ R/CF R/	-oma *tumor* oste/o- *bone* -sarc- *flesh*	Cancer arising in bone-forming cells
rhabdomyosarcoma	**RAB**-doh-**MY**-oh-sar-**KOH**-mah	S/ R/CF R/CF R/	-oma *tumor* rhabd/o- *rod-shaped* -my/o- *muscle* -sarc- *flesh*	Cancer derived from skeletal muscle
sarcoma	sar-**KOH**-mah	S/ R/	-oma *tumor* sarc- *flesh*	A malignant tumor originating in connective tissue

EXERCISES

Deconstruct the following **language of oncology** *into elements. These elements will form the basis for many additional oncologic terms. Fill in the table.*

Medical Term	Meaning of Prefix	Meaning of Root/ CF	Meaning of Suffix	Meaning of Medical Term
sarcoma				
adenocarcinoma				
chondrosarcoma				
osteosarcoma				
mesothelioma				
rhabdomyosarcoma				

Which of the following best describes *all* of the terms in the table above?

a. they are all malignant tumors

b. they are all cancerous neoplasms

c. they are all invasive

d. a, b, and c

e. only a and b

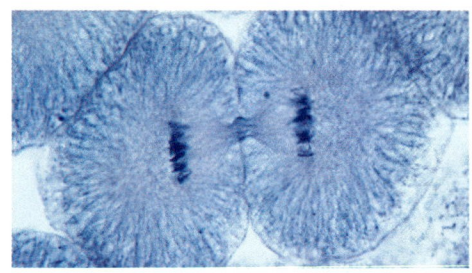

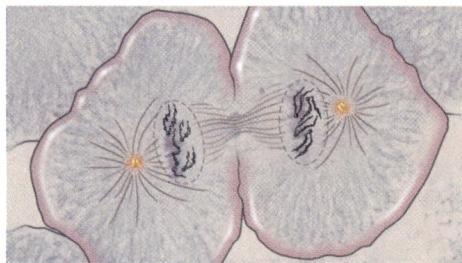

▲ **FIGURE 22.3 End Stage of Mitosis.**
For simplicity, the schematic drawing of the cell (*bottom*) is shown with only two chromosome pairs.

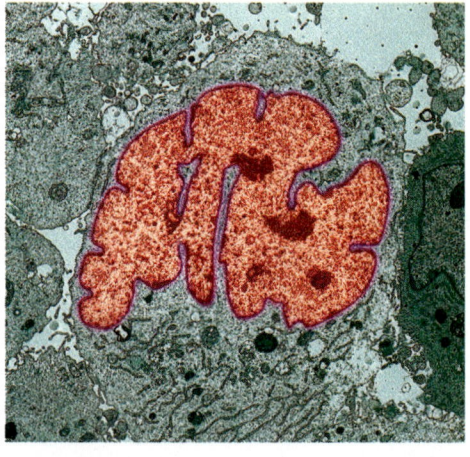

▲ **FIGURE 22.4 Cancer Cell Nucleus with Gene Mutations.**

Abbreviations

ETS	environmental tobacco smoke
PCD	programmed cell death
TS	tumor suppressor

Keynote

A pack-year equals the number of packs of cigarettes smoked per day multiplied by the number of years the person has smoked.

CARCINOGENESIS

Carcinogenesis, literally the creation of cancer, is the abnormal rate of cell division as a result of damaged DNA causing gene mutation. Normally, the balance between cell division and proliferation and cell death (**apoptosis,** or **programmed cell death [PCD]**) is tightly controlled to maintain the integrity of organs and tissues. Gene mutations that cause cancer disrupt this orderly process. Mutation in a single gene is usually not enough to cause cancer, and carcinogenesis requires multiple mutations in many genes.

Most normal cells cannot divide unless a **growth factor** binds to a receptor on its surface. This growth factor then stimulates the cell to undergo mitosis (*see Chapter 2*) and **differentiate** into mature, functional cells (*Figure 22.3*).

Two types of genes have been identified that play a part in the abnormal cell division and proliferation of cancer cells:

1. **Protooncogenes** are healthy genes that promote normal cell growth. Mutated **oncogenes** cause malfunctions in the normal growth mechanisms. For example, an oncogene called *SIS* stimulates blood vessels to grow into a tumor and provide the rich blood supply it needs to proliferate rapidly. An oncogene called *RAS* generates abnormal growth-factor receptors that switch on constant cell division signals. An oncogene called *HER-2* causes many cases of breast and ovarian cancer. The drug Herceptin is an antibody that targets the HER-2 receptors on the cancer cells. This cuts off the chemical signals that the cell needs to keep proliferating. It also marks the abnormal cells for destruction by the immune system.

2. **Tumor suppressor (TS) genes** normally suppress mitosis and are activated by DNA damage. Their function is to stop cell division so that the abnormal genetic structure cannot be passed on to daughter cells. **Mutated TS genes** cannot do this, so the abnormal cells can divide and proliferate. A mutated TS gene called *p53* is present in half of all cancers and is associated with a poor prognosis and resistance to chemotherapy.

Mutations in both types of genes are usually required for cancer to develop. The oncogenes turn on the abnormal cell growth, and the mutated TS genes cannot stop it (*Figure 22.4*).

Cancer is due to the accumulation of genetic injury and mutations. Agents that cause these mutations are called **mutagens,** and mutagens that cause cancer are called **carcinogens.** Particular carcinogens are linked to specific types of cancer. Examples are inhalation of asbestos fibers with mesothelioma, prolonged exposure to radiation and ultraviolet radiation with melanoma and other skin malignancies, and tobacco smoking with lung cancer. Although the link between cigarette smoking and lung cancer is well established, only 15 to 20% of smokers develop lung cancer. In addition, about 10% of the population carries a gene that protects against lung cancer.

Studies in 2004 and 2005 of the epithelial cells in the large bronchi found a large number of genes altered by cigarette smoking. The studies defined genes whose alteration correlated with cumulative pack-years of smoking and identified 13 genes whose alterations do not return to normal after smoking is stopped. This could explain the persistent risk of lung cancer in former smokers. In addition, a subset of smokers was identified whose gene alterations have a different profile to other smokers. It is possible that this subset is the group who develop lung cancer.

Second-hand smoke, called **environmental tobacco smoke (ETS),** contains the same chemicals and carcinogens as those inhaled by smokers. It is responsible for 3,000 lung cancer cases each year in America. The genetic mutations caused by the carcinogens are probably similar to the subset of smokers discussed above, even though the exposure to the carcinogens is much less than that for smokers.

Case Report 22.1 (continued)

Raquel Sacco probably developed her lung cancer as a result of inhaling secondhand smoke all her life (from her father and husband).

WORD	PRONUNCIATION	ELEMENTS		DEFINITION
apoptosis (**Note:** The second "p" is silent.)	AP-oh-**toe**-sis	P/ R/	**apo-** *from* **-ptosis** *falling*	Programmed normal cell death
carcinogen carcinogenic (adj) carcinogenesis	kar-**SIN**-oh-jen kar-**SIN**-oh-**JEN**-ik kar-**SIN**-oh-**JEN**-eh-sis	S/ R/CF S/	**-gen** *producing* **carcin/o-** *cancer* **-genesis** *source*	Cancer-producing agent Origin and development of cancer
mutagen	**MYU**-tah-jen	S/ R/	**-gen** *producing* **muta-** *change*	Agent that produces a mutation in a gene
oncogene oncogenic (adj)	**ONG**-koh-jeen **ONG**-koh-**JEN**-ik	S/ R/CF	**-gene** *producer, give birth* **onc/o-** *tumor*	One of a family of genes involved in cell growth that work in concert to cause cancer Capable of producing a neoplasm
protooncogene	pro-toe-**ON**-koh-jeen	S/ P/ R/CF	**-gene** *producer, give birth* **proto-** *first* **-onc/o-** *tumor*	A normal gene involved in normal cell growth

No patient with a cancer of any type passes through a hospital without it being recorded by the Tumor Registry. This enables cancer statistics to be maintained at a local level to facilitate such decisions as buying expensive equipment needed for treating certain types of cancer. The statistics are also fed into the national database.

> **Study Hint**
> **Ptosis** is a medical term in its own right. Another example is the term **hemolysis**, in which **lysis** is also a medical term in and of itself.

EXERCISES

*Build your knowledge of elements with this exercise in the **language of oncology**. The element is given to you in column 1, fill in the meaning of the element in column 2, and identify the type of element (prefix, root, combining form, or suffix) in column 3. The first one is done for you. Then, combine the correct elements to form one medical term from this WAD, and write a definition for that term on the following lines.*

Element	Meaning of Element	Type of Element (P, R, CF, S)
proto	*first*	P
apo		
muta		
genesis		
gen		
onco		
carcino		
ptosis		
gene		

1. Term: _____

2. Definition: _____

▲ **FIGURE 22.5 Woman Smoking.**

▲ **FIGURE 22.6 Air Pollution Over a Large City.**

▲ **FIGURE 22.7 Pesticide Spraying of Field of Vegetables.**

▲ **FIGURE 22.8 No Smoking Sign.**

ENVIRONMENTAL POLLUTION

Pollution is a trigger of many cancers. For example, cigarette smoke *(Figure 22.5)* causes 87% of all lung cancers and acts in the following ways:

- In the smoke are approximately 4,000 chemicals, some 60 of which are known to be carcinogenic and trigger genetic mutations that lead to cancer. Among the inhaled chemicals are cyanide, benzene, formaldehyde, acetylene, tar, arsenic, and ammonia, all of which can increase the risk for cancer.

- Inhaled nicotine was shown in one study to be converted into **aminoketone,** which has been linked to the development of lung cancer. Another study reports that inhaled nicotine triggers new blood vessel growth, which could promote growth of existing tumors.

Radon, a radioactive gas that you cannot see or smell, is the second leading cause of lung cancer (after smoking). It is produced by decaying **uranium** and is found in nearly all soils. In underground miners, it increases the risk of cancer to 40%. It gets into homes through cracks in the foundations or construction joints and is a problem in 1 out of 15 homes. Cigarette smoking on top of radon significantly increases the risk of lung cancer. Testing for radon is cheap and easy.

Air pollution may be the cause of the 10 to 40% increase in lung cancer mortality between urban and rural areas *(Figure 22.6)*. **Particulate matter,** especially very small particles, includes soot, organic material such as hydrocarbons, and metals such as arsenic, chromium, and nickel—all of which are known mutagens and carcinogens. It is not known whether a single carcinogen or the multiplicity of carcinogenic insults is responsible for lung cancer in city dwellers.

Chemical toxins are estimated to cause more than 75% of all cancers. Some 77,000 chemicals are used in this country. Over 3,000 are added to our food, and most Americans have between 400 and 800 chemicals stored in their bodies, mostly in fat cells. The toxins known to cause cancer include:

- **PCBs (polychlorinated biphenyls)**—These were banned years ago but still persist in the environment and are found in farmed salmon.

- **Pesticides**—According to the **Environmental Protection Agency (EPA),** 60% of herbicides, 90% of fungicides, and 30% of insecticides are known to be carcinogenic *(Figure 22.7)*. Farmers using pesticides have a 14% greater risk for developing prostate cancer than do organic farmers.

- **Dioxins**—chemical compounds produced by combustion processes from waste incineration and from burning fuels like wood, coal, and oil.

- **Asbestos**—an insulating material used in the 1950s to 1970s on floors, ceilings, water pipes, and heating ducts. When the material becomes old and crumbly, it releases fibers into the air. Inhalation of the fibers is the cause of mesothelioma.

- **Arsenic**—used by insecticide and herbicide sprayers and oil refinery workers.

Occupational Safety and Health Administration **(OSHA)** regulations are designed to protect workers from these environmental hazards.

Prevention of Cancer

More than 50% of cancers could be prevented by **changes in lifestyle and environment.** The same carcinogens that affect the lining of the respiratory tract cause cancer of the oral cavity, pharynx, larynx, and esophagus. They are also absorbed into the bloodstream and disseminated, thereby becoming factors that can cause cancer in the pancreas, stomach, kidney, bladder, prostate, and cervix. **Stopping smoking** alone would reduce the 30% of all cancer deaths due to lung cancer and reduce the incidence of many of the other cancers related to smoking *(Figure 22.8)*.

Clean air measures that are being implemented to reduce the more than 2 billion pounds of toxic air pollutants emitted into the atmosphere annually in this country can reduce the incidence of cancer.

Obesity is said to be linked to about 10% of breast and colorectal cancers and up to 40% of kidney, esophageal, and endometrial cancers. The mechanisms of obesity being linked to these cancers are not understood.

WORD	PRONUNCIATION	ELEMENTS		DEFINITION
aminoketone	ah-**ME**-no-**KEY**-tone	R/CF R/	amin/o- *from ammonia* -ketone *organic* *compound*	Byproduct of nicotine
dioxin	die-**OK**-sin	P/ R/	di- *two* -oxin *oxygen*	Carcinogenic contaminant in pesticides
environment environmental (adj)	en-**VI**-ron-ment en-**VI**-ron-ment-al	S/ R/ S/	-ment *resulting state* environ- *surroundings* -al *pertaining to*	All the external conditions affecting the life of an organism Pertaining to the environment
flavonoid	**FLAY**-vih-noid	S/ R/	-oid *resembling* flavin- *yellow*	A pigment found in fruit, wine, and tea
genistein	**JEN**-is-tine	R/CF R/	gen/i- *producing* -stein *stone*	Flavonoid found in soy
particle particulate (adj)	**PAR**-tih-kul par-**TIK**-you-late	 S/ R/	Latin *little piece* -ate *action* particul- *little piece*	A small piece of matter Relating to a fine particle
pesticide	**PES**-tih-side	S/ R/CF	-cide *to kill* pest/i- *nuisance*	Agent for destroying flies, mosquitoes, and other pests
phytochemical	fie-toe-**KEM**-ih-kal	S/ R/ R/CF	-al *pertaining to* -chemic- *chemistry* phyt/o- *plant*	Biologically active, nonnutrient plant chemical
pollution	poh-**LOO**-shun		Latin *dirty*	Condition that is unclean, impure, and a danger to health
uranium	you-**RAY**-nee-um		Greek mythological character, Uranus	Radioactive metallic element

Some **phytochemicals** may offer protection against cancer *(see Chapter 17)*. These include **isothiocyanates** (found in cruciferous vegetables like broccoli and cauliflower), **flavonoids** (found in apples and tea), **resveratrol** found in the skins of certain red grapes, **lycopene** (found in tomatoes), and soy protein, which contains the flavonoid **genistein** *(Figure 22.9)*.

FIGURE 22.9 Foods Containing Phytochemicals that May Offer Protection Against Cancer. ▶

EXERCISES

Demonstrate your knowledge of the following terminology by deconstructing the terms into their elements, and then using any one term in a sentence of your own choice (not directly from the text). Fill in the blanks.

1. phytochemical: _____ / _____ / _____
                  P   R/CF   S

2. environment: _____ / _____ / _____
                  P   R/CF   S

3. aminoketone: _____ / _____ / _____
                  P   R/CF   S

4. pesticide: _____ / _____ / _____
                  P   R/CF   S

5. genistein: _____ / _____ / _____
                  P   R/CF   S

6. dioxin: _____ / _____ / _____
                  P   R/CF   S

Pick any one of these terms, and use it in a sentence.

_____

_____

LESSON 22.2 Detecting and Treating Cancer

OBJECTIVES

All that is required for cancer to develop are genetic mutations in one cell, the mother or **progenitor** cell. The daughter cells can reproduce rapidly, but clinical detection by physical or radiographic means is rare for a tumor mass lower than 1 billion cancer cells (about 1 cm in diameter). The earlier the tumor is detected, the better the chance of cure. The information in this lesson will enable you to:

- **List methods of cancer prevention.**
- **Discuss methods of self-examination to detect cancer.**
- **Describe methods of screening for cancer.**
- **Explain therapies for treating cancer.**

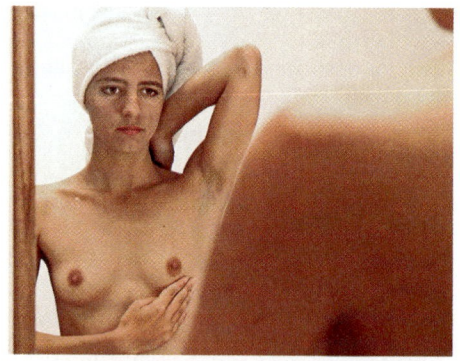

▲ **FIGURE 22.10 Breast Self-Examination.**

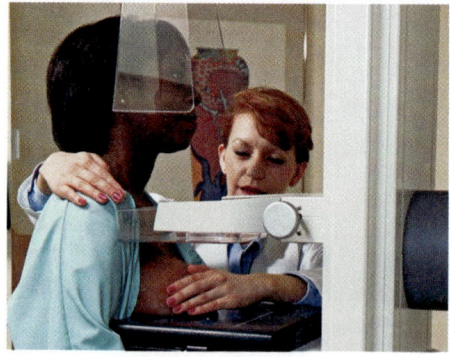

▲ **FIGURE 22.11 Mammography.**

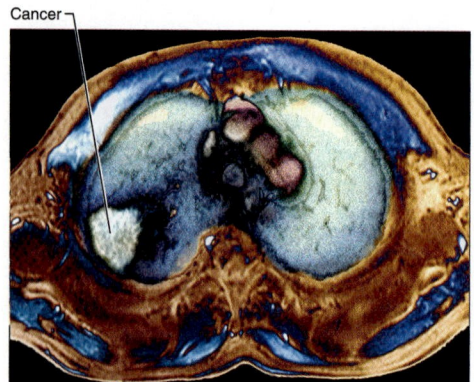

▲ **FIGURE 22.12 PET Scan Showing Cancer in Right Lung.**

DETECTING CANCERS OF THE REPRODUCTIVE SYSTEM

Breast, testicular, and prostate cancers are often detected by **palpation**. This is why **self-examination** of the breast and testes for adults should be done on a monthly basis *(Figure 22.10)*. For prostate cancer, men aged 50 and over should have an annual **digital rectal examination (DRE)** and **prostate specific antigen (PSA)** blood test.

Melanoma of the skin is a visible cancer and **self-examination of the skin** in front of a full-length mirror should also be performed monthly by adults.

All self-examinations should be performed in conjunction with health care provider examinations. For example, a **cancer-related clinical examination** should be performed every year for those aged over 40. Beginning at age 50, men and women should have a digital rectal examination annually, together with a **fecal occult blood test (FOBT)** as a screening for colon and rectal cancer. Every five years a **sigmoidoscopy** should be performed. For women, a **Pap test** should be performed annually to detect precancerous cells in the cervix *(see Chapter 13)*.

Screening for Breast Cancer

Mammograms should be performed every three years starting at age 20, every two years starting at age 40, and annually starting at age 50 *(Figure 22.11)* unless directed otherwise by your health care provider.

Digital mammography records x-ray images in computer code instead of on x-ray film. This technique allows the images to be manipulated to enhance subtle changes in tissue density. Studies are being performed to see if digital mammography is more effective than conventional mammography at finding cancer.

Computer-aided detection scans a mammogram with a laser beam and converts it into a digital signal that can be processed by a computer to highlight suspicious areas. The effectiveness of this technique is also being evaluated.

Magnetic resonance imaging (MRI) creates detailed images of the breast in different planes. This technique is being evaluated for screening women at high risk for breast cancer. MRI is also being used to screen for lung cancer in high-risk patients.

Positron emission tomography (PET) scan uses an injection of **radioactive sugar** to locate cancer *(Figure 22.12)*. Because of their rapid cell division and higher metabolism, cancer cells absorb sugar faster than do normal cells. The areas of increased sugar uptake can be seen on the scans. The scans are good at locating large (bigger than 8 mm), aggressive tumors and sites to which the tumor has metastasized. They are also useful in evaluating and staging recurrent cancer and tracking the response of a tumor to treatment.

Electrical impedance scanning is a technique based on the fact that electricity travels at different speeds through different tissues. Electricity travels rapidly through cancer tissue and appears as white spots on the computer screen of the

WORD	PRONUNCIATION		ELEMENTS	DEFINITION
digital	DIJ-ih-tal	S/ R/	-al *pertaining to* digit- *finger*	Pertaining to a finger or toe
impedance	im-PEE-dahns	S/ R/	-ance *forming* imped- *obstruct*	Resistance to the flow of an electric current
lavage	lah-VAHZH		Latin *to wash*	Washing out of a hollow cavity, tube, or organ
progenitor	pro-JEN-it-or	P/ R/	pro- *before* -genitor *offspring*	Founder; beginning of an ancestry
radioactive	RAY-dee-oh-AK-tiv	P/ R/	radio- *radiation* -active *getting things done*	Spontaneously emitting alpha, beta, or gamma rays
self-examination	SELF-ek-zam-ih-NAY-shun	S/ R/ R/	-ation *action* examin- *test, examine* self- *me*	Conduct an examination of one's own body
stereotactic	STER-ee-oh-TAK-tic	S/ R/CF R/	-ic *pertaining to* stere/o- *three-dimensional* -tact- *orderly arrangement*	A precise three-dimensional method to locate a lesion

scanning system. The device allows an abnormal area found on mammogram to be viewed from different angles and is being studied to see if its use can reduce the need for biopsy.

Image-guided breast biopsy techniques are important in helping doctors obtain biopsies from tumors that cannot be felt but are seen on conventional mammogram. **Stereotactic-guided biopsy** is the use of a computer and scanning devices to create three-dimensional images of lesions seen on a mammogram so that a needle can be inserted accurately into the lesion. Another type of needle biopsy uses a device called a mammatome to gently vacuum out suspicious tissue through a needle.

Ductal lavage collects samples of cells from breast ducts for microscopic analysis. Saline solution is introduced into a milk duct through a fine catheter inserted into the opening of the duct on the surface of the nipple. The solution is then aspirated out through the catheter, and cells in it are analyzed under the microscope to check for evidence of abnormal cells.

Abbreviations

DRE	digital rectal examination
FOBT	fecal occult blood test
MRI	magnetic resonance imaging
Pap	Papanicolaou cervical smear test
PET	positron emission tomography
PSA	prostate specific antigen

EXERCISES

Patient Documentation. *Apply the correct abbreviations in the following patient documentation. Fill in the blanks.*

1. The patient has been scheduled for a _____ test in the OB/GYN clinic at noon tomorrow.

2. This patient has an appointment in the radiology department at 3:15 p.m. for a _____ scan and

   an _____.

3. Screening for colon and rectal cancer should include a _____ and a _____.

4. Screening for prostate cancer can be done with a _____ blood test.

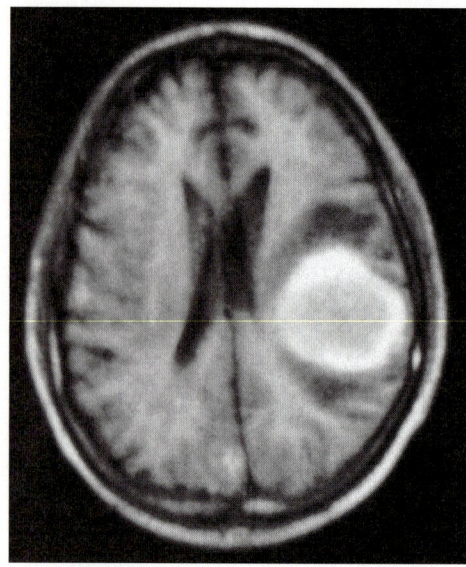

▲ **FIGURE 22.13 MRI Showing Brain Metastasis From a Lung Cancer.**

Case Report 22.1
(continued)

For Mrs. Raquel Sacco, because her cancer had metastasized to her brain, she is placed in stage IV, which only has a 2 percent 5-year survival rate.

DETECTING LUNG CANCER

Chest x-rays, as a screening tool, rarely provide the first indication of lung cancer. By the time lung cancer is diagnosed by chest x-ray, it often has spread beyond the lungs.

Computed tomography (CT) scans are more effective at identifying early tumors than are chest x-rays.

Positron emission tomography (PET) scans are expensive and not widely available, but they are the most accurate noninvasive test for identifying if the cancer has spread outside lung tissue. Its use may prevent unnecessary surgeries by identifying patients whose cancer had progressed beyond the stage at which surgery is beneficial.

Magnetic resonance imaging (MRI) can locate brain and bone metastases from lung cancer *(Figure 22.13)*.

Scintigraphy utilizes low-level radioactive agents that bind to cancer cells and can be tracked by special cameras to reveal the locations of cancer cells.

Bronchoscopy can locate cancers in the major airways of the lung. Specimens are obtained for biopsy by cutting tissue, using brushings, and using a washing process called **bronchoalveolar lavage (BAL).**

Needle biopsy of tumors in the **periphery** of the lungs is performed by inserting a needle between the ribs and guiding it to the tumor by **fluoroscopy** or CT scan. The biopsy can also be performed using **thoracoscopy,** in which a fiberoptic tube with a camera is inserted between the ribs into the pleural space to view the lungs and take a biopsy.

Mediastinoscopy uses a fiberoptic tube with a camera inserted into the mediastinum via the suprasternal notch to locate appropriate areas for biopsy if the cancer has spread to mediastinal lymph nodes.

Sputum analysis of coughed-up sputum can be a useful and cost-effective method of identifying cancer cells arising from the lining of the airways.

Biomarkers are substances that are released by specific cancers. They can be found in blood, sputum, and tissue samples. Biomarkers under investigation include **carcinoembryonic antigen (CEA)** that is found in 50% of cases of non–small cell lung cancer but is also found in colorectal, pancreatic, and breast cancer.

The blood test **anti-malignin antibody screen (AMAS)** is a general test for detecting any kind of cancer. Most cancers in their early stages secrete the antigen malignin; and, by using an antibody against malignin, the presence of the biomarker can be detected in the laboratory.

Alpha-fetoprotein levels are often elevated as a biomarker in cancer patients because cancer cells tend to revert to fetal characteristics.

Staging Lung Cancer

Staging defines how localized or how widespread the cancer is. Treatment and prognosis depend on the cancer's stage. The diagnostic tests described above are used to stage the cancer. In addition, brain metastases are identified by MRI and bone metastases by **technetium-99m (^{99m}Tc) radionuclide** bone scans.

The **TNM (tumor-node-metastasis) staging system** is used:

- "T" stands for tumor and describes its size and how far it has spread within the lung and to nearby tissues such as the pleura, diaphragm, and pericardium.
- "N" stands for spread to lymph nodes around the affected lung or around the other lung.
- "M" stands for metastasis to distant sites such as brain, liver, and bones.

Once the T, N, and M categories have been assigned, the information is combined (stage grouping) and given an overall stage of 0, I, II, III, or IV.

In many cancers, another measure of staging, called **grade,** is used. This depends on an assessment by a **pathologist** of the rate of growth of the cancer cells and how likely it is to spread. The most **virulent** cancers are given a grade of 4.

WORD	PRONUNCIATION	ELEMENTS		DEFINITION
biomarker	bi-oh-**MARK**-er	P/ R/	bio- *biological* -marker *sign*	A biological marker or product by which a cell can be identified
bronchoalveolar	**BRONG**-koh-al-**VEE**-oh-lar	S/ R/CF R/	-ar *pertaining to* bronch/o- *bronchus* -alveol- *alveolus*	Pertaining to the bronchi and alveoli
fluoroscopy	flor-**OS**-koh-pee	S/ R/CF	-scopy *to examine* fluor/o- *flux, flow*	Examination of the structures of the body by x-rays
grade	GRAYD		Latin *step*	In cancer pathology, a classification of the rate of growth of cancer cells
mediastinoscopy	**ME**-dee-as-tih-**NOS**-koh-pee	S/ R/CF	-scopy *to examine* mediastin/o- *middle septum*	Examination of the mediastinum using an endoscope
pathology pathologist	pa-**THOL**-oh-jee pa-**THOL**-oh-jist	S/ R/CF S/	-logy *study of* path/o- *disease* -logist *one who studies*	Medical specialty dealing with the structural and functional changes of a disease process A specialist in pathology
periphery peripheral (adj)	peh-**RIF**-eh-ree peh-**RIF**-eh-ral	P/ R/	peri- *around* -phery *edge*	Outer part of a structure away from the center
radionuclide	**RAY**-dee-oh-**NYU**-klide	S/ P/ R/	-ide *having a particular quality* radio- *radiation* -nucl- *nucleus*	Radioactive agent used in diagnostic imaging
scintigraphy	sin-**TIG**-rah-fee	S/ R/	-graphy *recording* scinti- *spark*	Recording of radioactivity with a special camera
stage staging	STAYJ **STAY**-jing		Latin *to stand*	Definition of extent and dissemination of a malignant neoplasm Process of determination of the extent of the distribution of a neoplasm
thoracoscopy	thor-ah-**KOS**-koh-pee	S/ R/CF	-scopy *to examine* thorac/o- *chest*	Examination of the pleural cavity with an endoscope
virulent	**VIR**-you-lent		Latin *poisonous*	Extremely toxic or pathogenic

EXERCISES

Language of Oncology. *Test your knowledge of the **language of oncology** with the following exercise. Circle the best answer(s). Some questions may have more than one correct answer.*

1. Which of the following terms contains a prefix?

   periphery   thoracoscopy   virulent   pathology

2. Which term means *one who studies?*

   nephrology   pathologist   pathology   fluroscopy

3. Which term would mean a recording with a special camera?

   biomarker   thoracoscopy   scintigraphy   mediastinoscopy

4. Which is the term for something extremely toxic or poisonous?

   virulent   scintigraphy   bronchoalveolar   peripheral

5. Which of the following terms means *to examine?*

   thoracoscopy   scintigraphy   mediastinoscopy   fluoroscopy

6. Which of the following terms would be a procedure on the chest?

   pathology   bronchoalveolar   biomarker   thoracoscopy

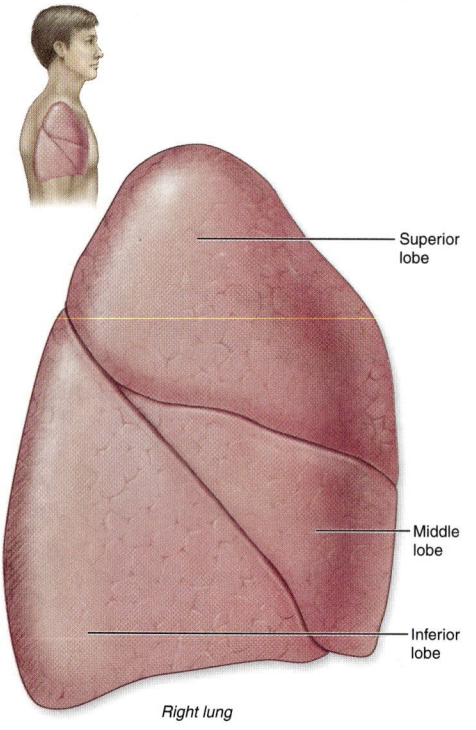

FIGURE 22.14 Lateral view of right lung showing lobes that could be removed surgically.

Superior lobe

Middle lobe

Inferior lobe

Right lung

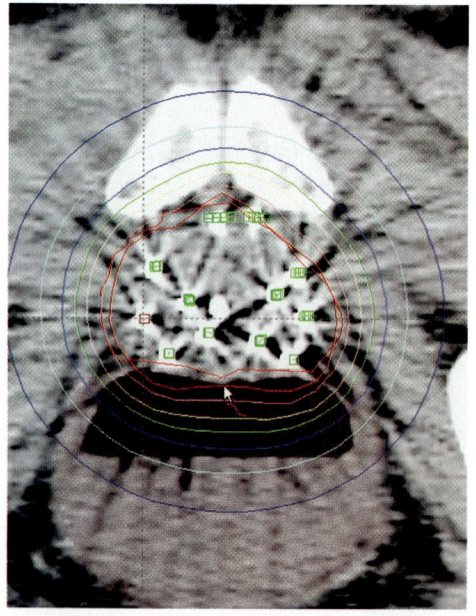

FIGURE 22.15 Radioactive Seeds Implanted in a Tumor.

TREATING CANCER

Treatment of any cancer depends on its location, its size, its localization or spread to surrounding tissues and lymph nodes, presence of metastases, and its aggressiveness (as determined by pathologic findings on biopsy or surgical removal).

If the cancer is still localized, it can be removed, and cure is possible. Unfortunately, few patients are diagnosed at such an early stage, particularly with lung cancer. Even if the original tumor is removed, cancer recurrence rates are high. Additional treatments with radiation and **chemotherapy** are used and can produce unpleasant side effects. A patient will have to balance a diminished quality of life against a chance for a modestly prolonged life.

In the elderly, studies have shown that survival rates are the same for therapies aimed at relieving pain as they are for aggressive, unpleasant treatment **regimens** with their diminished quality of life.

Surgical Procedures

Surgical procedures for specific body system cancers are discussed in those chapters. For example, surgery for breast cancer is in *Chapter 13* and for prostate cancer in *Chapter 12*.

The type of surgery for lung cancer depends on the amount of lung tissue that has to be removed.

Wedge resection (segmentectomy) removes only a small part of the lung and is used for carcinoma in situ, when the cancer is located in one local area.

Lobectomy is removal of one lobe of the lung and is used if the cancer has not spread beyond the lobe or into lymph nodes *(Figure 22.14)*.

Pneumonectomy removes an entire lung and has a mortality of 5 to 8%.

Case Report 22.1 (continued)

Lobectomy was the procedure performed on Mrs. Raquel Sacco. The respiratory therapy she is having is designed to enhance the function of her residual lung tissue.

Laser surgery enables small amounts of lung tissue to be removed and is used for improving symptoms in patients in whom more major surgery is not indicated.

Photodynamic therapy uses bronchoscopy and laser light beams combined with a photosensitive drug called porfimer sodium (Photofrin) to kill cancer cells in the lining of the bronchi in early stage disease.

Cryosurgery uses a probe chilled to below freezing to destroy early stage cancer cells.

Radiation Procedures (Radiotherapy)

Radiotherapy does not remove the lesion but distorts the DNA of the cancer cells so that they lose their ability to reproduce and to retain fluids; the cells shrink over time. Side effects of radiotherapy depend on the type of therapy used and occur when healthy cells are damaged during the treatment. Tiredness, nausea and loss of appetite, and sore skin in the treatment area can be short-term effects.

External-Beam Radiation focuses a beam of radiation directly on the tumor. It is generally used for metastasized cancer.

Brachytherapy implants radioactive seeds through thin tubes directly into the tumor to give high doses of radiation to the tumor, while reducing radiation exposure to the surrounding tissues *(Figure 22.15)*. It can be used for inoperable cancers.

Continuous Hyperfractionated Accelerated Radiotherapy (CHART) administers standard doses of radiation multiple times per day. It allows the total dose of radiation to be administered in a shorter period of time than the standard six weeks.

WORD	PRONUNCIATION	ELEMENTS		DEFINITION
brachytherapy	bra-kee-**THAIR**-ah-pee	S/ R/CF	-therapy *treatment* brach/y- *short*	Radiation therapy in which the source of irradiation is implanted in the tissue to be treated
chemotherapy	**KEY**-moh-**THAIR**-ah-pee	S/ R/CF	-therapy *treatment* chem/o- *chemistry*	Treatment using chemical agents
hyperfractionated	high-per-**FRAK**-shun-ay-ted	S/ P/ R/	-ated *action* hyper- *excessive* -fraction- *small amount*	Smaller fractions of a radiation dose given more frequently
lobectomy	low-**BECK**-toe-me	S/ R/	-ectomy *surgical excision* lob- *lobe*	Surgical removal of a lobe of the lungs
photodynamic	foh-toe-die-**NAM**-ik	S/ R/CF R/	-ic *pertaining to* phot/o- *light* -dynam- *power*	Use of a light-sensitive drug with a laser beam to destroy cells
pneumonectomy	**NEW**-moh-**NEK**-toe-me	S/ R/	-ectomy *surgical excision* pneumon- *lung*	Surgical removal of a whole lung
regimen	**REJ**-ih-men		Latin *direction*	Program of treatment
segmentectomy	seg-men-**TEK**-toe-me	S/ R/	-ectomy *surgical excision* segment- *section*	Surgical excision of a segment of a tissue or organ

Stereotactic radiosurgery (SRS) uses three-dimensional computer programming to deliver a precise, single high dose of radiation in a one-day session. The most common form of SRS used in the United States is a cobalt-60–based machine called the gamma knife. Though this technique is labeled and implied as "surgery," there is no actual surgery involved.

EXERCISES

Match the element in column 1 with its correct meaning in column 2. Some of these elements have appeared in earlier chapters as well.

_____ 1. phot/o-

_____ 2. pneumon-

_____ 3. brach/y-

_____ 4. hyper-

_____ 5. -ectomy

_____ 6. lob-

_____ 7. -therapy

_____ 8. -osis

_____ 9. chemo-

_____ 10. -otomy

A. condition

B. lobe

C. excessive

D. incision

E. lung

F. light

G. chemistry

H. surgical excision

I. treatment

J. short

Keynote

As well as affecting cancer cells, chemo-therapy alters the function of normal cells, causing side effects.

TREATING CANCER (continued)

Chemotherapy

Chemotherapy is the use of **cytotoxic agents,** the majority of which exert their effect by DNA damage that causes the cancer cells to be unable to reproduce and function so that they die. Unfortunately, these agents can also harm healthy cells, and that is what causes side effects. The kinds of side effects and their severity depend on the type and dose of chemotherapy. Fatigue, nausea, vomiting, and hair loss are common. Anemia and blood clotting problems can arise from the effects of the chemotherapy on the bone marrow.

Chemotherapy is usually given in regular cycles over several months. Platinum compounds, either cisplatin (Platinol) or carboplatin (Paraplatin) are the core of most treatment regimens. They are mostly used with other types of cytotoxic drugs in two-drug or three-drug combinations. Side effects are very common and often disabling.

For some cases, chemotherapy alone can be the treatment of choice, while others use a combination of chemotherapy and radiation. In many cases, surgery is performed prior to or following these forms of treatment.

Biologic Therapies

Biologic therapies use the body's immune system, directly or indirectly, to attack cancer cells or to lessen the side effects that can be caused by radiation and chemotherapy. **Biologic response modifiers** alter the immune system's response to cancer cells and include interferons, interleukins, monoclonal antibodies, vaccines, and gene therapy.

Monoclonal antibodies (MOABs) are antibodies produced by a single type of cell and are specific for a single antigen. Examples of MOABs are rituximab (Rituxan), used for non-Hodgkin lymphoma, and trastuzumab (Herceptin), used in breast cancer for tumors that produce a protein called HER-2. Other MOABs are in clinical trials for many different types of cancer.

Antiangiogenesis therapy interferes with the genetic mechanisms that increase blood supply for the active growth of cancer cells. The drug Avastin has lead to a great increase in the survival of patients with colon cancer and is also being used in lung and breast cancer.

Gene therapy is now a focus of cancer therapy. In 2005, the **National Cancer Institute (NCI)** and the **National Human Genome Research Institute (NHGRI)** announced a three-year pilot project to map the genetic alterations in cancer cells. New technologies called **microarrays** or **gene chips** (small slivers of glass or nylon that can be coated with genes) enable every gene that is active in a cancer cell to be identified.

Gene therapy involves introducing a normal gene into a person's cells to replace an abnormal disease-producing gene *(see Chapter 21)*. Numerous trials are underway to define gene therapy's applications in the biologic treatment of cancer.

Abbreviations

MOAB	monoclonal antibody
NCI	National Cancer Institute
NHGRI	National Human Genome Research Institute

Keynote

Gene therapy is an experimental treatment that can target healthy cells to enhance their ability to fight cancer or can target cancer cells to destroy them.

WORD	PRONUNCIATION	ELEMENTS		DEFINITION
angiogenesis	AN-jee-oh-JEN-eh-sis	S/ R/CF	-genesis *formation* angi/o- *blood vessel*	New formation of blood vessels
antiangiogenesis	anti-AN-jee-oh-JEN-eh-sis	P/	anti- *against*	The prevention of growth of new blood vessels
biology biologic (adj)	bi-OL-oh-jee BI-oh-LOJ-ik	S/ R/CF	-logy *study of* bi/o- *life*	Science concerned with life and living organisms
cytotoxic	sigh-toh-TOX-ik	S/ R/CF	-toxic *to kill* cyt/o- *cell*	Destructive to cells
microarray (also called gene chips)	MY-kroh-ah-RAY	P/ R/	micro- *small* -array *place in order*	Technique for studying one gene in one experiment
monoclonal	MON-oh-KLO-nal	S/ P/ R/	-al *pertaining to* mono- *one* -clon- *cutting used for propagation*	Derived from a single clone of cells

EXERCISES

Review the Word Analysis and Definition box on this page to find the answers for the following questions. Circle the best answer, then fill in the blanks.

1. The term containing a root that means *blood vessel* is:

   hemolysis   angiogenesis   environmental

2. The prefix in this term means *one:*

   biologic   dioxin   monoclonal

3. The suffix in this term means *study of:*

   microarray   biology   brachytherapy

4. The suffix in this term means *to kill:*

   cytotoxic   pnemonectomy   biologic

5. The term containing a word element that means *small* is:

   lobectomy   stereotactic   microarray

6. The term that does *not* contain a prefix is:

   biology   monoclonal   microarray

Test your recall of terms from previous chapters.

7. List as many terms as you can that have the suffix *-logy,* and give a brief definition of each term.

   _____ means _____

   _____ means _____

   _____ means _____

   _____ means _____

   _____ means _____

   _____ means _____

   _____ means _____

CANCER

CHALLENGE YOUR KNOWLEDGE

A. **Case Report:** The following exercise is based entirely on the scenario of Raquel Sacco, which was presented in this chapter.

1. Read this entire scenario out loud to yourself for pronunciation practice. The medical terms you should pay particular attention to have been underlined.

2. Utilize your knowledge of the *language of oncology* (and previous chapters) to answer the following questions based on the scenario. Fill in the blanks.

You are

. . . an advanced level <u>respiratory</u> <u>therapist</u> employed by Fulwood Medical Center, working with Tavis Senko, MD, a <u>pulmonologist.</u>

Your patient is

. . . Raquel Sacco, a 44-year-old mother of two teenage boys, who is the owner of a quilting fabrics store. She is two days postop from a <u>lobectomy</u> for non–small cell lung cancer. From her records, you see that she has two <u>secondary</u> <u>metastases</u> in her brain. She has been a nonsmoker all her life. Her 70-year-old father is a two-pack-a-day smoker, as is her husband. They both show no evidence of cancer on chest x-rays. Before Raquel is discharged, as part of her <u>postoperative</u> respiratory care plan, you are using <u>incentive spirometry</u>—also called <u>sustained maximal inspiration</u> (SMI)—to increase her <u>inspiratory</u> volume and improve her inspiratory muscle performance. You will also be taking an <u>arterial</u> blood sample to check her arterial oxygen pressure (PaO_2).

<u>Adenocarcinoma</u> was found in Raquel Sacco. It was <u>diagnosed</u> because she had a <u>seizure,</u> and <u>neurological</u> tests revealed the presence of two <u>metastases</u> in her brain, leading to a search for the primary tumor that was found in her lung. Raquel Sacco probably developed her lung cancer as a result of inhaling second-hand smoke all her life (from her father and husband). For Raquel Sacco, because her cancer had <u>metastasized</u> to her brain, she is placed in stage IV. The outlook for Mrs. Sacco is bleak.

Non–Small Cell Lung Cancer Survival

Stage	5-Year Relative Survival Rate
I	47%
II	26%
III	8%
IV	2%

1. What is the meaning of the term **postoperative**?

   _____

2. What type of procedure has Mrs. Sacco undergone?

   _____

3. Using your knowledge of word elements, deconstruct the procedure in question 2 and define it.

   _____

4. Define **metastases:**

   _____

5. Where did the metastases appear?

   _____

6. Are the metastases the 1° or 2° cancer? _____

7. Where does her 1° cancer originate? _____

8. What specific type of cancer is the 1° cancer? _____

9. What problem first brought Mrs. Sacco to the doctor? _____

10. What stage of cancer has Mrs. Sacco been diagnosed with? _____

11. Why is her prognosis bleak? _____

B. **Short answers based on the scenario:**

1. What is the purpose of the SMI?

   _____

   _____

   _____

2. Explain the phrase "secondhand smoke."

   _____

   _____

   _____

3. Explain the phrase "two-pack-a-day smoker."

   _____

   _____

   _____

4. How can a nonsmoker get lung cancer?

   _____

   _____

   _____

5. Record your thoughts or comments about this patient's case.

   _____

   _____

   _____

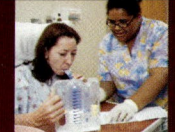
CANCER

C. **Correct Usage:** Demonstrate your knowledge of the *language of oncology*. These are similar medical terms but only have one correct use in the paragraph. Fill in the blanks.

carcinogen   carcinoma   carcinogenic   carcinogenesis

1. Raquel Sacco was unknowingly exposed to a(n) _____ in the form of secondhand smoke. This

   _____ substance brought about the _____ of her tumors. Her primary

   _____ had already metastasized; her prognosis is poor.

metastasis   metastasized   metastases   metastatic

2. The _____ of Raquel's primary cancer to a secondary site was discovered after diagnostic study.

   The _____ in her brain were not the site of her current surgery. Her _____

   lesions may require radiation therapy if they are inoperable. Since her cancer has already _____,
   her chances of survival are poor.

D. **Prefixes:** Not every medical term will have a prefix; but when they do, it is an extra clue for you in determining the meaning of the term. Fill in the meaning of the prefix, then give an example of a medical term with that prefix, and the meaning of the term. (You may also use terms from previous chapters, but be prepared to define them.)

Prefix	Meaning of Prefix	Medical Term with that Prefix	Meaning of the Term
apo-			
bio-			
di-			
hyper-			
meso-			
meta-			
micro-			
mono-			
neo-			
peri-			
pro-			
proto-			
radio-			

E. **Terminology Challenge:** All of the following medical terms have the same ending, but one term is slightly different in meaning than the others. Find the term, and explain why it is different, even though it appears the same.

lymphoma   melanoma   hematoma   carcinoma   sarcoma

The term is: _____

It is different because:

_____

_____

F. **Roots:** Deconstruct the following medical terms by slashing (/) the elements. Define only the roots/combining forms in every term. The first one is done for you. Fill in the blanks.

Medical Term	Root(s)/Combining Form	Meaning of Root(s)/Combining Form
adeno/carcin/oma	*adeno; carcin*	*gland; cancer*
stereotactic		
mediastinoscopy		
neoplastic		
cytotoxic		
bronchoalveolar		
chondrosarcoma		
digital		
monoclonal		
apoptosis		
lobectomy		
progenitor		

G. **Study Review:** Cancer is a class of diseases characterized by uncontrolled cell division. Using the *language of oncology*, fill in this mini-outline, and use it *for study review*. Fill in the blanks.

1. Uncontrolled cell division is caused by damage to a cell's _____ .

2. This damage produces _____ to the genes that cause cell division.

3. Damaged genes can be either _____ or _____.

4. Proliferation of damaged cells leads to _____ formation.

CANCER

H. Compare and contrast benign and malignant tumors to meet a lesson objective. You are given a statement about a tumor. Check in the appropriate column if it refers to a benign or malignant tumor. When you have finished the table, highlight all the statements that pertain to malignant tumors *only*.

Description of Tumor	Benign	Malignant
Grows slowly		
Invades the lymph system		
Does not metastasize to other organs		
Invades the bloodstream and travels to other organs		
Lipoma		
Surrounded by connective tissue capsule		
Can compress surrounding tissues and cause functional problems		
Does not invade or infiltrate adjacent tissues		
Unlimited, unregulated growth potential		
Invades or infiltrates adjacent tissues		
Does not spread to lymph nodes		
Mesothelioma		

I. Elements can provide a clue as to the origin of a tumor. Analyze the medical terms in column l, and match them to the cancer source in column 2.

Medical term

_____ 1. mesothelioma

_____ 2. sarcoma

_____ 3. adenocarcinoma

_____ 4. osteosarcoma

_____ 5. melanoma

_____ 6. chondrosarcoma

_____ 7. carcinoma

_____ 8. lymphoma

_____ 9. rhabdomyosarcoma

Cancer Arises From:

A. epithelial cells

B. lymph nodes

C. cells lining pleural cavity

D. connective tissue cells

E. glandular epithelial cells

F. skeletal muscle

G. bone-forming cells

H. pigment-producing skin cells

I. cartilage cells

J. **Deconstruct the following medical terms into basic elements.** These elements will be the basis for multiple terms in medical vocabulary. Fill in the table.

Medical Term	Meaning of Prefix	Meaning of Root/CF	Meaning of Suffix	Meaning of Medical Term
pathology				
neoplasm				
infiltrate				
carcinogen				
metastasis				
dioxin				
digital				
fluoroscopy				
oncology				

K. **Abbreviations must be used with care to ensure you are conveying precise information.** Demonstrate your knowledge of this chapter's abbreviations by matching them correctly.

_____ 1. genes normally suppress mitosis   A. PCD

_____ 2. injection of radioactive sugar   B. PSA

_____ 3. chemical toxin banned years ago   C. FOBT

_____ 4. general test for detecting cancer   D. PET

_____ 5. performed by respiratory therapist   E. AMAS

_____ 6. blood in stool   F. MRI

_____ 7. washing process with a scope   G. TS

_____ 8. apoptosis   H. PCB

_____ 9. detailed images in planes   I. BAL

_____ 10. blood test for men   J. SMI

CANCER

L. Procedures: There are many different procedures associated with cancer diagnosis and treatment. Can you correctly identify these procedures used for cancer patients? Circle the best choice.

1. Mrs. Sacco had this surgery at the site of her primary cancer:

    pneumonectomy   bronchoscopy   lobectomy

2. Examination of the pleural cavity with an endoscope:

    thoracoscopy   cystoscopy   bronchoscopy

3. Uses a chilled probe to destroy early cancer cells:

    brachytherapy   chemotherapy   cryosurgery

4. Fiberoptic tube with a camera is inserted into the chest:

    computed tomography   mediastinoscopy   fluoroscopy

5. Implants radioactive seeds into the tumor for direct radiation:

    brachytherapy   CHART   photodynamic therapy

6. Removes only a small part of the lung and used for carcinoma in situ:

    SRS   segmentectomy   pneumonectomy

7. Creates three-dimensional images of a lesion for accurate insertion of a needle:

    PET scan   stereotactic guided biopsy   ductal lavage

8. Removal of an entire lung:

    lobectomy   segmentectomy   pneumonectomy

9. Employed for cutting tissue, collecting brushings, and washings in the lung:

    bronchoscopy   scintigraphy   chest x-ray

10. More effective than chest x-rays at identifying early tumors:

    CT   PET   MRI

M. Suffixes can provide additional information about a medical term. Analyze the suffix in each of the following terms, and use it to provide a clue about the term. Fill in the blanks.

1. neoplasm: the suffix is _____ and means _____.

2. neoplasia: the suffix is _____ and means _____.

3. neoplastic: the suffix is _____ and means _____.

4. oncology: the suffix is _____ and means _____.

5. oncologist: the suffix is _____ and means _____.

6. pneumonectomy: the suffix is _____ and means _____.

7. chondrosarcoma: the suffix is _____ and means _____.

8. carcinogenesis: the suffix is _____ and means _____.

9. mediastinoscopy: the suffix is _____ and means _____.

10. scintigraphy: the suffix is _____ and means _____.

N. Recall and Review: How well do you remember these word elements from the previous chapter? Try to answer without first looking back to check. Fill in the blanks.

Element	Type of Element (P, R, CF, S)	Meaning of Element
1. auto	_____	_____
2. chromo	_____	_____
3. ist	_____	_____
4. hetero	_____	_____
5. dys	_____	_____

O. Commonalities: Analyze the following medical terms, and discover what they all have in common. Circle the correct answer.

1. Lobectomy, segmentectomy, and mastectomy are all:

   diagnoses   procedures   diagnostic tests

2. Chondrosarcoma, adenocarcinoma, and osteosarcoma are all:

   neoplasms   tumors   both of these

3. PET, MRI, and CT are all:

   blood tests   diagnostic tests   surgeries

4. Thoracoscopy, bronchoscopy, and mediastinoscopy are all:

   chest procedures   pelvic procedures   abdominal procedures

5. Pathologist, oncologist, and histologist are all:

   diseases   specialists   conditions

P. Procedures: An important distinction to learn about procedures is understanding which ones are diagnostic (used to determine a diagnosis) and which ones are therapeutic (carry out treatment). Analyze the following list of medical terms and abbreviations to determine whether they are diagnostic or therapeutic procedures. Fill in the table.

Procedure	Diagnostic	Therapeutic
segmentectomy		
BAL		
brachytherapy		
DRE		
stereotactic biopsy		
pneumonectomy		
ductal lavage		
mediastinoscopy		
CHART		

CANCER

Q. Cancer Quiz: Assess your knowledge of this chapter by correctly answering the following questions on cancer. The *language of oncology* will aid your understanding of the questions and possible answers. Circle the correct choice, and remember there is only one *best* answer.

1. Second leading cause of lung cancer (after smoking):

   a. air pollution

   b. radon

   c. chemical toxins

   d. PCBs

   e. particulate matter

2. Used to vacuum out suspicious breast tissue through a needle:

   a. gamma knife

   b. lavage

   c. bronchoscopy

   d. mammatome

   e. mammogram

3. In the TNM staging system for cancer, the "N" stands for:

   a. nothing

   b. normal

   c. neoplasm

   d. node

   e. noninvasive

4. A diagnostic test for female breast cancer is:

   a. mammogram

   b. FOBT

   c. Pap smear

   d. PSA blood test

   e. sigmoidoscopy

5. Tumor that has invaded or infiltrated has:

   a. grown into adjacent tissue

   b. died

   c. become weaker

   d. mutated

   e. necrotized

6. Healthy genes that promote normal cell growth are called:

   a. TS genes

   b. mutated TS genes

   c. protooncogenes

   d. mutated genes

   e. receptor genes

7. A benign tumor is:

   a. not harmful

   b. very weak

   c. metastatic

   d. necrotic

   e. harmful

8. An early form of carcinoma in which there is no invasion of surrounding tissues is:

   a. large cell carcinoma

   b. small cell carcinoma

   c. adenocarcinoma

   d. carcinoma in situ

   e. squamous cell carcinoma

9. The abbreviation PCD means the same as:

   a. protooncogene

   b. apoptosis

   c. oncogene

   d. polychlorinated biphenyls

   e. phytochemicals

10. Washing out of a hollow duct or cavity is:

   a. stereotactic biopsy

   b. lavage

   c. curettage

   d. aspiration

   e. gavage

CANCER

R. Elements: You are given the meaning of the element. Circle the correct term in which it appears.

1. The root meaning *surroundings* is in the term:

   environment   dioxin   pollution

2. The combining form meaning *producing* is in the term:

   genistein   pesticide   particle

3. The combining form meaning *plant* is in the term:

   phytochemical   particle   environment

4. The suffix meaning *to kill* is in the term:

   aminoketone   pollution   pesticide

5. The suffix meaning *pertaining to* is in the term:

   pollution   environmental   particulate

6. The prefix meaning *two* is in the term:

   pesticide   dioxin   genistein

7. The combining form meaning *chest* is in the term:

   fluoroscopy   thoracoscopy   endoscopy

8. The root meaning *flesh* is in the term:

   sarcoma   hematoma   carcinoma

S. Patient Education: Explain to your patient the difference between a benign and a malignant neoplasm.

Benign:

_____

_____

Malignant:

_____

_____

Note: This is an important distinction for coders to know as it may have a bearing on code choice.

T. **Abbreviations:** Transcribe into plain English the following physician orders using abbreviations. Patient safety depends on your precise interpretation of these orders. Fill in the blanks.

1. Patient's next yearly physical should include PSA, DRE, and FOBT.

   _____

   _____

   _____

   _____

   _____

2. Schedule this patient for a bronchoscopy with BAL.

   _____

   _____

   _____

   _____

   _____

3. Patient's blood work should include PSA, CEA, and AMAS analysis.

   _____

   _____

   _____

   _____

   _____

4. Treatment plan includes eventual CHART or SRS after conclusion of chemotherapy.

   _____

   _____

   _____

   _____

   _____

5. I am referring this patient to NCI for a clinical trial using MOABs for her CA.

   _____

   _____

   _____

   _____

   _____

CANCER

CHAPTER SUMMARY EXERCISE

1. *Listen to the pronunciation of the medical terms as given by your instructor.*
2. *Circle the correct spelling of the medical term.*
3. *Match the correctly spelled terms to the brief descriptions below.*
4. *Write a sentence for each of the 15 terms that appear in this exercise.*

A. SPELLING COMPREHENSION: CIRCLE THE CORRECT SPELLING OF THE TERM.

1. fluoroscopy	flueroscopy	fluorroscopy	foroscopy	floroscopy
2. apotosis	apoptosis	apoptossis	apotosus	apoptossus
3. regiment	regimen	regeemen	regimin	regimine
4. radionuclede	radionuklide	radeonuclide	rodeonuclide	radionuclide
5. levage	leevage	lavage	levege	laevage
6. porliferate	porlifferate	proliferate	proleferate	porleferate
7. metastasis	metassasis	mettasasis	meatus	metasasis
8. neoplasea	nioplasia	neoplasis	neoplasia	nioplassia
9. cytotoxic	sytotoxic	cyttotoxic	cytotoxsic	cytoxic
10. steeriotactic	stereotactic	steeriotaxic	steriotaxic	stereotaxic
11. sigmentektomy	segmentectomy	sigmentectomy	segmentictomy	segmintectomy
12. scentigraphy	sentigraphy	sentegraphy	scientigraphy	scintigraphy
13. osteosarrcoma	osteeosacoma	osteosarkoma	ostiosarcoma	osteosarcoma
14. pnueumonectomy	pneemonectomy	pneumonectomy	punectomy	numonectomy
15. virulent	vurulent	virulint	verulint	verulent

B. MATCH THE NUMBER OF THE CORRECT TERM IN PART A WITH THE BRIEF DESCRIPTION OF THE TERM BELOW.

a. radioactive agent used in diagnostic imaging _____

b. cancer arising in bone forming cells _____

c. examination of the body with x-rays _____

d. destructive to cells _____

e. extremely toxic _____

f. program of treatment _____

g. process and growth of a tumor _____

h. excision of a small section of lung tissue   _____

 i. to wash   _____

 j. recording of radioactivity with a special camera   _____

k. spread of cancer cells   _____

 l. removal of entire lung   _____

m. increase in number by reproducing   _____

n. PCD   _____

o. three-dimensional method of locating lesions   _____

C. USING YOUR KNOWLEDGE OF TERMS 1-15 IN PART A AND THEIR CORRECT SPELLING, WRITE A BRIEF SENTENCE FOR EACH OF THE TERMS AS IT MIGHT APPEAR IN PATIENT DOCUMENTATION.

1. _____

2. _____

3. _____

4. _____

5. _____

6. _____

7. _____

8. _____

9. _____

10. _____

11. _____

12. _____

13. _____

14. _____

15. _____

D. GO TO THE STUDENT CD. OPEN THE GLOSSARY AND PRACTICE YOUR PRONUNCIATION OF THE TERMS IN PART A OF THIS EXERCISE.

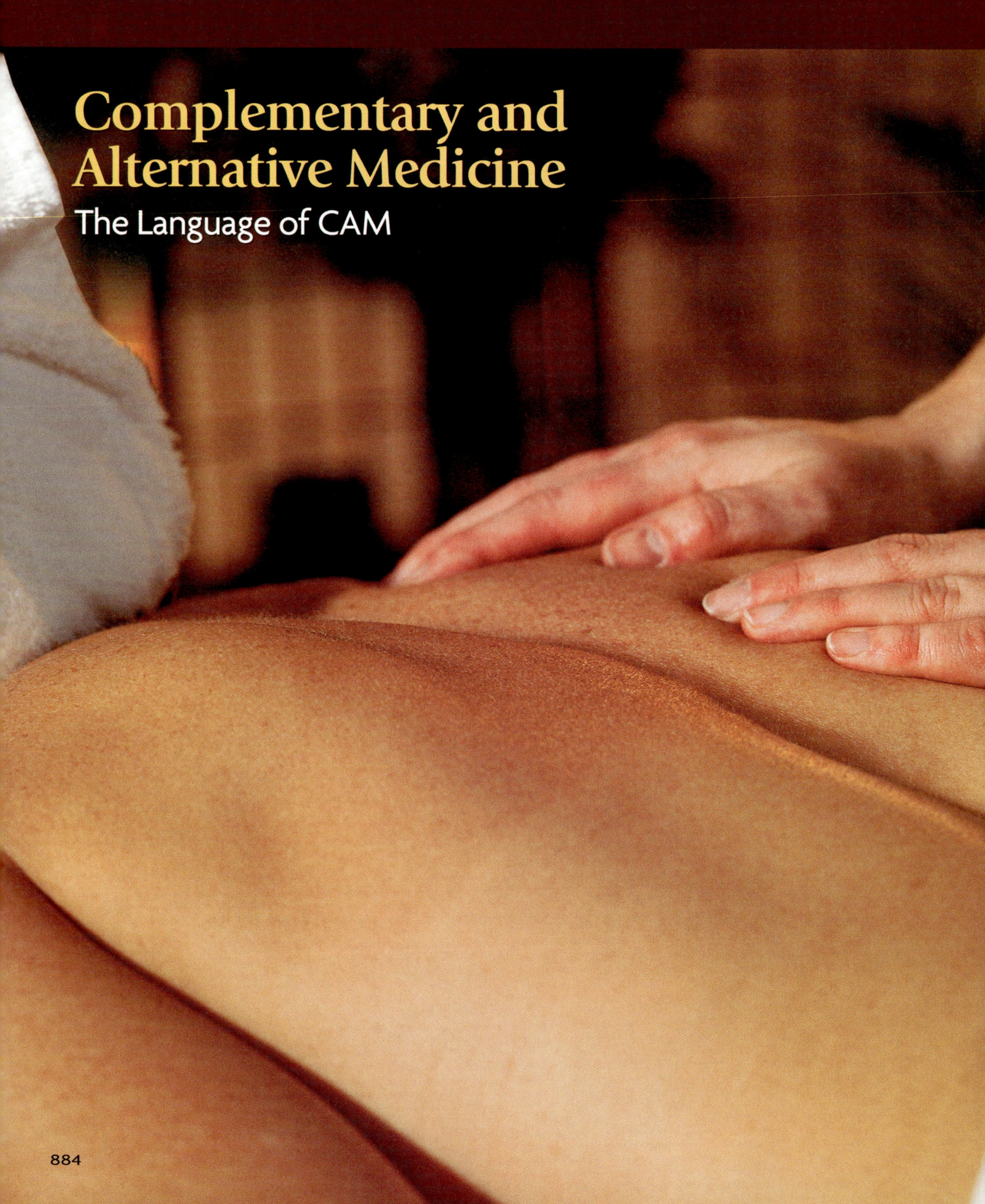

Complementary and Alternative Medicine

The Language of CAM

23

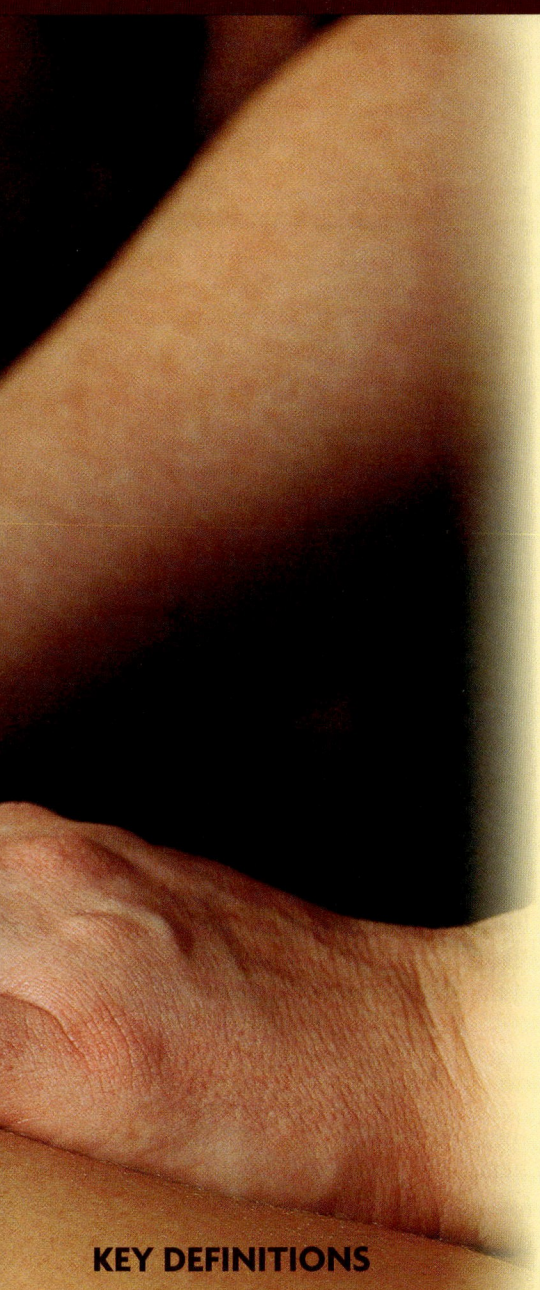

CASE REPORT 23.1

You are

. . . a **massage** therapist employed in the Pain Management Clinic at Fulwood Medical Center.

Your patient is

. . . Mrs. Mary Carr, a 65-year-old retired librarian who had been in good health until six months ago, when she had a sudden onset of severe pain in the muscles of her shoulders, upper arms, hips, and thighs. She was diagnosed as having polymyalgia rheumatica. Prednisone, 5 mg **t.i.d.,** has produced significant relief in the pain, but she is still having difficulty with such movements as turning over in bed and getting in and out of her car. Twice weekly, she is receiving massage therapy to the muscles of her shoulder and pelvic girdles. Once weekly, she is receiving acupuncture.

Learning Outcomes

CAM practices involve new terminology, not in anatomy and physiology, but in systems, techniques, and therapies. The information in this chapter will enable you to:

- Apply the language of complementary and alternative medicine to its different therapies, techniques, functions, and effects.

- Comprehend, analyze, spell, and write the medical terms of complementary and alternative medicine so that you communicate and document accurately and precisely in any health care setting.

- Recognize and pronounce the medical terms of complementary and alternative medicine so that you communicate verbally with accuracy and precision in any health care setting.

- Identify the known effects of complementary and alternative medicine on common disorders.

KEY DEFINITIONS

- **Complementary and alternative medicine (CAM)** is any medical practice, system, or product that is considered not to be part of conventional medicine and standard care.
- **Conventional medicine** is practiced by holders of MD or DO degrees and their allied health professionals such as registered nurses and therapists. Other terms for conventional medicine include **allopathic,** western, traditional, mainstream, or orthodox medicine.
- **Complementary medicine** is used together with standard or conventional medical treatments. An example is the use of **acupuncture** to help lessen the side effects of cancer treatment.
- **Alternative medicine** is used instead of standard or conventional medical treatments. An example is the use of a special diet to treat cancer instead of conventional surgery, radiation, or chemotherapy.
- **Integrative medicine,** a total approach to care, combines conventional medicine with CAM practices that involve the patient's body, mind, and spirit in the therapeutic process. An example is the use of meditation and relaxation techniques to reduce stress during treatment for hypertension and cardiovascular disease.

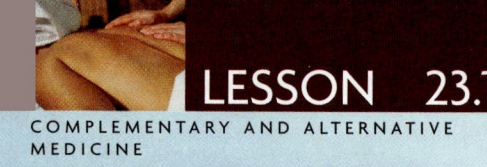

Complementary and Alternative Medicine Practices

OBJECTIVES

The **National Center for Complementary and Alternative Medicine (NCCAM)** was established by Congress in 1998 and is one of the 27 institutes and centers that make up the **National Institutes of Health (NIH).** Its missions are to explore CAM practices in the context of rigorous science, to integrate scientifically proven CAM practices into conventional medicine, and to disseminate authoritative information about CAM practices to the public and health professionals.

The information in this lesson will enable you to:

- **Identify the five major groups of CAM practices.**
- **Detail the use of complementary and alternative medicine in the United States.**
- **Describe frequently used manipulative and body-based techniques.**
- **Explain theories of energy fields in the body and therapeutic practices involving their use.**
- **Recognize the benefits of certain biologic-based products.**
- **Detail mind–body practices and their known effects.**
- **Recognize the philosophies and uses of certain whole medical systems.**

Abbreviations

CAM	complementary and alternative medicine
NCCAM	National Center for Complementary and Alternative Medicine
NIH	National Institutes of Health
t.i.d.	Latin *ter in die,* or three times a day

CAM PRACTICES

The NCCAM divides **CAM practices** into five major groups:

1. **Manipulative and body-based practices** are based on manipulation or movement of one or more body parts. Examples are:
   - **Massage**—manipulation of tissues with hands or special tools.
   - **Reflexology**—use of pressure points in the hands and feet to affect other parts of the body.

2. **Energy medicine practices** are based on the body being a web of energy fields that can be used to affect your health and well-being. Examples are:
   - **Reiki**—the balance of energy by placing hands on or near the patient and its transfer from one person to another.
   - **Therapeutic touch**—manipulation of a person's energy by a practitioner's hands.
   - **Acupuncture**—stimulation of specific energy points on the body to change or unblock energy fields and promote health.

3. **Biologic-based practices** use substances found in nature. These include dietary supplements, herbal products, and special diets. Examples are:
   - **Vitamins** such as vitamins C and E used with beta carotene to reduce the risk for age-related macular degeneration *(see Chapter 4).*
   - **Herbs** such as St. John's wort, used to treat depression.
   - **Special diets** such as a diet low in purine-rich foods to lower blood uric acid levels and reduce the risk of a gout attack.

4. **Mind–body practices** use a variety of techniques to enhance the mind's ability to affect body functions. Examples are:
   - **Biofeedback**—the patient learns how to affect certain body functions, such as heart rate, that are normally out of one's awareness.
   - **Hypnosis**—an altered state of consciousness in which suggestions can lead to changes in a person's behavior.
   - **Prayer and meditation**—practices that can slow the progression of cognitive impairment in Alzheimer disease.

5. **Whole medical systems** are healing systems that have evolved in different cultures and parts of the world. Examples are:

WORD	PRONUNCIATION	ELEMENTS		DEFINITION
acupuncture	ak-you-**PUNK**-chur	R/ R/	**acu-** *needle, sharp* **-puncture** *puncture*	Use of sterile, hair-thin needles to stimulate the energy pathways known as meridians
allopathic medicine	al-oh-**PATH**-ik **MED**-ih-sin	S/ P/ R/ R/	**-ic** *pertaining to* **allo-** *different from normal* **-path-** *disease* **medicine** *medicine*	Conventional medical practice
homeopathy homeopathic (adj)	ho-mee-**OP**-ah-thee **HO**-mee-oh-**PATH**-ik	S/ R/CF S/	**-pathy** *disease* **home/o-** *the same* **-ic** *pertaining to*	Treating disease with minute doses of substances
hypnosis hypnotic (adj) hypnotherapy	hip-**NOH**-sis hip-**NOT**-ic hip-noh-**THAIR**-ah-pee	S/ R/CF S/ S/	**-osis** *condition* **hypn/o-** *sleep* **-tic** *pertaining to* **-therapy** *treatment*	Changed state of consciousness Use of hypnosis in treatment of disorders
manipulation	mah-**NIP**-you-lay-shun	S/ R/	**-ation** *action* **manipul-** *handful*	Hands-on adjustment of joints, particularly of the spine
massage	mah-**SAHZH**		Greek *to knead, handle*	Application of pressure or vibration to soft body tissues
meditation	med-ih-**TAY**-shun		Latin *think over, contemplate*	Focusing attention or freeing the mind of thoughts as part of a formalized spiritual practice
naturopathic medicine	**NAH**-chur-oh-**PATH**-ik **MED**-ih-sin	S/ R/CF R/	**-ic** *pertaining to* **natur/o-** *nature* **-path-** *disease*	A system of healing based on the healing power of nature
reflexology	re-flek-**SOL**-oh-jee	S/ R/CF	**-logy** *study of* **reflex/o-** *to reflect*	Stimulation of reflexes in feet and hands, which correspond to other parts of the body
Reiki	**RAY**-kee		Japan *universal life force*	Transfer of energy by placing hands on or near a patient

- **Homeopathic** treatment is given with extremely small doses of substances that produce characteristic symptoms of illness in healthy people when given in larger doses.
- **Naturopathic medicine** emphasizes the treatment of disease through the stimulation of the inherent healing capabilities of the person's own vital force.
- **Oriental medicine** views health as a balance between yin and yang energies and disease as the physical expressions of an imbalance.

EXERCISES

*Elements will help you understand the **language of complementary and alternative medicine** (CAM). Identify the type of element, then give its meaning. Fill in the blanks.*

Element	Type of Element (P, R/CF, R)	Meaning of Element
acu	_____	_____
allo	_____	_____
naturo	_____	_____
homeo	_____	_____
hypno	_____	_____

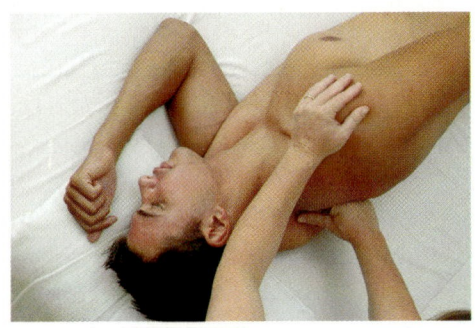

▲ FIGURE 23.1 Rolfing.

▲ FIGURE 23.2 Tai Chi.

▲ FIGURE 23.3 Yoga.

COMPLEMENTARY AND ALTERNATIVE MEDICINE IN THE UNITED STATES

A survey released by NCCAM indicates that, in a year, 48% of adults use at least one CAM therapy. If prayer specifically for health reasons is added, the figure increases to more than 60%. If **megavitamin** therapy is included, the figure increases to more than 70%. According to government estimates, at least $27 billion is being spent annually on CAM.

The majority of people (39%) used CAM to relieve pain; 16.8% used it to relieve back pain, 10% to relieve joint pain and arthritis, 6.6% to relieve neck pain, 3.1% for headache, and 2.4% for recurring pain elsewhere.

Many physicians are reluctant to accept CAM practices because they have not been shown to be effective in clinical trials. Once a CAM practice has been conclusively shown to be effective in a disorder, it will no longer be a CAM practice but will be incorporated into standard medical practice.

New procedures and drugs can only be approved after tests establish that their effect is significantly greater than that of a **placebo,** any treatment or intervention with no intrinsic therapeutic effect.

Manipulative and Body-Based Practices

Massage is not just a luxury found in spas and health clubs. As a complementary treatment, it can promote healing in muscles, tendons, and connective tissues; reduce stress, tension, and anxiety; and improve blood circulation.

The **National Certification Board for Therapeutic Massage and Bodywork (NCBTMB)** is a certifying group for massage therapists in the United States and awards the **NCTMB certification.** Many states do not recognize this, and there is no universally accepted licensure or certification.

There are more than 150 types of massage. The most commonly used are:

- **Swedish massage**—concentrates on increasing circulation to superficial soft tissues.
- **Deep massage**—focuses on increasing circulation to deep muscle tissues.
- **Sports massage**—aids in the recovery of injuries related to sports trauma.
- **Craniosacral therapy**—focuses on the bones of the cranium and sacrum.
- **Neuromuscular therapy**—an umbrella term that includes **trigger point therapy, myotherapy,** and other release techniques. These all focus on the normalization of muscles and the resting length of muscle through neural and muscular interventions.
- **Myofascial release**—uses manual techniques to stretch fascia with the aim of eliminating pain and balancing the body. One form of myofascial release is called **Rolfing,** a system of soft tissue manipulation and movement education *(Figure 23.1)*.
- **Thai massage** emphasizes practitioner assisted stretching and breathing.

Tai chi is a defined series of movements and postures that flow into each other without pause *(Figure 23.2)*. They are performed in a slow, graceful manner. Its physical and mental benefits include stress reduction, improved balance and coordination, and increased muscle strength and agility.

Progressive muscle relaxation is a mental technique to achieve total muscle relaxation, beginning at the toes and moving up your body to your head.

Relaxation breathing techniques that focus on the breathing are used to relax tense muscles and break cycles of negative thoughts about your health.

Yoga (unity) is a system of lifestyle measures to improve flexibility and muscle tone, develop breathing and relaxation techniques, and reduce stress *(Figure 23.3)*. It uses physical postures, called **asanas,** and controlled breathing exercises.

There are many different styles of yoga being practiced and taught today, including Hatha and Vinyasa.

Applied kinesiology involves testing muscle strength in response to a "question" that is presented to the body. It is used to identify substances and products

WORD	PRONUNCIATION	ELEMENTS		DEFINITION
Alexander technique	al-eg-**ZAN**-der tek-**NEEK**		Frederick Mathias Alexander, 1869–1955, Australian actor	The use of awareness and exercises to improve posture, breathing, and movement
asana	ah-**SAH**-nah		Hindu *posture*	Yoga posture or steady position of the body to open energy channels
craniosacral	**KRAY**-nee-oh-**SAY**-kral	S/ R/CF R/	-al *pertaining to* crani/o- *skull* -sacr- *sacrum*	Referring to the total length of the spine
Feldenkrais method	**FEL**-den-kries **METH**-od		Moshe Feldenkrais, 1904– 1984, Russian engineer	Series of exercises to discover new ways of pain-free movement
kinesiology	ki-**NEE**-see-**OL**-oh-jee	S/ R/CF	-logy *study of* kinesi/o- *movement*	Study of muscles and body parts involved in movement
megavitamin	meg-ah-**VIE**-tah-min	P/ R/ R/	mega- *enormous* -vita- *life* -min *amine*	Large dose of a vitamin
myofascial	**MY**-oh-**FASH**-ee-al	S/ R/CF R/	-al *pertaining to* my/o- *muscle* -fasci- *fascia*	Relating to the fascia surrounding and separating muscle tissue
myotherapy	**MY**-oh-**THAIR**-ah pee	S/ R/CF	-therapy *treatment* my/o- *muscle*	Treatment of muscles by massage
placebo	plah-**SEE**-boh		Latin *I shall please*	An inert compound with no innate therapeutic value
Rolfing	**ROLF**-ing		Ida Rolf, PhD, 1896–1979	Manipulation of connective tissue to realign and balance the whole body
tai chi	tie-**CHEE**		Chinese *supreme ultimate force*	Defined series of postures performed in fluid movement
yoga	**YOH**-gah		Hindu *unity*	A system of lifestyle measures

Case Report 23.1 (continued)

For Mrs. Mary Carr, with her diagnosis of polymyalgia rheumatica, predni-sone had produced marked pain relief, and massage therapy is being used to provide further pain relief and reduce associated muscle and joint stiffness.

Abbreviations

NCBTMB	National Certification Board for Therapeutic Massage and Bodywork
NCTMB	National Certificate for Therapeutic Massage and Bodywork

that can produce benefits or harm to the body.

The **Alexander technique** reviews the body's whole movement pattern to increase self-awareness about posture and movements. It is particularly concerned with the relationship of the head to the spine.

The **Feldenkrais method** also works with awareness to identify and adjust ineffective, painful movements and to help regain flexibility, coordination, and comfort in movement.

EXERCISES   *Complete the term with the correct missing element found in the Word Analysis and Definition box (WAD) on this page. Fill in the blanks.*

1. treatment of muscles by massage   _____ /therapy

2. study of body parts involved in movement   _____ /ology

3. large doses of vitamins, minerals, aminoacids   _____ /vitamin

4. pertaining to the total length of the spine   cranio/_____ /_____

5. relating to the fascia separating muscle tissue   myo/_____ /_____

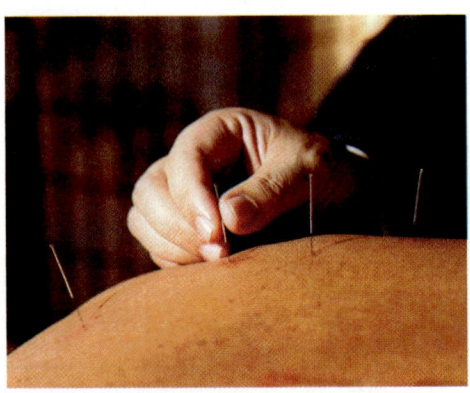

STANDARD MERIDIAN POINTS OF ACUPUNCTURE

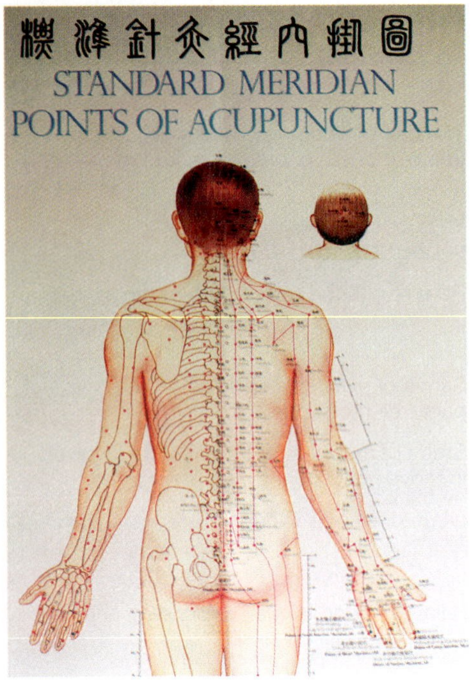

▲ **FIGURE 23.4** **Chinese Energy Pathways.**

![Acupuncture needles photo]

▲ **FIGURE 23.5** **Acupuncture Needles.**

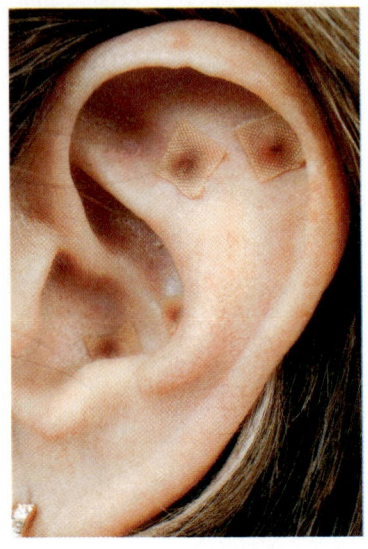

▲ **FIGURE 23.6** **Use of Magnets for Sleep Therapy.**

Energy Medicine

Modern science, particularly **quantum physics,** has shown that you are a web of energies that exists beneath your physical characteristics, connects your body–mind–spirit system, and gives life to your body. This concept is not new. It has been present in other cultures for thousands of years. The energy is called **qi** or **chi** in China, **prana** in India, **ki** in Japan and Korea, and **spirit** in many modern western healing teachings.

The term **subtle energy** is being used today by scientists to describe these energy forces in the body and environment. **Meridians** are energy pathways that carry energy into, through, and out of your body *(Figure 23.4)*. **Chakras** are seven energy centers that relate to specific organs.

Homeostasis *(see Chapter 2)* is the main essential in body chemistry. In energy medicine, balance and stability of the body's energy systems is the main essential. When the internal energy balance is disturbed, the body does not work well.

Energy psychology consists of mind–body interventions that involve the human energy matrix. This matrix includes the **biofield** of energy that envelops the body, the energy centers (chakras), and the energy pathways (meridians). Since 2006, the **Association for Comprehensive Energy Psychology (ACEP)** has offered certification programs for both licensed mental health professionals and other energy psychology practitioners.

Acupuncture originated in China more than 2000 years ago and is based on the meridians. **Acupuncture points (acupoints)** on the skin lead into the meridians and can be stimulated with needles or pressure **(acupressure)** to release or redistribute energy *(Figure 23.5)*.

In 1996, the FDA approved the use of sterile, nontoxic needles by licensed practitioners. It is frequently used as an **adjunct** or **ancillary treatment** in a comprehensive disease management program. It has been shown to be effective in treating postoperative dental pain, fibromyalgia, myofascial pain, osteoarthritis, lower back pain, carpal tunnel syndrome, and tennis elbow. It has also been effective in treating the nausea and vomiting related to chemotherapy or following anesthesia.

Biochemical and imaging studies have shown that acupuncture triggers the release of opioids in the same areas of the brain that are responsible for the beneficial effects of narcotic analgesics.

Bioelectrical acupuncture, in which the placed needles are attached to a low-voltage electrical stimulation system, is used by many practitioners to enhance the effect of acupuncture.

Therapeutic touch is being used extensively by nurses and other health practitioners for the relief of pain. The most common technique is to keep the hands a couple of inches from the patient's body to release energy into it. Its value is being keenly debated.

Reiki is a Japanese form of healing. The practitioner places hands on specific areas of the body, some of which can relate to the chakras, channeling energy for the body to use. Using its own innate intelligence, the body takes the energy it needs and directs it to where it is needed. It is a three-way partnership among the practitioner, client, and universal energy.

Electromagnetic fields (EMFs) are invisible lines of energy that are produced by the earth, sun, and by all electrical devices. We have learned to generate electromagnetic forces and saturate our environment with them. These forces influence your meridians, chakras, and subtle energy systems.

Electromagnetic therapy uses different devices to generate and open magnetic fields. These vary from strapping magnets to the skin *(Figure 23.6)*, to magnetic blankets, to machines used to stimulate the healing of bone fractures. Electromagnetic therapy has been used for numerous disorders. Scientific studies need to be done to define its efficacy.

Polarity therapy is based on the concept that the life-giving energy in the body is governed by opposite poles of positive and negative electromagnetic energy. When the flow of energy is blocked, disease results. Polarity therapy uses the practitioner's hands and fingers to balance the energy field.

WORD	PRONUNCIATION	ELEMENTS		DEFINITION
acupoint	AK-you-point	P/ R/	acu- *needle, sharp* -point *to pierce*	Point of entry in the skin to a meridian
acupressure	AK-you-presh-ur	S/ P/ R/	-ure *process* acu- *needle, sharp* -press- *to press*	Application of pressure to acupoints
adjunct	AJ-ungkt		Latin *joined to*	Something joined to another but is not an essential part
ancillary	AN-sil-air-ree		Latin *relating to a servant*	Accessory, adjunct
biofield	bi-oh-FIELD	R/CF R/	bi/o- *life* -field *definite area*	Area of energy in and surrounding the body
chakra	CHAK-rah		Hindu *center of energy*	One of seven centers of energy in the body
chi (also spelled qi)	CHEE		Chinese *force of energy*	Universal life force
electromagnetic	ee-LEK-troh-mag-NET-ik	S/ R/CF R/	-ic *pertaining to* electr/o- *electricity* -magnet- *magnet*	Energy propagated through matter and space
ki	KEY		Japanese *universal life force*	Universal energy of life
meridian	meh-RID-ee-an		Latin *midday*	Energy line connecting different anatomic sites
polarity	po-LAR-ih-tee		Latin *as the pole of the earth or a magnet*	Possession of opposite characteristics
prana	PRAH-nah		Hindu *universal life force*	Vital power
quantum physics	KWAHN-tum FIZ-iks		Latin *how much*	The study of subatomic particles

Light therapy is the use of natural or artificial light to treat depressive and sleep disorders. A bright-light box generates full-spectrum or white light and is used for treating the "winter blues" or **seasonal affective disorder (SAD)**.

Colored light therapy uses floodlights of different colors to treat migraines, and **cold laser therapy** uses low-intensity laser light to reduce inflammation and heal wounds.

Abbreviations

ACEP	Association for Comprehensive Energy Psychology
EMF	electromagnetic field
SAD	seasonal affective disorder

EXERCISES

Match the definitions in column 1 with the correct medical language of CAM in column 2. Check this spread if you are unsure of your answers to the questions.

_____ 1. point of entry in the skin to a meridian

_____ 2. area of energy in and around the body

_____ 3. means the same as ancillary

_____ 4. transcutaneous insertion of needles

_____ 5. energy line connecting anatomic sites

_____ 6. one of seven centers of energy in the body

_____ 7. energy sent through matter and space

_____ 8. application of pressure to acupoints

_____ 9. main essential in body chemistry

_____ 10. surrounding substance

A. electromagnetic

B. acupuncture

C. matrix

D. acupressure

E. biofield

F. homeostasis

G. adjunct

H. chakra

I. meridian

J. acupoint

CASE REPORT 23.2

Fulwood Medical Center

Mr. Mathew Hickman is a 74-year-old man recently diagnosed with prostate cancer. On a routine annual physical examination, a rectal examination revealed a slightly enlarged prostate with a small central nodule, and his **prostate-specific antigen (PSA)** was elevated. The only urinary symptom he has is occasional urgency.

In consultation with urologist Phillip Johnson, MD, Mr. Hickman learned that most prostate cancers are slow growing. With minimal symptoms and because of his age, he decided on "watchful waiting" with clinical examinations and PSA tests every six months. Dr. Johnson also recommended that a good nutrition program could reduce the progression of prostate cancer.

With the guidance of nutritionist Karen Goodrich, PhD, Mr. Hickman made a commitment to increase organic colorful vegetables and whole grains in his diet. This will provide vitamins, antioxidants, minerals, phytochemicals, and fiber. His supplements include an additional multivitamin, selenium, zinc, and fish oil (with omega-3). He also plans to drink green tea and to take the herb saw palmetto berry extract.

At his last examination by Dr. Johnson, his prostate had not enlarged, and his PSA was unchanged. He is continuing with his healthy lifestyle.

CAM IN THE UNITED STATES (continued)

Biologic-Based Practices

Dietary supplements are also called **nutritional supplements** or just **supplements.** They include:

- **Vitamins** *(see Chapter 22)*

- **Minerals** *(see Chapter 22)*

- **Herbs**—either as single herbs or mixtures

- **Botanicals**—another term for herbs

- **Spices**—such as garlic and turmeric

- **Amino acids**—such as arginine (a vasodilator) and lysine (helps form collagen)

- **Enzymes**—proteins that speed up chemical reactions in the body. For example, digestive enzymes such as lactaid (for lactose intolerance, *see Chapter 6*), bromelain, and papain.

- **Glandular products**—ingredients made from the glands of animals; for example, extracts from animal thyroid and thymus glands. Many CAM practitioners consider these products ineffective and even dangerous.

Dietary supplements cannot claim to prevent or treat any disease but can claim to maintain "normal structure and function" of body systems. Some dietary supplements have become part of conventional medicine because of their proven efficacy. For example, the vitamin folic acid taken early in pregnancy prevents certain **neural tube** birth defects; the use of the carotenoid lutein with vitamins C and E and the mineral zinc can slow the progression of the eye disease age-related macular degeneration *(see Chapter 4)*.

Herbal medicines are derived from natural sources. However, natural does not always mean safe. Some mushrooms that grow naturally in the wild are safe, while others are poisonous.

Many herbal medicines can interact with prescription drugs. Table 23.2 shows some of these interactions.

Supplement manufacturers must meet the requirements of the FDA's **Good Manufacturing Practices (GMPs)** to guarantee product quality and consistency. Unfortunately, what's in the bottle does not always match what's on the label. **Echinacea** is one of the most frequently used herbs to prevent or treat colds and to stimulate the immune system. One study analyzed 59 preparations of *Echinacea* and found half did not contain accurate information about the product. A study of **ginseng** products found that most contained less than half the amount of ginseng listed on the labels.

Keynote

The 1994 federal **Dietary Supplements Health and Education Act (DSHEA)** permits the sale of dietary supplements over-the-counter without requiring the products to be proven safe and effective—as is required for prescription or classic over-the-counter drugs licensed by the **U.S. Food and Drug Administration (FDA).**

Abbreviations

DSHEA	Dietary Supplements Health and Education Act
FDA	U.S. Food and Drug Administration
GMP	Good Manufacturing Practice

Keynote

"People who are allergic to the daisy family, which includes ragweed, are more likely to have allergic reactions to *Echinacea*."

WORD	PRONUNCIATION	ELEMENTS		DEFINITION
echinacea (common name) *Echinacea* (genus)	ek-ih-**NAY**-sha	S/ R/	-acea *condition* echin- *hedgehog*	Spiky North American herb
Ginkgo biloba	**GING**-koh **BIL**-oh-bah		Chinese tree with bilobed leaves	Extract of leaves used as a vasodilator
ginseng	**JIN**-seng		Chinese *man root or image*	Extract made from the root of a Chinese plant
neural tube	**NYU**-ral TYUB	S/ R/	-al *pertaining to* neur- *nerve*	Embryologic tubelike structure that forms the brain and spinal cord
supplement	**SUH**-pleh-ment	R/	supplement *supply a deficiency*	Substance taken to remedy or prevent a deficiency

TABLE 23.2 Herbal Interactions with Prescription Drugs

Herb	Prescription Drug	Effect of Interaction
Ginkgo biloba	Anticoagulants (e.g., coumadin)	Increased risk of bleeding
Ginseng	Diabetes medications (e.g., insulin, tolbutamide)	Lower blood sugar levels
St. John's wort	a) antidepressives b) anticancer drugs c) birth control drugs d) HIV protease inhibitor	a) increases effects b) reduces effects c) reduces effects d) reduces effects
Echinacea	Immunosuppressant drugs	Decreases effectiveness
Garlic	Anticoagulants (e.g., coumadin)	Increased risk of bleeding

EXERCISES

Suffixes. *Underline the suffix in each of the following terms, and give a meaning for each element. Fill in the blanks.*

1. Neural: the suffix is _____ and means _____ .

2. *Echinacea:*   the suffix is _____ and means _____ .

Write a sentence for each of these terms as it might appear in patient documentation:

3. _____

   _____

   _____

4. _____

   _____

   _____

Mind–Body Medicine

Mind–body medicine is based on the interactions between your mind (as expressed by the brain), body, and behavior. It shows the powerful ways in which mental, emotional, and spiritual interventions can affect behavior and health. It also emphasizes each person's individual responsibility for self-care and health.

Biofeedback is a method of taking information from a variety of monitoring procedures and equipment to learn how to control certain involuntary body responses. These responses include:

- muscle tension
- blood pressure
- heart rate
- brain activity

The machines and techniques used in biofeedback include:

- **Electromyogram (EMG)** uses electrodes to measure muscle tension. Early recognition of the tension enables relaxation of the muscles to be actively generated. It is used for headaches, neck pain, back pain, and **bruxism** (grinding your teeth).

- **Temperature biofeedback** uses sensors attached to fingers to measure skin temperature *(Figure 23.7)*. Stress often drops skin temperature due to vasoconstriction, and this technique prompts relaxation and vasodilation. It is used in peripheral vascular disease and to reduce the frequency of migraine attacks.

- **Galvanic skin response (GSR) training** uses sensors to measure the amount of perspiration on your skin, thus alerting you to anxiety. It is used in treating emotional disorders such as anxiety and phobias.

The **Biofeedback Certification Institute of America (BCIA)** certifies biofeedback therapists, who must be licensed in another area of health care or working under the guidance of a health care professional.

Meditation has been practiced for thousands of years, mostly in the Eastern cultures in spiritual and mystical contexts. Its technique is to concentrate on the moment and clear the mind of chattering thoughts and worries. It is used to prevent or reduce stress and for anxiety, depression, hypertension, and coronary artery disease.

Recent studies have shown that meditation increases brain activity and size in areas associated with positive emotional states and areas involved in control of the autonomic nervous system.

Prayer can be defined as an active process of appealing to a higher power. It is frequently used for health reasons on behalf of yourself or for others.

Spirituality can be defined as your sense of purpose or meaning to life, beyond material values. Spirituality can be practiced in many ways, including through religion.

The effect of prayer and spirituality on health outcomes is being studied extensively, particularly for their effect on the quality of life for patients with HIV/AIDS and cancer.

Hypnosis (hypnotherapy) aims to reach an altered state of consciousness in which the mind is relaxed and susceptible to suggestions to change behavior or to explore unconscious memories.

Studies of hypnotherapy have suggested a benefit for different types of chronic pain and for postprocedural pain. It is sometimes used with cognitive-behavioral therapy *(see Chapter 19)* to treat anxiety, insomnia, smoking cessation, **irritable bowel syndrome (IBS)**, and **posttraumatic stress disorder (PTSD)**.

Visualization (imagery) is based on the theory that the controlled use of mental images to evoke strong emotions or fantasy can help a number of health conditions. You clearly imagine what you want to occur or heal and focus on it frequently to make it part of your life. The results of using this self-help technique are very personal and inconsistent.

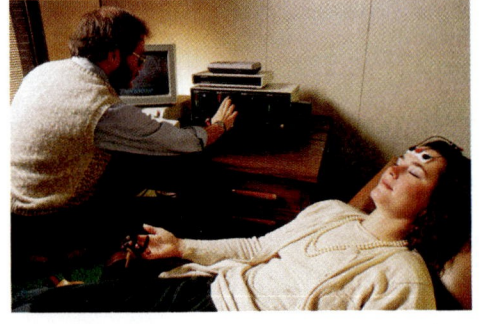

▲ **FIGURE 23.7** **Patient Undergoing Biofeedback.**

Keynote

A study in 1986 by insurance companies looked at 2000 meditators in Iowa and found them to be much healthier than the rest of the population in 17 major areas of disease.

A study of AIDS patients found that frequency of prayer was related to longer survival.

A study in Iowa linked church attendance with living longer.

Abbreviations

BCIA Biofeedback Certification Institute of America
EMG electromyogram
GSR galvanic skin response
IBS irritable bowel syndrome
PTSD posttraumatic stress disorder

Keynote

Ten to 15% of adults are highly hypnotizable, and 20% are highly resistant. The rest are in between these extremes.

Creative therapists are usually part of a team that includes doctors, physical therapists, speech therapists, and occupational therapists.

S = Suffix   P = Prefix   R = Root   R/CF = Combining Form

WORD	PRONUNCIATION	ELEMENTS		DEFINITION
electromyogram	ee-lek-troh-**MY**-oh-gram	S/ R/CF R/CF	**-gram** *record* **electr/o-** *electric* **-my/o-** *muscle*	Recording of electric currents associated with muscle action
galvanic	gal-**VAN**-ik	S/ R/	**-ic** *pertaining to* **galvan-** from Luigi Galvani, 1737–1798, Italian physician and anatomist	Low-voltage electric current
imagery	**IM**-aj-ree	S/ R/	**-ery** *condition* **imag-** *likeness*	Visualization of pleasant fantasies
spirituality	**SPEAR**-ih-choo-**AL**-ity	S/ S/ R/CF	**-ity** *condition* **-al-** *pertaining to* **spirit/u-** *spirit*	Meaning to life that comes from the spirit or soul rather than the physical body
visualization	**VIH**-zhoo-wah-lih-**ZAY**-shun	S/ S/ R/	**-ation** *action* **-iz-** *subject to* **visual-** *sight*	Form mental images or pictures

Note: Not a single term in this WAD has a prefix. Roots or combining forms can appear at the beginning of a term. *Their place in the term does not change their identity.*

Creative therapies, such as dance, music, drama, or art, allow patients to express difficult emotions such as anger or grief and to express what cannot be said. Originally designed for people with physical and mental disabilities, they are also being used in the rehabilitation phase of many illnesses and in dealing with stress and bereavement.

EXERCISES

Build your knowledge of elements with the following exercise. The term and the meaning of one of its elements are given to you. Find the correct element in the given term as defined by the meaning. The first one is done for you. Fill in the blanks and then answer the questions.

Term	Meaning of One Element in This Term	Defined Element
1. hypnotherapy	treatment	*therapy*
2. electromyogram	record	
3. visualization	sight	
4. galvanic	pertaining to	
5. spirituality	condition	
6. imagery	condition	

7. Which two terms pertain to electric current?_____ and _____

8. Which term relates to forming mental images?_____

9. Which term means visualization of pleasant fantasies?_____

10. Which term provides a meaning to life?_____

Mrs. Andrea Turpin is a 39-year-old civil servant, married with three children between 12 and 7 years. Since adolescence, she has had a moderate scoliosis of her spine, producing recurrent back pain (Figure 23.8). Her orthopedic surgeon prescribed Vioxx and suggested spinal surgery with the placement of rods.

Her Web research showed that Vioxx had significant side effects, with an increased risk of heart attacks and strokes, and that the surgery did not guarantee relief of pain and had a long and difficult rehabilitation.

She explored CAM alternatives, visited a chiropractor, and now also has acupuncture and neuromuscular massage. She has minimal pain and is able to manage her life and enjoy skiing. Vioxx has since been taken off the market.

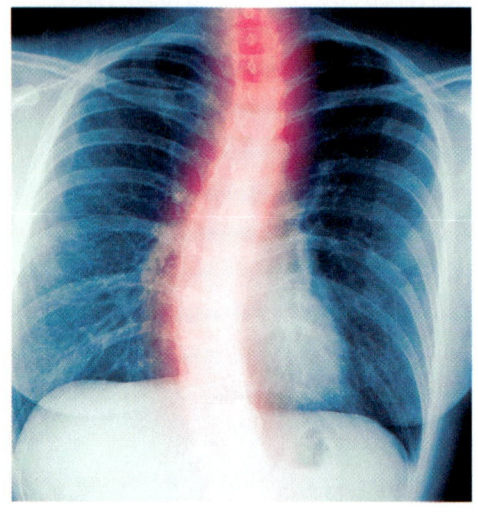

▲ **FIGURE 23.8   X-Ray of Scoliosis of the Spine.**

Keynote

The results of controlled trials of homeopathy are contradictory. In some trials, homeopathy is no more effective than a placebo. In others, the results were greater than from a placebo.

Licensed naturopathic physicians have completed four years of education in basic and clinical sciences.

There is no national standard for licensing Ayurvedic practitioners in the United States.

Abbreviation

NCCAOM   National Certification Commission for Acupuncture and Oriental Medicine

▲ **FIGURE 23.9   Qigong.**

WHOLE-MEDICINE SYSTEMS

Chiropractic medicine has its primary focus on the detection, reduction, and correction of spinal misalignments and resulting pain and nervous system dysfunction, as in Andrea Turpin's case. **Chiropractors** frequently use **manipulation** to move tissue. Gentle manipulations are referred to as mobilization or **adjustment.** Chiropractors in training spend five years in basic and clinical sciences and most complete postgraduate training in radiology and musculoskeletal therapeutics.

Osteopathic medicine began in 1892 in a similar belief to chiropractic medicine. However, it has evolved progressively towards allopathic medicine. Today, the training, practice, and licensure of osteopathic physicians **(osteopaths)** are identical to those of allopathic physicians.

Homeopathic medicine practitioners are frequently called **homeopaths.** Most **homeopathy** in the United States is practiced as part of another health care practice, such as allopathic medicine, naturopathy, or chiropractic medicine.

Homeopathy is based on the belief that every person has energy called a vital force that, when out of balance, produces health problems. Homeopathic treatment uses minuscule (extremely small) doses of substances (called remedies) that produce the characteristic symptoms of an illness in healthy people when given in larger doses. The intent is to stimulate the body's own defense mechanisms and healing responses.

The remedies used are derived from natural substances that come from plants, minerals, or animals. Because they are so dilute, they do not require FDA approval and testing for safety and efficacy.

Naturopathic medicine is a **holistic** approach to health and healing to recognize the integrity of the whole person. The **naturopath's** role is to facilitate the **inherent** capacity of the body to establish, maintain, and restore health. Symptoms are expressions of the body's attempts to heal, and the root causes of illness at the physical, genetic, mental, emotional, and spiritual level must be sought.

Naturopathic practices include nutrition, herbal medicine, homeopathic medicine, physical medicine, and acupuncture.

Oriental medicine or **Chinese medicine** is based on the concept that the body's vital energy (chi, or qi) circulates through channels called meridians that have branches to organs. Illness is a blockage or imbalance of chi. Acupuncture, herbal remedies, massage, and **Qigong** are used to restore balance. Qigong consists of numerous exercises and breathing routines performed daily to improve the function of the qi *(Figure 23.9).* Acupuncture is discussed in the energy medicine section of this chapter.

The **National Certification Commission for Acupuncture and Oriental Medicine (NCCAOM)** has licensed more than 13,000 practitioners.

Ayurvedic medicine is based on ideas from Hinduism and aims to integrate the body, mind, and spirit into a holistic unit. Disease arises when the person is out of harmony with the universe.

Three qualities, called **doshas,** control the body's activities and are associated with different body and personality types. Ayurvedic treatments require changes in lifestyle, diet, and habits. Herbs, spices, and oils are used frequently. For example, the spice **turmeric** is used to treat rheumatoid arthritis, Alzheimer disease, and for wound healing. **Aromatherapy,** in which the essential oils extracted from plants are inhaled or applied to the skin, is also used. For example, frankincense is used to enhance meditation, and myrrh is used for positive thinking.

WORD ANALYSIS AND DEFINITION

S = Suffix   P = Prefix   R = Root   R/CF = Combining Form

WORD	PRONUNCIATION	ELEMENTS		DEFINITION
adjustment (also called **manipulation**)	ah-**JUST**-ment	S/ R/	-ment *resulting state* adjust- *alter*	The action of bringing a body part into alignment with the others
aromatherapy	ah-**ROH**-mah-**THAIR**-ah-pee	S/ R/	-therapy *treatment* aroma- *smell, sweet herb*	Use of essential oils to promote well-being
aromatic (adj)	ah-roh-**MAT**-ik	S/	-tic *pertaining to*	Having an agreeable spicy odor, or one of a group of vegetable drugs
Ayurvedic (adj) **Ayurveda** (noun)	ah-yur-**VED**-ik ah-yur-**VAY**-duh	S/ P/ R/	-ic *pertaining to* ayur- *life* -ved- *knowledge*	A system of medicine arising from Hindu culture
chiropractic	kye-roh-**PRAK**-tik	S/ R/CF R/	-ic *pertaining to* chir/o- *hand* -pract- *practical*	Diagnosis, treatment, and prevention of mechanical disorders of the musculoskeletal system
chiropractor	kye-roh-**PRAK**-tor	S/	-or *a person who produces*	Practitioner of chiropractic
dosha	**DOH**-sha		Sanskrit *fault*	Psychophysical constitution of the body in Ayurvedic medicine
holistic	ho-**LIS**-tik	S/ R/	-ic *pertaining to* holist- *entire*	Pertaining to the care of the whole person in physical, mental, emotional, and spiritual dimensions
homeopathy	ho-mee-**OP**-ah-thee	S/ R/CF R/	-pathy *disease* home/o- *the same* -path *disease*	Treating disease with minute doses of substances
homeopath **homeopathic** (adj)	**HO**-mee-oh-path **HO**-mee-oh-**PATH**-ik	S/	-ic *pertaining to*	Practitioner of homeopathy
inherent	in-**HAIR**-ent		Latin *innate, inbred*	Occurring as a natural part of something
naturopathy	nah-chur-**OP**-ah-thee	S/ R/CF R/	-pathy *disease* natur/o- *nature* -path *disease*	Holistic system of medicine with a natural approach to healing
naturopath **naturopathic** (adj)	**NAH**-chur-oh-path nah-chur-oh-**PATH**-ik			Practitioner of naturopathy
osteopathy	**OS**-tee-**OP**-ah-thee	S/ R/CF R/	-pathy *disease* oste/o- *bone* -path *disease*	Medical practice based on maintaining the balance of the body
osteopath	**OS**-tee-oh-path			Practitioner of osteopathy
Qigong	**CHEE**-gong	R/ R/	qi- *vital force* -gong *daily practice*	Exercises and breathing routines performed daily
turmeric	ter-**MER**-ik		Yellow root	Spice used in Ayurvedic medicine

EXERCISES

Suffixes. *The suffix will tell you the difference between a practitioner and a practice. Choose the correct answers from among the following terms to fill in the blanks. There are more answers than questions.*

holistic	naturopathy	homeopathy	osteopath	naturopath
chiropractor	homeopath	osteopathy	aromatherapy	chiropractic

1. Holistic system of medicine with a natural approach to healing: _____

   One who practices this type of medicine: _____

2. Diagnosis, treatment, and prevention of mechanical disorders of the musculoskeletal system: _____

   One who practices this type of medicine: _____

3. Treating disease with small doses of drugs: _____

   One who practices this type of medicine: _____

4. Medical science close to conventional medicine: _____

   One who practices this type of medicine: _____

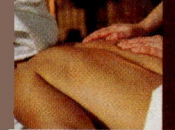

COMPLEMENTARY AND ALTERNATIVE MEDICINE
CHALLENGE YOUR KNOWLEDGE

A. **Case Report:** The following exercise is based entirely on the scenario of Andrea Turpin, which was presented in this chapter.

1. Read this scenario out loud to yourself for pronunciation practice.
2. Read it to yourself again and *underline* the medical terms.
3. Utilize your knowledge of the *language of complementary and alternative medicine* (and previous chapters) to answer the following questions based on the scenario.

> Mrs. Andrea Turpin is a 39-year-old civil servant, married with three children between 12 and 7 years. Since adolescence, she has had a moderate scoliosis of her spine, producing recurrent back pain. Her orthopedic surgeon prescribed Vioxx and suggested spinal surgery with the placement of rods. Her Web research showed that Vioxx had significant side effects, with an increased risk of heart attacks and strokes, and that the surgery did not guarantee relief of pain and had a long and difficult rehabilitation. She explored CAM alternatives, visited a chiropractor, and now also has acupuncture and neuromuscular massage. She has minimal pain and is able to manage her life and enjoy skiing. Vioxx has since been taken off the market.

1. Describe "scoliosis of the spine."

   _____

   _____

2. What is *recurrent* back pain?

   _____

3. What does an orthopedic surgeon treat?

   _____

   _____

4. What type of surgical hardware did he want to place in Mrs. Turpin's back?

   _____

5. What abbreviation can be used for heart attack? _____

6. What is another name for a stroke? _____

7. What is the purpose of rehabilitation?

   _____

   _____

8. What type of therapy would be involved in Mrs. Turpin's rehabilitation if she had this surgery performed? _____

9. What types of complementary and alternative medicine options is Mrs. Turpin now using?

   _____

10. Is a chiropractor a medical doctor? _____

   _____

B. **Combining Forms:** Know your elements. A root + combining vowel = combining form. Identify the combining forms in each of the following terms, then provide a meaning for each element. Fill in the chart, then answer the questions.

Medical Term	Combining Form	Combining Form Means
chiropractic		
electromyogram		
homeopathy		
myofascial		
naturopathic		
osteopath		
reflexology		

1. Which term is a practitioner? _____

2. Which term is a diagnostic test? _____

3. Which terms are whole-medicine systems?

   _____

4. Which term practices adjustments? _____

Now take any three terms from the chart above and use each of them in a sentence that would appear in patient documentation.

5. _____

   _____

6. _____

   _____

7. _____

   _____

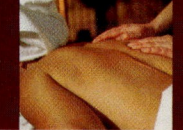

COMPLEMENTARY AND ALTERNATIVE MEDICINE

C. **CAM practices can be divided into the following five major groups.** Each group has been assigned a number. From the definition, identify the CAM technique, then assign it a number from its correct group. Fill in the blanks. The first one is done for you.

CAM Group
1. Manipulative and body-based practices
2. Energy medicine
3. Biologic-based practices
4. Mind–body practices
5. Whole-medicine systems

Definition	CAM Technique	CAM Group
1. based on the healing power of nature	*naturopathic*	5
2. stimulates energy points on the body		
3. to *think over* — to *contemplate*		
4. uses pressure points in the hands and feet		
5. treating disease with minute doses of substances		
6. transfer of energy; hands on/near a patient		
7. manipulation of tissues with the hands/tools		
8. adjustment of joints, especially spine		
9. training technique affects body functions		
10. substances found in nature		

D. **Terminology Challenge:** *Kinesiology*

Name at least three types of occupations that would need to study kinesiology in their formal educational training, and answer (a) why they would need that knowledge, and (b) how they would use that knowledge. (Occupations can be outside of medicine.)

1. _____

_____

_____

2. _____

_____

_____

3. _____

_____

_____

E. **Prefixes and Suffixes:** Expand your knowledge of prefixes and suffixes from the *language of CAM*. Column 1 contains the element. In column 2, you must identify it as either a prefix or a suffix. In column 3 you must write the meaning of the element.

Element	Prefix/Suffix	Meaning of Element
1. allo		
2. ation		
3. acu		
4. osis		
5. gram		
6. oid		
7. al		
8. mega		
9. ure		
10. acea		

F. **Patient Education:** Your patient has just been told that "biochemical and imaging studies have shown that acupuncture triggers the release of opioids in the same areas of the brain that are responsible for the beneficial effects of narcotic analgesics." Can you explain this to your patient in layman's terms?

_____

_____

_____

_____

_____

G. **Elements:** Deconstruct the following medical terminology into its basic elements and their meanings. Fill in the table.

Medical Term	Meaning of Prefix	Meaning of Root/CF	Meaning of Suffix
acupuncture			
allopathic			
chiropractic			
craniosacral			
electromyogram			
homeopathy			
hypnosis			
kinesiology			
myofascial			
neural			

COMPLEMENTARY AND ALTERNATIVE MEDICINE

H. **The Language of CAM:** Test what you have learned about *complementary and alternative medicine* by answering the following questions correctly. Circle the best answer.

1. A Japanese form of healing is:

    a. tai chi

    b. Rolfing

    c. yoga

    d. Reiki

    e. acupuncture

2. St. John's wort is a(n):

    a. disease

    b. inflammation

    c. herb

    d. megavitamin

    e. skin lesion

3. An allopathic physician practices:

    a. chiropractic medicine

    b. osteopathic medicine

    c. homeopathic medicine

    d. naturopathic medicine

    e. conventional medicine

4. The medical term **bruxism** means:

    a. fast heartbeat

    b. swelling

    c. tooth grinding

    d. high blood pressure

    e. inflammation

5. An altered state of consciousness is produced by:

    a. homeopathy

    b. hypnosis

    c. biofeedback

    d. oriental medicine

    e. reflexology

6. Homeopathic treatment uses minuscule doses of substances called:

   a. hormones

   b. vitamins

   c. enzymes

   d. minerals

   e. remedies

7. In addition to treating SAD, light therapy is also used for:

   a. depression

   b. pain relief

   c. stress relief

   d. muscle injury

   e. cancer

8. Therapeutic touch is an example of:

   a. energy medicine

   b. manipulative practice

   c. biologic-based practice

   d. mind–body practice

   e. whole-medicine system

9. What term comes from the Greek *to knead, to handle:*

   a. matrix

   b. massage

   c. meditate

   d. manipulate

   e. myofascial

10. Which of these responses can be controlled by biofeedback:

    a. muscle tension

    b. blood pressure

    c. sweating

    d. a and b

    e. a and c

COMPLEMENTARY AND ALTERNATIVE MEDICINE

I. **The Language of CAM:** Test what you have learned about complementary and alternative medicine by answering the following questions correctly. Circle the best answer.

1.   Trigger point therapy is also known as:

   a. neuromuscular therapy

   b. sleep therapy

   c. myotherapy

   d. a and c

   e. a and b

2.   Essential oils extracted from plants are inhaled or applied to the skin in:

   a. Reiki

   b. hypnotherapy

   c. sleep therapy

   d. Ayurvedic medicine

   e. aromatherapy

3.   Which product is *not* a dietary supplement:

   a. vitamins

   b. minerals

   c. hormones

   d. enzymes

   e. herbs

4.   **Mobilization** and **adjustment** are two terms used by a(n):

   a. homeopath

   b. pediatrician

   c. chiropractor

   d. naturopath

   e. otolaryngologist

5.   **Qi, chi, prana,** and **ki** all refer to:

   a. diseases

   b. yoga postures

   c. energy

   d. herbs

   e. tai chi

J. **Abbreviations:** Some, but not all, of the sentences in this exercise contain medical terms that have abbreviations. Rewrite each sentence, substituting the correct abbreviation where applicable. Fill in the blanks.

1. Light therapy was prescribed for her seasonal affective disorder.

   _____

   _____

2. The national certification board for therapeutic massage and bodywork is the accredited entity that issues the national certificate for therapeutic massage and bodywork.

   _____

   _____

3. Creative therapists are usually part of a team that includes medical doctors, physical therapists, speech therapists, and occupational therapists.

   _____

   _____

4. Reiki, therapeutic touch, and acupuncture are all examples of energy medicine.

   _____

   _____

5. Dietary supplements must meet the requirements of the food and drug administration's good manufacturing practices for product quality and consistency.

   _____

   _____

6. The patient was referred to the national institutes of health special center for complementary and alternative medicine known as the national center for complementary and alternative medicine.

   _____

   _____

7. Her electrocardiogram and electromyogram both were reported as normal, but her computed tomography scan and magnetic resonance imaging were rescheduled because of equipment problems.

   _____

   _____

COMPLEMENTARY AND ALTERNATIVE MEDICINE

K. **Key Words:** Key definitions can contain key words that are the basic core of the statement. Understanding the essential difference in the statements will help you make a distinction in their meanings. The following definitions are taken from the first page of this chapter. Underline the key word or words in each definition, then fill in the blanks.

Definitions:

1. Complementary medicine is used together with standard or conventional medical treatments.

2. Alternative medicine is used instead of conventional medical treatments.

3. Integrative medicine is a total approach to care that combines conventional medicine with CAM practices that involve the patient's body, mind, and spirit in the therapeutic process.

Now, utilizing the key words in the definitions, write yourself a shortcut for remembering how to tell the different systems apart.

Complementary medicine: _____

Alternative medicine: _____

Integrative medicine: _____

L. **The Terminology of CAM contains Latin, Greek, and Eastern terms.** These cannot be further deconstructed into prefix, root, or suffix. You must know them for what they are. Test your knowledge of these terms with this exercise. Match the meaning in column l with the correct medical term in column 2.

_____	1. to knead, handle	A. Reiki
_____	2. joined to	B. meditation
_____	3. supreme ultimate force	C. yoga
_____	4. force of energy	D. ancillary
_____	5. vital power	E. tai chi
_____	6. to contemplate	F. prana
_____	7. unity	G. massage
_____	8. posture	H. chi or qi
_____	9. relating to a servant	I. adjunct
_____	10. universal life force	J. asana

M. **Recall and Review:** How well do you remember these word elements from the previous chapter? Try to answer without first looking back to check. Fill in the blanks.

Element	Type of Element (P, R, CF, S)	Meaning of Element
adeno	_____	_____
ectomy	_____	_____
meso	_____	_____
stasis	_____	_____
ptosis	_____	_____

N. Short Answer: Recap what you have learned in this chapter by employing medical language to give some examples of dietary or herbal supplements, and explain why it is important to tell your doctor about any dietary or herbal supplements you are taking.

Give at least one example of an interaction between drugs and supplements that could be dangerous to the patient.

_____

_____

_____

_____

_____

_____

_____

O. Research and Discuss: Clinical trials and research studies often make use of placebos with their patient groups. Visit the school library or go online to research the role of _placebos_ in clinical trials, and be prepared to discuss your findings in class. You should be able to answer the following questions:

- What is a clinical trial?
- How and where do you find a clinical trial?
- What is the purpose of a clinical trial?
- How are patients picked for a clinical trial?
- What is a placebo?
- What is a placebo-controlled study?
- What is a control group?
- What is the "placebo effect"?

P. Elements: Knowledge of elements will always be your best clue to analyzing a medical term. Test your command of elements with the following exercise. Fill in the table.

Element	Element is (P, R, CF, S)	Meaning of Element	Medical Term Containing this Element
acu	_____	_____	_____
allo	_____	_____	_____
bio	_____	_____	_____
cranio	_____	_____	_____
holist	_____	_____	_____
ine	_____	_____	_____
kinesio	_____	_____	_____
myo	_____	_____	_____
osteo	_____	_____	_____
sacr	_____	_____	_____

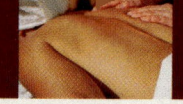

CHAPTER 23 REVIEW

COMPLEMENTARY AND ALTERNATIVE MEDICINE

CHAPTER SUMMARY EXERCISE

1. *Listen to the pronunciation of the medical terms as given by your instructor.*
2. *Circle the correct spelling of the medical term.*
3. *Match the correctly spelled terms to the brief descriptions below.*
4. *Write a sentence for each of the 15 terms that appear in this exercise.*

A. SPELLING COMPREHENSION: CIRCLE THE CORRECT SPELLING OF THE TERM.

1. manipulative	manipilative	mannipulative	manupilative	manepulative
2. polearity	polarity	pollarity	polarrity	polaritty
3. myofacial	myofascial	miofascial	miofacial	myofassial
4. vizulation	visualization	vizulliation	visualation	visuelation
5. creniosacral	craniosaccral	craniosacral	craniosacrul	creniosackrul
6. meridian	merridian	maridean	meridean	maridian
7. hipnossis	hypnosis	hypnossis	hipnosis	hypnoses
8. adjunct	addjunckt	adjunkt	addjunkt	adjunckt
9. Rulfing	Rolffing	Rollfing	Rolfling	Rolfing
10. placebbo	placibo	placeboo	plasebo	placebo
11. asanas	assanas	asannas	asanus	asanes
12. holestic	hollistic	holistic	holisteck	holeistick
13. alopathic	alopatic	allopathic	alopathetic	allopethic
14. ekinacea	echinacea	echinacia	ekinachia	echanacea
15. kenisiology	kinnesiology	kennesiology	kinesiology	kinessiology

B. MATCH THE NUMBER OF THE CORRECT TERM IN PART A WITH THE BRIEF DESCRIPTION OF THE TERM BELOW.

a. traditional medicine _____

b. total length of spine _____

c. action performed by a chiropractor _____

d. study of movement of muscles and body parts _____

e. energy line connecting anatomic sites _____

f. concentrates on connective tissue _____

g. possession of opposite characteristics _____

h. physical postures in yoga _____

i. care of the whole person _____

j. suggestions can change behavior _____

k. no therapeutic value   _____

l. not an essential part   _____

m. surrounds and separates muscle tissue _____

n. commonly used to treat colds _____

o. to form mental images   _____

C. USING YOUR KNOWLEDGE OF TERMS 1-15 IN PART A AND THEIR CORRECT SPELLING, WRITE A BRIEF SENTENCE FOR EACH OF THE TERMS AS IT MIGHT APPEAR IN PATIENT DOCUMENTATION.

1. _____

2. _____

3. _____

4. _____

5. _____

6. _____

7. _____

8. _____

9. _____

10. _____

11. _____

12. _____

13. _____

14. _____

15. _____

D. GO TO THE STUDENT CD. OPEN THE GLOSSARY AND PRACTICE YOUR PRONUNCIATION OF THE TERMS IN PART A OF THIS EXERCISE.

This chapter marks the end of the text. You have applied yourself to learning medical terminology, and what you take away from this course is commensurate with what you have put into learning this subject.

Remember: Every day on the job is a test of another kind—a test of your communication skills and professionalism. It is also an opportunity to continue your learning—which is a hallmark of a professional.

Appendices

End-of-Book Exercises

The following exercises draw from all the previous chapters in the text and will help you review some of the basic elements of medical terminology. Fill in the blanks.

Use these for study review!

A. Elements associated with body systems: The body systems are listed for you in the first column. Write five different roots/combining forms for each body system, with the meaning of the element, and an example of a medical term using that element. Fill in the table.

	Body System	Root/Combining Form	Meaning of Element	Medical Term Using This Element
	integumentary			
1.				
2.				
3.				
4.				
5.				
	musculoskeletal			
6.				
7.				
8.				
9.				
10.				
	nervous			
11.				
12.				
13.				
14.				
15.				
	endocrine			
16.				
17.				
18.				
19.				
20.				

	Body System	Root/Combining Form	Meaning of Element	Medical Term Using This Element
	cardiovascular			
21.				
22.				
23.				
24.				
25.				
	lymphatic			
26.				
27.				
28.				
29.				
30.				
	digestive			
31.				
32.				
33.				
34.				
35.				
	respiratory			
36.				
37.				
38.				
39.				
40.				
	urinary			
41.				
42.				
43.				
44.				
45.				
	reproductive			
46.				
47.				
48.				
49.				
50.				

ELEMENTS BY GROUPING

B. List all the elements that denote a color.

	Element	Color
1.	leuk/o	white
2.		
3.		
4.		
5.		
6.		
7.		
8.		

C. List all the elements that denote a location or direction (above, below, etc.).

	Element	Location
1.	epi	above
2.		
3.		
4.		
5.		
6.		
7.		
8.		
9.		
10.		
11.		
12.		

D. List all the elements that denote a number.

	Element	Number
1.	mono	one
2.		
3.		
4.		
5.		
6.		
7.		
8.		

E. **Difference between elements:** Many elements sound and look similar but have very different meanings. Be precise in your communication—patient safety depends on you!

	Element	Type of Element (P/R/CF/S)	Meaning of Element	Medical Term from Any Chapter Containing This Element
1.	pheresis			
2.	phoresis			
3.	uretero			
4.	urethro			
5.	acro			
6.	acromio			
7.	homeo			
8.	hemo			
9.	bi			
10.	bio			
11.	inter			
12.	intra			
13.	colo			
14.	colpo			
15.	echo			
16.	ecto			
17.	radiculo			
18.	reticulo			
19.	metacarpo			
20.	metatarso			
21.	vaso			
22.	veno			
23.	thymo			
24.	thyro			
25.	diplo			
26.	dipso			
27.	necro			
28.	narco			
29.	lipo			
30.	litho			
31.	sacro			
32.	sarco			
33.	oro			
34.	orcho			
35.	brady			
36.	brachy			

	Element	Type of Element (P/R/CF/S)	Meaning of Element	Medical Term from Any Chapter Containing This Element
37.	plexy			
38.	pexy			
39.	stalsis			
40.	stasis			

F. Elements: Reinforce your knowledge of the elements with this comprehensive list. Identify the element as to type, give its meaning, and then use it in an appropriate medical term. Fill in the table. The first one is done for you.

	Element	Type of Element (P/R/CF/S)	Meaning of Element	Medical Term Containing This Element
1.	*A, an*	*P*	*without*	*anencephaly*
2.	adeno			
3.	algesia			
4.	angio			
5.	brachio			
6.	broncho			
7.	bucco			
8.	cerumino			
9.	chole			
10.	coagulo			
11.	de			
12.	denti			
13.	dia			
14.	echo			
15.	ectasis			
16.	emesis			
17.	flex			
18.	fluoro			
19.	flux			
20.	gen			
21.	gingiv			
22.	glosso			
23.	hepat			
24.	hist			
25.	hydro			
26.	iasis			
27.	ion			
28.	isch			
29.	jaundo			
30.	jejuno			

	Element	Type of Element (P/R/CF/S)	Meaning of Element	Medical Term Containing This Element
31.	karyo			
32.	kerato			
33.	kinesio			
34.	laparo			
35.	lith			
36.	lysis			
37.	malacia			
38.	morpho			
39.	myelo			
40.	naso			
41.	necro			
42.	neo			
43.	olfact			
44.	oligo			
45.	os			
46.	penia			
47.	procto			
48.	psycho			
49.	rrhaphy			
50.	rrhea			
51.	rrhoid			
52.	stasis			
53.	stetho			
54.	stomy			
55.	terato			
56.	thrombo			
57.	tripsy			
58.	ule			
59.	um			
60.	uria			
61.	vascul			
62.	viscer			
63.	xeno			

G. Spelling demons: Precision in communication and professionalism require correct spelling of all medical terms. Circle the correct spelling of each term, then on the line below, deconstruct the correct spelling of the term with slashes, and write a brief explanation of the medical term.

1. acondroplasia   achondroplasia   acondroplesia

_____

2. hemorrhage   hemmorrhage   hemorhage

3. escultation   auscaltation   auscultation

4. cirrosis   sirosis   cirrhosis

5. aneurism   aneurysm   anerysm

6. antiarrythmics   antiarrhthmics   antiarrhythmics

7. hysterectomy   histerectomy   hystirectomy

8. systocele   cystocele   cystosele

9. osteomyelitis   osteomylitis   osteomyeletis

10. hernioraphy   herniorraphy   herniorrhaphy

11. preeclampsia   preclampsia   preklampsia

12. bronchopneumonia   broncopneumonia   bronchopeumonia

13. jundice   jaundice   jaunndice

14. diverticulosis   deverticulosis   diverticculosis

15. cholesterol   colesterol   cholesteral

16. malleolus   maleolus   malleolis

17. eustachian   eustacian   eushtacian

18. nephrilithiasis   nephrolithiasis   nephralithiasis

19. cholecystectomy   colecystectomy   collecystectomy

_____

20. ketoacidosis   ketoneacidosis   kettoacidosis

_____

21. epididimis   epididymus   epididymis

_____

22. immunosuppression   imunosupresion   immunosupression

_____

23. laryngapharnix   laryngopharynx   laryngopharnix

_____

24. exophthalmos   exopthalamos   exophtalamos

_____

25. galactorhea   gallactorea   galactorrhea

_____

26. rhabdomyosarcoma   rabdomyosarcoma   rhabomyosarcoma

_____

27. paresthesia   parasthesia   parresthesia

_____

28. fallopian   falopian   faalopian

_____

29. nosocomial   nosoccomial   nossocomial

_____

30. proptosis   protosis   proptossis

_____

31. thrombophlebitis   thembophlebitis   thrombopelpitis

_____

32. percutaneous   purcutaneous   perkutaneous

_____

33. gastroesophageal   gastroesopageal   gastroesophagial

_____

34. pneumonitis   penummonitis   pneumonnitis

_____

35. oophorectomy   ophorectomy   ooporectomy

_____

| 36. | uvula | uuvla | uvulla |

| 37. | tonsillectomy | tonsilectomy | tonssilectomy |

| 38. | streptococcus | striptococcus | streptococus |

| 39. | vasovasostomy | vasovesostomy | vesovasostomy |

| 40. | thyrotoxicosis | thyroidtoxicosis | thyrotoxicossis |

H. Review of Latin/Greek terms that do not deconstruct into elements. You must know these terms for what they are. The first one is done for you.

	Medical Term	Meaning of Term in Latin/Greek	Application to Medical Terminology
	cruciate	*cross*	*anterior cruciate ligament*
1.	integument		
2.	viscous		
3.	hirsutism		
4.	calculus		
5.	patent		
6.	zygote		
7.	Calorie		
8.	cognitive		
9.	lymph		
10.	vector		
11.	lavage		
12.	ptosis		
13.	gonad		
14.	matrix		
15.	apex		
16.	modality		
17.	ganglion		
18.	benign		
19.	cartilage		
20.	toxin		
21.	labium		
22.	node		
23.	bronchus		

I. Body systems: Use your knowledge of medical terminology to fill in the following chart with terms applicable to each specific body system. There may not be an appropriate answer for every blank. The first one is done for you.

	Body System	Study of (practice)	One Who Studies (practitioner)	Disease	Procedure
1.	*integumentary*	*dermatology*	*dermatologist*	*eczema*	*excisional biopsy*
2.	musculoskeletal				
3.	nervous				
4.	endocrine				
5.	cardiovascular				
6.	lymphatic				
7.	digestive				
8.	respiratory				
9.	urinary				
10.	reproductive				

J. Symptoms/chief complaint: The patients of Fulwood Medical Center have come into the various clinics with the following complaints. Use the correct medical terminology to enter the chief complaint in the patient's chart.

	Patient Complains of	Correct Medical Terminology for Chart
1.	double vision	
2.	blood in urine	
3.	ringing in ears	
4.	painful breathing	
5.	pus in gums	
6.	sore throat	
7.	earache	
8.	pink eye	
9.	fear of heights	
10.	low blood pressure	
11.	hair loss	
12.	inability to urinate	
13.	fainting	
14.	lack of bowel movements	
15.	broken wrist	
16.	nosebleeds	
17.	impacted earwax	
18.	bed-wetting	
19.	heavy menstrual bleeding	
20.	stomach ache	

K. Transcription exercises: The following paragraphs from patient documentation and office forms contain errors. Circle the errors in the paragraph, then rewrite the correct medical terminology on the lines below.

1. This 65-year-old male with a prior history of an appendectomy awoke on the day of admission with crampy addominal pain which was accompanied by destention, nausea, and vomitting.

   _____

2. Sections show an increased number of cysstically dilated glands with the lining epithelium composed primarily of muccous secreting glands. Diagnosis: Low-grade mucoepidimoid carcinomma.

   _____

3. Hemmostasis was accomplished using electrocogulation. The patient had a slight commuted fracture of the medial maleolus. The wound was irrigated and debris was removed.

   _____

4. The patient is a 58-year-old black female with an osteosarcoma of the hemipelvis who underwent successful wide resuction and reconstruction; however, two weeks later her wound became infected and perforated the rectim, which resulted in gross contammination.

   _____

5. Under general anesthesia it was clear that the patient had a grade II disruption of the latteral colateral ligament as well as an anterior and posterior cruxiate ligament disruption.

   _____

6. PA/lateral CXR: the heart size is normal. There is bilateral atellectasis noted. There is density within the overlying soft tissues of the right chest consistent with recent right-sided breast biopsie. There is no evidence of plural efusion or pneumothorax.

   _____

7. Numerous enlarged, abnormal appearing limph nodes in the right axila, with markedly thickened cortices and hillar effacement. Concerning for lympoma or metastaic disease. Further followup is recommended.

   _____

8. There is diffuse fatty infiltration of the liver. The spleen is unremarkable as well as kidneys and adrennal glands. There is no retroperitonial adenopathy or abdominal aortic aneursm. There are multiple calcifications within the galbladder consistent with choleithiasis.

   _____

9. Increased activity at the ankles and feet is seen bilateraly, likely related to degenerative/hypertopic changes. There is minimal increase activity at both shoulders and at the right sternocavicular joint, likely related to arthritic changes. No other significant abnormality is identified.

   _____

10. Past Medical History: childhood diseases

diphtheria   smallpox   scarlet fever   rhumatic fever
chorea   tyhphoid   whoping cough   chickenbox
mumps   meseles   tonsilitis   rubela

_____

11. Past Medical Illness: (within the last two years)

punmonia   plurisy   arthralgia   migrain headaches
malaria   sleep apnia   broncitis   cardiomyopathy
conjunctivetis   gout   otitus media   anemmia

_____

12. The gastriscope was advanced into the distal esopagus which was essentially normal. Advancement of the scope into the stomach showed evidence of erytema and gasritis. The pylorus was intubated and the duodenal bulb was visualized.

_____

L. **Coding exercises:** Solid knowledge of medical terminology will make you a better coder. Volumes I and II of ICD-9-CM contain diagnosis codes. CPT codes are billed for procedures and services. In the following exercise, choose whether the medical term requires an ICD-9-CM code or a CPT code (put a √ in the appropriate column).

	Medical Term	ICD-9-CM	CPT
1.	nephrectomy		
2.	CVA		
3.	carditis		
4.	blepharoplasty		
5.	thoracotomy		
6.	neurolysis		
7.	nephrosis		
8.	herniorrhaphy		
9.	conjunctivitis		
10.	osteoporosis		
11.	lithotripsy		
12.	LEEP		
13.	osteotomy		
14.	amniocentesis		
15.	anastomosis		
16.	embolus		
17.	IVF		
18.	rhinitis		
19.	fluoroscopy		
20.	embolectomy		
21.	fistula		
22.	MI		

	Medical Term	ICD-9-CM	CPT
23.	hematuria		
24.	hysterolysis		
25.	neoplasm		
26.	gingivectomy		
27.	arthrodesis		
28.	CF		
29.	leiomyoma		
30.	hemogram		

M. Diagnoses: The definition of the diagnosis is given to you. Assign an ICD-9-CM code from the code bank to the definition. Fill in the blanks.

CODE BANK

Medical Term	ICD-9-CM Code
acromegaly	253.0
anaphylaxis	995.61
anencephaly	740.0
blepharitis	373.00
cholera	001.9
Jakob-Creutzfeldt disease	046.1
DVT	453.40
eczema	692.9
endocarditis	424.90
enuresis	788.30
hyperkalemia	276.7
meningitis	322.9
osteoporosis	733.00
Peyronie disease	607.85
pneumothorax	512.8
pyromania	312.33
rickets	268.0
rubeola	055.9
Sjögren syndrome	710.2
Tay-Sachs disease	330.1
thrombocytopenia	287.5
toxic shock syndrome	040.82
urticaria	708.9

1. inflammation of the eyelid   _____
2. air in the pleural cavity   _____

3. rash of itchy wheals (hives) _____
4. inflammation of the lining of the heart _____
5. acute, contagious disease of childhood _____
6. inflammation of the brain and spinal cord covering _____
7. brittle, porous, fragile bones _____
8. vitamin D deficiency _____
9. caused by an exotoxin and associated with tampon use _____
10. enlargement of head and extremities due to excess growth
    hormone _____
11. autoimmune disease that attacks tear and salivary glands _____
12. human spongiform encephalopathy _____
13. involuntary bed-wetting _____
14. inflammatory skin disease often with a serous discharge _____
15. excessive amount of potassium in the blood _____
16. morbid impulse to set fires _____
17. deficiency of platelets _____
18. congenital, fatal disorder of fat metabolism _____
19. born without cerebral hemispheres _____
20. acute, endemic, infectious disease _____
21. penile bending and pain on erection _____
22. blood clot in a vein _____
23. immediate, severe, allergic reaction to peanuts _____

N. Surgical suffixes: The following suffixes are all associated with surgical procedures.
CPT codes are specific as to type of procedure—you can't code and bill a nephrotomy if
the patient actually had a nephrectomy. You must code what is documented in the medical
record. Know your suffixes!

This table contains surgical suffixes. Give the meaning of the suffix, an example of the suffix
in a term, and the definition of the term. The first one is done for you.

	Suffix	Suffix Meaning	Example of Term	Meaning of the Term
1.	*ectomy*	*removal of*	*nephrectomy*	*removal of the kidney*
2.	centesis			
3.	cision			
4.	desis			
5.	ostomy			
6.	pexy			
7.	plasty			
8.	rrhaphy			
9.	tomy			
10.	tripsy			

O. Work with more surgical terms. Can you identify the type of procedure these terms represent? You will see these terms in Volume III of ICD-9 and the CPT codes. Fill in the table.

	Medical Term	Brief Description of Procedure
1.	abdominocentesis	
2.	ablation	
3.	allograft	
4.	amputation	
5.	aspiration	
6.	catheterization	
7.	cauterization	
8.	curettage	
9.	debridement	
10.	dilation	
11.	excision	
12.	ligation	
13.	incision	
14.	manipulation	
15.	resection	

P. The following are code ranges for CPT codes. Notice that they are divided by body system. Analyze the medical term for the procedure, then decide which code range applies. The first one is done for you.

CODE RANGE

From–To

	From–To
integumentary system	10040–19499
musculoskeletal system	20000–29999
respiratory system	30000–32999
cardiovascular system	33010–39599
digestive system	40490–49999
urinary system	50010–53899
male genital system	54000–55980
female genital system and maternity care and delivery	56405–59899
endocrine system	60000–60699
nervous system	61000–64999
eye and ocular adnexa	65091–68899
auditory system	69000–69979

	Procedure	Meaning of Medical Term	Term Found in this Code Range
	arthrodesis	*surgical repair of a joint*	*20000–29999*
	GROUP ONE		
1.	cryosurgery		
2.	palatoplasty		
3.	biopsy of the uvula		
4.	amputation of a digit		
5.	myringotomy		
6.	vulvectomy		
7.	rhinoplasty		
8.	excision of decubitus ulcer		
9.	CABG		
10.	dermabrasion		
11.	gastrectomy		
12.	osteoplasty		
13.	percutaneous nephrolithotomy		
14.	vasectomy		
15.	adrenalectomy		
16.	bronchopulmonary lavage		
17.	C-section		
18.	ESWL (ureteral)		
19.	iridectomy		
20.	pulmonary lobectomy		
	GROUP TWO		
21.	keratoplasty		
22.	arthrotomy with meniscus repair		
23.	bilateral salpingo-oophorectomy		
24.	insertion of pacemaker		
25.	esophagogastroduodenoscopy		
26.	arteriovenous anastomosis		
27.	gingivectomy		
28.	meatotomy		
29.	neuroendoscopy		
30.	embolectomy		
31.	tympanostomy		
32.	herniorrhaphy (umbilical)		
33.	orchiopexy		
34.	colposcopy		
35.	neurorrhaphy		

	Procedure	Meaning of Medical Term	Term Found in this Code Range
36.	LASIK		
37.	appendectomy		
38.	THR		
39.	carotid endarterectomy		
40.	LEEP		

Q. Abbreviations: Reading patient documentation to extract/abstract information for coding purposes requires that you understand what you are reading. Identify the following abbreviations in the chart. Check (√) whether the abbreviation is a diagnosis, a procedure, or something else. In the last column, write the meaning of the abbreviation.

	Abbreviation	Diagnosis	Procedure	Other	Meaning of Abbreviation
1.	EBV				
2.	q.i.d.				
3.	BOM				
4.	SOB				
5.	PCL				
6.	SP				
7.	CPR				
8.	PDA				
9.	UTI				
10.	O.D.				
11.	CSF				
12.	ABG				
13.	PT				
14.	DJD				
15.	NSAID				
16.	p.r.n.				
17.	MI				
18.	CMA				
19.	CBC				
20.	ARDS				
21.	C5				
22.	URI				
23.	GI				
24.	WNV				
25.	CAD				
26.	AU				
27.	COPD				

	Abbreviation	Disease	Procedure	Other	Meaning of Abbreviation
28.	DEXA				
29.	WBC				
30.	EEG				
31.	ROM				
32.	STAT				
33.	LFT				
34.	CXR				
35.	AP				
36.	MRI				
37.	GYN				
38.	Hct				
39.	PVC				
40.	Pap				

Congratulations on a job well done!

Word Parts

B

Note: For easy identification, the word parts in this appendix appear in the same colors as in the Word Analysis and Definition boxes: suffix, prefix, root, root/combining form. Any term that is used in the text in both root and combining form is shown only in this appendix as a combining form.

WORD PART	DEFINITION
-ac	pertaining to
-al	pertaining to
-ar	pertaining to
-ary	pertaining to
a-	not, without
ab-	away from
abdomin/o	abdomen
ability	competence
ablat	take away
-able	capable
abort	fail at onset, expel nonviable fetus
absorpt	to swallow
ac-	toward
-ac	pertaining to
-acea	condition, remedy
acid	acid, low pH
acin	grape
acous	hearing
acr/o	peak, topmost, extremities
acromi/o	acromion
act	to do, perform, performance
activ	movement
acu	needle

WORD PART	DEFINITION
acu-	sharp
acumin	to sharpen
ad-	to, toward
adapt	to adjust
-ade	process
aden/o	gland
adenoid	adenoid
adip	fat
adjust	alter
adjuv	give help
adolesc	beginning of adulthood
adren/o	adrenal gland
aer/o	air, gas
ag-	to
-age	related to
agglutin	sticking together, clumping
-ago	disease
agor/a	marketplace
-agra	severe pain
-al	pertaining to
alanine	an amino acid, protein synthesized in muscle
albin/o	white

WORD PART	DEFINITION
albumin	albumin
ald/o	organic compound
-ale	pertaining to
alges	sensation of pain
-algia	pain, painful condition
aliment	nourishment
-alis	pertaining to
alkal	base
all/o	strange, other
alopec-	baldness, mange
alpha-	first letter in Greek alphabet
alveol	alveolus, air sac
-aly	condition
ambly-	dull
ambulat	to walk, walking
amin/o	nitrogen compound
-amine	nitrogen containing
ammon	ammonia
amni/o	amnion, fetal membrane
amph-	around
ampull	bottle-shaped
amput	to prune, lop off
amyl	starch
an-	not, lack of, without
-an	pertaining to
an/o	anus
ana-	away from, excessive
anabol	build up
analysis	process to study whole in terms of its parts
analyst	one who separates
anastom	join together
-ance	condition, state of
-ancy	state of
andr/o	male, masculine
aneurysm	dilation
angi/o	blood vessel, lymph vessel

WORD PART	DEFINITION
angina	sore throat, chest pain radiating to throat
ankyl	stiff
-ant	forming, pertaining to
ant-	against
ante-	before, forward
anthrac	coal
anti-	against
aort	aorta
apo-	different from, separation from
append	appendix
aqu-	water
-ar	pertaining to
arachn	cobweb, spider
-arche	beginning
aria	air
-arian	one who is
-aris	pertaining to
aroma	smell, sweet herb
array	place in order
arteri/o	artery
arteriosus	like an artery
arthr/o	joint
articul	joint
-ary	pertaining to
asbest	asbestos
ascit	fluid in the belly
-ase	enzyme
aspartate	an amino acid
aspergill	aspergillus
aspirat	to breathe
assay	evaluate
assist	aid, help
astr/o	star
-ata	action, place, use
-ate	composed of, pertaining to
-ated	process, composed of

S = Suffix   P = Prefix   R = Root   R/CF = Combining Form

WORD PART	DEFINITION
atel	incomplete
ather	porridge, gruel, fatty substance
athet	without position, uncontrolled
-atic	pertaining to
-ation	process
-ative	pertaining to, quality of
-ator	agent, instrument, person or thing that does something
-atric	treatment
atri/o	entrance, atrium
attent	awareness
attenu	to weaken
audi/o	hearing
audit	hearing
aur-	ear
auscult	listen to
auto-	self, same
avail	useful
axill	armpit
ayur-	life
azot	nitrogen
-back	back, toward the starting point
bacteri/o	bacteria
balan	glans penis
bar	pressure
bari	weight
bas/o	base, opposite of acid
basal	deepest part
be	life
behav	activity, mental
beta	second letter of Greek alphabet
bi-	two, twice, double
bi/o	life
-bil	able
bil/i	bile
-blast	embryo, germ cell
blast/o	embryonic, immature

WORD PART	DEFINITION
blephar/o	eyelid
body	body, mass, substance
bov	cattle
brachi/o	arm
brachii	of the arm
brachy-	short
brady-	slow
bride	rubbish, rubble
bronch/i	bronchus
bronch/o	bronchus
brucell	from pathologist David Bruce
bucc	cheek
buccinat	cheek
bulb/o	bulb
burs	bursa
calc/i	calcium
calcul	stone, little stone
callos	thickening
calor	heat
cancer	cancer
candid	Candida
capill	hairlike, capillary
capit	head
capn	carbon dioxide
caps	box, cover, shell
capsul	little box
carb/o	carbon
carboxy	group of organic compounds
carcin/o	cancerous
cardia	heart
cardi/o	heart
carotene	yellow-red pigment
carotid	large neck artery
carp/o	bones of the wrist
cartilag	cartilage
cata-	down
catabol	break down

S = Suffix   P = Prefix   R = Root   R/CF = Combining Form

WORD PART	DEFINITION
cathet	insert, catheter
caud	tail
cava	cave
cavern	cave
cec	cecum
-cele	cave, hernia, swelling
celi	abdomen
cellul	small cell
cent-	hundred
-centesis	to puncture
centr/o	central
cephal/o	head
-cephalus	head
-cephaly	condition of the head
-ceps	head
cept	to receive
cerebell	little brain, cerebellum
cerebr/o	brain
cervic	neck
cess	going forward
chancr	chancre
chem/o	chemical
chemic	chemical
-chete	hair
-chezia	pass a stool
chir/o	hand
chlor	green
cholangi	bile duct
chol/e	bile
choledoch/o	common bile duct
cholecyst	gallbladder
chondr/o	cartilage, rib
chorio	chorion, membrane
chrom/o	color
chromat	color
chron/o	time
chym/o	chyme

WORD PART	DEFINITION
-cidal	pertaining to killing
cide	to kill
cili	hairlike structure
circum-	around
cirrh	yellow
cis	to cut
cit/i	cell
-clast	break, break down
claudicat	limp
claustr/o	confined space
clav	clavicle
clave	lock
clavicul	clavicle
-cle	small
clitor	clitoris
clon	cutting used for propagation, tumult
-clonus	violent action
co-	with, together
coagul/o	clotting, clump
coarct	press together, narrow
cobal	cobalt
coccus	berry, spherical bacterium
cochle	cochlear
code	information system
cognit	thinking
coit	sexual intercourse
col	colon
colon/o	colon
coll	collect, glue
coll/a	glue
coloniz	form a colony
colp/o	vagina
com	take care of
com-	with, together
combin	combine
commodat	adjust
compat	tolerate

S = Suffix   P = Prefix   R = Root   R/CF = Combining Form

S = Suffix   P = Prefix   R = Root   R/CF = Combining Form

WORD PART	DEFINITION
compet	strive together
complex	woven together
compli	fulfill
compress	press together
compuls	drive, compel
con-	with, together
concav	arched, hollow
concept	become pregnant
concuss	shake violently
condyl	knuckle
confus	bewildered
coni	dust
coniz	cone
conjunctiv	conjunctiva
constipat	press together
constrict	narrow, to narrow
contagi	transmissible by contact
contaminat/o	to corrupt, make unclean
contin	hold together
contra-	against
contract	draw together, pull together
contus	bruise
convalesc	recover
cor	heart
cori	skin
corne/o	cornea
coron	crown, coronary
corpor/e	body
corpus	body
cortic/o	cortex, cortisone
cortis	cortisone
cost	rib
crani/o	cranium, skull
crease	groove
creat	flesh
creatin	creatine
cret	to separate

WORD PART	DEFINITION
cretin	cretin
crimin	distinguish
crine	secrete
-crine	secrete
crista	crest
-crit	to separate
cry/o	cold
crypt-	hidden
cub	cube
cubit	elbow
cubitus	lying down
cune/l	wedge
cur	cleanse, cure
curat	to care for
curett	to cleanse
cursor	run
cusp	point
cutan/e	skin
cyan/o	dark blue
-cyst	bladder
cyst/o	bladder, sac, cyst
cysteine	an amino acid
cyt/o	cell
-cyte	cell
dacry/o	tears, lacrimal duct
de-	from, take away, removal, without
defec	clear out waste
defici	failure, lacking, inadequate
degenerat	deteriorate
deglutit	to swallow
del	visible
deliri	confusion, disorientation
delus	deceive
dem	the people
demi-	half
dendr/o	treelike
dent	tooth

WORD PART	DEFINITION
dependent	relying on
depress	press down
derm	skin
derma	skin
-derma	skin
dermat/o	skin
dermis	skin
-desis	bind together, fixation of bone or joint
di-	two, complete
dia-	complete, through
diabet	diabetes
diagnost	decision
dialectic	argument
dialy	separate
diaphoret	sweat
diaphragmat	diaphragm
dict	consent, surrender
didym/o	testis
didymis	testis
diet	a way of life
different	not identical
digest	to break down, break up
digit	finger or toe
dilat	open up, expand, open out
dips	thirst
dis-	apart, away from
discipl	understand
disciplin	disciple, instruction
dist	away from the center
-dium	appearance
diuret	increase urine output
diverticul	by-road
dorm	sleep
dors	back
dorsi	back
drome	running
drop	liquid globule

WORD PART	DEFINITION
duce	to lead
ducer	to lead, leader
duct	to lead, lead
ductus	leading
duoden	twelve, duodenum
dur	dura mater
dwarf	miniature
dynam	power
dynam/o	power
-dynia	pain
dys-	bad, difficult, painful
e-	out of, from
-eal	pertaining to
ease	normal function, freedom from pain
ec-	out, outside
ech/o	sound wave
echin	hedgehog
eclamps	shining forth
eco-	environment
-ectasis	dilation
-ectomy	excision, surgical excision
ectop	on the outside, displaced
eczemat	eczema
edema	edema, swelling
efface	wipe out
effus	pour out
ejacul	shoot out
ejaculat	shoot out
elasma	plate
elect	choice
electr/o	electric, electricity
elimin	throw away, expel
-elle	small
-em	condition
em-	in, into
-ema	result
emac/i	make thin

S = Suffix   P = Prefix   R = Root   R/CF = Combining Form

WORD PART	DEFINITION
embol	plug
embry/o	embryo, fertilized egg
emet	to vomit
emesis	vomiting
-emesis	to vomit, vomiting
-emia	blood, blood condition
-emic	in the blood
emmetr-	measure
emuls	milk
en-	in
-ence	forming, quality of, state of
encephal/o	brain
encephaly	condition of the brain
-ency	condition, state of, quality, quality of
end-	inside, within
endo-	inner, inside, within
-ent	end result, pertaining to, state of, end, forming
enter/o	intestine
entery	condition of the bowels
enur	urinate
environ	surroundings
-eon	one who does
eosin/o	dawn
ependym	lining membrane
epi-	above, upon, over
epilept	seizure
epiphys/i	growth
episi/o	vulva
equi-	equal
equin	horse
equip	to fit out
-er	agent, one who does
erect	straight, to set up
erg/o	work
-ergy	process of working
-ery	condition, process of

WORD PART	DEFINITION
erysi-	red
erythemat	redness
erythr/o	red
-escent	process
-esis	abnormal condition
eso-	inward
esophag	esophagus
essent	existence
esthesia	sensation, feeling
esthet	sensation, perception
estr/o	woman
ethm	sieve
-etic	pertaining to
-etics	pertaining to
eti/o	cause
-ette	little
eu-	good, normal
ex-	away from, out, out of
exacerbat	increase, aggravate
examin	test, examine
excret	separate, discharge
exo-	outside, outward
expect	await
expir	breathe out
extra-	out of, outside
faci	face
factor	maker
farct	stuff
fasci/o	fascia
febr	fever
fec	feces
feed	to give food, nourish
femor	femur
fer	to bear
ferrit	iron
fertil	able to conceive
fertiliz	to bear

WORD PART	DEFINITION
fet/o	fetus
fibr/o	fiber, fibrous
fibril	small fiber
fibrin/o	fibrin
-fication	process of forming
fida	split
field	definite area
filar	roundworm
filtr	strain through
fiss	split
fistul	tube, pipe
flat	flatus
flatul	excessive gas
flavin	yellow
flex	bend
fluid	flowing
fluo-	fluorine
fluor/o	flux, flow
flux	flow
foc	center, focus
follicul	follicle
foramin	opening, foramen
fore-	in front
-form	appearance of, resembling
format	to form
fract	break
fraction	small amount
free	free
frequ	repeated, often
front	front, forehead
fructos	fruit sugar
function	perform
fund/o	fundus
fung/i	fungus
fusion	to pour
galact/o	milk
gall	bile

WORD PART	DEFINITION
gastr/o	stomach
gastrin	stomach hormone
gastrocnem	calf of leg
gemin	twin, double
gen	produce, create, origin
-gen	create, produce, form
gen-	birth
-gene	production, give birth
genesis	origin, creation, production
-genesis	creation, origin, formation, source
genet	origin
-genic	creation, producing
genit	bring forth, birth, primary male or female sex organ
genitor	offspring
ger	old age
geront/o	old age
gest	gestation, pregnancy, produce
gestat	gestation, pregnancy, to bear
gigant	giant
gingiv	gums
gland	gland
glauc	lens opacity, grey
gli/o	glue, supportive tissue of nervous system
-glia	glue, supportive tissue of nervous system
globin/o	protein
globul	globular, protein
glomerul/o	glomerulus
gloss/o	tongue
glott	mouth of windpipe
glottis	windpipe
gluc/o	glucose, sugar
glutin	glue, stick
glyc/o	glycogen, glucose, sugar
glycer	glycerol, sweet

WORD PART	DEFINITION
gnath	jaw
gnosis	knowledge
gomph	bolt, nail
gon/o	seed
gonad/o	gonads, testes or ovaries
gong	daily practice
-grade	going
graft	splice, transplant
-graft	tissue for transplant
graine	head pain
-gram	a record, drawing, recording
grand-	big
granul	small grain
granul/o	granule, small grain
-graph	to record, write
-grapher	one who records
-graphy	process of recording
-gravida	pregnant
gravis	serious
gru	to move
guan	dung
gurgit	flood
gynec/o	woman, female
habilitat	restore
halit	breath
hallucin	imagination
hallux	big toe
heme	red iron-containing pigment
hem/o	blood
hemangi/o	blood vessel
hemat/o	blood
hemi-	half
hepar	liver
hepato	liver
herb/i	plant
herni/o	hernia, rupture
herp	blister

WORD PART	DEFINITION
heter/o	different
hist/o	tissue
holist	entire, whole
hom/i	man
home/o	the same
homo-	same, alike
hormone	chemical messenger
humor	fluid
hyal	glass
hydr/o	water
hyp-	below
hyper-	above, beyond, excess, excessive
hypn/o	sleep
hypo-	below, deficient, smaller, low, under
hyster	uterus
hyster/o	uterus
-ia	abnormal condition
-iac	pertaining to
-ial	pertaining to
-ian	one who does, specialist
-ias	condition
-iasis	abnormal condition, state of
iatr	medical treatment, treatment
-iatric	relating to medicine, medical knowledge
-iatrics	field of medicine, healing
-iatrist	practitioner, one who treats
-iatry	treatment, field of medicine
-ible	can do, able to
-ic	pertaining to
-ica	pertaining to
-ical	pertaining to
ict	seizure
icterus	jaundice
-id	having a particular quality, pertaining to
-ide	having a particular quality
idi/o	personal, distinct
ifer	to bear, carry

S = Suffix   P = Prefix   R = Root   R/CF = Combining Form

WORD PART	DEFINITION
-ify	to become
-il	capability
-ile	capable, capability
ile/o	ileum
im-	not
imag	likeness
immun/o	immune, immune response, immunity
immune	immune response
immuniz	make immune
impair	worsen
impede	obstruct
-imus	most
in-	in
-in	chemical, chemical compound
in-	not, into
incub	sit on, lie on, hatch
index	to declare
-ine	pertaining to, substance
infant	infant
infect	corrupt, internal invasion, infection
infer	below, beneath
infest	invade, attack
inflammat	set on fire
inflat	blow up
infra-	below, beneath
-ing	quality of, doing
ingest	carry in
inguin	groin
inhal	breathe in
inhibit	repress
inject	force in
ino	sinew
insect/i	insect
insert	put together
inspir	breathe in
integr	whole
inter-	between

WORD PART	DEFINITION
intestin	gut, intestine
intra-	inside, within
intrins	on the inside
intus-	within
iod	violet, iodine
-ion	action, condition, process
-ior	pertaining to, suffix for comparatives
-iosum	pertaining to
-ious	pertaining to
-is	belonging to, pertaining to
isch	to keep back
-ism	action, condition, process
-ismus	take action
iso-	equal
-ist	agent, specialist
-isy	inflammation
-ites	associated with
-ition	process
-itis	inflammation, infection
-ity	condition, state
-ium	structure
-ius	pertaining to
-ive	nature of, quality of, pertaining to
-iz	subject to
-ization	process of creating, process of affecting in a specific way
-ize	action, affect in a specific way, policy
-ized	affected in a specific way
-izer	affects in a particular way, line of action
jejun	jejunum
jugul	throat
junct	joining together
juxta-	beside, near, close to
kal	potassium
kary/o	nucleus
kel/o	tumor
kerat/o	cornea

S = Suffix   P = Prefix   R = Root   R/CF = Combining Form

WORD PART	DEFINITION
keratin/o	keratin
kern	nucleus
ket/o	ketone
keton	ketone
ketone	organic compound
kin	motion
kinase	enzyme
kinesi/o	movement
kinet	motion
-kinin	move in
klept/o	to steal
kyph/o	bent
labi	lip
lacer	to tear
lacrim	tears, tear duct
lact	milk
lactat	secrete milk
lapar/o	abdomen in general
lapse	clasp, fall together
-lapse	fall together, slide
laryng/o	larynx
lash	end of whip
lat	to take
later	side
latiss	wide
-le	small
lei/o	smooth
-lemma	covering
-lepsy	seizure
lept	thin, small
-let	small
leuk/o	white
lex	word
librium	balance
ligament	ligament
ligat	tie up, tie off
lign	line

WORD PART	DEFINITION
-ling	small
lingu	tongue
lipid	fat
lip/o	fat
lith/o	stone
liv	life
load	to carry
lob	lobe
locat	a place
-logist	one who studies, one who specializes
logous	relation
-logy	to study, study of
longev	long life
lord	curve, swayback
lubric	make slippery
lucid	bright, clear
lumb	lower back, loin
lump	piece
lun	moon
-lus	small
luxat	dislocate
ly	break down, separate
-ly	going toward
lymph/o	lymph
lymphaden/o	lymph node
lymphangi/o	lymphatic vessels
lys/o	decompose, decomposition, dissolve
lysis	destruction
-lysis	destroy, destruction, dissolve, separate
lyt	dissolve
-lyte	soluble
-lytic	relating to destruction
lyze	destruct, dissolve
macro-	large
macul	spot
magnet	magnet
mak	makes

S = Suffix   P = Prefix   R = Root   R/CF = Combining Form

WORD PART	DEFINITION
-maker	one who makes
mal-	bad
-malacia	abnormal softness
malign	harmful, bad
malleol	small hammer, malleolus
mamm/o	breast
mandibul	mandible
mania	frenzy
-mania	frenzy, madness
manic	affected by frenzy
manipul	handful, use of hands
mano	pressure
marker	sign
mast	breast
mastic	chew
mastoid	mastoid process
matern	mother
matur	ripe, ready
medi	middle
media-	middle
mediastin/o	mediastinum, middle septum
medic	medicine
medulla	middle
mega-	enormous
-megaly	enlargement
mei	lessening
melan	black
melan/o	melanin, black pigment
mellit	sweetened with honey
membran/o	cover, skin
men/o	menses, monthly, month
mening/o	meninges, membranes
menisc	crescent, meniscus
menstru	menses, occurring monthly
ment	mind, chin
-ment	action, state, resulting state
mere	part

WORD PART	DEFINITION
mero-	partial
meso-	middle
meta-	after, behind, between, beyond, change
metabol	change
metacarp	bones of the hand
metatars	bones of the foot
-meter	measure, instrument to measure
metr/o	uterus
-metrist	skilled in measurement
mi-	derived from hemi, half
micr/o	small
micro-	small
mictur	make urine
mid-	middle
mileusis	lathe
milli-	one-thousandth
miner	mines
mineral	inorganic materials
miss	send
mit	threadlike structure
mito-	thread
mitr-	having two points
mitt	to send
mod	nature, form, method
molec	mass
mon	single
monas	unit
monil	type of fungus
mono-	one, single
morbid	disease
morph/o	shape
mort	death
mot	move
motiv	move
muc/o	mucous membrane, mucus
mucosa	lining of a cavity
multi-	many

WORD PART	DEFINITION
mune	in service
muscul/o	muscle
mut	silent
muta	genetic change
mutil	to maim
myc/o	fungus
myel/o	spinal cord, bone marrow
myelin	in the spinal cord, myelin
myo	muscle
myo-	to blink
my/o	muscle
myring/o	tympanic membrane, eardrum
myx-	mucus
narc/o	stupor
nas	nose
nas/o	nose
nat	born
nate	birth, born
natr	sodium
natr/i	sodium
natur/o	nature
nebul	cloud
necrot	death
neo-	new
nephr/o	kidney
nerv	nerve
neur	nerve, nerve tissue
neur/o	nerve, nervous tissue
neutr/o	neutral
nitr/o	nitrogen
noct-	night
noia	to think
nom	law
non-	no
norm-	normal
nos/o	disease
nucle/o	nucleus

WORD PART	DEFINITION
nucleol	small nucleus
nutri	nourish
nutrit	nourishment
o/o	egg
oblong	elongated
obsess	besieged by thoughts
obstetr	midwifery
occipit	back of head
occulta	hidden
ocul/o	eye
-ode	way, road, path
odont	tooth
odyn/o	pain
-oid	appearance of, resemble, resembling
-ol	alcohol, chemical substance
-ola	small
olfact	smell
olig/o-	scanty, too little
-oma	tumor, mass
om/o	body, tumor
onc/o	tumor
-one	chemical substance, hormone
onych/o	nail
ophthalm/o	eye
-opia	sight
opportun	take advantage of
-opsis	vision
-opsy	to view
opt/o	vision
-or	a doer, one who does, that which does something
or/o	mouth
orbit	orbit
orch/o	testicle
ordin	arrange
orex	appetite
organ	organ, tool, instrument

S = Suffix   P = Prefix   R = Root   R/CF = Combining Form

WORD PART	DEFINITION
or/o	mouth
orth/o	straight
orthot	correct
-orum	function of
-ory	having the function of
os	mouth
-osa	like
-ose	full of
-osis	condition
osmo	push
osmol	concentration
oss/e	bone
oste/o	bone
-osus	condition
ot/o	ear
-otomy	incision
-ous	pertaining to
ov/i	egg
ovari	ovary
ovul	ovum, egg
ox	oxygen
ox/y	oxygen
-oxia	oxygen condition
oxid	oxidize
palat	palate
palliat	reduce suffering
palpit	throb
pan-	all
pancreat	pancreas
panto-	entire
papill/o	pimple
par-	abnormal, beside
-para	to bring forth
para-	adjacent to, alongside, beside, abnormal
pareun	lying beside, sexual intercourse
pariet	wall
paroxysm	irritate

WORD PART	DEFINITION
particul	little piece
-partum	childbirth, to bring forth
patell	patella
-path	disease
path/o	disease
pathet	suffering
-pathic	pertaining to a disease
pathy	emotion, disease
-pathy	disease
pat	lie open
paus	cessation
-pause	cessation
pector	chest
ped	child, foot
pedicul	louse
pelas	skin
pelv	pelvis
pen	penis
-penia	deficient, deficiency
peps	digestion
pepsin/o	pepsin
peptid	digestion
per-	intense, through
perforat	bore through
peri-	around
perine	perineum
peripher	external boundary, outer part
peritone	stretch over, peritoneum
perm/e	pass through
pes	foot
pesti	pest
petit-	small
-pexy	fixation, surgical fixation
phaco-	lens
phag/o	to eat
-phage	to eat
-phagia	swallowing, eating

S = Suffix   P = Prefix   R = Root   R/CF = Combining Form

WORD PART	DEFINITION
phalang/e	phalanx
pharmac/o	drug
pharyng	pharynx
pharyng/e	pharynx
pharynx	throat
phenol	benzene derivative
phenyl	chemical group
pheo-	gray
pher/o	to carry
-pheresis	removal
peripher	outer edge
-phil	attraction
-phile	attraction
-philia	attraction
phim	muzzle
phleb/o	vein
phob	fear
-phobia	fear
phon/o	sound, voice
phor	bear, carry
phosphat	phosphorus
phot/o	light
phren	mind
phylac	protect
phylaxis	protection
-phyll	leaf
physema	blowing
physi/o	body
physis	growth
phyt/o	plant
pituit	pituitary
pituitar	pituitary
plak	plate, plaque
plant	insert, plant
planus	flat surface
plas	molding, formation
-plasia	formation

WORD PART	DEFINITION
-plasm	something formed
plasm/o	to form
-plasty	formation, repair, surgical repair
plate	flat
pleg	paralysis
plete	filled
pleur	pleura
plexy	stroke
pnea	breathe
pneum/o	air, lung
pneumat	structure filled with air
pneumon	air, lung
pod	foot
-poiesis	to make
-poiet	the making
-poietin	the maker
poikilo-	irregular
point	to pierce
pol	pole
polio-	gray matter
poly-	excessive, many, much
poplit/e	ham, back of knee
por/o	opening
post-	after
poster	coming behind
pract	efficient, practical
prand/i	breakfast
pre-	before, in front of
precis	accurate
pregn	with child, pregnant
presby	old man
press	press close, press down, squeeze
prevent	prevent
primi-	first
pro-	before, in front, projecting forward
proct/o	anus and rectum
product	lead forth

WORD PART	DEFINITION
prolifer	bear offspring
pronat	bend down
prostat	prostate
prot/e	first
protein	protein
proto-	first
proxim	nearest
prurit	itch
pseudo-	false
psych/o	mind, soul
psyche	mind, soul
pteryg	wing
ptosis	drooping, falling
-ptosis	drooping
ptysis	spit
pub	pubis
puer	child
pulmon/o	lung
puls	to drive
pump	pump
punct	puncture
pur	pus
purific	make pure
purul	pus
py/o	pus
pyel/o	renal pelvis
pylor	gate, pylorus
pyr/o	fire, heat, fever
pyrid	heat
qi	vital force
quadr	four
quadri-	four
radi/o	ray, radiation
radial	radius
radic	root
re-	again, back, backward
recept	receive

WORD PART	DEFINITION
rect/o	rectum
reflex	bend back
remiss	send back, give up
ren	kidney
replic	reply
rescein	resin
resect/o	cut off
resid/u	left over, what is left over
restor	renew
reticul	fine net, network
retinacul	hold back
retin/o	retina
retro-	backward
rhabd/o	rod shaped, striated
rheumat	a flow, rheumatism
rhin/o	nose
rhythm	rhythm
rib/o	like a rib
ribo	pentose, a sugar
ribo-	from gum Arabic
rigid	stiff
rose	rose
rotat	rotate
-rrhagia	excessive flow, discharge
-rrhaphy	suture
-rrhea	flow, discharge
-rrhoid	flow
rryth	rhythm
-rubin	rust colored
rumin	throat
sacchar	sugar
sacr	sacrum
sagitt	arrow
salping/o	fallopian tube, uterine tube
salpinx	trumpet
san	sound, healthy
sanit	health

S = Suffix   P = Prefix   R = Root   R/CF = Combining Form

WORD PART	DEFINITION
sapon	soap
sarc	flesh, sarcoma
satur	to fill
schiz/o	to split, cleave
scintill	spark
scler/o	hard, white of eye
-scope	instrument for viewing
-scopy	to examine, to view
scorb	scurvy
scrot	scrotum
seb/o	sebum
sebum	wax
secret	secrete, produce, separate
sect	cut off
sedent	sitting
segment	section
seiz	to grab
self	me, own individual
semi-	half
semin/i	semen, sperm
seminat	scatter seed
sen	old age
sens	feel
sensor/i	sensation, sensory
separat	move apart
seps	decay, infection
sept/o	septum, partition
sib	relative
-side	glycoside
sigm	Greek letter "S"
silic	silicon, glass
simi	ape, monkey
simul	imitate
sin/o	sinus
sipid	flavor
-sis	abnormal condition, process
sit/u	place

WORD PART	DEFINITION
skelet	skeleton
smear	spread
soc	partner
soci	partner, ally
soma	body
somat/o	body
-some	body
somn/o	sleep
son/o	sound
sorbit	fruit of a tree
sorpt	swallow
spad	tear or cut
spasm	spasm, sudden involuntary tightening
spast	tight
specif	species
sperm/i	sperm
spermat	sperm
sphen	wedge
spher/o	sphere
sphygm/o	pulse
spin/o	spine
spir/o	to breathe
spirat	breathe
spirit/u	spirit
spiro-	spiral, coil
splen/o	spleen
spong/i	sponge
spor	spore
stable	steady
stag	standing place
-stalsis	constrict, constriction
staphyl/o	bunch of grapes
-stasis	control; stop; to stand
-static	to make stand; stop
-statin	inhibit
stax	fall in drops
steat	fat

APPENDIX B

WORD PART	DEFINITION
stein	stone
sten/o	narrow, contract
ster	solid, steroid
stere/o	three-dimensional
stern	chest, breastbone
-steroid	steroid
-sterol	steroid
-sterone	steroid
stetho	chest
sthen	strength
stigmat	focus
stimul	excite, strengthen
stin	partition
stip	press
stiti	space
stoma	mouth
-stomy	new opening
stone	stone, pebble
storm	crisis
strab	squint
strat	layer
strept/o	twisted
study	inquiry
su/i	self
sub-	below, under, slightly, underneath
suffic/e	enough
sulf	sulfur
super-	above, excessive
supinat	bend backward
supplement	supply to remedy a deficiency
suppress	pressed under, push under
supra-	above
surfact	surface
surg	operate
suscept	to take up
-sylated	linked
sym-	together

WORD PART	DEFINITION
symptomat	symptom
syn-	together
syn/o	synovial membrane
syndesm	bind together
syring/o	tube, pipe
system	body system
systol	contraction
tachy-	rapid
tact	orderly arrangement
tag	touch
tain	hold
talip	ankle bone
tamin	touch
tampon	plug
tangent	touch
tax	coordination
tempor	time, temple
ten/o	tendon
tendin	tendon
tens	pressure
-tensin	tense, taut
terat/o	monster, malformed fetus
test/o	testis, testicle
testicul	testicle, testis
tetra-	four
thalam	thalamus
thalass	sea
thel	nipple
then	motion
thenar	palm
-therapist	one who treats
therap/o	healing, treatment
therapeut	healing, treatment
therm/o	heat
thesis	arrange, place
thi	sulfur
thora	chest

S = Suffix   **P = Prefix**   **R = Root**   **R/CF = Combining Form**

WORD PART	DEFINITION
thorac/o	chest
thromb/o	blood clot, clot
thym	thymus gland
thyr/o	thyroid
-tic	pertaining to
-tion	process, being
toc	labor, birth
toler	endure
tom/o	incise, cut
-tome	instrument to cut
-tomy	surgical incision
ton	tone
ton/o	pressure, tension
tonsil	tonsil
tonsill/o	tonsil
tope	part, location
topic	local
-tous	pertaining to
tox	poison
-toxic	able to kill
toxic/o	poison
trache/o	trachea, windpipe
tract	draw, pull
tranquil	calm
trans-	across, through
traumat	wound, injury
tri-	three
trich/o	hair
-tripsy	crush
-tripter	crusher
trochle	pulley
trop	turn, turning
troph	development, nourishment
trophy	development, nourishment
-tropic	a turning, change
-tropin	nourishing, stimulation
tryps	friction

WORD PART	DEFINITION
tub	tube
tubercul	swelling, tuberculosis
tubul	small tube
tuss/i	cough
tympan/o	eardrum, tympanic membrane
-type	model, particular kind
typh	typhus
ulcer	a sore
-ule	little, small
-ulent	abounding in
ultra-	higher, beyond
-um	tissue, structure
umbilic	belly button, navel, umbilicus
un	one
un-	not
uni-	one
ur/o	urine
-ure	process, result of
uresis	to urinate
uret	ureter, urine, urination
ureter/o	ureter
urethr/o	urethra
-uria	urine
urin	urine
urin/a	urine
uter	uterus
uve	uvea
uvul	uvula
vaccin	vaccine, giving a vaccine
vag	vagus nerve
vagin	sheath, vagina
valgus	turn out
valv	valve
varic/o	varicosity; dilated, tortuous vein
vas/o	blood vessel, duct
vascul	blood vessel
ved	knowledge

WORD PART	DEFINITION
vegetat	growth
veget	plants
ven/o	vein
ventil	wind
ventr	belly
ventricul	ventricle
vers	turn
-version	change
vert	to turn
vertebr	vertebra
vesic	sac containing fluid
vestibul/o	vestibule of inner ear
via	the way
violet	bluish purple
viril	masculine
virus	poison
viscer	an internal organ
visc/o	sticky
visu	sight

WORD PART	DEFINITION
vit/a	life
voc	voice
volunt	willing
volut	shrink, roll up
-volut	rolled up
volute	shrink, roll up
vuls	tear, pull
vulv/o	vulva
whip	to swing
xanth	yellow
xen/o	foreign material
-xis	condition
-yl	substance
zea-	to live
zeno-	foreign
-zoa	animal
zyg	zygote
zyme	fermenting, enzyme, transform

Abbreviations

ABBREVIATION	DEFINITION
μg	microgram; one-millionth of a gram
↑	increase/ above
↓	decrease/ below
1°	primary
2°	secondary
ABGs	arterial blood gases
ABI	ankle/brachial index
ABO	a blood group system
AC	acromioclavicular
ACE	angiotensin-converting enzyme
ACEP	Association for Comprehensive Energy Psychology
ACL	anterior cruciate ligament
ACTH	adrenocorticotropic hormone
AD	right ear
ADD	attention deficit disorder
ADH	antidiuretic hormone
ADHD	attention deficit hyperactivity disorder
ADL	activities of daily living
AED	automatic external defibrillator
AFP	alpha-fetoprotein
AI	adequate intake
AIDS	acquired immunodeficiency syndrome
ALL	acute lymphocytic leukemia
ALP	alkaline phosphatase
ALS	amyotrophic lateral sclerosis
ALT	alanine aminotransferase
AMAS	anti-malignin antibody screen

ABBREVIATION	DEFINITION
ANS	autonomic nervous system
AOM	acute otitis media
AP	antero-posterior
aPTT	activated partial thromboplastin time
ARDS	adult respiratory distress syndrome
ARF	acute respiratory failure
ARF	acute renal failure
AROM	active range of motion
AS	left ear
ASD	atrial septal defect
ASD	autism spectrum disorder
ASHD	arteriosclerotic heart disease
AST	aspartate aminotransferase
AU	both ears
AV	atrioventricular
AVM	arteriovenous malformation
BAL	bronchoalveolar lavage
BBB	blood brain barrier
BCIA	Biofeedback Certification Institute of America
BD	brain death
BKA	below knee amputation
BM	bowel movement
BMD	bone mineral density
BMR	basal metabolic rate
BNP	B-type natriuretic peptide
BOM	bilateral otitis media
BP	blood pressure

ABBREVIATION	DEFINITION
BPD	borderline personality disorder
BPH	benign prostatic hypertrophy
BPPV	benign paroxysmal positional vertigo
BRCA 1	genetic mutation responsible for breast and ovarian cancer (*BR*east *CA*ncer *1*)
BRCA 2	genetic mutation responsible for breast cancer (*BR*east *CA*ncer *2*)
BSE	bovine spongiform encephalopathy
BSE	breast self-examination
BSI	Body Substance Isolation
c/o	complains of
CA	cancer
CABG	coronary artery bypass graft
CAD	coronary artery disease
CAM	Complementary and Alternative Medicine
CAO	chronic airway obstruction
CAPD	continuous ambulatory peritoneal dialysis
CBC	complete blood count
CBT	cognitive behavioral therapy
CD	cluster domain; corecepters of cell membranes to recognize specific antigens
CD	conduct disorder
CD8	helper T-cell
CDC	Centers for Disease Control and Prevention
CEA	carcinoembryonic antigen
CF	cystic fibrosis
CHART	continuous hyperfractionated accelerated radiotherapy
CHD	congenital heart disease
CHES	Certified Health Education Specialist
CHF	congestive heart failure
CIS	carcinoma in situ
CJD	Creutzfeldt-Jakob disease
CK	creatine kinase
CKD	chronic kidney disease

ABBREVIATION	DEFINITION
CMA	Certified Medical Assistant
CMV	cytomegalovirus
CNA	Certified Nurse Assistant
CNS	central nervous system
CO_2	carbon dioxide
COPD	chronic obstructive pulmonary disease
COT	Certified Occupational Therapist
COTA	Certified Occupational Therapist Assistant
CP	cerebral palsy
CPAP	continuous positive airway pressure
CPR	cardiopulmonary resuscitation
CPT	cognitive processing therapy
CRF	chronic renal failure
CRP	C-reactive protein
C-section	cesarean section
CSF	cerebrospinal fluid
CT	computed tomography
CVA	cerebrovascular accident
CVP	central venous pressure
CVS	cardiovascular system
CVT	Cardiovascular Technologist
CXR	chest x-ray
D & C	dilation and curettage
DASH	Dietary Approaches to Stop Hypertension
DDAVP	synthetic ADH
DEXA	dual-energy x-ray absorptiometry
DI	diabetes insipidus
DIC	disseminated intravascular coagulation
DID	dissociative identity disorder
DIFF	differential white blood cell count
DJD	degenerative joint disease
DKA	diabetic ketoacidosis
dL	deciliter; one-tenth of a liter
DM	diabetes mellitus
DMD	Duchenne muscular dystrophy

ABBREVIATION	DEFINITION
DNA	deoxyribonucleic acid
DNR	do not resuscitate
DRE	digital rectal examination
DSHEA	Dietary Supplements Health and Education Act
DSM-IV	*Diagnostic and Statistical Manual of Mental Disorders,* fourth edition
DUB	dysfunctional uterine bleeding
DVT	deep vein thrombosis
E. coli	*Escherichia coli*
EBT	electron beam tomography
EBV	Epstein-Barr virus
ECG	electrocardiogram
ECT	electroconvulsive therapy
ED	erectile dysfunction
EEG	electroencephalogram
EFA	essential fatty acid
EKG	electrocardiogram
ELISA	enzyme-linked immunosorbent assay
EMDR	eye movement desensitization and reprocessing
EMF	electromagnetic field
EMG	electromyography
EMT	Emergency Medical Technician
EMT-P	Emergency Medical Technician–Paramedic
EP	evoked potential
EPA	Environmental Protection Agency
ER	emergency room
ERCP	endoscopic retrograde cholangiopancreatography
ESR	erythrocyte sedimentation rate
ESRD	end-stage renal disease
ESWL	extracorporeal shock wave lithotripsy
ETS	environmental tobacco smoke
FAS	fetal alcohol syndrome
FDA	U.S. Food and Drug Administration
FEV1	forced expiratory volume in one second

ABBREVIATION	DEFINITION
fL	femtoliter; one-quadrillionth of a liter
FOBT	fecal occult blood test
FSH	follicle-stimulating hormone
FTT	failure to thrive
FUS	focused ultrasound surgery
FVC	forced vital capacity
Fx	fracture
g	gram
GAD	generalized anxiety disorder
GDM	gestational diabetes mellitus
GERD	gastroesophageal reflux disease
GFR	glomerular filtration rate
GGT	gamma-glutamyl transpeptidase
GH	growth hormone, somatotropin
GI	gastrointestinal
GI	glycemic index
GL	glycemic load
GMP	Good Manufacturing Practice
GnRH	gonadotropin-releasing hormone
GSR	galvanic skin response
GTT	glucose tolerance test
GYN	gynecology
H/O	history of
H$_2$-blocker	histamine-2 receptor antagonist
HAV	hepatitis A virus
Hb	hemoglobin
Hb A1c	glycosylated hemoglobin A1c
HBOT	hyperbaric oxygen therapy
HBV	hepatitis B virus
HCG	human chorionic gonadotropin
HCL	hydrochloric acid
Hct	hematocrit
HCV	hepatitis C virus
HDL	high-density lipoprotein
HDN	hemolytic disease of the newborn
Hgb	hemoglobin

ABBREVIATION	DEFINITION
HIPAA	Health Insurance Portability and Accountability Act
HIV	human immunodeficiency virus
HLA	human leukocyte antigen
HLD	high-level disinfection
HMD	hyaline membrane disease
HPI	history of present illness
HPV	human papilloma virus
HRT	hormone replacement therapy
HSV	herpes simplex virus
HSV-1	herpes simplex virus, type 1
HUS	hemolytic uremic syndrome
IADL	instrumental activity of daily living
IBS	irritable bowel syndrome
ICD	implantable cardioverter/defibrillator
IDDM	Insulin-dependent diabetes mellitus
Ig	immunoglobulin
IgA	immunoglobulin A
IgD	immunoglobulin D
IgE	immunoglobulin E
IGF-1	insulin-like growth factor 1
IgG	immunoglobulin G
IgM	immunoglobulin M
IM	intramuscular
INR	international normalized ratio
ITP	idiopathic (or immunologic) thrombocytopenic purpura
IU	international unit(s)
IUD	intrauterine device
IV	intravenous
IVC	inferior vena cava
IVF	in vitro fertilization
IVP	intravenous pyelogram
JCAHO	Joint Commission on Accreditation of Healthcare Organizations
JRA	juvenile rheumatoid arthritis

ABBREVIATION	DEFINITION
KUB	x-ray of abdomen to show kidneys, ureters, and bladder
LASER	light amplification by stimulated emission of radiation
LCC-ST	Certified Surgical Technologist
LD	learning disability
LDL	low-density lipoprotein
LED	light emission diode
LEEP	loop electrosurgical excision procedure
LFT	liver function test
LH	luteinizing hormone
LLQ	left lower quadrant
LOC	loss of consciousness
LPN	Licensed Practical Nurse
LSD	lysergic acid diethylamide (acid)
LUQ	left upper quadrant
LVN	Licensed Vocational Nurse
MAOI	monoamine oxidase inhibitor
mcg	microgram; one-millionth of a gram
MCH	mean corpuscular hemoglobin (the average amount of hemoglobin in the average red blood cell)
MCHC	mean corpuscular hemoglobin concentration (the average concentration of hemoglobin in a given volume of red blood cells)
MCP	metacarpophalangeal
MCS	minimally conscious state
MCV	mean corpuscular volume (the average volume of a red blood cell)
MD	Doctor of Medicine
MDMA	methylenedioxymethamphetamine (ecstasy)
mg	milligram
MHC	major histocompatibility complex
MI	myocardial infarction
mL	milliliter
mm^3	cubic millimeter

ABBREVIATION	DEFINITION
MOAB	monoclonal antibody
MODY	mature-onset diabetes of the young
MPD	multiple personality disorder
MRA	magnetic resonance angiography
MRI	magnetic resonance imaging
mRNA	messenger RNA
MRSA	methicillin-resistant *Staphylococcus aureus*
MS	multiple sclerosis
NCBTMB	National Certification Board for Therapeutic Massage and Bodywork
NCCAM	National Center for Complementary and Alternative Medicine
NCCAOM	National Certifying Commission for Acupuncture and Oriental Medicine
NCI	National Cancer Institute
NCTMB	National Certificate for Therapeutic Massage and Bodywork
NHGRI	National Human Genome Research Institute
NHLBI	National Heart, Lung, and Blood Institute
NIDDM	non-insulin-dependent diabetes mellitus
NIH	National Institutes of Health
NKA	no known allergies
NMS	neurally mediated syncope
NO	nitric oxide
NPH	neutral protamine Hagedorn insulin
NRDS	neonatal respiratory distress syndrome
NSAID	nonsteroidal anti-inflammatory drug
O.D.	right eye
O.S.	left eye
O.U.	both eyes
O_2	oxygen
OA	osteoarthritis
OB	obstetrics
OCD	obsessive compulsive disorder
OD	Doctor of Osteopathy
ODD	oppositional defiant disorder

ABBREVIATION	DEFINITION
OGTT	oral glucose tolerance test
OME	otitis media with effusion
OSHA	Occupational Safety and Health Administration
OT	Ophthalmic Technician
OT	oxytocin
OT	Occupational Therapist
OTC	over-the-counter
P	pulse (rate)
p.r.n.	when necessary
PA	posteroanterior
PaO_2	partial pressure of arterial oxygen
Pap	Papanicolaou (Pap test, Pap smear)
PAT	paroxysmal atrial tachycardia
PCBs	polychlorinated biphenyls
PCD	programmed cell death
PCL	posterior cruciate ligament
PCOS	polycystic ovarian syndrome
PCP	phencyclidine (angel dust)
PDA	patent ductus arteriosus
PDD-NOS	pervasive developmental disorder–not otherwise specified
PDT	postural drainage therapy
PE	pressure equalization (tube)
PEEP	positive end-expiratory pressure
PEFR	peak expiratory flow rate
PET	positron emission tomography
PFTs	pulmonary function tests
pg	picogram, one-trillionth of a gram
PGY	pregnancy
pH	hydrogen ion concentration
PhD	Doctor of Philosophy
PID	pelvic inflammatory disease
PIP	proximal interphalangeal
PKD	polycystic kidney disease
PKU	phenylketonuria
PMDD	premenstrual dysphoric disorder

ABBREVIATION	DEFINITION
PMNL	polymorphonuclear leukocyte
PMS	premenstrual syndrome
PNS	peripheral nervous system
PO	by mouth
Polio	poliomyelitis
PPH	postpartum hemorrhage
PPI	proton pump inhibitor
PPS	postpolio syndrome
PRL	prolactin
PSA	prostate-specific antigen
PsyD	Doctor of Psychology
PT	physiotherapy
PT	prothrombin time
PT	physical therapy, Physical Therapist
PTA	Physical Therapy Assistant
PTCA	percutaneous transluminal coronary angioplasty
PTH	parathyroid hormone
PTSD	posttraumatic stress disorder
PVC	premature ventricular contractions
PVD	peripheral vascular disease
PVS	persistent vegetative state
q.4.h.	every four hours
q.i.d.	four times a day
R	respiration (rate)
R.I.C.E.	rest, ice, compression, elevation
RA	rheumatoid arthritis
RBC	red blood cell
RDA	recommended dietary allowance
RDS	respiratory distress syndrome
RF	radio frequency
Rh	Rhesus
RhoGAM	Rhesus immune globulin
RLQ	right lower quadrant
RN	Registered Nurse
RNA	ribonucleic acid
ROM	range of motion

ABBREVIATION	DEFINITION
RSV	respiratory syncytial virus
RT	Radiology Technician
RU-486	mifepristone
RUQ	right upper quadrant
SA	sinoatrial
SAD	seasonal affective disorder
SARS	severe acute respiratory syndrome
SBS	shaken baby syndrome
SC	subcutaneous
SCI	spinal cord injury
SET	self-examination of the testes
SFD	small for dates
SG	specific gravity
SGA	small for gestational age
SGOT	serum glutamic-oxaloacetic acid trans-aminase (AST)
SGPT	serum glutamic-pyruvic transaminase (ALT)
SI	sacroiliac
SIDS	sudden infant death syndrome
SLE	systemic lupus erythematosus
SMI	sustained maximal inspiration
SNRI	serotonin and norepinephrine reuptake inhibitors
SOB	short(ness) of breath
SP	Standard Precautions
SRS	stereotactic radiosurgery
SSA	Sjögren syndrome antibodies A
SSB	Sjögren syndrome antibodies B
SSRI	selective serotonin reuptake inhibitor
STAT	immediately
STD	sexually transmitted disease
SVC	superior vena cava
T	temperature
t.i.d.	(Latin *ter in die*) three times a day
T1	first thoracic vertebra or nerve
T_3	triiodothyronine

ABBREVIATION	DEFINITION
T_4	tetraiodothyronine (thyroxine)
TB	tuberculosis
TBI	traumatic brain injury
TCA	tricyclic antidepressant
TED	thromboembolic deterrent
TEE	trans-esophageal echocardiography
TENS	transcutaneous electrical nerve stimulation
THC	tetrahydrocannabinol (marijuana)
THR	total hip replacement
TIA	transient ischemic attack
TIBC	total iron binding capacity
TMJ	temporomandibular joint
TNM	tumor-node-metastasis (staging system for cancer)
TOF	tetralogy of Fallot
TPA	tissue plasminogen activator
TPN	total parenteral nutrition
TS	tumor suppressor
TSH	thyroid-stimulating hormone
TTM	trichotillomania
TTN	transient tachypnea of the newborn

ABBREVIATION	DEFINITION
TTP	thrombotic thrombocytopenic purpura
TURP	transurethral resection of the prostate
UA	urinalysis
μg	microgram, one-millionth of a gram
UP	Universal Precautions
URI	upper respiratory infection
USDA	U.S. Department of Agriculture
UTI	urinary tract infection
UV	ultraviolet
VCUG	voiding cystourethrogram
VEP	visual evoked potential
V-fib	ventricular fibrillation
VS	vital signs
VSD	ventricular septal defect
vWD	von Willebrand disease
vWF	von Willebrand factor
WAD	Word Analysis and Definition (box)
WBC	white blood cell; white blood (cell) count
WNL	within normal limits
WNV	West Nile virus

A

abdomen (AB-doh-men) Part of the trunk between the thorax and the pelvis.

abdominopelvic (ab-DOM-ih-no-PEL-vik) Pertaining to the abdomen and pelvis.

abducens (ab-DYU-senz) Sixth (VI) cranial nerve; responsible for eye movement.

abduction (ab-DUCK-shun) Action of moving away from the midline.

ablation (ab-LAY-shun) Removal of tissue to destroy its function.

abortion (ah-BOR-shun) Unnatural expulsion from the uterus at 20 weeks or less.

abortus (ah-BOR-tus) Product of abortion.

abrasion (ah-BRAY-shun) Area of skin or mucous membrane that has been scraped off.

abruptio (ab-RUP-she-oh) Placenta abruptio is the premature detachment of the placenta.

absorption (ab-SORP-shun) Uptake of nutrients and water by cells in the GI tract.

accessory (ack-SESS-oh-ree) Eleventh (XI) cranial nerve; supplying neck muscles, pharynx, and larynx.

accommodation (ah-kom-oh-DAY-shun) The act of adjusting something to make it fit the needs; in this case, the lens of the eye adjusts itself.

acetabulum (as-eh-TAB-you-lum) The cup-shaped cavity of the hipbone that receives the head of the femur to form the hip joint.

acetaminophen (ah-seat-ah-MIN-oh-fen) Medication that is an analgesic and an antipyretic.

acetone (ASS-eh-tone) Ketone that is found in blood, urine, and breath when diabetes mellitus is out of control.

acetylcholine (AS-eh-til-KOH-leen) Parasympathetic neurotransmitter.

Achilles tendon (ah-KILL-eeze) A tendon formed from gastrocnemius and soleus muscles and inserted into the calcaneus. Also called *calcaneal tendon*.

achondroplasia (a-kon-dro-PLA-ze-ah) Condition with abnormal conversion of cartilage into bone, leading to dwarfism.

acid (ASS-id) Substance with a pH below 7.0.

acinar cells (ASS-in-ar SELLS) Enzyme-secreting cells of the pancreas.

acne (AK-nee) Inflammatory disease of sebaceous glands and hair follicles.

acoustic (ah-KOOS-tik) Pertaining to hearing.

acquired (ah-KWIRED) A condition that arises from environmental influences and is not inherited.

acquired immunodeficiency syndrome (AIDS) (ah-KWIRED IM-you-noh-de-FISH-en-see SIN-drome) Infection with the HIV virus.

acromegaly (ak-roe-MEG-ah-lee) Enlargement of the head, face, hands, and feet due to excess growth hormone in an adult.

acromioclavicular (AC) (ah-CROW-mee-oh-kla-VICK-you-lar) The joint between the acromion and the clavicle.

acromion (ah-CROW-mee-on) Lateral end of the scapula, extending over the shoulder joint.

acrophobia (ak-roh-FO-be-ah) Pathologic fear of heights.

activities of daily living (ADLs) (ak-TIV-ih-tees of DAY-lee LIV-ing) Daily routines for mobility and personal care, bathing, dressing, eating, and moving.

acuminata (a-KYU-min-ah-ta) Tapering to a point.

acupoint (AK-you-point) Point of entry in the skin to a meridian.

acupressure (AK-you-presh-ur) Application of pressure to acupoints.

acupuncture (ak-you-PUNK-chur) Use of sterile, hair-thin needles to stimulate the energy pathways known as meridians.

acute (ah-KYUT) Disease of sudden onset.

adapt (a-DAPT) To adjust to different conditions.

adaptation (ad-ap-TAY-shun) Change in function or structure of an organ to meet new conditions.

adaptive equipment (a-DAP-tive ee-KWIP-ment) Devices and supplies that enable a disabled individual to perform specific functions.

addict (ADD-ikt) One who cannot live without a substance or practice.

addiction (ah-DIK-shun) Habitual psychologic and physiologic dependence on a substance or practice.

addictive (ah-DIK-tiv) Producing or causing addiction.

Addison disease (AD-ih-son diz-EEZ) An autoimmune disease leading to decreased production of adrenocortical steroids.

adduction (ah-DUCK-shun) Action of moving toward the midline.

adenine (AD-eh-neen) One of the chemicals found in both DNA and RNA.

adenocarcinoma (AD-eh-noh-kar-sih-NOH-mah) A cancer arising from glandular epithelial cells.

adenohypophysis (AD-en-oh-hi-POF-ih-sis) Anterior lobe of the pituitary gland.

adenoid (ADD-eh-noyd) Single mass of lymphoid tissue in the midline at the back of the throat.

adenomyosis (AD-en-oh-my-OH-sis) The implantation of endometrial glandular tissue in the myometrium.

adherence (ad-HERE-ents) The act of sticking to something.

adipose (ADD-i-pose) Containing fat.

adiposity (ad-ih-POSS-ih-tee) Excessive accumulation of fat in a site or organ.

adjunct (AJ-ungkt) Something joined to another but is not an essential part.

adjustment (ah-JUST-ment) The action of bringing a body part into alignment with the others. Also called *manipulation*.

adjuvant (AD-joo-vant) Additional treatment after a primary treatment has been used.

adnexa (ad-**NEK**-sa) Parts accessory to an organ or structure. Singular *adnexum*.

adnexal (ad-**NEK**-sal) Pertaining to accessory structures; for example, structures alongside the uterus.

adolescence (ad-oh-**LESS**-ents) Stage that begins with puberty and ends with physical maturity.

adolescent (ad-oh-**LESS**-ent) Pertaining to adolescence or a person in that stage.

adrenal gland (ah-**DREE**-nal GLAND) The suprarenal, or adrenal, gland on the upper pole of each kidney.

adrenalectomy (ah-dree-nal-**ECK**-to-me) Removal of part or whole of an adrenal gland.

adrenaline (ah-**DREN**-ah-lin) One of the catecholamines. Also called *epinephrine*.

adrenergic (ad-re-**NER**-jik) Relating to the autonomic nervous system.

adrenocortical (ah-dree-noh-**KOR**-tih-kal) Pertaining to the cortex of the adrenal gland.

adrenocorticotropic (ah-**DREE**-noh-**KOR**-tih-koh-**TROH**-pik) Hormone of the anterior pituitary that stimulates the cortex of the adrenal gland to produce its own hormones.

adrenogenital syndrome (ah-**DREE**-no-**JEN**-it-al **SIN**-drome) Hypersecretion of androgens from the adrenal gland.

advance medical directive (ad-**VANTS** **MED**-ih-kal die-**REK**-tiv) Legal document signed by the patient dealing with issues of prolonging or ending life in the event of life-threatening illness.

adventitia (ad-ven-**TISH**-ah) Outer layer of connective tissue covering blood vessels or organs.

aerobic (air-**OH**-bik) An organism capable of living in the presence of oxygen.

affect (**AF**-fekt) External display of feelings, thoughts, and emotions.

afferent (**AF**-eh-rent) Conduct nerve impulses toward a center; in this case, the spinal cord or brain.

aged (**A**-jid) Having lived to an advanced age.

agenesis (a-**JEN**-eh-sis) Failure to develop any organ or any part.

agglutinate (ah-**GLUE**-tin-ate) Stick together to form clumps.

agglutination (ah-glue-tih-**NAY**-shun) Process by which cells or other particles adhere to each other to form clumps.

aging (**A**-jing) The process of human maturation and decline.

agonist (**AG**-on-ist) Agent combines with receptors to initiate drug actions.

agoraphobia (ah-gor-ah-**FO**-be-ah) Pathologic fear of being trapped in a public place.

agranulocyte (a-**GRAN**-you-lo-site) A white blood cell without any granules in its cytoplasm.

alanine aminotransferase (ALT) (**AL**-ah-neen ah-**ME**-no-**TRANS**-fer-aze) Enzyme that is found in liver cells and leaks out into the bloodstream when the cells are damaged, enabling liver damage to be diagnosed.

albinism (**AL**-bih-nizm) Genetic disorder with lack of melanin.

albino (al-**BY**-no) Person with albinism.

albumin (al-**BYU**-min) Simple, soluble protein.

aldosterone (al-**DOS**-ter-own) Mineralocorticoid hormone of the adrenal cortex.

aldosteronism (al-**DOS**-ter-on-izm) Condition caused by excessive secretion of aldosterone. Also called *Conn syndrome*.

aldosteronoma (al-**DOS**-ter-on-oma) Benign adenoma of the adrenal cortex.

Alexander technique (al-eg-**ZAN**-der tek-**NEEK**) The use of awareness and exercises to improve posture, breathing, and movement.

alignment (a-**LINE**-ment) Having a structure in its correct position relative to other structures.

alimentary (al-ih-**MEN**-tar-ee) Pertaining to the digestive tract.

alkaline (**AL**-kah-line) Substance with a pH above 7.0. Also called *basic*.

alkaloid (**AL**-ka-loyd) Alkaline substances with pharmacological activity synthesized from plants.

allele (ah-**LEEL**) Genetic variant found on the same locus of a pair of chromosomes.

allergen (**AL**-er-jen) Substance producing a hypersensitivity (allergic) reaction.

allergy (**AL**-er-jee) Hypersensitivity to an allergen.

allogen (**AL**-oh-jen) Antigen from someone else in the same species.

allograft (**AL**-oh-graft) Skin graft from another person or cadaver.

alloimmune (**AL**-oh-im-**YUNE**) Reaction directed against foreign tissue.

allopathic medicine (al-oh-**PATH**-ic **MED**-ih-sin) Conventional medical practice.

allyl sulfides (**AL**-il **SUL**-fides) Group of substances found in garlic and onions that can reduce blood cholesterol.

alopecia (al-oh-**PEE**-shah) Partial or complete loss of hair, naturally or from medication.

alpha-fetoprotein (**AL**-fah fee-toe-**PRO**-teen) Protein normally produced only by the fetus.

alveolus (al-**VEE**-oh-lus) Terminal element of the respiratory tract. Plural *alveoli*.

Alzheimer disease (**AWLZ**-high-mer diz-**EEZ**) Common form of dementia.

amblyopia (am-blee-**OH**-pee-ah) Failure or incomplete development of the pathways of vision to the brain.

amenorrhea (a-men-oh-**REE**-ah) Absence or abnormal cessation of menstrual flow.

amino acid (ah-**ME**-no **ASS**-id) The basic building block for protein.

aminoketone (ah-**ME**-no-**KEY**-tone) By-product of nicotine.

ammonia (ah-**MOAN**-ih-ah) Toxic breakdown product of amino acids.

amniocentesis (**AM**-nee-oh-sen-tee-sis) Removal of amniotic fluid for diagnostic purposes.

amnion (**AM**-nee-on) Membrane around the fetus that contains amniotic fluid.

amniotic (am-nee-OT-ic) Pertaining to the amnion.

amoeba (ah-ME-bah) Single-celled organism that changes shape as it moves.

amoebiasis (ah-me-BY-ah-sis) Infection with *Amoeba*.

ampulla (am-PULL-ah) Dilated portion of a canal or duct.

amputation (am-pyu-TAY-shun) Process of removing a limb, part of a limb, a breast, or other projecting part.

amputee (AM-pyu-tee) A person with an amputation.

amylase (AM-il-aze) One of a group of enzymes that breaks down starch.

amyotrophic (a-my-oh-TRO-fik) Pertaining to muscular atrophy.

anabolism (an-AB-oh-lizm) The buildup of complex substances in the cell from simpler ones as a part of metabolism.

anaerobic (an-air-OH-bik) An organism capable of growing in the absence of oxygen.

analgesia (an-al-JEE-ze-ah) State in which pain is reduced.

analgesic (an-al-JEE-sic) Substance that reduces the response to pain.

anaphylaxis (AN-ah-fi-LAK-sis) Immediate severe allergic response.

anastomosis (ah-NAS-to-MO-sis) A surgically made union between two tubular structures. Plural *anastomoses*.

ancillary (AN-sil-air-ree) Accessory, adjunct.

androgen (AN-droh-jen) Hormone that promotes masculine characteristics.

anemia (ah-NEE-me-ah) Decreased number of red blood cells.

anencephaly (AN-en-SEF-ah-lee) Born without cerebral hemispheres.

anesthesia (an-es-THEE-zee-ah) Complete loss of sensation.

anesthesiologist (AN-es-thee-zee-OL-oh-jist) Medical specialist in anesthesia.

anesthesiology (AN-es-thee-zee-OL-oh-jee) Medical specialty related to anesthesia.

anesthetic (an-es-THET-ic) Substance that takes away feeling and pain.

aneurysm (AN-yur-izm) Small, circumscribed dilation of an artery or cardiac chamber.

angiogenesis (AN-jee-oh-JEN-eh-sis) New formation of blood vessels.

angiogram (AN-jee-oh-gram) Radiograph obtained after injection of radiopaque contrast material into blood vessels.

angiography (an-jee-OG-rah-fee) Radiography of vessels after injection of contrast material.

angioplasty (AN-jee-oh-PLAS-tee) Recanalization of a blood vessel by surgery.

angiotensin (an-jee-oh-TEN-sin) A vasoconstrictor.

anomaly (ah-NOM-ah-lee) Structural abnormality present at birth.

Anopheles (ah-NOF-eh-leez) A type of mosquito.

anorchism (an-OR-kizm) Absence of testes.

anorexia (an-oh-RECK-see-ah) Without an appetite; or having an aversion to food.

anoscopy (A-nos-koh-pee) Endoscopic examination of the anus.

anoxia (an-OCK-see-ah) Without oxygen.

antacid (ant-ASS-id) Agent that neutralizes acidity.

antagonism (an-TAG-oh-nizm) Situation of opposing.

antagonist (an-TAG-oh-nist) An opposing structure, agent, disease, or process.

antagonistic (an-TAG-oh-nist-ik) Having an opposite function.

anterior (an-TER-ee-or) Front surface of body; situated in front.

antevert (an-teh-VERT) Tilted forward.

anthracosis (an-thra-KOH-sis) Lung disease caused by the inhalation of coal dust.

anthrax (AN-thraks) A severe, malignant infectious disease.

antiangiogenesis (anti-AN-jee-oh-JEN-eh-sis) The prevention of growth of new blood vessels.

antibiotic (AN-tih-bye-OT-ik) A substance that has the capacity to destroy bacteria and other microorganisms.

antibody (AN-tee-body) Protein produced in response to an antigen. Plural *antibodies*.

anticoagulant (AN-tee-ko-AG-you-lant) Substance that prevents clotting.

antidiuretic (AN-tih-die-you-RET-ik) An agent that decreases urine production.

antidiuretic hormone (ADH) (AN-tih-die-you-RET-ik HOR-mohn) Posterior pituitary hormone that decreases urine output by acting on the kidney. Also called *vasopressin*.

antiepileptic (AN-tee-epih-LEP-tik) A pharmacologic agent capable of preventing or arresting epilepsy.

antigen (AN-tee-jen) Molecule capable of triggering an immune response

antimicrobial (AN-tee-my-KROH-bee-al) Agent to destroy or prevent multiplication of organisms.

antioxidant (an-tee-OKS-ih-dant) Substance that can prevent cell damage by neutralizing free radicals.

antipruritic (AN-tee-pru-RIT-ik) Medication against itching.

antipyretic (AN-tee-pie-RET-ik) Agent that reduces fever.

antisepsis (an-tih-SEP-sis) Inhibiting the growth of infectious agents.

antisocial personality disorder (AN-tee-SOH-shal per-son-AL-ih-tee dis-OR-der) Describes people who lie, cheat, and steal, and have no guilt about their behavior.

antithyroid (an-tee-THIGH-royd) A substance that inhibits production of thyroid hormones.

antrum (AN-trum) A closed cavity.

anuria (an-YOU-ree-ah) Absence of urine production.

anus (A-nus) Opening of the digestive tract through which feces are discharged.

anxiety (ang-ZI-eh-tee) Distress caused by fear

aorta (a-OR-tuh) Main trunk of the systemic arterial system.

apex (A-peks) Tip or end of cone-shaped heart.

Apgar score (AP-gar SKOR) Evaluation of newborn status.

apheresis (a-fer-EE-sis) Extraction of one element from donated blood.

aphonia (a-FO-nee-ah) Loss of voice.

aphthous (AF-thus) Painful small oral ulcers (canker sores).

apnea (AP-nee-ah) Absence of spontaneous respiration.

apocrine (AP-oh-krin) Apocrine sweat glands open into the hair follicle.

apoptosis (AP-oh-TOE-sis) Programmed normal cell death.

appendicitis (ah-pen-dih-SIGH-tis) Inflammation of the appendix.

appendix (ah-PEN-dicks) Small blind projection from the pouch of the cecum.

aqueous humor (ACHE-we-us HEW-mor) Watery liquid in the anterior and posterior chambers of the eye.

arachnoid mater (ah-RACK-noyd MAY-ter) Weblike middle layer of the three meninges.

areola (ah-REE-oh-luh) Circular reddish area surrounding the nipple.

aromatherapy (ah-ROH-mah-THAIR-ah-pee) Use of essential oils to promote well-being.

aromatic (ah-roh-MAT-ik) Having an agreeable spicy odor, or one of a group of vegetable drugs.

arrhythmia (a-RITH-me-ah) Condition when heart rhythm is abnormal.

arteriography (ar-teer-e-OG-reh-fee) X-ray visualization of an artery after injection of contrast material.

arteriole (ar-TER-ee-ole) Small terminal artery leading into the capillary network

arteriosclerosis (ar-TIER-e-oh-skler-OH-sis) Hardening of the arteries.

arteriovenous malformation (ar-TEER-e-o-VE-nus mal-for-MAY-shun) An abnormal communication between an artery and a vein.

artery (AR-ter-ee) Thick-walled blood vessel carrying blood away from the heart.

arthrocentesis (AR-throw-sen-TEE-sis) Withdrawal of fluid from a joint through a needle.

arthrodesis (ar-THROW-dee-sis) Fixation or stiffening of a joint by surgery.

arthrography (ar-THROG-ra-fee) X-ray of a joint taken after the injection of a contrast medium into the joint.

arthroplasty (AR-throw-plas-tee) Surgery to restore as far as possible the function of a joint.

arthroscope (AR-thro-skope) Endoscope used to examine the interior of a joint.

arthroscopy (ar-THROS-koh-pee) Visual examination of the interior of a joint.

articulate (ar-TIK-you-late) Two bones have formed a joint. The joint formed permits movement between two parts.

articulation (ar-tic-you-LAY-shun) A joint.

asana (ah-SAH-nah) Yoga posture or steady position of the body to open energy channels.

asbestosis (as-bes-TOE-sis) Lung disease caused by the inhalation of asbestos particles.

Ascaris lumbricoides (AS-kah-ris lum-bri-KOY-deez) Large roundworm parasite.

ascites (ah-SIGH-teez) Accumulation of fluid in the abdominal cavity.

ascorbic acid (as-KOR-bic ASS-id) Vitamin C, which prevents scurvy.

asepsis (a-SEP-sis) Absence of living pathogenic organisms.

Ashkenazi (ASH-ke-NAZ-ih) Jews of eastern European ancestry.

aspartate aminotransferase (AST) (as-PAR-tate ah-me-no-TRANS-fer-aze) Enzyme that is found in liver cells and leaks out into the bloodstream when the cells are damaged, enabling liver damage to be diagnosed.

Asperger syndrome (AHS-per-ger SIN-drome) Developmental disorder of children.

aspergilloma (AS-per-ji-LOH-mah) Infectious granuloma.

aspergillosis (AS-per-ji-LOH-sis) Presence of *Aspergillus* in the body.

Aspergillus (as-per-JILL-us) A type of fungus.

aspiration (AS-pih-RAY-shun) Removal by suction of fluid or gas from a body cavity.

assistive device (ah-SIS-tiv de-VICE) Tool, software, or hardware to assist in performing daily activities.

assistive therapy (ah-SIS-tiv THAIR-ah-pee) Use of methods, technology, and devices to help people with disabilities achieve specific functions.

asthma (AZ-mah) Episodes of breathing difficulty due to narrowed or obstructed airways.

astigmatism (ah-STIG-mah-tism) Inability to focus light rays that enter the eye in different planes.

astrocyte (ASS-troh-site) Star-shaped connective tissue cell in the nervous system.

astrocytoma (ASS-troh-sigh-TOE-mah) Brain tumor derived from astrocytes.

asystole (a-SIS-toe-lee) Absence of contractions of the heart.

ataxia (a-TAK-see-ah) Inability to coordinate muscle activity, leading to jerky movements.

atelectasis (at-el-ECK-tah-sis) Collapse of part of a lung.

attenuate (ah-TEN-you-ate) Weaken the ability of an organism to produce disease.

atherectomy (ath-er-EK-toe-me) Surgical removal of the atheroma.

atheroma (ath-er-ROE-mah) Lipid deposit in the lining of an artery.

atherosclerosis (ATH-er-oh-skler-OH-sis) Atheroma in arteries.

athetosis (ath-eh-TOE-sis) Slow, writhing involuntary movements.

atom (AT-om) A small unit of matter.

atonic (a-TOHN-ik) Without normal muscular tone.

atopy (AY-toh-pee) State of hypersensitivity to an allergen—allergic.

atrioventricular (AV) (a-tree-oh-ven-TRICK-you-lar) Pertaining to both the atrium and ventricle.

atrium (A-tree-um) Chamber where blood enters the heart on both right and left sides. Plural *atria*.

atrophy (AT-roh-fee) Wasting or diminished volume of a tissue or organ.

atropine (AT-ro-peen) Pharmacologic agent used to dilate pupils.

attenuate (Ah-TEN-you-ate) Weaken the ability of an organism to produce disease.

atypical (a-TIP-ih-kal) Something that does not conform to the normal type.

audiologist (aw-dee-OL-oh-jist) Specialist in evaluation of hearing function.

audiology (aw-dee-OL-oh-jee) Study of hearing disorders.

audiometer (aw-dee-OM-ee-ter) Instrument to measure hearing.

audiometric (AW-dee-oh-MET-rik) Pertaining to the measurement of hearing.

auditory (AW-dih-tor-ee) Pertaining to the sense or the organs of hearing.

aura (AWE-rah) Sensory experience preceding an epileptic seizure or a migraine headache.

auricle (AW-ri-kul) The shell-like external ear.

auscultation (aws-kul-TAY-shun) Diagnostic method of listening to body sounds with a stethoscope.

autism (AW-tizm) Developmental disorder of children.

autoantibody (aw-toe-AN-tee-bod-ee) Antibody produced in response to an antigen in the host's own tissue.

autoclave (AW-toe-klayv) Apparatus for sterilization by steam under pressure.

autograft (AWE-toe-graft) A graft using tissue taken from the same individual who is receiving the graft.

autoimmune (aw-toe-im-YUNE) Immune reaction directed against a person's own tissue.

autologous (awe-TOL-oh-gus) Blood transfusion with the same person as donor and recipient.

autolysis (awe-TOL-ih-sis) Destruction of cells by enzymes within the cells.

autonomic (awe-toh-NOM-ik) Self-governing visceral motor division of the peripheral nervous system.

autopsy (AWE-top-see) Examination of the body and organs of a dead person to determine the cause of death.

autosome (AWE-toe-soam) Any chromosome other than a sex chromosome.

avascular (a-VAS-cue-lar) Without a blood supply.

avian (A-vee-an) Pertaining to birds.

avulsion (a-VUL-shun) Forcible separation or tearing away, often of a tendon from bone.

axilla (AK-sill-ah) Medical name for the armpit. Plural *axillae*.

axon (ACK-son) Single process of a nerve cell carrying nervous impulses away from the cell body.

Ayurvedic (ah-yur-VED-ik) A system of medicine arising from Hindu culture.

azotemia (azo-TEE-me-ah) Excess nitrogenous waste products in the blood.

B

Babinski sign (bah-BIN-skee SINE) Abnormal neurological response to plantar reflex.

bacillus (ba-SIL-us) Spore-forming, gram-positive rod. Plural *bacilli*.

bacterial (bak-TEER-ee-al) Pertaining to bacteria.

bacterium (bak-TEER-ee-um) A unicellular simple organism. Plural *bacteria*.

balanitis (bal-ah-NIE-tis) Inflammation of the glans and prepuce.

bariatric (bar-ee-AT-rik) Treatment of obesity.

basal metabolic rate (BAY-sal met-ah-BOL-ic RATE) Energy the body requires to function at rest.

basilar (BAS-ih-lar) Pertaining to the base of a structure.

basophil (BAY-so-fill) A basophil's granules attract a basic blue stain in the laboratory.

Bell palsy (BELL PAWL-ze) Paresis or paralysis of one side of the face.

benign (bee-NINE) The nonmalignant character of a neoplasm or illness

beriberi (BER-ee-BER-ee) Disease produced by thiamine deficiency.

beta (BAY-tah) Second letter in the Greek alphabet.

beta carotene (BAY-tah KAR-oh-teen) Yellow-red pigment in fruits and vegetables.

biceps brachii (BYE-sepz BRAY-key-eye) A muscle of the upper arm that has two heads or points of origin on the scapula.

biconcave (bi-KON-cave) Hollowed surface on both sides of a structure.

bicuspid (by-KUSS-pid) Having two points; a bicuspid heart valve has two flaps; a bicuspid (premolar) tooth has two points.

bifid (BI-fid) Separated into two parts.

bilateral (by-LAT-er-al) On two sides; for example, in both ears.

bile (BILE) Fluid secreted by the liver into the duodenum.

bile acids (BILE AH-sids) Steroids synthesized from cholesterol.

bilirubin (bill-ee-RU-bin) Bile pigment formed from hemoglobin.

binge eating (BINJ EE-ting) Eating with periods of excessive intake.

bioavailable (BI-oh-ah-VAIL-ah-bul) Capable of being absorbed into the bloodstream.

biofeedback (bi-oh-FEED-back) Training techniques to achieve voluntary control of responses to stimuli.

biofield (bi-oh-FIELD) Area of energy in and surrounding the body.

biology (bi-OL-oh-jee) Science concerned with life and living organisms.

biomarker (bi-oh-MARK-er) A biological marker or product by which a cell can be identified.

biopsy (BI-op-see) Removing tissue from a living person for laboratory examination.

biopsy removal (BI-op-see re-MUV-al) Used for small tumors when complete removal provides tissue for a biopsy and cures the lesion. Also called *excisional biopsy*.

biotin (BI-oh-tin) Vitamin B_2.

bipolar disorder (bi-PO-lar dis-OR-der) A mood disorder with alternating episodes of depression and mania

bladder (BLAD-er) Hollow sac that holds fluid; for example, urine or bile.

blastocyst (BLAS-toe-sist) First two weeks of the developing embryo.

blepharitis (blef-ah-RYE-tis) Inflammation of the eyelid.

blepharoplasty (BLEF-ah-ro-plas-tee) Surgical repair of the eyelid.

blepharoptosis (BLEF-ah-ROP-toe-sis) Drooping of the upper eyelid.

blood-brain barrier (BBB) (BLUD BRAYN BAIR-ee-er) A selective mechanism that protects the brain from toxins and infections.

bolus (BOH-lus) Single mass of a substance.

bonding (BON-ding) Formation of a close and lasting emotional attachment.

Botox (BO-tox) Neurotoxin injected into the muscles of the face to prevent the muscles from contracting and causing wrinkles.

botulism (BOT-you-lizm) Food poisoning caused by the neurotoxin produced by *Clostridium botulinum*.

bovine spongiform encephalopathy (BO-vine SPON-jee-form en-sef-ah-LOP-ah-thee) Disease of cattle that can be transmitted to humans, causing Creutzfeldt-Jakob disease. Also called *mad cow disease*.

bowel (BOUGH-el) Another name for intestine.

brace (BRACE) Appliance to support a part of the body in its correct position.

brachial (BRAY-kee-al) Pertaining to the arm.

brachialis (BRAY-kee-al-is) Muscle that lies underneath the biceps and is the strongest flexor of the forearm.

brachiocephalic (BRAY-kee-oh-seh-FAL-ik) Pertaining to, in this case, an artery supplying the head and arm.

brachioradialis (BRAY-kee-oh-RAY-dee-al-is) Muscle that helps flex the forearm.

brachytherapy (bra-kee-THAIR-ah-pee) Radiation therapy in which the source of irradiation is implanted in the tissue to be treated.

bradycardia (brad-ee-KAR-dee-ah) Slow heart rate (below 60 beats per minute).

bradypnea (brad-ip-NEE-ah) Slow breathing.

brainstem (BRAYNSTEM) Comprises the thalamus, pineal gland, pons, fourth ventricle, and the medulla oblongata.

breech (BREECH) Buttocks-first presentation of the fetus at delivery.

bronchiectasis (brong-kee-ECK-tah-sis) Chronic dilation of the bronchi following inflammatory disease and obstruction.

bronchiole (BRONG-key-ole) Increasingly smaller subdivisions of bronchi.

bronchiolitis (brong-kee-oh-LYE-tis) Inflammation of the small bronchioles.

bronchoalveolar (BRONG-koh-al-VEE-oh-lar) Pertaining to the bronchi and alveoli.

bronchoconstriction (BRONG-koh-kon-STRIK-shun) Reduction in diameter of a bronchus.

bronchodilator (BRONG-koh-die-LAY-tor) Agent that increases the diameter of a bronchus.

bronchogenic (brong-koh-JEN-ik) Arising from a bronchus.

bronchopneumonia (BRONG-koh-new-MOH-nee-ah) Acute inflammation of the walls of smaller bronchioles with spread to lung parenchyma.

bronchopulmonary dysplasia (BRONG-koh-PUL-moh-nair-ee dis-PLAY-zee-ah) Chronic lung disorder in premature infants after prolonged mechanical ventilation.

bronchoscope (BRONG-koh-skope) Endoscope used for bronchoscopy.

bronchoscopy (brong-KOS-koh-pee) Examination of the interior of the tracheobronchial tree with an endoscope.

bronchus (BRONG-kuss) One of two subdivisions of the trachea. Plural *bronchi*.

brucellosis (brew-sel-OH-sis) Undulant fever.

bubo (BYU-bo) Swollen, inflamed lymph node. Plural *buboes*.

buccal smear (BUCK-al SMEER) Use of a small brush or cotton swab to collect cells from the inside surface of the cheek.

buccinator (BUCK-sin-a-tor) Buccinator muscle is the muscle in the cheek.

buffer (BUFF-er) Substance that resists a change in pH.

bulbourethral (BUL-boh-you-REE-thral) Pertaining to the bulbous penis and urethra.

bulimia (byu-LEEM-ee-ah) Episodic bouts of excessive eating with compensatory throwing up.

bulla (BULL-ah) Bubblelike dilated structure. Plural *bullae*.

bundle of His (HISS) Part of the electrical conduction system of the heart, connecting the atria to the ventricles.

bunion (BUN-yun) A swelling at the base of the big toe.

bursa (BURR-sah) A closed sac containing synovial fluid.

bursitis (burr-SIGH-tis) Inflammation of a bursa.

C

café-au-lait (KAF-ay-oh-LAY) Color of skin macules in neurofibromatosis.

calcaneus (kal-**KAY**-knee-us) Bone of the tarsus that forms the heel.

calcitonin (kal-sih-**TONE**-in) Thyroid hormone that moves calcium from blood to bones.

calcitriol (**KAL**-sih-**TRY**-ol) Potent form of vitamin D that acts as a hormone.

calculus (**KAL**-kyu-lus) Small stone. Plural *calculi.*

callus (**KAL**-us) The mass of fibrous connective tissue that forms at a fracture site and becomes the foundation for the formation of new bone.

caloric (kah-**LOR**-ik) Pertaining to calories.

Calorie (**KAL**-oh-ree) An expression of the energy content of food; capitalize "C" always.

calyx (**KAY**-licks) Funnel-shaped structure. Plural *calyces.*

cancellous (**KAN**-sell-us) Bone that has a spongy or latticelike structure.

cancer (**KAN**-ser) General term for a malignant neoplasm.

cancerous (**KAN**-ser-ous) Pertaining to a malignant neoplasm.

Candida (**KAN**-did-ah) A yeastlike fungus.

candidiasis (can-dih-**DIE**-ah-sis) Infection with the yeastlike fungus, *Candida.* Also called *thrush.*

canker (**KANG**-ker) Nonmedical term for aphthous ulcer. Also called *mouth ulcer.*

cannula (**KAN**-you-lah) Tube inserted into a blood vessel or cavity as a channel for fluid.

canthus (**KAN**-thus) Corner of the eye where upper and lower lid meet. Plural *canthi.*

capillary (**KAP**-ih-lair-ee) Minute blood vessel between the arterial and venous systems.

capsid (**KAP**-sid) Protein shell surrounding the nucleic acid in the core of a virus.

capsule (**KAP**-syul) Fibrous tissue layer surrounding a joint or other structure.

carbohydrate (kar-boh-**HIGH**-drate) Group of organic food compounds that includes sugars, starch, glycogen, and cellulose.

carboxypeptidase (kar-box-ee-**PEP**-tide-ase) Enzyme that breaks down protein.

carbuncle (**KAR**-bunk-ul) Infection of many furuncles in a small area, often on the back of the neck.

carcinogen (kar-**SIN**-oh-jen) Cancer-producing agent.

carcinogenesis (kar-**SIN**-oh-**JEN**-eh-sis) Origin and development of cancer.

carcinoma (kar-sih-**NOH**-mah) A malignant and invasive epithelial tumor.

carcinoma in situ (kar-sih-**NOH**-mah in **SIGH**-too) Carcinoma that has not invaded surrounding tissues.

cardiac (**KAR**-dee-ak) Pertaining to the heart.

cardiogenic (**KAR**-dee-oh-**JEN**-ik) Of cardiac origin.

cardiologist (kar-dee-**OL**-oh-jist) A medical specialist in diagnosis and treatment of the heart (cardiology).

cardiology (kar-dee-**OL**-oh-jee) Medical specialty of diseases of the heart.

cardiomegaly (**KAR**-dee-oh-**MEG**-ah-lee) Enlargement of the heart.

cardiomyopathy (**KAR**-dee-oh-my-**OP**-ah-thee) Disease of heart muscle, the myocardium.

cardiopulmonary resuscitation (**KAR**-dee-oh-**PUL**-mo-nary ree-sus-ih-**TAY**-shun) The attempt to restore cardiac and pulmonary function.

cardiovascular (**KAR**-dee-oh-**VAS**-kyu-lar) Pertaining to the heart and blood vessels.

cardioversion (**KAR**-dee-oh-**VER**-shun) Use of electric shock to change abnormal heart rhythm back to normal rhythm. Also called *defibrillation.*

cardioverter (**KAR**-dee-oh-**VER**-ter) Device used to generate electric shock for cardioversion.

caries (**KARE**-eez) Bacterial destruction of teeth.

carotenoid (kah-**ROT**-en-oyd) Organic pigment occurring naturally in plants.

carotid (kah-**ROT**-id) Main artery of the neck.

carotid endarterectomy (kah-**ROT**-id **END**-ar-ter-**EK**-toe-me) Surgical removal of diseased lining from the carotid artery to leave a smooth lining.

carpal (**KAR**-pal) Pertaining to the wrist.

carpus (**KAR**-pus) Collective term for the eight carpal bones of the wrist.

carrier (**KAH**-ree-er) In this setting, a person with an autosomal recessive gene for a disease. Also called *heterozygote.*

cartilage (**KAR**-tih-lage) Nonvascular, firm connective tissue found mostly in joints.

cast (**KAST**) A cylindrical mold formed by materials in kidney tubules.

catabolism (kah-**TAB**-oh-lizm) Breakdown of complex substances into simpler ones as a part of metabolism.

cataplexy (**KAT**-ah-plek-see) Sudden loss of muscle tone with brief paralysis.

cataract (**KAT**-ah-ract) Complete or partial opacity of the lens.

catatonia (kat-ah-**TOE**-nee-ah) A period of physical immobility.

catecholamine (kat-eh-**COAL**-ah-meen) Major element in stress response.

catheter (**KATH**-eh-ter) Hollow tube to allow passage of fluid into or out of a body cavity, organ, or vessel.

catheterization (**KATH**-eh-ter-ih-**ZAY**-shun) Introduction of a catheter.

catheterize (**KATH**-eh-teh-**RIZE**) To introduce a catheter.

cauda equina (**KAW**-dah eh-**KWY**-nah) Bundle of spinal nerves in the vertebral canal below the ending of the spinal cord.

caudal (**KAW**-dal) Pertaining to or nearer to the tail.

cautery (**KAW**-ter-ee) Agent or device used to burn or scar a tissue.

cavernosa (kav-er-**NO**-sah) Resembling a cave.

cavity (**KAV**-ih-tee) Hollow space or body compartment. Plural *cavities.*

cecum (SEE-kum) Blind pouch that is the first part of the large intestine.

celiac (SEE-lee-ack) Relating to the abdominal cavity.

celiac disease (SEE-lee-ak diz-EEZ) Disease caused by sensitivity to gluten.

cell (SELL) The smallest unit capable of independent existence.

cellular (SELL-you-lar) Pertaining to a cell.

cellulitis (sell-you-LIE-tis) Infection of subcutaneous connective tissue.

cellulose (SELL-you-lohse) Major constituent of cell walls of plants.

centromere (SEN-troh-mere) Junction that holds the two chromatids together to form a chromosome.

cephalic (se-FAL-ik) Pertaining to or nearer to the head.

cerebellum (ser-eh-BELL-um) Posterior brain located between the midbrain and the cerebral hemispheres.

cerebrospinal (SER-ee-bro-SPY-nal) Pertaining to the brain and spinal cord.

cerebrospinal fluid (CSF) (SER-ee-bro-SPY-nal FLU-id) Fluid formed in the ventricles of the brain; surrounds the brain and spinal cord.

cerebrum (SER-ee-brum) Cerebral hemispheres.

cerumen (seh-ROO-men) Waxy secretion of the ceruminous glands of the external ear.

cervical (SER-vih-kal) Pertaining to the cervix or to the neck region.

cervix (SER-viks) The lower part of the uterus.

cesarean section (seh-ZAH-ree-an SEK-shun) Extraction of the fetus through an incision in the abdomen and uterine wall. Also called *C-section*.

chakra (CHAK-rah) One of seven centers of energy in the body.

chalazion (kah-LAY-zee-on) Cyst on the outer edge of an eyelid.

chancre (SHAN-ker) Primary lesion of syphilis.

chancroid (SHAN-kroyd) Infectious, painful, ulcerative STD not related to syphilis.

Charcot joint (SHAR-koh JOYNT) Bone and joint destruction secondary to a neuropathy and loss of sensation.

chemoprophylaxis (KEEM-oh-PRO-fil-ak-sis) Prevent infection by use of chemicals or drugs.

chemotherapy (KEY-moh-THAIR-ah-pee) Treatment using chemical agents.

chi (CHEE) Universal life force. Also spelled *qi*.

chiasm (KYE-asm) X-shaped crossing of the two optic nerves at the base of the brain. Alternative term *chiasma*.

chickenpox (CHICK-en-pocks) Acute, contagious viral disease. Also called *varicella*.

chiropractic (kye-roh-PRAK-tik) Diagnosis, treatment, and prevention of mechanical disorders of the musculoskeletal system.

chiropractor (kye-roh-PRAK-tor) Practitioner of chiropractic.

chlamydia (kla-MID-ee-ah) An STD caused by infection with *Chlamydia*, a type of bacteria.

chlorophyll (KLOR-oh-fil) Light-absorbing pigments in plants.

cholangiography (KOH-lan-jee-OG-rah-fee) Use of a contrast medium to radiographically visualize the bile ducts.

cholecystectomy (KOH-leh-sis-TECK-toe-me) Surgical removal of the gallbladder.

cholecystitis (KOH-leh-sis-TIE-tis) Inflammation of the gallbladder.

cholecystokinin (KOH-leh-sis-toe-KIE-nin) Hormone secreted by the lining of the intestine that stimulates secretion of pancreatic enzymes and contraction of the gallbladder.

choledocholithiasis (koh-leh-DOH-koh-li-THIGH-ah-sis) Presence of a gallstone in the common bile duct.

cholelithiasis (KOH-leh-lih-THIGH-ah-sis) Condition of having bile (gall) stones.

cholera (KOL-er-ah) Acute endemic infectious disease.

cholestatic (koh-les-TAT-ik) Stopping the flow of bile.

cholesteatoma (koh-less-tee-ah-TOE-mah) Yellow, waxy tumor arising in the middle ear.

cholesterol (koh-LESS-ter-ol) Formed in liver cells; is the most abundant steroid in tissues and circulates in the plasma attached to proteins of different densities.

choline (KOH-leen) An amine found in most tissues; a precursor for acetylcholine.

chondromalacia (KON-dro-mah-LAY-she-ah) Softening and degeneration of cartilage.

chondrosarcoma (KON-dro-sar-KOH-mah) Cancer arising from cartilage cells.

chordae tendineae (KOR-dee ten-DIN-ee) Tendinous cords attaching the bicuspid and tricuspid valves to the heart wall.

chorea (kor-EE-ah) Involuntary, irregular spasms of limb and facial muscles.

choriocarcinoma (KOH-ree-oh-kar-sih-NOH-mah) Highly malignant cancer in a testis or ovary.

chorion (KOH-ree-on) The fetal membrane that forms the placenta.

chorionic (koh-ree-ON-ick) Pertaining to the chorion.

chorionic villus (koh-ree-ON-ik VILL-us) Vascular process of the embryonic chorion to form the placenta.

choroid (KOR-oid) Region of the retina and uvea.

chromatid (KROH-ma-tid) One of the two strands of a chromosome.

chromatin (KROH-ma-tin) Composed of DNA and RNA and forms chromosomes during cell division.

chromosome (KROH-moh-sohm) Body in the nucleus that contains DNA and genes.

chronic (KRON-ik) Term to describe a persistent, long-term disease.

chronotropic (KRONE-oh-TROH-pic) Agents that affect the heart rate.

chyle (KYLE) A milky fluid that results from the digestion and absorption of fats in the small intestine.

chyme (KYME) Semifluid, partially digested food passed from the stomach into the duodenum.

chymotrypsin (kye-moh-**TRIP**-sin) Trypsin found in chyme.

ciliary body (**SILL**-ee-ary **BOD**-ee) Muscles that make the eye lens thicker and thinner.

cilium (**SILL**-ee-um) Hairlike motile projection from the surface of a cell. Plural *cilia*.

circulation (**SER**-kyu-**LAY**-shun) Continuous movement of blood through the heart and blood vessels.

circumcision (ser-kum-**SIZH**-un) To remove part or all of the prepuce.

circumduction (ser-kum-**DUCK**-shun) Movement of an extremity in a circular motion.

cirrhosis (sir-**ROE**-sis) Extensive fibrotic liver disease.

claudication (klaw-dih-**KAY**-shun) Arterial blockage causing intermittent leg pain and limping.

claustrophobia (klaw-stroh-**FOH**-be-ah) Pathologic fear of being trapped in a confined space.

clavicle (**KLAV**-ih-kul) Curved bone that forms the anterior part of the pectoral girdle.

clean (KLENE) Free from visible contamination.

cleft lip (KLEFT LIP) Congenital defect of the upper lip.

cleft palate (KLEFT **PAL**-ate) Congenital defect of the upper palate.

clitoris (**KLIT**-oh-ris) Erectile organ of the vulva.

clonic (**KLON**-ik) State of rapid successions of muscular contractions and relaxations.

closed fracture (KLOSD **FRAK**-chur) A bone is broken but the skin over it is intact.

Clostridium botulinum (klos-**TRID**-ee-um bot-you-**LIE**-num) Bacterium that causes food poisoning.

Clostridium difficile (klos-**TRID**-ee-um dif-ih-**SEE**-il) Gram-positive rod producing powerful exotoxins that cause colitis.

clot (KLOT) The mass of fibrin and cells that is produced in a wound.

coagulate (koh-**AG**-you-late) Form a clot.

coagulation (koh-ag-you-**LAY**-shun) The process of blood clotting.

coagulopathy (koh-ag-you-**LOP**-ah-thee) Disorder of blood clotting. Plural *coagulopathies*.

coarctation (koh-ark-**TAY**-shun) Constriction, stenosis, particularly of the aorta.

coccus (**KOK**-us) Round, spheroid bacterium. Plural *cocci*.

coccyx (**KOK**-sicks) Small tailbone at the lower end of the vertebral column.

cochlea (**KOK**-lee-ah) An intricate combination of passages; used to describe the part of the inner ear used in hearing.

cochlear (**KOK**-lee-ar) Pertaining to the cochlea.

coenzyme (koh-**EN**-zime) Substance required for an enzyme to function.

cognition (kog-**NIH**-shun) Process of acquiring knowledge through thinking, learning, and memory.

cognitive (**KOG**-nih-tiv) Pertaining to the mental activities of thinking and learning.

cognitive-behavioral therapy (CBT) (**KOG**-nih-tiv be-**HAYV**-yur-al **THAIR**-ah-pee) Psychotherapy that emphasizes thoughts and attitudes in one's behavior.

cognitive processing therapy (**KOG**-nih-tiv **PROS**-es-ing **THAIR**-ah-pee) Psychotherapy to build skills to deal with effects of the trauma in other areas of life.

coitus (**KOH**-it-us) Sexual intercourse.

colic (**KOL**-ik) Spasmodic, crampy pains in the abdomen. In young infants, persistent crying and irritability thought to be arising from pain in the intestines.

colitis (koh-**LIE**-tis) Inflammation of the colon.

collagen (**KOL**-ah-jen) Major protein of connective tissue, cartilage, and bone.

collateral (koh-**LAT**-er-al) Situated at the side to bypass an obstruction.

colloid (**COLL**-oyd) Liquid containing suspended particles.

colon (**KOH**-lon) The large intestine, extending from the cecum to the rectum.

colonization (**KOL**-on-ih-**ZAY**-shun) Formation of a population of microorganisms.

colonoscopy (koh-lon-**OSS**-koh-pee) Examination of inside of the colon by endoscopy.

color Doppler ultrasonography (**DOP**-ler **UL**-trah-soh-**NOG**-rah-fee) Computer-generated color image to show directions of blood flow.

colostomy (ko-**LOSS**-toe-me) Artificial opening from the colon to the outside of the body.

colostrum (ko-**LOSS**-trum) The first breast secretion at the end of pregnancy.

colpopexy (**KOL**-po-peck-see) Surgical fixation of the vagina.

coma (**KOH**-mah) State of deep unconsciousness.

comatose (**KOH**-mah-toes) Being in a coma.

comedo (**KOM**-ee-doh) A whitehead or blackhead caused by too much sebum and too many keratin cells blocking the hair follicle.

comminuted fracture (**KOM**-ih-nyu-ted **FRAK**-chur) A fracture in which the bone is broken into pieces.

comorbidity (koh-mor-**BID**-ih-tee) Presence of two or more diseases at the same time.

competent (**KOM**-peh-tent) Capable of performing a task or function.

complement (**KOM**-pleh-ment) Group of proteins in serum that finish off the work of antibodies to destroy bacteria and other cells.

complete (kom-**PLEET**) Whole, entire, total.

complete fracture (kom-**PLEET FRAK**-chur) A bone is fractured into two separate pieces.

compliance (kom-**PLY**-ance) Measure of the capacity of a chamber or hollow viscus to expand; in this case, the lungs.

compression (kom-**PRESH**-un) Squeeze together to increase density or decrease a dimension of a structure.

compression fracture (kom-PRESH-un FRAK-chur) Fracture of a vertebra causing loss of height of the vertebra.

compulsion (kom-PULL-shun) Uncontrollable impulses to perform an act repetitively.

compulsive (kom-PULL-siv) Possessing uncontrollable impulses to perform an act repetitively.

conception (kon-SEP-shun) Fertilization of the egg by sperm to form a zygote.

concha (KON-kah) Shell-shaped bone on the medial wall of the nasal cavity. Plural *conchae*.

concussion (kon-KUSH-un) Mild head injury.

condom (KON-dom) A sheath or cover for the penis or vagina to prevent conception and infection.

conduction (kon-DUCK-shun) Process of transmitting energy.

conductive hearing loss (kon-DUK-tiv) Hearing loss caused by lesions in the outer ear or middle ear.

condyle (KON-dile) Large, smooth rounded expansion of the end of a bone to form a joint with another bone.

condyloma (kon-dih-LOW-ma) Warty growth on external genitalia. Plural *condylomata*.

confusion (kon-FEW-zhun) Mental state in which environmental stimuli are not processed appropriately.

congenital (kon-JEN-ih-tal) Present at birth, either inherited or due to an event during gestation up to the moment of birth.

congruent (KON-gru-ent) Coinciding or agreeing with.

conization (koh-nih-ZAY-shun) Surgical excision of a cone-shaped piece of tissue.

conjunctiva (kon-junk-TIE-vah) Inner lining of the eyelids.

conjunctivitis (kon-junk-tih-VI-tis) Inflammation of the conjunctiva.

Conn syndrome (KON SIN-drom) Condition caused by excessive secretion of aldosterone. Also called *aldosteronism*.

constipation (kon-sti-PAY-shun) Hard, infrequent bowel movements.

contagiosum (kon-TAY-jee-oh-sum) Infection spread from one person to another by direct contact.

contagious (kon-TAY-jus) Infection can be transmitted from person to person or from a person to a surface to a person.

contaminate (kon-TAM-in-ate) To cause the presence of an infectious agent to be on any surface.

contamination (KON-tam-ih-NAY-shun) Presence of an infectious agent on a surface or in substances.

contraception (kon-trah-SEP-shun) Prevention of conception.

contraceptive (kon-trah-SEP-tiv) An agent that prevents conception.

contract (kon-TRAKT) Draw together or shorten.

contracture (kon-TRAK-chur) Muscle shortening due to spasm or fibrosis.

contrecoup (KON-tre-koo) Injury to the brain at a point directly opposite the point of original contact.

contusion (kon-TOO-zhun) Bruising of a tissue, including the brain.

conversion disorder (kon-VER-shun dis-OR-der) An unconscious emotional conflict is expressed by a severe physical problem.

convulsion (kon-VUL-shun) Alternative name for seizure.

coordinate (ko-OR-din-ate) To bring together different structures into a harmonious function.

cor pulmonale (KOR pul-moh-NAH-lee) Right-sided heart failure arising from chronic lung disease.

coreceptor (koh-ree-SEP-tor) Cell surface protein to enhance the sensitivity of an antigen receptor.

cornea (KOR-nee-ah) The central, transparent part of the outer coat of the eye covering the iris and pupil.

coronal (KOR-oh-nal) Vertical plane dividing the body into anterior and posterior portions.

coronal plane (KOR-oh-nal PLAIN) Vertical plane dividing the body into anterior and posterior portions.

coronary circulation (KOR-oh-nair-ee SER-kyu-LAY-shun) Blood vessels supplying the heart.

corpus (KOR-pus) Major part of a structure. Plural *corpora*.

corpus albicans (KOR-pus AL-bih-kanz) An atrophied corpus luteum.

corpus callosum (KOR-pus kah-LOW-sum) Bridge of nerve fibers connecting the two cerebral hemispheres.

corpus luteum (KOR-pus LOO-teh-um) Yellow structure at the site of a ruptured ovarian follicle.

corpuscle (KOR-pus-ul) A blood cell.

cortex (KOR-teks) Outer portion of an organ, such as bone. Gray covering of cerebral hemispheres. Plural *cortices*.

corticoid (KOR-tih-koyd) One of the steroid hormones produced by the adrenal cortex. Also called *corticosteroid*.

corticosteroid (KOR-tih-koh-STEHR-oyd) A hormone produced by the adrenal cortex.

corticotropin (KOR-tih-koh-TROH-pin) Pituitary hormone that stimulates the adrenal gland to secrete corticosteroids.

cortisol (KOR-tih-sol) One of the glucocorticoids produced by the adrenal cortex; has anti-inflammatory effects. Also called *hydrocortisone*.

coryza (ko-RYE-zah) Viral inflammation of the mucous membrane of the nose. Also called *rhinitis*.

counseling (KOWN-sel-ing) Professional relationship to transmit advice to direct the judgment of another.

coup (KOO) Injury to the brain occurring directly under the skull at the point of impact.

coxa (COCK-sah) Hipbone. Plural *coxae*.

cranial (KRAY-nee-al) Pertaining to the skull.

craniofacial (KRAY-nee-oh-FAY-shal) Pertaining to both the face and cranium.

craniosacral (KRAY-nee-oh-SAY-kral) Referring to the total length of the spine.

cranium (KRAY-nee-um) The upper part of the skull that encloses and protects the brain.

craving (KRAY-ving) Deep longing or desire.

creatine kinase (**KREE**-ah-teen **KI**-naze) Enzyme elevated in plasma following heart muscle damage in myocardial infarction.

creatinine (kree-**AT**-ih-neen) Breakdown product of the skeletal muscle protein creatine.

cretin (**KREH**-tin) A person with severe congenital hypothyroidism.

cretinism (**KREH**-tin-izm) Condition of severe congenital hypothyroidism.

Creutzfeldt-Jakob disease (**KROITS**-felt-**YAK**-op diz-**EEZ**) Progressive incurable neurologic disease caused by infectious prions.

cricoid (**CRY**-koyd) Ring-shaped cartilage in the larynx.

crista ampullaris (**KRIS**-tah am-**PULL**-air-is) Mound of hair cells and gelatinous material in the ampulla of a semicircular canal.

criterion (kri-**TEER**-ee-on) Standard or rule for judging. Plural *criteria*.

Crohn disease (**KRONE** diz-**EEZ**) Narrowing and thickening of terminal small bowel. Also called *regional enteritis*.

croup (**KROOP**) Infection of the upper airways in children; characterized by a barking cough. Also called *laryngotracheobonchitis*.

crown (**KROWN**) Part of tooth above the gum.

crowning (**KROWN**-ing) During childbirth, when the maximum diameter of the baby's head comes through the vulval ring.

cruciate (**KRU**-she-ate) Shaped like a cross.

cryokinetics (**CRY**-oh-kih-**NET**-iks) Combination of cold therapy with exercise.

cryoneurolysis (cry-oh-**NYUR**-oh-lie-sis) Temporary deactivation of nerve tissue using extreme cold.

cryopexy (cry-oh-**PEX**-ee) Fix the detached retina by freezing it to surrounding tissue.

cryosurgery (cry-oh-**SUR**-jer-ee) Use of liquid nitrogen or argon gas in a probe to freeze and kill abnormal tissue.

cryotherapy (**CRY**-oh-**THAIR**-ah-pee) The use of cold in the treatment of injury.

cryptorchism (krip-**TOR**-kizm) Failure of one or both testes to descend into the scrotum.

curative (**KYUR**-ah-tiv) That which heals or cures.

curettage (kyu-reh-**TAHZH**) Scraping the interior of a cavity.

curette (kyu-**RET**) Scoop-shaped instrument for scraping the interior of a cavity or removing new growths.

Cushing syndrome (**KUSH**-ing **SIN**-drom) Hypersecretion of cortisol by the adrenal cortex.

cuspid (**KUSS**-pid) Tooth with one point.

cutaneous (kyu-**TAY**-nee-us) Pertaining to the skin.

cuticle (**KEW**-tih-cul) Nonliving epidermis at the base of the finger and toe nails.

cyanocobalamin (**SIGH**-an-oh-koh-**BAL**-ah-min) Vitamin B_{12}.

cyanosis (sigh-ah-**NO**-sis) Blue discoloration of the skin, lips, and nail beds due to low levels of oxygen in the blood.

cyanotic (sigh-ah-**NOT**-ik) Marked by cyanosis.

cyst (**SIST**) An abnormal, fluid-containing sac.

cystic (**SIS**-tik) Relating to a cyst.

cystic fibrosis (CF) (**SIS**-tik fie-**BRO**-sis) Genetic disease in which excessive viscid mucus obstructs passages, including bronchi.

cystocele (**SIS**-toh-seal) Hernia of the bladder into the vagina.

cystopexy (**SIS**-toh-pek-see) Surgical procedure to support the urinary bladder.

cystoscope (**SIS**-toh-skope) An endoscope inserted to view the inside of the bladder.

cystoscopy (sis-**TOS**-koh-pee) The process of using a cystoscope.

cystourethrogram (sis-toh-you-**REETH**-roe-gram) X-ray image during voiding to show the structure and function of the bladder and urethra.

cytokine (**SIGH**-toh-kine) Proteins produced by different cells that communicate with other cells in the immune system.

cytology (**SIGH**-tol-oh-gee) Study of the cell.

cytomegalovirus (sigh-toh-**MEG**-ah-loh-**VIE**-rus) A group of herpesviruses that can cause congenital infections.

cytoplasm (**SIGH**-toh-plazm) Clear, gelatinous substance that forms the substance of a cell except for the nucleus.

cytosine (**SIGH**-toh-seen) One of the chemicals found in both DNA and RNA.

cytotoxic (sigh-toh-**TOX**-ik) Destructive to cells.

D

dacryocystitis (**DAK**-re-oh-sis-**TIE**-tis) Inflammation of the lacrimal sac.

dacryostenosis (**DAK**-re-oh-ste-**NO**-sis) Narrowing of the nasolacrimal duct.

dandruff (**DAN**-druff) Seborrheic scales from the scalp.

death (**DETH**) Total and permanent cessation of all vital functions.

debridement (day-**BREED**-mon) The removal of injured or necrotic tissue.

decubitus ulcer (de-**KYU**-bit-us **UL**-ser) Sore caused by lying down for long periods of time.

decussate (**DEE**-kuss-ate) Cross over like the arms of an "X."

defecation (def-eh-**KAY**-shun) Evacuation of feces from the rectum and anus.

defect (**DEE**-fect) An absence, malformation, or imperfection.

defective (dee-**FEK**-tiv) Imperfect.

defibrillation (de-fib-rih-**LAY**-shun) Restoration of uncontrolled twitching of cardiac muscle fibers to normal rhythm.

defibrillator (de-fib-rih-**LAY**-tor) Instrument for defibrillation.

deformity (de-**FOR**-mih-tee) A permanent structural deviation from the normal.

degenerative (dee-**JEN**-er-a-tiv) Relating to the deterioration of a structure.

deglutition (dee-glue-**TISH**-un) The act of swallowing.

dehydroepiandrosterone (DHEA) (de-**HIGH**-droh-epee-an-**DROS**-ter-own) Precursor to testosterone; produced in the adrenal cortex.

delirium (de-**LIR**-ee-um) Acute altered state of consciousness with agitation and disorientation; condition is reversible.

deltoid (**DEL**-toyd) Large, fan-shaped muscle connecting the scapula and clavicle to the humerus.

delusion (de-**LOO**-zhun) Fixed, unyielding, false belief or judgment held despite strong evidence to the contrary.

dementia (de-**MEN**-she-ah) Chronic, progressive, irreversible loss of the mind's cognitive and intellectual functions.

demyelination (dee-**MY**-eh-lin-**A**-shun) Process of losing the myelin sheath of a nerve fiber.

dendrite (**DEN**-dright) Branched extension of the nerve cell body that receives nervous stimuli.

dental (**DEN**-tal) Pertaining to the teeth.

dentin (**DEN**-tin) Dense, ivorylike substance located under enamel in a tooth.

dentist (**DEN**-tist) Legally qualified specialist in dentistry.

dentistry (**DEN**-tis-tree) Evaluation, diagnosis, prevention, and treatment of conditions of the oral cavity and associated structures.

deoxyribonucleic acid (DNA) (dee-**OCK**-see-**RYE**-boh-noo-**KLEE**-ik **ASS**-id) Source of hereditary characteristics found in chromosomes.

dependence (de-**PEN**-dense) State of needing someone or something.

dependent (de-**PEN**-dent) Having to rely on someone else.

depressant (de-**PRESS**-ant) Substance that diminishes activity, sensation, or tone.

depression (de-**PRESH**-un) Mental disorder with feelings of deep sadness and despair.

dermatitis (der-mah-**TYE**-tis) Inflammation of the skin.

dermatologist (der-mah-**TOL**-oh-jist) Medical specialist in diseases of the skin.

dermatology (der-mah-**TOL**-oh-jee) Medical specialty concerned with disorders of the skin.

dermatome (**DER**-mah-tome) The area of skin supplied by a single spinal nerve; alternatively, an instrument used for cutting thin slices.

dermatomyositis (**DER**-mah-toe-**MY**-oh-site-is) Inflammation of the skin and muscles.

dermis (**DER**-miss) Connective tissue layer of the skin beneath the epidermis.

detoxification (de-**TOKS**-ih-fi-**KAY**-shun) Remove poison from a tissue or substance.

deviation (de-ve-**A**-shun) Turn aside from normal course.

diabetes insipidus (dye-ah-**BEE**-teez in-**SIP**-ih-dus) Excretion of large amounts of dilute urine as a result of inadequate ADH production.

diabetes mellitus (dye-ah-**BEE**-teez **MEL**-ih-tus) Metabolic syndrome caused by absolute or relative insulin deficiency and/or insulin ineffectiveness.

diabetic (dye-ah-**BET**-ik) Pertaining to or suffering from diabetes.

dialectic (die-ah-**LEK**-tik) Logical argumentation.

dialysis (die-**AL**-ih-sis) An artificial method of filtration to remove excess waste materials and water from the body.

dialyzer (**DIE**-ah-lie-zer) Machine for dialysis.

diaphoretic (**DIE**-ah-fo-**RET**-ic) Pertaining to sweat or perspiration.

diaphragm (**DIE**-ah-fram) A ring and dome-shaped material inserted in the vagina to prevent pregnancy, or the musculo-ligamentous partition separating the abdominal and thoracic cavities.

diaphragmatic (**DIE**-ah-frag-**MAT**-ic) Pertaining to the diaphragm.

diaphysis (die-**AF**-ih-sis) The shaft of a long bone.

diarrhea (die-ah-**REE**-ah) Rapid flow of feces through the intestine followed by its discharge through the anus.

diastasis (die-**ASS**-tah-sis) Separation of normally joined parts.

diastole (die-**AS**-toe-lee) Dilation of heart cavities, during which they fill with blood.

diet (**DIE**-et) Specific course of eating and drinking.

dietetics (die-eh-**TET**-iks) Application of diet to prevention and treatment of disease.

dietician (die-eh-**TISH**-un) Licensed professional in dietetics. Alternative spelling: *dietitian.*

differential (dif-er-**EN**-shal) A differential white blood cell count lists percentages of the different leukocytes in a blood sample.

diffuse (di-**FUSE**) To disseminate or spread out.

diffusion (di-**FYU**-zhun) The means by which small particles move between tissues.

DiGeorge syndrome (dee-**JORJ SIN**-drome) Congenital absence of the thymus gland.

digestion (die-**JEST**-shun) Breakdown of food into elements suitable for cell metabolism.

digestive (die-**JEST**-iv) Relating to digestion.

digital (**DIJ**-ih-tal) Pertaining to a finger or toe.

diglyceride (die-**GLISS**-eh-ride) Has two fatty acids.

dilation (die-**LAY**-shun) Stretching or enlarging an opening.

diode (**DIE**-ode) Allows electrical current to flow in one direction only.

dioxin (die-**OK**-sin) Carcinogenic contaminant in pesticides.

diphtheria (dif-**THEER**-ee-ah) Disease with a thick, membranous (leathery) coating of the pharynx.

diplegia (die-**PLEE**-jee-ah) Paralysis of all four limbs with the two legs affected most severely.

disability (dis-ah-**BILL**-ih-tee) Diminished capacity to perform certain activities or functions.

disaccharide (die-SACK-ah-ride) A combination of two monosaccharides; for example, table sugar.

discipline (DIS-ih-plin) Training for proper conduct or action.

discrimination (DIS-krim-ih-NAY-shun) Ability to distinguish between different things.

disinfectant (dis-in-FEK-tant) Agent that disinfects.

disinfection (dis-in-FEK-shun) Process of destruction of microorganisms by chemical agents.

dislocation (dis-low-KAY-shun) Completely out of joint.

displaced fracture (dis-PLAYSD FRAK-chur) A fracture in which the fragments are separated and are not in alignment.

disseminate (dih-SEM-in-ate) Widely scattered throughout the body or an organ.

dissociative identity disorder (di-SO-see-ah-tiv eye-DEN-tih-tee dis-OR-der) Part of an individual's personality is separated from the rest, leading to multiple personalities.

distal (DISS-tal) Situated away from the center of the body.

diuresis (die-you-REE-sis) Excretion of large volumes of urine.

diuretic (die-you-RET-ik) Agent that increases urine output.

diverticulitis (DIE-ver-tick-you-LIE-tis) Inflammation of the diverticula.

diverticulosis (DIE-ver-tick-you-LOW-sis) Presence of a number of small pouches in the wall of the large intestine.

diverticulum (die-ver-TICK-you-lum) A pouchlike opening or sac from a tubular structure (e.g., gut). Plural *diverticula*.

dizygotic (die-zye-GOT-ik) Twins from two separate zygotes.

dominant gene (DOM-ih-nant JEEN) Single allele that is expressed as a trait or characteristic.

dopamine (DOH-pah-meen) Neurotransmitter in small areas of the brain.

Doppler (DOP-ler) Diagnostic instrument that sends an ultrasonic beam into the body.

Doppler ultrasonography (DOP-ler UL-trah-soh-NOG-rah-fee) Detects direction, velocity, and turbulence of blood flow; used in workup of stroke patients.

dormant (DOR-mant) Inactive.

dorsal (DOR-sal) Pertaining to the back or situated behind.

dorsum (DOR-sum) Upper, posterior, or back surface.

dosha (DOH-sha) Psychophysical constitution of the body in Ayurvedic medicine.

Down syndrome (DOWN SIN-drome) A syndrome with variable abnormalities associated with three chromosomes 21.

droplet (DROP-let) Globule of liquid; for example, that which is ejected from the mouth during speaking, coughing, sneezing.

Duchenne muscular dystrophy (DOO-shen MUSS-kyu-lar DISS-troh-fee) Symmetrical weakness and wasting of pelvic, shoulder, and proximal limb muscles.

ductus arteriosus (DUK-tus ar-TEER-ih-OH-sus) Fetal vessel that connects the descending aorta with the left pulmonary artery.

ductus deferens (DUK-tus DEH-fuh-renz) Tube that receives sperm from the epididymis. Also known as *vas deferens*.

duodenum (du-oh-DEE-num) The duodenum is the first part of the small intestine and is approximately twelve finger-breadths (9 to 10 inches) in length.

Dupuytren (du-pwe-TRAHN) Dupuytren contracture is thickening and shortening of fibrous bands in the palm of the hand.

dura mater (DYU-rah MAY-ter) Hard, fibrous outer layer of the meninges.

dwarfism (DWORF-izm) Short stature due to underproduction of growth hormone.

dysentery (DIS-en-tare-ee) Disease with diarrhea, bowel spasms, fever, and dehydration.

dysfunctional (dis-FUNK-shun-al) Difficulty in performing.

dyslexia (dis-LEK-see-ah) Impaired reading and writing ability below the person's level of intelligence.

dyslipidemia (DIS-li-pi-DEE-me-ah) Abnormal (and "bad") levels of blood lipids.

dysmenorrhea (dis-men-oh-REE-ah) Painful and difficult menstruation.

dyspareunia (dis-pah-RUE-nee-ah) Pain during sexual intercourse.

dyspepsia (dis-PEP-see-ah) "Upset stomach," epigastric pain, nausea, and gas.

dysphagia (dis-FAY-jee-ah) Difficulty in swallowing.

dysplasia (dis-PLAY-zee-ah) Abnormal tissue formation.

dyspnea (disp-NEE-ah) Difficulty breathing.

dysrhythmia (dis-RITH-me-ah) An abnormal heart rhythm.

dysuria (dis-YOU-ree-ah) Difficulty or pain with urination.

E

eccrine (EK-rin) Coiled sweat gland that occurs in skin all over the body.

echinacea (ek-ih-NAY-sha) Spiky North American herb.

echocardiography (EK-oh-kar-dee-OG-rah-fee) Ultrasound recording of heart function.

echoencephalography (EK-oh-en-sef-ah-LOG-rah-fee) Use of ultrasound in the diagnosis of intracranial lesions.

eclampsia (ek-LAMP-see-uh) Convulsions in a patient with preeclampsia.

ecologic (ee-koh-LOJ-ik) Pertaining to the study of the environment.

ecology (ee-KOL-oh-jee) Interrelationship between living organisms.

ectopic (ek-TOP-ik) Out of place, not in a normal position.

eczema (EK-zeh-mah) Inflammatory skin disease often with a serous discharge.

edema (ee-DEE-mah) Excessive accumulation of fluid in cells and tissues.

edematous (ee-DEM-ah-tus) Marked by edema.

effacement (ee-FACE-ment) Thinning of the cervix in relation to labor.

efferent (**EF**-eh-rent) Conduct nerve impulses away from the brain or spinal cord.

effusion (eh-**FYU**-shun) Collection of fluid that has escaped from blood vessels into a cavity or tissues.

ejaculate (ee-**JACK**-you-late) To expel suddenly, or the semen expelled in ejaculation.

ejaculation (ee-**JACK**-you-**LAY**-shun) Process of expelling semen suddenly.

elective (e-**LEK**-tiv) Surgery that is not urgent or vital.

electrocardiogram (**ECG or EKG**) (ee-lek-troh-**KAR**-dee-oh-gram) Record of the electrical signals of the heart.

electrocardiograph (ee-lek-troh-**KAR**-dee-oh-graf) Machine that makes the electrocardiogram.

electrocardiography (ee-**LEK**-troh-kar-dee-**OG**-rah-fee) Interpretation of electrocardiograms.

electroconvulsive therapy (ee-**LEK**-troh-kon-**VUL**-siv **THAIR**-ah-pee) Passage of electric current through the brain to produce convulsions and treat persistent depression.

electrode (ee-**LEK**-trode) A device for conducting electricity.

electroencephalogram (**EEG**) (ee-**LEK**-troh-en-**SEF**-ah-low-gram) Record of the electrical activity of the brain.

electroencephalograph (ee-**LEK**-troh-en-**SEF**-ah-low-graf) Device used to record the electrical activity of the brain.

electroencephalography (ee-**LEK**-troh-en-**SEF**-ah-**LOG**-rah-fee) The process of recording the electrical activity of the brain.

electrolyte (ee-**LEK**-troh-lite) Substance that, when dissolved in a suitable medium, forms electrically charged particles.

electromagnetic (ee-**LEK**-troh-mag-**NET**-ik) Energy propagated through matter and space.

electromyogram (ee-lek-troh-**MY**-oh-gram) Recording of electric currents associated with muscle action.

electromyography (ee-**LEK**-troh-my-**OG**-rah-fee) Recording of electrical activity in muscle.

electroneurodiagnostic (ee-**LEK**-troh-**NYUR**-oh-die-ag-**NOS**-tik) Pertaining to the use of electricity in the diagnosis of a neurological disorder.

elimination (e-lim-ih-**NAY**-shun) Removal of waste material from the digestive tract.

emaciation (ee-may-see-**AY**-shun) Abnormal thinness.

embolus (**EM**-bo-lus) Detached piece of thrombus, a mass of bacteria, quantity of air, or foreign body that blocks a vessel.

embryo (**EM**-bree-oh) Developing organism from conception until the end of the second month.

embryology (em-bree-**OL**-oh-jee) Science of the origin and early development of an organism.

embryonic (em-bree-**ON**-ic) Pertaining to the embryo.

emesis (**EM**-eh-sis) Vomit.

eminence (**EM**-ih-nens) A higher place or part.

emmetropia (emm-eh-**TROH**-pee-ah) Normal refractive condition of the eye.

empathy (**EM**-pa-thee) Ability to place yourself into the feelings, emotions, and reactions of another person.

emphysema (em-fih-**SEE**-mah) Dilation of respiratory bronchioles and alveoli.

empyema (**EM**-pie-**EE**-mah) Pus in a body cavity, particularly in the pleural cavity.

emulsify (eh-**MUL**-sih-fye) Break up into very small droplets to suspend in a solution (emulsion).

enamel (ee-**NAM**-el) Hard substance covering a tooth.

encephalitis (en-**SEF**-ah-**LIE**-tis) Inflammation of the brain parenchyma.

encephalocele (en-**SEF**-ah-loh-seal) Congenital defect of the cranium with herniation of brain tissue.

encephalomyelitis (en-**SEF**-ah-loh-**MY**-eh-lie-tis) Inflammation of the brain and spinal cord.

encode (en-**KODE**) Convert information.

encopresis (en-koh-**PREE**-sis) Repeated soiling with feces.

endarterectomy (**END**-ar-ter-**EK**-toe-me) Surgical removal of plaque from an artery.

endemic (en-**DEM**-ik) Disease always present in a community.

endocarditis (**EN**-doh-kar-**DIE**-tis) Inflammation of the lining of the heart.

endocardium (**EN**-doh-kar-**DEE**-um) The lining of the heart.

endocrine (**EN**-doh-krin) A gland that produces an internal or hormonal secretion.

endocrinologist (**EN**-doh-kri-**NOL**-oh-jist) A medical specialist in endocrinology.

endocrinology (**EN**-doh-kri-**NOL**-oh-jee) Medical specialty concerned with the production and effects of hormones.

endogenous (en-**DOJ**-en-us) Produced within the organism.

endometrial (en-doh-**ME**-tree-al) Pertaining to the inner lining of the uterus.

endometriosis (**EN**-doh-me-tree-**OH**-sis) Endometrial tissue outside the uterus.

endometrium (en-doh-**ME**-tree-um) Inner lining of the uterus.

endoplasmic reticulum (**EN**-doh-**PLAZ**-mik reh-**TIC**-you-lum) Structure inside a cell that synthesizes steroids, detoxifies drugs, and manufactures cell membranes.

endorphin (en-**DOR**-fin) Natural substance in the brain that has same effect as opium.

endoscope (**EN**-doh-skope) Instrument to examine the inside of a tubular or hollow organ.

endoscopy (en-**DOS**-koh-pee) The use of an endoscope.

endospore (**EN**-doh-spor) Spore produced inside a cell and capable of resisting heat, freezing, radiation, and chemicals.

endosteum (en-**DOSS**-tee-um) A membrane of tissue lining the inner (medullary) cavity of a long bone.

endotracheal (en-doh-**TRAY**-kee-al) Pertaining to being inside the trachea.

enema (**EN**-eh-mah) An injection of fluid into the rectum.

enteric (en-**TEHR**-ik) Pertaining to the intestine.

enteroscope (**EN**-ter-oh-**SKOPE**) Slender, tubular instrument with light source and camera to visualize the digestive tract.

enteroscopy (en-ter-**OSS**-koh-pee) The examination of the lining of the digestive tract.

enuresis (en-you-**REE**-sis) Bed-wetting, urinary incontinence.

environment (en-**VI**-ron-ment) All the external conditions affecting the life of an organism.

environmental (en-**VI**-ron-ment-al) Pertaining to the environment.

enzyme (**EN**-zime) Protein that induces changes in other substances.

eosinophil (ee-oh-**SIN**-oh-fill) An eosinophil's granules attract a rosy-red color on staining.

ependyma (ep-**EN**-dih-mah) Membrane lining the central canal of the spinal cord and the ventricles of the brain.

ependymoma (eh-pen-dih-**MOH**-mah) Benign tumor arising from cells lining the ventricles.

epicondyle (ep-ih-**KON**-dile) Projection above the condyle for attachment of a ligament or tendon.

epidemic (ep-ih-**DEM**-ik) Outbreak in a community of a disease or a health-related behavior.

epidermis (ep-ih-**DER**-miss) Top layer of the skin.

epididymis (**EP**-ih-**DID**-ih-miss) Coiled tube attached to the testis.

epididymitis (**EP**-ih-did-ih-**MY**-tis) Inflammation of the epididymis.

epididymoorchitis (ep-ih-**DID**-ih-mo-or-**KIE**-tis) Inflammation of the epididymis and testicle. Also called *orchitis*.

epidural (ep-ih-**DYU**-ral) Above the dura.

epidural space (ep-ih-**DYU**-ral SPASE) Space between the dura mater and the wall of the vertebral canal.

epigastric (ep-ih-**GAS**-trik) Abdominal region above the stomach.

epiglottis (ep-ih-**GLOT**-is) Leaf-shaped plate of cartilage that shuts off the larynx during swallowing.

epiglottitis (ep-ih-**GLOT**-eye-tis) Inflammation of the epiglottis.

epilepsy (**EP**-ih-**LEP**-see) Chronic brain disorder due to paroxysmal excessive neuronal discharges.

epinephrine (ep-ih-**NEF**-rin) Main catecholamine produced by the adrenal medulla. Also called *adrenaline*.

epiphyseal plate (eh-**PIF**-ih-see-al PLATE) Layer of cartilage between the epiphysis and metaphysis where bone growth occurs.

epiphysis (eh-**PIF**-ih-sis) Expanded area at the proximal and distal ends of a long bone to provide increased surface area for attachment of ligaments and tendons.

episiotomy (eh-piz-ee-**OT**-oh-me) Surgical incision of the vulva.

epispadias (ep-ih-**SPAY**-dee-as) Condition in which the urethral opening is on the dorsum of the penis.

epistaxis (ep-ih-**STAK**-sis) Nosebleed.

epithelium (ep-ih-**THEE**-lee-um) Tissue that covers surfaces or lines cavities.

equilibrium (ee-kwi-**LIB**-ree-um) Being evenly balanced.

erectile (ee-**REK**-tile) Capable of erection or being distended with blood.

erection (ee-**REK**-shun) Distended and rigid state of an organ.

ergonomic (err-go-**NOM**-ick) Describes a workplace tool or equipment designed to prevent worker injury and discomfort.

erosion (ee-**ROE**-shun) Form a shallow ulcer in the lining of a structure.

erythema infectiosum (er-ih-**THEE**-mah in-fek-she-**OH**-sum) Mild infectious disease of childhood with a flushed cheek appearance. Also called *fifth disease*.

erythroblast (eh-**RITH**-ro-blast) Precursor to a red blood cell.

erythroblastosis (eh-**RITH**-ro-blast-oh-sis) Condition of many immature red cells in blood.

erythrocyte (eh-**RITH**-ro-site) Another name for a red blood cell.

erythropoiesis (eh-**RITH**-ro-poy-**EE**-sis) The formation of red blood cells.

erythropoietin (eh-**RITH**-ro-**POY**-ee-tin) Protein secreted by the kidney that stimulates red blood cell production.

eschar (**ESS**-kar) The burnt, dead tissue lying on top of third-degree burns.

Escherichia coli (esh-eh-**RIK**-ee-ah **KOH**-lie) Organism in the intestine; releases an exotoxin that causes diarrhea.

esophagitis (ee-**SOF**-ah-**JI**-tis) Inflammation of the lining of the esophagus.

esophagus (ee-**SOF**-ah-gus) Tube linking the pharynx and the stomach.

esotropia (es-oh-**TROH**-pee-ah) Turning the eye inward toward the nose.

essential (eh-**SEN**-shal) Amino acids that cannot be synthesized by the body.

estrogen (**ES**-troh-jen) Generic term for hormones that stimulate female secondary sex characteristics.

ethmoid (**ETH**-moyd) Forms the back of the nose and encloses numerous air cells.

euphoria (yoo-**FOR**-ee-ah) Exaggerated feeling of well-being.

eupnea (yoop-**NEE**-ah) Normal breathing.

eustachian tube (you-**STAY**-shun TYUB) Tube that connects the middle ear to the nasopharynx. Also called the *auditory tube*.

euthyroid (you-**THIGH**-royd) Normal thyroid function.

eversion (ee-**VER**-shun) Turn outward.

evolve (ee-**VOLV**) To develop gradually.

exacerbation (ek-zas-er-**BAY**-shun) Period when there is an increase in the severity of a disease.

exanthem (ek-**ZAN**-them) Skin eruption or rash occurring as the outward sign of a viral or bacterial disease.

excoriate (eks-**KOR**-ee-ate) To scratch.

excoriation (eks-**KOR**-ee-**AY**-shun) Scratch marks.

excrement (**EKS**-kreh-ment) Waste matter such as feces.

excrete (eks-**KREET**) To pass out of the body waste products of metabolism.

excretion (eks-**KREE**-shun) Removal of waste products of metabolism out of the body.

exhale (**EKS**-hail) Breathe out.

exocrine (**EK**-soh-krin) A gland that secretes outwardly through excretory ducts.

exogenous (ex-**OJ**-en-us) Originating outside the organism.

exophthalmos (ek-sof-**THAL**-mos) Protrusion of the eyeball.

exotropia (ek-soh-**TROH**-pee-ah) Turning the eye outward away from the nose.

expectorate (ek-**SPEC**-toh-rate) Cough up and spit out mucus from the respiratory tract.

expiration (**EKS**-pih-**RAY**-shun) Breathe out.

extension (eks-**TEN**-shun) Straighten a joint to increase its angle.

extracorporeal (**EKS**-tra-kor-**PO**-ree-al) Outside the body.

extravasate (eks-**TRAV**-ah-sate) To ooze out from a vessel into the tissues.

extrinsic (eks-**TRIN**-sik) Extrinsic eye muscles are located on the outside of the eye, as opposed to intrinsic muscles, which are located inside the eye.

F

facet (**FAS**-et) Small smooth area around a pain-producing nerve.

facial (**FAY**-shal) Seventh (VII) cranial nerve; supplying the forehead, nose, eyes, mouth, and jaws.

facies (**FASH**-eez) Facial expression and features.

fallopian tubes (fah-**LOW**-pee-an) Uterine tubes connected to the fundus of the uterus.

Fallot (fah-**LOW**) First described this tetralogy of congenital heart defects.

fascia (**FASH**-ee-ah) Sheet of fibrous connective tissue

fascicle (**FAS**-ih-kull) Bundle of muscle fibers.

fasciectomy (fash-ee-**EK**-toe-me) Surgical removal of fascia.

fasciotomy (fash-ee-**OT**-oh-me) An incision through a band of fascia, usually to relieve pressure on underlying structures.

fat (FAT) Lipid that is solid at room temperature.

fatty acid (**FAT**-ee **ASS**-id) An acid obtained from the hydrolysis of fats.

febrile (**FEB**-ril or **FEB**-rile) Denoting or pertaining to fever.

fecal (**FEE**-kal) Pertaining to feces.

feces (**FEE**-sees) Undigested, waste material discharged from the bowel.

Feldenkrais method (**FEL**-den-kries **METH**-od) Series of exercises to discover new ways of pain-free movement.

femoral (**FEM**-oh-ral) Pertaining to the femur.

femur (**FEE**-mur) The thigh bone.

ferritin (**FER**-ih-tin) Iron-protein complex that regulates iron storage and transport.

fertilization (**FER**-til-eye-**ZAY**-shun) Union of a male sperm and a female egg.

fertilize (**FER**-til-ize) Penetration of the oocyte by sperm.

fertilizer (**FER**-tih-lie-zer) Substance used to increase the yield of crops.

festinant (**FES**-tih-nant) Shuffling, falling forward gait.

fetal (**FEE**-tal) Pertaining to the fetus.

fetalis (fee-**TAH**-lis) Erythroblastosis fetalis is a hemolytic disease of the newborn.

fetus (**FEE**-tus) Human organism from the end of the eighth week after conception to birth.

fever (**FEE**-ver) Increased body temperature that is a physiologic response to disease.

fiber (**FIE**-ber) Carbohydrate not digested by intestinal enzymes, or a strand or filament.

fibrillation (fi-brih-**LAY**-shun) Uncontrolled quivering or twitching of the heart muscle.

fibrin (**FIE**-brin) Stringy protein fiber that is a component of a blood clot.

fibrinogen (fie-**BRIN**-oh-jen) Precursor of fibrin in blood-clotting process.

fibroadenoma (**FIE**-bro-ad-en-**OH**-muh) Benign tumor containing much fibrous tissue.

fibroblast (**FIE**-bro-blast) Cell that forms collagen fibers.

fibrocartilage (fie-bro-**KAR**-til-age) Cartilage containing collagen fibers.

fibrocystic disease (fie-bro-**SIS**-tik diz-**EEZ**) Benign breast disease with multiple tiny lumps.

fibroid (**FIE**-broyd) Uterine tumor resembling fibrous tissue.

fibromyalgia (fie-bro-my-**AL**-jee-ah) Pain in the muscle fibers.

fibromyoma (**FIE**-bro-my-**OH**-mah) Benign neoplasm derived from smooth muscle containing fibrous tissue.

fibrosis (fie-**BRO**-sis) Repair of dead tissue cells by formation of fibrous tissue.

fibrous (**FIE**-brus) Tissue containing fibroblasts and fibers.

fibula (**FIB**-you-lah) The smaller of the two bones of the lower leg.

filtrate (**FIL**-trate) That which has passed through a filter.

filtration (fil-**TRAY**-shun) Process of passing liquid through a filter.

fimbria (**FIM**-bree-ah) A fringelike structure on the surface of a cell or microorganism. Plural *fimbriae.*

fissure (**FISH**-ur) Deep furrow or cleft. Plural *fissures.*

fistula (**FIS**-tyu-lah) Abnormal passage.

flagellum (fla-**JELL**-um) Tail of a sperm. Plural *flagella.*

flatulence (**FLAT**-you-lents) Excessive amount of gas in the stomach and intestines.

flatus (**FLAY**-tus) Gas or air expelled through the anus.

flavonoid (**FLAY**-vih-noid) A pigment found in fruit, wine, and tea.

flex (FLEKS) To bend a joint so that the two parts come together.

flexion (**FLEK**-shun) Bend a joint to decrease its angle.

flexor (**FLEK**-sor) Muscle or tendon that flexes a joint.

flexure (**FLEK**-shur) A bend in a structure.

flora (FLO-rah) Microorganisms covering the exterior and interior of a healthy animal.

fluidized therapy (FLU-id-ized THAIR-ah-pee) Use of suspended particles in hot air stream to apply heat.

fluidotherapy (FLU-id-oh-THAIR-ah-pee) A form of heat therapy.

fluorescein (flor-ESS-ee-in) Dye that produces a vivid green color under a blue light to diagnose corneal abrasions and foreign bodies.

fluoride (FLOR-ide) Chemical found in bones and teeth.

fluoroscopy (flor-OS-koh-pee) Examination of the structures of the body by x-rays.

folate (FO-late) Natural B vitamin.

folic acid (FO-lik ASS-id) Synthetic B vitamin.

follicle (FOLL-ih-kull) Spherical mass of cells containing a cavity or a small cul-de-sac, such as a hair follicle.

follicular (fo-LIK-you-lar) Pertaining to a follicle.

fomites (FO-mites) Bedding, clothing, towels, etc., that can harbor and transmit a disease agent.

foramen (fo-RAY-men) An opening through a structure. Plural *foramina.*

forceps extraction (FOR-seps ek-STRAK-shun) Assisted delivery of the baby by an instrument that grasps the head of the baby.

foreskin (FOR-skin) Skin that covers the glans penis.

fornix (FOR-niks) Arch-shaped, blind-ended part of the vagina behind and around the cervix. Plural *fornices.*

fovea centralis (FOH-vee-ah sen-TRAH-lis) Small pit in the center of the macula that has the highest visual acuity.

free radical (FREE RAD-ih-kal) Short-lived product of oxidation in a cell that can be damaging to the cell.

frenulum (FREN-you-lum) Fold of mucous membrane between the glans and prepuce.

frequency (FREE-kwen-see) The number of times something happens in a given time (e.g., passing urine).

frontal (FRON-tal) Vertical plane dividing the body into anterior and posterior portions.

frontal lobe (FRON-tal LOBE) Area of brain behind the frontal bone.

fructosamine (FRUK-toe-sah-meen) Organic compound with fructose as its base.

fructose (FRUK-toes) Sugar found in fruits and honey.

function (FUNK-shun) The ability of an organ or tissue to perform its special work.

fundoscopy (fun-DOS-koh-pee) Examination of the fundus (retina) of the eye.

fundus (FUN-dus) Part farthest from the opening of a hollow organ.

fungicide (FUN-jee-side) Agent to destroy fungi.

fungus (FUN-gus) General term used to describe yeasts and molds. Plural *fungi.*

furuncle (FU-rung-kel) An infected hair follicle that spreads into the tissues around the follicle.

G

galactorrhea (ga-LAK-toe-REE-ah) Abnormal flow of milk from the breasts.

gallbladder (GAWL-blad-er) Receptacle on the inferior surface of the liver for bile.

gallstone (GAWL-stone) Hard mass of cholesterol, calcium, and bilirubin that can be formed in the gallbladder and bile duct.

galvanic (gal-VAN-ik) Low-voltage electric current.

ganglion (GANG-lee-on) Collection of nerve cell bodies outside the CNS, or a fluid-containing swelling attached to the synovial sheath of a tendon. Plural *ganglia.*

gastric (GAS-trik) Pertaining to the stomach.

gastrin (GAS-trin) Hormone secreted in the stomach that stimulates secretion of HCl and increases gastric motility.

gastritis (gas-TRY-tis) Inflammation of the lining of the stomach.

gastrocnemius (gas-trok-NEE-me-us) Major muscle in back of the lower leg (the calf).

gastrocolic reflex (gas-troh-KOL-ik RE-fleks) Taking food into the stomach leads to mass movement of feces in the colon and the desire to defecate.

gastroenterologist (GAS-troh-en-ter-OL-oh-jist) Medical specialist in gastroenterology.

gastroenterology (GAS-troh-en-ter-OL-oh-gee) Medical specialty of the stomach and intestines.

gastroesophageal (GAS-troh-ee-sof-ah-JEE-al) Pertaining to the stomach and esophagus.

gastrointestinal (GI) (GAS-troh-in-TESS-tin-al) Relating to the stomach and intestines.

gastroscope (GAS-troh-skope) Endoscope for examining the inside of the stomach.

gastroscopy (gas-TROS-koh-pee) Endoscopic examination of the stomach.

Gaucher disease (go-SHAY diz-EEZ) Congenital disorder of fat metabolism.

gavage (guh-VAHZH) To feed by a stomach tube.

gene (JEEN) Functional segment of the DNA molecule.

geneticist (jeh-NET-ih-sist) A specialist in genetics.

genetics (jeh-NET-iks) Science of the inheritance of characteristics.

genistein (JEN-is-tine) Flavonoid found in soy.

genital (JEN-ih-tal) Relating to reproduction or to the male or female sex organs.

genitalia (JEN-ih-TAY-lee-ah) External and internal organs of reproduction.

genome (JEE-nome) Complete set of genes.

genomics (jee-NOME-iks) Study of the interaction of genes.

genotype (jee-NOH-type) Specific genetic constitution of an individual.

geriatrician (jer-ee-ah-TRISH-an) Medical specialist in geriatrics.

geriatrics (jer-ee-AT-riks) Medical specialty that deals with the problems of old age.

gerontologist (jer-on-TOL-oh-jist) Medical specialist in gerontology.

gerontology (jer-on-TOL-oh-jee) Study of the process and problems of aging.

gestation (jes-TAY-shun) From conception to birth.

Giardia (jee-AR-dee-ah) Parasite in the small intestine.

giardiasis (jee-ar-DIE-ah-sis) Infection with *Giardia*, causing diarrhea.

gigantism (JI-gan-tizm) Abnormal height and size of the entire body.

gingiva (JIN-jih-vah) Tissue surrounding teeth and covering the jaw.

gingivectomy (jin-jih-VEC-toe-me) Surgical removal of diseased gum tissue.

gingivitis (jin-jih-VI-tis) Inflammation of the gums.

Ginkgo biloba (GING-koh BIL-oh-bah) Extract of leaves used as a vasodilator.

ginseng (JIN-seng) Extract made from the root of a Chinese plant.

glans (GLANZ) Head of the penis or clitoris.

glaucoma (glau-KOH-mah) Increased intraocular pressure.

glia (GLEE-ah) Connective tissue that holds a structure together.

glioma (gli-OH-mah) Tumor of a glial cell.

globulin (GLOB-you-lin) Family of blood proteins.

glomerulonephritis (glo-MER-you-low-nef-RYE-tis) Infection of the glomeruli of the kidney.

glomerulus (glo-MER-you-lus) Plexus of capillaries; part of a nephron. Plural *glomeruli*.

glossodynia (gloss-oh-DIN-ee-ah) Painful, burning tongue.

glossopharyngeal (GLOSS-oh-fah-RIN-jee-al) Ninth (IX) cranial nerve; supplying the tongue and pharynx.

glottis (GLOT-is) Vocal apparatus of the larynx.

glucagon (GLU-kah-gon) Pancreatic hormone that supports blood glucose levels.

glucocorticoid (glu-co-KOR-tih-koyd) Hormone of the adrenal cortex that helps regulate glucose metabolism.

gluconeogenesis (GLU-ko-nee-oh-JEN-eh-sis) Formation of glucose from noncarbohydrate sources.

glucose (GLU-koes) The final product of carbohydrate digestion and the main sugar in the blood.

gluten (GLU-ten) Insoluble protein found in wheat, barley, and oats.

gluteus (GLU-tee-us) Refers to a muscle in the buttocks.

glycemic index (glye-SEE-mic IN-deks) Measure of the rapidity in rise of blood glucose after ingestion of carbohydrates.

glycemic load (glye-SEE-mic LOHD) Takes into account the amount of sugar available in the food to cause the rise in blood sugar.

glycogen (GLYE-koh-gen) The body's principal carbohydrate reserve, stored in the liver and skeletal muscle.

glycogenolysis (GLYE-koh-jen-oh-LYE-sis) Conversion of glycogen to glucose.

glycoprotein (GLYE-koh-PRO-teen) Combination of carbohydrate and protein.

glycosuria (GLYE-koh-SYU-ree-ah) Presence of glucose in urine.

glycosylated hemoglobin (Hb A1c) (GLYE-koh-sih-lay-ted HE-moh-GLOW-bin) Hemoglobin A fraction linked to glucose; used as index of glucose control.

goiter (GOY-ter) Enlargement of the thyroid gland.

Golgi complex (GOAL-jee KOM-pleks) Organelle involved in synthesis of carbohydrates and glycoproteins.

gomphosis (gom-FOE-sis) Joint formed by a peg and socket. Plural *gomphoses*.

gonad (GO-nad) Testis or ovary. Plural *gonads*.

gonadotropin (GO-nad-oh-TROH-pin) Hormone capable of promoting gonad function.

gonorrhea (gon-oh-REE-ah) Specific contagious sexually transmitted infection.

grade (GRAYD) In cancer pathology, a classification of the rate of growth of cancer cells.

graft (GRAFT) Transplantation of living tissue.

Gram stain (GRAM STAYN) A method for differential staining of bacteria.

grand mal (GRAHN MAL) Generalized tonic-clonic seizure.

granulation (gran-you-LAY-shun) New fibrous tissue formed during wound healing.

granulocyte (GRAN-you-loh-site) A white blood cell that contains multiple small granules in its cytoplasm.

granulosa cell (gran-you-LOH-sa SELL) Cell lining the ovarian follicle.

Graves disease (GRAVZ diz-EEZ) Hyperthyroidism with toxic goiter.

gravida (GRAV-ih-dah) A pregnant woman.

gravidarum (gra-vih-DAR-um) Relating to pregnant women.

gray matter (GRAY MATT-er) Regions of the brain and spinal cord occupied by cell bodies and dendrites.

greenstick fracture (GREEN-stik FRAK-chur) A fracture in which one side of the bone is partially broken and the other side is bent. Occurs mostly in children.

guanine (GWAH-neen) One of the chemicals found in both DNA and RNA.

Guillain-Barré syndrome (GEE-yan-bah-RAY SIN-drom) Disorder in which the body makes antibodies against myelin, disrupting nerve conduction.

gynecologist (guy-nih-KOL-oh-jist) Specialist in gynecology.

gynecology (guy-nih-KOL-oh-jee) Medical specialty of diseases of the female.

gynecomastia (GUY-nih-koh-MAS-tee-ah) Enlargement of the breast.

gyrus (JI-rus) Rounded elevation on the surface of the cerebral hemispheres. Plural *gyri*.

H

hairline fracture (**HAIR**-line **FRAK**-chur) A fracture without separation of the fragments.

halitosis (hal-ih-**TOE**-sis) Bad odor of the breath.

hallucination (hah-loo-sih-**NAY**-shun) Perception of an object or event when there is no such thing present.

hallux valgus (**HAL**-uks **VAL**-gus) Deviation of the big toe toward the lateral side of the foot.

handicap (**HAND**-ee-cap) Condition that interferes with a person's ability to function normally.

hapten (**HAP**-ten) Small molecule that has to bind to a larger molecule to form an antigen.

Hashimoto disease (hah-shee-**MO**-toe diz-**EEZ**) Autoimmune disease of the thyroid gland. Also called *Hashimoto thyroiditis*.

haversian canals (hah-**VER**-shan ka-**NALS**) Vascular canals in bone. Also called *central canals*.

head (HED) The rounded extremity of a bone.

helix (**HE**-liks) A line in the shape of a coil.

hemangioma (he-**MAN**-jee-o-mah) Mass of proliferating blood vessels.

hematemesis (he-mah-**TEM**-eh-sis) Vomiting of red blood.

hematochezia (he-mat-oh-**KEY**-zee-ah) The passage of red, bloody stools.

hematocrit (Hct) (**HE**-mat-oh-krit) Percentage of red blood cells in blood.

hematologist (he-mah-**TOL**-oh-jist) Specialist in hematology.

hematology (he-mah-**TOL**-oh-jee) Medical specialty of disorders of blood.

hematoma (he-mah-**TOH**-mah) Collection of blood that has escaped from the blood vessels into tissue. Also called *bruise*.

hematopoietic (**HE**-mah-toh-poy-**ET**-ick) Pertaining to the making of red blood cells.

hematuria (he-mah-**TYU**-ree-ah) Blood in the urine.

heme (HEEM) The iron-based component of hemoglobin that carries oxygen.

hemifacial (hem-ee-**FAY**-shal) Pertaining to one side of the face.

hemiparesis (**HEM**-ee-pah-**REE**-sis) Weakness of one side of the body.

hemiplegia (hem-ee-**PLEE**-jee-ah) Paralysis of one side of body.

helminth (**HELL**-minth) Any intestinal wormlike parasite.

Hemoccult test (**HEEM**-o-kult TEST) *Hemoccult* (trade name for a fecal occult blood test).

hemochromatosis (**HE**-mah-krom-ah-**TOE**-sis) Dangerously high levels of iron in the body with deposition of iron pigments in tissues.

hemodialysis (**HE**-moh-die-**AL**-ih-sis) An artificial method of filtration to remove excess waste materials and water directly from the blood.

hemodynamics (**HE**-moh-die-**NAM**-iks) The science of the motion of blood through the circulation.

hemoglobin (**HE**-moh-**GLOW**-bin) Red-pigmented protein that is the main component of red blood cells.

hemoglobinopathy (**HE**-moh-**GLOW**-bih-**NOP**-ah-thee) Disease caused by the presence of an abnormal hemoglobin in the red blood cells.

hemolysis (he-**MOL**-ih-sis) Destruction of red blood cells so that hemoglobin is liberated.

hemolytic (he-moh-**LIT**-ik) Pertaining to the process of destruction of red blood cells.

hemophilia (he-moh-**FILL**-ee-ah) An inherited disease from a deficiency of clotting factor VIII.

hemoptysis (he-**MOP**-tih-sis) Bloody sputum.

hemorrhage (**HEM**-oh-raj) To bleed profusely.

hemorrhoid (**HEM**-oh-royd) Dilated rectal vein producing painful anal swelling. Plural *hemorrhoids*.

hemorrhoidectomy (**HEM**-oh-roy-**DEK**-toh-me) Surgical removal of hemorrhoids.

hemostasis (he-moh-**STAY**-sis) Control of or stopping bleeding.

hemothorax (he-moh-**THOR**-ax) Blood in the pleural cavity.

heparin (**HEP**-ah-rin) An anticoagulant secreted particularly by liver cells.

hepatic (hep-**AT**-ik) Pertaining to the liver.

hepatitis (hep-ah-**TIE**-tis) Inflammation of the liver.

hepatocellular (**HEP**-ah-toe-**SELL**-you-lar) Pertaining to liver cells.

herbicide (**ER**-bih-side) Agent to destroy plants.

heredity (heh-**RED**-ih-tee) Transmission of characteristics from parents to offspring through genes.

herniate (**HER**-nee-ate) To protrude.

hernia (**HER**-nee-ah) Protrusion of a structure through the tissue that normally contains it.

herniation (**HER**-nee-ay-shun) Protrusion of an anatomical structure from its normal location.

herniorrhaphy (**HER**-nee-**OR**-ah-fee) Repair of a hernia.

herpangina (her-**PAN**-ji-nah) Ulcerative disease of the throat.

herpes simplex virus (HSV) (**HER**-peez **SIM**-pleks **VIE**-rus) Manifests with painful, watery blisters on the skin and mucous membranes.

herpes zoster (**HER**-pees **ZOS**-ter) Painful eruption of vesicles that follows a dermatome or nerve root on one side of the body. Also called *shingles*.

heterograft (**HET**-er-oh-graft) A graft using tissue taken from another species. Also known as *xenograft*.

heterophile (**HET**-er-oh-file) Antibodies not directed against the causative organism but seen during the disease.

heterozygous (**HET**-er-oh-**ZIE**-gus) Carries a different version (allele) of a specific gene on each of the two corresponding chromosomes.

hiatus (high-**AY**-tus) An opening through a structure.

hilum (**HIGH**-lum) The site where the nerves and blood vessels enter and leave an organ. Plural *hila*.

hirsutism (**HER**-sue-tizm) Excessive body and facial hair.

histamine (HISS-tah-mean) Compound liberated in tissues as a result of injury or an allergic response.

histology (his-TOL-oh-jee) Structure and function of cells, tissues, and organs.

holistic (ho-LIS-tik) Pertaining to the care of the whole person in physical, mental, emotional, and spiritual dimensions.

homeopath (HO-mee-oh-path) Practitioner of homeopathy.

homeopathy (ho-mee-OP-ah-thee) Treating disease with minute doses of substances.

homeostasis (ho-mee-oh-STAY-sis) Maintaining the stability or equilibrium of a system or the body's internal environment.

homicidal (hom-ih-SIDE-al) Having a tendency to commit homicide.

homicide (HOM-ih-side) Killing of one human by another.

homocysteine (ho-moh-SIS-teen) An amino acid similar to cysteine.

homograft (HOH-moh-graft) Skin graft from another person or cadaver.

homozygous (hoh-moh-ZIE-gus) Carries two identical copies of a specific gene on the two corresponding chromosomes.

hordeolum (hor-DEE-oh-lum) Abscess in an eyelash follicle. Also called *stye*.

hormone (HOR-mohn) Chemical formed in one tissue or organ and carried by the blood to stimulate or inhibit a function of another tissue or organ.

Horner syndrome (HOR-ner SIN-drome) Disorder of the sympathetic nerves to the face and eye.

hospice (HOS-pis) Provides care to the dying and their families.

host (HOST) Organism on which organisms live.

human immunodeficiency virus (HIV) (HYU-man IM-you-noh-dee-FISH-en-see VIE-rus) Etiologic agent of acquired immunodeficiency syndrome.

human papilloma virus (HPV) (HYU-man pap-ih-LOW-mah VIE-rus) Causes warts on the skin and genitalia and can increase the risk for cervical cancer.

humerus (HYU-mer-us) Single bone of the upper arm.

humoral immunity (HYU-mor-al ih-MYU-nih-tee) Defense mechanism arising from antibodies in the blood.

Huntington disease (HUN-ting-ton diz-EEZ) Progressive inherited, degenerative, incurable neurologic disease. Also called *Huntington chorea*.

hyaline (HIGH-ah-line) Cartilage that looks like frosted glass and contains fine collagen fibers.

hyaline membrane disease (HIGH-ah-line MEM-brain diz-EEZ) Respiratory distress syndrome of the newborn.

hydrocele (HIGH-droh-seal) Collection of fluid in the space of the tunica vaginalis.

hydrocephalus (high-droh-SEF-ah-lus) Enlarged head due to excess CSF in the cerebral ventricles.

hydrochloric acid (HCl) (high-droh-KLOR-ic ASS-id) HCl is the acid of gastric juice.

Hydrocollator (high-droh-KOLL-ay-tor) Synthetic hot or cold gel to stimulate a rise or fall in tissue temperature.

hydrocortisone (high-droh-KOR-tih-sohn) Potent glucocorticoid with anti-inflammatory properties. Also called *cortisol*.

hydrogenated (HIGH-droh-jeh-NAY-ted) Addition of hydrogen to unsaturated oils to solidify them and produce trans fats.

hydronephrosis (HIGH-droh-neh-FRO-sis) Dilation of the pelvis and calyces of a kidney.

hymen (HIGH-men) Thin membrane partly occluding the vaginal orifice.

hyperactivity (HIGH-per-ac-TIV-ih-tee) Excessive restlessness and movement.

hyperbaric (high-per-BAR-ik) Pressure greater than atmospheric pressure.

hypercalcemia (HIGH-per-cal-SEE-me-ah) Excessive level of calcium in the blood.

hypercapnia (HIGH-per-KAP-nee-ah) Abnormal increase of carbon dioxide in the arterial bloodstream.

hypercarotenemia (HIGH-per-KAR-o-teh-NEE-me-ah) Excessive level of the yellow-red pigment carotene in the blood.

hyperemesis (high-per-EM-ee-sis) Excessive vomiting.

hyperflexion (high-per-FLEK-shun) Flexion of a limb or part beyond the normal limits.

hyperfractionated (high-per-FRAK-shun-ay-ted) Smaller fractions of a radiation dose given more frequently.

hyperglycemia (HIGH-per-gly-SEE-me-ah) High level of glucose (sugar) in blood.

hyperglycemic (HIGH-per-gly-SEE-mik) Pertaining to high blood sugar.

hyperimmune globulin (HIGH-per-im-YUNE GLOB-you-lin) Immunoglobulin prepared from serum of people with a high antibody titer to a specific virus.

hyperinflation (HIGH-per-in-FLAY-shun) Overdistension of pulmonary alveoli with air resulting from airway obstruction.

hyperkalemia (HIGH-per-kah-LEE-me-ah) High level of potassium in the blood.

hypernatremia (HIGH-per-nah-TREE-me-ah) High level of sodium in the blood.

hyperopia (high-per-OH-pee-ah) Able to see distant objects, but unable to see close objects.

hyperosmolar (HIGH-per-os-MOH-lar) Marked hyperglycemia without ketoacidosis.

hyperparathyroidism (HIGH-per-para-THIGH-royd-ism) Excessive levels of parathyroid hormone.

hyperpnea (high-perp-NEE-ah) Deeper and more rapid breathing than normal.

hypersecretion (HIGH-per-se-KREE-shun) Excessive secretion of mucus (or enzymes or waste products).

hypersensitivity (HIGH-per-sen-sih-TIV-ih-tee) Exaggerated abnormal reaction to an allergen.

hypersplenism (high-per-SPLEN-izm) Condition in which the spleen removes blood components at an excessive rate.

hypertension (HIGH-per-TEN-shun) Persistent high arterial blood pressure.

hyperthyroidism (high-per-**THIGH**-royd-ism) Excessive production of thyroid hormones.

hypertrophy (high-**PER**-troh-fee) Increase in size, but not in number, of an individual tissue element.

hypha (**HIGH**-fah) Branching tubular fungal cell. Plural *hyphae*.

hypnosis (hip-**NOH**-sis) Changed state of consciousness.

hypnotherapy (hip-noh-**THAIR**-ah-pee) Use of hypnosis in treatment of disorders.

hypochondriac (high-poh-**KON**-dree-ack) A person who exaggerates the significance of symptoms.

hypochondriasis (**HIGH**-poh-kon-**DRY**-ah-sis) Belief that a minor symptom indicates a severe disease.

hypochromic (high-poh-**CROW**-mik) Pale in color, as in RBCs when hemoglobin is deficient.

hypodermis (high-poh-**DER**-miss) Tissue layer below the dermis.

hypogastric (high-poh-**GAS**-trik) Abdominal region below the stomach.

hypoglossal (high-poh-**GLOSS**-al) Twelfth (XII) cranial nerve; supplying muscles of the tongue.

hypoglycemia (**HIGH**-poh-glie-**SEE**-me-ah) Low level of glucose (sugar) in the blood.

hypogonadism (**HIGH**-poh-**GOH**-nad-izm) Deficient gonad production of sperm or eggs or hormones.

hypokalemia (**HIGH**-poh-kah-**LEE**-me-ah) Low level of potassium in the blood.

hyponatremia (**HIGH**-poh-nah-**TREE**-me-ah) Low level of sodium in the blood.

hypoparathyroidism (**HIGH**-poh-para-**THIGH**-royd-ism) Deficient levels of parathyroid hormone.

hypophysis (high-**POF**-ih-sis) Another name for the pituitary gland.

hypopituitarism (**HIGH**-poh-pih-**TYU**-ih-tah-rizm) Condition of one or more deficient pituitary hormones.

hypospadias (high-poh-**SPAY**-dee-as) Urethral opening more proximal than normal on the ventral surface of the penis.

hypotension (**HIGH**-poh-**TEN**-shun) Persistent low arterial blood pressure.

hypothalamus (high-poh-**THAL**-ah-muss) Area of gray matter lying below the thalamus.

hypothenar (high-poh-**THAY**-nar) Eminence at the base of the little finger.

hypothermia (high-poh-**THER**-me-ah) Very low core body temperature.

hypothyroidism (high-poh-**THIGH**-royd-ism) Deficient production of thyroid hormones.

hypotonia (high-poh-**TOE**-nee-ah) Diminished muscle tone.

hypoxia (high-**POCK**-see-ah) Below normal levels of oxygen in tissues, gases, or blood.

hypoxic (high-**POCK**-sik) Deficient in oxygen.

hysterectomy (his-ter-**EK**-toe-me) Surgical removal of the uterus.

hysterosalpingogram (**HIS**-ter-oh-sal-**PING**-oh-gram) Radiograph of the uterus and uterine tubes after injection of contrast material.

hysteroscopy (his-ter-**OS**-koh-pee) Visual inspection of the uterine cavity using an endoscope.

I

ictal (**ICK**-tal) Pertaining to, or condition caused by, a stroke or epilepsy.

idiopathic (**ID**-ih-oh-**PATH**-ik) Pertaining to a disease of unknown etiology.

ileocecal (**ILL**-ee-oh-**SEE**-cal) Junction of the ileum and cecum.

ileoscopy (ill-ee-**OS**-koh-pee) Endoscopic examination of the ileum.

ileostomy (ill-ee-**OS**-toe-me) Artificial opening from the ileum to the outside of the body.

ileum (**ILL**-ee-um) Third portion of the small intestine.

iliac (**ILL**-ee-ack) A structure related to the ilium (pelvic bone).

ilium (**ILL**-ee-um) Large wing-shaped bone at the upper and posterior part of the pelvis. Plural *ilia*.

imagery (**IM**-aj-ree) Visualization of pleasant fantasies.

immune (im-**YUNE**) Protected from an infectious disease.

immunity (im-**YOU**-nih-tee) State of being protected.

immunization (im-you-nih-**ZAY**-shun) Administration of an agent to provide immunity.

immunize (**IM**-you-nize) To make resistant to an infectious disease.

immunoassay (**IM**-you-noh-**ASS**-ay) Biochemical test to measure the amount of a substance in a liquid, using the reaction of an antibody to its antigen.

immunodeficiency (**IM**-you-noh-dee-**FISH**-en-see) Failure of the immune system.

immunoglobulin (**IM**-you-noh-**GLOB**-you-lin) Specific protein evoked by an antigen. All antibodies are immunoglobulins.

immunologist (im-you-**NOL**-oh-jist) Medical specialist in immunology.

immunology (im-you-**NOL**-oh-jee) The science and practice of immunity and allergy.

immunosuppression (**IM**-you-noh-suh-**PRESH**-un) Failure of the immune system caused by an outside agent.

immune serum (im-**YUNE SEER**-um) Serum taken from another human or animal that has antibodies to a disease. Also called *antiserum*.

impacted (im-**PAK**-ted) Immovably wedged, as with ear wax blocking the external canal.

impacted fracture (im-**PAK**-ted **FRAK**-chur) A fracture in which one bone fragment is driven into the other.

impairment (im-**PAIR**-ment) Diminishing of normal function.

impedance (im-**PEE**-dahns) Resistance to the flow of an electric current.

impermeable (im-**PER**-me-ah-bull) Does not allow passage of anything.

impetigo (im-peh-**TIE**-go) Infection of the skin producing thick, yellow crusts.

implant (im-**PLANT**) To insert material into tissues, or the material inserted into tissues.

implantable (im-**PLAN**-tah-bul) A device that can be inserted into tissues.

implantation (im-plan-**TAY**-shun) Attachment of a fertilized egg to the endometrium.

impotence (**IM**-poh-tence) Inability to achieve an erection.

impulsive (im-**PUL**-siv) Inability to resist performing inappropriate actions.

in situ (IN **SIGH**-tyu) In the correct place.

in utero (in **YOU**-ter-oh) Within the womb; not yet born.

in vitro fertilization (IVF) (IN **VEE**-tro **FER**-til-ih-**ZAY**-shun) Process of combining sperm and egg in a laboratory dish and placing the resulting embryos inside the uterus.

inattention (**IN**-ah-**TEN**-shun) Lack of concentration and direction.

incisor (in-**SIGH**-zor) Chisel-shaped tooth.

incompatible (in-kom-**PAT**-ih-bul) Substances that interfere with each other physiologically.

incompetence (in-**KOM**-peh-tense) Failure of valves to close completely.

incomplete (in-kom-**PLEET**) Lacking some part.

incomplete fracture (in-kom-**PLEET FRAK**-chur) A fracture that does not extend across the bone, as in a hairline fracture.

incontinence (in-**KON**-tin-ence) Inability to prevent discharge of urine or feces.

incubation (in-kyu-**BAY**-shun) Process to develp an infection.

incus (**IN**-cuss) Middle one of the three ossicles in the middle ear; shaped like an anvil.

independent (in-de-**PEN**-dent) Able to fend for themselves.

index (**IN**-deks) A standard indicator of measurement. Plural *indices*.

indole (**IN**-dole) A phytochemical that makes estrogen less effective.

infancy (**IN**-fan-see) The first year of life.

infant (**IN**-fant) Child in the first year of life.

infant formula (**IN**-fant **FOR**-myu-lah) Commercial product for infants manufactured from cows' milk or soy milk.

infarct (in-**FARKT**) Area of cell death resulting from an infarction.

infarction (in-**FARK**-shun) Sudden blockage of an artery.

infect (in-**FEKT**) To invade an organism by a microorganism.

infection (in-**FEK**-shun) Invasion of the body by disease-producing microorganisms.

infectious (in-**FEK**-shus) Capable of being transmitted, or a disease caused by the action of a microorganism.

inferior (in-**FEE**-ree-or) Situated below.

infertility (in-fer-**TIL**-ih-tee) Failure to conceive.

infestation (in-fes-**TAY**-shun) Act of being invaded on the skin by a troublesome other species, such as a parasite.

infiltrate (**IN**-fil-trate) To penetrate and invade into a tissue or cell.

infiltration (in-fil-**TRAY**-shun) The invasion into a tissue or cell.

inflate (in-**FLAYT**) Expand with air.

inflation (in-**FLAY**-shun) Process of expanding with air.

infundibulum (**IN**-fun-**DIB**-you-lum) Funnel-shaped structure. Plural *infundibula*.

infusion (in-**FYU**-zhun) Introduction of a substance other than blood intravenously.

ingestion (in-**JEST**-shun) Intake of food, either by mouth or through a nasogastric tube.

inhale (**IN**-hail) Breathe in.

inherent (in-**HAIR**-ent) Occurring as a natural part of something.

inherited (in-**HAIR**-it-ed) Acquired through the genetic code.

innate (ih-**NATE**) Present at birth; arising from the intellect.

inotropic (**IN**-oh-**TROH**-pic) Agent that affects the contractility of cardiac muscle.

insanity (in-**SAN**-ih-tee) Nonmedical term for a person unable to be responsible for their actions.

insecticide (in-**SEK**-tih-side) Agent to destroy insects.

insemination (in-sem-ih-**NAY**-shun) Introduction of semen into the vagina.

insertion (in-**SIR**-shun) The insertion of a muscle is the attachment of a muscle to a more movable part of the skeleton, as distinct from the origin.

insomnia (in-**SOM**-nee-ah) Inability to sleep.

inspiration (in-spih-**RAY**-shun) Breathe in.

instability (in-stah-**BIL**-ih-tee) Abnormal tendency of a joint to partially or fully dislocate.

insufficiency (in-suh-**FISH**-en-see) Lack of completeness of function; in this case, for a valve to close properly.

insulin (**IN**-syu-lin) A hormone secreted by the pancreas.

integrate (**IN**-teh-grate) To bring together into a complete and harmonious whole.

integument (in-**TEG**-you-ment) Organ system that covers the body, the skin being the main organ within the system.

intellectual (in-teh-**LEK**-chu-al) Pertaining to the capacity for thinking and acquiring knowledge.

interatrial (**IN**-ter-**AY**-tree-al) Between the atria of the heart.

intercostal (**IN**-ter-**KOS**-tal) The space between two ribs.

intermittent (**IN**-ter-**MIT**-ent) Alternately ceasing and beginning again.

interosseous (in-ter-**OSS**-ee-us) A structure between bones, in this case muscles.

interphalangeal (**IN**-ter-fay-**LAN**-jee-al) Finger or toe joint between two phalanges.

interstitial (in-ter-**STISH**-al) Pertaining to spaces between cells in a tissue or organ.

interventricular (**IN**-ter-ven-**TRIK**-you-lar) Between the ventricles of the heart.

longevity (lon-JEV-ih-tee) Duration of life beyond the normal expectation.

loop of Henle (LOOP of HEN-lee) Part of the renal tubule where reabsorption occurs.

lordosis (lore-DOH-sis) An exaggerated forward curvature of the lumbar spine.

louse (LOWSE) Parasitic insect. Plural *lice*.

lubricant (LOO-bri-cant) Substance for reducing friction.

lumbar (LUM-bar) Region in the back and sides between the ribs and pelvis.

lumen (LOO-men) The interior space of a tubelike structure.

lumpectomy (lump-ECK-toe-me) Removal of a lesion with preservation of surrounding tissue.

luteal (LOO-tee-al) Pertaining to a corpus luteum.

lutein (LOO-tee-in) Yellow pigment.

luteum (LOO-tee-um) Corpus luteum is the yellow (lutein) body formed after an ovarian follicle ruptures.

lycopene (LIE-koh-peen) Carotenoid that gives tomatoes their red color.

Lyme disease (LIME diz-EEZ) Disease transmitted by the bite of an infected deer tick.

lymph (LIMF) A clear fluid collected from tissues and transported by vessels to the venous circulation.

lymphadenectomy (lim-FAD-eh-NECK-toe-me) Surgical excision of a lymph node.

lymphadenitis (lim-FAD-eh-neye-tis) Inflammation of a lymph node.

lymphadenopathy (lim-FAD-eh-NOP-ah-thee) Any disease process affecting a lymph node.

lymphangiogram (lim-FAN-jee-oh-gram) Radiographic images of lymph vessels and nodes following injection of contrast material.

lymphatic (lim-FAT-ic) Pertaining to lymph.

lymphedema (LIMF-e-dee-mah) Tissue swelling due to lymphatic obstruction.

lymphocyte (LIM-fo-site) Small white blood cell with a large nucleus.

lymphoid (LIM-foid) Resembling lymphatic tissue.

lymphoma (lim-FO-muh) Any neoplasm of lymphatic tissue.

lysis (LIE-sis) Destruction of a cell.

lysosome (LIE-soh-sohm) Enzyme that digests foreign material.

lysozyme (LIE-soh-zime) Enzyme that dissolves the cell walls of bacteria.

M

macrocyte (MAK-roh-site) Large red blood cell.

macrocytic (mak-roh-SIT-ik) Pertaining to macrocytes.

macrophage (MAK-roh-fayj) Large white blood cell that removes bacteria, foreign particles, and dead cells.

macula (MAK-you-lah) Small area of special function; in this case, a sensory receptor. Plural *maculae*.

macula lutea (MAK-you-lah LOO-tee-ah) Yellowish spot on the back of the retina; contains the fovea centralis.

macule (MAK-yul) Small, flat spot or patch on the skin.

majus (MAY-jus) Bigger or greater; for example, labia majora. Plural *majora*.

malabsorption (mal-ab-SORP-shun) Inadequate gastrointestinal absorption of nutrients.

malaria (mah-LAIR-ee-ah) Disease transmitted by the bite of a female *Anopheles* mosquito.

malfunction (mal-FUNK-shun) Inadequate or abnormal function.

malignancy (mah-LIG-nan-see) Able to be malignant.

malignant (mah-LIG-nant) Tumor that invades surrounding tissues and metastasizes to distant organs.

malleus (MAL-ee-us) Outer (lateral) one of the three ossicles in the middle ear; shaped like a hammer.

malnutrition (mal-nyu-TRISH-un) Inadequate nutrition from poor diet or inadequate absorption of nutrients.

malunion (mal-YOU-nee-un) When the two bony ends of the fracture fail to heal together correctly.

mammary (MAM-ah-ree) Relating to the lactating breast.

mandible (MAN-di-bel) Lower jawbone.

mania (MAY-nee-ah) Mood disorder with hyperactivity, irritability, and rapid speech.

manic-depressive disorder (MAN-ik de-PRESS-iv dis-OR-der) An outdated name for bipolar disorder.

manipulation (mah-NIP-you-lay-shun) Hands-on adjustment of joints, particularly of the spine.

Marfan syndrome (mahr-FAN SIN-drome) Genetic condition with malformation of elastic connective tissue.

marijuana (mar-ih-HWAN-ah) Dried, flowering leaves of the plant *Cannabis sativa*.

marrow (MAH-roe) Fatty, blood-forming tissue in the cavities of long bones.

massage (mah-SAHZH) Application of pressure or vibration to soft body tissues.

masseter (MASS-eh-ter) Muscle that closes the mouth.

mastalgia (mass-TAL-jee-uh) Pain in the breast.

mastectomy (mass-TECK-toe-me) Surgical excision of the breast.

masticate (MAS-tih-kate) To chew.

mastitis (mass-TIE-tis) Inflammation of the breast.

mastoid (MASS-toyd) Small bony protrusion immediately behind the ear.

matrix (MAY-triks) Substance that surrounds cells, is manufactured by the cells, and holds them together.

maturation (mat-you-RAY-shun) Process to achieve full development.

maxilla (mak-SILL-ah) Upper jawbone, containing right and left maxillary sinuses.

maximus (MAKS-ih-mus) The gluteus maximus muscle is the largest muscle in the body, covering a large part of each buttock.

McBurney point (mack-BUR-nee POYNT) One-third the distance from the anterior superior iliac spine to the umbilicus.

measles (ME-zelz) Acute, contagious disease of childhood. Also known as *rubeola*.

meatus (me-AY-tus) Passage or channel; also used to denote the external opening of a passage.

meconium (meh-KOH-nee-um) The first bowel movement of the newborn.

media (ME-dee-ah) Middle layer of a structure, particularly a blood vessel.

medial (ME-dee-al) Nearer to the middle of the body.

mediastinoscopy (ME-dee-ass-tih-NOS-koh-pee) Examination of the mediastinum using an endoscope.

mediastinum (ME-dee-ass-TIE-num) Area between the lungs containing the heart, aorta, venae cavae, esophagus, and trachea.

mediate (ME-dee-ate) Effect by means of an intermediary substance or person.

meditation (med-ih-TAY-shun) Focusing attention or freeing the mind of thoughts as part of a formalized spiritual practice.

medius (ME-dee-us) The gluteus medius muscle is partly covered by the gluteus maximus; it originates on the ilium and is inserted into the femur.

medulla (meh-DULL-ah) Central portion of a structure surrounded by cortex.

medulla oblongata (meh-DULL-ah ob-lon-GAH-tah) Most posterior subdivision of the brainstem, continuation of the spinal cord.

megakaryocyte (MEG-ah-kair-ee-oh-site) Large cell with a large nucleus. Parts of the cytoplasm break off to form platelets.

megavitamin (meg-ah-VIE-tah-min) Large dose of a vitamin.

meiosis (my-OH-sis) Two rapid cell divisions, resulting in half the number of chromosomes.

melanin (MEL-ah-nin) Black pigment found in the skin, hair, and retina.

melanocyte (MEL-ann-oh-cyte) Cell that forms melanin.

melanoma (mel-ah-NO-mah) Malignant neoplasm formed from cells that produce melanin.

melatonin (mel-ah-TONE-in) Hormone formed by the pineal gland.

melena (mel-EN-ah) The passage of black, tarry stools.

membrane (MEM-brain) Thin layer of tissue covering a structure or cavity.

menarche (meh-NAR-key) First menstrual period.

Mendelian (men-DEE-lee-an) Described by Gregor Mendel.

Ménière disease (men-YEAR diz-EEZ) Disorder of the inner ear with cluster of symptoms of acute attacks of tinnitus, vertigo, and hearing loss.

meninges (meh-NIN-jeez) Three-layered covering of the brain and spinal cord.

meningioma (meh-NIN-jee-OH-mah) Tumor arising from the arachnoid layer of the meninges.

meningitis (men-in-JIE-tis) Acute infectious disease of children and young adults.

meningocele (meh-NING-oh-seal) Protrusion of the meninges from the spinal cord or brain through a defect in the vertebral column or cranium.

meningococcal (meh-nin-goh-KOK-al) Relating to the meningococcus.

meningomyelocele (meh-NIN-goh-MY-el-oh-seal) Protrusion of the spinal cord and meninges through a defect in the vertebral arch of one or more vertebrae.

meniscectomy (men-ih-SEK-toh-me) Excision (cutting out) of all or part of a meniscus.

meniscus (meh-NISS-kuss) Disc of connective tissue cartilage between the bones of a joint; for example, in the knee joint. Plural *menisci*.

menopausal (MEN-oh-paws-al) Pertaining to the menopause.

menopause (MEN-oh-paws) Permanent ending of menstrual periods.

menorrhagia (men-oh-RAY-jee-ah) Excessive menstrual bleeding.

menses (MEN-seez) Monthly uterine bleeding.

menstruate (MEN-stru-ate) The act of menstruation.

menstruation (men-stru-AY-shun) Synonym of menses.

meridian (meh-RID-ee-an) Energy line connecting different anatomic sites.

merocrine (MARE-oh-krin) Another name for eccrine.

mesentery (MESS-en-ter-ree) A double layer of peritoneum enclosing the abdominal viscera.

mesothelioma (MEZ-oh-thee-lee-OH-mah) Cancer arising from the cells lining the pleura or peritoneum.

metabolic acidosis (met-ah-BOL-ik ass-ih-DOE-sis) Decreased pH in the blood and body tissues as a result of an upset in metabolism.

metabolism (meh-TAB-oh-lizm) The constantly changing physical and chemical processes occurring in the cell.

metacarpal (MET-ah-KAR-pal) The five bones between the carpus and the fingers.

metacarpophalangeal (MET-ah-KAR-poh-fay-LAN-jee-al) The articulations (joints) between the metacarpal bones and phalanges.

metaphysis (meh-TAF-ih-sis) Region between the diaphysis and the epiphysis where bone growth occurs.

metastasis (meh-TAS-tah-sis) Spread of a disease from one part of the body to another. Plural *metastases*.

metatarsus (MET-ah-TAR-sus) A collective term referring to the five parallel bones of the foot between the tarsus and the phalanges.

metrorrhagia (MEH-tro-RAY-jee-ah) Irregular uterine bleeding between menses.

microalbuminuria (MY-kroh-al-byu-min-YOU-ree-ah) Presence of very small quantities of albumin in urine that cannot be detected by conventional urine testing.

microaneurysm (my-kroh-AN-yu-rizm) Focal dilation of retinal capillaries.

microangiopathy (MY-kroh-an-jee-OP-ah-thee) Disease of the very small blood vessels (capillaries).

microarray (MY-kroh-ah-RAY) Technique for studying one gene in one experiment. Also called *gene chips*.

microbe (MY-krohb) Short for microorganism.

microcephaly (MY-kroh-SEF-ah-lee) An abnormally small head.

microcytic (my-kroh-SIT-ik) Pertaining to a small cell.

microglia (my-KROH-glee-ah) Small nervous tissue cells that are phagocytes.

microorganism (MY-kroh-OR-gan-izm) Any organism too small to be seen by the naked eye.

microscope (MY-kroh-skope) Instrument for viewing something small that cannot be seen in detail by the naked eye.

microscopic (MY-kroh-SKOP-ik) Visible only with the aid of a microscope.

micturate (MIK-choo-rate) Pass urine.

micturition (mik-choo-RISH-un) Act of passing urine.

migraine (MY-grain) Paroxysmal severe headache confined to one side of the head.

mineral (MIN-er-al) Inorganic compound usually found in earth's crust.

mineralocorticoid (MIN-er-al-oh-KOR-tih-koyd) Hormone of the adrenal cortex that influences sodium and potassium metabolism.

minimus (MIN-ih-mus) The gluteus minimus is the smallest of the gluteal muscles and lies under the gluteus medius.

minus (MY-nus) Smaller or lesser; for example, labia minora. Plural *minora*.

mitochondrion (my-toe-KON-dree-on) Organelle that generates, stores, and releases energy for cell activities. Plural *mitochondria*.

mitosis (my-TOE-sis) Cell division to create two identical cells, each with 46 chromosomes.

mitral (MY-tral) Shaped like the headdress of a Catholic bishop.

modality (moh-DAL-ih-tee) A form of therapeutic agent or regimen.

modify (MOD-ih-fie) Change the form or qualities of something.

molar (MO-lar) One of six teeth in each jaw that grind food.

molasses (mo-LASS-iz) Dark-colored syrups produced during the refining of sugar.

mold (MOLD) Filamentous fungus.

mole (MOLE) Benign localized area of melanin-producing cells.

molecule (MOLL-eh-kyul) Very small particle.

molluscum (moh-LUS-kum) Soft, round tumor of the skin caused by a virus.

molluscum contagiosum (moh-LUS-kum kon-TAY-jee-oh-sum) STD caused by a virus.

monoclonal (MON-oh-KLO-nal) Derived from a single clone of cells.

monocyte (MON-oh-site) Large white blood cell with a single nucleus.

monoglyceride (mon-oh-GLISS-eh-ride) A fatty substance with a single fatty acid.

mononeuropathy (MON-oh-nyu-ROP-ah-thee) Disorder affecting a single nerve.

mononucleosis (MON-oh-nyu-klee-OH-sis) Presence of large numbers of mononuclear leukocytes.

monoplegia (MON-oh-PLEE-jee-ah) Paralysis of one limb.

monosaccharide (MON-oh-SACK-ah-ride) Simplest form of sugar; for example, glucose.

Monospot test (MON-oh-spot TEST) Detects heterophile antibodies in infectious mononucleosis.

monozygotic (MON-oh-zye-GOT-ik) Twins from a single zygote.

mons pubis (MONZ PYU-bis) Fleshy pad with pubic hair, overlying the pubic bone.

Moro reflex (MOR-oh RE-fleks) Neonatal brainstem reflex. Also called *startle reflex*.

morphine (MOR-feen) Derivative of opium used as an analgesic or sedative.

morula (MOR-you-lah) Ball of cells formed from divisions of a zygote.

mosquito (mos-KEY-toe) Blood-sucking insect. Plural *mosquitoes*.

motile (MOH-til) Capable of spontaneous movement.

motility (moh-TILL-ih-tee) The ability for spontaneous movement.

motivation (moh-tih-VAY-shun) Force that enables a person to meet a need or achieve a goal.

motor (MOH-tor) Structures of the nervous system that send impulses out to cause muscles to contract or glands to secrete.

mouth (MOWTH) External opening of a cavity or canal.

mucin (MYU-sin) Protein element of mucus.

mucociliary (MY-koh-SIL-ih-ah-ree) Pertaining to the ciliated epithelium lining the bronchial tree.

mucolytic (MYU-koh-LIT-ik) Agent capable of dissolving or liquefying mucus.

mucopurulent (myu-koh-PYUR-you-lent) Mixture of pus and mucus.

mucosa (myu-KOH-sah) Lining of a tubular structure. Another name for *mucous membrane*.

mucous (MYU-kus) Relating to mucus or the mucosa.

mucus (MYU-kus) Sticky secretion of cells in mucous membranes.

multidisciplinary (mul-tee-DIS-ih-plih-NAR-ee) Involving health care providers from more than one profession

multifocal (mul-tee-FOH-kal) Arising from many centers.

multimodal (mul-tee-MOH-dal) Using many methods.

multipara (mul-TIP-ah-ruh) Woman who has given birth to two or more children.

murmur (**MUR**-mur) Abnormal heart sound heard with a stethoscope when a valve closes or opens abnormally.

Murphy sign (**MUR**-fee SINE) Tenderness in the right subcostal area on inspiration associated with acute cholecystitis.

muscle (**MUSS**-el) A tissue consisting of contractile cells.

muscularis (muss-kyu-**LAR**-is) The muscular layer of a hollow organ or tube.

musculoskeletal (**MUSS**-kyu-loh-**SKEL**-eh-tal) Pertaining to the muscles and the bony skeleton.

mutagen (**MYU**-tah-jen) Agent that produces a mutation in a gene.

mutation (myu-**TAY**-shun) Change in the chemistry of a gene.

mute (**MYUT**) Unable or unwilling to speak.

mutism (**MY**-tizm) Absence of speech.

myasthenia gravis (my-as-**THEE**-nee-ah **GRA**-vis) Disorder of fluctuating muscle weakness.

mycelium (my-**SEE**-lee-um) Mass of hyphae forming a colony of fungi.

mycologist (my-**KOL**-oh-jist) Specialist in mycology.

mycology (my-**KOL**-oh-jee) Study of fungi.

myelin (**MY**-eh-lin) Material of the sheath around the axon of a nerve.

myelocele (**MY**-eh-low-seal) Protrusion of the spinal cord through a defect in the vertebral arch.

myelography (my-eh-**LOG**-rah-fee) Radiography of the spinal cord and nerve roots after injection of contrast medium into the subarachnoid space.

myeloid (**MY**-eh-loyd) Resembling cells derived from bone marrow.

myelomeningocele (**MY**-eh-low-meh-**NING**-oh-seal) Protrusion of the spinal cord and meninges through a defect in the vertebral arch of one or more vertebrae.

myocarditis (**MY**-oh-kar-**DIE**-tis) Inflammation of the heart muscle.

myocardium (**MY**-oh-**KAR**-dee-um) All the heart muscle.

myofascial (**MY**-oh-**FASH**-ee-al) Relating to the fascia surrounding and separating muscle tissue.

myoglobin (**MY**-oh-**GLOW**-bin) Protein of muscle that stores and transports oxygen.

myoma (my-**OH**-mah) Benign tumor of muscle.

myomectomy (my-oh-**MEK**-toe-me) Surgical removal of a myoma (fibroid).

myometrium (my-oh-**ME**-tree-um) Muscle wall of the uterus.

myopia (my-**OH**-pee-ah) Able to see close objects but unable to see distant objects.

myotherapy (**MY**-oh-**THAIR**-ah-pee) Treatment of muscles by massage.

myringotomy (mir-in-**GOT**-oh-me) Incision in the tympanic membrane.

myxedema (miks-eh-**DEE**-muh) Severe hypothyroidism.

N

narcissism (**NAR**-sih-sizm) Self-love; person interprets everything purely in relation to themselves.

narcolepsy (**NAR**-coh-lep-see) Involuntary falling asleep.

narcotic (nar-**KOT**-ik) Drug derived from opium or a synthetic drug with similar effects.

naris (**NAH**-ris) Nostril. Plural *nares.*

nasal (**NAY**-zal) Pertaining to the nose.

nasogastric (**NAY**-zoh-**GAS**-trik) Pertaining to the nose and stomach.

nasolacrimal duct (**NAY**-zoh-**LAK**-rim-al DUKT) Passage from the lacrimal sac to the nose.

nasopharynx (**NAY**-zoh-**FAIR**-inks) Region of the pharynx at the back of the nose and above the soft palate.

natriuretic peptide (**NAH**-tree-you-**RET**-ik **PEP**-tide) Protein that increases the excretion of sodium.

naturopath (**NAH**-chur-oh-path) Practitioner of naturopathy.

naturopathic medicine (**NAH**-chur-oh-**PATH**-ik **MED**-ih-sin) A system of healing based on the healing power of nature.

naturopathy (nah-chur-**OP**-ah-thee) Holistic system of medicine with a natural approach to healing.

nebulizer (**NEB**-you-liz-er) Device used to deliver liquid medicine in a fine mist.

necrosis (neh-**KROH**-sis) Pathologic death of cells or tissue.

necrotic (neh-**KROT**-ik) Affected by necrosis.

Neisseria gonorrhoeae (ni-**SEE**-ree-ah gon-oh-**REE**-ee) Bacterium that causes gonorrhea.

neonatal (**NEE**-oh-**NAY**-tal) Pertaining to the newborn infant.

neonate (**NEE**-oh-nate) A newborn infant.

neoplasia (**NEE**-oh-**PLAY**-zee-ah) Process that results in formation of a tumor.

neoplasm (**NEE**-oh-plazm) A new growth, either a benign or malignant tumor.

neoplastic (**NEE**-oh-**PLAS**-tic) Pertaining to a neoplasm.

nephrectomy (neh-**FREK**-toe-me) Surgical removal of a kidney.

nephritis (neh-**FRY**-tis) Inflammation of the kidney.

nephrolithiasis (**NEF**-roe-lih-**THIGH**-ah-sis) Presence of a kidney stone.

nephrolithotomy (**NEF**-roe-lih-**THOT**-oh-me) Incision for removal of a stone.

nephrologist (neh-**FROL**-oh-jist) Medical specialist in disorders of the kidney.

nephrology (neh-**FROL**-oh-jee) Medical specialty of diseases of the kidney.

nephron (**NEF**-ron) Filtration unit of the kidney; glomerulus + renal tubule.

nephropathy (neh-**FROP**-ah-thee) Any disease of the kidney.

nephroscope (**NEF**-roe-skope) Endoscope to view the inside of the kidney.

nephroscopy (neh-**FROS**-koh-pee) To examine the kidney.

nephrotic syndrome (neh-**FROT**-ik **SIN**-drome) Glomerular disease with marked loss of protein. Also known as *nephrosis*.

nerve (**NERV**) A cord of nerve fibers bound together by connective tissue.

nerve conduction study (**NERV** kon-**DUK**-shun **STUD**-ee) Procedure to measure the speed at which an electrical impulse travels along a nerve.

neural (**NYU**-ral) Pertaining to nervous tissue.

neural tube (**NYU**-ral **TYUB**) Embryologic tubelike structure that forms the brain and spinal cord.

neuralgia (nyu-**RAL**-jee-ah) Pain in the distribution of a nerve.

neurilemma (nyu-ri-**LEM**-ah) Covering of a nerve around the myelin sheath.

neuroglia (nyu-roh-**GLEE**-ah) Connective tissue holding nervous tissue together.

neurohypophysis (**NYUR**-oh-high-**POF**-ih-sis) Posterior lobe of the pituitary gland.

neurologist (nyu-**ROL**-oh-jist) Medical specialist in disorders of the nervous system.

neurology (nyu-**ROL**-oh-jee) Medical specialty of disorders of the nervous system.

neuromuscular (**NYUR**-oh-**MUSS**-kyu-lar) A junction where a nerve supplies muscle tissue.

neuron (**NYUR**-on) Technical term for a nerve cell; consists of the cell body with its dendrites and axons.

neuropathy (nyu-**ROP**-ah-thee) Any disorder affecting the nervous system.

neurosurgeon (**NYU**-roh-**SUR**-jun) Specialist in operating on the nervous system.

neurosurgery (**NYU**-roh-**SUR**-jer-ee) Operating on the nervous system.

neurotoxin (**NYUR**-oh-tock-sin) Agent that poisons the nervous system.

neurotransmitter (**NYUR**-oh-trans-**MIT**-er) Chemical agent that relays messages from one nerve cell to the next.

neutropenia (**NEW**-troh-**PEE**-nee-uh) A deficiency of neutrophils.

neutrophil (**NEW**-troh-fill) A neutrophil's granules take up (purple) stain equally, whether the stain is acid or alkaline.

neutrophilia (**NEW**-troh-**FILL**-ee-ah) An increase in neutrophils.

nevus (**NEE**-vus) Congenital lesion of the skin. Plural *nevi*.

niacin (**NI**-ah-sin) Vitamin B₃.

nipple (**NIP**-el) Projection from the breast into which the lactiferous ducts open.

nitrite (**NI**-trite) Chemical formed in urine by *E. coli* and other microorganisms.

nitrogenous (ni-**TROJ**-en-us) Containing or generating nitrogen.

nocturia (nok-**TYU**-ree-ah) Excessive urination at night.

node (**NOHD**) A circumscribed mass of tissue.

nodule (**NOD**-yule) Small node or knotlike swelling.

nonessential (**NON**-ee-**SEN**-shal) Can be synthesized by the body.

nonunion (non-**YOU**-nee-un) Total failure of healing of a fracture.

norepinephrine (**NOR**-ep-ih-**NEFF**-rin) Parasympathetic neurotransmitter. Also called *noradrenaline*.

nosocomial (noh-soh-**KOH**-mee-al) Acquired while in the hospital.

nuchal cord (**NYU**-kul **KORD**) Loops of umbilical cord around the fetal neck.

nucleolus (nyu-**KLEE**-oh-lus) Small mass within the nucleus.

nucleus (**NYU**-klee-us) Functional center of a cell or structure.

null cells (**NULL SELLS**) Lymphocytes with no surface markers, unlike T cells or B cells.

nutrient (**NYU**-tree-ent) A substance in food required for normal physiological function.

nutrition (nyu-**TRISH**-un) Food and liquid requirements for normal function of the human body.

nutritionist (nyu-**TRISH**-un-ist) Certified professional in nutrition science.

nutritive (**NYU**-trih-tiv) Providing nourishment.

O

obesity (oh-**BEE**-sih-tee) Excessive amount of fat in the body.

oblique fracture (ob-**LEEK FRAK**-chur) A diagonal fracture across the long axis of the bone.

obsession (ob-**SESH**-un) Persistent, recurrent, uncontrollable thoughts or impulses.

obsessive (ob-**SES**-iv) Possessing persistent, recurrent, uncontrollable thoughts or impulses.

obstetrician (ob-steh-**TRISH**-un) Medical specialist in obstetrics.

obstetrics (**OB**) (ob-**STET**-ricks) Medical specialty for the care of women during pregnancy and the postpartum period.

occipital (ock-**SIP**-it-al) The back of the skull.

occipital lobe (ock-**SIP**-it-al **LOBE**) Posterior area of the cerebral hemispheres.

occlude (o-**KLUDE**) To close, plug, or completely obstruct.

occult (o-**KULT**) Not visible on the surface.

occupational therapy (**OCK**-you-**PAY**-shun-al **THAIR**-ah-pee) Use of work and recreational activities to increase independent function.

ocular (**OCK**-you-lar) Pertaining to the eye.

oculomotor (**OCK**-you-loh-**MOH**-tor) Third (III) cranial nerve; moves the eye.

olfaction (ol-**FAK**-shun) Sense of smell.

olfactory (ol-**FAK**-toh-ree) First (I) cranial nerve; carries information related to the sense of smell.

oligodendrocyte (**OL**-ih-goh-**DEN**-droh-site) Connective tissue cell of the central nervous system that forms a myelin sheath.

oligodendroglioma (OL-ih-goh-**DEN**-droh-gly-**OH**-mah) A slow-growing tumor in the cerebral hemisphere of an adult.

oligohydramnios (OL-ih-goh-high-**DRAM**-nee-os) Too little amniotic fluid.

oliguria (ol-ih-**GYUR**-ee-ah) Scanty production of urine.

omentum (oh-**MEN**-tum) Membrane that encloses the bowels.

oncogene (**ONG**-koh-jeen) One of a family of genes involved in cell growth that work in concert to cause cancer.

oncogenic (**ONG**-koh-**JEN**-ik) Capable of producing a neoplasm.

oncologist (on-**KOL**-oh-jist) Medical specialist in oncology.

oncology (on-**KOL**-oh-jee) The science dealing with cancer.

onychomycosis (oh-ni-koh-my-**KOH**-sis) Condition of a fungus infection in a nail.

oocyte (**OH**-oh-site) Female egg cell.

oogenesis (oh-oh-**JEN**-eh-sis) Development of female egg cell.

open fracture (**OH**-pen **FRAK**-chur) The skin over the fracture is broken.

ophthalmia neonatorum (off-**THAL**-me-ah ne-oh-nay-**TOR**-um) Conjunctivitis of the newborn.

ophthalmologist (off-thal-**MALL**-oh-jist) Medical specialist in ophthalmology.

ophthalmology (off-thal-**MALL**-oh-jee) Diagnosis and treatment of diseases of the eye.

ophthalmoscope (off-**THAL**-moh-skope) Instrument for viewing the retina.

ophthalmoscopic (**OFF**-thal-**MOS**-koh-pik) Pertaining to the use of an ophthalmoscope.

ophthalmoscopy (**OFF**-thal-**MOS**-koh-pee) The process of viewing the retina.

opiate (**OH**-pee-ate) A drug derived from opium.

opportunistic (**OP**-or-tyu-**NIS**-tik) An organism or a disease in a host with lowered resistance.

opportunistic infection (**OP**-or-tyu-**NIS**-tik in-**FEK**-shun) An infection that causes disease when the immune system is compromised for other reasons.

opposition (op-oh-**SIH**-shun) The movement of the thumb across the palm of the hand to touch the tips of the other fingers.

optic (**OP**-tick) Pertaining to the eye; second (II) cranial nerve; carries visual information.

optometrist (op-**TOM**-eh-trist) Someone skilled in the measurement of vision but who cannot treat eye diseases or prescribe medication.

oral (**OR**-al) Pertaining to the mouth.

orbit (**OR**-bit) The bony socket that holds the eyeball.

orchiectomy (or-kee-**ECK**-toe-me) Removal of one or both testes.

orchiopexy (**OR**-kee-oh-**PEK**-see) Surgical fixation of a testis in the scrotum.

orchitis (or-**KIE**-tis) Inflammation of the testis. Also called *epididymoorchitis.*

organ (**OR**-gan) Structure with specific functions in a body system.

organelle (**OR**-gah-nell) Part of a cell having specialized function(s).

organic (or-**GAN**-ik) Compound with carbon atoms. Food produced without using chemicals.

organism (**OR**-gan-izm) Any whole, living individual whether animal or plant.

organophosphate (**OR**-ga-no-**FOS**-fate) Organic phosphorus compound used as an insecticide.

orifice (**OR**-ih-fis) Any opening or aperture.

origin (**OR**-ih-gin) Fixed source of a muscle at its attachment to bone.

oropharynx (**OR**-oh-fair-inks) Region at the back of the mouth between the soft palate and the tip of the epiglottis.

orthopedic (or-tho-**PEE**-dik) Pertaining to the correction and cure of deformities and diseases of the musculoskeletal system; originally, most of the deformities treated were in children. Also spelled *orthopaedic.*

orthopedist (or-tho-**PEE**-dist) Specialist in orthopedics.

orthotic (or-**THOT**-ik) Orthopedic appliance to correct an abnormality.

orthotist (or-**THOT**-ist) Maker and fitter of orthopedic appliances

os (OS) Opening into a canal; for example, the cervix.

osmosis (oz-**MO**-sis) The passage of water across a cell membrane.

ossicle (**OS**-ih-kel) A small bone, particularly relating to the three bones in the middle ear.

osteoarthritis (**OS**-tee-oh-ar-**THRI**-tis) Chronic inflammatory disease of the joints with pain and loss of function.

osteoblast (**OS**-tee-oh-blast) Bone-forming cell.

osteoclast (**OS**-tee-oh-klast) Bone-removing cell.

osteocyte (**OS**-tee-oh-site) Bone-maintaining cell.

osteogenesis (**OS**-tee-oh-**JEN**-eh-sis) Creation of new bone.

osteogenesis imperfecta (**OS**-tee-oh-**JEN**-eh-sis im-per-**FEK**-tah) Inherited condition when bone formation is incomplete, leading to fragile, easily broken bones.

osteogenic sarcoma (**OS**-tee-oh-**JEN**-ik sar-**KOH**-mah) Malignant tumor originating in bone-producing cells.

osteomalacia (**OS**-tee-oh-mah-**LAY**-she-ah) Soft, flexible bones lacking in calcium (rickets).

osteomyelitis (**OS**-tee-oh-my-eh-**LIE**-tis) Inflammation of bone tissue.

osteopath (**OS**-tee-oh-path) Practitioner of osteopathy.

osteopathy (**OS**-tee-**OP**-ah-thee) Medical practice based on maintaining the balance of the body.

osteopenia (**OS**-tee-oh-**PEE**-nee-ah) Decreased calcification of bone.

osteoporosis (**OS**-tee-oh-poh-**ROE**-sis) Condition in which the bones become more porous, brittle, fragile, and more likely to fracture.

osteosarcoma (OS-tee-oh-sar-**KOH**-mah) Cancer arising in bone-forming cells.

ostomy (OS-toe-me) Artificial opening into a tubular structure.

otitis media (oh-**TIE**-tis **ME**-dee-ah) Inflammation of the middle ear.

otolith (**OH**-toe-lith) A calcium particle in the vestibule of the inner ear.

otologist (oh-**TOL**-oh-jist) Medical specialist in diseases of the ear.

otology (oh-**TOL**-oh-jee) Study of the function and diseases of the ear.

otomycosis (**OH**-toe-my-**KOH**-sis) Fungal infection of the external ear.

otorhinolaryngologist (oh-toe-rhino-lah-rin-**GOL**-oh-jist) Ear, nose, and throat medical specialist.

otosclerosis (oh-toe-sklair-**OH**-sis) Hardening at the junction of the stapes and oval window that causes loss of hearing.

otoscope (**OH**-toe-skope) Instrument for examining the ear.

otoscopy (oh-**TOS**-koh-pee) Examination of the ear.

ovarian (oh-**VAIR**-ee-an) Pertaining to the ovary.

ovary (**OH**-va-ree) One of the paired female egg-producing glands.

ovulation (**OV**-you-**LAY**-shun) Release of an oocyte from a follicle.

ovum (**OH**-vum) Egg. Also called *oocyte.* Plural *ova.*

oxygen (**OCK**-see-jen) The gas essential for life.

oxyhemoglobin (**OCK**-see-he-moh-**GLOW**-bin) Hemoglobin in combination with oxygen.

oxytocin (**OCK**-see-toe-sin) Pituitary hormone that stimulates the uterus to contract.

P

pacemaker (**PACE**-may-ker) Device that regulates cardiac electrical activity.

pain threshold (PANE **THRESH**-old) The point at which pain is first noticed.

palate (**PAL**-uht) Roof of the mouth.

palatine (**PAL**-ah-tine) Bone that forms the hard palate and parts of the nose and orbits.

palliative care (**PAL**-ee-ah-tiv KAIR) To relieve symptoms and pain without curing.

pallor (**PAL**-or) Paleness of the skin.

palm (PAHLM) Palm of the hand.

palpate (**PAL**-pate) To examine with the fingers and hands.

palpitation (pal-pih-**TAY**-shun) Forcible, rapid beat of the heart felt by the patient.

palsy (**PAWL**-zee) Paralysis or paresis from brain damage.

pancreas (**PAN**-kree-as) Lobulated gland, the head of which is tucked into the curve of the duodenum.

pancreatitis (**PAN**-kree-ah-**TIE**-tis) Inflammation of the pancreas.

pancytopenia (**PAN**-site-oh-**PEE**-nee-uh) Deficiency of all types of blood cells.

pandemic (pan-**DEM**-ik) Disease attacking the population of a very large area.

panhypopituitarism (pan-**HIGH**-poh-pih-**TYU**-ih-tah-rizm) Deficiency of all the pituitary hormones.

pantothenic acid (**PAN**-toh-**THEN**-ik **ASS**-id) Coenzyme essential for cell function; vitamin B_5.

Pap test (**PAP** TEST) Examination of cells taken from the cervix.

papilla (pah-**PILL**-ah) Any small projection. Plural *papillae.*

papilledema (pah-pill-eh-**DEE**-mah) Swelling of the optic disc in the retina.

papilloma (pap-ih-**LOH**-mah) Benign projection of epithelial cells.

papule (**PAP**-yul) Small, circumscribed elevation on the skin.

para (**PAH**-rah) Abbreviation for number of deliveries.

paralysis (pah-**RAL**-ih-sis) Loss of voluntary movement.

paralytic (par-ah-**LYT**-ik) Suffering from paralysis.

paralyze (**PAR**-ah-lyze) To make incapable of movement.

parameter (pah-**RAM**-eh-ter) Evaluation or way of measuring.

paranasal (**PAR**-ah **NAY**-zal) Adjacent to the nose.

paranoia (par-ah-**NOY**-ah) Presence of persecutory delusions.

paranoid (**PAR**-ah-noyd) Having delusions of persecution.

paraphimosis (**PAR**-ah-fi-**MOH**-sis) Condition in which a retracted prepuce cannot be pulled forward to cover the glans.

paraplegia (par-ah-**PLEE**-jee-ah) Paralysis of both lower extremities.

parasite (**PAR**-ah-site) An organism that attaches itself to, lives on or in, and derives its nutrition from another species.

parasympathetic (par-ah-sim-pah-**THET**-ik) Division of the autonomic nervous system; has opposite effects of the sympathetic division.

parathyroid (par-ah-**THY**-royd) Endocrine gland embedded in the back of the thyroid.

paraurethral (**PAR**-ah-you-**REE**-thral) Situated around the urethra.

parenchyma (pah-**RENG**-kih-mah) Characteristic functional cells of a gland or organ that are supported by the connective tissue framework.

parenteral (pah-**REN**-ter-al) Giving medication by any means other than the gastrointestinal tract.

paresis (par-**EE**-sis) Partial paralysis.

paresthesia (par-es-**THEE**-ze-ah) An abnormal sensation; for example, tingling, burning, pricking. Plural *parasthesias.*

parietal (pah-**RYE**-eh-tal) Pertaining to the outer layer of the pericardium and other body cavities, or the two bones forming the sidewalls and roof of the cranium.

parietal lobe (pah-**RYE**-eh-tal LOBE) Area of brain under the parietal bone.

parity (**PAIR**-ih-tee) Number of deliveries.

Parkinson disease (PAR-kin-son diz-EEZ) Disease of muscular rigidity, tremors, and a masklike facial expression.

paronychia (par-oh-NICK-ee-ah) Infection alongside the nail.

parotid (pah-ROT-id) Parotid gland is the salivary gland beside the ear.

paroxysmal (par-ock-SIZ-mal) Occurring in sharp, spasmodic episodes.

particle (PAR-tih-kul) A small piece of matter.

particulate (par-TIK-you-late) Relating to a fine particle.

pasteurization (PAS-tyur-ih-ZAY-shun) The heating of fluids to moderate temperatures to destroy microorganisms.

patella (pah-TELL-ah) Thin, circular bone in front of the knee joint and embedded in the patellar tendon. Also called the *kneecap*.

patent (PAY-tent) Open.

patent ductus arteriosus (PAY-tent DUK-tus ar-TER-ee-oh-sus) An open channel between the aorta and the pulmonary artery.

pathogen (PATH-oh-jen) A disease-causing microorganism.

pathologic gambling (path-oh-LOJ-ik GAM-bling) Morbid, constant, uncontrollable, destructive gambling.

pathologist (pa-THOL-oh-jist) A specialist in pathology.

pathology (pa-THOL-oh-jee) Medical specialty dealing with the structural and functional changes of a disease process, or the cause, development, and structural changes in disease

pectin (PEK-tin) Plant fiber with the ability to thicken and solidify to a gel.

pectoral (PEK-tor-al) Pertaining to the chest.

pectoral girdle (PEK-tor-al GIR-del) Incomplete bony ring that attaches the upper limb to the axial skeleton.

pedal (PEED-al) Pertaining to the foot.

pediatrician (PEE-dee-ah-TRISH-an) Medical specialist in pediatrics.

pediatrics (pee-dee-AT-riks) Medical specialty of treating children during development from birth through adolescence.

pediculosis (peh-dick-you-LOH-sis) An infestation with lice.

peer (PEER) A person at the same level or standing.

pellagra (peh-LAG-rah) Disease due to dietary deficiency of niacin.

pelvis (PEL-vis) A cup-shaped cavity, as in the pelvis of the kidney, or a cup-shaped ring of bone.

penile (PEE-nile) Pertaining to the penis.

penis (PEE-nis) Conveys urine and semen to the outside.

pepsin (PEP-sin) Enzyme produced by the stomach that breaks down protein.

pepsinogen (pep-SIN-oh-jen) Converted by HCl in stomach to pepsin.

peptic (PEP-tik) Relating to the stomach and duodenum.

percentile (per-SEN-tile) One of a hundred groups in a distribution of variables.

perforated (PER-foh-ray-ted) Punctured with one or more holes.

perforation (per-foh-RAY-shun) Erosion that progresses to become a hole through the wall of a structure.

perfuse (per-FYUSE) To force blood to flow through a lumen or a vascular bed.

pericarditis (PER-ih-kar-DIE-tis) Inflammation of the pericardium, the covering of the heart.

pericardium (per-ih-KAR-dee-um) The tissue covering the heart.

perimeter (peh-RIM-eh-ter) An edge or border.

perimetrium (per-ih-ME-tree-um) The covering of the uterus; part of the peritoneum.

perineal (PER-ih-NEE-al) Pertaining to the perineum.

perineum (PER-ih-NEE-um) Area between the thighs, extending from the coccyx to the pubis.

periodontal (PER-ee-oh-DON-tal) Around a tooth.

periodontics (PER-ee-oh-DON-tiks) Branch of dentistry specializing in disorders of tissues around the teeth.

periodontist (PER-ee-oh-DON-tist) Specialist in periodontics.

periodontitis (PER-ee-oh-don-TIE-tis) Inflammation of tissues around a tooth.

periorbital (per-ee-OR-bit-al) Pertaining to tissues around the orbit.

periosteum (PER-ee-OSS-tee-um) Fibrous membrane covering a bone.

peripheral (peh-RIF-er-al) Pertaining to the periphery or external boundary.

peripheral vision (peh-RIF-er-al VIZH-un) Ability to see objects as they come into the outer edges of the visual field.

periphery (peh-RIF-eh-ree) Outer part of a structure away from the center.

peristalsis (per-ih-STAL-sis) Wave of alternate contraction and relaxation of the intestinal wall to move food along.

peritoneal (PER-ih-toe-NEE-al) Pertaining to the peritoneum.

peritoneum (per-ih-toe-NEE-um) Membrane that lines the abdominal cavity.

peritonitis (PER-ih-toe-NIE-tis) Inflammation of the peritoneum.

peritubular (PER-ih-too-BYU-lar) Surrounding the small renal tubules.

permeable (PER-me-ah-bull) Allows passage of substances through a membrane.

pernicious anemia (per-NISH-us ah-NEE-me-ah) Chronic anemia due to lack of vitamin B_{12}.

pertussis (per-TUSS-is) Infectious disease with a spasmodic, intense cough ending on a whoop (stridor). Also known as *whooping cough*.

pes planus (PES PLAY-nuss) A flat foot with no plantar arch.

pessary (PES-ah-ree) Appliance inserted into the vagina to support the uterus.

pesticide (PES-tih-side) Agent for destroying flies, mosquitoes, and other pests.

petechia (peh-TEE-kee-ah) Pinpoint capillary hemorrhagic spot in the skin. Plural *petechiae*.

petit mal (peh-**TEE** MAL) Type of seizure.

Peyronie disease (pay-**ROH**-nee diz-**EEZ**) Penile bending and pain on erection.

phacoemulsification (fake-oh-ee-**MUL**-sih-fih-**KAY**-shun) Fragment the center of the lens into very tiny pieces and suck them out of the eye.

phagocyte (**FAG**-oh-site) Blood cell that ingests and destroys foreign particles and cells.

phagocytosis (**FAG**-oh-sigh-**TOE**-sis) Process of ingestion and destruction.

phalanx (**FAY**-lanks) A bone of a finger or toe. Plural *phalanges.*

pharmacist (**FAR**-mah-sist) Person licensed by the state to prepare and dispense drugs.

pharmacology (far-mah-**KOLL**-oh-jee) Science of the preparation, uses, and effects of drugs.

pharmacy (**FAR**-mah-see) Facility licensed to prepare and dispense drugs.

pharyngitis (fair-in-**JIE**-tis) Inflammation of the pharynx.

pharynx (**FAIR**-inks) Air tube from the back of the nose to the larynx.

phenotype (**FEE**-noh-type) A characteristic of genetic selection.

phenylalanine (fen-il-**AL**-ah-neen) An amino acid.

phenylketonuria (**FEN**-il-**KEE**-toe-**NYU**-ree-ah) Hereditary disease with accumulation of phenylalanine and urinary excretion of its metabolites; leads to mental retardation if not controlled.

pheochromocytoma (fee-oh-**KRO**-moh-sigh-**TOE**-muh) Adenoma of the adrenal medulla secreting excessive catecholamines.

pheromone (**FER**-oh-moan) Substance that carries and generates a physical attraction for other people.

phimosis (fi-**MOH**-sis) Prepuce cannot be retracted.

phlebitis (fleh-**BIE**-tis) Inflammation of a vein.

phlebotomist (fleh-**BOT**-oh-mist) Person skilled in taking blood from veins.

phlebotomy (fleh-**BOT**-oh-me) Taking blood from a vein.

phlegm (FLEM) Abnormal amounts of mucus expectorated from the respiratory tract.

phobia (**FOH**-bee-ah) Pathologic fear or dread

phonophoresis (foh-noh-for-**EE**-sis) Transport of one substance across the skin through the use of ultrasound.

phosphatase (**FOS**-fah-tase) Enzyme that liberates phosphorus.

photocoagulation (foh-toe-koh-ag-you-**LAY**-shun) Using light (laser beam) to form a clot.

photodynamic (foh-toe-die-**NAM**-ik) Use of a light-sensitive drug with a laser beam to destroy cells.

photophobia (foh-toe-**FOH**-bee-ah) Fear of the light because it hurts the eyes.

photoreceptor (foh-toe-ree-**SEP**-tor) A photoreceptor cell receives light and converts it into electrical impulses.

photosensitivity (foh-toe-**SEN**-sih-tiv-ih-tee) When light produces pain in the eye.

phototherapy (foh-toe-**THAIR**-ah-pee) Treatment using light rays.

physiatrist (fih-**ZIE**-ah-trist) Specialist in physical medicine.

physiatry (fih-**ZIE**-ah-tree) Physical medicine.

physical medicine (**FIZ**-ih-cal **MED**-ih-sin) Diagnosis and treatment by means of remedial agents, such as exercises, manipulation, heat, etc.

physical therapy (**FIZ**-ih-cal **THAIR**-ah-pee) Use of remedial processes to overcome a physical defect. Also known as *physiotherapy.*

physiotherapy (**FIZ**-ee-oh-**THAIR**-ah-pee) Another term for physical therapy.

phytic acid (**FIE**-tik **ASS**-id) Component of fiber that can limit absorption of some minerals.

phytochemical (fie-toe-**KEM**-ih-kal) Biologically active, nonnutrient plant chemical.

pia mater (**PEE**-ah **MAY**-ter) Delicate inner layer of the meninges.

pica (**PIE**-kah) Eating substances not considered to be food.

pineal (**PIN**-ee-al) Pertaining to the pineal gland.

pink eye (PINK EYE) Conjunctivitis.

pinna (**PIN**-ah) Another name for auricle. Plural *pinnae.*

pinworm (**PIN**-worm) Intestinal parasite.

pitting edema (ee-**DEE**-mah) An indentation made by a finger in an edematous area persists for a long time.

pituitary (pih-**TYU**-ih-tary) Pertaining to the pituitary gland.

placebo (plah-**SEE**-boh) An inert compound with no innate therapeutic value.

placenta (plah-**SEN**-tah) Organ that allows metabolic interchange between the mother and fetus.

plague (PLAYG) Infectious disease causing excessive mortality.

plantar reflex (**PLAN**-tar re-**FLEKS**) Neurological response to stimulation of the sole of the foot.

plaque (PLAK) Patch of abnormal tissue.

plasma (**PLAZ**-mah) Fluid, noncellular component of blood.

plasma cell (**PLAZ**-mah SELL) Cell derived from B lymphocytes and active in formation of antibodies.

Plasmodium (plaz-**MOH**-dee-um) Causal agent for malaria.

platelet (**PLAYT**-let) Cell fragment involved in clotting process. Also called *thrombocyte.*

pleura (**PLUR**-ah) Membrane covering the lungs and lining the ribs in the thoracic cavity. Plural *pleurae.*

pleurisy (**PLUR**-ih-see) Inflammation of the pleura.

plexus (**PLEK**-sus) A weblike network of joined nerves. Plural *plexuses.*

plica (**PLEE**-cah) Fold in a mucous membrane. Plural *plicae.*

pneumatic (new-**MAT**-ik) Pertaining to a structure filled with air.

pneumococcus (new-moh-**KOK**-us) Gram-positive cocci associated with respiratory infection. Plural *pneumococci.*

pneumoconiosis (new-moh-koh-nee-**OH**-sis) Fibrotic lung disease caused by the inhalation of different dusts.

pneumonectomy (NEW-moh-NEK-toe-me) Surgical removal of a whole lung.

pneumonia (new-MOH-nee-ah) Inflammation of the lung parenchyma.

pneumonic (new-MON-ik) Relating to pneumonia.

pneumothorax (new-moh-THOR-ax) Air in the pleural cavity.

podiatrist (po-DIE-ah-trist) Practitioner of podiatry.

podiatry (po-DIE-ah-tree) The diagnosis and treatment of disorders and injuries of the foot.

poikilocytic (POY-key-low-SIT-ik) Pertaining to an irregular-shaped RBC.

polarity (po-LAR-ih-tee) Possession of opposite characteristics.

poliomyelitis (POE-lee-oh-MY-eh-lie-tis) Inflammation of the gray matter of the spinal cord, leading to paralysis of the limbs and muscles of respiration.

pollutant (poh-LOO-tant) Substance that makes the environment unclean or impure.

pollution (poh-LOO-shun) Condition that is unclean, impure, and a danger to health.

polycystic (pol-ee-SIS-tik) Composed of many cysts.

polycythemia vera (POL-ee-sigh-THEE-me-ah) Chronic disease with bone marrow hyperplasia, increase in number of RBCs, and in blood volume.

polydipsia (pol-ee-DIP-see-ah) Excessive thirst.

polyhydramnios (POL-ee-high-DRAM-nee-os) Too much amniotic fluid.

polymenorrhea (POL-ee-men-oh-REE-ah) More than normal frequency of menses.

polymorphonuclear (POL-ee-more-foh-NEW-klee-ur) White blood cell with a multi-lobed nucleus.

polymyalgia rheumatica (poll-ee-my-AL-jee-ah rue-MAT-ick-ah) Pain in several muscle groups with systemic symptoms.

polyneuropathy (POL-ee-nyu-ROP-ah-thee) Disorder affecting many nerves.

polyp (POL-ip) Mass of tissue that projects into the lumen of the bowel.

polypectomy (pol-ip-ECK-toh-mee) Excision or removal of a polyp.

polyphagia (pol-ee-FAY-jee-ah) Excessive eating.

polyphenol (pol-ee-FEE-nol) Antioxidant found in grapes and tea.

polyposis (pol-ih-POH-sis) Presence of several polyps.

polysaccharide (pol-ee-SACK-ah-ride) A combination of many saccharides; for example, starch.

polysomnography (pol-ee-som-NOG-rah-fee) Test to monitor brain waves, muscle tension, eye movement, and oxygen levels in the blood as the patient sleeps.

polyuria (pol-ee-YOU-ree-ah) Excessive production of urine.

pons (PONZ) Part of the brainstem.

popliteal (pop-LIT-ee-al) Pertaining to the back of the knee.

popliteal fossa (pop-LIT-ee-al FOSS-ah) The hollow at the back of the knee.

portal (POR-tal) The vein that brings blood from the intestines to the liver.

postcoital (post-KOH-eye-tal) After sexual intercourse.

posterior (pos-TER-ee-or) Back surface of the body; situated behind.

postictal (post-IK-tal) Transient neurologic deficit after a seizure.

postmature (post-mah-TYUR) Infant born after 42 weeks of gestation.

postmaturity (post-mah-TYUR-ih-tee) Condition of being postmature.

postpartum (post-PAR-tum) After childbirth.

postpolio syndrome (PPS) (post-POE-lee-oh SIN-drome) Progressive muscle weakness in a person previously affected by polio.

postprandial (post-PRAN-dee-al) Following a meal.

postpubescent (post-pyu-BESS-ent) After the period of puberty.

posttraumatic (post-traw-MAT-ik) Occurring after and caused by trauma.

Pott fracture (POT FRAK-shur) Fracture of the lower end of the fibula, often with fracture of the tibial malleolus.

prana (PRAH-nah) Vital power.

precancerous (pree-KAN-sir-us) Lesion from which a cancer can develop.

precipitate (pree-SIP-ih-tate) Precipitate labor is a very rapid labor and delivery.

precision (pree-SIH-zhun) Quality of being clearly defined or stated.

precursor (pree-KUR-sir) Cell or substance formed earlier in the development of the cell or substance.

preeclampsia (pree-eh-KLAMP-see-uh) Hypertension, edema, and proteinuria during pregnancy.

preemie (PREE-me) Slang for *premature baby.*

pregnancy (PREG-nan-see) State of being pregnant.

pregnant (PREG-nant) Having conceived.

prehypertension (pree-HIGH-per-TEN-shun) Precursor to hypertension.

premature (pree-mah-TYUR) Occurring before the expected time; for example, an infant born before 37 weeks of gestation.

prematurity (pree-mah-TYUR-ih-tee) Condition of being premature.

premenstrual (pree-MEN-stru-al) Pertaining to the time immediately before the menses.

prenatal (pree-NAY-tal) Before birth.

prepatellar (pree-pah-TELL-ar) In front of the patella.

prepuce (PREE-puce) Fold of skin that covers the glans penis.

presbyopia (prez-bee-OH-pee-ah) Difficulty in nearsighted vision occurring in middle and old age.

preterm (PREE-term) Baby delivered before 37 weeks of gestation. Also called *premature.*

prevention (pree-VEN-shun) Process to prevent occurrence of a disease or health problem

previa (PREE-vee-ah) Anything blocking the fetus during its birth; for example, an abnomally situated placenta, *placenta previa.*

priapism (PRY-ah-pizm) Persistent erection of the penis.

primigravida (pree-mih-GRAV-ih-dah) First pregnancy.

primipara (pree-MIP-ah-ruh) Woman giving birth for the first time.

prion (PREE-on) Small infectious protein particle.

proctitis (prok-TIE-tis) Inflammation of the lining of the rectum.

proctoscopy (prok-TOSS-koh-pee) Examination of the inside of the anus by endoscopy.

prodromal (pro-DRO-mal) Beginning of disease before the signs become overt.

progenitor (pro-JEN-it-or) Founder; beginning of an ancestry.

progesterone (pro-JESS-ter-own) Hormone that prepares the uterus for pregnancy.

progestin (pro-JESS-tin) A synthetic form of progesterone.

prognathism (PROG-nah-thizm) Condition of a forward projecting jaw.

prognosis (prog-NO-sis) Forecasting of the probable course of a disease.

prolactin (pro-LAK-tin) Pituitary hormone that stimulates production of milk.

prolactinoma (pro-lak-tih-NO-muh) Prolactin-producing tumor.

prolapse (pro-LAPS) An organ slips out of its normal position.

proliferate (pro-LIF-eh-rate) To increase in number through reproduction.

pronate (PRO-nate) Rotate the forearm so that the surface of the palm faces posteriorly in the anatomic position.

pronation (pro-NAY-shun) Process of lying face down or of turning a hand or foot with the volar (palm or sole) surface down.

prone (PRONE) Lying face down, flat on your belly.

prophylactic (pro-fih-LAK-tik) The act or the agent that prevents a disease.

prophylaxis (pro-fih-LAX-is) Prevention of disease.

prostaglandin (PROS-tah-GLAN-din) Hormone present in many tissues, but first isolated from the prostate gland.

prostate (PROS-tate) Organ surrounding the beginning of the urethra.

prostatectomy (pross-tah-TEK-toe-me) Surgical removal of the prostate.

prostatic (pros-TAT-ik) Pertaining to the prostate.

prostatitis (pross-tah-TIE-tis) Inflammation of the prostate.

prosthesis (PROS-thee-sis) Manufactured substitute for a missing part of the body.

protease (PRO-tee-aze) Group of enzymes that break down protein.

protection (pro-TEK-shun) Defense against attack or invasion.

protein (PRO-teen) Class of food substances based on amino acids.

proteinuria (pro-tee-NYU-ree-ah) Presence of protein in urine.

prothrombin (pro-THROM-bin) Protein formed by the liver and converted to thrombin in the blood-clotting mechanism.

protocol (PRO-toe-kol) Detailed plan; in this case, for a regimen of therapy.

proton pump inhibitor (PPI) (PRO-ton PUMP in-HIB-ih-tor) Agent that blocks production of gastric acid.

protooncogene (pro-toe-ON-koh-jeen) A normal gene involved in normal cell growth.

proximal (PROK-sih-mal) Situated nearest the center of the body.

pruritic (proo-RIT-ik) Itchy.

pruritus (proo-RYE-tus) Itching.

Pseudomonas (soo-doh-MOH-nas) Gram-negative aerobic rods.

psoriasis (so-RYE-ah-sis) Rash characterized by reddish, silver-scaled patches.

psychedelic (sigh-keh-DEL-ik) Agent that intensifies sensory perception.

psychiatric (sigh-kee-AH-trik) Pertaining to psychiatry.

psychiatrist (sigh-KIGH-ah-trist) Licensed medical specialist in psychiatry.

psychiatry (sigh-KIGH-ah-tree) Diagnosis and treatment of mental disorders.

psychoactive (sigh-koh-AK-tiv) An agent able to alter mood, behavior, and/or cognition.

psychoanalysis (sigh-koh-ah-NAL-ih-sis) Method of psychotherapy.

psychoanalyst (sigh-koh-AN-ah-list) Practitioner of psychoanalysis.

psychologic (sigh-koh-LOJ-ik) Pertaining to psychology.

psychological (sigh-koh-LOJ-ik-al) Pertaining to psychology.

psychologist (sigh-KOL-oh-jist) Licensed specialist in psychology.

psychology (sigh-KOL-oh-jee) Science concerned with the behavior of the human mind.

psychopath (SIGH-koh-path) Person with antisocial personality disorder.

psychopharmacotherapy (SIGH-koh-FAR-mah-koh-THAIR-ah-pee) Drug treatment of mental disorders.

psychosis (sigh-KOH-sis) Disorder causing mental disruption and loss of contact with reality.

psychosocial (sigh-koh-SOH-shal) Involving both the mind and various social and community aspects of life.

psychosomatic (sigh-koh-soh-MAT-ik) Disorders of the body influenced by the mind.

psychotherapist (sigh-koh-THAIR-ah-pist) Practitioner of psychotherapy.

psychotherapy (sigh-koh-THAIR-ah-pee) Treatment of mental disorders through communication.

psychotic (sigh-KOT-ik) Pertaining to or affected by psychosis.

pterygoid (TER-ih-goyd) Pterygoid muscles are two wing-shaped muscles that open and close the mouth.

ptosis (TOE-sis) Sinking down of an eyelid or an organ.

pubarche (pyu-BAR-key) Development of pubic and axillary hair.

puberty (PYU-ber-tee) Process of maturing from child to young adult.

pubis (PYU-bis) Alternative name for the pubic bone.

puerperium (pyu-er-PEE-ree-um) Six-week period after birth in which the uterus involutes.

pulmonary (PULL-moh-NAR-ee) Pertaining to the lungs and their blood supply.

pulmonologist (PULL-moh-NOL-oh-jist) Medical specialist in pulmonary disorders.

pulmonology (PULL-moh-NOL-oh-gee) Study of the lungs, or the medical specialty of disorders of the respiratory tract.

pulp (PULP) Dental pulp is the connective tissue in the cavity in the center of the tooth.

pupil (PYU-pill) The opening in the center of the iris that allows light to reach the lens. Plural *pupillae*.

purge (PURJ) Consciously throw up, or cause bowel evacuation.

purification (PYUR-if-ih-kay-shun) Make free from pathogens.

Purkinje fibers (per-KIN-jee fi-BERS) Network of nerve fibers in the myocardium.

purpura (PUR-pyou-rah) Skin hemorrhages that are red initially, then turn purple.

purulent (PURE-you-lent) Showing or containing a lot of pus.

pustule (PUS-tyul) Small protuberance on the skin that contains pus.

pyelitis (pie-eh-LYE-tis) Inflammation of the renal pelvis.

pyelonephritis (PIE-eh-loh-neh-FRY-tis) Inflammation of the kidney and renal pelvis.

pylorus (pie-LOR-us) Exit area of the stomach.

pyogenes (PIE-o-jen-ese) Producing pus.

pyrexia (pie-REK-see-ah) An abnormally high body temperature or fever.

pyridoxine (pir-ih-DOK-seen) Vitamin B_6.

pyromania (pie-roh-MAY-nee-ah) Morbid impulse to set fires

Q

Qigong (CHEE-gong) Exercises and breathing routines performed daily.

quadrant (KWAD-rant) One-quarter of a circle.

quadrantectomy (kwad-ran-TEK-toe-me) Surgical excision of a quadrant of the breast.

quadriceps femoris (KWAD-rih-seps FEM-or-is) An anterior thigh muscle with four heads.

quadriplegia (kwad-rih-PLEE-jee-ah) Paralysis of all four limbs.

quantum physics (KWAHN-tum FIZ-iks) The study of subatomic particles.

quiescent (kwi-ESS-ent) Latent, dormant.

quinoa (kee-NO-ah) Plant with edible seeds high in protein.

R

rabid (RAB-id) Suffering from rabies.

rabies (RAY-beez) Highly fatal infectious disease transmitted by the bite of infected animals.

radial (RAY-dee-al) Pertaining to the forearm.

radiation (ray-dee-AY-shun) To spread out.

radical (RAD-ih-cal) Extensive removal of disease process.

radioactive (RAY-dee-oh-AK-tiv) Spontaneously emitting alpha, beta, or gamma rays.

radioactive iodine (RAY-dee-oh-AK-tiv EYE-oh-dine) Iodine-emitting alpha, beta, or gamma rays.

radionuclide (RAY-dee-oh-NYU-klide) Radioactive agent used in diagnostic imaging.

radius (RAY-dee-us) The forearm bone on the thumb side.

rale (RAHL) Crackle heard through a stethoscope when air bubbles through liquid in the lungs. Plural *rales*.

raphe (RAY-fee) Line separating two symmetrical structures.

rash (RASH) Cutaneous eruption.

reabsorption (ree-ab-SORP-shun) Take back into the blood substances that had previously been filtered out from it.

recessive gene (ree-SESS-iv JEEN) Allele that does not manifest as a trait or characteristic.

recombinant DNA (ree-KOM-bin-ant dee-en-a) DNA (deoxyribonucleic acid) altered by inserting a new sequence of DNA into the chain.

rectocele (REK-toe-seal) Hernia of the rectum into the vagina.

rectum (RECK-tum) Terminal part of the colon from the sigmoid to the anal canal.

reduction (ree-DUCK-shun) Restore a structure to its normal position.

reflex (REE-fleks) An involuntary response to a stimulus.

reflexology (ree-flek-SOL-oh-jee) Stimulation of reflexes in the feet and hands, which correspond to other parts of the body.

reflux (REE-fluks) Backward flow.

refract (ree-FRACT) Make a change in the direction of, or to bend, a ray of light.

regenerate (ree-JEN-eh-rate) Reconstitution of a lost part.

regimen (REJ-ih-men) Program of treatment.

regulation (reg-you-LAY-shun) Control of the way in which a process progresses.

regurgitate (ree-GUR-jih-tate) To flow backward; in this case, through a heart valve.

regurgitation (ree-gur-jih-TAY-shun) Expel contents of the stomach into the mouth, short of vomiting.

rehabilitation (REE-hah-bill-ih-**TAY**-shun) Therapeutic restoration of an ability to function as before.

Reiki (**RAY**-kee) Transfer of energy by placing hands on or near a patient.

remission (ree-**MISH**-un) Period when there is a lessening or absence of the symptoms of a disease.

remit (ree-**MIT**) To diminish in intensity.

renal (**REE**-nal) Pertaining to the kidney.

renin (**REE**-nin) Enzyme secreted by the kidney that causes vasoconstriction.

replication (rep-lih-**KAY**-shun) Reproduction to produce an exact copy.

reproductive (ree-pro-**DUC**-tiv) Relating to the process by which organisms produce offspring.

resection (ree-**SEK**-shun) Removal of a specific part of an organ or structure.

resectoscope (ree-**SEK**-toe-skope) Endoscope for transurethral removal of lesions.

residual (re-**ZID**-you-al) Pertaining to anything left over.

resistance (ree-**ZIS**-tants) Ability of an organism to withstand the effects of an antagonistic agent.

resistant (ree-**ZIS**-tant) Able to resist.

resorption (ree-**SORP**-shun) Loss of substance; in this case, bone.

respiration (RES-pih-**RAY**-shun) Fundamental process of life used to exchange oxygen and carbon dioxide.

respirator (RES-pir-**AY**-tor) Another name for *ventilator*.

restorative rehabilitation (ree-STOR-ah-tiv REE-hah-bill-ih-**TAY**-shun) Promote renewal of health and strength.

rete testis (**REE**-teh **TES**-tis) Network of tubules between the seminiferous tubules and the epididymis.

retention (ree-**TEN**-shun) Holding back in the body what should normally be discharged (e.g., urine).

reticulum (reh-**TIK**-you-lum) Fine network of cells in the medulla oblongata.

retina (**RET**-ih-nah) Light-sensitive innermost layer of the eyeball.

retinaculum (ret-ih-**NACK**-you-lum) Fibrous ligament that keeps the tendons in place on the wrist so that they do not "bowstring" when the forearm muscles contract.

retinoblastoma (**RET**-in-oh-blas-**TOE**-mah) Malignant neoplasm of primitive retinal cells.

retinoid (**RET**-ih-noyd) A class of keratolytic agents.

retinopathy (ret-ih-**NOP**-ah-thee) Degenerative disease of the retina.

retraction (ree-**TRAK**-shun) To pull back; in this case, the intercostal spaces and the neck above the clavicle.

retrograde (**RET**-roh-grade) Reversal of a normal flow; for example, back from the bladder into the ureters.

retroversion (reh-troh-**VER**-shun) Tipping backward of the uterus.

retrovert (**REH**-troh-vert) Tilted backward.

retrovirus (**REH**-troh-vie-rus) Virus with an RNA core.

Reye syndrome (RAY **SIN**-drome) Encephalopathy and liver damage in children following an acute viral illness; linked to aspirin use.

rhabdomyolysis (RAB-doh-my-oh-**LIE**-sis) Destruction of muscle to produce myoglobin.

rhabdomyosarcoma (RAB-doh-**MY**-oh-sar-**KOH**-mah) Cancer derived from skeletal muscle.

rheumatism (**RU**-mat-izm) Pain in various parts of the musculoskeletal system.

rheumatoid arthritis (RA) (**RU**-mah-toyd ar-**THRI**-tis) Disease of connective tissue, with arthritis as a major manifestation.

rhinitis (rye-**NI**-tis) Inflammation of the nasal mucosa. Also called *coryza*.

rhoncus (**RONG**-kuss) Wheezing sound heard on auscultation of the lungs; made by air passing through a constricted lumen. Plural *rhonci*.

riboflavin (**RYE**-boh-flay-vin) Vitamin B_2.

ribonucleic acid (RNA) (**RYE**-boh-nyu-**KLEE**-ik **ASS**-id) Information carrier from DNA in the nucleus to the ribosome to produce protein molecules.

ribosome (**RYE**-bo-sohm) Structure in the cell that assembles amino acids into protein.

rickets (**RICK**-ets) Disease due to vitamin D deficiency, producing soft, flexible bones.

rigidity (ri-**JID**-ih-tee) Increased muscle tone at rest.

Rinne test (**RIN**-eh TEST) Test for conductive hearing loss.

ritual (**RITCH**-you-al) An activity or set of activities established and repeated.

Rolfing (**ROLF**-ing) Manipulation of connective tissue to realign and balance the whole body.

root (ROOT) Fundamental or beginning part of a structure.

rooting (rue-**TING**) A neonatal reflex to turn toward and open the mouth when a nipple is placed on the cheek.

rosacea (roh-**ZAY**-she-ah) Persistent erythematous rash of the central face.

roseola infantum (roh-**ZEE**-oh-lah in-**FAN**-tum) Disease of infants and young children caused by a herpesvirus.

rotator cuff (roh-**TAY**-tor CUFF) Part of the capsule of the shoulder joint.

Roux-en-Y (**ROO**-on-Y) Surgical procedure to reduce the size of the stomach.

ruga (**ROO**-ga) A fold, ridge, or crease. Plural *rugae*.

rumination (**ROO**-min-ay-shun) To bring back food into the mouth to chew over and over.

rupture (**RUP**-tyur) Break or tear of any organ or body part.

S

sacral (**SAY**-kral) In the neighborhood of the sacrum.

sacroiliac joint (say-kroh-**ILL**-ih-ak JOINT) The joint between the sacrum and ilium.

sacrum (**SAY**-crum) Segment of the vertebral column that forms part of the pelvis.

sagittal (SAJ-ih-tal) Plane vertically through the body dividing it into right and left portions.

saliva (sa-LIE-vah) Secretion in mouth from salivary glands.

Salmonella (sal-moh-NELL-ah) Pathogenic gram-negative rods causing dysentery.

salpingitis (sal-pin-JIE-tis) Inflammation of the uterine tube.

sanitization (SAN-ih-tih-ZAY-shun) Process of using chemicals to remove pathogens from surfaces.

saphenous (SAPH-ih-nus) Relating to the saphenous vein in the thigh.

saponins (SAP-oh-nins) Phytochemicals that can prevent cancer cell replication.

sarcoidosis (sar-koy-DOH-sis) Granulomatous lesions of the lungs and other organs; cause is unknown.

sarcoma (sar-KOH-mah) A malignant tumor originating in connective tissue.

saturated fatty acid (satch-you-RAY-ted FAT-ee ASS-id) Incapable of absorbing any more hydrogen.

scab (SKAB) Crust that forms over a wound or sore during healing.

scabies (SKAY-bees) Skin disease produced by mites.

scapula (SKAP-you-lah) Shoulder blade. Plural *scapulae.*

scar (SKAR) Fibrotic seam that forms when a wound heals.

schizoid (SKITZ-oyd) Withdrawn, socially isolated.

schizophrenia (skitz-oh-FREE-nee-ah) Disorder of perception, thought, emotion, and behavior.

Schwann cell (SHWANN SELL) Connective tissue cell of the peripheral nervous system that forms a myelin sheath.

scintigraphy (sin-TIG-rah-fee) Recording of radioactivity with a special camera.

sclera (SKLAIR-ah) Fibrous outer covering of the eyeball and the white of the eye.

scleritis (sklair-RI-tis) Inflammation of the sclera.

scleroderma (sklair-oh-DERM-ah) Thickening and hardening of the skin due to new collagen formation.

sclerotherapy (SKLAIR-oh-THAIR-ah-pee) Injection of a solution into a vein to thrombose it.

scoliosis (sko-lee-OH-sis) An abnormal lateral curvature of the vertebral column.

scrotal (SKRO-tal) Pertaining to the scrotum.

scrotum (SKRO-tum) Sac containing testes.

scurvy (SKUR-vee) Deficiency of vitamin C.

seasonal affective disorder (see-ZON-al af-FEK-tiv dis-OR-der) Depression that occurs at the same time every year, often in winter.

sebaceous glands (se-BAY-shus GLANZ) Glands in the dermis that open into hair follicles and secrete an oily fluid called sebum.

seborrhea (seb-oh-REE-ah) Excessive amount of sebum.

sebum (SEE-bum) Waxy secretion of the sebaceous glands.

secrete (se-KREET) To produce a chemical substance in a cell and release it from the cell.

secretin (se-KREE-tin) Hormone produced by the duodenum to stimulate pancreatic juice.

sedation (se-DAY-shun) State of being calmed.

sedative (SED-ah-tiv) Agent that calms nervous excitement.

sedentary (sed-en-TER-ee) Accustomed to little exercise or movement.

sediment (SED-ih-ment) Insoluble material that settles to the bottom of a liquid.

sedimentation (SED-ih-men-TAY-shun) Formation of a sediment.

segment (SEG-ment) A section of an organ or structure.

segmentectomy (seg-men-TEK-toe-me) Surgical excision of a segment of a tissue or organ.

seizure (SEE-zhur) Event due to excessive electrical activity in the brain.

self-examination (SELF-ek-zam-ih-NAY-shun) Conduct an examination of one's own body.

self-mutilation (self-myu-tih-LAY-shun) Injury or disfigurement made to one's own body.

semen (SEE-men) Penile ejaculate containing sperm and seminal fluid.

semilunar (sem-ee-LOO-nar) Appear like a half moon.

seminal vesicle (SEM-in-al VES-ih-kull) Sac of the ductus deferens that produces seminal fluid.

seminiferous (sem-ih-NIF-er-us) Pertaining to carrying semen.

seminiferous tubule (sem-ih-NIF-er-us TU-byul) Coiled tubes in the testes that produce sperm.

seminoma (sem-ih-NO-mah) Neoplasm of germ cells of a testis.

semipermeable (sem-ee-PER-me-ah-bull) Freely permeable to water but not to solutes.

semipermeable membrane (sem-ee-PER-me-ah-bull MEM-brain) A membrane that allows only certain substances to pass through it.

senescence (se-NES-ens) The state of being old.

senile (SEE-nile) Characteristic of old age.

senility (se-NIL-ih-tee) Old age.

sensation (sen-SAY-shun) The conscious feeling of the effects of a stimulation.

sensorineural hearing loss (SEN-sor-ih-NYUR-al) Hearing loss caused by lesions of the inner ear or the auditory nerve.

sensory (SEN-so-ree) Pertaining to sensation; structures of the nervous system that carry impulses to the brain.

sepsis (SEP-sis) Presence of pathogenic organisms or their toxins in blood or tissues.

septicemia (sep-tih-SEE-mee-ah) Microorganisms circulating in, and infecting, the blood (blood poisoning).

septum (SEP-tum) A wall dividing two cavities. Plural *septa.*

sequence (SEE-kwens) The succession of one event after another.

sequential (see-KWEN-shal) One event following after another.

serosa (seh-ROH-sa) Outermost covering of the alimentary tract.

serotonin (ser-oh-**TOE**-nin) A neurotransmitter in the central and peripheral nervous systems.

serous (**SEER**-us) Thicker and less transparent than water.

serum (**SEER**-um) Fluid remaining after removal of cells and fibrin clot.

sewage (**SOO**-aje) Waste matter from populated areas.

sharps (**SHARPS**) Any medical instrument capable of puncturing skin.

sharps container (**SHARPS** kon-**TAY**-ner) Puncture-resistant container for disposal of sharps.

Shigella (she-**GEL**-ah) Genus of gram-negative rods.

shigellosis (shig-eh-**LOH**-sis) Dysentery caused by *Shigella*.

shock (**SHOCK**) Sudden physical or mental collapse or circulatory collapse.

shunt (**SHUNT**) A bypass or diversion of fluid; in this case, blood.

sibling (**SIB**-ling) Brother or sister.

sigmoid (**SIG**-moyd) Sigmoid colon is shaped like an "S."

sigmoidoscopy (sig-moi-**DOS**-koh-pee) Endoscopic examination of the sigmoid colon.

silicosis (sil-ih-**KOH**-sis) Fibrotic lung disease from inhaling silica particles.

simian crease (sih-**ME**-an **KREES**) Single crease across the palm of the hand; found in monkeys.

simulate (**SIM**-you-late) To imitate a disease process.

sinoatrial (SA) node (sigh-noh-**AY**-tree-al **NODE**) The mass of modified cardiac muscle fibers in the wall of the right atrium that acts as the pacemaker for the heart rhythm.

sinus rhythm (**SIGH**-nus **RITH**-um) The normal (optimal) heart rhythm arising from the sinoatrial node.

Sjögren syndrome (**SHOW**-gren **SIN**-drome) Autoimmune disease that attacks the glands that produce saliva and tears.

Skene glands (**SKEEN GLANZ**) Paraurethral glands in the anterior wall of the vagina. Also called *paraurethral glands.*

smegma (**SMEG**-ma) Oily material produced by the glans and prepuce.

Snellen letter chart (**SNEL**-en) Test for acuity of distant vision.

snore (**SNOR**) Noise produced by vibrations in the structures of the nasopharynx.

sociopath (**SO**-see-oh-path) Person with antisocial personality disorder.

soleus (**SO**-lee-us) Large muscle of the calf.

somatic (soh-**MAT**-ik) Relating to the body in general, or a division of the periperal nervous system serving the skeletal muscles.

somatoform (soh-**MAT**-oh-form) Physical symptoms occurring without identifiable physical cause.

somatostatin (**SO**-mah-toh-**STAT**-in) Hormone that inhibits release of growth hormone and insulin.

somatotropin (**SO**-mah-toh-**TROH**-pin) Hormone of the anterior pituitary that stimulates growth of body tissues. Also called *growth hormone.*

sonogram (**SON**-oh-gram) Image obtained by using a sonograph.

sonograph (**SON**-oh-graf) Instrument that uses sound waves to create images of structures.

sonographer (so-**NOG**-rah-fer) The technician who performs a sonogram.

sorbitol (**SOR**-bih-tol) Alcohol derivative of glucose.

spasm (**SPASM**) Sudden involuntary contraction of a muscle group.

spasmodic (spaz-**MOD**-ik) Intermittent contractions.

spastic (**SPAZ**-tik) Increased muscle tone on movement.

species (**SPEE**-sheez) A group of organisms that bear a strong resemblance to each other.

specific (speh-**SIF**-ik) Relating to a particular entity.

specificity (spes-ih-**FIS**-ih-tee) State of having a fixed relation to a particular entity.

sperm (**SPERM**) Mature male sex cell. Also called *spermatozoon.*

spermatid (**SPER**-ma-tid) A cell late in the development process of sperm.

spermatocele (**SPER**-mat-oh-seal) Cyst of the epididymis that contains sperm.

spermatogenesis (**SPER**-mat-oh-**JEN**-eh-sis) The process by which male germ cells differentiate into sperm.

spermatozoa (**SPER**-mat-oh-**ZOH**-ah) Sperm (plural of spermatozoon).

spermicide (**SPER**-mih-side) Agent that destroys sperm.

sphenoid (**SFEE**-noyd) Wedge-shaped bone at the base of the skull.

spherocyte (**SFEAR**-oh-site) A spherical cell.

spherocytosis (**SFEAR**-oh-site-oh-sis) Presence of spherocytes in the blood.

sphincter (**SFINK**-ter) Band of muscle that encircles an opening; when it contracts, the opening squeezes closed.

sphygmomanometer (**SFIG**-moh-mah-**NOM**-ih-ter) Instrument for measuring arterial blood pressure.

spina bifida (**SPY**-nah **BIH**-fi-dah) Failure of one or more vertebral arches to close during fetal development.

spina bifida cystica (**SIS**-tik-ah) Meninges and spinal cord protruding through the absent vertebral arch and having the appearance of a cyst.

spina bifida occulta (**OH**-kul-tah) The deformity is not apparent from the surface.

spinal tap (**SPY**-nal **TAP**) Placement of a needle through an intervertebral space into the subarachnoid space to withdraw CSF.

spine (**SPINE**) Vertebral column *or* a short projection from a bone.

spiral fracture (**SPY**-ral **FRAK**-chur) A fracture in the shape of a coil.

spirituality (**SPEAR**-ih-choo-**AL**-ity) Meaning to life that comes from the spirit or soul rather than the physical body.

spirochete (**SPY**-roh-keet) Spiral-shaped bacterium causing a sexually transmitted disease (syphilis).

spirometer (spy-**ROM**-eh-ter) An instrument used to measure respiratory volumes.

spirometry (spy-**ROM**-eh-tree) Use of a spirometer.

spirulina (spy-roo-**LEE**-nah) Commercial product of blue-green algae containing 60 to 70% protein.

spleen (SPLEEN) Vascular, lymphatic organ in the left upper quadrant of the abdomen.

splenectomy (sple-**NECK**-toe-me) Surgical removal of the spleen.

splenomegaly (sple-noh-**MEG**-ah-lee) Enlarged spleen.

spondylosis (spon-dih-**LOH**-sis) Degenerative osteoarthritis of the spine.

spongiform (**SPON**-jih-form) Looking like a sponge.

spongiosum (spun-jee-**OH**-sum) Spongelike tissue.

spore (SPOR) Generic term for any tiny compact cell produced during reproduction by bacteria.

sprain (SPRAIN) A wrench or tear in a ligament.

sputum (**SPYU**-tum) Matter coughed up and spat out by individuals with respiratory disorders.

squamous cell (**SKWAY**-mus SELL) Flat, scalelike epithelial cell.

stage (STAYJ) Definition of the extent and dissemination of a malignant neoplasm.

staging (**STAY**-jing) Process of determination of the extent of the distribution of a neoplasm.

stapes (**STAY**-peas) Inner (medial) one of the three ossicles of the middle ear; shaped like a stirrup.

Staphylococcus (**STAF**-ih-loh-**KOK**-us) Genus of gram-positive bacteria that divide in more than one plane to form clusters. Plural *staphylococci.*

starch (STARCH) Complex carbohydrate made of multiple units of glucose attached together.

status (**STAT**-us) A state or condition

status epilepticus (**STAT**-us ep-ih-**LEP**-tik-us) Latin phrase for being in a prolonged or recurrent seizure for longer than a specific time frame.

stem cell (STEM SELL) Undifferentiated cell found in a differentiated tissue that can divide to yield the specialized cells in that tissue.

stenosis (ste-**NOH**-sis) Narrowing of a passage.

stent (STENT) Wire mesh tube used to keep arteries open.

stereopsis (ster-ee-**OP**-sis) Three-dimensional vision.

stereotactic (**STER**-ee-oh-**TAK**-tic) A precise three-dimensional method to locate a lesion.

stereotype (**STER**-ee-oh-tipe) An image held in common by members of a group.

sterile (**STER**-isle) Free from all living organisms and their spores, or unable to fertilize or reproduce.

sterility (steh-**RIL**-ih-tee) Inability to reproduce.

sterilization (**STER**-ih-lih-**ZAY**-shun) Process of making sterile.

sterilize (**STER**-ih-lize) To make sterile.

sternum (**STIR**-num) Long, flat bone forming the center of the anterior wall of the chest.

steroid (**STER**-oyd) Large family of chemical substances found in many drugs, hormones, and body components.

stethoscope (**STETH**-oh-skope) Instrument for listening to cardiac and respiratory sounds.

stimulant (**STIM**-you-lant) Agent that excites or strengthens functional activity.

stimulation (stim-you-**LAY**-shun) Arousal to increased functional activity.

stoma (**STOW**-mah) Artificial opening.

strabismus (strah-**BIZ**-mus) Turning of an eye away from its normal position.

strain (STRAIN) Overstretch or tear in a muscle or tendon.

stratum basale (**STRAH**-tum ba-**SAL**-eh) Deepest layer of the epidermis, from which the other cells originate and migrate.

Streptococcus (strep-toe-**KOK**-us) Genus of gram-positive bacteria that grow in chains. Plural *streptococci.*

streptokinase (strep-toe-**KI**-nase) An enzyme that dissolves clots.

striated muscle (**STRI**-ay-ted **MUSS**-el) Another term for skeletal muscle.

striation (stri-**AY**-shun) Stripes.

stricture (**STRICK**-shur) Narrowing of a tube.

stridor (**STRY**-door) High-pitched noise made when there is a respiratory obstruction in the larynx or trachea.

stroke (STROHK) Acute clinical event caused by an impaired cerebral circulation.

stroma (**STROH**-mah) Connective tissue framework that supports the parenchyma of an organ or gland.

subarachnoid space (sub-ah-**RACK**-noyd SPASE) Space between the pia mater and the arachnoid membrane.

subclavian (sub-**CLAY**-vee-an) Underneath the clavicle.

subcutaneous (sub-kew-**TAY**-nee-us) Below the skin. Also known as *hypodermic.*

sublingual (sub-**LING**-wal) Underneath the tongue.

subluxation (sub-luck-**SAY**-shun) An incomplete dislocation when some contact between the joint surfaces remains.

submandibular (sub-man-**DIB**-you-lar) Underneath the mandible.

submucosa (sub-mew-**KOH**-sa) Tissue layer underneath the mucosa.

substernal (sub-**STER**-nal) Under the sternum or breastbone.

sucrose (**SUE**-krose) Table sugar.

suction (**SUK**-shun) Use of a catheter to clear the upper airway or other tubes.

sugar (**SHUH**-gar) Basic carbohydrate; term sometimes used for glucose or sucrose.

suicidal (**SOO**-ih-**SIGH**-dal) Wanting to kill oneself.

suicide (**SOO**-ih-side) Kill oneself.

sulcus (**SUL**-cuss) Groove on the surface of the cerebral hemispheres that separates gyri. Plural *sulci.*

superior (soo-**PEE**-ree-or) Situated above.

supinate (SOO-pih-nate) Rotate the forearm so that the surface of the palm faces anteriorly in the anatomic position.

supination (soo-pih-NAY-shun) Process of lying face upward or turning an arm or foot so that the palm or sole is facing up.

supine (soo-PINE) Lying face up, flat on your spine.

supplement (SUH-pleh-ment) Substance taken to remedy or prevent a deficiency.

suprapubic (SOO-prah-pyu-bik) Above the symphysis pubis.

surfactant (ser-FAK-tant) A protein and fat compound that creates surface tension to hold lung alveolar walls apart.

susceptible (suh-SEP-tih-bill) Capable of being affected by.

suture (SOO-chur) Two bones are joined together by a fibrous band continuous with their periosteum, as in the skull, or stitch to hold the edges of a wound together. Plural *sutures*.

swab (SWOB) Wad of cotton used to remove or apply something from/to a surface.

sympathetic (sim-pah-THET-ik) Division of the autonomic nervous system operating at an unconscious level.

sympathy (SIM-pa-thee) Appreciation and concern for another person's mental and emotional state.

symphysis (SIM-feh-sis) Two bones joined by fibrocartilage. Plural *symphyses*.

symptom (SIMP-tum) Departure from the normal experienced by a patient.

symptomatic (simp-toe-MAT-ik) Relating to the symptoms of a disease.

synapse (SIN-aps) Junction between two nerve cells, or a nerve fiber and its target cell where electrical impulses are transmitted between the cells.

synchondrosis (sin-kon-DROH-sis) Binding together of joint with cartilage. Plural *synchondroses*.

syncytium (sin-SISH-ee-um) A multinucleated mass not separated into cells.

syndesmosis (sin-dez-MOH-sis) Binding together of two bones with ligaments. Plural *syndesmoses*.

synergist (SIN-er-jist) Agent or process that aids the action of another.

synovial (si-NOH-vee-al) Pertaining to synovial fluid and synovial membrane.

synthesis (SIN-the-sis) The process of building a compound from different elements.

synthetic (sin-THET-ik) Built up or put together from simpler compounds.

syphilis (SIF-ih-lis) Sexually transmitted disease caused by a spirochete.

syringomyelia (si-RING-oh-my-EE-lee-ah) Abnormal longitudinal cavities in the spinal cord cause paresthesias and muscle weakness.

systemic (sis-TEM-ik) Relating to the entire organism.

systemic lupus erythematosus (sis-TEM-ik LOO-pus er-ih-THEE-mah-toe-sus) Inflammatory connective tissue disease affecting the whole body.

systole (SIS-toe-lee) Contraction of the heart muscle.

T

tachycardia (tak-ih-KAR-dee-ah) Rapid heart rate (above 100 beats per minute).

tachypnea (tak-ip-NEE-ah) Rapid breathing.

tactile (TAK-tile) Relating to touch.

tai chi (tie-CHEE) Defined series of postures performed in fluid movement.

talipes (TAL-ip-eze) Deformity of the foot involving the talus.

talus (TAY-luss) The tarsal bone that articulates with the tibia to form the ankle joint.

tampon (TAM-pon) Plug or pack in a cavity to absorb or stop bleeding.

tamponade (tam-po-NAID) Pathologic compression of an organ such as the heart.

tangent (TAN-jent) Sudden change of course.

tangentiality (tan-jen-she-AL-ih-tee) Thought processes move rapidly and superficially from one topic to another.

tapeworm (TAPEWORM) Intestinal parasitic worm.

tarsus (TAR-sus) The collection of seven bones in the foot that form the ankle and instep, or the flat fibrous plate that gives shape to the outer edges of the eyelids.

tartar (TAR-tar) Calcified deposit at the gingival margin of the teeth.

taste (TAYST) Sensation from chemicals on the taste buds.

Tay-Sachs disease (TAY-SAKS diz-EEZ) Congenital fatal disorder of fat metabolism.

temperament (TEM-per-ah-ment) Predisposition to character or personality.

temporal (TEM-por-al) Bone that forms part of the base and sides of the skull.

temporal lobe (TEM-por-al LOBE) Posterior two-thirds of the cerebral hemispheres.

temporalis muscle (tem-poh-RAHL-is MUSS-el) Muscle attached to the temporal bone that opens and closes the jaw.

temporomandibular joint (TMJ) (TEM-por-oh-man-DIB-you-lar JOYNT) The joint between the temporal bone and the mandible.

tendinitis (ten-dih-NYE-tis) Inflammation of a tendon. Also spelled *tendonitis*.

tendon (TEN-dun) Fibrous band that connects muscle to bone.

tenosynovitis (TEN-oh-sin-oh-VIE-tis) Inflammation of a tendon and its surrounding sheath.

teratogen (TER-ah-toe-jen) Agent that produces fetal deformities.

teratogenesis (TER-ah-toe-JEN-eh-sis) Process involved in producing fetal deformities.

teratoma (ter-ah-TOE-mah) Neoplasm of a testis or ovary containing multiple tissues from other sites in the body.

testicle (TES-tih-kul) One of the male reproductive glands. Also called *testis*.

testicular (tes-TICK-you-lar) Pertaining to the testicle.

testis (TES-tis) A synonym for testicle. Plural *testes*.

testosterone (tes-TOSS-ter-own) Powerful androgen produced by the testes.

tetany (TET-ah-nee) Severe muscle twitches, cramps, and spasms.

tetralogy (te-TRAL-oh-jee) A set of four congenital heart defects.

tetralogy of Fallot (TOF) (te-TRAL-oh-jee of fah-LOW) Set of four congenital heart defects occurring together.

thalamus (THAL-ah-mus) Mass of gray matter underneath the ventricle in each cerebral hemisphere.

thalassemia (thal-ah-SEE-mee-ah) Group of inherited blood disorders that produce a hemolytic anemia.

thelarche (thee-LAR-key) Onset of breast development.

thenar (THAY-nar) The thenar eminence is the fleshy mass at the base of the thumb.

therapeutic (THAIR-ah-PYU-tik) Relating to the treatment of a disease or disorder.

therapy (THAIR-ah-pee) Systematic treatment of a disease, dysfunction, or disorder.

thermotherapy (THER-moh-THAIR-ah-pee) The use of heat in treatment.

thiamine (THIGH-ah-min) Vitamin B_1.

thoracentesis (THOR-ah-sen-TEE-sis) Insertion of a needle into the pleural cavity to withdraw fluid or air. Also called *pleural tap*.

thoracic (THOR-ass-ik) Relating to the chest (thorax).

thoracoscopy (thor-ah-KOS-koh-pee) Examination of the pleural cavity with an endoscope.

thoracotomy (thor-ah-KOT-oh-me) Incision through the chest wall.

thorax (THO-racks) The part of the trunk between the abdomen and neck.

thrombin (THROM-bin) Enzyme that forms fibrin.

thrombocyte (THROM-boh-site) Another name for a platelet.

thrombocytopenia (THROM-boh-site-oh-PEE-nee-uh) Deficiency of platelets in circulating blood.

thromboembolism (THROM-boh-EM-boh-lizm) A piece of detached blood clot (embolus) blocking a distant blood vessel.

thrombolysis (throm-BOL-ih-sis) Dissolving a thrombus (clot).

thrombophlebitis (THROM-boh-fleh-BY-tis) Inflammation of a vein with clot formation.

thrombosis (throm-BOH-sis) Formation of a thrombus.

thrombus (THROM-bus) A clot attached to a diseased blood vessel or heart lining.

thrush (THRUSH) Infection with *Candida albicans*.

thymectomy (thigh-MEK-toe-me) Surgical removal of the thyroid gland.

thymine (THIGH-meen) Chemical found in DNA but not RNA.

thymoma (thigh-MOH-mah) Benign tumor of the thymus.

thyroid (THIGH-royd) Gland in the neck, or a cartilage of the larynx.

thyroid hormone (THIGH-royd HOR-mohn) Collective term for the two thyroid hormones, T_3 and T_4.

thyroid storm (THIGH-royd STORM) Medical crisis and emergency due to excess thyroid hormones.

thyroidectomy (thigh-roy-DEK-toe-me) Surgical removal of the thyroid gland.

thyroiditis (thigh-roy-DIE-tis) Inflammation of the thyroid gland.

thyrotoxicosis (THIGH-roe-toks-ih-KOH-sis) Disorder produced by excessive thyroid hormone production.

thyrotropin (thigh-roe-TROH-pin) Hormone from the anterior pituitary gland that stimulates function of the thyroid gland.

thyroxine (thigh-ROCK-sin) Thyroid hormone, T_4, tetraiodothyronine.

tibia (TIB-ee-ah) The larger bone of the lower leg.

tic (TIK) Sudden, involuntary, repeated contraction of muscles.

tic douloureux (tik duh-luh-RUE) Painful, sudden, spasmodic involuntary contractions of the facial muscles supplied by the trigeminal nerve. Also called *trigeminal neuralgia*.

tinea (TIN-ee-ah) General term for a group of related skin infections caused by different species of fungi.

tinnitus (TIN-ih-tus) Persistent ringing, whistling, clicking, or booming noise in the ears.

tissue (TISH-you) Collection of similar cells.

titer (TIE-ter) The strength of a substance in a solution as compared to a standard.

tolerance (TOL-er-ants) Become accustomed to a stimulus or drug.

tomography (toe-MOG-rah-fee) Radiographic image of a selected slice of tissue.

tone (TONE) Tension present in resting muscles.

tongue (TUNG) Mobile muscle mass in the mouth; bears the taste buds.

tonic (TON-ik) State of muscular contraction.

tonic-clonic (TON-ik KLON-ik) The body alternates between excessive muscular rigidity (tonic) and jerking muscular contractions (clonic).

tonic-clonic seizure (TON-ik-KLON-ik SEE-zhur) Generalized seizure due to epileptic activity in all or most of the brain.

tonometer (toe-NOM-eh-ter) Instrument for determining intraocular pressure.

tonometry (toe-NOM-eh-tree) The measurement of intraocular pressure.

tonsil (TON-sill) Mass of lymphoid tissue on either side of the throat at the back of the tongue.

tonsillectomy (ton-sih-LEC-toh-me) Surgical removal of the tonsils.

tonsillitis (ton-sih-LIE-tis) Inflammation of the tonsils.

topical (TOP-ih-kal) Medication applied to the skin to obtain a local effect.

torsion (TOR-shun) The act or result of twisting.

villus (**VILL**-us) Thin, hairlike projection, particularly of a mucous membrane lining a cavity. Plural *villae*.

virilism (**VIR**-ih-lizm) Development of masculine characteristics by a woman or girl.

virulence (**VIR**-you-lence) The power of a toxin or pathogen.

virulent (**VIR**-you-lent) Extremely toxic or pathogenic.

virus (**VIE**-rus) Group of infectious agents that require living cells for growth and reproduction.

viscera (**VISS**-er-ah) Internal organs, particularly in the abdomen.

visceral (**VISS**-er-al) Pertaining to the internal organs.

viscosity (vis-**KOS**-ih-tee) The resistance of a fluid to flow.

viscous (**VISS**-kus) Sticky fluid that is resistant to flow.

viscus (**VISS**-kus) Hollow, walled, internal organ.

visual acuity (**VIH**-zhoo-wal ah-**KYU**-ih-tee) Sharpness and clearness of vision.

visualization (**VIH**-zhoo-wah-lih-**ZAY**-shun) Form mental images or pictures.

vitamin (**VYE**-tah-min) Essential organic substance necessary in small amounts for normal cell function.

vitiligo (vit-ill-**EYE**-go) Nonpigmented white patches on otherwise normal skin.

vitreous (**VIT**-ree-us) Vitreous humor is a gelatinous liquid in the posterior cavity of the eyeball with the appearance of glass.

vocal (**VOH**-kal) Pertaining to the voice.

void (VOYD) To evacuate urine or feces.

voluntary muscle (**VOL**-un-tare-ee **MUSS**-el) Muscle that is under the control of the will.

vomer (**VOH**-mer) Lower nasal septum.

vulva (**VUL**-vah) Female external genitalia.

vulvodynia (vul-voh-**DIN**-ee-uh) Chronic vulvar pain.

vulvovaginal (**VUL**-voh-**VAJ**-ih-nal) Pertaining to the vulva and vagina.

vulvovaginitis (**VUL**-voh-vaj-ih-**NIE**-tis) Inflammation of the vagina and vulva.

W

warfarin (**WAR**-fuh-rin) Anticoagulant; also used as rat poison, tradename Coumadin.

Weber test (**VA**-ber TEST) Test for sensorineural hearing loss.

wheal (WHEEL) Small, itchy swelling of the skin. Wheals raised by an injection do not itch. Also called *hives*.

white matter (WITE **MATT**-er) Regions of the brain and spinal cord occupied by bundles of axons.

whooping cough (**WHO**-ping KAWF) Infectious disease with spasmodic, intense cough ending on a whoop (stridor). Also called *pertussis*.

Wilms tumor (WILMZ **TOO**-mor) Cancerous kidney tumor of childhood. Also known as *nephroblastoma*.

wound (WOOND) Any injury that interrupts the continuity of skin or a mucous membrane.

X

xenograft (**ZEN**-oh-graft) A graft from another species. Also known as *heterograft*.

Y

yeast (YEEST) Microscopic fungus.

yoga (**YOH**-gah) A system of lifestyle measures.

yolk sac (YOKE SACK) Source of blood cells and future sex cells for the fetus.

Z

zeaxanthine (**ZEE**-ah-**ZAN**-thin) Carotenoid found in pepper, corn, and spinach.

zygoma (zye-**GOH**-mah) Bone that forms the prominence of the cheek.

zygote (**ZYE**-goat) Cell resulting from the union of the sperm and egg.

PHOTOS

FRONT MATTER

Opener: © The McGraw-Hill Companies, Inc./Rick Brady, photographer; **pg. iii (top right):** © Autumn Paul; (center right): © Feragne Portrait Studio; **pg. xix (bottom right):** © BananaStock/Jupiter Images; **pg. xvi (right):** © Royalty-Free/Corbis; **pg. xvii (top left):** © Vol. 69 PhotoDisc/Getty; **pg. xviii (top right):** © Vol. 107 PhotoDisc/Getty.

WELCOME CHAPTER

Opener, W.1-W.7, W.9, W.12, W.14: © The McGraw-Hill Companies, Inc./Rick Brady, photographer; **W.11:** © Corbis RF; **W.1-CR (pg.W.10):** © Vol. 115 PhotoDisc/Getty; **W.13:** © Vol. 66 PhotoDisc/Getty; **W.15:** © Dynamicgraphics/Jupiter RF; **W.16:** © Vol. 15 PhotoDisc/Getty.

CHAPTER 1

Opener: © The McGraw-Hill Companies, Inc./Rick Brady, photographer.

CHAPTER 2

Opener: © Corbis RF; **2.2:** © Francis Leroy, BIOCOSMOS/Photo Researchers Inc.; **2.7:** © The McGraw-Hill Companies, Inc./Al Telser, photographer; **2.10, 2.11:** © The McGraw-Hill Companies, Inc./Eric Wise, photographer; **2.12, 2.14a, 2.14b:** © The McGraw-Hill Companies, Inc./Joe DeGrandis.

CHAPTER 3

Opener: © The McGraw-Hill Companies, Inc./Rick Brady, photographer; **3.4, 3.5:** © BioPhoto Associates/Photo Researchers Inc.; **3.6:** © James Stevenson/Photo Researchers Inc.; **3.8:** © The McGraw-Hill Companies, Inc./Dennis Strete, photographer; **3.11:** © Medical-on-line/Alamy; **3.12:** © Dr. P. Marazzi/SPL/Photo Researchers Inc.; **3.13:** © Kenneth Greer/Visuals Unlimited; **3.14:** © Logical Images/Custom Medical Stock Photos; **3.15:** © SPL/Photo Researchers Inc.; **3.16:** © Dr. P. Marazzi/SPL/Photo Researchers Inc.; **3.17:** ©Meckes/Ottawa/Photo Researchers Inc.; **3.18:** © Diepgen T.L., Yihume G., et al. *Dermatology Online Atlas* published online at www.dermis.net. Reprinted by permissions; **3.19:** Courtesy Dr. Maureen Mayes; **3.20:** © Mediscan/Visuals Unlimited; **3.21:** © Medical-on-line/Alamy; **3.23:** © Kenneth Greer/Visuals Unlimited; **3.25(all):** © The McGraw-Hill Companies, Inc./Joe DeGrandis, photographer; **3.28:** Reprinted from J. Walter Wilson, *Fungous Diseases of Man*, Plate 42 (middle right), © 1965, The Regents of the University of California; **3.29:** © Logical Images/Custom Medical Stock Photo; **3.30a:** © Sheila Terry/Photo Researchers Inc.; **3.30b:** © Dr. P. Marazzi/SPL/Photo Researchers Inc.; **3.30c:** © John Radcliffe Hospital/Photo Researchers Inc.; **3.39:** © Kenneth Greer/Visuals Unlimited.

CHAPTER 4

Opener: © The McGraw-Hill Companies, Inc./Rick Brady, photographer; **4.1b:** © The McGraw-Hill Companies, Inc./Joe DeGrandis, photographer; **4.3:** PHOTOTAKE Inc./Alamy; **4.4:** © Western Ophthamolic Hospital/Photo Researchers Inc.; **4.5:** Levin AV, Rootman D, Heon E, and Buncic JR. Ophthamology.

In *Atlas of Pediatrics*, Edited by Laxer RM, Ford-Jones EL, Friedman JN and Gerstle JT. Current Medicine, Philadelphia, 2005: 205; **4.6:** © Mediscan; **4.7:** © ISM/Phototake; **4.9:** © BioPhoto Associates/Photo Researchers Inc.; **4.10:** © Matt Harris photography/Alamy; **4.18:** PHOTOTAKE Inc./Alamy; **4.19:** National Eye Institute, National Institutes of Health; **4.20:** © Dr. P. Marazzi/Photo Researchers Inc.; **4.21:** National Eye Institute, National Institutes of Health; **4.22:** © Paul Parker/Photo Researchers Inc; **4.23:** © Vol. 58/PhotoDisc/Getty; **4.24:** © Chris Barry/Phototake; **4.25:** National Eye Institute, National Institutes of Health; **4.26:** © Lisa Klancher; **4.29a:** © The McGraw-Hill Companies, Inc./Rick Brady, photographer; **4.29b:** Courtesy Richmond Products Inc.; **4.30:** © St. Bartholomew's Hospital/Photo Researchers, Inc.; **4.35:** © ISM/Phototake; **4.37:** © Lester V. Bergman/Corbis; **4.38:** © ISM/Phototake; **4.39:** © Collection CNRI/Phototake; **4.40:** © ISM/Phototake.

CHAPTER 5

Opener: © The McGraw-Hill Companies, Inc./Rick Brady, photographer; **5.2a:** © The McGraw-Hill Companies, Inc./Christine Eckel, photographer; **5.4:** © Dr. Michael Klein/Peter Arnold Inc.; **5.5:** © The McGraw-Hill Companies, Inc./Joe DeGrandis, photographer; **5.6:** Dr. Francis Collins; **5.8:** © SPL/Photo Researchers Inc.; **5.9:** © SIU/Visuals Limited; **5.14(all):** © The McGraw-Hill Companies, Inc./Tim Vacula, photographer; **5.15(all):** © The McGraw-Hill Companies, Inc./Eric Wise, photographer; **5.16a:** Du Cane Medical Imaging Ltd/Photo Researchers Inc; **5.16b:** British Columbia Institute of Technology, Medical Radiography Technology; **5.16c:** © Logical Images/Custom Medical Stock Photo; **5.16d:** © Dr. Richard Anderson; **5.19:** © The McGraw-Hill Companies, Inc./Rick Brady, photographer; **5.31:** © Zephyr/Photo Researchers Inc; **5.32a:** © The McGraw-Hill Companies, Inc./Christine Eckel, photographer; **5.33:** © The McGraw-Hill Companies, Inc./Eric Wise, photographer; **5.34:** © Dr. P. Marazzi/SPL/Science Photo Library; **5.35:** © Ralph Hutchings/Visuals Unlimited; **5.36:** © Dr. P. Marazzi/ Science Photo Library; **5.40:** © Mediscan/Visuals Unlimited; **5.41:** © AJPhoto/Photo Researchers Inc.; **5.44:** © Charles McRae, M.D./Visuals Unlimited; **5.47:** © Sovereign/Phototake Inc; **5.48:** © Jim Stevenson/SPL/Photo Researchers Inc.

CHAPTER 6

Opener: © The McGraw-Hill Companies, Inc./Rick Brady, photographer; **6.8:** © Photo Network Stock/Grant Heilman Photography Inc.; **6.9:** ISM/Phototake; **6.10:** © Medical-on-line/Alamy; **6.11:** © Mediscan/Visuals Unlimited; **6.19:** © CNRI/SPL/Photo Researchers Inc.; **6.24:** © Dr. Joseph William/Phototake; **6.26:** © SIU Biomedical/Photo Researchers Inc.; **6.29:** © Medical-on-line/Alamy; **6.32:** © Phototake Inc./Alamy; **6.33:** © CNRI/Photo Researchers Inc.; **6.35:** © Susan Leavine/Photo Researchers Inc.; **6.36:** From Leonard V. Crowley, *An Introduction to Human Disease: Pathology & Pathophysiology Correlations*, 3e, fig 23.22. © 1992, Jones & Bartlett Publishers, Sudbury, MA **www. jbpub.com**. Reprinted by permission; **6.37:** © Dr. P. Marazzi/SPL/Photo Researchers Inc.

CHAPTER 7

Opener: © Vol. 40/PhotoDisc/Getty; **7.1:** © The McGraw-Hill Companies, Inc./Eric Wise, photographer; **7.2:** © Bill Longcore/

Photo Researchers, Inc.; **7.5 (both):** © Ed Reschke; **7.6:** Dr. E. Walker/Photo Researchers Inc.; **7.7:** © Meckes/Ottawa/Photo Researchers Inc.; **7.8-7.12:** © Ed Reschke; **7.13:** © Andrew Syred/ SPL/Photo Researchers, Inc.; **7.15:** © Oliver Meckes/Photo Researchers, Inc.; **7.16a:** © Medical-on-line/Alamy; **7.16b:** © Dr. P. Marazzi/SPL/Photo Researchers Inc.; **7.16c:** © Paul Cox/ Alamy.

CHAPTER 8

Opener: © The McGraw-Hill Companies, Inc./Rick Brady, photographer; **8.11:** © The McGraw-Hill Companies, Inc./Rick Brady, photographer; **8.13 (both):** © Ed Reschke; **8.14:** © Pasieka/ Science Photo Library; **8.16:** © Wellcome Photo Library; **8.23:** © Carolina Biological/Visuals Unlimited; **8.24:** © Dr. P. Marazzi/ Photo Researchers Inc.

CHAPTER 9

Opener: © The McGraw-Hill Companies, Inc./Rick Brady, photographer; **9.8:** © Phototake; **9.14:** © SIU/Visuals Unlimited; **9.15, 9.17 (both):** © Ralph Hutchings/Visuals Unlimited; **9.19:** © Collection CNRI/Phototake; **9.20:** © Wellcome Photo Library; **9.21:** © Garo/Photo Researchers Inc.

CHAPTER 10

Opener: © The McGraw-Hill Companies, Inc./Rick Brady, photographer; **10.10b (1-4):** © Dr. Marcus E. Raichle; **10.18 (both):** © Phototake Inc/Alamy; **10.19a:** © Wellcome Photo Library; **10.19b:** © R. Spencer Phippen/Phototake Inc.; **10.20:** © Rachel Epstein/The Image Works; **10.21:** © Simon Fraser/ Photo Researchers Inc.; **10.24a:** © ISM/Phototake Inc.; **10.24b:** © Scott Camazine/Alamy; **10.25:** © NIH/Phototake Inc.; **10.26:** © Mediscan; **10.27:** © James Cavallini/Photo Researchers Inc.; **10.28a:** © Wellcome Photo Library; **10.28b:** © Simon Fraser/ Newcastle Hospitals NHS/Science Photo Library; **10.29:** © Bart's Medical Library/Phototake Inc.; **10.31:** © O.J. Staats/Custom Medical Stock Photography; **10.32:** © Dr. M.A. Ansary/Custom Medical Stock Photography; **10.33b:** © NMSB/Custom Medical Stock; **10.35 (both):** © Phototake Inc./Alamy; **10.36:** © Marcus E. Raichle.

CHAPTER 11

Opener: © The McGraw-Hill Companies, Inc./Rick Brady, photographer; **11.1b:** © CNRI/SPL/Photo Researchers Inc.; **11.4:** © Lester V. Bergman/The Bergman Collection; **11.5:** © Per H. Kjeldsen; **11.8:** ©Medical-on-Line/Alamy; **11.12:** © Saturn Stills/ SPL/Photo Researchers Inc.; **11.13:** © SPL/Photo Researchers Inc.

CHAPTER 12

Opener: © The McGraw-Hill Companies, Inc./Rick Brady, photographer; **12.7:** Brian Evans/Photo Researchers Inc.; **12.8a:** © Carolina Biological/Visuals Unlimited; **12.8b:** © The McGraw-Hill Companies, Inc./Al Telser, photographer; **12.11:** © Wellcome Photo Library; **12.12:** © English/Custom Medical Stock Photo.

CHAPTER 13

Opener: © The McGraw-Hill Companies, Inc./Rick Brady, photographer; **13.3:** © Carroll Weiss/Camera M.D. Studios; **13.4:** © Charles Stoer/Camera M.D. Studios; **13.5:** © Carroll Weiss/

Camera M.D. Studios; **13.6, 13.7:** © Kenneth Greer/Visuals Unlimited; **13.8:** © Carroll Weiss/Camera M.D. Studios; **13.11:** © SPL/Photo Researchers Inc.; **13.14:** © Dr. Landrum Shettles; **13.16:** The William Boyd Museum, Dept. of Pathology and Laboratory Medicine, The University of British Columbia; **13.17:** © Wellcome Photo Library; **13.18:** The William Boyd Museum, Dept. of Pathology and Laboratory Medicine, The University of British Columbia; **13.19:** © Parviz M. Pour/Photo Researchers Inc.; **13.20:** © Phototake Inc./Alamy.; **13.21:** © Corbis RF; **13.23:** © Getty RF; **13.28:** © BrandX Pictures/Punchstock; **13.30:** © Photo Researchers Inc.; **13.34:** © Visuals Unlimited; **13.36:** © EP Vol. 90/Getty Images; **13.37:** © Wellcome Photo Library; **13.38:** ©ALIX/Phanie/Photo Researchers Inc; **13.39:** © TSI/ Getty Images; **13.40, 13.41:** © Biophoto Associates/Photo Researchers Inc.

CHAPTER 14

Opener: © The McGraw-Hill Companies, Inc./Rick Brady, photographer; **14.5:** © Eric Robert/Corbis; **14.6:** Reprinted by permission of publisher from Albert Mendeloff, "Acromegaly, diabetes, hypermetabolism, proteinuia and heart failure" *American Journal of Medicine*, 20:1, 01-56, p. 135. © by Excerpta Medica Inc.; **14.7:** © Frank Trapper/Corbis; **14.10:** © L.V. Bergman/Project Masters Inc.; **14.11:** Dr. P. Marazzi/Science Photo Library; **14.9:** © John Watney; **14.12:** © Mediscan; **14.15:** © Bettmann/Corbis; **14.17 (both):** From *Atlas of Pediatric Physical Diagnosis*, 3/e by Zitelli and Davis, fig. 19.17, 1997. Mosby-Wolfe Europe Limited, London, UK.; **14.18a:** © AP/Wide World Photos; **14.18b:** © Bettmann/ Corbis.

CHAPTER 15

Opener: © The McGraw-Hill Companies, Inc./Rick Brady, photographer; **15.4:** © The McGraw-Hill Companies, Inc./Dennis Strete, photographer; **15.6:** © NYU Franklin New Fund/ Phototake; **15.7:** © Science VU/Visuals Unlimited; **15.8:** © SPL/ Photo Researchers, Inc.

CHAPTER 16

Opener: © The McGraw-Hill Companies, Inc./Rick Brady, photographer; **16.3:** © St. Bartholomew's Hospital, London/Alamy; **16.4:** © Sally and Richard Greenhill/Alamy; **16.5:** © Scott Camazine/Alamy; **16.6:** © Medical-on-Line/Alamy; **16.7:** © NMSB/Custom Medical Stock Photo; **16.8:** © Susan Leavine/ Photo Researchers Inc.; **16.9:** © Wellcome Medical Trust Library; **16.10:** David Parker/Photo Researchers Inc; **16.11:** © Barry Slaven, MD, PhD/Phototake; **16.12 (lower):** From *The 1974 Science Year*, © 1973 Filed Enterprises Educational Corporation. By permission of Worldbook, Inc.; **16.12 (upper):** © John Launois/Stock Photo; **16.13:** © Pasieka/Science Photo Library.

CHAPTER 17

Opener: © The McGraw-Hill Companies, Inc./Rick Brady, photographer; **17.1:** © Vol. 12/PhotoLink/Getty Images; **17.2:** © The McGraw-Hill Companies, Inc./Elite Images; **17.3:** © Vol. 83/ Corbis; **17.4:** © OS 49 PhotoDisc/Getty; **17.5:** © Biophoto Associates/Photo Researchers Inc; **17.6:** © Wellcome Photo Library; **17.7:** © Vol. 20/PhotoDisc/Getty; **17.8 (both):** © Vol. OS 49/PhotoDisc/Getty; **17.9:** © Photo Network Stock/Grant

Heilman Photography Inc.; **17.11:** © Garry D. McMichael/Photo Researchers Inc.

CHAPTER 18

Opener: © The McGraw-Hill Companies, Inc./Rick Brady, photographer; **18.1 (both):** © Courtesy of North Coast Medical; **18.2a:** © Mediscan/Visuals Unlimited; **18.2b:** © AJPhoto/Photo Researchers Inc.; **18.3:** © The McGraw-Hill Companies, Inc./Rick Brady, photographer; **18.4:** © Roger Ressmeyer/Corbis; **18.5:** © Mona Reeder/Dallas Morning News/Corbis; **18.6, 18.7, 18.8, 18.9, 18.10:** © The McGraw-Hill Companies, Inc./Rick Brady, photographer.

CHAPTER 19

Opener: © The McGraw-Hill Companies, Inc./Rick Brady, photographer; **19.1:** © Vol. 15 PhotoDisc/Getty; **19.2:** © Javier Pierini/Getty Images; **19.3:** © Will & Deni McIntyre/Photo Researchers Inc; **19.4:** © Paul Almasy/Corbis; **19.5:** © Dr. P. Marazzi/Photo Researchers Inc; **19.6:** © Royalty-Free/Corbis; **19.7:** © Masterfile.

CHAPTER 20

Opener: © Mark Pearson/Alamy; **20.4:** © Kathy Park Talaro; **20.5, 20.6:** Centers for Disease Control and Prevention; **20.7:** © Custom Medical Stock Photo; **20.9:** © Dr. Jack M. Bostrack/Visuals Unlimited; **20.10:** © Kathy Park Talaro; **20.11:** CNRI/SPL/Photo Researchers Inc.; **20.12:** ©Phototake Inc/Alamy; **20.13:** Courtesy of Dr. Patricia Abbitt; **20.14:** Courtesy Dr. S. Knutton from D.R. Lloyd and S. Knutton, *Infection and Immunity*, January 1987, p. 86-92. © ASM; **20.15, 20.16:** Centers for Disease Control and Prevention; **20.17:** © Vol. 18 PhotoDisc/Getty; **20.18 (both):** Dr. Judy A. Murphy, San Joaquin Delta College, Department of Microscopy, Stockton, CA; **20.19:** © Dr. P. Marazzi/Photo Researchers Inc; **20.20:** © ISM/Phototake Inc; **20.21:** National Genome New Institute/NIH; **20.22:** Centers for Disease Control and Prevention; **20.23:** Katz et al., *Parasitic Diseases*,© Springer-Verlag; **20.24:** © Henry Westheim Photography/Alamy; **20.25:** © Taylor Jorjorian/Alamy; **20.26:** © The McGraw-Hill Companies, Inc./Rick Brady, photographer.

CHAPTER 21

Opener: © Lauren Shear/Photo Researchers, Inc; **21.2:** © CNRI/Photo Researchers Inc; **21.8:** © Hattie Young/Photo Researchers Inc.

CHAPTER 22

Opener: © The McGraw-Hill Companies, Inc./Rick Brady, photographer; **22.2:** © BSIP/Phototake Inc; **22.3:** © Ed Reschke; **22.4:** Steve Gschmeissner/SPL/Photo Researchers Inc.; **22.5:** © The McGraw-Hill Companies, Inc./Jill Braaten, photographer; **22.6:** © Getty RF; **22.7:** © Garry D. McMichael/Photo Researchers Inc; **22.8:** © Medical Elements PhotoDisc/Getty Images; **22.9:** © Dynamic Graphics RF/Jupiter; **22.10:** © Tomas del Amo/Alamy; **22.11:** © Vol. 40 PhotoDisc/GettyImages; **22.12:** © ISM/Phototake Inc; **22.13:** © Wellcome Photo Library; **22.15:** Courtesy Varian Medical Systems.

CHAPTER 23

Opener: © Corbis RF; **23.1:** © garythephotographer; **23.2:** © Vol. 189 Corbis RF; **23.3:** © Vol. 67 PhotoDisc/Getty Images; **23.4:** © Image Source/Alamy; **23.5:** © Vol.189 Corbis RF; **23.6:** © The McGraw-Hill Companies, Inc./Rick Brady, photographer; **23.7:** © Will & Deni McIntyre/Photo Researchers Inc; **23.8:** © Scott Camazine/Photo Researchers Inc.; **23.9:** © Dag Sundberg/Alamy.

ILLUSTRATIONS

CHAPTER 4

4.31: Near vision chart, Courtesy of Richmond Products, Albuquerque, NM

CHAPTER 8

page 322: Courtesy of Bibbeo Systems, Inc., Petaluma, CA

CHAPTER 17

17.13: Waist Circumference Measurement, NIH Publication; **17.17:** Anatomy of a Pyramid, U.S. Department of Agriculture (USDA)

A

Abdomen, 5
Abdominal aorta, 324
Abdominal cavity, 40
Abdominal quadrants, 40–41
Abdominopelvic cavity, 40, 41
Abducens nerve, 402, 403
Abduct, 163
Abduction, 162, 163
ABG, 351, 352
ABI, 330
Ablation, 321, 419, 531
Abnormal spinal curvatures, 171
Abortion, 541
Abortus, 540, 541
Abrasion, 80, 81, 113
Abruptio, 547
Absence seizure, 412
Absorb, 217, 682
Absorption, 216, 217, 240, 244, 683
    disorders of, 242–243
Accessory glands, 482, 490–491
Accessory nerve, 402, 403
Accessory organs, 214
Accommodate, 105
Accommodation, 105, 106
Accommodative esotropia, 104
ACE, 320
ACEP, 891
Acesulfame-K, 684
Acetabulum, 184, 185, 186
Acetaminophen, 119, 121
Acetone, 590, 591
Acetylcholine, 394, 395, 698
Achilles tendinitis, 192
Achilles tendon, 192, 193
Achondroplasia, 154, 155, 840
Acid, 270, 271
Acidification, 122
Acinar cells, 238, 239
ACL, 32, 188, 190
Acne, 72, 73
Acoustic, 739
Acquired, 834, 835
Acquired immunodeficiency, 618
Acquired immunodeficiency syndrome (AIDS), 516,
    517, 618, 620–621
Acromegaly, 572, 573
Acromioclavicular (AC), 174, 175
Acromion, 174, 175
Acrophobia, 764, 765
ACTH, 570
Activated partial thromboplastin time (aPTT), 282
Active range of motion (AROM), 736
Activities of daily living (ADL), 416, 417, 730
Acuminata, 495
Acupoint, 890, 891
Acupressure, 890, 891
Acupuncture, 886, 887, 890
Acute, 121
Acute bronchitis, 366
Acute epiglottitis, 358
Acute glomerulonephritis, 456
Acute labyrinthitis, 130
Acute lymphoblastic leukemia (ALL), 278
Acute otitis media (AOM), 126
Acute renal failure (ARF), 458
Acute respiratory failure (ARF), 368
Acute retention, 462
Acute transverse myelitis, 424
A.D., 129
Adapt, 638, 639, 735
Adaptation, 639
Adaptive equipment, 734, 735
ADD, 656
Addict, 433, 769
Addiction, 433, 768, 769, 770

Addictive, 432, 433
Addison disease, 582, 583, 584
Adduct, 163
Adduction, 162, 163
Adductor, 186
Adenine, 696, 697, 832, 833
Adenocarcinoma, 856, 857
Adenohypophysis, 570, 571
Adenoid, 124, 125, 356, 357, 611
Adequate Intake (AI), 683
ADH, 568, 570, 656
ADHD, 656
Adhere, 791
Adherence, 790, 791
Adipose, 65
Adipose tissue, 64
Adiposity, 708, 709
Adjunct, 890, 891
Adjustment, 896, 897
Adjuvant, 580, 581
ADL, 416, 730
Adnexa, 520, 521
Adnexal, 521
Adnexum, 521
Adolescence
    developmental disorders of, 656–659
    eating disorders in, 658
    as stage, 654–655
Adolescent, 655
Adrenal cortex, 582
Adrenal cortical hyperfunction, 584
Adrenal cortical hypofunction, 584
Adrenalectomy, 585
Adrenal gland, 571
    anatomy and function of, 582–583
    disorders of, 584–585
Adrenaline, 582, 583
Adrenal medulla, 582
Adrenal virilism, 584
Adrenergic, 321
Adrenocortical, 583
Adrenocortical hormone, 582
Adrenocorticotropic, 571
Adrenocorticotropic hormone (ACTH), 570
Adrenogenital syndrome, 584, 585
Adulthood
    stages of, 660–661
Adult respiratory distress syndrome (ARDS), 368
Advance medical directive, 664, 665
Adventitia, 329
AED, 310
Aerobe, 798, 799
Aerobic, 799
Affect, 766, 767
Affective disorders, 760–761
Afferent, 393
Afferent nerve, 392
AFP, 838
Aged, 661
Agenesis, 247, 646
Age spots, 662
Agglutinate, 274, 275, 617
Agglutination, 284, 285, 616, 617
Aging, 660, 661
    senescence of organ systems, 662–663
Agonist, 531
Agoraphobia, 764, 765
Agranulocyte, 276, 277
AI, 682
AIDS, 516, 618, 620–621
Air pollution, 860
Alanine aminotransferase (ALT), 234, 235
Alarm reaction, 584
Albinism, 74, 75, 841
Albino, 75, 841
Albumin, 268, 269
Aldosterone, 582, 583, 584
Aldosteronism, 584, 585

Aldosteronoma, 585
Alexander technique, 889
Alignment, 156, 157
Alimentary, 215
Alimentary canal, 214–215
Alkaline, 270, 271
Alkaline phosphatase (ALP), 234
ALL, 278
Allele, 834, 835
Allergen, 66, 67, 112, 113, 607, 609
Allergenic, 67
Allergic, 66, 113
Allergic conjunctivitis, 112
Allergic rhinitis, 354
Allergy, 67, 113, 618
Allogen, 619
Allogenic, 619
Allograft, 79, 190, 191, 618, 619
Alloimmune, 619
Alloimmune disorder, 618
Allopathic, 885
Allopathic medicine, 887
Allyl sulfide, 698, 699
Alopecia, 74, 75
ALP, 234
Alpha cell, 586
Alpha-fetoprotein (AFP), 838, 839, 864
Alpha-hemolytic streptococci, 800
Alpha-linolenic acid, 688
ALS, 424
ALT, 234
Alternative medicine, 885. See also Complementary and
    alternative medicine (CAM)
Alternative sweeteners, 684
Alveolar, 353, 363
Alveoli, 352, 353, 548
Alveolus, 353, 363
Alzheimer disease, 406, 407
AMAS, 864
Amblyopia, 105
Ambulatory blood pressure monitor, 318
Amenorrhea, 527
Amino acid, 240, 241, 690, 691
Aminoketone, 861
Ammonia, 450, 451
Amniocentesis, 428, 540, 541, 838
Amnion, 540, 541
Amniotic, 541
Amniotic fluid abnormalities, 544
Amoeba, 807
Amoebiasis, 806, 807
Amphetamine, 432
Ampulla, 130, 131, 488, 489
Amputate, 183, 735
Amputation, 183, 418, 419
    rehabilitation, 734–735
Amputee, 183, 735
Amylase, 216, 217, 220, 238
Amyotrophic, 425
Amyotrophic lateral sclerosis (ALS), 424
Anabolic steroids, 168
Anabolism, 30, 31
Anaerobe, 798, 799
Anaerobic, 799
Anal, 245
Anal canal, 244
    disorders of, 246
Anal columns, 244
Anal fissure, 246
Anal fistulas, 246, 247
Analgesia, 121, 419
Analgesic, 121, 418, 419
Anaphylactic, 619
Anaphylactic shock, 618
Anaphylactoid purpura, 282
Anaphylaxis, 618, 619
Anastomoses, 249, 493, 537
Anastomosis, 248, 249, 492, 493, 537